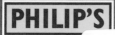

PHILIP'S

STR............................5

Nortn Essex

C000180624

First published in 1999 by

Philip's, a division of
Octopus Publishing Group Ltd
2–4 Heron Quays, London E14 4JP

Second edition 2003
First impression 2003

ISBN 0-540-08286-4 (pocket)

© Philip's 2003

Ordnance Survey®

This product includes mapping data licensed from Ordnance Survey® with the permission of the Controller of Her Majesty's Stationery Office. © Crown copyright 2003. All rights reserved. Licence number 100011710.

No part of this publication may be reproduced, stored in a retrieval system or transmitted in any form or by any means, electronic, mechanical, photocopying, recording or otherwise, without the permission of the Publishers and the copyright owner.

To the best of the Publishers' knowledge, the information in this atlas was correct at the time of going to press. No responsibility can be accepted for any errors or their consequences.

The representation in this atlas of a road, track or path is no evidence of the existence of a right of way.

Ordnance Survey and the OS Symbol are registered trademarks of Ordnance Survey, the national mapping agency of Great Britain

Printed and bound in Spain
by Cayfosa-Quebecor

Contents

III	**Key to map symbols**	
IV	**Key to map pages**	
VI	**Route planning**	
VIII	**Administrative and Postcode boundaries**	
1	**Street maps** at 2½ inches to 1 mile	
222	**Index** of towns and villages	
223	**Index** of streets, hospitals, industrial estates, railway stations, schools, shopping centres, universities and places of interest	

Digital Data

The exceptionally high-quality mapping found in this atlas is available as digital data in TIFF format, which is easily convertible to other bitmapped (raster) image formats.

The index is also available in digital form as a standard database table. It contains all the details found in the printed index together with the National Grid reference for the map square in which each entry is named.

For further information and to discuss your requirements, please contact Philip's on 020 7644 6932 or james.mann@philips-maps.co.uk

Key to map symbols

III

Symbol	Description
(22a)	**Motorway** with junction number
	Primary route – dual/single carriageway
	A road – dual/single carriageway
	B road – dual/single carriageway
	Minor road – dual/single carriageway
	Other minor road – dual/single carriageway
	Road under construction
	Tunnel, covered road
	Rural track, private road or narrow road in urban area
	Gate or obstruction to traffic (restrictions may not apply at all times or to all vehicles)
	Path, bridleway, byway open to all traffic, road used as a public path
	Pedestrianised area
DY7	**Postcode boundaries**
	County and unitary authority boundaries
	Railway, tunnel, railway under construction
	Tramway, tramway under construction
	Miniature railway
Walsall	**Railway station**
	Private railway station
South Shields	**Metro station**
	Tram stop, tram stop under construction
	Bus, coach station

Symbol	Description
♦	**Ambulance station**
♦	**Coastguard station**
♦	**Fire station**
♦	**Police station**
✚	**Accident and Emergency entrance to hospital**
Ⓗ	**Hospital**
✛	**Place of worship**
𝒊	**Information Centre** (open all year)
Ⓟ	**Parking**
P&R	**Park and Ride**
PO	**Post Office**
Ⱦ	**Camping site**
⊕	**Caravan site**
⚑	**Golf course**
⍓	**Picnic site**
Prim Sch	**Important buildings, schools, colleges, universities and hospitals**
River Medway	**Water name**
	River, weir, stream
	Canal, lock, tunnel
	Water
	Tidal water
	Woods
	Built up area
Church	**Non-Roman antiquity**
ROMAN FORT	**Roman antiquity**
87 / 58	**Adjoining page indicators**

Abbr	Full	Abbr	Full	Abbr	Full
Acad	**Academy**	Inst	**Institute**	Recn Gd	**Recreation Ground**
Allot Gdns	**Allotments**	Ct	**Law Court**		
Cemy	**Cemetery**	L Ctr	**Leisure Centre**	Resr	**Reservoir**
C Ctr	**Civic Centre**	LC	**Level Crossing**	Ret Pk	**Retail Park**
CH	**Club House**	Liby	**Library**	Sch	**School**
Coll	**College**	Mkt	**Market**	Sh Ctr	**Shopping Centre**
Crem	**Crematorium**	Meml	**Memorial**	TH	**Town Hall/House**
Ent	**Enterprise**	Mon	**Monument**	Trad Est	**Trading Estate**
Ex H	**Exhibition Hall**	Mus	**Museum**	Univ	**University**
Ind Est	**Industrial Estate**	Obsy	**Observatory**	W Twr	**Water Tower**
IRB Sta	**Inshore Rescue**	Pal	**Royal Palace**	Wks	**Works**
	Boat Station	PH	**Public House**	YH	**Youth Hostel**

■ The small numbers around the edges of the maps identify the 1 kilometre National Grid lines

■ The dark grey border on the inside edge of some pages indicates that the mapping does not continue onto the adjacent page

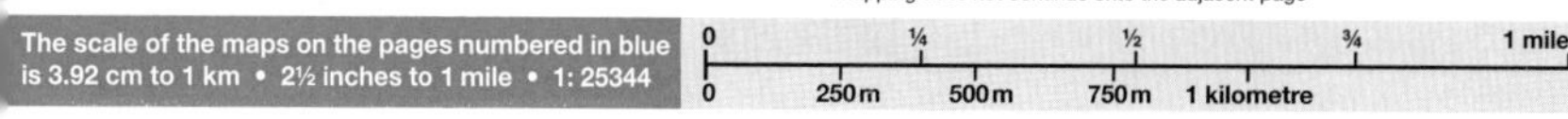

The scale of the maps on the pages numbered in blue is 3.92 cm to 1 km • 2½ inches to 1 mile • 1: 25344

0	¼	½	¾	1 mile
0	250 m	500 m	750 m	1 kilometre

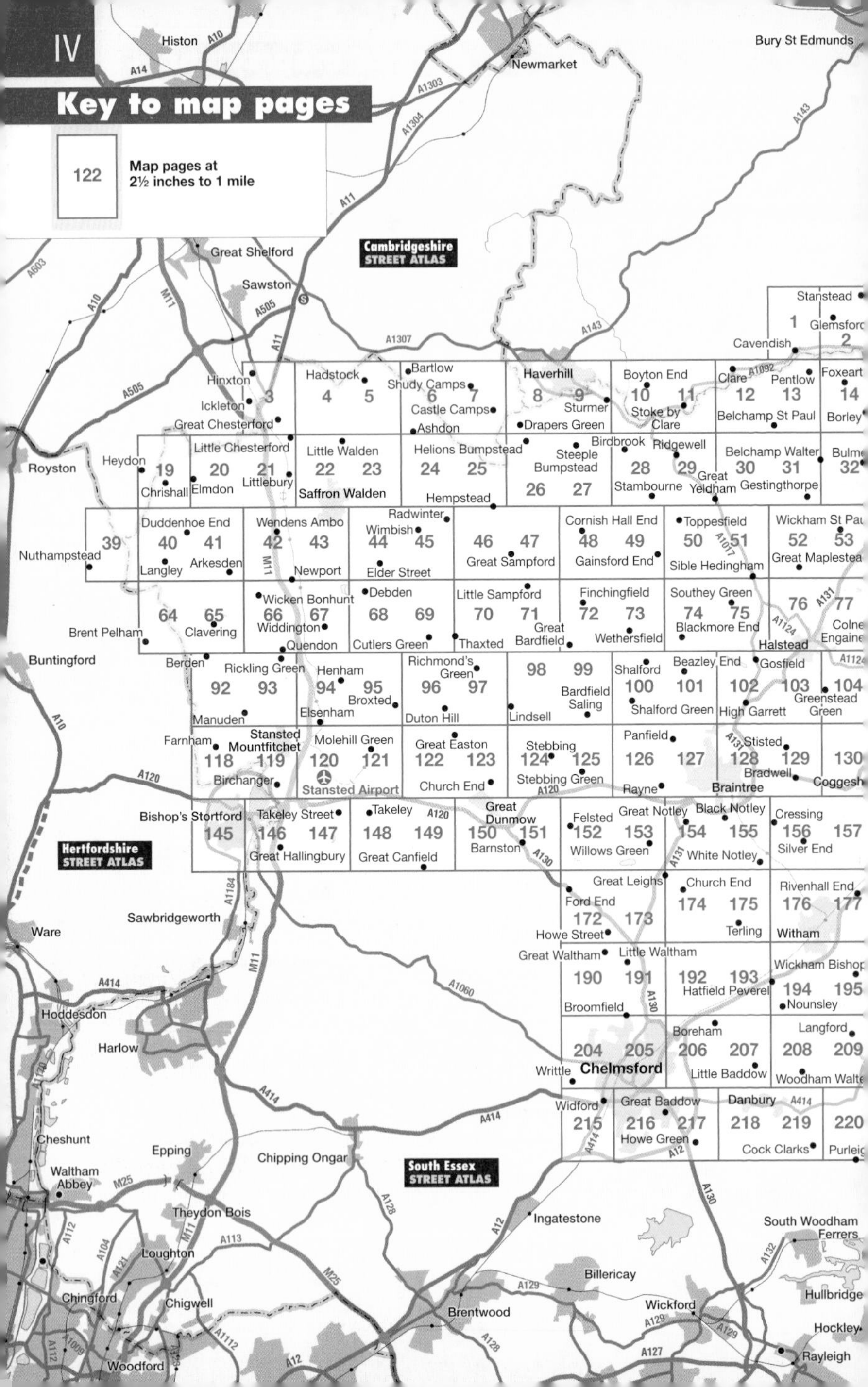

IV

| 122 | Map pages at 2½ inches to 1 mile |

Cambridgeshire STREET ATLAS

Hertfordshire STREET ATLAS

South Essex STREET ATLAS

Bury St Edmunds

Histon

Newmarket

Great Shelford

Sawston

Stanstead
1
Glemsford
2

Cavendish

Hinxton
Ickleton
Great Chesterford

Hadstock
4   5

Bartlow
Shudy Camps
6
Castle Camps
Ashdon   7

Haverhill
8   9

Boyton End
10   11

Clare
12

Pentlow
13

Foxearth
14

Sturmer
Stoke by Clare
Drapers Green

Belchamp St Paul

Borley

Heydon
Royston

Little Chesterford
19   20   21
Chrishall   Elmdon   Littlebury

Little Walden
22   23
Saffron Walden

Helions Bumpstead
24   25
Hempstead

Birdbrook
Steeple
Bumpstead
26   27

Ridgewell
28
Stambourne

Great
29
Yeldham

Belchamp Walter
30   31
Gestingthorpe

Bulme
32

Nuthampstead
39

Duddenhoe End
40   41
Langley   Arkesden

Wendens Ambo
42   43
Newport

Radwinter
Wimbish
44   45
Elder Street

46   47
Great Sampford

Cornish Hall End
48   49
Gainsford End

Toppesfield
50   51
Sible Hedingham

Wickham St Pau
52   53
Great Maplestea

64   65
Brent Pelham   Clavering

Wicken Bonhunt
66   67
Widdington
Quendon

Debden
68   69
Cutlers Green

Little Sampford
70   71
Great
Bardfield
Thaxted

Finchingfield
72   73
Wethersfield

Southey Green
74   75
Blackmore End

76   77
Colne
Engaine
Halstead

Buntingford

Bergen
92   93
Manuden

Rickling Green
94   95
Broxted
Elsenham

Henham
96   97
Duton Hill

Richmond's
Green
98   99
Bardfield
Saling
Lindsell

Shalford
100   101
Shalford Green

Beazley End
102   103
High Garrett

Gosfield
104
Greenstead
Green

Farnham
118   119
Birchanger

Stansted
Mountfitchet
Molehill Green
120   121
Stansted Airport
Church End

Great Easton
122   123

Stebbing
124   125
Stebbing Green
Rayne

Panfield
126   127

Stisted
128   129
Bradwell
Braintree

130
Coggesh

Bishop's Stortford
145

Takeley Street
146   147
Great Hallingbury

Takeley
148   149
Great Canfield

Great
Dunmow
150   151
Barnston
Willows Green

Felsted
152   153
White Notley

Great Notley
154   155

Black Notley

Cressing
156   157
Silver End

Ware
Sawbridgeworth

Great Leighs
Ford End
172   173
Howe Street

Church End
174   175
Terling

Rivenhall End
176   177
Witham

Hoddesdon
Harlow

Great Waltham
190   191
Broomfield

Little Waltham
192   193
Hatfield Peverel

Wickham Bishop
194   195
Nounsley

Writtle
204   205
Chelmsford

Boreham
206   207
Little Baddow

Langford
208   209
Woodham Walte

Cheshunt

Widford
215

Great Baddow
216   217
Howe Green

Danbury
218   219
Cock Clarks

220
Purleig

Waltham
Abbey
Epping
Chipping Ongar

Theydon Bois
Loughton

Ingatestone

South Woodham
Ferrers

Chingford   Chigwell

Billericay

Wickford

Hullbridge

Woodford

Brentwood

Hockley

Rayleigh

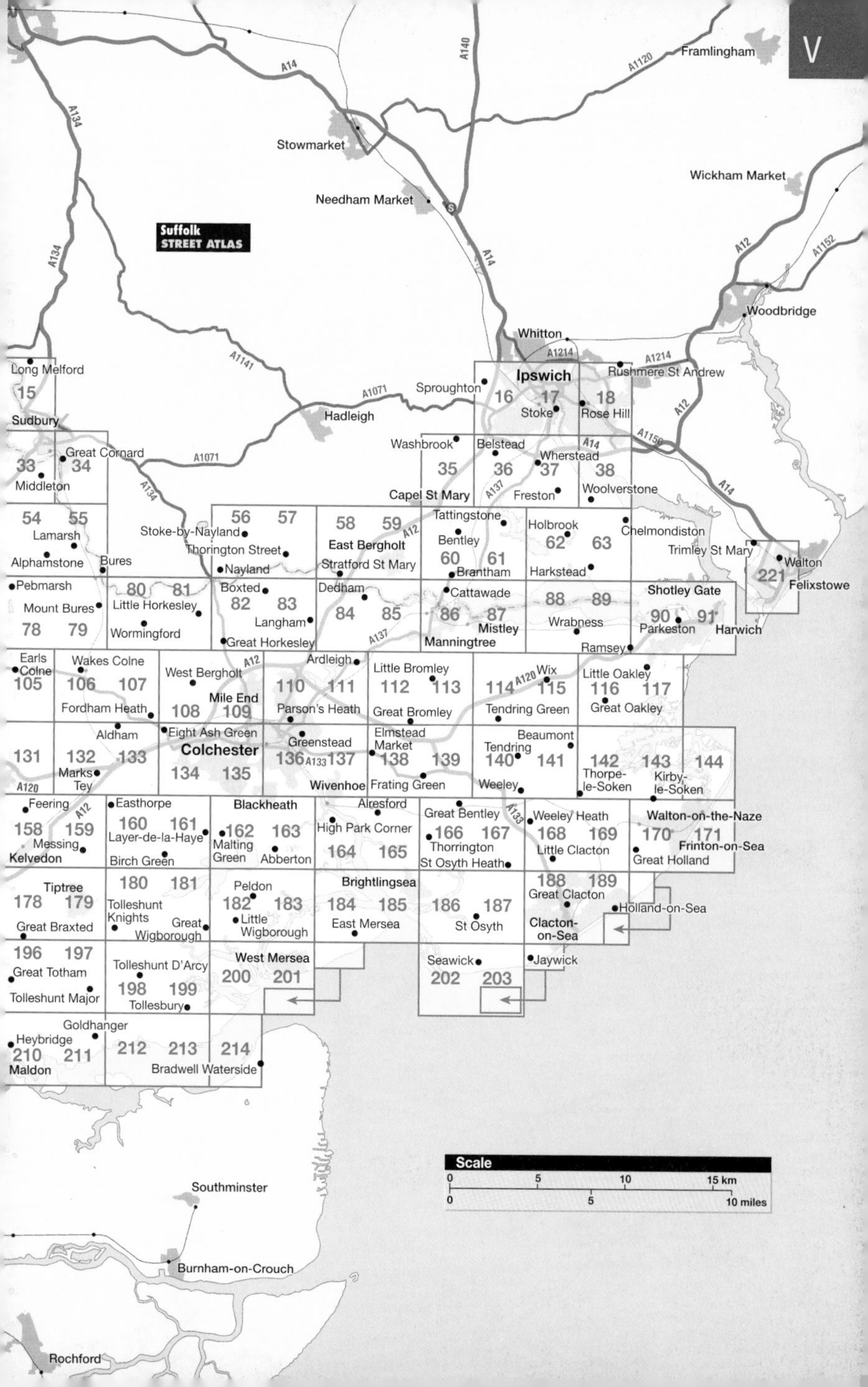

V

Framlingham

A14

A140

A1120

Stowmarket

Needham Market

Wickham Market

Suffolk
STREET ATLAS

A134

A1152

A12

Whitton

Woodbridge

A1214

A1214

A1156

A14

Long Melford

A1141

Sproughton

Ipswich

16 17 18

Rushmere St Andrew

15

A1071

Hadleigh

Stoke Rose Hill

Sudbury

33 34

Great Cornard

A1071

Washbrook

Belstead

35 36

Wherstead

37 38

Middleton

A134

Capel St Mary

A137

Freston

Woolverston

54 55

Stoke-by-Nayland

56 57

Tattingstone

58 59

Holbrook

Chelmondiston

Lamarsh

Thorington Street

East Bergholt

Bentley

62 63

Trimley St Mary

Alphamstone

Bures

Nayland

Stratford St Mary

60 61

Harkstead

Walton

221

Pebmarsh

80 81

Boxted

Dedham

Brantham

Cattawade

88 89

Shotley Gate

Felixstowe

Mount Bures

Little Horkesley

82 83

Langham

84 85

86 87

Wrabness

90 91

78 79

Wormingford

Great Horkesley

A137

Manningtree

Mistley

Ramsey

Parkeston Harwich

Earls
Colne

Wakes Colne

West Bergholt

Ardleigh

Little Bromley

A120 Wix

Little Oakley

105 106 107

110 111

112 113

114 115

116 117

Fordham Heath

108

Mile End
109

Parson's Heath

Great Bromley

Tendring Green

Great Oakley

Aldham

Eight Ash Green

Greenstead

Elmstead
Market

Beaumont

142 143 144

131 132 133

Colchester

136 137

138 139

Tendring

140 141

Thorpe-
le-Soken

Kirby-
le-Soken

Marks
Tey

134 135

Wivenhoe

Frating Green

Weeley

A120

A133

Feering

A12

Easthorpe

Blackheath

Alresford

Great Bentley

A133

Weeley Heath

Walton-on-the-Naze

158 159

160 161

162 163

High Park Corner

166 167

168 169

170 171

Messing

Layer-de-la-Haye

Malting
Green

Thorrington

Little Clacton

Frinton-on-Sea

Kelvedon

Birch Green

Abberton

164 165

St Osyth Heath

Great Holland

Tiptree

180 181

Peldon

Brightlingsea

188 189

178 179

Tolleshunt
Knights

182 183

184 185

186 187

Great Clacton

Holland-on-Sea

Great Braxted

Great
Wigborough

Little
Wigborough

East Mersea

St Osyth

Clacton-
on-Sea

196 197

Tolleshunt D'Arcy

West Mersea

Seawick

Jaywick

Great Totham

198 199

200 201

202 203

Tolleshunt Major

Tollesbury

Heybridge

Goldhanger

210 211

212 213

214

Maldon

Bradwell Waterside

Southminster

Scale

0   5   10   15 km
0   5   10 miles

Burnham-on-Crouch

Rochford

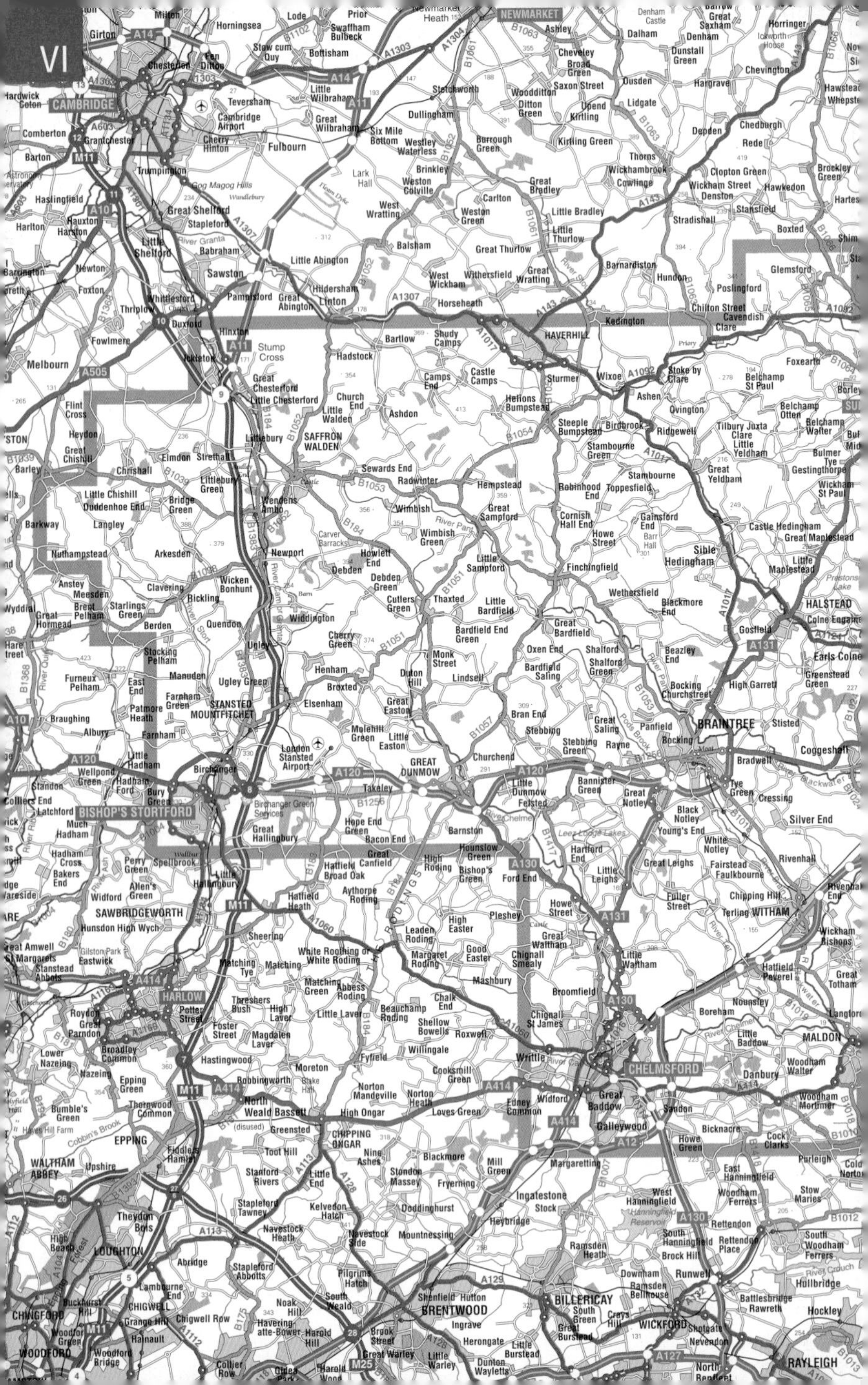

VI
Milton
Horningsea
Lode
Prior
Swaffham Bulbeck
Newmarket Heath
NEWMARKET
Denham Castle
Great Saxham
Horringer
Ickworth House
Girton
A14
Stow cum Quy
Bottisham
A1303
A1304
B1063
Ashley
Dalham
Denham
Fen Ditton
Chesterton
Cheveley
Broad Green
Dunstall Green
Chevington
Hardwick
Coton
CAMBRIDGE
A1303
Teversham
Little Wilbraham
Stetchworth
Woodditton
Ditton Green
Saxon Street
Ousden
Hargrave
Hawstead
Whepstead
Cambridge Airport
Great Wilbraham
Six Mile Bottom
Dullingham
Upend
Kirtling
Lidgate
Chedburgh
Comberton
Grantchester
A603
Cherry Hinton
Fulbourn
Westley Waterless
Burrough Green
Kirtling Green
Depden
Rede
Barton
M11
Trumpington
A1134
Brinkley
Thorns
Wickhambrook
Cowlinge
Clopton Green
Brockley Green
Gog Magog Hills
Wandlebury
Lark Hall
Weston Colville
Great Bradley
Wickham Street
Denston
Hawkedon
Haslingfield
A10
Great Shelford
Stapleford
West Wratting
Carlton
Little Bradley
Stansfield
Hartest
Harlton
Hauxton
Harston
A1307
Weston Green
Stradishall
Little Thurlow
Boxted
River Granta
Little Shelford
Babraham
Balsham
Great Thurlow
B1061
A143
Barrington
Newton
Sawston
Little Abington
West Wickham
Withersfield
Great Wratting
Barnardiston
Hundon
Glemsford
Foxton
Pampisford
Great Abington
Hildersham
Linton
A1307
Horseheath
Poslingford
Thriplow
Whittlesford
Duxford
Chilton Street
Cavendish
Clare
A1092
Hinxton
Bartlow
Shudy Camps
HAVERHILL
Kedington
Fowlmere
A11
Stump Cross
A1017
Ickleton
Hadstock
Camps End
Castle Camps
Sturmer
Wixoe
Stoke by Clare
Foxearth
Melbourn
A505
Great Chesterford
Little Chesterford
Helions Bumpstead
Ashen
Belchamp St Paul
Flint Cross
Church End
Little Walden
Ashdon
Ovington
Belchamp Otten
Heydon
Littlebury
SAFFRON WALDEN
Steeple Bumpstead
Birdbrook
Ridgewell
Tilbury Juxta Clare
Belchamp Walter
Great Chishill
Elmdon
Strethall
B1052
B1054
Stambourne Green
Little Yeldham
Bulmer Tye
Barley
B1039
Chrishall
Sewards End
Radwinter
Hempstead
Stambourne
Great Yeldham
Gestingthorpe
Little Chishill
Littlebury Green
B1053
Robinhood End
Toppesfield
Wickham St Paul
Duddenhoe End
Bridge Green
Wendens Ambo
Wimbish
Great Sampford
Barkway
Langley
River Pant
Cornish Hall End
Gainsford End
Castle Hedingham
Carver Barracks
Wimbish Green
Howe Street
Barr Hall
Great Maplestead
Nuthampstead
Arkesden
B1383
Newport
Howlett End
Little Sampford
Sible Hedingham
Little Maplestead
Debden
Finchingfield
Anstey
Meesden
Clavering
Wicken Bonhunt
Debden Green
B1051
Wethersfield
HALSTEAD
Wyddial
Brent Pelham
Rickling
Cutlers Green
Thaxted
Little Bardfield
Blackmore End
Colne Engaine
Great Hormead
Starlings Green
Widdington
A1017
Berden
Quendon
Bardfield End Green
Great Bardfield
Gosfield
Cherry Green
A1124
Ugley
Stocking Pelham
Monk Street
Oxen End
Shalford
Beazley End
Earls Colne
B1368
Furneux Pelham
Manuden
Henham
Duton Hill
Lindsell
Shalford Green
Greenstead Green
East End
Ugley Green
Broxted
Bardfield Saling
Bocking Churchstreet
High Garrett
Farnham Green
STANSTED MOUNTFITCHET
Elsenham
Great Easton
Patmore Heath
Braughing
Bran End
Great Saling
Panfield
BRAINTREE
Stisted
Albury
Farnham
Molehill Green
Little Easton
B1057
Stebbing
Stebbing Green
Rayne
Bocking
Coggeshall
A120
Little Hadham
London Stansted Airport
GREAT DUNMOW
Churchend
Wellpond Green
Birchanger
A120
Bradwell
Standon
Hadham Ford
Takeley
Little Dunmow
Bannister Green
Tye Green
Colliers End
Bury Green
Felsted
Great Notley
Cressing
Latchford
BISHOP'S STORTFORD
B1256
Birchanger Green Services
Black Notley
Silver End
Much Hadham
Hope End Green
Barnston
Young's End
Great Hallingbury
Bacon End
Leez Lodge Lakes
White Notley
B1004
Hounslow Green
Hartford End
Rivenhall
Hadham Cross
Perry Green
Spellbrook
Great Canfield
Hatfield Broad Oak
High Roding
A130
Great Leighs
Fairstead
Faulkbourne
Bakers End
Allen's Green
Little Hallingbury
Bishop's Green
Ford End
Little Leighs
Widford
Aythorpe Roding
Fuller Street
Chipping Hill
Rivenhall End
SAWBRIDGEWORTH
M11
Hatfield Heath
Howe Street
A131
Terling
WITHAM
Hunsdon
High Wych
High Easter
Pleshey
Wickham Bishops
A1060
Leaden Roding
Sheering
Great Waltham
Great Amwell
Gilston Park
White Roothing or White Roding
Good Easter
St Margarets
Eastwick
Matching
Margaret Roding
Chignall Smealy
Little Waltham
Hatfield Peverel
Stanstead Abbotts
A414
Matching Tye
Mashbury
Great Totham
HARLOW
Matching Green
Abbess Roding
Broomfield
Roydon
Potter Street
Threshers Bush
High Laver
Little Laver
Beauchamp Roding
Chalk End
A130
Nounsley
Boreham
Great Parndon
Foster Street
Shellow Bowells
Roxwell
Chignall St James
Langford
Magdalen Laver
Little Baddow
Broadley Common
Willingale
MALDON
Lower Nazeing
Hastingwood
Fyfield
Writtle
CHELMSFORD
Nazeing
Moreton
Cooksmill Green
Danbury
Woodham Walter
Epping Green
Bobbingworth
Stake Hall
M11
A414
A414
Norton Mandeville
Norton Heath
Great Baddow
Woodham Mortimer
Bumble's Green
Thornwood Common
North Weald Bassett
High Ongar
Loves Green
Edney Common
Widford
Sandon
Galleywood
Bicknacre
EPPING
(disused)
Greensted
CHIPPING ONGAR
A414
Howe Green
Cock Clarks
Cobbin's Brook
Fiddlers Hamlet
Toot Hill
Nine Ashes
Blackmore
Mill Green
Margaretting
A12
Purleigh
WALTHAM ABBEY
Upshire
Stanford Rivers
Little End
Stondon Massey
Fryerning
East Hanningfield
B1007
Stow Maries
B1393
A128
Theydon Bois
Stapleford Tawney
Kelvedon Hatch
Doddinghurst
Ingatestone
Stock
West Hanningfield
Woodham Ferrers
A113
Navestock Heath
Heybridge
Hanningfield Reservoir
A130
Rettendon
South Woodham Ferrers
High Beach
LOUGHTON
Navestock Side
Mountnessing
South Hanningfield
Rettendon Place
Abridge
Ramsden Heath
Brock Hill
Epping Forest
A104
Stapleford Abbotts
Pilgrims Hatch
Downham
Ramsden Bellhouse
Runwell
River Crouch
Hullbridge
Lambourne End
A129
CHIGWELL
South Weald
Shenfield
Hutton
BILLERICAY
A132
Battlesbridge
Rawreth
Hockley
CHINGFORD
Buckhurst Hill
Grange Hill
Chigwell Row
Noak Hill
BRENTWOOD
South Green
Crays Hill
WICKFORD
Shotgate
Hainault
Havering-atte-Bower
Harold Hill
Brook Street
Ingrave
Great Burstead
Nevendon
Woodford Green
M11
A1112
Herongate
Little Burstead
WOODFORD
Woodford Bridge
Great Warley
Little Warley
Dunton Wayletts
A127
RAYLEIGH
M25
Collier Row
Gidea Park
Harold Wood
North Benfleet

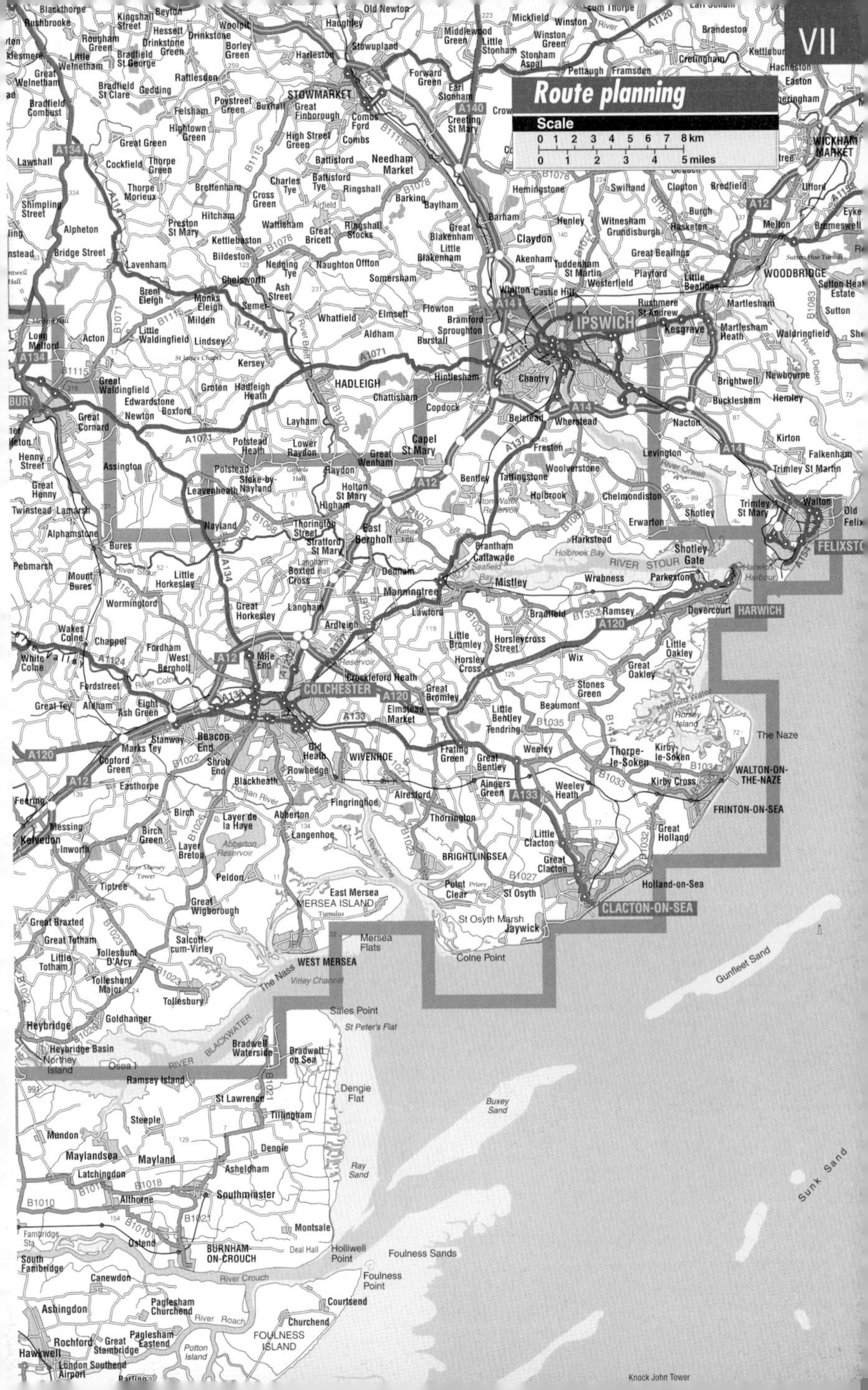
Route planning
Scale
0 1 2 3 4 5 6 7 8 km
0 1 2 3 4 5 miles
STOWMARKET
IPSWICH
WICKHAM MARKET
WOODBRIDGE
HADLEIGH
FELIXSTOWE
HARWICH
COLCHESTER
WIVENHOE
BRIGHTLINGSEA
CLACTON-ON-SEA
WALTON-ON-THE-NAZE
FRINTON-ON-SEA
WEST MERSEA
BURNHAM-ON-CROUCH
FOULNESS ISLAND
MERSEA ISLAND
Lavenham
Long Melford
Needham Market
Kesgrave
Martlesham
Nacton
Levington
Shotley Gate
Dovercourt
Manningtree
Mistley
Dedham
East Bergholt
Capel St Mary
Nayland
Bures
Tiptree
Kelvedon
Heybridge
Tollesbury
Southminster
Rochford
Hawkwell
Ashingdon
South Fambridge
Mayland
Maylandsea
Jaywick
St Osyth
Holland-on-Sea
Thorpe-le-Soken
Kirby-le-Soken
The Naze
River Stour
River Orwell
River Colne
River Crouch
River Roach
River Blackwater
Holbrook Bay
Hamford Water
Alton Water Reservoir
Abberton Reservoir
Gunfleet Sand
Buxey Sand
Ray Sand
Foulness Sands
Sunk Sand
Dengie Flat
Knock John Tower
London Southend Airport

Major administrative and Postcode boundaries

County and unitary authority boundaries
District boundaries
Postcode boundaries
Area covered by this atlas

Scale

0   5   10   15 km
0   5   10 miles

Suffolk

Cambridgeshire

Hertfordshire

Essex

Colchester

Tendring

Braintree

Uttlesford

Harlow

Epping Forest

Brentwood

Chelmsford

Maldon

Rochford

Basildon

Castle Point

Southend-on-Sea

London

Kent

Medway

IP11 Felixstowe
IP1 Ipswich
IP4 IP5
IP2 IP3
IP10
IP9
IP7
Harwich
CO14
CO12 Great Oakley
Walton-on-the-Naze
Frinton-on-Sea
CO13
Clacton-on-Sea
CO15
Holbrook
Manningtree
CO11
CO16
St Osyth
Brightlingsea
Wivenhoe
CO7
East Bergholt
Ardleigh
CO1
CO2
CO3
Colchester
Layer-de-la-Haye
CO5
West Mersea
CO4
CO6
Bures
Tollesbury
CO9
Tiptree
CM9
Witham
CM8
Maldon
CM0
Southminster
Burnham-on-Crouch
Tillingham
SS3 Great Wakering
Canewdon
SS4
Rochford
SS5
Rayleigh
SS6
Hatfield Peverel
Danbury
CM3
East Hanningfield
Cold Norton
SS11
Wickford
SS12
SS13
SS14 Basildon
SS16
SS15
SS7
Hadleigh
SS8
Canvey Island
SS9
Southend-on-Sea
SS1
SS2
SS0
Stanford-le-Hope
SS17
Glemsford
Clare
Sudbury
Haverhill
Belchamp St Paul
CO10
Castle Hedingham
CO8
Steeple Bumpstead
CB9
CB1
Halstead
Earls Colne
Coggeshall
CM77
Braintree
CM7
Great Bardfield
Stebbing
Great Dunmow
CM6
Great Samford
Thaxted
Great Leighs
CM1
Broomfield
Chelmsford
CM2
CM4
Stock
Billericay
CM12
Ingrave
CM13
Brentwood
CM14
CM15
Chipping Ongar
CM5
Hatfield Heath
CM17
CM24
Elsenham
Stansted Mountfitchet
CM22
CM23
Bishop's Stortford
CM21
Sawbridgeworth
SG12
Harlow
CM20
CM19
CM18
CM16
Epping
EN9
Waltham Abbey
EN11
EN10
EN8
EN3
Loughton
IG10
Abridge
RM4
IG7
Chingford
E4
E17
Woodford
IG8
IG9
IG6
IG5
IG4
IG3
IG2
IG1
Barking
IG11
RM9
RM8
RM10
Romford
RM7
RM5
RM6
RM1
RM2
RM3
RM11
Upminster
RM14
RM12
RM13
RM15
RM16
RM17
RM18
Tilbury
RM19
RM20
DA1
DA2
DA9
DA8
DA11
DA12
DA17
DA18
Great Chesterford
CB11
Saffron Walden
Newport
Clavering
CM10
Ive Green
SG9
SG8

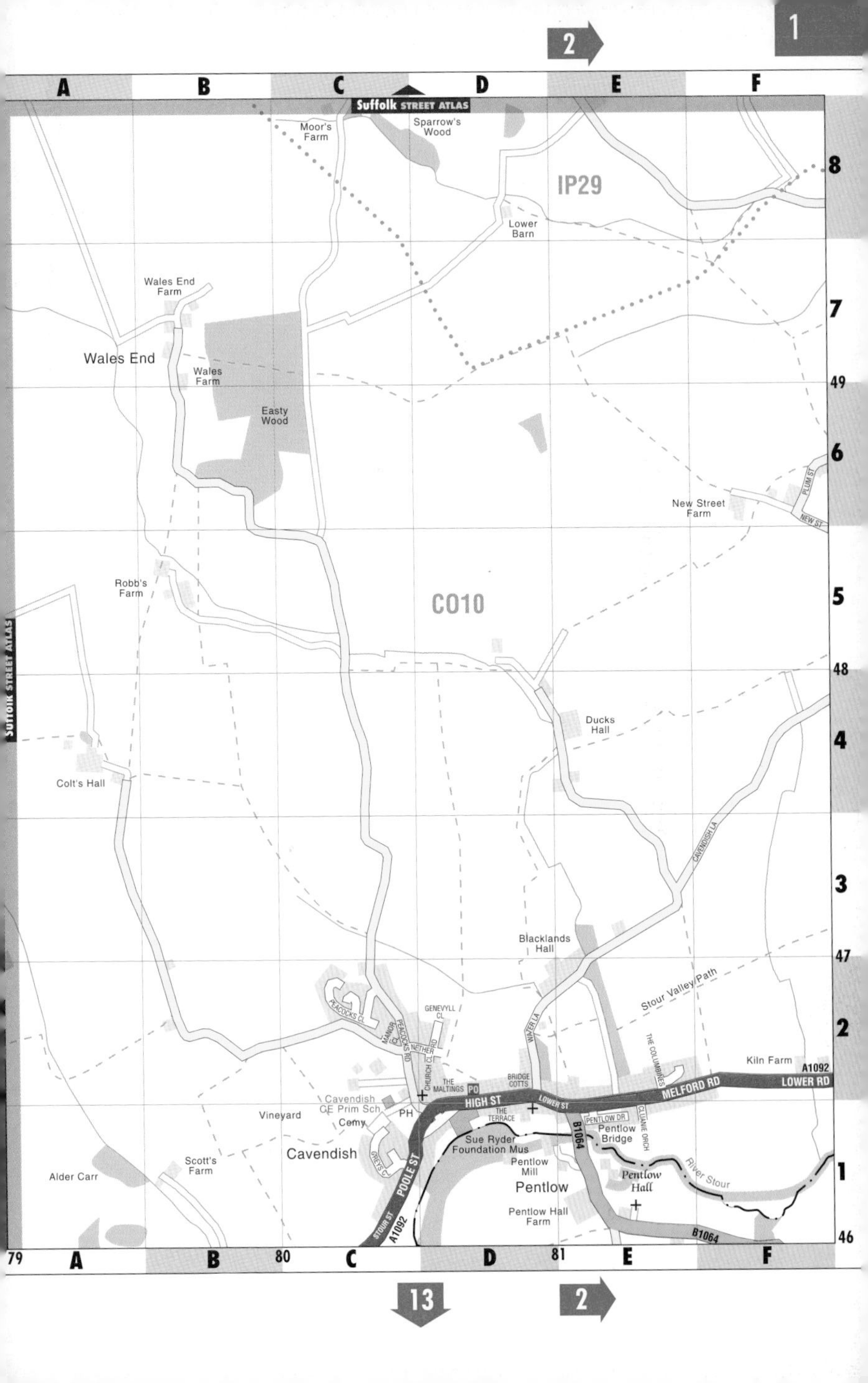

Suffolk STREET ATLAS

A   B   C   D   E   F

Moor's Farm

Sparrow's Wood

IP29

Lower Barn

8

Wales End Farm

7

Wales End

Wales Farm

49

Easty Wood

6

New Street Farm

R LAM ST

NEW ST

Robb's Farm

CO10

5

48

Ducks Hall

4

CAVENDISH LA

Colt's Hall

3

47

Blacklands Hall

Stour Valley Path

GENEYVLL CL

2

Kiln Farm

A1092

THE COLNMBRES

MELFORD RD

LOWER RD

PLACE CL

MANSE TER

NETHER

CHURCH

THE MALTINGS

PO

HIGH ST

BRIDGE COTTS

LOWER ST

PENTLOW DR

B1064

Cavendish CE Prim Sch

Vineyard

PH

Cemy

THE TERRACE

Pentlow Bridge

COLNE ORCH

River Stour

1

Sue Ryder Foundation Mus

Pentlow Mill

Pentlow Hall

Scott's Farm

Cavendish

POOLE ST

Pentlow

Alder Carr

RIDING ST

A1092

Pentlow Hall Farm

B1064

46

79   A   B   80   C   D   81   E   F

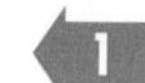

1

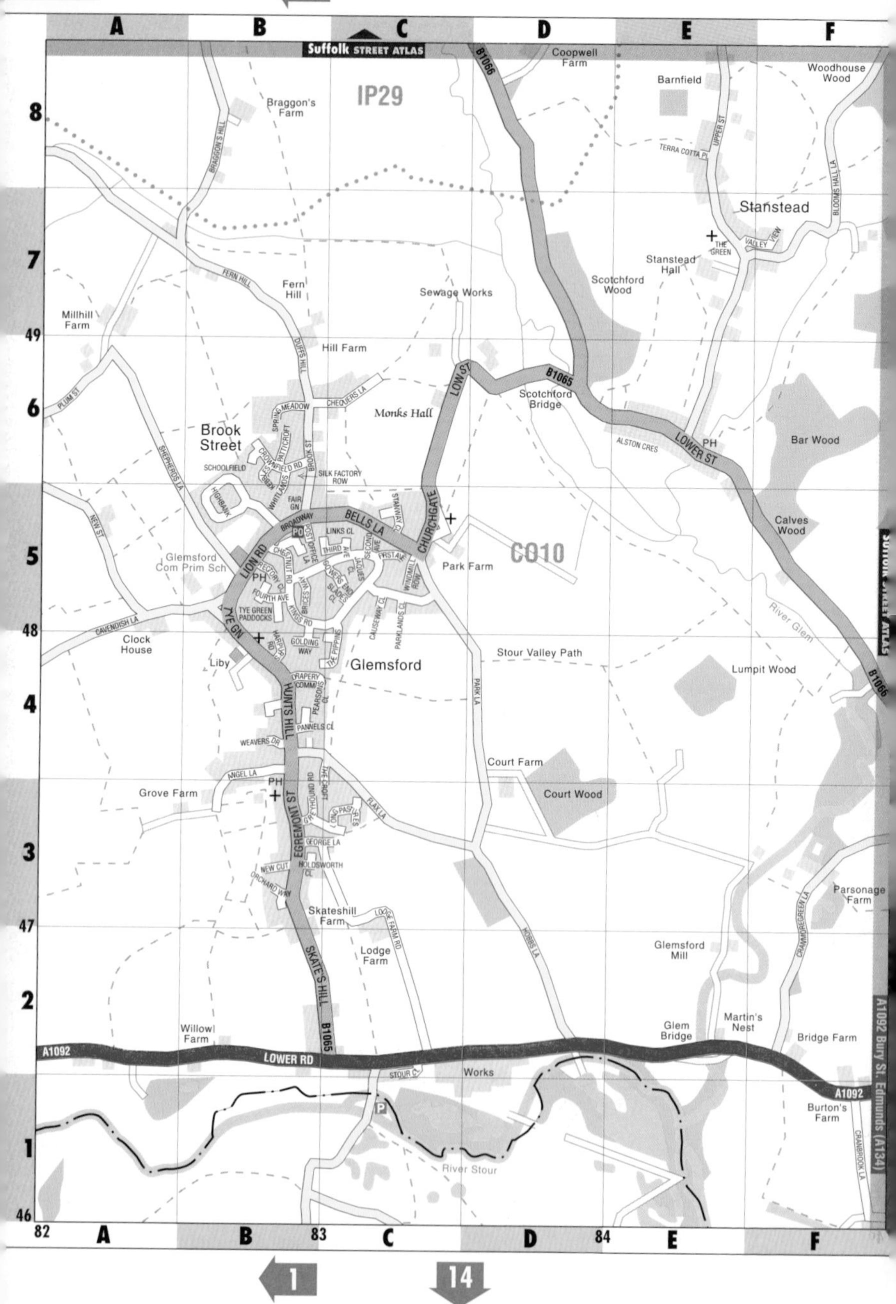

Suffolk STREET ATLAS
A
B
C
D
E
F
8
7
6
5
4
3
2
1
49
48
47
46
82
83
84
IP29
CO10
Coopwell Farm
Barnfield
Woodhouse Wood
Braggon's Farm
BRAGGON'S HILL
B1066
UPPER ST
TERRA COTTA PL
BLOOMS HALL LA
Stanstead
THE GREEN
VALLEY VIEW
Stanstead Hall
Scotchford Wood
FERN HILL
Fern Hill
Sewage Works
Millhill Farm
Hill Farm
DUFFS HILL
LOW ST
B1065
Scotchford Bridge
PLUM ST
CHEQUERS LA
MEADOW
Monks Hall
Brook Street
SPRING
PATTICROFT
BROOK ST
SCHOOLFIELD
CROWNFIELD RD
SILK FACTORY ROW
ALSTON CRES
LOWER ST
PH
Bar Wood
SHEPHERDS LA
HIGHBANK
WHITLANDS
FAIR GN
BROADWAY
BELLS LA
STAIRWAY CL
CHURCHGATE
NEW ST
PO
LINKS CL
THIRD AVE
SECOND AVE
FIRST AVE
Calves Wood
Glemsford Com Prim Sch
LION RD
CHESTNUT RD
POST OFFICE LA
JACQUES CL
Park Farm
RECTORY CL
WINDMILL ROW
FOURTH AVE
TYE GREEN PADDOCKS
KINGS RD
CAUSEWAY CL
PARKLANDS CL
River Glem
CAVENDISH LA
TYE GN
48
Clock House
HARPUR RD
GOLDING WAY
THE PIPPINS
Stour Valley Path
Liby
Glemsford
Lumpit Wood
DRAPERY COMM
PARK LA
HUNTS HILL
PEARSONS CL
PANNELS CL
WEAVERS DR
Court Farm
ANGEL LA
Grove Farm
GREYHOUND RD
THE CROFT
Court Wood
FLAX LA
LONG PASTURES
EGREMONT ST
GEORGE LA
HOLDSWORTH CL
NEW CUT
ORCHARD WAY
Parsonage Farm
Skateshill Farm
LODGE FARM RD
Lodge Farm
HOBBS LA
Glemsford Mill
CRANMOREGREEN LA
SKATE'S HILL
B1065
Willow Farm
Glem Bridge
Martin's Nest
Bridge Farm
A1092
LOWER RD
STOUR CL
Works
A1092 Bury St. Edmunds (A134)
P
Burton's Farm
River Stour
CRANBROOK LA
14

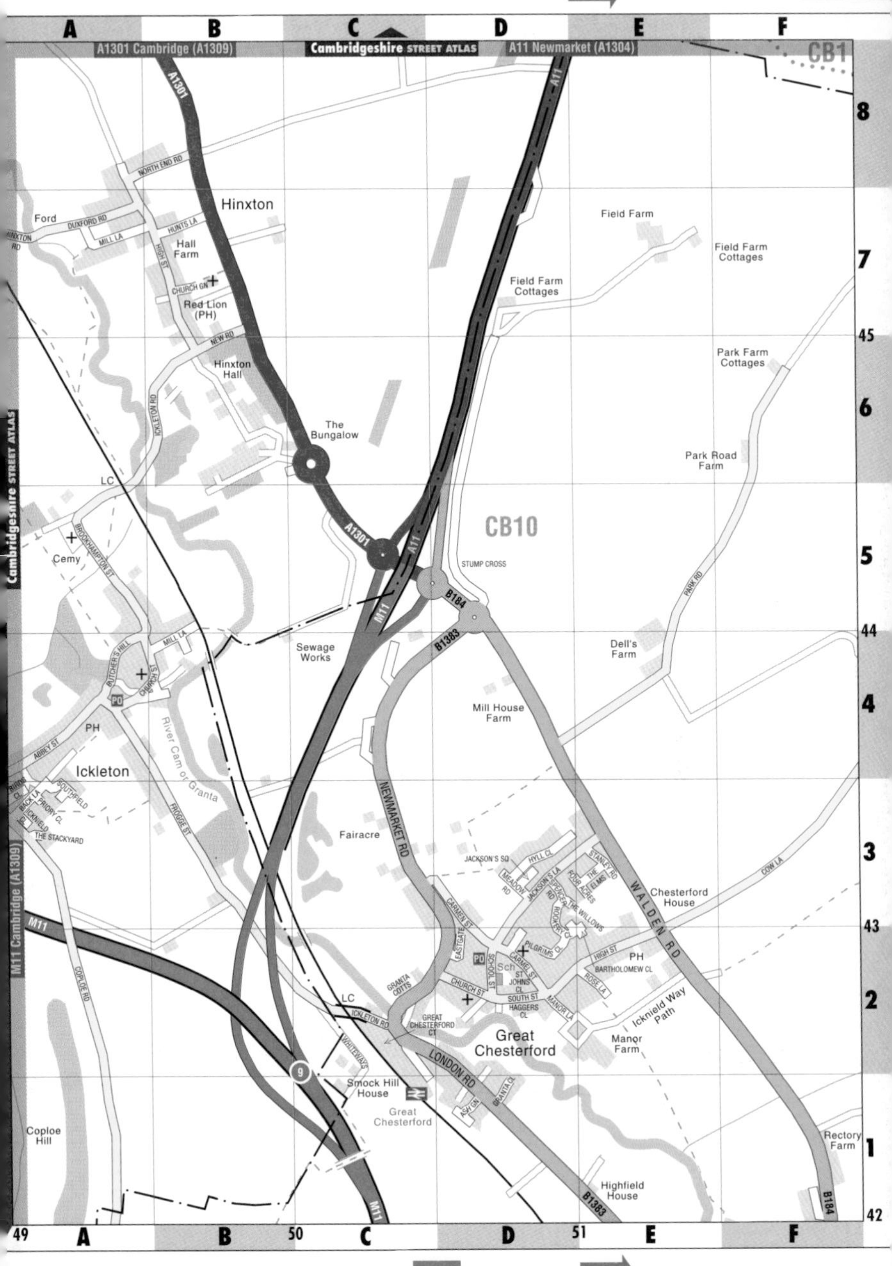

A1301 Cambridge (A1309)
A11 Newmarket (A1304)
CB1

Cambridgeshire STREET ATLAS

M11 Cambridge (A1309)

A1301

A11

Ford

Hinxton

Field Farm

Field Farm Cottages

DUXFORD RD

MILL LA

HINXTON RD

NORTH END RD

HUNTS LA

Hall Farm

CHURCH LN

Red Lion (PH)

NEW RD

Field Farm Cottages

Park Farm Cottages

Hinxton Hall

The Bungalow

Park Road Farm

LC

A1301

AVE

CB10

STUMP CROSS

Cemy

B184

Dell's Farm

FRINE RD

B1383

Sewage Works

Mill House Farm

MILL LA

BUTCHER'S HILL

PO

River Cam or Granta

PH

NEWMARKET RD

Ickleton

Fairacre

JACKSON'S SQ

RYTE CL

WALDEN RD

Chesterford House

COW LA

MINT ST

THE ELMS

THE WILLOWS

CASTLE ST

M11

COLLIER RD

BACK LA

PRIORY CL

THE STACKYARD

LC

ROCHESTER

CASTLE END

HIGH ST

BARTHOLOMEW CL

PH

ICKLETON RD

GT CHESTERFORD CT

PO

JOHN'S

Sch

CHURCH ST

SOUTH ST

HAGGERS CL

Icknield Way Path

GRANTA COTTS

WHITTAKERS

NEWARK RD

HILL ST

MANOR LA

Great Chesterford

Manor Farm

LONDON RD

Smock Hill House

Great Chesterford

Coploe Hill

Highfield House

B1383

Rectory Farm

B184

Cambridgeshire STREET ATLAS

	A	B	C	D	E	F

8

Hildersham Wood

Mast

Park Farm

7

CB1

45

Catley Park

6

Grumble Hall

Crave Hall Farm

5

COW LA

Icknield Way Path

44

Burtonwood Farm

4

Burton Wood

Great Chesterford Common

Little Paddocks

Icknield Way Path

3

CB10

Paddock Wood

43

Park Farm

Bassingbourne Wood

Burntwood End

2

Lady Plantation

Fishpond Plantation

Home Farm

Sewage Works

Ashwell's Grove

1

Chesterford Park

42

52	A	B	53	C	D	54	E	F

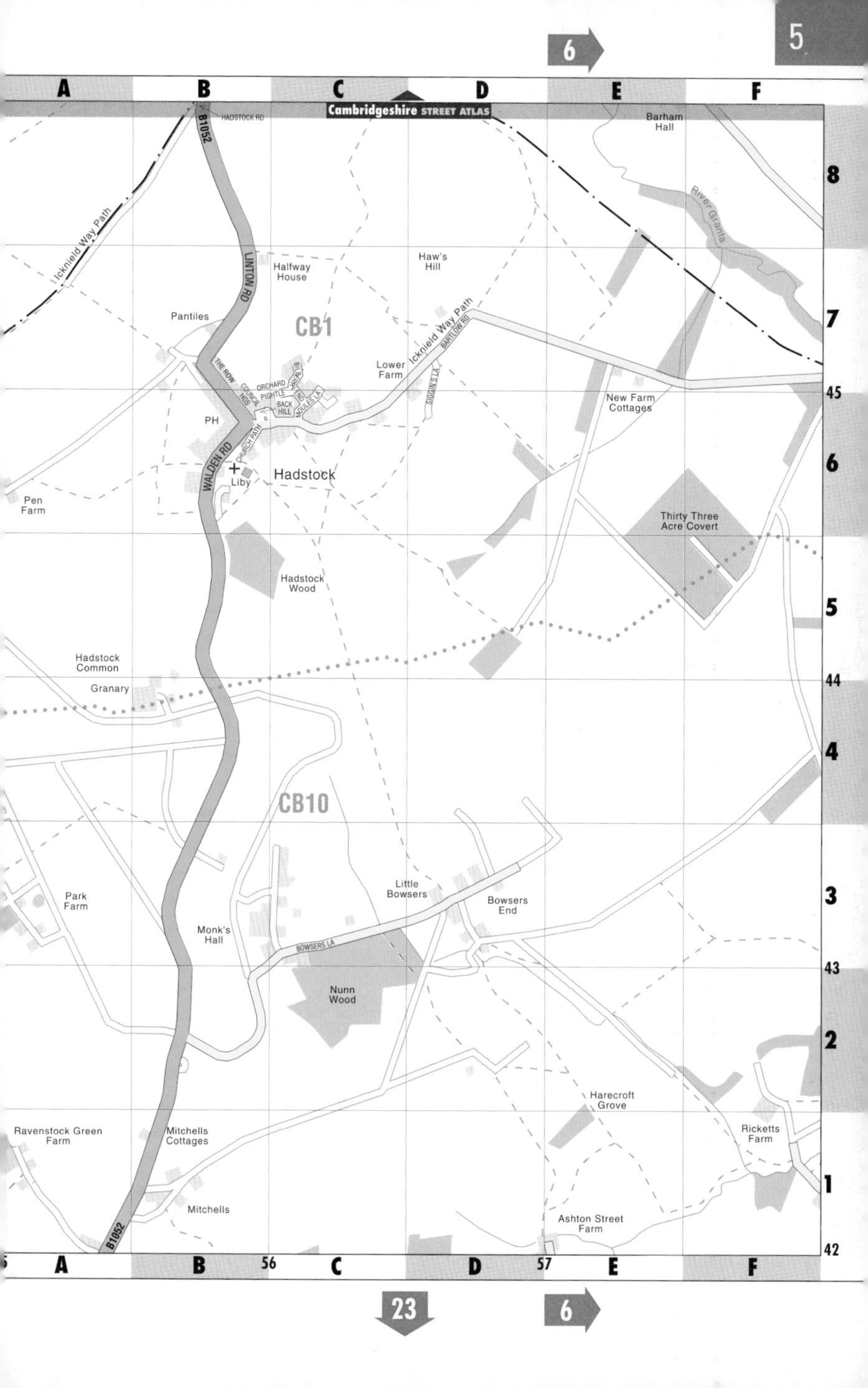

A B C D E F

8

7

45

6

5

44

4

3

43

2

1

42

Barham Hall

River Granta

Icknield Way Path

HADSTOCK RD

B1052

LINTON RD

Halfway House

Haw's Hill

CB1

Pantiles

Icknield Way Path

BRIDEWELL

THE BOW

CHURCH PATH

ORCHARD

PIGHTLE

Lower Farm

SUGDEN'S LA

BACK HILL

ENDEAVOUR

New Farm Cottages

PH

PINCH PATH

WALDEN RD

✠
Liby

Hadstock

Pen Farm

Thirty Three Acre Covert

Hadstock Wood

Hadstock Common

Granary

CB10

Park Farm

Monk's Hall

Little Bowsers

Bowsers End

BOWSERS LA

Nunn Wood

Harecroft Grove

Ravenstock Green Farm

Mitchells Cottages

Ricketts Farm

Mitchells

B1052

Ashton Street Farm

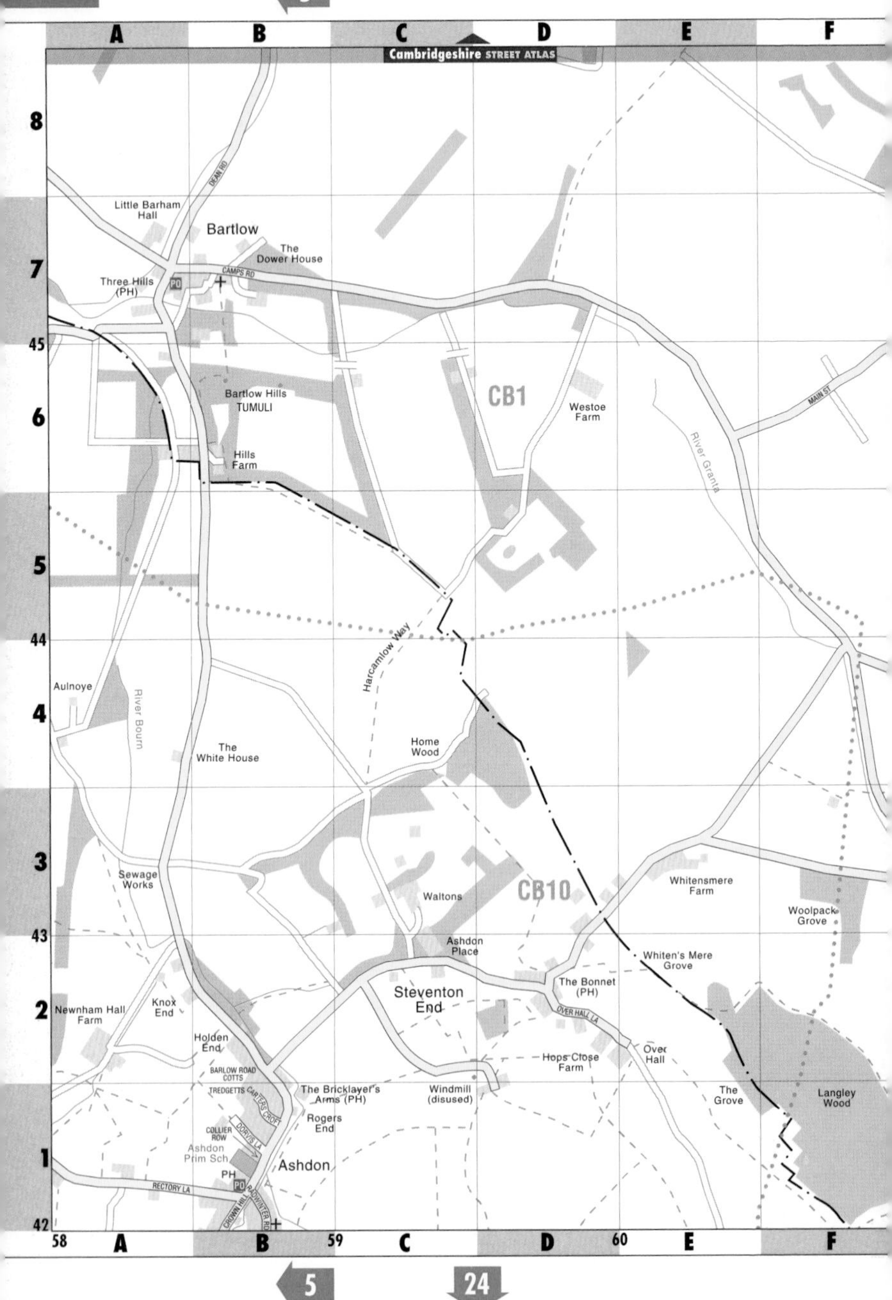

A B C D E F

8

Little Barham
Hall

Bartlow

The
Dower House

7

Three Hills
(PH)

CAMPS RD

45

Bartlow Hills
TUMULI

CB1

Westoe
Farm

6

Hills
Farm

River Granta

MAIN ST

5

Harcamlow Way

44

Aulnoye

River Bourn

4

The
White House

Home
Wood

3

Sewage
Works

Waltons

CB10

Whitensmere
Farm

Woolpack
Grove

43

Ashdon
Place

Newnham Hall
Farm

Knox
End

Steventon
End

The Bonnet
(PH)

Whiten's Mere
Grove

2

OVER HALL LA

Holden
End

BARLOW ROAD
COTTS

Over
Hall

TREDGETTS

The Bricklayer's
Arms (PH)

Rogers
End

Windmill
(disused)

Hops Close
Farm

The
Grove

Langley
Wood

COLLIER
ROW

1

Ashdon Prim Sch

PH

RECTORY LA

Ashdon

42

58 A B 59 C D 60 E F

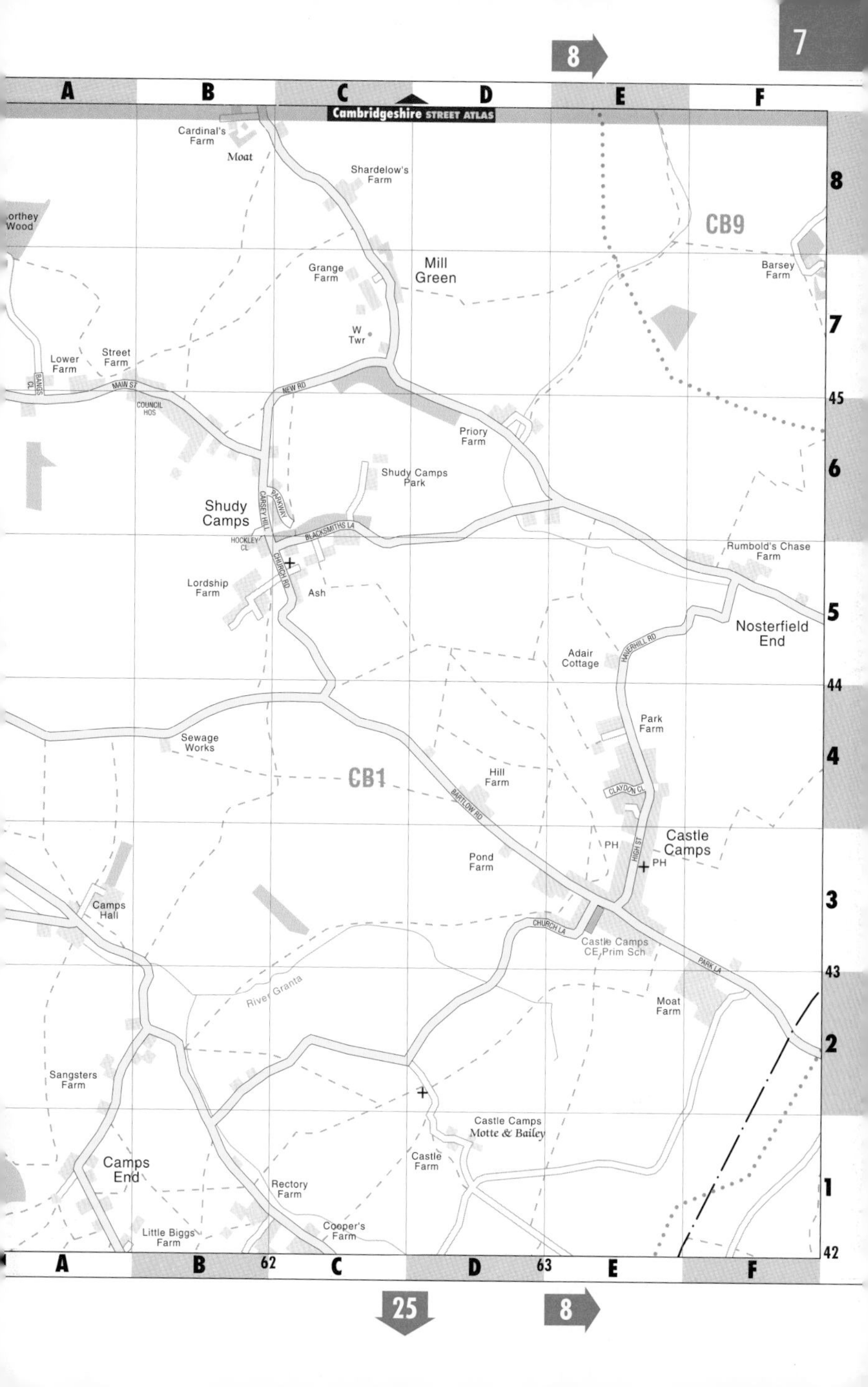

CAMBRIDGESHIRE STREET ATLAS

A **B** **C** **D** **E** **F**

8

CB9

orthey
Wood

Cardinal's
Farm

Moat

Shardelow's
Farm

Grange
Farm

Mill
Green

Barsey
Farm

7

Lower
Farm

Street
Farm

W
Twr

MAWS ST

NEW RD

45

COUNCIL
HOS

Priory
Farm

6

Shudy Camps
Park

Shudy
Camps

CASSELL

BLACKSMITHS LA

Rumbold's Chase
Farm

HOCKLEY
CL

Lordship
Farm

Ash

CHURCH RD

Nosterfield
End

5

Adair
Cottage

HAVERHILL RD

44

Sewage
Works

Park
Farm

CB1

Hill
Farm

CLAYTON LA

4

BARTLOW RD

PH

HIGH ST

Castle
Camps

PH

Pond
Farm

3

Camps
Hall

CHURCH LA

Castle Camps
CE Prim Sch

PARK LA

43

River Granta

Moat
Farm

2

Sangsters
Farm

Castle Camps
Motte & Bailey

Camps
End

Castle
Farm

1

Rectory
Farm

Little Biggs
Farm

Cooper's
Farm

42

A **B** 62 **C** **D** 63 **E** **F**

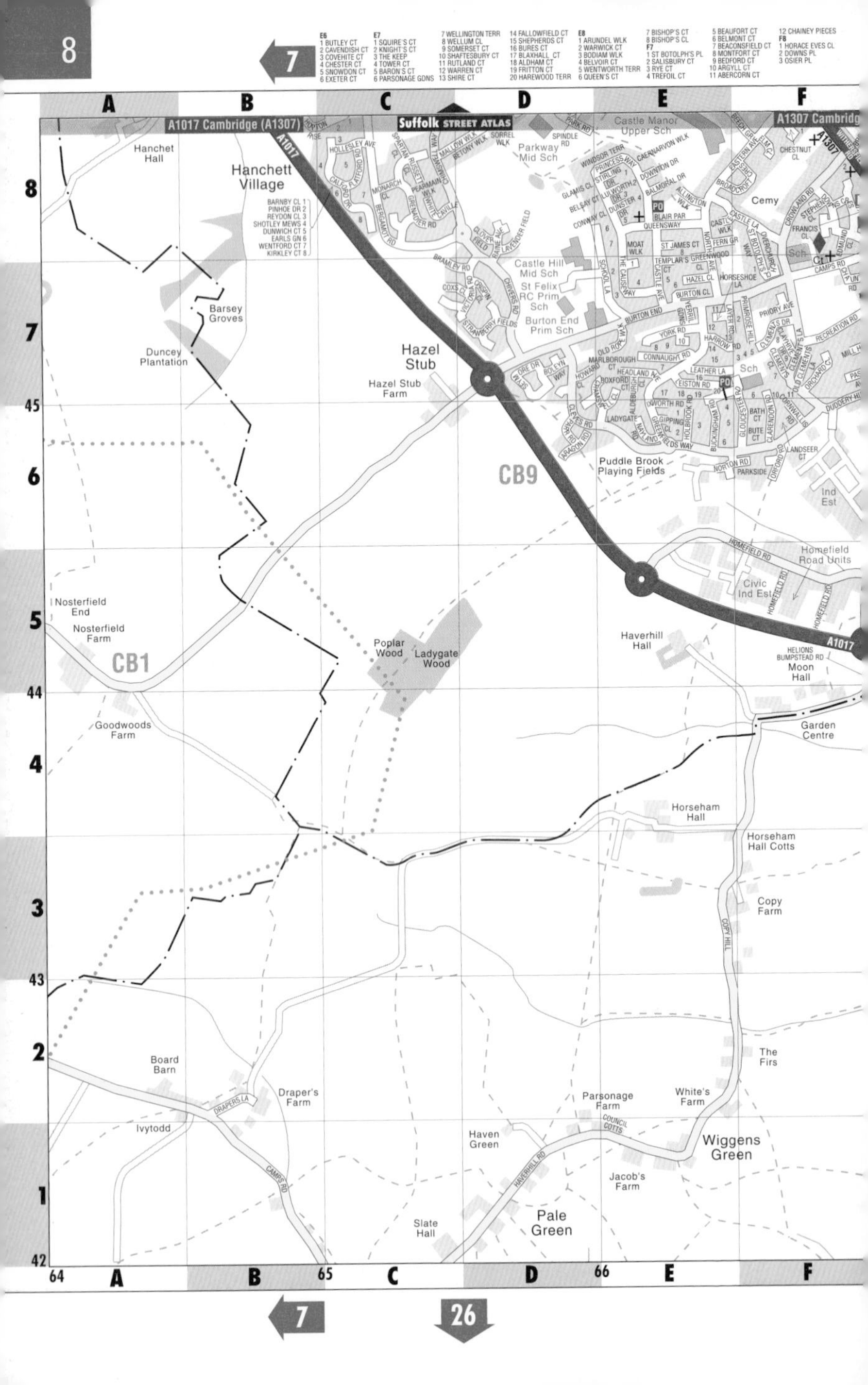

7

E6
1 BUTLEY CT
2 CAVENDISH CT
3 COVEHITE CT
4 CHESTER CT
5 SNOWDON CT
6 EXETER CT

E7
1 SQUIRE'S CT
2 KNIGHT'S CT
3 THE KEEP
4 TOWER CT
5 BARON'S CT
6 PARSONAGE GDNS

7 WELLINGTON TERR
8 WELLUM CL
9 SOMERSET CT
10 SHAFTESBURY CT
11 RUTLAND CT
12 WARREN CT
13 SHIRE CT

14 FALLOWFIELD CT
15 SHEPHERDS CT
16 BURES CT
17 BLAXHALL CT
18 ALDHAM CT
19 FRITTON CT
20 HAREWOOD TERR

E8
1 ARUNDEL WLK
2 WARWICK CT
3 BODIAM WLK
4 BELVOIR CT
5 WENTWORTH TERR
6 QUEEN'S CT

7 BISHOP'S CT
8 BISHOP'S CL
F7
1 ST BOTOLPH'S PL
2 SALISBURY CT
3 RYE CT
4 TREFOIL CT

5 BEAUFORT CT
6 BELMONT CT
7 BEACONSFIELD CT
8 MONTFORT CT
9 BEDFORD CT
10 ARGYLL CT
11 ABERCORN CT

12 CHAINEY PIECES
F8
1 HORACE EVES CL
2 DOWNS PL
3 OSIER PL

Suffolk STREET ATLAS

A1017 Cambridge (A1307)

A1307 Cambridge

Hanchet Hall

Hanchett Village

Hanchet Hall

BARNBY CL 1
PINHOE DR 2
REYDON CL 3
SHOTLEY MEWS 4
DUNWICH CT 5
EARLS GN 6
WENTFORD CT 7
KIRKLEY CT 8

Castle Manor Upper Sch

Cemy

Barsey Groves

Parkway Mid Sch

Duncey Plantation

Castle Hill Mid Sch
St Felix RC Prim Sch

Hazel Stub

Burton End Prim Sch

Hazel Stub Farm

CB9

Puddle Brook Playing Fields

Ind Est

Homefield Road Units

Civic Ind Este

Nosterfield End

Nosterfield Farm

CB1

Poplar Wood

Ladgate Wood

Haverhill Hall

HELIONS BUMPSTEAD RD
Moon Hall

A1017

Garden Centre

Goodwoods Farm

Horseham Hall

Horseham Hall Cotts

Copy Farm

Board Barn

Draper's Farm

The Firs

Ivytodd

Parsonage Farm

White's Farm

Haven Green

Wiggens Green

Jacob's Farm

Slate Hall

Pale Green

64
65
66

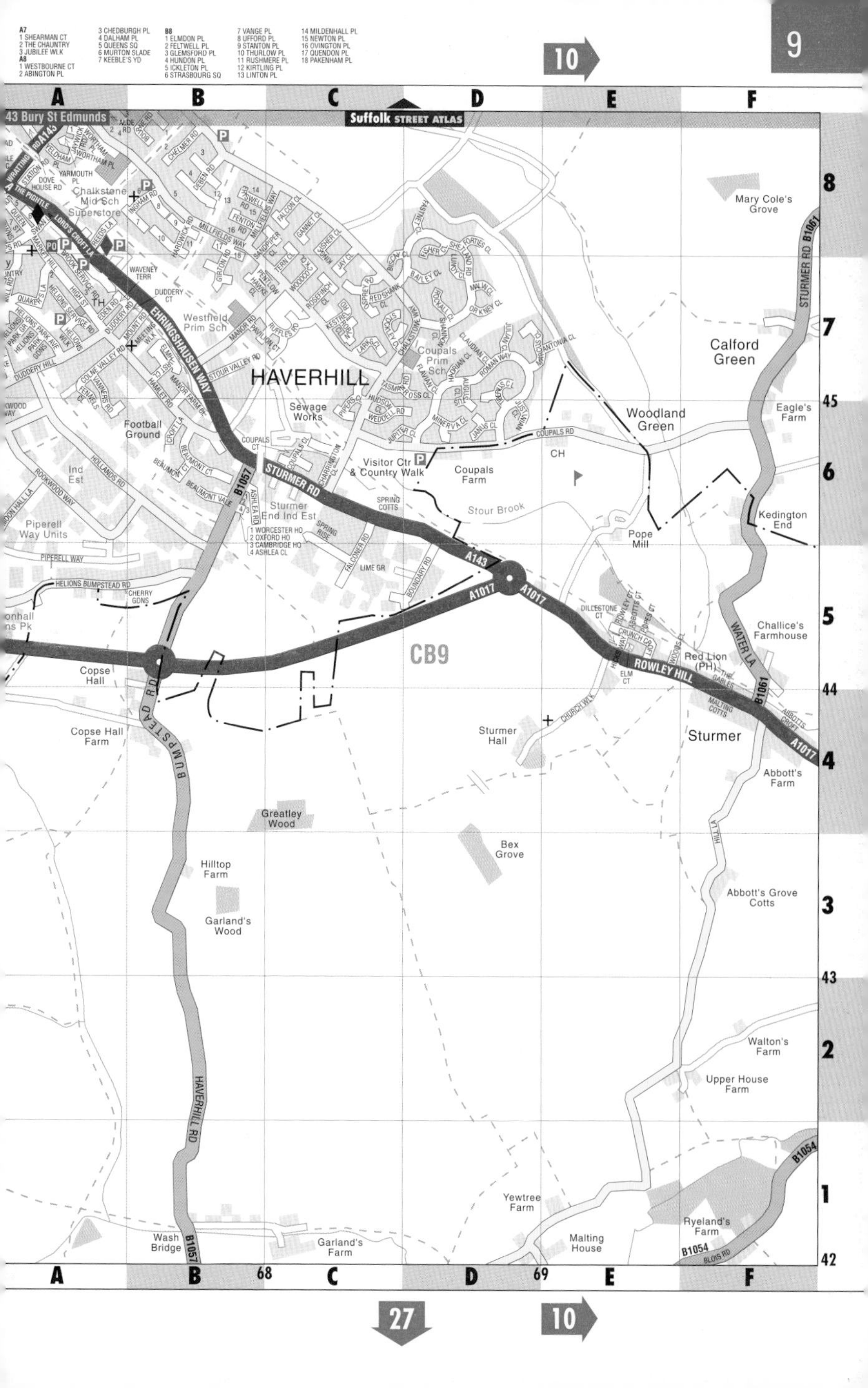
A7
1 SHEARMAN CT
2 THE CHAUNTRY
3 JUBILEE WLK
A8
1 WESTBOURNE CT
2 ABINGTON PL
3 CHEDBURGH PL
4 DALHAM PL
5 QUEENS SQ
6 MURTON SLADE
7 KEEBLE'S YD
B8
1 ELMDON PL
2 FELTWELL PL
3 GLEMSFORD PL
4 HUNDON PL
5 ICKLETON PL
6 STRASBOURG SQ
7 VANGE PL
8 UFFORD PL
9 STANTON PL
10 THURLOW PL
11 RUSHMERE PL
12 KIRTLING PL
13 LINTON PL
14 MILDENHALL PL
15 NEWTON PL
16 OVINGTON PL
17 QUENDON PL
18 PAKENHAM PL
10
9
43 Bury St Edmunds
Suffolk STREET ATLAS
Chalkstone Mid Sch
Superstore
WAVENEY TERR
DUDDERY CT
Westfield Prim Sch
EHRINGSHAUSEN WAY
STOUR VALLEY RD
HAVERHILL
Sewage Works
Coupals Prim Sch
Football Ground
Ind Est
Piperell Way Units
PIPERELL WAY
HELIONS BUMPSTEAD RD
CHERRY GDNS
COUPALS CT
STURMER RD
B1057
Sturmer End Ind Est
1 WORCESTER HO
2 OXFORD HO
3 CAMBRIDGE HO
4 ASHLEA CL
SPRING COTTS
SPRING RISE
LIME GR
FALCONER RD
BOUNDARY RD
Visitor Ctr & Country Walk
Coupals Farm
COUPALS RD
CH
Stour Brook
Woodland Green
Pope Mill
A143
A1017
CB9
Copse Hall
Copse Hall Farm
BUMPSTEAD RD
Mary Cole's Grove
STURMER RD B1061
Calford Green
Eagle's Farm
Kedington End
Challice's Farmhouse
WATER LA
Red Lion (PH)
ROWLEY HILL
DILLESTONE CT
ELM CT
CHURCH WLK
Sturmer Hall
Sturmer
MALTING COTTS
ABBOTTS CROFT
Abbott's Farm
Greatley Wood
Bex Grove
Hilltop Farm
Garland's Wood
Abbott's Grove Cotts
HILL LA
Walton's Farm
Upper House Farm
HAVERHILL RD
B1054
Yewtree Farm
Ryeland's Farm
Malting House
BLOIS RD
Wash Bridge
Garland's Farm
A B C D E F
8 7 45 6 5 44 4 3 43 2 1 42
68 69
27
10

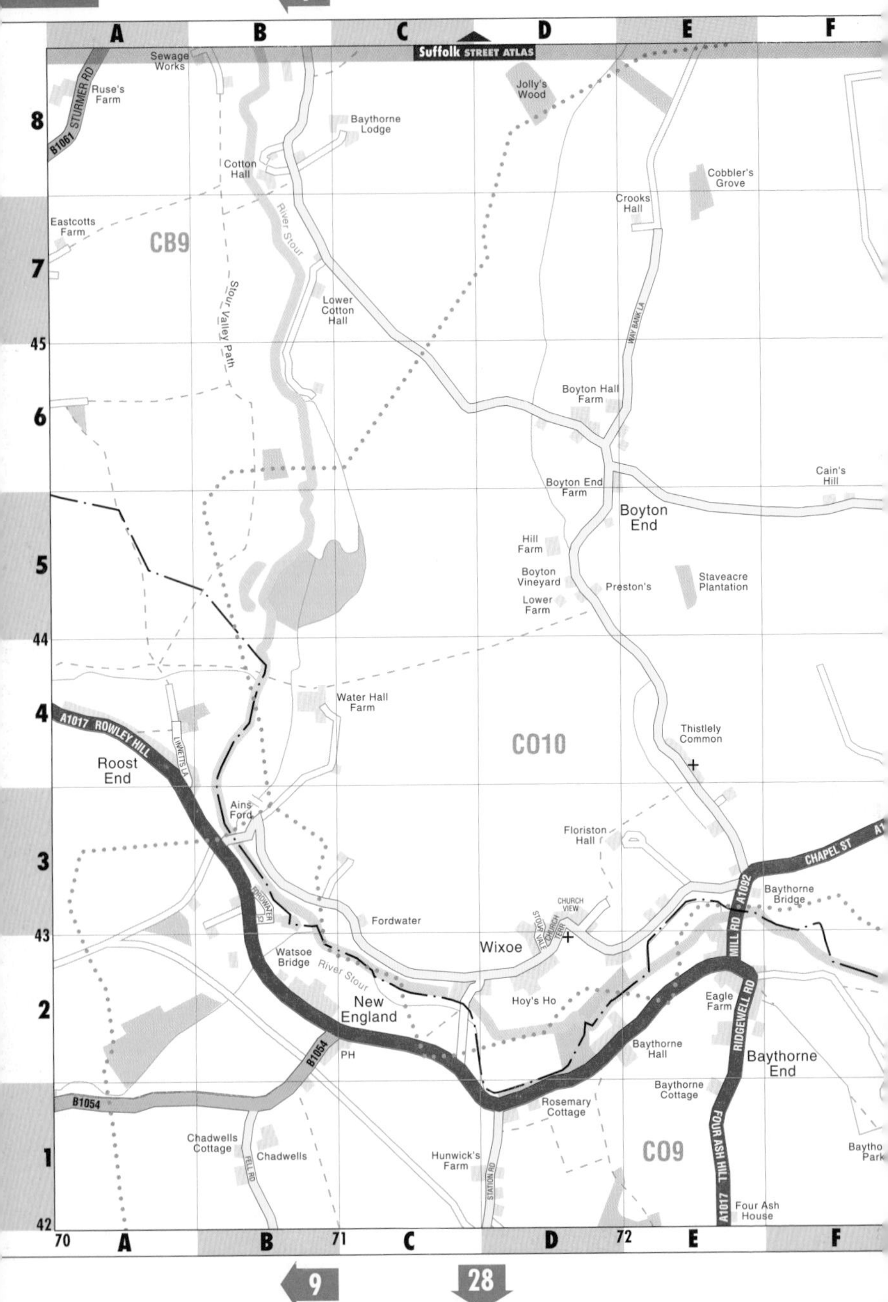

A B C D E F

8

Sewage
Works

Ruse's
Farm

Baythorne
Lodge

Jolly's
Wood

Cotton
Hall

Crooks
Hall

Cobbler's
Grove

Eastcotts
Farm

CB9

7

45

B1061 STURMER RD

River Stour

Stour Valley Path

Lower
Cotton
Hall

WAY BACK LA

Boyton Hall
Farm

6

Boyton End
Farm

Boyton
End

Cain's
Hill

5

Hill
Farm

Boyton
Vineyard

Preston's

Staveacre
Plantation

44

Lower
Farm

Water Hall
Farm

4

A1017 ROWLEY HILL

CO10

Thistlely
Common

Roost
End

LIMETREE

Ains
Ford

Floriston
Hall

Baythorne
Bridge

3

CHAPEL ST

A1092

A1

43

CHURCH
VIEW

STOUR CRES

Fordwater

Wixoe

MILL RD

Watsoe
Bridge

River Stour

Hoy's Ho

Eagle
Farm

2

New
England

B1054

Baythorne
Hall

RIDGEWELL RD

Baythorne
End

B1054

PH

Baythorne
Cottage

Baytho
Park

FOUR ASH HILL

Rosemary
Cottage

CO9

1

Chadwells
Cottage

Chadwells

Hunwick's
Farm

Four Ash
House

A1017

42

70 A B 71 C D 72 E F

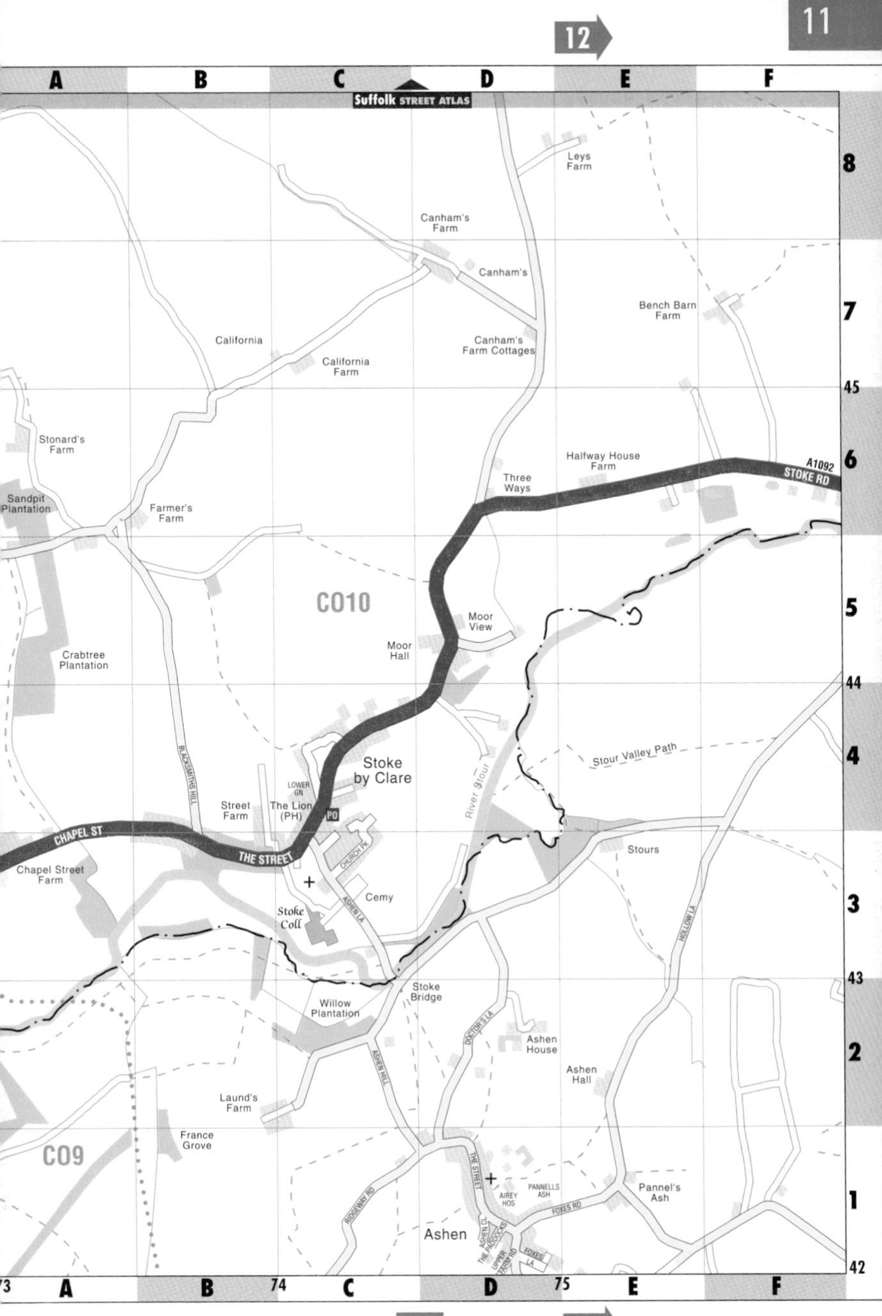

Suffolk STREET ATLAS

A   B   C   D   E   F

8

Leys Farm

Canham's Farm

7

Canham's

California

California Farm

Canham's Farm Cottages

Bench Barn Farm

45

Stonard's Farm

A1092

6

Sandpit Plantation

Farmer's Farm

Three Ways

Halfway House Farm

STOKE RD

CO10

Moor View

5

Crabtree Plantation

Moor Hall

44

Stour Valley Path

4

BLACKSMITHS HILL

Stoke by Clare

River Stour

Street Farm

LOWER GN

The Lion (PH)

PO

Chapel Street Farm

CHAPEL ST

THE STREET

Stours

AGNES LA

CHURCH PK

Cemy

3

Stoke Coll

+

43

Willow Plantation

Stoke Bridge

2

Ashen House

Ashen Hall

Laund's Farm

POTTER LA

AGNES HALL

France Grove

RIDGEMENT RD

THE BOSTOCK

PANNELLS ASH

Pannel's Ash

1

+

AIREY HOS

FOXES RD

LOWERE LA

Ashen

FOXES LA

42

CO9

'3 A   B 74 C   D 75 E   F

11

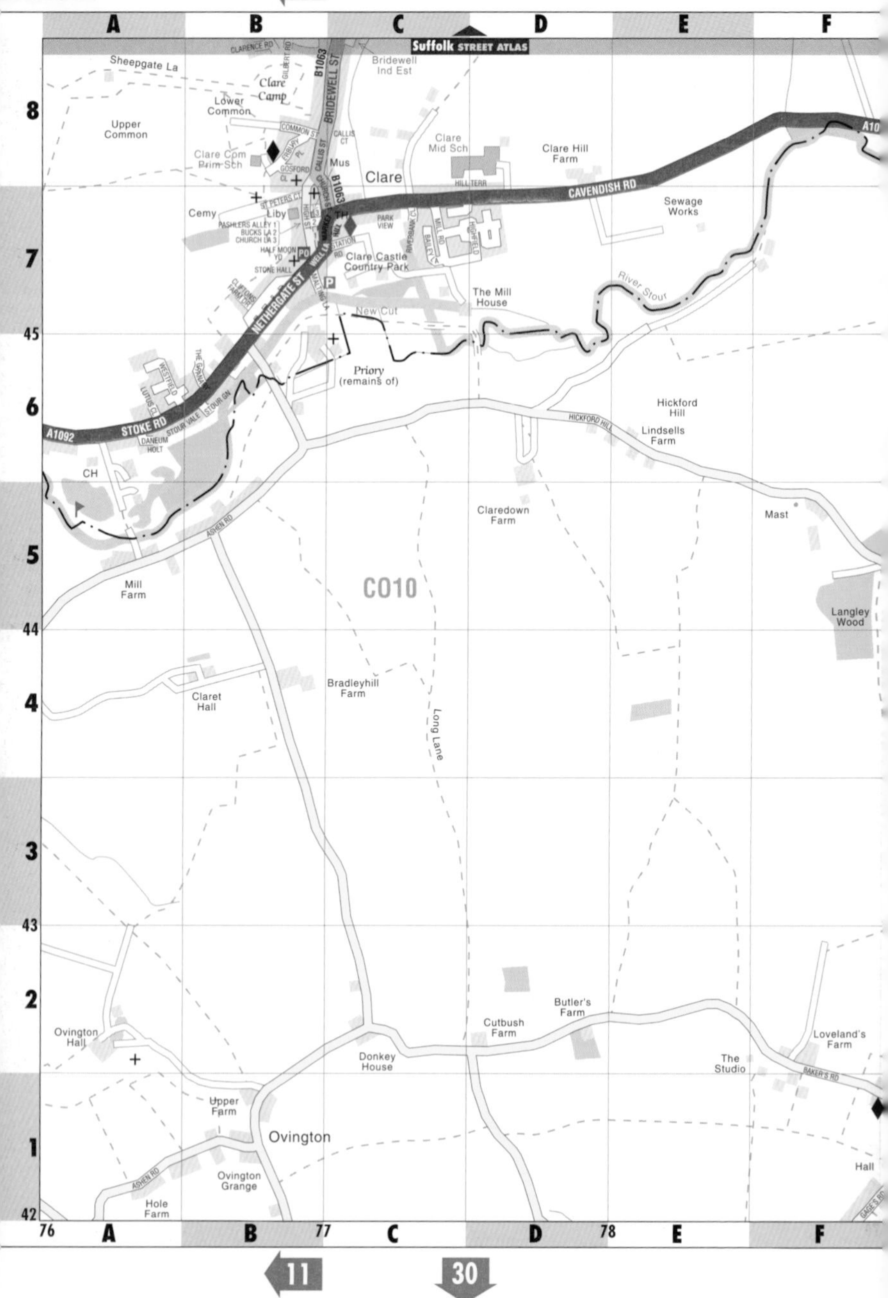
Suffolk STREET ATLAS
Sheepgate La
Clare Camp
Lower Common
Upper Common
Clare Com Prim Sch
Bridewell Ind Est
BRIDEWELL ST
B1063
Clare Mid Sch
Clare Hill Farm
Mus
Clare
CAVENDISH RD
Sewage Works
Cemy
Liby
TH
PASHLERS ALLEY 1
BUCKS LA 2
CHURCH LA 3
Clare Castle Country Park
NETHERGATE ST
The Mill House
River Stour
New Cut
Priory (remains of)
STOKE RD
A1092
STOUR VALE
STOUR GN
DANEUM HOLT
Hickford Hill
HICKFORD HILL
Lindsells Farm
CH
Claredown Farm
Mast
ASHEN RD
Mill Farm
CO10
Langley Wood
Bradleyhill Farm
Claret Hall
Long Lane
Butler's Farm
Cutbush Farm
Ovington Hall
Donkey House
Loveland's Farm
The Studio
BAKER'S RD
Upper Farm
Ovington
Ovington Grange
Hole Farm
Hall
GAGE'S RD
A B C D E F
8 7 6 5 4 3 2 1
45 44 43 42
76 77 78

11
30

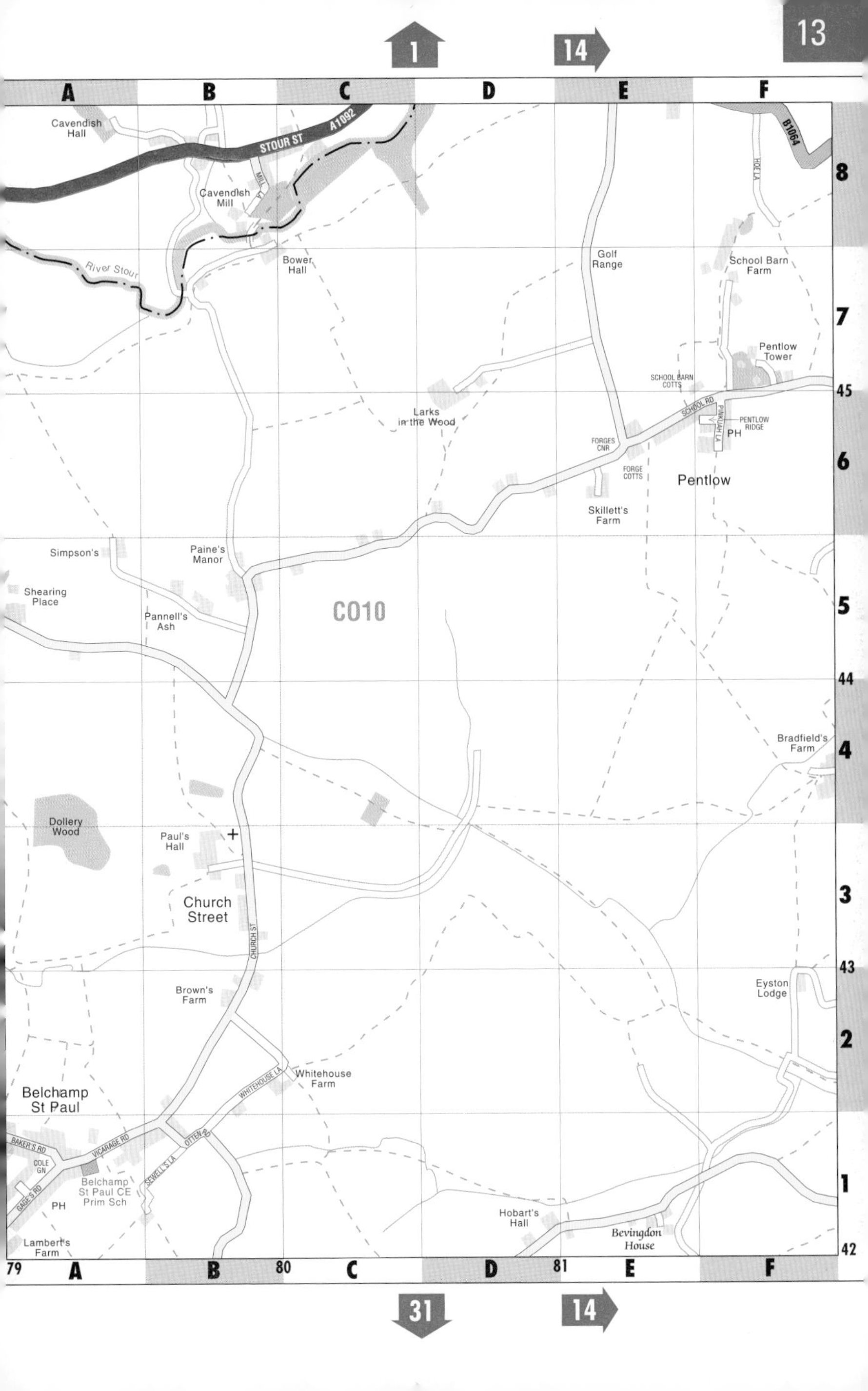
1
14
A
B
C
D
E
F
Cavendish Hall
STOUR ST
A1092
B1064
HOE LA
MILL LA
Cavendish Mill
River Stour
Bower Hall
Golf Range
School Barn Farm
Pentlow Tower
SCHOOL BARN COTTS
SCHOOL RD
PINKUAH LA
PENTLOW RIDGE
PH
Larks in the Wood
FORGES CNR
FORGE COTTS
Pentlow
Skillett's Farm
Simpson's
Paine's Manor
Shearing Place
Pannell's Ash
CO10
Bradfield's Farm
Dollery Wood
Paul's Hall
Church Street
CHURCH ST
Eyston Lodge
Brown's Farm
Whitehouse Farm
WHITEHOUSE LA
Belchamp St Paul
BAKER'S RD
VICARAGE RD
COLE GN
GAGE'S RD
OTTEN RD
SEWELL'S LA
Belchamp St Paul CE Prim Sch
PH
Hobart's Hall
Bevingdon House
Lambert's Farm
8
7
45
6
5
44
4
3
43
2
1
42
79
80
81
31
14

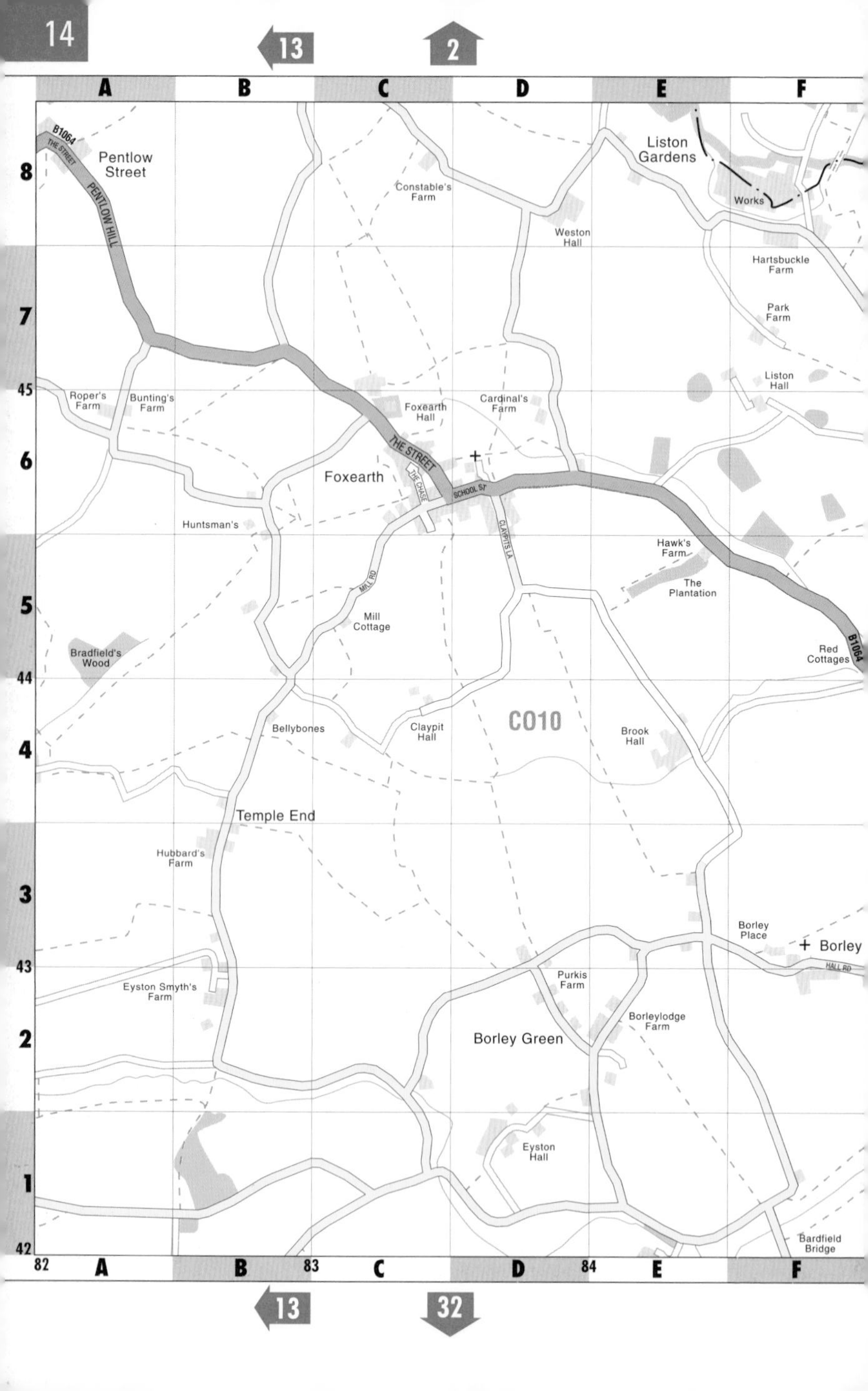

13
2
A
B
C
D
E
F
B1064
THE STREET
Pentlow Street
PENTLOW HILL
Constable's Farm
Liston Gardens
Works
Weston Hall
Hartsbuckle Farm
Park Farm
Liston Hall
Roper's Farm
Bunting's Farm
Foxearth Hall
Cardinal's Farm
THE STREET
THE CHASE
SCHOOL ST
Foxearth
Huntsman's
CLAYPITS LA
Hawk's Farm
The Plantation
MILL RD
Mill Cottage
Bradfield's Wood
Red Cottages
B1064
Bellybones
Claypit Hall
CO10
Brook Hall
Temple End
Hubbard's Farm
Borley Place
Borley
HALL RD
Eyston Smyth's Farm
Purkis Farm
Borleylodge Farm
Borley Green
Eyston Hall
Bardfield Bridge
8
7
45
6
5
44
4
3
43
2
1
42
82
83
84
13
32

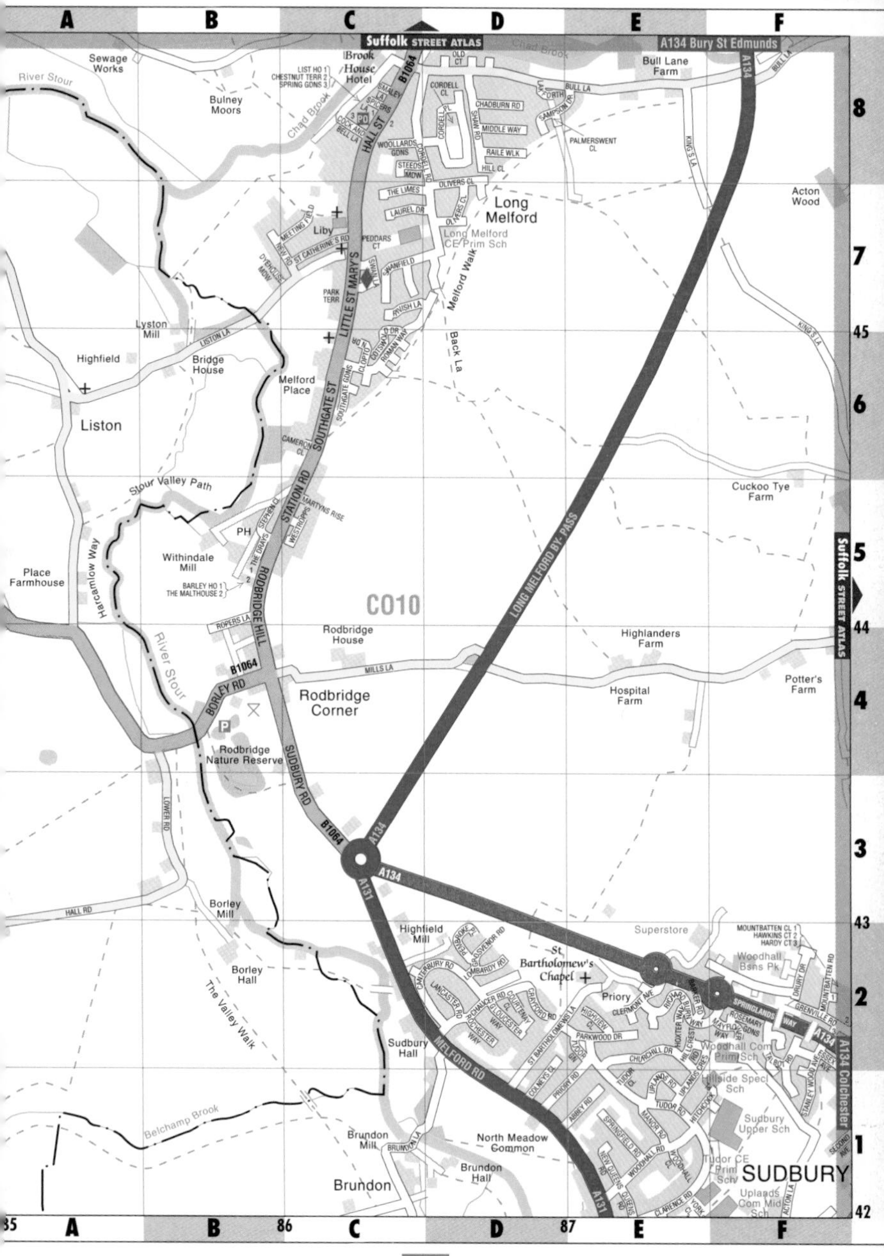

A134 Bury St Edmunds

Sewage Works

River Stour

Bulney Moors

Brook House Hotel

LIST HO
CHESTNUT TERR
SPRING GDNS

OLD CT

CORDELL CL

CHADBURN RD

MIDDLE WAY

RAILE WLK

HILL CL

PALMERSWENT CL

Bull Lane Farm

Acton Wood

WOODLANDS GDNS

STEEDS MDW

THE LIMES

LAUREL DR

OLIVERS CL

Long Melford

Liby

Long Melford CE Prim Sch

PEDDARS CT

PARK TERR

WINFIELD

RYSH LA

Melford Walk

Lyston Mill

Highfield

Bridge House

Melford Place

Back La

Liston

CAMBRIDGE CL

Stour Valley Path

PH

ST MARTYNS RISE

Withindale Mill

BARLEY HO 1
THE MALTHOUSE 2

CO10

Rodbridge House

Highlanders Farm

Cuckoo Tye Farm

ROPERS LA

B1064

BORLEY RD

Rodbridge Corner

MILLS LA

Hospital Farm

Potter's Farm

Place Farmhouse

Hardwicke Way

River Stour

LOWER RD

SUDBURY RD

B1064

Rodbridge Nature Reserve

A134

A131

Long Melford By-Pass

Superstore

MOUNTBATTEN CL 1
HAWKINS CT 2
HARDY CT 3

Woodhall Bsns Pk

HALL RD

Borley Mill

Borley Hall

The Valley Walk

Highfield Mill

St. Bartholomew's Chapel

Priory

CLERMONT AV

SPRINGLANDS WAY

Woodhall Com Prim Sch

Sudbury Hall

MELFORD RD

PARKWOOD DR

CHURCHILL DR

Uplands Spec Sch

A134

A134 Colchester

Belchamp Brook

Brundon Mill

Brundon Hall

North Meadow Common

Sudbury Upper Sch

Tudor CE Prim Sch

Uplands Com Mid Sch

Brundon

SUDBURY

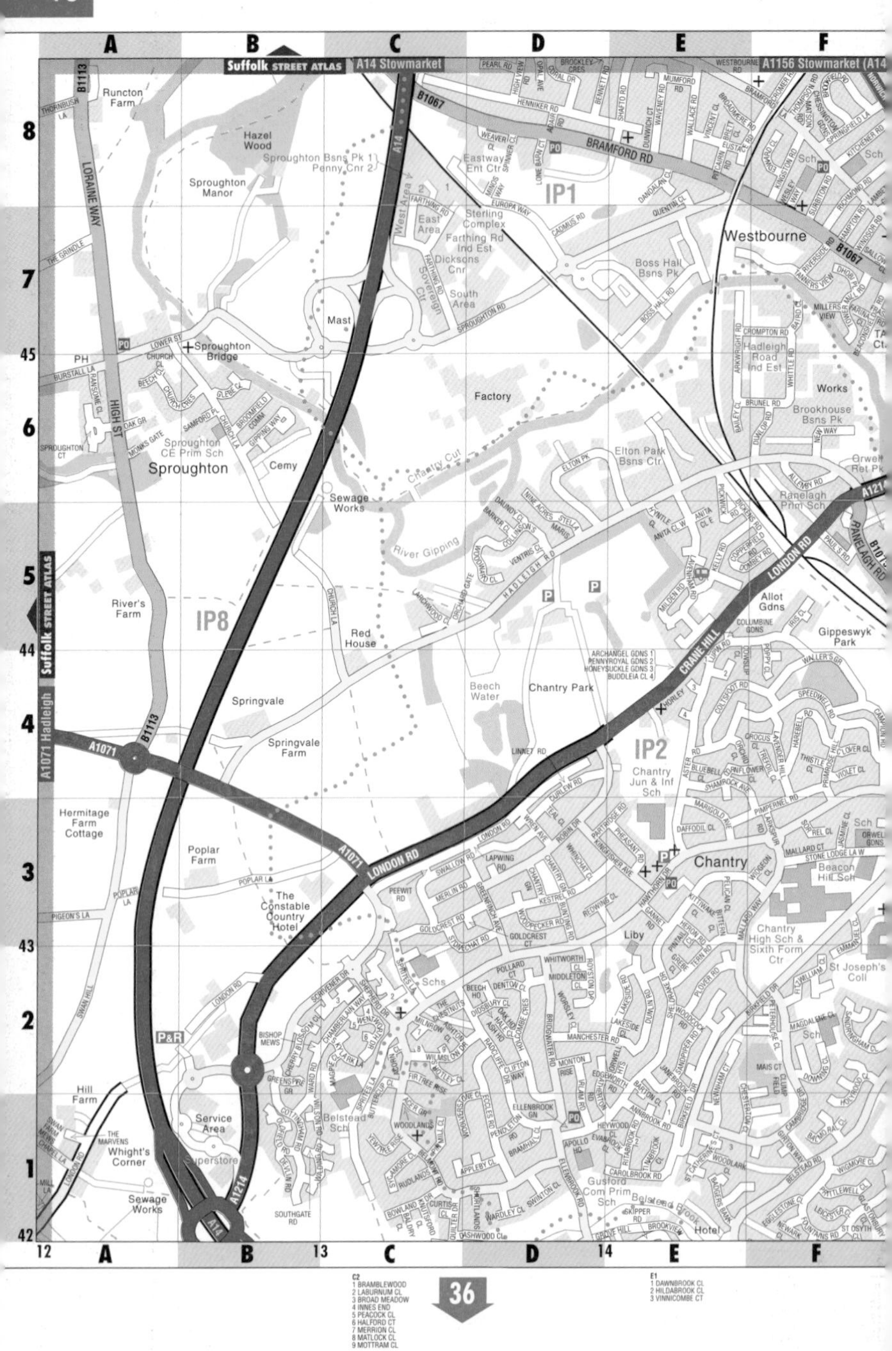

C2
1 BRAMBLEWOOD
2 LABURNUM CL
3 BROAD MEADOW
4 INNES END
5 PEACOCK CL
6 HALFORD CT
7 MERRION CL
8 MATLOCK CL
9 MOTTRAM CL

E1
1 DAWNBROOK CL
2 HILDABROOK CL
3 VINNICOMBE CT

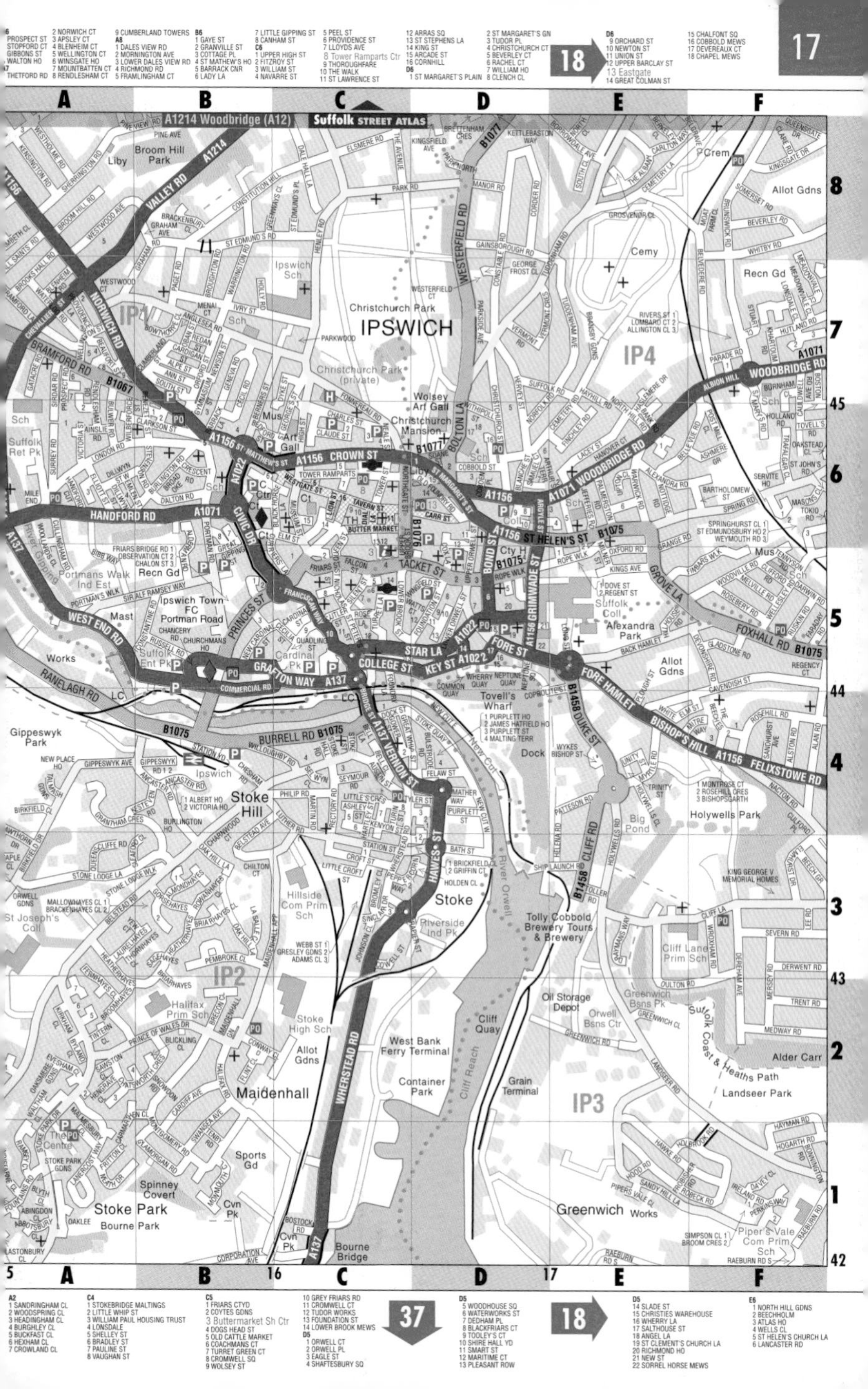

A8
PROSPECT ST
STOPFORD CT
GIBBONS ST
WALTON HO
THETFORD RD

2 NORWICH CT
3 APSLEY CT
4 BLENHEIM CT
5 WELLINGTON CT
6 WINSGATE HO
7 MOUNTBATTEN CT
8 RENDLESHAM CT

9 CUMBERLAND TOWERS
A8
1 DALES VIEW RD

B6
1 GAYE ST
2 GRANVILLE ST
3 COTTAGE PL
4 MORNINGTON AVE
5 LOWER DALES VIEW RD
6 RICHMOND RD
7 FRAMLINGHAM CT

7 LITTLE GIPPING ST
8 CANHAM ST

C6
1 HIGH HIGH ST
2 FITZROY ST
3 WILLIAM ST
4 NAVARRE ST

5 PEEL ST
6 PROVIDENCE ST
7 LLOYDS AVE
8 ARCADE ST
9 THOROUGHFARE
10 THE WALK
11 ST LAWRENCE ST

12 ARRAS SQ
13 ST STEPHENS LA
14 KING ST
15 ARCADE ST
16 CORNHILL
C6
1 ST MARGARET'S PLAIN

2 ST MARGARET'S GN
3 TUDOR PL
4 CHRISTCHURCH CT
5 BEVERLEY CT
6 RACHEL CT
7 WILLIAM HO
8 CLENCH CL

D6
9 ORCHARD ST
10 NEWTON ST
11 UNION ST
12 UPPER BARCLAY ST
13 Eastgate
14 GREAT COLMAN ST

15 CHALFONT SQ
16 COBBOLD MEWS
17 DEVERAUX CT
18 CHAPEL MEWS

18

IPSWICH

37

18

A2
1 SANDRINGHAM CL
2 WOODSPRING CL
3 HEADINGHAM CL
4 BURGHLEY CL
5 BUCKFAST CL
6 HEXHAM CL
7 CROWLAND CL

C4
1 STOKEBRIDGE MALTINGS
2 LITTLE WHIP ST
3 WILLIAM PAUL HOUSING TRUST
4 LONSDALE
5 SHELLEY ST
6 BRADLEY ST
7 PAULINE ST
8 VAUGHAN ST

C5
1 FRIARS CTYD
2 COYTES GDNS
3 Buttermarket Sh Ctr

B5
1 DOGS HEAD ST
2 OLD CATTLE MARKET
3 COACHMANS CT
4 TURRET GREEN CT
5 CROMWELL SQ
6 WOLSEY SQ

10 GREY FRIARS RD
11 CROMWELL CT
12 TUDOR WORKS
13 FOUNDATION ST
14 LOWER BROOK MEWS

C6
1 ORWELL CT
2 ORWELL PL
3 EAGLE ST
4 SHAFTESBURY SQ

D5
1 WOODHOUSE SQ
2 WATERWORKS ST
3 DEDHAM PL
4 BLACKFRIARS CT
5 TOOLEY'S CT
6 SHIRE HALL YD
7 SMART ST
8 MARITIME CT
9 PLEASANT ROW

E5
14 SLADE ST
15 CHRISTIES WAREHOUSE
16 WHERRY LA
17 SALTHOUSE ST
18 ANGEL LA
19 ST CLEMENT'S CHURCH LA
20 RICHMOND HO
21 NEW ST
22 SORREL HORSE MEWS

E6
1 NORTH HILL GDNS
2 BEECHHOLM
3 ATLAS HO
4 WELLS CL
5 ST HELEN'S CHURCH LA
6 LANCASTER RD

17

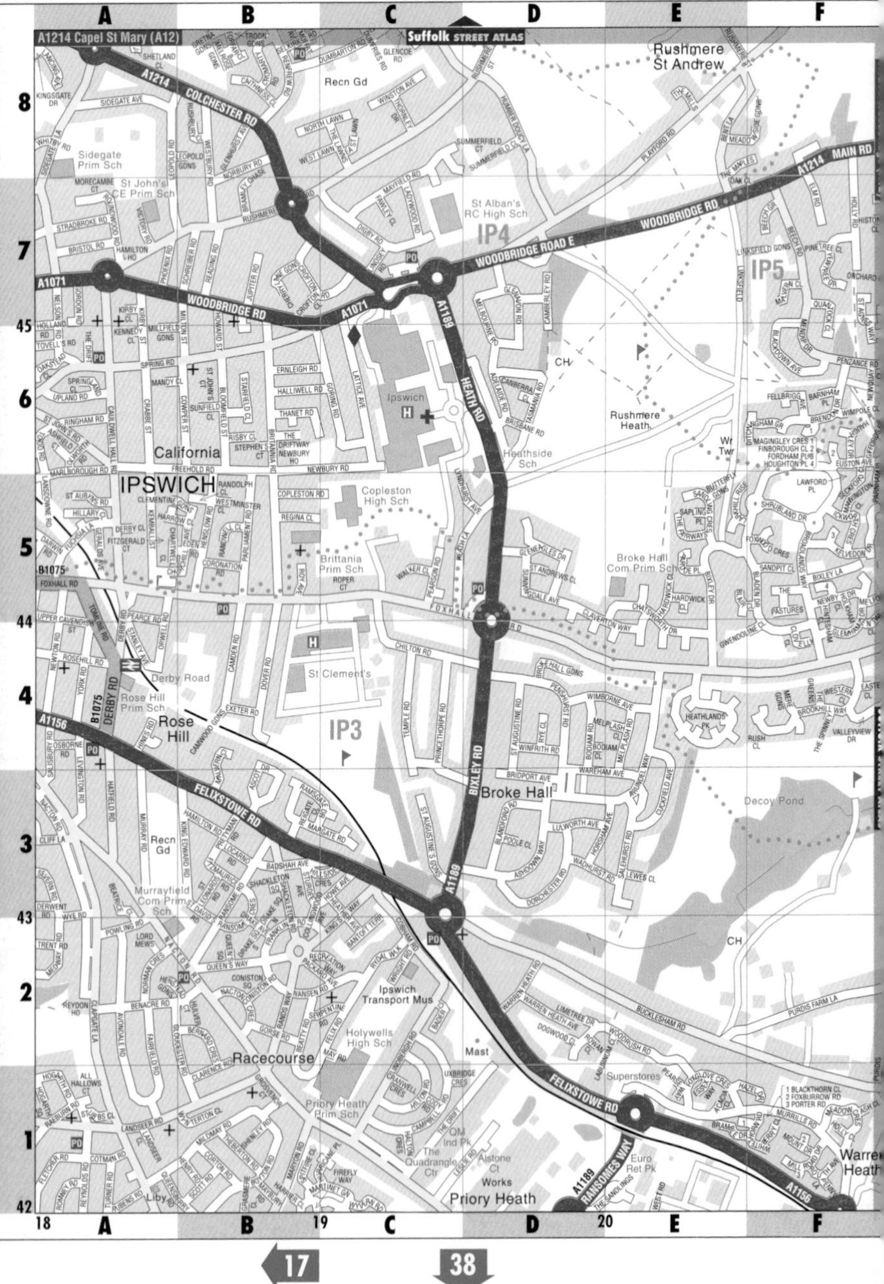
A1214 Capel St Mary (A12)
Suffolk STREET ATLAS
A
B
C
D
E
F
8
7
6
5
4
3
2
1
45
44
43
42
18
19
20
Rushmere St Andrew
Recn Gd
KINGSGATE DR
SIDEGATE AVE
Sidegate Prim Sch
St John's CE Prim Sch
A1214
COLCHESTER RD
SHETLAND CL
DUMBARTON RD
GLENCOE RD
WINSTON AVE
NORTH LAWN
WEST LAWN
SUMMERFIELD CT
SUMMERFIELD CL
HUMBER DOUCY LA
PLAYFORD RD
THE MILLS
MAIN RD
A1214
WOODBRIDGE RD
WOODBRIDGE ROAD E
St Alban's RC High Sch
IP4
IP5
MAYFIELD RD
LADYWOOD RD
DIGBY RD
STRADBROKE RD
BRISTOL RD
MORECAMBE CT
HAMILTON HO
A1071
WOODBRIDGE RD
A1071
A1189
HEATH RD
NORBURY RD
RUSHMERE RD
LINKSFIELD GDNS
PINETREE CL
ORCHARD
HOLLAND RD
TOVELL'S RD
THE DRIFT
KIRBY CL
KENNEDY CL
MILLFIELD GDNS
SPRING RD
MANDY CL
ERNLEIGH RD
HALLIWELL RD
THANET RD
GORING RD
LATTICE AVE
Ipswich
H
MELBOURNE RD
ADELAIDE RD
CANBERRA CL
TASMANIA RD
BRISBANE RD
CH
Rushmere Heath
Wr Twr
PENZANCE RD
BARNHAM PL
FELLBRIGG AVE
UPLAND RD
RINGHAM RD
CRABBE ST
SUNFIELD CL
RISBY CL
STEPHEN'S CT
THE DRIFTWAY
NEWBURY HO
California
IPSWICH
FREEHOLD RD
NEWBURY RD
Heathside Sch
MAGINGLEY CRES 1
FINBOROUGH CL 2
FORDHAM PL 3
HOUGHTON PL 4
EUSTON AVE
LAWFORD PL
MARLBOROUGH RD
ST AUBYNS RD
HILLARY CL
RANDOLPH CL
CLEMENTINE GDNS
WESTMINSTER CL
COPLESTON RD
REGINA CL
Copleston High Sch
BUTTERFLY GDNS
SAPLING PL
THE FAIRWAYS
SHRUBLAND DR
FOXWOOD CRES
KELVEDON DR
DERBY CL
FITZGERALD CT
CORONATION RD
Brittania Prim Sch
ROPER CT
WALKER CL
PEARSON RD
GLENEAGLES DR
ST ANDREWS CL
Broke Hall Com Prim Sch
SANDPIT CL
BIXLEY LA
B1075
FOXHALL RD
PO
FOXHALL RD
CLAVERTON WAY
CHATSWORTH DR
HARDWICK CL
BIXLEY DR
THE PASTURES
GWENDOLINE CL
UPPER CAVENDISH ST
PEARCE RD
ROSEHILL RD
CHILTON RD
BROKE HALL GDNS
PENSHURST RD
WIMBORNE AVE
MELPLASH CL
HEATHLANDS PK
Derby Road
St Clement's
Rose Hill Prim Sch
Rose Hill
B1075 DERBY RD
EXETER RD
CAMDEN RD
DOVER RD
IP3
TEMPLE RD
PRINCETHORPE RD
ST AUGUSTINE RD
WINFRITH RD
RYE CL
BODIAM RD
BODIAM CL
RUSH CL
VALLEYVIEW DR
WESTERN CL
BROOKHILL WAY
A1156
OSBORNE RD
LEVINGTON RD
HATFIELD RD
FELIXSTOWE RD
RAMSGATE DR
MARGATE RD
BIXLEY RD
Broke Hall
BRIDPORT AVE
WAREHAM AVE
ARUNDEL WAY
CUCKFIELD AVE
Decoy Pond
NACTON RD
CLIFF LA
HAMILTON RD
Recn Gd
KING EDWARD RD
BLANDFORD RD
POOLE CL
LULWORTH AVE
HORSHAM AVE
SALEHURST RD
WADHURST RD
LEWES CL
ASHDOWN WAY
DORCHESTER RD
ST AUGUSTINE'S GDNS
A1189
BADSHAH AVE
SHACKLETON RD
Murrayfield Com Prim Sch
DERWENT RD
WYE RD
BEATRICE
POWLING RD
LORD MEWS
TRENT RD
MEDWAY RD
RANSOME RD
QUEEN'S WAY
RECREATION WAY
PACKARD AVE
COBHAM RD
RYDAL WLK
WRIGHT RD
CH
NACTON RD
CONISTON SQ
NANSEN RD
Ipswich Transport Mus
WARREN HEATH RD
WARREN HEATH AVE
LIMETREE DR
BUCKLESHAM RD
PURDIS FARM LA
REYDON HO
CLAPGATE LA
BENACRE RD
AVONDALE RD
FAIRFIELD RD
GLOUCESTER RD
BERNARD CRES
CLARENCE RD
Racecourse
GORSE RD
Holywells High Sch
Mast
DOGWOOD CL
ROWAN CL
WOODRUSH RD
Superstores
HAZEL DR
1 BLACKTHORN CL
2 FOXBURROW RD
3 PORTER RD
ALL HALLOWS CT
HOGARTH RD
RAEBURN RD
STUBBS CL
UXBRIDGE CRES
FELIXSTOWE RD
MURRILLS RD
BRAMBLE DR
Priory Heath Prim Sch
LANDSEER RD
GROSVENOR CT
THE DRIFT
QM Ind Pk
Alstone Ct
The Quadrangle Ctr
Works
Priory Heath
Euro Ret Pk
A1189
RANSOMES WAY
THE SANDLINGS
A1156
Warren Heath
FLETCHER RD
COTMAN RD
TURNER RD
REYNOLDS RD
RUBENS RD
MILDMAY RD
HENRY RD
SCOTT RD
Liby
GRASMERE CL
MAYBURY RD
MARTINET GN
FIREFLY WAY

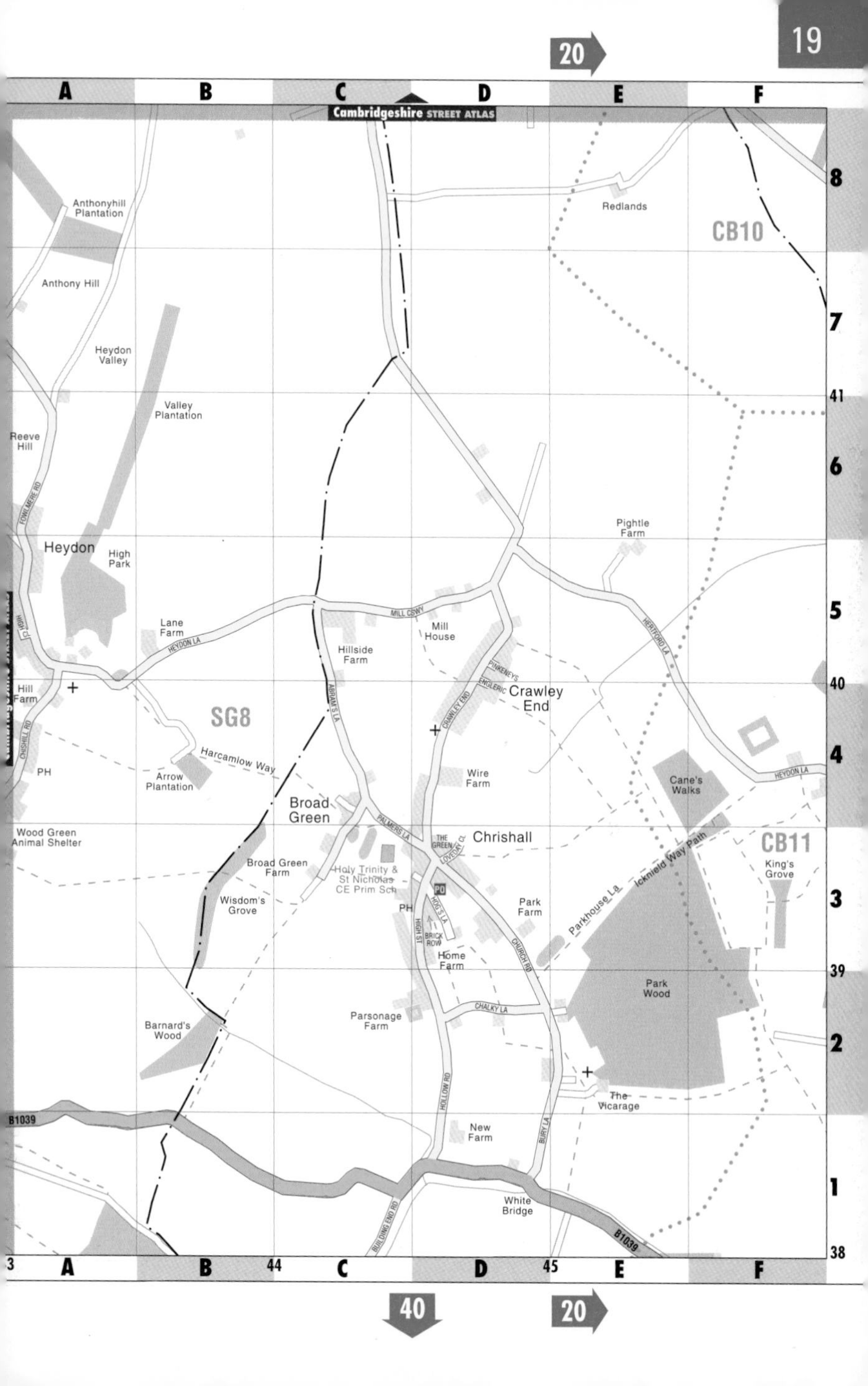

A **B** **C** **D** **E** **F**

8

Anthonyhill Plantation

Redlands

CB10

Anthony Hill

7

Heydon Valley

41

Valley Plantation

Reeve Hill

6

Heydon

High Park

Pightle Farm

5

Lane Farm

HEYDON LA

MILL CNR

Mill House

Hillside Farm

THORNEYS

EXCHANGE RD

HEYDON LA

Crawley End

40

Hill Farm

SG8

COURT RD

Wire Farm

Cane's Walks

4

PH

Arrow Plantation

Harcamlow Way

ARROW LA

Broad Green

Parkhouse La

Icknield Way Path

HEYDON LA

CB11

King's Grove

3

Wood Green Animal Shelter

Broad Green Farm

Wisdom's Grove

PALMERS LA

Holy Trinity & St Nicholas CE Prim Sch

THE GREEN

PH

Chrishall

PO

BRICK ROW

HIGH ST

CHURCH RD

Park Farm

Park Wood

39

Barnard's Wood

Parsonage Farm

Home Farm

CHALKY LA

2

The Vicarage

B1039

HOLLOW RD

BURY LA

New Farm

BUILDING END RD

B1039

White Bridge

1

38

A **B** 44 **C** **D** 45 **E** **F**

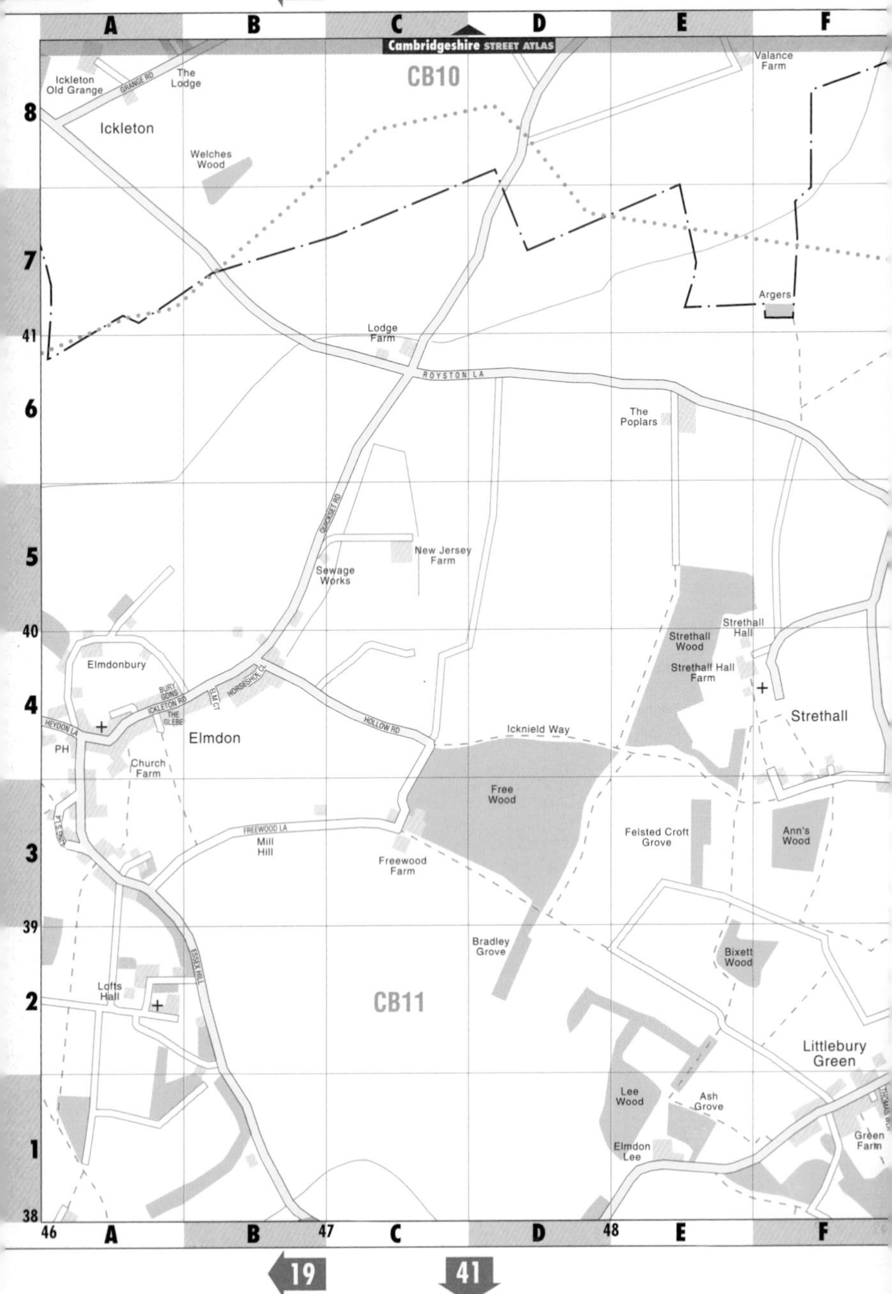

A   B   C   D   E   F

Cambridgeshire STREET ATLAS

CB10

8

Ickleton Old Grange
The Lodge
GRANGE RD
Ickleton
Welches Wood
Valance Farm

7

Argers

41

Lodge Farm
ROYSTON LA

6

The Poplars

5

New Jersey Farm
Sewage Works

40

Elmdonbury
Strethall Wood
Strethall Hall

4

Elmdon
BURY GREEN
ICKLETON RD
THE GLEBE
ELM CT
HORNSGATE CL
HEYDON LA
HOLLOW RD
Icknield Way
Strethall Hall Farm
Strethall

PH
Church Farm
Free Wood

3

FREEWOOD LA
Mill Hill
Freewood Farm
Felsted Croft Grove
Ann's Wood

39

Bradley Grove
Bixett Wood

2

Lofts Hall
CB11
Littlebury Green

1

Lee Wood
Ash Grove
Green Farm
Elmdon Lee

38

46   A   B   47   C   D   48   E   F

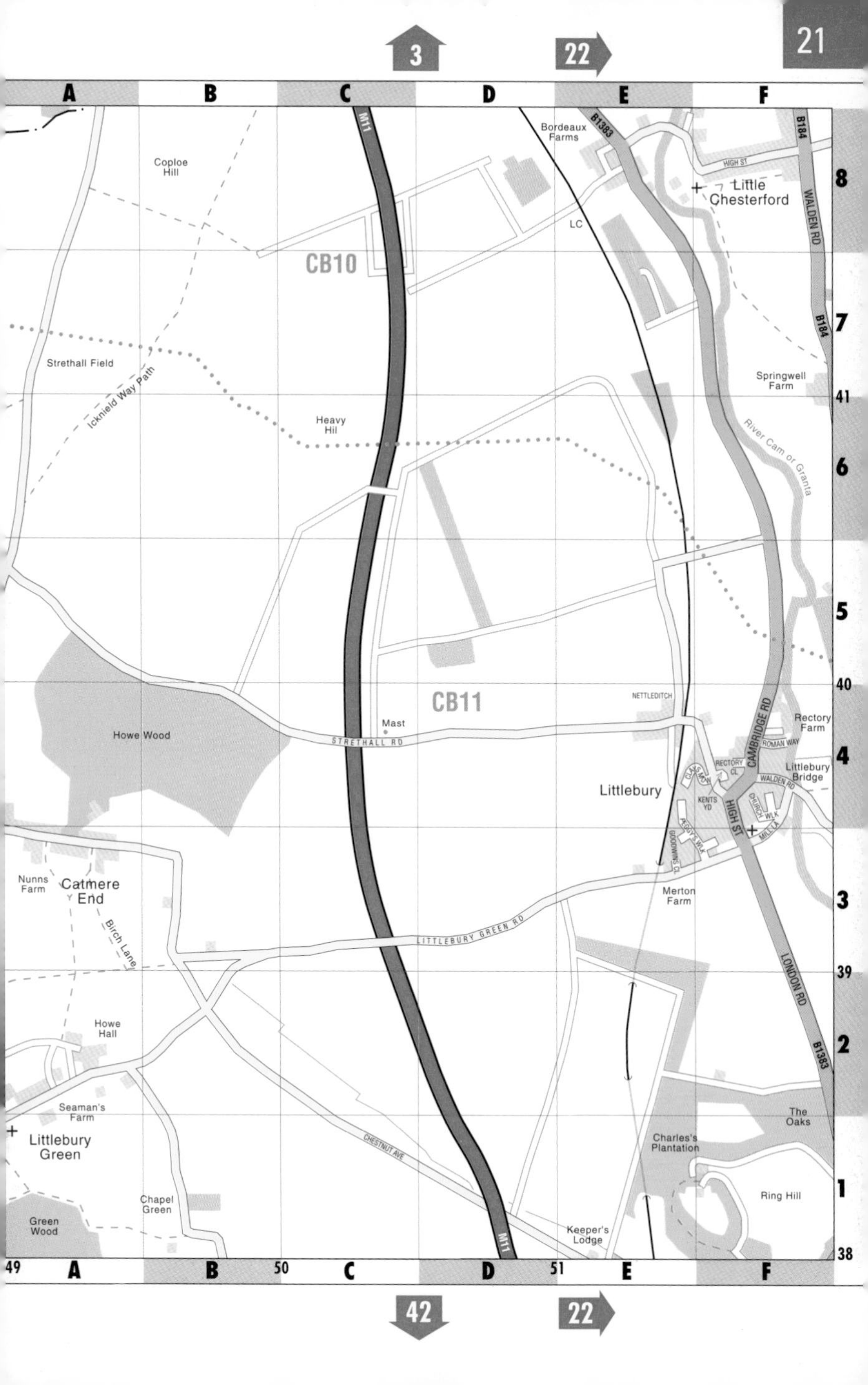

A B C D E F

8
7
41
6
5
40
4
3
39
2
1
38

49 50 51

Coploe Hill

CB10

Bordeaux Farms

Little Chesterford

HIGH ST

LC

WALDEN RD

B184

B184

B1383

Strethall Field

Icknield Way Path

Heavy Hill

Springwell Farm

River Cam or Granta

CB11

Mast

NETTLEDITCH

Howe Wood

STRETHALL RD

Rectory Farm

CAMBRIDGE RD

ROMAN WAY

RECTORY

Littlebury Bridge

Littlebury

WALDEN RD

KENTS YD

HIGH ST

Nunns Farm

Catmere End

Birch Lane

LITTLEBURY GREEN RD

Merton Farm

LONDON RD

B1383

Howe Hall

Seaman's Farm

Littlebury Green

The Oaks

Charles's Plantation

Chapel Green

Green Wood

CHESTNUT AVE

Keeper's Lodge

Ring Hill

M11

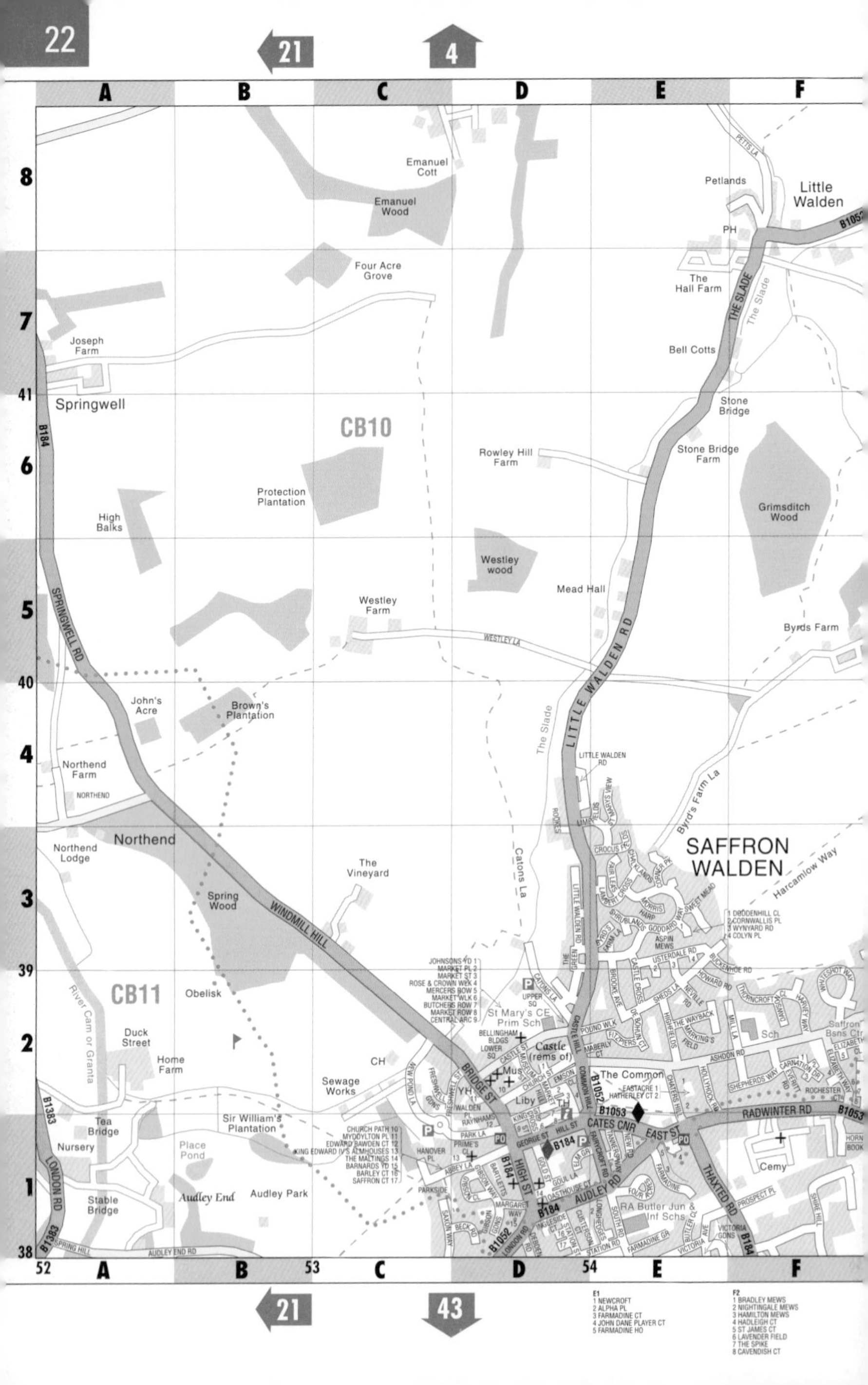
21
4
A B C D E F
8 7 41 6 5 40 4 3 39 2 1 38
Emanuel Cott
Emanuel Wood
Petlands
Little Walden
B1052
PH
Four Acre Grove
The Hall Farm
THE SLADE
The Slade
Joseph Farm
Bell Cotts
Springwell
CB10
Stone Bridge
B184
Rowley Hill Farm
Stone Bridge Farm
Protection Plantation
Grimsditch Wood
High Balks
Westley wood
Mead Hall
SPRINGWELL RD
Westley Farm
Byrds Farm
WESTLEY LA
LITTLE WALDEN RD
John's Acre
Brown's Plantation
The Slade
Northend Farm
NORTHEND
LITTLE WALDEN RD
Byrd's Farm La
Northend
Northend Lodge
SAFFRON WALDEN
Harcamlow Way
The Vineyard
Catons La
Spring Wood
WINDMILL HILL
CB11
Obelisk
River Cam or Granta
Duck Street
Home Farm
CH
Sewage Works
The Common
B1383
Tea Bridge
Sir William's Plantation
Nursery
Place Pond
LONDON RD
Stable Bridge
Audley End
Audley Park
RA Butler Jun & Inf Schs
SPRING HILL
AUDLEY END RD
BRIDGE ST
HIGH ST
CATES CNR
EAST ST
RADWINTER RD
B1053
THAXTED RD
AUDLEY RD
St Mary's CE Prim Sch
Castle (rems of)
Mus
Liby
YH
TH
Sch
Cemy
Saffron Bsns Ctr
JOHNSONS YD 1
MARKET PL 2
MARKET ST 3
ROSE & CROWN WLK 4
MERCERS ROW 5
MARKET WLK 6
BUTCHERS ROW 7
MARKET ROW 8
CENTRAL ARC 9
CHURCH PATH 10
MYDDYLTON PL 11
EDWARD BAWDEN CT 12
KING EDWARD IV'S ALMHOUSES 13
THE MALTINGS 14
BARNARDS YD 15
BARLEY CT 16
SAFFRON CT 17
1 DODDENHILL CL
2 CORNWALLIS PL
3 WYNYARD RD
4 COLYN PL
52 53 54
21
43
E1
1 NEWCROFT
2 ALPHA PL
3 FARMADINE CT
4 JOHN DANE PLAYER CT
5 FARMADINE HO
F2
1 BRADLEY MEWS
2 NIGHTINGALE MEWS
3 HAMILTON MEWS
4 HADLEIGH CT
5 ST JAMES CT
6 LAVENDER FIELD
7 THE SPIKE
8 CAVENDISH CT

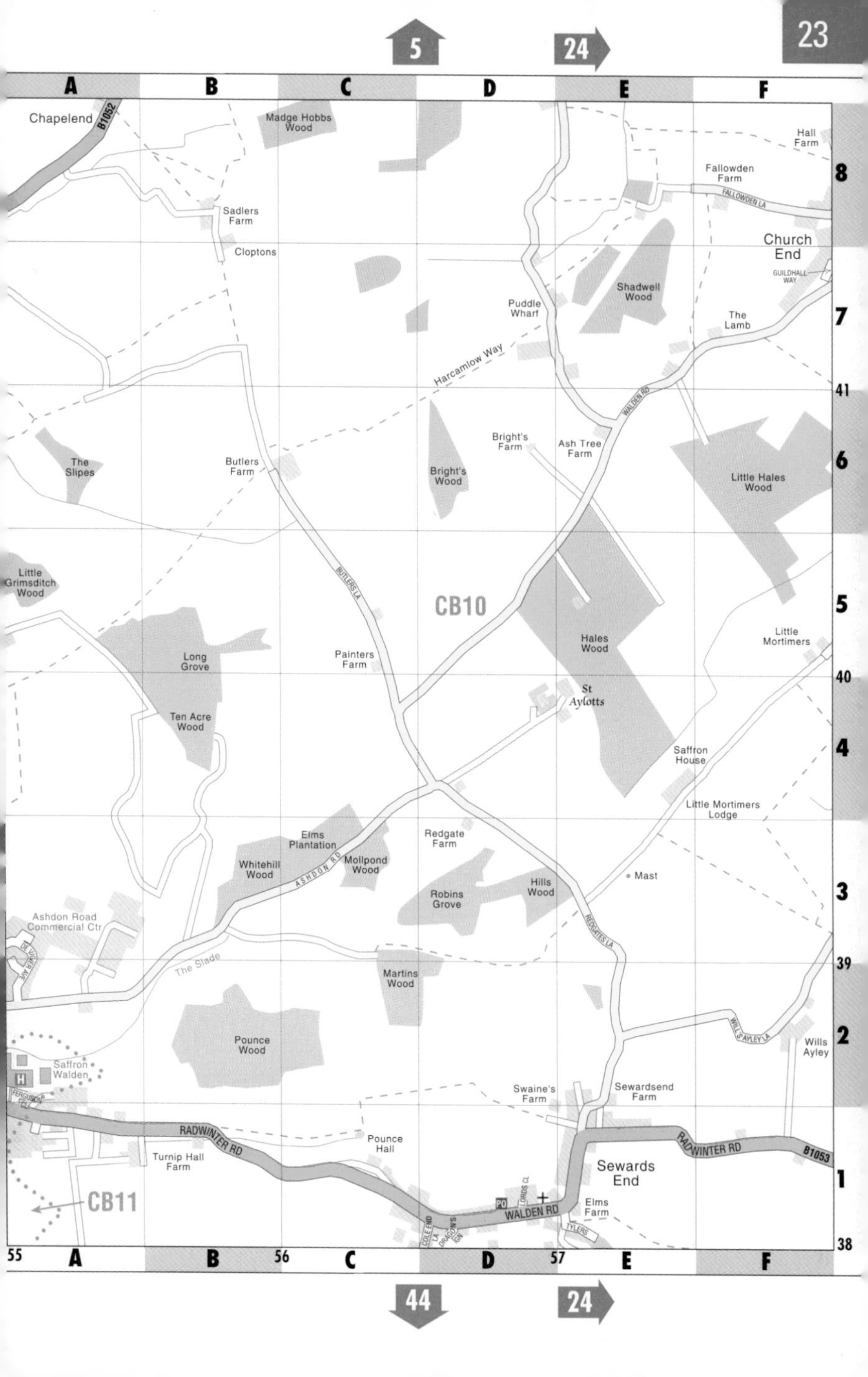
5
24
A
B
C
D
E
F
Chapelend
B1052
Madge Hobbs Wood
Hall Farm
Fallowden Farm
FALLOWDEN LA
8
Sadlers Farm
Cloptons
Church End
GUILDHALL WAY
Shadwell Wood
Puddle Wharf
The Lamb
7
Harcamlow Way
41
WALDEN RD
Bright's Farm
Ash Tree Farm
The Slipes
Butlers Farm
Bright's Wood
6
Little Hales Wood
Little Grimsditch Wood
BUTLERS LA
CB10
5
Hales Wood
Little Mortimers
Long Grove
Painters Farm
40
St Aylotts
Ten Acre Wood
Saffron House
4
Little Mortimers Lodge
Elms Plantation
Redgate Farm
Whitehill Wood
Mollpond Wood
ASHDON RD
Mast
Robins Grove
Hills Wood
3
Ashdon Road Commercial Ctr
DE VIGIER AVE
REDGATES LA
The Slade
39
Martins Wood
Pounce Wood
WILLS AYLEY LA
2
Wills Ayley
Saffron Walden
H
FERGUSON CL
Swaine's Farm
Sewardsend Farm
RADWINTER RD
Pounce Hall
RADWINTER RD
B1053
Turnip Hall Farm
Sewards End
1
LORDS CL
CB11
PO
WALDEN RD
Elms Farm
COLE END LA
DRAGON'S GN
TYLERS
38
55
A
B
56
C
D
57
E
F
44
24

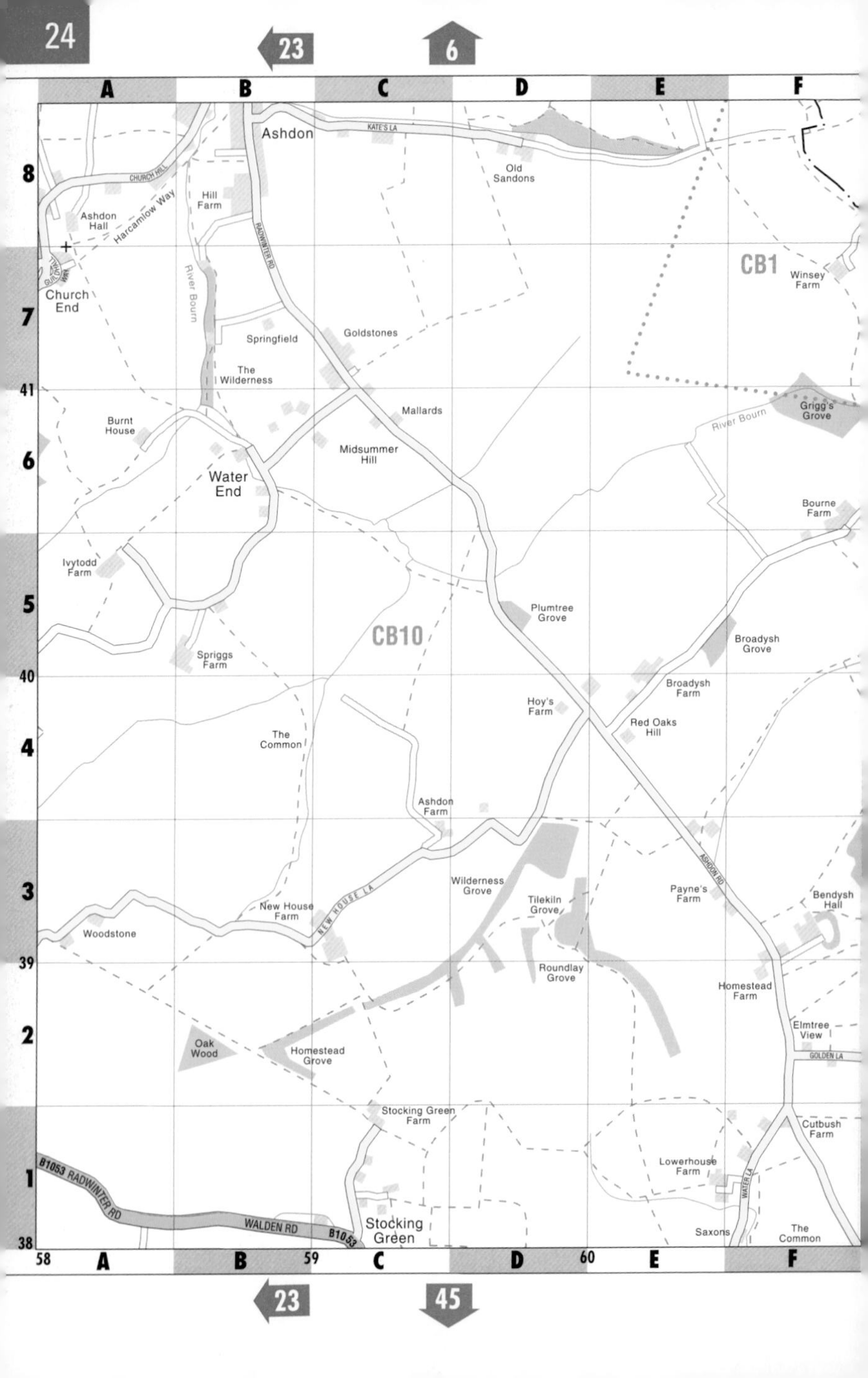
23
6
A
B
C
D
E
F
Ashdon
KATE'S LA
CHURCH HILL
Old
Sandons
Hill
Farm
Ashdon
Hall
Harcamlow Way
RADWINTER RD
CB1
Winsey
Farm
Church
End
River Bourn
Springfield
Goldstones
The
Wilderness
Burnt
House
Mallards
Grigg's
Grove
River Bourn
Midsummer
Hill
Water
End
Bourne
Farm
Ivytodd
Farm
Plumtree
Grove
CB10
Broadysh
Grove
Spriggs
Farm
Broadysh
Farm
Hoy's
Farm
Red Oaks
Hill
The
Common
Ashdon
Farm
ASHDON RD
Wilderness
Grove
Payne's
Farm
Bendysh
Hall
New House
Farm
NEW HOUSE LA
Tilekiln
Grove
Woodstone
Roundlay
Grove
Homestead
Farm
Elmtree
View
GOLDEN LA
Oak
Wood
Homestead
Grove
Stocking Green
Farm
Cutbush
Farm
Lowerhouse
Farm
WATER LA
B1053 RADWINTER RD
WALDEN RD
B1053
Stocking
Green
Saxons
The
Common
8
7
41
6
5
40
4
3
39
2
1
38
58
59
60
23
45

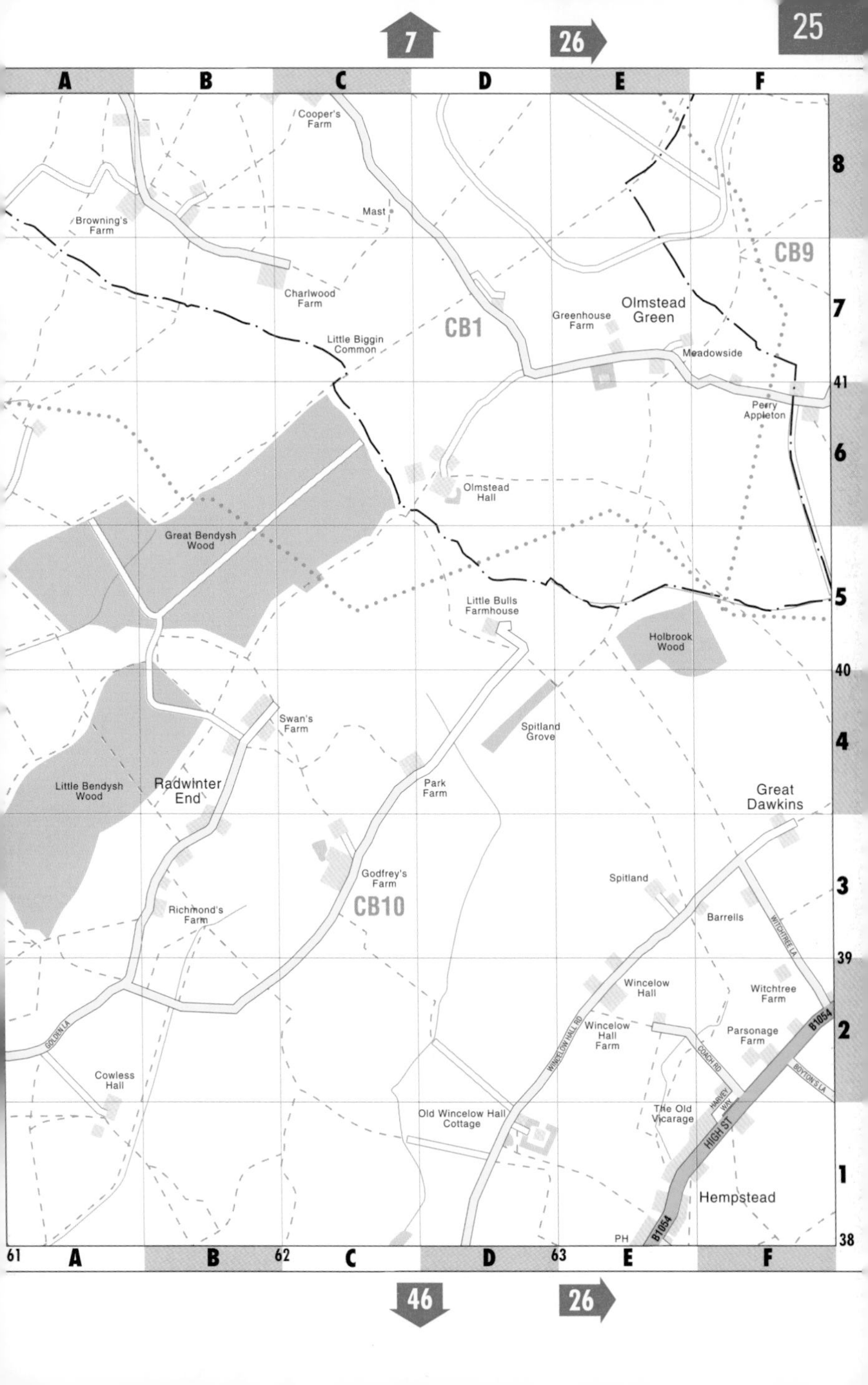

A B C D E F

8
CB9
7
41
6
5
40
4
3
39
2
1
38

Cooper's Farm
Mast
Browning's Farm
Charlwood Farm
Little Biggin Common
CB1
Greenhouse Farm
Olmstead Green
Meadowside
Peery Appleton
Great Bendysh Wood
Olmstead Hall
Little Bulls Farmhouse
Holbrook Wood
Swan's Farm
Spitland Grove
Little Bendysh Wood
Radwinter End
Park Farm
Great Dawkins
Godfrey's Farm
CB10
Spitland
Richmond's Farm
Barrells
Wincelow Hall
Witchtree Farm
Parsonage Farm
B1054
Cowless Hall
Wincelow Hall Farm
GOULDS LA
WINCELOW HALL RD
COACH RD
The Old Vicarage
HIGH ST
Old Wincelow Hall Cottage
BOYTON LA
Hempstead
PH
B1054

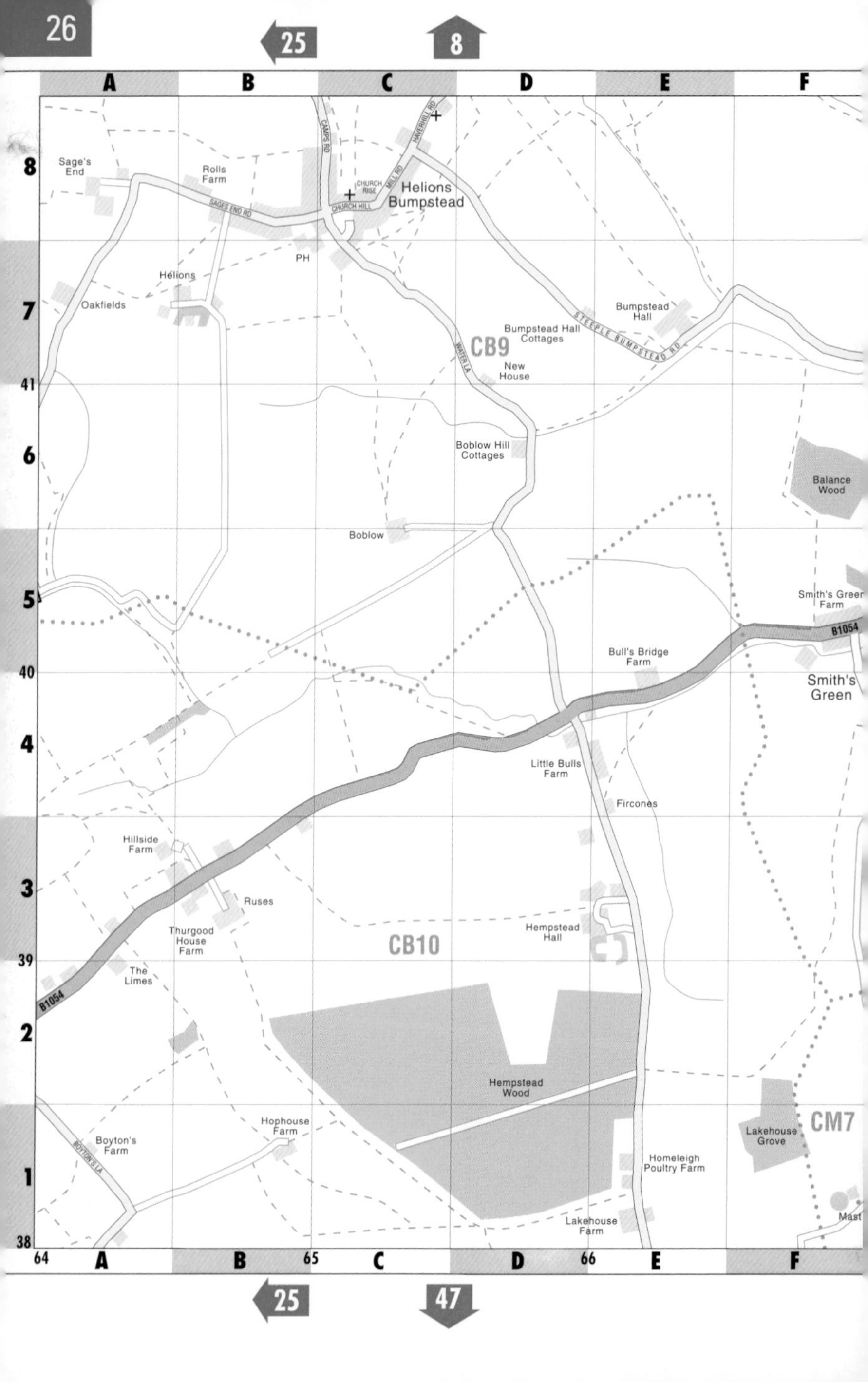

A   B   C   D   E   F

8 Sage's End

Rolls Farm

CHALK RD
HAVERILL RD

CHURCH RISE
Helions Bumpstead

CHURCH HILL
SAGES END RD

Helions

PH

Oakfields

7 Bumpstead Hall

Bumpstead Hall Cottages

CB9

New House

STEEPLE BUMPSTEAD RD

WIXOE LA

41

6 Boblow Hill Cottages

Balance Wood

Boblow

Smith's Green Farm

5

B1054

Bull's Bridge Farm

Smith's Green

40

4 Little Bulls Farm

Fircones

Hillside Farm

3 Ruses

Hempstead Hall

CB10

Thurgood House Farm

39

The Limes

B1054

2

Hempstead Wood

Hophouse Farm

Lakehouse Grove

CM7

1 Boyton's Farm

BOYTON'S LA

Homeleigh Poultry Farm

Lakehouse Farm

Mast

38

64   A   B   65   C   D   66   E   F

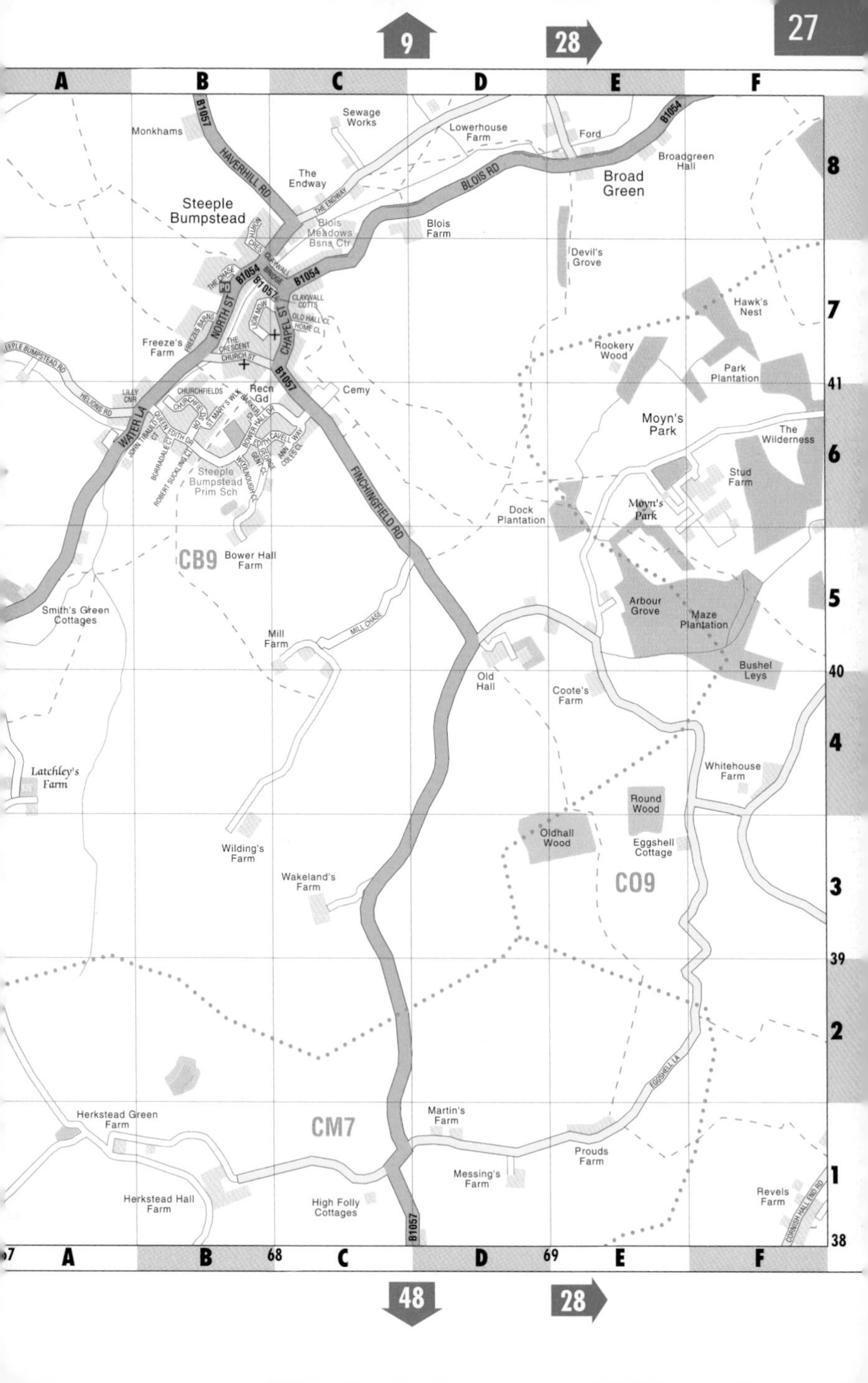
9
28
A
B
C
D
E
F
8
7
41
6
5
40
4
3
39
2
1
38
Monkhams
Sewage Works
Lowerhouse Farm
Ford
Broadgreen Hall
Broad Green
The Endway
Steeple Bumpstead
HAVERHILL RD
THE ENDWAY
BLOIS RD
B1057
B1054
Blois Meadows Bsns Ctr
Blois Farm
Devil's Grove
HURON CRES
CLAYWALL BRIDGE
THE CHASE
PO
NORTH ST
CHAPEL ST
CLAYWALL COTTS
OLD HALL CL
HOME CL
LION MDW
FREEZES BARNS
Freeze's Farm
THE CRESCENT
CHURCH ST
Hawk's Nest
Rookery Wood
Park Plantation
STEEPLE BUMPSTEAD RD
HELIONS RD
LILLY CNR
CHURCHFIELDS
Recn Gd
Cemy
Moyn's Park
The Wilderness
WATER LA
JOHN TIBAULD CT
QUEEN EDITH DR
ST MARY'S WLK
BARKER CL
BOWER HALL DR
CAVELL WAY
EDITH GDN
GEORGE CL
ANN COLES CL
BORRADALE CT
ROBERT SUCKLING CT
WOOLNOUGH CL
Steeple Bumpstead Prim Sch
FINCHINGFIELD RD
Stud Farm
Dock Plantation
CB9
Bower Hall Farm
Arbour Grove
Maze Plantation
Smith's Green Cottages
Mill Farm
MILL CHASE
Old Hall
Bushel Leys
Coote's Farm
Latchley's Farm
Whitehouse Farm
Round Wood
Oldhall Wood
Eggshell Cottage
Wilding's Farm
Wakeland's Farm
CO9
EGGSHELL LA
Herkstead Green Farm
CM7
Martin's Farm
Prouds Farm
Messing's Farm
Revels Farm
CORNISH HALL END RD
Herkstead Hall Farm
High Folly Cottages
67
68
69
48
28

27
10

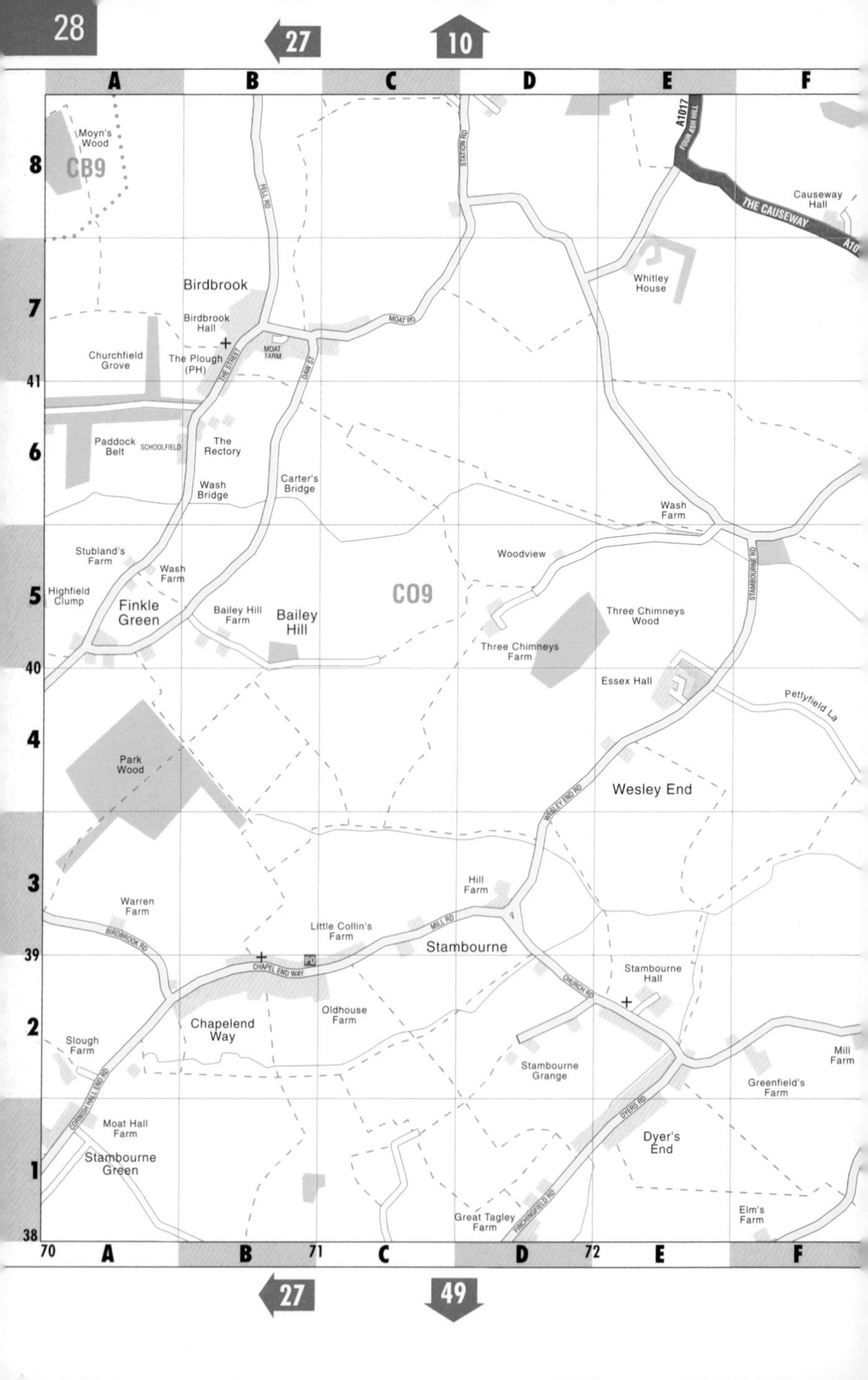
A
B
C
D
E
F
Moyn's Wood
CB9
8
FELL RD
STATION RD
A1017
FOUR ASH HILL
Causeway Hall
THE CAUSEWAY
Birdbrook
Whitley House
7
Birdbrook Hall
MOAT RD
Churchfield Grove
The Plough (PH)
THE STREET
MOAT FARM
DAW ST
41
Paddock Belt
SCHOOLFIELD
The Rectory
6
Wash Bridge
Carter's Bridge
Wash Farm
Stubland's Farm
Woodview
Wash Farm
Highfield Clump
5
Finkle Green
Bailey Hill Farm
Bailey Hill
CO9
Three Chimneys Wood
STAMBOURNE RD
Three Chimneys Farm
40
Essex Hall
Pettyfield La
4
Park Wood
Wesley End
WESLEY END RD
3
Hill Farm
Warren Farm
BIRDBROOK RD
Little Collin's Farm
MILL RD
Stambourne
39
PO
CHAPEL END WAY
Stambourne Hall
CHURCH RD
2
Chapelend Way
Oldhouse Farm
Slough Farm
Mill Farm
Stambourne Grange
Greenfield's Farm
CORNISH HALL END RD
DYERS RD
Moat Hall Farm
Dyer's End
1
Stambourne Green
Elm's Farm
Great Tagley Farm
FINCHINGFIELD RD
38
70
71
72

27
49

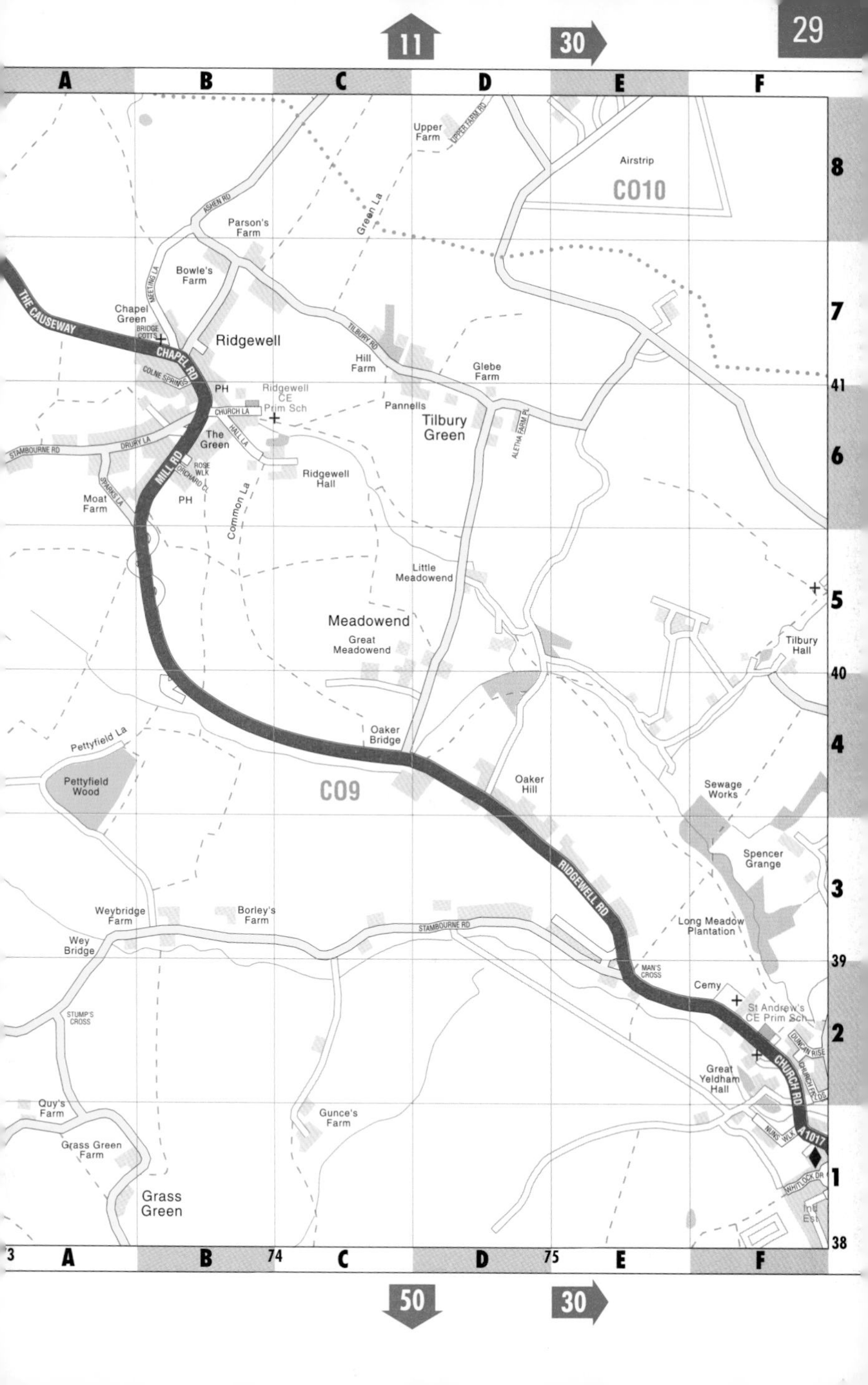
11
30
A
B
C
D
E
F
Upper Farm
UPPER FARM RD
Airstrip
CO10
8
ASHEN RD
Parson's Farm
Green La
Bowle's Farm
MEETING LA
7
Chapel Green
THE CAUSEWAY
BRIDGE COTTS
CHAPEL RD
Ridgewell
TILBURY RD
Hill Farm
Glebe Farm
COLNE SPRINGS
41
PH
Ridgewell CE Prim Sch
Pannells
CHURCH LA
Tilbury Green
ALETHA FARM PL
HALL LA
The Green
STAMBOURNE RD
DRURY LA
6
MILL RD
ROSE WLK
ORCHARD CL
Ridgewell Hall
SPARKS LA
Moat Farm
PH
Common La
Little Meadowend
5
Meadowend
Great Meadowend
Tilbury Hall
40
Oaker Bridge
Pettyfield La
4
Pettyfield Wood
CO9
Oaker Hill
Sewage Works
Spencer Grange
RIDGEWELL RD
3
Weybridge Farm
Borley's Farm
Long Meadow Plantation
STAMBOURNE RD
Wey Bridge
MAN'S CROSS
39
Cemy
St Andrew's CE Prim Sch
STUMP'S CROSS
2
DUNCAN RISE
Great Yeldham Hall
CHURCH RD
CHURCH FIELDS
Quy's Farm
Gunce's Farm
NUNS WLK
A1017
Grass Green Farm
1
WHITLOCK DR
Grass Green
Ind Est
38
3
74
75
50
30

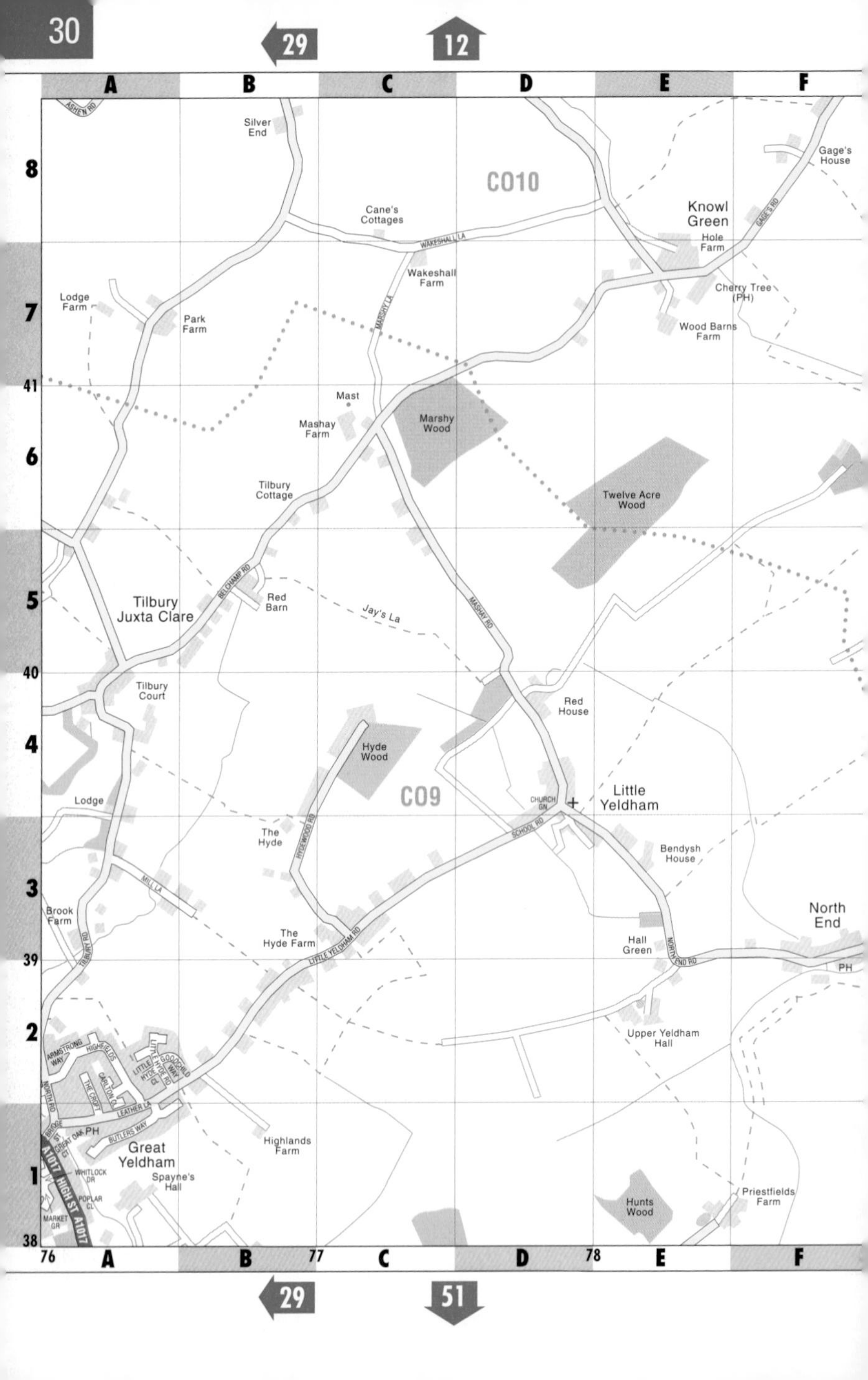
29
12
A
B
C
D
E
F
ASHEN RD
Silver End
8
CO10
Gage's House
Cane's Cottages
Knowl Green
GAGE'S RD
WAKESHALL LA
Hole Farm
Wakeshall Farm
Cherry Tree (PH)
Lodge Farm
7
Park Farm
MARSHY LA
Wood Barns Farm
41
Mast
Marshy Wood
Mashay Farm
6
Tilbury Cottage
Twelve Acre Wood
BELCHAMP RD
Red Barn
5
Tilbury Juxta Clare
Jay's La
MASHAY RD
40
Tilbury Court
Red House
4
Hyde Wood
CO9
Little Yeldham
CHURCH GN
Lodge
The Hyde
HYDEWOOD RD
SCHOOL RD
Bendysh House
3
MILL LA
Brook Farm
North End
The Hyde Farm
LITTLE YELDHAM RD
Hall Green
NORTH END RD
39
TILBURY RD
PH
2
ARMSTRONG WAY
HIGHFIELDS
LITTLE HYDE RD
GOODCHILD WAY
LITTLE HYDE CL
CARLTON CL
THE CROFT
Upper Yeldham Hall
NORTH RD
LEATHER LA
BRIDGE ST
GREAT OAK CT
PH
BUTLERS WAY
Highlands Farm
Great Yeldham
1
A1017 HIGH ST A1017
WHITLOCK DR
Spayne's Hall
POPLAR CL
Priestfields Farm
Hunts Wood
MARKET GR
38
76
77
78
A
B
C
D
E
F
29
51

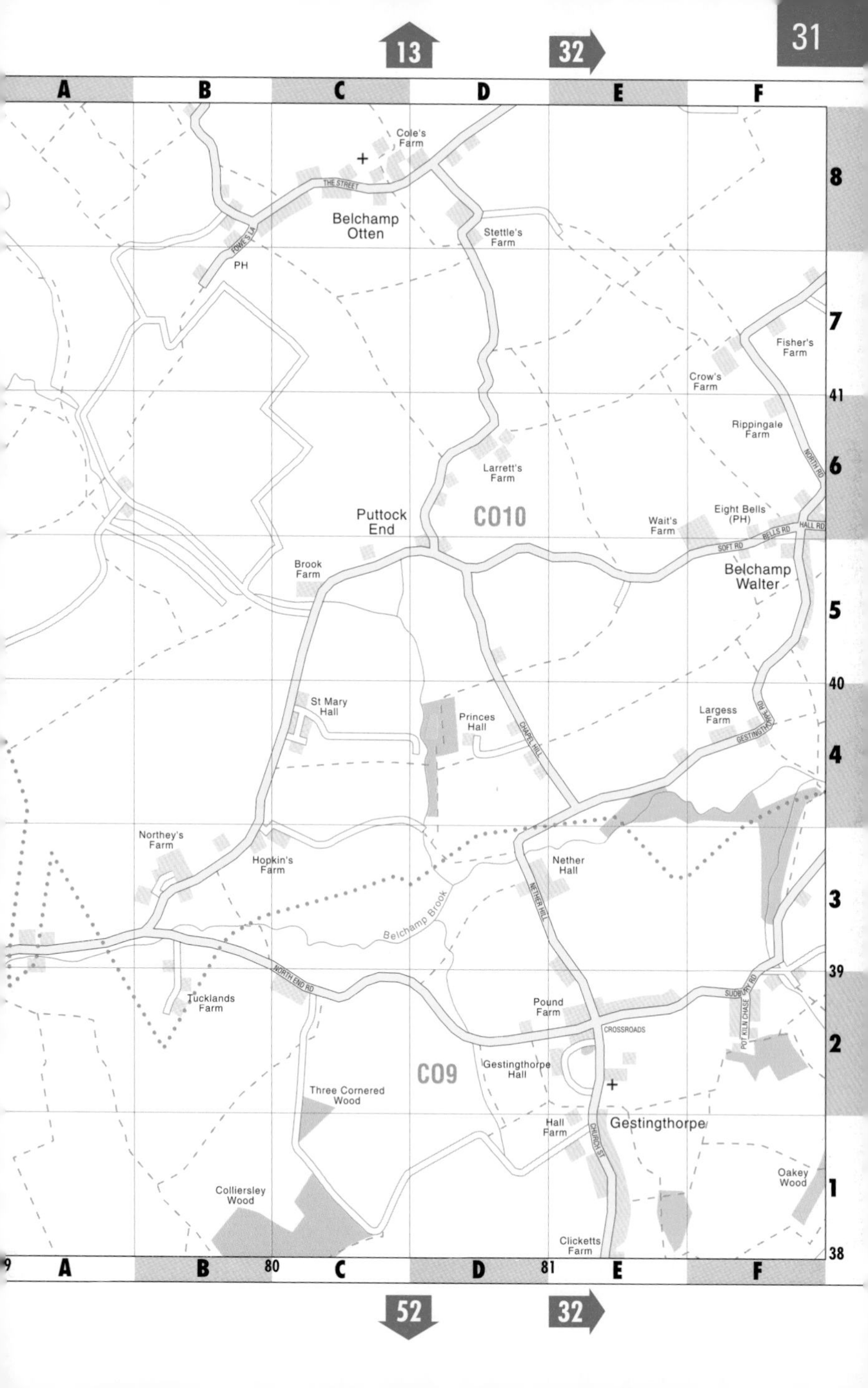

A B C D E F

8

Cole's
Farm

THE STREET

Belchamp
Otten

Stettle's
Farm

FORE ST N

PH

7

Fisher's
Farm

Crow's
Farm

41

NORTH RD

Rippingale
Farm

6

Larrett's
Farm

Wait's
Farm

Eight Bells
(PH)

HALL RD

CO10

Puttock
End

SOFT RD

BELLS RD

Belchamp
Walter

Brook
Farm

5

40

St Mary
Hall

Princes
Hall

CHAPEL HILL

Largess
Farm

GESTINGTHORPE RD

RD SOUTH

4

Northey's
Farm

Nether
Hall

Hopkin's
Farm

NETHER HILL

Belchamp Brook

3

39

Tucklands
Farm

NORTH END RD

Pound
Farm

CROSSROADS

SUDBURY RD

PUT KILN CHASE

2

CO9

Gestingthorpe
Hall

Three Cornered
Wood

Hall
Farm

CHURCH ST

Gestingthorpe

Oakey
Wood

1

Colliersley
Wood

Clicketts
Farm

38

9 A B 80 C D 81 E F

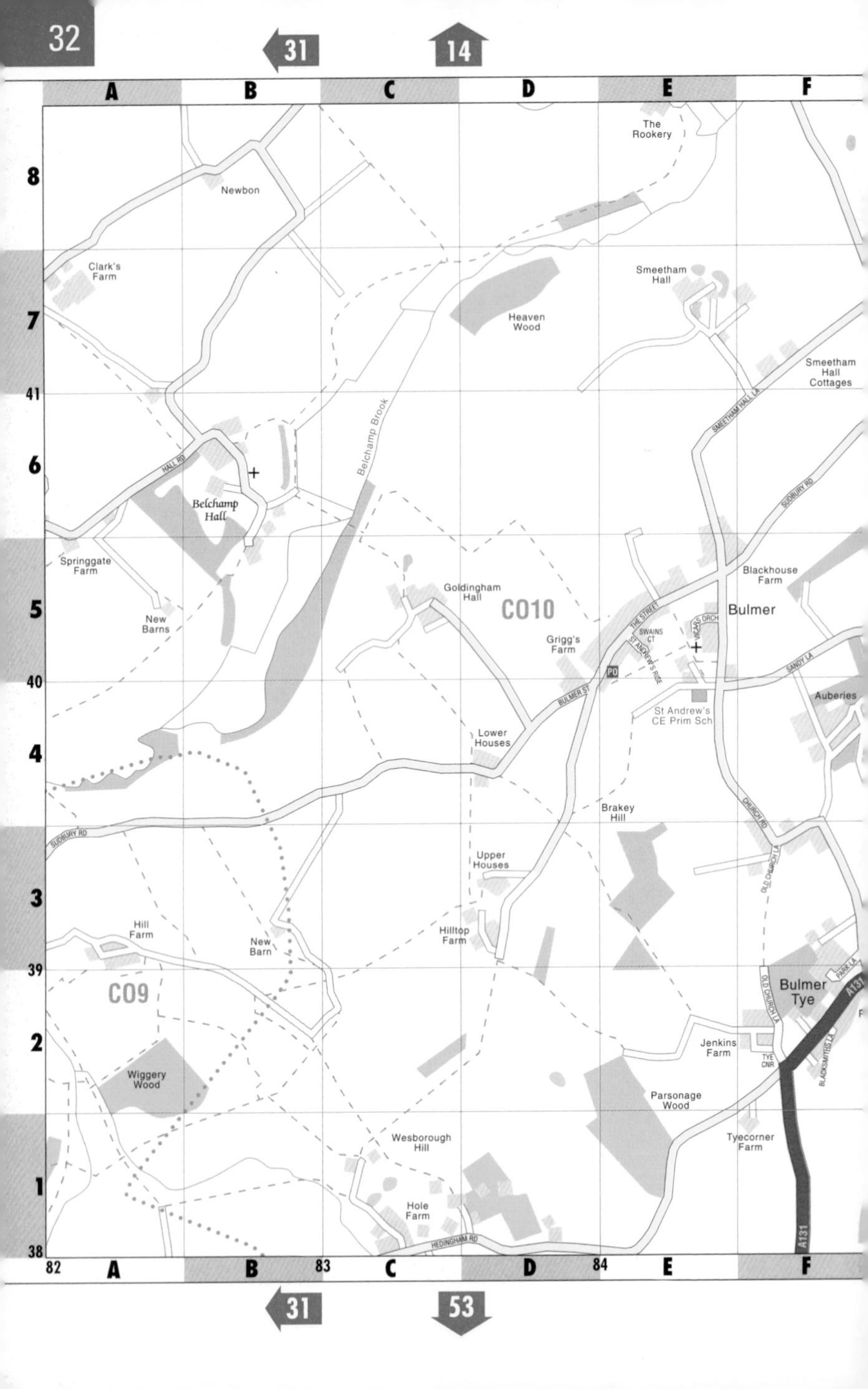

8

7

41

6

5

40

4

3

39

2

1

38

A   B   C   D   E   F

The Rookery

Newbon

Clark's Farm

Smeetham Hall

Heaven Wood

Smeetham Hall Cottages

HALL RD

Belchamp Brook

Belchamp Hall

SUDBURY RD

SMEETHAM HALL LA

Springgate Farm

Goldingham Hall

CO10

Blackhouse Farm

New Barns

Grigg's Farm

THE STREET

SWAINS CT

ST ANDREW'S RISE

Bulmer

ST ANDS ORCH

SANDY LA

Auberies

PO

BULMER ST

St Andrew's CE Prim Sch

Lower Houses

Brakey Hill

CHURCH RD

OLD CHAPEL RD

Hill Farm

New Barn

CO9

Upper Houses

Hilltop Farm

PARK LA

Bulmer Tye

A131

SUDBURY RD

Wiggery Wood

Jenkins Farm

TYE CNR

OLD CHURCH RD

BLACKSMITHS LA

Parsonage Wood

Wesborough Hill

Tyecorner Farm

Hole Farm

PEDLINGHAM RD

A131

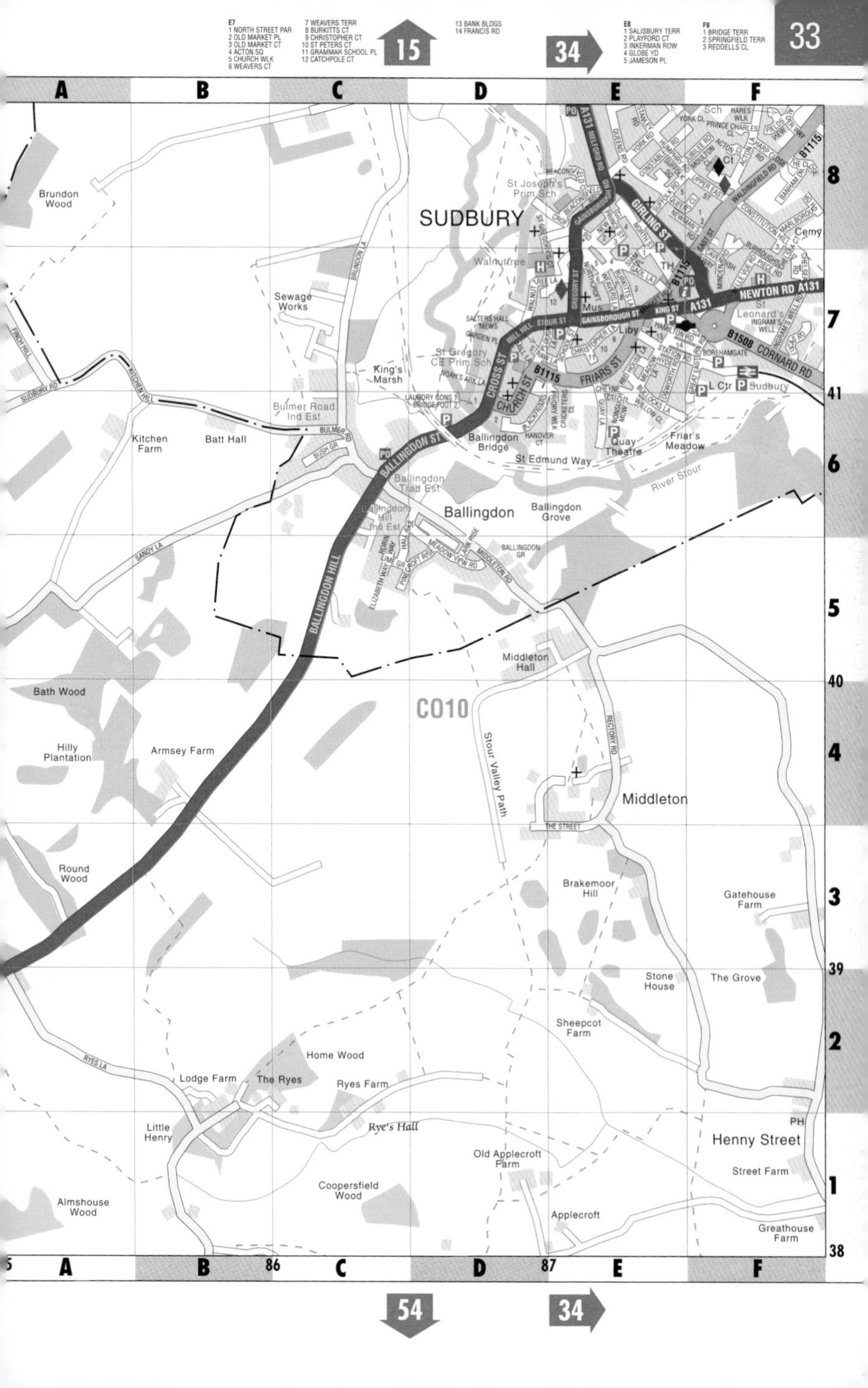
E7
1 NORTH STREET PAR
2 OLD MARKET PL
3 OLD MARKET CT
4 ACTON SQ
5 CHURCH WLK
6 WEAVERS CT
7 WEAVERS TERR
8 BURKITTS CT
9 CHRISTOPHER CT
10 ST PETERS CT
11 GRAMMAR SCHOOL PL
12 CATCHPOLE CT
13 BANK BLDGS
14 FRANCIS RD
15
34
E8
1 SALISBURY TERR
2 PLAYFORD CT
3 INKERMAN ROW
4 GLOBE YD
5 JAMESON PL
F8
1 BRIDGE TERR
2 SPRINGFIELD TERR
3 REDDELLS CL
SUDBURY
Brundon Wood
Sewage Works
King's Marsh
Bulmer Road Ind Est
Kitchen Farm
Batt Hall
St Joseph's Prim Sch
Walnuttree
St Gregory CE Prim Sch
Ballingdon Bridge
St Edmund Way
Quay Theatre
Friar's Meadow
River Stour
Ballingdon Trad Est
Ballingdon
Ballingdon Grove
Ballingdon Hill Ind Est
Middleton Hall
CO10
Bath Wood
Hilly Plantation
Armsey Farm
Stour Valley Path
Middleton
Round Wood
Brakemoor Hill
Gatehouse Farm
Stone House
The Grove
Sheepcot Farm
Home Wood
Lodge Farm
The Ryes
Ryes Farm
Rye's Hall
Little Henry
Henny Street
Old Applecroft Farm
Street Farm
Coopersfield Wood
Almshouse Wood
Applecroft
Greathouse Farm
A131
B1115
B1508
CROSS ST
CHURCH ST
FRIARS ST
GIRLING ST
NEWTON RD
CORNARD RD
GAINSBOROUGH ST
BALLINGDON ST
BALLINGDON HILL
SUDBURY RD
KITCHEN HILL
BULMER RD
SANDY LA
RECTORY RD
THE STREET
RYES LA
Sudbury
54
34

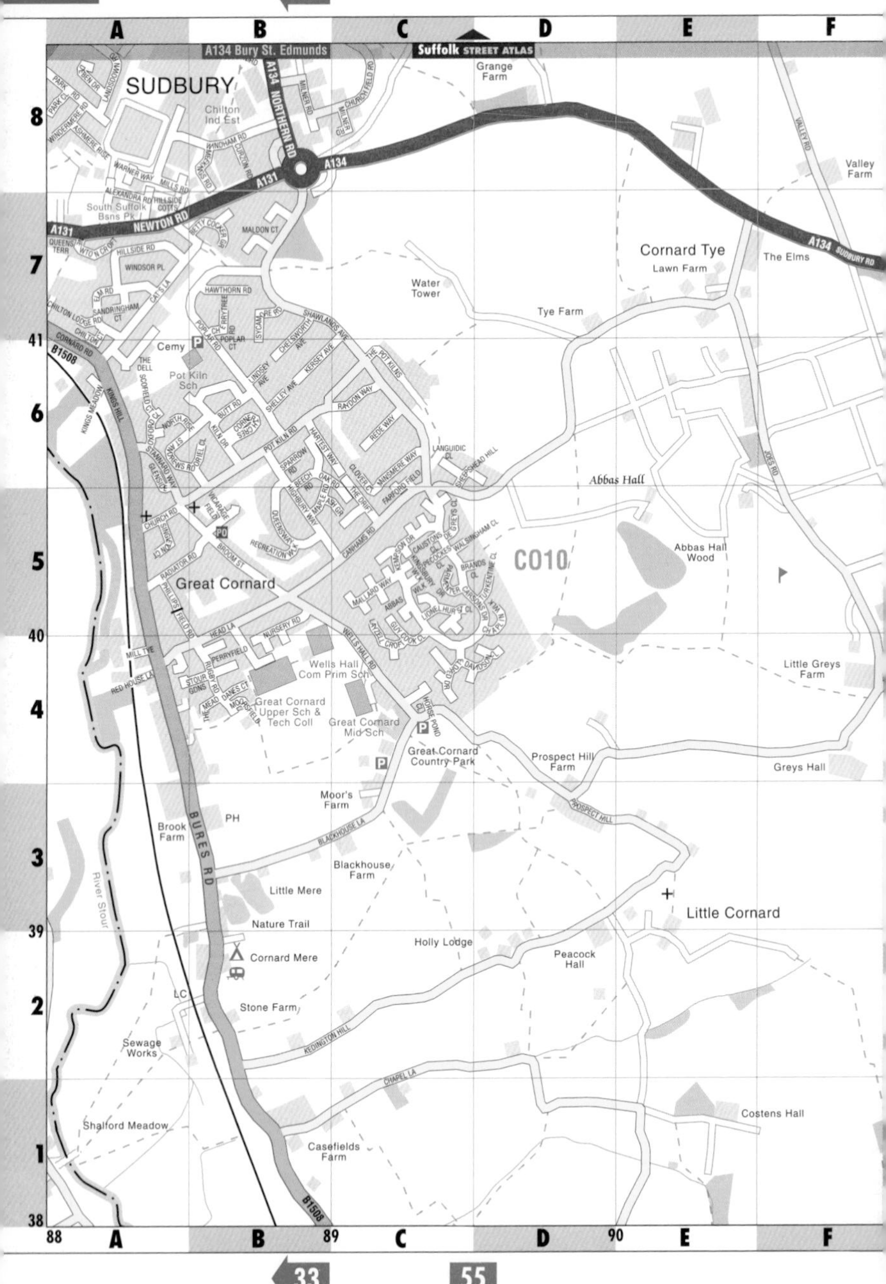

A B C D E F

8

SUDBURY

A134 Bury St. Edmunds

Chilton Ind Est

Grange Farm

Valley Farm

South Suffolk Bsns Pk

A131

A134

NEWTON RD

7

MALDON CT

QUEENS TERR

WINDSOR PL

B150B

CORNARD RD

Cornard Tye

Lawn Farm

The Elms

A134 SUDBURY RD

Water Tower

Tye Farm

41

Cemy

THE DELL

Pot Kiln Sch

HAWTHORN RD

POPLAR

CHELSFORD RD

KERSEY AVE

RAYDON WAY

Abbas Hall

6

PO

LANGUIDIC CL

SPRINGHILL

Abbas Hall Wood

5

Great Cornard

CO10

40

Wells Hall Com Prim Sch

Little Greys Farm

4

Great Cornard Upper Sch & Tech Coll

Great Cornard Mid Sch

Great Cornard Country Park

PD

Prospect Hill Farm

Greys Hall

PROSPECT HILL

Moor's Farm

3

Brook Farm

PH

BURES RD

BLACKHOUSE LA

Blackhouse Farm

Little Mere

Little Cornard

39

Nature Trail

Cornard Mere

Holly Lodge

Peacock Hall

2

LC

Stone Farm

KEDINGTON HILL

Sewage Works

CHAPEL LA

Shalford Meadow

Costens Hall

1

River Stout

Casefields Farm

B150B

38

88 A B 89 C D 90 E F

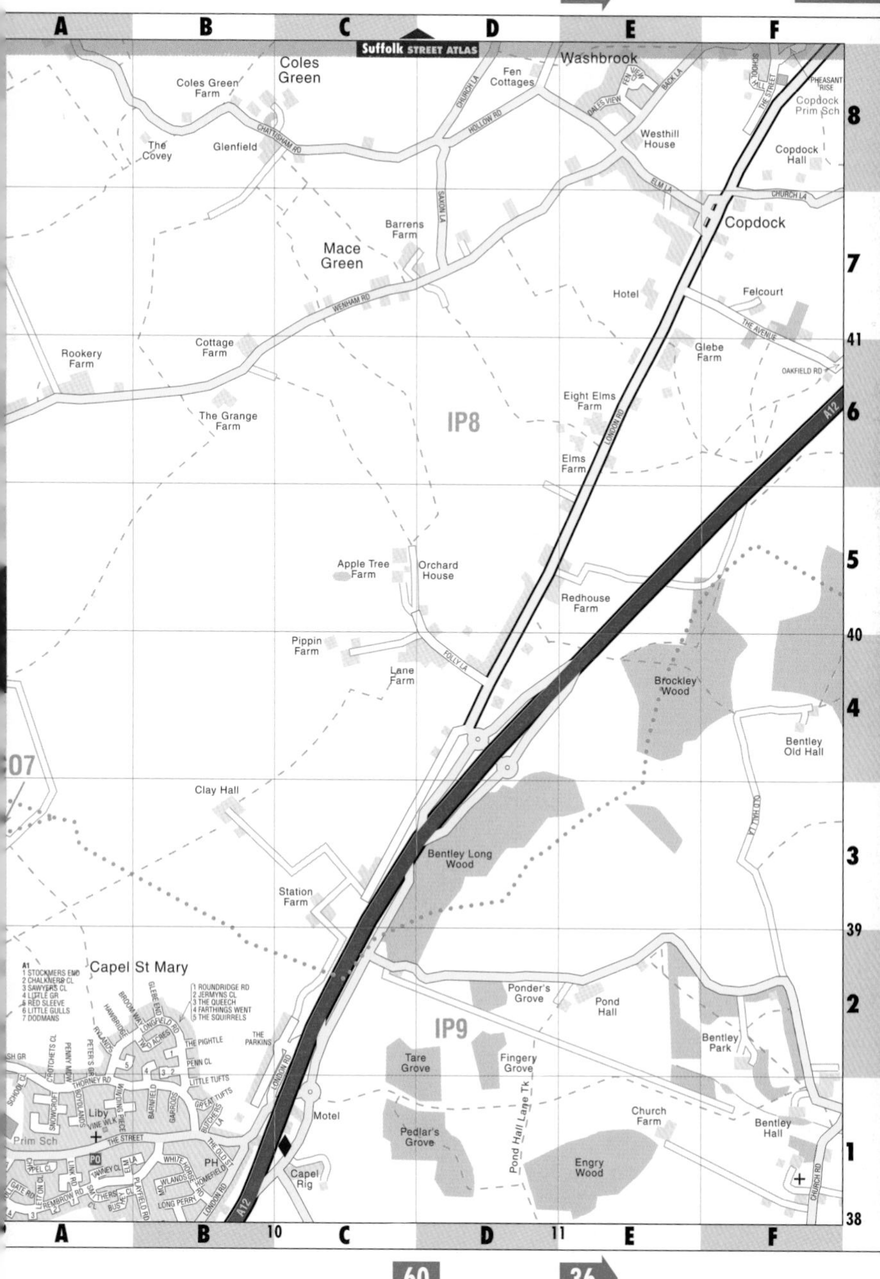

Suffolk STREET ATLAS

Coles
Green

Washbrook

PHEASANT
RISE

Copdock
Prim Sch

8

Coles Green
Farm

Fen
Cottages

WALES VIEW

MILL LA

Copdock
Hall

The
Covey

Glenfield

CHATTISHAM RD

CHURCH LA

HELLOW RD

SAXON LA

Westhill
House

ELM LA

THE GRANGE

CHURCH LA

Copdock

Barrens
Farm

7

Mace
Green

Hotel

Felcourt

Rookery
Farm

WENHAM RD

Glebe
Farm

THE AVENUE

41

Cottage
Farm

OAKFIELD RD

Eight Elms
Farm

A12

6

The Grange
Farm

IP8

LONDON RD

Elms
Farm

5

Apple Tree
Farm

Orchard
House

Redhouse
Farm

Pippin
Farm

FOLLY LA

40

Brockley
Wood

Lane
Farm

Bentley
Old Hall

4

C07

Clay Hall

A12 TREE RD

Station
Farm

Bentley Long
Wood

3

39

Capel St Mary

A1
1 STOCKMERS END
2 CHALKNER RD
3 SAWYER'S CL
4 LITTLE GR
5 RED SLEEVE
6 LITTLE GULLS
7 DODMANS

1 ROUNDRIDGE RD
2 JERMYNS CL
3 THE QUEECH
4 FARTHINGS WENT
5 THE SQUIRRELS

Ponder's
Grove

Pond
Hall

Bentley
Park

2

IP9

Tare
Grove

Fingery
Grove

THE PIGHTLE

PENN CL

LITTLE TUFTS

THE PARKINS

Prim Sch

PO

PH

Motel

Pedlar's
Grove

Pond Hall Lane Tk

Church
Farm

Bentley
Hall

CHURCH RD

1

Capel
Rig

A12

LONDON RD

Engry
Wood

38

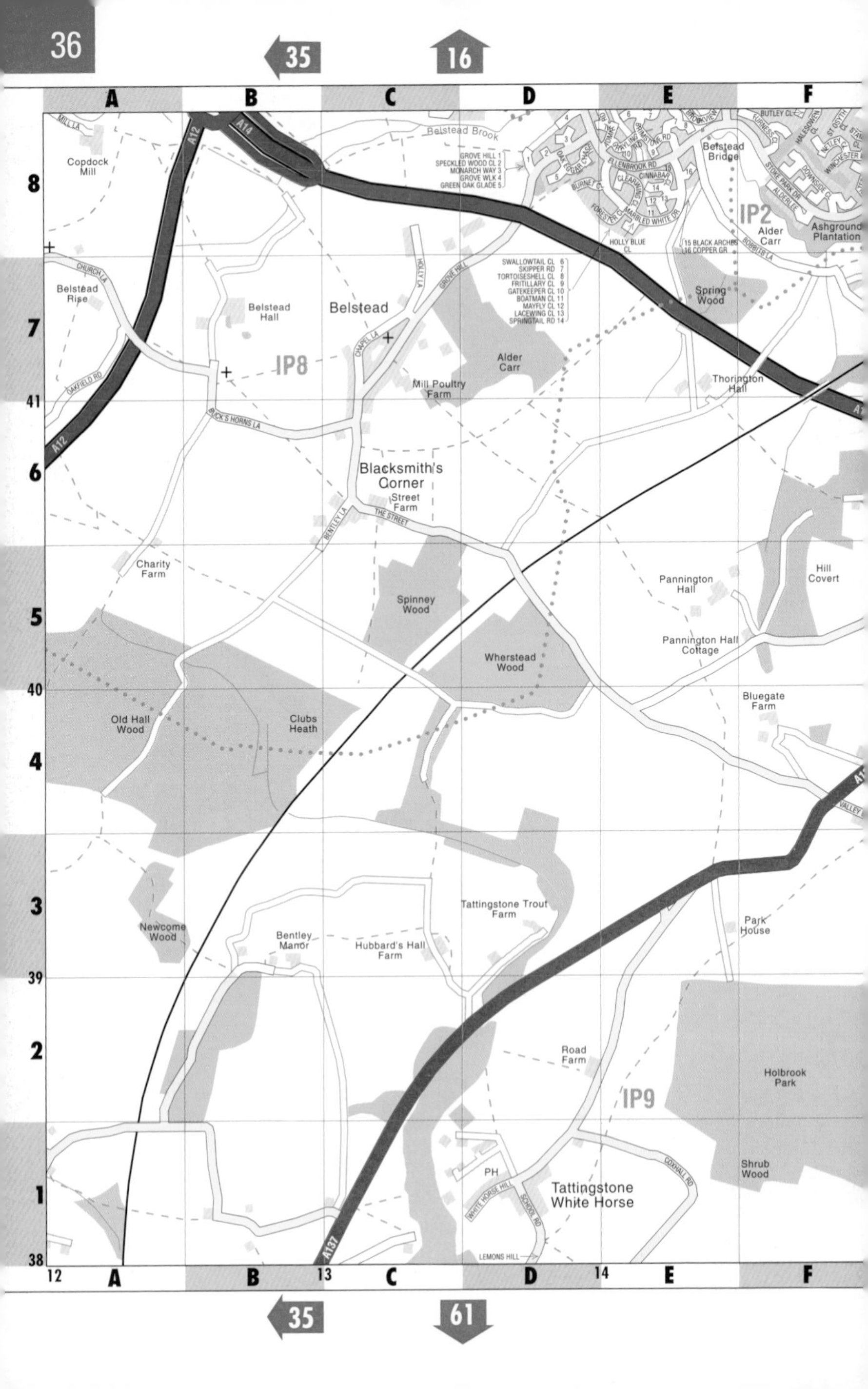

35
16
A
B
C
D
E
F
MILL LA
Copdock Mill
A12
A14
Belstead Brook
GROVE HILL 1
SPECKLED WOOD CL 2
MONARCH WAY 3
GROVE WLK 4
GREEN OAK GLADE 5
ELLENBROOK RD
CINNABAR
CLEARWING CL
BURNEY CL
FORESTER CL
MARBLED WHITE DR
HOLLY BLUE CL
Belstead Bridge
BUTLEY CL
FURNESS CL
HALESOWEN CL
NETLEY CL
STOKE PARK DR
DOWNSIDE CL
ALDERLEE
WINCHESTER
IP2
Alder Carr
Ashground Plantation
15 BLACK ARCHES
16 COPPER GR
BOBBITS LA
SWALLOWTAIL CL 6
SKIPPER RD 7
TORTOISESHELL CL 8
FRITILLARY CL 9
GATEKEEPER CL 10
BOATMAN CL 11
MAYFLY CL 12
LACEWING CL 13
SPRINGTAIL RD 14
CHURCH LA
Belstead Rise
Belstead Hall
Belstead
HOLLY LA
GROVE HILL
CHAPEL LA
Spring Wood
IP8
Alder Carr
Mill Poultry Farm
Thorington Hall
OAKFIELD RD
BUCK'S HORNS LA
Blacksmith's Corner
Street Farm
THE STREET
BENTLEY LA
Charity Farm
Spinney Wood
Pannington Hall
Hill Covert
Wherstead Wood
Pannington Hall Cottage
Old Hall Wood
Clubs Heath
Bluegate Farm
VALLEY
Newcome Wood
Tattingstone Trout Farm
Bentley Manor
Hubbard's Hall Farm
Park House
Road Farm
Holbrook Park
IP9
PH
COXHALL RD
Shrub Wood
WHITE HORSE HILL
SCHOOL RD
Tattingstone White Horse
A137
LEMONS HILL
8
7
41
6
5
40
4
3
39
2
1
38
12
13
14

17
38

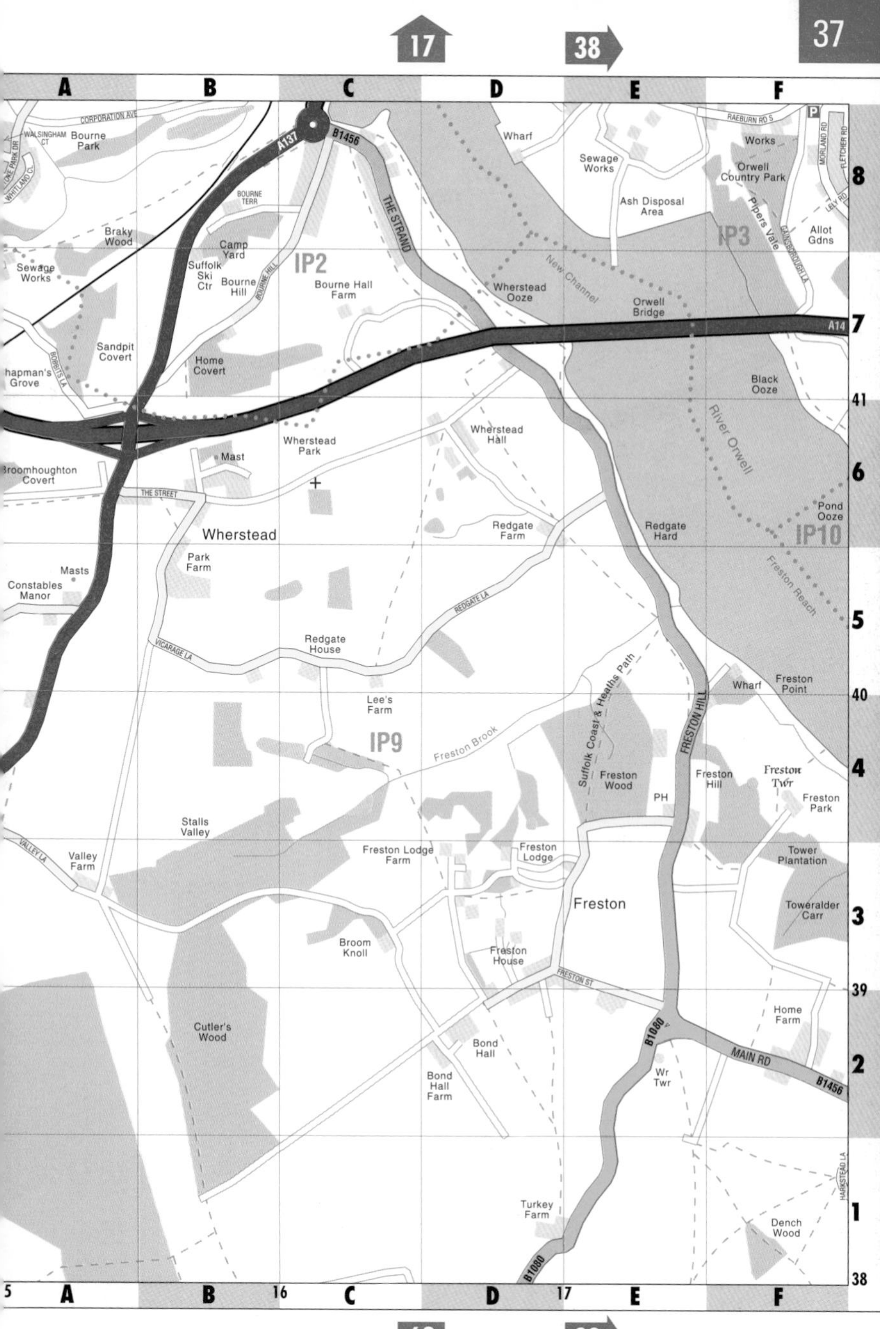
A
B
C
D
E
F
CORPORATION AVE
WALSINGHAM CT
Bourne Park
WHITLAND CL
A137
B1456
Wharf
RAEBURN RD S
Sewage Works
Works
Orwell Country Park
MORLAND RD
FLETCHER RD
8
BOURNE TERR
THE STRAND
Ash Disposal Area
LELY RD
Braky Wood
Camp Yard
IP3
Pipers Vale
Allot Gdns
Sewage Works
Suffolk Ski Ctr
Bourne Hill
BOURNE HILL
IP2
Bourne Hall Farm
New Channel
Wherstead Ooze
Orwell Bridge
GAINSBOROUGH LA
7
A14
Sandpit Covert
Home Covert
hapman's Grove
BOBBITS LA
Black Ooze
41
Wherstead Park
Wherstead Hall
River Orwell
Mast
Broomhoughton Covert
6
THE STREET
Wherstead
Redgate Farm
Redgate Hard
Pond Ooze
IP10
Park Farm
Masts
Constables Manor
Freston Reach
REDGATE LA
5
Redgate House
VICARAGE LA
Wharf
Freston Point
40
Lee's Farm
Suffolk Coast & Heaths Path
IP9
Freston Brook
FRESTON HILL
Freston Twr
4
Freston Wood
Freston Hill
PH
Freston Park
Stalls Valley
VALLEY LA
Valley Farm
Freston Lodge Farm
Freston Lodge
Tower Plantation
Freston
Toweralder Carr
3
Broom Knoll
Freston House
FRESTON ST
39
Cutler's Wood
B1080
Home Farm
Bond Hall
MAIN RD
2
Bond Hall Farm
Wr Twr
B1456
HARKSTEAD LA
Turkey Farm
1
Dench Wood
B1080
38
5
16
17

62
38

37
18

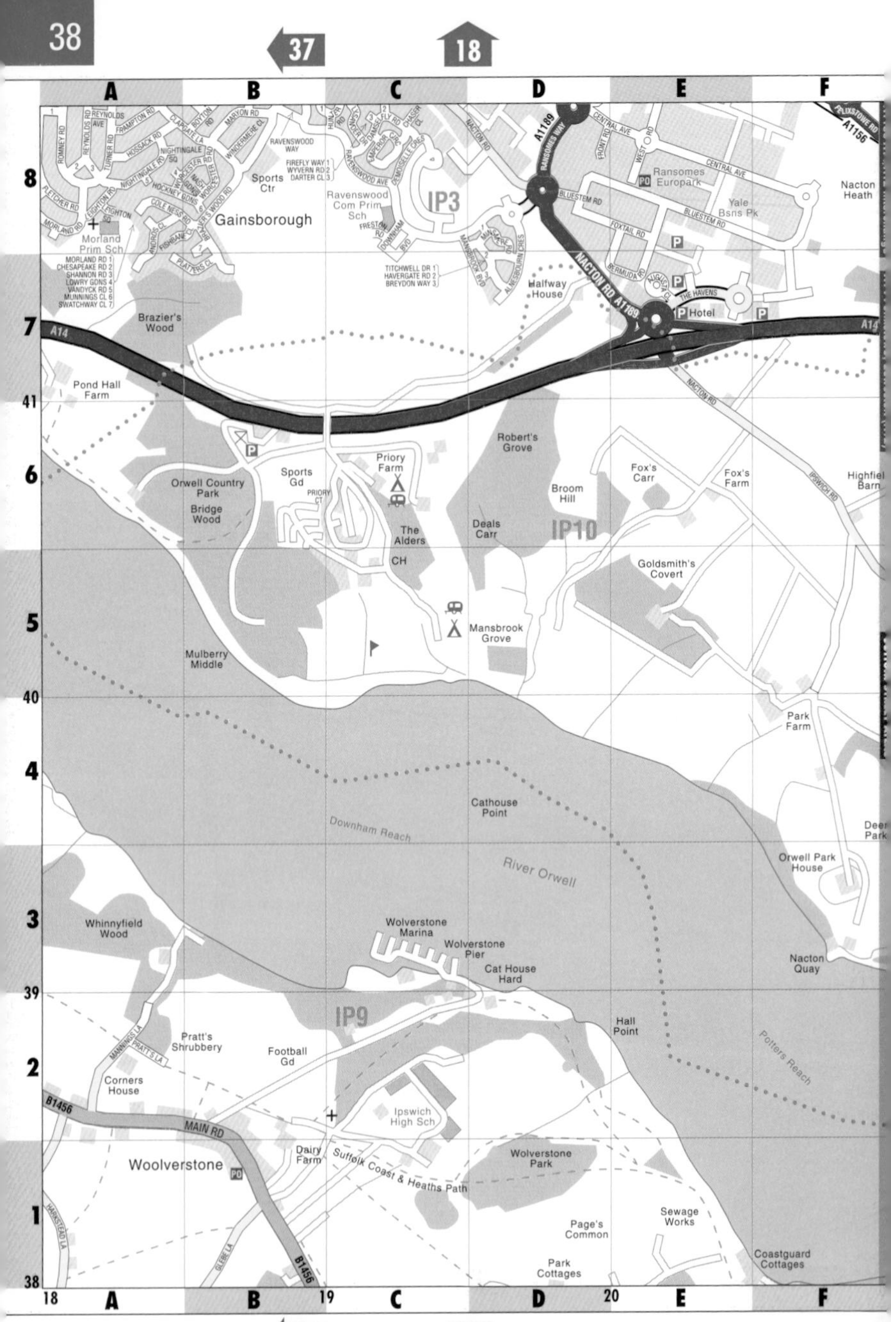
A
B
C
D
E
F
8
7
6
5
4
3
2
1
41
40
39
38
18
19
20
Gainsborough
Sports Ctr
Ravenswood Com Prim Sch
IP3
Ransomes Europark
Nacton Heath
Yale Bsns Pk
Morland Prim Sch
MORLAND RD 1
CHESAPEAKE RD 2
SHANNON RD 3
LOWRY GDNS 4
VANDYCK RD 5
MUNNINGS CL 6
SWATCHWAY CL 7
TITCHWELL DR 1
HAVERGATE RD 2
BREYDON WAY 3
FIREFLY WAY 1
WYVERN RD 2
DARTER CL 3
RAVENSWOOD WAY
Halfway House
Hotel
Brazier's Wood
A14
A1189
A1156
NACTON RD A1189
RANSOMES WAY
BLUESTEM RD
CENTRAL AVE
Pond Hall Farm
Robert's Grove
Priory Farm
Sports Gd
Orwell Country Park
Bridge Wood
The Alders
CH
Deals Carr
Broom Hill
IP10
Fox's Carr
Fox's Farm
Highfield Barn
Goldsmith's Covert
Mansbrook Grove
Mulberry Middle
Park Farm
Cathouse Point
Downham Reach
River Orwell
Deer Park
Orwell Park House
Whinnyfield Wood
Wolverstone Marina
Wolverstone Pier
Cat House Hard
Nacton Quay
IP9
Hall Point
Potters Reach
Pratt's Shrubbery
Football Gd
Corners House
Ipswich High Sch
B1456
MAIN RD
Woolverstone
Dairy Farm
Suffolk Coast & Heaths Path
Wolverstone Park
Page's Common
Sewage Works
Park Cottages
Coastguard Cottages

37
63

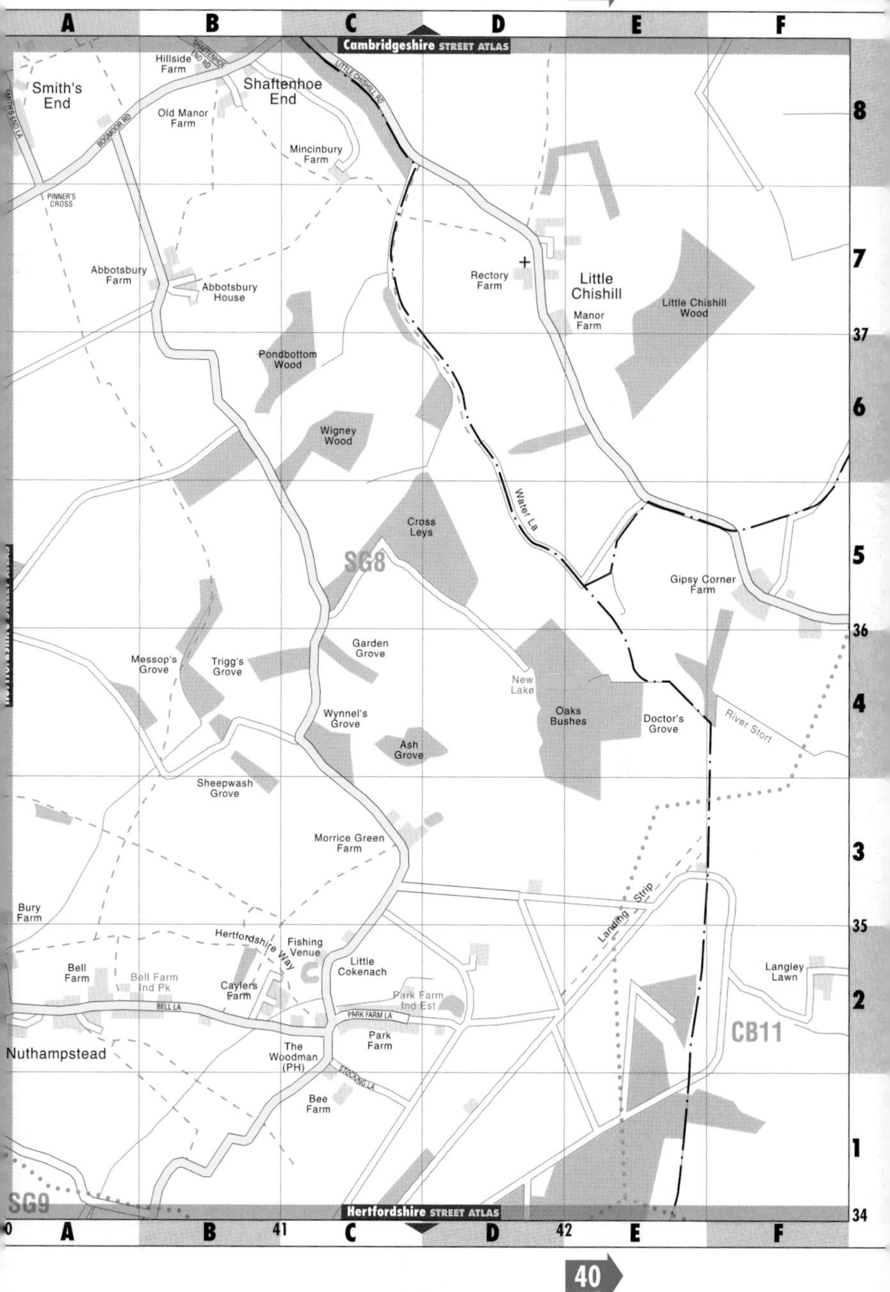

A | B | C | D | E | F

8

Smith's End

Hillside Farm

Old Manor Farm

Shaftenhoe End

Mincinbury Farm

PINNER'S CROSS

Abbotsbury Farm

Abbotsbury House

7

Rectory Farm

Little Chishill

Little Chishill Wood

37

Manor Farm

Pondbottom Wood

6

Wigney Wood

Water La

Cross Leys

SG8

5

Gipsy Corner Farm

36

Messop's Grove

Trigg's Grove

Garden Grove

New Lake

Doctor's Grove

River Stort

4

Wynnel's Grove

Ash Grove

Oaks Bushes

Sheepwash Grove

Morrice Green Farm

3

Landing Strip

Bury Farm

35

Hertfordshire Way

Fishing Venue

Little Cokenach

Langley Lawn

Bell Farm

Bell Farm Ind Pk

Cayler's Farm

Park Farm Ind Est

CB11

2

BELL LA

PARK FARM LA

Nuthampstead

The Woodman (PH)

Park Farm

BROOKED LA

Bee Farm

1

SG9

34

0 | A | B | 41 | C | D | 42 | E | F

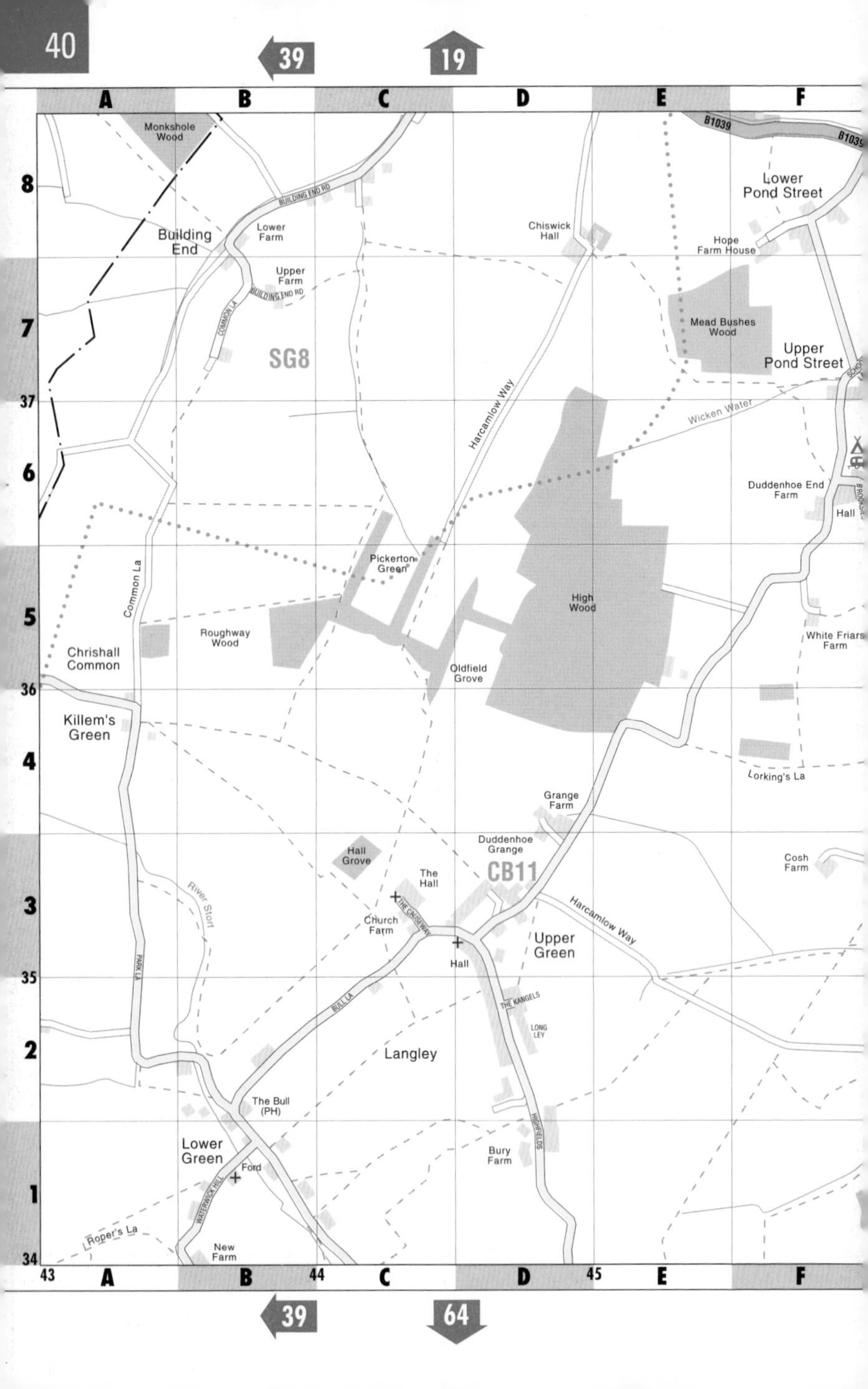
39
19
A
B
C
D
E
F
Monkshole Wood
BUILDING END RD
Building End
Lower Farm
Upper Farm
BUILDING END RD
COMMON LA
SG8
Chiswick Hall
B1039
B1039
Lower Pond Street
Hope Farm House
Mead Bushes Wood
Upper Pond Street
Harcamlow Way
Wicken Water
Duddenhoe End Farm
Hall
Pickerton Green
Common La
High Wood
Roughway Wood
Chrishall Common
Oldfield Grove
White Friars Farm
Killem's Green
Lorking's La
Grange Farm
Duddenhoe Grange
Hall Grove
The Hall
CB11
Cosh Farm
River Stort
Church Farm
THE CAUSEWAY
Harcamlow Way
Hall
Upper Green
PARK LA
BULL LA
THE KANGELS
LONG LEY
Langley
The Bull (PH)
HIGHFIELDS
Lower Green
Ford
Bury Farm
WATERWICK HILL
Roper's La
New Farm
8
7
37
6
5
36
4
3
35
2
1
34
43
44
45
39
64

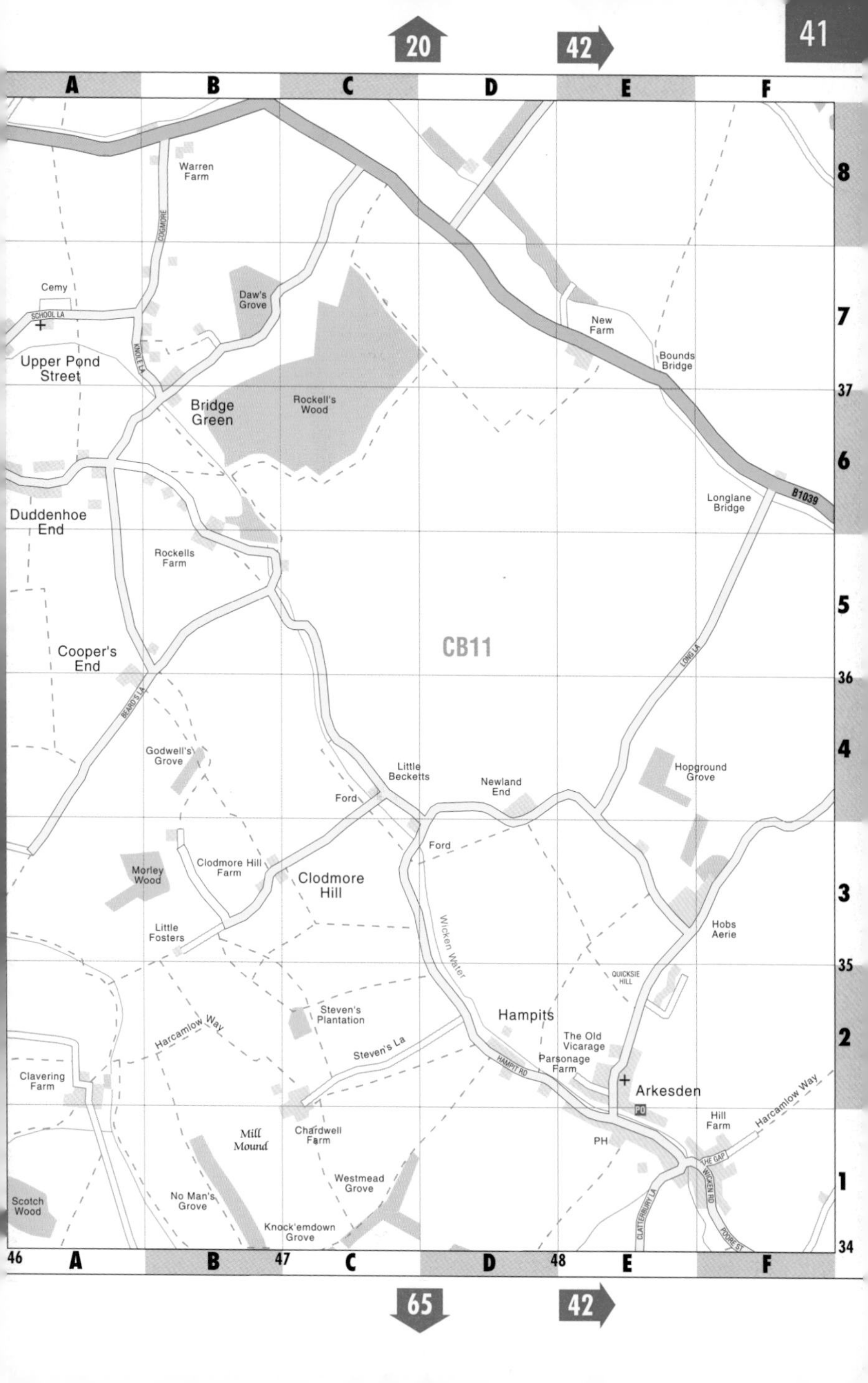
20
42
A
B
C
D
E
F
Warren Farm
COGMORE
Cemy
SCHOOL LA
Daw's Grove
New Farm
Bounds Bridge
Upper Pond Street
KNOLE LA
Bridge Green
Rockell's Wood
Duddenhoe End
Longlane Bridge
B1039
Rockells Farm
Cooper's End
CB11
LONG LA
BEARD'S LA
Godwell's Grove
Little Becketts
Newland End
Hopground Grove
Ford
Ford
Morley Wood
Clodmore Hill Farm
Clodmore Hill
Little Fosters
Wicken Water
Hobs Aerie
QUICKSIE HILL
Steven's Plantation
Hampits
Harcamlow Way
The Old Vicarage
Steven's La
Parsonage Farm
HAMPIT RD
Clavering Farm
Arkesden
PO
Hill Farm
Harcamlow Way
Mill Mound
Chardwell Farm
PH
THE GAP
Westmead Grove
WICKEN RD
CLATTERBURY LA
Scotch Wood
No Man's Grove
Knock'emdown Grove
POORE ST
8
7
37
6
5
36
4
3
35
2
1
34
46
47
48
65
42

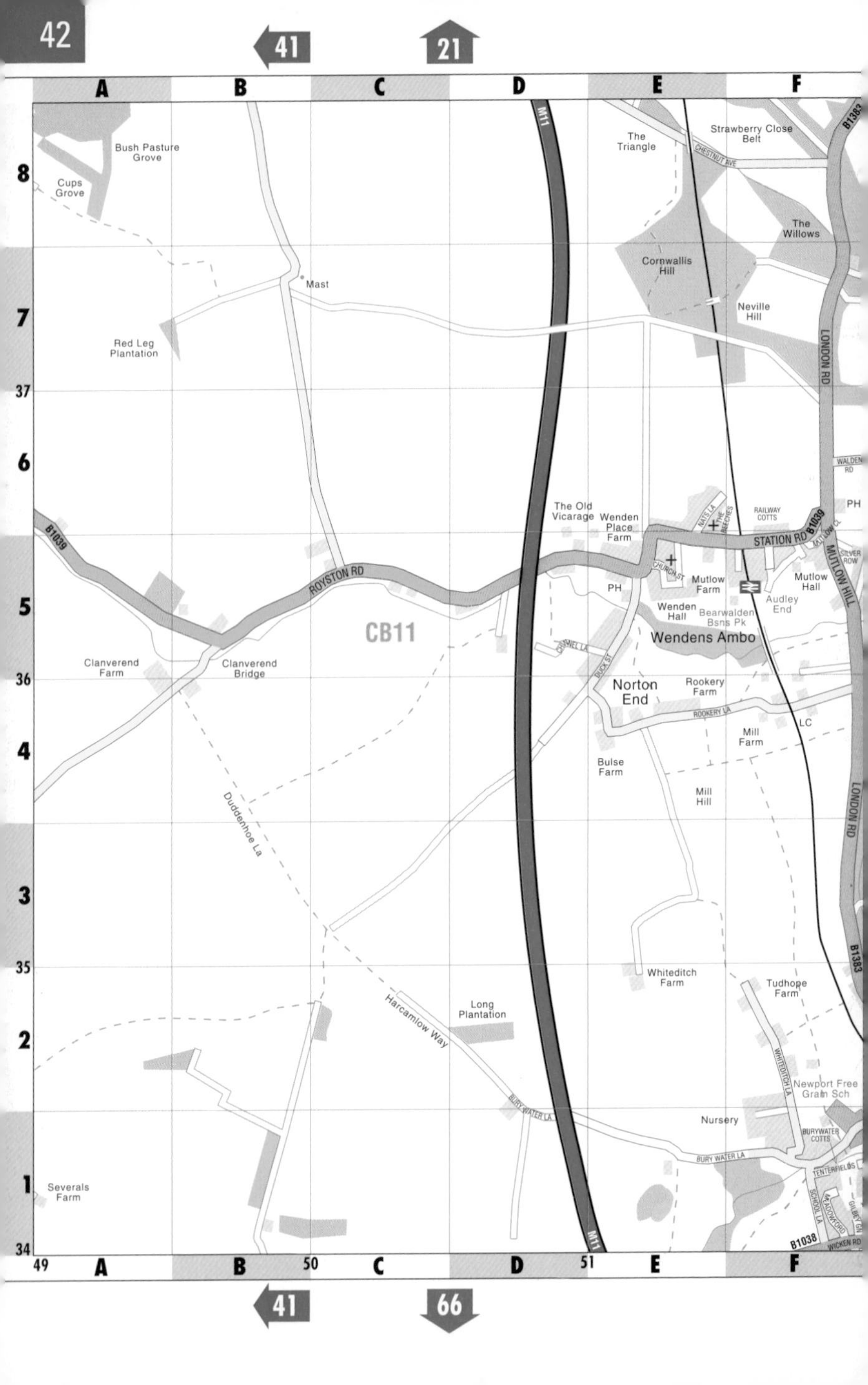

8

Cups
Grove

Bush Pasture
Grove

The
Triangle

Strawberry Close
Belt

CHESTNUT AVE

The
Willows

Cornwallis
Hill

7

Mast

Red Leg
Plantation

Neville
Hill

LONDON RD

37

6

WALDEN
RD

PH

The Old
Vicarage

Wenden
Place
Farm

NUTS

RAILWAY
COTTS

STATION RD

B1039

PH

ROYSTON RD

5

PH

Mutlow
Farm

Mutlow
Hall

STRIER
ROW

MUTLOW HILL

CB11

Wenden
Hall

Bearwalden
Bsns Pk

Audley
End

Wendens Ambo

Clanverend
Farm

Clanverend
Bridge

36

Norton
End

Rookery
Farm

ROOKERY LA

LC

4

Mill
Farm

LONDON RD

B1383

Bulse
Farm

Mill
Hill

Durdenhoe La

3

35

Whiteditch
Farm

Tudhope
Farm

2

Harcamlow Way

Long
Plantation

WHITEDITCH LA

Newport Free
Grain Sch

BURYWATER
COTTS

Nursery

BURY WATER LA

TENTERHELDS

1

Severals
Farm

BURY WATER LA

SCHOOL LA

B1038

WICKEN RD

34

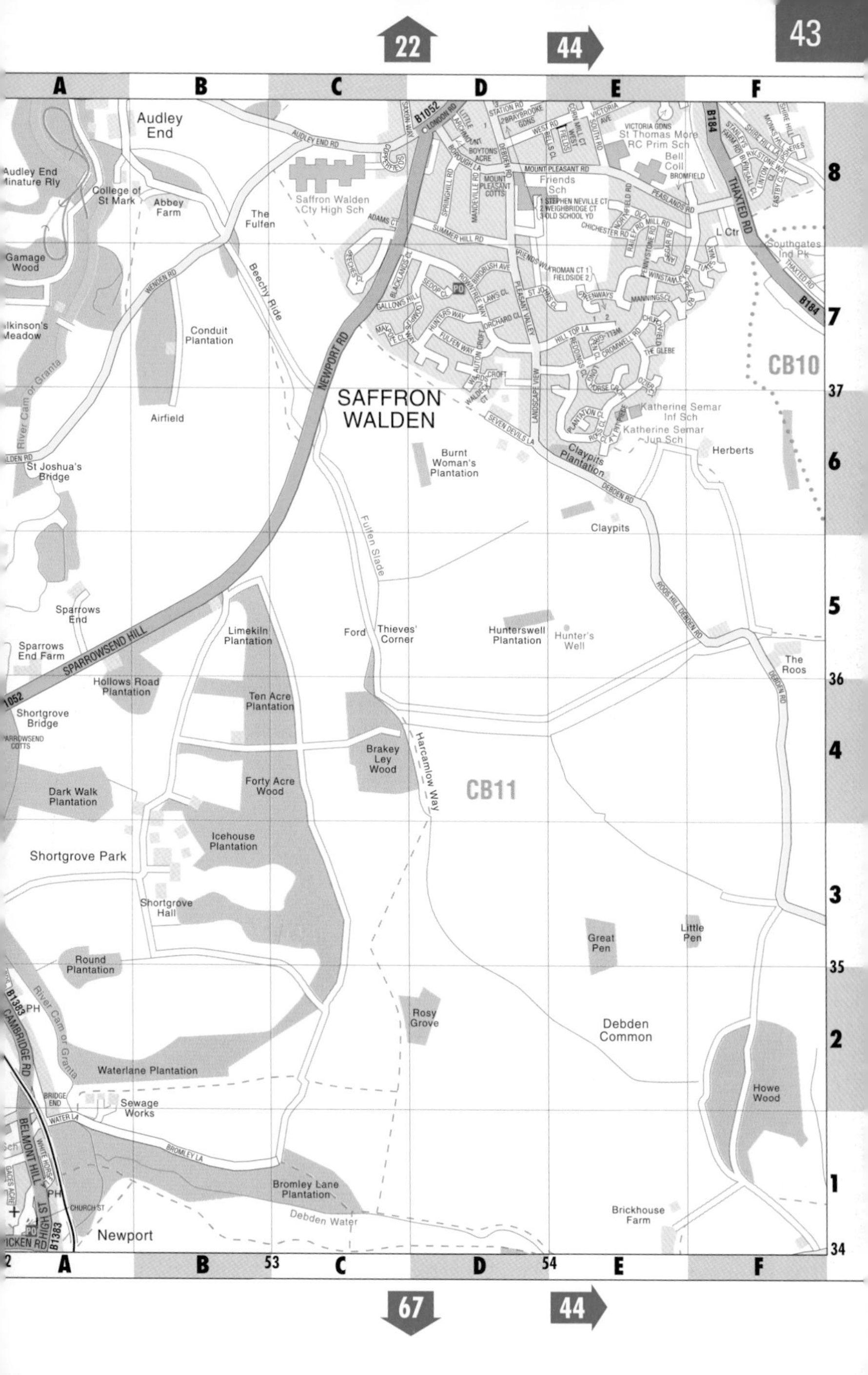
22
44
A
B
C
D
E
F
Audley End
Audley End Minature Rly
College of St Mark
Abbey Farm
The Fulfen
Saffron Walden Cty High Sch
Gamage Wood
Conduit Plantation
Airfield
Beechy Ride
NEWPORT RD
SAFFRON WALDEN
Friends Sch
St Thomas More RC Prim Sch
Bell Coll
L Ctr
Southgates Ind Pk
THAXTED RD
B184
B1052
CB10
Katherine Semar Inf Sch
Katherine Semar Jun Sch
Herberts
Claypits Plantation
Burnt Woman's Plantation
St Joshua's Bridge
River Cam or Granta
Fulfen Slade
Claypits
Sparrows End
Sparrows End Farm
SPARROWSEND HILL
Limekiln Plantation
Ford
Thieves' Corner
Hunterswell Plantation
Hunter's Well
The Roos
Hollows Road Plantation
Shortgrove Bridge
Ten Acre Plantation
Brakey Ley Wood
Harcamlow Way
CB11
Dark Walk Plantation
Forty Acre Wood
Icehouse Plantation
Shortgrove Park
Shortgrove Hall
Great Pen
Little Pen
Round Plantation
Rosy Grove
Debden Common
Waterlane Plantation
Sewage Works
Howe Wood
Bromley Lane Plantation
Debden Water
Brickhouse Farm
Newport
BELMONT HILL
CAMBRIDGE RD
B1383
WATER LA
BROMLEY LA
CHURCH ST
DEBDEN RD
ROOS HILL DEBDEN RD
SEVEN DEVILS LA
LANDSCAPE VIEW
PLEASANT VALLEY
AUDLEY END RD
WENDEN RD
MOUNT PLEASANT RD
PEASLANDS RD
SUMMER HILL RD
ADAMS CT
GALLOWS HILL
FULFEN WAY
HUNTERS WAY
ORCHARD CL
ROWNTREE WAY
BIRDBUSH AVE
HILL TOP LA
CROMWELL RD
WINSTANLEY RD
MANNINGS CL
THE GLEBE
CHICHESTER RD
MILL RD
1 STEPHEN NEVILLE CT
2 WEIGHBRIDGE CT
3 OLD SCHOOL YD
ROMAN CT 1
FIELDSIDE 2
VICTORIA GDNS
WEST RD
SOUTH RD
STATION RD
LONDON RD
BOROUGH LA
SHIRE HILL
PH
PO
1
2
3
4
5
6
7
8
34
35
36
37
53
54
67
44

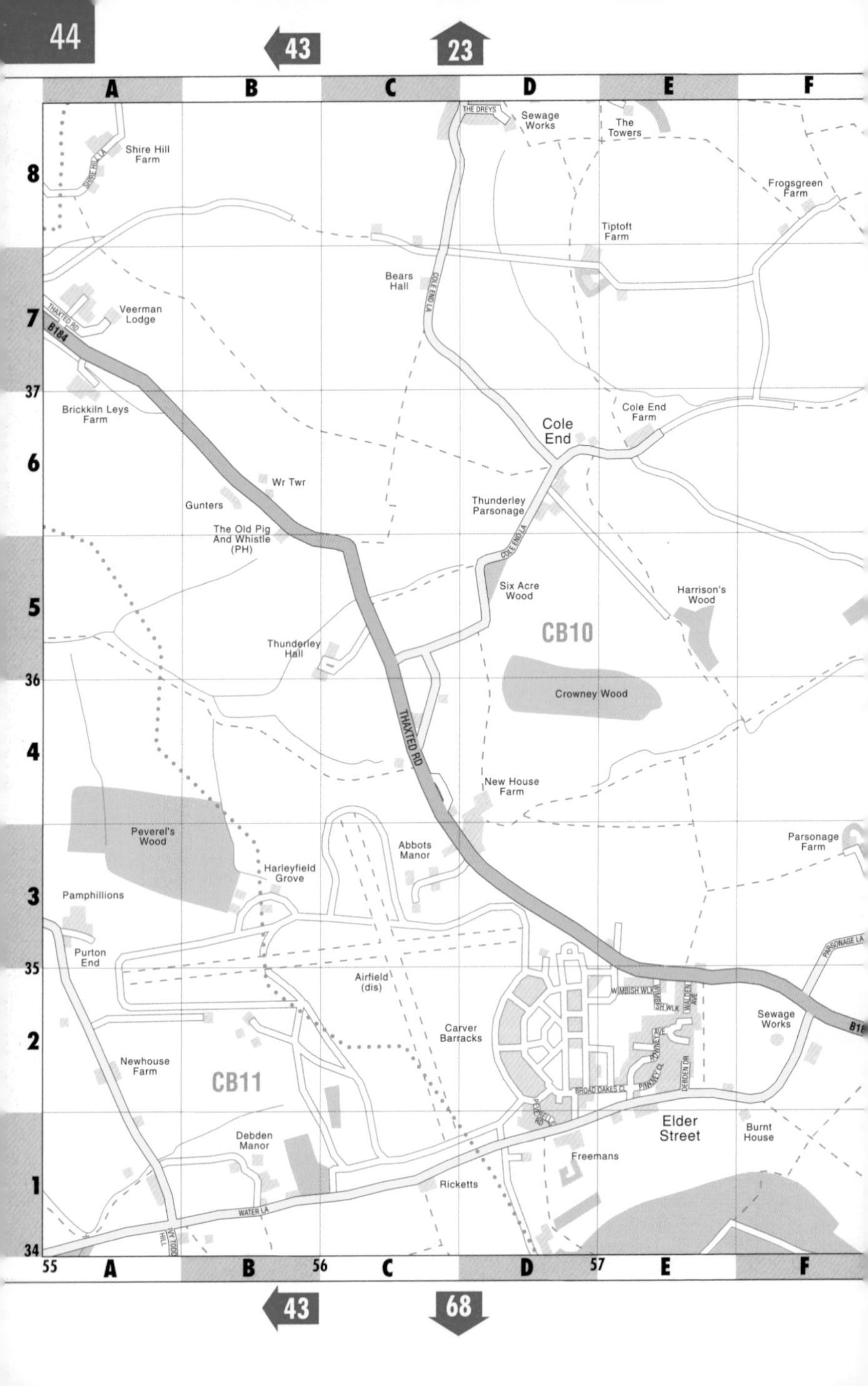

43
23
A
B
C
D
E
F
8
7
37
6
5
36
4
3
35
2
1
34
55
56
57
The Dreys
Sewage Works
The Towers
Shire Hill Farm
Shire Hill La
Frogsgreen Farm
Tiptoft Farm
Bears Hall
Cole End La
Veerman Lodge
Thaxted Rd
B184
Brickkiln Leys Farm
Cole End Farm
Cole End
Wr Twr
Gunters
Thunderley Parsonage
The Old Pig And Whistle (PH)
Cole End La
Six Acre Wood
Harrison's Wood
CB10
Thunderley Hall
Crowney Wood
Thaxted Rd
New House Farm
Peverel's Wood
Abbots Manor
Parsonage Farm
Harleyfield Grove
Pamphillions
Purton End
Parsonage La
Airfield (dis)
Wimbish Wlk
Walden Ave
Sewage Works
Carver Barracks
Rowney Ave
Newhouse Farm
Pinkney Cl
Debden Dr
Broad Oakes Cl
CB11
Elder Street
Burnt House
Debden Manor
Freemans
Ricketts
Water La
Ivy Todd Hill
43
68

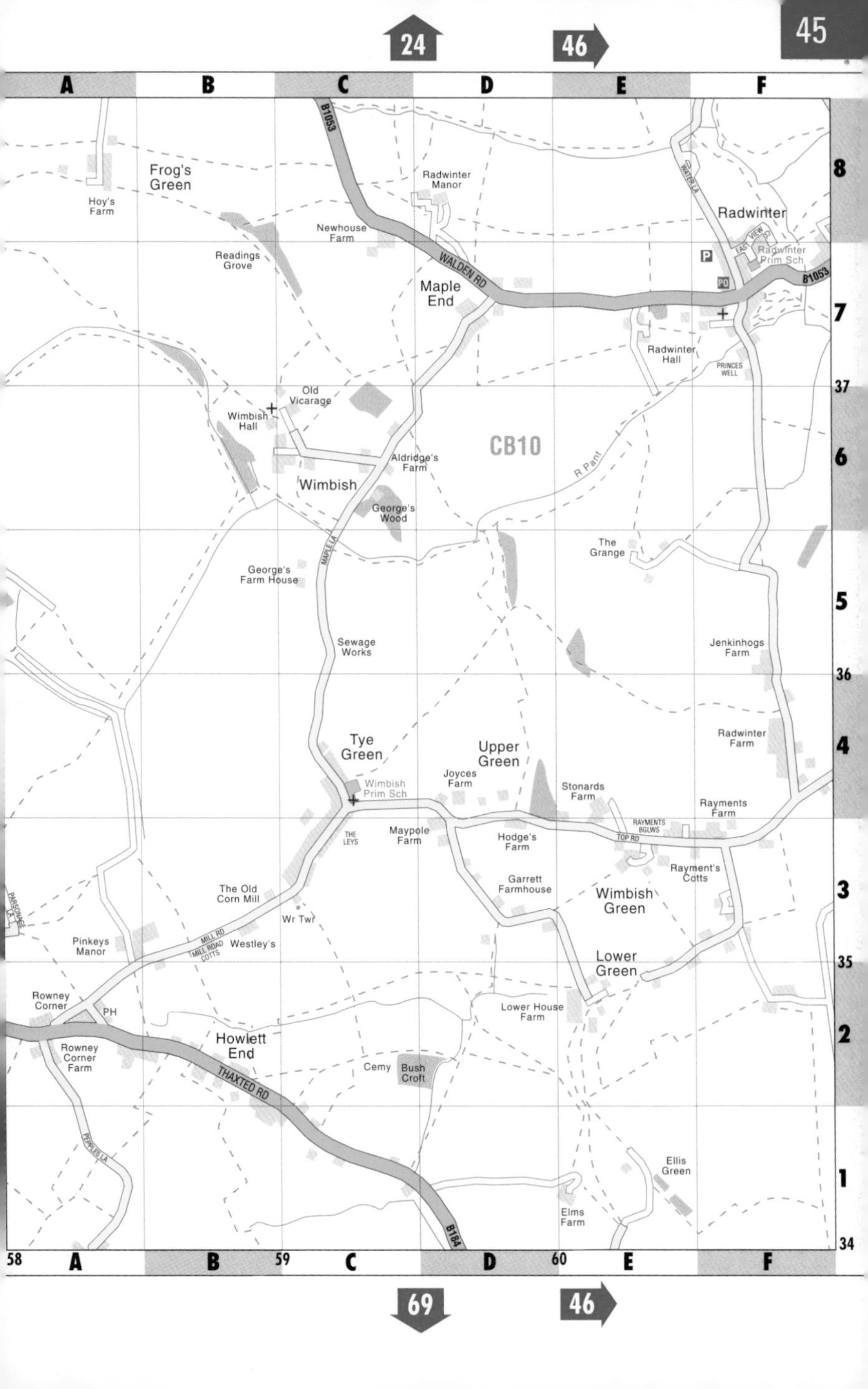
24
46
A
B
C
D
E
F
B1053
Frog's Green
Hoy's Farm
Radwinter Manor
Newhouse Farm
Readings Grove
Radwinter
WATER LA
EAST VIEW CL
Radwinter Prim Sch
P
PO
B1053
WALDEN RD
Maple End
Radwinter Hall
PRINCES WELL
Old Vicarage
Wimbish Hall
CB10
Aldridge's Farm
R Pant
Wimbish
George's Wood
The Grange
MAPLE LA
George's Farm House
Sewage Works
Jenkinhogs Farm
Radwinter Farm
Tye Green
Upper Green
Joyces Farm
Wimbish Prim Sch
Stonards Farm
Rayments Farm
RAYMENTS BGLWS
THE LEYS
Maypole Farm
Hodge's Farm
TOP RD
Rayment's Cotts
Garrett Farmhouse
Wimbish Green
The Old Corn Mill
Wr Twr
PARSONAGE LA
Pinkeys Manor
MILL RD
MILL ROAD COTTS
Westley's
Lower Green
Rowney Corner
PH
Lower House Farm
Howlett End
Rowney Corner Farm
THAXTED RD
Cemy
Bush Croft
PEPPLES LA
Ellis Green
Elms Farm
B184
8
7
37
6
5
36
4
3
35
2
1
34
58
59
60
A
B
C
D
E
F
69
46

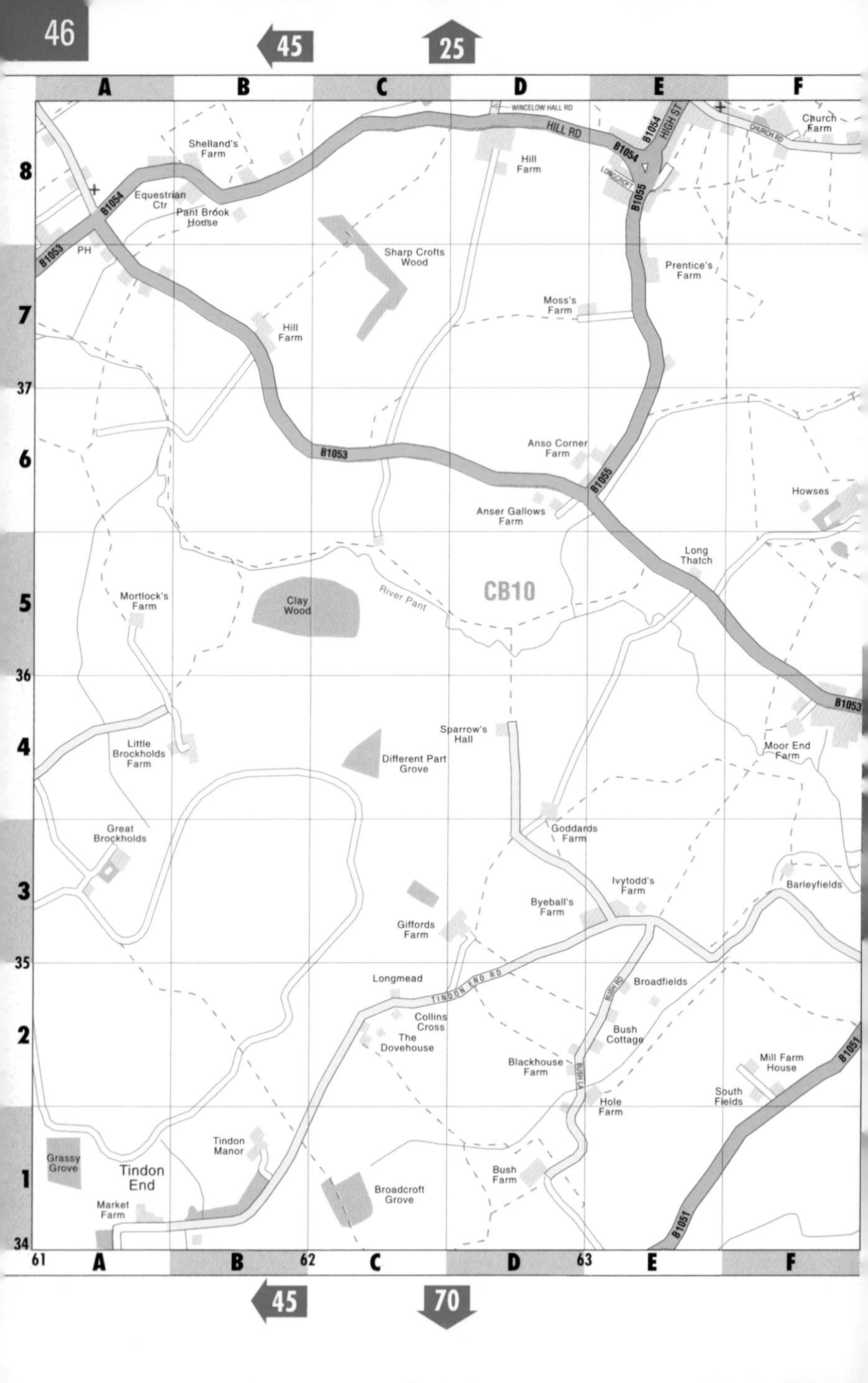

45

25

| | A | B | C | D | E | F |

8

WINCELOW HALL RD
HILL RD
B1054
B1054 HIGH ST
Church
Farm
CHURCH RD
Shelland's
Farm
Hill
Farm
+
LONGROW
Equestrian
Ctr
B1054
B1055
Pant Brook
House
+
B1053
PH

7
Sharp Crofts
Wood
Prentice's
Farm
Hill
Farm
Moss's
Farm

37

6
B1053
Anso Corner
Farm
B1055
Howses
Anser Gallows
Farm
Long
Thatch

5
Mortlock's
Farm
Clay
Wood
River Pant
CB10

36
B1053

4
Little
Brockholds
Farm
Sparrow's
Hall
Moor End
Farm
Different Part
Grove

Great
Brockholds
Goddards
Farm

3
Ivytodd's
Farm
Barleyfields
Byeball's
Farm
Giffords
Farm

35
Longmead
TINDON END RD
Broadfields
Collins
Cross
BUSH RD
Bush
Cottage

2
The
Dovehouse
Mill Farm
House
Blackhouse
Farm
BUSH LA
B1051
South
Fields
Hole
Farm

1
Grassy
Grove
Tindon
Manor
Tindon
End
Bush
Farm
Market
Farm
Broadcroft
Grove
B1051

34
| 61 | A | B | 62 | C | D | 63 | E | F |

45

70

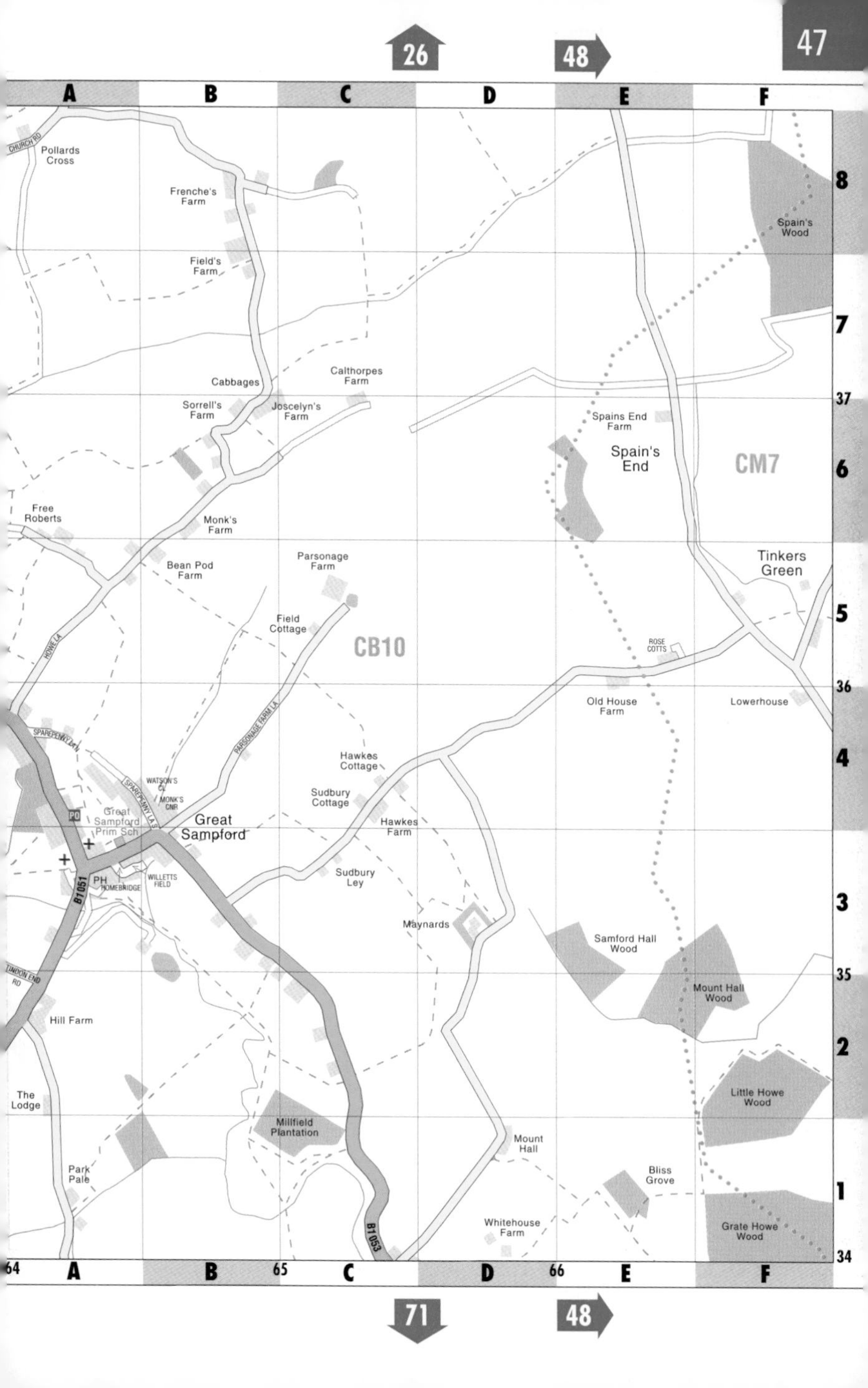

A   B   C   D   E   F

8

CHURCH RD
Pollards
Cross

Frenche's
Farm

Field's
Farm

Spain's
Wood

7

37

Cabbages
Calthorpes
Farm

Sorrell's
Farm
Joscelyn's
Farm

Spains End
Farm

Spain's
End

CM7

6

Free
Roberts

Monk's
Farm

Bean Pod
Farm

Parsonage
Farm

Tinkers
Green

5

Field
Cottage

CB10

ROSE
COTTS

Lowerhouse

36

Old House
Farm

Hawkes
Cottage

Sudbury
Cottage

Hawkes
Farm

WATSON'S
MONK'S GNR

Great
Sampford Prim Sch

PO

Great
Sampford

4

+

PH
HOMEBRIDGE

WILLETTS
FIELD

Sudbury
Ley

B1051

Maynards

Samford Hall
Wood

3

Mount Hall
Wood

35

Hill Farm

TINDON END
RD

The
Lodge

Little Howe
Wood

2

Park
Pale

Millfield
Plantation

Mount
Hall

Bliss
Grove

1

B1053

Whitehouse
Farm

Grate Howe
Wood

34

64   A   B   65   C   D   66   E   F

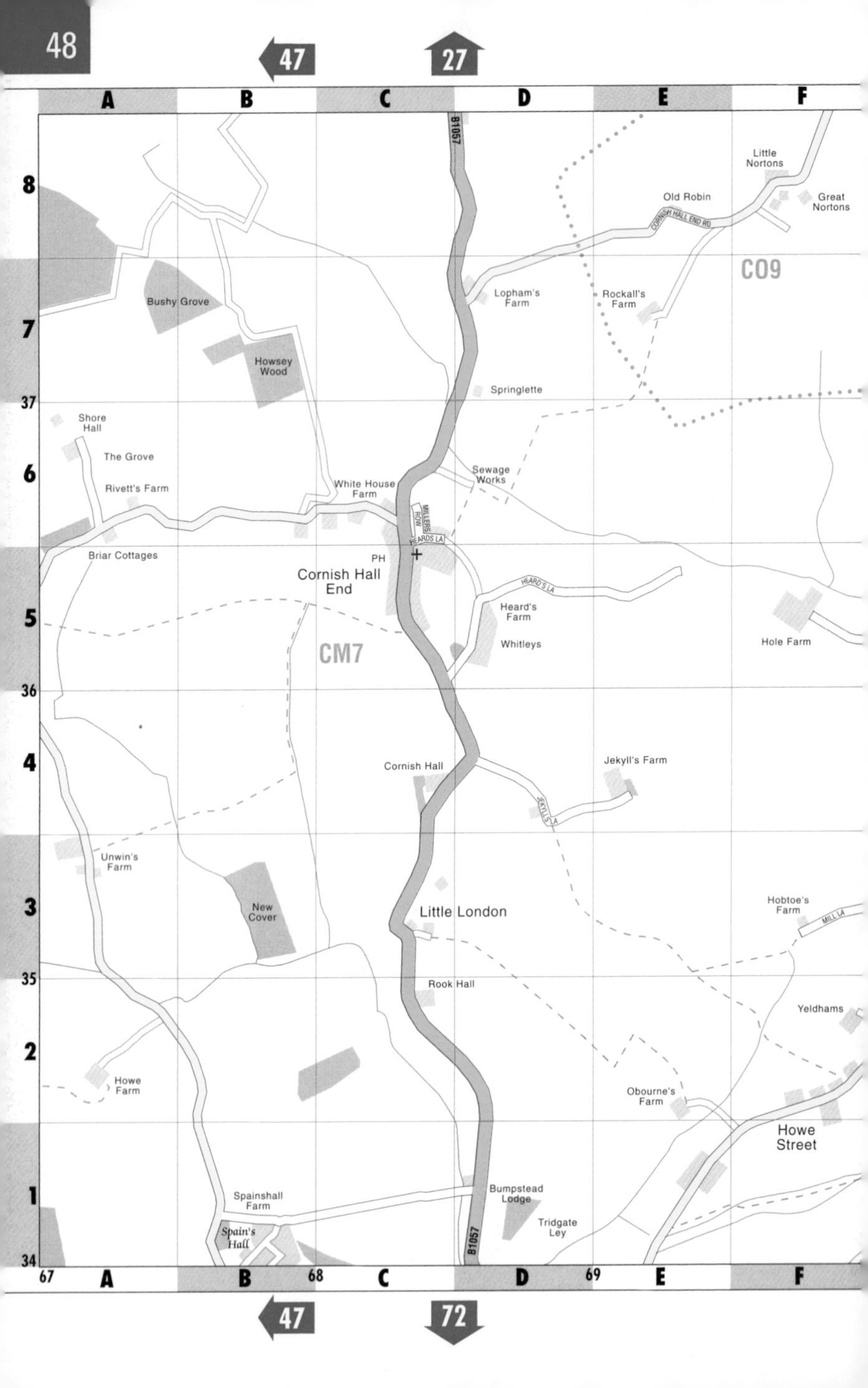
47
27
A
B
C
D
E
F
8
7
37
6
5
36
4
3
35
2
1
34
B1057
Little
Nortons
Old Robin
Great
Nortons
CORNISH HALL END RD
CO9
Bushy Grove
Lopham's
Farm
Rockall's
Farm
Howsey
Wood
Springlette
Shore
Hall
The Grove
Sewage
Works
White House
Farm
Rivett's Farm
MILLERS
ROW
HEARDS LA
Briar Cottages
PH
Cornish Hall
End
HEARD'S LA
Heard's
Farm
Whitleys
Hole Farm
CM7
Cornish Hall
Jekyll's Farm
JEKYLL'S LA
Unwin's
Farm
New
Cover
Little London
Hobtoe's
Farm
MILL LA
Rook Hall
Yeldhams
Howe
Farm
Obourne's
Farm
Howe
Street
Spainshall
Farm
Bumpstead
Lodge
Tridgate
Ley
Spain's
Hall
B1057
67
68
69
47
72

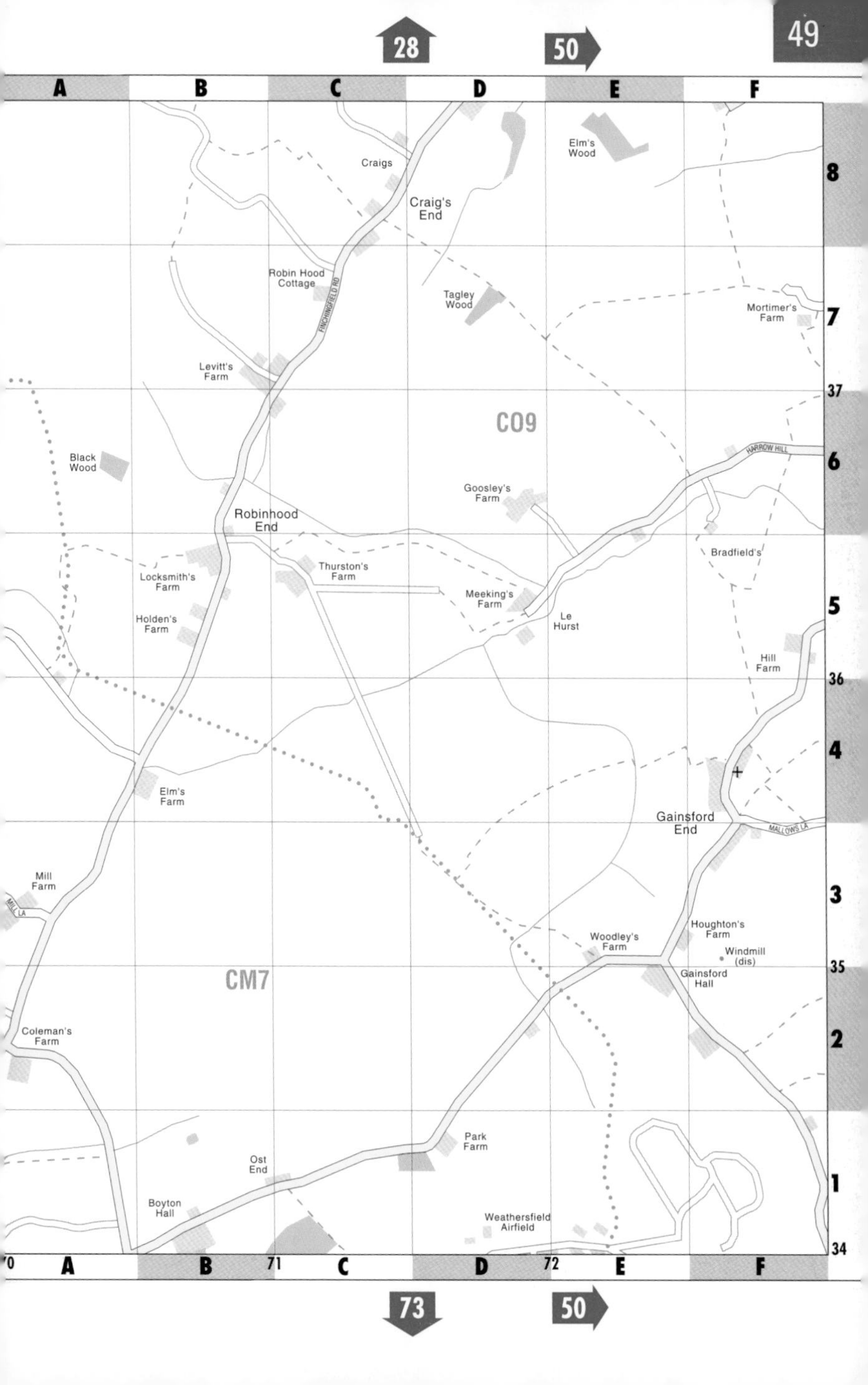

A B C D E F

8

Elm's Wood

Craigs

Craig's End

7

Robin Hood Cottage

Tagley Wood

Mortimer's Farm

Levitt's Farm

37

CO9

HARROW HILL

6

Black Wood

Goosley's Farm

Robinhood End

Bradfield's

Locksmith's Farm

Thurston's Farm

Meeking's Farm

Le Hurst

5

Holden's Farm

Hill Farm

36

4

Elm's Farm

Gainsford End

MALLOWS LA

Mill Farm

3

Houghton's Farm

MILL LA

Woodley's Farm

Windmill (dis)

35

CM7

Gainsford Hall

Coleman's Farm

2

Park Farm

1

Ost End

Boyton Hall

Weathersfield Airfield

34

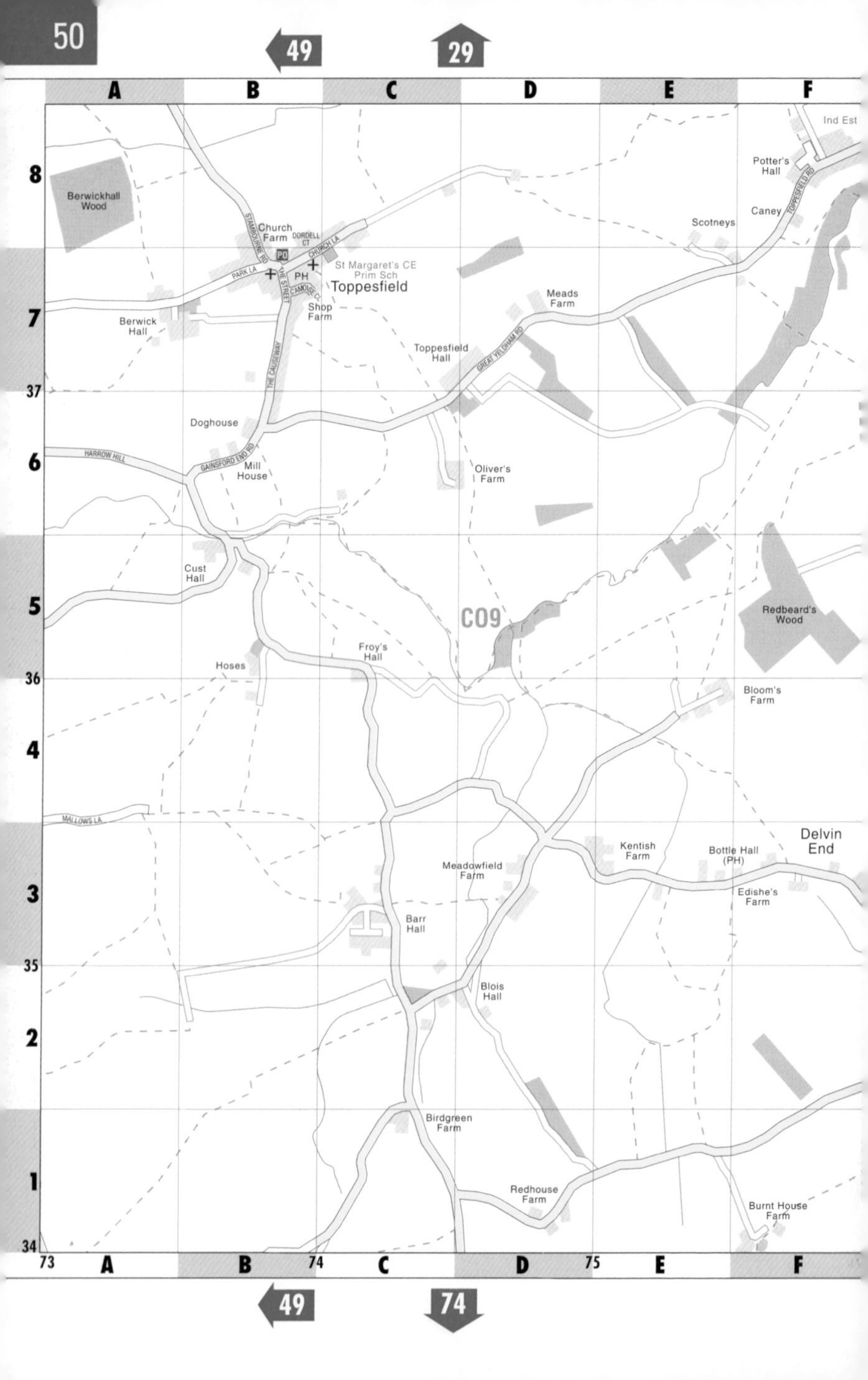

8

Berwickhall Wood

Potter's Hall

Ind Est

Scotneys

Caney

Church Farm

PO

Dürdell Ct

St Margaret's CE Prim Sch

Toppesfield

PH

Shop Farm

PARK LA

THE CAUSEWAY

CHURCH LA

Meads Farm

7

Berwick Hall

Toppesfield Hall

37

GREAT YELDHAM RD

Doghouse

HARROW HILL

GAINSFORD END RD

Mill House

Oliver's Farm

6

Cust Hall

CO9

Redbeard's Wood

5

Froy's Hall

Hoses

Bloom's Farm

36

MALLOWS LA

4

Kentish Farm

Bottle Hall (PH)

Delvin End

Meadowfield Farm

Edishe's Farm

3

Barr Hall

35

Blois Hall

2

Birdgreen Farm

1

Redhouse Farm

Burnt House Farm

34

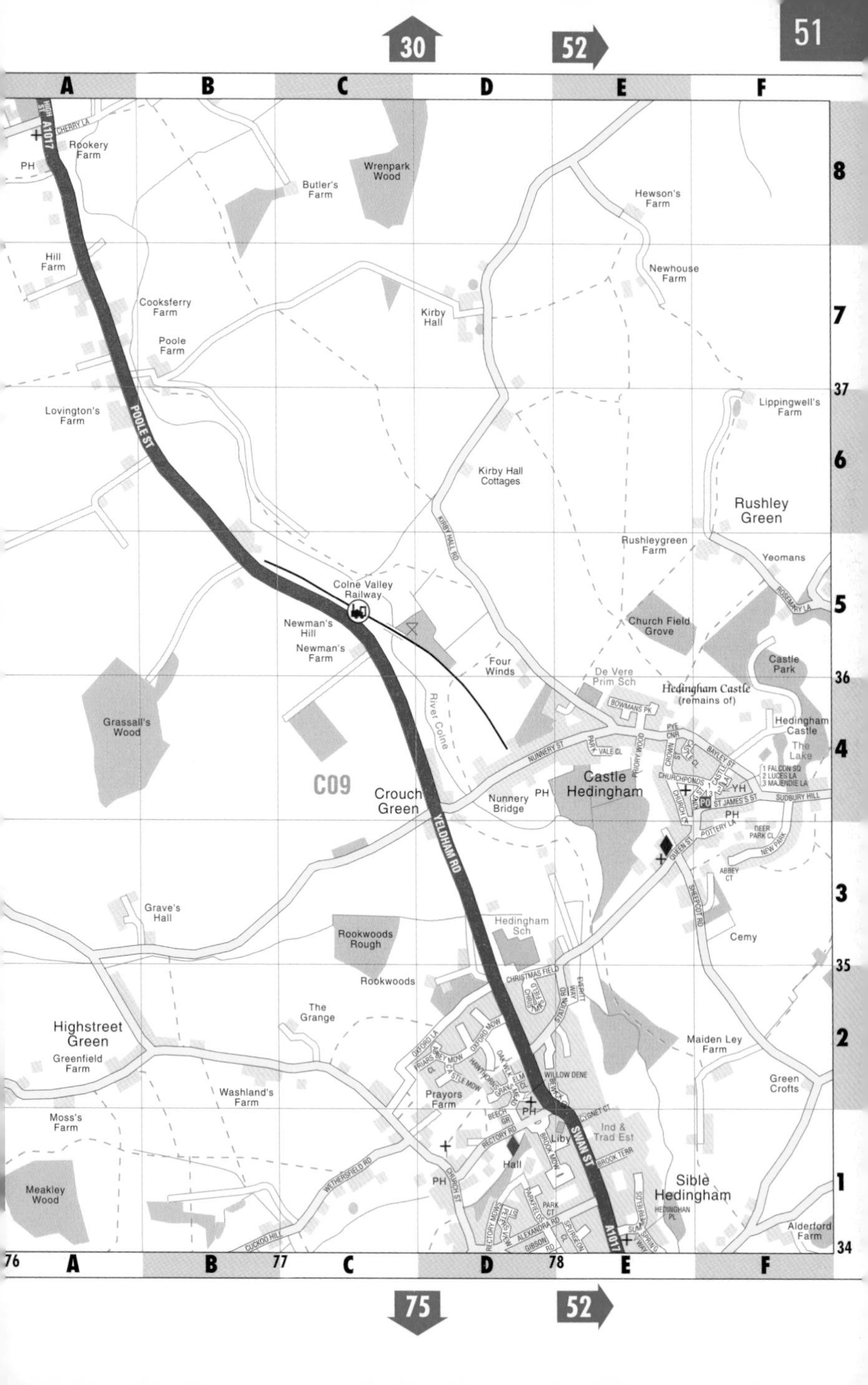

30
52

A **B** **C** **D** **E** **F**

8

7

37

6

5

36

4

3

35

2

1

34

75
52

76 **A** **B** 77 **C** **D** 78 **E** **F**

Rookery Farm
PH
Hill Farm
Cooksferry Farm
Poole Farm
Lovington's Farm
POOLE ST
Butler's Farm
Wrenpark Wood
Kirby Hall
Hewson's Farm
Newhouse Farm
Lippingwell's Farm
RUSHLEY GREEN
Kirby Hall Cottages
Rushleygreen Farm
Yeomans
Colne Valley Railway
Newman's Hill
Newman's Farm
Four Winds
River Colne
Church Field Grove
De Vere Prim Sch
Hedingham Castle (remains of)
Hedingham Castle
The Lake
Castle Park
Grassall's Wood
C09
Crouch Green
Nunnery Bridge
Castle Hedingham
YELDHAM RD
Grave's Hall
Rookwoods Rough
Hedingham Sch
Rookwoods
Cemy
Highstreet Green
Greenfield Farm
Washland's Farm
Moss's Farm
Meakley Wood
The Grange
Prayors Farm
Christmas Field
WILLOW DENE
SWAN ST
Hall
PH
Liby
Ind & Trad Est
Sible Hedingham
Maiden Ley Farm
Green Crofts
Alderford Farm

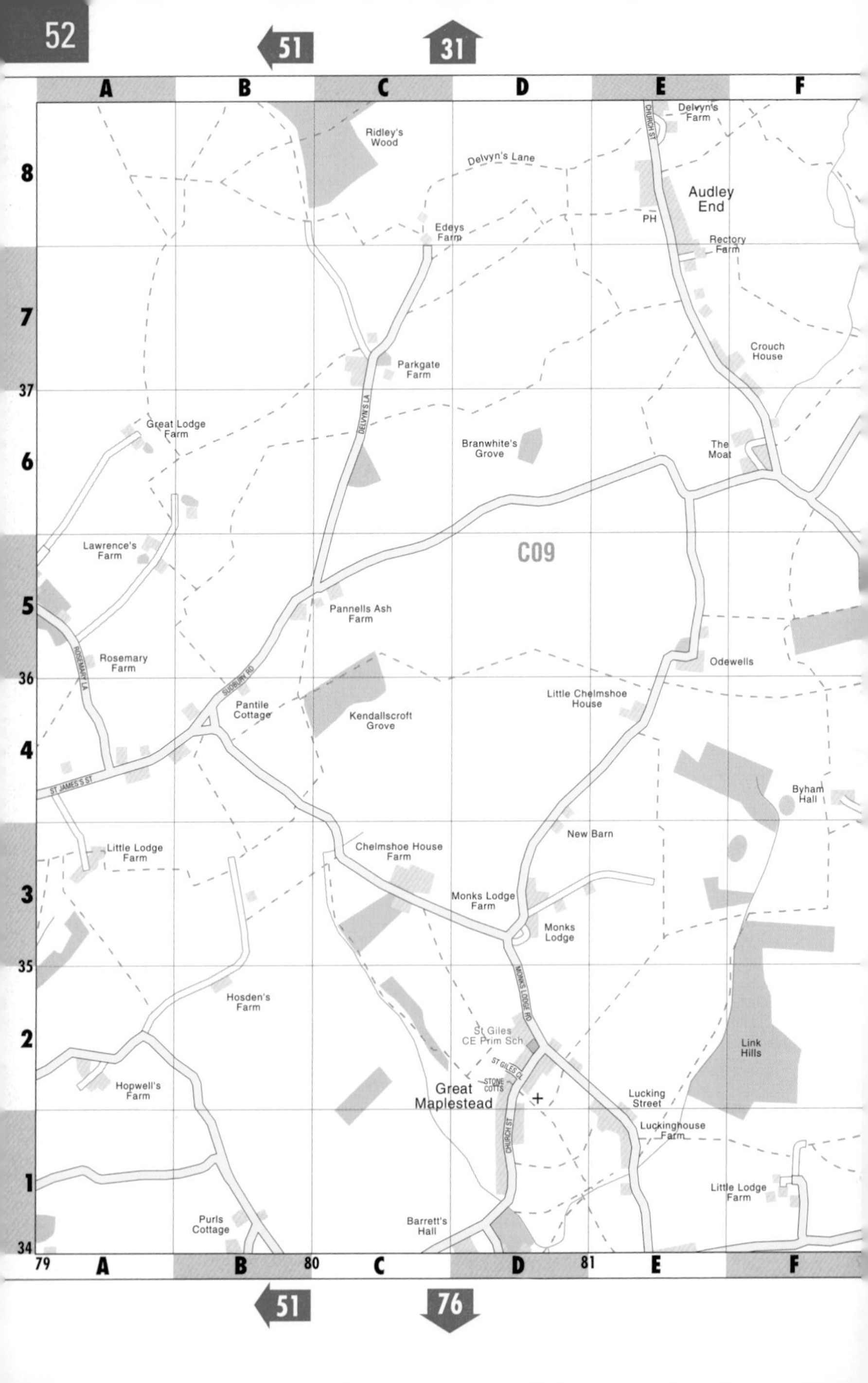

A B C D E F

8

Ridley's
Wood

Delvyn's Lane

Delvyn's
Farm

CHURCH ST

Audley
End

PH

Edeys
Farm

Rectory
Farm

7

37

Parkgate
Farm

Crouch
House

Great Lodge
Farm

Branwhite's
Grove

The Moat

6

C09

Lawrence's
Farm

Pannells Ash
Farm

Odewells

5

36

Rosemary
Farm

Pantile
Cottage

Kendallscroft
Grove

Little Chelmshoe
House

4

ST JAMES'S ST

Byham
Hall

Little Lodge
Farm

Chelmshoe House
Farm

New Barn

3

Monks Lodge
Farm

Monks
Lodge

35

Hosden's
Farm

St Giles
CE Prim Sch

Link
Hills

2

Hopwell's
Farm

STONE
COTTS

Great
Maplestead

ST GILES RD

MONKS LODGE RD

Lucking
Street

Luckinghouse
Farm

CHURCH RD

Little Lodge
Farm

1

34

Purls
Cottage

Barrett's
Hall

79 A B 80 C D 81 E F

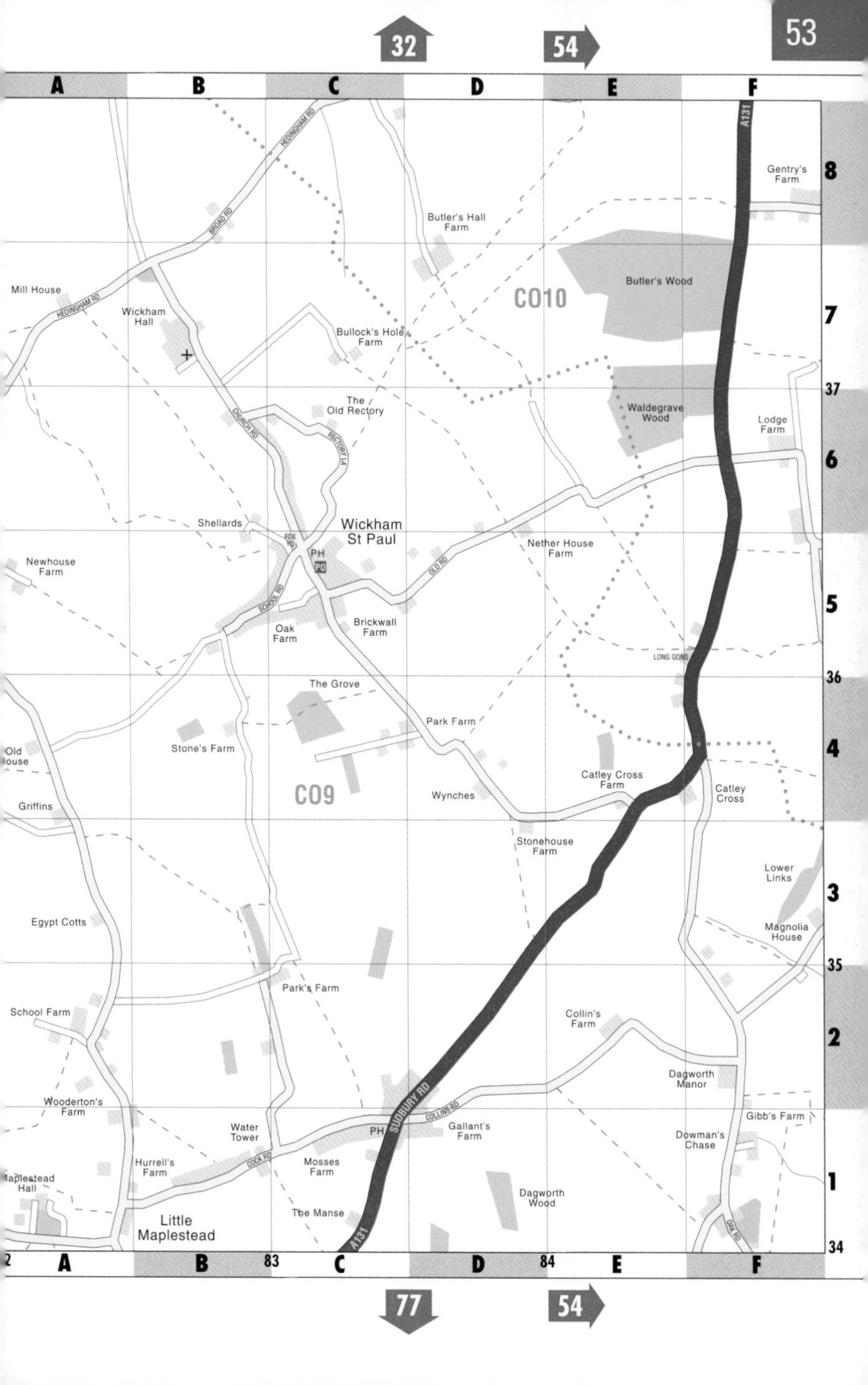
32
54
A
B
C
D
E
F
8
7
37
6
5
36
4
3
35
2
1
34
83
84
77
54
A131
Gentry's Farm
Butler's Hall Farm
Butler's Wood
CO10
Mill House
HEDINGHAM RD
BROAD RD
Wickham Hall
Bullock's Hole Farm
The Old Rectory
Waldegrave Wood
Lodge Farm
CHURCH RD
RECTORY LA
Shellards
FOX YD
Wickham St Paul
PH
PO
Nether House Farm
Newhouse Farm
OLD RD
SCHOOL RD
Oak Farm
Brickwall Farm
LONG GDNS
The Grove
Park Farm
Old House
Stone's Farm
Catley Cross Farm
Catley Cross
CO9
Wynches
Griffins
Stonehouse Farm
Lower Links
Egypt Cotts
Magnolia House
Park's Farm
School Farm
Collin's Farm
Dagworth Manor
Wooderton's Farm
SUDBURY RD
COLLINS RD
Gibb's Farm
Water Tower
PH
Gallant's Farm
Dowman's Chase
COCK RD
Hurrell's Farm
Mosses Farm
Maplestead Hall
Dagworth Wood
Little Maplestead
The Manse
OAK RD

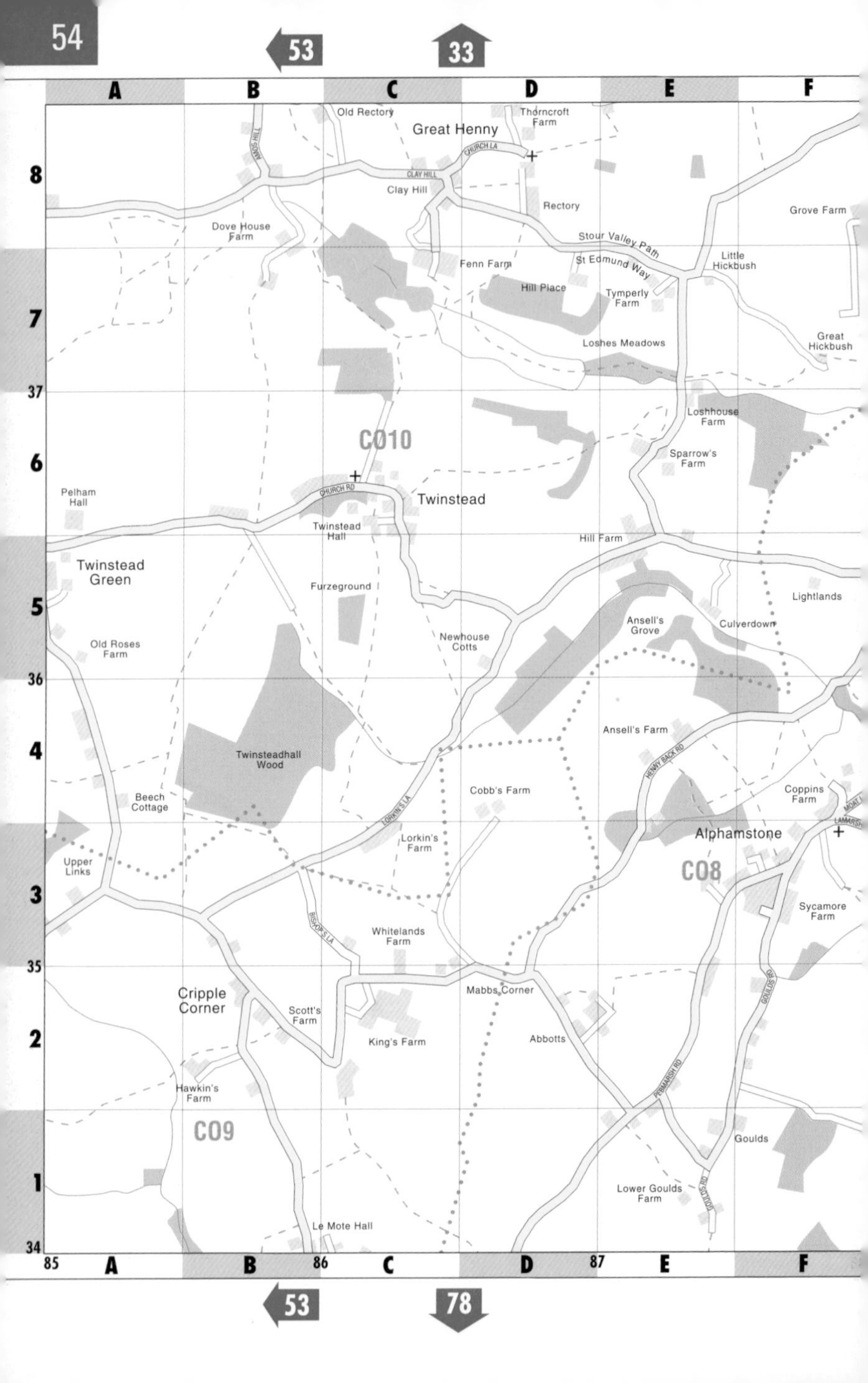
53
33
A
B
C
D
E
F
Old Rectory
Great Henny
Thorncroft Farm
AMOS HILL
CHURCH LA
CLAY HILL
Clay Hill
Rectory
Grove Farm
Dove House Farm
Stour Valley Path
St Edmund Way
Little Hickbush
Fenn Farm
Hill Place
Tymperly Farm
Great Hickbush
Loshes Meadows
Loshhouse Farm
CO10
Sparrow's Farm
Pelham Hall
CHURCH RD
Twinstead
Twinstead Hall
Hill Farm
Twinstead Green
Furzeground
Lightlands
Ansell's Grove
Culverdown
Newhouse Cotts
Old Roses Farm
Ansell's Farm
Twinsteadhall Wood
HENNY BACK RD
Cobb's Farm
Coppins Farm
Beech Cottage
LORKIN'S LA
MOAT LA
LAMARSH
Lorkin's Farm
Alphamstone
Upper Links
CO8
Sycamore Farm
BISHOP'S LA
Whitelands Farm
Cripple Corner
Mabbs Corner
GOULDS RD
Scott's Farm
King's Farm
Abbotts
PEBMARSH RD
Hawkin's Farm
CO9
Goulds
Lower Goulds Farm
Le Mote Hall
8
7
37
6
5
36
4
3
35
2
1
34
85
86
87
53
78

34

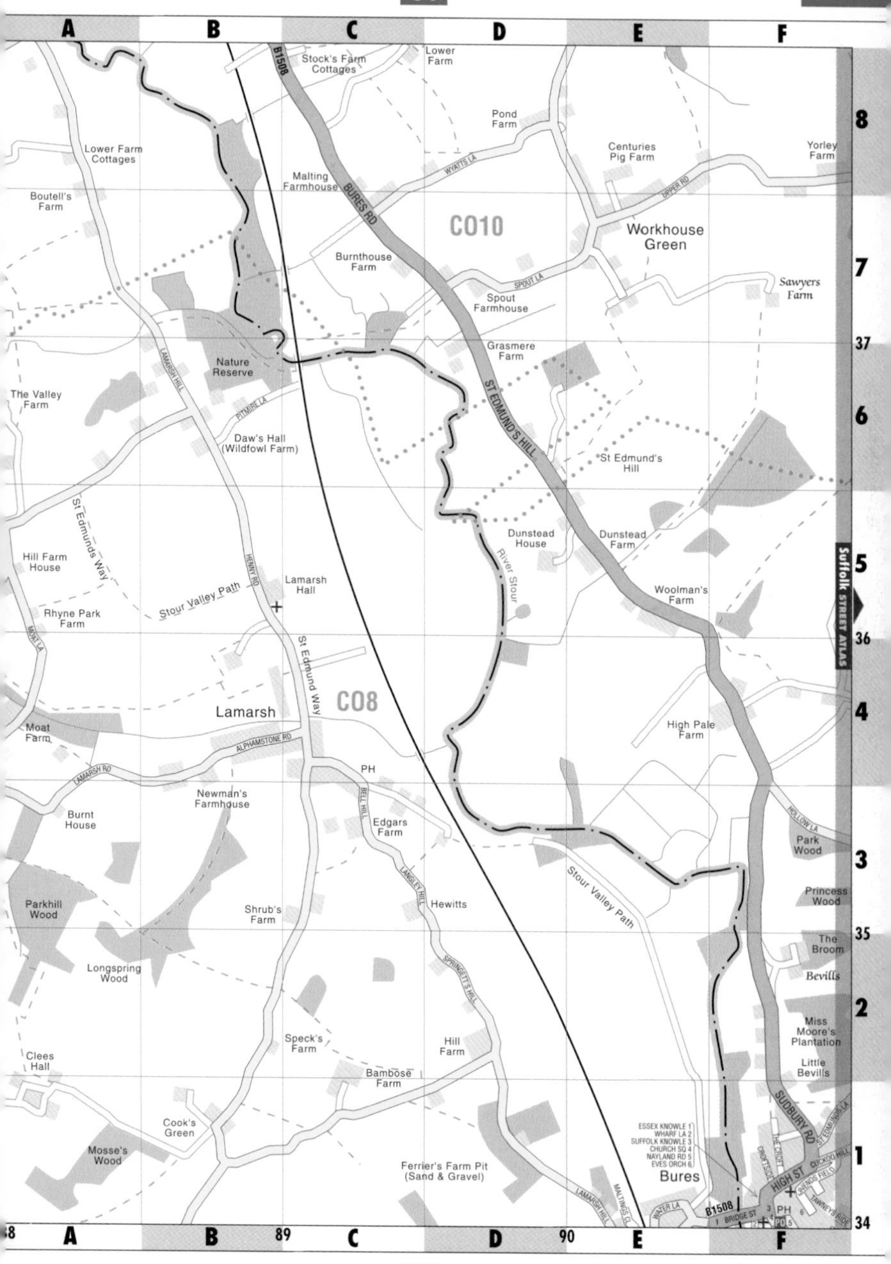
A
B
C
D
E
F
B1508
Stock's Farm Cottages
Lower Farm
Pond Farm
Centuries Pig Farm
Yorley Farm
Lower Farm Cottages
Boutell's Farm
Malting Farmhouse
BURES RD
WYATTS LA
UPPER RD
CO10
Workhouse Green
Burnthouse Farm
Spout Farmhouse
SPOUT LA
Sawyers Farm
Grasmere Farm
Nature Reserve
LAMARSH HILL
PITMIRE LA
The Valley Farm
Daw's Hall (Wildfowl Farm)
ST EDMUND'S HILL
St Edmund's Hill
St Edmunds Way
Hill Farm House
Dunstead House
Dunstead Farm
River Stour
HENNY RD
Lamarsh Hall
Stour Valley Path
Woolman's Farm
Rhyne Park Farm
MOAT LA
St Edmund Way
CO8
Lamarsh
High Pale Farm
Moat Farm
ALPHAMSTONE RD
LAMARSH RD
PH
BELL HILL
Newman's Farmhouse
Burnt House
Edgars Farm
HOLLOW LA
Park Wood
Princess Wood
Parkhill Wood
Shrub's Farm
LANGLEY HILL
Hewitts
Stour Valley Path
The Broom
Longspring Wood
Bevills
SPRINGETT'S HILL
Miss Moore's Plantation
Speck's Farm
Hill Farm
Little Bevills
Clees Hall
Bambose Farm
SUDBURY RD
ESSEX KNOWLE 1
WHARF LA 2
SUFFOLK KNOWLE 3
CHURCH SQ 4
NAYLAND RD 5
EVES ORCH 6
Cook's Green
Mosse's Wood
Ferrier's Farm Pit (Sand & Gravel)
LAMARSH HILL
MALTINGS CL
Bures
WATER LA
B1508
BRIDGE ST
HIGH ST
CROFTSIDE
THE CROFT
ST EDMUNDS LA
CUCKOO HILL
TAWNEYS RIDE
PO
Suffolk STREET ATLAS
8
7
37
6
5
36
4
3
35
2
1
34
88
89
90

79

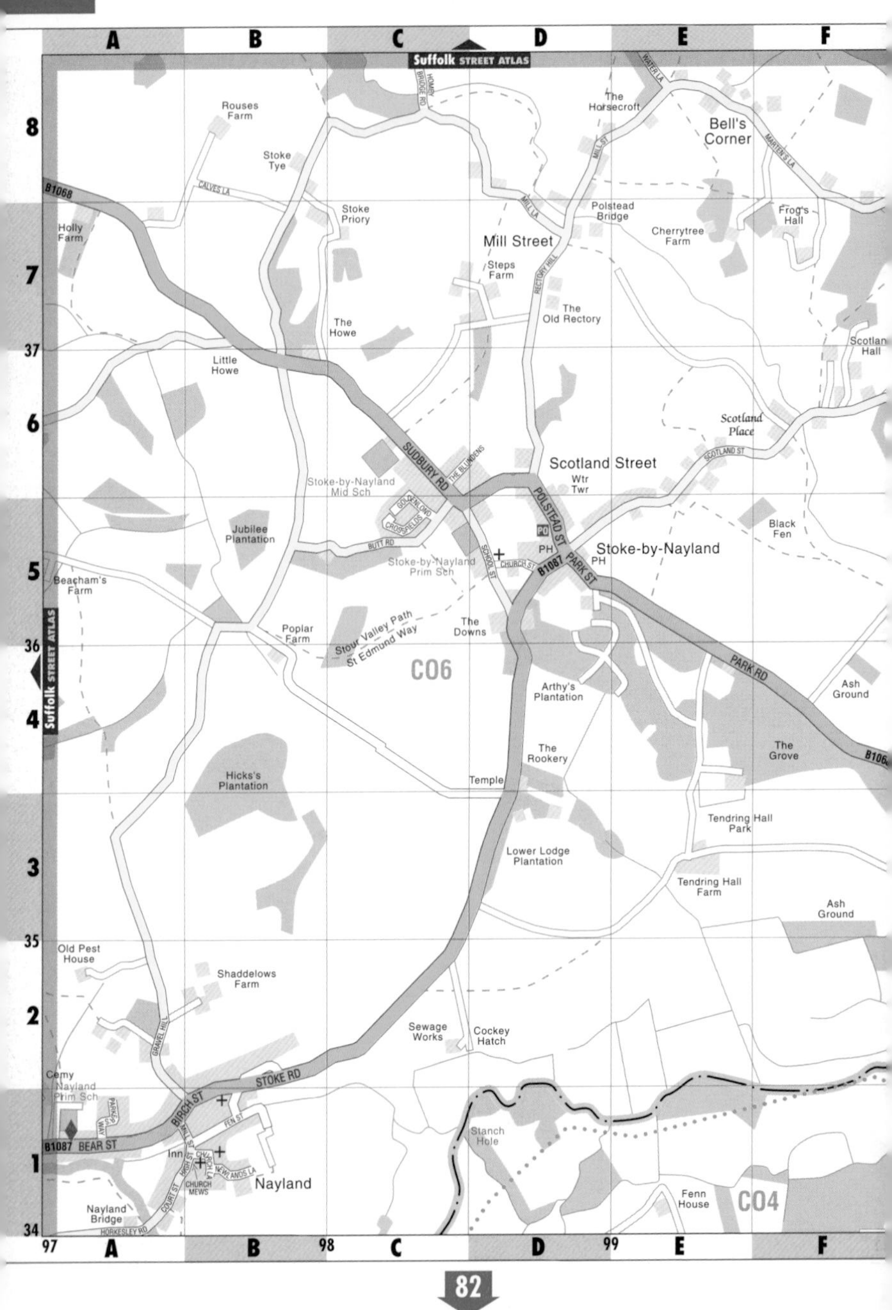

A **B** **C** **D** **E** **F**

8

Rouses
Farm

The
Horsecroft

Bell's
Corner

Stoke
Tye

B1068

Stoke
Priory

Polstead
Bridge

Frog's
Hall

CALVES LA

Mill Street

Cherrytree
Farm

Holly
Farm

7

Steps
Farm

Scotlan
Hall

The Howe

37

The
Old Rectory

Little
Howe

Scotland
Place

6

SUDBURY RD

Scotland Street

SCOTLAND ST

Stoke-by-Nayland
Mid Sch

Wtr
Twr

Jubilee
Plantation

Scotland Street

POLSTEAD ST

PO

Black
Fen

PH

Stoke-by-Nayland

BUTT RD

B1087

PH

PARK ST

PARK RD

5

Beacham's
Farm

Stoke-by-Nayland
Prim Sch

Poplar
Farm

Stour Valley Path
St Edmund Way

The
Downs

Ash
Ground

36

The Grove

CO6

4

Arthy's
Plantation

Hicks's
Plantation

The
Rookery

The
Grove

B106

Temple

Tendring Hall
Park

3

Lower Lodge
Plantation

Tendring Hall
Farm

Ash
Ground

35

Old Pest
House

Shaddelows
Farm

GRANGE HILL

2

Sewage
Works

Cockey
Hatch

Cemy
Nayland
Prim Sch

BIRCH ST

STOKE RD

1

B1087

BEAR ST

Inn

Stanch
Hole

Fenn
House

CO4

Nayland

CHURCH
MEWS

Nayland
Bridge

34

97 **A** **B** **98** **C** **D** **99** **E** **F**

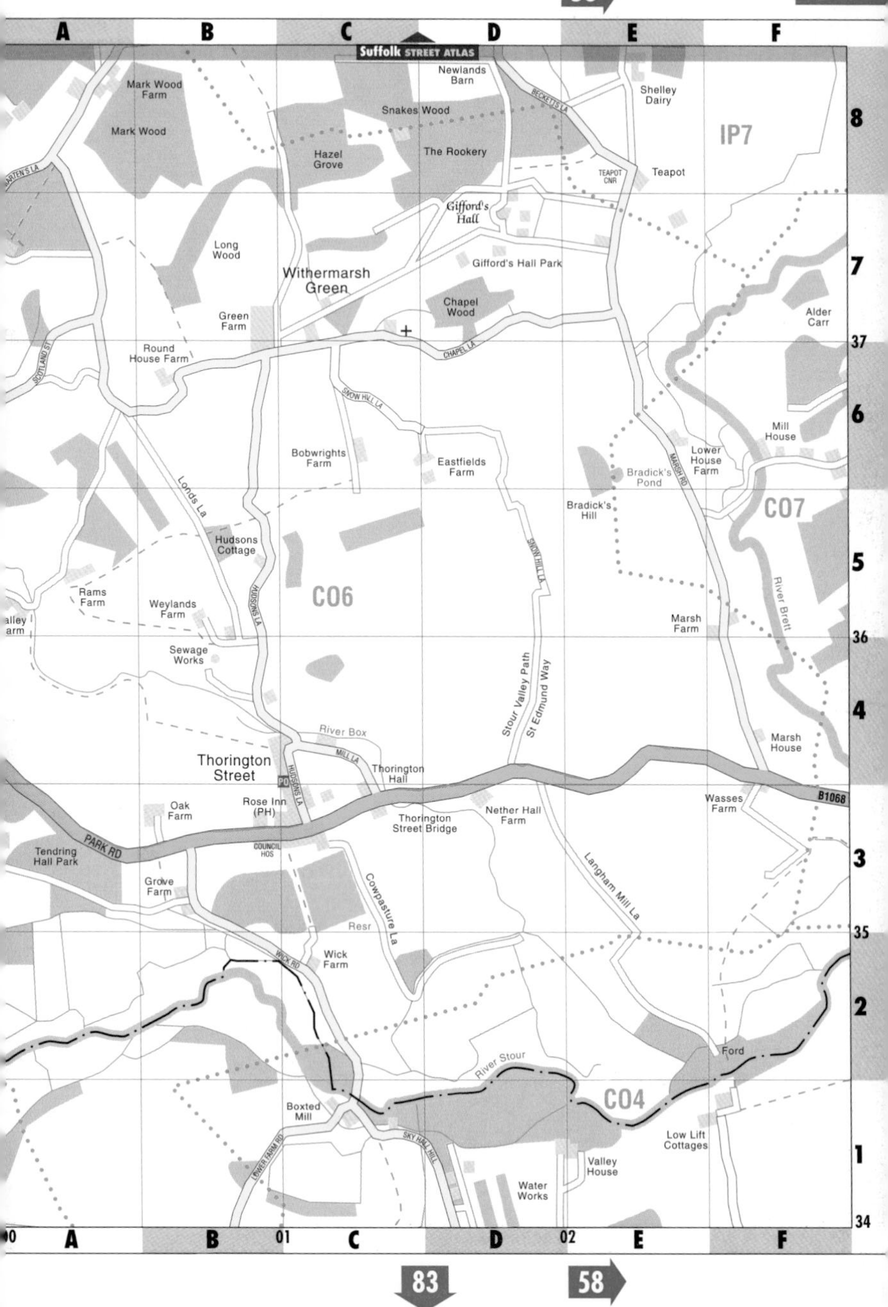

A **B** **C** **D** **E** **F**

8

IP7

Mark Wood Farm
Mark Wood
Newlands Barn
Snakes Wood
Shelley Dairy

Hazel Grove
The Rookery
TEAPOT CNR
Teapot

7

Gifford's Hall

Long Wood
Withermarsh Green
Gifford's Hall Park
Alder Carr

Green Farm
Chapel Wood

37

Round House Farm
CHAPEL LA

6

SNOW HILL LA
Mill House

Bobwrights Farm
Eastfields Farm
Lower House Farm

Bradick's Pond
CO7

Bradick's Hill

Hudsons Cottage

5

Rams Farm
Weylands Farm
CO6

River Brett

36

Sewage Works
Marsh Farm

4

River Box
Marsh House

MILL LA
Thorington Hall

Thorington Street
Stour Valley Path St Edmund Way
Wasses Farm
B1068

Rose Inn (PH)
Oak Farm
Thorington Street Bridge
Nether Hall Farm

3

PARK RD
COUNCIL HOS

Tendring Hall Park
Grove Farm
Cowpasture La
Langham Mill La

35

Resr
Wick Farm

2

Ford

River Stour
CO4

Boxted Mill
Low Lift Cottages

1

Water Works
Valley House

34

A **B** **C** **D** **E** **F**

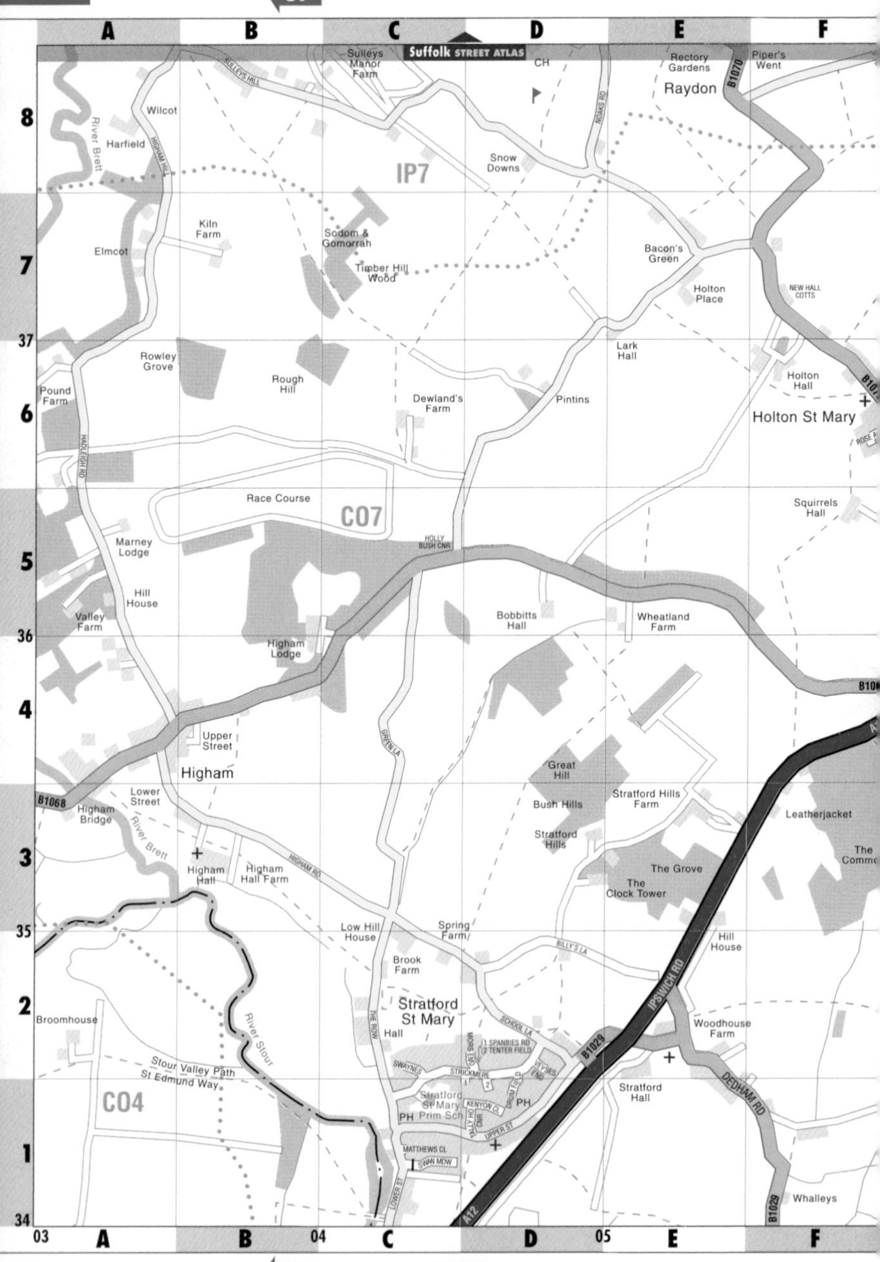

Suffolk STREET ATLAS

A   B   C   D   E   F

8

Wilcot

Sulleys Manor Farm

CH

Rectory Gardens

Piper's Went

Raydon

Harfield

River Brett

Snow Downs

IP7

Kiln Farm

Elmcot

Sodom & Gomorrah

Timber Hill Wood

Bacon's Green

Holton Place

NEW HALL COTTS

7

37

Rowley Grove

Rough Hill

Dewland's Farm

Pintins

Lark Hall

Holton Hall

6

Pound Farm

Holton St Mary

MORE 2

Race Course

CO7

HOLLY BUSH CNR

Squirrels Hall

5

Marney Lodge

Hill House

Bobbitts Hall

Wheatland Farm

36

Valley Farm

Higham Lodge

4

Upper Street

Higham

Great Hill

Bush Hills

Stratford Hills Farm

Leatherjacket

The Common

B1068

Lower Street

Higham Bridge

River Brett

Higham Hall

Higham Hall Farm

Stratford Hills

The Grove

The Clock Tower

3

Low Hill House

Spring Farm

BILLY'S LA

Hill House

35

Brook Farm

Stratford St Mary

Broomhouse

Stour Valley Path
St Edmund Way

River Stour

Stratford St Mary Hall

1 SPANBIES RD
2 TENTER FIELD

Woodhouse Farm

2

CO4

Stratford St Mary Prim Sch

PH

PH

Stratford Hall

DEDHAM RD

IPSWICH RD

B1029

1

MATTHEWS CL

34

03   A   B   04   C   D   05   E   F

Suffolk STREET ATLAS

Sewage Works

Springhill

Capelgrove

Wenham Place

8

The Robins

Hill House Farm

Wenham Hill

A12

7

Orchard Farm

Manor House

Bradfield Farm

IP9

37

Boydland Farm

Old London Rd

Three Elms

Lattinford Bridge

Oaks Farm

Brick Kiln Farm

Lattinford Hill

6

Hill Farm

Highfields

Hassocks

Chaplin's Farm

The Four Sisters

Stratford House

FOUR SISTERS

B1070

Kiln Cottage

5

CO7

Woodgates Farm

IPSWICH RD

Hustlers Grove

36

Rookery

HUGHES CNR

Road Covert

High Trees Farm

Rookery Farm

4

xhall verts

The Lodge

QUINTONS CNR
East Bergholt High Sch

Parkfield

Lodge Plantation

Allen's Farm

GASTON END

HEATH RD

L Ctr

Elm Farm

3

Ackworth House

East Bergholt CE Prim Sch

PH

Richardson's Farm

35

Gatton House Farm

East Bergholt

Old Mill House

Dead La

Vale Farm

Cemy

P

Willow Farm

Warren House

2

CEMETERY LA

Highlands

Fishpond Wood

Old Hall

RECTORY HILL

PH

BURNT OAK CNR

WHITE HORSE RD

East Bergholt Place Gdn

Warren Wood

1

DAZELEY'S LA

MANNINGTREE RD

B1070

34

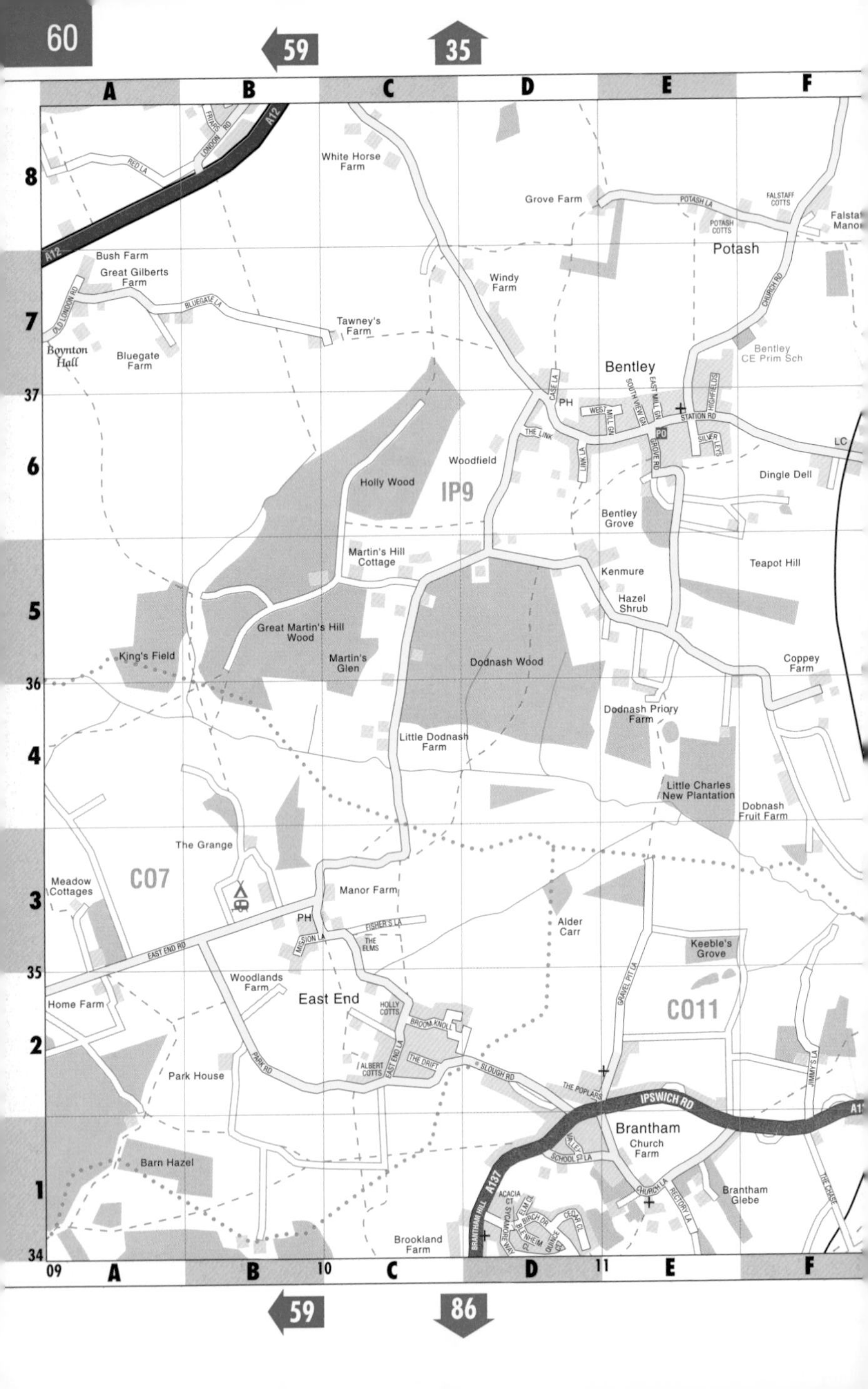
60
59
35
A
B
C
D
E
F
8
7
37
6
5
36
4
3
35
2
1
34
09
10
11
A12
RED LA
FRIARS RD
LONDON RD
White Horse Farm
Grove Farm
POTASH LA
FALSTAFF COTTS
POTASH COTTS
Potash
Bush Farm
Great Gilberts Farm
OLD LONDON RD
BLUEGATE LA
Tawney's Farm
Windy Farm
CHURCH RD
Boynton Hall
Bluegate Farm
Bentley
Bentley CE Prim Sch
CASE LA
SOUTH VIEW GN
EAST MILL GN
HIGHFIELDS
PH
WEST MILL GN
STATION RD
THE LINK
PO
SILVER LEYS
LC
Woodfield
LINK LA
GROVE RD
Holly Wood
IP9
Dingle Dell
Bentley Grove
Martin's Hill Cottage
Teapot Hill
Kenmure
Hazel Shrub
Great Martin's Hill Wood
Martin's Glen
King's Field
Dodnash Wood
Coppey Farm
Dodnash Priory Farm
Little Dodnash Farm
Little Charles New Plantation
Dobnash Fruit Farm
The Grange
Meadow Cottages
CO7
Manor Farm
PH
FISHER'S LA
MISSION LA
THE ELMS
Alder Carr
Keeble's Grove
EAST END RD
Woodlands Farm
GRAVEL PIT LA
Home Farm
East End
HOLLY COTTS
BROOM KNOLL
CO11
PARK RD
THE DRIFT
ALBERT COTTS
EAST END LA
SLOUGH RD
Park House
JIMMY'S LA
THE POPLARS
IPSWICH RD
A1
Brantham
Church Farm
VALLEY CL
SCHOOL LA
Barn Hazel
A137
ACACIA CT
ELM CL
CHURCH LA
RECTORY LA
Brantham Glebe
THE CHASE
SYCAMORE WAY
BIRCH DR
BLENHEIM CL
CEDAR CL
QUINCE CL
BRANTHAM HILL
Brookland Farm
59
86

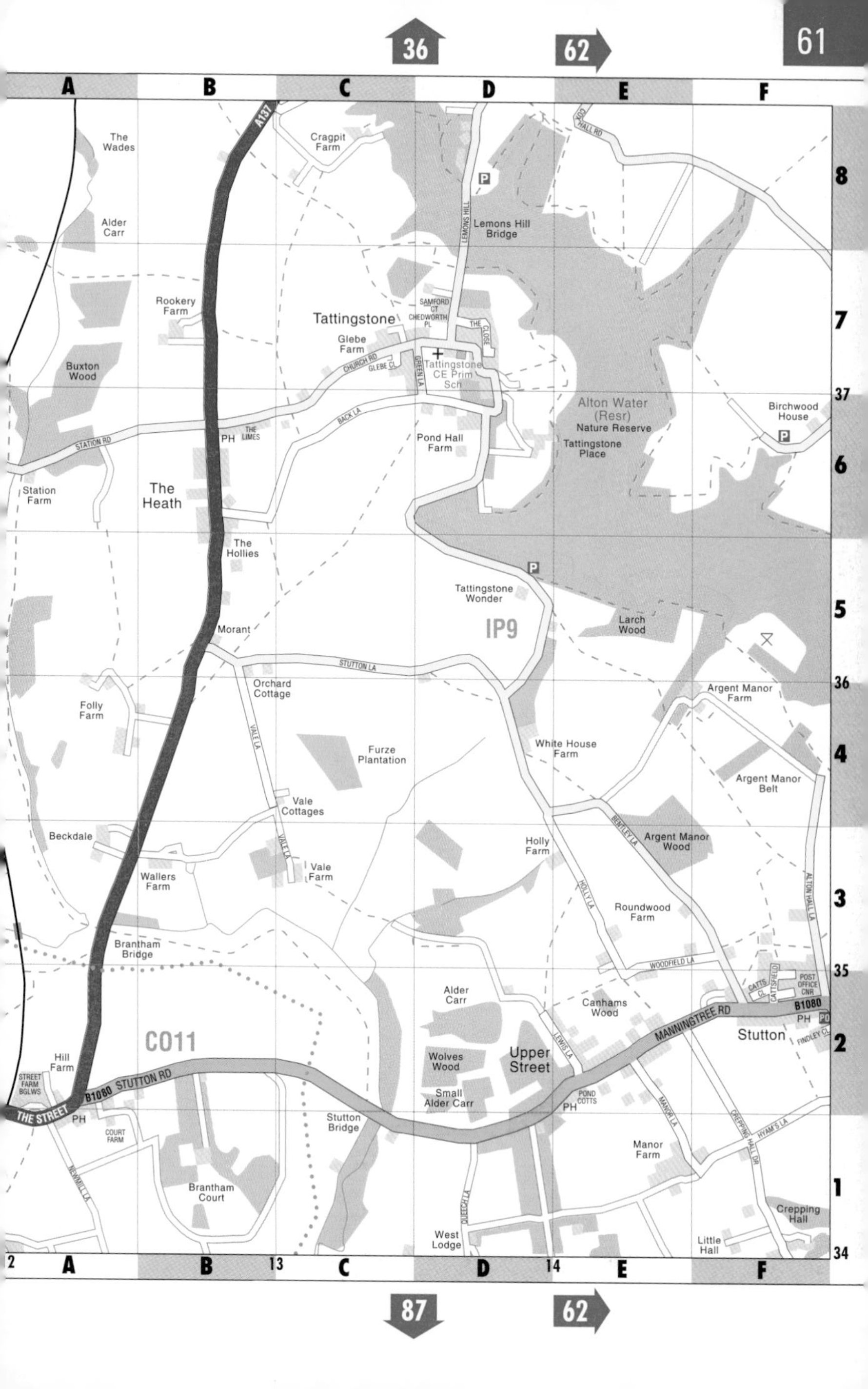
36
62
A
B
C
D
E
F
8
7
37
6
5
36
4
3
35
2
1
34
The Wades
Alder Carr
Rookery Farm
Buxton Wood
Cragpit Farm
Lemons Hill Bridge
LEMONS HILL
Tattingstone
Glebe Farm
SAMFORD CT
CHEDWORTH PL
THE CLOSE
CHURCH RD
GLEBE CL
GREEN LA
Tattingstone CE Prim Sch
COX HALL RD
A137
Alton Water (Resr)
Nature Reserve
Tattingstone Place
Birchwood House
STATION RD
PH
THE LIMES
BACK LA
Pond Hall Farm
Station Farm
The Heath
The Hollies
Tattingstone Wonder
IP9
Larch Wood
Morant
STUTTON LA
Orchard Cottage
Argent Manor Farm
Folly Farm
VALE LA
Furze Plantation
White House Farm
Argent Manor Belt
Vale Cottages
BENTLEY LA
Argent Manor Wood
Beckdale
Holly Farm
Wallers Farm
Vale Farm
HOLLY LA
Roundwood Farm
ALTON HALL LA
Brantham Bridge
WOODFIELD LA
CATTS CL
CATTSFIELD
POST OFFICE CNR
Alder Carr
Canhams Wood
B1080
MANNINGTREE RD
Stutton
FINDLEY CL
CO11
LEWIS LA
Wolves Wood
Upper Street
Hill Farm
STREET FARM BGLWS
B1080
STUTTON RD
THE STREET
Small Alder Carr
POND COTTS
COURT FARM
Stutton Bridge
MANOR LA
CREPPING HALL DR
HYAM'S LA
Manor Farm
NEWMILL LA
Brantham Court
QUEECH LA
Crepping Hall
West Lodge
Little Hall
2
13
14
87
62

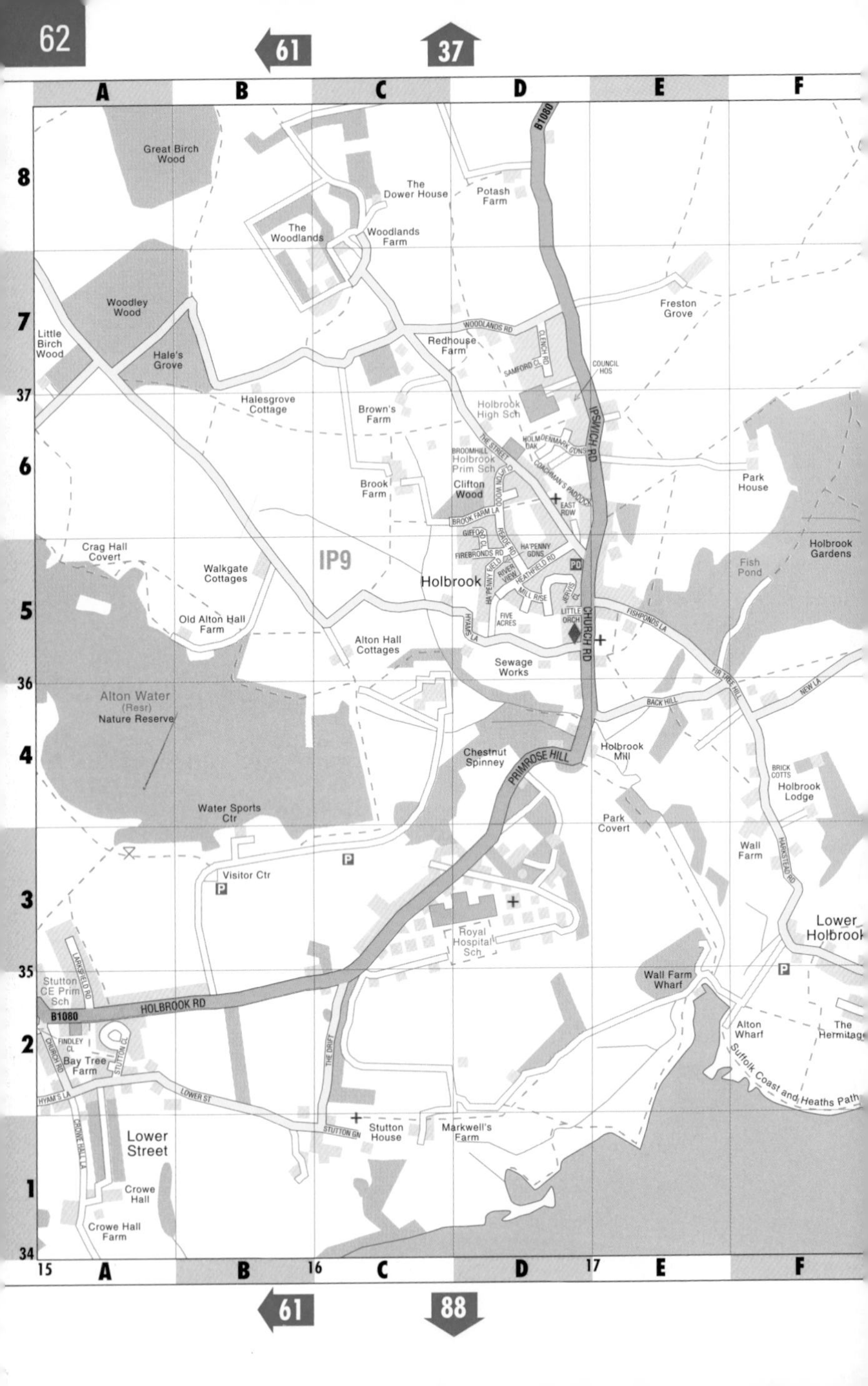
61
37
A
B
C
D
E
F
8
7
37
6
5
36
4
3
35
2
1
34
15
16
17
Great Birch Wood
The Dower House
Potash Farm
The Woodlands
Woodlands Farm
B1080
Woodley Wood
Little Birch Wood
Hale's Grove
WOODLANDS RD
Redhouse Farm
Freston Grove
CLENCH RD
SAMFORD CL
COUNCIL HOS
Halesgrove Cottage
Brown's Farm
Holbrook High Sch
IPSWICH RD
HOLM OAK
DENMARK GDNS
BROOMHILL
THE STREET
Holbrook Prim Sch
COACHMAN'S PADDOCK
Park House
Brook Farm
Clifton Wood
CLIFTON WOOD
EAST ROW
BROOK FARM LA
GIFFORD CL
READE RD
HA'PENNY GDNS
Crag Hall Covert
FIREBRONDS RD
HEATHFIELD RD
Holbrook Gardens
Walkgate Cottages
IP9
RIVER VIEW
PO
Fish Pond
Holbrook
HA'PENNY FIELD
MILL RISE
JERVIS CL
FIVE ACRES
LITTLE ORCH
CHURCH RD
FISHPONDS LA
Old Alton Hall Farm
HYAMS LA
Alton Hall Cottages
Sewage Works
Alton Water (Resr) Nature Reserve
FIR TREE HILL
BACK HILL
NEW LA
Chestnut Spinney
Holbrook Mill
PRIMROSE HILL
BRICK COTTS
Holbrook Lodge
Water Sports Ctr
Park Covert
Wall Farm
HARKSTEAD RD
P
Visitor Ctr
P
Royal Hospital Sch
Lower Holbrook
LARKSFIELD RD
Stutton CE Prim Sch
Wall Farm Wharf
P
HOLBROOK RD
B1080
FINDLEY CL
CHURCH RD
Bay Tree Farm
STUTTON CL
THE DRIFT
Alton Wharf
The Hermitage
Suffolk Coast and Heaths Path
HYAM'S LA
LOWER ST
STUTTON GN
Stutton House
Markwell's Farm
Lower Street
CROWE HALL LA
Crowe Hall
Crowe Hall Farm
61
88

38

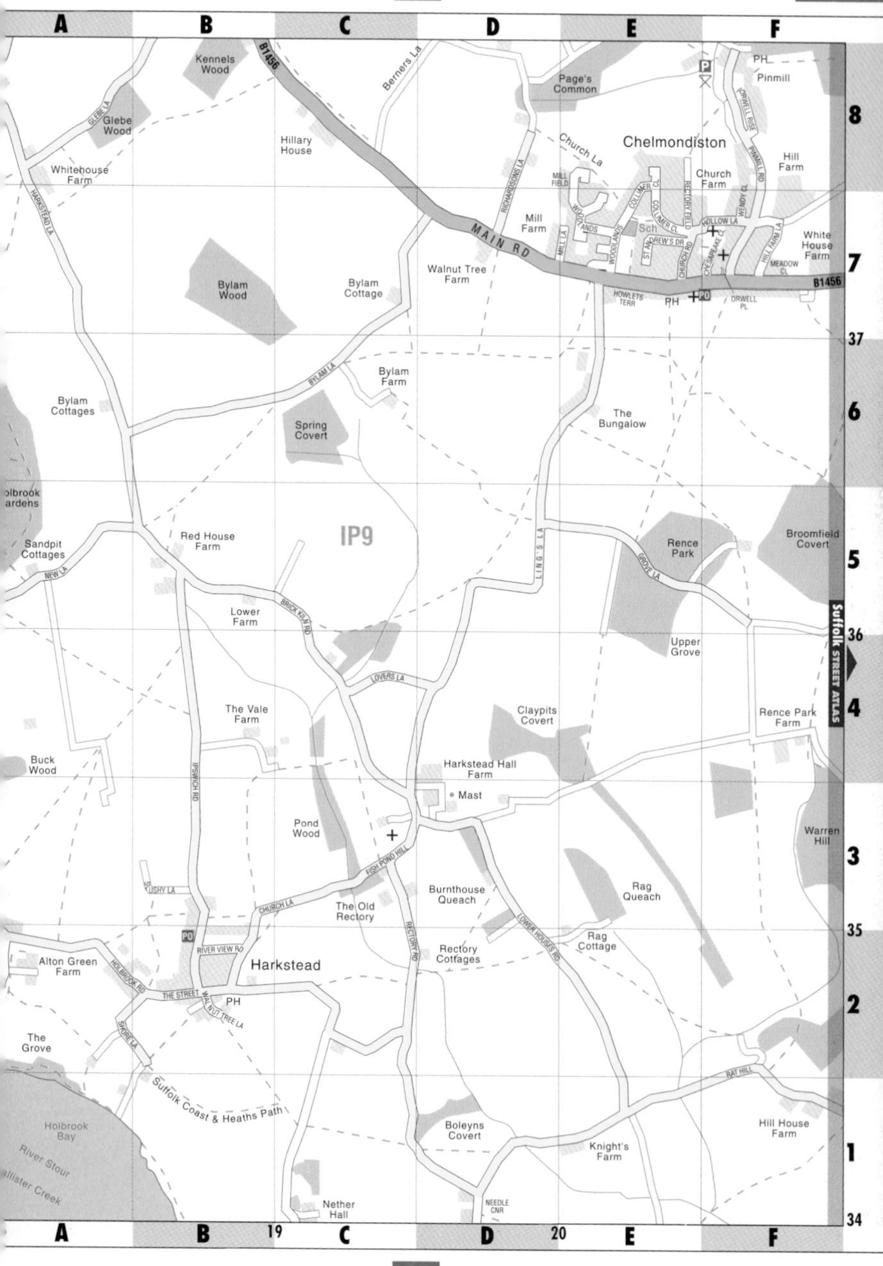

A
B
C
D
E
F
Kennels Wood
B1456
Berners La
Page's Common
PH
Pinmill
Glebe La
Glebe Wood
Hillary House
Church La
Chelmondiston
Pinmill Rd
Hill Farm
Whitehouse Farm
Church Farm
Harkstead La
Richardsons La
Mill Field
Colliner Cl
Rectory Field
Woodlands
Mill Farm
Hollow La
Main Rd
Sch
St Andrew's Dr
Church Rd
Chesapeake Cl
Hill Farm La
White House Farm
Mill La
Meadow Cl
Bylam Wood
Bylam Cottage
Walnut Tree Farm
B1456
Howlets Terr
PH
PO
Orwell Pl
Bylam La
Bylam Farm
Bylam Cottages
The Bungalow
Spring Covert
Holbrook Gardens
IP9
Red House Farm
Rence Park
Broomfield Covert
Sandpit Cottages
Ling's La
Grove La
New La
Lower Farm
Brick Kiln Rd
Upper Grove
Suffolk STREET ATLAS
Lovers La
The Vale Farm
Claypits Covert
Rence Park Farm
Buck Wood
Harkstead Hall Farm
Mast
Ipswich Rd
Pond Wood
Warren Hill
Fish Pond Hill
Slushy La
Burnthouse Queach
Rag Queach
Church La
The Old Rectory
PO
Lower Houses Rd
Rag Cottage
Rectory Rd
River View Rd
Rectory Cottages
Alton Green Farm
Harkstead
Holbrook Rd
The Street
PH
Walnut Tree La
Shore La
The Grove
Rat Hill
Suffolk Coast & Heaths Path
Holbrook Bay
Hill House Farm
River Stour
Boleyns Covert
Knight's Farm
Stallister Creek
Nether Hall
Needle Cnr
8
7
37
6
5
36
4
3
35
2
1
34
19
20

89

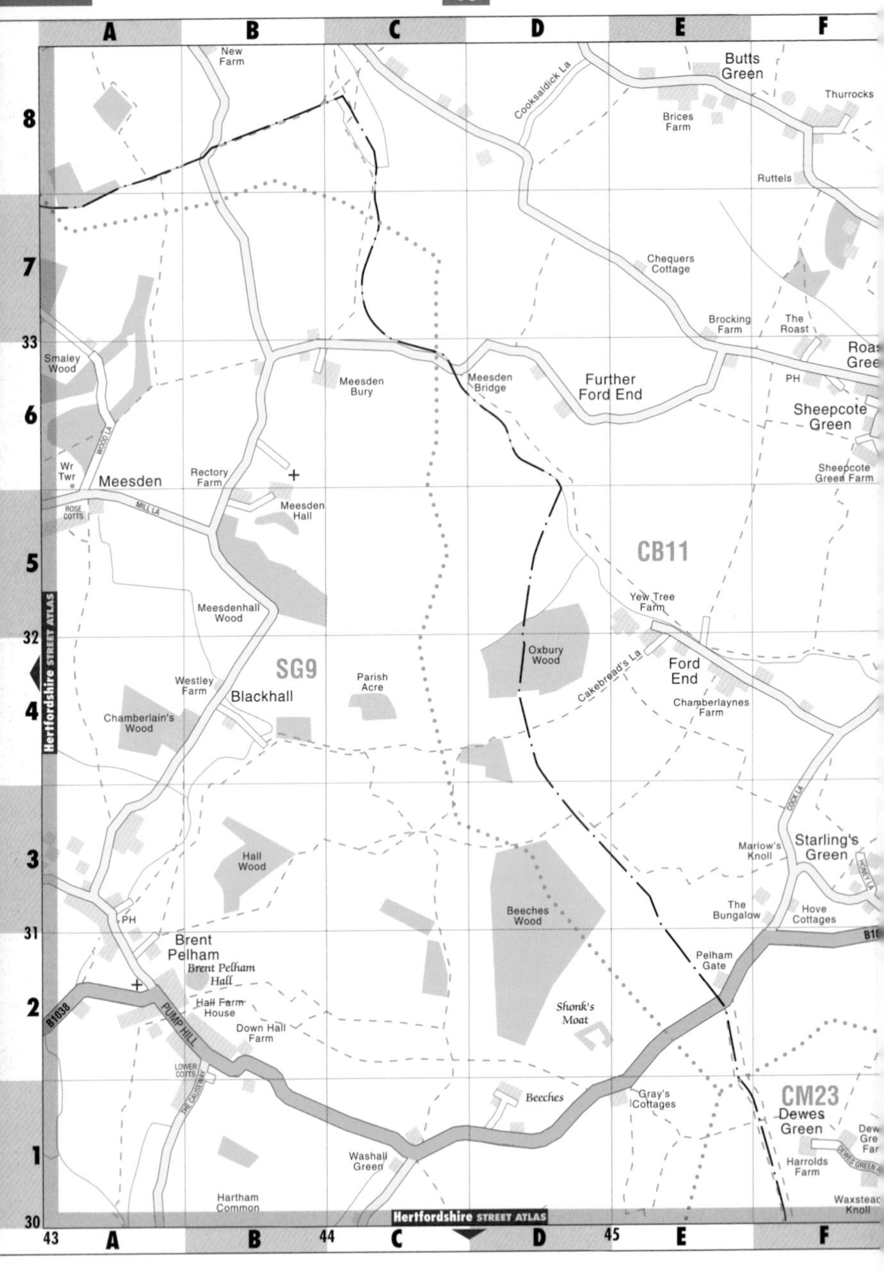

New Farm

Cooksdick La

Butts Green

Thurrocks

Brices Farm

Ruttels

Chequers Cottage

Brocking Farm

The Roast

Roas Gree

Smaley Wood

Meesden Bury

Meesden Bridge

Further Ford End

Sheepcote Green

PH

Wr Twr

Meesden

Rectory Farm

Meesden Hall

Sheepcote Green Farm

ROSE COTTS

MILL LA

CB11

Meesdenhall Wood

Yew Tree Farm

SG9

Westley Farm

Blackhall

Parish Acre

Oxbury Wood

Ford End

Chamberlaynes Farm

Chamberlain's Wood

Hall Wood

Marlow's Knoll

Starling's Green

PH

Beeches Wood

The Bungalow

Hove Cottages

Brent Pelham

Brent Pelham Hall

Pelham Gate

B16

Hall Farm House

Down Hall Farm

Shonk's Moat

B1038

LOWER COTTS

PUMP HILL

CM23

Dewes Green

Beeches

Gray's Cottages

Washall Green

Harrolds Farm

Dew Gre Far

Hartham Common

Waxstead Knoll

43   A   B   44   C   D   45   E   F

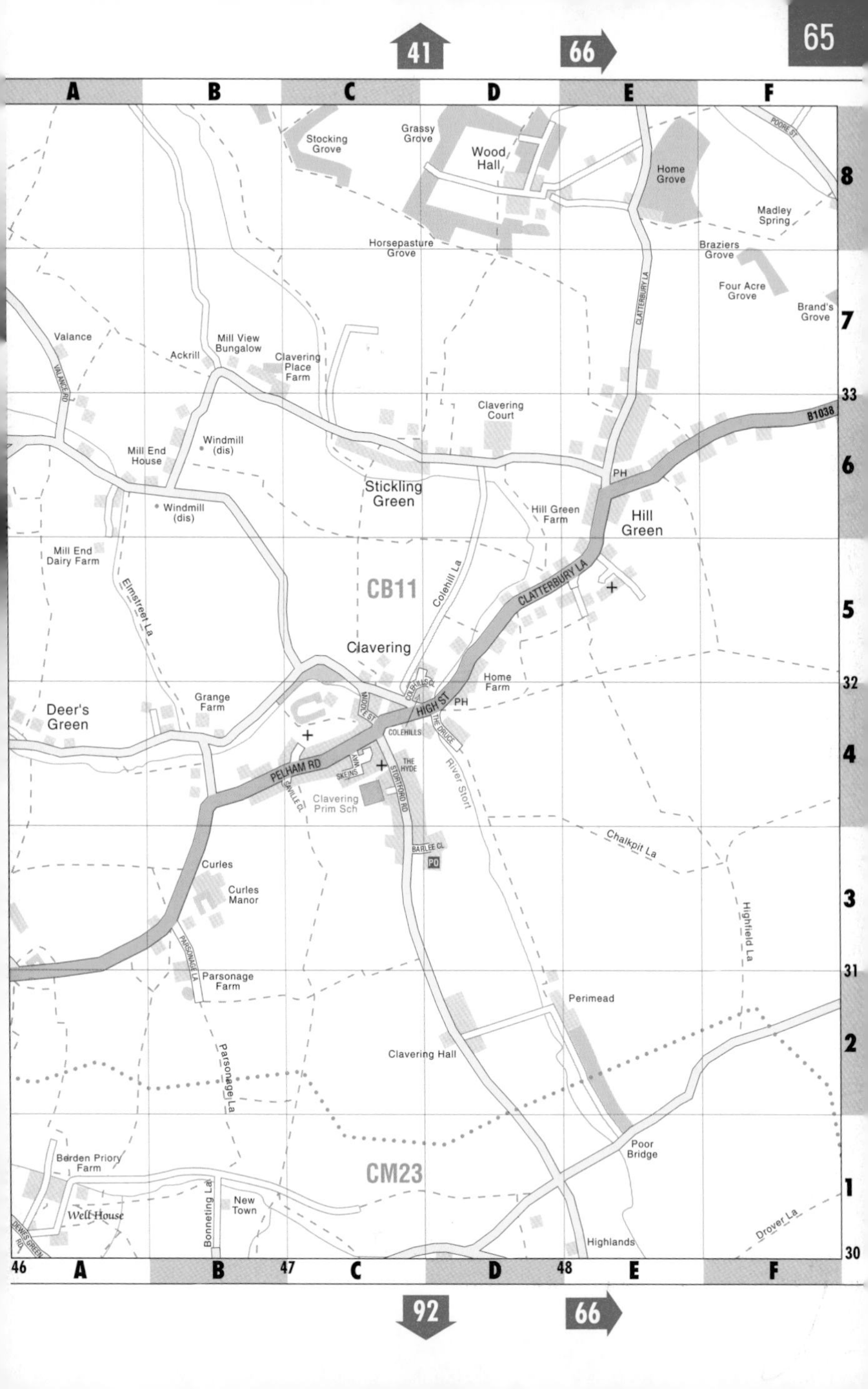

A B C D E F

8

Wood Hall

Stocking Grove

Grassy Grove

Home Grove

Madley Spring

Horsepasture Grove

Braziers Grove

Four Acre Grove

Brand's Grove

7

Valance

Ackrill

Mill View Bungalow

Clavering Place Farm

Clavering Court

B1038

33

Mill End House

Windmill (dis)

Stickling Green

PH

6

Hill Green Farm

Hill Green

Mill End Dairy Farm

Windmill (dis)

CB11

Colehill La

CLATTERBURY LA

5

Clavering

32

Home Farm

Deer's Green

Grange Farm

HIGH ST

PH

4

PELHAM RD

COLEHILLS

THE HYDE

Clavering Prim Sch

STORTFORD RD

River Stort

Chalkpit La

Highfield La

Curles

BAILLIE CL

PO

3

Curles Manor

31

Parsonage Farm

Perimead

2

Parsonage La

Clavering Hall

Poor Bridge

Barden Priory Farm

CM23

1

Well House

Bonnetting La

New Town

Highlands

Drover La

30

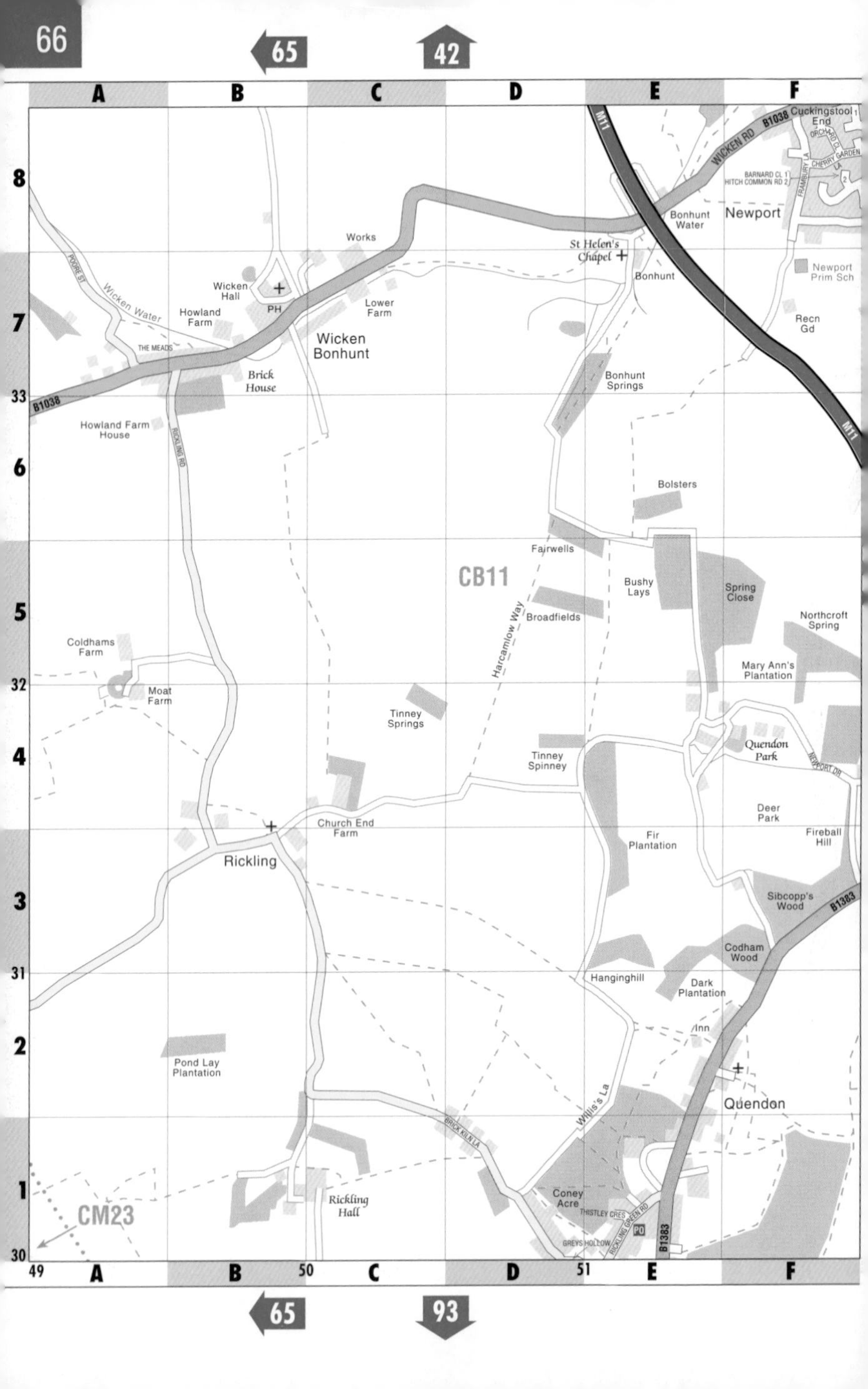
65
42
A
B
C
D
E
F
8
7
33
6
5
32
4
3
31
2
1
30
49
50
51
M11
B1038
WICKEN RD
Cuckingstool End
ORCHARD CL
CHERRY GARDEN LA
FRAMBURY LA
BARNARD CL 1
HITCH COMMON RD 2
Bonhunt Water
Newport
St Helen's Chapel
Bonhunt
Newport Prim Sch
Recn Gd
Works
Wicken Hall
PH
Lower Farm
Howland Farm
POORE ST
Wicken Water
THE MEADS
Wicken Bonhunt
Brick House
Howland Farm House
RICKLING RD
Bonhunt Springs
Bolsters
Fairwells
CB11
Bushy Lays
Spring Close
Northcroft Spring
Harcamlow Way
Broadfields
Coldhams Farm
Moat Farm
Mary Ann's Plantation
Tinney Springs
Tinney Spinney
Quendon Park
NEWPORT DR
Deer Park
Church End Farm
Rickling
Fir Plantation
Fireball Hill
Sibcopp's Wood
B1383
Codham Wood
Hanginghill
Dark Plantation
Inn
Pond Lay Plantation
Willis's La
Quendon
BRICK KILN LA
Coney Acre
THISTLEY CRES
RICKLING GREEN RD
PO
GREYS HOLLOW
Rickling Hall
CM23
65
93

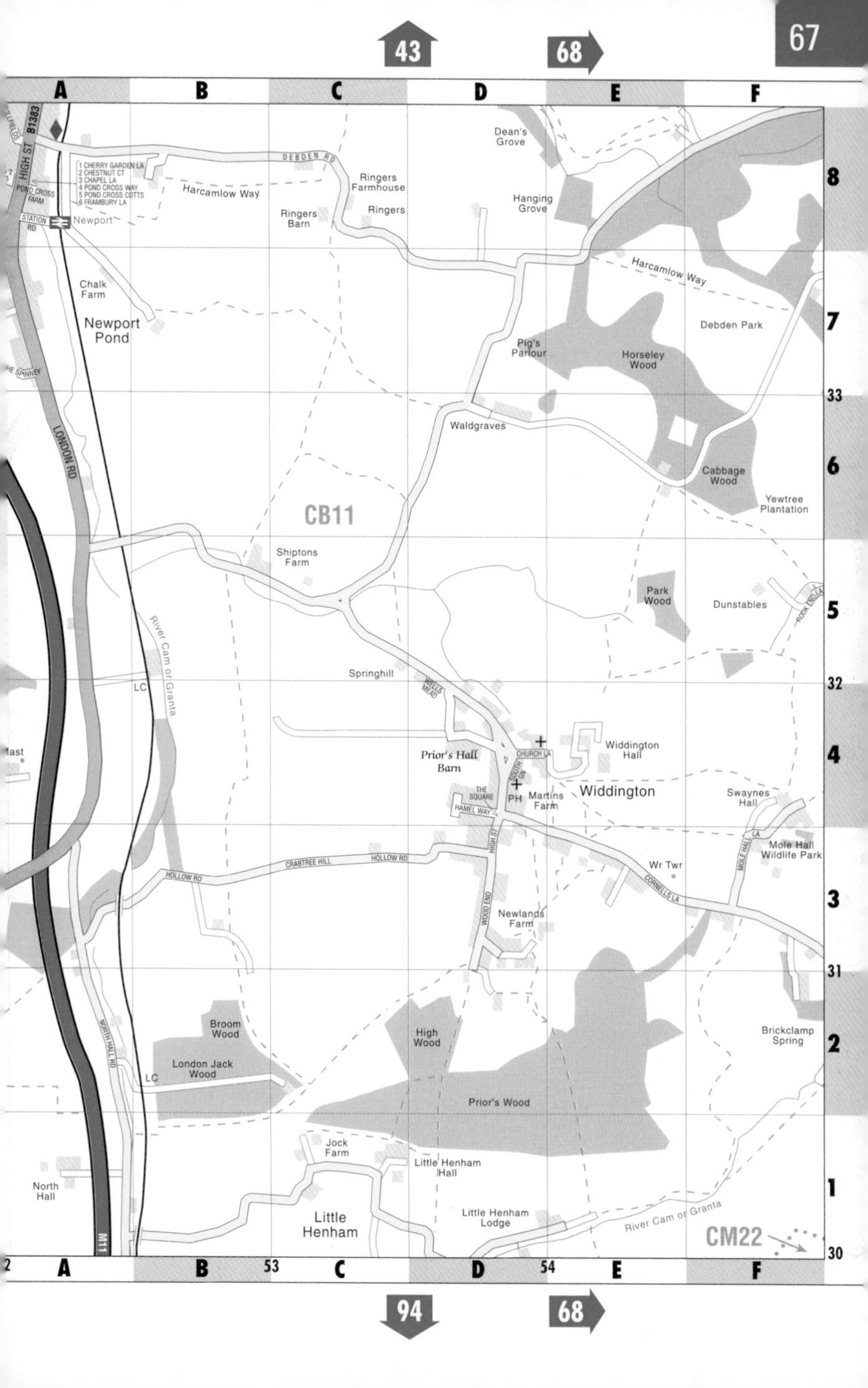
43
68
A
B
C
D
E
F
8
7
33
6
5
32
4
3
31
2
1
30
53
54
94
68
B1383
HIGH ST
POND CROSS FARM
STATION RD
Newport
1 CHERRY GARDEN LA
2 CHESTNUT CT
3 CHAPEL LA
4 POND CROSS WAY
5 POND CROSS COTTS
6 FRAMBURY LA
DEBDEN RD
Harcamlow Way
Ringers Barn
Ringers Farmhouse
Ringers
Dean's Grove
Hanging Grove
Harcamlow Way
Chalk Farm
Newport Pond
THE SPINNEY
LONDON RD
Pig's Parlour
Horseley Wood
Debden Park
Waldgraves
Cabbage Wood
Yewtree Plantation
CB11
Shiptons Farm
Park Wood
Dunstables
ROOK END LA
River Cam or Granta
LC
Springhill
WELLS MEAD
Mast
Prior's Hall Barn
CHURCH LA
SOUTH GN
Widdington Hall
THE SQUARE
HAMEL WAY
PH
Martins Farm
Widdington
Swaynes Hall
HIGH ST
HOLLOW RD
CRABTREE HILL
HOLLOW RD
Wr Twr
CORNELLS LA
MOLE HALL LA
Mole Hall Wildlife Park
WOOD END
Newlands Farm
NORTH HALL RD
Broom Wood
London Jack Wood
LC
High Wood
Brickclamp Spring
Prior's Wood
Jock Farm
Little Henham Hall
North Hall
Little Henham
Little Henham Lodge
River Cam or Granta
CM22
M11

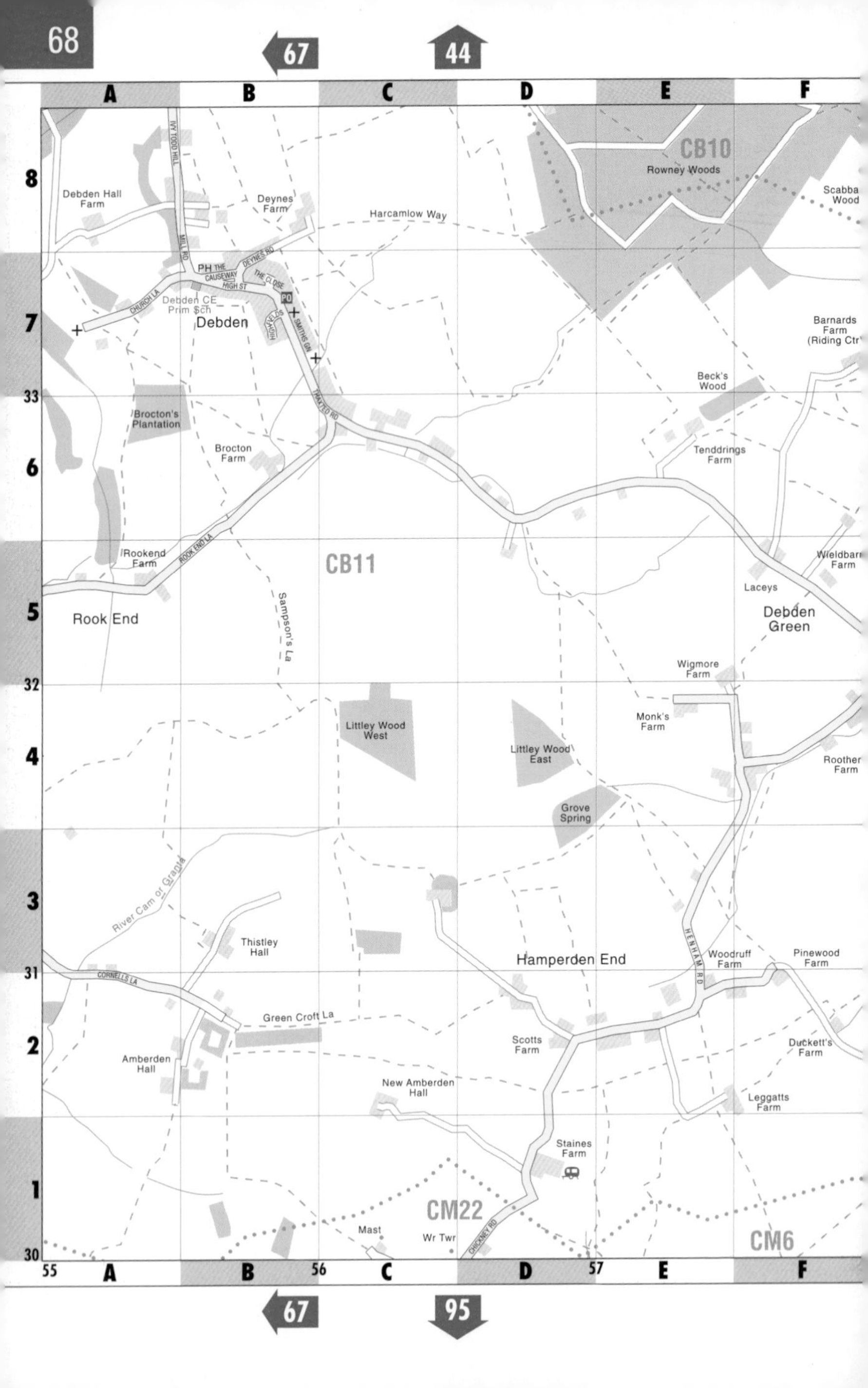

A | **B** | **C** | **D** | **E** | **F**

8

Debden Hall Farm

Deynes Farm

Harcamlow Way

CB10
Rowney Woods

Scabba Wood

7

PH THE CAUSEWAY
CHURCH LA
HIGH ST
DEYNES RD
THE CO DYKE
Debden CE Prim Sch
PO
SMITHS GRN
Debden

Barnards Farm (Riding Ctr)

33

Brocton's Plantation

Beck's Wood

6

Brocton Farm

Tenddrings Farm

CB11

Rookend Farm

ROOK END LA

Wieldbarn

5

Sampson's La

Rook End

Laceys

Debden Green

32

Wigmore Farm

Monk's Farm

4

Littley Wood West

Littley Wood East

Roother Farm

Grove Spring

3

River Cam or Granta

Thistley Hall

Hamperden End

Woodruff Farm

DEERS LA

Pinewood Farm

31

CORNELLS LA

Green Croft La

Scotts Farm

Duckett's Farm

2

Amberden Hall

New Amberden Hall

Leggatts Farm

Staines Farm

1

CM22

ORCHARD RD

Mast   Wr Twr

CM6

30

55   **A**   **B**   56   **C**   **D**   57   **E**   **F**

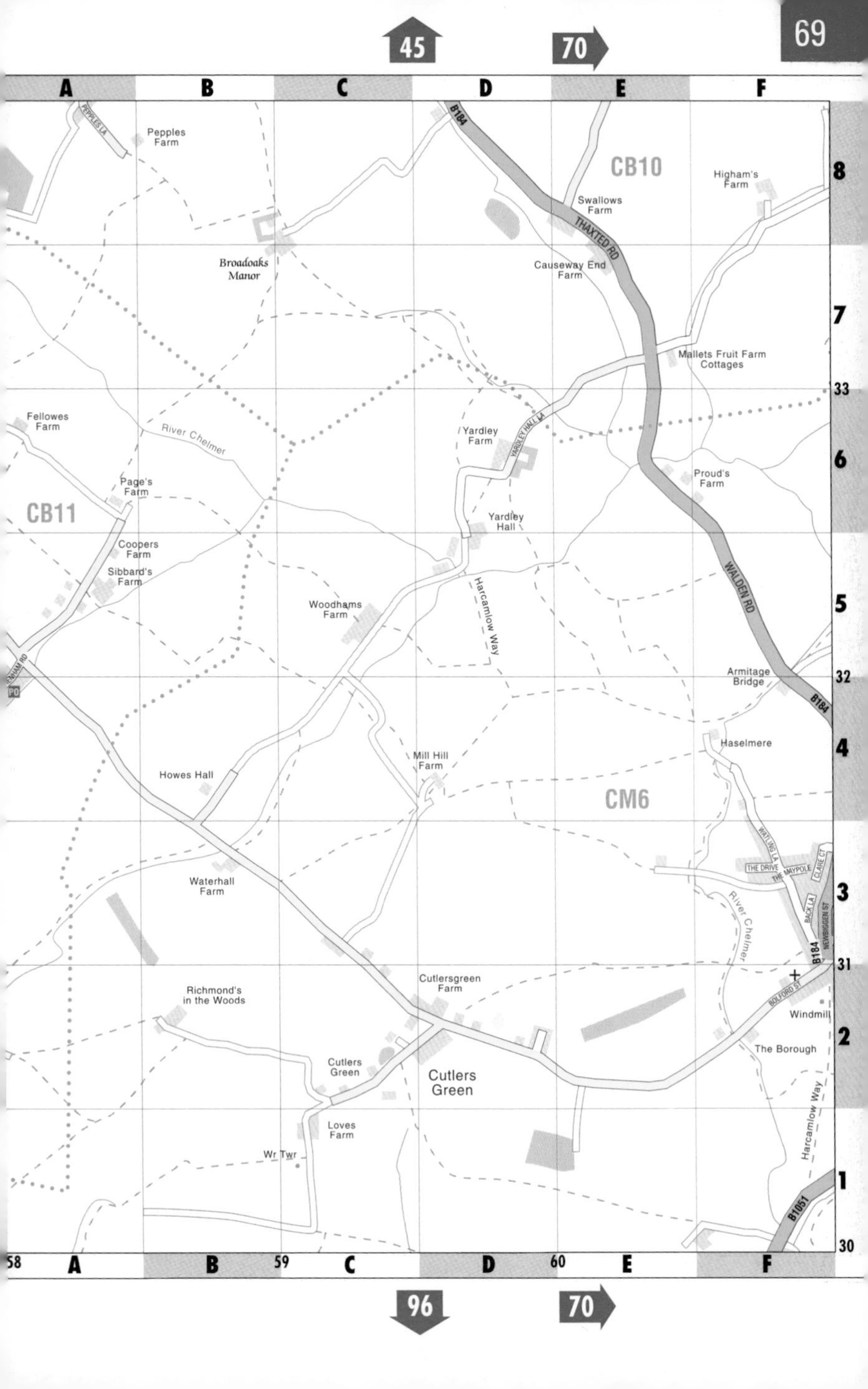
45
70
A
B
C
D
E
F
8
7
6
5
4
3
2
1
33
32
31
30
58
59
60
96
70
PEPPLES LA
Pepples Farm
B184
CB10
Higham's Farm
Swallows Farm
THAXTED RD
Broadoaks Manor
Causeway End Farm
Mallets Fruit Farm Cottages
Fellowes Farm
River Chelmer
Yardley Farm
YARDLEY HALL LA
Proud's Farm
Page's Farm
CB11
Yardley Hall
Coopers Farm
Sibbard's Farm
WALDEN RD
Woodhams Farm
Harcamlow Way
Armitage Bridge
B184
PO
Haselmere
Mill Hill Farm
Howes Hall
CM6
WATLING LA
THE DRIVE
THE MAYPOLE
CLARE CT
BACK LA
NEWBIGGEN ST
Waterhall Farm
River Chelmer
B184
Richmond's in the Woods
Cutlersgreen Farm
BOLFORD ST
Windmill
The Borough
Cutlers Green
Cutlers Green
Harcamlow Way
Loves Farm
Wr Twr
B1051

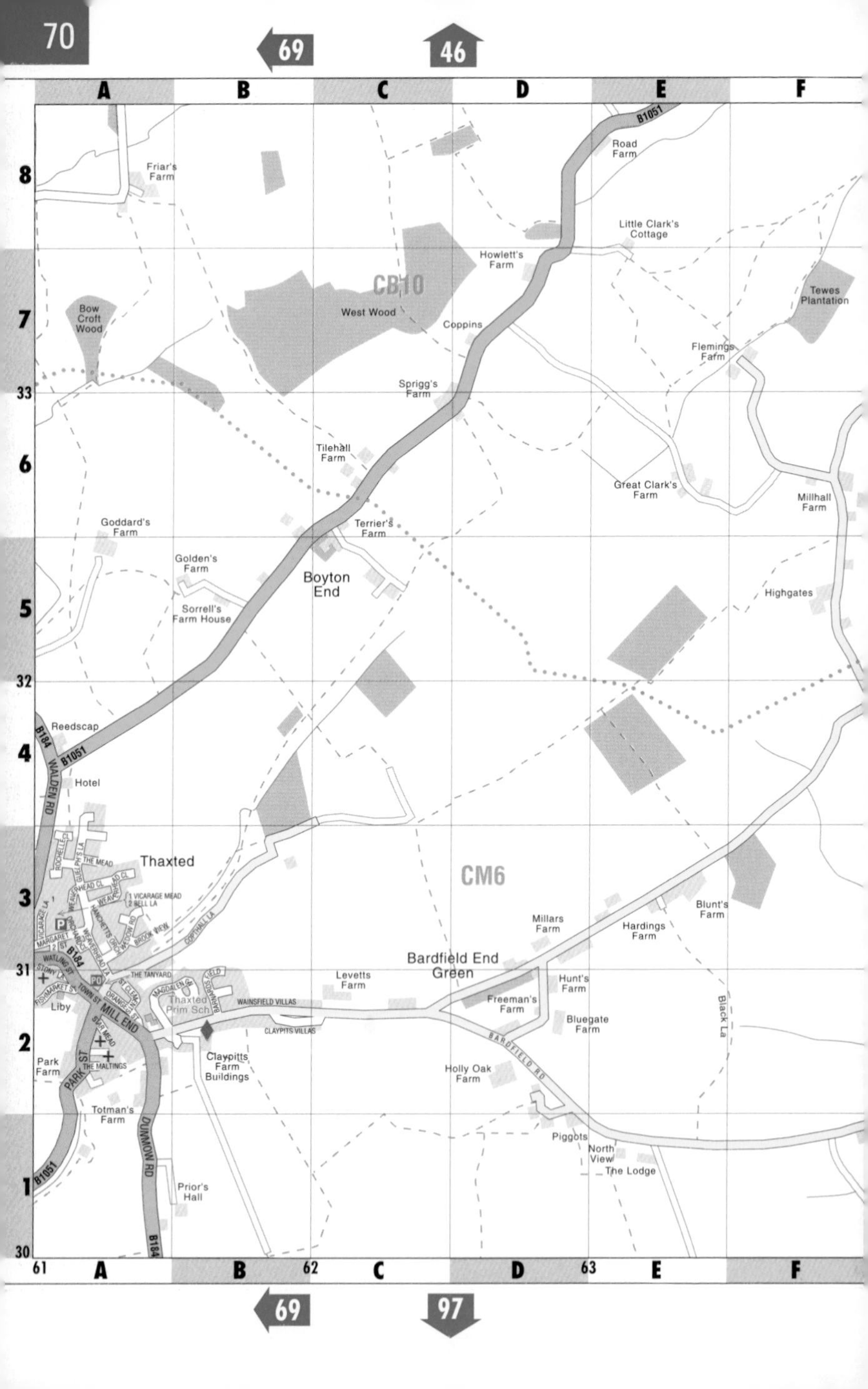

69

46

A B C D E F

8

7

33

6

5

32

4

3

31

2

1

30

B1051

Road Farm

Little Clark's Cottage

Howlett's Farm

CB10

West Wood

Coppins

Tewes Plantation

Flemings Farm

Sprigg's Farm

Tilehall Farm

Great Clark's Farm

Millhall Farm

Terrier's Farm

Friar's Farm

Bow Croft Wood

Goddard's Farm

Golden's Farm

Boyton End

Highgates

Sorrell's Farm House

Reedscap

B184 B1051

HALDEN RD

Hotel

Thaxted

THE MEAD

1 VICARAGE MEAD
2 MILL LA

MILL LA

COPPIELD LA

CM6

Millars Farm

Hardings Farm

Blunt's Farm

P

B184

THE TANYARD

MAGDALEN ST

31

Liby

MILL END

Levetts Farm

Bardfield End Green

Hunt's Farm

Freeman's Farm

Bluegate Farm

Black La

WAINSFIELD VILLAS

Thaxted Prim Sch

CLAYPITTS VILLAS

BARDFIELD RD

Park Farm

THE HALTINGS

Claypitts Farm Buildings

Holly Oak Farm

DUNMOW RD

PARK ST

Totman's Farm

Piggots

North View

The Lodge

B1051

Prior's Hall

B184

61 A B 62 C D 63 E F

69

97

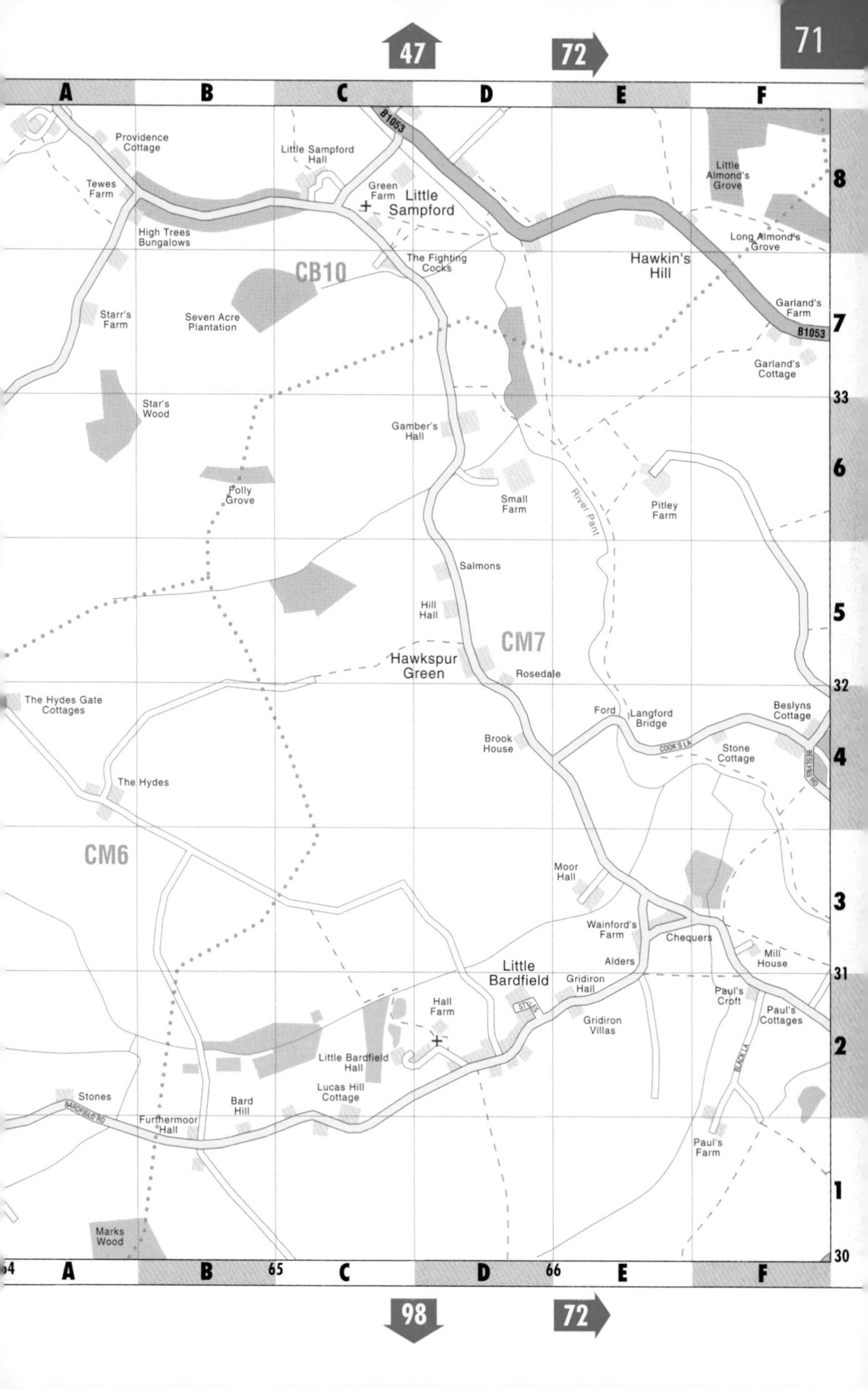
47
72
A
B
C
D
E
F
B1053
Providence Cottage
Little Sampford Hall
Tewes Farm
Green Farm
Little Sampford
Little Almond's Grove
8
High Trees Bungalows
Long Almond's Grove
The Fighting Cocks
Hawkin's Hill
CB10
Starr's Farm
Seven Acre Plantation
Garland's Farm
7
Garland's Cottage
33
Star's Wood
Gamber's Hall
6
Polly Grove
Small Farm
River Pant
Pitley Farm
Salmons
Hill Hall
5
CM7
Hawkspur Green
Rosedale
32
The Hydes Gate Cottages
Ford
Langford Bridge
Beslyns Cottage
Brook House
COOK'S LA
Stone Cottage
BESLYNS RD
4
The Hydes
CM6
Moor Hall
3
Wainford's Farm
Chequers
Alders
Mill House
Little Bardfield
Gridiron Hall
31
STYLES
Hall Farm
Paul's Croft
Paul's Cottages
Gridiron Villas
2
Little Bardfield Hall
BLACK LA
Lucas Hill Cottage
Stones
Bard Hill
BARDFIELD RD
Furthermoor Hall
Paul's Farm
1
Marks Wood
30
64
65
66
98
72

71
48

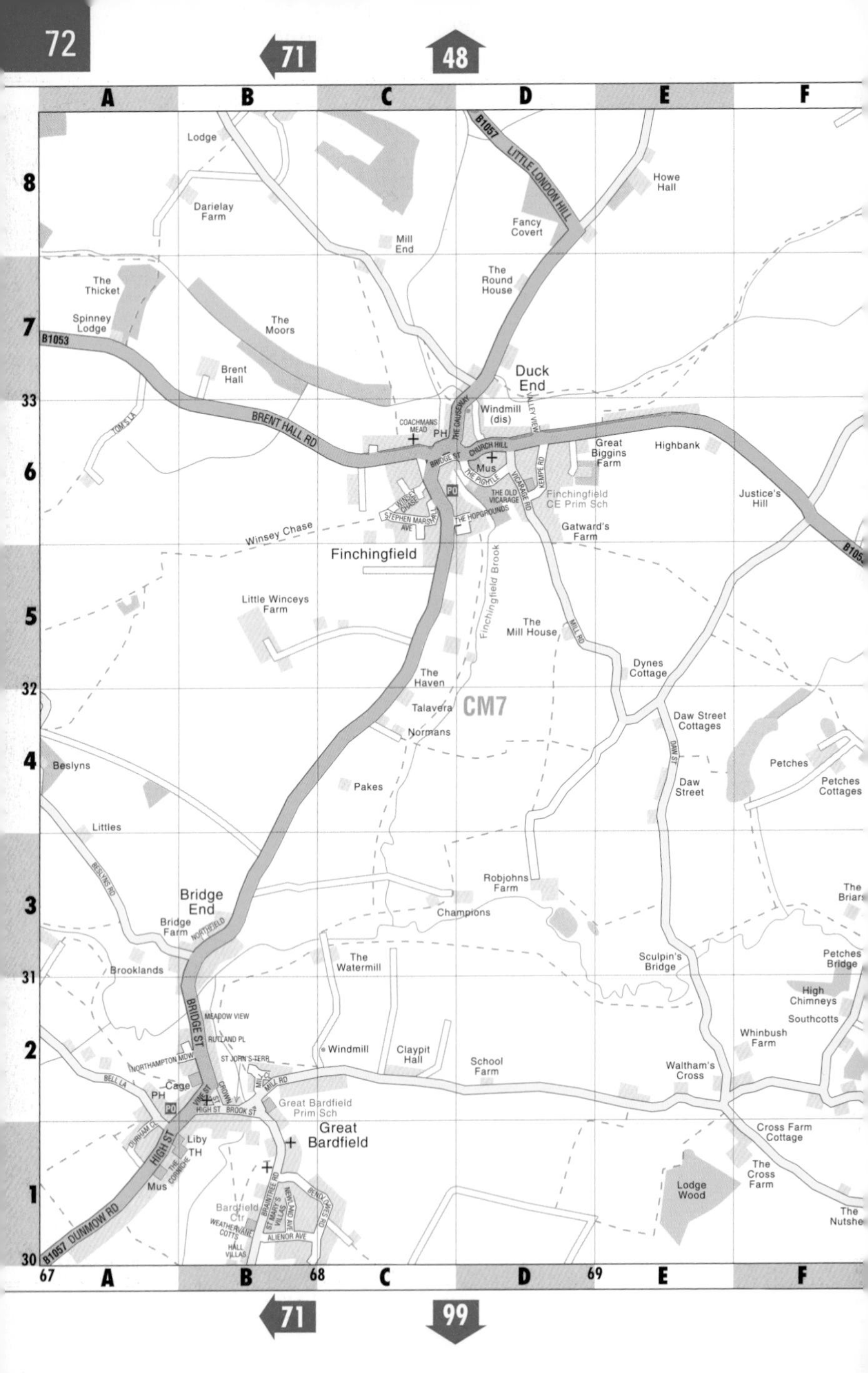
A
B
C
D
E
F
8
7
33
6
5
32
4
3
31
2
1
30
67
68
69
Lodge
Darielay Farm
Mill End
B1057
LITTLE LONDON HILL
Howe Hall
Fancy Covert
The Thicket
Spinney Lodge
The Moors
The Round House
B1053
Brent Hall
Duck End
BRENT HALL RD
TOM'S LA
COACHMANS MEAD
PH
THE CAUSEWAY
Windmill (dis)
VALLEY VIEW
CHURCH HILL
BRIDGE ST
Mus
THE PIGHTLE
Great Biggins Farm
Highbank
KEMPE RD
VICARAGE RD
THE OLD VICARAGE
Finchingfield CE Prim Sch
Justice's Hill
WINSEY CHASE
STEPHEN MARSHALL AVE
THE HOPGROUNDS
Winsey Chase
Gatward's Farm
Finchingfield
Finchingfield Brook
Little Winceys Farm
The Mill House
MILL RD
Dynes Cottage
The Haven
Talavera
CM7
Normans
Daw Street Cottages
DAW ST
Beslyns
Petches
Petches Cottages
Pakes
Daw Street
Littles
BESLYNS RD
Robjohns Farm
Bridge End
The Briars
Champions
Bridge Farm
NORTHFIELD
The Watermill
Sculpin's Bridge
Petches Bridge
Brooklands
High Chimneys
Southcotts
BRIDGE ST
MEADOW VIEW
RUTLAND PL
Windmill
Claypit Hall
School Farm
Whinbush Farm
ST JOHN'S TERR
NORTHAMPTON MDW
Waltham's Cross
BELL LA
Cage
MILL CL
MILL RD
PH
VINE ST
CROWN ST
PO
HIGH ST
BROOK ST
Great Bardfield Prim Sch
DURHAM CL
Great Bardfield
Cross Farm Cottage
HIGH ST
Liby
TH
THE CORNICHE
The Cross Farm
Mus
BRAINTREE RD
ST MARY'S VILLAS
NEWLAND AVE
BENDY CLOSE RD
Lodge Wood
B1057 DUNMOW RD
Bardfield Ctr
WEATHERVANE COTTS
ALIENOR AVE
HALL VILLAS
The Nutshell

71
99

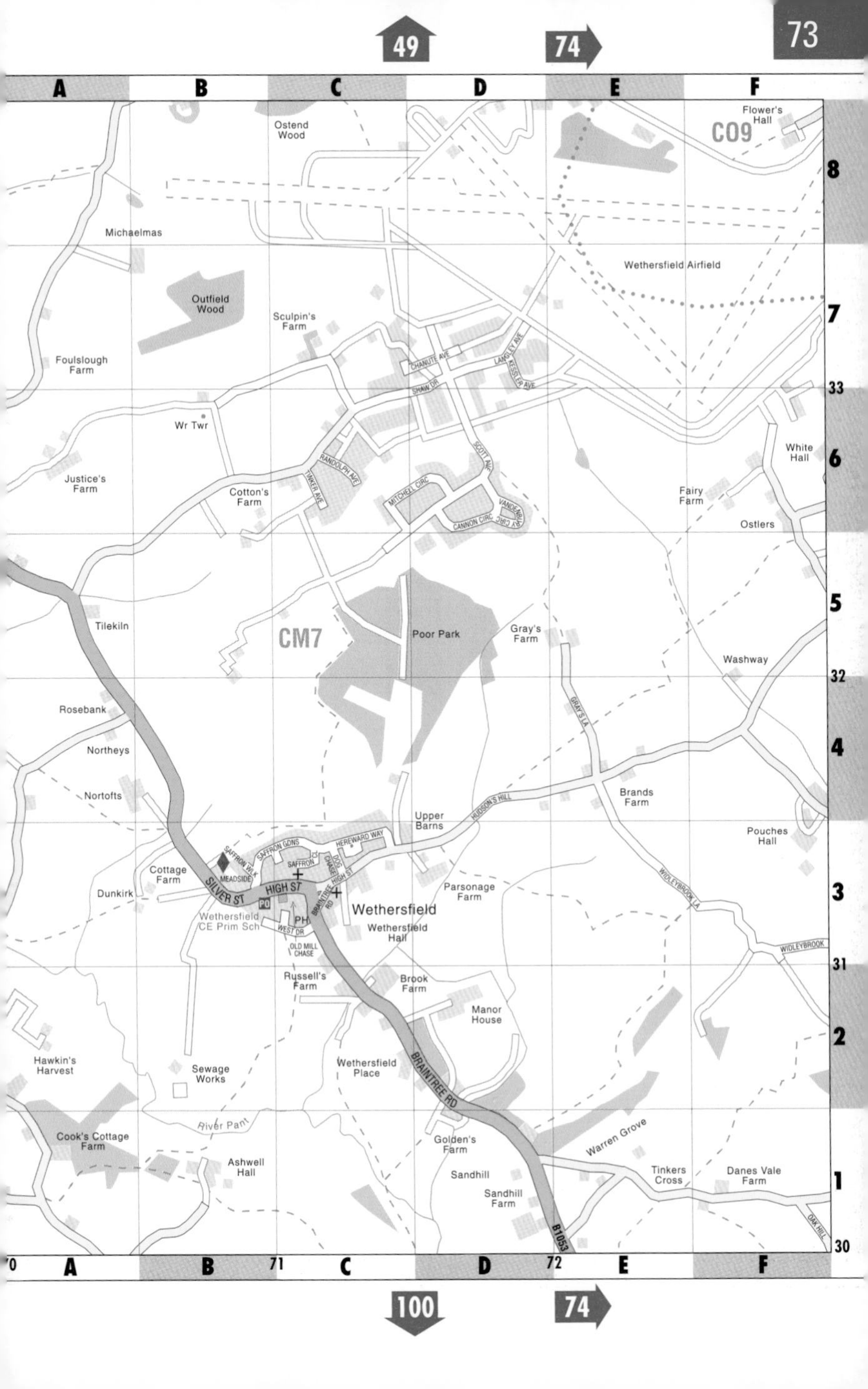

CO9

Flower's Hall

Ostend Wood

Michaelmas

Wethersfield Airfield

Outfield Wood

Sculpin's Farm

Foulslough Farm

CHANTREY AVE
SPANN CTR
LANE HOUSE LA.
LANE HOUSE AVE.

Wr Twr

Justice's Farm

Cotton's Farm

HANGER MILTON WAY
DAVEY DRIVE
MITCHELL CIRC.
SCOTT RD.
VANGUARD
CANNON CIRC.
2ND DR.

White Hall

Fairy Farm

Ostlers

CM7

Poor Park

Gray's Farm

Tilekiln

EAST ST.

Washway

Rosebank

Northeys

Nortofts

Brands Farm

HIGGINS HILL

Pouches Hall

WIDLEYBROOK LA

Upper Barns

WIDLEYBROOK

Cottage Farm

SAFFRON GDNS
MEADSIDE
SAFFRON
HEREWARD WAY
HIGH ST.
WEST DR.

SILVER ST

HIGH ST

PH

Wethersfield /CE Prim Sch

OLD MILL CHASE

Parsonage Farm

Wethersfield Hall

Wethersfield

Dunkirk

Russell's Farm

Brook Farm

Manor House

Hawkin's Harvest

Sewage Works

River Pant

Wethersfield Place

BRAINTREE RD

Cook's Cottage Farm

Ashwell Hall

Golden's Farm

Sandhill

Sandhill Farm

Warren Grove

Tinkers Cross

Danes Vale Farm

OAK HILL

B1053

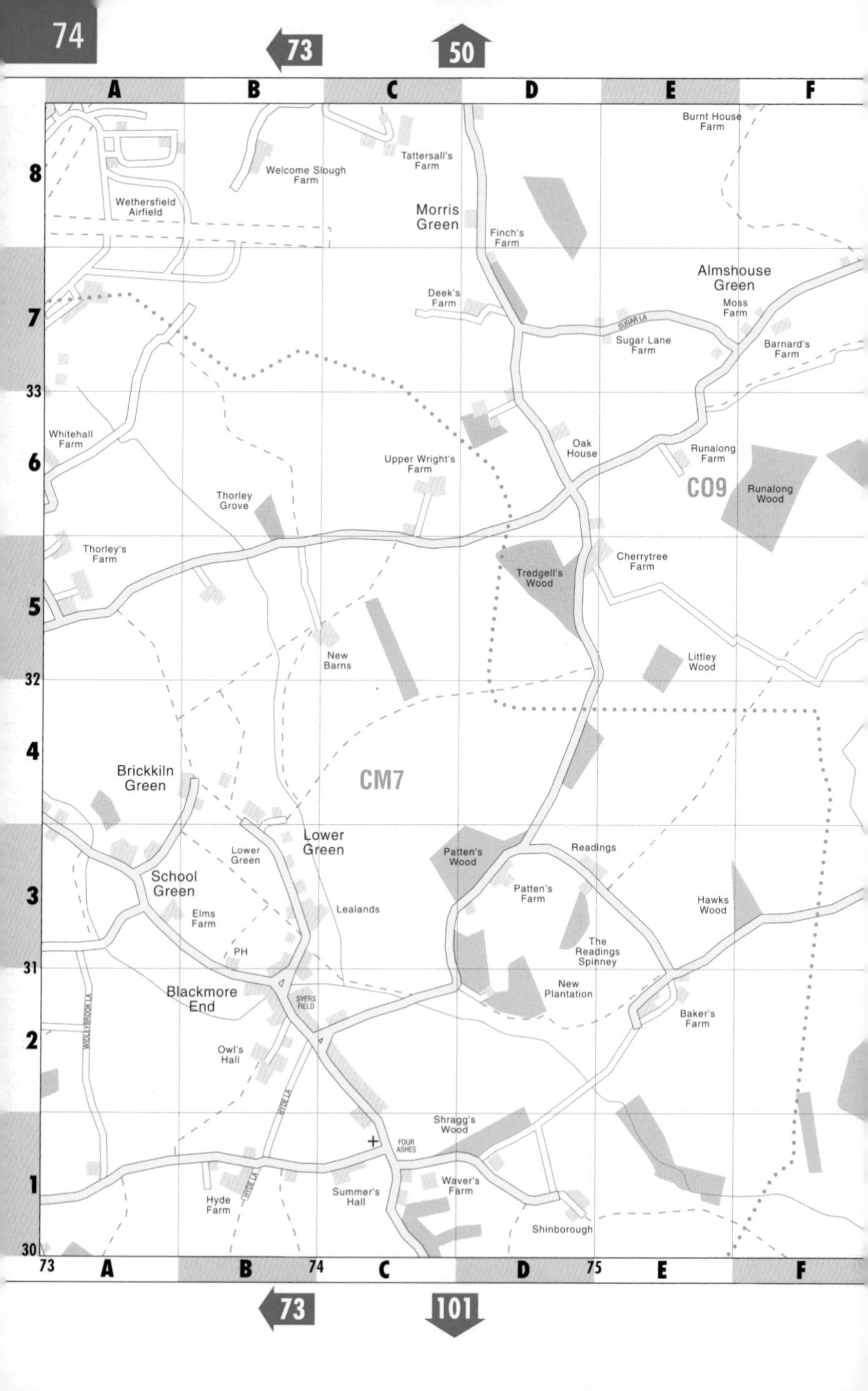
73
50
A
B
C
D
E
F
Burnt House Farm
Welcome Slough Farm
Tattersall's Farm
Wethersfield Airfield
Morris Green
Finch's Farm
Almshouse Green
Deek's Farm
SUGAR LA
Moss Farm
Sugar Lane Farm
Barnard's Farm
Whitehall Farm
Oak House
Runalong Farm
Upper Wright's Farm
CO9
Runalong Wood
Thorley Grove
Thorley's Farm
Cherrytree Farm
Tredgell's Wood
New Barns
Littley Wood
Brickkiln Green
CM7
Lower Green
Lower Green
Patten's Wood
Readings
School Green
Patten's Farm
Elms Farm
Lealands
Hawks Wood
The Readings Spinney
PH
Blackmore End
SYERS FIELD
New Plantation
Baker's Farm
WIDLEYBROOK LA
Owl's Hall
HYDE LA
Shragg's Wood
FOUR ASHES
Waver's Farm
Hyde Farm
HYDE LA
Summer's Hall
Shinborough
8
7
33
6
5
32
4
3
31
2
1
30
73
74
75
73
101

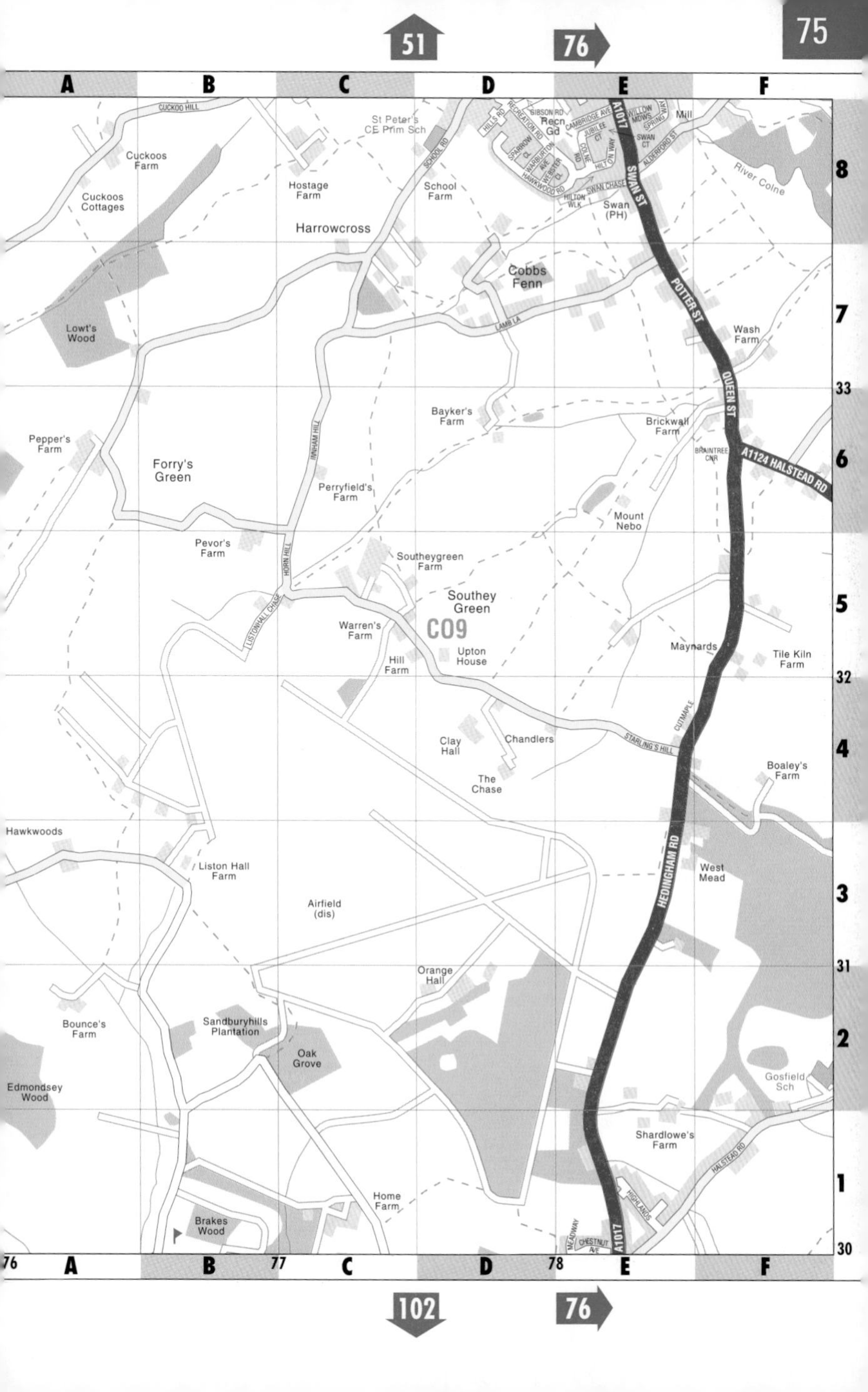
51
76
A
B
C
D
E
F
CUCKOO HILL
Cuckoos Farm
Cuckoos Cottages
St Peter's CE Prim Sch
SCHOOL RD
Hostage Farm
School Farm
Harrowcross
HILLS RD
RECREATION RD
SIBSON RD
Recn Gd
CAMBRIDGE AVE
JUBILEE CT
WILLOW MDWS
SPRING WAY
Mill
SWAN CT
ALDERFORD ST
SPARROW CL
NARBURTON AVE
WEBSTER CL
HAWKWOOD RD
COLNE RD
HILTON WAY
SWAN CHASE
HILTON WLK
Swan (PH)
A1017
SWAN ST
River Colne
Cobbs Fenn
Lowt's Wood
LAMB LA
POTTER ST
Wash Farm
QUEEN ST
Bayker's Farm
Brickwall Farm
BRAINTREE CNR
A1124 HALSTEAD RD
Pepper's Farm
Forry's Green
INHAM HILL
Perryfield's Farm
Mount Nebo
Pevor's Farm
HORN HILL
Southeygreen Farm
Southey Green
LISTONHALL CHASE
Warren's Farm
CO9
Hill Farm
Upton House
Maynards
Tile Kiln Farm
CUTMAPLE
Clay Hall
Chandlers
STARLING'S HILL
The Chase
Boaley's Farm
Hawkwoods
Liston Hall Farm
HEDINGHAM RD
West Mead
Airfield (dis)
Orange Hall
Bounce's Farm
Sandburyhills Plantation
Oak Grove
Edmondsey Wood
Gosfield Sch
Shardlowe's Farm
HALSTEAD RD
HIGHLANDS
Home Farm
Brakes Wood
MEADWAY
CHESTNUT AVE
8
7
33
6
5
32
4
3
31
2
1
30
76
77
78
102

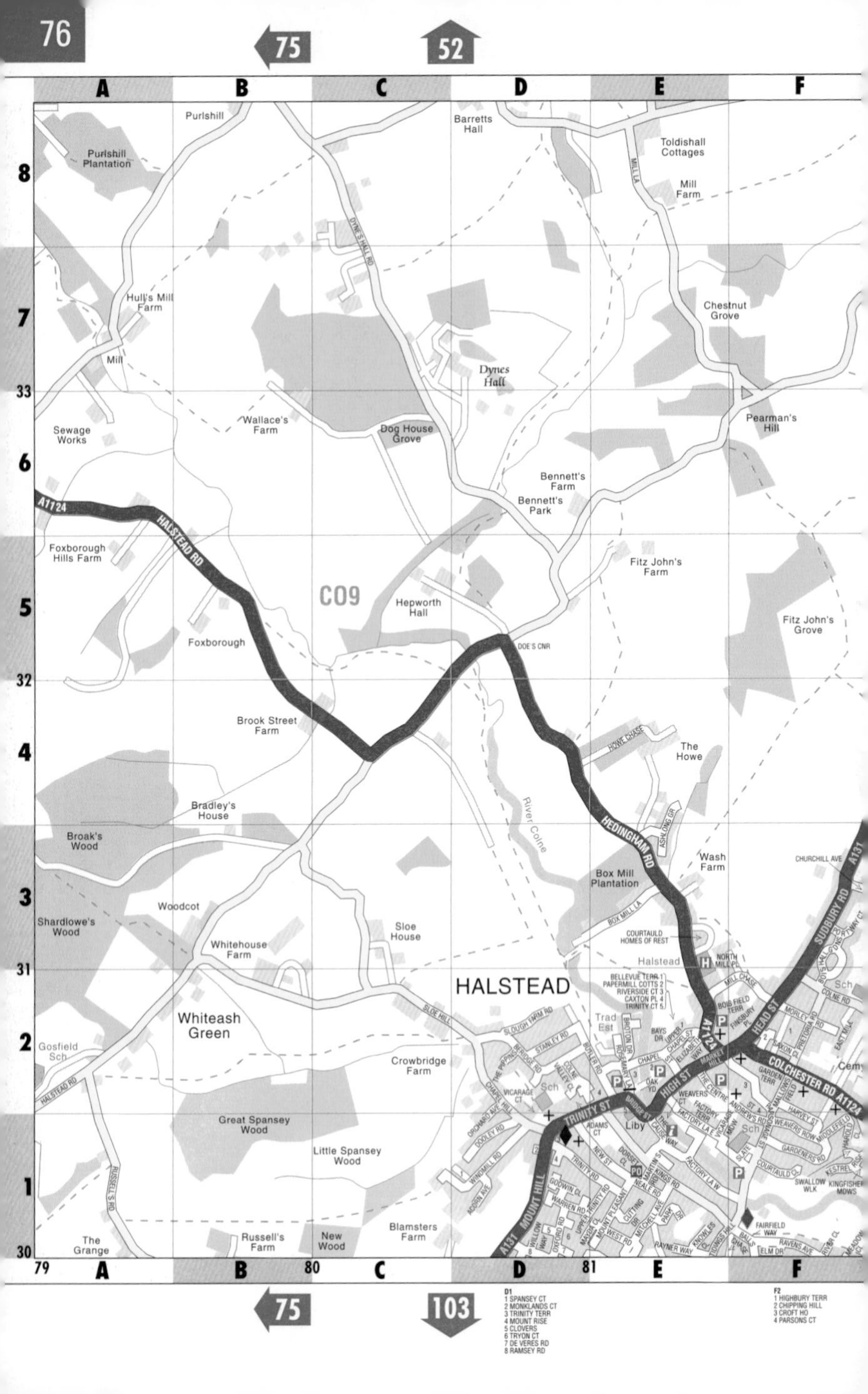
75
52
A B C D E F
Purlshill
Purlshill Plantation
Barretts Hall
Toldishall Cottages
Mill Farm
MILL LA
DYNES HALL RD
Hull's Mill Farm
Mill
Chestnut Grove
Dynes Hall
Sewage Works
Wallace's Farm
Dog House Grove
Pearman's Hill
Bennett's Farm
Bennett's Park
A1124
HALSTEAD RD
Foxborough Hills Farm
Fitz John's Farm
CO9
Hepworth Hall
Fitz John's Grove
Foxborough
DOE'S CNR
Brook Street Farm
HOWE CHASE
The Howe
Bradley's House
River Colne
ASHLONG GR
HEDINGHAM RD
Broak's Wood
Wash Farm
CHURCHILL AVE
A131
Box Mill Plantation
Woodcot
Shardlowe's Wood
BOX MILL LA
SUDBURY RD
Sloe House
COURTAULD HOMES OF REST
Whitehouse Farm
Halstead
NORTH MILL PL
HALSTEAD
BELLEVUE TERR 1
PAPERMILL COTTS 2
RIVERSIDE CT 3
CAXTON PL 4
TRINITY CT 5
MILL CHASE
Whiteash Green
SLOE HILL
SLOUGH FARM RD
Trad Est
BOIS FIELD TERR
FINSBURY PL
HEAD ST
Gosfield Sch
STANLEY RD
BAYS DR
MORLEY RD
PRETORIA RD
EAST MILL
Crowbridge Farm
CHAPEL ST
HIGH ST
MARKET HILL
COLCHESTER RD A1124
Cem
HALSTEAD RD
VICARAGE CT
Sch
OAK YD
WEAVERS CT
FACTORY TERR
THE CENTRE
Great Spansey Wood
TRINITY ST
BRIDGE ST
FACTORY LA E
HARVEY ST
Liby
ADAMS CT
WEAVERS ROW
Little Spansey Wood
DOOLEY RD
NEW ST
DORSEY CL
GARDENERS RD
RUSSELL'S RD
TRINITY RD
KINGS RD
FACTORY LA W
COURTAULD CT
KESTREL RISE
WINDMILL RD
MOUNT HILL
GODWIN CL
NEALE RD
SWALLOW WLK
KINGFISHER MDWS
ACORN AVE
WARREN RD
MOUNT PLEASANT
CUTTING DR
MITCHELL AVE
PARK DR
FAIRFIELD WAY
The Grange
Russell's Farm
New Wood
Blamsters Farm
WEST RD
RAYNER WAY
KNOWLES CL
TIDINGS HILL
ELM DR
RAVENS AVE
RIVER CL
8 7 6 5 4 3 2 1
33 32 31 30
79 80 81
75
103
D1
1 SPANSEY CT
2 MONKLANDS CT
3 TRINITY TERR
4 MOUNT RISE
5 CLOVERS
6 TRYON CT
7 DE VERES RD
8 RAMSEY RD
F2
1 HIGHBURY TERR
2 CHIPPING HILL
3 CROFT HO
4 PARSONS CT

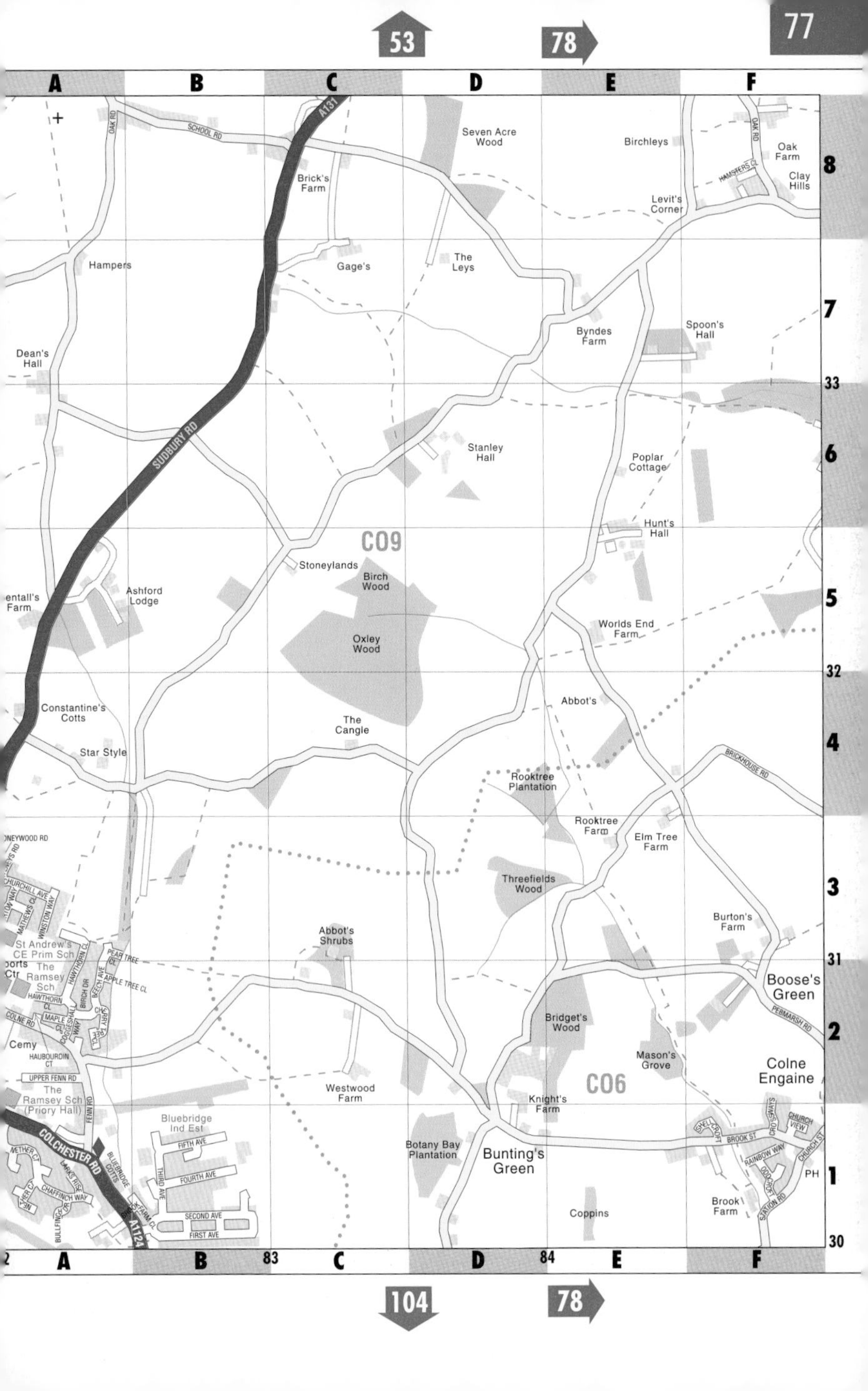
53
78
A
B
C
D
E
F
SCHOOL RD
OAK RD
A131
Seven Acre Wood
Birchleys
Oak Farm
HAMSTERS CL
Clay Hills
8
Brick's Farm
Levit's Corner
Hampers
Gage's
The Leys
7
Byndes Farm
Spoon's Hall
Dean's Hall
33
SUDBURY RD
Stanley Hall
Poplar Cottage
6
Hunt's Hall
CO9
Stoneylands
Birch Wood
Ashford Lodge
entall's Farm
5
Oxley Wood
Worlds End Farm
32
Abbot's
Constantine's Cotts
The Cangle
Star Style
4
BRICKHOUSE RD
Rooktree Plantation
Rooktree Farm
Elm Tree Farm
Threefields Wood
3
Burton's Farm
Abbot's Shrubs
St Andrew's CE Prim Sch
The Ramsey Sch
31
Boose's Green
PEAR TREE CL
APPLE TREE CL
HAWTHORN CL
MAPLE CL
COLNE RD
COGGESHALL WAY
CHURCHILL AVE
MATHEWS CL
WINSTON WAY
Bridget's Wood
PEBMARSH RD
2
Cemy
HAUBOURDIN CT
Mason's Grove
Colne Engaine
UPPER FENN RD
The Ramsey Sch (Priory Hall)
FENN RD
Westwood Farm
CO6
Knight's Farm
Bluebridge Ind Est
FIFTH AVE
COLCHESTER RD
BLUEBRIDGE COTTS
THIRD AVE
FOURTH AVE
SECOND AVE
FIRST AVE
NETHER CT
LARKS RISE
CHAFFINCH WAY
BULLFINCH DR
A1124
Botany Bay Plantation
Bunting's Green
SHELL CROFT
BROOK ST
CHURCH VIEW
RAINBOW WAY
CHURCH ST
STATION RD
PH
1
Coppins
Brook Farm
30
83
84
104
78

77
54

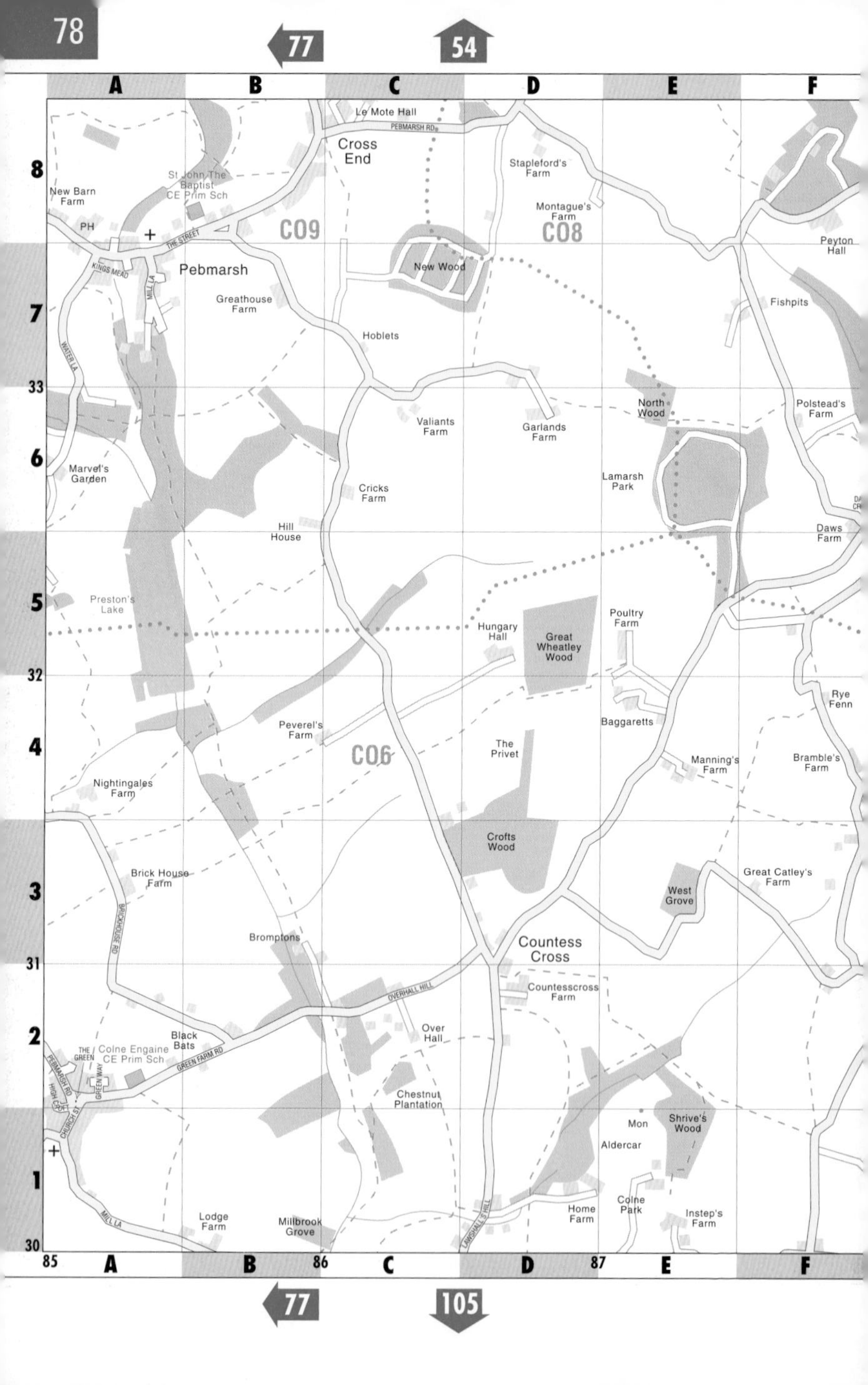

	A	B	C	D	E	F

8

New Barn Farm

St John The Baptist CE Prim Sch

PH

Pebmarsh

KINGS MEAD

THE STREET

C09

Cross End

Le Mote Hall

PEBMARSH RD

Stapleford's Farm

Montague's Farm

C08

Peyton Hall

7

Greathouse Farm

MILL LA

WHEELY RD

New Wood

Hoblets

Fishpits

33

Marvel's Garden

Valiants Farm

Garlands Farm

North Wood

Polstead's Farm

6

Cricks Farm

Lamarsh Park

Daws Farm

Hill House

5

Preston's Lake

Hungary Hall

Great Wheatley Wood

Poultry Farm

32

Baggaretts

Rye Fenn

4

Peverel's Farm

C06

The Privet

Manning's Farm

Bramble's Farm

Nightingales Farm

Crofts Wood

3

Brick House Farm

West Grove

Great Catley's Farm

31

Bromptons

Countess Cross

OVERHALL HILL

Countesscross Farm

2

Colne Engaine CE Prim Sch

THE GREEN

GREEN WAY

Black Bats

GREEN FARM RD

Over Hall

Chestnut Plantation

Aldercar

Mon

Shrive's Wood

1

Lodge Farm

Millbrook Grove

Home Farm

Colne Park

Instep's Farm

30

HILL LA

85 A 86 B C 87 D E F

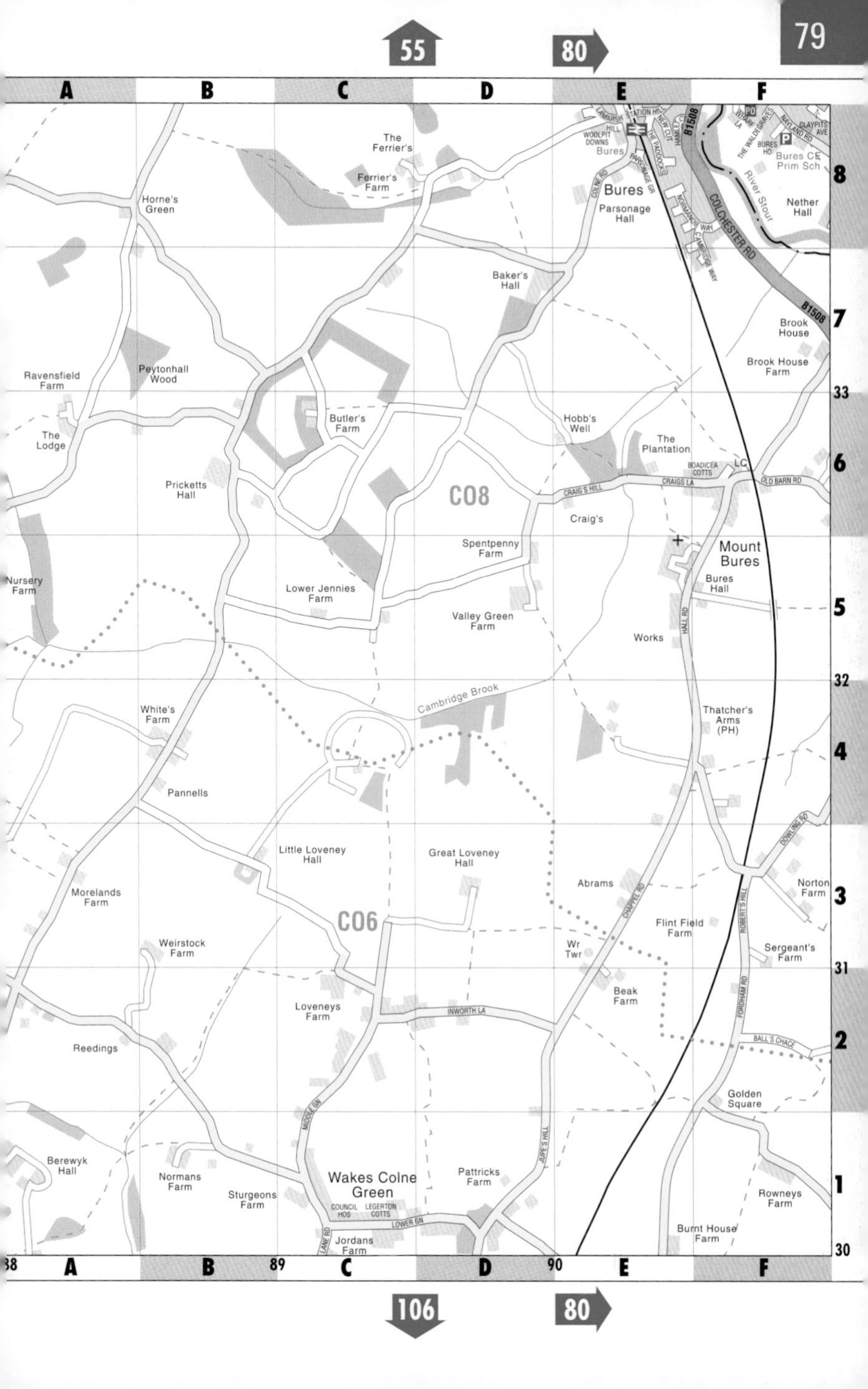
55
80
A
B
C
D
E
F
The Ferrier's
Ferrier's Farm
Horne's Green
Bures
Bures
Parsonage Hall
Nether Hall
Bures CE Prim Sch
River Stour
COLCHESTER RD
B1508
Baker's Hall
Brook House
Brook House Farm
Ravensfield Farm
Peytonhall Wood
Butler's Farm
Hobb's Well
The Plantation
The Lodge
Pricketts Hall
CO8
CRAIG'S HILL
CRAIGS LA
OLD BARN RD
BOADICEA COTTS
Craig's
Spentpenny Farm
Mount Bures
Bures Hall
Nursery Farm
Lower Jennies Farm
Valley Green Farm
Works
HALL RD
Cambridge Brook
White's Farm
Thatcher's Arms (PH)
Pannells
Little Loveney Hall
Great Loveney Hall
Abrams
DOWLING RD
Morelands Farm
CO6
CHAPPEL RD
Norton Farm
Flint Field Farm
ROBERT'S HILL
Weirstock Farm
Wr Twr
Sergeant's Farm
Beak Farm
Loveneys Farm
INWORTH LA
FORDHAM RD
Reedings
BALL'S CHACE
Golden Square
MIDDLE GN
JUPE'S HILL
Berewyk Hall
Normans Farm
Sturgeons Farm
Wakes Colne Green
COUNCIL HOS
LEGERTON COTTS
LOWER GN
Pattricks Farm
Rowneys Farm
Burnt House Farm
Jordans Farm
8
7
33
6
5
32
4
3
31
2
1
30
88
89
90
106
80

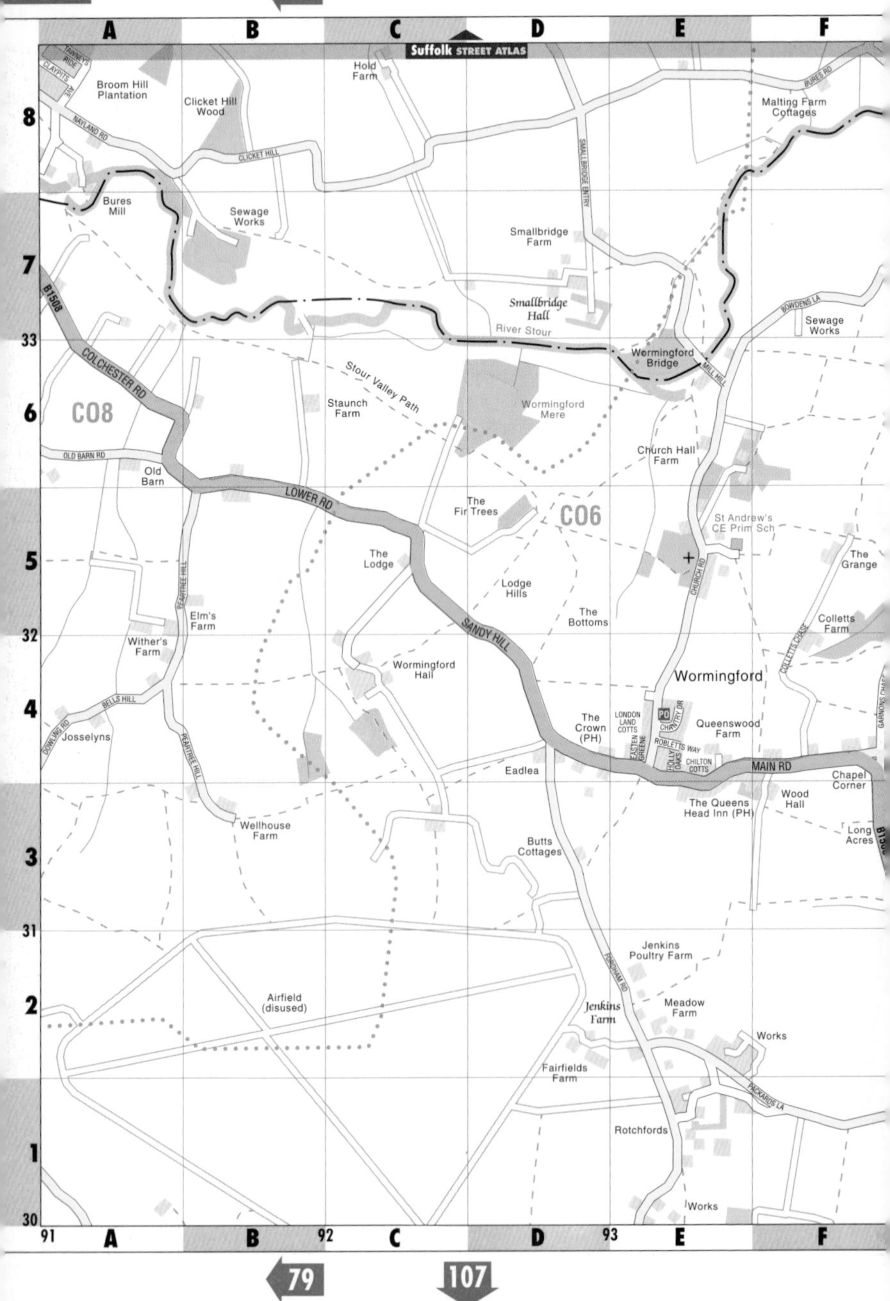

79

Suffolk STREET ATLAS

A B C D E F

8

7

33

6 CO8

5

32

4

3

31

2

1

30

Bridget's Dale
Clayple
NAYLAND RD
Broom Hill Plantation
Clicket Hill Wood
CLICKET HILL
Hold Farm
Malting Farm Cottages
SMALL BRIDGE ENTRY
Bures Mill
Sewage Works
Smallbridge Farm
BORDENS LA
Sewage Works
B508
COLCHESTER RD
Smallbridge Hall
River Stour
Wormingford Bridge
BELL HILL
Stour Valley Path
Staunch Farm
Wormingford Mere
Church Hall Farm
St Andrew's CE Prim Sch
OLD BARN RD
Old Barn
LOWER RD
The Fir Trees
CO6
CHURCH RD
The Grange
PEARTREE HILL
The Lodge
Lodge Hills
The Bottoms
Collets Farm
PARLETTS CHASE
Elm's Farm
SANDY HILL
Wormingford Hall
Wormingford
Wither's Farm
BELLS HILL
The Crown (PH)
LONDON LAND COTTS
PD
CHAPEL ST
Queenswood Farm
BARNAGE CHASE
Josselyns
PEARTREE HILL
Eadlea
PARLETTS WAY
CHILTON COTTS
MAIN RD
Chapel Corner
Wood Hall
B1508
Wellhouse Farm
The Queens Head Inn (PH)
Long Acres
Butts Cottages
Airfield (disused)
Jenkins Poultry Farm
Meadow Farm
SANDY HILL
Works
Jenkins Farm
Fairfields Farm
PACKARDS LA
Rotchfords
Works

91 A B 92 C D 93 E F

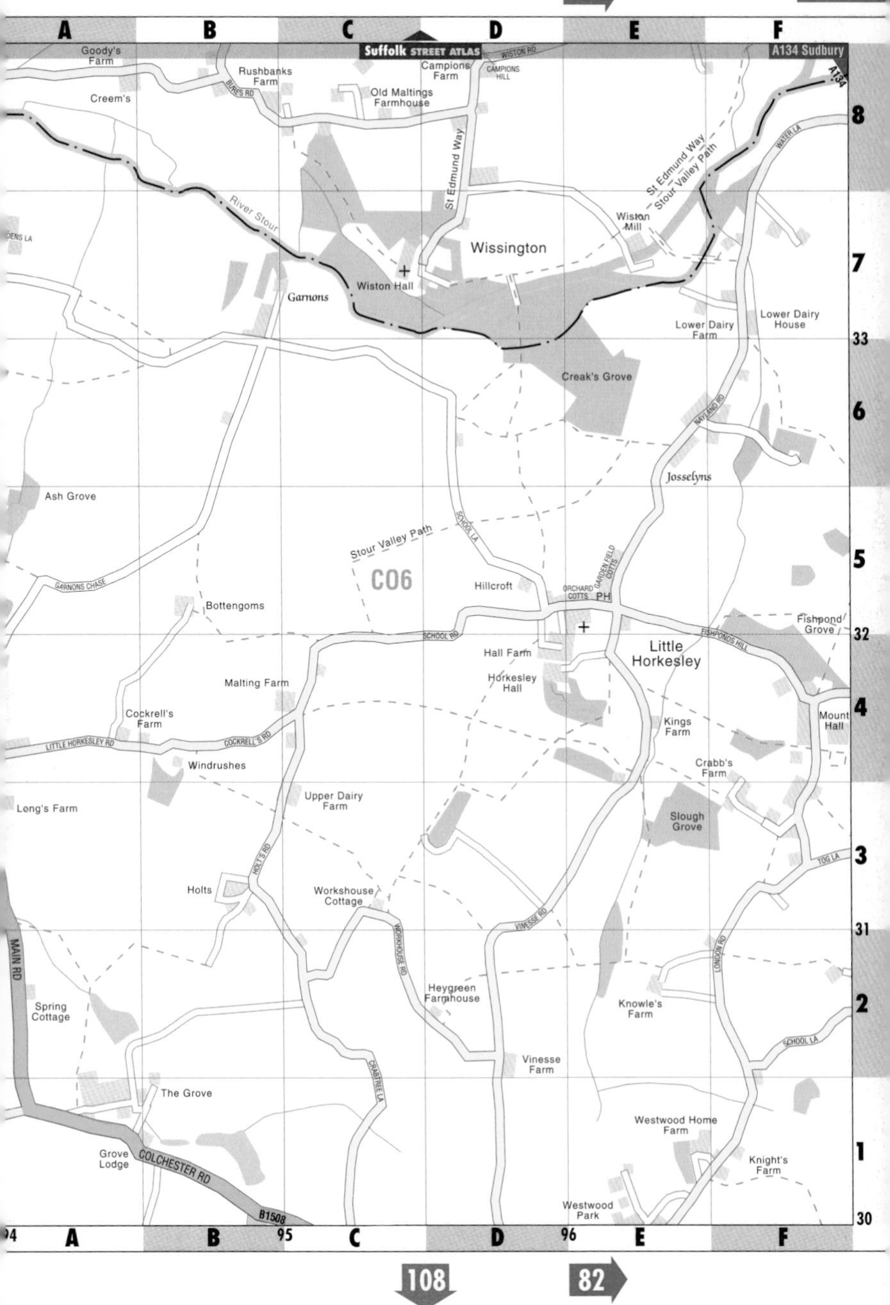

Suffolk STREET ATLAS

A134 Sudbury

Grid references (left column, top to bottom): A, B, C, D, E, F

Row numbers (right margin): 8, 7, 33, 6, 5, 32, 4, 3, 31, 2, 1, 30

Goody's Farm

Creem's

Rushbanks Farm

BURE'S RD

Old Maltings Farmhouse

Campions Farm

CAMPIONS HILL

BRISTON RD

St Edmund Way

St Edmund Way
Stour Valley Path

WATER LA

River Stour

Garnons

Wiston Hall

Wissington

Wiston Mill

Lower Dairy Farm

Lower Dairy House

Creak's Grove

GDENS LA

Ash Grove

MITERS RD

Josselyns

GARNONS CHASE

Stour Valley Path

SCHOOL LA

CO6

Hillcroft

ORCHARD COTTS

GARDEN FIELD COTTS

PH

Fishpond Grove

Bottengoms

SCHOOL RD

Hall Farm

Little Horkesley

FISHPONDS HILL

Malting Farm

Horkesley Hall

Mount Hall

Cockrell's Farm

LITTLE HORKESLEY RD

COCKRELL'S RD

Kings Farm

Crabb's Farm

Windrushes

Leng's Farm

Upper Dairy Farm

Slough Grove

TOG LA

CARTERS LA

Holts

Workshouse Cottage

WORKHOUSE RD

VINESSE RD

MAIN RD

Spring Cottage

Heygreen Farmhouse

Knowle's Farm

SCHOOL LA

The Grove

Vinesse Farm

Westwood Home Farm

Grove Lodge

COLCHESTER RD

Knight's Farm

B1508

Westwood Park

94

95

96

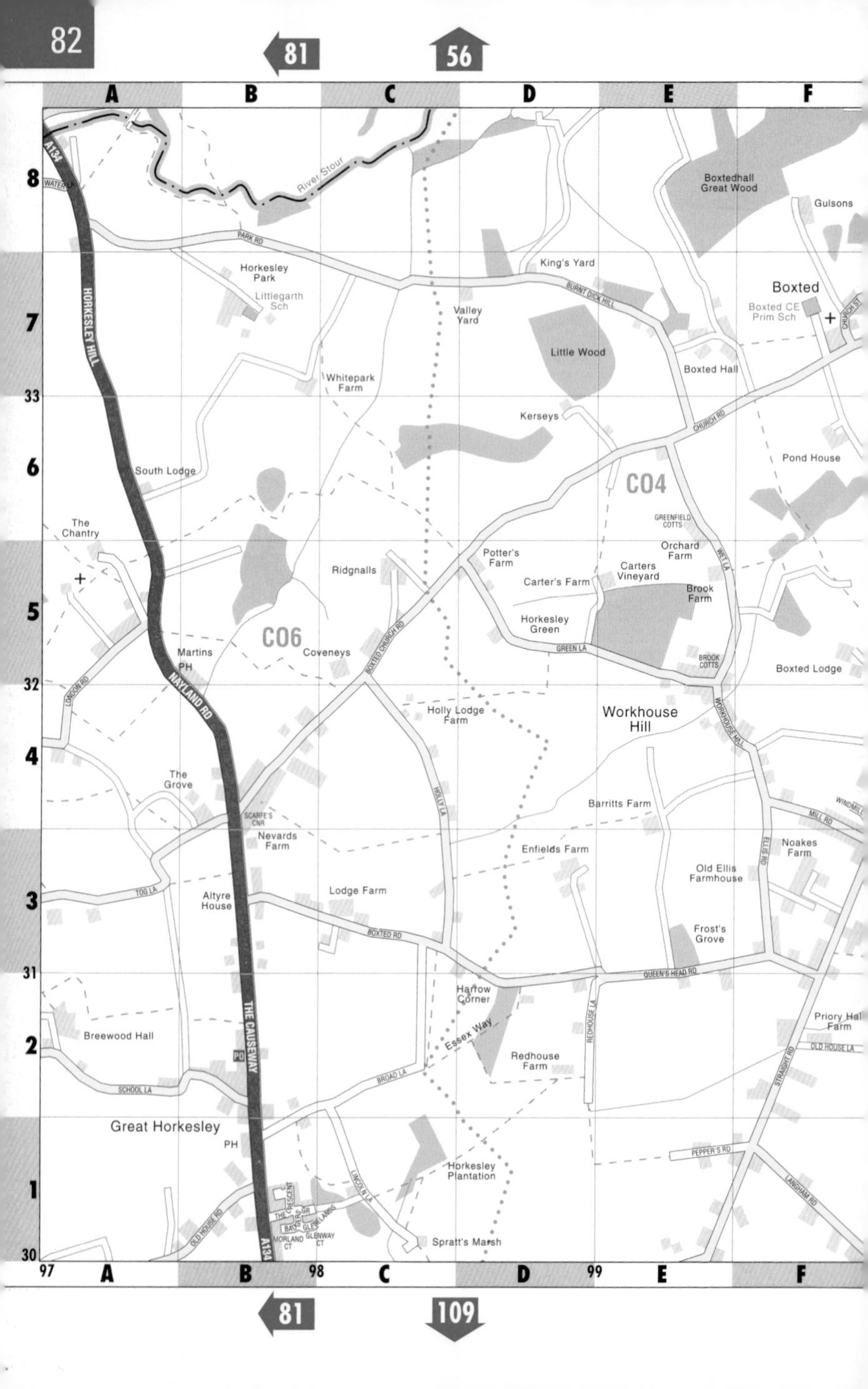
81
56
River Stour
WATER LA
PARK RD
Horkesley Park
Littlegarth Sch
King's Yard
BURNT DICK HILL
Boxtedhall Great Wood
Gulsons
Boxted
Boxted CE Prim Sch
CHURCH ST
Valley Yard
Little Wood
Boxted Hall
HORKESLEY HILL
Whitepark Farm
Kerseys
CHURCH RD
Pond House
South Lodge
CO4
GREENFIELD COTTS
Orchard Farm
The Chantry
Potter's Farm
Ridgnalls
Carters Vineyard
Carter's Farm
Brook Farm
WET LA
Horkesley Green
CO6
Coveneys
Martins PH
GREEN LA
BROOK COTTS
Boxted Lodge
BOXTED CHURCH RD
NAYLAND RD
LONDON RD
Holly Lodge Farm
Workhouse Hill
WORKHOUSE HILL
The Grove
HOLLY LA
Barritts Farm
WINDMILL
MILL RD
SCARFE'S CNR
Nevards Farm
Enfields Farm
ELLIS RD
Noakes Farm
Old Ellis Farmhouse
TOG LA
Altyre House
Lodge Farm
BOXTED RD
Frost's Grove
QUEEN'S HEAD RD
Harrow Corner
Priory Hall Farm
OLD HOUSE LA
Breewood Hall
Essex Way
REDHOUSE LA
Redhouse Farm
STRAIGHT RD
PO
THE CAUSEWAY
BROAD LA
SCHOOL LA
Great Horkesley
PH
PEPPER'S RD
Horkesley Plantation
LANGHAM RD
LINCOLN LA
OLD HOUSE RD
THE CRESCENT
MORLAND CT
GLENWAY CT
Spratt's Marsh
A134
A B C D E F
8 7 6 5 4 3 2 1
33 32 31 30
97 98 99
81
109

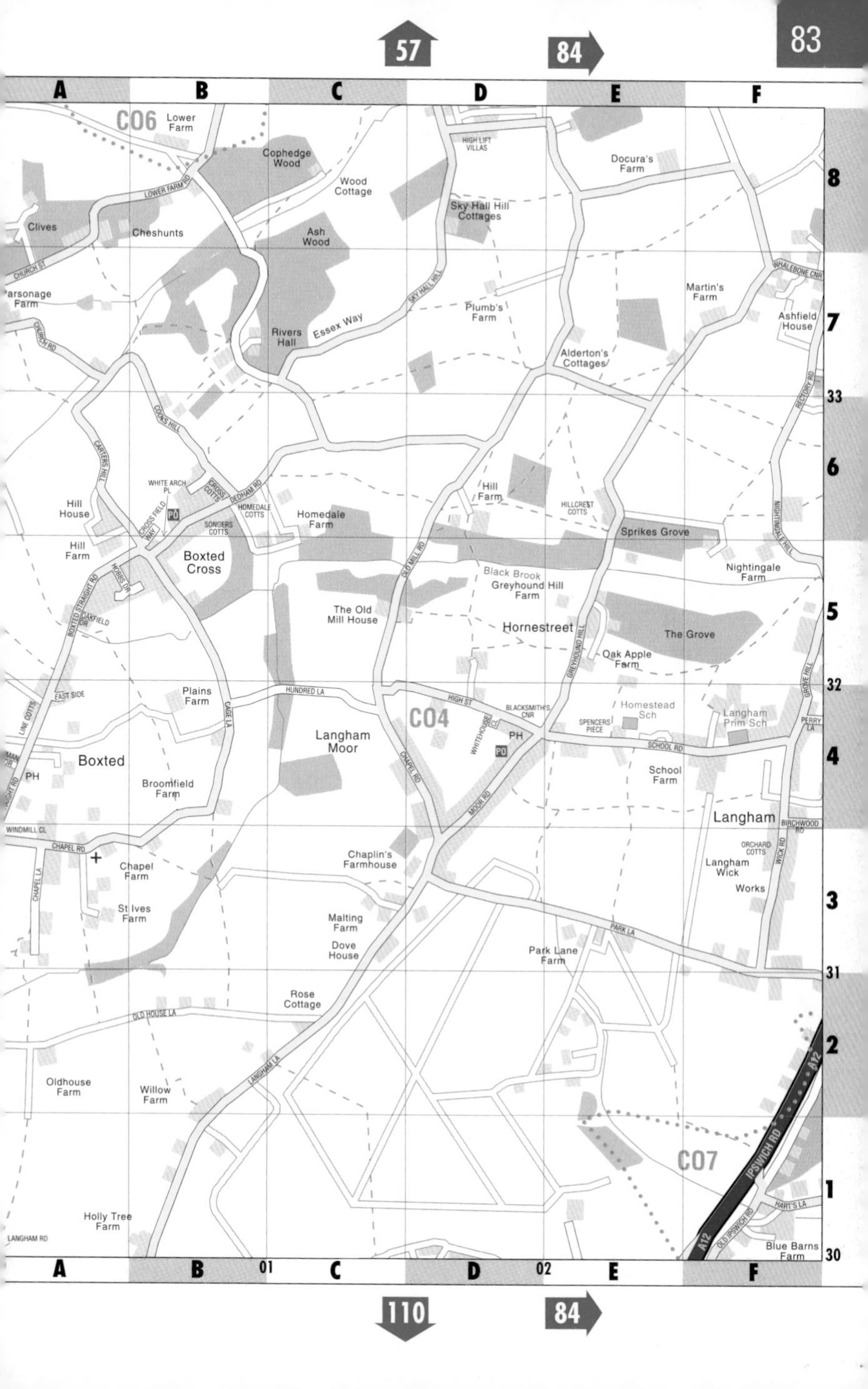

A   B   C   D   E   F

CO6

Lower Farm

Cophedge Wood

Wood Cottage

HIGH LIFT VILLAS

Docura's Farm

Sky Hall Hill Cottages

Clives

Cheshunts

Ash Wood

8

CHURCH ST

Parsonage Farm

Rivers Hall

Essex Way

SKY HALL RD

Plumb's Farm

Martin's Farm

Ashfield House

WHALEBONE CNR

7

CHURCH RD

Alderton's Cottages

33

COAL HILL

6

Hill House

WHITE ARCH

BECHAM RD

EASTFIELD RD

CROSS FIELD

PO

HOMEDALE COTTS

Hill Farm

Homedale Farm

SONOERS COTTS

Hill Farm

Black Brook

HILLCREST COTTS

Sprikes Grove

Nightingale Farm

NIGHTINGALE HILL

PERRY LA

BEECH RD

Boxted Cross

The Old Mill House

Greyhound Hill Farm

Hornestreet

The Grove

5

CARR LA

Plains Farm

HUNDRED LA

HIGH ST

CO4

Oak Apple Farm

GREYHOUND HILL

32

EAST SIDE

Langham Moor

BLACKSMITHES CNR

WHITEHOUSE RD

SCHOOL RD

Homestead Sch

SPENCERS PIECE

Langham Prim Sch

4

MAN LA

PH

Boxted

Broomfield Farm

CABLE LA

PH

PO

School Farm

Langham

BIRCHWOOD RD

WINDMILL CL

CHAPEL RD

MOORS RD

ORCHARD COTTS

Langham Wick

PACK RD

Works

3

Chapel Farm

St Ives Farm

Chaplin's Farmhouse

Malting Farm

Dove House

PARK LA

Park Lane Farm

31

Rose Cottage

OLD HOUSE LA

2

Oldhouse Farm

Willow Farm

LANGHAM LA

CO7

IPSWICH RD

A12

1

Holly Tree Farm

LANGHAM RD

A12

OLD IPSWICH RD

HARTS LA

Blue Barns Farm

30

A   B   01   C   D   02   E   F

83
58

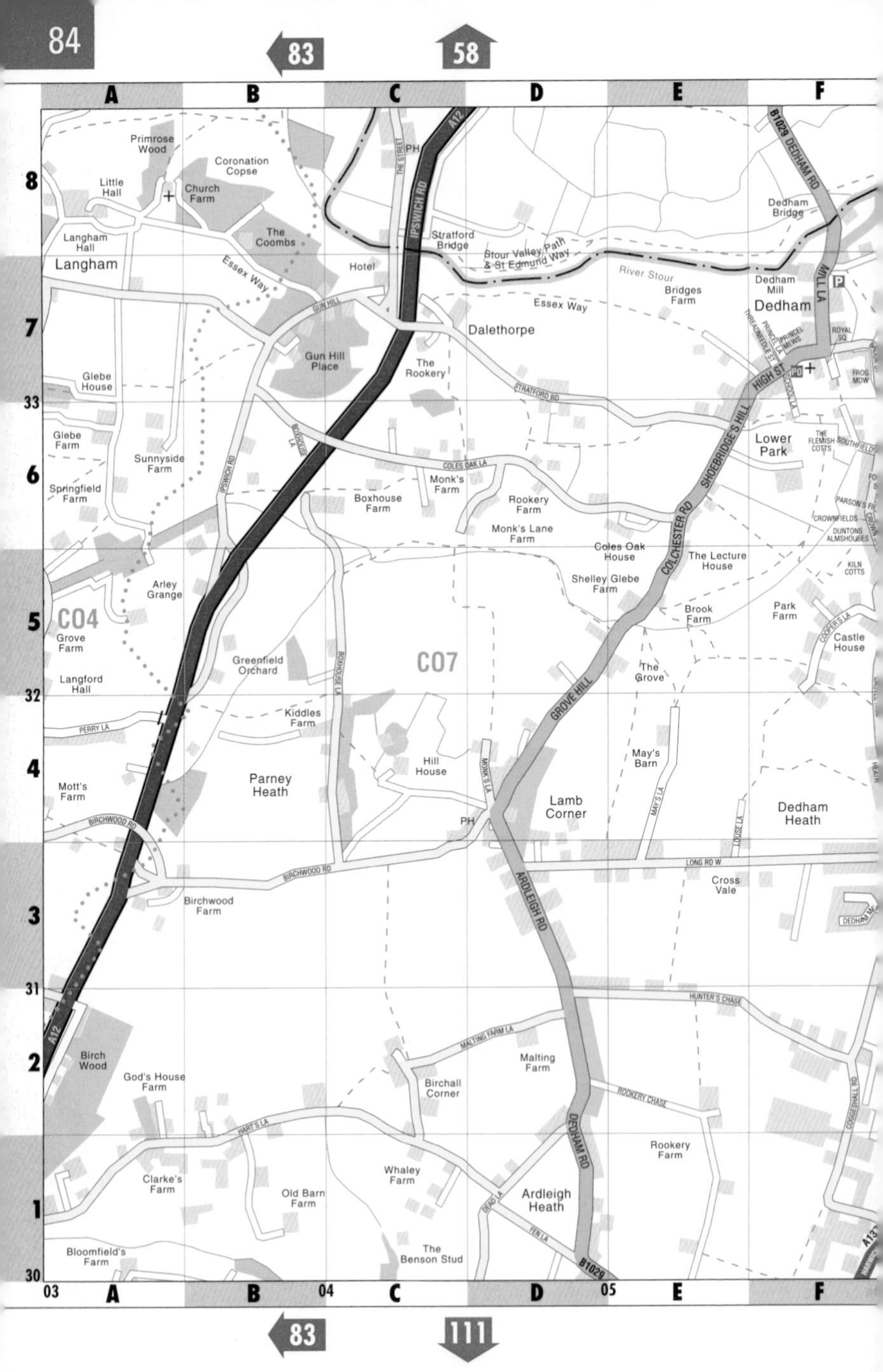
A
B
C
D
E
F
8
7
33
6
5
32
4
3
31
2
1
30
03
04
05
Primrose Wood
Coronation Copse
Little Hall
Church Farm
Langham Hall
The Coombs
Langham
Essex Way
Hotel
PH
THE STREET
A12
IPSWICH RD
Stratford Bridge
Stour Valley Path & St Edmund Way
River Stour
B1029 DEDHAM RD
Dedham Bridge
Dedham Mill
MILL LA
Dedham
Bridges Farm
Essex Way
GUN HILL
Dalethorpe
Gun Hill Place
The Rookery
Glebe House
STRATFORD RD
HIGH ST
ROYAL SQ
FROG MDW
Glebe Farm
BOXHOUSE LA
Lower Park
THE FLEMISH COTTS
SOUTHFIELDS
Sunnyside Farm
COLES OAK LA
Springfield Farm
IPSWICH RD
Monk's Farm
Boxhouse Farm
Rookery Farm
SHOEBRIDGE'S HILL
Monk's Lane Farm
COLCHESTER RD
CROWNFIELDS
DUNTONS ALMSHOUSES
Coles Oak House
The Lecture House
KILN COTTS
Arley Grange
Shelley Glebe Farm
Brook Farm
Park Farm
CO4
Grove Farm
COOPER'S LA
Castle House
Greenfield Orchard
CO7
The Grove
Langford Hall
GROVE HILL
PERRY LA
Kiddles Farm
May's Barn
Hill House
MONK'S LA
Mott's Farm
Parney Heath
MAY'S LA
Lamb Corner
LOUSE LA
Dedham Heath
BIRCHWOOD RD
PH
LONG RD W
BIRCHWOOD RD
Cross Vale
Birchwood Farm
ARDLEIGH RD
HUNTER'S CHASE
MALTING FARM LA
Birch Wood
Malting Farm
God's House Farm
Birchall Corner
ROOKERY CHASE
COGGESHALL RD
HART'S LA
DEDHAM RD
Rookery Farm
Clarke's Farm
Whaley Farm
Old Barn Farm
DEAD LA
Ardleigh Heath
FEN LA
Bloomfield's Farm
The Benson Stud
B1029

83
111

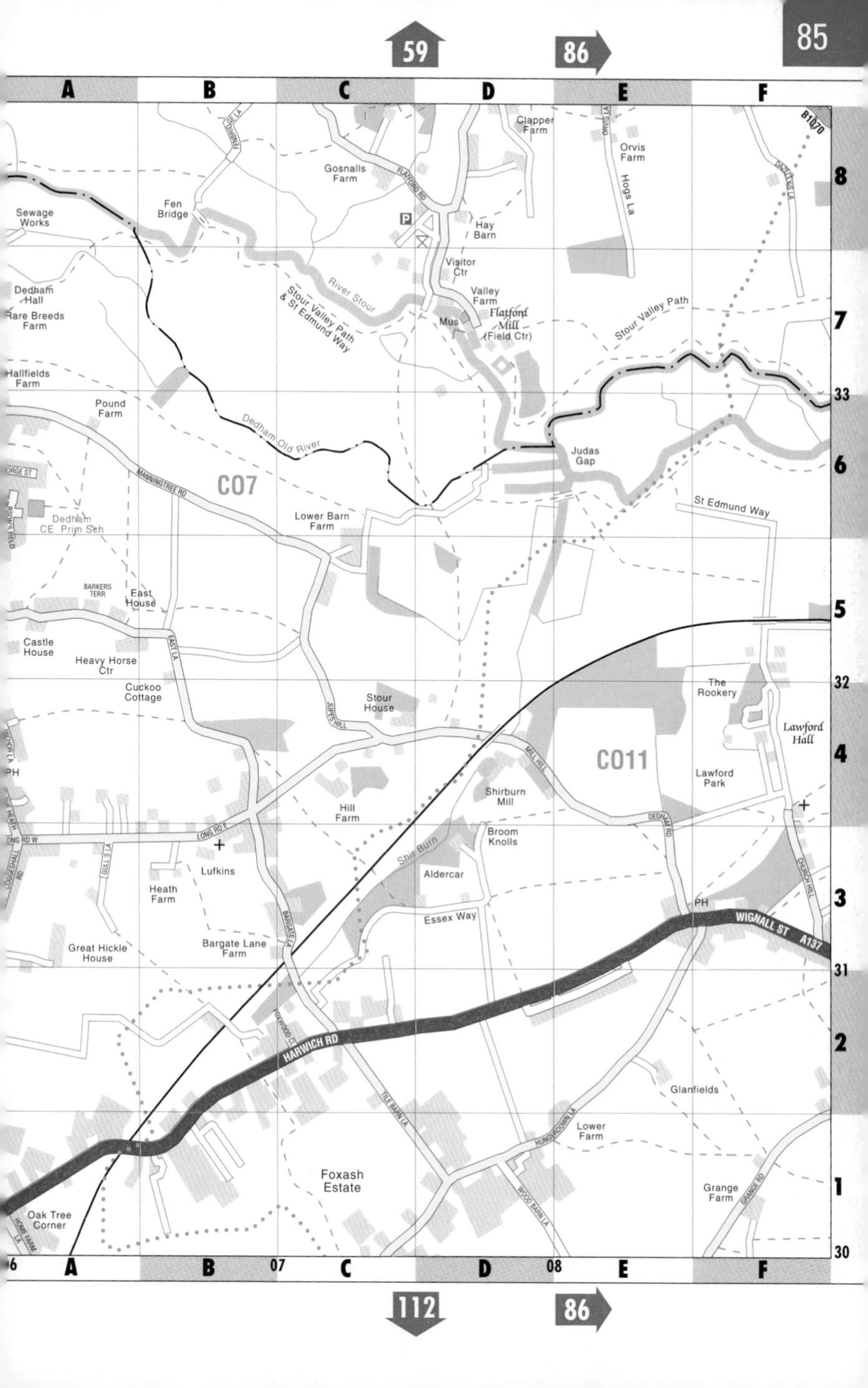
59
86
A
B
C
D
E
F
8
7
33
6
5
32
4
3
31
2
1
30
Clapper Farm
Orvis Farm
Hogs La
ORVIS LA
B1070
DAZELEYS LA
FENBRIDGE LA
Gosnalls Farm
FLATFORD RD
Fen Bridge
Sewage Works
Hay Barn
Visitor Ctr
Valley Farm
Flatford Mill (Field Ctr)
Mus
River Stour
Stour Valley Path & St Edmund Way
Stour Valley Path
Dedham Hall
Rare Breeds Farm
Hallfields Farm
Pound Farm
Dedham Old River
Judas Gap
CO7
MANNINGTREE RD
St Edmund Way
Dedham CE Prim Sch
Lower Barn Farm
BARKERS TERR
East House
Castle House
Heavy Horse Ctr
EAST LA
Cuckoo Cottage
JUPES HILL
Stour House
The Rookery
Lawford Hall
MILL HILL
CO11
Lawford Park
Shirburn Mill
Hill Farm
LONG RD E
LONG RD W
Broom Knolls
DEDHAM RD
GULL'S LA
Lufkins
Shir Burn
Aldercar
CHURCH HILL
Heath Farm
Essex Way
PH
WIGNALL ST
A137
BARGATE LA
Great Hickle House
Bargate Lane Farm
FOXWOOD CT
HARWICH RD
Glanfields
TILE BARN LA
HUNGERDOWN LA
Lower Farm
Foxash Estate
WOOD BARN LA
Grange Farm
GRANGE RD
Oak Tree Corner
HOME FARM LA
07
08
112
86

A B C D E F

8

B1070

MANNINGTREE RD

Spooners Wood

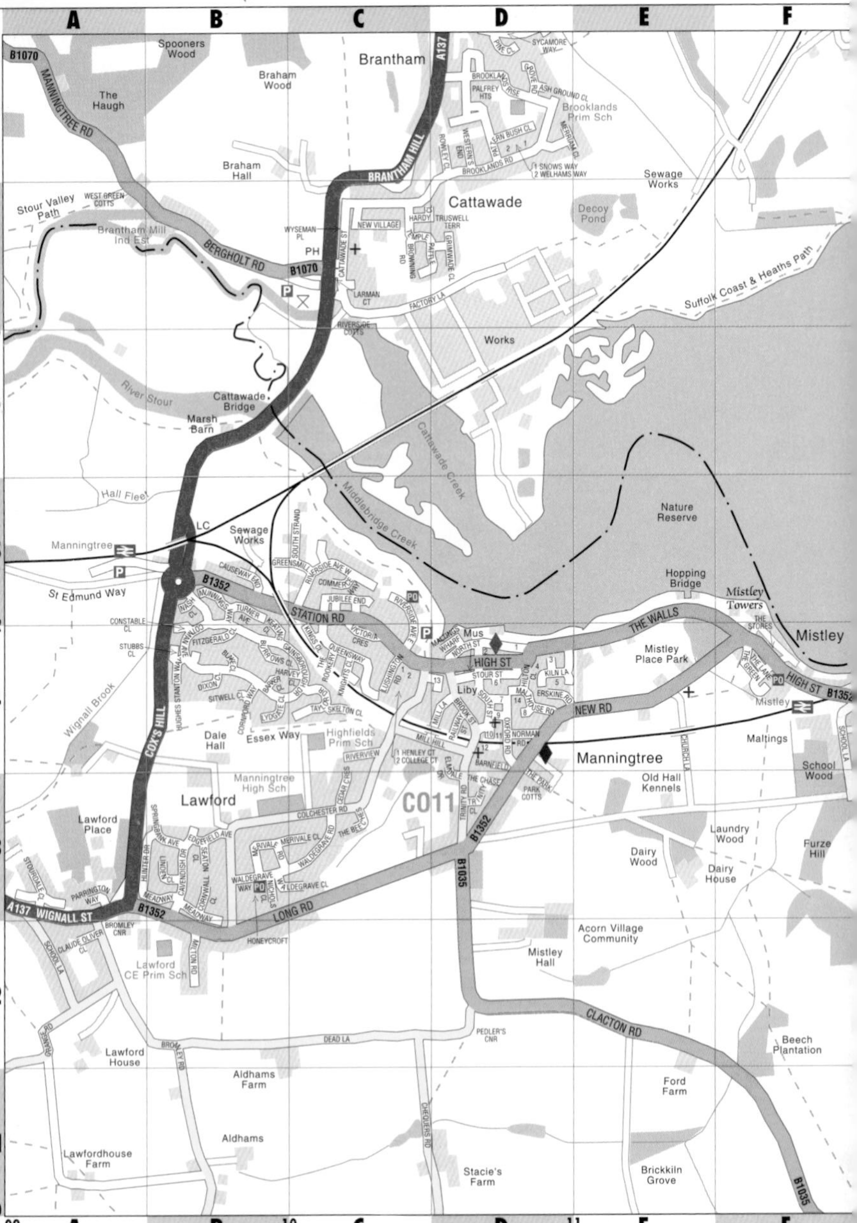

Braham Wood

Brantham

The Haugh

SYCAMORE WAY

A137

BROOKLAND RISE

ASH GROUND CL

PALFREY HTS

JON BUSH CL

Brooklands Prim Sch

BROOKLANDS RD

Braham Hall

BRANTHAM HILL

1 SNOWS WAY
2 WELHAMS WAY

Sewage Works

Cattawade

7

Stour Valley Path

WEST GREEN COTTS

Brantham Mill Ind Est

BERGHOLT RD

WYSEMAN PL

NEW VILLAGE

CATTAWADE ST

PH
B1070

HARDY
TRUSWELL TERR

BROWNING

Decoy Pond

LARMAN CT

FACTORY LA

33

RIVERSIDE

River Stour

Works

6

Cattawade Bridge

Cattawade Creek

Marsh Barn

Hall Fleet

Nature Reserve

5

Manningtree

P

LC

Sewage Works

GREENHAYES

Middlebridge Creek

Hopping Bridge

Mistley Towers

THE STONES

St Edmund Way

B1352

STATION RD

COMMERCE

JUBILEE END

P

Mistley

32

CONSTABLE CL

STUBBS CL

Wignall Brook

FITZGERALD'S

TURNER

HAILS

FACTORY CRES

MASTING RD

Mus

THE WALLS

Mistley Place Park

THE STOUR

HIGH ST B1352

DIXON

SITWELL CL

TATE

CARLTON CL

HIGH ST

Lib

KILN LA

ERSKINE

Mistley

SCHOOL RD

4

COW'S HILL

Dale Hall

Essex Way

Highfields Prim Sch

RIVERVIEW

MILL HILL

NORMAN

NEW RD

Maltings

School Wood

Manningtree High Sch

1 HENLEY CT
2 COLERNE CT

BARNFIELD

Manningtree

Old Hall Kennels

Furze Hill

3

Lawford Place

COLCHESTER RD

THE BLD

CO11

THE CHASE

PARK COTTS

B1352

Laundry Wood

Dairy Wood

Lawford

RIVAL

MERIVALE CT

B1035

Dairy House

A137 WIGNALL ST

BROMLEY CNR

WALDEGRAVE WAY

1 DEGRAVE CL

LONG RD

Dairy Wood

Acorn Village Community

31

CLAUDE OLIVER

HONEYCROFT

Lawford CE Prim Sch

Mistley Hall

2

Lawford House

BROOK

DEAD LA

PEDLER'S CNR

CLACTON RD

Beech Plantation

Aldhams Farm

Ford Farm

1

Lawfordhouse Farm

Aldhams

CHEQUERS RD

Stacie's Farm

Brickkiln Grove

B1035

30

09 A B 10 C D 11 E F

D4
1 QUAY ST
2 QUAY CTYD
3 BROOKS MALTING
4 ALMA SQ
5 THE CENTRAL MALTINGS
6 ST MICHAELS CT
7 YORK ST
8 FALKLANDS DR
9 REGENT ST
10 PARSONS YD
11 RAILWAY TERR
12 TRINITY FARM CT
13 BENDALLS CT
14 GASFIELD

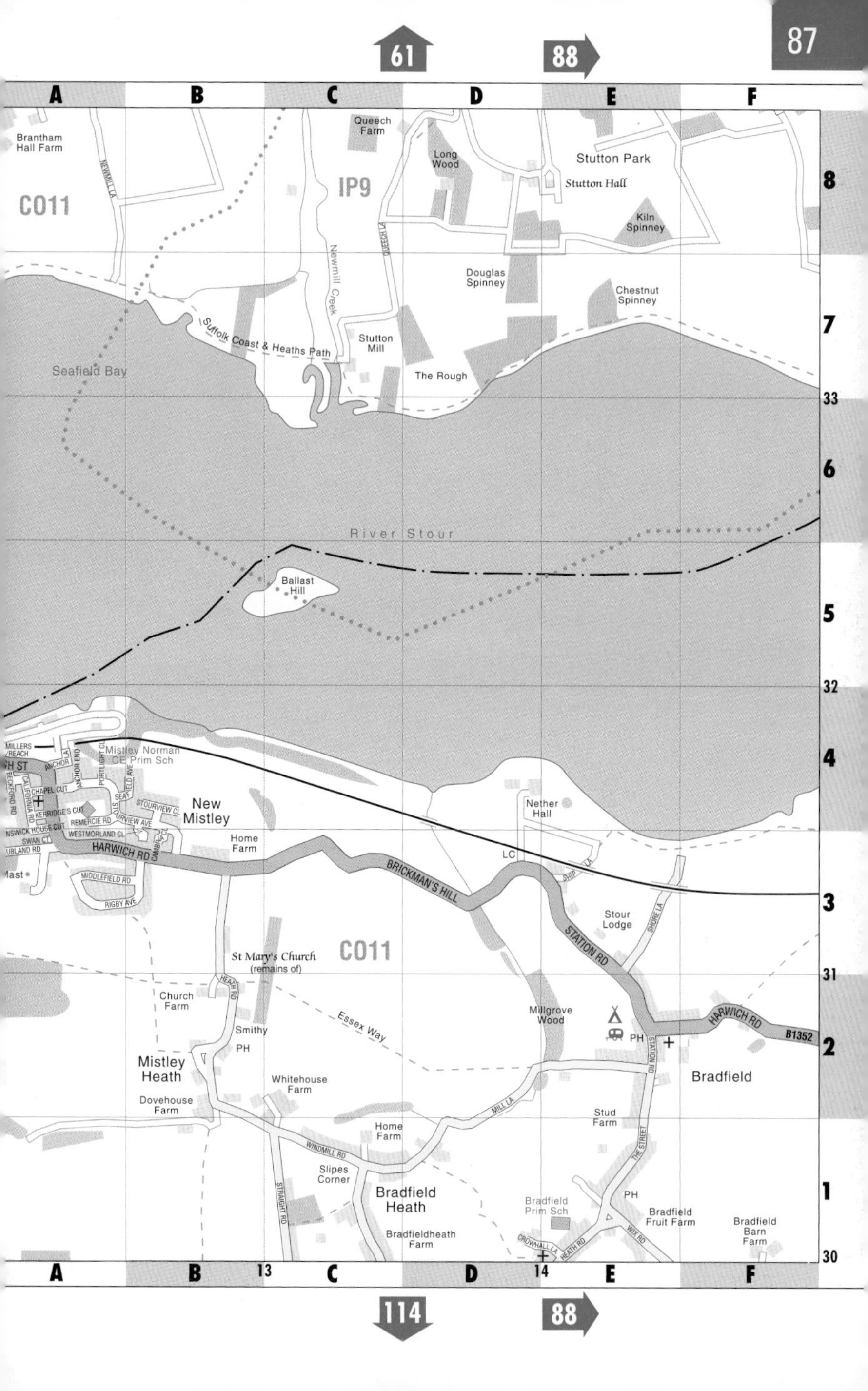
61
88
A
B
C
D
E
F
Brantham Hall Farm
NEWMILL LA
CO11
Queech Farm
IP9
Long Wood
Stutton Park
Stutton Hall
Kiln Spinney
QUEECH LA
Newmill Creek
Douglas Spinney
Chestnut Spinney
Suffolk Coast & Heaths Path
Stutton Mill
Seafield Bay
The Rough
River Stour
Ballast Hill
MILLERS REACH
ANCHOR LA
ANCHOR END
PORTLIGHT CL
Mistley Norman CE Prim Sch
CALIFORNIA RD
BECKFORD RD
CHAPEL CUT
KERRIDGE'S CUT
STOURVIEW CL
STOURVIEW AVE
REMERCIE RD
WESTMORLAND CL
SWAN CT
New Mistley
Home Farm
HARWICH RD
Nether Hall
LC
BRICKMAN'S HILL
SHIP LA
MIDDLEFIELD RD
RIGBY AVE
Stour Lodge
SHORE LA
STATION RD
St Mary's Church (remains of)
CO11
HEATH RD
Church Farm
Essex Way
Millgrove Wood
HARWICH RD
B1352
Smithy
PH
PH
Mistley Heath
Whitehouse Farm
Bradfield
Dovehouse Farm
MILL LA
Stud Farm
Home Farm
WINDMILL RD
THE STREET
Slipes Corner
Bradfield Heath
STRAIGHT RD
PH
Bradfield Prim Sch
Bradfield Fruit Farm
Bradfield Barn Farm
Bradfieldheath Farm
CROWHALL LA
HEATH RD
WIX RD
8
7
33
6
5
32
4
3
31
2
1
30
13
14
114
88

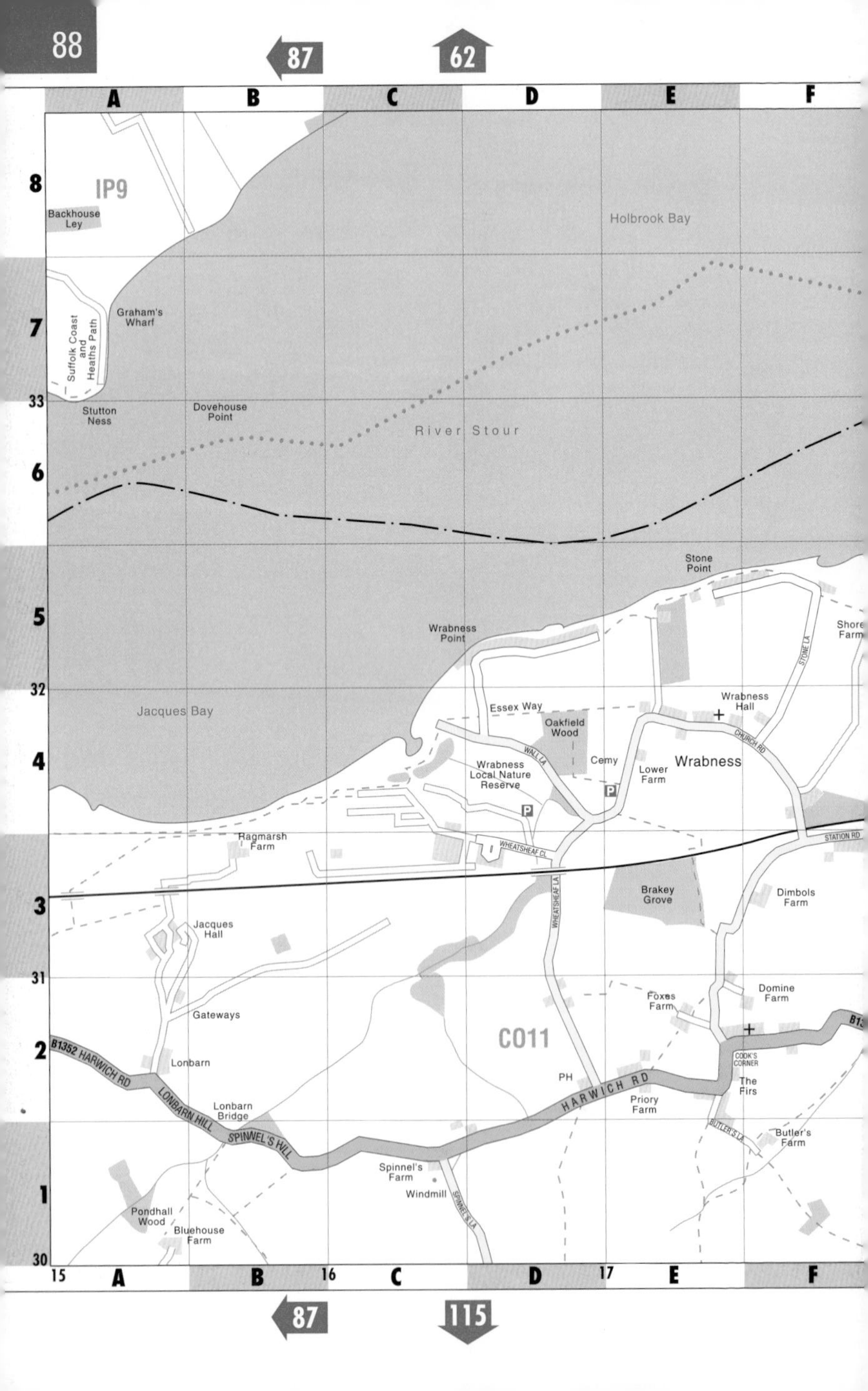

87
62
A
B
C
D
E
F
8
IP9
Backhouse Ley
Holbrook Bay
7
Graham's Wharf
Suffolk Coast and Heaths Path
33
Stutton Ness
Dovehouse Point
River Stour
6
Stone Point
5
Wrabness Point
Shore Farm
STONE LA
32
Jacques Bay
Essex Way
Wrabness Hall
Oakfield Wood
CHURCH RD
4
WALL LA
Wrabness Local Nature Reserve
Cemy
Lower Farm
Wrabness
P
Ragmarsh Farm
WHEATSHEAF CL
STATION RD
3
WHEATSHEAF LA
Brakey Grove
Dimbols Farm
Jacques Hall
31
Foxes Farm
Domine Farm
Gateways
2
B1352 HARWICH RD
CO11
COOK'S CORNER
Lonbarn
PH
HARWICH RD
The Firs
LONBARN HILL
Lonbarn Bridge
Priory Farm
SPINNEL'S HILL
BUTLER'S LA
Butler's Farm
Spinnel's Farm
1
Windmill
SPINNEL'S LA
Pondhall Wood
Bluehouse Farm
30
15
16
17
87
115

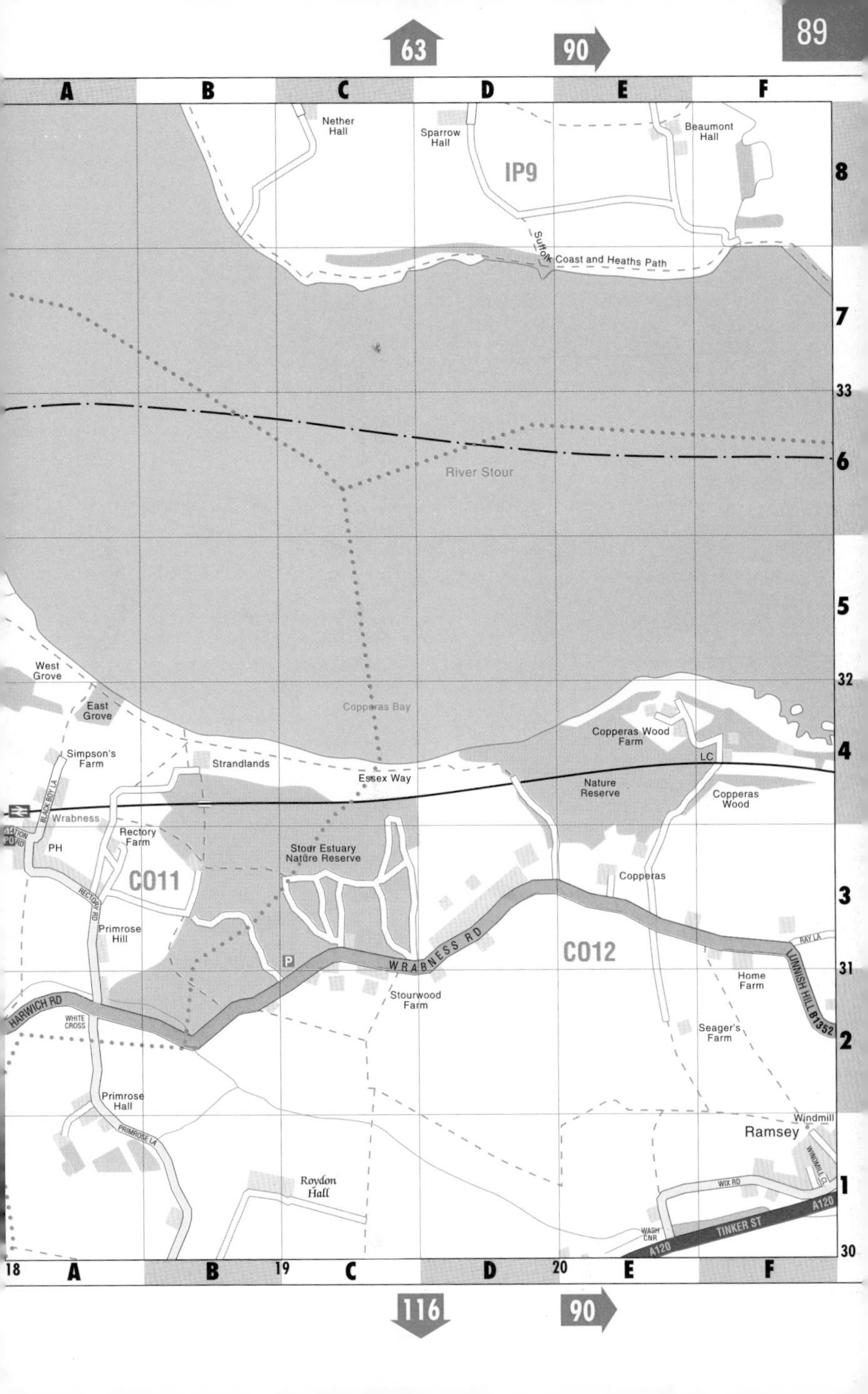
63
90
A
B
C
D
E
F
Nether Hall
Sparrow Hall
Beaumont Hall
IP9
8
Suffolk Coast and Heaths Path
7
33
6
River Stour
5
West Grove
East Grove
32
Copperas Bay
Copperas Wood Farm
4
Simpson's Farm
Strandlands
LC
Essex Way
Nature Reserve
Copperas Wood
BLACK BOY LA
Wrabness
STATION RD
Rectory Farm
PH
Stour Estuary Nature Reserve
CO11
Copperas
3
RECTORY RD
Primrose Hill
WRABNESS RD
CO12
RAY LA
P
31
LUNNISH HILL B1352
Home Farm
HARWICH RD
Stourwood Farm
WHITE CROSS
Seager's Farm
2
Primrose Hall
Windmill
Ramsey
PRIMROSE LA
WINDMILL CL
1
WIX RD
Roydon Hall
A120
WASH CNR
TINKER ST
A120
30
18
A
B
19
C
D
20
E
F
116
90

89

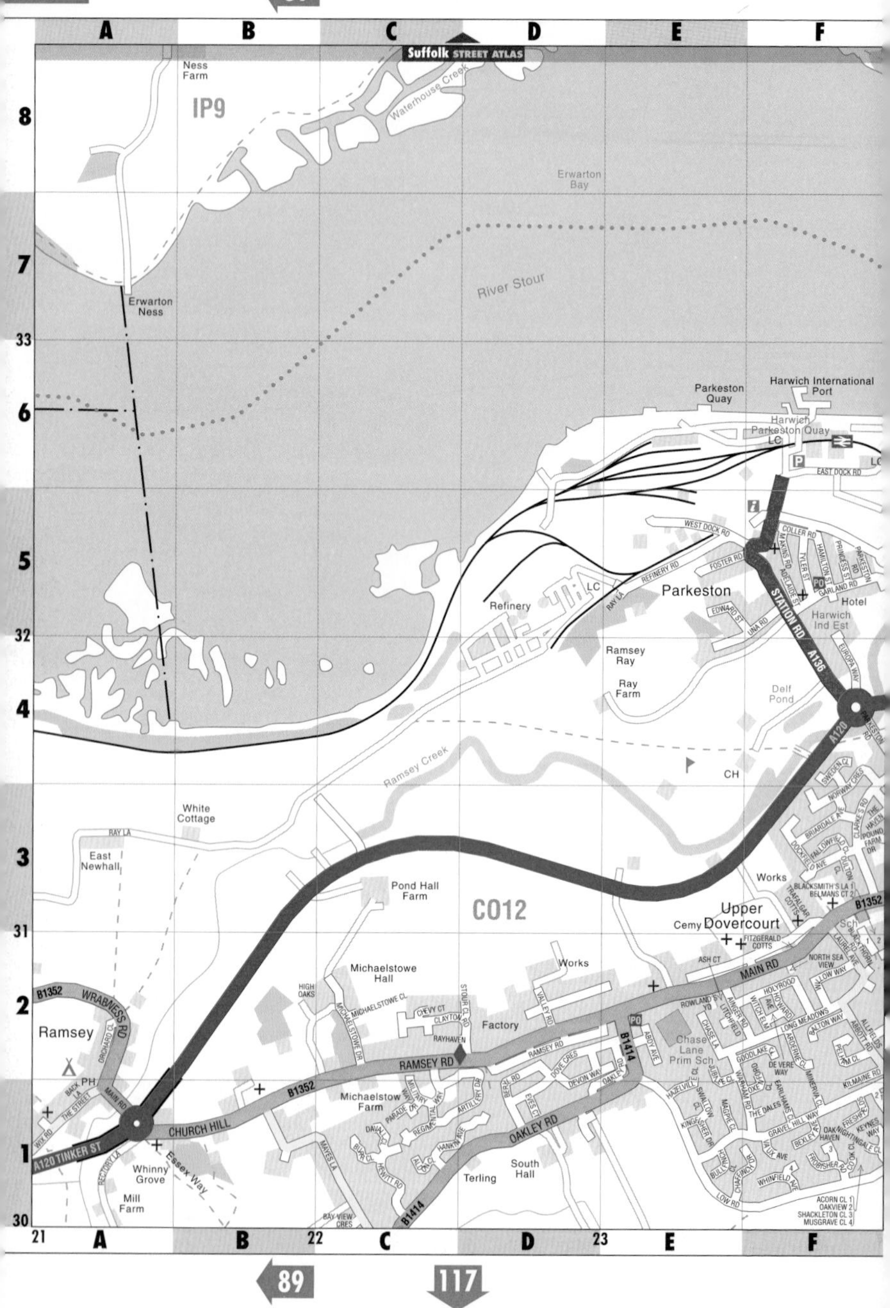

Suffolk STREET ATLAS
Ness Farm
IP9
Waterhouse Creek
Erwarton Bay
River Stour
Erwarton Ness
Parkeston Quay
Harwich International Port
Harwich Parkeston Quay
EAST DOCK RD
WEST DOCK RD
COLLER RD
MAKINS RD
FOSTER RD
REFINERY RD
RAY LA
Refinery
Parkeston
Hotel
Harwich Ind Est
STATION RD
A136
EUROPA WAY
Ramsey Ray
Ray Farm
Delf Pond
A120
Ramsey Creek
CH
White Cottage
RAY LA
East Newhall
Pond Hall Farm
CO12
Works
Upper Dovercourt
Cemy
FITZGERALD COTTS
B1352
MAIN RD
Michaelstowe Hall
Works
HIGH OAKS
MICHAELSTOWE CL
CHEVY CT
CLAYTON RD
STOUR CL
VALLEY RD
Factory
RAYHAVEN
RAMSEY RD
B1414
ABDY AVE
Chase Lane Prim Sch
Ramsey
WRABNESS RD
ORCHARD CL
BACK LA
PH
THE STREET
MAIN RD
WIX RD
A120 TINKER ST
CHURCH HILL
B1352
Michaelstow Farm
OAKLEY RD
South Hall
Terling
Whinny Grove
Essex Way
Mill Farm
RECTORY LA
MAYES LA
BAY VIEW CRES
B1414
ACORN CL 1
OAKVIEW 2
SHACKLETON CL 3
MUSGRAVE CL 4
21
22
23

89
117

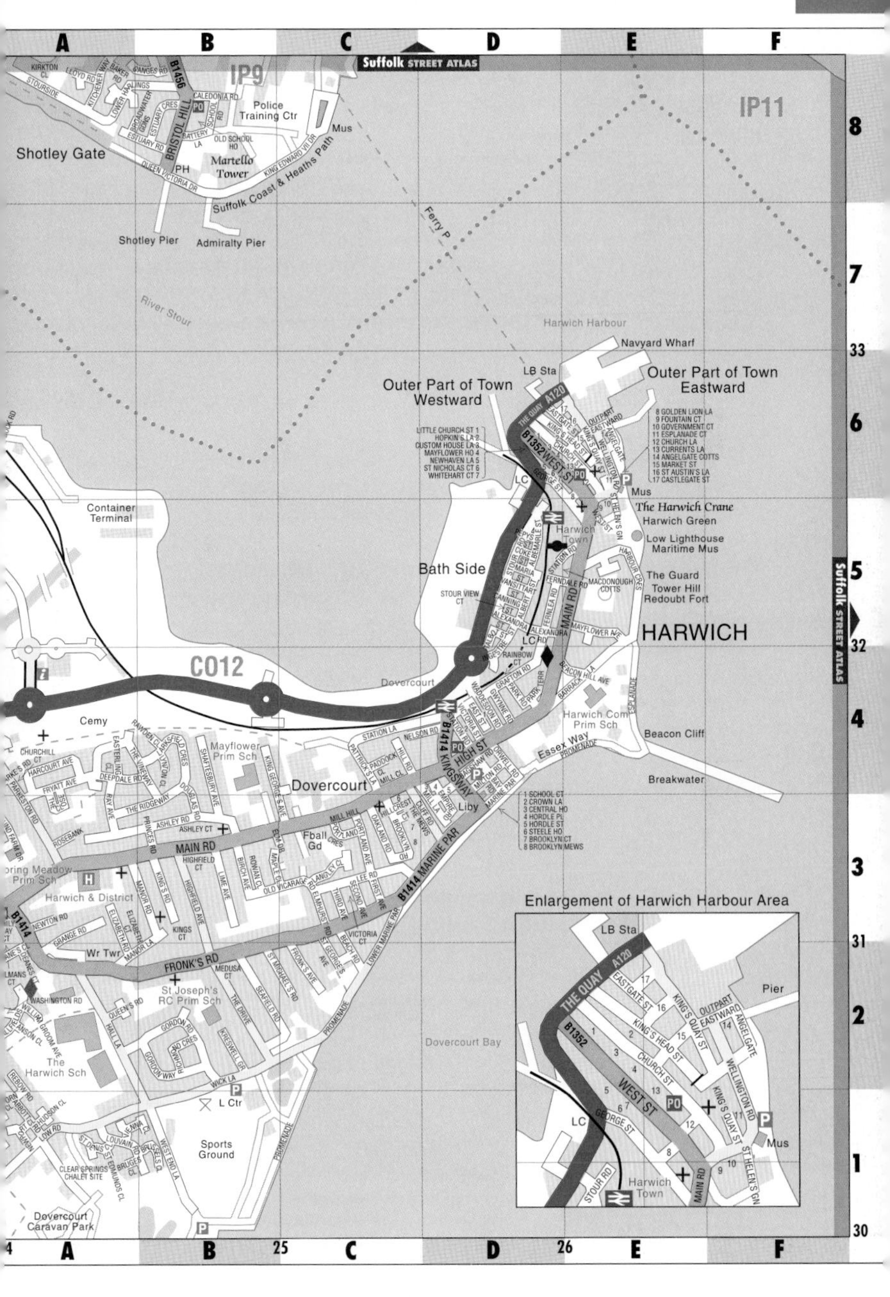

Suffolk STREET ATLAS

IP9

IP11

Shotley Gate

Police Training Ctr

Mus

Martello Tower

Suffolk Coast & Heaths Path

Shotley Pier   Admiralty Pier

River Stour

Harwich Harbour

Navyard Wharf

Outer Part of Town Westward

LB Sta

Outer Part of Town Eastward

8 GOLDEN LION LA
9 FOUNTAIN CT
10 GOVERNMENT CT
11 ESPLANADE CT
12 CHURCH LA
13 CURRENTS LA
14 ANGELGATE COTTS
15 MARKET ST
16 ST AUSTIN'S LA
17 CASTLEGATE ST

LITTLE CHURCH ST 1
HOPKIN LA 2
CUSTOM HOUSE LA 3
MAYFLOWER HO 4
NEWHAVEN LA 5
ST NICHOLAS CT 6
WHITEHART CT 7

Mus

Container Terminal

The Harwich Crane
Harwich Green

Low Lighthouse
Maritime Mus

Bath Side

STOUR VIEW CT

The Guard
Tower Hill
Redoubt Fort

HARWICH

Dovercourt

Cemy

Harwich Com Prim Sch

CO12

Mayflower Prim Sch

Dovercourt

Beacon Cliff

Breakwater

Essex Way PROMENADE

1 SCHOOL CT
2 CROWN LA
3 CENTRAL RD
4 HORDLE CT
5 STEELE HO
6 BROOKLYN CT
7 BROOKLYN MEWS

Liby

Harwich & District

MAIN RD

HIGHFIELD

Football Gd

Enlargement of Harwich Harbour Area

FRONK'S RD

St Joseph's RC Prim Sch

LB Sta

Pier

THE QUAY

EASTGATE ST

KING'S HEAD ST

OUTPART EASTWARD
ANGEL GATE

The Harwich Sch

WEST ST

CHURCH ST

KING'S QUAY ST

WELLINGTON RD

Dovercourt Bay

PO

GEORGE ST

LC

STOUR RD

Mus

Harwich Town

Sports Ground

Dovercourt Caravan Park

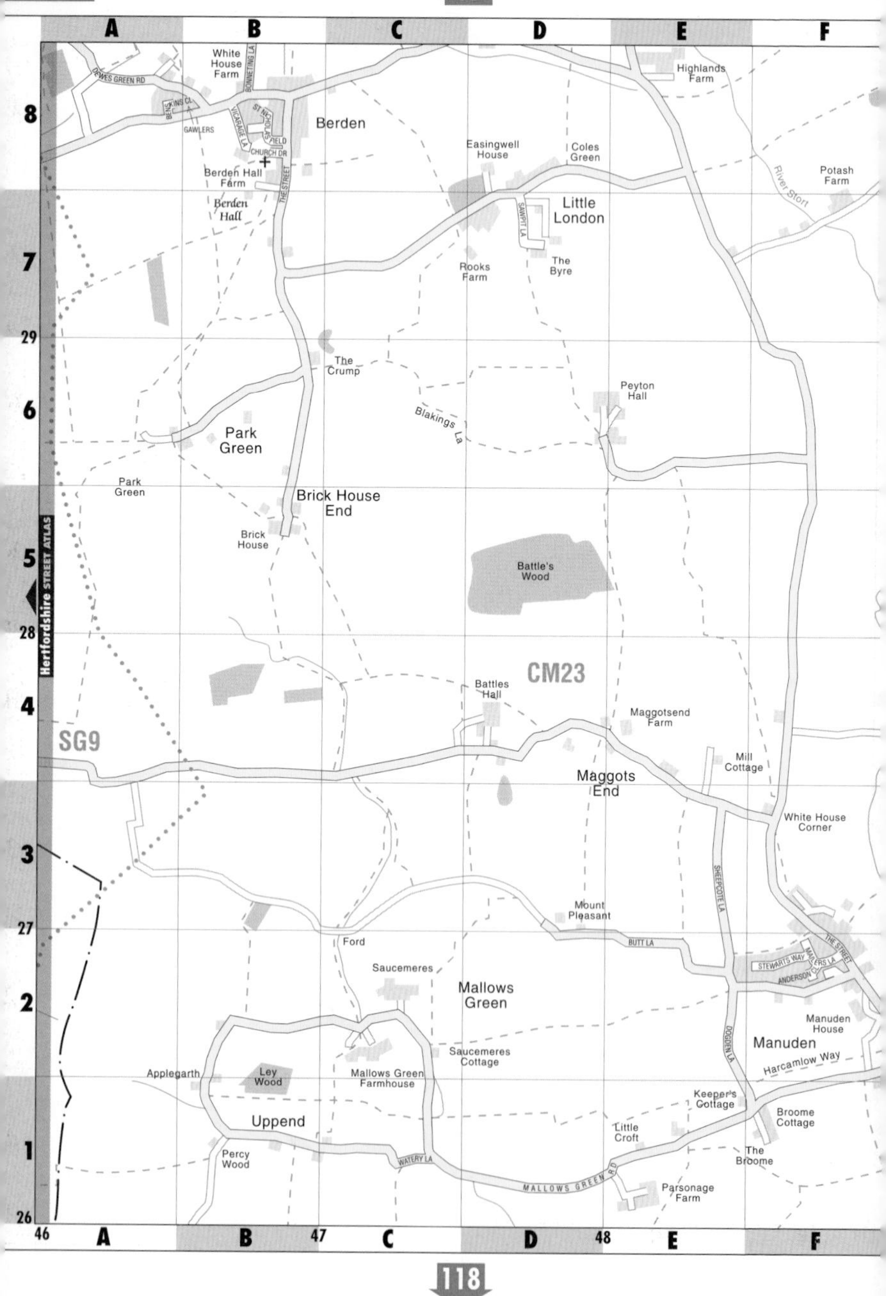

A **B** **C** **D** **E** **F**

Herfordshire STREET ATLAS

8

7

29

6

5

28

4

3

27

2

1

26

White House Farm

PINKS GREEN RD

PINKS GL

GAWLERS

Berden

VICARAGE LA

ST JOHNS

CHURCH DR

FIELD

Berden Hall Farm

Berden Hall

THE STREET

The Crump

Park Green

Park Green

Brick House End

Brick House

Easingwell House

Coles Green

Highlands Farm

River Stort

Potash Farm

Little London

The Byre

Rooks Farm

QUENDEN LA

Blakings La

Peyton Hall

Battle's Wood

CM23

Battles Hall

Maggotsend Farm

Maggots End

Mill Cottage

White House Corner

SG9

Mount Pleasant

Ford

Saucemeres

Mallows Green

Saucemeres Cottage

Applegarth

Ley Wood

Mallows Green Farmhouse

Uppend

Percy Wood

WATERY LA

MALLOWS GREEN

Little Croft

Keeper's Cottage

Parsonage Farm

The Broome

Broome Cottage

Manuden House

Manuden

Harcamlow Way

SHELFORDS LA

BUTT LA

STEWART'S WAY

ANDERSON

THE STREET

PINKS LA

BROOM LA

46 **A** 47 **B** **C** 48 **D** **E** **F**

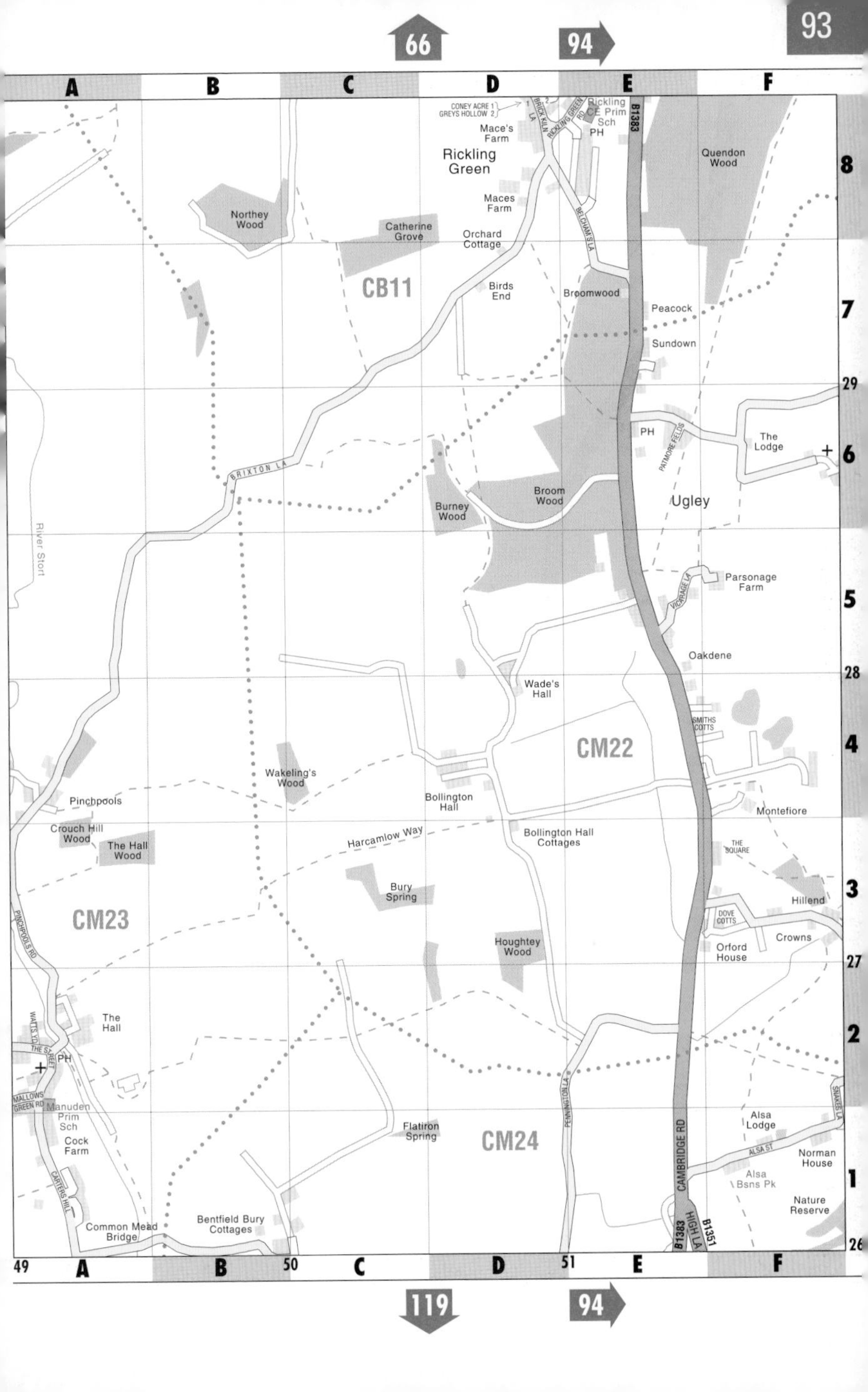

A | **B** | **C** | **D** | **E** | **F**

CONEY ACRE 1
GREYS HOLLOW 2
Mace's Farm
Rickling Prim Sch
PH

Rickling Green
Quendon Wood

8

Northey Wood
Catherine Grove
Maces Farm
Orchard Cottage

CB11

Birds End
Broomwood

7

Peacock

Sundown

29

PH
The Lodge

6

Burney Wood
Broom Wood

Ugley

BRIXTON LA

River Stort

Parsonage Farm

5

Oakdene

28

Wade's Hall
SMITHS COTTS

CM22

4

Wakeling's Wood
Montefiore

Pinchpools
Bollington Hall
THE SQUARE

Crouch Hill Wood
Harcamlow Way
Bollington Hall Cottages
Hillend

3

The Hall Wood
Bury Spring
DOVE COTTS
Crowns

CM23

Houghtey Wood
Orford House

27

The Hall
PH

2

MALLOWS
Manuden Prim Sch
Cock Farm
Flatiron Spring

CM24

Alsa Lodge
Norman House

CAMBRIDGE RD

Alsa Bsns Pk
Nature Reserve

1

Common Mead Bridge
Bentfield Bury Cottages

B1383
HIGH LA
B1351

26

49 | **A** | **B** | **C** 50 | **C** | **D** | 51 **E** | **F**

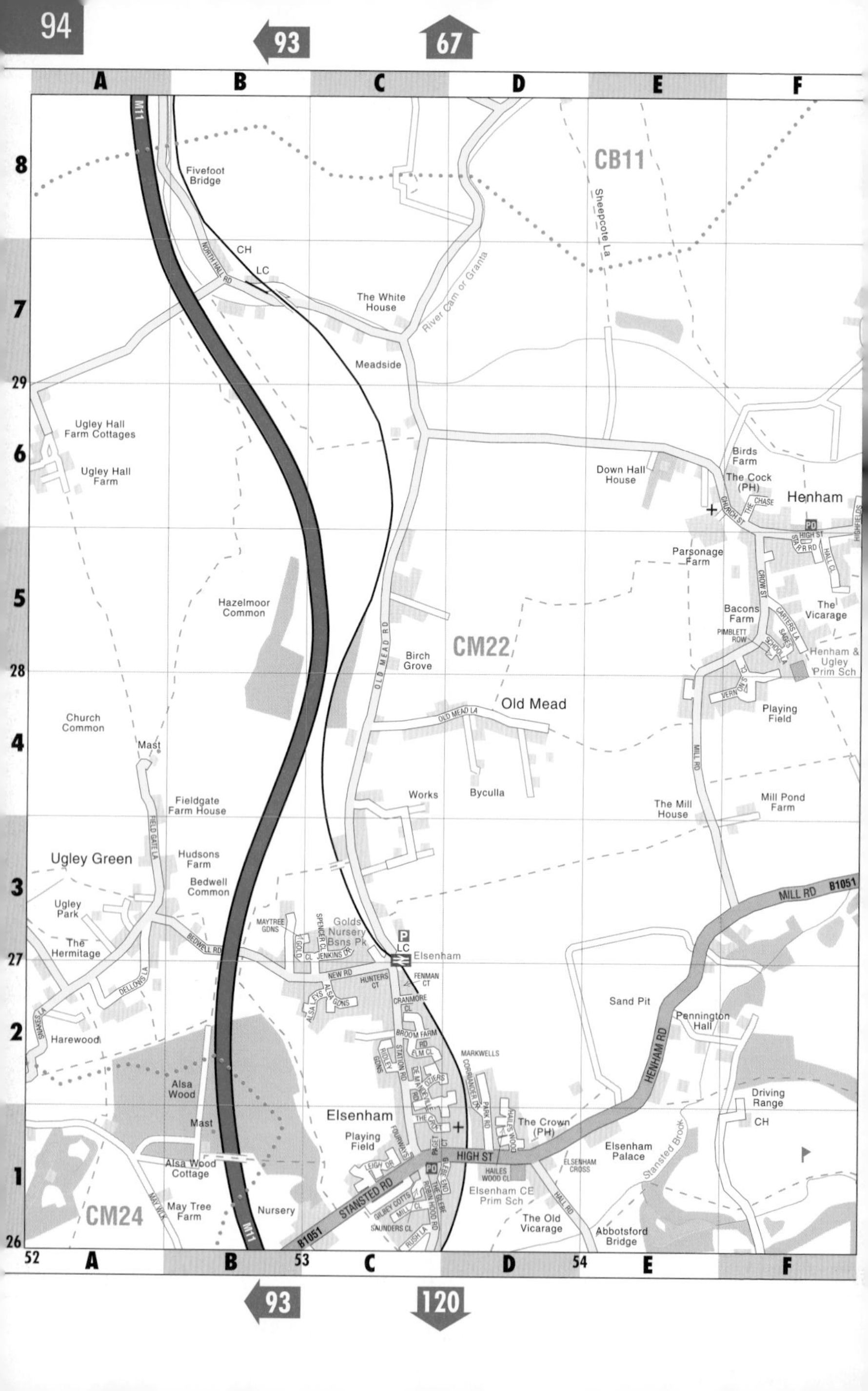
93
67
A
B
C
D
E
F
8
7
29
6
5
28
4
3
27
2
1
26
52
53
54
M11
Fivefoot Bridge
CH
LC
NORTH HALL RD
The White House
River Cam or Granta
Meadside
CB11
Sheepcote La
Ugley Hall Farm Cottages
Ugley Hall Farm
Down Hall House
Birds Farm
The Cock (PH)
Henham
CHURCH ST
THE CHASE
HIGH ST
STARR RD
HALL CL
HIGHFIELDS
Parsonage Farm
CROW ST
Bacons Farm
The Vicarage
CARTERS LA
PIMBLETT ROW
SAGES
SCHOOL LA
Henham & Ugley Prim Sch
VERNONS CL
Playing Field
Hazelmoor Common
OLD MEAD RD
Birch Grove
CM22
Old Mead
OLD MEAD LA
Church Common
Mast
Works
Byculla
MILL RD
The Mill House
Mill Pond Farm
Fieldgate Farm House
FIELD GATE LA
Hudsons Farm
Ugley Green
Bedwell Common
Ugley Park
MAYTREE GDNS
GOLD CL
SPENCER CL
JENKINS DR
Golds Nursery Bsns Pk
P
LC
Elsenham
MILL RD
B1051
The Hermitage
BEDWELL RD
NEW RD
HUNTERS CT
FENMAN CT
DELLOWS LA
ALSA LEYS
ALSA GDNS
CRANMORE CL
Sand Pit
SNAKES LA
Pennington Hall
Harewood
BROOM FARM RD
ELM CL
STATION RD
RIDLEY GDNS
MARKWELLS
CORRIANDER DR
HENHAM RD
Alsa Wood
DE MANDEVILLE RD
QUIERS
PARK RD
Driving Range
CH
Mast
Elsenham
THE CROFT
HAILES WOOD
The Crown (PH)
Playing Field
FOURWAYS
PAGET CT
HIGH ST
Elsenham Palace
Stansted Brook
LEIGH DR
PO
ELSENHAM CROSS
Alsa Wood Cottage
HAILES WOOD CL
STANSTED RD
ROBIN HOOD RD
THE GLEBE
Elsenham CE Prim Sch
HALL RD
May Tree Farm
MAY WLK
GILBEY COTTS
MILL CL
The Old Vicarage
CM24
Nursery
B1051
SAUNDERS CL
RUSH LA
Abbotsford Bridge
M11
93
120

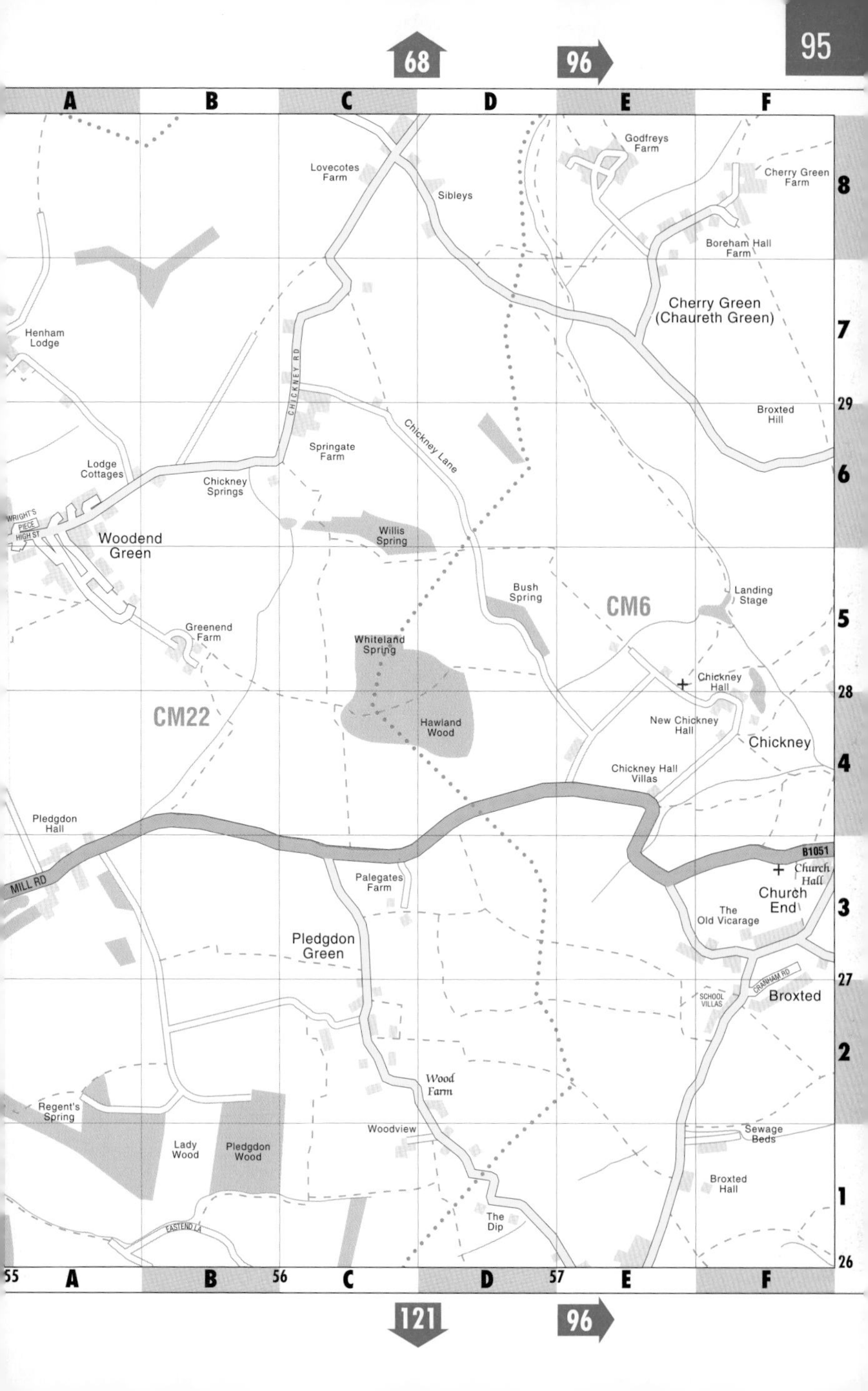

A   B   C   D   E   F

Godfreys Farm

Lovecotes Farm

Sibleys

Cherry Green Farm

8

Boreham Hall Farm

Cherry Green (Chaureth Green)

7

Henham Lodge

Broxted Hill

29

CHICKNEY RD

Chickney Lane

6

Lodge Cottages

Springate Farm

Chickney Springs

WRIGHT'S PIECE
HIGH ST

Woodend Green

Willis Spring

Bush Spring

CM6

Landing Stage

5

Greenend Farm

Whiteland Spring

Chickney Hall

28

CM22

New Chickney Hall

Chickney

4

Hawland Wood

Chickney Hall Villas

Pledgdon Hall

B1051

Church Hall

MILL RD

Palegates Farm

The Old Vicarage

Church End

3

Pledgdon Green

OAKHAM RD

27

SCHOOL VILLAS

Broxted

Regent's Spring

2

Wood Farm

Lady Wood

Pledgdon Wood

Woodview

Sewage Beds

Broxted Hall

1

EASTEND LA

The Dip

26

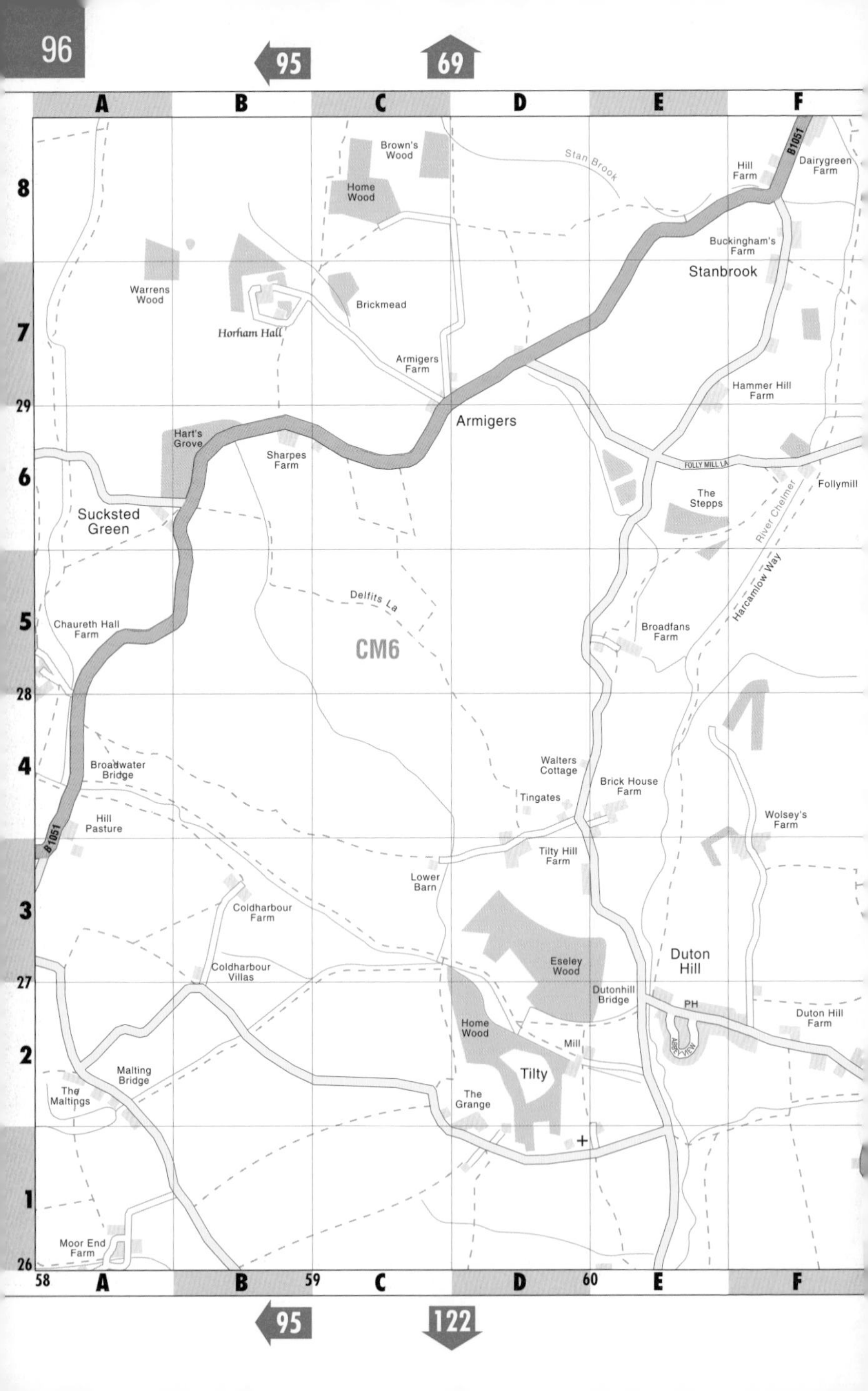

A B C D E F

8

Brown's
Wood

Home
Wood

Stan Brook

Hill
Farm

Dairygreen
Farm

B1051

Buckingham's
Farm

Stanbrook

7

Warrens
Wood

Brickmead

Horham Hall

Armigers
Farm

Hammer Hill
Farm

29

Armigers

6

Hart's
Grove

Sharpes
Farm

FOLLY MILL LN

The
Stepps

Follymill

Sucksted
Green

River Chelmer

5

Chaureth Hall
Farm

Delfits La

CM6

Broadfans
Farm

Harcamlow Way

28

4

Broadwater
Bridge

Walters
Cottage

Brick House
Farm

Wolsey's
Farm

Hill
Pasture

Tingates

Tilty Hill
Farm

B1051

3

Lower
Barn

Coldharbour
Farm

Eseley
Wood

Duton
Hill

27

Coldharbour
Villas

Dutonhill
Bridge

PH

Duton Hill
Farm

2

Malting
Bridge

Home
Wood

Mill

Tilty

The
Maltings

The
Grange

+

1

Moor End
Farm

26

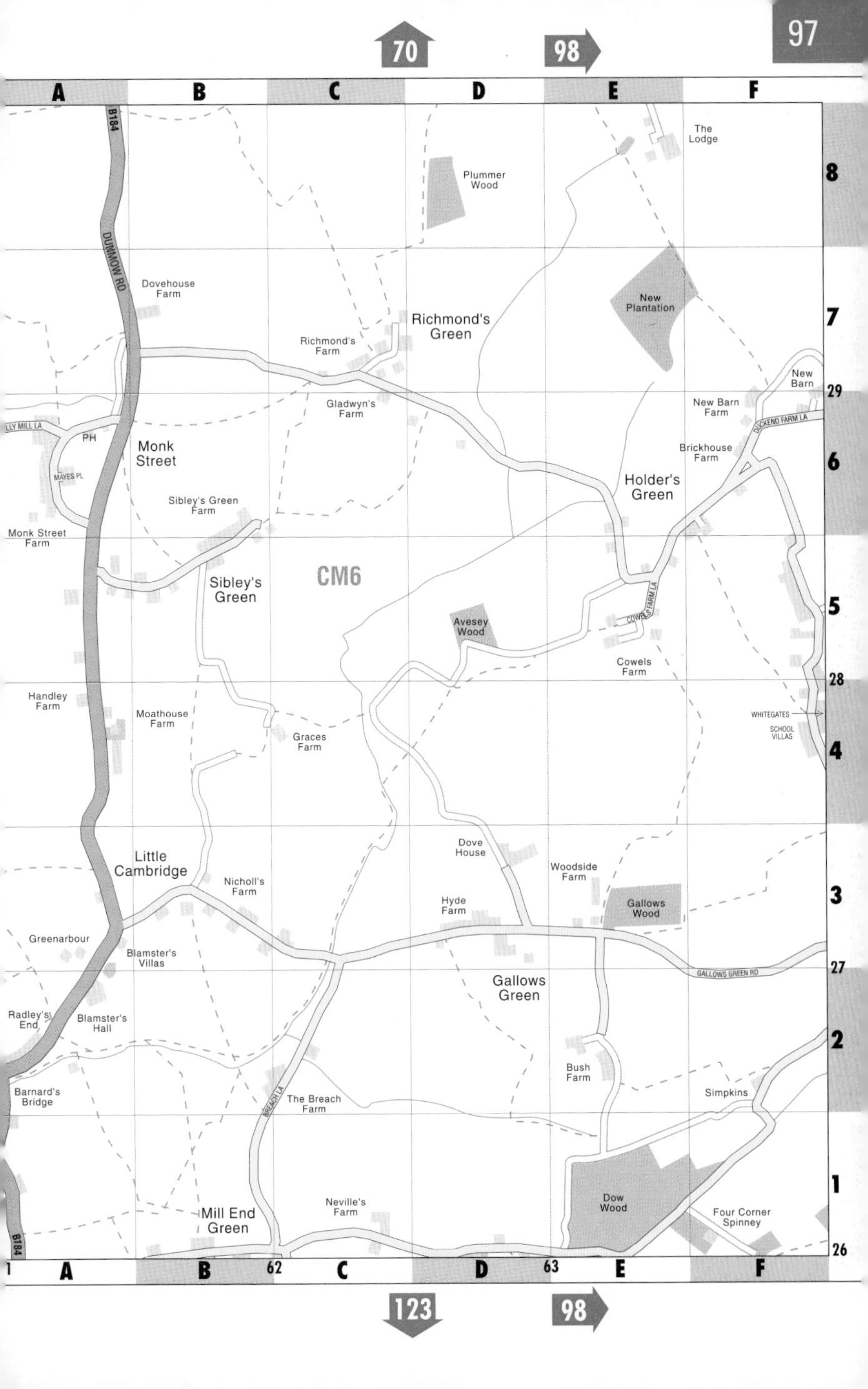
70
98
A
B
C
D
E
F
B184
DUMMOW RD
The Lodge
Plummer Wood
8
Dovehouse Farm
New Plantation
Richmond's Green
7
Richmond's Farm
New Barn
29
Gladwyn's Farm
New Barn Farm
LLY MILL LA
DUCKEND FARM LA
PH
Monk Street
Brickhouse Farm
MAYES PL
6
Holder's Green
Sibley's Green Farm
Monk Street Farm
CM6
Sibley's Green
5
Avesey Wood
COWELS FARM LA
Cowels Farm
28
Handley Farm
Moathouse Farm
WHITEGATES
SCHOOL VILLAS
Graces Farm
4
Dove House
Little Cambridge
Woodside Farm
Nicholl's Farm
3
Gallows Wood
Hyde Farm
Greenarbour
Blamster's Villas
27
GALLOWS GREEN RD
Gallows Green
Radley's End
Blamster's Hall
2
Bush Farm
Barnard's Bridge
Simpkins
BREACH LA
The Breach Farm
1
Dow Wood
Neville's Farm
Four Corner Spinney
Mill End Green
B184
26
62
63
123
98

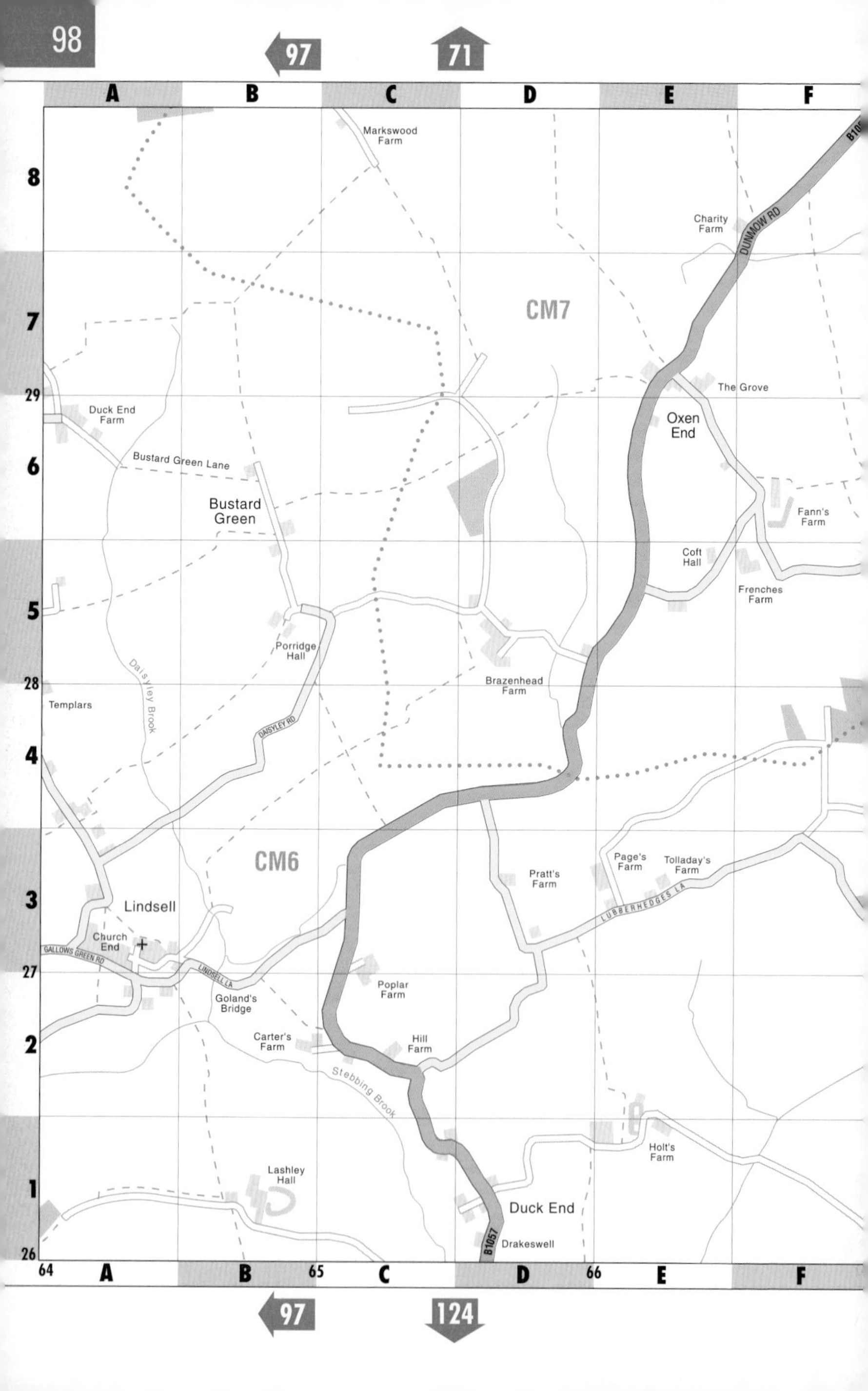

A B C D E F

8

7

CM7

29

6

B1110

DUNMOW RD

Markswood Farm

Charity Farm

The Grove

Oxen End

Duck End Farm

Bustard Green Lane

Bustard Green

Fann's Farm

Coft Hall

5

Daisley Brook

Porridge Hall

Brazenhead Farm

Frenches Farm

28

Templars

LADSLEY RD

4

CM6

Page's Farm

Tolladay's Farm

Pratt's Farm

3

Lindsell

LUBBENHEDGES LA

27

Church End

GALLOWS GREEN RD

LINDSELL LA

Goland's Bridge

Poplar Farm

2

Carter's Farm

Hill Farm

Stebbing Brook

Holt's Farm

1

Lashley Hall

Duck End

B1057

26

Drakeswell

64 A B 65 C D 66 E F

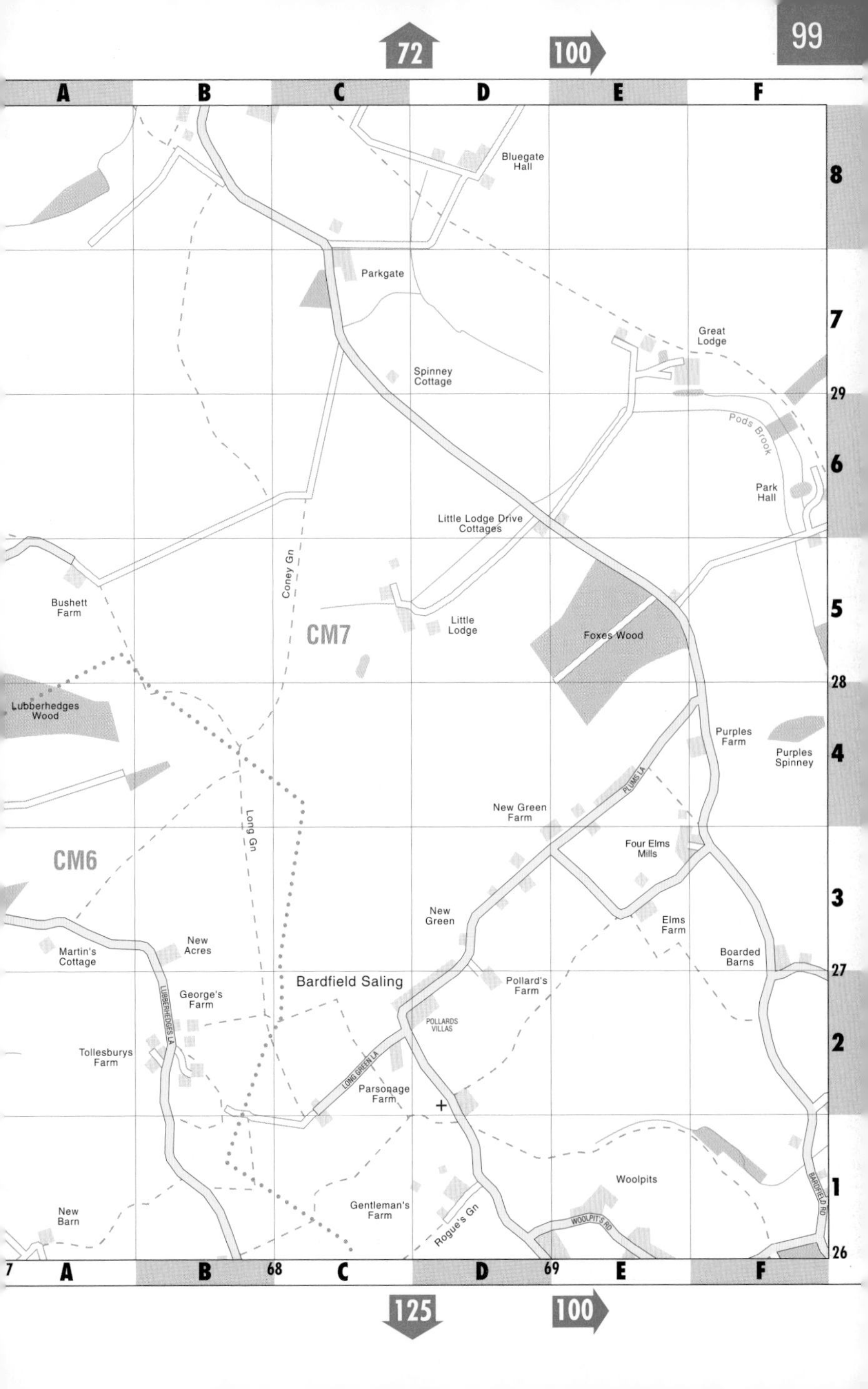
72
100
A
B
C
D
E
F
8
7
6
5
4
3
2
1
29
28
27
26
Bluegate Hall
Parkgate
Great Lodge
Spinney Cottage
Pods Brook
Park Hall
Little Lodge Drive Cottages
Coney Gn
Bushett Farm
CM7
Little Lodge
Foxes Wood
Lubberhedges Wood
Purples Farm
Purples Spinney
PLUMS LA
New Green Farm
Long Gn
Four Elms Mills
CM6
New Green
Elms Farm
Martin's Cottage
New Acres
Boarded Barns
Bardfield Saling
Pollard's Farm
George's Farm
LUBBERHEDGES LA
POLLARDS VILLAS
Tollesburys Farm
LONG GREEN LA
Parsonage Farm
Woolpits
BARDFIELD RD
New Barn
Gentleman's Farm
Rogue's Gn
WOOLPIT'S RD
7
68
69
125
100

99
73

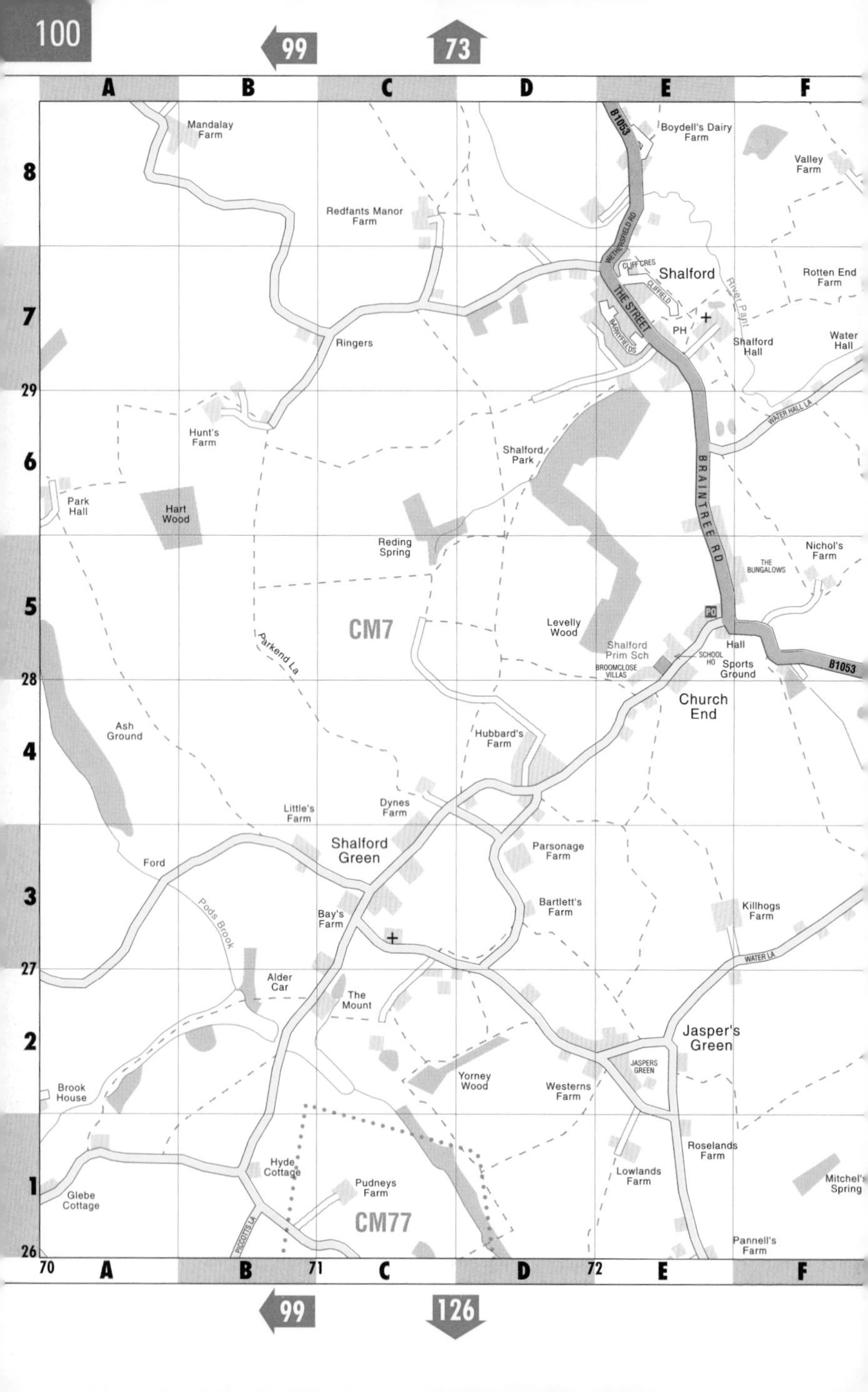
A
B
C
D
E
F
8
7
29
6
5
28
4
3
27
2
1
26
70
71
72
Mandalay Farm
Redfants Manor Farm
Boydell's Dairy Farm
Valley Farm
B1053
WETHERSFIELD RD
CLIFF CRES
CLIFFIELD
Shalford
THE STREET
BARRYFIELDS
PH
River Pant
Rotten End Farm
Water Hall
Shalford Hall
Ringers
WATER HALL LA
Hunt's Farm
Shalford Park
Park Hall
Hart Wood
BRAINTREE RD
Reding Spring
Nichol's Farm
THE BUNGALOWS
CM7
Levelly Wood
PO
Parkend La
Shalford Prim Sch
SCHOOL HO
Hall
Sports Ground
BROOMCLOSE VILLAS
B1053
Church End
Ash Ground
Hubbard's Farm
Little's Farm
Dynes Farm
Shalford Green
Parsonage Farm
Ford
Pods Brook
Bartlett's Farm
Killhogs Farm
Bay's Farm
WATER LA
Alder Car
The Mount
Jasper's Green
JASPERS GREEN
Yorney Wood
Westerns Farm
Brook House
Roselands Farm
Hyde Cottage
Lowlands Farm
Pudneys Farm
Glebe Cottage
CM77
PICCOTTS LA
Pannell's Farm

99
126

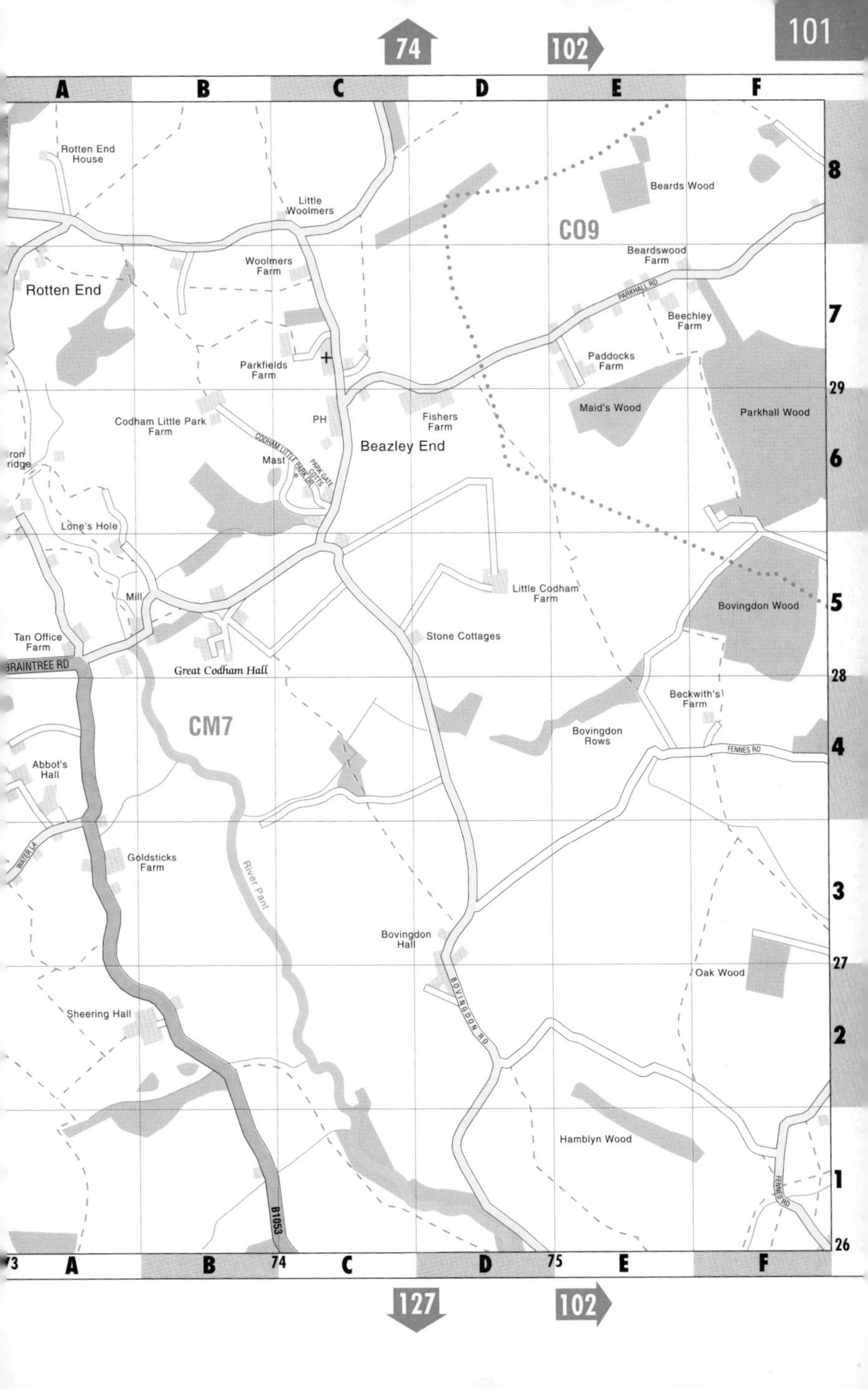

A   B   C   D   E   F

8

Rotten End
House

Little
Woolmers

Beards Wood

CO9

Beardswood
Farm

7

Woolmers
Farm

PARKHALL RD

Beechley
Farm

Rotten End

Paddocks
Farm

29

Parkfields
Farm

+

Codham Little Park
Farm

PH

Fishers
Farm

Maid's Wood

Parkhall Wood

Iron
ridge

Mast

CODHAM LITTLE PARK LANE

HARGATES

Beazley End

6

Lone's Hole

Mill

Little Codham
Farm

Bovingdon Wood

5

Tan Office
Farm

Great Codham Hall

Stone Cottages

Beckwith's
Farm

28

BRAINTREE RD

CM7

Bovingdon
Rows

FENNES RD

4

Abbot's
Hall

RIVER LA

Goldsticks
Farm

River Pant

Bovingdon
Hall

BOVINGDON RD

Oak Wood

27

3

Sheering Hall

2

Hamblyn Wood

FENNES RD

1

B1053

26

101 75

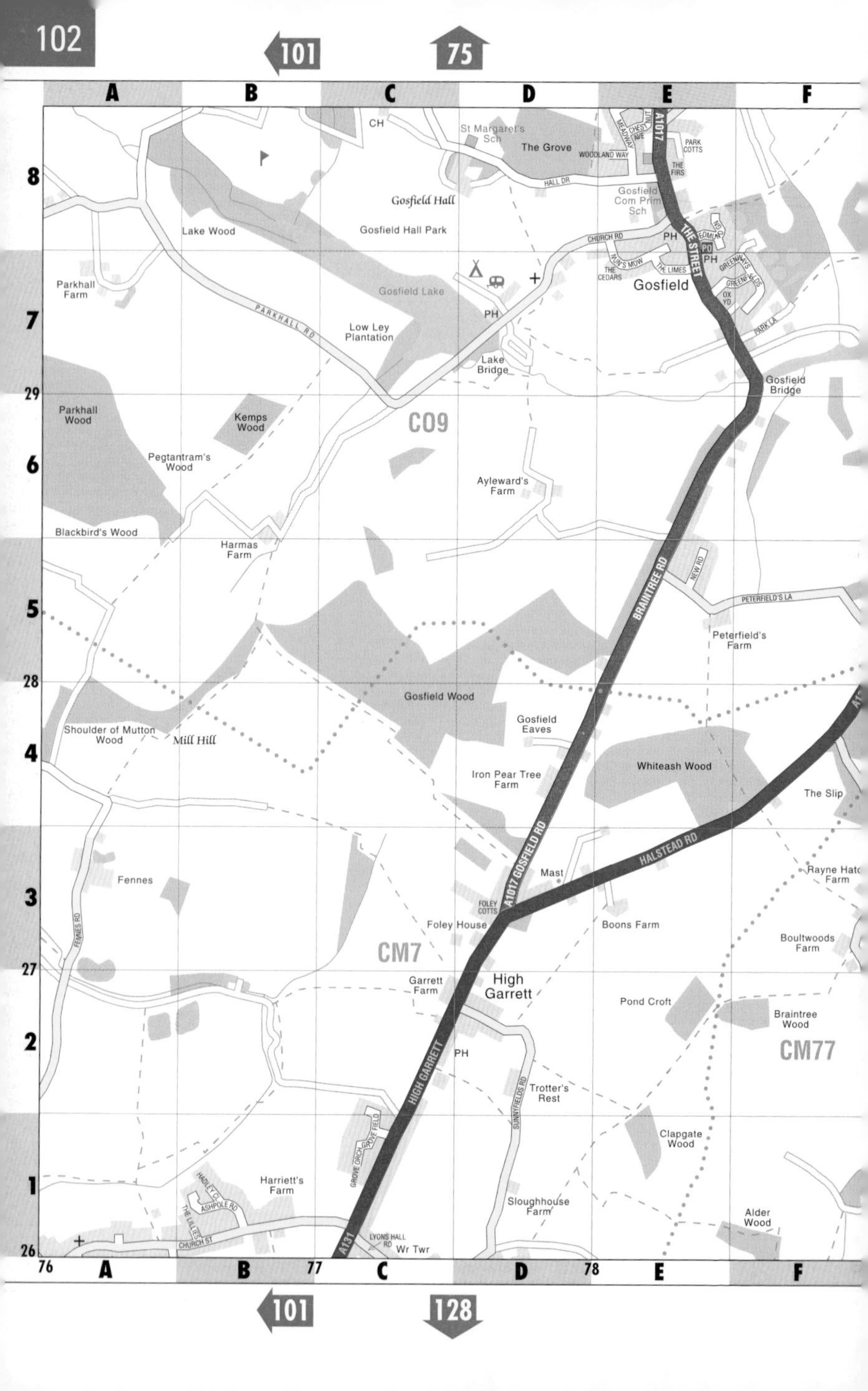
A
B
C
D
E
F
8
7
29
6
5
28
4
3
27
2
1
26
76
77
78
CH
St Margaret's Sch
The Grove
WOODLAND WAY
HALL DR
A1017
PARK COTTS
THE FIRS
Gosfield Hall
Gosfield Com Prim Sch
Lake Wood
Gosfield Hall Park
CHURCH RD
PH
THE STREET
PO
NUN'S MDW
THE LIMES
THE CEDARS
Parkhall Farm
Gosfield Lake
Gosfield
PARKHALL RD
Low Ley Plantation
PH
PARK LA
Lake Bridge
Gosfield Bridge
Parkhall Wood
Kemps Wood
CO9
Pegtantram's Wood
Ayleward's Farm
Blackbird's Wood
Harmas Farm
BRAINTREE RD
NEW RD
PETERFIELD'S LA
Peterfield's Farm
Gosfield Wood
Gosfield Eaves
Shoulder of Mutton Wood
Mill Hill
Whiteash Wood
Iron Pear Tree Farm
The Slip
A1017 GOSFIELD RD
HALSTEAD RD
Mast
Fennes
FOLEY COTTS
Foley House
Boons Farm
FENNES RD
CM7
Boultwoods Farm
Garrett Farm
High Garrett
Pond Croft
Braintree Wood
PH
CM77
HIGH GARRETT
SUNNYFIELDS RD
Trotter's Rest
Clapgate Wood
GROVE ORCH
GROVE FIELD
Harriett's Farm
HADLEY CL
ASHPOLE RD
THE LILLIES
CHURCH ST
A131
LYONS HALL RD
Wr Twr
Sloughhouse Farm
Alder Wood

101 128

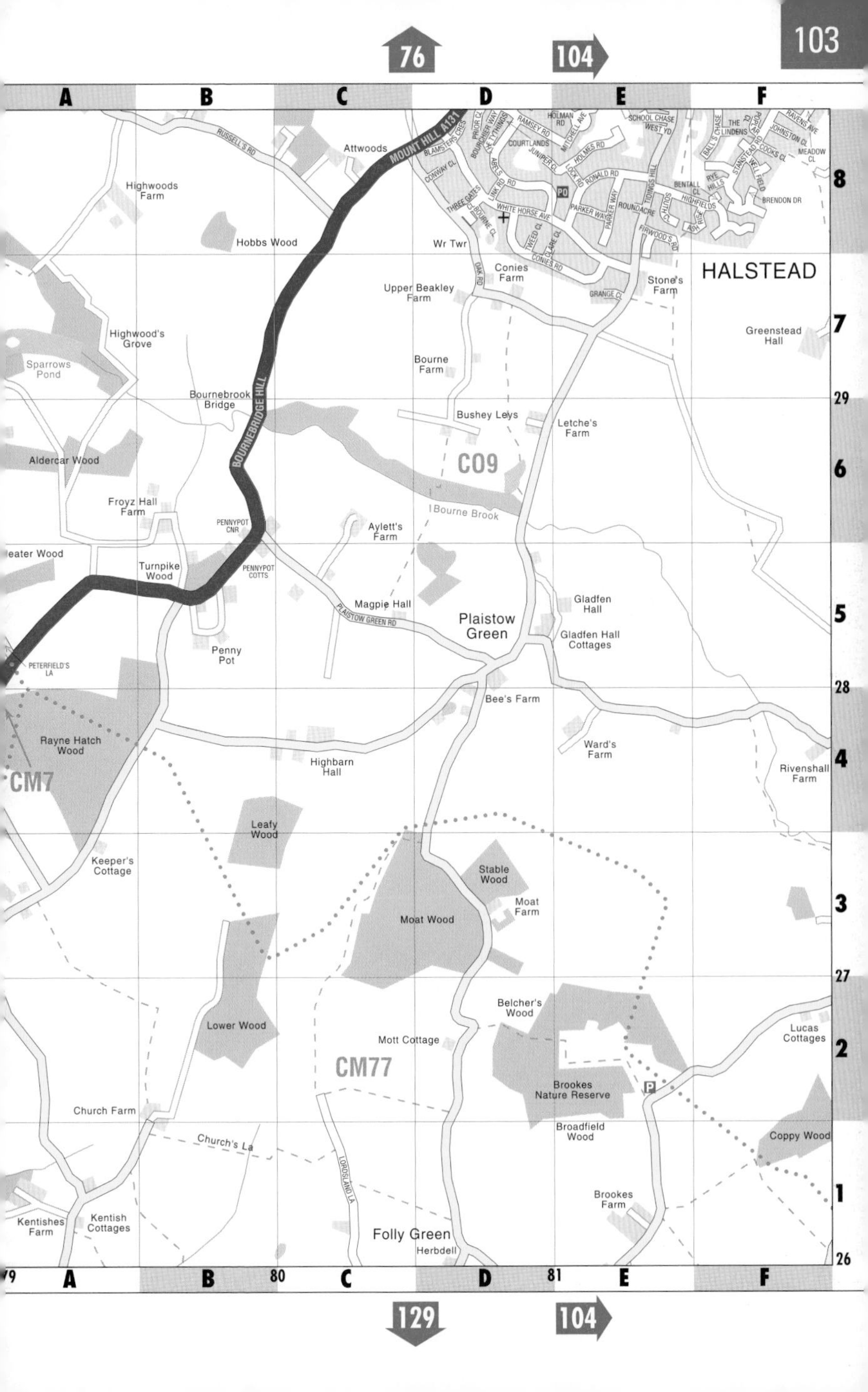

76
104

A **B** **C** **D** **E** **F**

8

Highwoods Farm

Attwoods

MOUNT HILL A131

RUSSELL'S RD

Hobbs Wood

HALSTEAD

Wr Twr

Upper Beakley Farm

Conies Farm

Stone's Farm

Highwood's Grove

Bourne Farm

Greenstead Hall

7

Sparrows Pond

Bournebrook Bridge

Bushey Leys

Letche's Farm

29

Aldercar Wood

BOURNEBRIDGE HILL

CO9

Bourne Brook

6

Froyz Hall Farm

PENNYPOT CNR

Aylett's Farm

eater Wood

Turnpike Wood

PENNYPOT COTTS

Magpie Hall

PLAISTOW GREEN RD

Plaistow Green

Gladfen Hall

Gladfen Hall Cottages

5

Penny Pot

28

PETERFIELD'S LA

Bee's Farm

Rayne Hatch Wood

Ward's Farm

Rivenshall Farm

CM7

Highbarn Hall

4

Leafy Wood

Stable Wood

Keeper's Cottage

Moat Wood

Moat Farm

3

27

Lower Wood

Belcher's Wood

Lucas Cottages

2

Mott Cottage

CM77

Brookes Nature Reserve

P

Broadfield Wood

Coppy Wood

Church Farm

Church's La

LORDSLAND LA

Brookes Farm

1

Kentishes Farm

Kentish Cottages

Folly Green

Herbdell

26

129
104

103
77

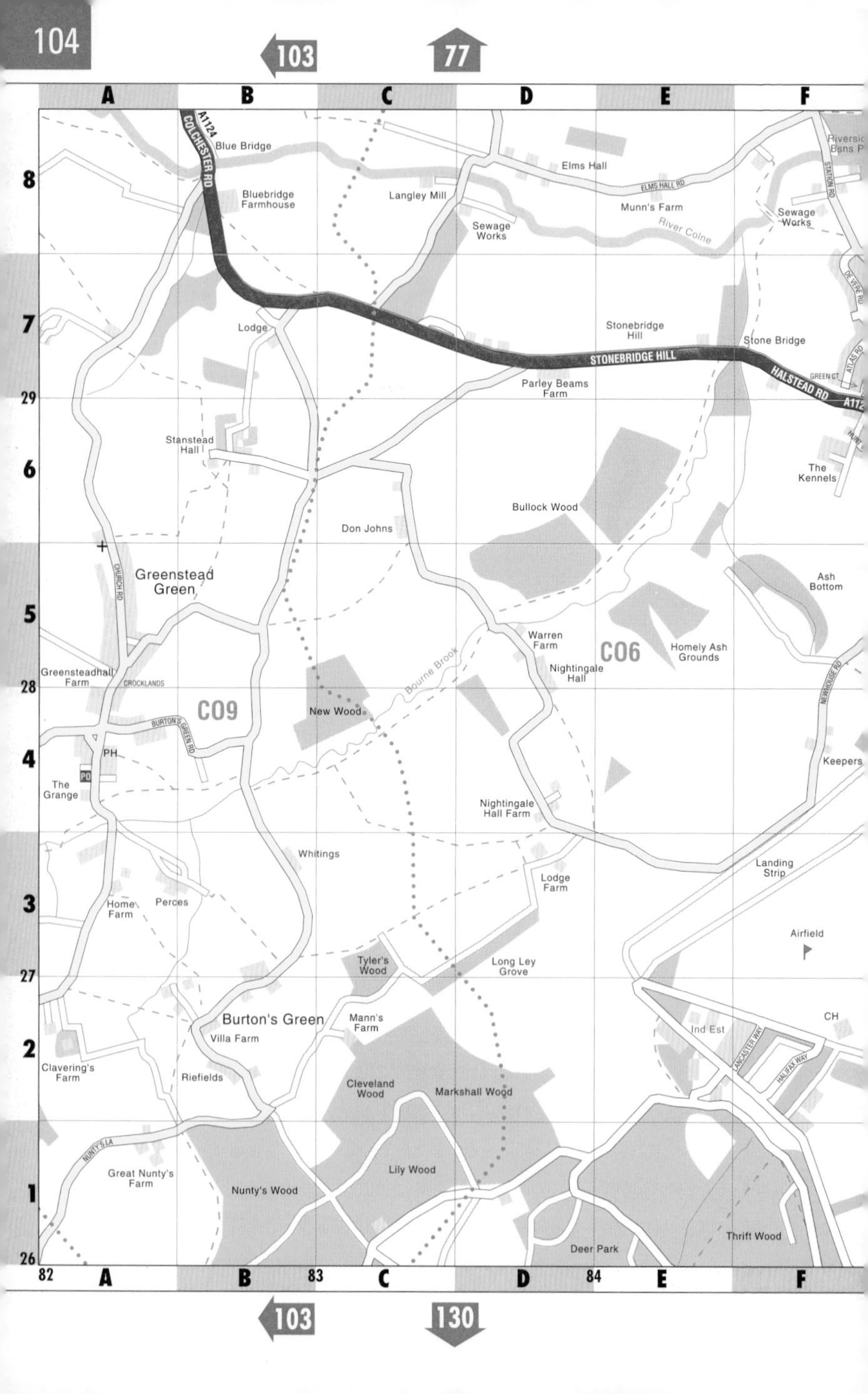
A
B
C
D
E
F
A1124
COLCHESTER RD
Blue Bridge
Bluebridge Farmhouse
Langley Mill
Elms Hall
ELMS HALL RD
Munn's Farm
Sewage Works
River Colne
Sewage Works
STATION RD
DE VERE RD
Lodge
Stonebridge Hill
Stone Bridge
STONEBRIDGE HILL
HALSTEAD RD
GREEN CT
ATLAS RD
Parley Beams Farm
Stanstead Hall
The Kennels
Bullock Wood
Don Johns
CHURCH RD
Greenstead Green
Ash Bottom
Warren Farm
CO6
Homely Ash Grounds
Nightingale Hall
Bourne Brook
Greensteadhall Farm
CROCKLANDS
CO9
New Wood
NEWHOUSE RD
BURTON'S GREEN RD
PH
PO
Keepers
The Grange
Nightingale Hall Farm
Whitings
Landing Strip
Lodge Farm
Home Farm
Perces
Airfield
Tyler's Wood
Long Ley Grove
Burton's Green
Mann's Farm
CH
Ind Est
LANCASTER WAY
HALIFAX WAY
Villa Farm
Clavering's Farm
Riefields
Cleveland Wood
Markshall Wood
NUNTY'S LA
Great Nunty's Farm
Lily Wood
Nunty's Wood
Deer Park
Thrift Wood
8
7
29
6
5
28
4
3
27
2
1
26
82
83
84

103
130

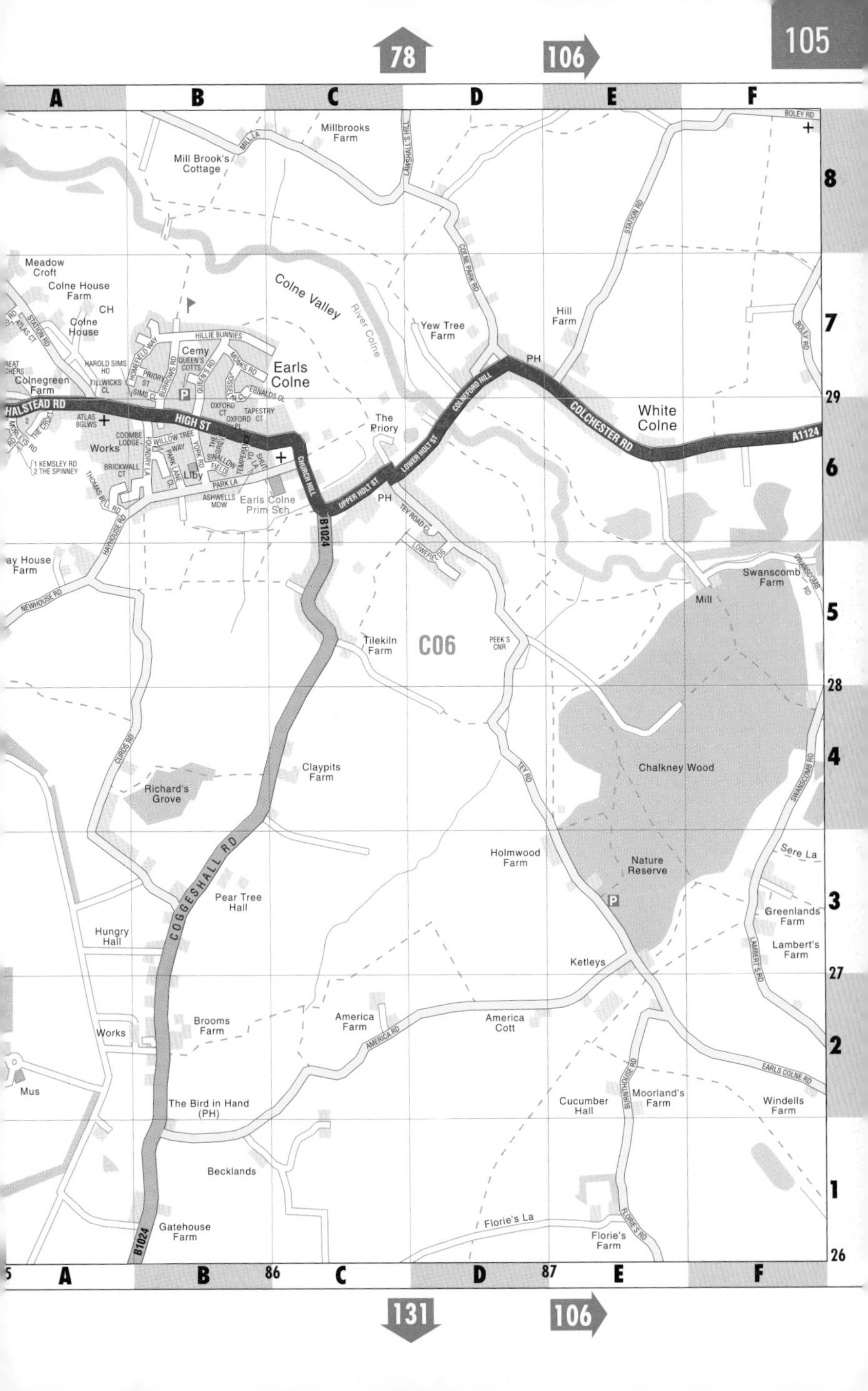

A B C D E F

8

Millbrooks
Farm

Mill Brook's
Cottage

Meadow
Croft

Colne House
Farm

7

CH

Colne
House

Colne Valley

River Colne

Yew Tree
Farm

Hill
Farm

GREAT
CHERRY

HILLIE BUNNIES

Cemy

Earls Colne

PH

29

Colnegreen
Farm

HAROLD SIMS HO

QUEEN'S
COTTS

PRIORY
ST

FERNALDS CL

P

HALSTEAD RD

ATLAS
BGLWS

HIGH ST

OXFORD
CT

OXFORD CT

TAPESTRY
CT

The Priory

COLNEFORD HILL

PH

White
Colne

A1124

COLCHESTER RD

COOMBE
LODGE

Works

WILLOW TREE

WAY

SWALLOW

LARNER HOLT ST

1 KEMSLEY RD
2 THE SPINNEY

BRICKWALL
CT

Lby

PARK LA

6

ASHWELLS
MDW

Earls Colne
Prim Sch

CHURCH HILL

UPPER HOLT ST

PH

TEE ROAD CL

LOWFIELD

ay House
Farm

NEWHOUSE RD

B1024

Swanscomb
Farm

5

Tilekiln
Farm

C06

PEEK'S
CNR

Mill

28

Chalkney Wood

4

Claypits
Farm

Richard's
Grove

COGGESHALL RD

Holmwood
Farm

Nature
Reserve

Sere La

3

Pear Tree
Hall

Greenlands
Farm

Hungry
Hall

P

Lambert's
Farm

LAMBERT RD

Ketleys

27

Works

Brooms
Farm

America
Farm

AMERICA RD

America
Cott

EARLS COLNE RD

2

Mus

The Bird in Hand
(PH)

Cucumber
Hall

Moorland's
Farm

Windells
Farm

B1024

Becklands

1

Gatehouse
Farm

Florie's La

Florie's
Farm

26

A B C D E F

86 87

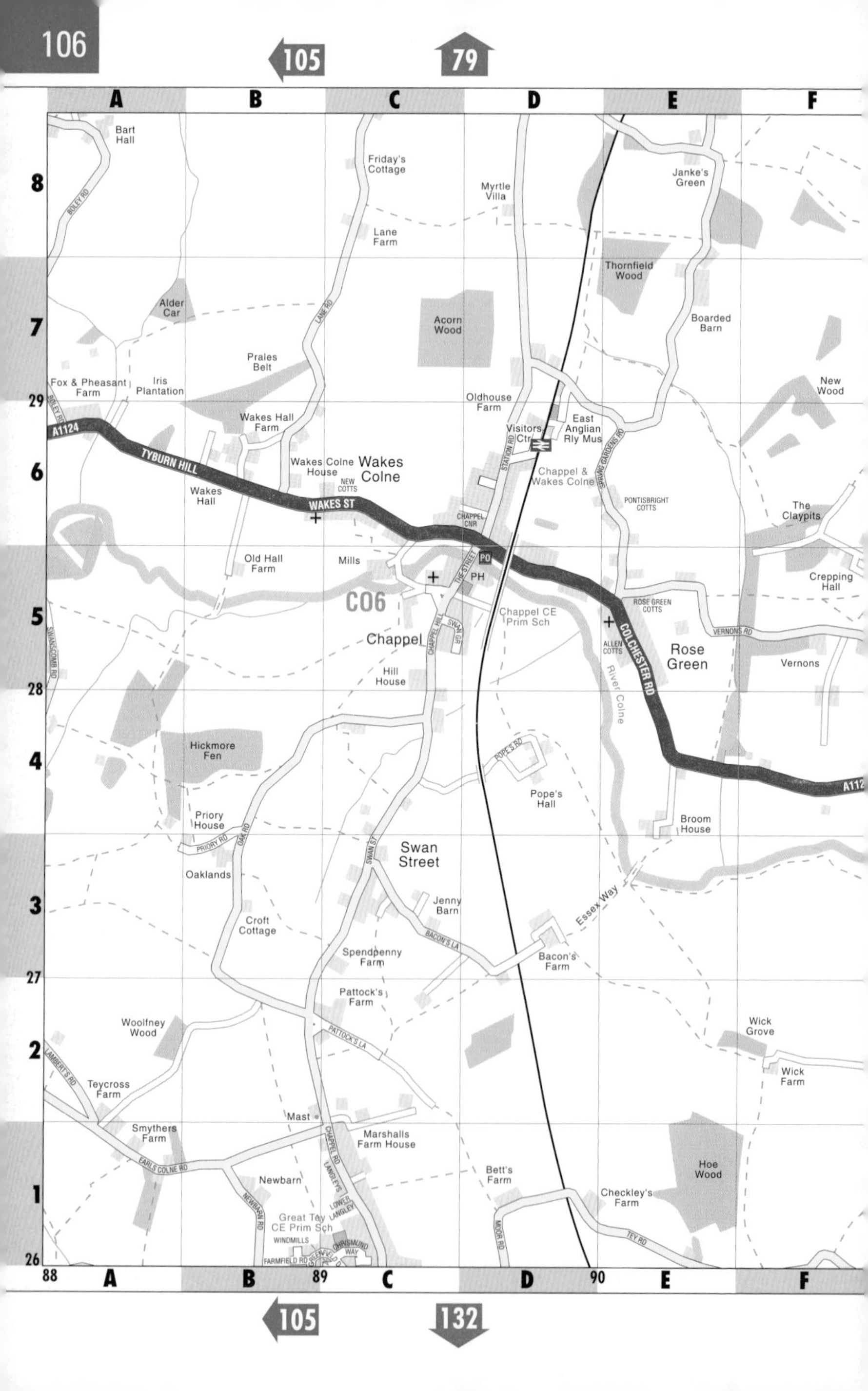
105
79
A
B
C
D
E
F
8
7
29
6
5
28
4
3
27
2
1
26
Bart Hall
Friday's Cottage
Myrtle Villa
Janke's Green
Lane Farm
Thornfield Wood
Alder Car
Acorn Wood
Boarded Barn
Prales Belt
Fox & Pheasant Farm
Iris Plantation
Oldhouse Farm
New Wood
Wakes Hall Farm
Visitors Ctr
East Anglian Rly Mus
A1124
TYBURN HILL
Wakes Colne House
Wakes Colne
NEW COTTS
Chappel & Wakes Colne
Wakes Hall
WAKES ST
PONTISBRIGHT COTTS
The Claypits
CHAPPEL CNR
Old Hall Farm
Mills
PO
PH
Crepping Hall
CO6
ROSE GREEN COTTS
Chappel CE Prim Sch
Chappel
ALLEN COTTS
COLCHESTER RD
Rose Green
Vernons
VERNONS RD
River Colne
Hill House
Hickmore Fen
POPE'S RD
Pope's Hall
A1124
Priory House
PRIORY RD
OAK RD
Broom House
Swan Street
SWAN ST
Oaklands
Jenny Barn
Essex Way
Croft Cottage
BACON'S LA
Spendpenny Farm
Bacon's Farm
Pattock's Farm
Woolfney Wood
PATTOCK'S LA
Wick Grove
Wick Farm
Teycross Farm
Mast
Smythers Farm
Marshalls Farm House
EARLS COLNE RD
Bett's Farm
Hoe Wood
Newbarn
Checkley's Farm
Great Tey CE Prim Sch
NEWBARN RD
MOOR RD
TEY RD
WINDMILLS
FARMFIELD RD
BOLEY RD
LANE RD
STATION RD
SPRING GARDENS RD
THE STREET
CHAPPEL HILL
SWAN GR
SWANSCOMB RD
LAMBERT'S RD
CHAPPEL RD
LANGLEY'S
LOWER LANGLEY
CHRISMUND WAY
88
89
90
132

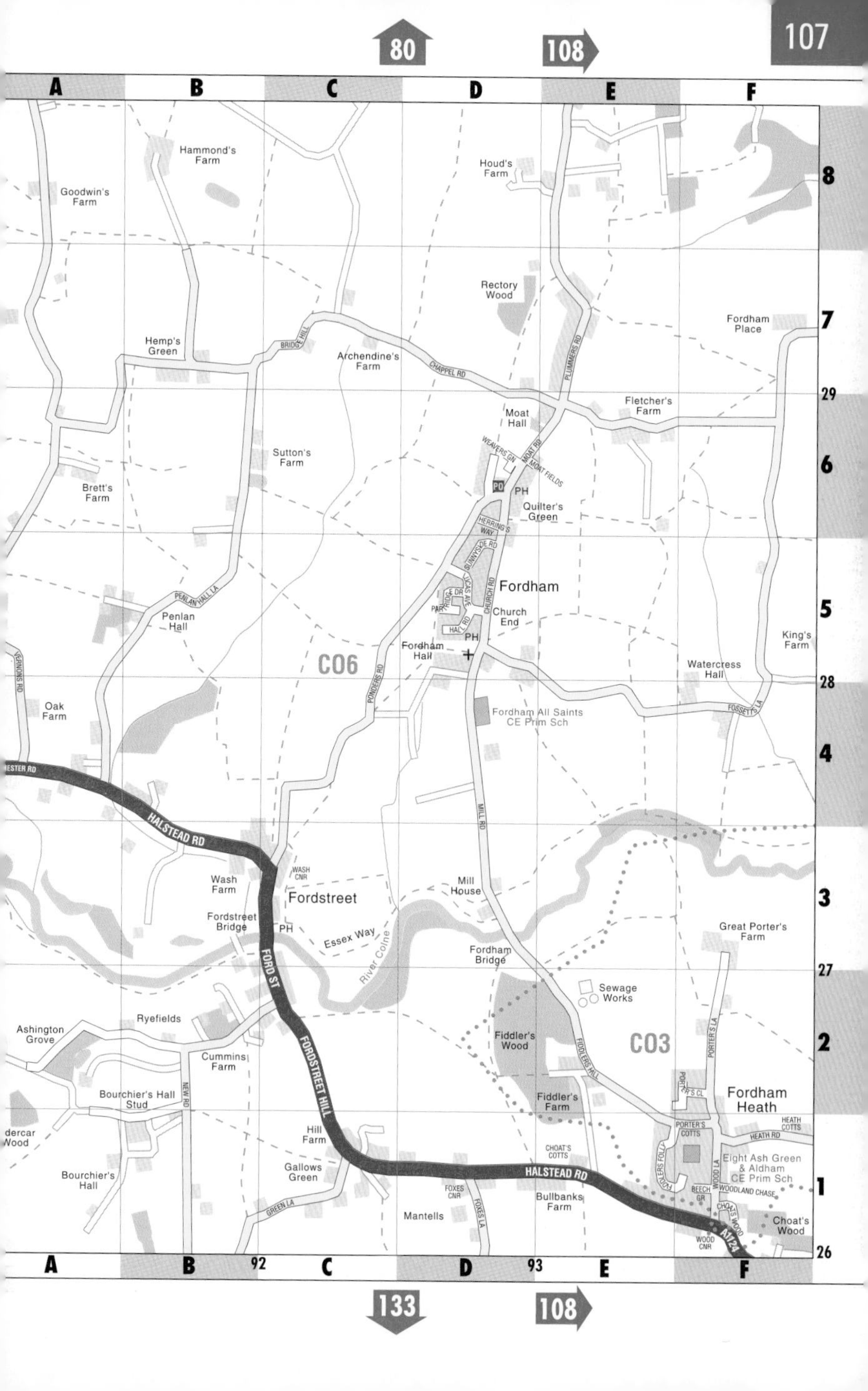

8

Goodwin's Farm

Hammond's Farm

Houd's Farm

Hemp's Green

BRIDG RD

Archendine's Farm

CHAPPEL RD

Rectory Wood

PLUMMERS RD

Fordham Place

7

29

Moat Hall

WEAVERS DR

MOAT FIELDS

Fletcher's Farm

Brett's Farm

Sutton's Farm

PO PH

Quilter's Green

6

PULHAM'S LA

Penlan Hall

CO06

HEDDING'S WAY

KNIGHTS CL

Fordham

PARK SIDE DR

PARK

Church End

HALL

PH

King's Farm

5

Oak Farm

KENNING RD

SPRINGS RD

Fordham Hall

✠

Watercress Hall

FOSSETT'S

28

Fordham All Saints CE Prim Sch

MILL RD

4

HALSTEAD RD

CHESTER RD

Wash Farm

WASH CNR

Mill House

Great Porter's Farm

3

Fordstreet

Fordham Bridge

Fordstreet Bridge

PH

Essex Way

River Colne

PORTER'S LA

FORD ST

27

Ashington Grove

Ryefields

NEW RD

Cummins Farm

FORDSTREET HILL

Sewage Works

Fiddler's Wood

CO03

2

dercar Wood

Bourchier's Hall Stud

Fiddler's Farm

FODDER'S HILL

PORTER'S CL

Porter's Cotts

Fordham Heath

HEATH CL

HEATH COTTS

HEATH RD

T DOWN

Bourchier's Hall

Hill Farm

Gallows Green

CHOAT'S COTTS

Eight Ash Green & Aldham CE Prim Sch

WOODLAND CHASE

1

GREEN LA

FOXES CNR

FOXES LA

Mantells

Bullbanks Farm

HALSTEAD RD

BEECH GR

COCK RD

CROFT RD

A1124

Choat's Wood

WOOD CNR

26

A   B   C   D   E   F

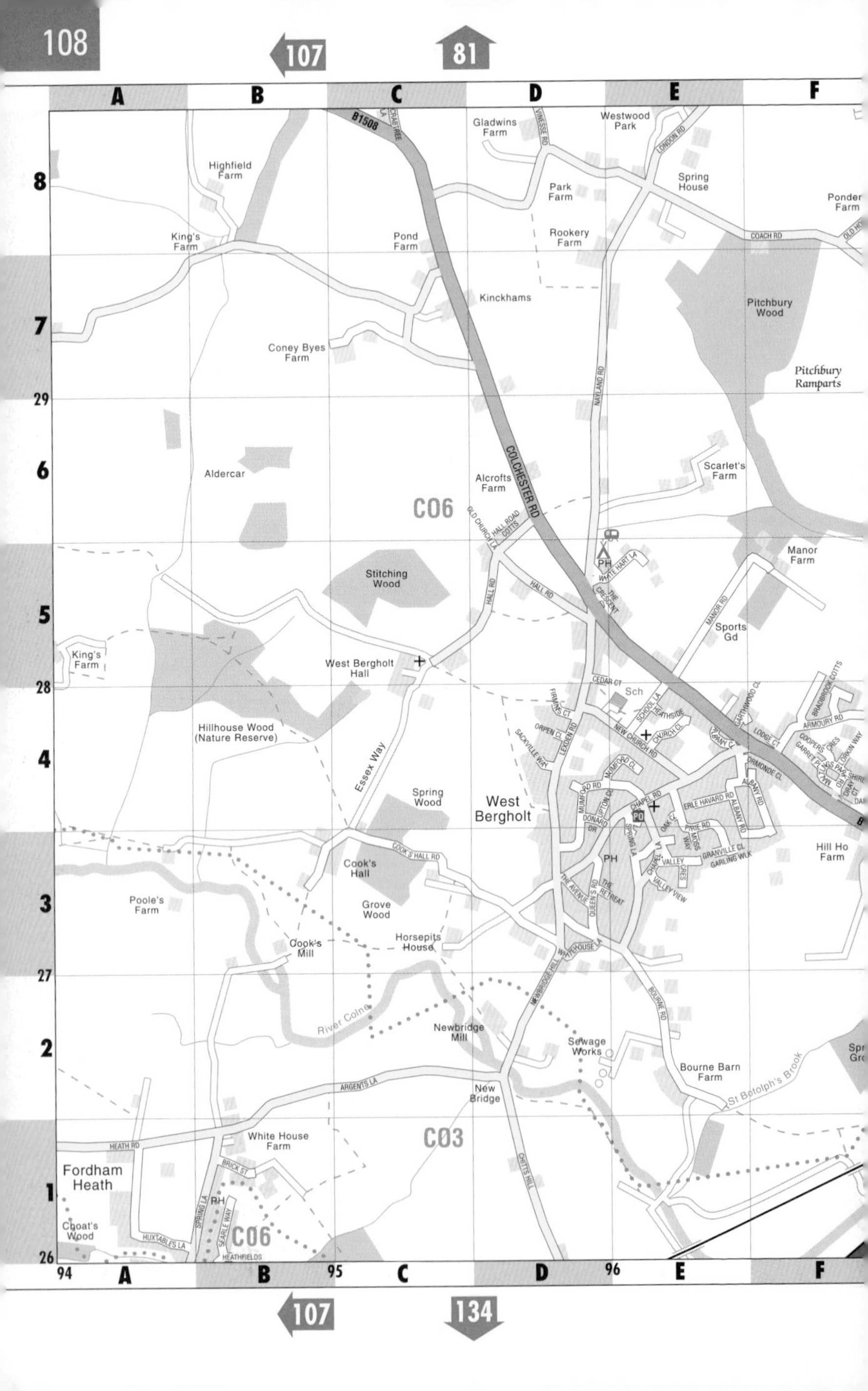
107
81
A
B
C
D
E
F
8
7
29
6
5
28
4
3
27
2
1
26
94
95
96
B1508
CRABTREE
Gladwins Farm
VINESSE RD
Westwood Park
LONDON RD
Highfield Farm
Park Farm
Spring House
Ponder Farm
King's Farm
Pond Farm
Rookery Farm
COACH RD
Kinckhams
Pitchbury Wood
Coney Byes Farm
Pitchbury Ramparts
NAYLAND RD
Aldercar
Alcrofts Farm
Scarlet's Farm
CO6
COLCHESTER RD
OLD CHURCH LA
HALL ROAD COTTS
PH
WHITE HART LA
Manor Farm
Stitching Wood
HALL RD
THE CRESCENT
MANOR RD
Sports Gd
King's Farm
West Bergholt Hall
CEDAR CT
Sch
FIRMINS CT
SCHOOL LA
HEATHSIDE
GARTHWOOD CL
BRADBROOK COTTS
ARMOURY RD
Hillhouse Wood (Nature Reserve)
ORPEN CL
LEXDEN RD
NEW CHURCH RD
CHURCH CL
ALBANY CL
LODGE CT
COOPERS CRES
SACKVILLE WAY
MUMFORD CL
ORMONDE CL
Essex Way
Spring Wood
West Bergholt
MUMFORD RD
UPTON CL
CHAPEL RD
PO
ERLE HAVARD RD
ALBANY RD
DONARD DR
OAK CL
PIRIE RD
MOSS WAY
SPRING LA
Hill Ho Farm
COOK'S HALL RD
PH
GRANVILLE CL
GARLING WLK
Cook's Hall
VALLEY CRES
CHAPEL LA
Poole's Farm
THE AVENUE
QUEEN'S RD
THE RETREAT
VALLEY VIEW
Grove Wood
Cook's Mill
Horsepits House
WATERHOUSE LA
River Colne
Newbridge Mill
NEWBRIDGE HILL
BOURNE RD
Sewage Works
Bourne Barn Farm
ARGENTS LA
New Bridge
St Botolph's Brook
HEATH RD
White House Farm
CO3
BRICK ST
Fordham Heath
CHITTS HILL
PH
SPRING LA
SEARLE WAY
Choat's Wood
HUXTABLES LA
CO6
HEATHFIELDS
107
134

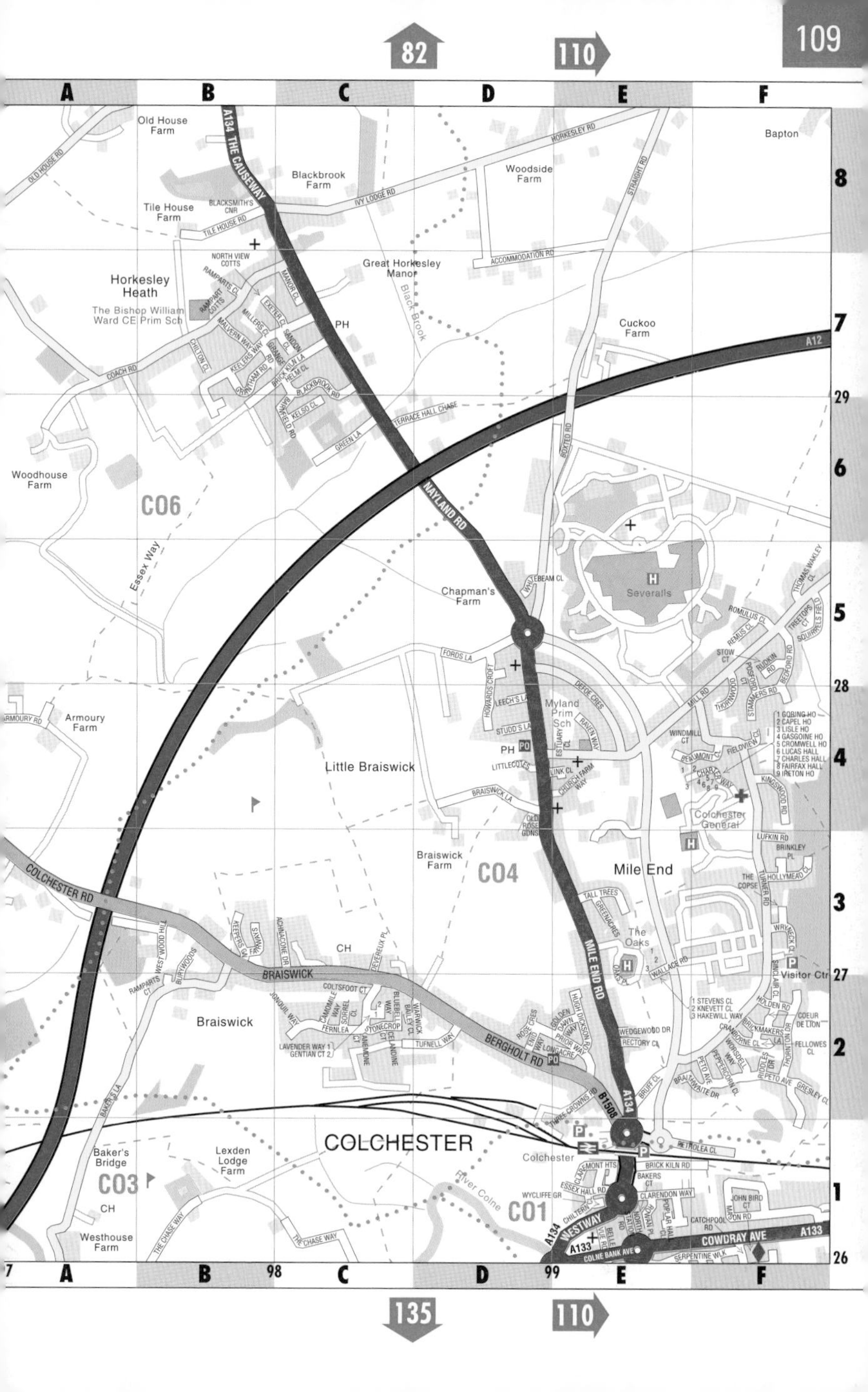
82
110
A
B
C
D
E
F
Old House Farm
Blackbrook Farm
Woodside Farm
Bapton
Tile House Farm
Horkesley Heath
The Bishop William Ward CE Prim Sch
Great Horkesley Manor
Black Brook
Cuckoo Farm
PH
Woodhouse Farm
CO6
Essex Way
Severalls
Chapman's Farm
Armoury Farm
Myland Prim Sch
Little Braiswick
Colchester General
Braiswick Farm
CO4
Mile End
The Oaks
Visitor Ctr
CH
Braiswick
COLCHESTER
Baker's Bridge
Lexden Lodge Farm
Colchester
CO3
CO1
River Colne
Westhouse Farm
A134 THE CAUSEWAY
NAYLAND RD
MILE END RD
COLCHESTER RD
BRAISWICK
BERGHOLT RD
COWDRAY AVE
A12
A133
B1508
8
7
6
5
4
3
2
1
29
28
27
26
98
99
135
110

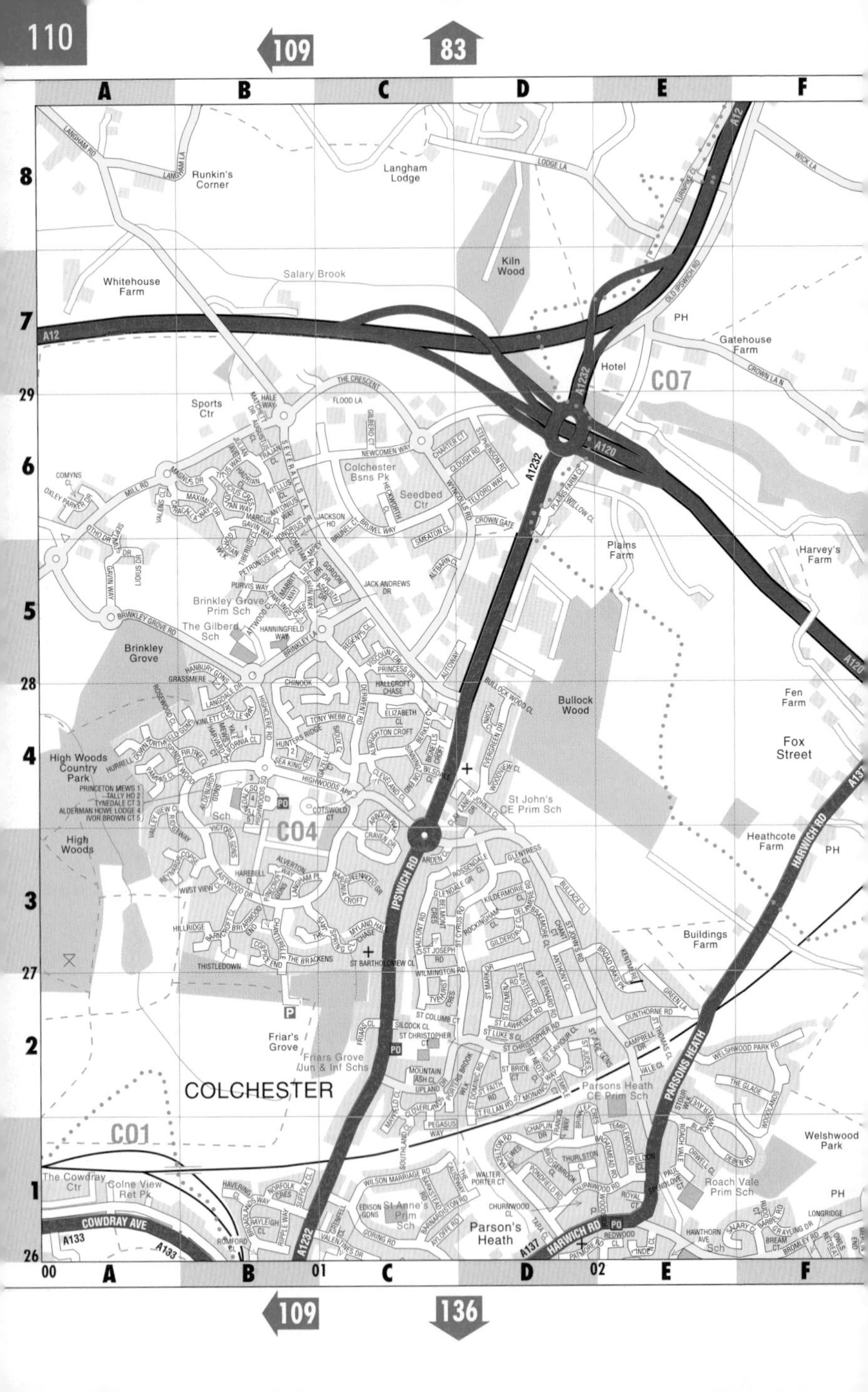
109
83
Runkin's Corner
Langham Lodge
Kiln Wood
Whitehouse Farm
Salary Brook
A12
Gatehouse Farm
Hotel
CO7
Sports Ctr
Colchester Bsns Pk
Seedbed Ctr
Plains Farm
Harvey's Farm
Brinkley Grove Prim Sch
The Gilberd Sch
Brinkley Grove
Bullock Wood
Fen Farm
Fox Street
High Woods Country Park
St John's CE Prim Sch
CO4
High Woods
Heathcote Farm
Buildings Farm
Friar's Grove
Friars Grove Jun & Inf Schs
COLCHESTER
Parsons Heath CE Prim Sch
Welshwood Park
CO1
The Cowdray Ctr
Colne View Ret Pk
COWDRAY AVE
St Anne's Prim Sch
Parson's Heath
Roach Vale Prim Sch
IPSWICH RD
HARWICH RD
PARSONS HEATH
A1232
A120
A133
A137
109
136

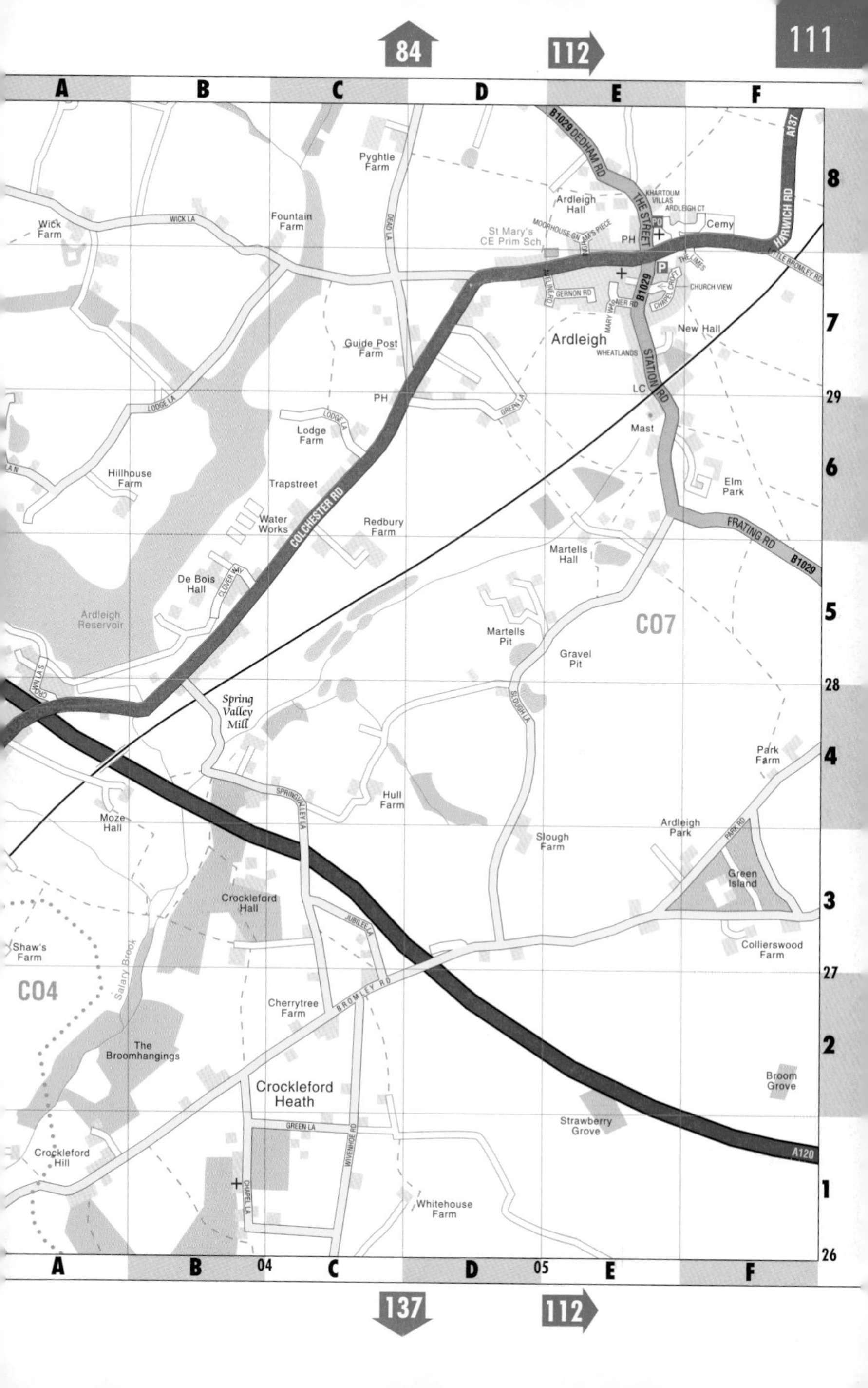
84
112
A
B
C
D
E
F
8
7
29
6
5
28
4
3
27
2
1
26
04
05
Pyghtle Farm
Wick Farm
WICK LA
Fountain Farm
DEAD LA
B1029 DEDHAM RD
Ardleigh Hall
THE STREET
KHARTOUM VILLAS
ARDLEIGH CT
Cemy
HARWICH RD
A137
St Mary's CE Prim Sch
MOORHOUSE GN
PH
PO
P
THE LIMES
LITTLE BROMLEY RD
GERNON RD
CHURCH VIEW
CHAPEL CROFT
B1029
Ardleigh
New Hall
WHEATLANDS
STATION RD
Guide Post Farm
LC
PH
LODGE LA
Lodge Farm
GREEN LA
Mast
Hillhouse Farm
Trapstreet
Elm Park
Water Works
COLCHESTER RD
Redbury Farm
FRATING RD
B1029
Martells Hall
De Bois Hall
CLOVER WAY
Ardleigh Reservoir
CO7
Martells Pit
Gravel Pit
Spring Valley Mill
SLOUGH LA
Park Farm
Hull Farm
SPRINGVALLEY LA
Moze Hall
Ardleigh Park
PARK RD
Slough Farm
Green Island
Crockleford Hall
JUBILEE LA
Shaw's Farm
Collierswood Farm
CO4
Salary Brook
Cherrytree Farm
BROMLEY RD
The Broomhangings
Crockleford Heath
Broom Grove
GREEN LA
Strawberry Grove
WIVENHOE RD
A120
Crockleford Hill
CHAPEL LA
Whitehouse Farm

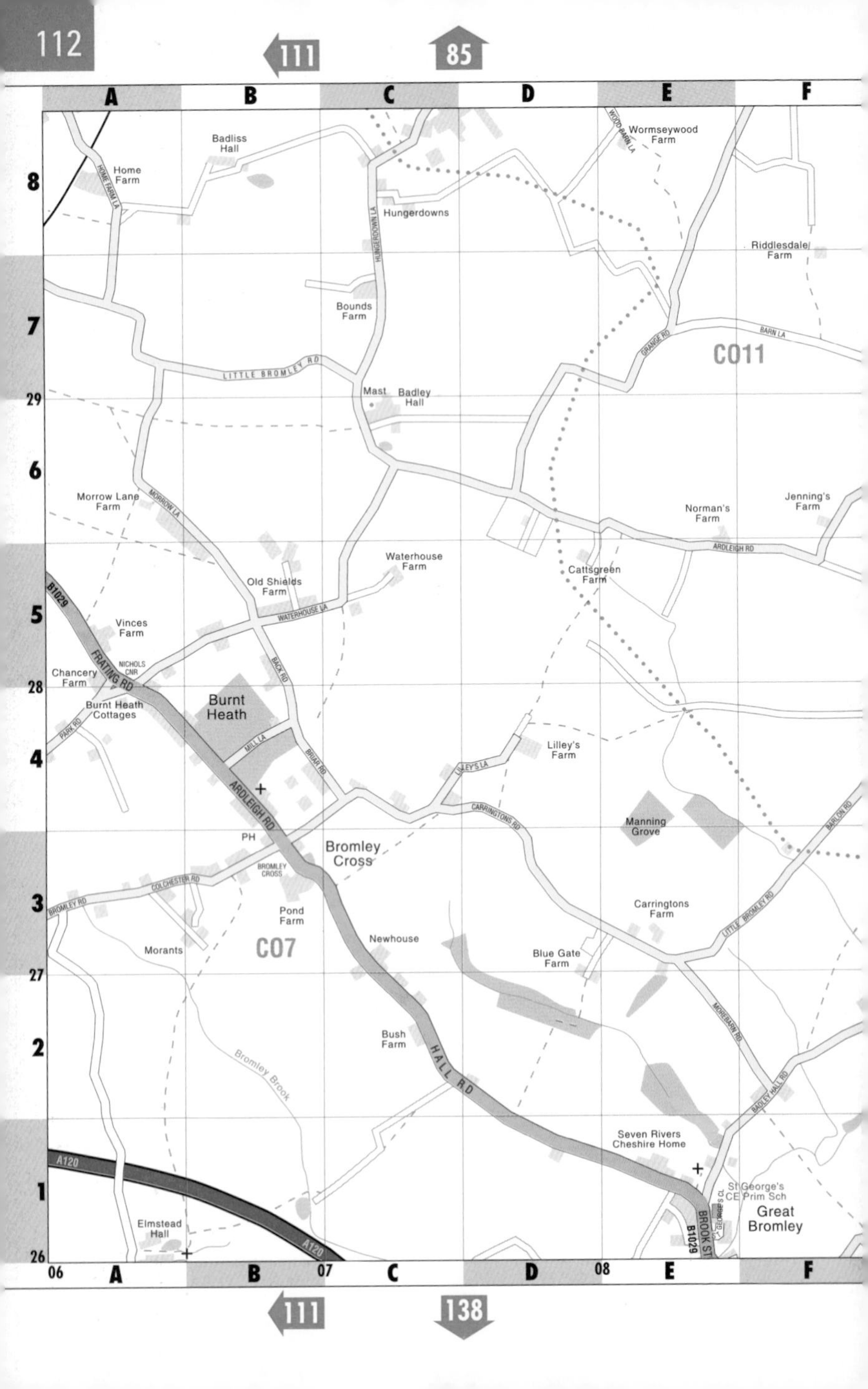
A
B
C
D
E
F
8
7
29
6
5
28
4
3
27
2
1
26
06
07
08
Badliss Hall
Home Farm
HOME FARM LA
Hungerdowns
HUNGERDOWN LA
Wormseywood Farm
WOOD BARN LA
Riddlesdale Farm
Bounds Farm
GRANGE RD
BARN LA
CO11
LITTLE BROMLEY RD
Mast
Badley Hall
Morrow Lane Farm
MORROW LA
Norman's Farm
Jenning's Farm
ARDLEIGH RD
Waterhouse Farm
Old Shields Farm
Cattsgreen Farm
B1029
WATERHOUSE LA
Vinces Farm
NICHOLS CNR
Chancery Farm
FRATING RD
BACK RD
Burnt Heath Cottages
Burnt Heath
PARK RD
MILL LA
BRIAR RD
Lilley's Farm
LILLEY'S LA
ARDLEIGH RD
CARRINGTONS RD
Manning Grove
BARLON RD
PH
Bromley Cross
BROMLEY CROSS
COLCHESTER RD
BROMLEY RD
Pond Farm
Carringtons Farm
LITTLE BROMLEY RD
Morants
CO7
Newhouse
Blue Gate Farm
MOREBARN RD
Bush Farm
HALL RD
Bromley Brook
BADLEY HALL RD
Seven Rivers Cheshire Home
A120
St George's CE Prim Sch
Great Bromley
ST GEORGE'S CL
Elmstead Hall
BROOK ST
B1029

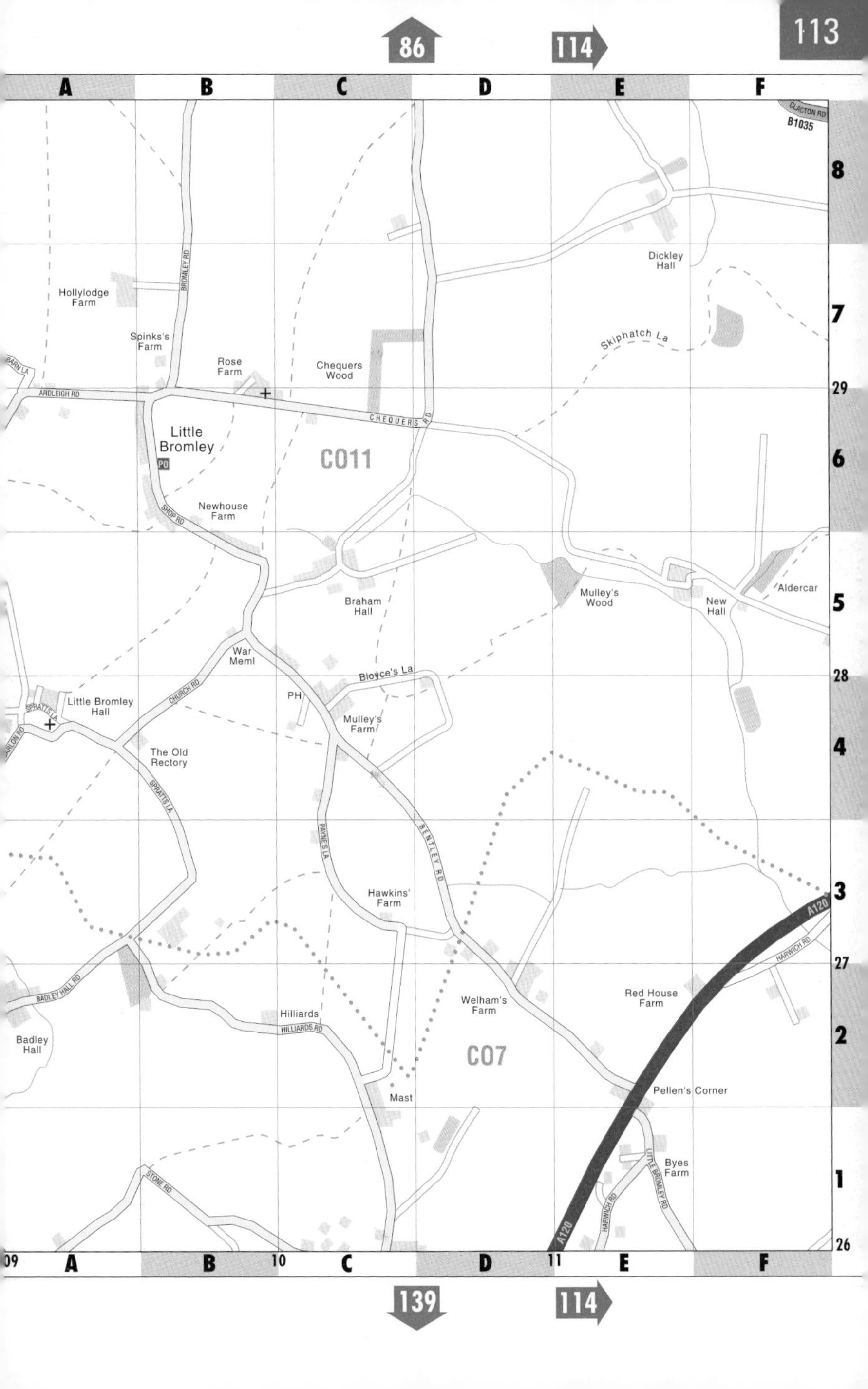
86
114
A
B
C
D
E
F
CLACTON RD
B1035
8
Dickley Hall
Hollylodge Farm
BROMLEY RD
7
Skiphatch La
Spinks's Farm
BARN LA
Rose Farm
Chequers Wood
29
ARDLEIGH RD
CHEQUERS RD
Little Bromley
PO
CO11
6
Newhouse Farm
SHOP RD
Mulley's Wood
Aldercar
Braham Hall
New Hall
5
War Meml
Bloyce's La
28
PH
Little Bromley Hall
SPRATTS LA
CHURCH RD
Mulley's Farm
The Old Rectory
4
SPRATTS LA
PAYNE'S LA
BENTLEY RD
Hawkins' Farm
3
A120
HARWICH RD
27
BADLEY HALL RD
Welham's Farm
Red House Farm
Hilliards
HILLIARDS RD
2
Badley Hall
CO7
Pellen's Corner
Mast
Byes Farm
1
LITTLE BROMLEY RD
STONE RD
HARWICH RD
A120
26
09
10
11
139
114

113
87

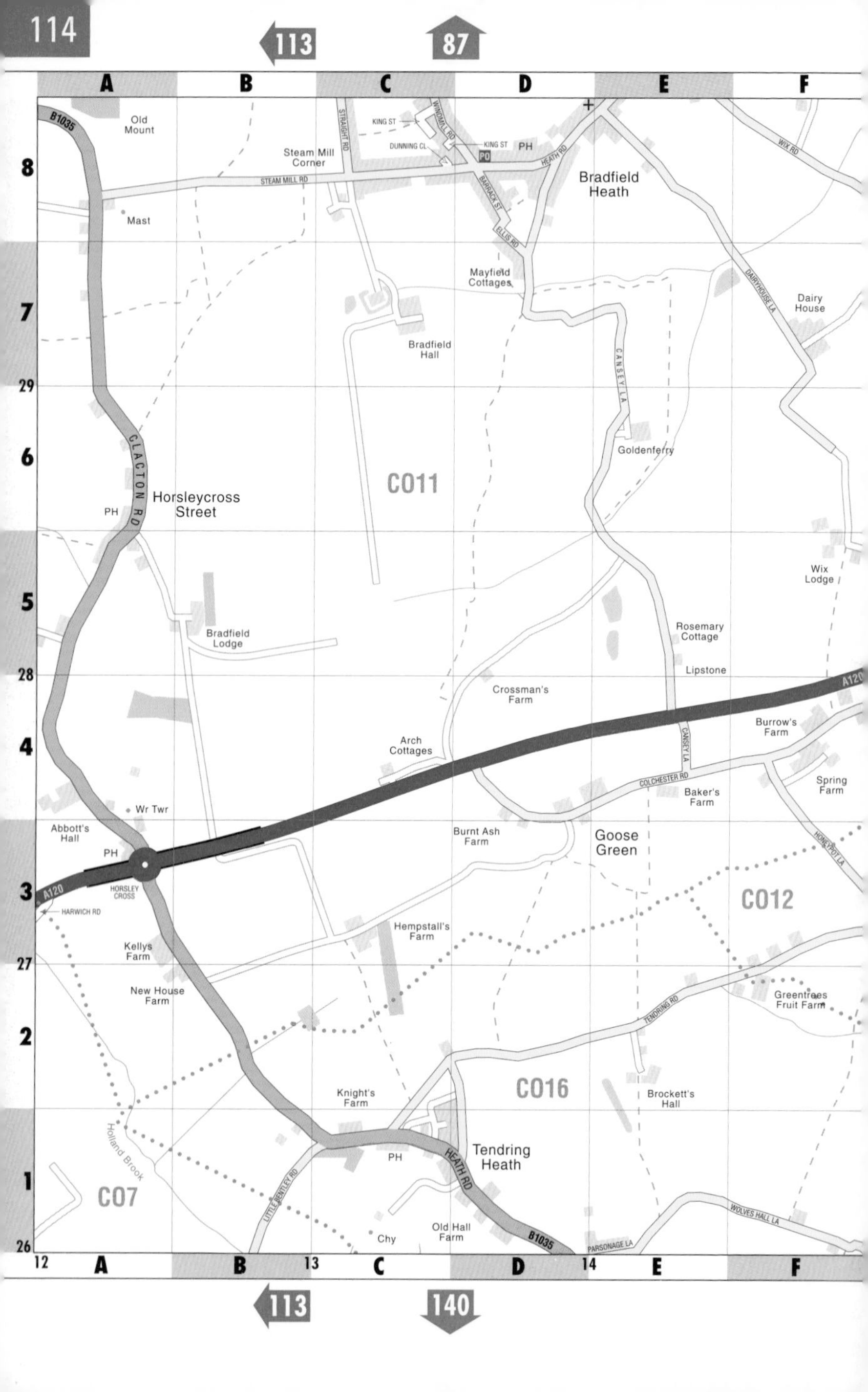
A
B
C
D
E
F
8
7
29
6
5
28
4
3
27
2
1
26
12
13
14
B1035
Old Mount
Steam Mill Corner
STRAIGHT RD
KING ST
DUNNING CL
WINDMILL RD
KING ST
PH
PO
HEATH RD
STEAM MILL RD
BARRACK ST
Bradfield Heath
WIX RD
Mast
ELLIS RD
Mayfield Cottages
DAIRYHOUSE LA
Dairy House
Bradfield Hall
CANSEY LA
Goldenferry
CLACTON RD
CO11
Horsleycross Street
PH
Wix Lodge
Bradfield Lodge
Rosemary Cottage
Lipstone
A120
Crossman's Farm
Burrow's Farm
Arch Cottages
CANSEY LA
Spring Farm
COLCHESTER RD
Baker's Farm
Wr Twr
Abbott's Hall
Burnt Ash Farm
Goose Green
PH
HONEYPOT LA
A120
HORSLEY CROSS
HARWICH RD
CO12
Hempstall's Farm
Kellys Farm
New House Farm
TENDRING RD
Greentrees Fruit Farm
CO16
Knight's Farm
Brockett's Hall
Holland Brook
PH
Tendring Heath
HEATH RD
LITTLE BENTLEY RD
CO7
WOLVES HALL LA
Chy
Old Hall Farm
B1035
PARSONAGE LA

113
140

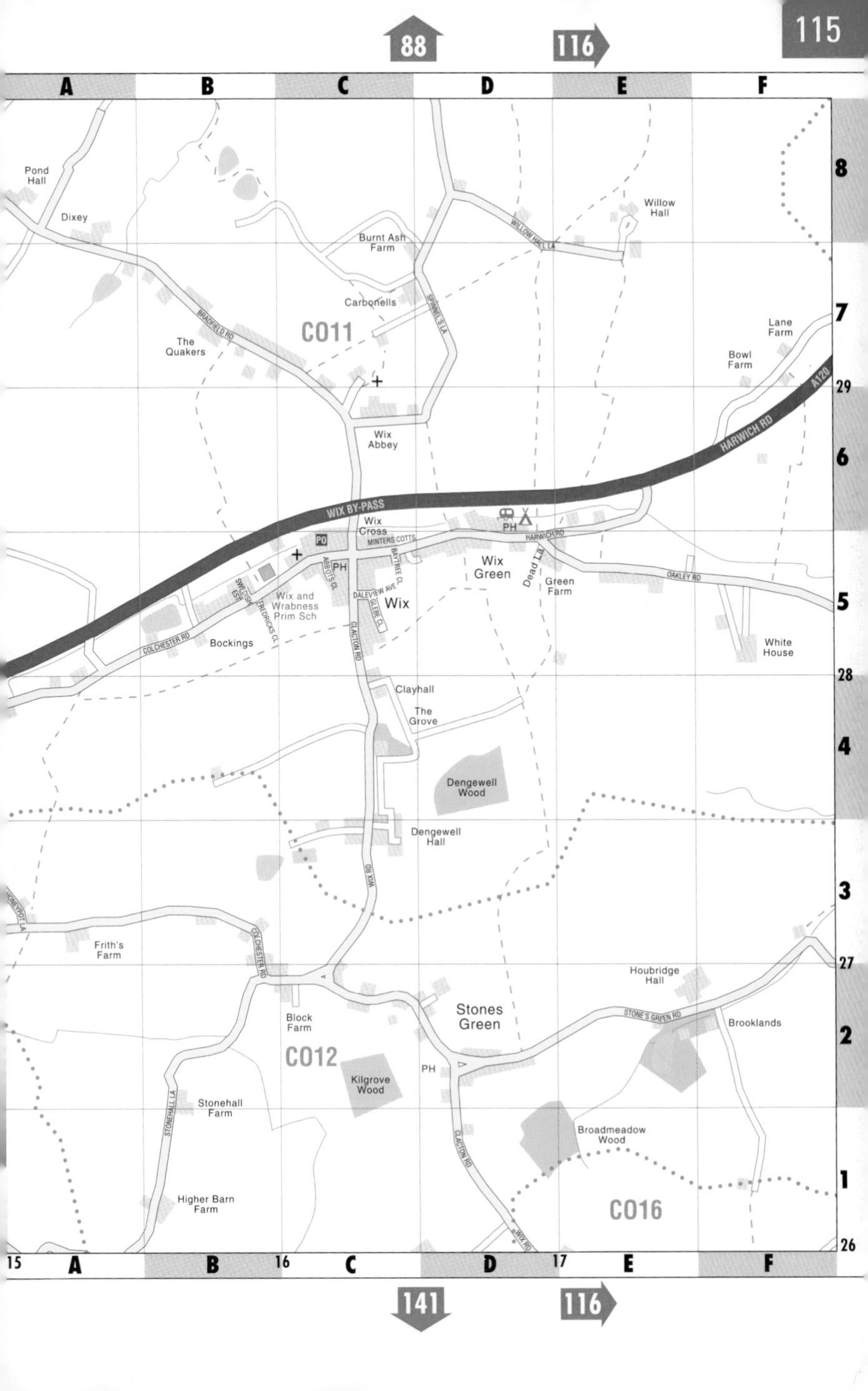

88
116

8

Pond Hall

Dixey

Willow Hall

Burnt Ash Farm

Carbonells

CO11

7

Lane Farm

The Quakers

BRADFIELD RD

SPRING ST LA

WILLOW PACE LA

Bowl Farm

29

A120

Wix Abbey

+

HARWICH RD

6

WIX BY-PASS

Wix Cross

MINTERS COTTS

PH

HARWICH RD

Wix Green

Dead La

Green Farm

OAKLEY RD

PO

PH

MINTERS CL

PARTRIDGE CL

Wix and Wrabness Prim Sch

SPRINGFIELD ESTATE

+

DALE VIEW AVE CL

CLACTON RD

Wix

5

White House

COLCHESTER RD

Bockings

28

Clayhall

The Grove

4

Dengewell Wood

THE HAM

Dengewell Hall

3

27

DORCHESTER LA

Frith's Farm

COLCHESTER RD

Houbridge Hall

Block Farm

Stones Green

STONE'S GREEN RD

Brooklands

2

CO12

Kilgrove Wood

PH

CLACTON RD

Broadmeadow Wood

Stonehall Farm

HILL THORNS RD

Higher Barn Farm

1

CO16

BULL'S RD

26

141
116

115
89

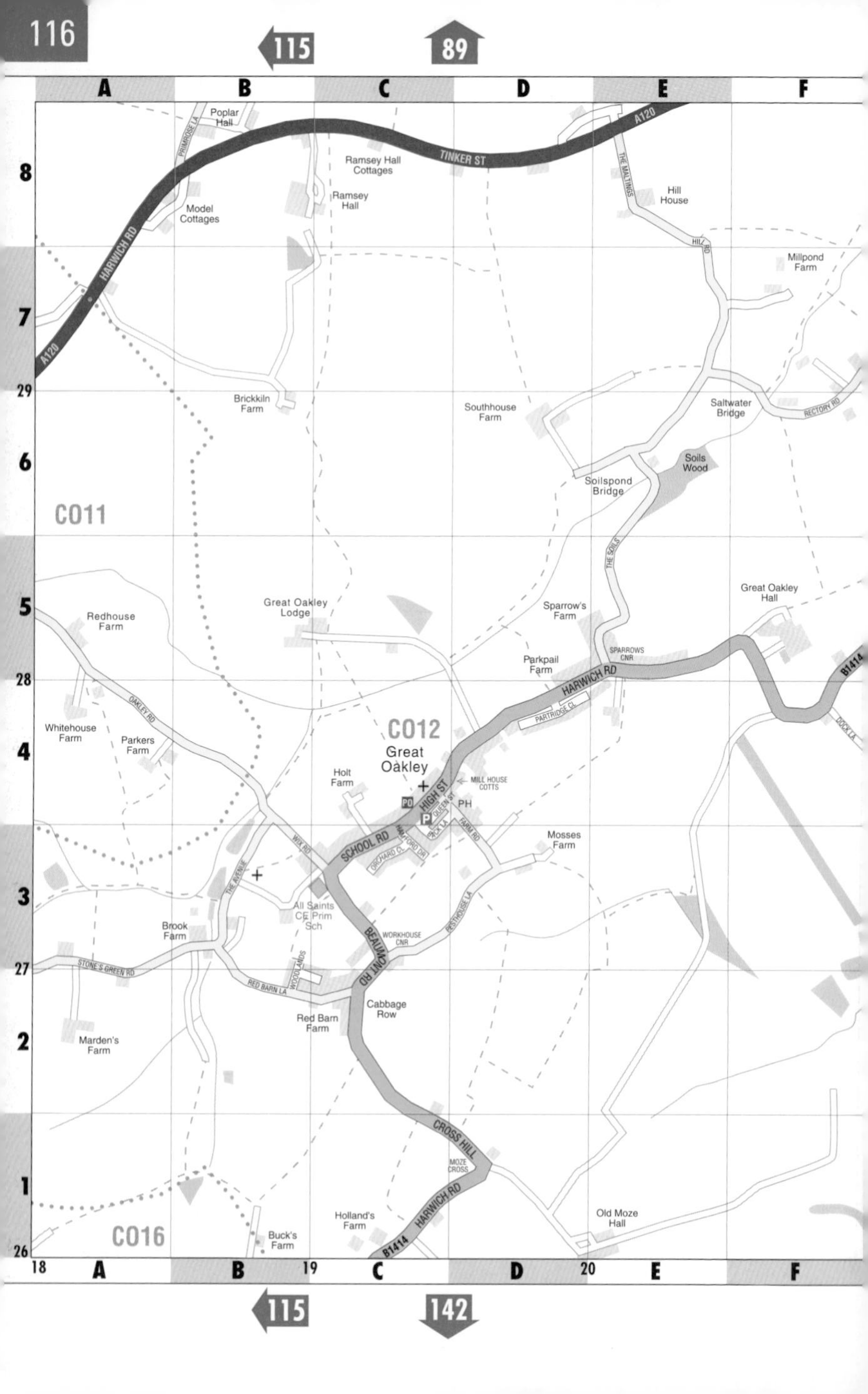
A
B
C
D
E
F
8
7
29
6
5
28
4
3
27
2
1
26
18
19
20
Poplar Hall
PRIMROSE LA
TINKER ST
A120
Ramsey Hall Cottages
Ramsey Hall
THE MALTINGS
Hill House
Model Cottages
HARWICH RD
HILL RD
Millpond Farm
A120
Brickkiln Farm
Southhouse Farm
Saltwater Bridge
RECTORY RD
Soils Wood
Soilspond Bridge
CO11
THE SOILS
Great Oakley Hall
Great Oakley Lodge
Sparrow's Farm
Redhouse Farm
SPARROWS CNR
Parkpail Farm
HARWICH RD
B1414
OAKLEY RD
PARTRIDGE CL
DOCK LA
Whitehouse Farm
Parkers Farm
CO12
Great Oakley
Holt Farm
MILL HOUSE COTTS
HIGH ST
PH
QUEEN ST
WIX RD
SCHOOL RD
HALFORD DR
BACK LA
FARM RD
Mosses Farm
ORCHARD CL
THE AVENUE
All Saints CE Prim Sch
BEAUMONT RD
PESTHOUSE LA
WORKHOUSE CNR
Brook Farm
STONE'S GREEN RD
WOODLANDS
RED BARN LA
Cabbage Row
Red Barn Farm
Marden's Farm
CROSS HILL
MOZE CROSS
HARWICH RD
Holland's Farm
Old Moze Hall
CO16
Buck's Farm
B1414

115
142

90

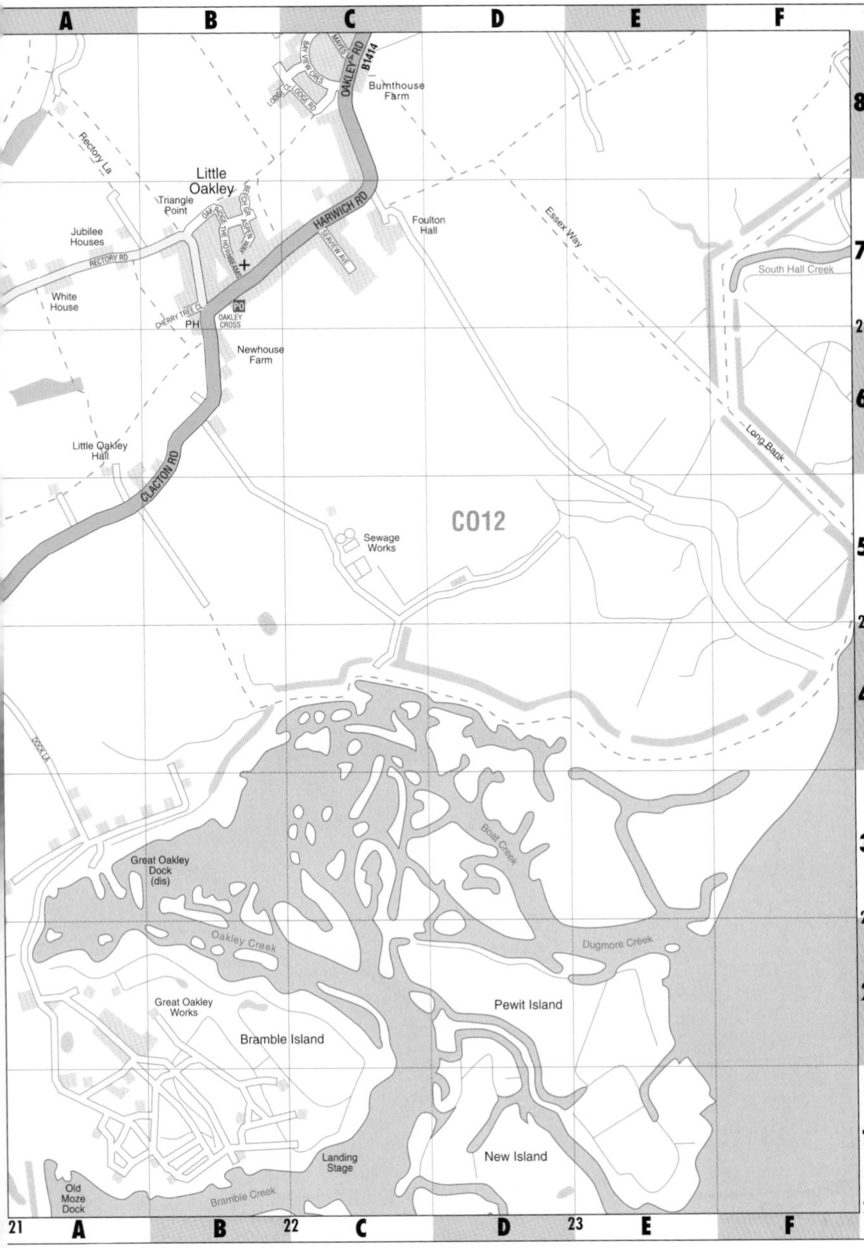

A
B
C
D
E
F
8
7
29
6
5
28
4
3
27
2
1
26
21
22
23
MAYES LA
BAY VIEW CRES
LODGE CL
LODGE RD
OAKLEY RD
B1414
Burnthouse Farm
Rectory La
Little Oakley
Triangle Point
BEECH GR
ASPEN WAY
OAK RIDGE
THE HORNBEAMS
HARWICH RD
SEAVIEW AVE
Foulton Hall
Essex Way
Jubilee Houses
RECTORY RD
White House
CHERRY TREE CL
PH
PO
OAKLEY CROSS
Newhouse Farm
South Hall Creek
Long Bank
Little Oakley Hall
CLACTON RD
CO12
Sewage Works
DOCK LA
Boat Creek
Great Oakley Dock (dis)
Oakley Creek
Dugmore Creek
Pewit Island
Great Oakley Works
Bramble Island
New Island
Landing Stage
Old Moze Dock
Bramble Creek

143

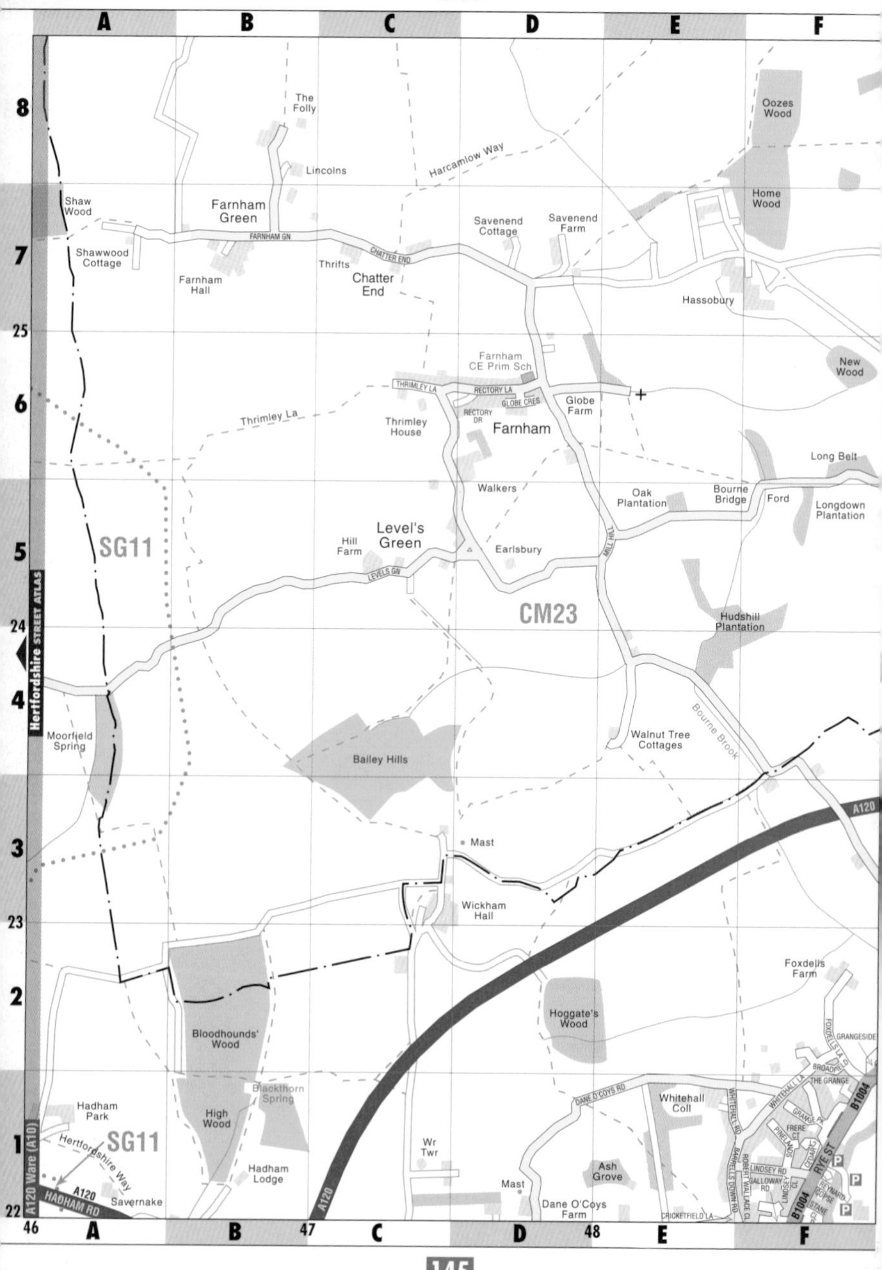

A **B** **C** **D** **E** **F**

8

7

25

6

5

24

4

3

23

2

1

22

Hertfordshire STREET ATLAS

Oozes Wood

The Folly

Lincolns

Home Wood

Harcamlow Way

Shaw Wood

Farnham Green

Savenend Cottage

Savenend Farm

Shawwood Cottage

FARNHAM GN

CHATTER END

Thrifts

Hassobury

New Wood

Farnham Hall

Chatter End

Farnham CE Prim Sch

THRIMLEY LA

RECTORY LA

GLOBE CRES

Thrimley La.

Thrimley House

RECTORY DR

Farnham

Globe Farm

Long Belt

Walkers

Oak Plantation

Bourne Bridge

Ford

Longdown Plantation

SG11

Level's Green

Hill Farm

Earlsbury

MILL END

CM23

Hudshill Plantation

Moorfield Spring

Walnut Tree Cottages

Bourne Brook

Bailey Hills

A120

Mast

Wickham Hall

Foxdells Farm

Bloodhounds' Wood

Hoggate's Wood

GRANGESIDE

THE GRANGE

BROADLEAF

WHITEHALL LA.

B1004

Hadham Park

Blackthorn Spring

SG11

High Wood

Wr Twr

Whitehall Coll

WHITEHALL RD

FRERE

Hertfordshire Way

Hadham Lodge

Mast

Ash Grove

LINDSEY RD

GALLOWAY RD

PYE ST

P

A120 Ware (A10)

HADHAM RD

Savernake

Dane O'Coys Farm

DANE O'COYS RD

CRICKFIELD LA.

B1004

P

P

46 **A** **B** 47 **C** **D** 48 **E** **F**

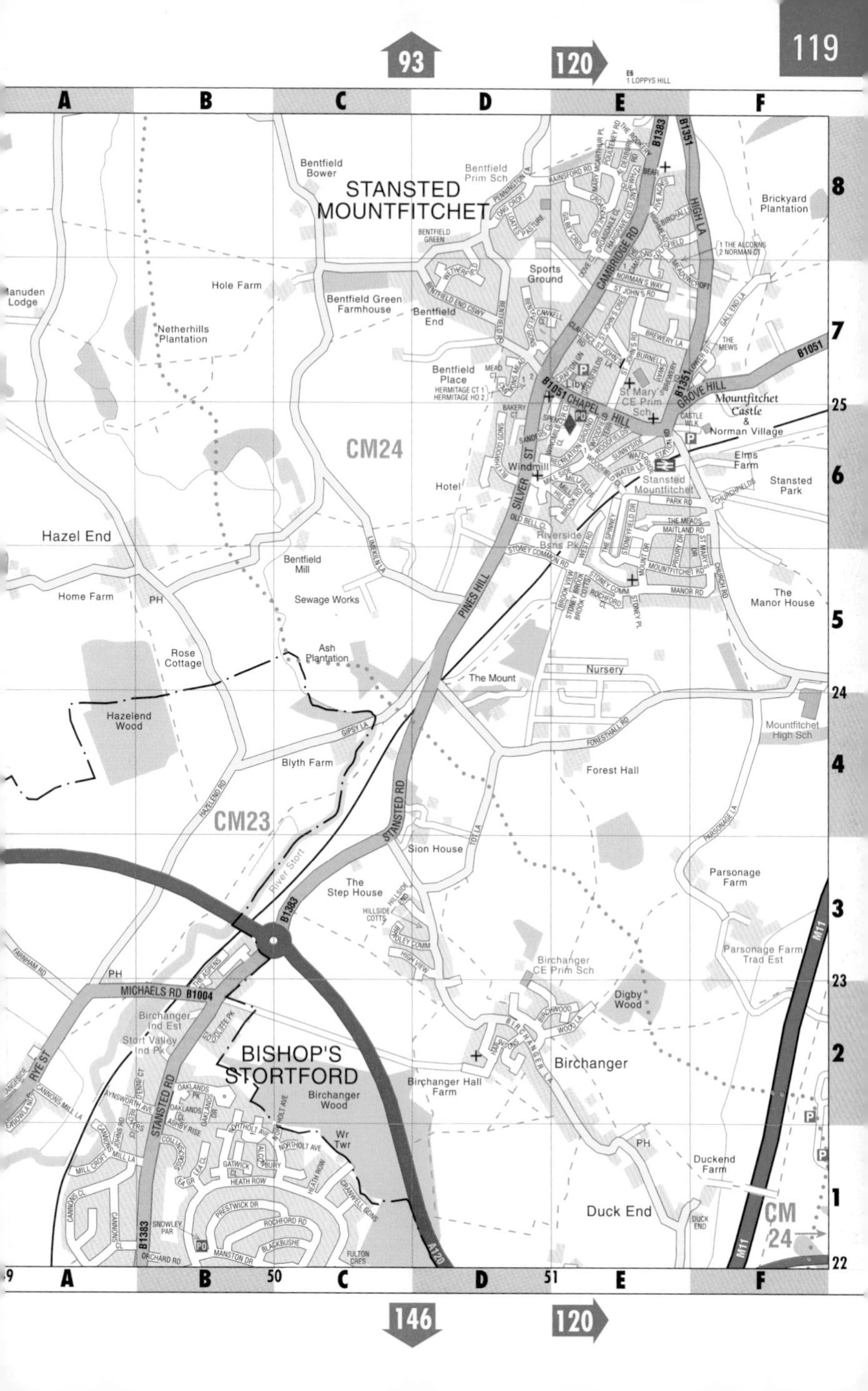
93
120
E6
1 LOPPYS HILL
STANSTED MOUNTFITCHET
Bentfield Bower
Bentfield Prim Sch
Brickyard Plantation
Hole Farm
Bentfield Green Farmhouse
Bentfield End
Sports Ground
Netherhills Plantation
Bentfield Place
Mountfitchet Castle & Norman Village
CM24
Elms Farm
Stansted Park
Hotel
Windmill
Stansted Mountfitchet
Hazel End
Bentfield Mill
Riverside Bsns Pk
Home Farm
PH
Sewage Works
The Manor House
Rose Cottage
Ash Plantation
The Mount
Nursery
Hazelend Wood
Mountfitchet High Sch
Blyth Farm
Forest Hall
CM23
Sion House
Parsonage Farm
The Step House
Parsonage Farm Trad Est
Birchanger CE Prim Sch
Digby Wood
BISHOP'S STORTFORD
Birchanger
Birchanger Hall Farm
Birchanger Wood
Birchanger Ind Est
Stort Valley Ind Pk
Duckend Farm
Duck End
CM 24
146
120

119
94

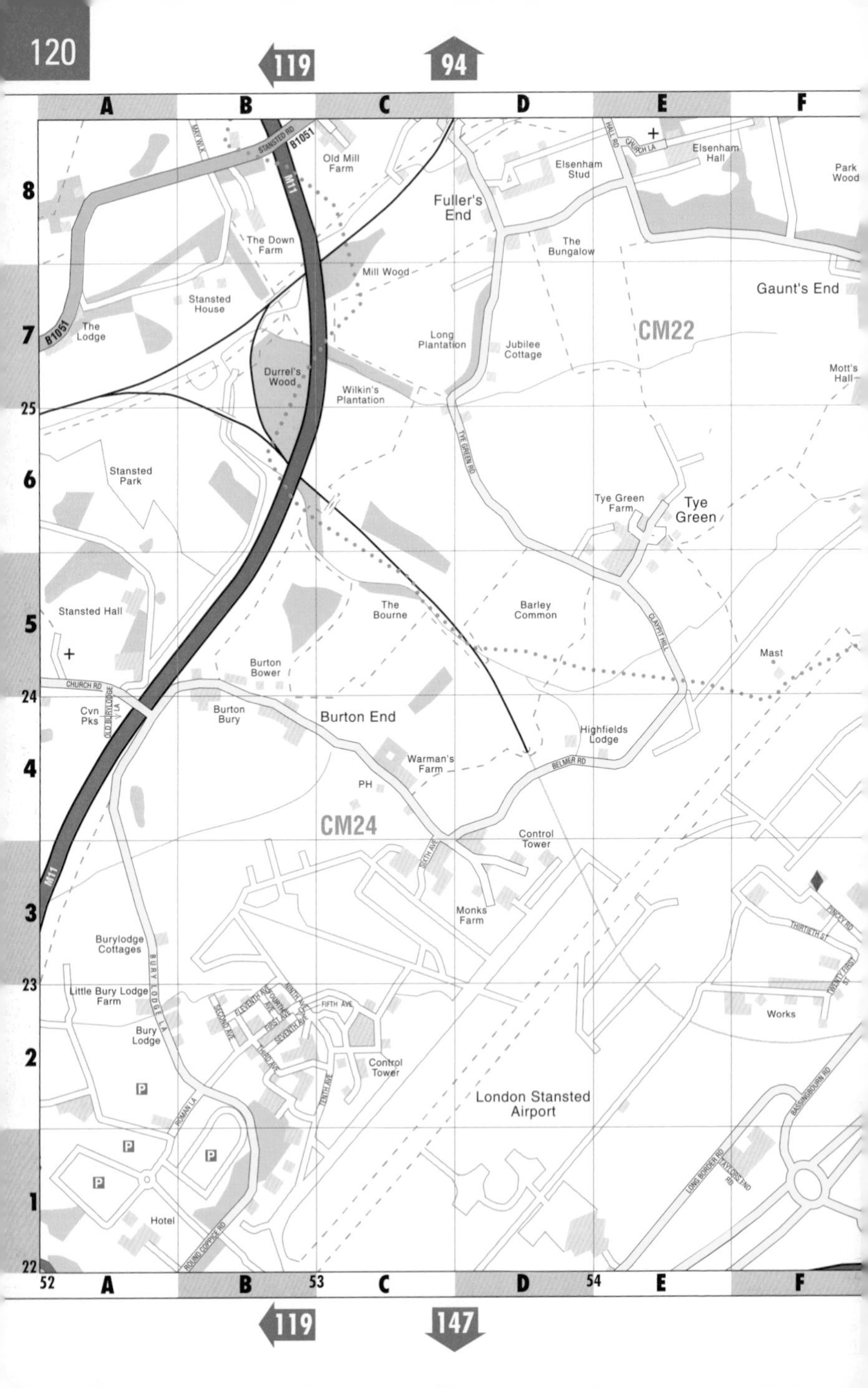
Old Mill Farm
Elsenham Stud
Elsenham Hall
Park Wood
Fuller's End
The Down Farm
The Bungalow
Mill Wood
Gaunt's End
Stansted House
The Lodge
Long Plantation
Jubilee Cottage
CM22
Durrel's Wood
Wilkin's Plantation
Mott's Hall
Stansted Park
Tye Green Farm
Tye Green
Stansted Hall
The Bourne
Barley Common
Mast
Burton Bower
Burton Bury
Burton End
Highfields Lodge
Cvn Pks
Warman's Farm
PH
CM24
Control Tower
Monks Farm
Burylodge Cottages
Little Bury Lodge Farm
Bury Lodge
Control Tower
Works
London Stansted Airport
Hotel
B1051
STANSTED RD
M11
MAY WLK
HALL RD
CHURCH LA
TYE GREEN RD
CLAYPIT HILL
BELMER RD
CHURCH RD
OLD BURYLODGE LA
SIXTH AVE
PINCEY RD
THIRTIETH ST
TWENTY FIRST ST
BURY LODGE LA
ELEVENTH AVE
FOURTH AVE
NINTH AVE
FIFTH AVE
FIRST AVE
SEVENTH AVE
SECOND AVE
THIRD AVE
TENTH AVE
ROMAN LA
ROUND COPPICE RD
BASSINGBOURN RD
LONG BORDER RD
TAYLORS END RD
A
B
C
D
E
F
8
7
6
5
4
3
2
1
25
24
23
22
52
53
54

119
147

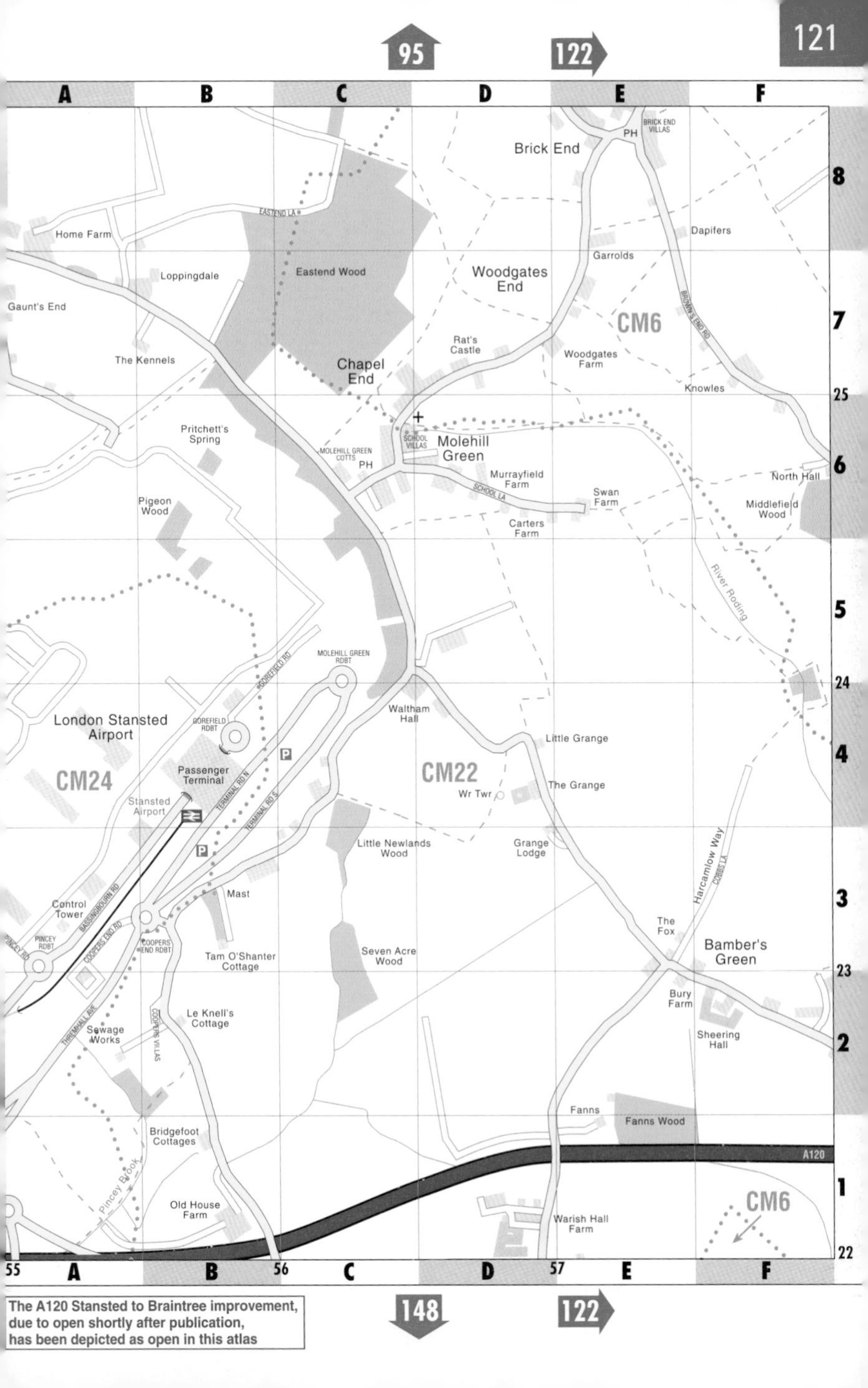

95
122

| A | B | C | D | E | F |

8

Brick End

PH

BRICK END VILLAS

Home Farm

EASTEND LA

Loppingdale

Eastend Wood

Dapifers

Woodgates End

Garrolds

Gaunt's End

CM6

7

The Kennels

Rat's Castle

Chapel End

Woodgates Farm

Knowles

25

Pritchett's Spring

SCHOOL VILLAS

Molehill Green

MOLEHILL GREEN COTTS

PH

6

North Hall

Pigeon Wood

Murrayfield Farm

SCHOOL LA

Swan Farm

Middlefield Wood

Carters Farm

5

River Roding

MOLEHILL GREEN RDBT

DOSPERS END RD

24

London Stansted Airport

GOREFIELD RDBT

Waltham Hall

Little Grange

4

CM24

Passenger Terminal

TERMINAL RD E

CM22

The Grange

P

Stansted Airport

TERMINAL RD S

Wr Twr

Little Newlands Wood

Grange Lodge

Harcamlow Way

COBES LA

3

Control Tower

MASONBOURGH RD

P

Mast

COOPERS WEND RDBT

The Fox

Bamber's Green

PINCEY RDBT

COOPERS END RD

Tam O'Shanter Cottage

Seven Acre Wood

23

Bury Farm

COOPERS VILLAS

THREMHALL RD

Le Knell's Cottage

Sheering Hall

2

Sewage Works

Bridgefoot Cottages

Fanns

Fanns Wood

A120

1

PINCEY BROOK

Old House Farm

Warish Hall Farm

CM6

22

| A | B | C | D | E | F |

55 56 57

148
122

The A120 Stansted to Braintree improvement, due to open shortly after publication, has been depicted as open in this atlas

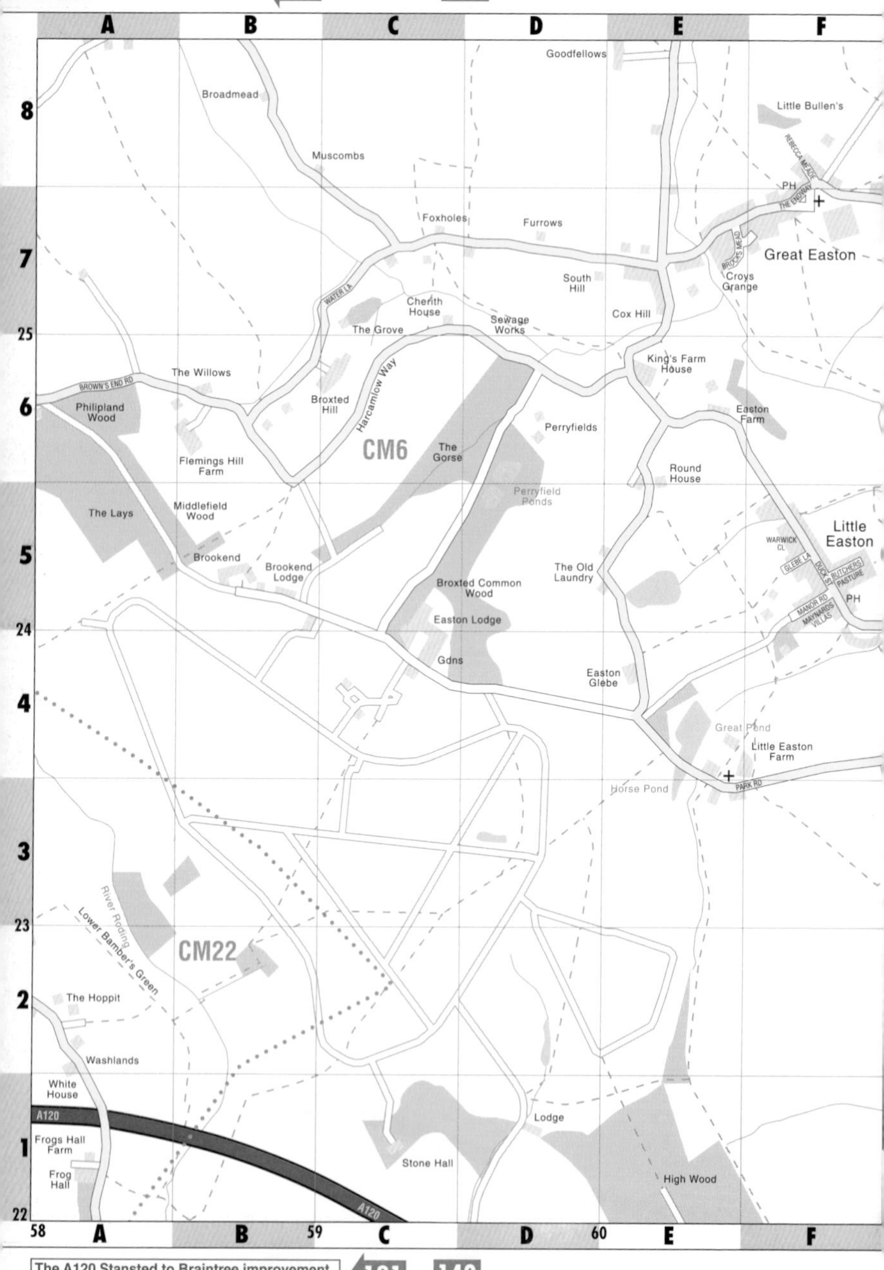

The A120 Stansted to Braintree improvement, due to open shortly after publication, has been depicted as open in this atlas

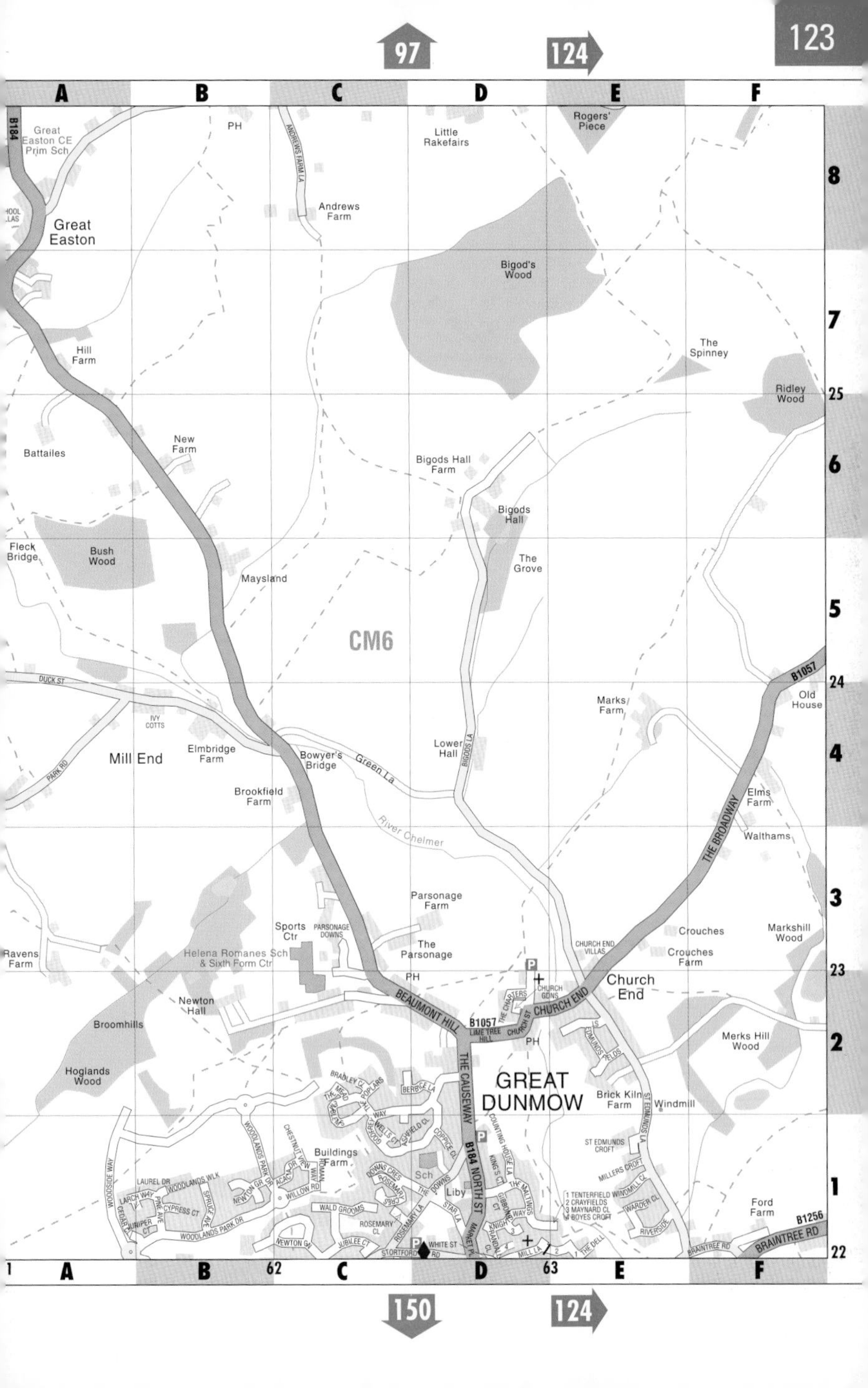
97
124
A B C D E F
Great Easton CE Prim Sch
PH
Little Rakefairs
Rogers' Piece
Andrews Farm
Great Easton
Bigod's Wood
Hill Farm
The Spinney
Ridley Wood
Battailes
New Farm
Bigods Hall Farm
Bigods Hall
Fleck Bridge
Bush Wood
The Grove
Maysland
CM6
Duck St
Marks Farm
Old House
Ivy Cotts
Mill End
Elmbridge Farm
Bowyer's Bridge
Green La
Lower Hall
Bigods La
Park Rd
Brookfield Farm
Elms Farm
River Chelmer
Walthams
The Broadway
Parsonage Farm
Sports Ctr
Parsonage Downs
Crouches
Markshill Wood
Ravens Farm
Helena Romanes Sch & Sixth Form Ctr
The Parsonage
Church End Villas
Crouches Farm
Church End
Newton Hall
Beaumont Hill
B1057
Lime Tree Hill
Church St
Broomhills
Merks Hill Wood
Hoglands Wood
The Causeway
GREAT DUNMOW
Brick Kiln Farm
Windmill
St Edmunds La
St Edmunds Croft
Buildings Farm
Sch
Millers Croft
Liby
B184 North St
1 Tenterfield
2 Crayfields
3 Maynard Cl
4 Boyes Croft
Ford Farm
B1256
Braintree Rd
Woodlands Park Dr
Woodside Way
Laurel Dr
Woodlands Wlk
Cypress Ct
Larch Way
Pine Ave
Spruce Ave
Juniper Ct
Cedar Ct
Newton Gn
Wald Grooms
Rosemary Cl
Rosemary La
Jubilee Ct
Stortford Rd
White St
Market Pl
Mill La
The Dell
Riverside
Warder Cl
Windmill Cl
The Maltings
Counting House La
King's Ct
Star La
The Downs
Coppice Cl
Ashfield Cl
Berbice La
Bradley Cl
The Mead
The Poplars
Willow Rd
Chestnut View
Newton Gr
Acacia Dr
Braintree Rd
St Edmunds Fields
The Charters
Church Gdns
B184
B1057
8 7 6 5 4 3 2 1
25 24 23 22
62 63
150
124

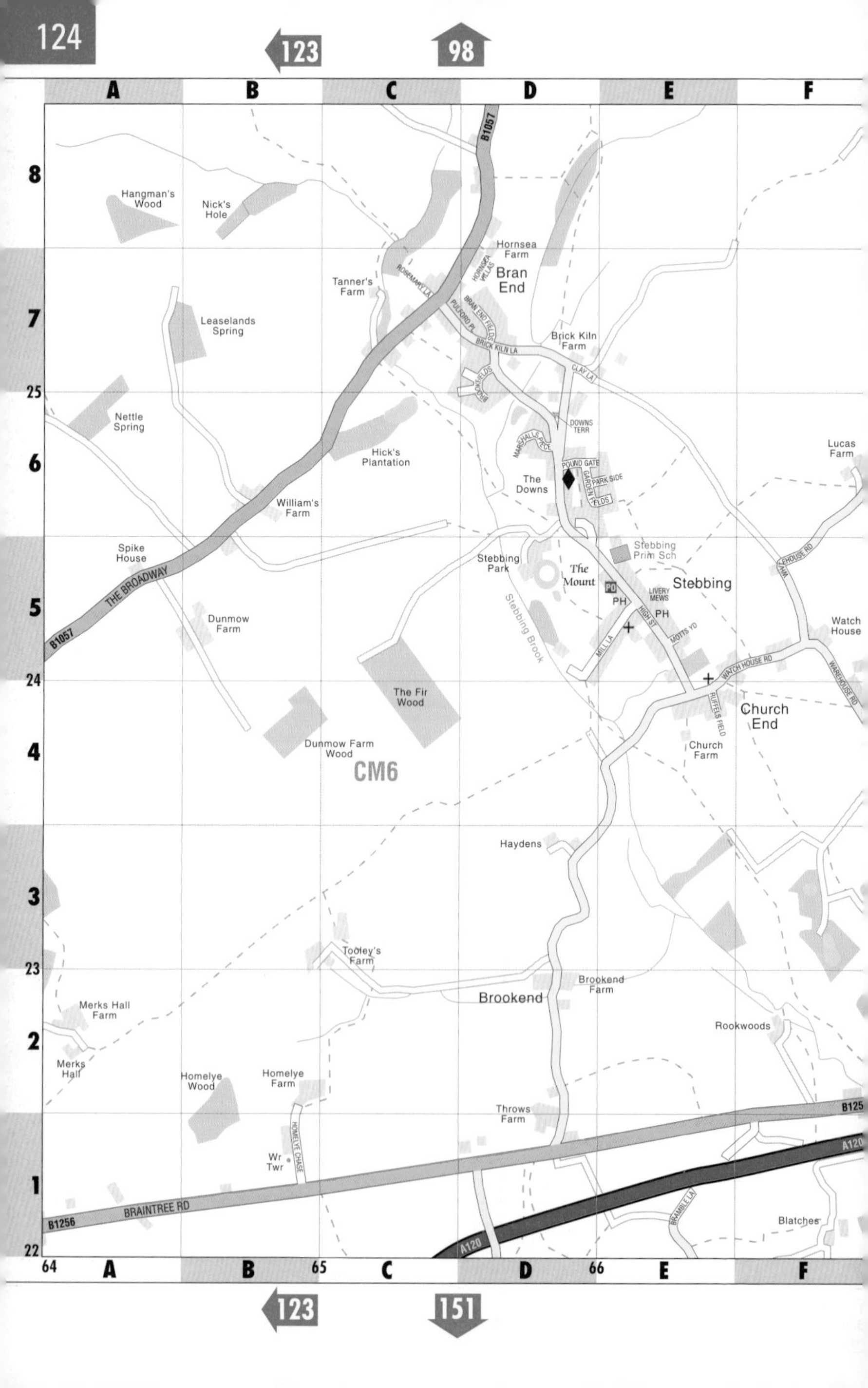
Hangman's Wood
Nick's Hole
Hornsea Farm
Bran End
Tanner's Farm
Leaselands Spring
Brick Kiln Farm
Nettle Spring
Hick's Plantation
The Downs
Lucas Farm
William's Farm
Spike House
Stebbing Prim Sch
Stebbing Park
The Mount
Stebbing
Dunmow Farm
Watch House
Stebbing Brook
The Fir Wood
Church End
Dunmow Farm Wood
Church Farm
CM6
Haydens
Tooley's Farm
Brookend
Brookend Farm
Merks Hall Farm
Rookwoods
Merks Hall
Homelye Wood
Homelye Farm
Throws Farm
Wr Twr
Blatches
B1057
THE BROADWAY
ROSEMARY LA
HORNSEA VILLAS
BRAN END FIELDS
PULFORD PL
BRICK KILN LA
CLAY LA
BROOKFIELDS
DOWNS TERR
MARSHALLS PIECE
POUND GATE
GARDEN FLDS
PARK SIDE
LIVERY MEWS
HIGH ST
MOTTS YD
MILL LA
WATCH HOUSE RD
RUFFELS FIELD
WAREHOUSE RD
PO
PH
B1256
BRAINTREE RD
HOMELYE CHASE
BRAMBLE LA
A120
B125
8
7
25
6
5
24
4
3
23
2
1
22
64
65
66

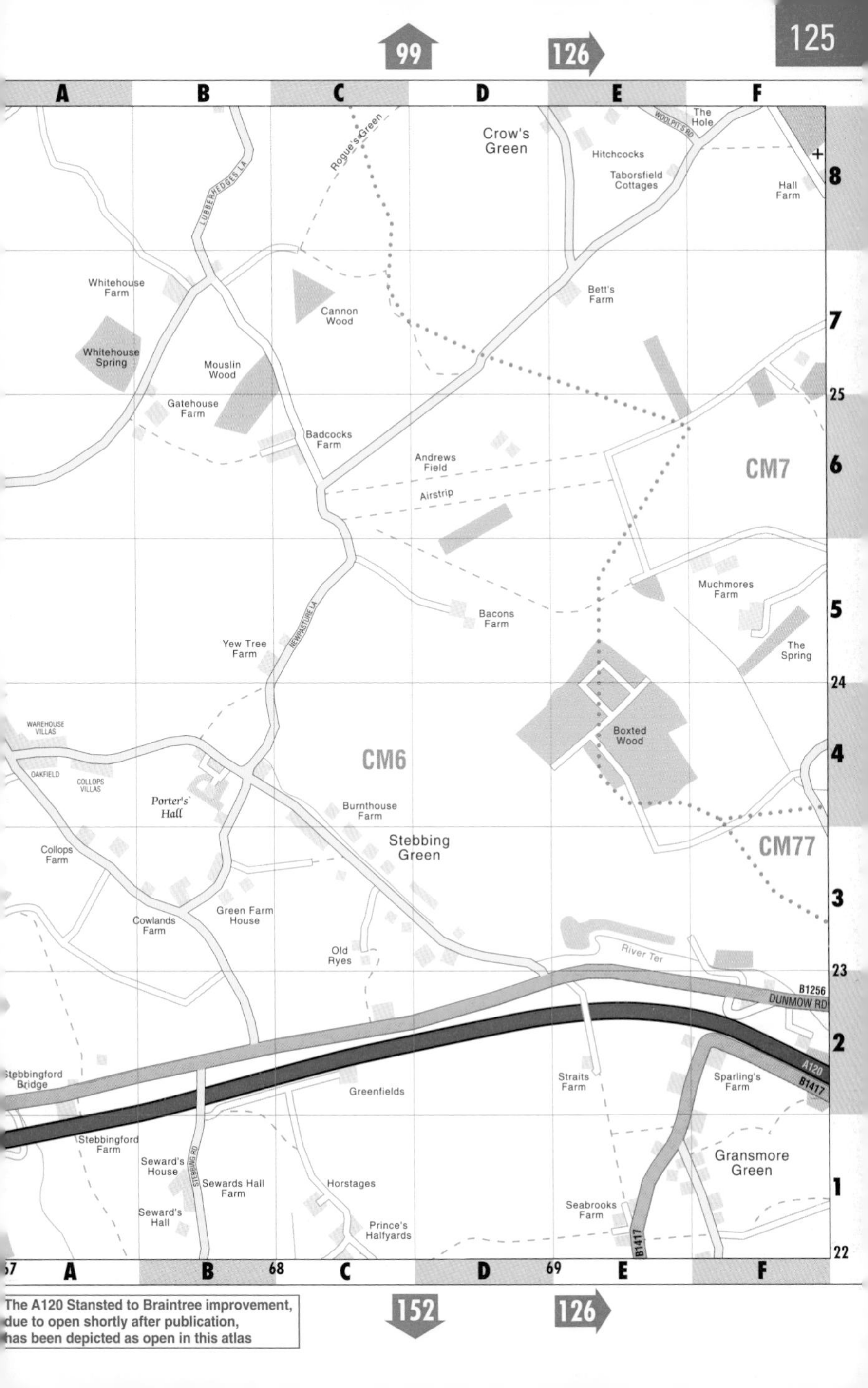

A	B	C	D	E	F

8

Crow's Green

The Hole
WOOLPITS RD

Hitchcocks
Taborsfield
Cottages

Hall
Farm

+

Whitehouse
Farm

LIEBERSPREGELS LN

Rogue's Green

Bett's
Farm

7

25

Whitehouse
Spring

Mouslin
Wood

Cannon
Wood

Gatehouse
Farm

Badcocks
Farm

Andrews
Field

Airstrip

CM7

6

Bacons
Farm

Muchmores
Farm

The
Spring

5

Yew Tree
Farm

KEWSFIELD LA

24

WAREHOUSE
VILLAS

Boxted
Wood

4

OAKFIELD

COLLOPS
VILLAS

Porter's
Hall

CM6

Burnthouse
Farm

Stebbing
Green

CM77

Collops
Farm

3

Cowlands
Farm

Green Farm
House

Old
Ryes

River Ter

23

B1256
DUNMOW RD

Stebbingford
Bridge

Straits
Farm

Sparling's
Farm

A120

B1417

2

Stebbingford
Farm

Greenfields

Gransmore
Green

Seward's
House

Sewards Hall
Farm

Horstages

Seabrooks
Farm

1

Seward's
Hall

Prince's
Halfyards

B1417

22

A	B	C	D	E	F

67   68   69

The A120 Stansted to Braintree improvement,
due to open shortly after publication,
has been depicted as open in this atlas

	A	B	C	D	E	F

8

Saling Hall Gardens
Great Saling
GROVE VILLAS
PO
Cold Hall Farm
Ivy Hall
KYNASTON RD
PH
THE MEWS
PICCOTTS LA
Piccotts Farm
Chapel Hill
Kynaston's Farm

7

Saling Grove
CM7
HALL RD

25

Mount's Farm
Lightwaters Farm
Perry Childs Farm

6

CM7
New Spinney
Jubilee Spinney
Park's Farm

5

Onchor's Farm
Golden Grove
Old Hall
POD'S BROOK

24

Rumley Wood

4

3

Blackbush Wood
Blake House Farm
Craft Ctr
Moor's Farm
Pound Farm
Pound Farmhouse
Gould's Farm
Duckend Green
MOORS LA
Moor's Spinney
CM77
SHALFORD RD
Rayne Prim Sch

23

Rayne
B1256
PH
B1417
DUNMOW RD
POD'S LA
Havering's Farm

2

Blake End
A120
B1417
Broadfield Farm
THE STREET
B1256

1

CM6
Hazelmere Farm
Gatewoods Farm
Fairy Hall
Little Paddocks
DUNMOW RD
A120

22

Graunt Courts
Sorrell's Farm
MILL LA
DRAPERS CHASE

| 70 | A | B | 71 | C | D | 72 | E | F |

The A120 Stansted to Braintree improvement, due to open shortly after publication, has been depicted as open in this atlas

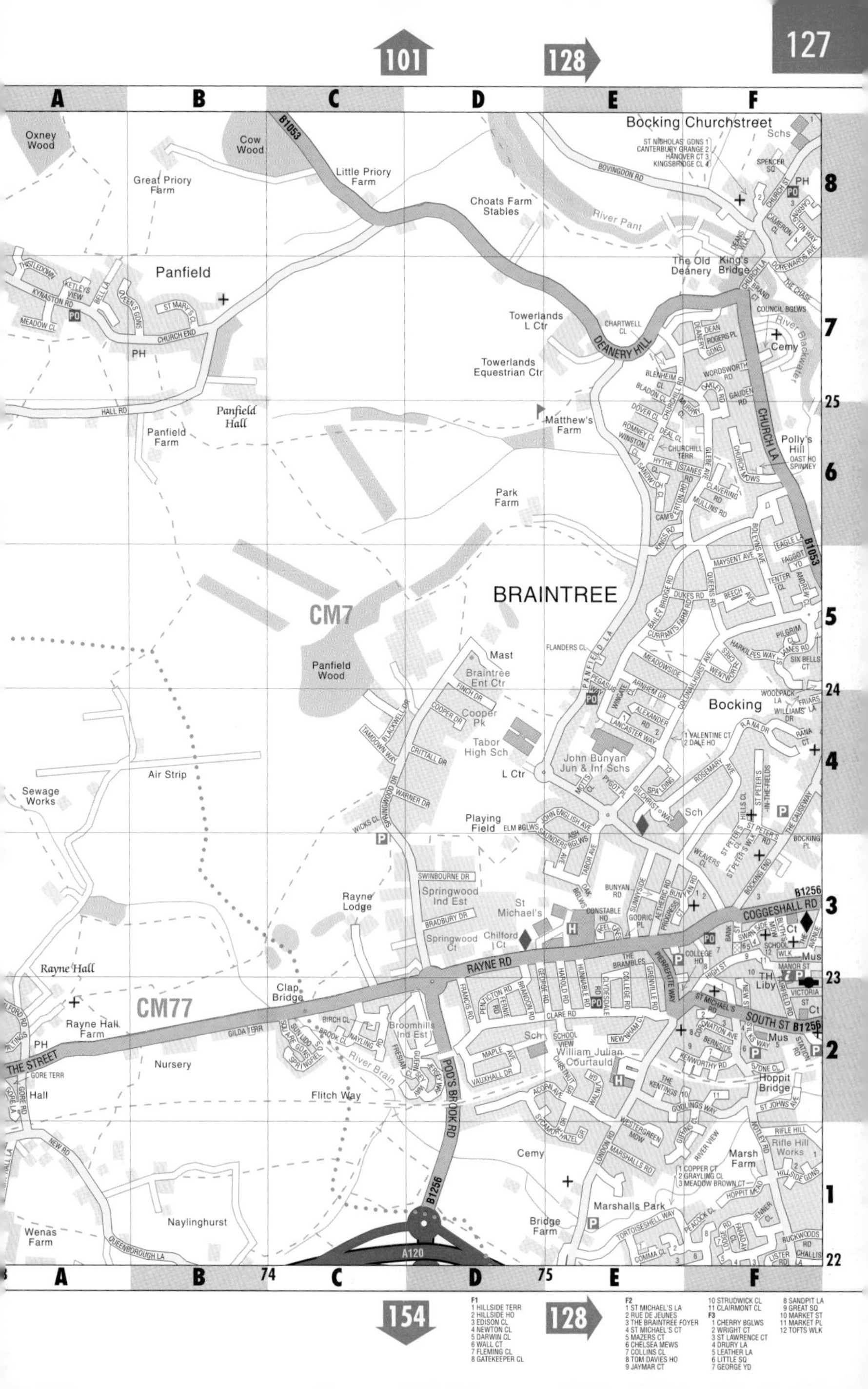

101 128 154 128

BRAINTREE

CM7

CM77

Bocking Churchstreet

Bocking

Panfield

127
102

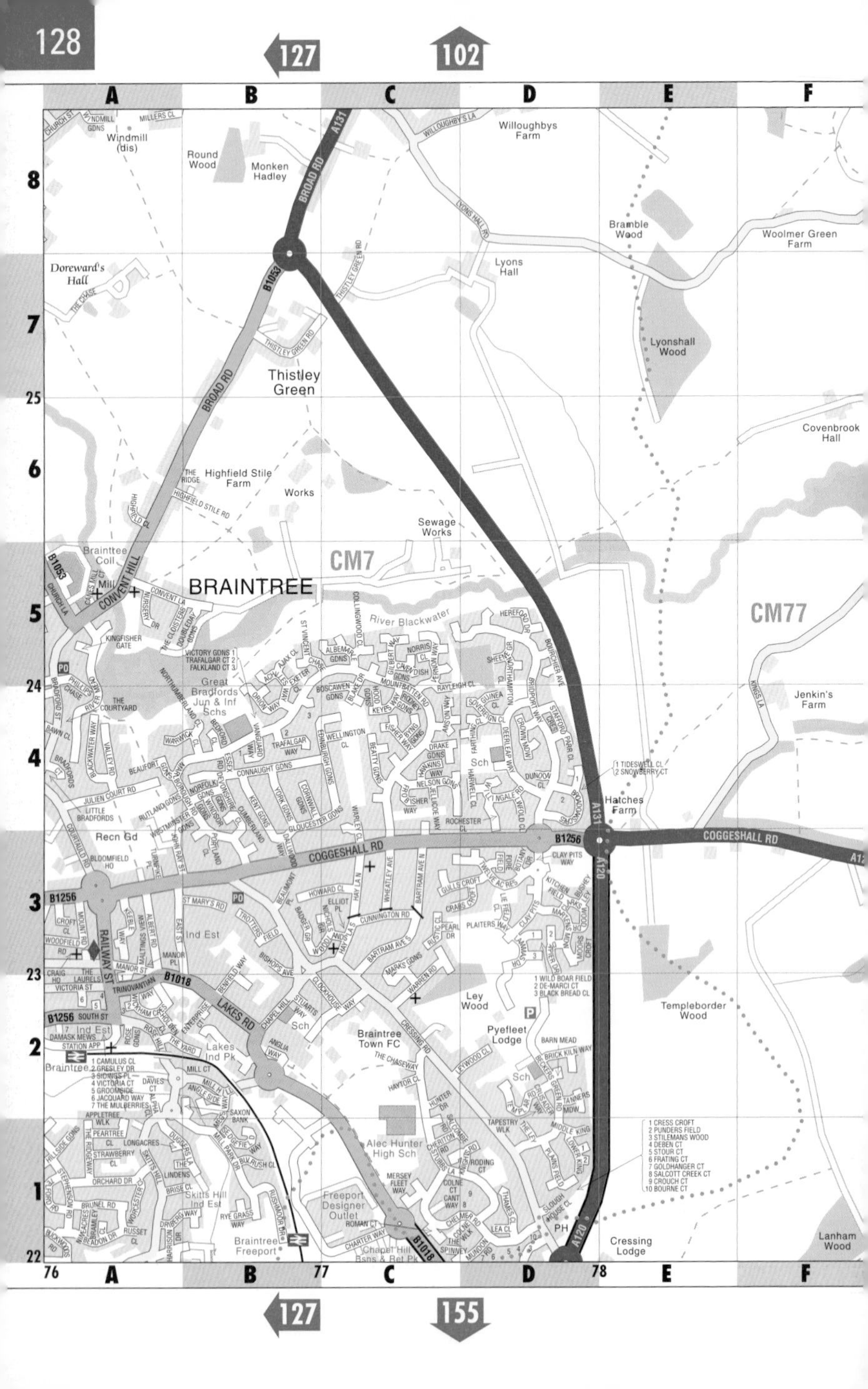
A
B
C
D
E
F
8
7
25
6
5
24
4
3
23
2
1
22
76
77
78
Windmill (dis)
Round Wood
Monken Hadley
BROAD RD
A131
Willoughbys Farm
WILLOUGHBYS LA
LYONS HALL RD
Bramble Wood
Woolmer Green Farm
Doreward's Hall
THE CHASE
B1053
THISTLEY GREEN RD
Lyons Hall
Lyonshall Wood
Thistley Green
Covenbrook Hall
Highfield Stile Farm
THE RIDGE
HIGHFIELD STILE RD
HIGHFIELD CL
Works
Sewage Works
Braintree Coll
CM7
BRAINTREE
CONVENT HILL
CONVENT LA
CHURCH LA
Mill
River Blackwater
CM77
KINGFISHER GATE
Great Bradfords Jun & Inf Schs
Jenkin's Farm
KINGS LA
THE COURTYARD
NORTHUMBERLAND CL
COLLINGWOOD CL
MOUNTBATTEN RD
RAYLEIGH CL
HEREFORD DR
BOURCHIER AVE
WELLINGTON CL
TRAFALGAR WAY
CONNAUGHT GDNS
VALLEY RD
BLACKWATER WAY
JULIEN COURT RD
LITTLE BRADFORDS
Sch
1 TIDESWELL CL
2 SNOWBERRY CT
Hatches Farm
A120
B1256
COGGESHALL RD
Recn Gd
BLOOMFIELD HO
GLOUCESTER GDNS
ROCHESTER CL
CLAY PITS WAY
TWELVE ACRES
GULLS CROFT
CRABS CROFT
PLAITERS WAY
RAILWAY ST
MOUNT RD
CROFT CL
WOODFIELD RD
KEEBLE WAY
MALTINGS
ALBERT RD
EAST ST
ST MARY'S RD
Ind Est
TROTTERS FIELD
HOWARD CL
CUNNINGTON RD
BARTRAM AVE S
BARTRAM AVE N
WHEATLEY AVE
HAY LA N
BISHOPS AVE
CLOCKHOUSE WAY
MANOR ST
TRINOVANTIAN WAY
B1018
LAKES RD
CHAPEL HILL
STUARTS WAY
1 WILD BOAR FIELD
2 DE-MARCI CT
3 BLACK BREAD CL
Ley Wood
Pyefleet Lodge
Templeborder Wood
CRAIG HO
THE LAURELS
VICTORIA ST
SOUTH ST
Ind Est
DAMASK MEWS
STATION APP
Braintree
Lakes Ind Pk
ANGLIA WAY
Braintree Town FC
THE CHASEWAY
CRESSING RD
LEYWOOD CL
BARN MEAD
BRICK KILN WAY
1 CAMULUS CL
2 GRESLEY DR
3 SIDINGS PL
4 VICTORIA CT
5 GROOMSIDE
6 JACQUARD WAY
7 THE MULBERRIES
MILL CT
HAYTOR CL
HUNTER DR
TAPESTRY WLK
APPLETREE WLK
PEARTREE CL
LONGACRES
STRAWBERRY CL
ORCHARD DR
SAXON BANK
Alec Hunter High Sch
1 CRESS CROFT
2 PUNDERS FIELD
3 STILEMANS WOOD
4 DEBEN CT
5 STOUR CT
6 FRATING CT
7 GOLDHANGER CT
8 SALCOTT CREEK CT
9 CROUCH CT
10 BOURNE CT
BRUNEL RD
RUSSET CL
Skitts Hill Ind Est
RYE GRASS WAY
Freeport Designer Outlet
ROMAN CT
CHARTER WAY
Braintree Freeport
Chapel Hill Bsns & Ret Pk
MERSEY FLEET WAY
COLNE CT
CHELMER RD
THAMES CL
LEA CL
SLOUGH HOUSE CL
PH
Cressing Lodge
Lanham Wood

127
155

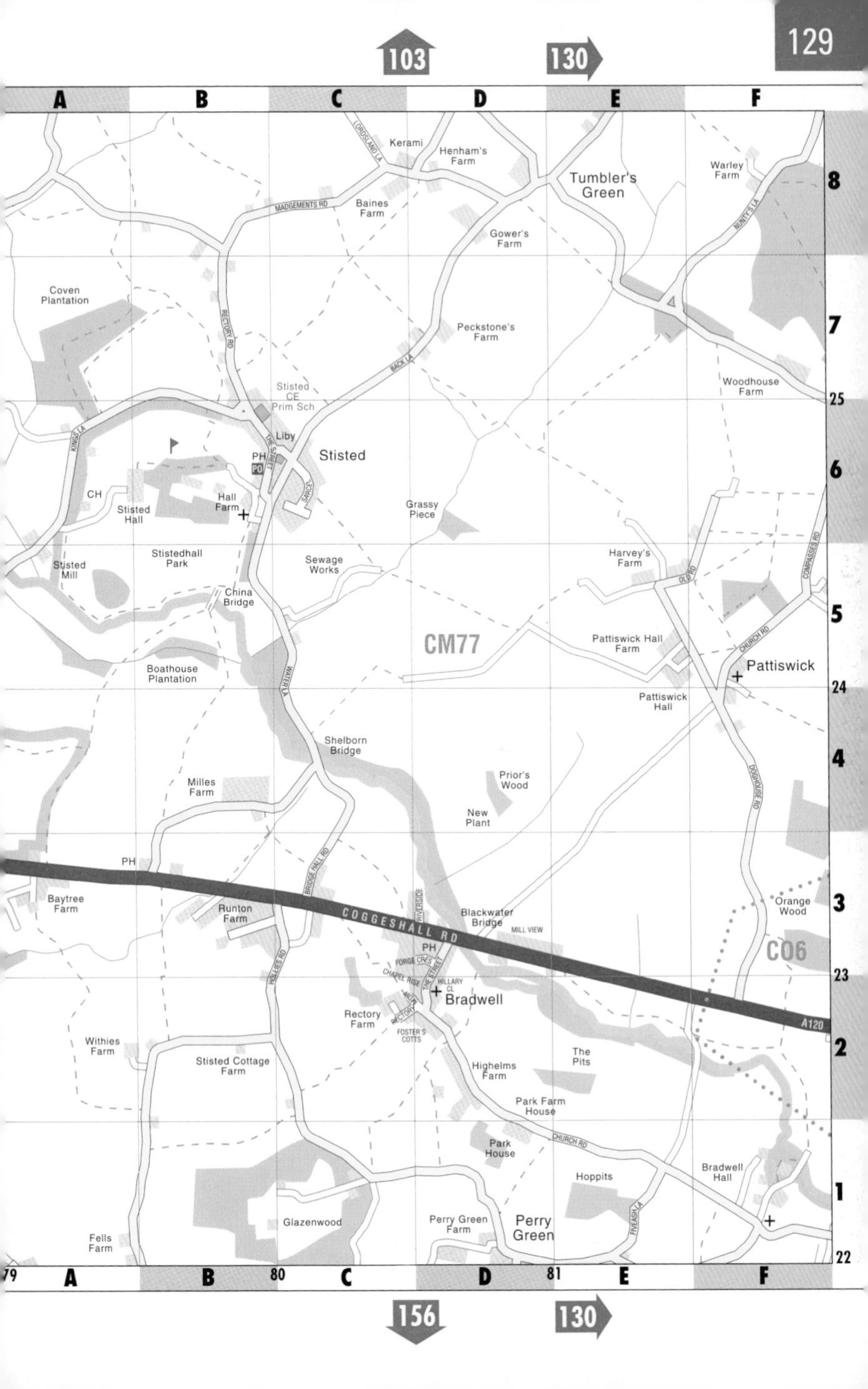
103
130
A
B
C
D
E
F
8
7
25
6
5
24
4
3
23
2
1
22
79
80
81
156
130
Kerami
Henham's Farm
LORDSLAND LA
MADGEMENTS RD
Baines Farm
Tumbler's Green
Warley Farm
NUNTY'S LA
Gower's Farm
Coven Plantation
RECTORY RD
Peckstone's Farm
BACK LA
Woodhouse Farm
Stisted CE Prim Sch
KINGS LA
Liby
THE STREET
Stisted
PH
PO
SARCEL
CH
Stisted Hall
Hall Farm
Grassy Piece
Stisted Mill
Stistedhall Park
Sewage Works
Harvey's Farm
OLD RD
COMPASSES RD
China Bridge
CM77
Pattiswick Hall Farm
CHURCH RD
Pattiswick
Boathouse Plantation
WATER LA
Pattiswick Hall
Shelborn Bridge
Prior's Wood
DOGHOUSE RD
Milles Farm
New Plant
PH
BRIDGE HALL RD
RIVERSIDE
Baytree Farm
Runton Farm
COGGESHALL RD
Blackwater Bridge
MILL VIEW
Orange Wood
CO6
HOLLIES RD
PH
FORGE CRES
CHAPEL RISE
THE STREET
HILLARY CL
Bradwell
A120
Rectory Farm
RECTORY
FOSTER'S COTTS
Withies Farm
Stisted Cottage Farm
Highelms Farm
The Pits
Park Farm House
Park House
CHURCH RD
Hoppits
Bradwell Hall
Glazenwood
Perry Green Farm
Perry Green
FINEASH LA
Fells Farm

129
104

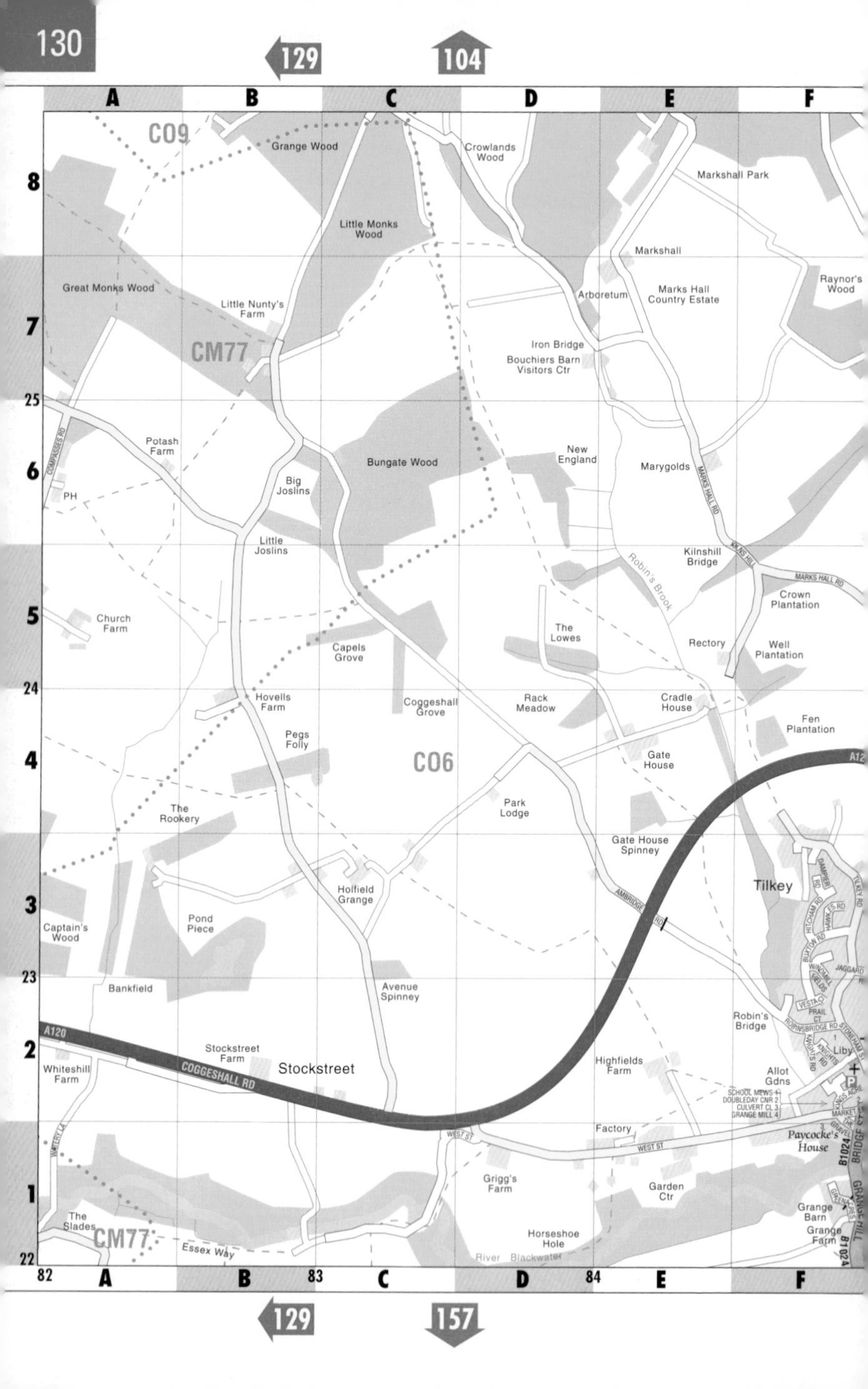
A
B
C
D
E
F
CO9
Grange Wood
Crowlands Wood
Markshall Park
Little Monks Wood
Markshall
Great Monks Wood
Little Nunty's Farm
Arboretum
Marks Hall Country Estate
Raynor's Wood
CM77
Iron Bridge
Bouchiers Barn Visitors Ctr
COMPASSES RD
Potash Farm
Bungate Wood
New England
Marygolds
MARKS HALL RD
PH
Big Joslins
Little Joslins
Kilnshill Bridge
Robin's Brook
MARKS HALL RD
Crown Plantation
Church Farm
The Lowes
Rectory
Well Plantation
Capels Grove
Hovells Farm
Coggeshall Grove
Rack Meadow
Cradle House
Fen Plantation
Pegs Folly
CO6
Gate House
A120
The Rookery
Park Lodge
Gate House Spinney
Tilkey
AMBRIDGE RD
Holfield Grange
Captain's Wood
Pond Piece
Bankfield
Avenue Spinney
JAGGARD
Robin's Bridge
A120
Stockstreet Farm
Highfields Farm
Whiteshill Farm
COGGESHALL RD
Stockstreet
Liby
Allot Gdns
SCHOOL MEWS 1
DOUBLEDAY CNR 2
CULVERT CL 3
GRANGE MILL 4
Factory
WEST ST
WEST ST
Paycocke's House
B1024
WATER LA
Grigg's Farm
Garden Ctr
Grange Barn
The Slades
CM77
Horseshoe Hole
Grange Farm
Essex Way
River Blackwater
B1024
8
7
25
6
5
24
4
3
23
2
1
22
82
83
84

129
157

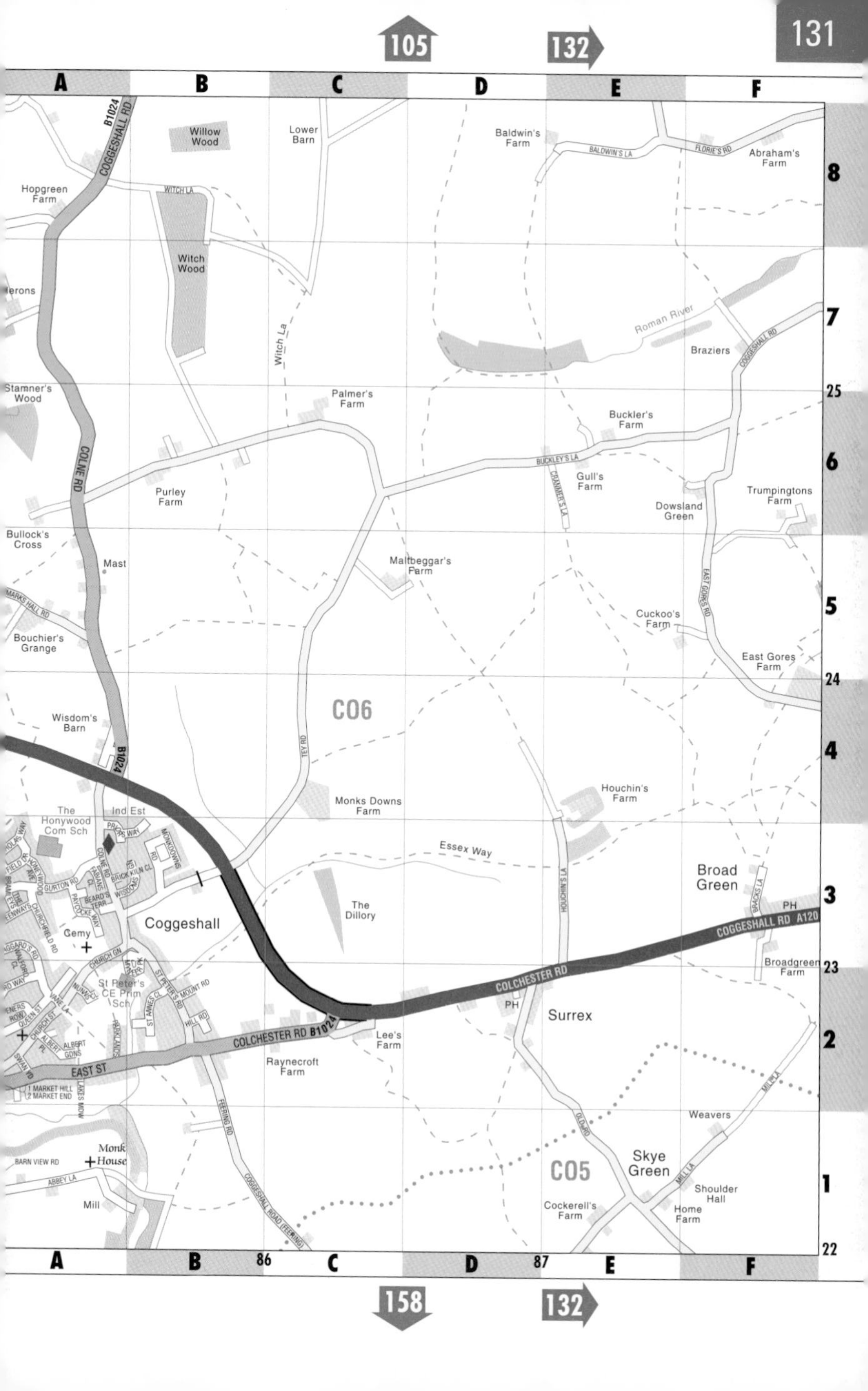
131
105
132
A
B
C
D
E
F
8
7
25
6
5
24
4
3
23
2
1
22
86
87
158
132
Willow Wood
Lower Barn
Baldwin's Farm
BALDWIN'S LA
FLORIE'S RD
Abraham's Farm
B1024
COGGESHALL RD
Hopgreen Farm
WITCH LA
Witch Wood
Herons
Witch La
Roman River
Braziers
COGGESHALL RD
Stamner's Wood
Palmer's Farm
Buckler's Farm
COLNE RD
BUCKLEY'S LA
Gull's Farm
CRANMER'S LA
Purley Farm
Dowsland Green
Trumpingtons Farm
Bullock's Cross
Mast
Maltbeggar's Farm
MARKS HALL RD
EAST GORES RD
Cuckoo's Farm
Bouchier's Grange
East Gores Farm
CO6
Wisdom's Barn
B1024
TEY RD
Houchin's Farm
Monks Downs Farm
The Honywood Com Sch
Ind Est
PRIORS WAY
MONKDOWNS RD
COLNE RD
BRICK KILN CL
Essex Way
HOUCHIN'S LA
Broad Green
BRACKS LA
GURTON RD
BEARD'S TERR
PAYCOCKE WAY
CHURCHFIELD RD
Coggeshall
The Dillory
PH
COGGESHALL RD A120
Gemy
CHURCH GN
Broadgreen Farm
St Peter's CE Prim Sch
ST PETER'S RD
MOUNT RD
COLCHESTER RD
PH
Surrex
QUEEN ST
CHURCH ST
ALBERT PL
ALBERT GDNS
HILL RD
COLCHESTER RD B1024
Lee's Farm
Raynecroft Farm
EAST ST
1 MARKET HILL
2 MARKET END
FEERING RD
OLD RD
Weavers
MILL LA
Monk House
BARN VIEW RD
ABBEY LA
CO5
Skye Green
MILL LA
Shoulder Hall
Mill
COGGESHALL ROAD (FEERING)
Cockerell's Farm
Home Farm

131
106

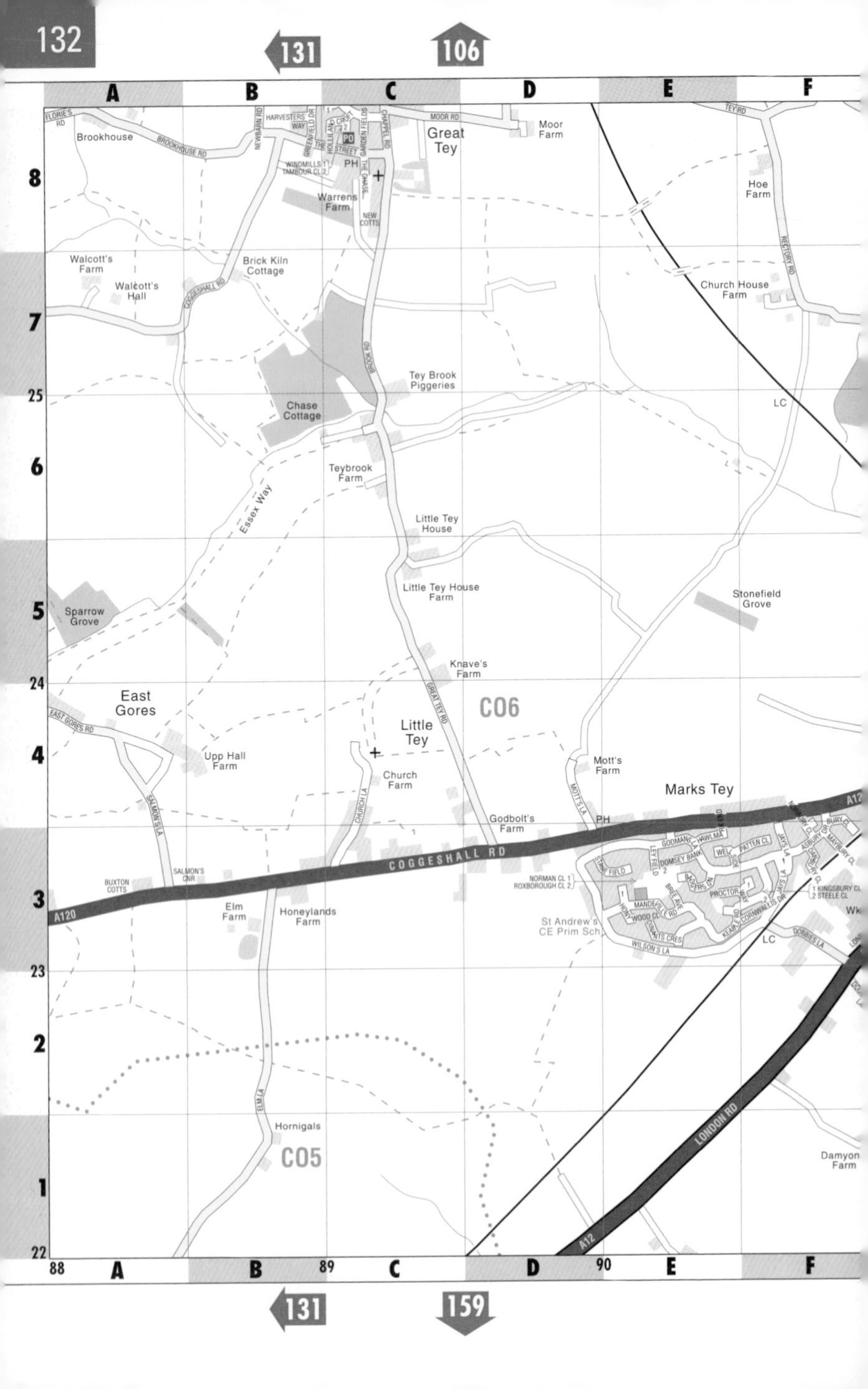
A
B
C
D
E
F
Brookhouse
BROOKHOUSE RD
NEWBARN RD
HARVESTERS WAY
MOOR RD
Great
Tey
Moor
Farm
PH
PO
Warrens
Farm
NEW COTTS
THE CHASE
CHAPPEL RD
Hoe
Farm
RECTORY RD
TEY RD
Walcott's
Farm
Walcott's
Hall
Brick Kiln
Cottage
COGGESHALL RD
Church House
Farm
Tey Brook
Piggeries
Chase
Cottage
LC
Teybrook
Farm
Essex Way
Little Tey
House
Little Tey House
Farm
Stonefield
Grove
Sparrow
Grove
Knave's
Farm
East
Gores
EAST GORES RD
GREAT TEY RD
CO6
Little
Tey
Upp Hall
Farm
Church
Farm
CHURCH LA
Mott's
Farm
MOTT'S LA
Marks Tey
SALMON'S LA
Godbolt's
Farm
PH
COGGESHALL RD
SALMON'S CNR
BUXTON COTTS
A120
Elm
Farm
Honeylands
Farm
St Andrew's
CE Prim Sch
WILSON'S LA
LC
DOBBIES LA
Hornigals
ELM LA
CO5
LONDON RD
A12
Damyon
Farm
8
7
25
6
5
24
4
3
23
2
1
22
88
89
90

131
159

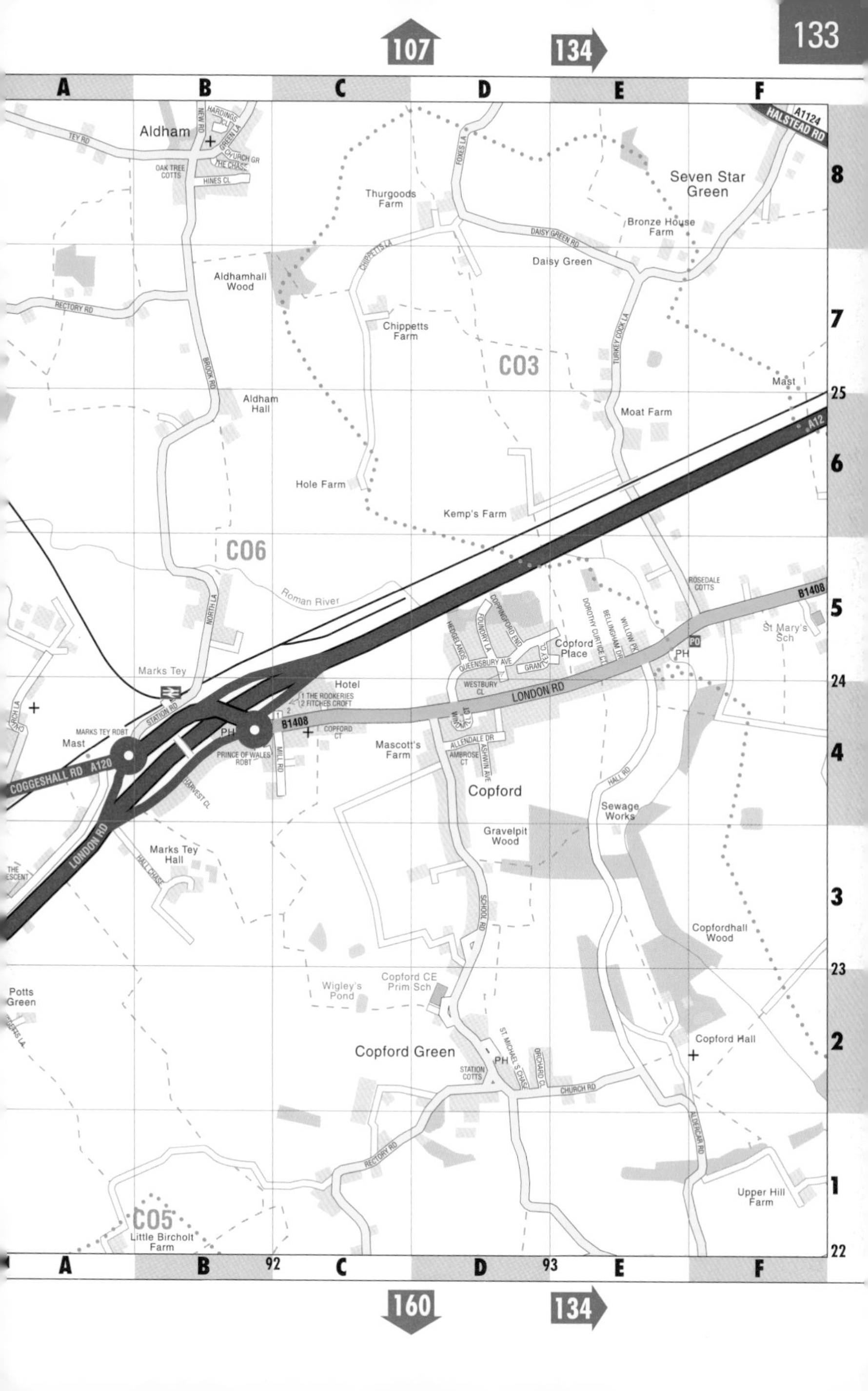
107
134
Aldham
TEY RD
NEW RD
HARDINGS CL
GREEN LA
CHURCH GR
THE CHASE
OAK TREE COTTS
HINES CL
Thurgoods Farm
FOXES LA
Seven Star Green
A1124
HALSTEAD RD
Bronze House Farm
DAISY GREEN RD
Daisy Green
CHIPPETTS LA
Aldhamhall Wood
RECTORY RD
Chippetts Farm
CO3
BROOK RD
TURKEY COCK LA
Mast
Aldham Hall
Moat Farm
A12
Hole Farm
Kemp's Farm
CO6
Roman River
NORTH LA
ROSEDALE COTTS
B1408
COPPINGFORD END
HEDGELANDS
FOUNDRY LA
DOROTHY CURTICE CT
BELLINGHAM DR
WILLOW PK
Copford Place
St Mary's Sch
QUEENSBURY AVE
GRANT CT
PH
PO
Marks Tey
Hotel
WESTBURY CL
LONDON RD
1 THE ROOKERIES
2 FITCHES CROFT
STATION RD
MARKS TEY RDBT
B1408
COPFORD CT
Mast
PH
Mascott's Farm
ALLENDALE DR
AMBROSE CT
ASHWIN AVE
PRINCE OF WALES RDBT
MILL RD
COGGESHALL RD
A120
HARVEST CL
Copford
HALL RD
Sewage Works
LONDON RD
Gravelpit Wood
Marks Tey Hall
HALL CHASE
SCHOOL RD
Copfordhall Wood
Potts Green
Wigley's Pond
Copford CE Prim Sch
Copford Hall
Copford Green
ST MICHAEL'S CHASE
ORCHARD CL
PH
STATION COTTS
CHURCH RD
ALDERCAR RD
RECTORY RD
Upper Hill Farm
CO5
Little Birchholt Farm
A
B
C
D
E
F
8
7
25
6
5
24
4
3
23
2
1
22
92
93
160
134

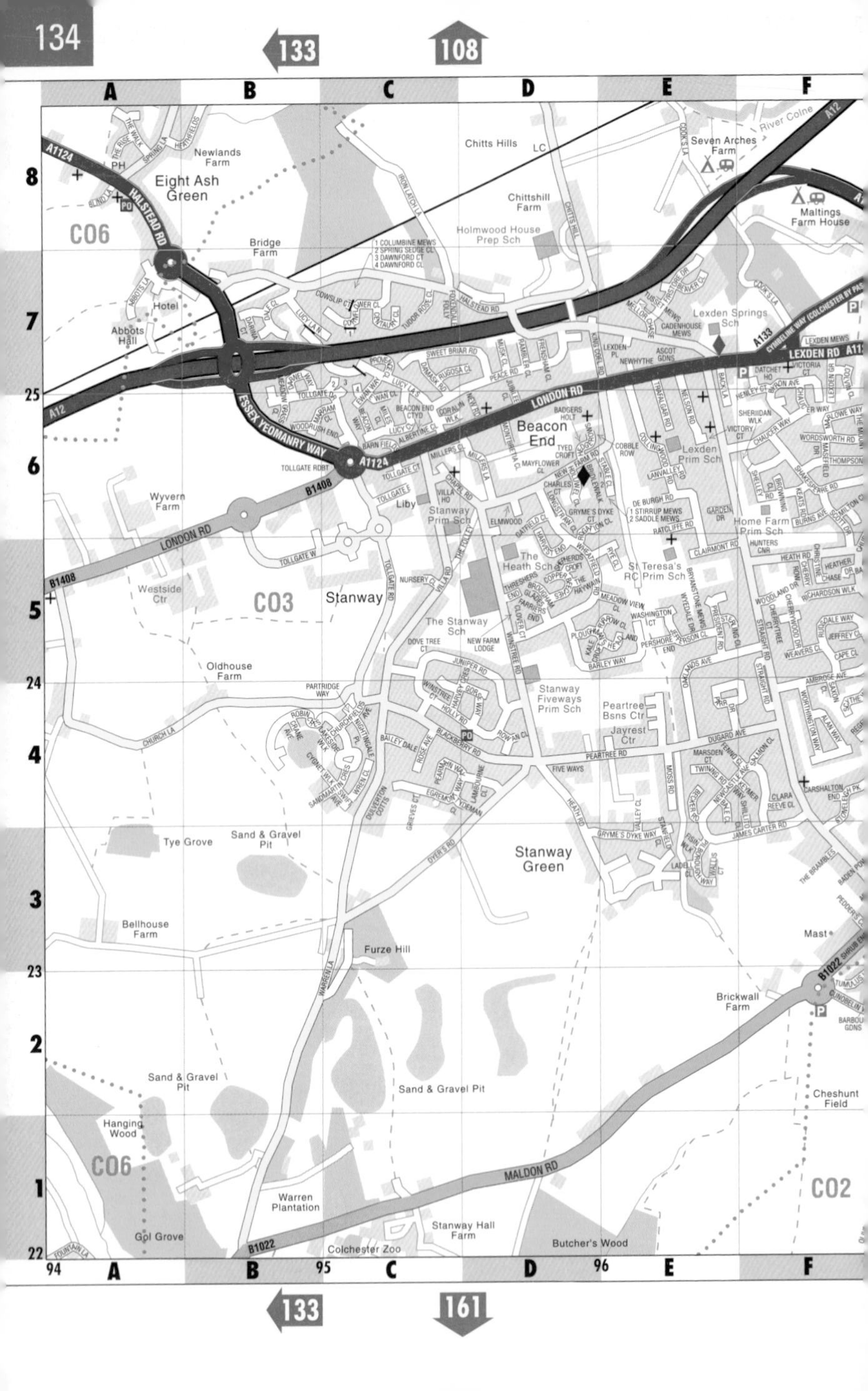
133
108
A
B
C
D
E
F
8
7
25
6
5
24
4
3
23
2
1
22
94
95
96
Newlands Farm
Eight Ash Green
PH
PO
HALSTEAD RD
A1124
CO6
Chitts Hills
LC
Seven Arches Farm
River Colne
A12
Maltings Farm House
Chittshill Farm
Holmwood House Prep Sch
Bridge Farm
1 COLUMBINE MEWS
2 SPRING SEDGE CL
3 DAWNFORD CT
4 DAWNFORD CL
Hotel
Abbots Hall
Lexden Springs Sch
CYMBELINE WAY (COLCHESTER BY PASS)
A133
LEXDEN RD
LONDON RD
ESSEX YEOMANRY WAY
Beacon End
TOLLGATE RDBT
Lexden Prim Sch
Wyvern Farm
B1408
Liby
Stanway Prim Sch
Home Farm Prim Sch
The Heath Sch
St Teresa's RC Prim Sch
Westside Ctr
CO3
Stanway
The Stanway Sch
Oldhouse Farm
Stanway Fiveways Prim Sch
Peartree Bsns Ctr
Jayrest Ctr
FIVE WAYS
PEARTREE RD
Tye Grove
Sand & Gravel Pit
Stanway Green
Bellhouse Farm
Furze Hill
Mast
Brickwall Farm
B1022
Sand & Gravel Pit
Sand & Gravel Pit
Hanging Wood
CO6
Cheshunt Field
MALDON RD
CO2
Warren Plantation
Stanway Hall Farm
Butcher's Wood
Gol Grove
Colchester Zoo
133
161

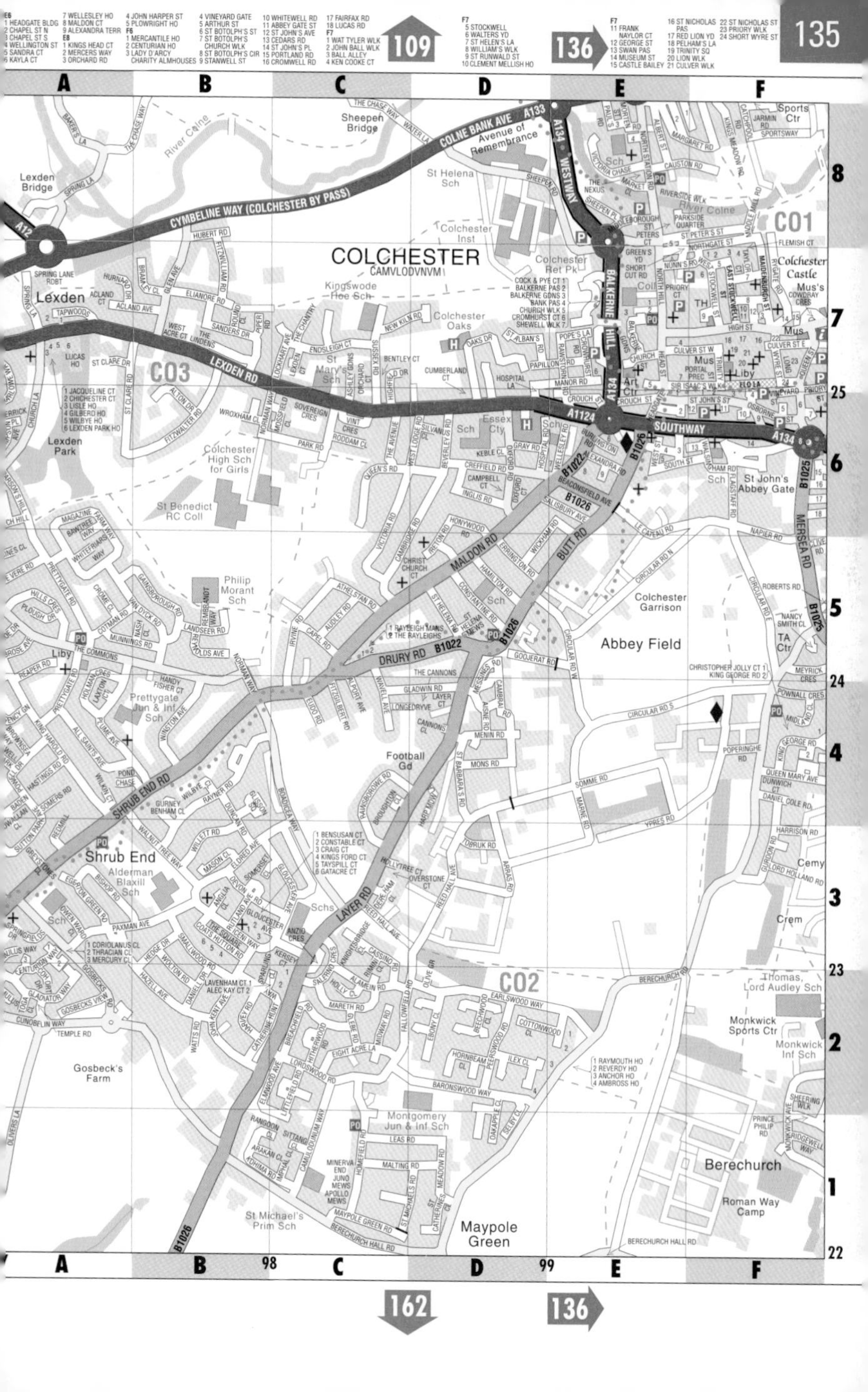
135
E6
1 HEADGATE BLDG
2 CHAPEL ST N
3 CHAPEL ST S
4 WELLINGTON ST
5 SANDRA CT
6 KAYLA CT
7 WELLESLEY HO
8 MALDON CT
9 ALEXANDRA TERR
E8
1 KINGS HEAD CT
2 MERCERS WAY
3 ORCHARD RD
4 JOHN HARPER ST
5 PLOWRIGHT HO
F6
1 MERCANTILE HO
2 CENTURIAN HO
3 LADY D'ARCY CHARITY ALMHOUSES
4 VINEYARD GATE
5 ARTHUR ST
6 ST BOTOLPH'S ST
7 ST BOTOLPH'S CHURCH WLK
8 ST BOTOLPH'S CIR
9 STANWELL ST
10 WHITEWELL RD
11 ABBEY GATE ST
12 ST JOHN'S AVE
13 CEDARS RD
14 ST JOHN'S PL
15 PORTLAND RD
16 CROMWELL RD
17 FAIRFAX RD
18 LUCAS RD
F7
1 WAT TYLER WLK
2 JOHN BALL WLK
3 BALL ALLEY
4 KEN COOKE CT
109
F7
5 STOCKWELL
6 WALTERS YD
7 ST HELEN'S LA
8 WILLIAM'S WLK
9 ST RUNWALD ST
10 CLEMENT MELLISH HO
136
F7
11 FRANK NAYLOR CT
12 GEORGE ST
13 SWAN PAS
14 MUSEUM ST
15 CASTLE BAILEY
16 ST NICHOLAS PAS
17 RED LION YD
18 PELHAM'S LA
19 TRINITY SQ
20 LION WLK
21 CULVER WLK
22 ST NICHOLAS ST
23 PRIORY WLK
24 SHORT WYRE ST
A B C D E F
8 7 25 6 5 24 4 3 23 2 1 22
COLCHESTER
CAMVLODVNVM
CO1
CO2
CO3
Lexden
Lexden Bridge
Lexden Park
Sheepen Bridge
Avenue of Remembrance
St Helena Sch
Colchester Inst
Colchester Ret Pk
Kingswode Hoe Sch
Colchester Oaks
St Mary's Sch
Essex Cty
Colchester High Sch for Girls
St Benedict RC Coll
Philip Morant Sch
Prettygate Jun & Inf Sch
Shrub End
Alderman Blaxill Sch
Gosbeck's Farm
Football Gd
Colchester Garrison
Abbey Field
St John's Abbey Gate
Colchester Castle
Mus's
Sports Ctr
TA Ctr
Cemy
Crem
Thomas, Lord Audley Sch
Monkwick Sports Ctr
Monkwick Inf Sch
Berechurch
Roman Way Camp
Maypole Green
Montgomery Jun & Inf Sch
St Michael's Prim Sch
CYMBELINE WAY (COLCHESTER BY PASS)
COLNE BANK AVE
LEXDEN RD
WESTWAY
BALKERNE HILL
SOUTHWAY
MALDON RD
BUTT RD
DRURY RD
SHRUB END RD
LAYER RD
MERSEA RD
BERECHURCH RD
BERECHURCH HALL RD
A12
A133
A134
A1124
B1022
B1025
B1026
River Colne
COCK & PYE CT 1
BALKERNE PAS 2
BALKERNE GDNS 3
BANK PAS 4
CHURCH WLK 5
CROMHURST CT 6
SHEWELL WLK 7
1 JACQUELINE CT
2 CHICHESTER CT
3 LISLE HO
4 GILBERD HO
5 WILBYE HO
6 LEXDEN PARK HO
1 RAYLEIGH MANS
2 THE RAYLEIGHS
CHRISTOPHER JOLLY CT 1
KING GEORGE RD 2
1 BENSUSAN CT
2 CONSTABLE CT
3 CRAIG CT
4 KINGS FORD CT
5 TAYSPILL CT
6 GATACRE CT
1 CORIOLANUS CL
2 THRACIAN CL
3 MERCURY CL
LAVENHAM CT 1
ALEC KAY CT 2
1 RAYMOUTH HO
2 REVERDY HO
3 ANCHOR HO
4 AMBROSS HO
98
99
162
136

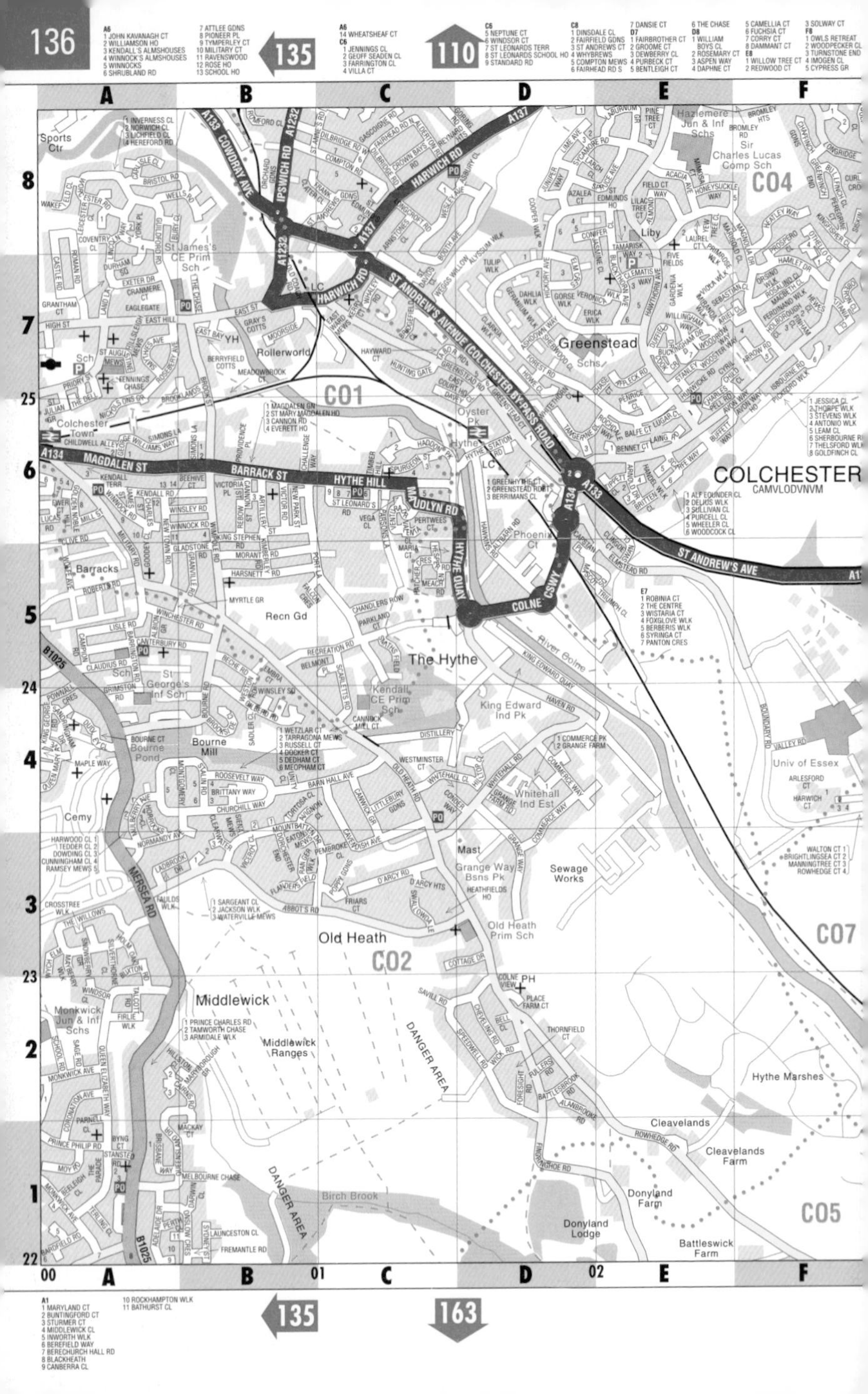

136
A6
1 JOHN KAVANAGH CT
2 WILLIAMSON HO
3 KENDALL'S ALMSHOUSES
4 WINNOCK'S ALMSHOUSES
5 WINNOCKS
6 SHRUBLAND RD
7 ATTLEE GDNS
8 PIONEER PL
9 TYMPERLEY CT
10 MILITARY CT
11 RAVENSWOOD
12 ROSE HO
13 SCHOOL HO
135
A6
14 WHEATSHEAF CT
C6
1 JENNINGS CL
2 GEOFF SEADEN CL
3 FARRINGTON CL
4 VILLA CT
110
C6
5 NEPTUNE CT
6 WINDSOR CT
7 ST LEONARDS TERR
8 ST LEONARDS SCHOOL HO
9 STANDARD RD
C8
1 DINSDALE CL
2 FAIRFIELD GDNS
3 ST ANDREWS CT
4 WHYBREWS
5 COMPTON MEWS
6 FAIRHEAD RD S
7 DANSIE CT
D7
1 FAIRBROTHER CT
2 GROOME CT
3 DEWBERRY CL
4 PURBECK CT
5 BENTLEIGH CT
6 THE CHASE
D8
1 WILLIAM BOYS CL
2 ROSEMARY CT
3 ASPEN WAY
4 DAPHNE CT
5 CAMELLIA CT
6 FUCHSIA CT
7 CORRY CT
8 DAMMANT CT
E8
1 WILLOW TREE CT
2 REDWOOD CT
3 SOLWAY CT
F8
1 OWLS RETREAT
2 WOODPECKER CL
3 TURNSTONE END
4 IMOGEN CL
5 CYPRESS GR
A B C D E F
8 7 6 5 4 3 2 1
25 24 23 22
00 01 02
COLCHESTER
CAMVLODVNVM
CO1 CO2 CO4 CO5 CO7
A133 A1232 A137 A134 B1025
COWDRAY AVE
IPSWICH RD
HARWICH RD
ST ANDREW'S AVENUE (COLCHESTER BY-PASS ROAD)
ST ANDREW'S AVE
MAGDALEN ST
BARRACK ST
HYTHE HILL
MAUDLYN RD
HYTHE QUAY
COLNE CSWY
MERSEA RD
Sports Ctr
St James's CE Prim Sch
Rollerworld
Colchester Town
Barracks
Recn Gd
The Hythe
Kendall CE Prim Sch
St George's Inf Sch
Bourne Mill
Bourne Pond
Cemy
King Edward Ind Pk
Whitehall Ind Est
Grange Way Bsns Pk
Sewage Works
Old Heath Prim Sch
Old Heath
Middlewick
Middlewick Ranges
DANGER AREA
Monkwick Jun & Inf Schs
Birch Brook
Donyland Lodge
Donyland Farm
Battleswick Farm
Cleavelands
Cleavelands Farm
Hythe Marshes
Univ of Essex
Greenstead
Greenstead Schs
Hazlemere Jun & Inf Schs
Sir Charles Lucas Comp Sch
Oyster Pk
Hythe
Phoenix Ct
River Colne
Five Fields
Liby
1 INVERNESS CL
2 NORWICH CL
3 LICHFIELD CL
4 HEREFORD RD
1 MAGDALEN GN
2 ST MARY MAGDALEN HO
3 CANNON RD
4 EVERETT HO
1 GREENHYTHE CT
2 GREENSTEAD RDBT
3 BERRIMANS CL
1 JESSICA CL
2 THORPE WLK
3 STEVENS WLK
4 ANTONIO WLK
5 LEAM CL
6 SHERBOURNE RD
7 THELSFORD WLK
8 GOLDFINCH CL
1 ALF EOUNDER CL
2 DELIUS WLK
3 SULLIVAN CL
4 PURCELL CL
5 WHEELER CL
6 WOODCOCK CL
E7
1 ROBINIA CT
2 THE CENTRE
3 WISTARIA CT
4 FOXGLOVE WLK
5 BERBERIS WLK
6 SYRINGA CT
7 PANTON CRES
1 WETZLAR CT
2 TARRAGONA MEWS
3 RUSSELL CT
4 DOCKER CT
5 DEDHAM CT
6 MEOPHAM CT
1 COMMERCE PK
2 GRANGE FARM
HARWOOD CL 1
TEDDER CL 2
DOWDING CL 3
CUNNINGHAM CL 4
RAMSEY MEWS 5
1 SARGEANT CL
2 JACKSON WLK
3 WATERVILLE MEWS
WALTON CT 1
BRIGHTLINGSEA CT 2
MANNINGTREE CT 3
ROWHEDGE CT 4
1 PRINCE CHARLES RD
2 TAMWORTH CHASE
3 ARMIDALE WLK
135
163
A1
1 MARYLAND CT
2 BUNTINGFORD CT
3 STURMER CT
4 MIDDLEWICK CL
5 INWORTH WLK
6 BEREFIELD WAY
7 BERECHURCH HALL RD
8 BLACKHEATH
9 CANBERRA CL
10 ROCKHAMPTON WLK
11 BATHURST CL

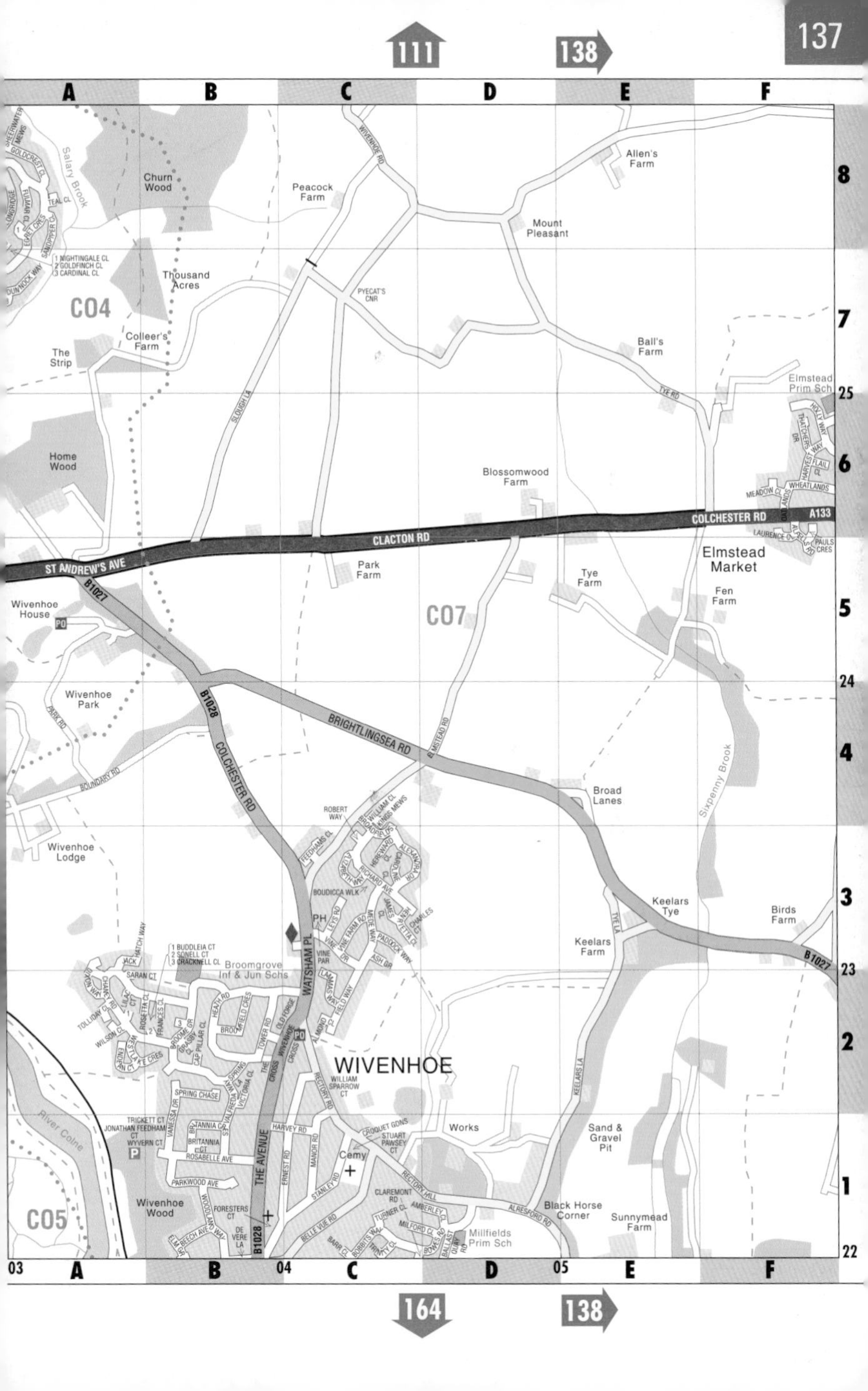
111
138
A
B
C
D
E
F
8
7
25
6
5
24
4
3
23
2
1
22
03
04
05
Churn Wood
Salary Brook
Peacock Farm
Allen's Farm
Mount Pleasant
Thousand Acres
CO4
PYECAT'S CNR
Colleer's Farm
The Strip
Ball's Farm
Elmstead Prim Sch
SLOUGH LA
TYE RD
WIVENHOE RD
Home Wood
Blossomwood Farm
COLCHESTER RD
A133
CLACTON RD
ST ANDREW'S AVE
B1027
Park Farm
Elmstead Market
Tye Farm
Fen Farm
Wivenhoe House
CO7
Wivenhoe Park
B1028
BRIGHTLINGSEA RD
ELMSTEAD RD
COLCHESTER RD
BOUNDARY RD
PARK RD
Broad Lanes
Sixpenny Brook
Wivenhoe Lodge
Keelars Tye
Birds Farm
Keelars Farm
TYE LA
Broomgrove Inf & Jun Schs
1 BUDDLEIA CT
2 SONELL CT
3 CRACKNELL CL
WATSHAM PL
WIVENHOE
Works
Sand & Gravel Pit
KEELARS LA
River Colne
Cemy
THE AVENUE
Wivenhoe Wood
CO5
Black Horse Corner
Sunnymead Farm
ALRESFORD RD
RECTORY HILL
Millfields Prim Sch
1 NIGHTINGALE CL
2 GOLDFINCH CL
3 CARDINAL CL
MEADOW CL
WHEATLANDS
HARVEST WAY
THATCHERS DR
LAURENCE CL
PAULS CRES
FLAIL CL
HOLLY WAY
ROBERT WAY
FEEDHAMS CL
WILLIAM CL
KINGS MEWS
BOUDICCA WLK
RICHARD AVE
ALEXANDRA DR
HEREWARD CL
VINE FARM RD
VINE PAR
PADDOCK WAY
ASH GR
LEYS RD
FIELD WAY
ALMOND CL
HATCH WAY
JACK CT
SARAN CT
TOLLIDAY CL
WILSON CL
ROSETTA CL
FRANCES CL
CAP PILLAR CL
HEATH RD
BROOMFIELD CRES
TOWER RD
OLD FORGE
THE CROSS
SPRING CHASE
VANESSA DR
VICTORIA CL
TRICKETT CT
JONATHAN FEEDHAM CT
WYVERN CT
TANNIA CT
BRITANNIA CT
ROSABELLE AVE
PARKWOOD AVE
WOODLAND WAY
FORESTERS CT
DE VERE LA
BEECH AVE
ELM GR
ERNEST RD
MANOR RD
HARVEY RD
STANLEY RD
RECTORY RD
WILLIAM SPARROW CT
CROQUET GDNS
STUART PAWSEY CT
CLAREMONT RD
AMBERLEY CL
TURNER CL
MILFORD CL
BELLE VUE RD
BARR CL
BOBBITS WAY
BOWES RD
BALLAST QUAY
PH
PO
P
164
138

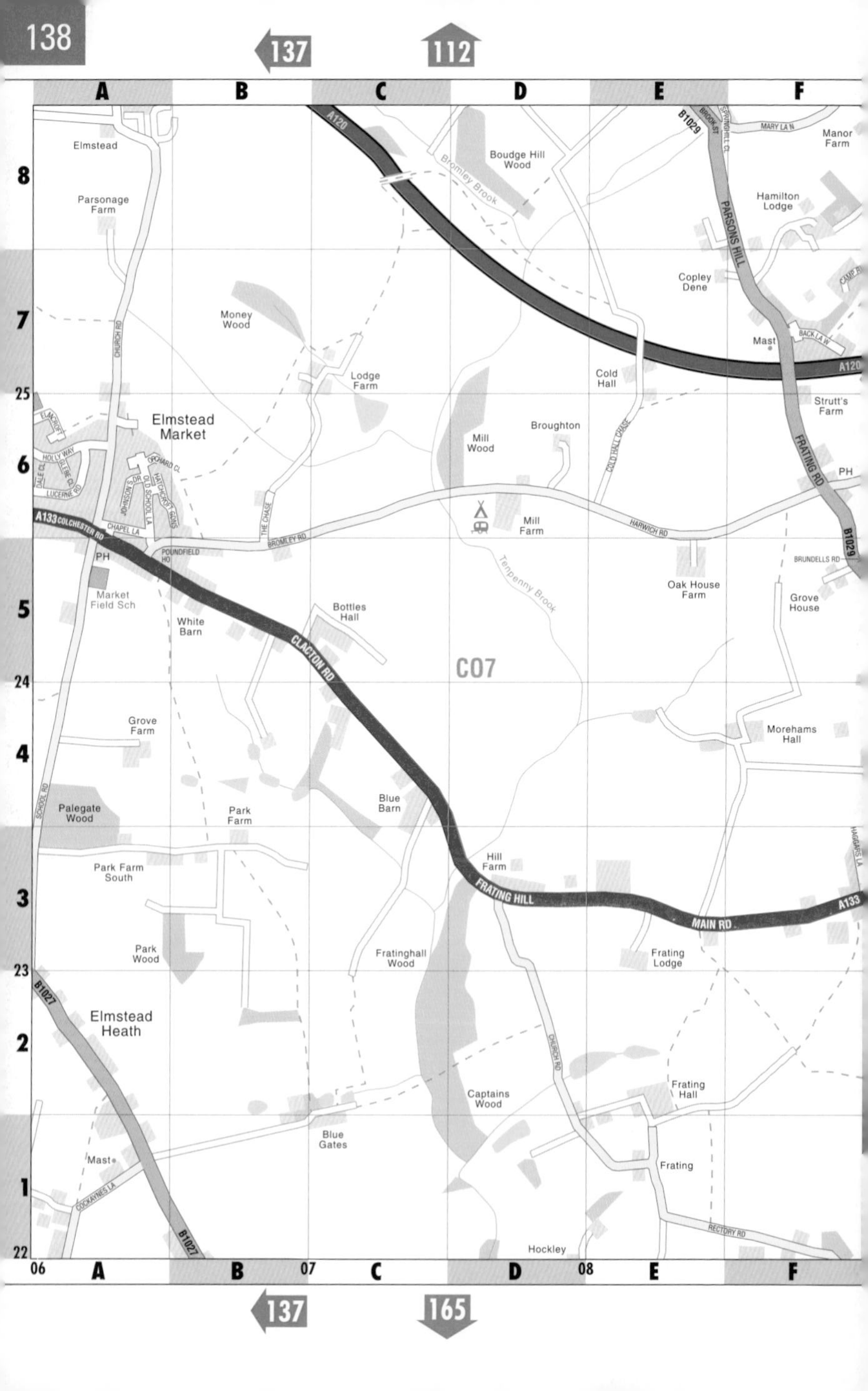

137
112
A
B
C
D
E
F
8
7
25
6
5
24
4
3
23
2
1
22
06
07
08
Elmstead
Parsonage Farm
Money Wood
Lodge Farm
Boudge Hill Wood
Bromley Brook
A120
B1029
BROOK ST
SPRINGHILL CL
MARY LA N
Manor Farm
Hamilton Lodge
PARSONS HILL
Copley Dene
CAMP RD
Mast
BACK LA W
Cold Hall
Strutt's Farm
CHURCH RD
Elmstead Market
ELMCROFT
HOLLY WAY
GLEBE CL
DALE CL
LUCERNE RD
ORCHARD CL
JOHNSON'S DR
HATCHCROFT GDNS
OLD SCHOOL LA
CHAPEL LA
A133 COLCHESTER RD
POUNDFIELD HO
PH
Market Field Sch
THE CHASE
BROMLEY RD
Mill Wood
Broughton
COLD HALL CHASE
Mill Farm
HARWICH RD
FRATING RD
PH
B1029
BRUNDELLS RD
Oak House Farm
Grove House
Tenpenny Brook
White Barn
Bottles Hall
CLACTON RD
CO7
Grove Farm
Morehams Hall
PH
SCHOOL RD
Palegate Wood
Park Farm
Blue Barn
Park Farm South
Hill Farm
FRATING HILL
MAIN RD
A133
HAGGARS LA
Park Wood
Fratinghall Wood
Frating Lodge
B1027
Elmstead Heath
CHURCH RD
Captains Wood
Frating Hall
Blue Gates
Mast
Frating
COCKAYNES LA
B1027
RECTORY RD
Hockley
137
165

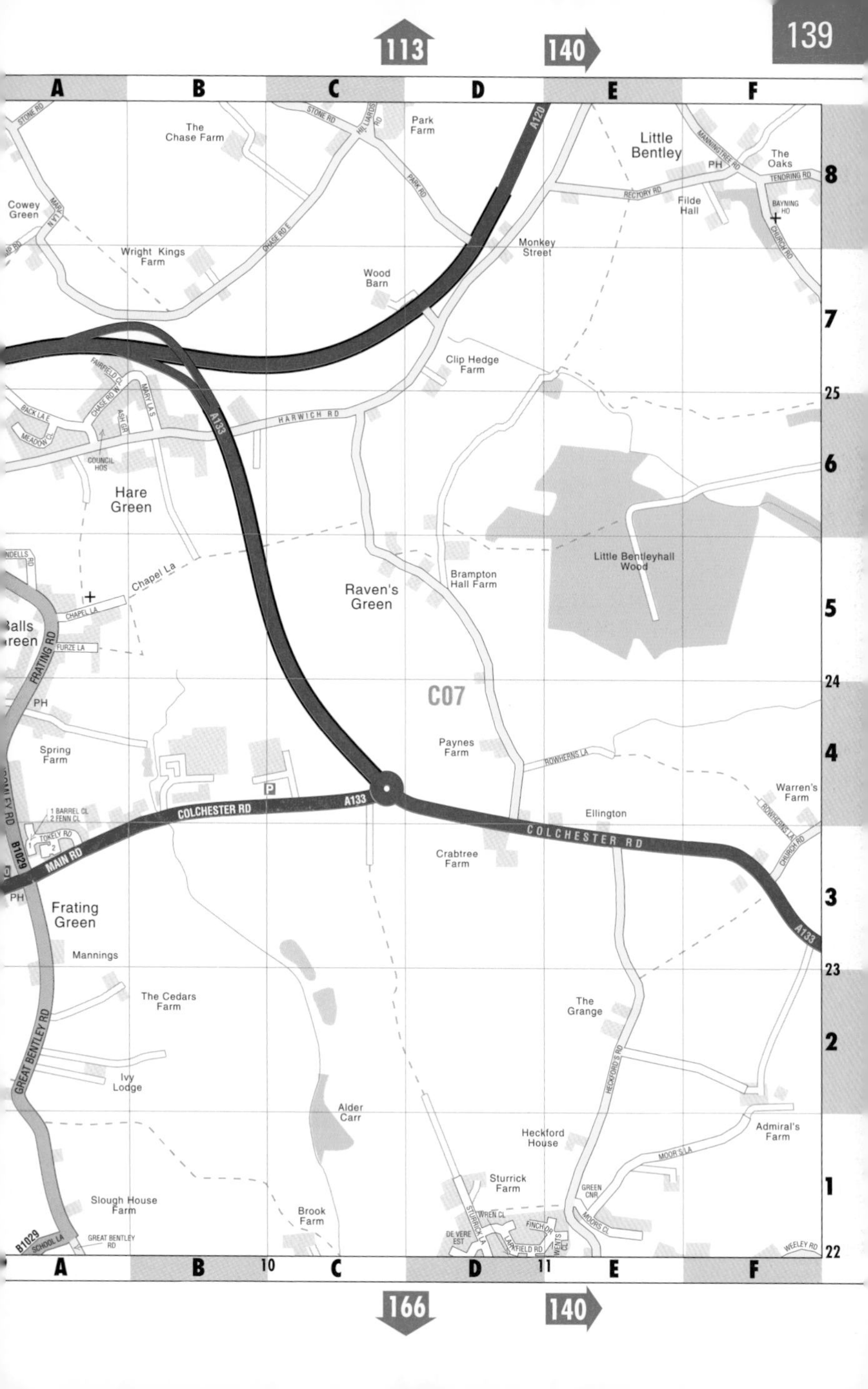
113
140
A B C D E F
The Chase Farm
Park Farm
Little Bentley
The Oaks
Cowey Green
Wright Kings Farm
Filde Hall
Monkey Street
Wood Barn
Clip Hedge Farm
HARWICH RD
Hare Green
Chapel La
Raven's Green
Brampton Hall Farm
Little Bentleyhall Wood
Balls Green
FRATING RD
C07
Spring Farm
Paynes Farm
ROWHERNS LA
Warren's Farm
COLCHESTER RD
A133
Ellington
MAIN RD
Crabtree Farm
Frating Green
Mannings
The Cedars Farm
The Grange
GREAT BENTLEY RD
HECKFORD'S RD
Ivy Lodge
Alder Carr
Admiral's Farm
Heckford House
MOOR'S LA
Sturrick Farm
Slough House Farm
Brook Farm
B1029
SCHOOL LA
WEELEY RD
A120
STONE RD
CHASE RD E
PARK RD
RECTORY RD
TENDRING RD
MANNINGTREE RD
CHURCH RD
BAYNING HO
PH
8 7 6 5 4 3 2 1
25 24 23 22
10 11
166
140

139
114

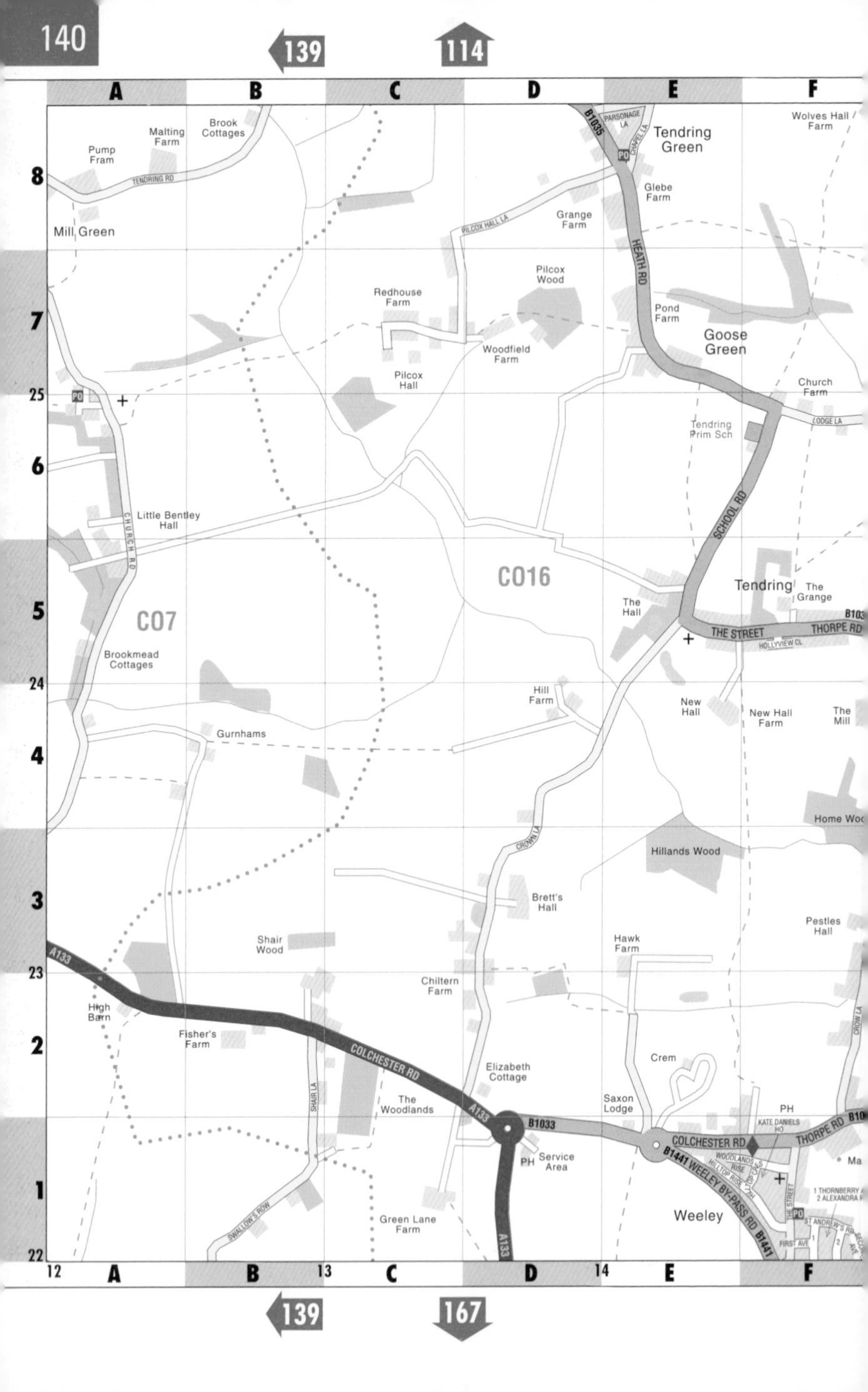
A
B
C
D
E
F
8
7
25
6
5
24
4
3
23
2
1
22
12
13
14
Pump Fram
Malting Farm
Brook Cottages
TENDRING RD
Mill Green
B1035
PARSONAGE LA
CHAPEL LA
PO
Tendring Green
Wolves Hall Farm
Glebe Farm
Grange Farm
PILCOX HALL LA
HEATH RD
Pilcox Wood
Redhouse Farm
Pond Farm
Goose Green
Woodfield Farm
Pilcox Hall
Church Farm
LODGE LA
Tendring Prim Sch
Little Bentley Hall
CHURCH RD
SCHOOL RD
CO16
Tendring
The Grange
The Hall
CO7
THE STREET
THORPE RD
B1033
HOLLYVIEW CL
Brookmead Cottages
Hill Farm
New Hall
New Hall Farm
The Mill
Gurnhams
Home Wo
CROWN LA
Hillands Wood
Brett's Hall
Pestles Hall
Shair Wood
Hawk Farm
A133
Chiltern Farm
High Barn
Fisher's Farm
Crem
COLCHESTER RD
Elizabeth Cottage
SHAIR LA
The Woodlands
Saxon Lodge
PH
KATE DANIELS HO
COLCHESTER RD
THORPE RD
B1441 WEELEY BY-PASS RD
WOODLANDS RISE
HILLTOP RISE
HILLTOP CRES
Service Area
1 THORNBERRY
2 ALEXANDRA
Weeley
THE STREET
ST ANDREW'S RD
FIRST AVE
SWALLOW'S ROW
Green Lane Farm

139
167

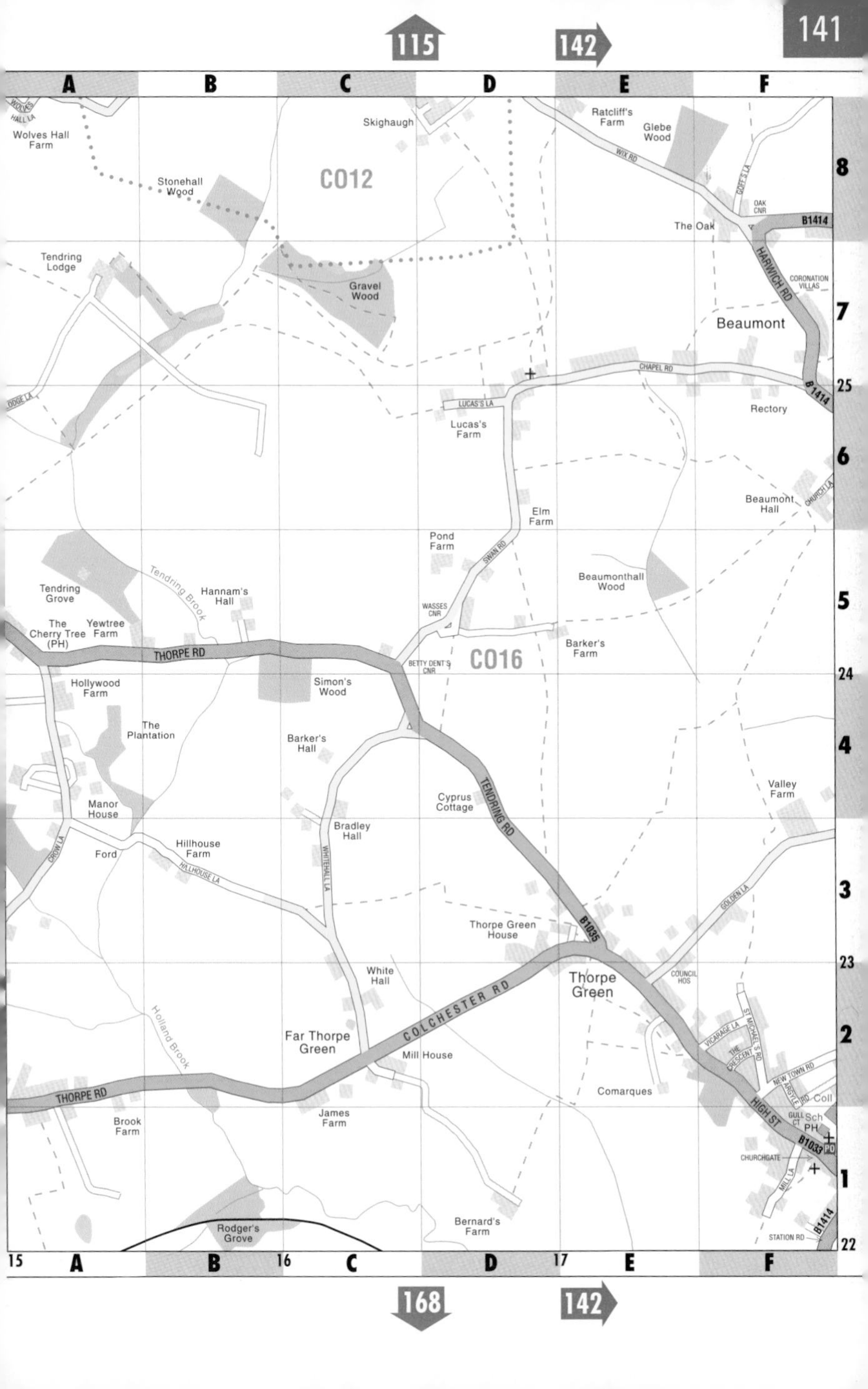

115
142

A **B** **C** **D** **E** **F**

Wolves Hall Farm

Skighaugh

Ratcliff's Farm

Glebe Wood

8

CO12

Stonehall Wood

The Oak

B1414

Tendring Lodge

Gravel Wood

CORONATION VILLAS

7

Beaumont

HARWICH RD

OAK CNR

WIX RD

DALE LA

CHAPEL RD

B1414

25

LUCAS'S LA

Lucas's Farm

Rectory

6

Beaumont Hall

Elm Farm

CHURCH LA

Pond Farm

SWAN RD

Beaumonthall Wood

Tendring Grove

Hannam's Hall

5

Tendring Brook

The Cherry Tree (PH)

Yewtree Farm

WASSES CNR

Barker's Farm

THORPE RD

CO16

Hollywood Farm

BETTY DENT'S CNR

24

Simon's Wood

The Plantation

Barker's Hall

4

Valley Farm

Manor House

Bradley Hall

Cyprus Cottage

TENDRING RD

Ford

Hillhouse Farm

GOLDEN LA

CROSS LA

WHITEHALL LA

HILLHOUSE LA

3

Thorpe Green House

B1035

White Hall

COLCHESTER RD

Thorpe Green

COUNCIL HOS

23

Far Thorpe Green

Mill House

2

Comarques

VICARAGE LA

THE STREET

NEW TOWN RD

Co-Coll

THORPE RD

Brook Farm

James Farm

HIGH ST

GULL PH

Sch

B1035

Holland Brook

CHURCHGATE

MILL LA

1

Bernard's Farm

STATION RD

Rodger's Grove

B1414

22

15 **A** **B** 16 **C** **D** 17 **E** **F**

141
116

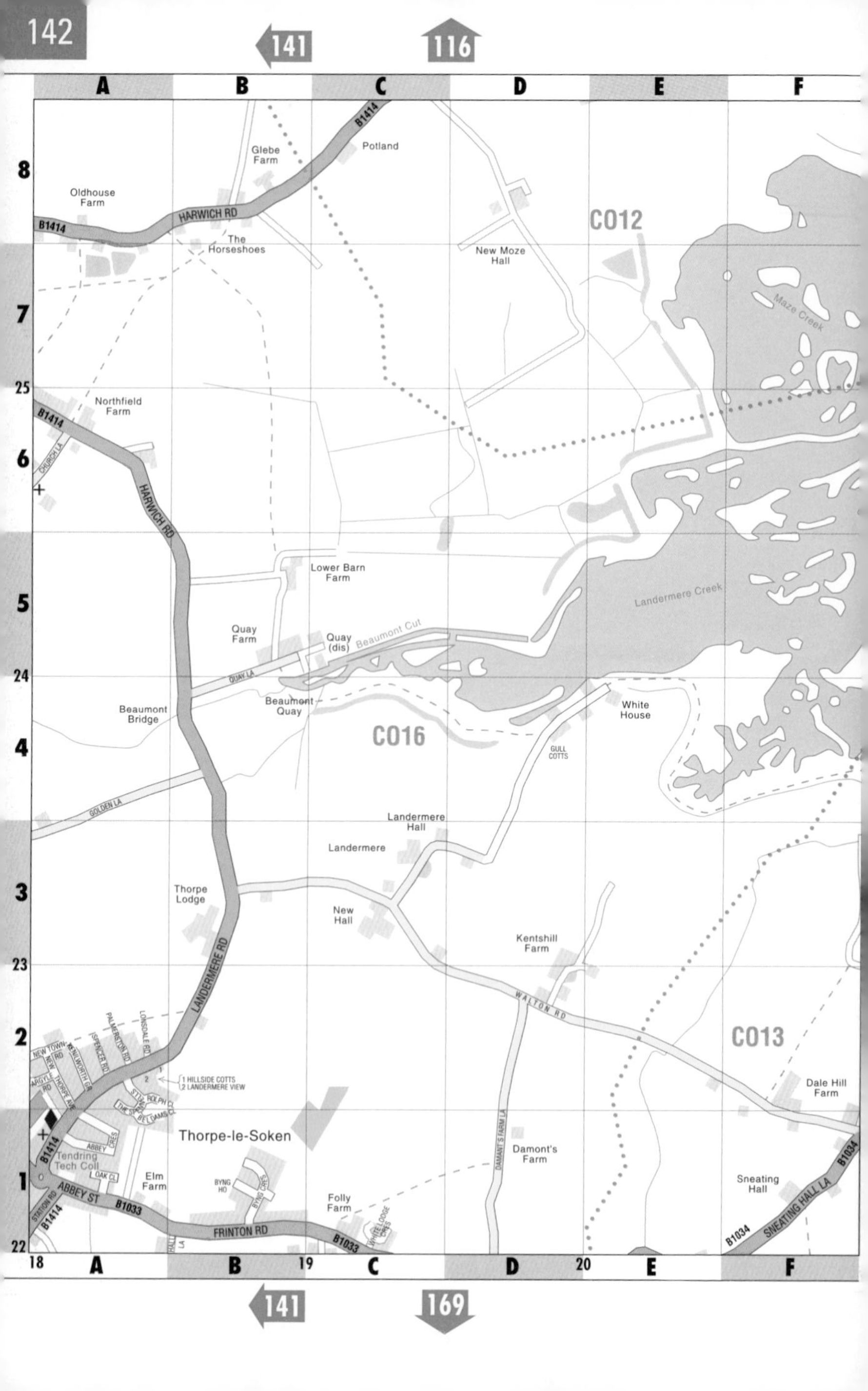
A
B
C
D
E
F
8
7
25
6
5
24
4
3
23
2
1
22
18
19
20
Oldhouse Farm
Glebe Farm
Potland
B1414
HARWICH RD
The Horseshoes
New Moze Hall
CO12
Maze Creek
Northfield Farm
CHURCH LA
Lower Barn Farm
Landermere Creek
Quay Farm
Quay (dis)
Beaumont Cut
QUAY LA
Beaumont Bridge
Beaumont Quay
CO16
White House
GULL COTTS
GOLDEN LA
Landermere Hall
Landermere
Thorpe Lodge
New Hall
LANDERMERE RD
Kentshill Farm
WALTON RD
CO13
Dale Hill Farm
NEW TOWN RD
SPENCER RD
PALMERSTON RD
LONSDALE RD
KENILWORTH GR
ARGYLE RD
THORPE AVE
1 HILLSIDE COTTS
2 LANDERMERE VIEW
ROLPH CL
ADAMS CL
Thorpe-le-Soken
ABBEY CRES
Tendring Tech Coll
OAK CL
Elm Farm
ABBEY ST
B1033
STATION RD
BYNG HO
BYNG CRES
FRINTON RD
Folly Farm
WHITE LODGE CRES
DAMANT'S FARM LA
Damont's Farm
Sneating Hall
B1034
SNEATING HALL LA
HALL LA

141
169

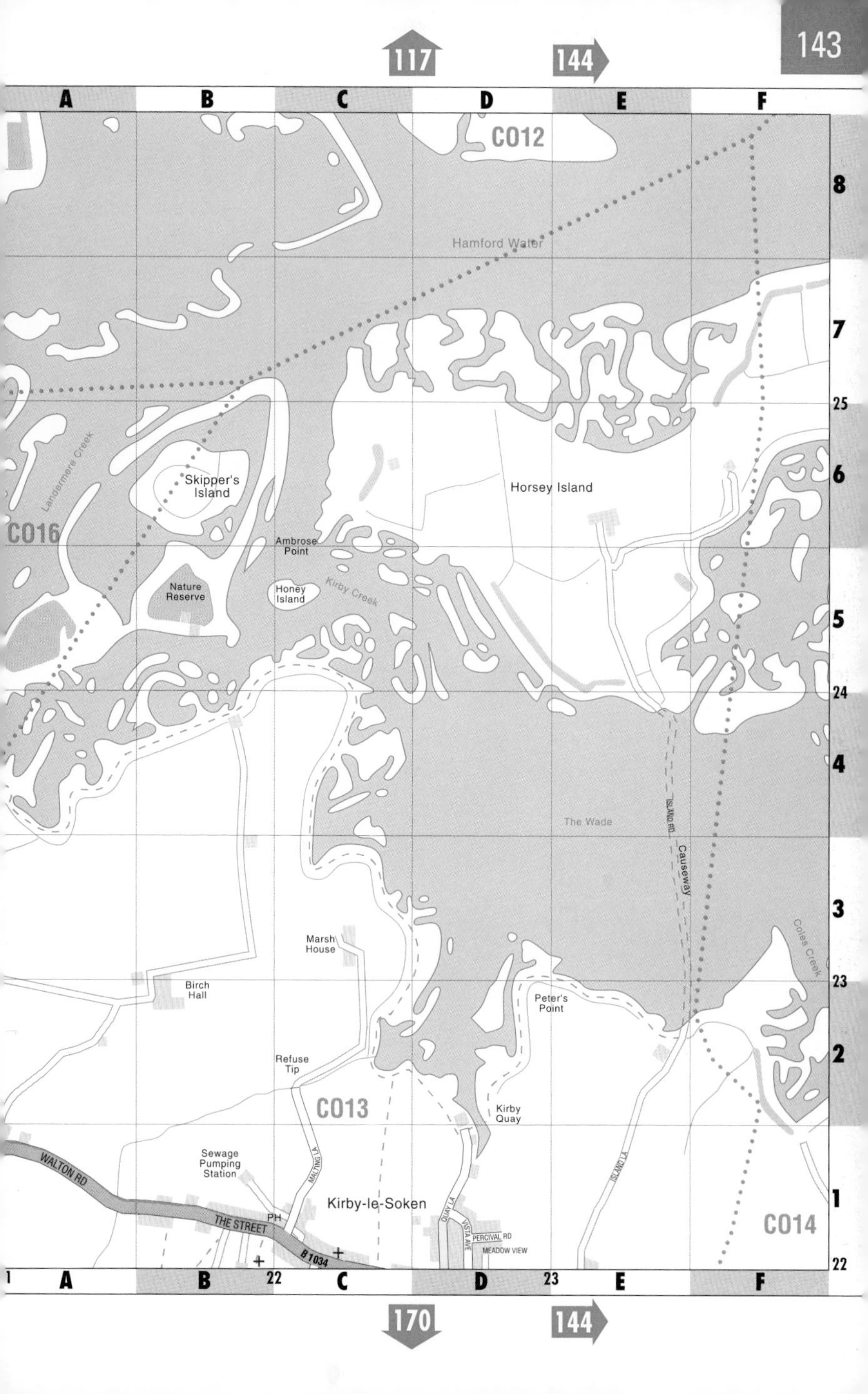

A B C D E F

CO12

Hamford Water

8

7

25

Landermere Creek

CO16

Skipper's
Island

6

Ambrose
Point

Horsey Island

Nature
Reserve

Honey
Island

Kirby Creek

5

24

4

The Wade

Badly Rd.

Causeway

Coles Creek

3

23

Marsh
House

Birch
Hall

Peter's
Point

2

Refuse
Tip

CO13

Kirby Quay

Island La.

CO14

WALTON RD

Sewage
Pumping
Station

MALTING LA

Kirby-le-Soken

Quay La.

VILLAGE

PERCIVAL RD

MEADOW VIEW

PH

THE STREET

B 1034

1

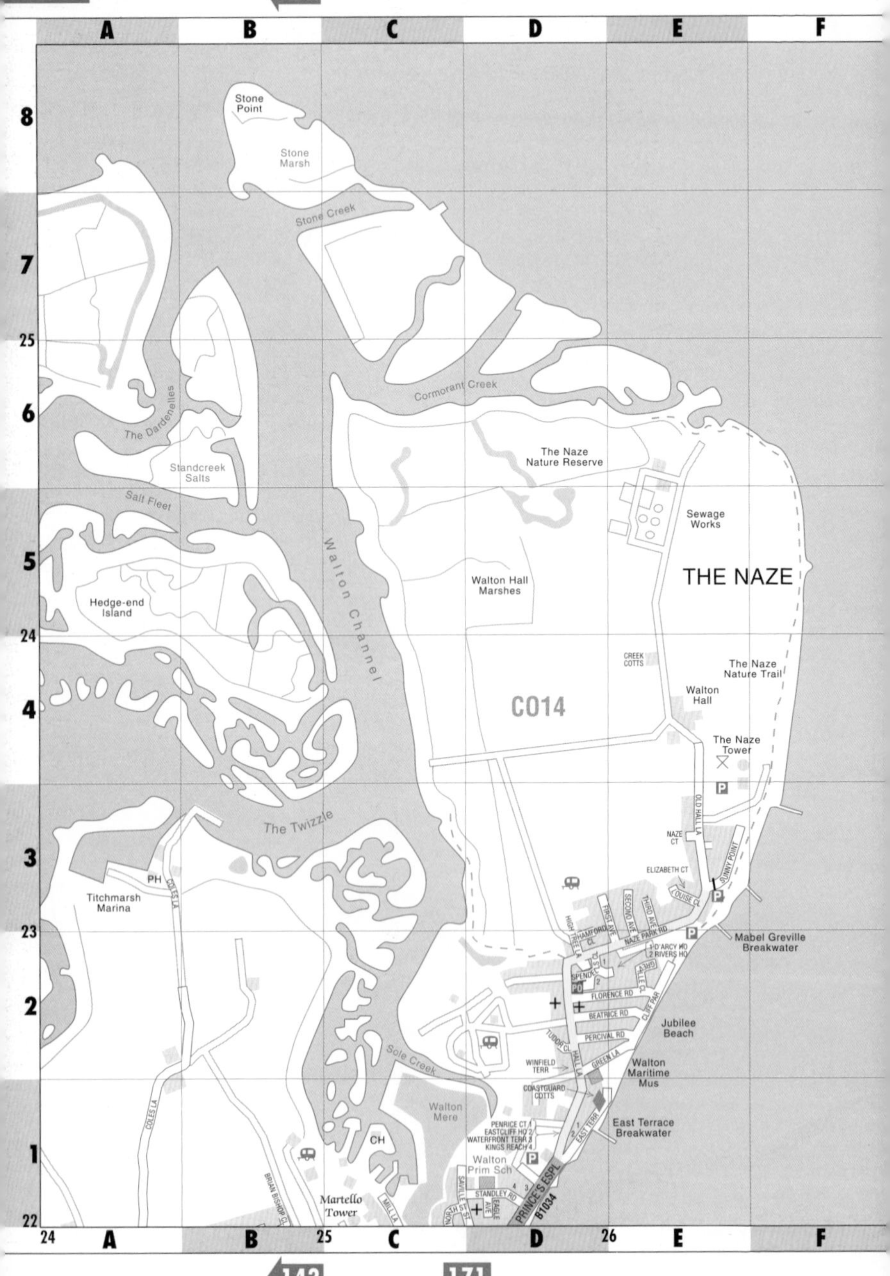

A   B   C   D   E   F

8

Stone
Point

Stone
Marsh

7

Stone Creek

25

Cormorant Creek

6

The Dardanelles

Standcreek
Salts

The Naze
Nature Reserve

Salt Fleet

Sewage
Works

5

Walton Hall
Marshes

THE NAZE

Hedge-end
Island

24

CREEK
COTTS

The Naze
Nature Trail

Walton
Hall

4

CO14

The Naze
Tower

P

NAZE
CT

3

ELIZABETH CT

SUNNY POINT

Titchmarsh
Marina

PH

The Twizzle

P

Mabel Greville
Breakwater

23

HIGH ST

NORMAN RD
NAZE PARK RD

OLD HALL

D'ARCY RD
2 RIVERS RD

SAXON RD

FLORENCE RD

2

BEATRICE RD

PERCIVAL RD

Jubilee Beach

WINFIELD TERR
LORING RD
GREVILLE

Walton
Maritime
Mus

COASTGUARD
COTTS

East Terrace
Breakwater

1

PENRICE CT
EASTCLIFF HO
WATERFRONT TERR
KINGS REACH

Walton
Mere

CH

P

EASTCLIFF RD

Walton
Prim Sch

STANDLEY RD

PRINCES ESPL

22

Martello
Tower

MELT ST

B1034

24   A   B   25   C   D   26   E   F

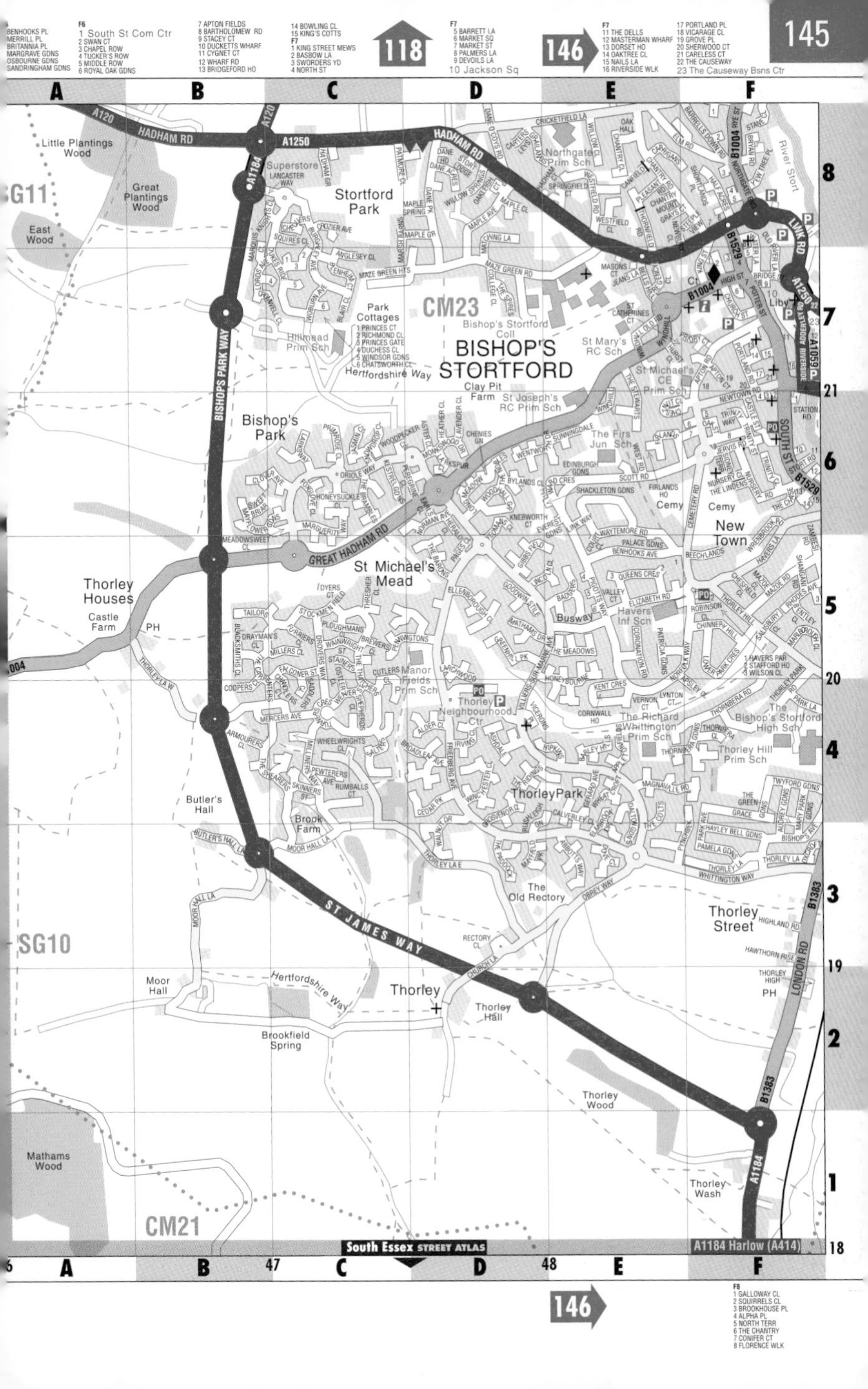

BENHOOKS PL
MERRILL PL
BRITANNIA PL
MARGRAVE GDNS
OSBOURNE GDNS
SANDRINGHAM GDNS
F6
1 South St Com Ctr
2 SWAN CT
3 CHAPEL ROW
4 TUCKER'S ROW
5 MIDDLE ROW
6 ROYAL OAK GDNS
7 APTON FIELDS
8 BARTHOLOMEW RD
9 STACEY CT
10 DUCKETTS WHARF
11 CYGNET CT
12 WHARF RD
13 BRIDGEFORD HO
14 BOWLING CL
15 KING'S COTTS
F7
1 KING STREET MEWS
2 BASBOW LA
3 SWORDERS YD
4 NORTH ST
118
F7
5 BARRETT LA
6 MARKET SQ
7 MARKET ST
8 PALMERS LA
9 DEVOILS LA
10 Jackson Sq
146
F7
11 THE DELLS
12 MASTERMAN WHARF
13 DORSET HO
14 OAKTREE CL
15 NAILS LA
16 RIVERSIDE WLK
17 PORTLAND PL
18 VICARAGE CL
19 GROVE PL
20 SHERWOOD CT
21 CARELESS CT
22 THE CAUSEWAY
23 The Causeway Bsns Ctr
145
A
B
C
D
E
F
Little Plantings Wood
Great Plantings Wood
East Wood
SG11
HADHAM RD
A120
A1250
A1184
Superstore
Stortford Park
Northgate Prim Sch
River Stort
B1004
B1529
LINK RD
HIGH ST
Park Cottages
1 PRINCES CT
2 RICHMOND CL
3 PRINCES GATE
4 DUCHESS CL
5 WINDSOR GDNS
6 CHATSWORTH CL
Hillmead Prim Sch
Hertfordshire Way
CM23
Bishop's Stortford Coll
BISHOP'S STORTFORD
St Mary's RC Sch
St Michael's CE Prim Sch
Clay Pit Farm
St Joseph's RC Prim Sch
BISHOPS PARK WAY
Bishop's Park
The Firs Jun Sch
SOUTH ST
Cemy
New Town
GREAT HADHAM RD
St Michael's Mead
Thorley Houses
Castle Farm
PH
Busway
Havers Inf Sch
Manor Fields Prim Sch
Thorley Neighbourhood Ctr
The Richard Whittington Prim Sch
The Bishop's Stortford High Sch
Thorley Hill Prim Sch
1 HAVERS PAR
2 STAFFORD HO
3 WILSON CL
Butler's Hall
Brook Farm
ThorleyPark
The Old Rectory
ST JAMES WAY
Thorley Street
LONDON RD
B1383
SG10
Moor Hall
Hertfordshire Way
Thorley
Thorley Hall
Brookfield Spring
Thorley Wood
Mathams Wood
Thorley Wash
CM21
South Essex STREET ATLAS
A1184 Harlow (A414)
8
7
21
6
5
20
4
3
19
2
1
18
47
48
146
F8
1 GALLOWAY CL
2 SQUIRRELS CL
3 BROOKHOUSE PL
4 ALPHA PL
5 NORTH TERR
6 THE CHANTRY
7 CONIFER CT
8 FLORENCE WLK

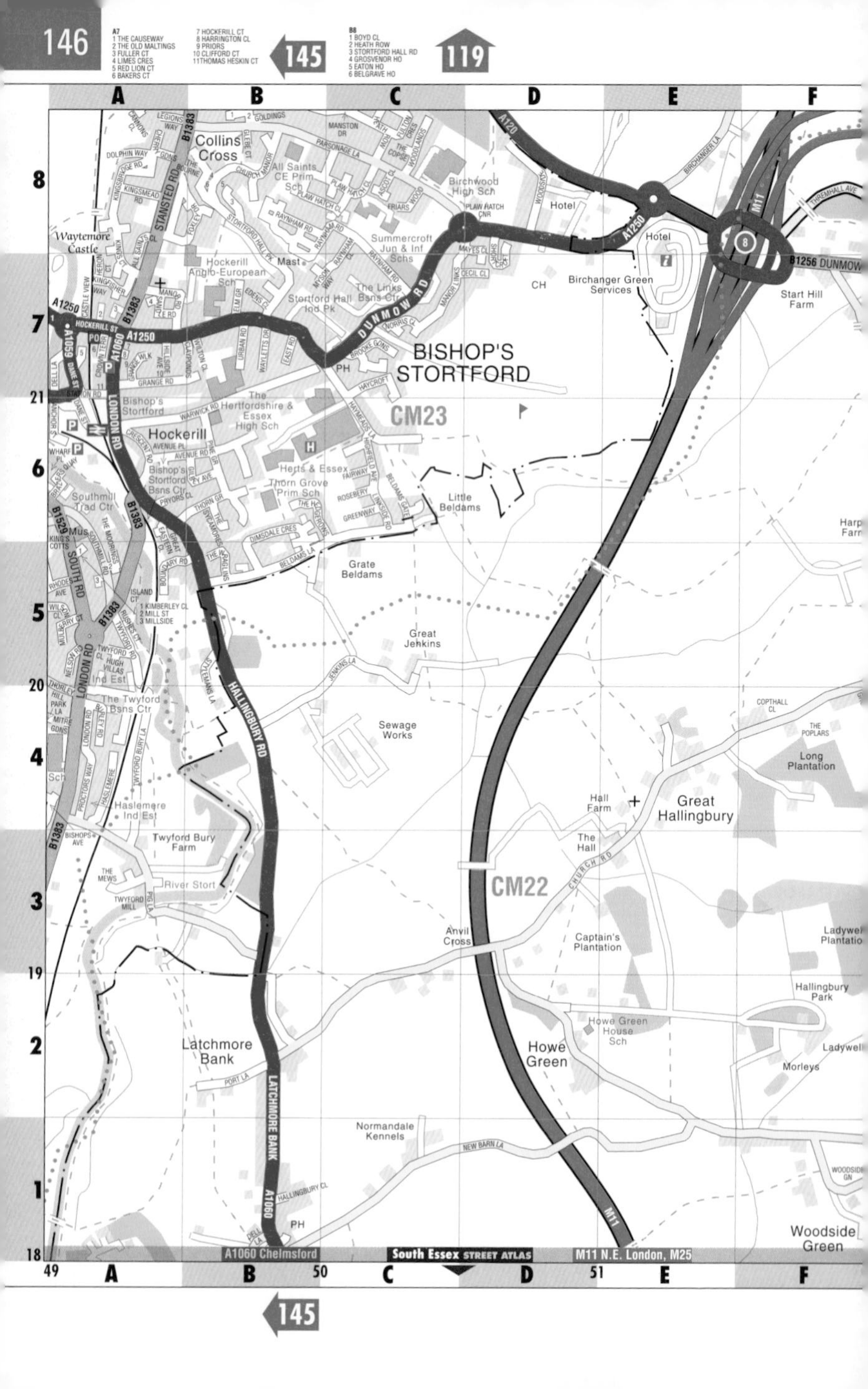
Collins Cross
All Saints CE Prim Sch
Birchwood High Sch
Hotel
Waytemore Castle
Hockerill Anglo-European Sch
Mast
Summercroft Jun & Inf Schs
The Links Bsns Ctr
Stortford Hall Ind Pk
Birchanger Green Services
CH
Start Hill Farm
BISHOP'S STORTFORD
DUNMOW RD
B1256 DUNMOW
A1250
A120
M11
A1060
B1383
A1059
STANSTED RD
LONDON RD
HOCKERILL ST
Bishop's Stortford
Hockerill
The Hertfordshire & Essex High Sch
CM23
Herts & Essex
Thorn Grove Prim Sch
Bishop's Stortford Bsns Ctr
Southmill Trad Ctr
Mus
Little Beldams
Grate Beldams
B1529
SOUTH RD
1 KIMBERLEY CL
2 MILL ST
3 MILLSIDE
Great Jenkins
Ind Est
The Twyford Bsns Ctr
HALLINGBURY RD
Sewage Works
Sch
Haslemere Ind Est
Twyford Bury Farm
River Stort
Hall Farm
Great Hallingbury
The Hall
Long Plantation
CM22
CHURCH RD
Anvil Cross
Captain's Plantation
Ladywell Plantation
Hallingbury Park
Howe Green House Sch
Latchmore Bank
Howe Green
Ladywell
Morleys
LATCHMORE BANK
Normandale Kennels
NEW BARN LA
PH
Woodside Green
Harp Farm

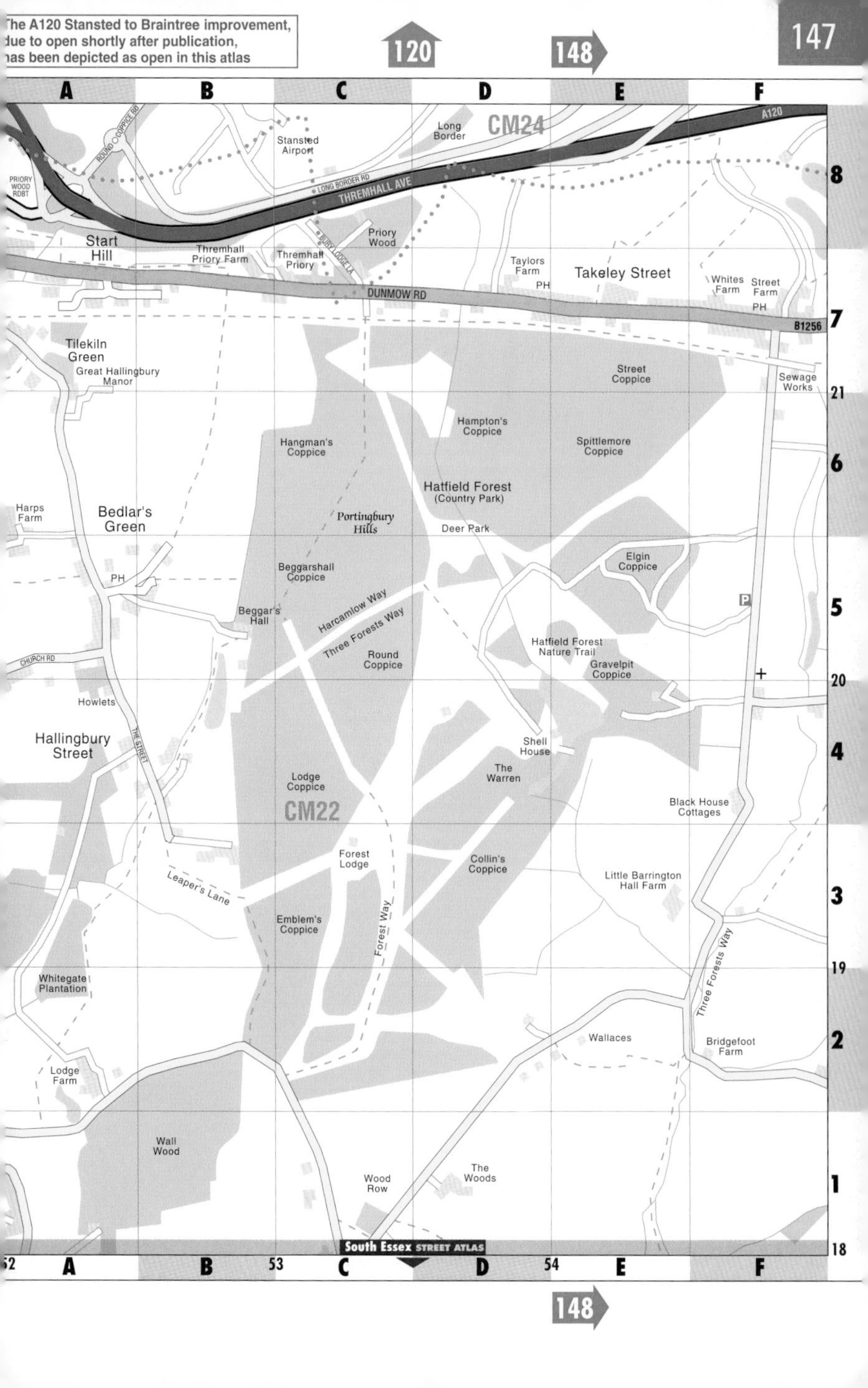

The A120 Stansted to Braintree improvement, due to open shortly after publication, has been depicted as open in this atlas

120   148

A   B   C   D   E   F

8

Long Border   CM24
Stansted Airport
A LONG BORDER RD
THREMHALL AVE
PRIORY WOOD RDBT
A120
PRIORY WOOD RD
Priory Wood
Taylors Farm
PH
Takeley Street
Whites Farm
Street Farm PH

Start Hill
Thremhall Priory Farm
Thremhall Priory
DUNMOW RD
B1256
7

Tilekiln Green
Great Hallingbury Manor
Street Coppice
Sewage Works
21

Hampton's Coppice
Hangman's Coppice
Spittlemore Coppice
6

Harps Farm
Bedlar's Green
Hatfield Forest (Country Park)
Portingbury Hills
Deer Park
Elgin Coppice
P

Beggarshall Coppice
Hatfield Forest Nature Trail
+
5

Beggar's Hall
Hargamlow Way
Three Forests Way
Round Coppice
Gravelpit Coppice
20

CHURCH RD
Howlets
Shell House
The Warren
Black House Cottages
4

Hallingbury Street
THE STREET
Lodge Coppice
CM22
Collin's Coppice
Little Barrington Hall Farm
3

Leaper's Lane
Forest Lodge
Forest Way
Whitegate Plantation
Emblem's Coppice
Three Forests Way
19

Wallaces
Bridgefoot Farm
2

Lodge Farm
Wall Wood
Wood Row
The Woods
1

South Essex STREET ATLAS
18

52   **A**   **B**   53   **C**   **D**   54   **E**   **F**

148

147
121

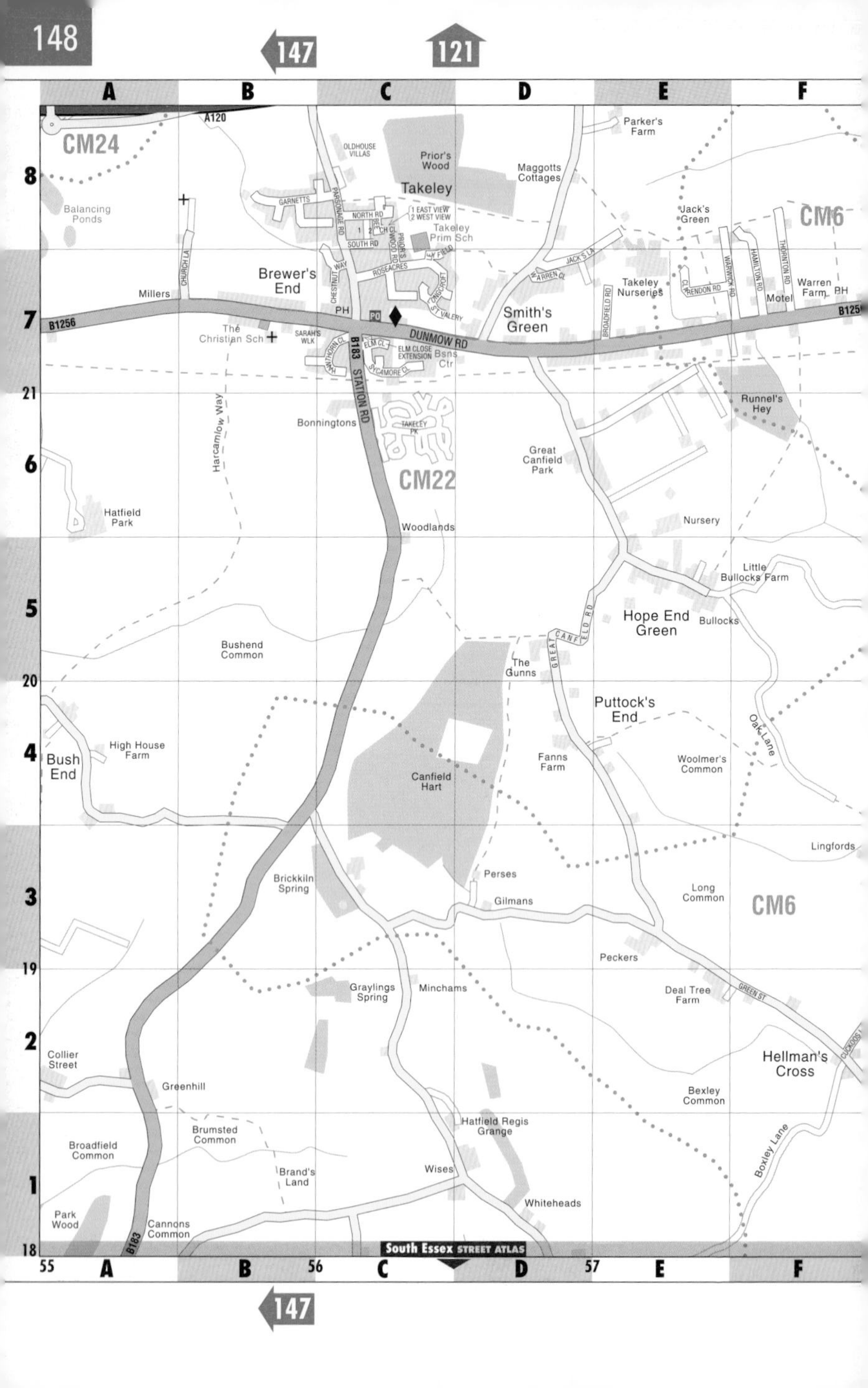
A
B
C
D
E
F
A120
CM24
8
Balancing Ponds
OLDHOUSE VILLAS
Prior's Wood
Takeley
Maggotts Cottages
Parker's Farm
GARNETTS
PARSONAGE RD
NORTH RD
1 EAST VIEW
2 WEST VIEW
Takeley Prim Sch
SOUTH RD
Jack's Green
CM6
CHURCH LA
Brewer's End
CHESTNUT WAY
ROSEACRES
JACK'S LA
WARREN CL
Takeley Nurseries
CLARENDON RD
WARWICK RD
HAMILTON RD
THORNTON RD
Warren Farm
PH
Motel
Millers
7
B1256
PH
PO
ST VALERY
Smith's Green
The Christian Sch
SARAH'S WLK
HAWTHORN CL
ELM CL
ELM CLOSE EXTENSION
Bsns Ctr
DUNMOW RD
BROADFIELD RD
B1256
B183
STATION RD
SYCAMORE CL
21
Harcamlow Way
Bonningtons
TAKELEY PK
Runnel's Hey
Great Canfield Park
6
CM22
Hatfield Park
Woodlands
Nursery
Little Bullocks Farm
5
Hope End Green
Bullocks
GREAT CANFIELD RD
Bushend Common
The Gunns
20
Puttock's End
Oak Lane
4
Bush End
High House Farm
Fanns Farm
Woolmer's Common
Canfield Hart
Lingfords
Perses
Brickkiln Spring
3
Gilmans
Long Common
CM6
Peckers
19
Graylings Spring
Minchams
Deal Tree Farm
GREEN ST
2
Collier Street
Hellman's Cross
CUCKOOS LA
Greenhill
Bexley Common
Hatfield Regis Grange
Brumsted Common
Broadfield Common
Boxley Lane
1
Brand's Land
Wises
Whiteheads
Park Wood
Cannons Common
B183
18
55
56
57

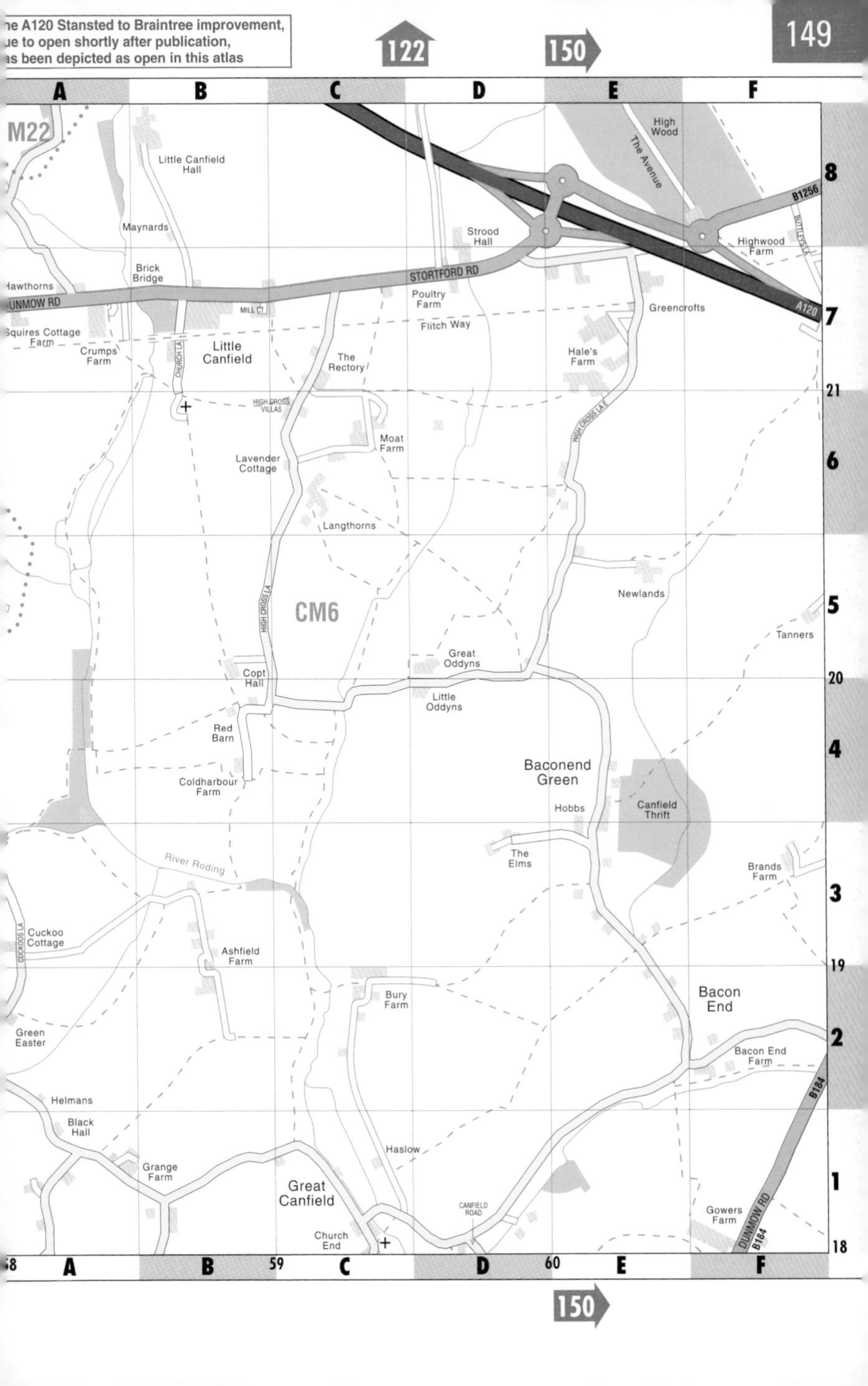

The A120 Stansted to Braintree improvement,
ue to open shortly after publication,
as been depicted as open in this atlas

122   150

M22

8

Little Canfield
Hall

B1256

Maynards

Strood
Hall

Highwood
Farm

Hawthorns
UNMOW RD

Brick
Bridge

STORTFORD RD

Poultry
Farm

Greencrofts

A120

7

MILL CT

Flitch Way

Squires Cottage
Farm

Little
Canfield

The
Rectory

Hale's
Farm

21

Crumps
Farm

HIGH CROSS
VILLAS

CHURCH LA

HIGH CROSS LA

6

Lavender
Cottage

Moat
Farm

Langthorns

CM6

Newlands

5

Tanners

HIGH CROSS LA

Great
Oddyns

20

Copt
Hall

Little
Oddyns

Red
Barn

Baconend
Green

4

Coldharbour
Farm

Hobbs

Canfield
Thrift

River Roding

The
Elms

Brands
Farm

3

Cuckoo
Cottage

Ashfield
Farm

19

Green
Easter

Bury
Farm

Bacon
End

2

Helmans

Bacon End
Farm

B184

Black
Hall

Grange
Farm

Great
Canfield

Haslow

CANFIELD
ROAD

Gowers
Farm

1

Church
End

DUNMOW RD
B184

18

58   A   B   59   C   D   60   E   F

150

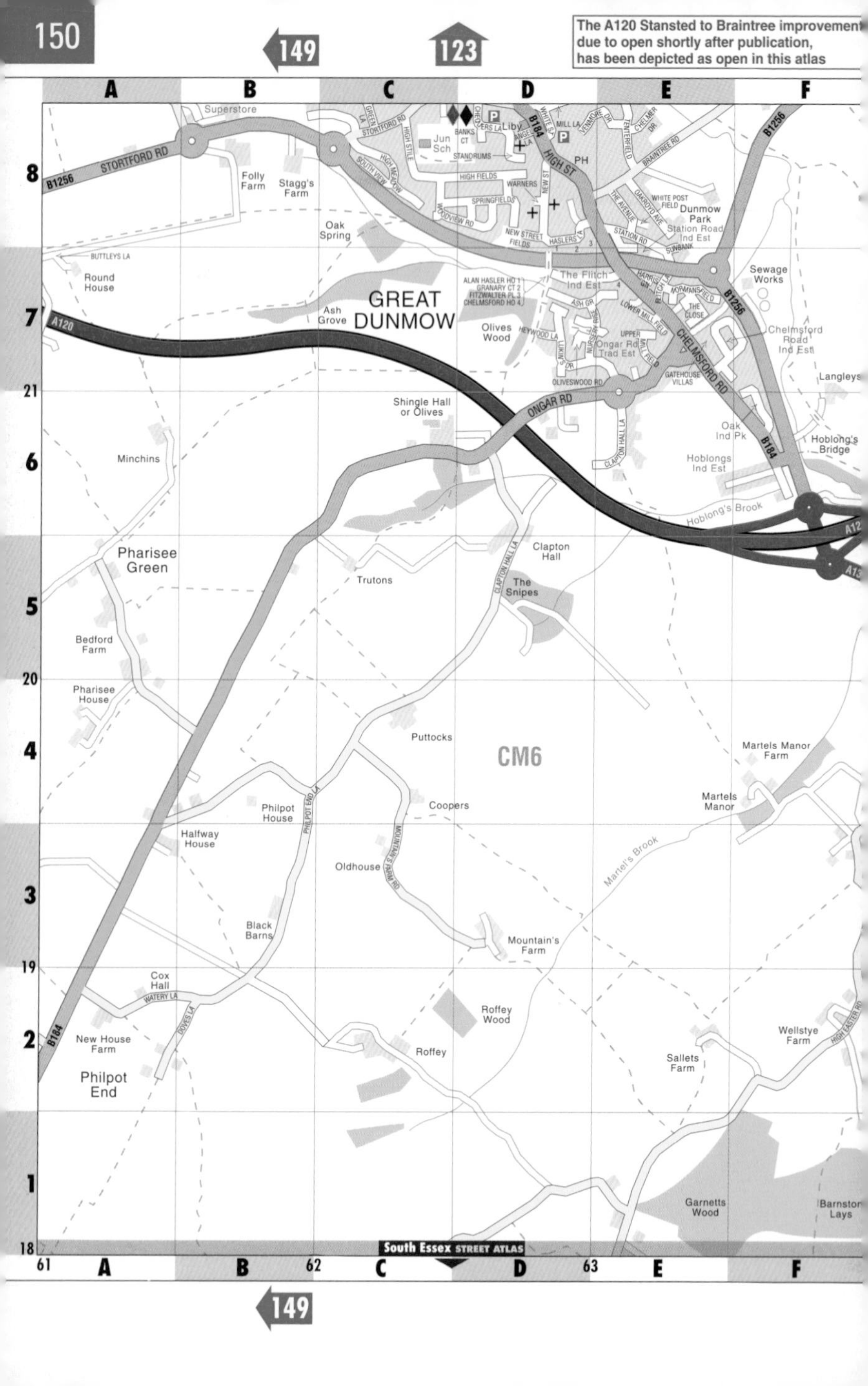

The A120 Stansted to Braintree improvement due to open shortly after publication, has been depicted as open in this atlas

149 123

8

B1256 STORTFORD RD

Superstore

Folly Farm

Stagg's Farm

Oak Spring

BUTTLEYS LA

Round House

7

A120

Ash Grove

GREAT DUNMOW

Olives Wood

GREENFIELDS RD
STORTFORD RD
HIGH STILE
SOUTH RD

BANKS CT
Jun Sch
STANDRUMS
HIGH FIELDS

WARNERS

SPRINGFIELD

NEW STREET FIELDS
HASLERS

B184 HIGH ST MILL LA

PH

LINDSELL
BRAINTREE RD

WHITE POST FIELD
Dunmow Park
Station Road Ind Est

ALAN HASLER HO
GRANARY CT
FITZWALTER PL
CHELMSFORD HO

The Flitch Ind Est

STATION RD

NEWHOUSE RD

Sewage Works

B1256

Chelmsford Road Ind Est

Langleys

21

Shingle Hall or Olives

ONGAR RD

CLAPTON HALL LA

UPPER
S Ongar Rd Trad Est
OLIVESWOOD RD
GATEHOUSE VILLAS

THE CLOSE
LOWER MILL LA
CHELMSFORD RD

Oak Ind Pk

Hoblongs Ind Est

Hoblong's Bridge

6

Minchins

Hoblong's Brook

A12

A13

Pharisee Green

Trutons

Clapton Hall

The Snipes

5

Bedford Farm

CLAPTON HALL LA

20

Pharisee House

Puttocks

4

Martels Manor Farm

CM6

Coopers

Martels Manor

Philpot House

MOUNTAINS FARM LA

PHILPOT END

Martel's Brook

Halfway House

Oldhouse

3

Black Barns

Mountain's Farm

19

Cox Hall

WATERY LA

DOVES LA

Roffey Wood

Roffey

Sallets Farm

Wellstye Farm

2

B184

New House Farm

Philpot End

1

Garnetts Wood

Barnston Lays

18

61 A B 62 C D 63 E F

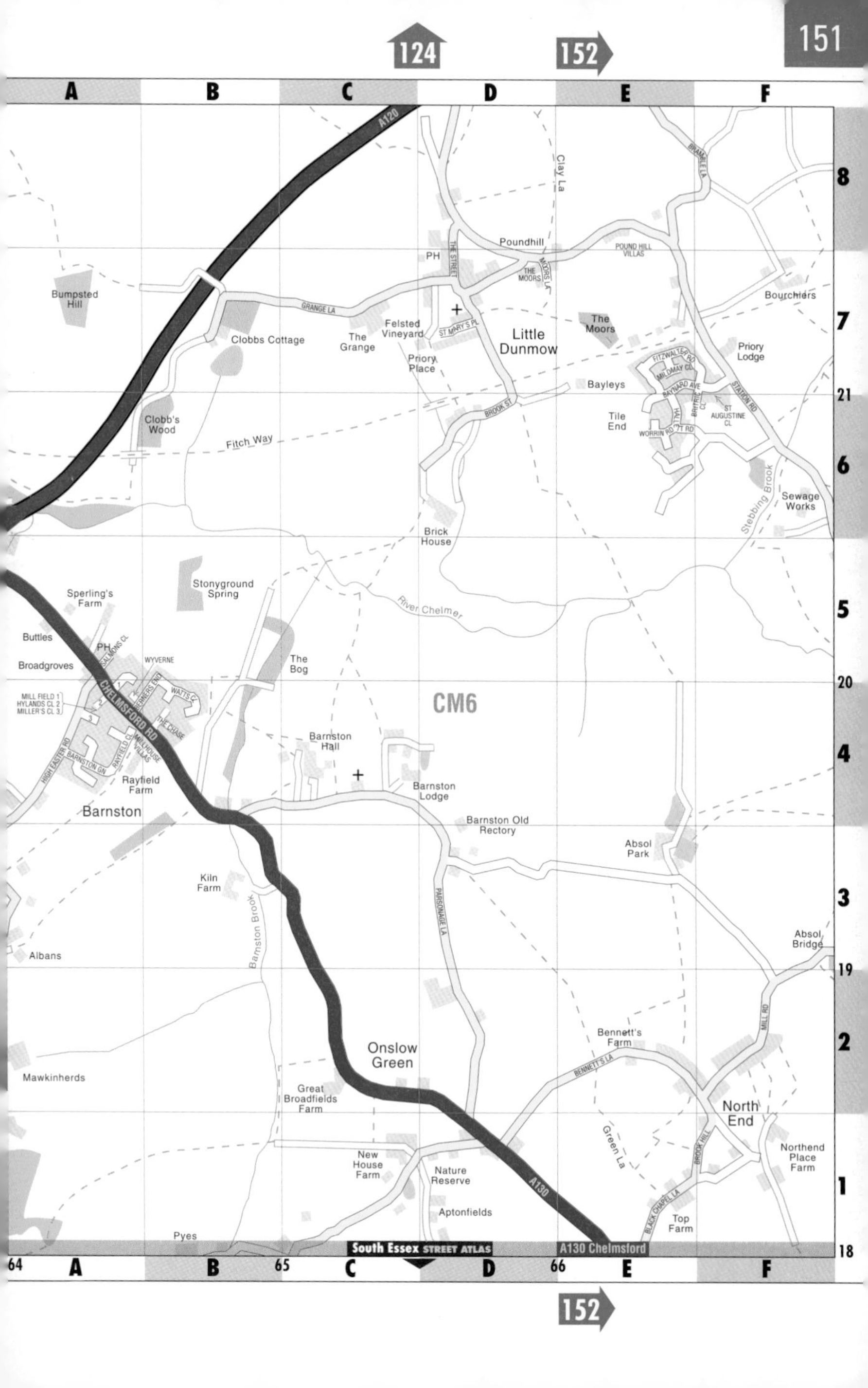
124
152
A
B
C
D
E
F
8
7
21
6
5
20
4
3
19
2
1
18
A120
Clay La
Poundhill
POUND HILL VILLAS
PH
THE STREET
THE MOORS
MOORS LA
Bumpsted Hill
GRANGE LA
Felsted Vineyard
ST MARY'S PL
Little Dunmow
The Moors
Bourchiers
Clobbs Cottage
The Grange
Priory Place
Priory Lodge
FITZWALTER RD
MILDMAY CL
BAYNARD AVE
Bayleys
BROOK ST
STATION RD
Clobb's Wood
Tile End
ST AUGUSTINE CL
WORRIN RD
Fitch Way
Stebbing Brook
Sewage Works
Brick House
Stonyground Spring
Sperling's Farm
River Chelmer
Buttles
PH
SALMONS CL
WYVERNE
Broadgroves
The Bog
MILL FIELD 1
HYLANDS CL 2
MILLER'S CL 3
CHELMSFORD RD
WATTS CL
THE CHASE
CM6
Barnston Hall
HIGH EASTER RD
BARNSTON GN
RAYFIELD CL
MILLHOUSE VILLAS
Rayfield Farm
Barnston Lodge
Barnston
Barnston Old Rectory
Absol Park
Kiln Farm
PARSONAGE LA
Barnston Brook
Absol Bridge
Albans
MILL RD
Bennett's Farm
Onslow Green
Mawkinherds
BENNETT'S LA
Great Broadfields Farm
North End
Green La
BROOK HILL
New House Farm
Nature Reserve
Northend Place Farm
A130
BLACK CHAPEL LA
Aptonfields
Top Farm
Pyes
South Essex STREET ATLAS
A130 Chelmsford
64
65
66
152

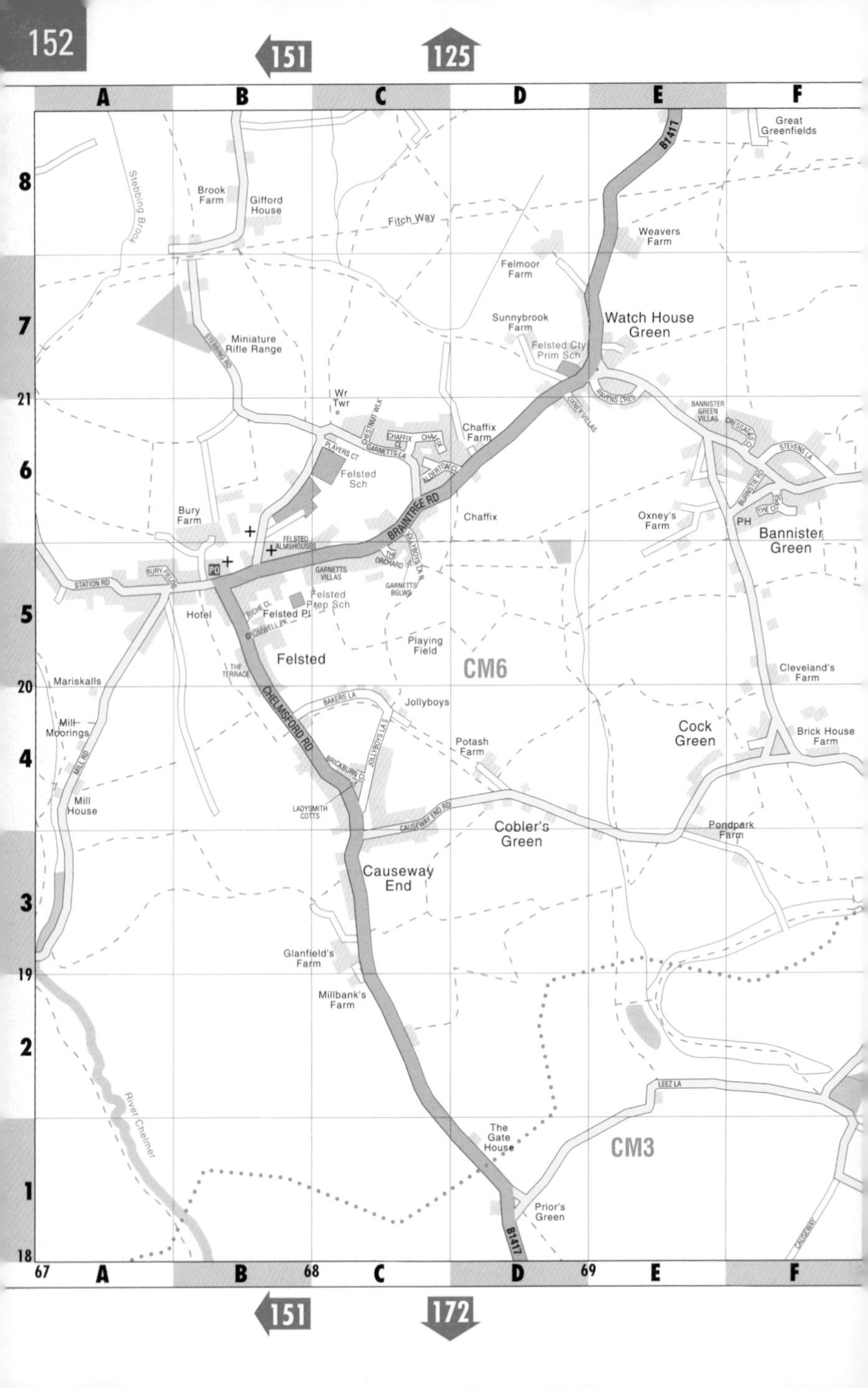

A   B   C   D   E   F

8

Great
Greenfields

Brook
Farm

Gifford
House

Fitch Way

Weavers
Farm

Felmoor
Farm

7

Miniature
Rifle Range

Sunnybrook
Farm

Felsted Cty
Prim Sch

Watch House
Green

21

Wr
Twr

Chaffix

Chaffix
Farm

Bannister
Green Villas

6

Felsted
Sch

Oxney's
Farm

PH

Bannister
Green

Bury
Farm

Chaffix

FELSTED
ALMSHOUSES

PO

Garnetts
Villas

The
Orchard

GARNETTS
BGLWS

5

STATION RD

Hotel

Felsted Pl.

Felsted Prep Sch

Playing
Field

CM6

Cleveland's
Farm

Felsted

20

Mariskalls

THE TERRACE

Jollyboys

Cock
Green

Brick House
Farm

Mill
Moorings

Potash
Farm

4

CHELMSFORD RD

BAKERS LA

BRICKBURN

LADYSMITH
COTTS

CAUSEWAY END RD

Cobler's
Green

Pondpark
Farm

Mill
House

Cobler's
Green

3

Glanfield's
Farm

Causeway
End

19

Millbank's
Farm

2

River Chelmer

LEEZ LA

CM3

The Gate
House

1

Prior's
Green

18

67   A   B   68   C   D   69   E   F

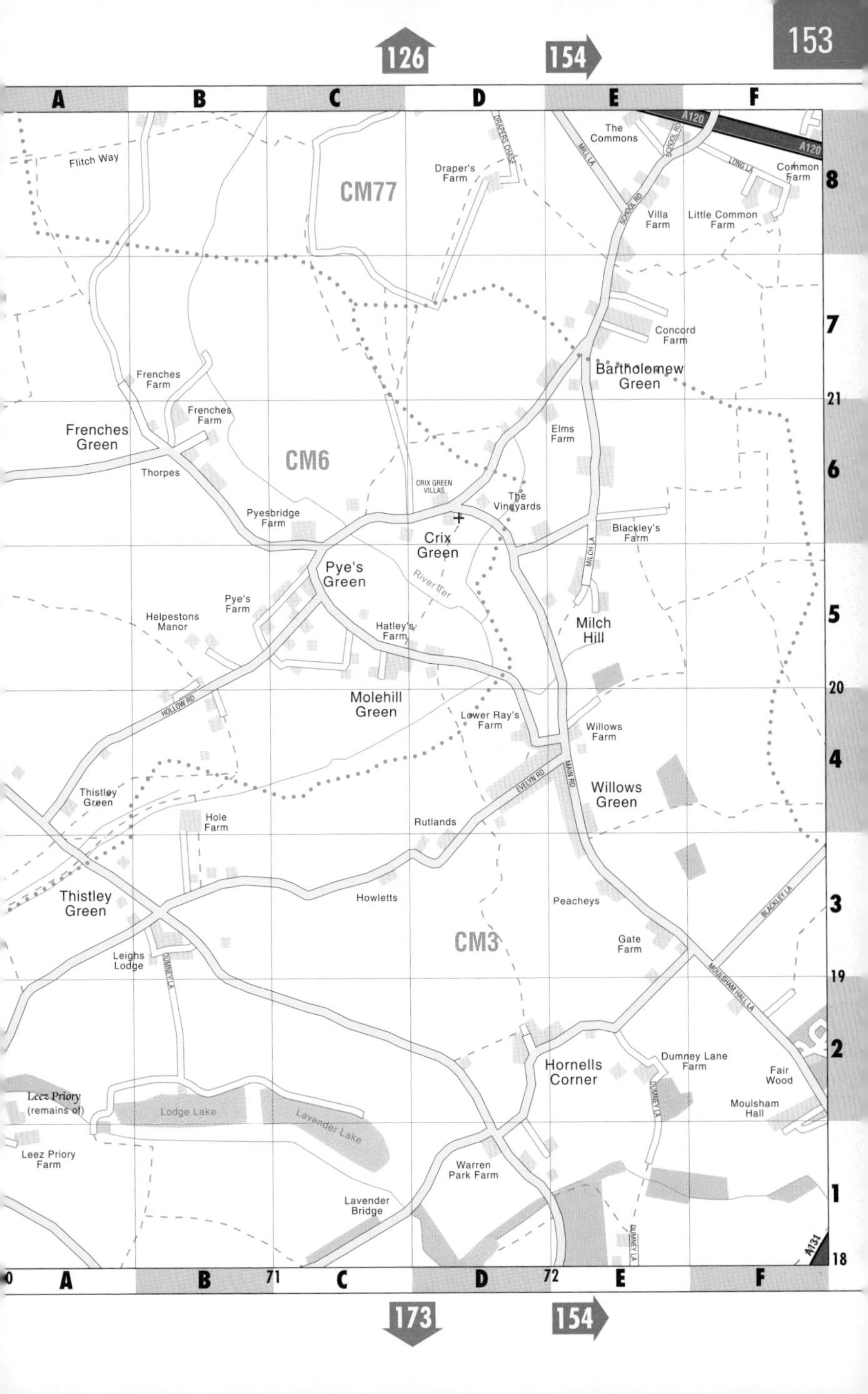
126
154
A
B
C
D
E
F
Flitch Way
CM77
Draper's Farm
DRAPERS CHASE
The Commons
MILL LA
SCHOOL RD
A120
LONG LA
Common Farm
Villa Farm
Little Common Farm
8
7
Concord Farm
Bartholomew Green
21
Frenches Farm
Frenches Farm
Frenches Green
Thorpes
CM6
Elms Farm
6
CRIX GREEN VILLAS
The Vineyards
Pyesbridge Farm
Crix Green
Blackley's Farm
MILCH LA
Pye's Green
River Ter
Pye's Farm
Helpestons Manor
Hatley's Farm
Milch Hill
5
HOLLOW RD
Molehill Green
Lower Ray's Farm
20
Willows Farm
4
EVELYN RD
MAIN RD
Willows Green
Thistley Green
Hole Farm
Rutlands
Thistley Green
Howletts
Peacheys
3
BLACKLEY LA
CM3
Gate Farm
Leighs Lodge
DUMNEY LA
MOULSHAM HALL LA
19
Hornells Corner
Dumney Lane Farm
2
Fair Wood
Leez Priory (remains of)
Lodge Lake
Lavender Lake
DUMNEY LA
Moulsham Hall
Leez Priory Farm
Warren Park Farm
1
Lavender Bridge
DUMNEY LA
A131
18
70
71
72
173
154

153 127

A B C D E F

8

A120
Lakes Farm
Stanford Farm
QUEENBOROUGH LA
STOCKMAN TERR
QUEENBOROUGH GR
A131
B1256
A120
THE LAURELS
TORTOISESHELL WAY
COPPERED YELLOW CL
John Ray Jun & Inf Schs
CM7
The Notley High Sch

Great Notley

7

DRAYMANS WAY
BLICKLING RD
Prim Sch
TAILORS WAY
COOPERS CRES
PH
Hill House Farm

FELBRIGG CL
SADDLERS CL
BUTTERMERE
SUMMERLEAZE CT
LUCHAM HALL LA
Hayeswood Farm

21

White Court Prim Sch
1 BURGHLEY CL
FRAMLINGHAM WAY
THORINGTON
BRANCASTER DR
PINTAIL CL
CALDBECK WAY
PICKPOCKET LA
CM77
Row Green
BAKER'S LA
Oak Farm
BUCK HILL
CHURCH RD

6

POCHARD WAY
SHELDUCK
MEADOW
WIGEON CL
MALLARD CL
TEAL CL

5

Abattoir
Card's Farm

20

Great Slampseys
BLACKLEY LA
PH
Friar's Farm
DAGNET'S LA

4

Young's End
Lynderswood Farm
Lynderswood Court
Wren Park
Dagnets Farm

3

CM8
Hazeltop

19

Essex Show Ground
Bushy Wood
Paul's Wood
Hazelton Wood

2

CM3
Bateman's Farm
MAIN RD
RANTELS LA

1

A131
North Whitehouse
Little Walley Hall

18

73 A B 74 C D 75 E F

153 174

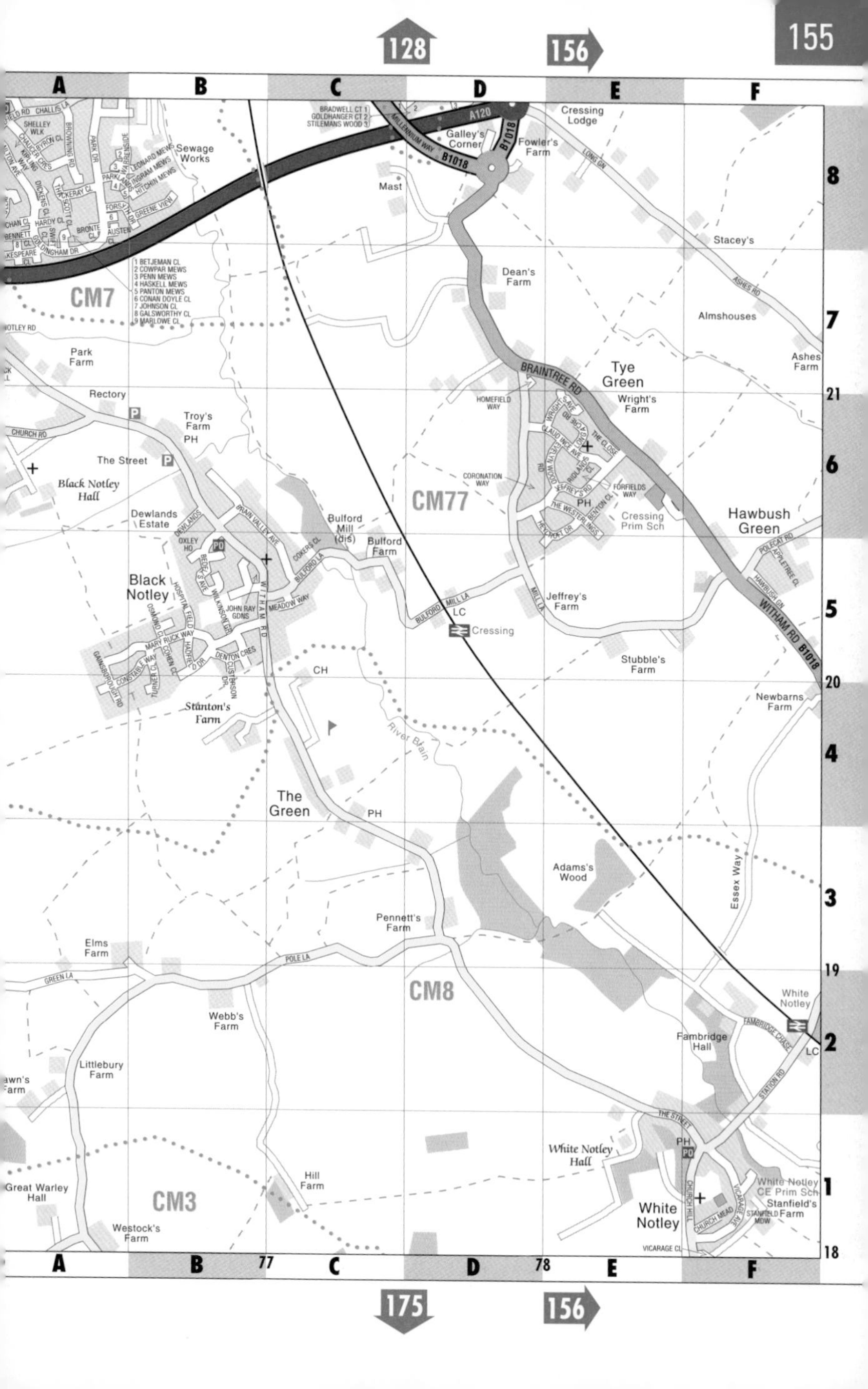
128
156
A
B
C
D
E
F
Sewage Works
Cressing Lodge
Galley's Corner
Fowler's Farm
A120
B1018
MILLENNIUM WAY
BRADWELL CT 1
GOLDHANGER CT 2
STILEMANS WOOD 3
LONG GN
Mast
Stacey's
Dean's Farm
ASHES RD
Almshouses
Ashes Farm
CM7
1 BETJEMAN CL
2 COWPAR MEWS
3 PENN MEWS
4 HASKELL MEWS
5 PANTON MEWS
6 CONAN DOYLE CL
7 JOHNSON CL
8 GALSWORTHY CL
9 MARLOWE CL
SHELLEY WLK
CHAUCER CRES
BYRON CL
KIPLING WAY
MILTON AVE
BROWNING RD
PARK DR
DICKENS CL
THACKERAY CL
HARDY CL
SWIFT CL
BRONTE CL
AUSTEN CL
GOLDINGHAM DR
LEONARD MEWS
INGRAM MEWS
HITCHIN MEWS
GREENE VIEW
FORSYTH DR
PARKLANDS
WARRENSIDE
CHALLIS LA
Park Farm
Rectory
Troy's Farm
PH
The Street
Black Notley Hall
CHURCH RD
Tye Green
Wright's Farm
BRAINTREE RD
HOMEFIELD WAY
CORONATION WAY
CM77
THE CLOSE
FORFIELDS WAY
PH
Cressing Prim Sch
Hawbush Green
THE WESTERLINGS
JEFFREY'S RD
BENTON CL
Dewlands Estate
DEWLANDS
OXLEY HO
PO
BRAIN VALLEY AVE
COKERS CL
BULFORD LA
Bulford Mill (dis)
Bulford Farm
Black Notley
HOSPITAL FIELD
WITHAM RD
MEADOW WAY
JOHN RAY GDNS
WILKINSON DR
BEDE'S AVE
BULFORD MILL LA
LC
Cressing
MILL LA
Jeffrey's Farm
POLECAT RD
APPLETREE CL
HAWBUSH GN
WITHAM RD
B1018
MARY RUCK WAY
HADFIELD DR
DENTON CRES
CUSTERSON DR
CONSTABLE WAY
TURNER CL
COHEN CL
GAINSBOROUGH RD
ORMOND CL
CH
Stubble's Farm
Newbarns Farm
Stanton's Farm
River Brain
The Green
PH
Adams's Wood
Essex Way
Pennett's Farm
Elms Farm
POLE LA
GREEN LA
CM8
White Notley
Webb's Farm
FAMBRIDGE CHASE
Fambridge Hall
LC
STATION RD
Littlebury Farm
THE STREET
PH
PO
White Notley Hall
CHURCH HILL
VICARAGE AVE
CHURCH MEAD
STANFIELD MDW
White Notley CE Prim Sch
Stanfield's Farm
White Notley
Great Warley Hall
CM3
Hill Farm
Westock's Farm
VICARAGE CL
8
7
21
6
5
20
4
3
19
2
1
18
77
78

155
129

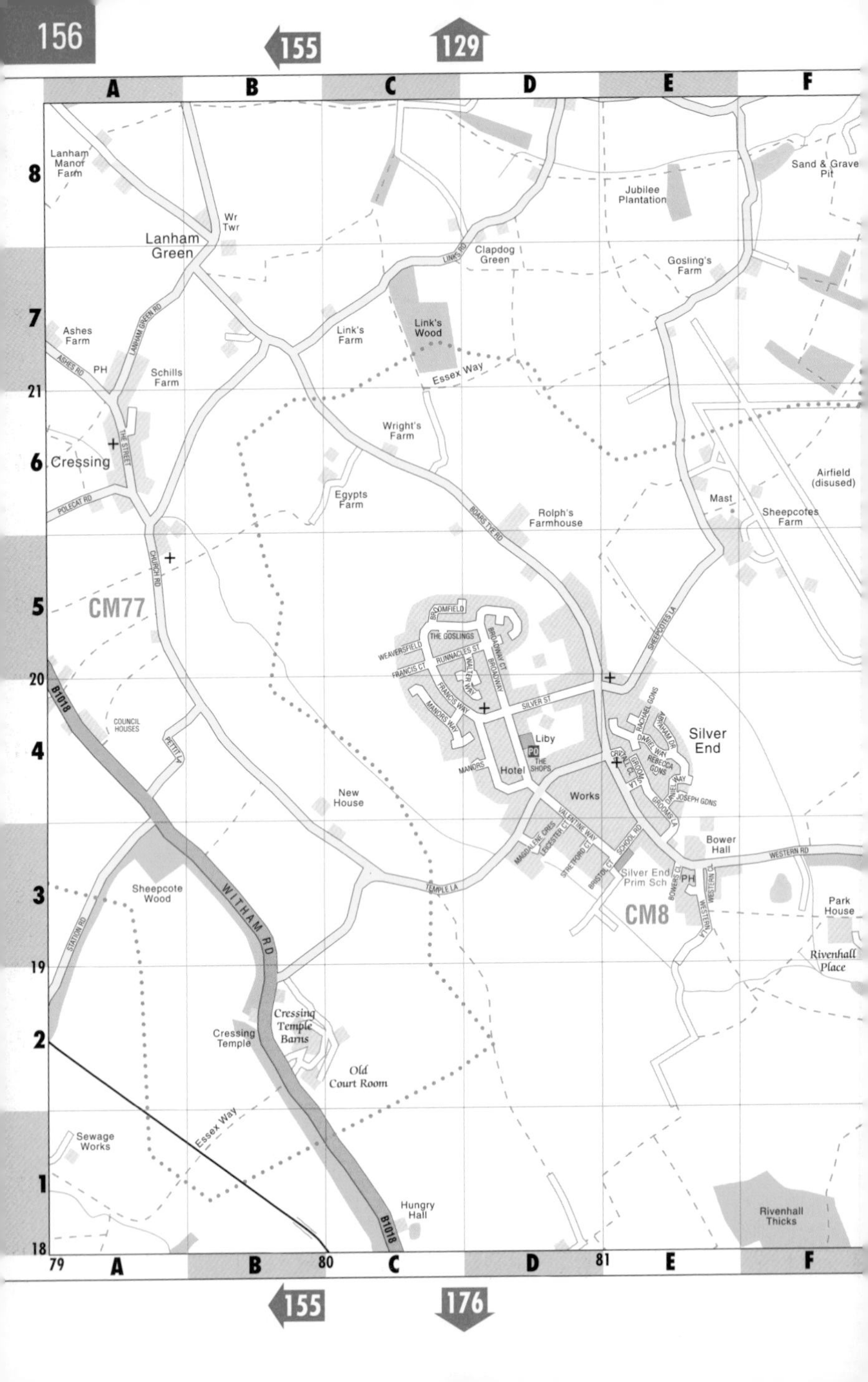
A
B
C
D
E
F
8
7
21
6
5
20
4
3
19
2
1
18
79
80
81
Lanham Manor Farm
Wr Twr
Lanham Green
LANHAM GREEN RD
Ashes Farm
ASHES RD
PH
Schills Farm
Cressing
THE STREET
POLECAT RD
CHURCH RD
CM77
B1018
COUNCIL HOUSES
PETTIT LA
STATION RD
Sheepcote Wood
WITHAM RD
Cressing Temple
Cressing Temple Barns
Old Court Room
Essex Way
Sewage Works
Hungry Hall
Link's Farm
LINKS RD
Link's Wood
Essex Way
Clapdog Green
Wright's Farm
Egypts Farm
BOARS TYE RD
Rolph's Farmhouse
New House
TEMPLE LA
Jubilee Plantation
Gosling's Farm
Sand & Gravel Pit
Airfield (disused)
Mast
Sheepcotes Farm
SHEEPCOTES LA
BROOMFIELD
THE GOSLINGS
WEAVERSFIELD
FRANCIS CT
RUNNACLES ST
WALTER WAY
BROADWAY
BROADWAY CT
FRANCIS WAY
MANORS WAY
SILVER ST
Liby
PO
THE SHOPS
Hotel
MANORS
Works
VALENTINE WAY
MAGDALENE CRES
LEICESTER CT
STRETFORD CT
BRISTOL CT
SCHOOL RD
Silver End Prim Sch
CM8
Silver End
RACHAEL GDNS
ABRAHAM DR
DANIEL WAY
REBECCA GDNS
CRITTALL CL
GROOMS LA
JOSEPH GDNS
Bower Hall
WESTERN RD
PH
BOWERS CL
WESTERN CL
WESTERN LA
Park House
Rivenhall Place
Rivenhall Thicks

155
176

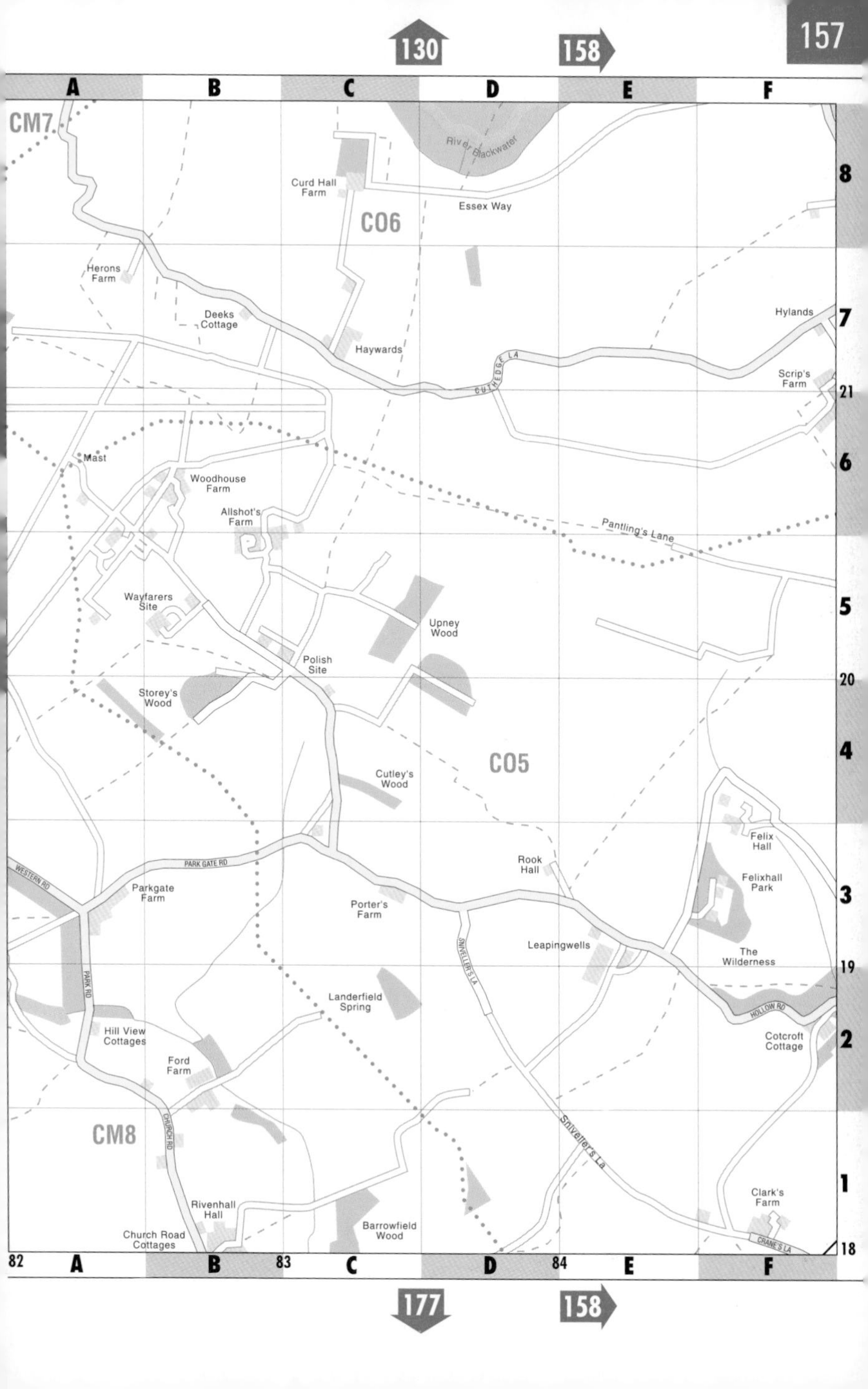

CM7

8

Curd Hall Farm

CO6

River Blackwater

Essex Way

Herons Farm

Deeks Cottage

Haywards

7

21

CUTLEDGE LA

Hylands

Scrip's Farm

6

Mast

Woodhouse Farm

Allshot's Farm

Pantling's Lane

Wayfarers Site

Upney Wood

5

Polish Site

Storey's Wood

20

Cutley's Wood

CO5

4

PARK GATE RD

Parkgate Farm

Porter's Farm

Rook Hall

Felix Hall

Felixhall Park

3

WESTERN RD

Leapingwells

The Wilderness

19

PARK RD

Hill View Cottages

Landerfield Spring

Cotcroft Cottage

HOLTON RD

2

Ford Farm

CHURCH RD

INTLEBE'S LA

SNIVELLER'S LA

CM8

Clark's Farm

1

Rivenhall Hall

Church Road Cottages

Barrowfield Wood

CRANE'S LA

18

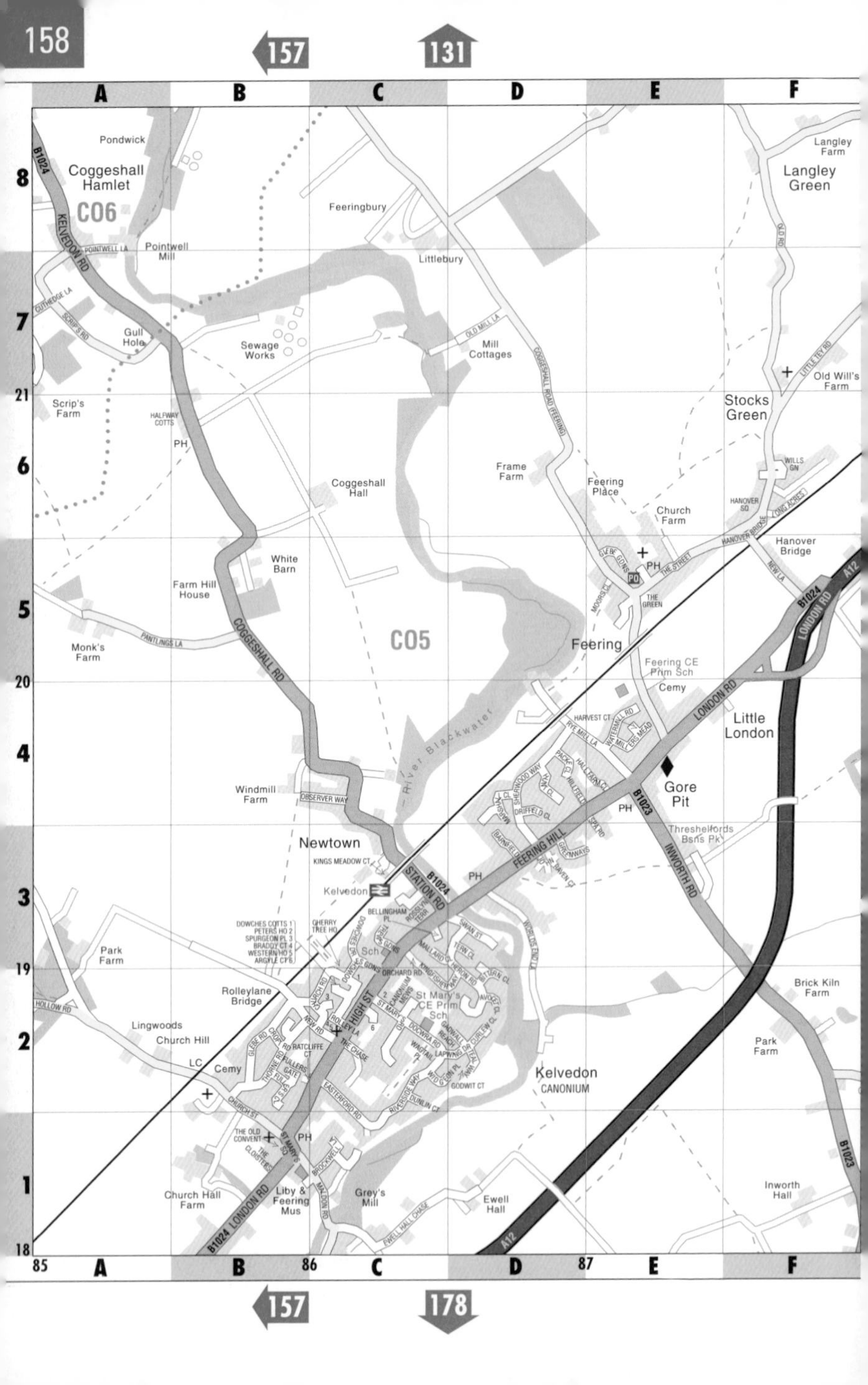

157 131

A **B** **C** **D** **E** **F**

Pondwick

Coggeshall
Hamlet

CO6

Feeringbury

Langley
Farm

Langley
Green

8

Pointwell
Mill

KELVEDON RD

COTTAGE LA

SCRIP'S RD

Gull
Hole

7

Littlebury

Mill
Cottages

Old Will's
Farm

Stocks
Green

21

Scrip's
Farm

Sewage
Works

HALFWAY
COTTS

PH

OLD MILL LA

COGGESHALL ROAD FEERING

WILLS
GN

HANOVER
SQ

LONG CROFTS

6

Coggeshall
Hall

Frame
Farm

Feering
Place

Church
Farm

Hanover
Bridge

HANOVER RD

A12

B1023

LONDON RD

Farm Hill
House

White
Barn

CO5

PANTLINGS LA

COGGESHALL RD

Feering

PH
PO

GLEBE AVE
GLEBE CL

THE
GREEN

MASON RD

NEW LA

5

Monk's
Farm

20

Feering CE
Prim Sch

Cemy

Little
London

River Blackwater

HARVEST CT

Gore
Pit

4

Windmill
Farm

OBSERVER WAY

Newtown

KINGS MEADOW CT

Kelvedon

B1024 STATION RD

PH

FEERING HILL

B1023

Thresherfords
Bsns Pk

INWORTH RD

Brick Kiln
Farm

3

Park
Farm

HOLLOW RD

Rolleylane
Bridge

Lingwoods
Church Hill

LC

Cemy

HIGH ST

DOWCHES COTTS 1
PETERS HO 2
SPURGEON PL 3
BRADY CT 4
WESTERN HO 5
ARGYLE CT 6

CHERRY
TREE HO

BELLINGHAM
PL

Sch

ORCHARD RD

St Mary's
CE Prim
Sch

GODWIT CT

Kelvedon
CANONIUM

Park
Farm

19

Park
Farm

2

RATCLIFFE

EASTFORD RD

'THE OLD
CONVENT'

THE CLOSE

PH

B1024 LONDON RD

Liby &
Feering
Mus

Grey's
Mill

EWEL MILL CHASE

Church Hall
Farm

Ewell
Hall

Inworth
Hall

B1023

1

A12

18

85 **A** **B** 86 **C** **D** 87 **E** **F**

157 178

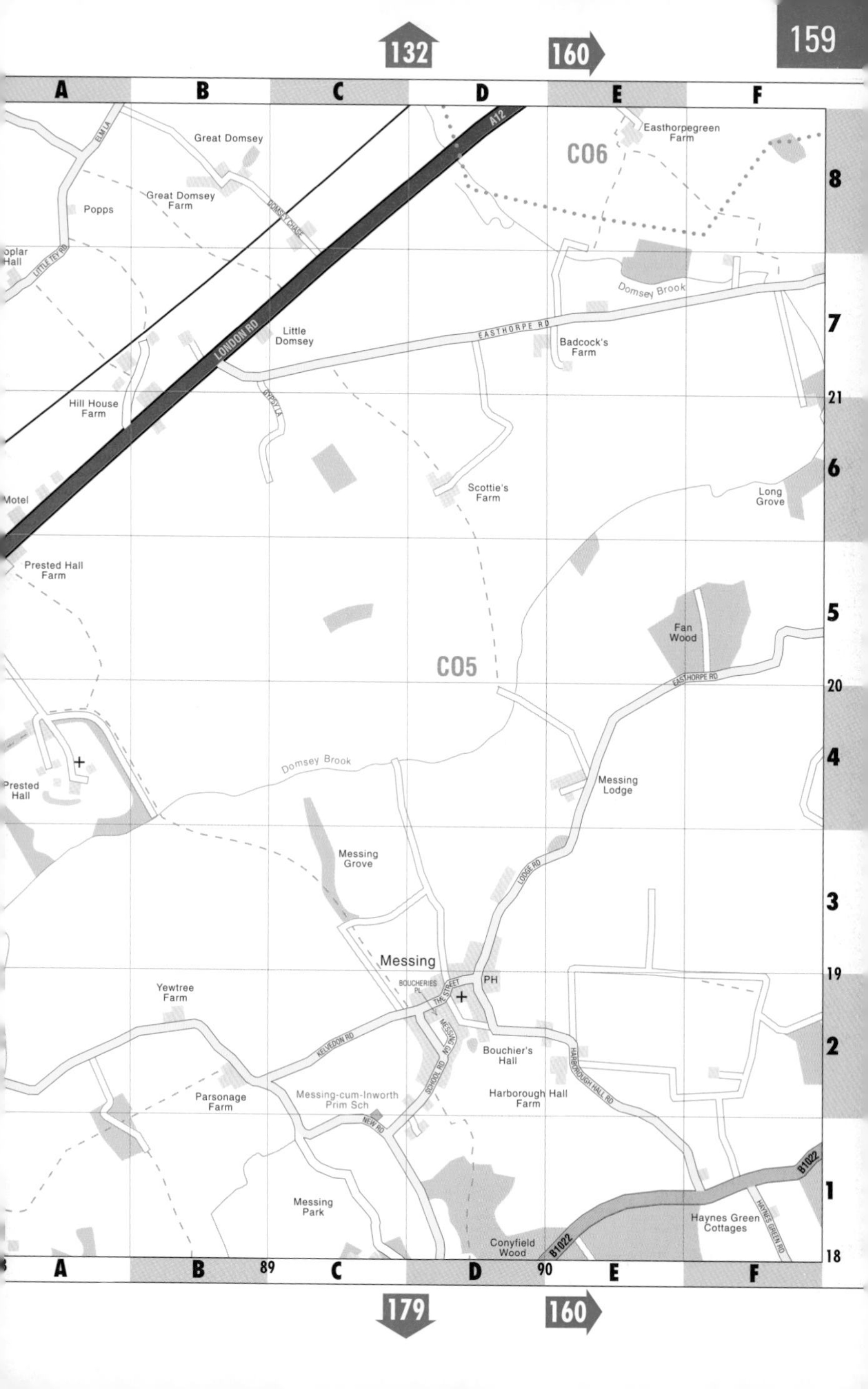

A B C D E F

8

CO6

Great Domsey

Easthorpegreen
Farm

Popps

Great Domsey
Farm

Poplar
Hall

LITTLE FEX RD

DOMSEY CHASE

A12

Domsey Brook

7

LONDON RD

Little
Domsey

EASTHORPE RD

Badcock's
Farm

21

Hill House
Farm

JOBS LA

6

Motel

Scottie's
Farm

Long
Grove

Prested Hall
Farm

5

Fan
Wood

CO5

20

EASTHORPE RD

Prested
Hall

+

Domsey Brook

Messing
Lodge

4

LODGE RD

Messing
Grove

3

Messing

Yewtree
Farm

BOUCHERIES
PL

THE STREET

PH

19

+

Bouchier's
Hall

2

Parsonage
Farm

KELVEDON RD

Messing-cum-Inworth
Prim Sch

SCHOOL RD

MILL RD

Harborough
Farm

Harborough
Hall
Farm

HARBOROUGH HALL RD

NEW RD

B1022

1

Messing
Park

Conyfield
Wood

B1022

Haynes Green
Cottages

JAMES GREEN RD

18

A B 89 C D 90 E F

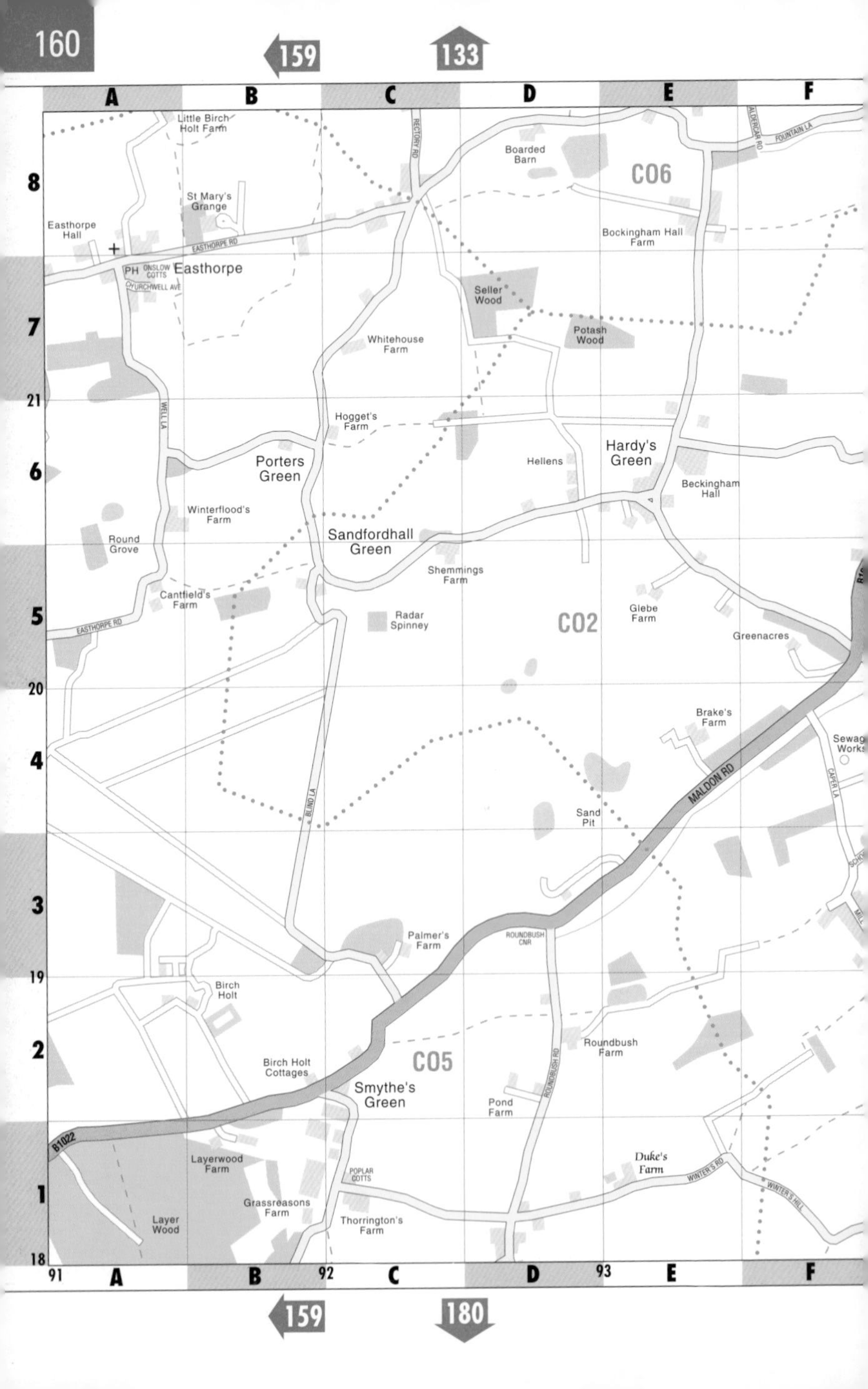

A   B   C   D   E   F

8

Little Birch Holt Farm

St Mary's Grange

Boarded Barn

CO6

Easthorpe Hall

ONSLOW COTTS

PH

EASTHORPE RD

Easthorpe

CHURCHWELL AVE

Bockingham Hall Farm

7

Seller Wood

Whitehouse Farm

Potash Wood

21

Hogget's Farm

Porters Green

Hardy's Green

6

Hellens

Beckingham Hall

Winterflood's Farm

Round Grove

Sandfordhall Green

Cantfield's Farm

Shemmings Farm

5

EASTHORPE RD

Radar Spinney

CO2

Glebe Farm

Greenacres

20

Brake's Farm

4

Sewage Works

BLIND LA

MALDON RD

Sand Pit

3

Palmer's Farm

ROUNDBUSH CNR

19

Birch Holt

2

Birch Holt Cottages

CO5

Roundbush Farm

Smythe's Green

Pond Farm

B1022

Layerwood Farm

POPLAR COTTS

Duke's Farm

1

WINTER'S RD

WINTER'S HILL

Grassreasons Farm

Layer Wood

Thorrington's Farm

18

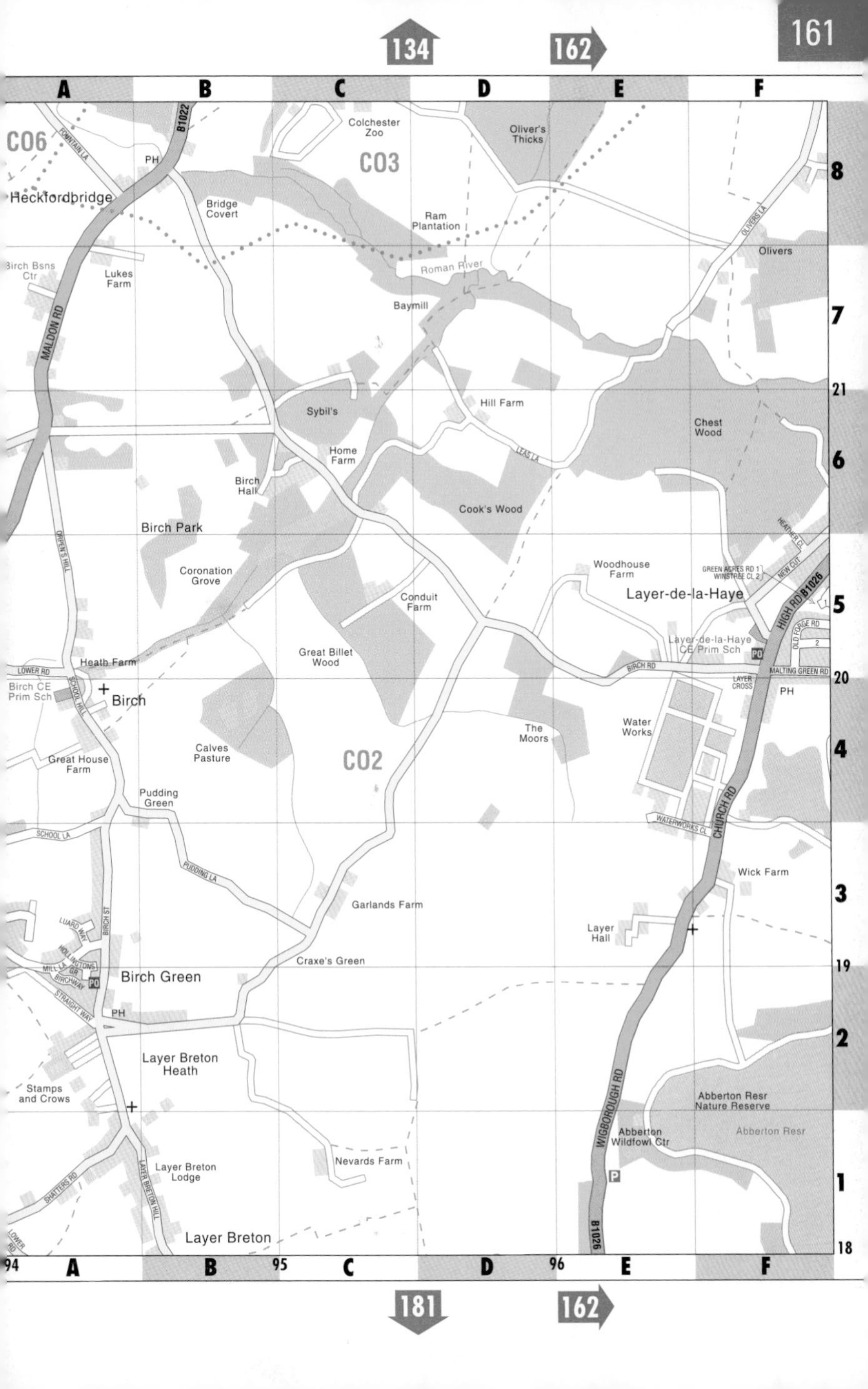
134
162
A
B
C
D
E
F
CO6
CO3
CO2
Heckfordbridge
Colchester Zoo
Oliver's Thicks
Bridge Covert
Ram Plantation
Roman River
Birch Bsns Ctr
Lukes Farm
Baymill
Olivers
MALDON RD
B1022
FOUNTAIN LA
OLIVERS LA
PH
Sybil's
Hill Farm
Chest Wood
Home Farm
LEAS LA
Birch Hall
Cook's Wood
Birch Park
Coronation Grove
Woodhouse Farm
Conduit Farm
Layer-de-la-Haye
GREEN ACRES RD
WINSTREE CL
HEATHER CL
NEW CUT
HIGH RD B1026
OLD FORGE RD
Layer-de-la-Haye CE Prim Sch
Heath Farm
Great Billet Wood
BIRCH RD
MALTING GREEN RD
LAYER CROSS
LOWER RD
Birch CE Prim Sch
SCHOOL HILL
ORPEN'S HILL
Birch
The Moors
Water Works
Calves Pasture
Great House Farm
Pudding Green
WATERWORKS CL
CHURCH RD
SCHOOL LA
PUDDING LA
Wick Farm
Garlands Farm
Layer Hall
LUARD WAY
BIRCH ST
HOLLINGTONS GR
MILL LA
BIRCHWAY
STRAIGHT WAY
Birch Green
Craxe's Green
PO
Layer Breton Heath
Stamps and Crows
Abberton Resr Nature Reserve
Abberton Resr
Abberton Wildfowl Ctr
WIGBOROUGH RD
Nevards Farm
Layer Breton Lodge
LAYER BRETON HILL
SHATTERS RD
LOWER RD
Layer Breton
B1026
P
8
7
21
6
5
20
4
3
19
2
1
18
94
95
96
181
162

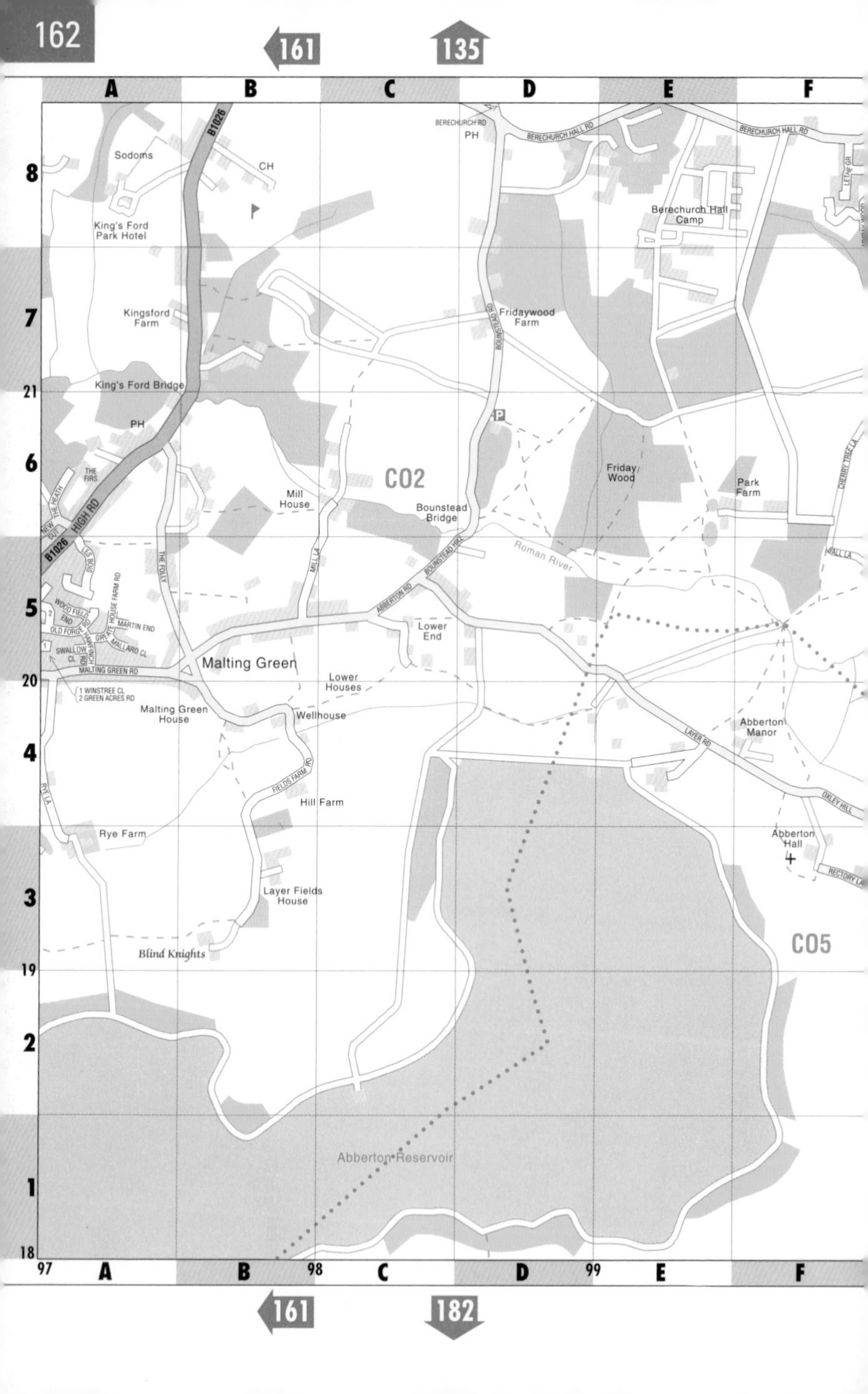

161
135

A **B** **C** **D** **E** **F**

8

Sodoms

CH

King's Ford
Park Hotel

BERECHURCH RD
PH

BERECHURCH HALL RD

BERECHURCH HALL RD

Berechurch Hall
Camp

7

Kingsford
Farm

Fridaywood
Farm

21

King's Ford Bridge

PH

CO2

6

THE FIRS

HIGH RD

B1026

Mill
House

Bounstead
Bridge

Friday
Wood

Park
Farm

CHERRY TREE LA

HALL LA

THE FOLLY

MILL LA

BOUNSTEAD HALL

Roman River

5

HOUSE FARM RD

MARTIN END

MALLARD CL

WINSTREE
END

OLD FORD

Abberton Rd

Lower
End

SWALLOW
CL

20

Malting Green

Lower
Houses

MALTING GREEN RD

1 WINSTREE CL
2 GREEN ACRES RD

Malting Green
House

Wellhouse

Abberton
Manor

LAYER RD

OXLEY HILL

4

PYE LA

FIELDS FARM RD

Hill Farm

3

Rye Farm

Layer Fields
House

Abberton
Hall
+

RECTORY LA

CO5

19

Blind Knights

2

1

Abberton Reservoir

18

97 **A** **B** 98 **C** **D** 99 **E** **F**

161
182

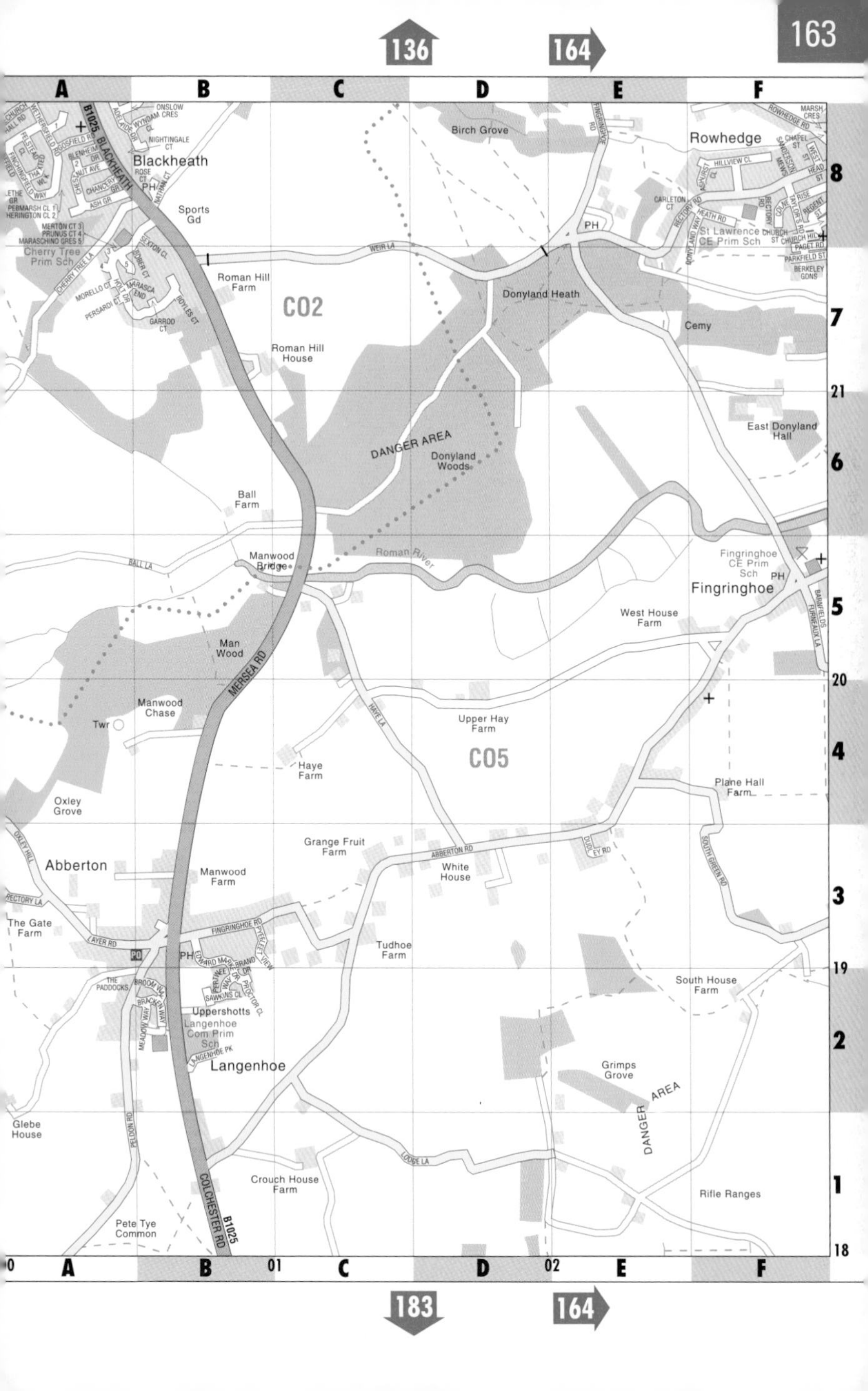
136
164
A
B
C
D
E
F
Blackheath
B1025 BLACKHEATH
Sports Gd
Cherry Tree Prim Sch
Roman Hill Farm
CO2
Roman Hill House
Birch Grove
Rowhedge
WEIR LA
Donyland Heath
Cemy
St Lawrence CE Prim Sch
DANGER AREA
Donyland Woods
East Donyland Hall
Ball Farm
BALL LA
Manwood Bridge
Roman River
Fingringhoe CE Prim Sch
Fingringhoe
West House Farm
Man Wood
MERSEA RD
Manwood Chase
Twr
Upper Hay Farm
HAYE LA
CO5
Haye Farm
Plane Hall Farm
Oxley Grove
Abberton
Grange Fruit Farm
ABBERTON RD
White House
Manwood Farm
The Gate Farm
LAYER RD
FINGRINGHOE RD
Tudhoe Farm
South House Farm
Uppershotts
Langenhoe Com Prim Sch
Langenhoe
Grimps Grove
DANGER AREA
Glebe House
PELDON RD
LODGE LA
Crouch House Farm
Rifle Ranges
COLCHESTER RD
B1025
Pete Tye Common
SOUTH GREEN RD
8
7
21
6
5
20
4
3
19
2
1
18
0
01
02
183
164

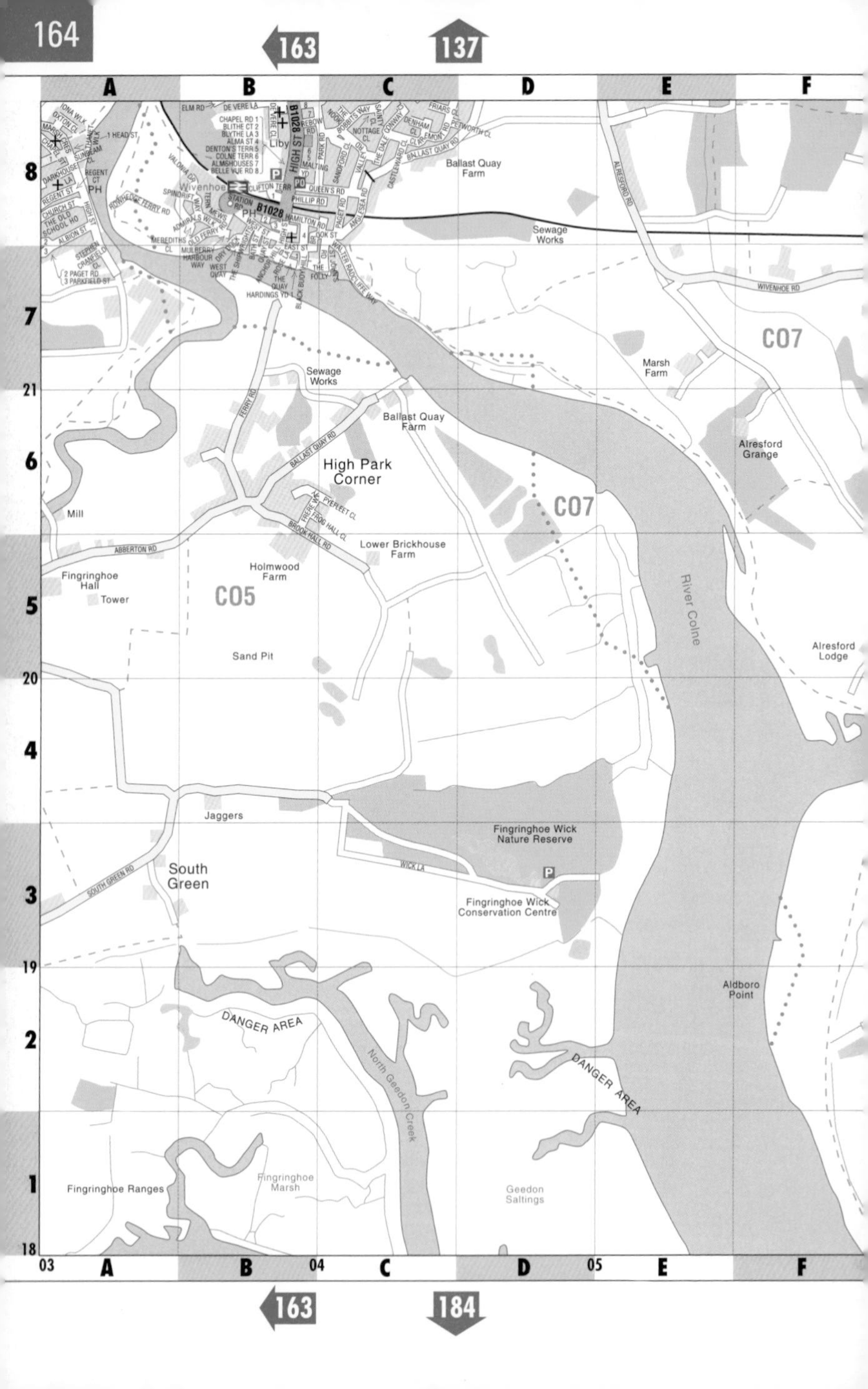

164
163
137
A
B
C
D
E
F
8
7
21
6
5
20
4
3
19
2
1
18
03
04
05
Wivenhoe
Liby
B1028
HIGH ST
Ballast Quay Farm
Sewage Works
WIVENHOE RD
ALRESFORD RD
CO7
Marsh Farm
Sewage Works
FERRY RD
BALLAST QUAY RD
Ballast Quay Farm
High Park Corner
Alresford Grange
Mill
ABBERTON RD
BROOK HALL RD
Lower Brickhouse Farm
Fingringhoe Hall
Tower
Holmwood Farm
CO5
River Colne
Sand Pit
Alresford Lodge
Jaggers
Fingringhoe Wick Nature Reserve
WICK LA
South Green
SOUTH GREEN RD
Fingringhoe Wick Conservation Centre
Aldboro Point
DANGER AREA
North Geedon Creek
DANGER AREA
Fingringhoe Ranges
Fingringhoe Marsh
Geedon Saltings
163
184

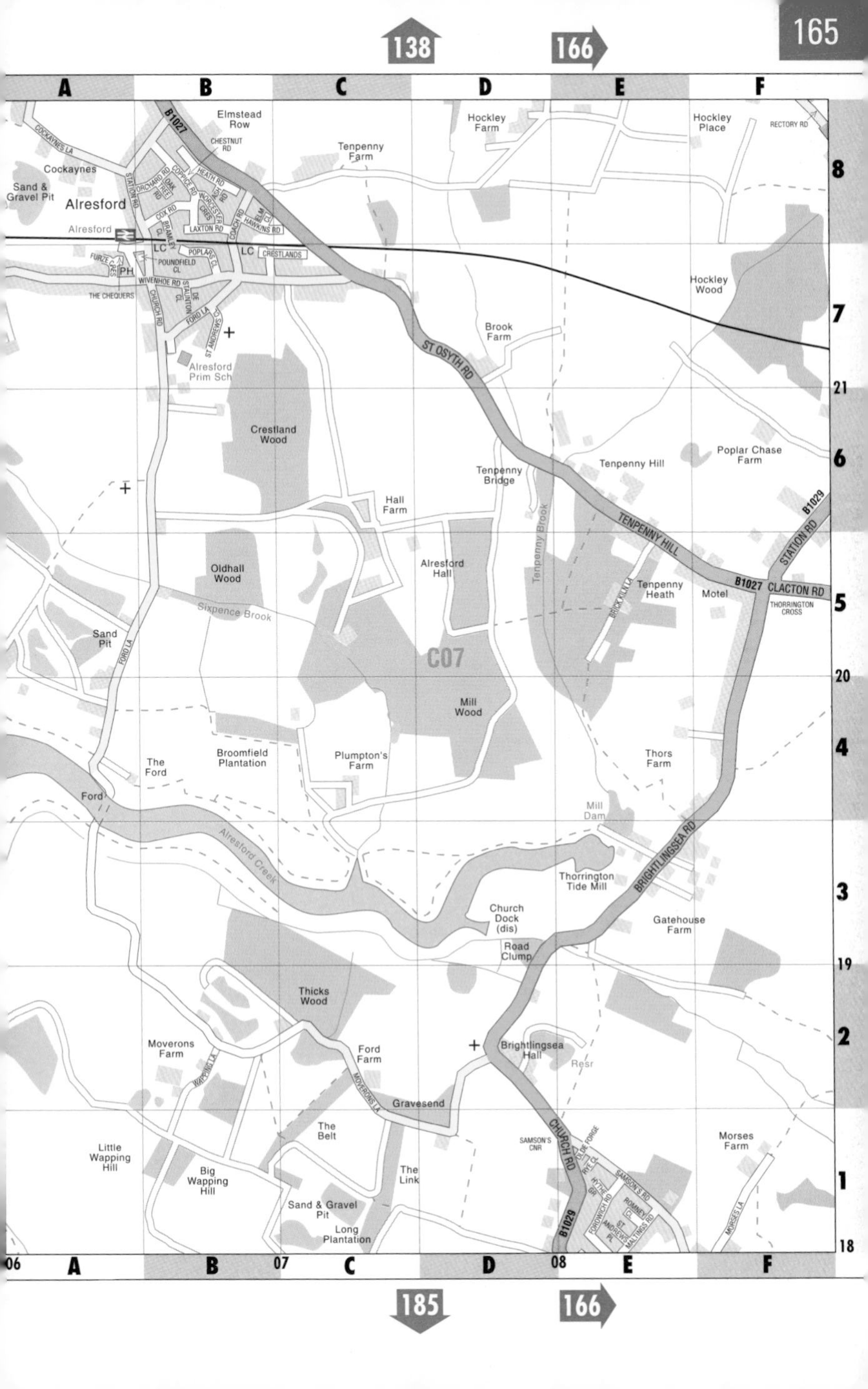

138
166
A
B
C
D
E
F
Elmstead Row
Cockaynes
Sand & Gravel Pit
Alresford
Hockley Farm
Tenpenny Farm
Hockley Place
Hockley Wood
Brook Farm
ST OSYTH RD
Alresford Prim Sch
Crestland Wood
Tenpenny Bridge
Tenpenny Hill
Poplar Chase Farm
Hall Farm
TENPENNY HILL
Oldhall Wood
Alresford Hall
Tenpenny Heath
Motel
CLACTON RD
STATION RD
Sixpence Brook
Sand Pit
CO7
Mill Wood
Tenpenny Brook
The Ford
Broomfield Plantation
Plumpton's Farm
Thors Farm
Ford
Mill Dam
Alresford Creek
Thorrington Tide Mill
BRIGHTLINGSEA RD
Church Dock (dis)
Gatehouse Farm
Road Clump
Thicks Wood
Moverons Farm
Ford Farm
Brightlingsea Hall
Resr
Gravesend
The Belt
CHURCH RD
Morses Farm
Little Wapping Hill
Big Wapping Hill
The Link
Sand & Gravel Pit
Long Plantation
185
166

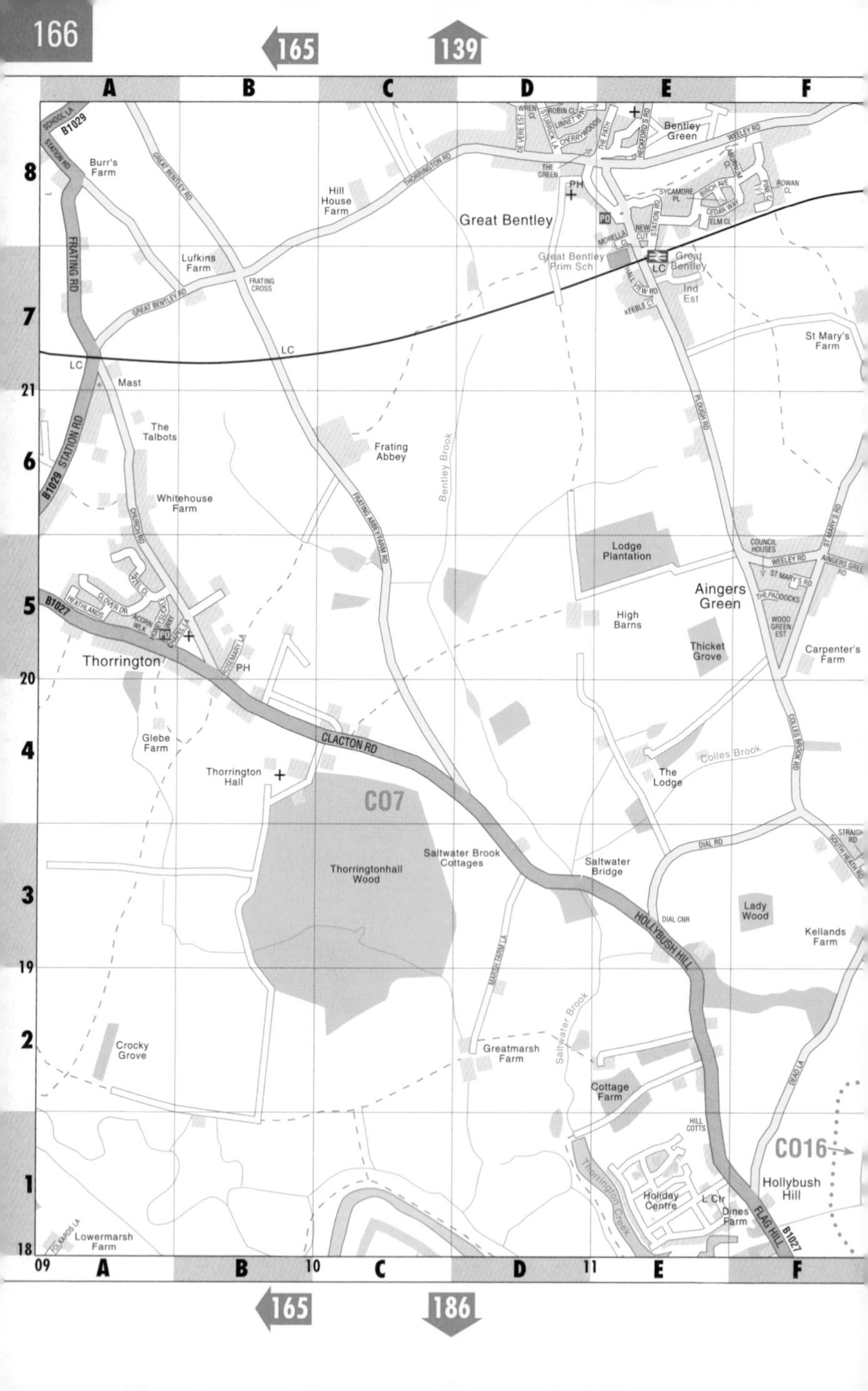
165
139
A
B
C
D
E
F
8
7
21
6
5
20
4
3
19
2
1
18
09
10
11
SCHOOL LA
B1029
STATION RD
Burr's
Farm
GREAT BENTLEY RD
FRATING RD
Hill
House
Farm
THORRINGTON RD
WREN CL
ROBIN CL
LINNEY WAY
DE VERE EST
STURRICK LA
CHERRYWOODS
THE PATH
HECKFORD'S RD
Bentley
Green
WEELEY RD
LABURNUM CL
ROWAN CL
PINE CL
THE GREEN
PH
SYCAMORE PL
BIRCH AVE
CEDAR WAY
ELM CL
Great Bentley
PO
MORELLA CL
NEW CUT
STATION RD
Great Bentley
Prim Sch
Great
Bentley
LC
Lufkins
Farm
FRATING
CROSS
HALL VIEW RD
KEEBLE CT
Ind
Est
GREAT BENTLEY RD
LC
St Mary's
Farm
LC
Mast
The
Talbots
B1029 STATION RD
Frating
Abbey
Bentley Brook
PLOUGH RD
Whitehouse
Farm
CHURCH RD
FRATING ABBEY FARM RD
ST MARY'S RD
COUNCIL
HOUSES
WEELEY RD
AINGERS GREEN RD
Lodge
Plantation
ST MARY'S RD
THE PADDOCKS
HAZEL CL
CLOVER DR
HEATHLANDS
B1027
ACORN WLK
HONEYSUCKLE WAY
CHAPEL LA
PO
ROSEMARY LA
Aingers
Green
High
Barns
WOOD
GREEN
EST
Thicket
Grove
Carpenter's
Farm
Thorrington
PH
Glebe
Farm
CLACTON RD
COLLES BROOK RD
Colles Brook
Thorrington
Hall
The
Lodge
CO7
DIAL RD
STRAIGHT RD
SOUTH HEATH RD
Saltwater Brook
Cottages
Thorringtonhall
Wood
Saltwater
Bridge
HOLLYBUSH HILL
DIAL CNR
Lady
Wood
Kellands
Farm
MARSH FARM LA
Saltwater Brook
Crocky
Grove
Greatmarsh
Farm
Cottage
Farm
DEAD LA
HILL
COTTS
CO16
Thorrington Creek
Holiday
Centre
L Ctr
Hollybush
Hill
Dines
Farm
FLAG HILL
B1027
FOLKARDS LA
Lowermarsh
Farm
165
186

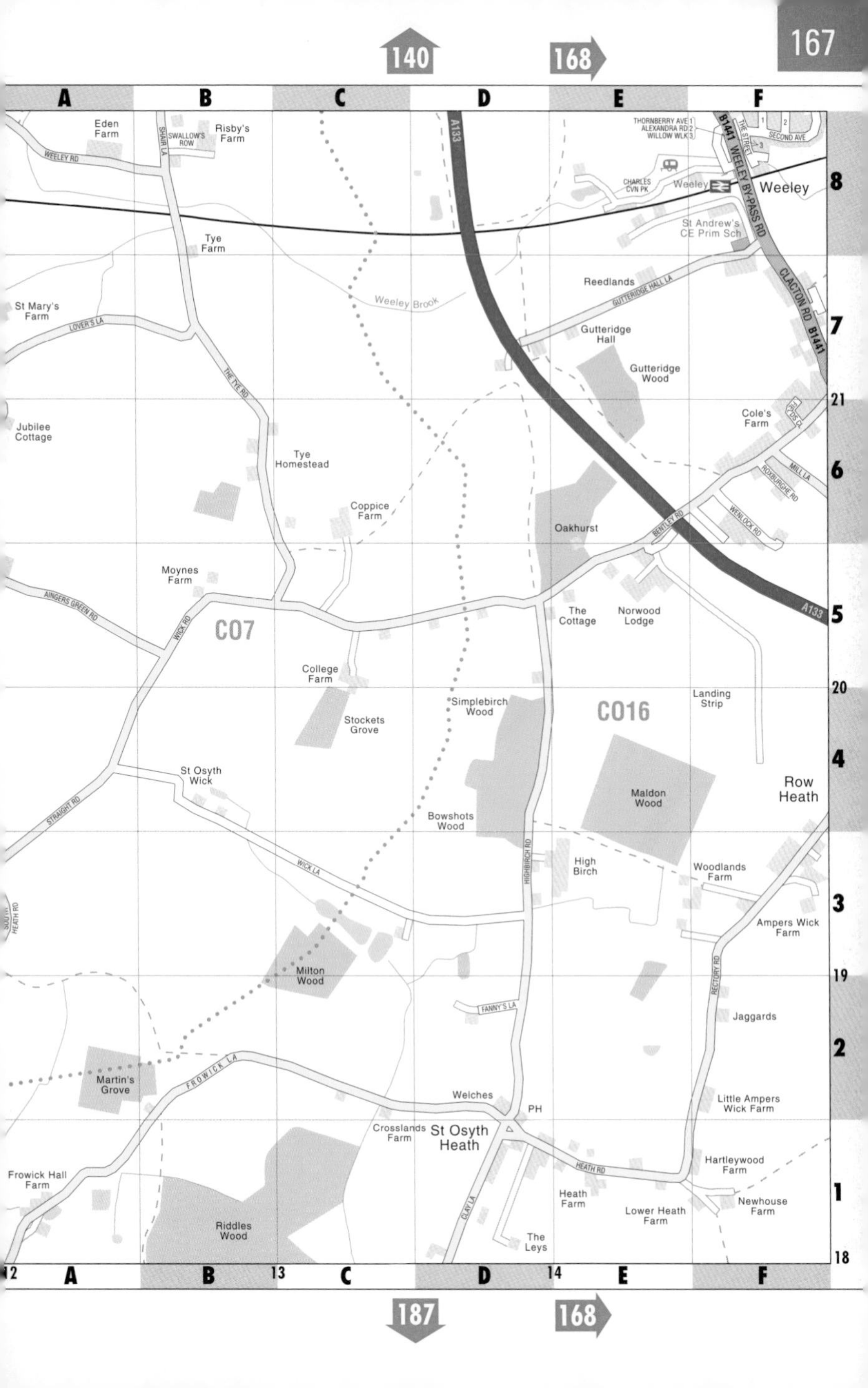
140
168
A
B
C
D
E
F
Eden Farm
Risby's Farm
SWALLOW'S ROW
SHAIR LA
WEELEY RD
A133
THORNBERRY AVE 1
ALEXANDRA RD 2
WILLOW WLK 3
B1441
THE STREET
SECOND AVE
CHARLES CVN PK
Weeley
WEELEY BY-PASS RD
8
Tye Farm
St Andrew's CE Prim Sch
Reedlands
CLACTON RD
B1441
GUTTERIDGE HALL LA
Weeley Brook
St Mary's Farm
LOVER'S LA
7
Gutteridge Hall
Gutteridge Wood
THE TYE RD
21
Cole's Farm
Jubilee Cottage
Tye Homestead
MILL LA
ROXBURGHE RD
6
Coppice Farm
Oakhurst
BENTLEY RD
WENLOCK RD
Moynes Farm
AINGERS GREEN RD
WICK RD
CO7
The Cottage
Norwood Lodge
A133
5
College Farm
Landing Strip
20
Simplebirch Wood
CO16
Stockets Grove
4
St Osyth Wick
Row Heath
Maldon Wood
STRAIGHT RD
Bowshots Wood
HIGHBIRCH RD
High Birch
Woodlands Farm
WICK LA
3
Ampers Wick Farm
SOUTH HEATH RD
Milton Wood
19
RECTORY RD
FANNY'S LA
Jaggards
2
Martin's Grove
FROWICK LA
Welches
PH
Little Ampers Wick Farm
Crosslands Farm
St Osyth Heath
HEATH RD
Hartleywood Farm
Frowick Hall Farm
Heath Farm
Newhouse Farm
1
CLAY LA
Lower Heath Farm
Riddles Wood
The Leys
18
12
A
B
13
C
D
14
E
F
187
168

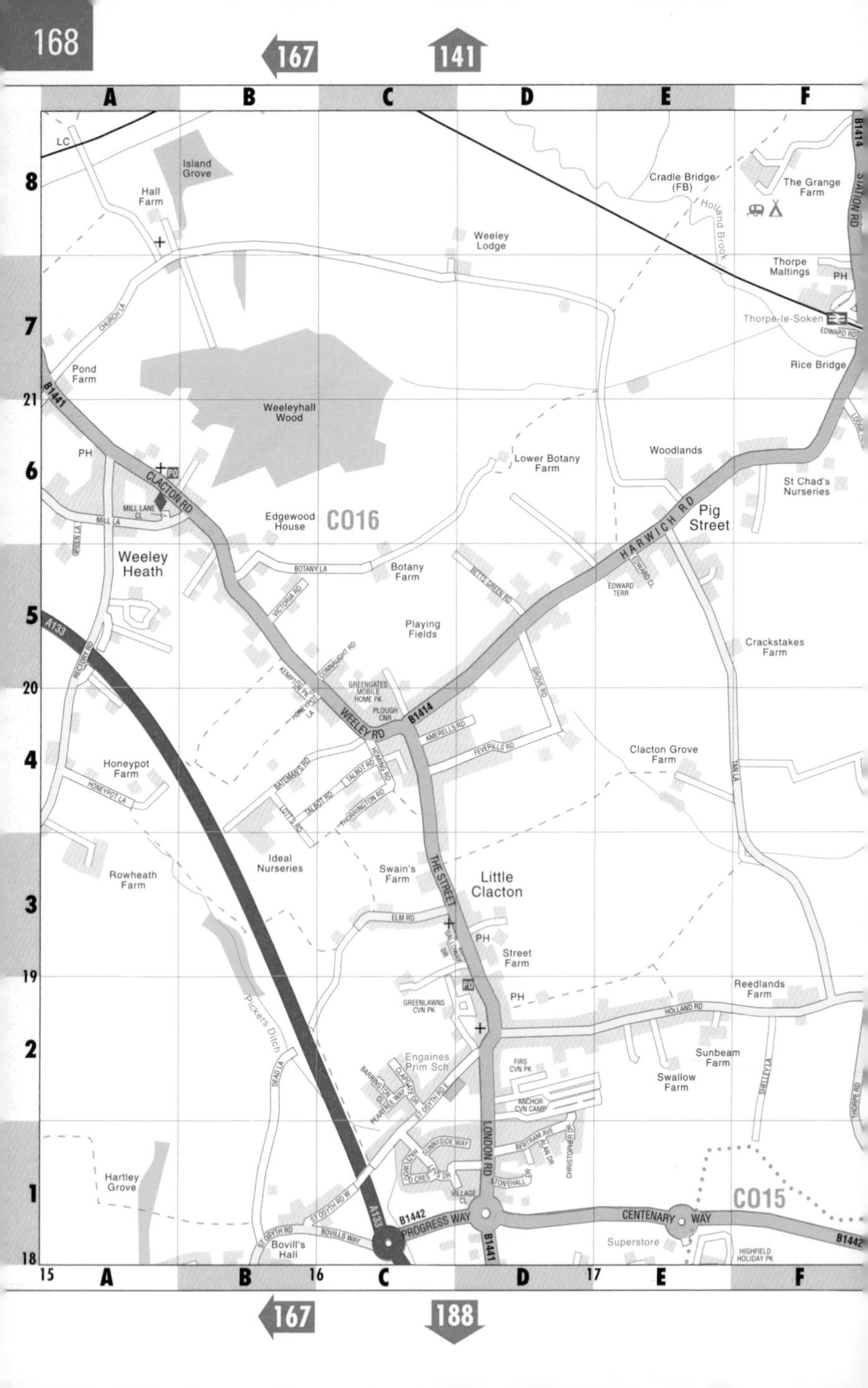
167
141
LC
Island Grove
Hall Farm
Cradle Bridge (FB)
Holland Brook
The Grange Farm
B1414
STATION RD
Weeley Lodge
Thorpe Maltings
PH
Thorpe-le-Soken
EDWARD RD
CHURCH LA
Pond Farm
Rice Bridge
B1441
Weeleyhall Wood
Woodlands
PH
Lower Botany Farm
St Chad's Nurseries
CLACTON RD
MILL LANE CL
MILL LA
Edgewood House
CO16
Pig Street
HARWICH RD
GREEN LA
Weeley Heath
BOTANY LA
Botany Farm
BETTS GREEN RD
EDWARD CL
EDWARD TERR
VICTORIA RD
A133
Playing Fields
Crackstakes Farm
RECTORY RD
CONNAUGHT RD
KEMPTON PK
GREENGATES MOBILE HOME PK
GROVE RD
HONEYPOT LA
PLOUGH CNR
WEELEY RD
B1414
AMERELLS RD
FEVERALLS RD
Clacton Grove Farm
Honeypot Farm
HONEYPOT LA
BATEMAN'S RD
TALBOT RD
HOMING RD
TAN LA
LOTTS RD
THORRINGTON RD
Ideal Nurseries
Swain's Farm
THE STREET
Little Clacton
Rowheath Farm
ELM RD
GALLOWAY DR
PH
Street Farm
Reedlands Farm
PH
GREENLAWNS CVN PK
HOLLAND RD
Pickers Ditch
Engaines Prim Sch
Sunbeam Farm
DEAD LA
BARRINGTON CL
CLAPGATE DR
FIRS CVN PK
Swallow Farm
SHELLEY LA
PEARTREE WAY
ST OSYTH RD E
ANCHOR CVN CAMP
THORPE RD
LONDON RD
SUNNYSIDE WAY
BERTRAM AVE
ALAN DR
CHRISTOPHER DR
Hartley Grove
LEYS DR
STONEHALL DR
CO15
VILLAGE CL
ST OSYTH RD W
B1442
PROGRESS WAY
CENTENARY WAY
B1442
ST OSYTH RD
BOVILLS WAY
Bovill's Hall
Superstore
B1441
HIGHFIELD HOLIDAY PK
15
16
17
A
B
C
D
E
F
8
7
21
6
5
20
4
3
19
2
1
18
167
188

142
170

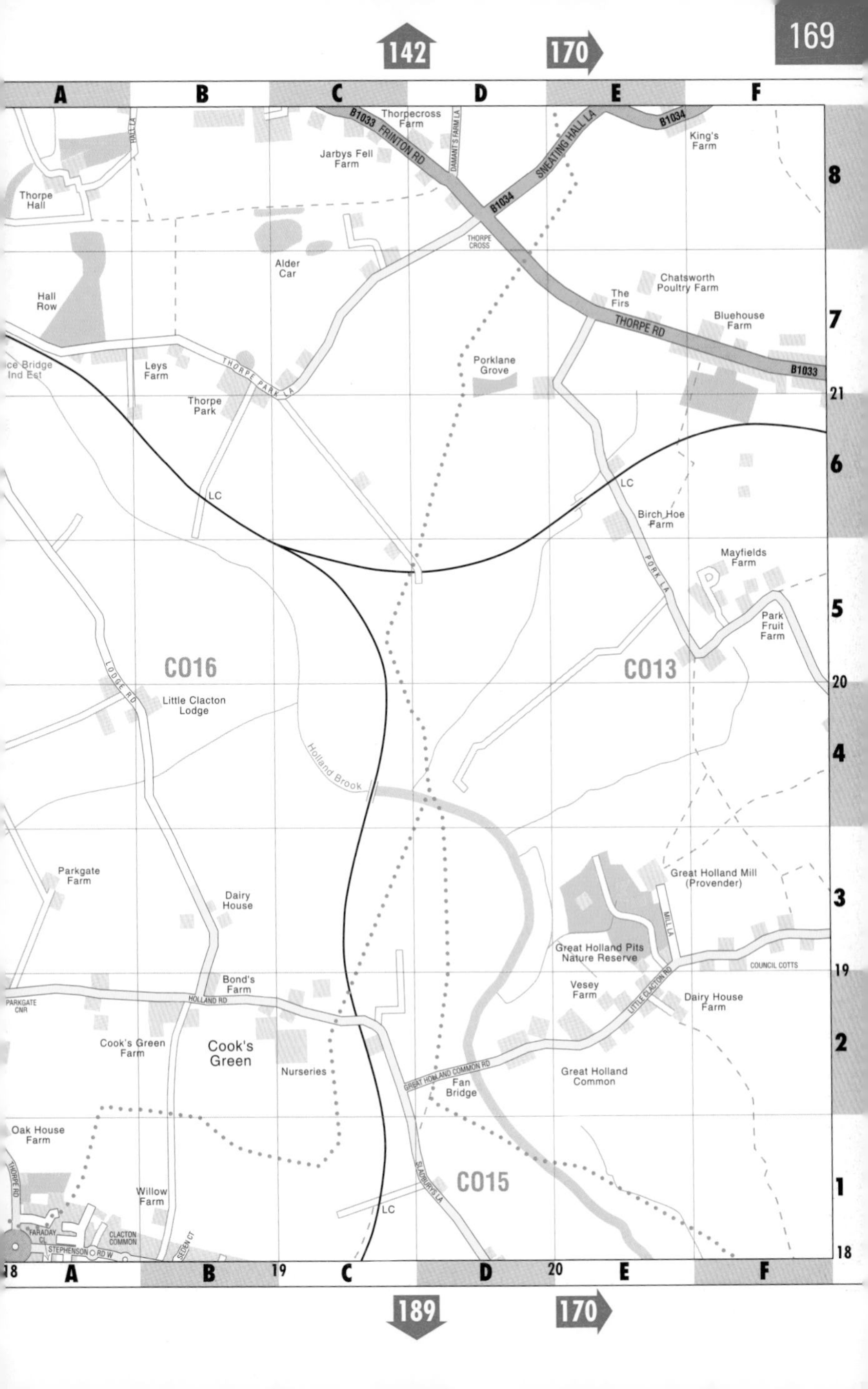
A
B
C
D
E
F
Thorpecross Farm
B1033 FRINTON RD
Jarbys Fell Farm
DAMANT'S FARM LA
SNEATING HALL LA
B1034
King's Farm
HALL LA
Thorpe Hall
B1034
THORPE CROSS
Alder Car
Hall Row
The Firs
Chatsworth Poultry Farm
Bluehouse Farm
THORPE RD
B1033
Porklane Grove
ce Bridge Ind Est
Leys Farm
THORPE PARK LA
Thorpe Park
LC
LC
Birch Hoe Farm
Mayfields Farm
PORK LA
Park Fruit Farm
CO16
CO13
LODGE RD
Little Clacton Lodge
Holland Brook
Parkgate Farm
Dairy House
Great Holland Mill (Provender)
MILL LA
Great Holland Pits Nature Reserve
COUNCIL COTTS
Bond's Farm
PARKGATE CNR
HOLLAND RD
Vesey Farm
LITTLE CLACTON RD
Dairy House Farm
Cook's Green Farm
Cook's Green
Nurseries
GREAT HOLLAND COMMON RD
Fan Bridge
Great Holland Common
Oak House Farm
THORPE RD
SLADBURYS LA
CO15
Willow Farm
LC
FARADAY CL
CLACTON COMMON
STEPHENSON RD W
SEDEN CT
8
7
21
6
5
20
4
3
19
2
1
18
18
19
20

189
170

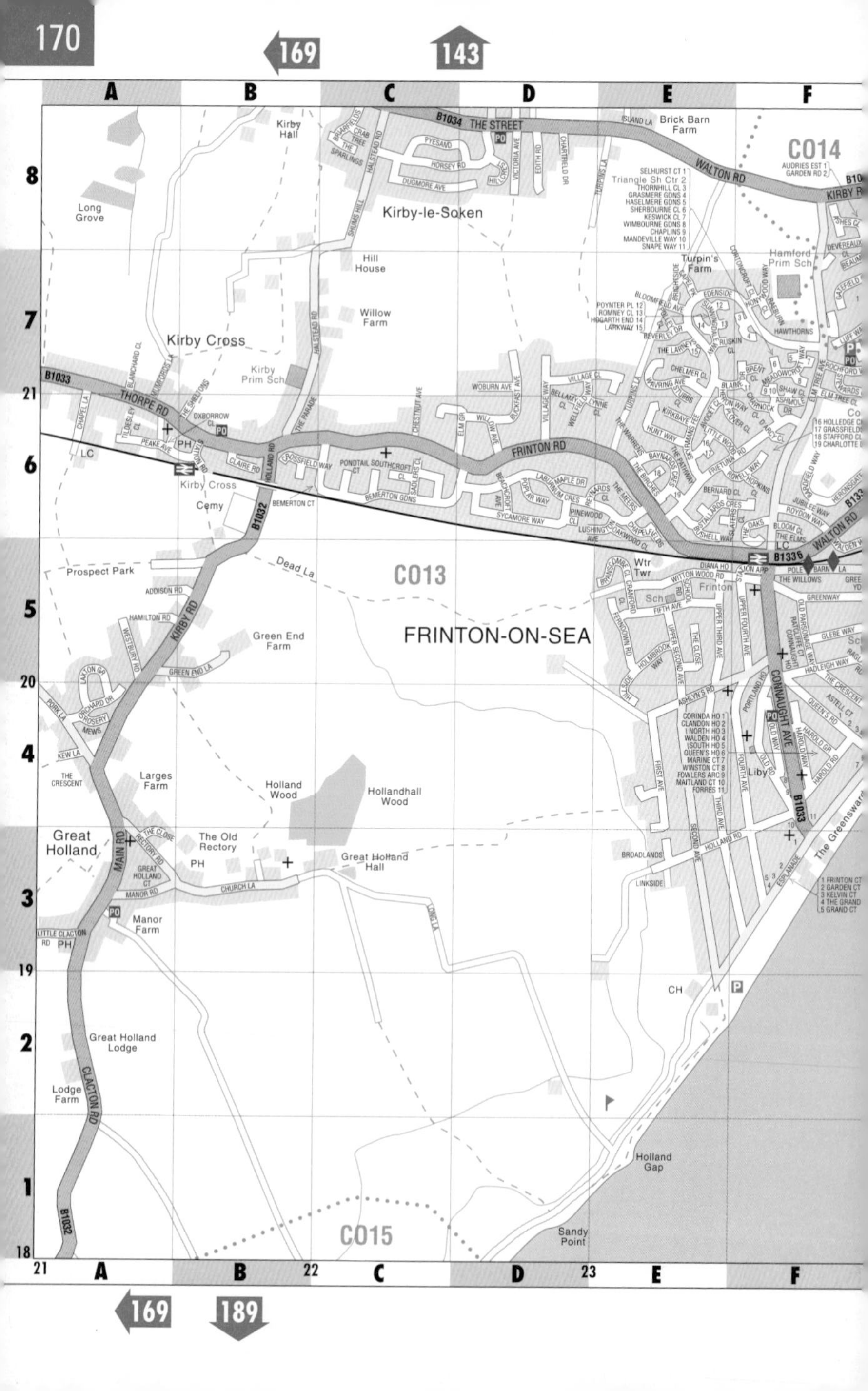
169
143
Kirby Hall
Long Grove
Kirby-le-Soken
Hill House
Willow Farm
Kirby Cross
Kirby Prim Sch
Brick Barn Farm
Turpin's Farm
Hamford Prim Sch
CO14
CO13
CO15
FRINTON-ON-SEA
Frinton
Prospect Park
Green End Farm
Larges Farm
Holland Wood
Hollandhall Wood
Great Holland
The Old Rectory
Great Holland Hall
Manor Farm
Great Holland Lodge
Lodge Farm
Holland Gap
Sandy Point
THE STREET
WALTON RD
THORPE RD
FRINTON RD
KIRBY RD
MAIN RD
CLACTON RD
CONNAUGHT AVE
CHURCH LA
LONG LA
Dead La
B1034
B1033
B1032
B1336
169
189

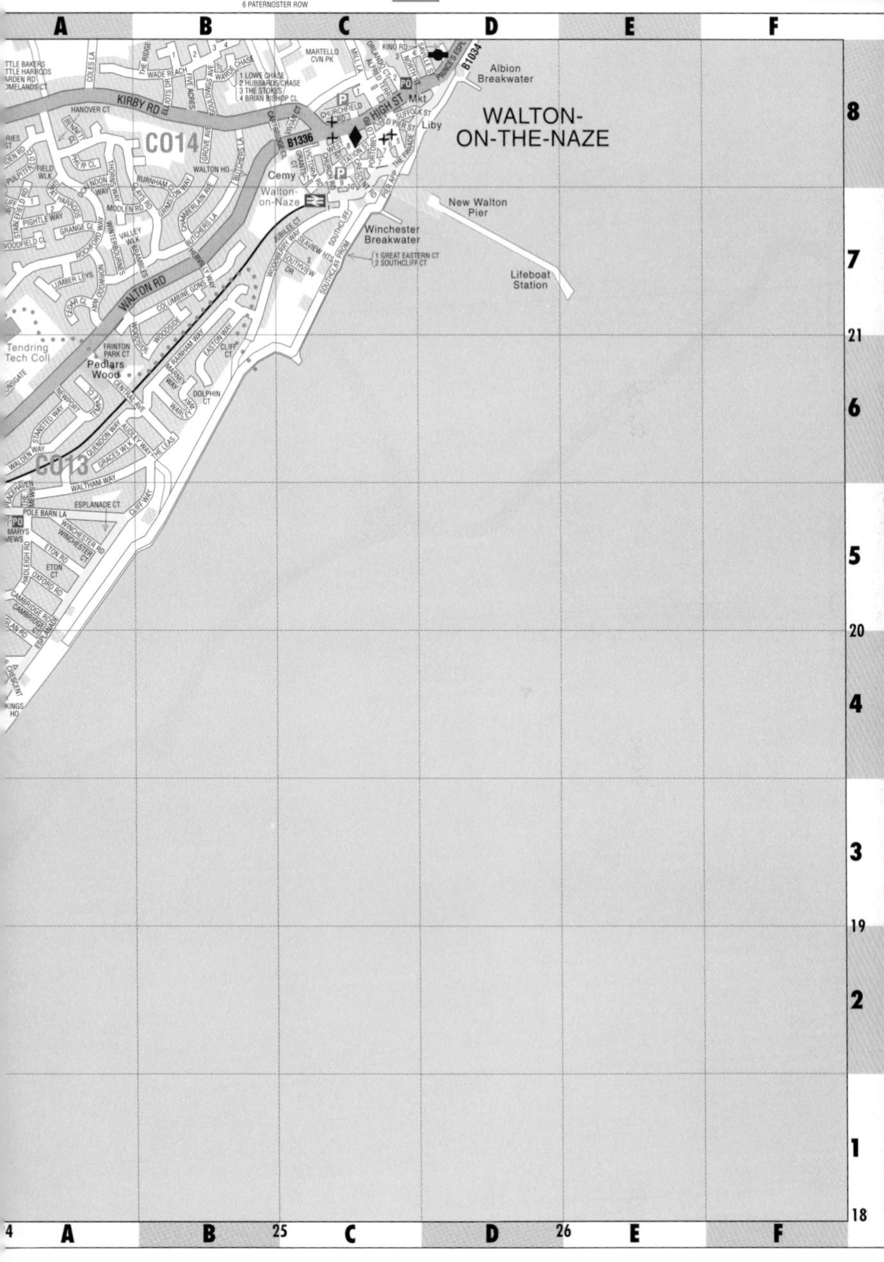

C8
1 MARINA MEWS
2 VICARAGE LA
3 HAVENCROFT CT
4 STRATFORD PL
5 NEWGATE ST
6 PATERNOSTER ROW

7 NEW PIER ST
8 MARTELLO RD
9 AGAR RD
10 AGAR ROAD APP
11 ST BOTOLPH'S TERR

144

WALTON-
ON-THE-NAZE

Albion
Breakwater

New Walton
Pier

Winchester
Breakwater

Lifeboat
Station

1 GREAT EASTERN CT
2 SOUTHCLIFF CT

CO14

CO13

Tendring
Tech Col

Pedlars
Wood

KIRBY RD

WALTON RD

HANOVER CT

Cemy

Walton-
on-Naze

| A | B | 25 | C | D | 26 | E | F |

152

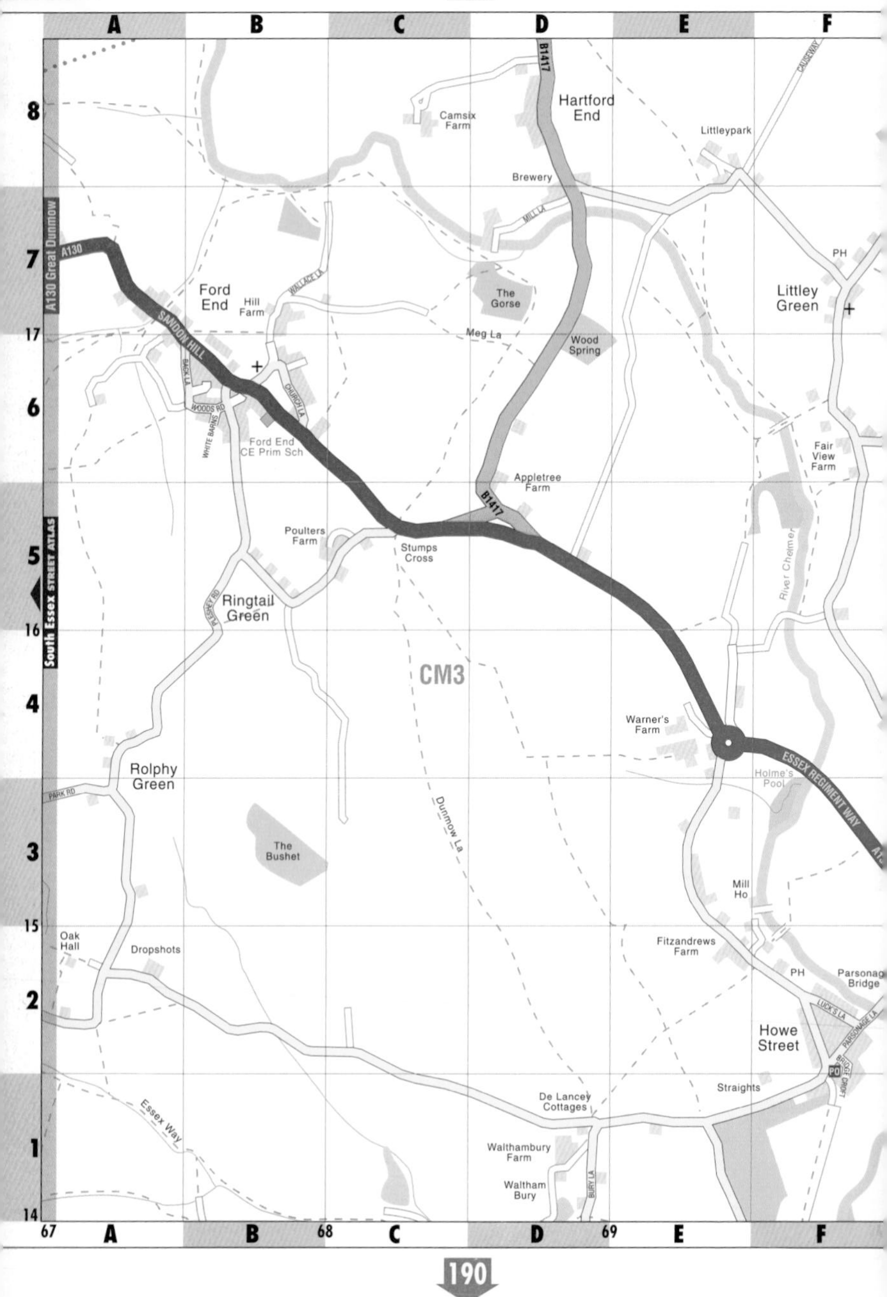
A
B
C
D
E
F
8
7
17
6
5
16
4
3
15
2
1
14
67
68
69
A130 Great Dunmow
A130
B1417
Hartford End
Camsix Farm
Littleypark
Brewery
MILL LA
Littley Green
PH
Ford End
Hill Farm
WALLACE LA
The Gorse
Meg La
Wood Spring
SANDON HILL
BACK LA
WOODS RD
WHITE BARNS
CHURCH LA
Ford End CE Prim Sch
Fair View Farm
Appletree Farm
Poulters Farm
Stumps Cross
Ringtail Green
PLESHEY RD
River Chelmer
CM3
Warner's Farm
ESSEX REGIMENT WAY
Holme's Pool
Rolphy Green
PARK RD
The Bushet
Dunmow La
Mill Ho
Oak Hall
Dropshots
Fitzandrews Farm
PH
Parsonage Bridge
LUCK'S LA
PARSONAGE LA
Howe Street
BRIDGE CROFT
PO
Straights
De Lancey Cottages
Essex Way
Walthambury Farm
Waltham Bury
BURY LA
South Essex STREET ATLAS

190

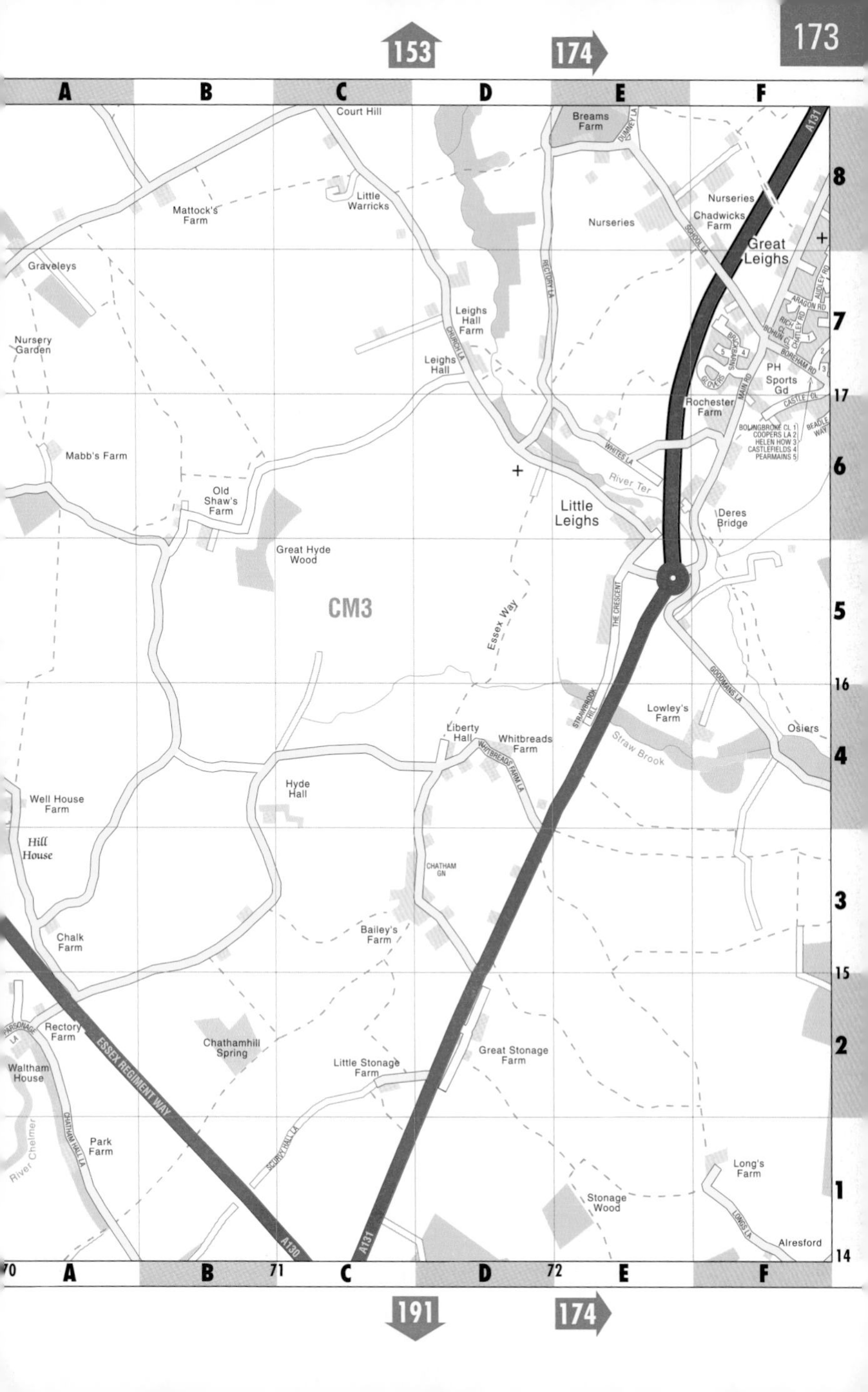
153
174
A
B
C
D
E
F
Court Hill
Breams Farm
DUMNEY LA
A131
8
Little Warricks
Mattock's Farm
Nurseries
Nurseries
Chadwicks Farm
SCHOOL LA
Great Leighs
Graveleys
RECTORY LA
Leighs Hall Farm
ARAGON RD
AUDLEY RD
7
Nursery Garden
CHURCH LA
RICH CL
BOHUN CL
CHATLEY RD
BROCKBARNS
BOREHAM RD
Leighs Hall
GLOVERS
MAIN RD
PH
Sports Gd
17
Rochester Farm
CASTLE CL
BOLINGBROKE CL 1
COOPERS LA 2
HELEN HOW 3
CASTLEFIELDS 4
PEARMAINS 5
BEADLE WAY
Mabb's Farm
WHITES LA
6
River Ter
Old Shaw's Farm
Little Leighs
Deres Bridge
Great Hyde Wood
CM3
THE CRESCENT
5
Essex Way
GOODMANS LA
16
STRAWBROOK HILL
Lowley's Farm
Liberty Hall
Whitbreads Farm
WHITBREADS FARM LA
Osiers
Straw Brook
4
Hyde Hall
Well House Farm
Hill House
CHATHAM GN
3
Bailey's Farm
Chalk Farm
15
Rectory Farm
PARSONAGE LA
ESSEX REGIMENT WAY
Chathamhill Spring
Great Stonage Farm
2
Waltham House
Little Stonage Farm
CHATHAM HALL LA
Park Farm
River Chelmer
SCURVY HALL LA
Long's Farm
1
Stonage Wood
LONGS LA
A130
A131
Alresford
14
70
71
72
191
174

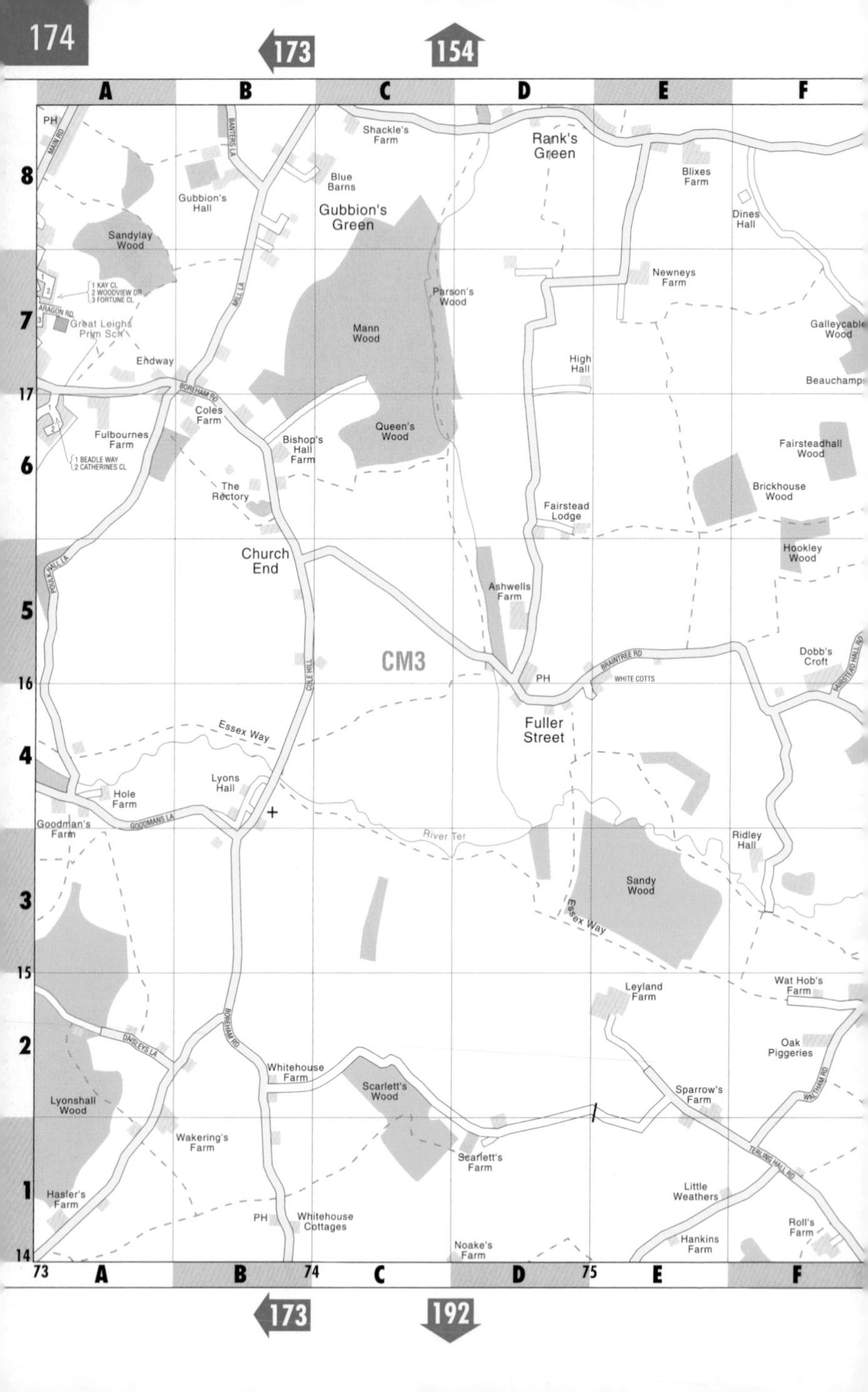
173
154
A
B
C
D
E
F
8
7
17
6
5
16
4
3
15
2
1
14
73
74
75
PH
MAIN RD
BANTERS LA
Shackle's Farm
Rank's Green
Blue Barns
Blixes Farm
Gubbion's Hall
Gubbion's Green
Dines Hall
Sandylay Wood
Newneys Farm
1 KAY CL
2 WOODVIEW DR
3 FORTUNE CL
MILL LA
Parson's Wood
ARAGON RD
Great Leighs Prim Sch
Mann Wood
Galleycable Wood
Endway
High Hall
Beauchamps
BOREHAM RD
Coles Farm
Fulbournes Farm
Queen's Wood
Bishop's Hall Farm
Fairsteadhall Wood
1 BEADLE WAY
2 CATHERINES CL
The Rectory
Brickhouse Wood
Fairstead Lodge
Church End
Hookley Wood
POULK HALL LA
Ashwells Farm
CM3
Dobb's Croft
COLE HILL
BRAINTREE RD
PH
WHITE COTTS
FAIRSTEAD HALL RD
Fuller Street
Essex Way
Lyons Hall
Hole Farm
Goodman's Farm
GOODMANS LA
River Ter
Ridley Hall
Sandy Wood
Essex Way
Leyland Farm
Wat Hob's Farm
BOREHAM RD
DAISLEYS LA
Oak Piggeries
Whitehouse Farm
Scarlett's Wood
Sparrow's Farm
WITHAM RD
Lyonshall Wood
Wakering's Farm
Scarlett's Farm
TERLING HALL RD
Little Weathers
Hasler's Farm
PH
Whitehouse Cottages
Roll's Farm
Noake's Farm
Hankins Farm
173
192

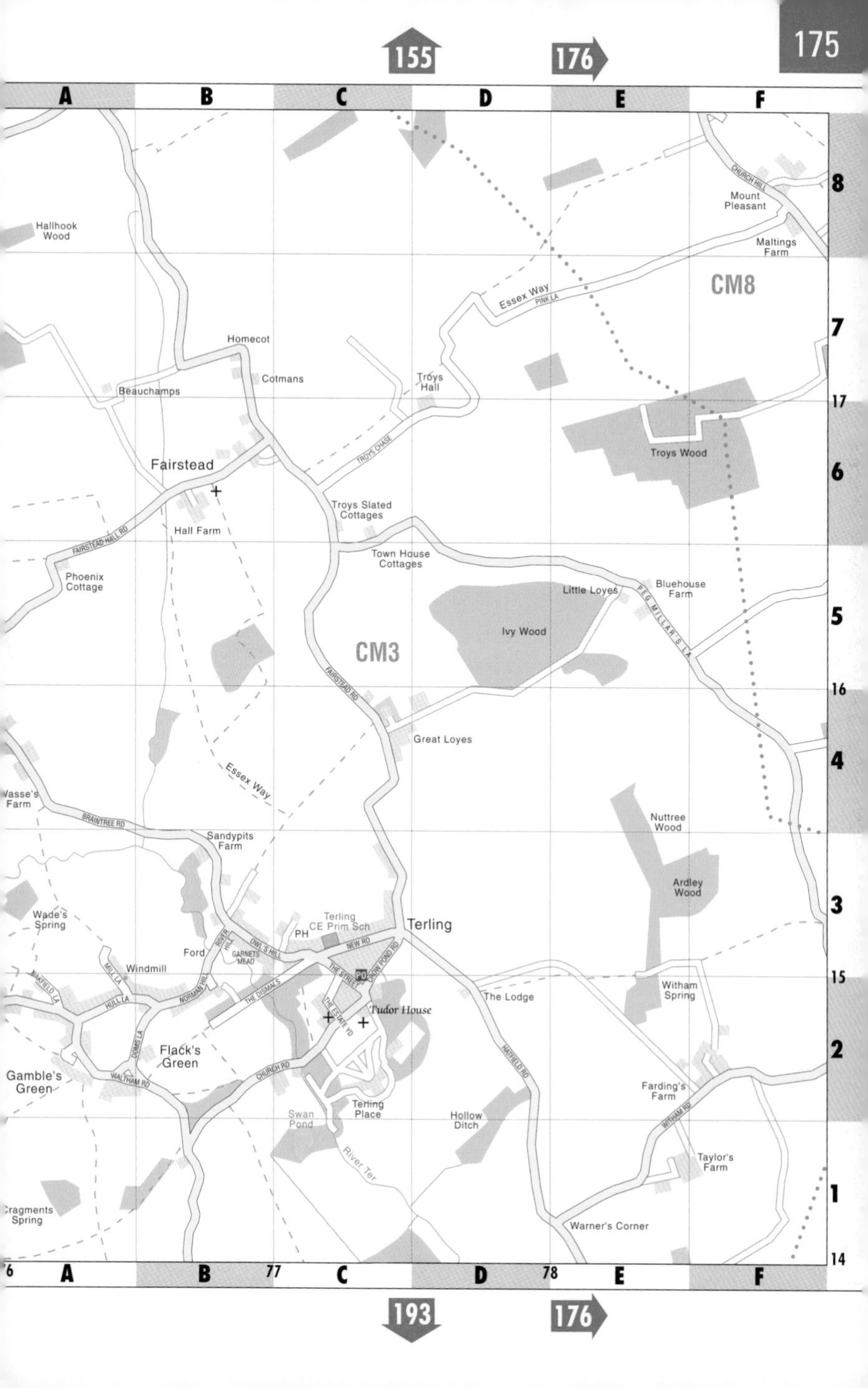

155
176

| A | B | C | D | E | F |

8

Hallhook Wood

Mount Pleasant

CHURCH HILL

Maltings Farm

CM8

7

Homecot

Cotmans

Beauchamps

Troys Hall

Essex Way

PINK LA

17

Fairstead

Troys Wood

6

Hall Farm

Troys Slated Cottages

Phoenix Cottage

Town House Cottages

Little Loyes

Bluehouse Farm

PER MILLER'S LA

5

Ivy Wood

CM3

16

Great Loyes

4

Wasse's Farm

BRAINTREE RD

Essex Way

Nuttree Wood

Sandypits Farm

Ardley Wood

3

Wade's Spring

Terling CE Prim Sch

PH

Terling

Ford

Windmill

GARNETS MEAD

NEW RD

Witham Spring

THE STREET

PO

15

Tudor House

The Lodge

Flack's Green

Gamble's Green

CHURCH RD

WALTHAM RD

Terling Place

Hollow Ditch

Farding's Farm

WITHAM RD

2

Swan Pond

River Ter.

Taylor's Farm

1

Cragments Spring

Warner's Corner

14

| A | B | C | D | E | F |

193
176

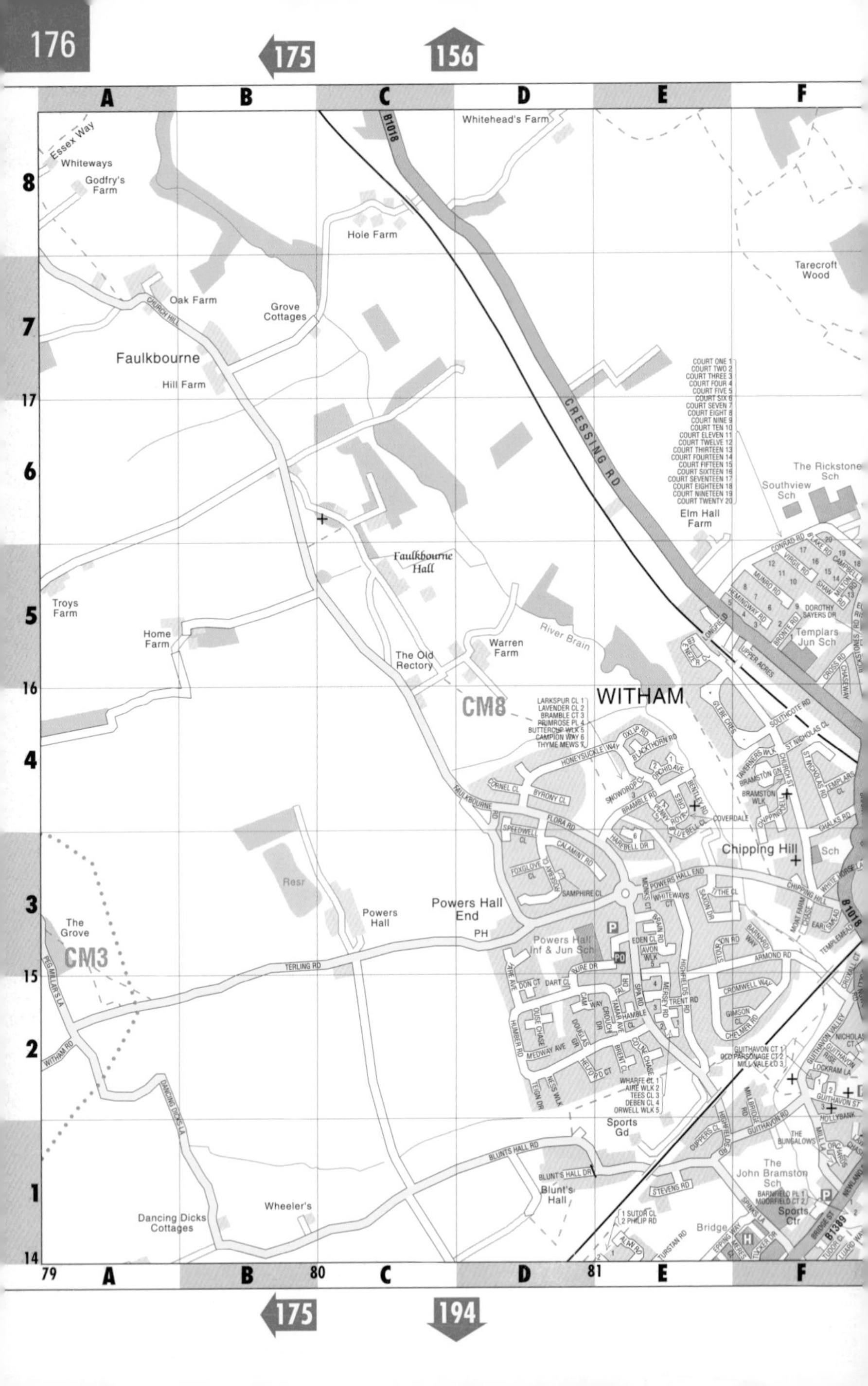
175
156
A
B
C
D
E
F
8
7
17
6
5
16
4
3
15
2
1
14
Essex Way
Whiteways
Godfry's Farm
Whitehead's Farm
B1018
Hole Farm
Oak Farm
Church Hill
Grove Cottages
Faulkbourne
Hill Farm
Tarecroft Wood
CRESSING RD
COURT ONE 1
COURT TWO 2
COURT THREE 3
COURT FOUR 4
COURT FIVE 5
COURT SIX 6
COURT SEVEN 7
COURT EIGHT 8
COURT NINE 9
COURT TEN 10
COURT ELEVEN 11
COURT TWELVE 12
COURT THIRTEEN 13
COURT FOURTEEN 14
COURT FIFTEEN 15
COURT SIXTEEN 16
COURT SEVENTEEN 17
COURT EIGHTEEN 18
COURT NINETEEN 19
COURT TWENTY 20
The Rickstones Sch
Southview Sch
Elm Hall Farm
Faulkbourne Hall
Troys Farm
Home Farm
The Old Rectory
Warren Farm
River Brain
Templars Jun Sch
CM8
WITHAM
LARKSPUR CL 1
LAVENDER CL 2
BRAMBLE CT 3
PRIMROSE PL 4
BUTTERCUP WLK 5
CAMPION WAY 6
THYME MEWS 7
HONEYSUCKLE WAY
FAULKBOURNE RD
CORNEL CL
BYRONY CL
FLORA RD
SPEEDWELL CL
CALAMINT RD
FOXGLOVE CL
SAMPHIRE CL
Resr
Chipping Hill
Sch
POWERS HALL END
WHITEWAYS CT
The Grove
CM3
Powers Hall
Powers Hall End
PH
Powers Hall Inf & Jun Sch
P
PO
TERLING RD
ARMOND RD
CROMWELL WAY
PEG MILLAR'S LA
WITHAM RD
HUMBER RD
MEDWAY AVE
DOUGLAS GR
CROUCH DR
TRENT RD
HIGHFIELDS RD
CHELMER RD
GUITHAVON CT 1
OLD PARSONAGE CT 2
MILL VALE LD 3
WHARFE CL 1
AIRE WLK 2
TEES CL 3
DEBEN CL 4
ORWELL WLK 5
TEIGN DR
NESS WLK
DANCING DICKS LA
Sports Gd
BLUNTS HALL RD
BLUNT'S HALL DR
Blunt's Hall
STEVENS RD
1 SUTOR CL
2 PHILIP RD
TURSTAN RD
Bridge
The John Bramston Sch
BARNFIELD PL 1
MOORFIELD CT 2
Sports Ctr
BRIDGE ST
B1389
Wheeler's
Dancing Dicks Cottages
79
80
81
175
194

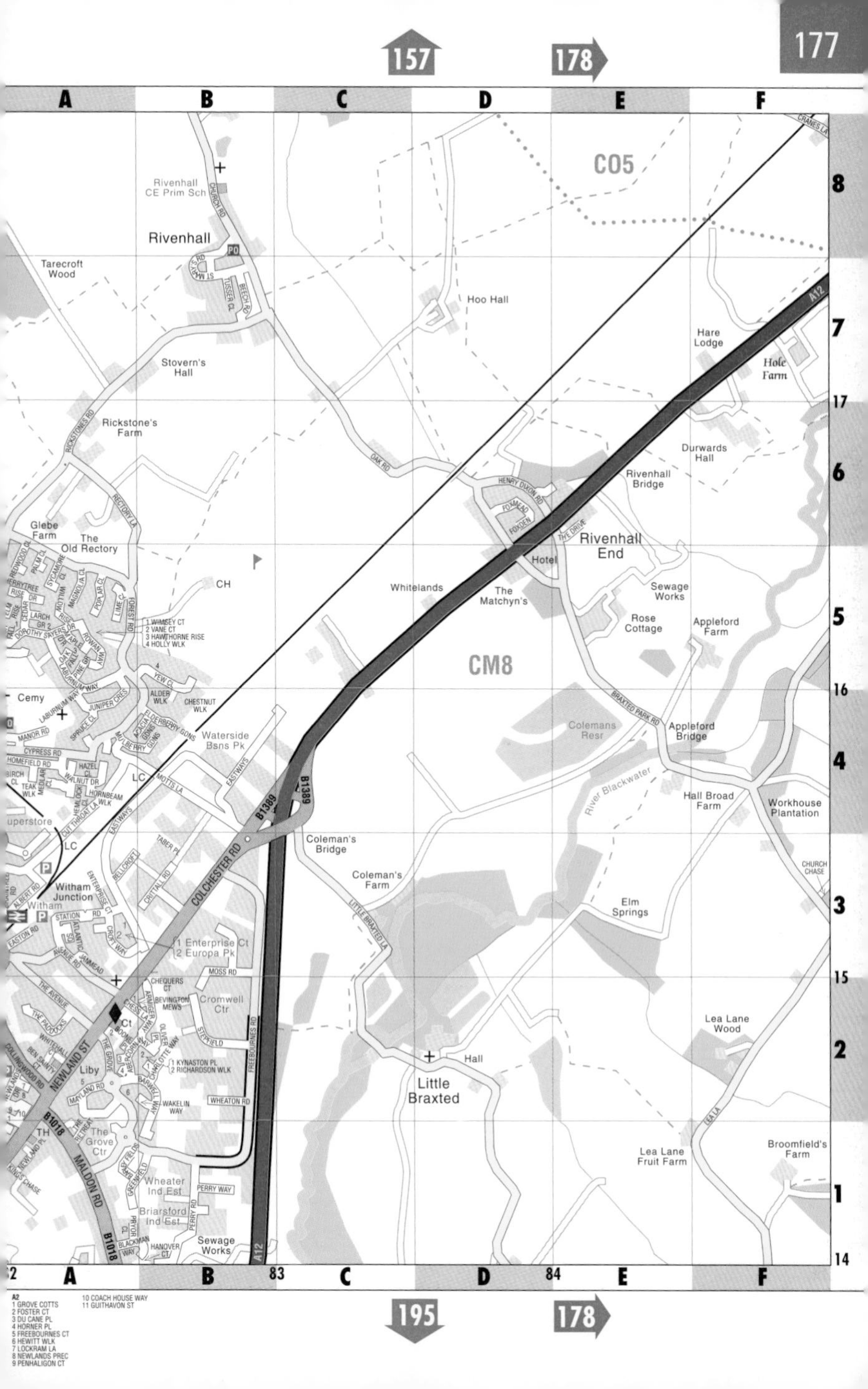
157
178
CO5
CM8
Rivenhall
Rivenhall CE Prim Sch
Tarecroft Wood
Hoo Hall
Hare Lodge
Hole Farm
Stovern's Hall
Rickstone's Farm
Durwards Hall
Rivenhall Bridge
Rivenhall End
Glebe Farm
The Old Rectory
Hotel
Whitelands
The Matchyn's
Sewage Works
Rose Cottage
Appleford Farm
Cemy
Waterside Bsns Pk
Colemans Resr
Appleford Bridge
River Blackwater
Hall Broad Farm
Workhouse Plantation
Coleman's Bridge
Coleman's Farm
Witham Junction
Witham
Elm Springs
1 Enterprise Ct
2 Europa Pk
Cromwell Ctr
Lea Lane Wood
Little Braxted
Hall
Liby
The Grove Ctr
Wheater Ind Est
Briarsford Ind Est
Sewage Works
Lea Lane Fruit Farm
Broomfield's Farm
1 WIMSEY CT
2 VANE CT
3 HAWTHORNE RISE
4 HOLLY WLK
1 KYNASTON PL
2 RICHARDSON WLK
A12
B1389
B1018
COLCHESTER RD
NEWLAND ST
MALDON RD
BRAXTED PARK RD
LITTLE BRAXTED LA
OAK RD
A2
1 GROVE COTTS
2 FOSTER CT
3 DU CANE PL
4 HORNER PL
5 FREEBOURNES CT
6 HEWITT WLK
7 LOCKRAM LA
8 NEWLANDS PREC
9 PENHALIGON CT
10 COACH HOUSE WAY
11 GUITHAVON ST
195
178

177 158

A B C D E F

Crabb's Farm

CRABB'S LA

LONDON RD B1024

MALDON RD

A12

Churchman's Farm

Inwort

8

LONDON RD

A12

Koorbaes

Ashman's Farm

Lucas's Croft

Highfields

New Barn

7

River Blackwater

BRETTS FIELD S LA

17

Kelvedon Hall Wood

Brickhouse Farm

Jubb's Row

6

Merlins

Kelvedon Hall Farm

Square Wood

The Glebe House

CO5

Fabian's Plantation

New Wood

5

Braxted Park

CH

KELVEDON HALL LA

Grange Farm House

Mason's Plantation

Inworth Grange

16

Howbridges Wood

4

Pinecroft

The Lake

Prodys

Orange Road

The Mount

Braxted Park House

Nursery Plantation

Ash Plantation

Tiptree Wood

BRETTS COTTS

WEST END RD

3

CH

LA LA

CM8

Pundicts Lodge

PRIORY RD

STONE L

15

Great Braxted Hall

NOAK'S CROSS

Hollytree Farm

2

Noak's Cross Farm

SEXTON'S LA

Priory Farm

Tiptree Priory

BRAXTED PARK RD

B1027

Broadfield Fruit Farm

1

West Hall Wood

Sexton's Farm

PH

TIPTREE RD

BRAXTED LA

PO

Great Braxted

Porter's Farm

Heathgate Farm

MALDON RD

GROVE FARM RD

GRANT HILL

White Rail Farm

B1022

14

BLING ROW

85 A B 86 C D 87 E F

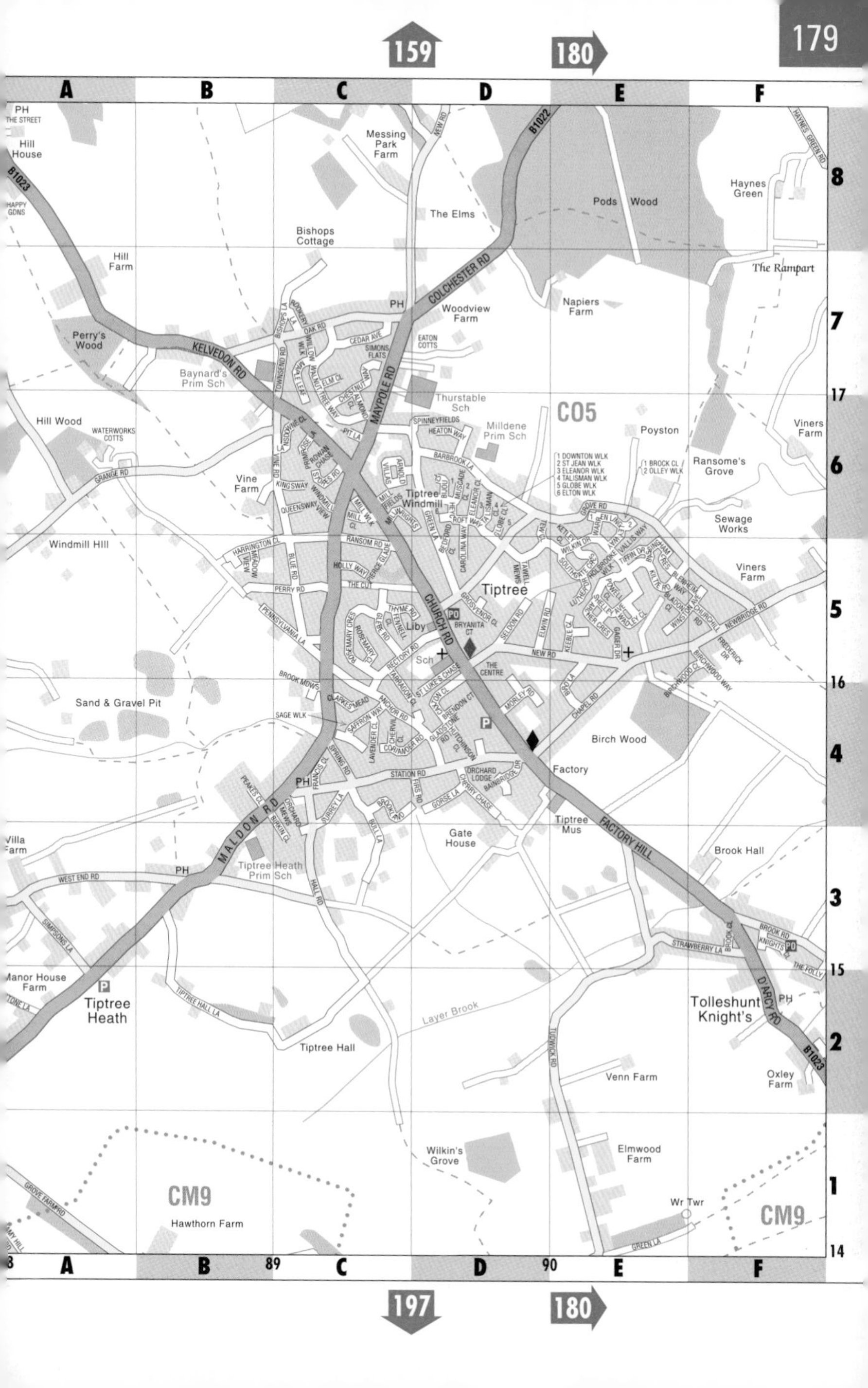
159
180
A
B
C
D
E
F
8
7
17
6
5
16
4
3
15
2
1
14
89
90
197
180
Tiptree
CO5
CM9
CM9
Messing Park Farm
The Elms
Bishops Cottage
Pods Wood
Haynes Green
The Rampart
Hill House
Hill Farm
Perry's Wood
Baynard's Prim Sch
Woodview Farm
Napiers Farm
Thurstable Sch
Milldene Prim Sch
Hill Wood
Waterworks Cotts
Vine Farm
Tiptree Windmill
Poyston
Ransome's Grove
Viners Farm
Sewage Works
Windmill Hill
Liby
Sch
Sand & Gravel Pit
Birch Wood
Factory
Gate House
Tiptree Mus
Villa Farm
Tiptree Heath Prim Sch
Brook Hall
Manor House Farm
Tiptree Heath
Tiptree Hall
Layer Brook
Tolleshunt Knight's
Venn Farm
Oxley Farm
Wilkin's Grove
Elmwood Farm
Hawthorn Farm
Wr Twr
1 DOWNTON WLK
2 ST JEAN WLK
3 ELEANOR WLK
4 TALISMAN WLK
5 GLOBE WLK
6 ELTON WLK
1 BROCK CL
2 OLLEY WLK
KELVEDON RD
COLCHESTER RD
MAYPOLE RD
CHURCH RD
MALDON RD
FACTORY HILL
D'ARCY RD
B1022
B1023
WEST END RD
GRANGE RD
NEW RD
STATION RD
GROVE RD
RANSOM RD
PERRY RD
THE CUT
CHAPEL RD
NEWBRIDGE RD
STRAWBERRY LA
TIPTREE HALL LA
TUDWICK RD
GREEN LA
HALL RD
GROVE FARM RD
SIMPSONS LA
KINGSWAY
QUEENSWAY
OAK RD
CEDAR AVE
EATON COTTS
SIMONS FLATS
BARBROOK LA
HEATON WAY
SPINNEYFIELDS
PIT LA
GROSVENOR CL
BRYANITA CT
THE CENTRE
BROOK MDWS
SAGE WLK
HAYNES GREEN RD
THE STREET
HAPPY GDNS
BROOK RD
KNIGHTS CL
THE FOLLY
BIRCHWOOD WAY
BIRCHWOOD CL
FREDERICK DR
CHURCHILL RD
BLENHEIM WAY
VALLIS WAY
SELDON RD
ELWIN RD
KEEBLE CL
GAGER DR
MORLEY RD
FIRS RD
GORSE LA
CHERRY CHASE
ORCHARD LODGE
BAINBRIDGE DR
BULL LA
SURREY LA
FRANCIS CL
SPRING RD
PEAKES CL
ORCHARD MEWS
BIRKIN CL
PENNSYLVANIA LA
HARRINGTON CL
MEADOW VIEW
BLUE RD
HOLLY WAY
HEDGE GLADE
ROSEMARY CRES
RECTORY RD
TARRAGON CL
ST LUKE'S CHASE
CLARKES MEAD
ANCHOR RD
SAFFRON WAY
CORIANDER RD
GLADSTONE RD
HUTCHINSON CL
BRENDON CT
THYME RD
FENNELL CL
BEDFORD CL
CAROLINA WAY
GREEN LA
HEYWOOD WAY
MUSCADE CL
ELEANOR CL
TALISMAN WLK
GLOBE CL
ARNOLD VILLAS
MILL FIELDS
MILLWRIGHTS
MILL CL
MILL WLK
WINDMILL VIEW
TOWNSEND RD
BISHOPS LA
ROOKERY LA
WILLOW WLK
WALNUT TREE WAY
MAPLE LEAF
ELM CL
CHESTNUT CL
ALMOND WAY
ROWAN CHASE
STORS RD
VINE RD
TEW CL
KETLEY CL
WILKIN DR
SOUTHGATE CRES
LUTHER RD
HOLBROOKE WLK
TIFFIN DR
POWELL CL
SHELLEY AVE
WADLEY CL
KILTIE RD
BLADON CL
WINSTON AVE
TAWELL MEWS
ELTON PARK

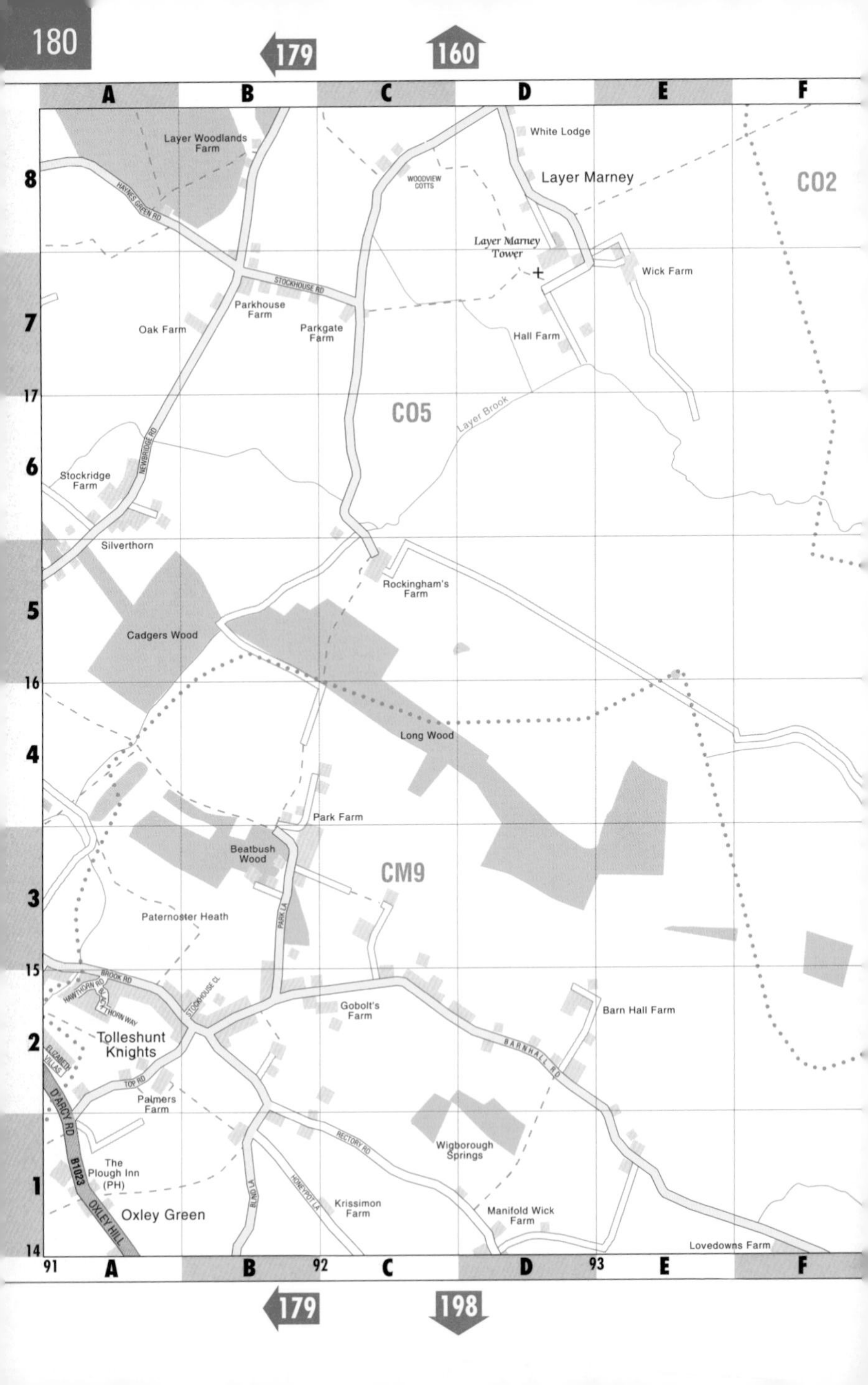
179
160
A
B
C
D
E
F
Layer Woodlands Farm
HAYNES GREEN RD
White Lodge
WOODVIEW COTTS
Layer Marney
CO2
Layer Marney Tower
Wick Farm
STOCKHOUSE RD
Parkhouse Farm
Oak Farm
Parkgate Farm
Hall Farm
CO5
Layer Brook
NEWBRIDGE RD
Stockridge Farm
Silverthorn
Rockingham's Farm
Cadgers Wood
Long Wood
Park Farm
Beatbush Wood
CM9
Paternoster Heath
PARK LA
BROOK RD
HAWTHORN RD
STOCKHOUSE CL
THORN WAY
Gobolt's Farm
Barn Hall Farm
Tolleshunt Knights
ELIZABETH VILLAS
BARNHALL RD
TOP RD
Palmers Farm
D'ARCY RD
RECTORY RD
Wigborough Springs
The Plough Inn (PH)
B1023
HONEYPOT LA
BLIND LA
Krissimon Farm
Manifold Wick Farm
Oxley Green
OXLEY HILL
Lovedowns Farm
8
7
17
6
5
16
4
3
15
2
1
14
91
92
93
179
198

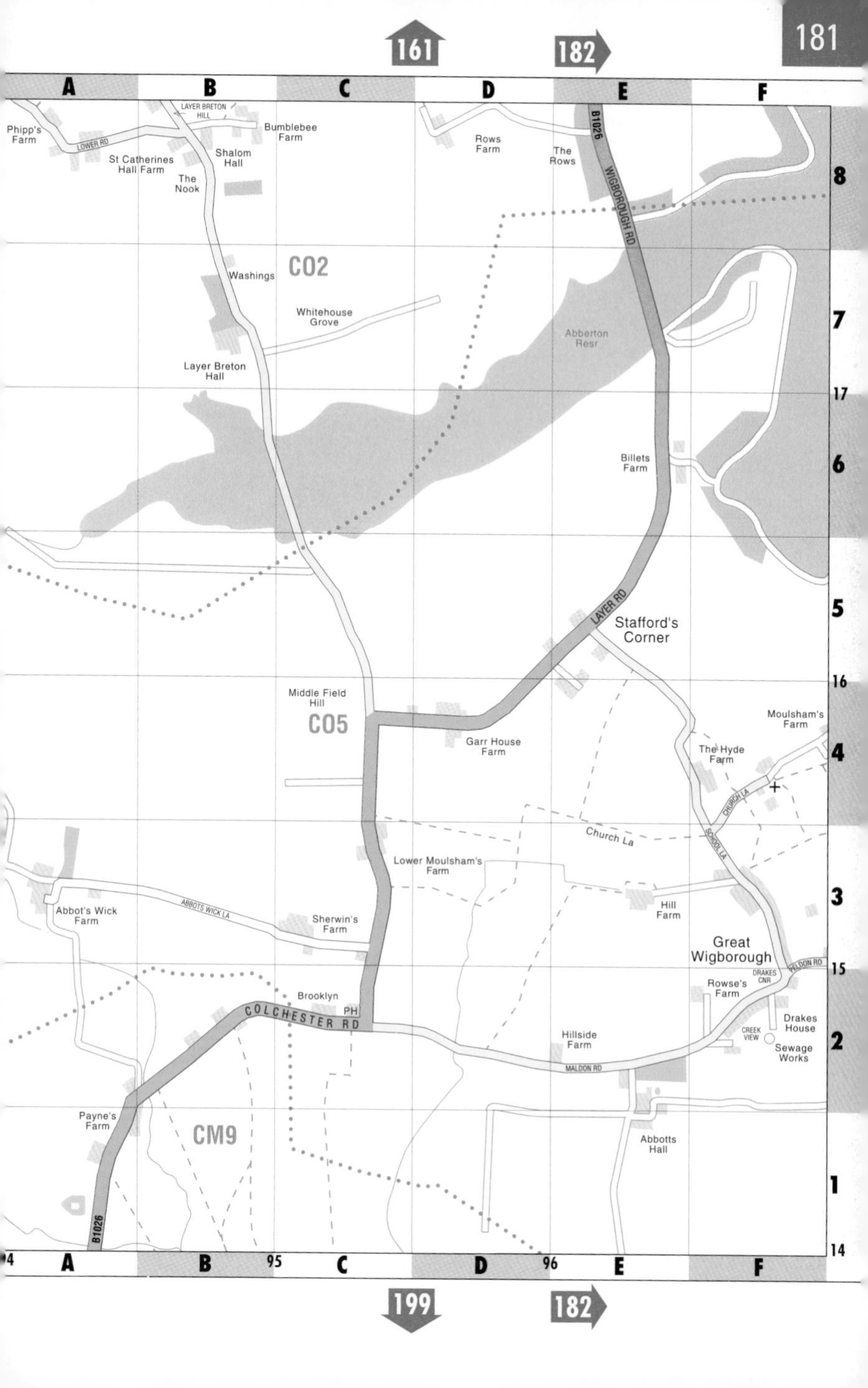

161
182

A B C D E F

Phipp's Farm
LOWER RD
St Catherines Hall Farm
LAYER BRETON HILL
Bumblebee Farm
Shalom Hall
The Nook
Rows Farm
The Rows
B1026
WIGBOROUGH RD

8

CO2
Washings
Whitehouse Grove
Abberton Resr

7

Layer Breton Hall

17

Billets Farm

6

LAYER RD

5

Stafford's Corner

Middle Field Hill
CO5

16

Garr House Farm
Moulsham's Farm
The Hyde Farm
CHURCH LA

4

Church La
CHURCH LA

Lower Moulsham's Farm

Abbot's Wick Farm
ABBOTS WICK LA
Sherwin's Farm
Hill Farm

Great Wigborough

3

MALDON RD

15

Brooklyn
PH
COLCHESTER RD
Rowse's Farm
DRAKES CNR
CREEK VIEW
Drakes House
Sewage Works

Hillside Farm
MALDON RD

2

Payne's Farm
CM9
Abbotts Hall

1

B1026

14

4
A B C 95 C D 96 E F

199
182

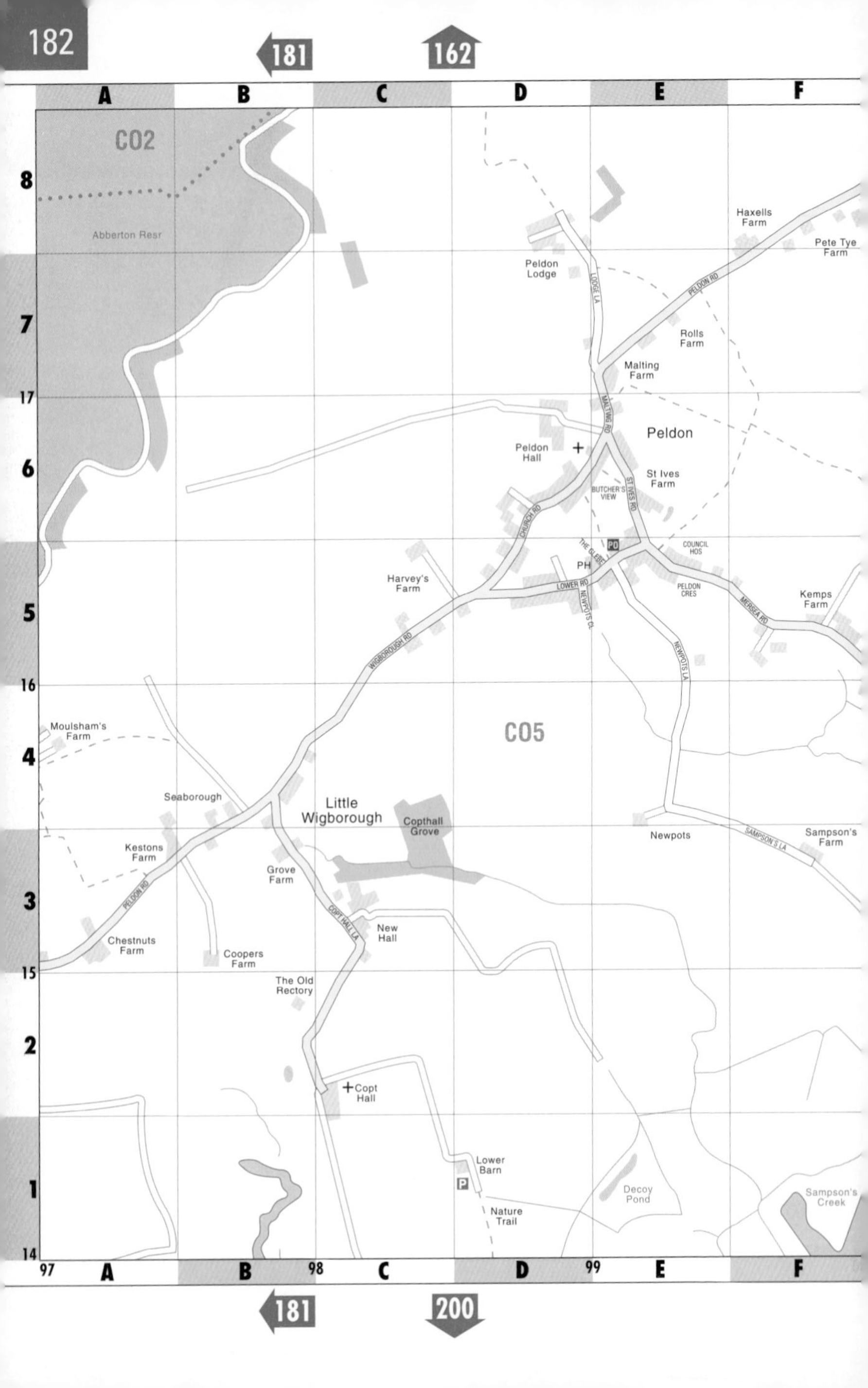
181
162
A
B
C
D
E
F
8
7
17
6
5
16
4
3
15
2
1
14
97
98
99
CO2
Abberton Resr
Haxells Farm
Pete Tye Farm
Peldon Lodge
LODGE LA
PELDON RD
Rolls Farm
Malting Farm
MALTING RD
Peldon
Peldon Hall
St Ives Farm
BUTCHER'S VIEW
ST IVES RD
CHURCH RD
THE GLEBE
PO
PH
COUNCIL HOS
Harvey's Farm
LOWER RD
NEWPOTS CL
PELDON CRES
MERSEA RD
Kemps Farm
WIGBOROUGH RD
NEWPOTS LA
CO5
Moulsham's Farm
Seaborough
Little Wigborough
Copthall Grove
Newpots
SAMPSON'S LA
Sampson's Farm
Kestons Farm
Grove Farm
PELDON RD
COPT HALL LA
New Hall
Chestnuts Farm
Coopers Farm
The Old Rectory
Copt Hall
Lower Barn
P
Nature Trail
Decoy Pond
Sampson's Creek
181
200

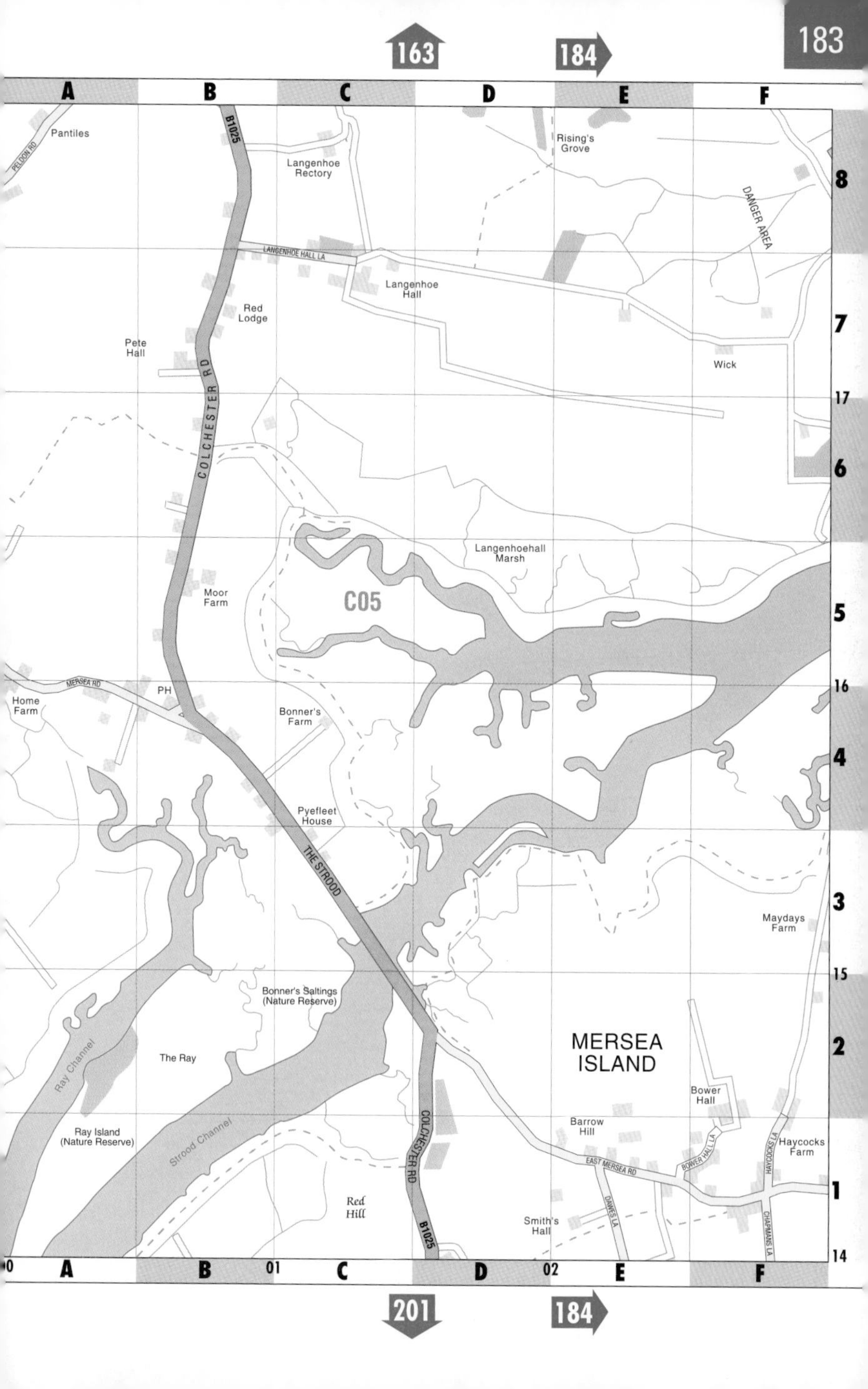

163
184
A
B
C
D
E
F
Pantiles
PELDON RD
B1025
Langenhoe Rectory
Rising's Grove
DANGER AREA
LANGENHOE HALL LA
Langenhoe Hall
Red Lodge
Pete Hall
Wick
COLCHESTER RD
Langenhoehall Marsh
CO5
Moor Farm
MERSEA RD
PH
Home Farm
Bonner's Farm
Pyefleet House
THE STROOD
Maydays Farm
Bonner's Saltings (Nature Reserve)
MERSEA ISLAND
The Ray
Ray Channel
Bower Hall
Barrow Hill
Ray Island (Nature Reserve)
Strood Channel
COLCHESTER RD
EAST MERSEA RD
BOWER HALL LA
HAYCOCKS LA
Haycocks Farm
Red Hill
DAWES LA
Smith's Hall
CHAPMANS LA
B1025
8
7
17
6
5
16
4
3
15
2
1
14
0
01
02
201
184

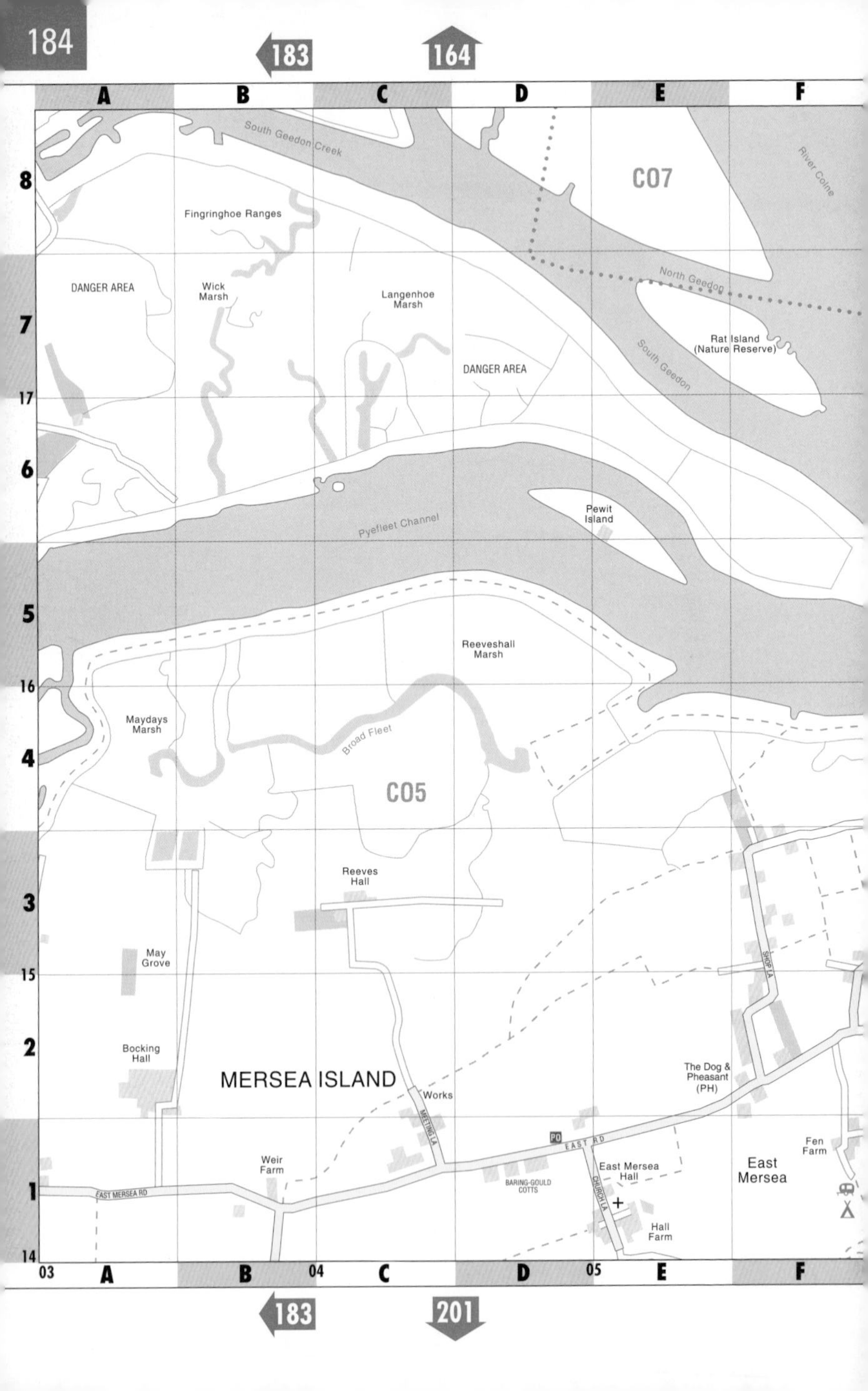

183
164

South Geedon Creek

CO7

River Colne

8

Fingringhoe Ranges

North Geedon

DANGER AREA

Wick Marsh

Langenhoe Marsh

South Geedon

Rat Island
(Nature Reserve)

7

DANGER AREA

17

6

Pyefleet Channel

Pewit Island

5

Reeveshall Marsh

16

Maydays Marsh

Broad Fleet

4

CO5

3

Reeves Hall

May Grove

15

2

Bocking Hall

MERSEA ISLAND

Works

The Dog & Pheasant (PH)

Fen Farm

East Mersea

1

EAST MERSEA RD

Weir Farm

PO

EAST RD

BARING-GOULD COTTS

East Mersea Hall

Hall Farm

14

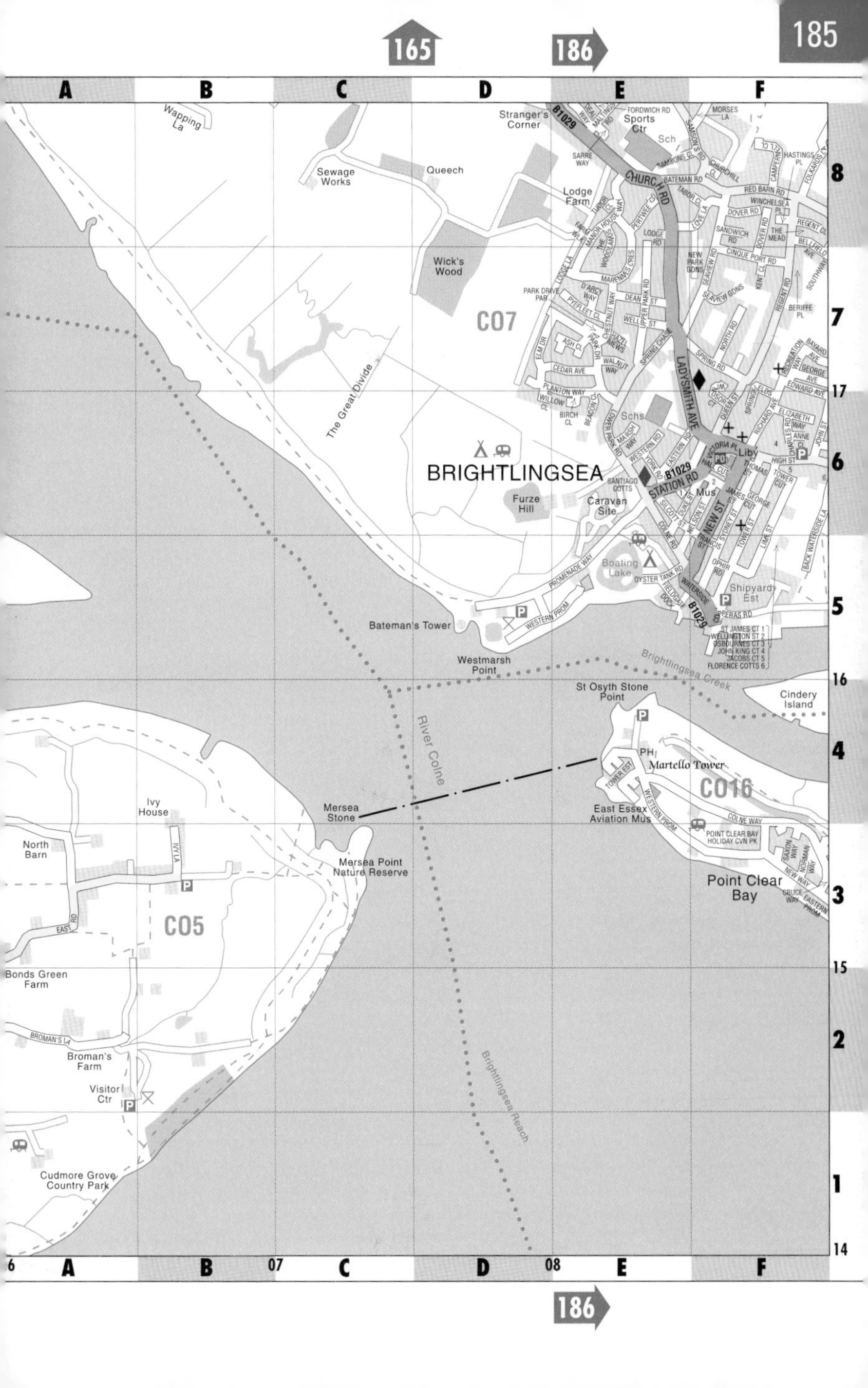
165
186
A
B
C
D
E
F
8
7
17
6
5
16
4
3
15
2
1
14
07
08
Wapping La
Sewage Works
Queech
Wick's Wood
Stranger's Corner
Sports Ctr
Sch
Lodge Farm
CO7
The Great Divide
BRIGHTLINGSEA
Furze Hill
Caravan Site
Schs
Mus
Liby
Boating Lake
Shipyard Est
Bateman's Tower
Westmarsh Point
Brightlingsea Creek
St Osyth Stone Point
Cindery Island
River Colne
Martello Tower
CO16
Mersea Stone
East Essex Aviation Mus
Ivy House
North Barn
Mersea Point Nature Reserve
Point Clear Bay
CO5
Bonds Green Farm
Broman's Farm
Visitor Ctr
Cudmore Grove Country Park
Brightlingsea Reach
B1029
CHURCH RD
LADYSMITH AVE
STATION RD
NEW ST
WESTERN PROM
PROMENADE WAY
OYSTER TANK RD
WATERSIDE
COLNE WAY
POINT CLEAR BAY HOLIDAY CVN PK
EAST RD
IVY LA
BROMAN'S LA
186

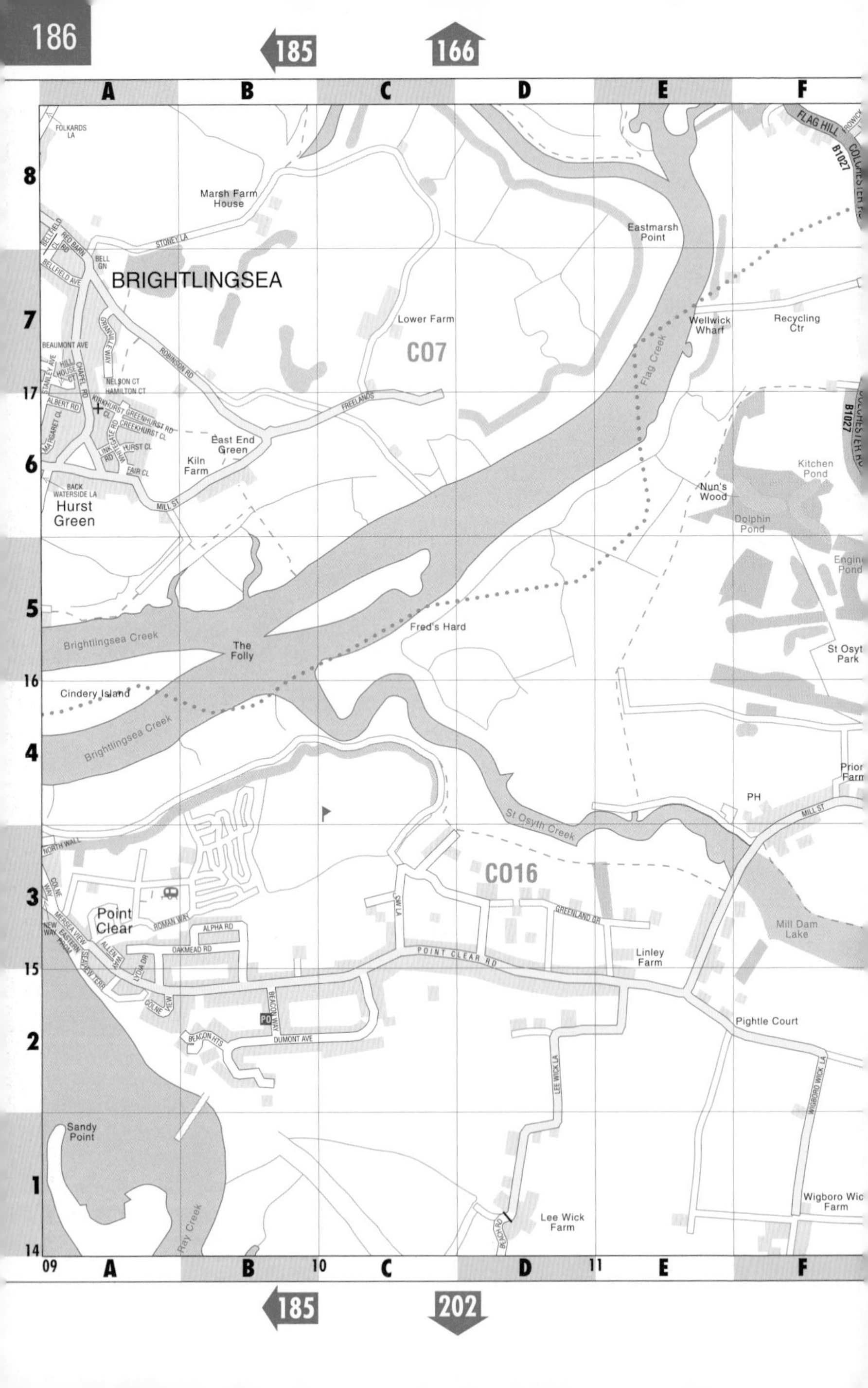

A   B   C   D   E   F

FOLKARDS LA

8

Marsh Farm House

STONEY LA

BELL GN

BRIGHTLINGSEA

Eastmarsh Point

7

Lower Farm

CO7

Wellwick Wharf

Recycling Ctr

Flag Creek

B1027

COLCHESTER RD

FLAG HILL

17

BEAUMONT AVE

NELSON CT

HAMILTON CT

FREELANDS

GREENHURST RD

Kitchen Pond

ALBERT RD

6

HURST CL

FAIR CL

East End Green

Kiln Farm

MILL LA

Nun's Wood

Dolphin Pond

BACK WATERSIDE LA

Hurst Green

Engine Pond

5

Brightlingsea Creek

The Folly

Fred's Hard

St Osyth Park

16

Cindery Island

Brightlingsea Creek

Prior Farm

4

St Osyth Creek

PH

MILL ST

NORTH WALL

Point Clear

ROMAN WAY

ALPHA RD

3

OAKMEAD RD

GREENLAND RD

CO16

Linley Farm

Mill Dam Lake

15

NEW EASTERN ESPL

POINT CLEAR RD

BEACON HTS

PO

DUMONT AVE

Pightle Court

2

LEE WICK LA

WIGBORO

Sandy Point

1

Lee Wick Farm

Wigboro Wick Farm

14

Ray Creek

09   A   B   10   C   D   11   E   F

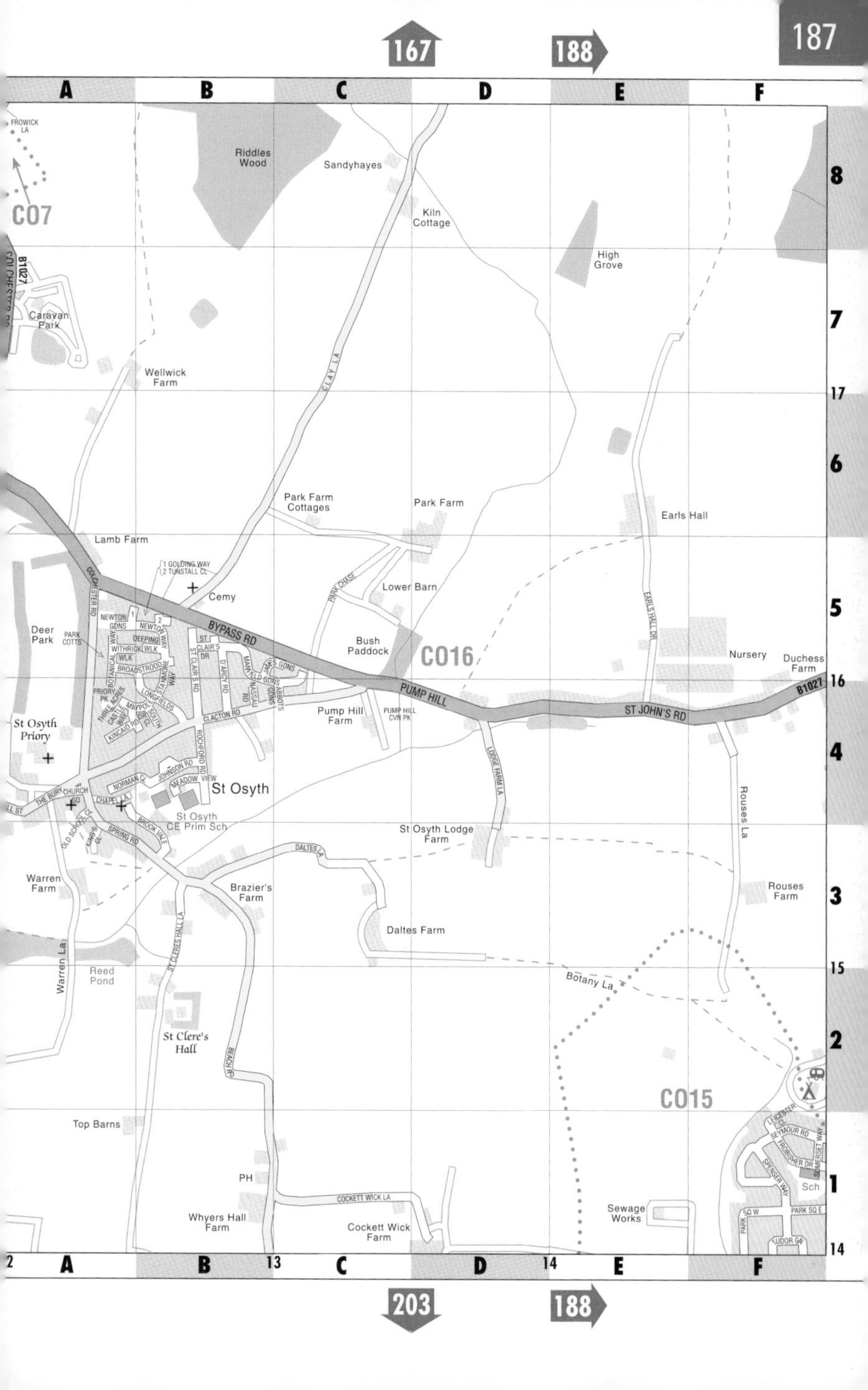

A B C D E F

FROWICK LA
CO7
B1027
COLCHESTER RD

Caravan Park

Riddles Wood

Sandyhayes

Kiln Cottage

High Grove

8

7

17

Wellwick Farm

CLAY LA

Park Farm Cottages

Park Farm

Earls Hall

6

Lamb Farm

Deer Park

PARK COTTS

COLCHESTER RD

1 GOLDING WAY
2 TUNSTALL CL
Cemy

NEWTON GDNS
NEWTON
DEEPING WK
WITHROW WLK
BROADSTROOD

CLAIR'S DR
CLAIR'S

BYPASS RD

Lower Barn

Bush Paddock

5

CO16

EARLS HALL DR

Nursery

Duchess Farm

PRIORY PK
THIRD AVE
KINGAD
NORMAN CT
BRICK CL
CHAPEL CL

PRIEST CL
MAIN RD
ST ALBANS
ST AGNES
ST DENIS
ST CLAIRS DR
CLACTON RD
ROCHFORD

MEADOW VIEW

St Osyth

PUMP HILL

St John's Rd

B1027

16

St Osyth Priory

THE BURY
CHURCH
HALL ST
OLD FERRY RD
SPRING RD

St Osyth CE Prim Sch

Pump Hill Farm

PUMP HILL CVN PK

LODGE FARM LA

Rouses La

4

Warren Farm

DALTER CL

St Osyth Lodge Farm

Rouses Farm

3

Brazier's Farm

ST CHEDESTALL LA

Daltes Farm

15

Warren La

Reed Pond

St Clere's Hall

BEACH RD

Botany La

2

CO15

Top Barns

PH

COCKETT WICK LA

Sewage Works

LECKFORD CL
SEYMOUR RD
SEYMOUR DR E

Sch

TUDOR GR
PARK SQ E
PARK SQ W

1

14

Whyers Hall Farm

Cockett Wick Farm

187
168

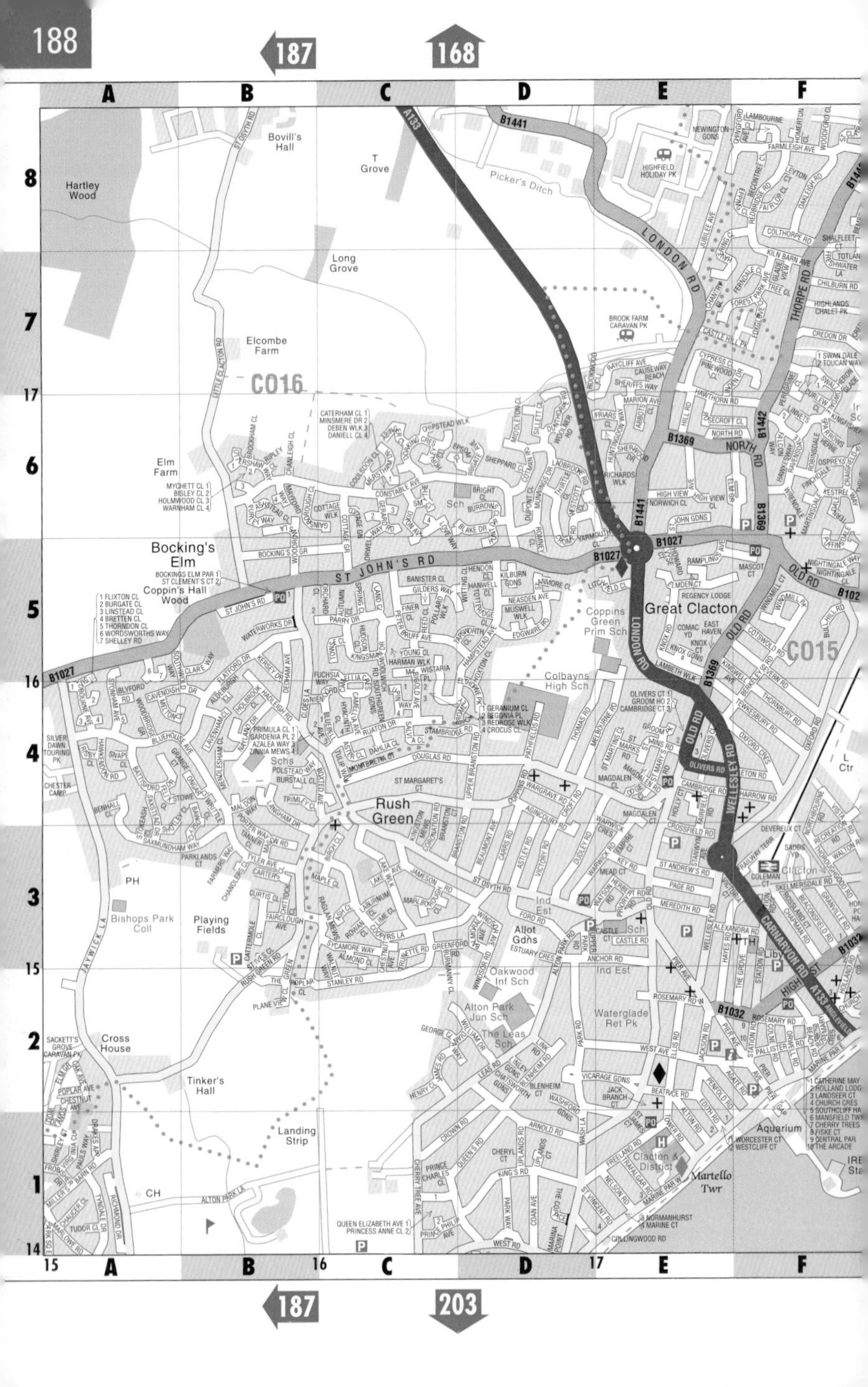
A
B
C
D
E
F
8
7
17
6
5
16
4
3
15
2
1
14
Hartley Wood
Bovill's Hall
T Grove
Long Grove
Picker's Ditch
HIGHFIELD HOLIDAY PK
BROOK FARM CARAVAN PK
Elcombe Farm
CO16
Elm Farm
Bocking's Elm
Coppin's Hall Wood
ST JOHN'S RD
B1027
B1441
B1369
B1442
A133
B1032
LONDON RD
THORPE RD
OLD RD
WELLESLEY RD
CARNARVON RD
HIGH ST
NORTH RD
Great Clacton
CO15
Coppins Green Prim Sch
Colbayns High Sch
Rush Green
Schs
Sch
Ind Est
Allot Gdns
Oakwood Inf Sch
Alton Park Jun Sch
The Leas Sch
Waterglade Ret Pk
SILVER DAWN TOURING PK
CHESTER CAMP
PH
Bishops Park Coll
Playing Fields
SACKETT'S GROVE CARAVAN PK
Cross House
Tinker's Hall
Landing Strip
CH
ALTON PARK LA
JAYWICK LA
Clacton & District
Martello Twr
Aquarium
Clacton
Liby
L Ctr
ST OSYTH RD
LITTLE CLACTON RD
MARINE PAR W
MARINE PAR E
WEST AVE
COLLINGWOOD RD
WEST RD

169

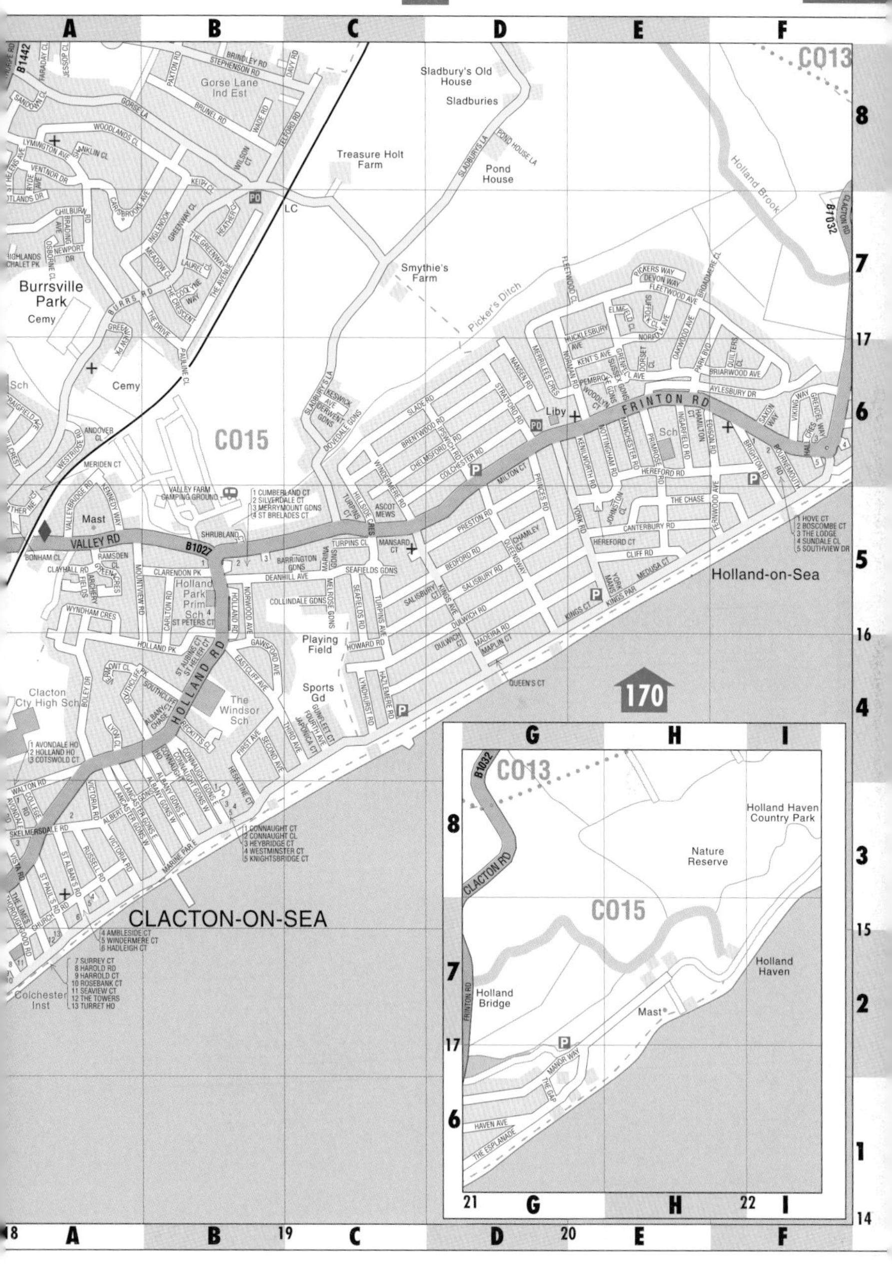

CO15
CO13
CLACTON-ON-SEA
Holland-on-Sea
Burrsville Park
Gorse Lane Ind Est
Sladbury's Old House
Sladburies
Treasure Holt Farm
Pond House
Smythie's Farm
Holland Brook
Picker's Ditch
FRINTON RD
VALLEY RD
HOLLAND RD
B1027
B1032
B1442
Valley Farm Camping Ground
Holland Park Prim Sch
The Windsor Sch
Playing Field
Sports Gd
Clacton Cty High Sch
Colchester Inst
Holland Haven Country Park
Nature Reserve
Holland Haven
Holland Bridge
Mast
CLACTON RD
FRINTON RD
MANOR WAY
THE GAP
HAVEN AVE
THE ESPLANADE

170

172

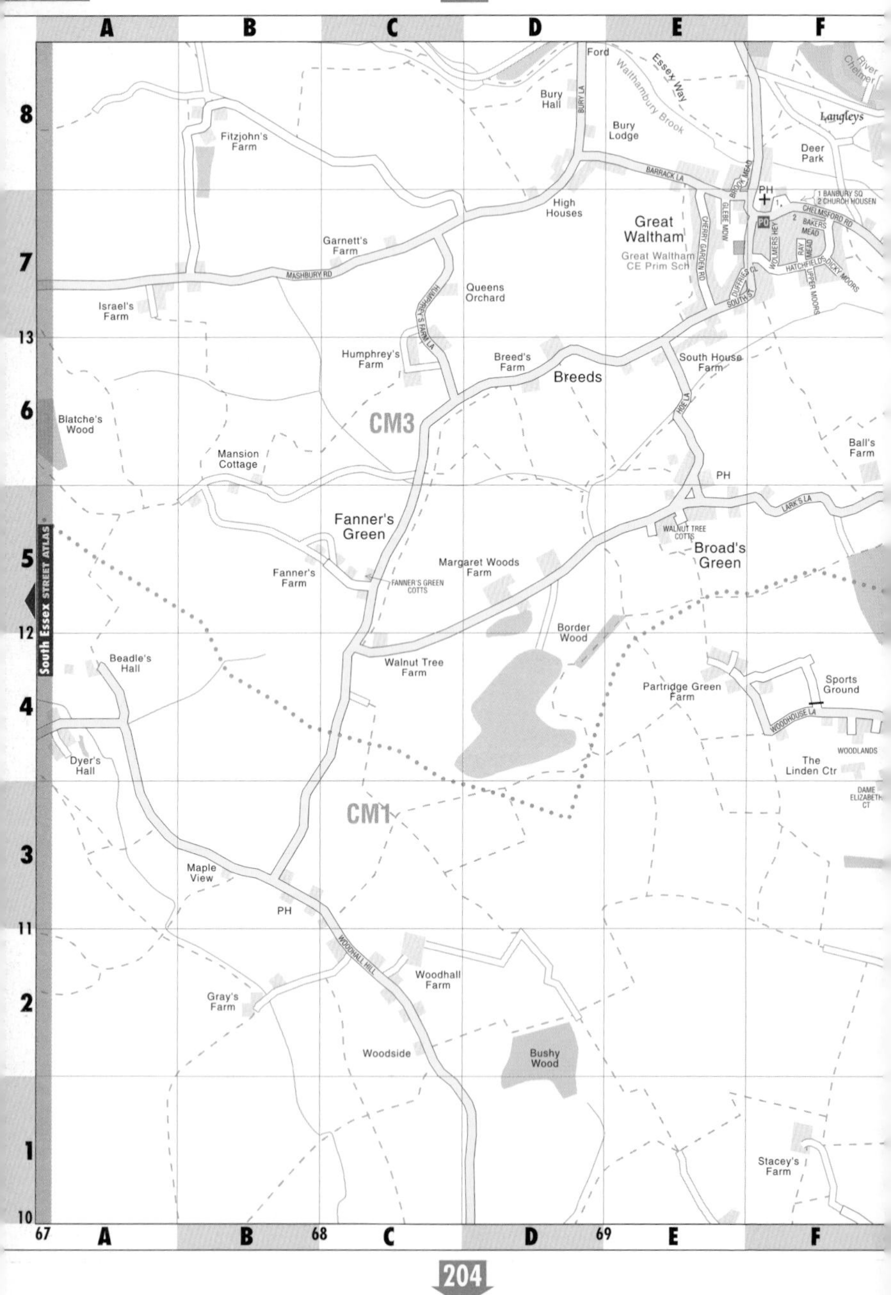
A
B
C
D
E
F
8
7
6
5
4
3
2
1
13
12
11
10
67
68
69
Ford
Essex Way
Walthambury Brook
Bury Hall
BURY LA
Bury Lodge
River Chelmer
Langleys
Deer Park
Fitzjohn's Farm
BARRACK LA
BROOK MEAD
PH
1 BANBURY SQ
2 CHURCH HOUSEN
CHELMSFORD RD
High Houses
Great Waltham
Great Waltham CE Prim Sch
GLEBE MDW
CHERRY GARDEN RD
PO
BAKERS MEAD
WOLMERS HEY
RAY MEAD
HATCHFIELDS
DICKY MOORS
UPPER MOORS
DUFFRIES CL
SOUTH ST
Garnett's Farm
MASHBURY RD
Queens Orchard
HUMPHREY'S FARM LA
Israel's Farm
Humphrey's Farm
Breed's Farm
Breeds
South House Farm
HOE LA
Blatche's Wood
CM3
Mansion Cottage
Ball's Farm
PH
LARK'S LA
Fanner's Green
WALNUT TREE COTTS
Broad's Green
Margaret Woods Farm
Fanner's Farm
FANNER'S GREEN COTTS
South Essex STREET ATLAS
Border Wood
Walnut Tree Farm
Beadle's Hall
Partridge Green Farm
Sports Ground
WOODHOUSE LA
WOODLANDS
Dyer's Hall
The Linden Ctr
DAME ELIZABETH CT
CM1
Maple View
PH
WOODHALL HILL
Woodhall Farm
Gray's Farm
Woodside
Bushy Wood
Stacey's Farm

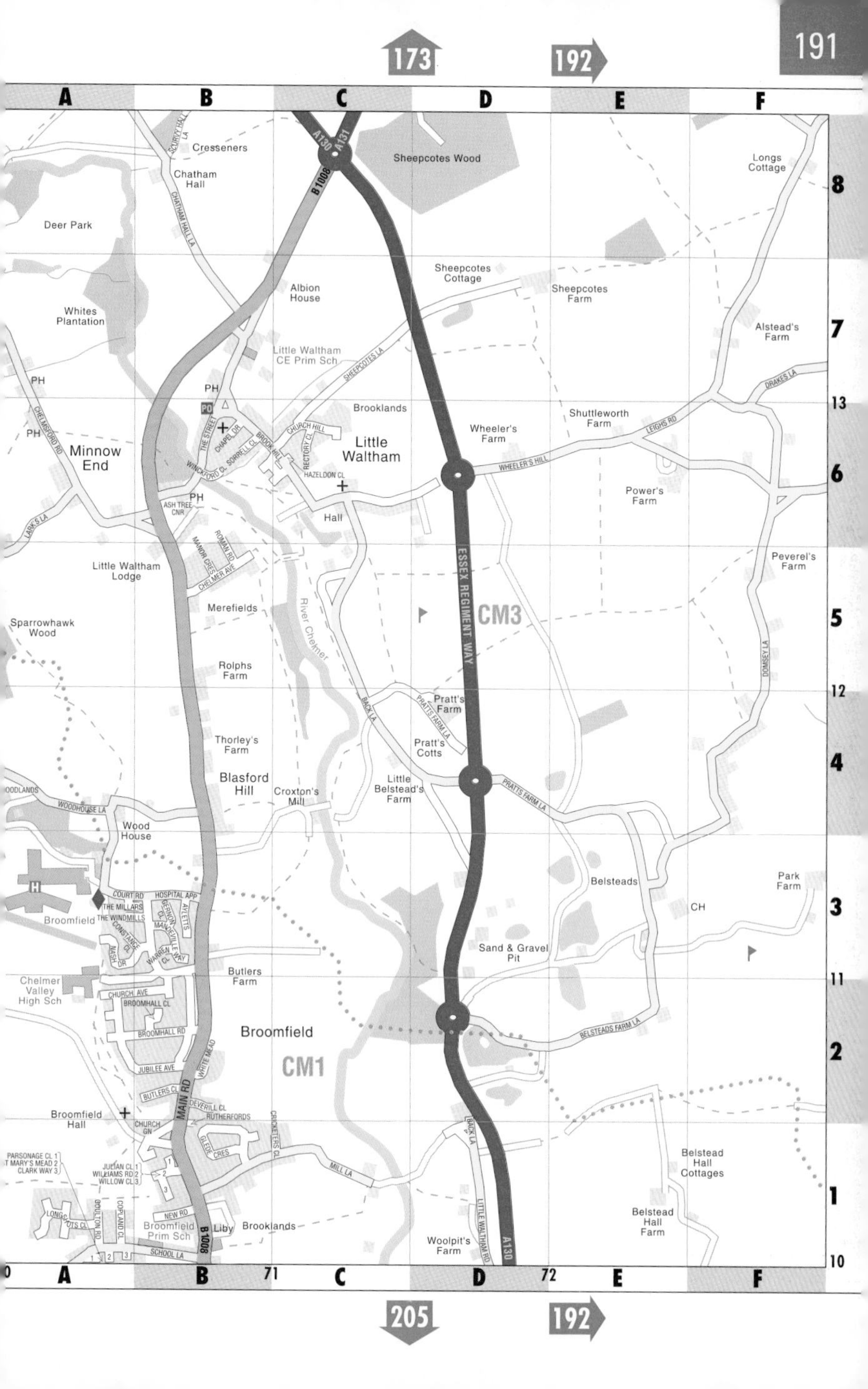

A   B   C   D   E   F

Cresseners

Chatham Hall

Sheepcotes Wood

Longs Cottage

8

Deer Park

Albion House

Sheepcotes Cottage

Sheepcotes Farm

Alstead's Farm

Whites Plantation

7

PH

Little Waltham CE Prim Sch

Brooklands

Wheeler's Farm

Shuttleworth Farm

13

PH

PH

PO

Minnow End

Little Waltham

WHEELER'S HILL

LEIGHS RD

Power's Farm

6

Ash Tree Cnr

Half

ESSEX REGIMENT WAY

Peverel's Farm

Little Waltham Lodge

CHELMER AVE

River Chelmer

CM3

DENNELY LA

5

Sparrowhawk Wood

Merefields

12

Rolphs Farm

Pratt's Farm

Thorley's Farm

Pratt's Cotts

4

WOODHOUSE LA

Blasford Hill

Croxton's Mill

Little Belstead's Farm

PRATTS FARM LA

WOODLANDS

Wood House

Belsteads

CH

Park Farm

3

H

THE WINDMILLS

Broomfield

Butlers Farm

Sand & Gravel Pit

11

Chelmer Valley High Sch

CHURCH GN

Broomfield

CM1

BELSTEADS FARM LA

2

JUBILEE AVE

Broomfield Hall

MAIN RD

RUTHERFORDS

BRACK LA

Belstead Hall Cottages

1

PARSONAGE CL
ST MARY'S MEAD
CLARK WAY
JULIAN CL
WILLIAMS RD
WILLOW CL

B 1008

Broomfield Prim Sch

Lrby

Brooklands

MILL LA

LITTLE WALTHAM RD

A 130

Woolpit's Farm

Belstead Hall Farm

10

A   B 71 C   D 72 E   F

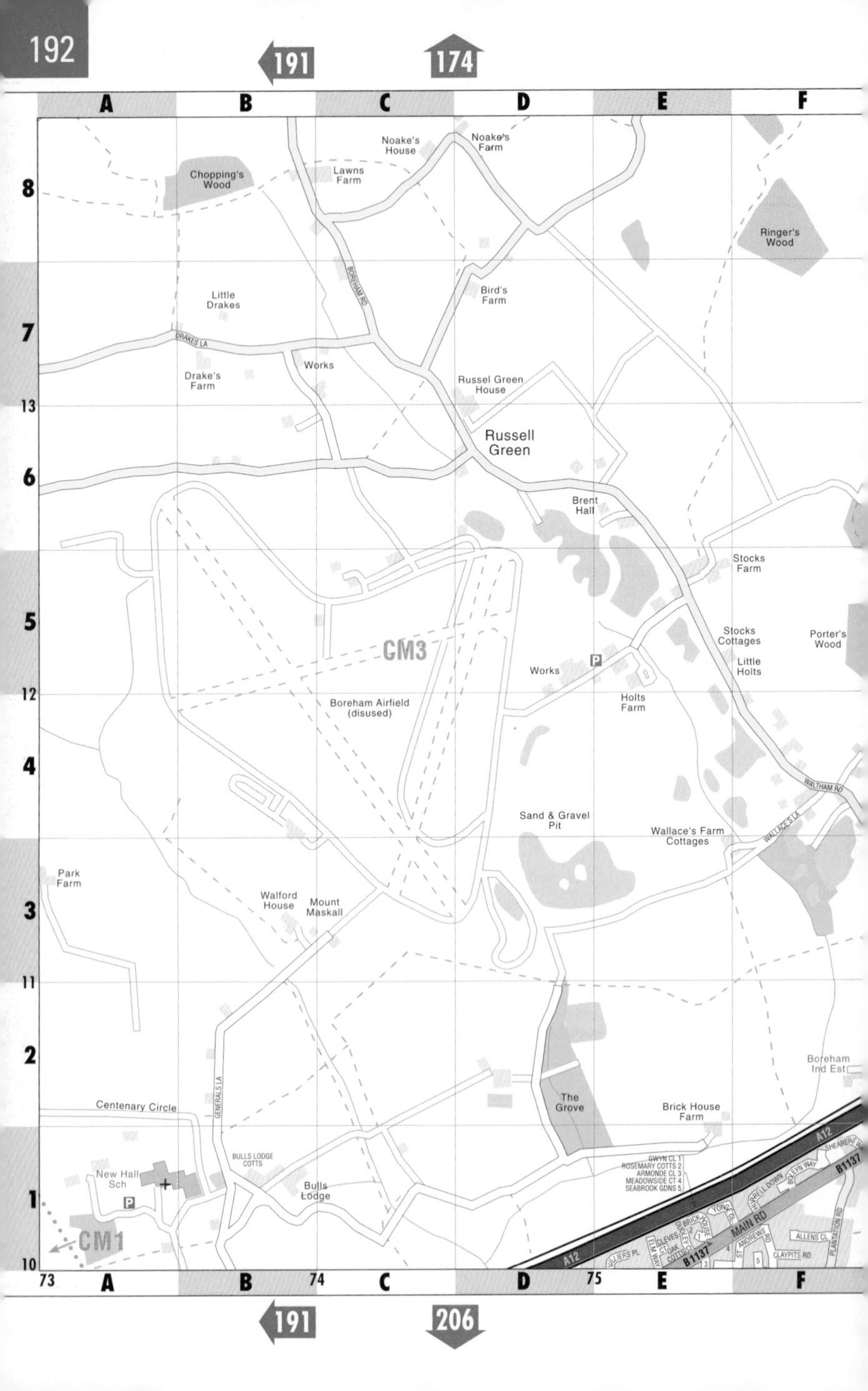

191
174

A   B   C   D   E   F

8

Chopping's
Wood

Noake's
House

Noake's
Farm

Ringer's
Wood

Little
Drakes

Lawns
Farm

Bird's
Farm

7

DRAKES LA

Drake's
Farm

Works

Russel Green
House

13

Russell
Green

6

Brent
Hall

Stocks
Farm

5

CM3

Stocks
Cottages

Little
Holts

Porter's
Wood

12

Boreham Airfield
(disused)

Works

Holts
Farm

4

BELTHAM RD

Sand & Gravel
Pit

Wallace's Farm
Cottages

WALLACE LA

Park
Farm

Walford
House

Mount
Maskall

3

11

Centenary Circle

GENERALS LA

The
Grove

Brick House
Farm

Boreham
Ind Est

2

A12

B1137

New Hall
Sch

BULLS LODGE
COTTS

Bulls
Lodge

GWYN CL 1
ROSEMARY COTTS 2
ARMONDE CL 3
MEADOWSIDE CT 4
SEABROOK GDNS 5

MAIN RD

1

CM1

A12

B1137

CLAYPITS RD

ALLENS CL

10

73   A   B   74   C   D   75   E   F

191
206

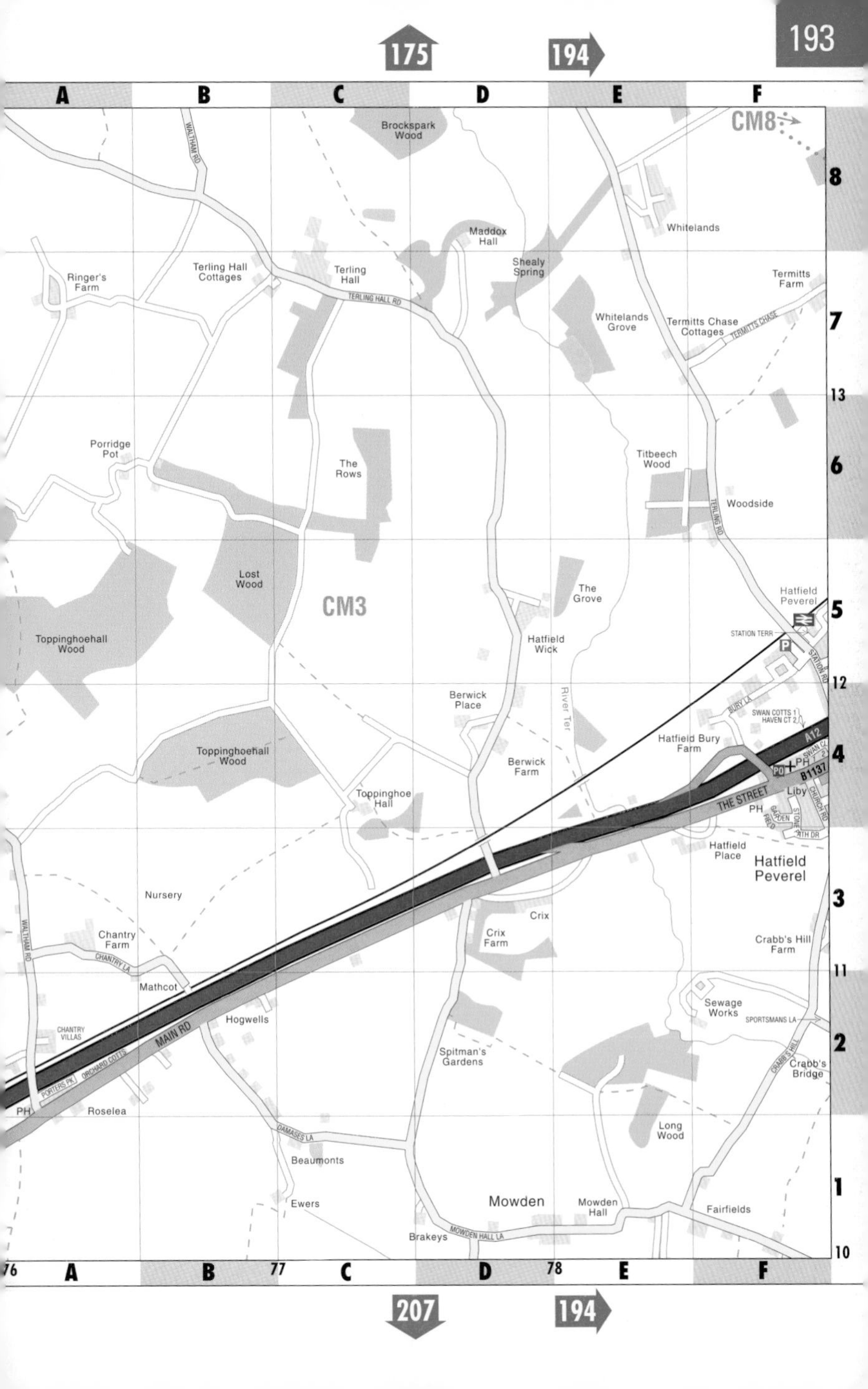
175
194
A
B
C
D
E
F
Brockspark Wood
CM8
8
Whitelands
Maddox Hall
WALTHAM RD
Terling Hall Cottages
Terling Hall
Shealy Spring
Ringer's Farm
TERLING HALL RD
Termitts Farm
Whitelands Grove
Termitts Chase Cottages
TERMITTS CHASE
7
13
Porridge Pot
The Rows
Titbeech Wood
6
Woodside
TERLING RD
Lost Wood
The Grove
Hatfield Peverel
CM3
5
Toppinghoehall Wood
Hatfield Wick
STATION TERR
STATION RD
12
River Ter
Berwick Place
BURY LA
SWAN COTTS 1
HAVEN CT 2
Hatfield Bury Farm
A12
Toppinghoehall Wood
Berwick Farm
SWAN CL
PH
PO
B1137
4
Toppinghoe Hall
THE STREET
Liby
PH
GARDEN FIELD
STONE
CHURCH RD
ATH DR
Hatfield Place
Hatfield Peverel
Nursery
3
Crix
Crix Farm
Chantry Farm
Crabb's Hill Farm
WALTHAM RD
CHANTRY LA
11
Mathcot
Sewage Works
CHANTRY VILLAS
Hogwells
SPORTSMANS LA
MAIN RD
2
Spitman's Gardens
CRABB'S HILL
Crabb's Bridge
ORCHARD COTTS
PORTERS PK
PH
Roselea
DAMASES LA
Long Wood
Beaumonts
1
Ewers
Mowden
Mowden Hall
Fairfields
Brakeys
MOWDEN HALL LA
10
76
A
B
77
C
D
78
E
F
207
194

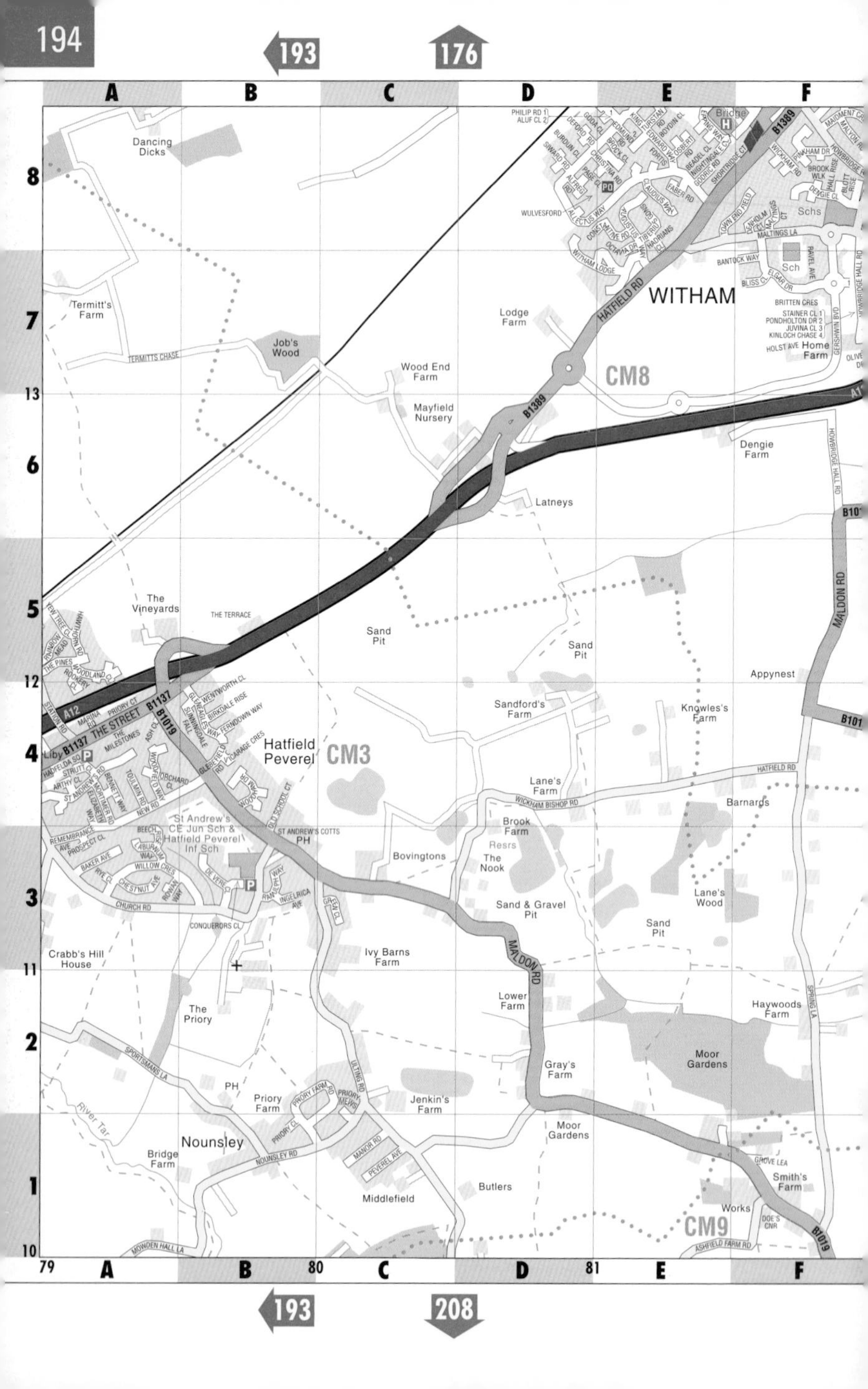
194
193
176
A
B
C
D
E
F
8
7
13
6
5
12
4
3
11
2
1
10
79
80
81
208
Dancing Dicks
Termitt's Farm
TERMITTS CHASE
Job's Wood
Wood End Farm
Mayfield Nursery
Lodge Farm
WITHAM
CM8
HATFIELD RD
B1389
WULVESFORD
WITHAM LODGE
Bridge
Schs
Sch
MALTINGS LA
BANTOCK WAY
BRITTEN CRES
STAINER CL
PONDHOLTON DR
JUVINA CL
KINLOCH CHASE
HOLST AVE
Home Farm
HOWBRIDGE HALL RD
Dengie Farm
Latneys
A12
The Vineyards
THE TERRACE
Sand Pit
Sand Pit
Appynest
MALDON RD
B1019
B1137
THE STREET
Hatfield Peverel
CM3
Sandford's Farm
Knowles's Farm
HATFIELD RD
Lane's Farm
WICKHAM BISHOP RD
Barnards
Brook Farm
Resrs
The Nook
Bovingtons
St Andrew's CE Jun Sch & Hatfield Peverel Inf Sch
PH
ST ANDREW'S COTTS
OLD SCHOOL CT
CHURCH RD
CONQUERORS CL
Sand & Gravel Pit
Lane's Wood
Sand Pit
Crabb's Hill House
Ivy Barns Farm
Lower Farm
The Priory
Haywoods Farm
SPRING LA
SPORTSMANS LA
Gray's Farm
Moor Gardens
PH
Priory Farm
Jenkin's Farm
ULTING RD
River Ter
Nounsley
Bridge Farm
NOUNSLEY RD
Moor Gardens
Butlers
Middlefield
Smith's Farm
GROVE LEA
Works
CM9
ASHFIELD FARM RD
MOWDEN HALL LA

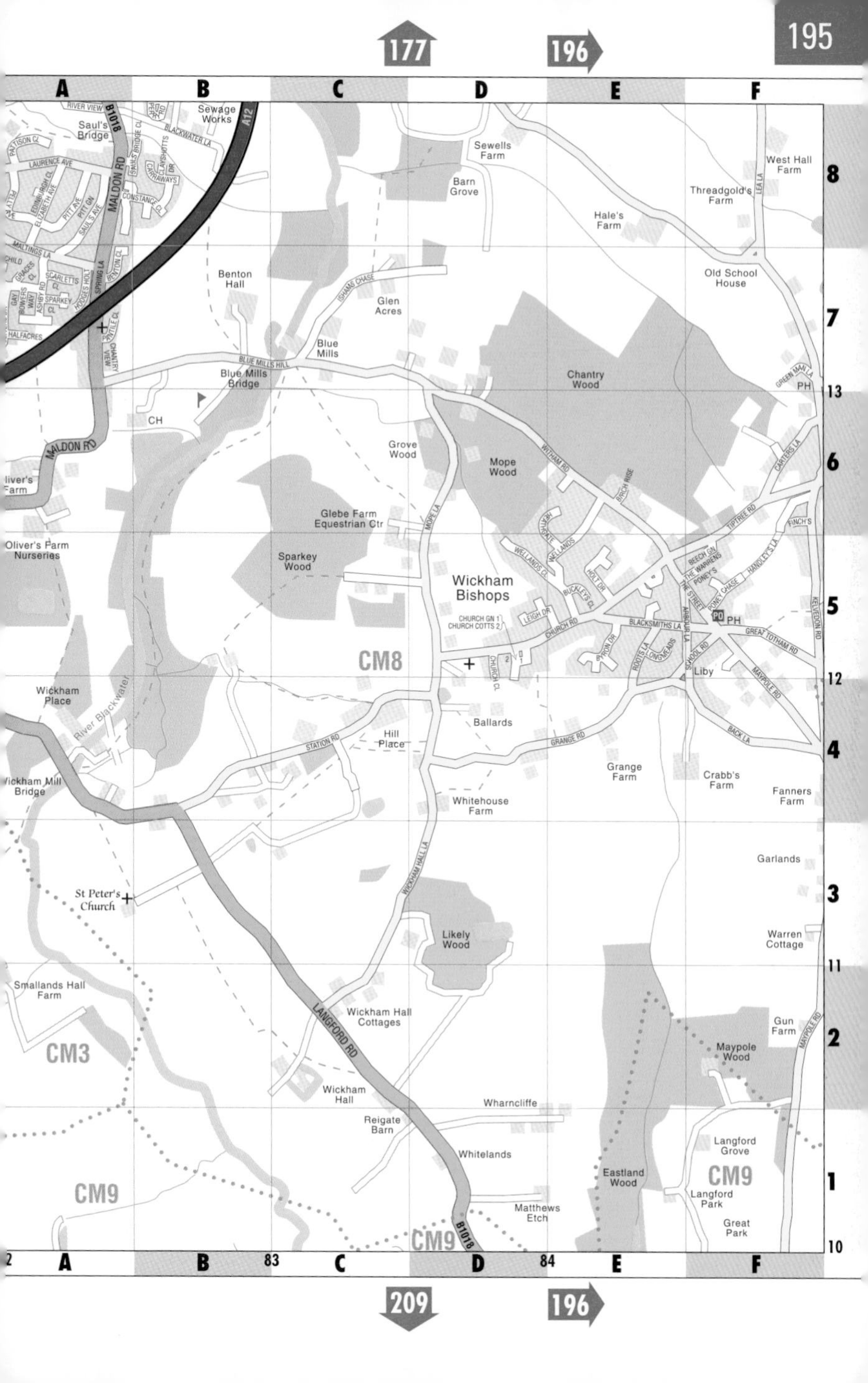
177
196
A
B
C
D
E
F
Sewage Works
Saul's Bridge
Sewells Farm
West Hall Farm
Barn Grove
Threadgold's Farm
Hale's Farm
Benton Hall
Old School House
Glen Acres
Blue Mills
Blue Mills Bridge
Chantry Wood
CH
PH
Grove Wood
Mope Wood
Oliver's Farm
Glebe Farm Equestrian Ctr
Oliver's Farm Nurseries
Sparkey Wood
Wickham Bishops
PO
CM8
Liby
Wickham Place
River Blackwater
Ballards
Hill Place
Grange Farm
Crabb's Farm
Fanners Farm
Wickham Mill Bridge
Whitehouse Farm
Garlands
St Peter's Church
Likely Wood
Warren Cottage
Smallands Hall Farm
Wickham Hall Cottages
Gun Farm
CM3
Maypole Wood
Wickham Hall
Wharncliffe
Reigate Barn
Langford Grove
Whitelands
Eastland Wood
CM9
CM9
Langford Park
Matthews Etch
Great Park
CM9
MALDON RD
B1018
A12
LANGFORD RD
WITHAM RD
STATION RD
GRANGE RD
CHURCH RD
MOPE LA
WICKHAM HALL LA
BLUE MILLS HILL
ISHAMS CHASE
BLACKSMITHS LA
GREAT TOTHAM RD
MAYPOLE RD
BACK LA
TIPTREE RD
KELVEDON RD
CARTERS LA
GREEN MAN LA
LEA LA
THE STREET
ARBOUR LA
SCHOOL RD
HANDLEY'S LA
FINCH'S
BIRCH RISE
WELLANDS
WELLANDS CL
HEATHGATE
HOLT DR
BUCKLEYS CL
LEIGH DR
BYRON DR
ROOTS LA
LONGMEADS
CHURCH GN 1
CHURCH COTTS 2
CHURCH CL
BEECH GN
THE WARRENS
PONEY'S
PONEY CHASE
RIVER VIEW
PATTISON CL
LAURENCE AVE
EDINBURGH CL
ELIZABETH AVE
PITT AVE
PITT GN
SAUL'S AVE
MALTINGS LA
SCARLETTS CL
SPARKEY CL
GRACES CL
BOWERS WAY
ASHBY RD
HODGES HOLT
SPRING LA
BENTON CL
HALFACRES
SAUL'S BRIDGE CL
CLAYSHOTTS DR
CARRAWAYS
CONSTANCE CL
BLACKWATER LA
PYTTLE CL
CHANTRY VIEW
8
7
13
6
5
12
4
3
11
2
1
10
83
84
209
196

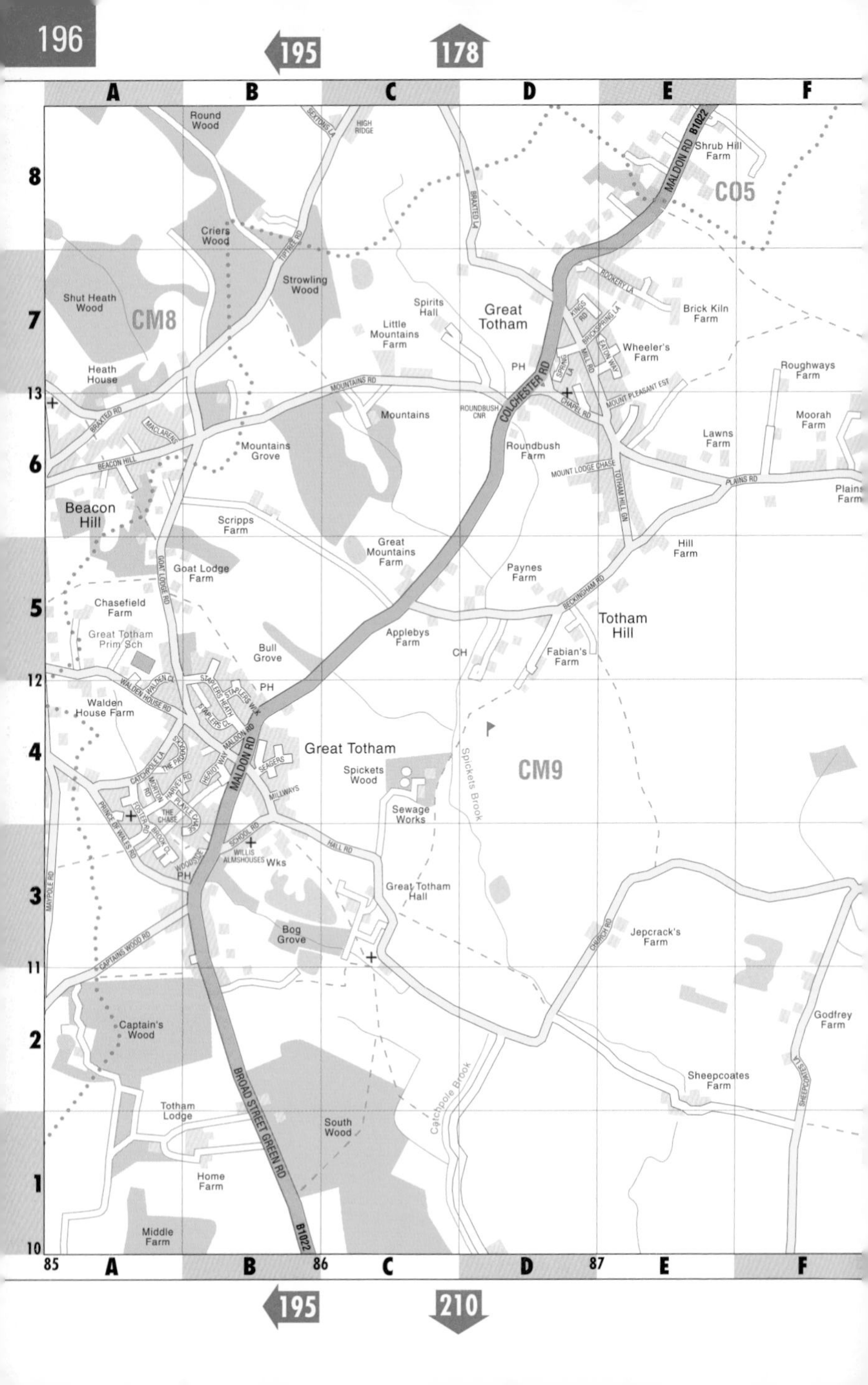
196
195
178
A
B
C
D
E
F
8
7
13
6
5
12
4
3
11
2
1
10
85
86
87
Round Wood
SEXTONS LA
HIGH RIDGE
B1022
MALDON RD
Shrub Hill Farm
CO5
BRAXTED LA
Criers Wood
TIPTREE RD
Strowling Wood
Shut Heath Wood
CM8
Spirits Hall
Great Totham
Little Mountains Farm
ROOKERY LA
Brick Kiln Farm
KINGS RD
BRICKSPRING LA
EATON WAY
MILL RD
SPRING LA
Wheeler's Farm
Roughways Farm
Heath House
PH
COLCHESTER RD
MOUNTAINS RD
MOUNT PLEASANT EST
BRAXTED RD
MACLARENS
Mountains
ROUNDBUSH CNR
CHAPEL RD
Moorah Farm
Lawns Farm
Mountains Grove
Roundbush Farm
BEACON HILL
MOUNT LODGE CHASE
TOTHAM HILL GN
PLAINS RD
Plains Farm
Beacon Hill
Scripps Farm
Hill Farm
Great Mountains Farm
Goat Lodge Farm
GOAT LODGE RD
Paynes Farm
BECKINGHAM RD
Chasefield Farm
Totham Hill
Applebys Farm
Great Totham Prim Sch
Bull Grove
CH
Fabian's Farm
WALDEN CL
STAPLERS HEATH
STAPLERS WK
WALDEN HOUSE RD
STAPLERS CL
Walden House Farm
Great Totham
CM9
Spickets Brook
Spickets Wood
SEAGERS
CATCHPOLE LA
THE PADDOCKS
HERIOT WAY
MALDON RD
MORTON RD
HARVEY RD
MILLWAYS
PLAYLE CHASE
Sewage Works
THE CHASE
PRINCE OF WALES RD
FOSTER RD
BROOK CL
SCHOOL RD
HALL RD
WILLIS ALMSHOUSES
Wks
WOODSIDE
MAYPOLE RD
Great Totham Hall
Jepcrack's Farm
CHURCH RD
Bog Grove
CAPTAINS WOOD RD
Godfrey Farm
Captain's Wood
Catchpole Brook
Sheepcoates Farm
SHEEPCOATES LA
BROAD STREET GREEN RD
Totham Lodge
South Wood
Home Farm
Middle Farm
210

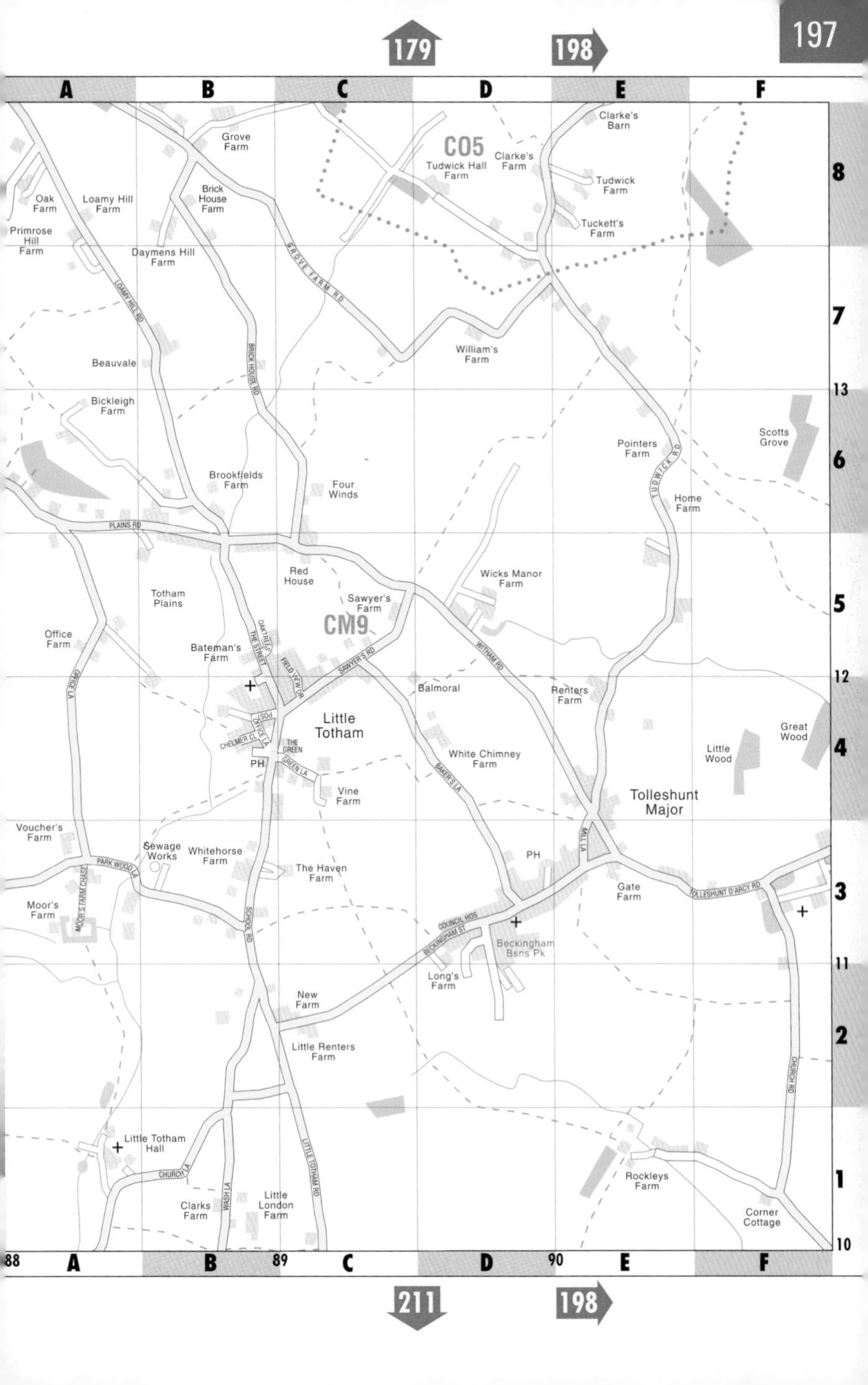

A B C D E F

8
7
13
6
5
12
4
3
11
2
1
10

Grove Farm

Oak Farm
Loamy Hill Farm
Primrose Hill Farm
Brick House Farm
Daymens Hill Farm

CO5
Tudwick Hall Farm
Clarke's Farm
Clarke's Barn
Tudwick Farm
Tuckett's Farm

William's Farm

Beauvale
Bickleigh Farm

Brookfields Farm
Four Winds

Pointers Farm
Scotts Grove
Home Farm

PLAINS RD

Red House
Sawyer's Farm
Wicks Manor Farm

Totham Plains
CM9

Office Farm
Bateman's Farm

Balmoral
Renters Farm
Little Wood
Great Wood

Little Totham
White Chimney Farm

PH
Tolleshunt Major

Vine Farm

Voucher's Farm
Sewage Works
Whitehorse Farm
The Haven Farm

PH
Gate Farm

TOLLESHUNT D'ARCY RD

Moor's Farm
PARK WOOD

COUNCIL HOS

Beckingham Bsns Pk

New Farm
Long's Farm

Little Renters Farm

Little Totham Hall
CHURCH LA

Clarks Farm
Little London Farm

Rockleys Farm

Corner Cottage

197
180

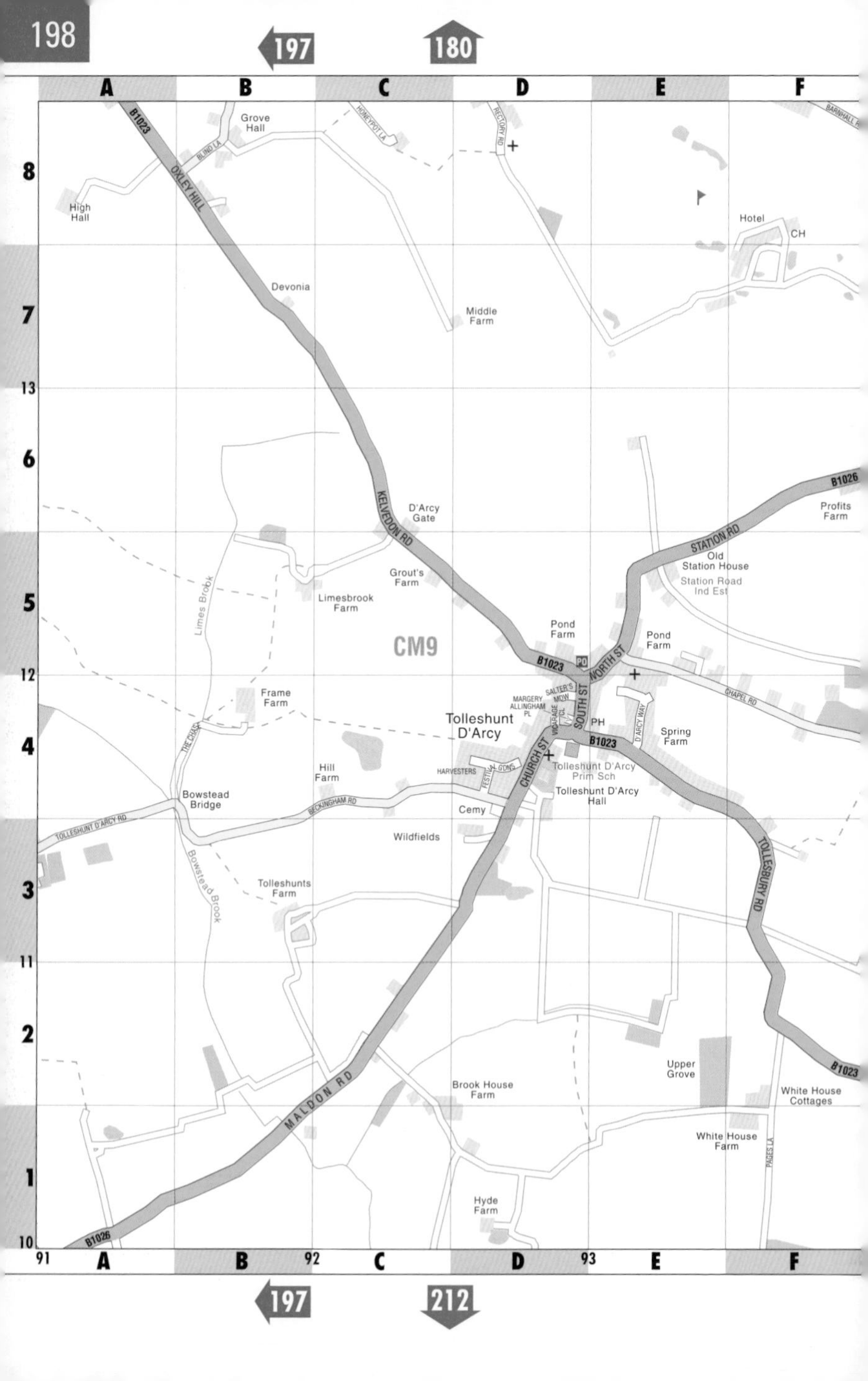
A
B
C
D
E
F
8
7
13
6
5
12
4
3
11
2
1
10
91
92
93
B1023
OXLEY HILL
BLIND LA
Grove Hall
High Hall
HONEYPOT LA
RECTORY RD
BARNHALL RD
Hotel
CH
Devonia
Middle Farm
KELVEDON RD
D'Arcy Gate
Grout's Farm
Limesbrook Farm
Limes Brook
CM9
B1026
STATION RD
Profits Farm
Old Station House
Station Road Ind Est
Pond Farm
Pond Farm
PO
NORTH ST
CHAPEL RD
SALTER'S MDW
MARGERY ALLINGHAM PL
VICARAGE CL
SOUTH ST
PH
D'ARCY WAY
Spring Farm
Tolleshunt D'Arcy
Frame Farm
THE CHASE
Hill Farm
HARVESTERS
FESTIVAL GDNS
CHURCH ST
Tolleshunt D'Arcy Prim Sch
Tolleshunt D'Arcy Hall
Bowstead Bridge
BECKINGHAM RD
TOLLESHUNT D'ARCY RD
Cemy
Wildfields
Bowstead Brook
Tolleshunts Farm
TOLLESBURY RD
MALDON RD
Brook House Farm
Upper Grove
White House Cottages
White House Farm
PAGES LA
Hyde Farm

197
212

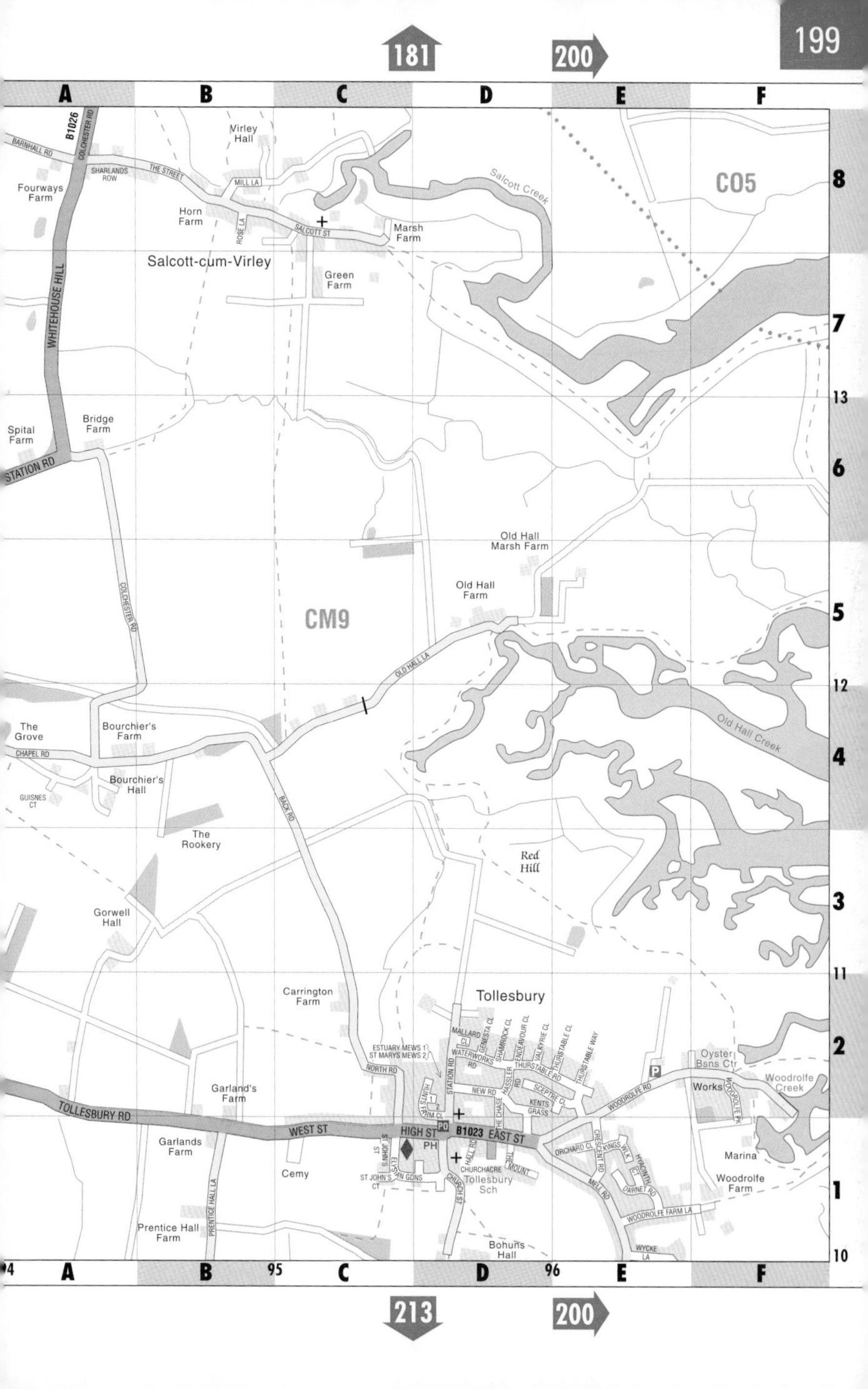
181
200
A
B
C
D
E
F
8
7
13
6
5
12
4
3
11
2
1
10
B1026
COLCHESTER RD
BARNHALL RD
SHARLANDS ROW
THE STREET
Virley Hall
MILL LA
Fourways Farm
Horn Farm
ROSE LA
SALCOTT ST
Marsh Farm
Salcott Creek
CO5
Salcott-cum-Virley
Green Farm
WHITEHOUSE HILL
Spital Farm
Bridge Farm
STATION RD
Old Hall Marsh Farm
Old Hall Farm
COLCHESTER RD
CM9
OLD HALL LA
Old Hall Creek
The Grove
Bourchier's Farm
CHAPEL RD
Bourchier's Hall
GUISNES CT
BACK RD
The Rookery
Red Hill
Gorwell Hall
Carrington Farm
Tollesbury
MALLARD CL
GENESTA CL
SHAMROCK CL
ENDEAVOUR CL
VALKYRIE CL
THURSTABLE CL
THURSTABLE WAY
ESTUARY MEWS 1
ST MARYS MEWS 2
WATERWORKS RD
THURSTABLE RD
NORTH RD
STATION RD
HUNTS FARM CL
NEW RD
HASSLER RD
THE CHASE
SCEPTRE CL
KENTS GRASS
WOODROLFE RD
Oyster Bsns Ctr
Works
WOODROLFE PK
Woodrolfe Creek
Garland's Farm
TOLLESBURY RD
WEST ST
HIGH ST
PO
B1023
EAST ST
PH
ST JOHN'S ST
ELYSIAN GDNS
HALL RD
CHURCHACRE
THE MOUNT
ORCHARD CL
CRESCENT RD
KINGS WLK
HYACINTH CT
DARNET RD
Marina
Garlands Farm
Cemy
ST JOHN'S CT
CHURCH ST
Tollesbury Sch
MELL RD
Woodrolfe Farm
WOODROLFE FARM LA
PRENTICE HALL LA
Prentice Hall Farm
Bohuns Hall
WYCKE LA
94
95
96
213
200

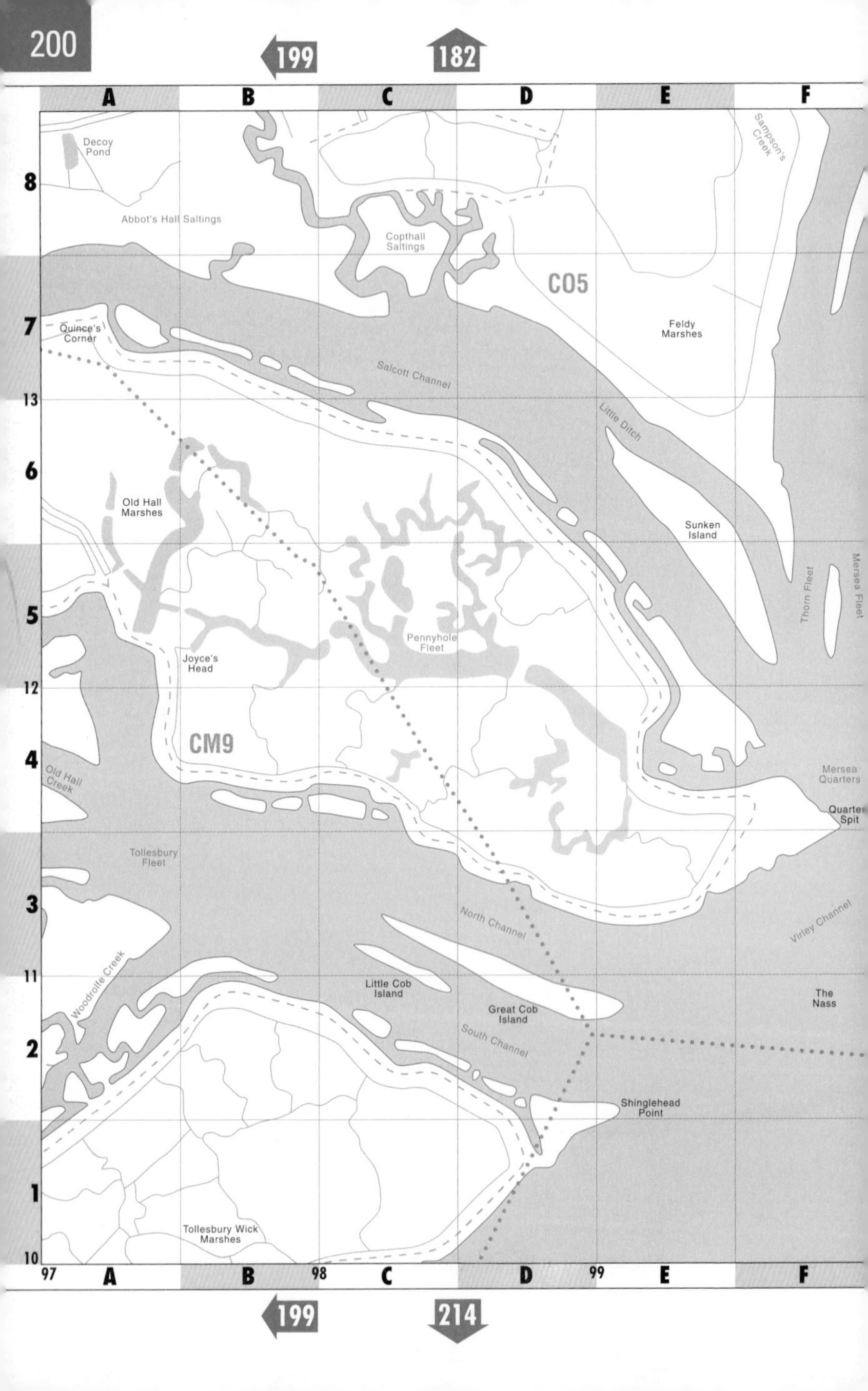

A   B   C   D   E   F

Decoy Pond

8

Abbot's Hall Saltings

Copthall Saltings

Sampson's Creek

CO5

Feldy Marshes

7

Quince's Corner

Salcott Channel

13

Little Ditch

6

Old Hall Marshes

Sunken Island

5

Pennyhole Fleet

Thorn Fleet

Mersea Fleet

12

Joyce's Head

CM9

4

Old Hall Creek

Mersea Quarters

Quarters Spit

3

Tollesbury Fleet

North Channel

Virley Channel

11

Woodrolfe Creek

Little Cob Island

Great Cob Island

The Nass

2

South Channel

Shinglehead Point

1

10

Tollesbury Wick Marshes

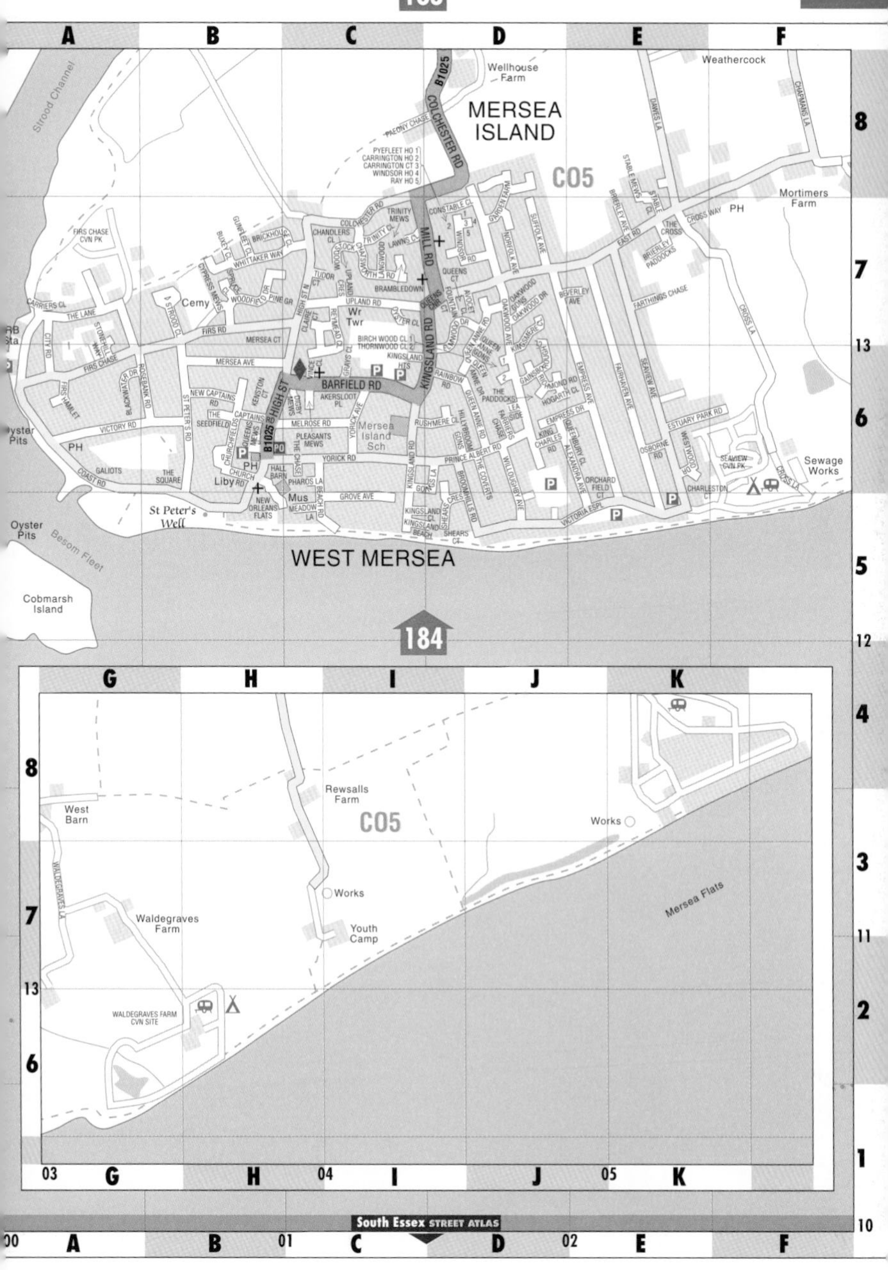

MERSEA ISLAND

CO5

Weathercock

Wellhouse Farm

Mortimers Farm

PYEFLEET HO 1
CARRINGTON HO 2
CARRINGTON CT 3
WINDSOR HO 4
RAY HO 5

TRINITY MEWS

CHANDLERS

BRAMBLEDOWN

QUEENS

BIRCH WOOD CL 1
THORNWOOD CL 2
KINGSLAND

Wr Twr

MERSEA CT

Cemy

THE LANE

FIRS CHASE CVN PK

BARFIELD RD

AKERSLOOT

Mus

PLEASANTS MEWS

YORICK RD

MELROSE RD

Merses Island Sch

GROVE AVE

PHAROS LA

SHEARS RD

KINGSLAND

MEADOW LA

NEW ORLEANS FLATS

HALL BARN

Liby

PH

THE SQUARE

VICTORY RD

GALIOTS

THE MARKET

St Peter's Well

COAST RD

WEST MERSEA

Oyster Pits

Cobmarsh Island

Besom Fleet

Strood Channel

Oyster Pits

Charleston

Sewage Works

Sea View Cvn Pk

Orchard Field

Farthings Chase

Stuart Park Rd

The Paddocks

West Barn

Waldegraves Farm

Rewsalls Farm

CO5

Works

Youth Camp

Works

Mersea Flats

WALDEGRAVES FARM CVN SITE

186

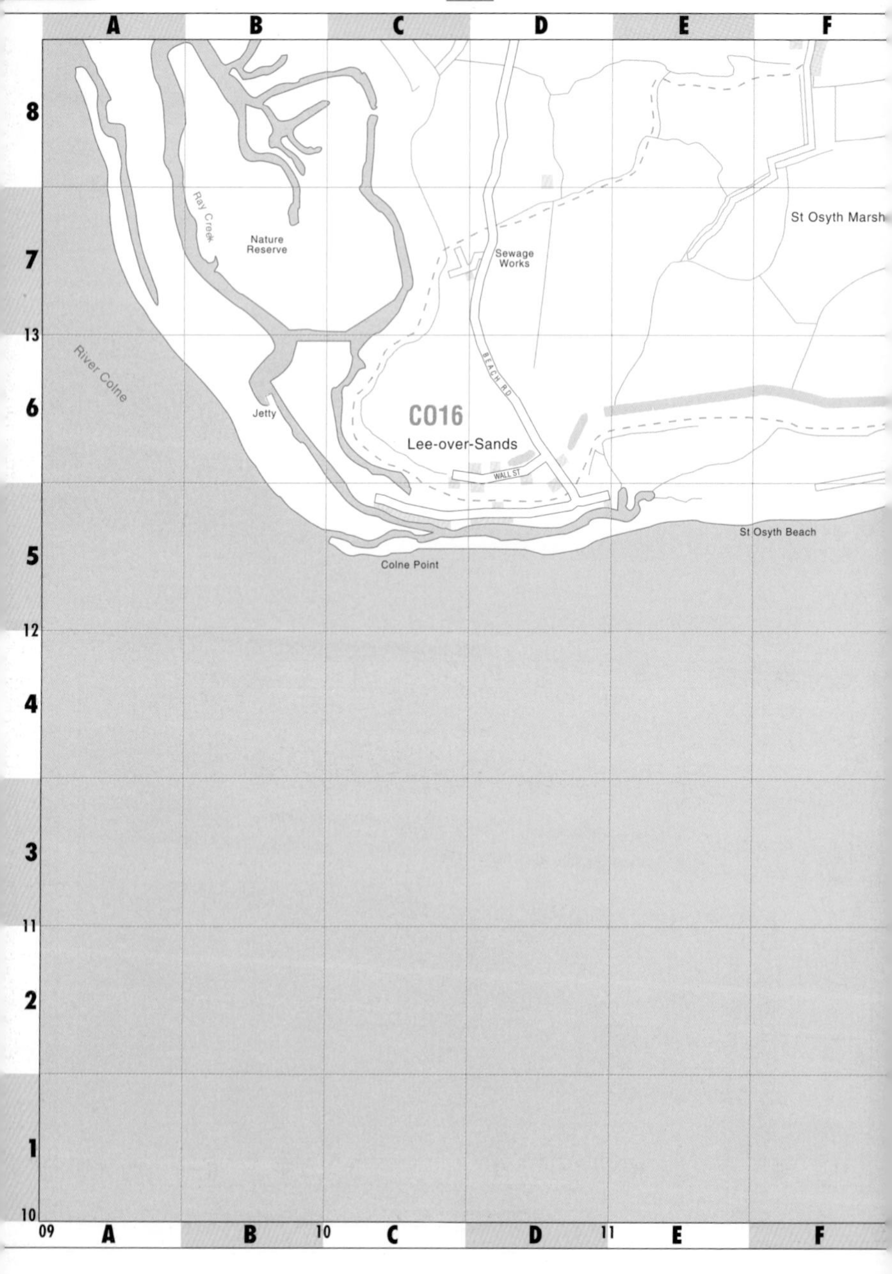

Ray Creek

River Colne

Nature
Reserve

Jetty

Sewage
Works

St Osyth Marsh

CO16
Lee-over-Sands

BEACH RD

WALL ST

Colne Point

St Osyth Beach

187

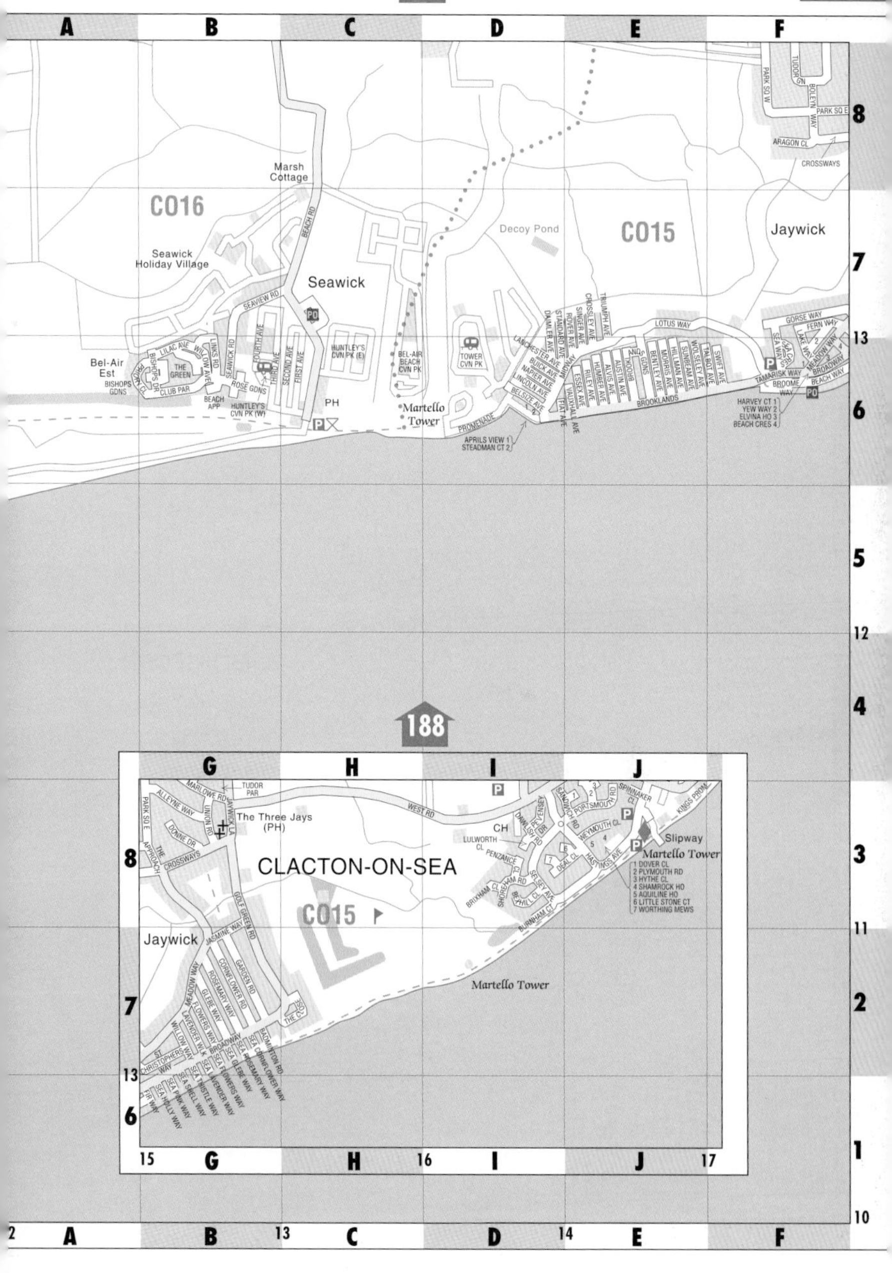

Marsh Cottage
CO16
Seawick Holiday Village
Seawick
Bel-Air Est
BISHOPS GDNS
THE GREEN
HUNTLEY'S CVN PK (E)
HUNTLEY'S CVN PK (W)
BEL-AIR BEACH CVN PK
TOWER CVN PK
Martello Tower
Decoy Pond
CO15
Jaywick
PROMENADE
BROOKLANDS
LOTUS WAY
APRILS VIEW 1
STEADMAN CT 2
HARVEY CT 1
YEW WAY 2
ELVINA HO 3
BEACH CRES 4
CROSSWAYS
ARAGON CL
188
The Three Jays (PH)
CLACTON-ON-SEA
CO15
Jaywick
WEST RD
Slipway
Martello Tower
1 DOVER CL
2 PLYMOUTH RD
3 HYTHE CL
4 SHAMROCK HO
5 AQUILINE HO
6 LITTLE STONE CT
7 WORTHING MEWS
Martello Tower

190

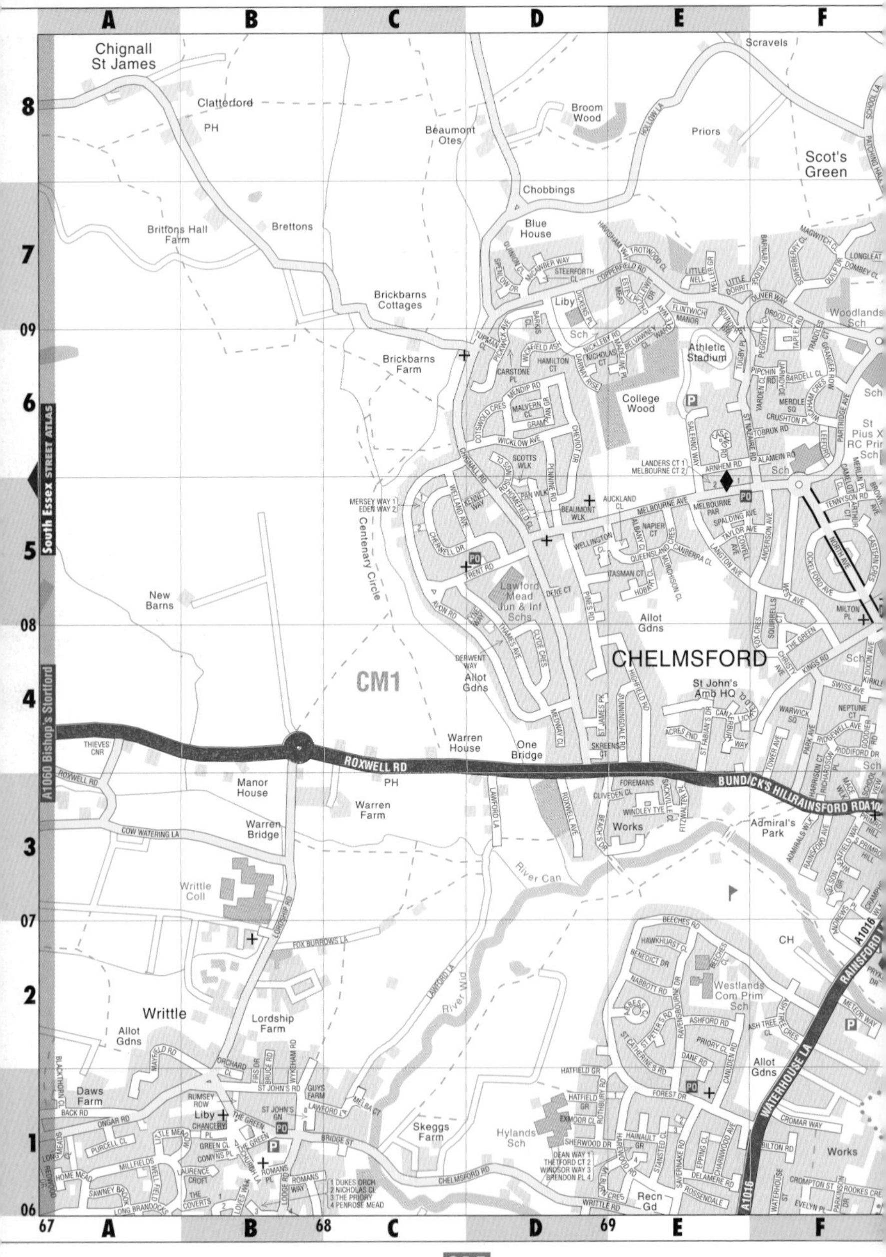

215

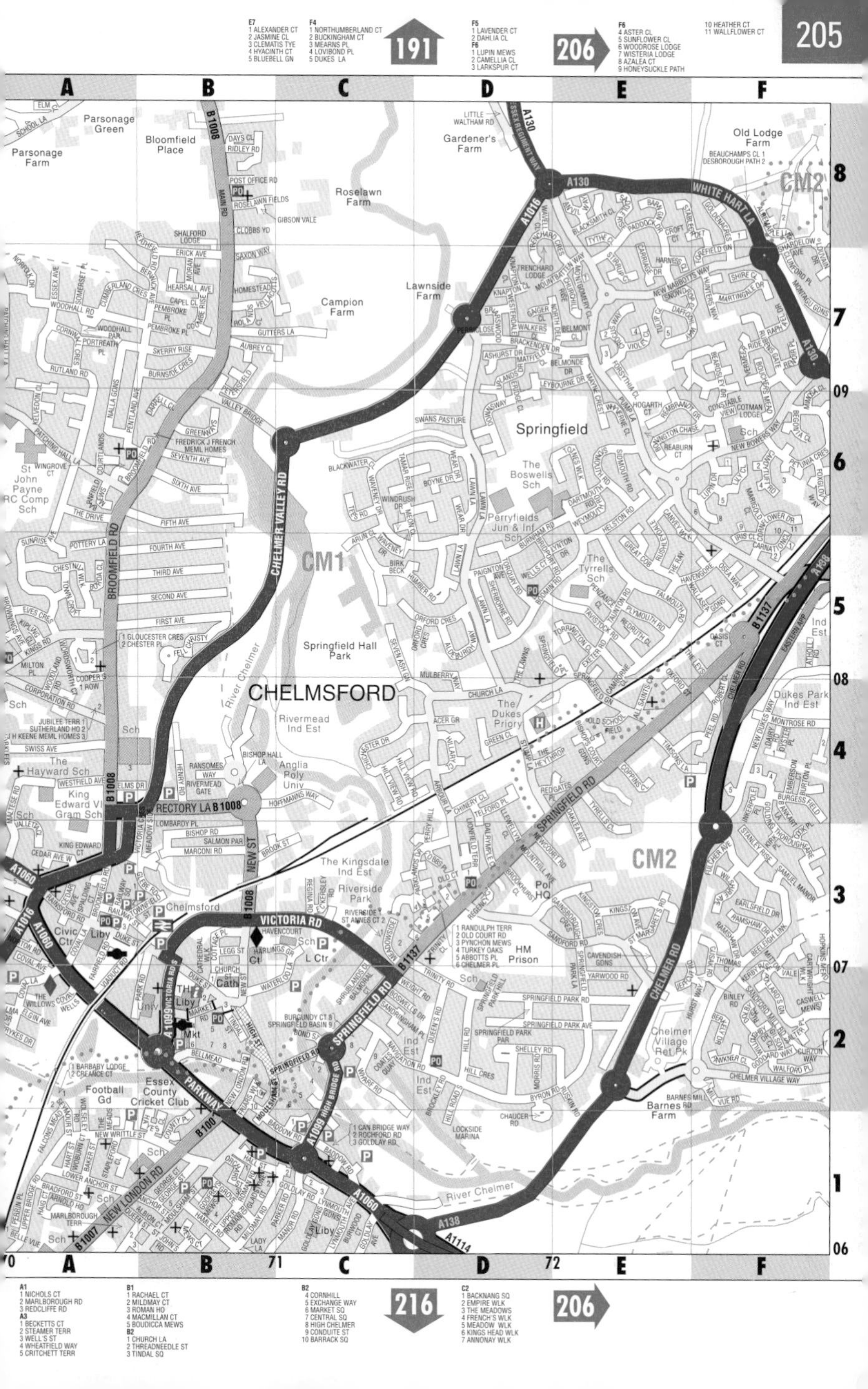
205
E7
1 ALEXANDER CT
2 JASMINE CL
3 CLEMATIS TYE
4 HYACINTH CT
5 BLUEBELL GN
F4
1 NORTHUMBERLAND CT
2 BUCKINGHAM CT
3 MEARNS PL
4 LOVIBOND PL
5 DUKES LA
191
F5
1 LAVENDER CT
2 DAHLIA CL
F6
1 LUPIN MEWS
2 CAMELLIA CL
3 LARKSPUR CT
206
F6
4 ASTER CL
5 SUNFLOWER CL
6 WOODROSE LODGE
7 WISTERIA LODGE
8 AZALEA CT
9 HONEYSUCKLE PATH
10 HEATHER CT
11 WALLFLOWER CT
A B C D E F
8 7 09 6 5 08 4 3 07 2 1 06
70 71 72
Parsonage Green
Parsonage Farm
Bloomfield Place
Roselawn Farm
Gardener's Farm
Old Lodge Farm
Campion Farm
Lawnside Farm
Springfield
The Boswells Sch
Perryfields Jun & Inf Sch
The Tyrrells Sch
CM1
CM2
St John Payne RC Comp Sch
Springfield Hall Park
CHELMSFORD
River Chelmer
Rivermead Ind Est
Anglia Poly Univ
The Dukes Priory
The Hayward Sch
King Edward VI Gram Sch
The Kingsdale Ind Est
Riverside Park
Pol HQ
HM Prison
Dukes Park Ind Est
Chelmer Village Ret Pk
Barnes Farm
Football Gd
Essex County Cricket Club
Lockside Marina
Chelmsford
Civic Ctr
Liby
Mkt
Cath
Univ
A130
A1016
A1060
A1099
A138
A1114
B1008
B1137
B1007
WHITE HART LA
CHELMER VALLEY RD
BROOMFIELD RD
SPRINGFIELD RD
VICTORIA RD
CHELMER RD
PARKWAY
NEW LONDON RD
RECTORY LA
NEW ST
MAIN RD
1 RANDULPH TERR
2 OLD COURT RD
3 PYNCHON MEWS
4 TURKEY OAKS
5 ABBOTTS PL
6 CHELMER PL
1 CAN BRIDGE WAY
2 ROCHFORD RD
3 GOLDLAY RD
1 GLOUCESTER CRES
2 CHESTER PL
1 BARBAY LODGE
2 CREANCE CT
A1
1 NICHOLS CT
2 MARLBOROUGH RD
3 REDCLIFFE RD
A3
1 BECKETTS CT
2 STEAMER TERR
3 WELL'S ST
4 WHEATFIELD WAY
5 CRITCHETT TERR
B1
1 RACHAEL CT
2 MILDMAY CT
3 ROMAN HO
4 MACMILLAN CT
5 BOUDICCA MEWS
B2
1 CHURCH LA
2 THREADNEEDLE ST
3 TINDAL SQ
B2
4 CORNHILL
5 EXCHANGE WAY
6 MARKET SQ
7 CENTRAL SQ
8 HIGH CHELMER
9 CONDUITE ST
10 BARRACK SQ
216
C2
1 BACKNANG SQ
2 EMPIRE WLK
3 THE MEADOWS
4 FRENCH'S WLK
5 MEADOW WLK
6 KINGS HEAD WLK
7 ANNONAY WLK
206

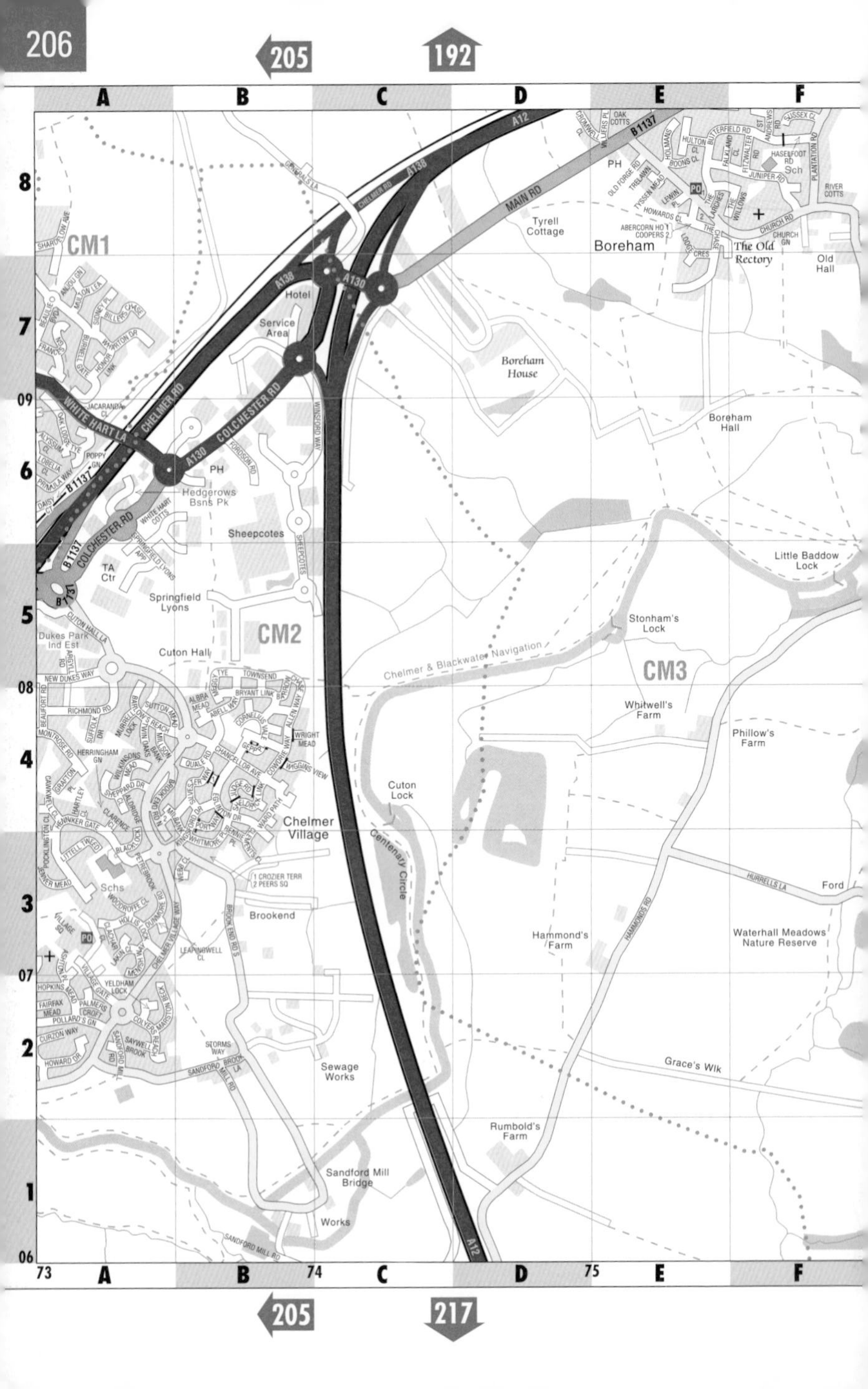

205
192

CM1

A12
B1137
Oak Cotts
PH
Tyrell Cottage
Main Rd
Boreham
The Old Rectory
Old Hall
River Cotts
Abercorn Ho
Coopers
Church
Cutton

Hotel
Service Area
A130
A130
Boreham House
Boreham Hall

White Hart La
Jacaranda Cl
Colchester Rd
Chelmer Rd
A130
Poppy
B1137
PH
Hedgerows Bsnh Pk
Little Baddow Lock

B131
TA Ctr
Colchester Rd
White Hart Cotts
Sheepcotes
Windsor Way

Dukes Park Ind Est
Springfield Lyons
CM2
Cuton Hall
Stonham's Lock
Chelmer & Blackwater Navigation
CM3

New Dukes Way
Richmond Rd
Tye
Townsend
Bryant Link
Whitwell's Farm
Phillow's Farm

Herringham Gn
Wright Mead
Shepperd Dr
Cuton Lock
Hurrell's La
Ford

Clarence
Chelmer Village
Centenary Circle
Waterhall Meadows Nature Reserve

Schs
1 Crozier Terr
2 Peers Sq
Brookend
Hammond's Farm
Sandon Rd

PO
Leafinwell Cl
Hopkins
Fairfax Mead
Palmers Croft
Pollard's Gn
Veldham Lock

Howard's
Curzon Way
Storms Way
Sandford Brook La
Sewage Works
Grace's Wik

Rumbold's Farm

Sandford Mill Bridge
Works

Sandford Mill Rd
A12

73
74
75

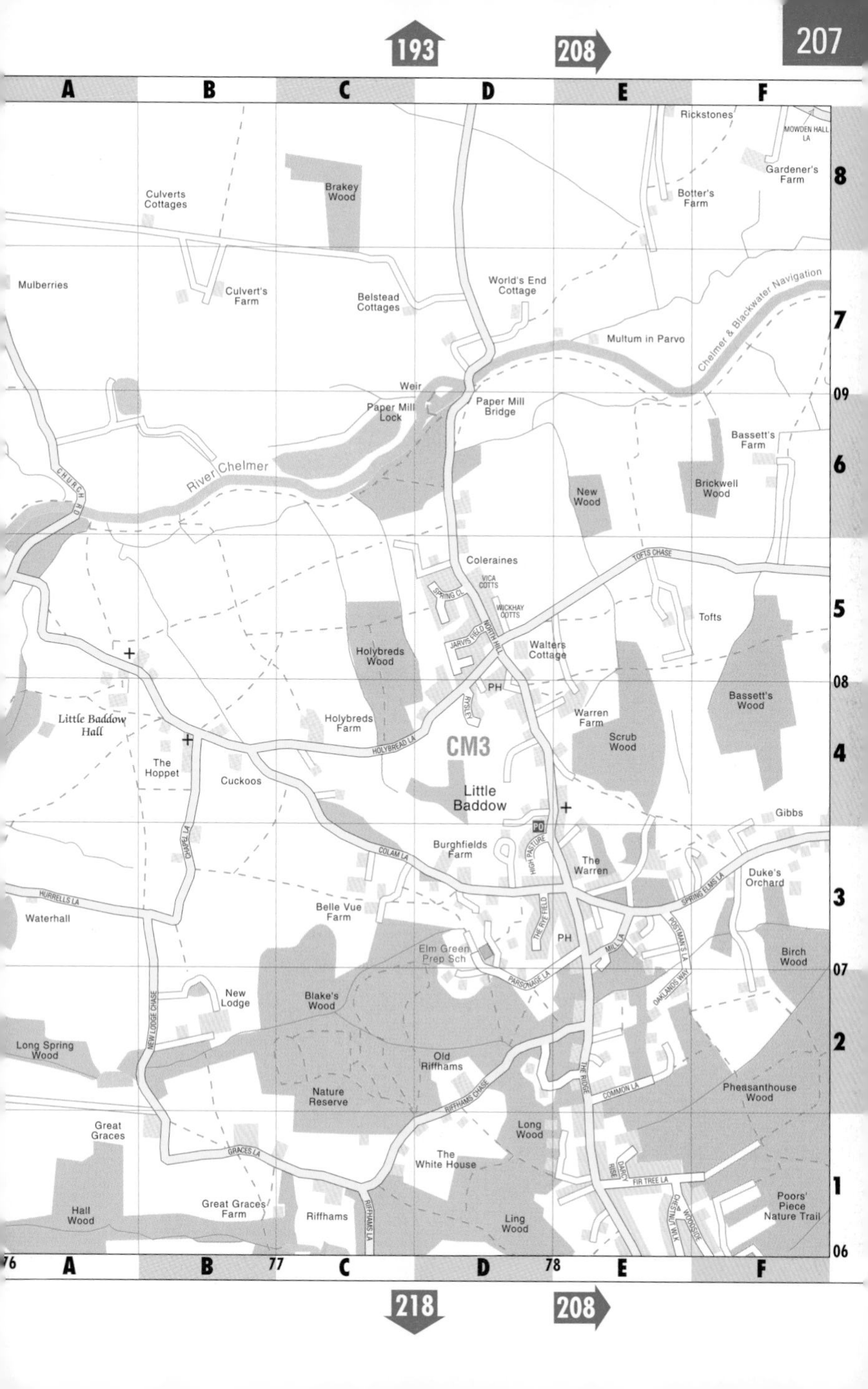

A B C D E F

8

Rickstones

MOWDEN HALL
LA

Gardener's
Farm

Culverts
Cottages

Brakey
Wood

Botter's
Farm

7

Mulberries

Culvert's
Farm

Belstead
Cottages

World's End
Cottage

Multum in Parvo

Chelmer & Blackwater Navigation

09

Weir

Paper Mill
Lock

Paper Mill
Bridge

Bassett's
Farm

6

River Chelmer

New
Wood

Brickwell
Wood

Coleraines

TOFTS CHASE

5

VICA
COTTS

RING CO

WICKHAY
COTTS

Tofts

JARVIS FIELD

Walters
Cottage

Bassett's
Wood

08

Holybreds
Wood

PH

Warren
Farm

CM3

Holybreds
Farm

Scrub
Wood

4

Little Baddow
Hall

HOLYBREAD LA

The
Hoppet

Cuckoos

Little
Baddow

Gibbs

PO

CHAPEL LA

Burghfields
Farm

The
Warren

Duke's
Orchard

HIGH FIELDS LA

SPRING LANE LA

HURRELLS LA

COLAM LA

3

Waterhall

Belle Vue
Farm

PH

Birch
Wood

THE RIDGE

Elm Green
Prep Sch

PARSONAGE LA

NEW LODGE CHASE

07

New
Lodge

Blake's
Wood

MILL LA

COMMON LA

2

Long Spring
Wood

Old
Riffhams

BETTHAMS CHASE

Pheasanthouse
Wood

Great
Graces

Nature
Reserve

Long
Wood

GRACES LA

The
White House

FIR TREE LA

1

Hall
Wood

Great Graces
Farm

Riffhams

Ling
Wood

WOODSIDE

Poors'
Piece
Nature Trail

76 A 77 B C 78 D E F 06

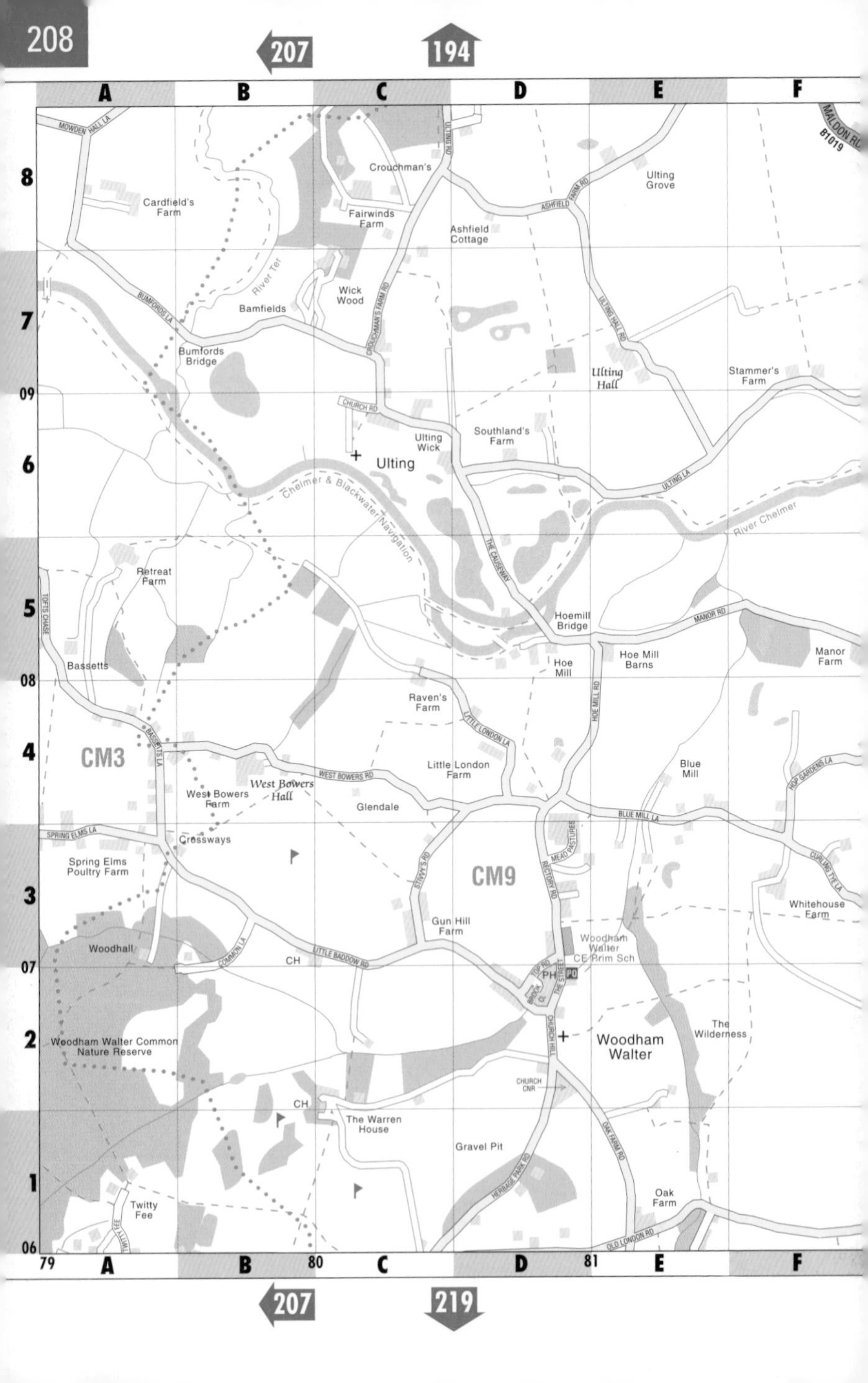

8

7

09

6

5

08

4

3

07

2

1

06

A B C D E F

MORRIS HALL LA

B1019 MALDON RD

Cardfield's Farm

Crouchman's

Fairwinds Farm

Ulting Grove

Ashfield Cottage

ASHFIELD FARM RD

River Ter

BUMFORDS LA

Bamfields

Wick Wood

WOODHAM HALL RD

Bumfords Bridge

ULTING HALL RD

Ulting Hall

Stammer's Farm

CHURCH RD

Ulting Wick

Ulting

Southland's Farm

ULTING LA

Chelmer & Blackwater Navigation

River Chelmer

TOFTS CHASE

Retreat Farm

Bassetts

THE CHASE

THE CHASE RD

Hoemill Bridge

Hoe Mill

Hoe Mill Barns

MANOR RD

Manor Farm

CM3

Raven's Farm

LITTLE LONDON LA

West Bowers Rd

West Bowers Farm

West Bowers Hall

Little London Farm

HOE MILL RD

Blue Mill

HOP GARDENS LA

Glendale

Blue Mill La

SPRING ELMS LA

Cressways

CM9

CURLING TYE LA

Spring Elms Poultry Farm

Gun Hill Farm

STAGS LA

MEAD PASTURES

Whitehouse Farm

Woodhall

COMMON LA

CH

LITTLE BADDOW RD

Woodham Walter CE Prim Sch

PH

PO

CHURCH HILL

The Wilderness

Woodham Walter

Woodham Walter Common Nature Reserve

CH

CHURCH CNR

OAK FARM RD

The Warren House

Gravel Pit

HEYBRIDGE RD

Twitty Fee

Oak Farm

OLD LONDON RD

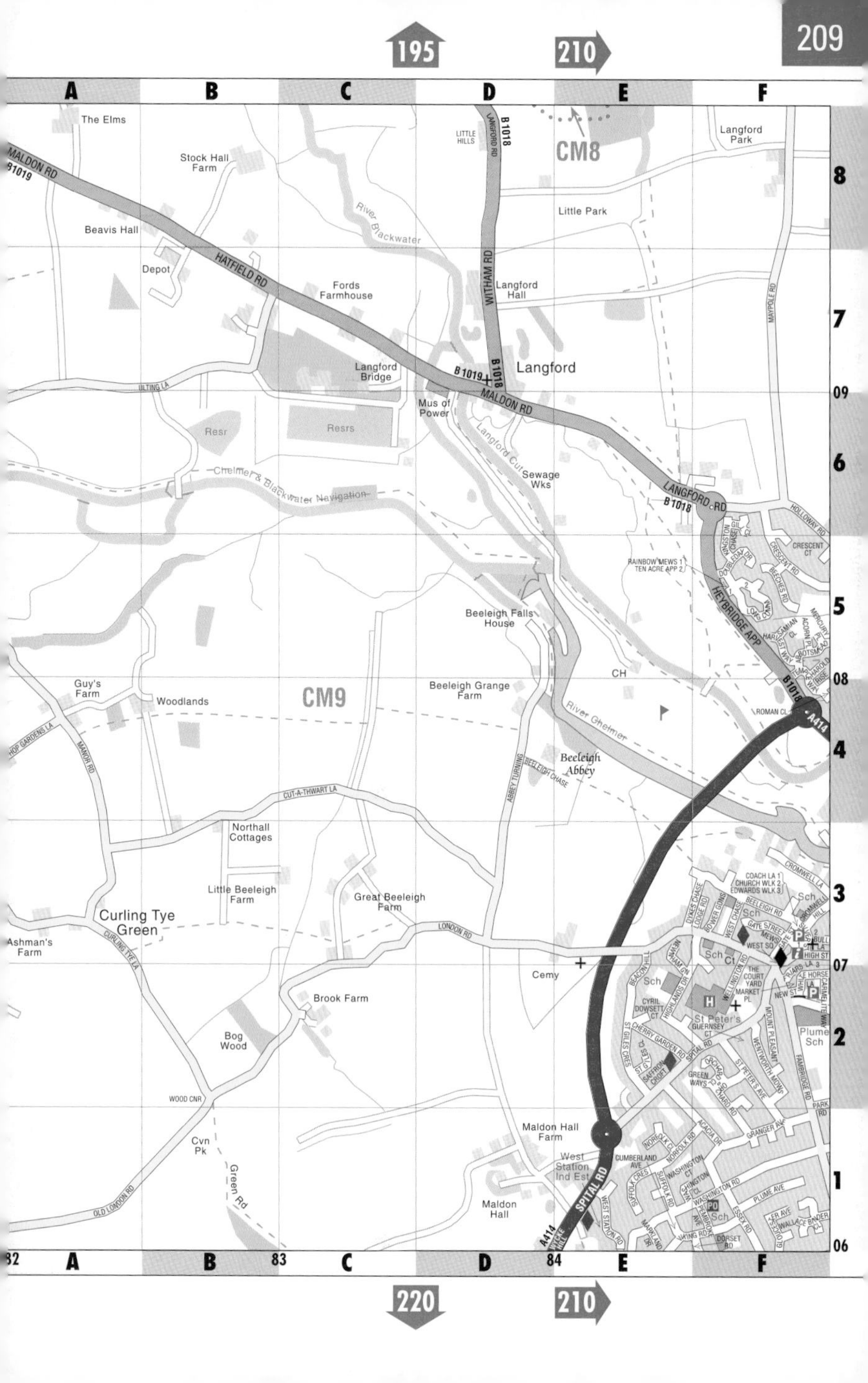

A | B | C | D | E | F

The Elms

Stock Hall Farm

MALDON RD
B1019

Beavis Hall

HATFIELD RD

Depot

LITTLE HILLS

B1018
LANGFORD RD

CM8

Langford Park

Little Park

River Blackwater

Fords Farmhouse

Langford Hall

8

7

ULTING LA

Langford Bridge

Mus of Power

Resr

Resrs

B1019

WITHAM RD

B1018

MALDON RD

Langford

Langford Cut

Sewage Wks

09

6

Chelmer & Blackwater Navigation

LANGFORD RD
B1018

HOLLOWAY RD

CRESCENT CT

MAYPOLE RD

Guy's Farm

Woodlands

CM9

Beeleigh Falls House

Beeleigh Grange Farm

CH

River Chelmer

RAINBOW MEWS 1
TEN ACRE APP 2

HYBRIDGE APP

B1018
A414

5

08

HOP GARDENS LA

BASIN RD

Beeleigh Abbey

BEELEIGH CHASE

River Chelmer

ROMAN CL

CROMWELL LA

4

CUT-A-THWART LA

Northall Cottages

Little Beeleigh Farm

Great Beeleigh Farm

LONDON RD

COACH LA 1
CHURCH WLK 2
ONWARDS WLK 3

Sch

WEST SQ

HIGH ST

3

07

Curling Tye Green

Ashman's Farm

CURLING TYE GREEN RD

Cemy

Sch

CYRIL DOWSETT CT

St Peter's
Guernsey

THE COURT YARD MARKET

NEW

H

GREEN WAYS

Plume Sch

2

Brook Farm

Bog Wood

WOOD CNR

Cvn Pk

Green Rd

Maldon Hall Farm

West Station Ind Est

CUMBERLAND RD

SPITAL RD

A414

PLUME AVE

DORSET RD

1

06

OLD LONDON RD

Maldon Hall

82 | A | B | 83 | C | D | 84 | E | F

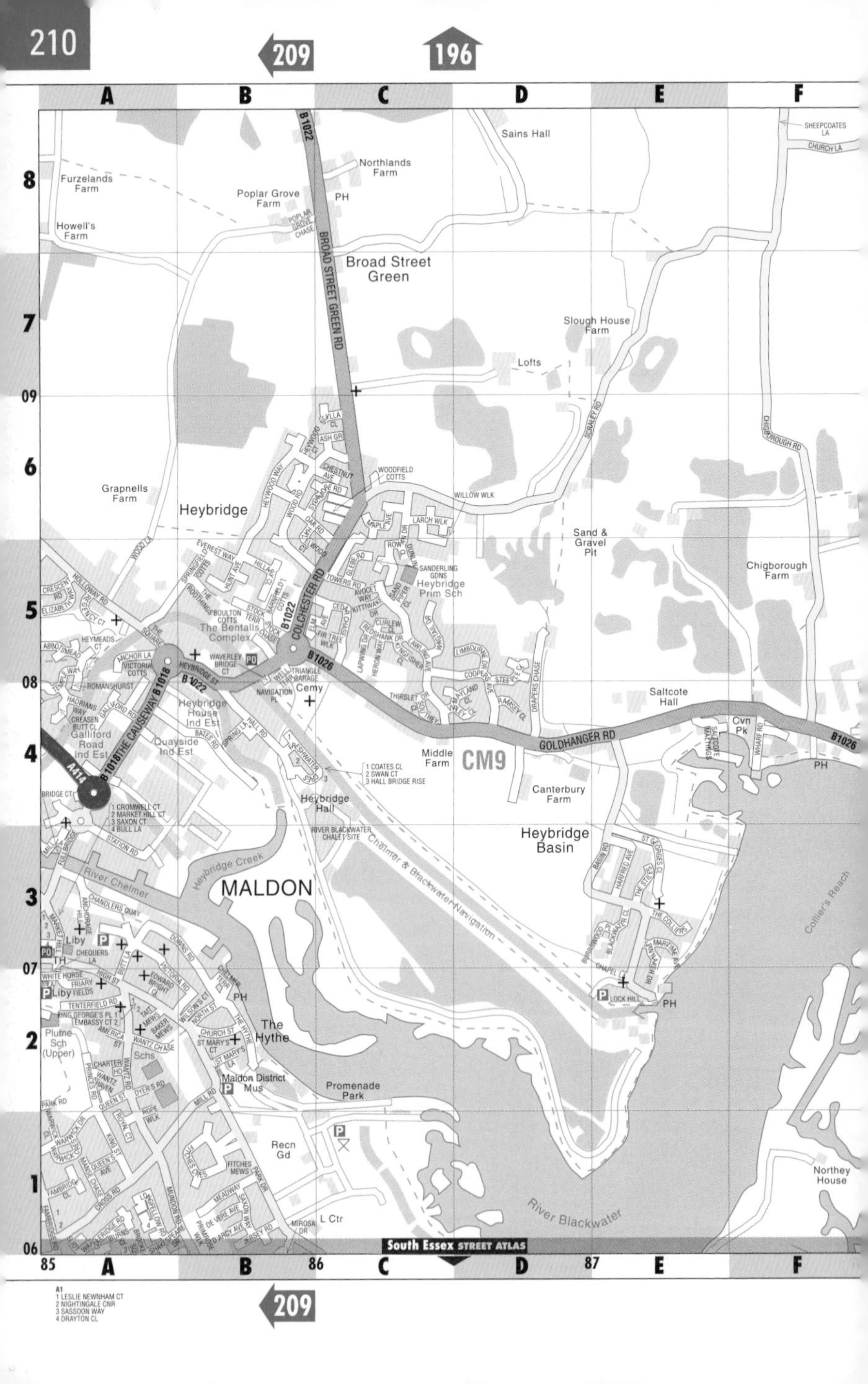

A B C D E F

8
7
09
6
5
08
4
3
07
2
1
06

85 A B 86 C D 87 E F

Furzelands Farm
Howell's Farm

Poplar Grove Farm

PH

Northlands Farm

Sains Hall

SHEEPCOATES LA
CHURCH LA

BROAD STREET GREEN RD
B1022

Broad Street Green

POPLAR GROVE CHASE

Slough House Farm

Lofts

SCANLEY RD

CHIGBOROUGH RD

Grapnells Farm

Heybridge

Woodfield Cotts

WILLOW WLK

CHESTNUT

LARCH WLK

Sand & Gravel Pit

Chigborough Farm

SANDERLING GDNS
Heybridge Prim Sch

B1022

The Bentalls Complex
The Boulton Cotts

CEMy

B1026

Saltcote Hall

ANCHOR LA
Romanshurst

HEYMEADS LA
VICTORIAN COTTS

NAVIGATION

Cvn Pk

B1026

Heybridge House Ind Est
Quayside Ind Est

Galliford Road Ind Est

A414

BRIDGE CT

HALL RD

Middle Farm

CM9

GOLDHANGER RD

Canterbury Farm

PH

1 COATES CL
2 SWAN CT
3 HALL BRIDGE RISE

Heybridge Hall

Heybridge Basin

1 CROMWELL CT
2 MARKET HILL
3 SAXON CT
4 BULL LA

RIVER BLACKWATER
CHALET SITE

Chelmer & Blackwater Navigation

Collier's Reach

River Chelmer

Heybridge Creek

MALDON

CHANDLERS QUAY

Liby

CHEQUERS LA

LOCK HILL

PH

Libry Fields

WHITE HORSE LA

TENTERFIELD RD

Plume Sch (Upper)

High George's Pl 1
Embassy Ct 2

MART CHASE

ST GILES AVE

Sch

CHURCH ST

St MARY'S CT

The Hythe

MILL RD

Maldon District Mus

Promenade Park

Recn Gd

P

MIROSA DR

L Ctr

River Blackwater

Northey House

A1
1 LESLIE NEWNHAM CT
2 NIGHTINGALE CNR
3 SASSOON WAY
4 DRAYTON CL

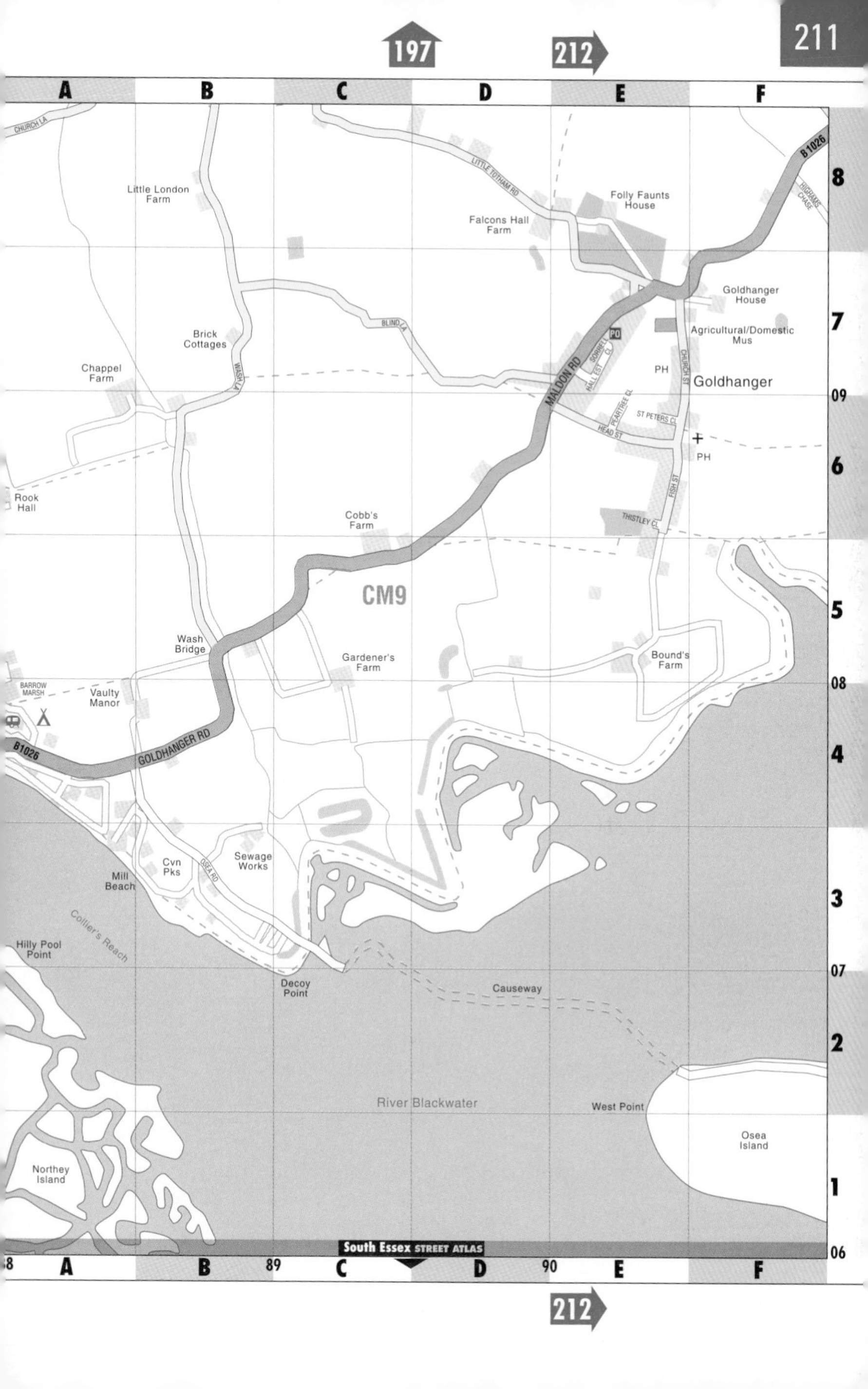

8

7

09

6

5

08

4

3

07

2

1

06

CHURCH LA

B1026

Little London
Farm

Folly Faunts
House

Falcons Hall
Farm

LITTLE TOTHAM RD

Goldhanger
House

BLIND LA

Brick
Cottages

PO

Agricultural/Domestic
Mus

Chappel
Farm

MALDON RD

PH

Goldhanger

ST PETERS CL

Rook
Hall

HEAD ST

PH

Cobb's
Farm

THISTLEY CL

CM9

Wash
Bridge

Gardener's
Farm

Bound's
Farm

BARROW
MARSH

Vaulty
Manor

B1026

GOLDHANGER RD

Cvn
Pks

Sewage
Works

OSEA RD

Mill
Beach

Hilly Pool
Point

Collier's Reach

Decoy
Point

Causeway

River Blackwater

West Point

Osea
Island

Northey
Island

88

A

B

89

C

D

90

E

F

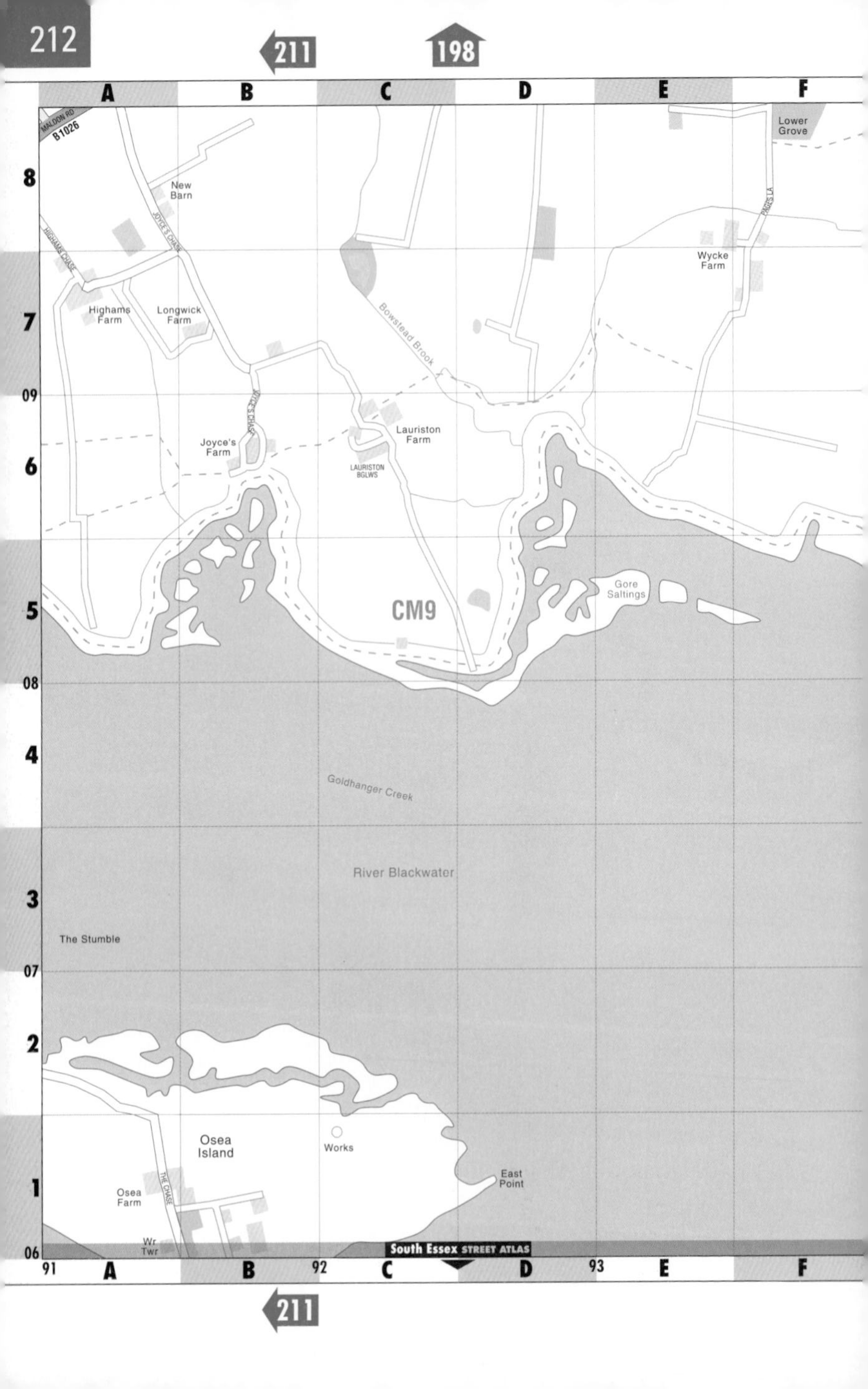

A   B   C   D   E   F

8

MALDON RD
B1026

New
Barn

JOYCE'S CRESS

JOYCE'S CROSS

Highams
Farm

Longwick
Farm

Lower
Grove

DARCYS LA

Wycke
Farm

7

09

Joyce's
Farm

JOYCE'S CROSS

Lauriston
Farm

LAURISTON
BGLWS

Bowstead Brook

6

CM9

Gore
Saltings

5

08

4

Goldhanger Creek

3

River Blackwater

The Stumble

07

2

Osea
Island

Works

East
Point

1

Osea
Farm

THE CAUSE

Wr
Twr

06

91   A   B   92   C   D   93   E   F

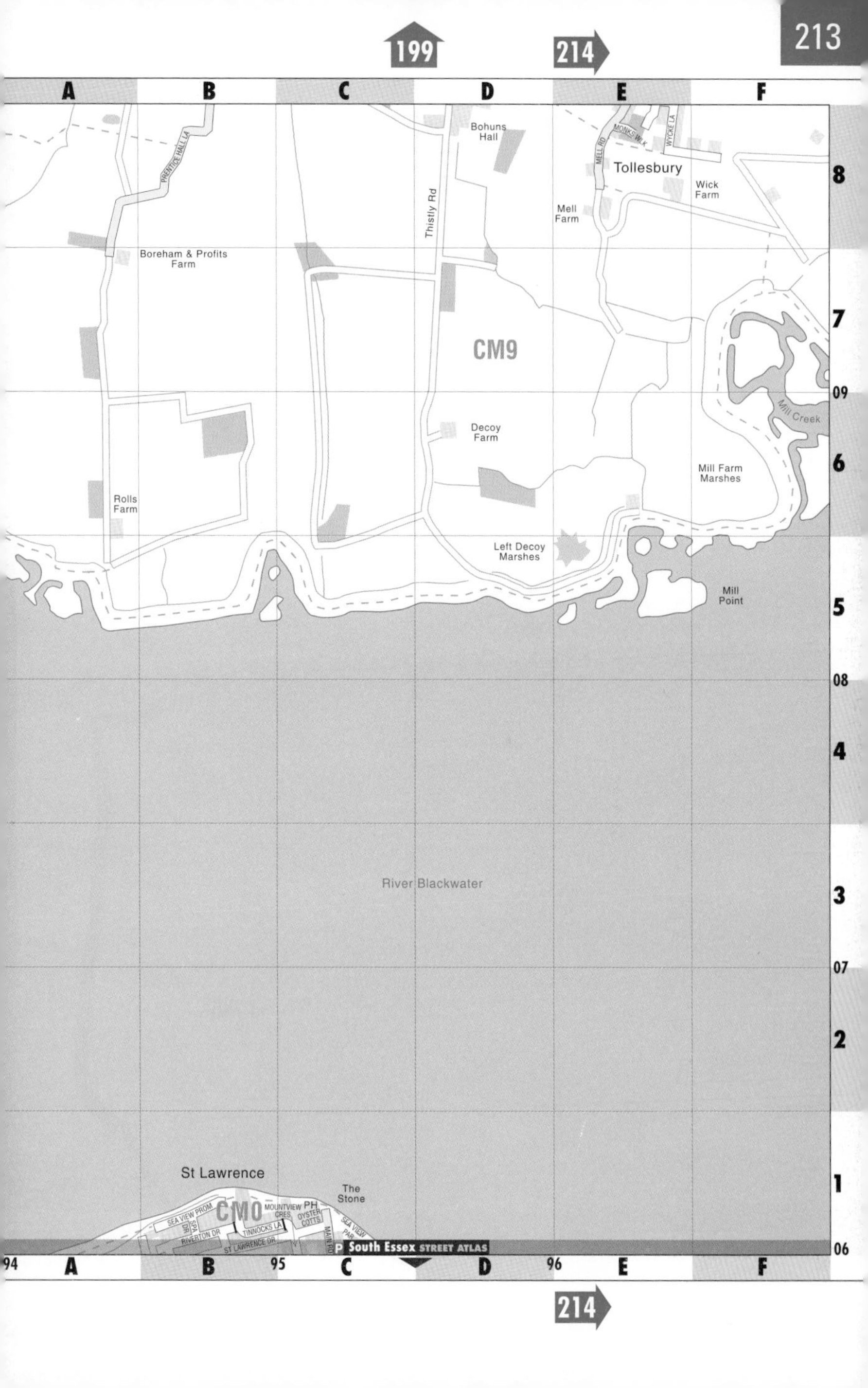

| A | B | C | D | E | F |

8

Bohuns
Hall

Tollesbury

Wick
Farm

Thistly Rd

Mell
Farm

WICK LA

MORRIS AV

MELL RD

Boreham & Profits
Farm

CM9

7

09

Decoy
Farm

Mill Farm
Marshes

Mill Creek

6

Rolls
Farm

Left Decoy
Marshes

Mill
Point

5

08

4

River Blackwater

3

07

2

1

St Lawrence

The
Stone

06

SEA VIEW PROM

MOUNTVIEW PH

CM0

OYSTER
COTTS

TINNOCKS LA

BOYTON DR

ST LAWRENCE DR

SEA WAY

| 94 | A | B | 95 | C | D | 96 | E | F |

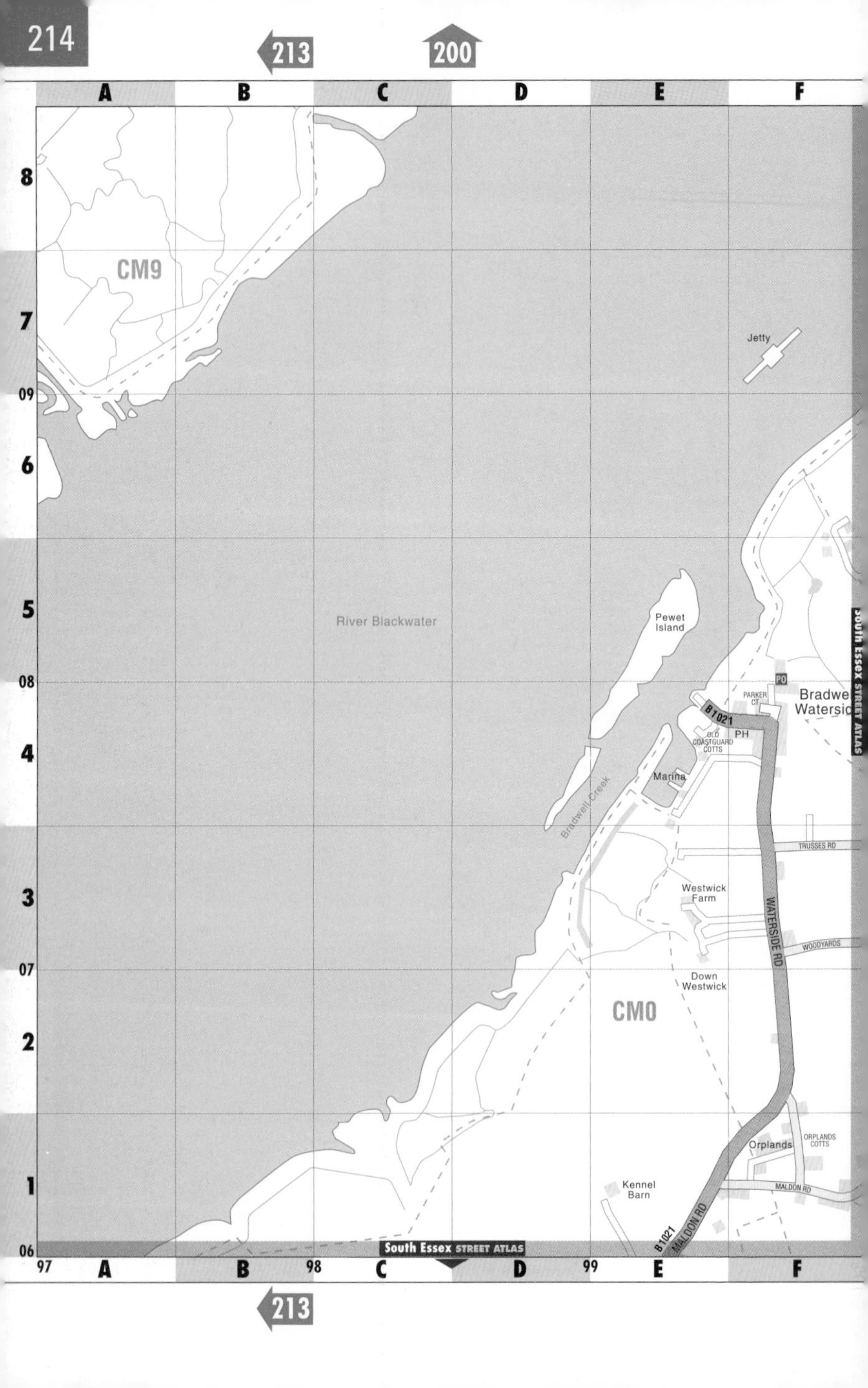

CM9

River Blackwater

Pewet
Island

Jetty

PO

PARKER
CT

Bradwe
Waterside

B1021

OLD
COASTGUARD
COTTS

PH

Marina

TRUSSES RD

Westwick
Farm

WATERSIDE RD

WOODYARDS

Down
Westwick

CM0

Bradwell Creek

Orplands
Cotts

Orplands

Kennel
Barn

MALDON RD

B1021

MALDON RD

South Essex STREET ATLAS

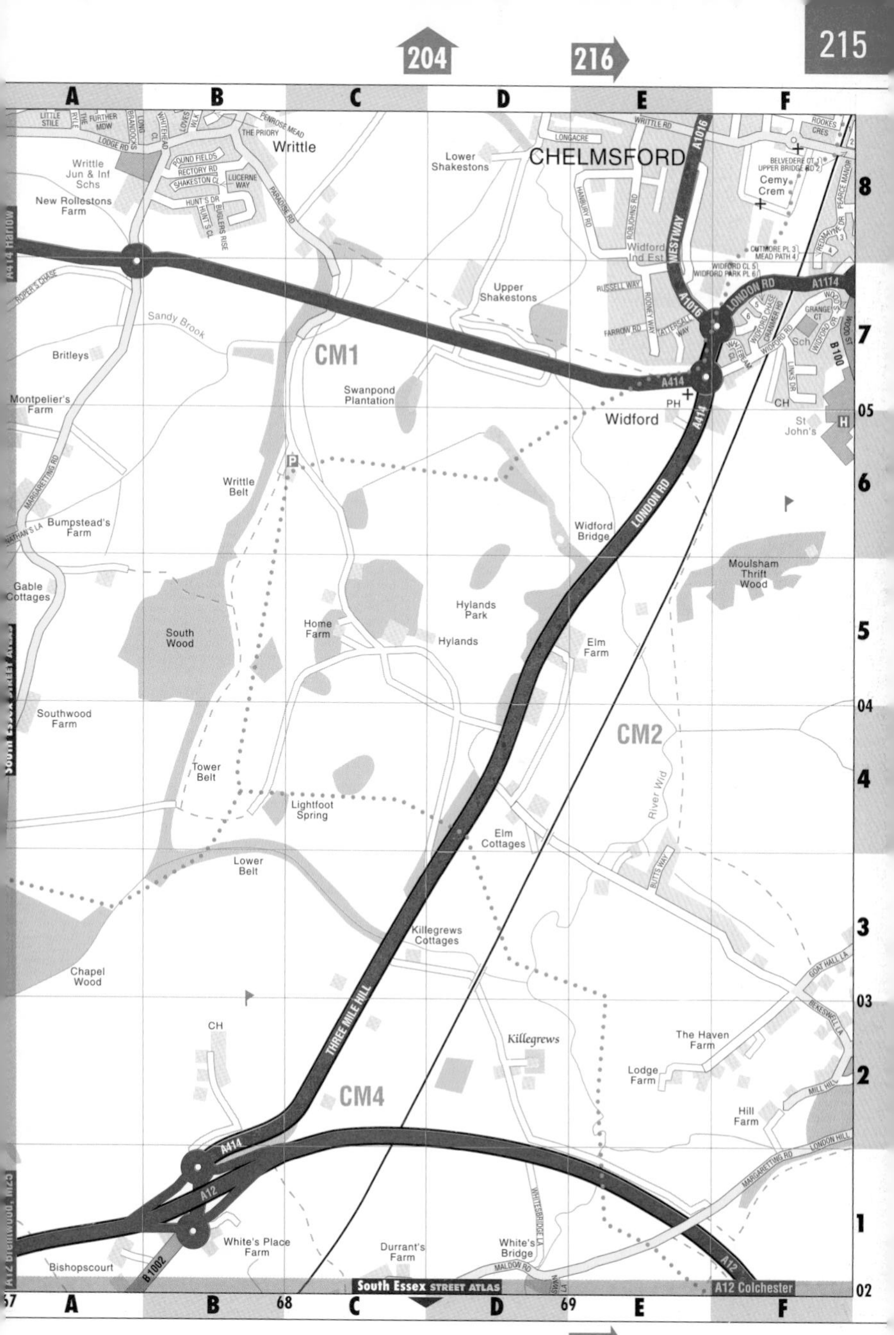
A
B
C
D
E
F
Writtle
CHELMSFORD
Writtle Jun & Inf Schs
New Rollestons Farm
Lower Shakestons
Cemy Crem
Widford Ind Est
Upper Shakestons
Sandy Brook
CM1
Britleys
Swanpond Plantation
Montpelier's Farm
Widford
St John's
Writtle Belt
Widford Bridge
Bumpstead's Farm
Moulsham Thrift Wood
Gable Cottages
Hylands Park
Home Farm
Hylands
South Wood
Elm Farm
Southwood Farm
CM2
Tower Belt
Lightfoot Spring
River Wid
Elm Cottages
Lower Belt
Killegrews Cottages
Chapel Wood
Killegrews
The Haven Farm
CH
Lodge Farm
CM4
Hill Farm
White's Place Farm
Durrant's Farm
White's Bridge
Bishopscourt
THREE MILE HILL
LONDON RD
A414
A12
A1016
A1114
B100
B1002
WESTWAY
A414 Harlow
A12 Brentwood, M25
A12 Colchester
8
7
6
5
4
3
2
1
05
04
03
02
67
68
69

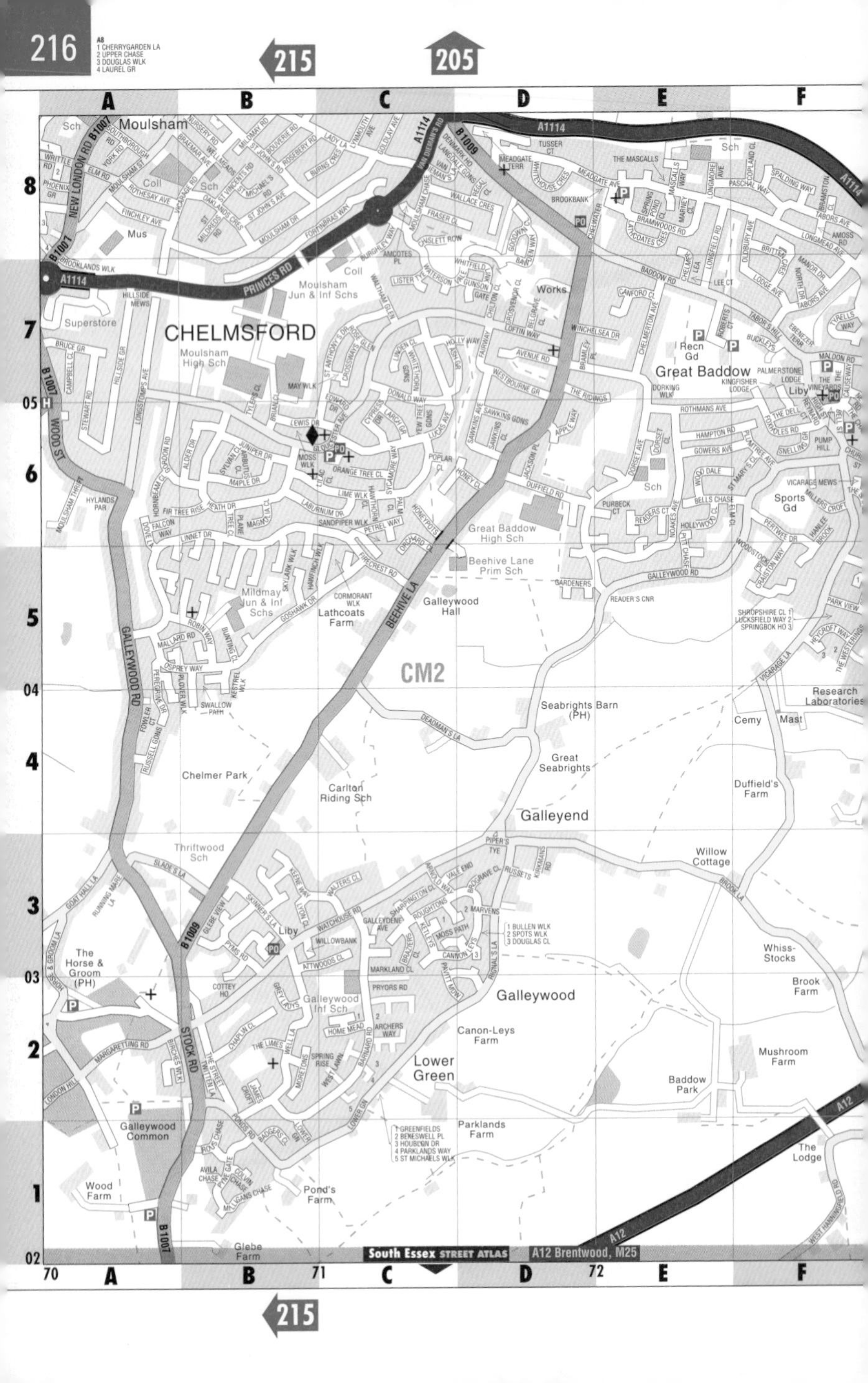
216
AB
1 CHERRYGARDEN LA
2 UPPER CHASE
3 DOUGLAS WLK
4 LAUREL GR
215
205
A
B
C
D
E
F
8
7
6
5
4
3
2
1
05
04
03
02
70
71
72
Moulsham
CHELMSFORD
Great Baddow
CM2
Galleyend
Galleywood
Lower Green
Moulsham Jun & Inf Schs
Moulsham High Sch
Great Baddow High Sch
Beehive Lane Prim Sch
Mildmay Jun & Inf Schs
Lathcoats Farm
Galleywood Hall
Seabrights Barn (PH)
Great Seabrights
Research Laboratories
Cemy
Mast
Duffield's Farm
Chelmer Park
Carlton Riding Sch
Thriftwood Sch
Willow Cottage
Whiss-Stocks
Brook Farm
The Horse & Groom (PH)
Galleywood Inf Sch
Canon-Leys Farm
Mushroom Farm
Baddow Park
Parklands Farm
The Lodge
Galleywood Common
Wood Farm
Pond's Farm
Glebe Farm
Superstore
Recn Gd
Sports Gd
Works
Coll
Mus
Liby
Sch
A1114
B1007
B1009
A12
PRINCES RD
NEW LONDON RD
WOOD ST
GALLEYWOOD RD
BEEHIVE LA
STOCK RD
BADDOW RD
GALLEYWOOD RD
VICARAGE LA
BROOK LA
DEADMAN'S LA
WATCHHOUSE RD
SLADE'S LA
GOAT HALL LA
MARGARETTING RD
LONDON HILL
WEST HANNINGFIELD RD
READER'S CNR
PIPER'S TYE
1 BULLEN WLK
2 SPOTS WLK
3 DOUGLAS CL
1 GREENFIELDS
2 BEESWELL PL
3 HOUBLON DR
4 PARKLANDS WAY
5 ST MICHAELS WLK
SHROPSHIRE CL 1
LUCKSFIELD WAY 2
SPRINGBOK HO 3
South Essex STREET ATLAS
A12 Brentwood, M25
215

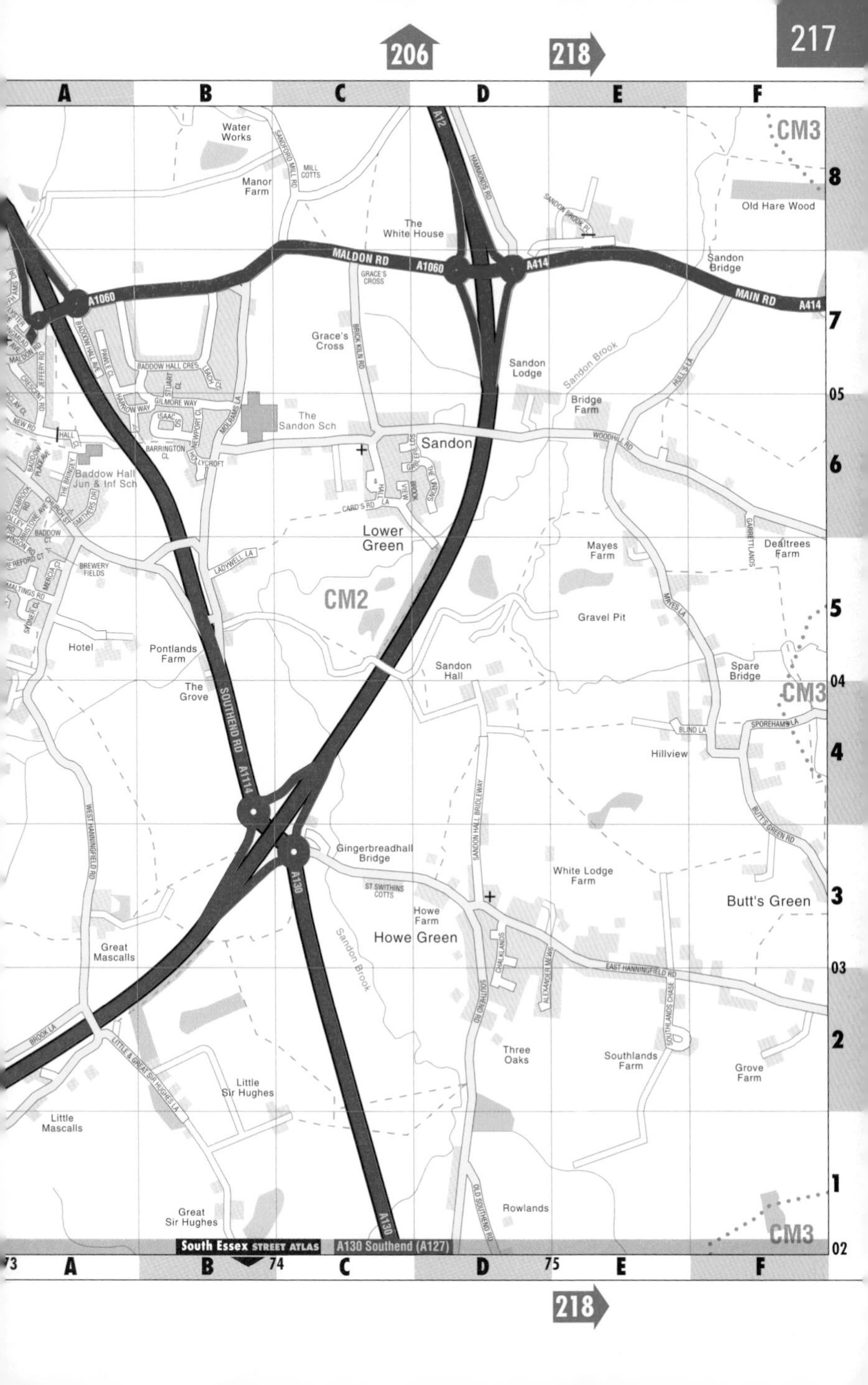
206
218
Water Works
Manor Farm
The White House
MALDON RD
A1060
A414
A12
MAIN RD
Old Hare Wood
Sandon Bridge
CM3
Grace's Cross
Sandon Lodge
Sandon Brook
Bridge Farm
The Sandon Sch
Sandon
Baddow Hall Jun & Inf Sch
Lower Green
CM2
Mayes Farm
Dealtrees Farm
Gravel Pit
Hotel
Pontlands Farm
The Grove
Sandon Hall
Spare Bridge
Hillview
SOUTHEND RD
A1114
A130
Gingerbreadhall Bridge
White Lodge Farm
Butt's Green
Howe Farm
Howe Green
Great Mascalls
Three Oaks
Southlands Farm
Grove Farm
Little Sir Hughes
Little Mascalls
Great Sir Hughes
Rowlands
South Essex STREET ATLAS
A130 Southend (A127)
218

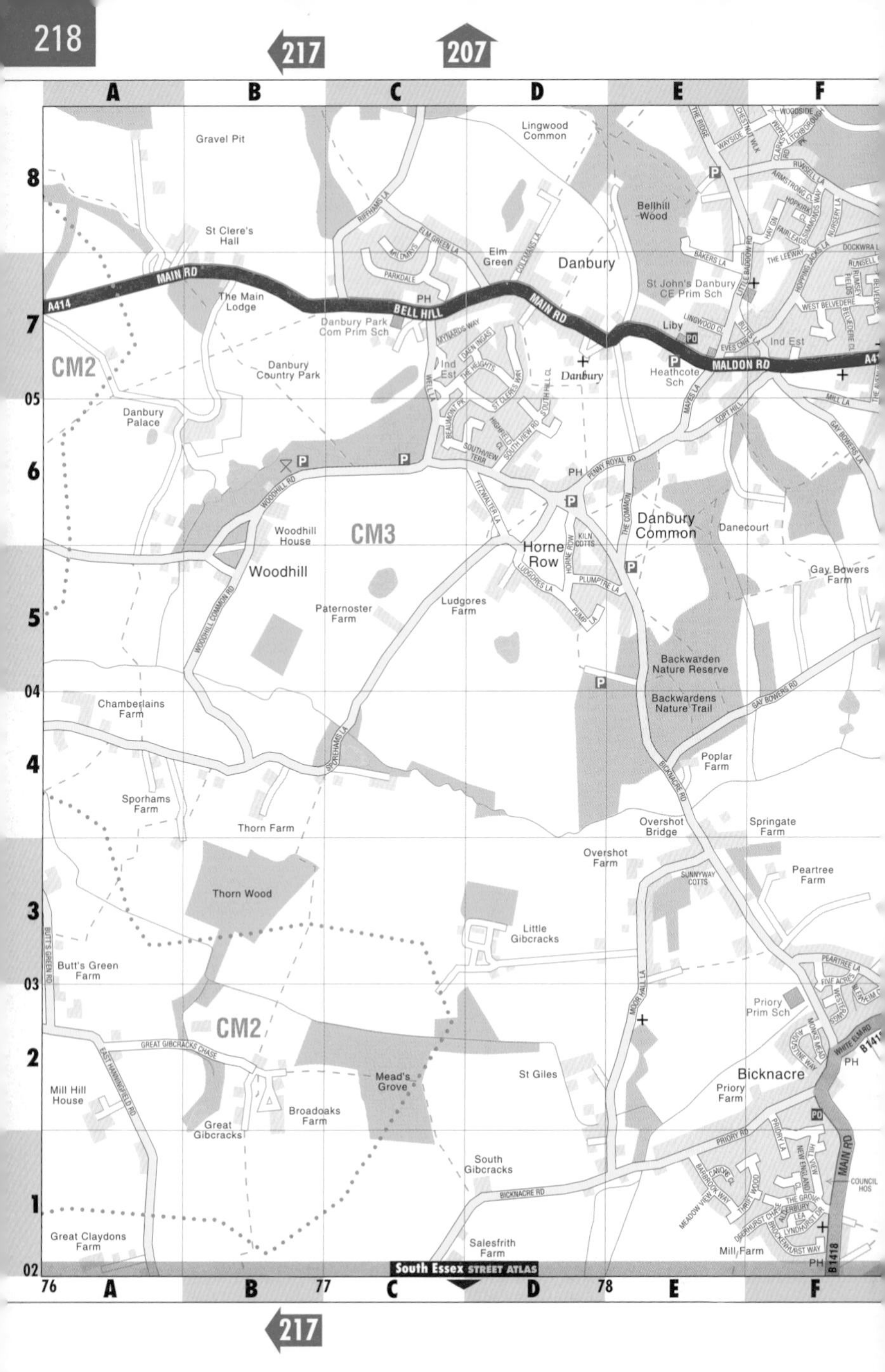

A B C D E F

8

7

05

6

04

4

03

2

1

02

76 A B 77 C D 78 E F

CM2

CM3

CM2

Gravel Pit

St Clere's Hall

Lingwood Common

Elm Green

Danbury

Bellhill Wood

St John's Danbury CE Prim Sch

MAIN RD

A414

The Main Lodge

BELL HILL

PH

MAIN RD

Liby

MALDON RD

A4

Danbury Park Com Prim Sch

Ind Est

Danbury Park Country Park

Ind Est

Danbury

Heathcote Sch

Ind Est

Danbury Palace

Danbury Palace

Woodhill House

CM3

Horne Row

PH

PVNT ROYAL RD

Danbury Common

Danecourt

Woodhill

Paternoster Farm

Ludgores Farm

KILN COTTS

THE COMMON

Gay Bowers Farm

Chamberlains Farm

Backwarden Nature Reserve

Backwardens Nature Trail

Poplar Farm

Sporhams Farm

Thorn Farm

Overshot Bridge

Overshot Farm

SUNNYWAY COTTS

Springate Farm

Peartree Farm

Thorn Wood

Little Gibcracks

Butt's Green Farm

Priory Prim Sch

CM2

GREAT GIBCRACKS CHASE

Mead's Grove

St Giles

Bicknacre

Priory Farm

PH

Mill Hill House

Great Gibcracks

Broadoaks Farm

South Gibcracks

MAIN RD

Great Claydons Farm

BICKNACRE RD

Salesfrith Farm

Mill Farm

B1418

PH

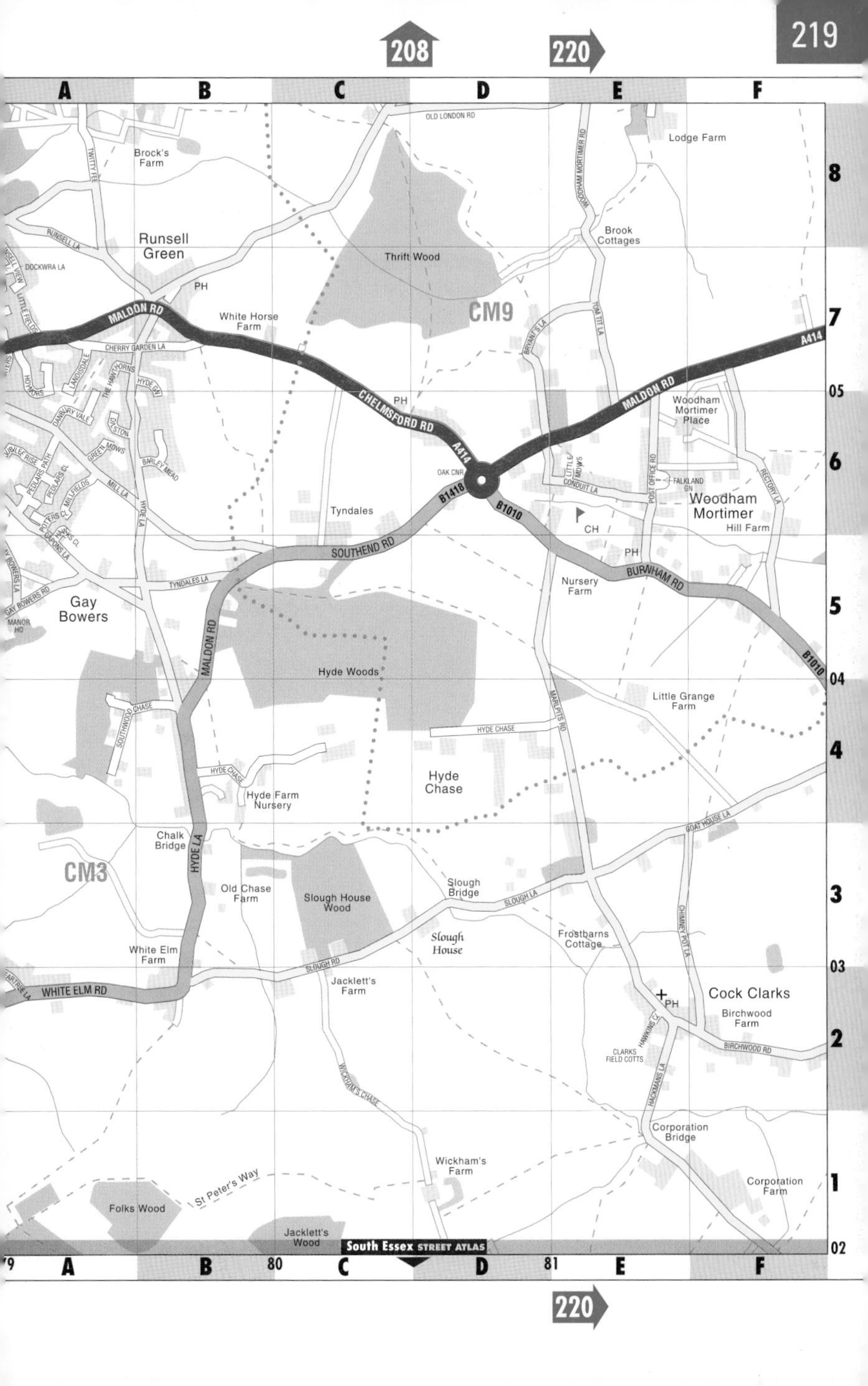
208
220
A
B
C
D
E
F
8
7
6
5
4
3
2
1
05
04
03
02
79
80
81
OLD LONDON RD
Lodge Farm
Brock's Farm
TWITTY FEE
WOODHAM MORTIMER RD
RUNSELL LA
Runsell Green
Brook Cottages
Thrift Wood
DOCKWRA LA
PH
CM9
White Horse Farm
MALDON RD
TOM TIT LA
BRYANT'S LA
CHERRY GARDEN LA
A414
MALDON RD
CHELMSFORD RD
Woodham Mortimer Place
PH
OAK CNR
B1418
B1010
LITTLE MDWS
CONDUIT LA
POST OFFICE RD
FALKLAND GN
RECTORY LA
Woodham Mortimer
Hill Farm
Tyndales
CH
SOUTHEND RD
PH
BURNHAM RD
Nursery Farm
TYNDALES LA
Gay Bowers
HYDE LA
MILL LA
MALDON RD
Hyde Woods
Little Grange Farm
SOUTHWOOD CHASE
HYDE CHASE
MARLPITS RD
Hyde Chase
Hyde Farm Nursery
GOAT HOUSE LA
Chalk Bridge
HYDE LA
CM3
Old Chase Farm
Slough House Wood
Slough Bridge
SLOUGH LA
Slough House
Frostbarns Cottage
CHIMNEY POT LA
White Elm Farm
SLOUGH RD
Jacklett's Farm
WHITE ELM RD
Cock Clarks
PH
Birchwood Farm
HAWKINS CL
BIRCHWOOD RD
CLARKS FIELD COTTS
HACKMANS LA
WICKHAM'S CHASE
Corporation Bridge
Wickham's Farm
St Peter's Way
Corporation Farm
Folks Wood
Jacklett's Wood
South Essex STREET ATLAS
220

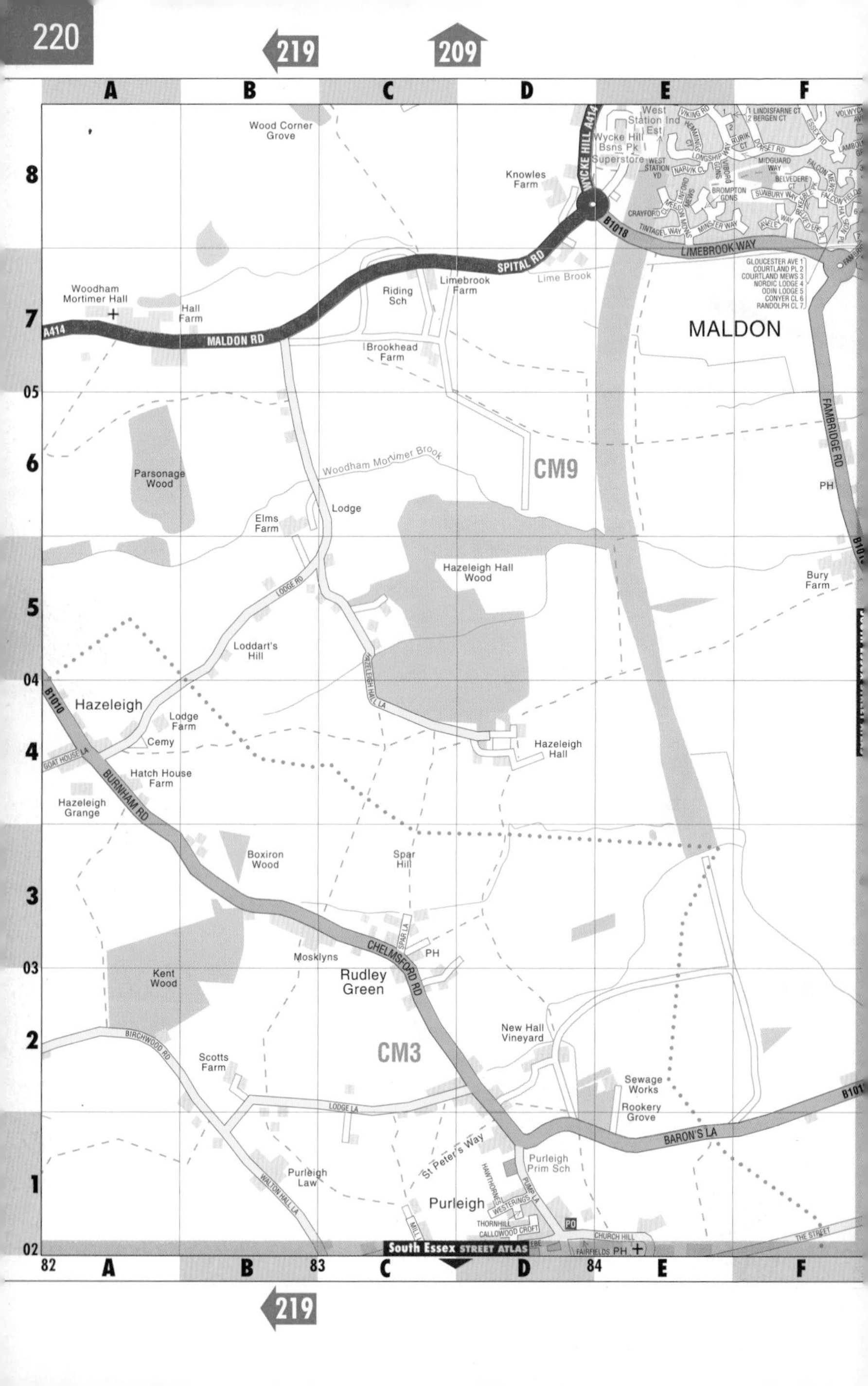

219
209

A B C D E F

Wood Corner
Grove

Knowles
Farm

West
Station Ind
Est

Wycke Hill
Bsns Pk
Superstore

VIKING RD

WEST
STATION
YD

BROMPTON
GDNS

CRAYFORD

LIMEBROOK WAY

LINDISFARNE CT 1
BERGEN CT 2

MIDGUARD
WAY
BELVEDERE
CT

SUNBURY WAY

8

Woodham
Mortimer Hall

Hall
Farm

Riding
Sch

Limebrook
Farm

Lime Brook

SPITAL RD

B1018

MALDON

GLOUCESTER AVE 1
COURTLAND PL 2
COURTLAND MEWS 3
NORDIC LODGE 4
ODIN LODGE 5
CONYER CL 6
RANDOLPH CL 7

7

A414

MALDON RD

Brookhead
Farm

05

6

Parsonage
Wood

Woodham Mortimer Brook

Lodge

CM9

FAMBRIDGE RD

PH

Elms
Farm

Hazeleigh Hall
Wood

Bury
Farm

5

LODGE RD

Loddart's
Hill

HAZELEIGH LA

04

Hazeleigh

B1010

Lodge
Farm

Cemy

Hazeleigh
Hall

4

GOAT HOUSE LA

BURNHAM RD

Hatch House
Farm

Hazeleigh
Grange

Boxiron
Wood

Spar
Hill

3

CHELMSFORD RD

Kent
Wood

Mosklyns

PH

Rudley
Green

03

New Hall
Vineyard

2

BIRCHWOOD RD

Scotts
Farm

CM3

LODGE LA

Sewage
Works

Rookery
Grove

BARON'S LA

B1010

Purleigh
Law

WALTON HALL LA

St Peter's Way

Purleigh
Prim Sch

1

HARTSWOOD

Thornhill
Callowood Croft

FAIRFIELDS

Purleigh

PH

CHURCH HILL

THE STREET

PO

02

South Essex STREET ATLAS

82 A B 83 C D 84 E F

219

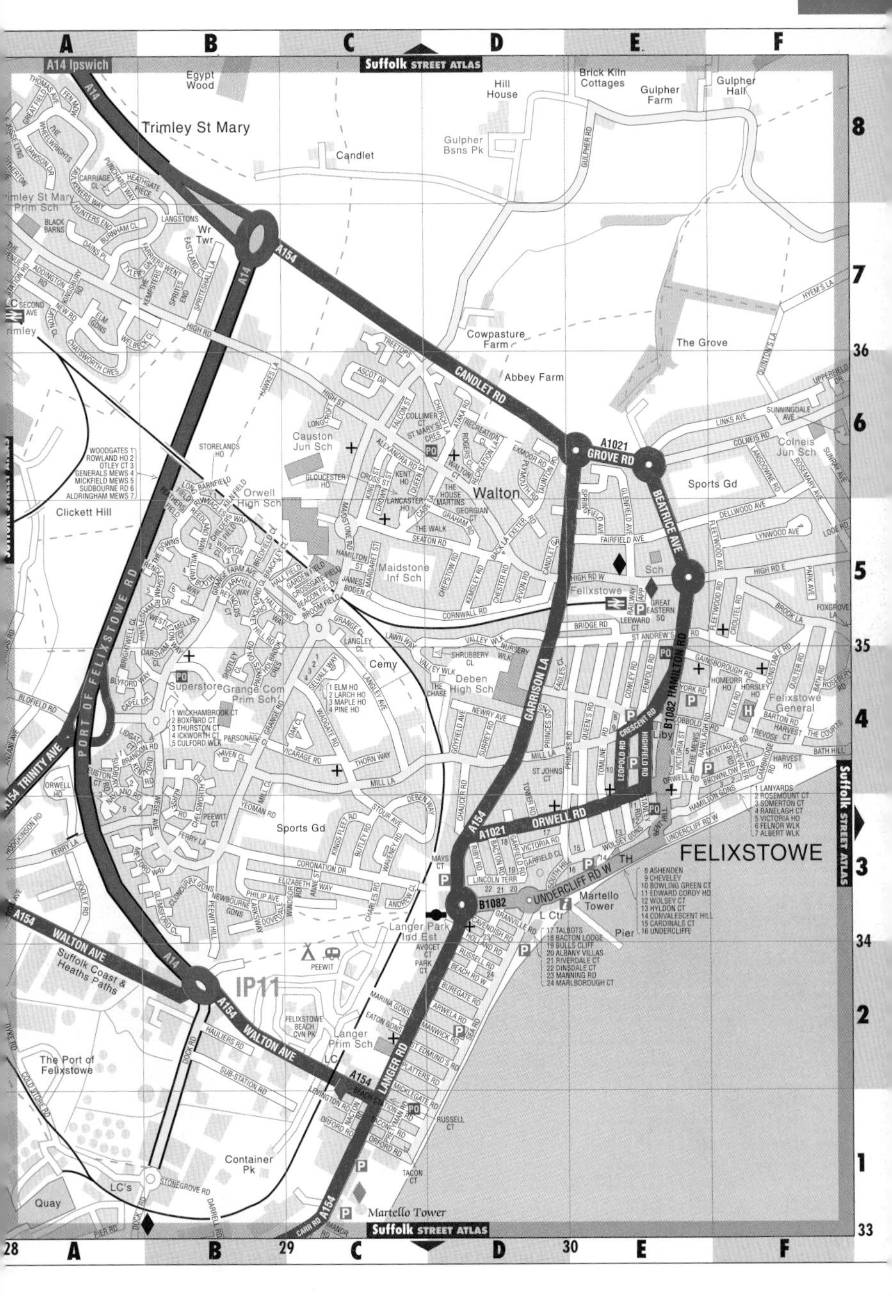

A14 Ipswich

Suffolk STREET ATLAS

Trimley St Mary

Egypt Wood

Candlet

Hill House

Brick Kiln Cottages

Gulpher Farm

Gulpher Half

Gulpher Bsns Pk

8

A154

7

Cowpasture Farm

Abbey Farm

The Grove

36

WOODGATES 1
ROWLAND HO 2
GENERALS MEWS 3
MICKFIELD MEWS 5
SUDBOURNE HO 6
ALDRINGHAM MEWS 7

Storelands Ho

Causton Jun Sch

St Mary's

CANDLET RD

A1021
GROVE RD

6

Colneis Jun Sch
Colnels

Links Ave

Sunningdale Ave

Sports Gd

Orwell High Sch

Clickett Hill

Maidstone Inf Sch

Walton

The Martins

BEATRICE AVE

Sch

Dellwood Ave

Lynwood Ave

Felixstowe

Great Eastern Sq

5

35

Cerny

1 ELM HO
2 LARCH HO
3 MAPLE HO
4 PINE HO

Deben High Sch

Superstore

Grange Com Prim Sch

1 WICKHAMBROOK CT
2 BOXFORD CT
3 THURSTON CT
4 ICKWORTH CT
5 GULFORD MEWS

PARSONAGE

GARRISON LA

ORWELL RD

Felixstowe General

The Courts

H

HAMILTON RD

A1021
ORWELL RD

FELIXSTOWE

1 LANYARDS
2 ROSEMOUNT CT
3 SOMERTON CT
4 RANELAGH CT
5 VICTORIA HO
6 FELNOR WLK
7 ALBERT WLK

3

Sports Gd

A154
WALTON AVE

IP11

Langer Park Ind Est

PEEWIT

Suffolk Coast & Heaths Paths

A154
WALTON AVE

UNDERCLIFF RD W

Martello Tower

Pier

B1082

8 ASHENDEN
9 CHEVELEY
10 BOWLING GREEN CT
11 EDWARD CORDY HO
12 WOLSEY CT
13 HYLDON CT
14 CONVALESCENT HILL
15 CARDINALS CT
16 UNDERCLIFFE

17 TALBOTS
18 BACTON LODGE
19 BULLS CLIFF
20 ALBANY VILLAS
21 RIVERDALE CT
22 DINSDALE CT
23 MANNING RD
24 MARLBOROUGH CT

34

The Port of Felixstowe

Felixstowe Beach Cvn Pk

Langer Prim Sch

LANGER RD

2

Container Pk

Quay

LC's

STONEGROVE RD

Martello Tower

A154
CARR RD

Suffolk STREET ATLAS

1

33

28   A   B   29   C   D   30   E   F

Index

Church Rd 6 Beckenham BR2..........53 C6

Place name	Location number	Locality, town or village	Postcode district	Page and grid square
May be abbreviated on the map	Present when a number indicates the place's position in a crowded area of mapping	Shown when more than one place has the same name	District for the indexed place	Page number and grid reference for the standard mapping

Public and commercial buildings are highlighted in magenta. Places of interest are highlighted in blue with a star★

Abbreviations used in the index

Abbreviation	Meaning
Acad	Academy
App	Approach
Arc	Arcade
Ave	Avenue
Bglw	Bungalow
Bldg	Building
Bsns, Bus	Business
Bvd	Boulevard
Cath	Cathedral
Cir	Circus
Cl	Close
Cnr	Corner
Coll	College
Com	Community
Comm	Common
Cott	Cottage
Cres	Crescent
Cswy	Causeway
Ct	Court
Ctr	Centre
Ctry	Country
Cty	County
Dr	Drive
Dro	Drove
Ed	Education
Emb	Embankment
Est	Estate
Ex	Exhibition
Gd	Ground
Gdn	Garden
Gn	Green
Gr	Grove
H	Hall
Ho	House
Hospl	Hospital
HQ	Headquarters
Hts	Heights
Ind	Industrial
Inst	Institute
Int	International
Intc	Interchange
Junc	Junction
L	Leisure
La	Lane
Liby	Library
Mdw	Meadow
Meml	Memorial
Mkt	Market
Mus	Museum
Orch	Orchard
Pal	Palace
Par	Parade
Pas	Passage
Pk	Park
Pl	Place
Prec	Precinct
Prom	Prom
Rd	Road
Recn	Recreation
Ret	Retail
Sh	Shopping
Sq	Square
St	Street
Sta	Station
Terr	Terrace
TH	Town Hall
Univ	University
Wk, Wlk	Walk
Wr	Water
Yd	Yard

Index of localities, towns and villages

Abberton 163 A3
Aldham 133 B8
Alphamstone 54 F3
Alresford 165 A8
Ardleigh 111 E7
Arkesden 41 E2
Ashdon 6 B1
Ashen 11 D1
Bardfield Saling 99 C2
Barnston 151 A4
Bartlow 6 B7
Beaumont 141 F7
Beazley End 101 C6
Belchamp St Paul 13 A2
Belchamp Walter 31 F5
Belstead 36 C7
Bentley 60 E7
Berden 92 C8
Bicknacre 218 F2
Birch 161 A4
Birchanger 119 E2
Birdbrook 28 B7
Bishop's Stortford 145 D7
Blackheath 163 B8
Black Notley 155 B5
Boreham 206 E8
Borley 14 F3
Boxted 82 F7
Bradfield 87 F2
Bradwell 129 D2
Bradwell Waterside 214 F4
Braintree 128 B5
Brantham 60 E1
Brightlingsea 185 E6
Broomfield 191 B2
Bulmer 32 E5
Bulmer Tye 32 F2
Bures 79 E8
Capel St Mary 35 B2
Castle Camps 7 E3
Castle Hedingham 51 E4
Cavendish 1 C1
Chappel 106 C5
Chelmondiston 63 E8
Chelmsford 205 C4
Chrishall 19 D3
Clacton-on-Sea 189 B3
Clare 12 C8
Clavering 65 C5
Cock Clarks 219 F2
Coggeshall 131 B3
Colchester 135 D7
Colne Engaine 77 F2
Copford 133 D4
Cressing 156 A6
Danbury 218 D7
Debden 68 B7
Dedham 84 F7
Duddenhoe End 41 A6
Earls Colne 105 C7
East Bergholt 59 C2
Easthorpe 160 A7
East Mersea 184 F1
Eight Ash Green 134 A8
Elder Street 44 E1
Elmdon 20 B4
Elmstead 138 A6
Elsenham 94 C1
Farnham 118 D6
Feering 158 E5
Felixstowe 221 F3
Felsted 152 B5
Finchingfield 72 C5
Fingringhoe 163 F5
Ford End 172 B7
Fordham 107 D5
Fordham Heath 107 F2
Foxearth 14 C6
Frating 139 A3
Frinton-on-Sea 170 D5
Galleywood 216 D2
Gestingthorpe 31 E1
Glemsford 2 C4
Goldhanger 211 F7
Gosfield 102 E8
Great Baddow 216 E7
Great Bardfield 72 C1
Great Bentley 166 D8
Great Braxted 178 C1
Great Bromley 112 F1
Great Canfield 149 C1
Great Chesterford 3 D2
Great Cornard 34 B5
Great Dunmow 150 C7
Great Easton 122 F7
Great Hallingbury 146 E4
Great Henny 54 C8
Great Holland 170 A3
Great Horkesley 82 B1
Great Leighs 173 F7
Great Maplestead 52 D2
Great Notley 154 B7
Great Oakley 116 C4
Great Sampford 47 B3
Great Tey 132 C8
Great Totham 196 B4
Great Waltham 190 E7
Great Wigborough 181 F3
Great Yeldham 30 A1
Greenstead Green 104 A5
Hadstock 5 C6
Halstead 76 D2
Harkstead 63 B2
Harwich 91 E5
Hatfield Peverel 194 B4
Haverhill 9 C7
Helions Bumpstead 26 C8
Hempstead 25 F1
Henham 94 F6
Heybridge 210 B6
Heybridge Basin 210 D3
Heydon 19 A5
Hinxton 3 B7
Holbrook 62 C5
Holland-on-Sea 189 F5
Howe Green 217 D3
Howe Street 172 F2
Ickleton 3 A4
Ipswich 17 C7
Jaywick 203 F7
Kelvedon 158 D2
Kirby Cross 170 B7
Kirby-le-Soken 170 C8
Lamarsh 55 B4
Langford 209 D7
Langham 83 F4
Langley 40 C2
Lawford 86 B3
Layer-de-la-Haye 161 F5
Lindsell 98 A3
Little Baddow 207 D4
Little Bentley 139 E8
Little Bromley 113 B6
Littlebury 21 E4
Little Clacton 168 D3
Little Dunmow 151 D7
Little Easton 122 F5
Little Horkesley 81 E4
Little Leighs 173 E6
Little Maplestead 53 B1
Little Oakley 117 B7
Little Totham 197 C4
Little Waltham 191 C6
Little Yeldham 30 E4
Long Melford 15 D7
Maldon 210 B3
Manningtree 86 E4
Manuden 92 F2
Marks Tey 132 E4
Messing 159 D3
Mistley 86 F4
Nayland 56 B1
New Mistley 87 B4
Newport 43 A1
North End 151 F2
Nuthampstead 39 A2
Panfield 127 B7
Pattiswick 129 F5
Pebmarsh 78 B7
Peldon 182 E6
Pentlow 13 F6
Point Clear Bay 185 F3
Purleigh 220 D1
Quendon 66 F2
Radwinter 45 F8
Ramsey 89 F1
Rayne 126 E2
Rickling Green 93 D8
Ridgewell 29 B7
Rivenhall 177 B8
Rowhedge 163 F8
Rushmere St Andrew 18 E8
Saffron Walden 22 E3
St Lawrence 213 B1
St Osyth 187 B4
Salcott-cum-Virley 199 B8
Seawick 203 C7
Sewards End 23 E1
Shalford 100 E7
Shotley Gate 91 A8
Shudy Camps 7 B6
Sible Hedingham 51 E1
Silver End 156 E4
Sproughton 16 B6
Stambourne 28 D3
Stanstead 2 F7
Stansted Mountfitchet 119 C8
Stebbing 124 E5
Steeple Bumpstead 27 B8
Stisted 129 C6
Stoke by Clare 11 C4
Stoke-by-Nayland 56 E5
Stratford St Mary 58 C2
Sturmer 9 F4
Stutton 61 F2
Sudbury 33 D8
Takeley 148 C8
Tattingstone 61 C7
Tendring 140 F5
Terling 175 C3
Thaxted 70 A3
Thorington Street 57 B4
Thorpe-le-Soken 142 B1
Thorrington 166 A5
Tiptree 179 D5
Tollesbury 199 D2
Tolleshunt D'arcy 198 D4
Tolleshunt Knights 180 A2
Tolleshunt Major 197 E4
Toppesfield 50 C7
Trimley St Mary 221 B8
Ugley 93 E6
Ulting 208 C6
Wakes Colne 106 C6
Walton-on-the-Naze 171 D8
Washbrook 35 E8
Weeley 140 E1
Weeley Heath 168 A5
Wendens Ambo 42 E5
West Bergholt 108 D4
West Mersea 201 C5
Wethersfield 73 C3
Wherstead 37 B6
White Colne 105 E6
White Notley 155 E1
Wicken Bonhunt 66 C7
Wickham Bishops 195 D5
Wickham St Paul 53 C5
Widdington 67 E4
Wimbish 45 C6
Witham 176 E4
Wivenhoe 137 C2
Wix 115 C5
Woodham Mortimer 219 F6
Woodham Walter 208 E2
Woolverstone 38 B1
Wormingford 80 E4
Wrabness 88 E4
Writtle 204 A2

A

Abbas Wlk CO10 34 C5
Abberton Rd
Fingringhoe CO5 163 D3
Layer-de-l-H CO2 162 C5
Abberton Resr Nature Reserve* CO2 161 F2
Abberton Wildfowl Ctr* CO2 161 E1
Abbess Cl CM1 204 E2
Abbey Cres CO16 142 A1
Abbey Ct CO9 51 F3
Abbey Gate St 11 CO2 135 F6
Abbey La Coggeshall CO6 131 A1
Saffron Walden CB10 22 D1
Abbey Mdw CO9 51 D2
Abbey Rd CO10 15 E1
Abbey St Ickleton CB10 3 A4
Thorpe-le-S CO16 142 A1
Abbey Turning CM9 209 D4
Abbey View CM6 96 E2
Abbot's Rd CO2 136 B3
Abbots Cl
Clacton-on-S CO15 188 E6
Wix CO11 115 C5
Abbots Gdns CO16 187 C4
Abbots La CO6 134 A7
Abbots Wick La CO5 181 B3
Abbotsbury Cl IP2 17 A1
Abbotsmead CM9 209 F5
Abbott Rd CO12 90 F2
Abbotts Croft CB9 9 F4
Abbotts Ct CB9 9 E5
Abbotts Pl CM2 205 D3
Abbotts Way CM23 145 E3
Abdy Ave CO12 90 E2
Abell Way CM2 206 B4
Abels Rd CO9 103 D8
Abercorn Ct 11 CB9 8 F7
Abercorn Ho CM3 206 E8
Abercorn Way CM8 177 A2
Abingdon Cl IP2 17 A1
Abinger Cl CO16 188 C6
Abington Pl 2 CB9 9 A8
Abraham Dr CM8 156 E4
Abram's La SG8 19 C4
Acacia Ave CO4 136 E8
Acacia Cl IP3 18 E1
Acacia Ct CO11 60 D1
Acacia Dr
Great Dunmow CM6 123 C1
Maldon CM9 209 F1
Acacia Gdns CM8 177 B4
Accommodation Rd CO4 109 D7
Acer Gr Chelmsford CM1 205 D4
Ipswich IP8 16 C1
Achilles Way CM7 128 B5
Achnacone Dr CO4 109 C3
Acland Ave CO3 135 B7
Acland Ct CO3 135 A7
Acorn Ave Braintree CM7 127 E2
Halstead CO9 76 D1
Acorn Cl Colchester CO4 110 D4
Harwich CO12 90 F1
Ipswich IP2 16 C2
Acorn Pl CM9 209 F5
Acorn Wlk CO7 166 A5
Acres End CM1 204 E4
Acton Cl CO10 33 F8
Acton Gn CO10 33 E7
Acton La CO10 33 F8
Acton Sq 4 CO10 33 E7
Adair Rd IP1 16 D8
Adams Cl IP2 17 C3
Adams Ct Halstead CO9 76 D2
Saffron Walden CB11 43 C8
Adderley Rd CM23 145 F7
Addington Rd IP11 221 A7
Addison Rd
Great Holland CO13 170 B5
Sudbury CO10 34 B8
Adelaide Dr CO2 136 A1
Adelaide Rd IP4 18 D6
Adelaide St CO12 90 F5
Admiral Rd IP8 36 E8
Admirals Wlk
Chelmsford CM1 204 F3
Wivenhoe CO7 164 B8
Aetheric Rd CM7 127 E3
Affleck Rd CO4 136 E7
Agar Rd 9 CO14 171 C8
Agar Road App 10 CO14 171 C8
Agate Rd CO15 188 F2
Agincourt Rd CO15 188 D4
Agricultural/Domestic Mus* CM9 211 E7
Ainger Rd CO12 90 E2
Aingers Green Rd CO7 167 A5
Ainslie Rd IP1 17 A6
Aire Wlk CM8 176 E2
Airey Hos CO10 11 D1
Aisne Rd CO2 135 D4
Ajax Cl CM7 128 B5
Akersloot Pl CO5 201 C6
Alamein Rd
Chelmsford CM1 204 F6
Colchester CO2 135 C2
Alan Dr CO16 168 D1
Alan Hasler Ho CM6 150 D7
Alan Rd Ipswich IP3 17 F4
Witham CM8 176 E1
Alan Way CO3 134 F4
Alanbrooke Rd CO2 136 D2
Albany Chase CO15 189 B4
Albany Cl
Chelmsford CM1 204 E5
West Bergholt CO6 108 E4
Albany Gdns E CO15 189 B3
Albany Gdns W CO15 189 B3
Albany Rd CO6 108 E4
Albany The IP4 17 E8
Albany Villas IP11 221 D3
Albemarle Gdns CM7 128 C5
Albemarle Link CM2 205 F8
Albemarle St CO12 91 D5
Albert Cotts CO7 60 C2
Albert Gdns
Clacton-on-S CO15 189 B3
Coggeshall CO6 131 A2
Albert Ho IP2 17 B4
Albert Pl CO6 131 A2
Albert Rd Braintree CM7 128 A3
Brightlingsea CO7 186 A6
Witham CM8 177 A3
Albert St Colchester CO1 135 E8
Harwich CO12 91 D5
Albert Wlk IP11 221 E4
Albertine Cl CO3 134 C6
Albion Ct CM2 205 B1
Albion Gr CO2 136 A5
Albion Hill IP4 17 F7
Albion St CO5 164 A8
Albra Mead CM2 206 B4
Albrighton Croft CO4 110 C4
Alconbury CM23 119 B1
Alcorns The CM24 119 E7
Alde Rd CB9 9 A8
Aldeburgh Cl
Clacton-on-S CO16 188 B4
Haverhill CB9 8 E7
Aldeburgh Gdns CO4 110 B4
Aldeburgh Way CM1 205 D5
Alder Cl CM23 145 D4
Alder Dr CM2 216 B6
Alder Way CO10 33 F8
Alder Wlk CM8 177 B4
Alderbury Lea CM3 218 F1
Alderbury Rd CM24 119 E8
Aldercar Rd CO6 133 F1
Alderford St CO9 75 E8
Alderlee IP2 36 F8
Alderman Blaxhill Sch CO2 135 B3
Alderman Howe Lodge CO4 110 B4
Alderman Rd IP1 17 B5
Alderton Cl CM6 152 C6
Alderton Rd CO4 136 C8
Aldham Ct 18 CB9 8 E7
Aldon Cl CO12 90 C1
Aldous Cl CO7 59 C3
Aldridge Cl CM2 206 A4
Aldringham Mews IP11 221 B5
Alec Hunter High Sch CM7 128 C1
Alec Kay Ct CO2 135 C2
Aletha Farm Pl CO9 29 D6
Alexander Ct 1 CM1 205 E7
Alexander Mews CM2 217 D2
Alexander Rd CM7 127 E4
Alexandra Ave CO5 201 E6
Alexandra Dr CO7 137 C3
Alexandra Rd
Clacton-on-S CO15 188 F3
Colchester CO3 135 E6
Felixstowe IP11 221 C6
Harwich CO12 91 D5
Ipswich IP4 17 E6
Sible Hedingham CO9 51 D1
Sudbury CO10 34 A7
Weeley CO16 140 F1
Alexandra St CO12 91 D5
Alexandra Terr 9 CO3 135 E6
Alf Eounder Cl CO4 136 E6
Alfells Rd CO7 137 F6
Alfred Terr CO14 171 C8
Alfreg Rd CM8 194 D8
Alienor Ave CM7 72 B1
All Hallows Ct IP3 18 A1
All Saints Ave CO3 135 A4
All Saints CE Prim Sch
Bishop's Stortford CM23 146 B8
Great Oakley CO12 116 C3
Harwich CO12 90 F3
All Saints Cl
Bishop's Stortford CM23 146 A8
Chelmsford CM1 205 E4
All Saints Maldon CE Prim Sch CM9 209 E2
All Saints' Rd IP1 17 A8
Allectus Way CM8 194 D8
Allen Cotts CO6 106 E5
Allen Way
Chelmsford CM2 206 B4
Point Clear B CO16 186 A3
Allenby Rd IP2 16 F6
Allendale Dr CO6 133 D4
Allens Cl CM3 192 F1
Alleyne Way CO15 203 G8
Allfields CO12 91 A2
Allington Cl IP4 17 F7
Allington Wlk CB9 8 E8
Alma Dr CM1 205 A2
Alma Sq 4 CO11 86 D4
Alma St CO7 164 B8
Almond Cl
Clacton-on-S CO15 188 C3
Tiptree CO5 179 C6
Wivenhoe CO7 137 C2
Almond Way CO4 136 E8
Almondhayes IP2 17 B3
Almshouses CO7 164 B8
Alnesbourn Cres IP3 38 D7
Alpe St IP1 17 B7
Alpha Cl CM7 128 A2
Alpha Pl
4 Bishop's Stortford CM23 145 F8
2 Saffron Walden CB11 22 E1
Alpha Rd CO16 186 B3
Alphamstone Rd CO8 55 B4
Alport Ave CO2 135 C4
Alresford Prim Sch CO7 165 B7
Alresford Rd CO7 164 E8
Alresford Sta CO7 165 A8
Alsa Bsns Pk CM24 93 F1
Alsa Gdns CM22 94 C2
Alsa Leys CM22 94 C2
Alsa St CM24 93 F1
Alston Cres CO10 2 E6
Alston Rd IP3 17 F4
Alstone Ct IP3 18 D1
Altbarn Cl CO4 110 C5
Altbarn Rd CO2 136 D5
Alton Dr CO3 135 B6
Alton Hall La IP9 61 F3
Alton Park Jun Sch CO15 188 D2
Alton Park La CO15 188 B1
Alton Park Rd CO15 188 D3
Alton Rd CO15 188 E1
Alton Water (Resr)* IP9 62 A4
Alton Water Visitor Ctr* IP9 62 B3
Aluf Cl CM8 194 E8
Alverton Cl CM77 154 B6
Alverton Way CO4 110 B3
Alvis Ave CO15 203 E6
Alyssum Cl CM1 206 A6
Alyssum Wlk CO4 136 D8
Amberley Cl CO7 137 D1
Ambleside Ct CO15 189 A3
Ambridge Rd CO6 130 E3
Ambrose Ave CO3 134 F4
Ambrose Ct CO6 133 D4
Ambross Ho CO2 135 D2
Amcotes Pl CM2 216 C8
Amerells Rd CO16 168 C4
America Rd CO6 105 C2
America St CM9 210 A2
Amos Hill CO10 54 B8
Amoss Rd CM2 216 F8
Ancaster Rd IP2 17 B4
Anchor Cvn Camp CO16 168 D2
Anchor End CO11 87 A4
Anchor Hill CO7 164 B7
Anchor Ho CO2 135 E2
Anchor La Dedham CO7 85 A4
Heybridge CM9 210 A5
New Mistley CO11 87 A4
Anchor Rd
Clacton-on-S CO15 188 E3
Tiptree CO5 179 C4
Anchor St
Bishop's Stortford CM23 146 A6
Chelmsford CM2 205 B1
Anchorage Hill CM9 210 A3
Anderson Ave CM1 204 F5
Anderson Cl CM23 92 F2
Andover Cl CO15 189 A6
Andrew Cl Braintree CM7 127 F5
Felixstowe IP11 221 C3
Andrews Farm La CM6 123 C8
Andrews Pl CM1 204 F3
Andros Cl IP3 38 A8
Anemone Ct CO4 109 C2
Angel La Glemsford CO10 2 B4
Great Dunmow CM6 150 D8
18 Ipswich IP4 17 D5
Angelgate CO12 91 E6
Angelgate Cotts CO12 91 E6
Angle Side CM7 128 B2
Anglefield CO15 188 F2
Anglesea Rd Ipswich IP1 17 B7
Wivenhoe CO7 164 C8
Anglesey Cl CM23 145 C7
Anglia Cl CO2 135 B3
Anglia Poly Univ
Chelmsford CM1 205 B2
Chelmsford CM1 205 B4
Anglia Way CM7 128 B2
Anita Cl E IP2 16 E5
Anita Cl W IP2 16 E5
Anjou Gn CM1 206 A7
Ann Coles Cl CB9 27 C6
Ann St IP1 17 B7
Annbrook Rd IP2 16 E1
Anne Cl CO7 185 F6
Anne St IP11 221 C3
Annonay Wlk 7 CM2 205 C2
Ansgar Rd CB11 43 E7
Anson Cl CO12 91 A2
Anson Way CM7 128 C4
Anthony Cl CO4 110 D2
Antonia Cl CB9 9 E7
Antonio Wlk CO4 136 F7
Antonius Way CO4 110 B6
Anvil Way CM1 205 E8
Anzani Ave IP11 221 A4
Anzio Cres CO2 135 C3
Apollo Ho IP2 16 D1
Apollo Mews CO2 135 C1
Apple Tree Cl CO9 77 A2
Apple Way CM2 216 D6
Appleby Cl IP2 16 D1
Appleton Fields CM23 145 E4
Appletree Cl CM77 155 F5
Appletree Wlk CM7 128 A1
Approach The CO15 203 G8
Aprils View CO15 203 D6
Apsley Cl CM23 145 F4
Apsley Ct 3 IP1 17 A7
Apton Ct CM23 145 F7
Apton Fields 7 CM23 145 F6
Apton Rd CM23 145 F7
Aquiline Ho CO15 203 J8
Aragon Cl CO15 203 F8
Aragon Rd
Great Leighs CM3 173 F7
Haverhill CB9 8 D6
Arakan Cl CO2 135 B1
Arbour La
Chelmsford CM1 205 D4
Wickham Bishops CM8 195 F5
Arbour Way CO4 110 C4
Arbutus Cl CM2 216 B6
Arcade St 15 IP1 17 C6
Arcade The CO15 188 F2
Archangel Gdns IP2 16 E4
Archer Cres CO5 179 E5
Archers Way CM2 216 C2
Archery Fields CO15 189 A5
Arden Cl CO4 110 C3
Arderne Cl CO12 90 F2
Ardleigh Ct CO7 111 E8
Ardleigh Rd Dedham CO7 84 D3
Great Bromley CO7 112 B4
Little Bromley CO11 112 E5
Argents La CO3 108 C2
Argyle Ct CO5 158 C2
Argyle Rd CO16 141 F2
Argyle St IP4 17 D6
Argyll Ct 10 CB9 8 F7
Argyll Rd CM2 206 A5
Ariel Cl CO4 136 F7
Arkwright Rd IP2 16 E7
Arlesford Ct CO4 136 F4
Armidale Wlk CO2 136 A2
Armiger Way CM8 177 B2
Armond Rd CM8 176 F3
Armonde Cl CM3 192 E1
Armourers Cl CM23 145 B4
Armoury Rd CO6 108 F4
Armstrong Cl CM3 218 F8
Armstrong Way CO9 30 A2
Arnhem Gr CM7 127 E5
Arnhem Rd CM1 204 E6
Arnold Dr CO4 136 E6
Arnold Ho CM2 205 A1
Arnold Rd CO15 188 D1
Arnold Villas CO5 179 C6
Arnold Way CM2 216 C3
Arnstones Cl CO4 136 C8
ARP Shelter Mus* IP4 17 F5
Arras Rd CO2 135 D3
Arras Sq 12 IP1 17 C6
Arrow Rd CO4 136 F7
Arthur Ct CM1 204 F5
Arthur St 5 CO2 135 F6
Arthur's Terr IP4 17 E6
Arthy Cl CM3 194 A4
Artillery Dr CO12 90 D1
Artillery St CO1 136 B6
Arun Cl CM1 205 C5
Arundel Way IP3 18 E3
Arundel Wlk 1 CB9 8 E8
Arwela Rd IP11 221 D2
Asbury Cl CO4 136 D8
Asbury Dr CO6 132 F3
Ascot Cl CM23 146 C8
Ascot Dr Felixstowe IP11 221 C6
Ipswich IP3 18 B4
Ascot Gdns CO3 134 E7
Ascot Mews CO15 189 C5
Ash Bglws CM7 127 E3
Ash Cl Brightlingsea CO7 185 E7
Clacton-on-S CO15 188 C3
Hatfield Peverel CM3 194 A4
Ipswich IP3 18 F1
Ash Ct CO12 90 E2
Ash Fall CM8 177 A5
Ash Gn CB10 3 D1
Ash Gr Blackheath CO2 163 A8
Capel St M IP9 35 A2
Chelmsford CM2 216 D7
Great Bromley CO7 139 A6
Great Cornard CO10 34 C5
Great Dunmow CM6 150 D7
Heybridge CM9 210 C6
Wivenhoe CO7 137 C3
Ash Ground Cl CO11 86 D8
Ash Ho IP2 16 D2
Ash Rd CO7 165 B8
Ash Rise CO9 103 F8
Ash Tree Cl CM1 204 F2
Ash Tree Cnr CM3 191 B6
Ash Tree Cres CM1 204 F2
Ash Way CO3 134 F3
Ashby Rd CM8 195 A7
Ashby Rise CM23 119 B1
Ashdale CM23 145 D4
Ashdon Prim Sch CB10 6 B1
Ashdon Rd Ashdon CB10 24 E3
Saffron Walden CB10 23 C3
Ashdon Road Commercial Ctr CB10 23 A3
Ashdown Cl CM77 154 B8
Ashdown Way
Colchester CO4 136 D7
Ipswich IP3 18 D3
Ashen Cl CO10 11 D1
Ashen Hill CO10 11 C2
Ashen La CO10 11 C3
Ashen Rd Ashen CO10 12 A1
Clare CO10 12 B5
Ridgewell CO9 29 B8
Ashenden IP11 221 E4
Ashes Cl CO14 170 F8
Ashes Rd CM77 155 F7
Ashfield Cl CM6 123 C1
Ashfield Ct IP4 18 A6
Ashfield Farm Rd CM9 208 D8
Ashford Rd CM1 204 E2
Ashlea Cl CB9 9 B6
Ashlea Rd CB9 9 B6
Ashley Ct CO12 91 B3
Ashley Gdns CO3 135 C6
Ashley Rd CO12 91 B3
Ashley St IP2 17 C4
Ashlong Gr CO9 76 E3
Ashlyn's Rd CO13 170 E4
Ashmere Gr IP4 17 F6
Ashmere Rise CO10 34 A8
Ashmole Dr CO13 170 F6
Ashpole Rd CM7 102 B1
Ashstead Cl CO16 188 B6
Ashton Cl IP2 16 C2
Ashton Pl CM2 206 A3
Ashurst Cl CO5 163 F8
Ashurst Dr CM1 205 D7
Ashwells Mdw CO6 105 B6
Ashwin Ave CO6 133 D4
Askins Rd CO7 59 C3
Aspen Way
3 Colchester CO4 136 D8
Little Oakley CO12 117 B7
Aspens The CM23 119 B3
Aspin Mews CB10 22 E3
Asquith Dr CO4 110 C5
Astell Ct CO13 170 F4
Aster Cl
Bishop's Stortford CM23 145 D6
4 Chelmsford CM1 205 F6
Clacton-on-S CO16 188 C4
Aster Rd IP2 16 E4
Astley Rd CO15 188 D3
Ataka Rd IP11 221 D6
Athelstan Rd CO3 135 C5
Atherton Rd IP2 16 D2
Atholl Rd CM2 205 F5
Atlantic Sq CM8 177 A3
Atlas Bglws CO6 105 A6
Atlas Ct CO6 105 A7
Atlas Ho 3 IP4 17 E6
Atlas Rd CO6 104 F7
Attlee Gdns 7 CO1 136 A6
Attwood Cl CO4 110 B5
Attwoods Cl CM2 216 C3
Aubrey Cl CM1 205 B7
Auckland Cl CM1 204 E5
Audley Cl CM77 154 B7
Audley End* CB11 22 B1
Audley End Miniature Rly* CB11 43 A8
Audley End Rd CB11 43 C8
Audley End Sta CB11 42 F5
Audley Rd
Colchester CO3 135 C5
Great Leighs CM3 173 F7
Saffron Walden CB11 22 E1
Audley Way CO13 171 B6
Audrey Gdns CM23 145 F4
Audries Est CO14 171 A8
Augusta Cl IP3 38 E7
Augustine Way CM3 218 F2
Augustus Cl
Colchester CO4 110 B6
Haverhill CB9 9 D7
Augustus Way CM8 194 E8
Austen Cl CM7 155 A8
Austin Ave CO15 203 E6
Austin St IP2 17 C4
Auton Croft CB11 43 D7
Autoway CO4 110 C5
Autumn Cl CO16 188 C5
Aveley Way CM9 220 F8
Aveline Rd CO7 111 E7
Avenue Pl CM23 146 A6
Avenue Rd
Bishop's Stortford CM23 146 B6
Chelmsford CM2 216 D7
Witham CM8 177 A3
Avenue The
Braintree CM7 127 F3
Clacton-on-S CO15 189 B7
Colchester CO3 135 C6
Danbury CM3 218 F7
Great Braxted CM8 178 A3
Great Dunmow CM6 150 E8
Great Oakley CO12 116 B3
Ipswich IP1 17 C8
Trimley St M IP11 221 A7
Washbrook IP8 35 F7
West Bergholt CO6 108 D3
Witham CM8 177 A2
Wivenhoe CO7 137 B1
Avignon Cl CO2 136 B4
Avila Chase CM2 216 B1
Avocet Cl
Frinton-on-S CO13 170 E6
Kelvedon CO5 158 D2
West Mersea CO5 201 D7
Avocet Ct IP11 221 D2
Avocet Way CM9 210 C5
Avon Rd CM1 204 C5
Avon Way CO4 136 F6
Avon Way Ho CO4 136 F6
Avon Wlk CM8 176 E3
Avondale Ho CO15 189 A3
Avondale Rd
Clacton-on-S CO15 189 A3
Ipswich IP3 18 A2

Aylesbury Dr
Great Notley CM77 154 C5
Holland-on-S CO15 189 F6
Ayletts CM1 191 B3
Ayloffe Rd CO4 110 C1
Aynsworth Ave CM23 119 B2
Azalea Ct
8 Chelmsford CM1 205 F6
Colchester CO4 136 D8
Azalea Way CO16 188 C4

B

Back Hamlet IP3 17 E5
Back Hill Hadstock CB1 5 B6
Holbrook IP9 62 E4
Back La Broomfield CM1 191 D1
Colchester CO3 134 E7
Felixstowe IP11 221 D5
Ford End CM3 172 B6
Great Oakley CO12 116 C4
Ickleton CB10 3 A3
Little Waltham CM3 191 C4
Ramsey CO12 90 A1
Stisted CM7 129 C7
Tattingstone IP9 61 C6
Thaxted CM6 69 F3
Washbrook IP8 35 E8
Wickham Bishops CM8 195 F4
Back La E CO7 139 A6
Back La W CO7 138 F7
Back Rd Ardleigh CO7 112 B5
Tollesbury CM9 199 C4
Writtle CM1 204 A1
Back Waterside La CO7 185 F5
Backnang Sq 1 CM2 205 C2
Backwarden Nature Reserve* CM3 218 E5
Backwardens Nature Trail* CM3 218 E4
Bacon's La CO6 106 C3
Bacton Lodge IP11 221 D3
Bacton Rd IP11 221 D3
Baddow Ct CM2 217 A6
Baddow Hall Ave CM2 217 A7
Baddow Hall Cres CM2 217 B7
Baddow Hall Jun & Inf Sch CM2 217 A6
Baddow Place Ave CM2 217 A6
Baddow Rd
Chelmsford CM2 205 C1
Great Baddow CM2 216 E7
Baden Powell Dr CO3 135 A4
Bader Cl IP3 18 C2
Badger Gr CM7 128 B3
Badgers CM23 145 E5
Badgers Bank IP2 16 E1
Badgers Cl CM2 216 B1
Badgers Gn CO6 132 E3
Badgers Gr CO6 82 B1
Badgers Holt CO3 134 D6
Badley Hall Rd CO7 112 F2
Badminton Rd CO15 203 G7
Badshah Ave IP3 18 B3
Bagshaw Rd CO12 91 D4
Bailey Bridge Rd CM7 127 E5
Bailey Cl Haverhill CB9 9 D7
Ipswich IP2 16 E6
Bailey Dale CO3 134 C4
Bailey La CO10 12 C7
Bainbridge Dr CO5 179 D4
Baines Cl CO3 135 A5
Baird Cl IP2 16 F7
Baker Ave CM3 194 A3
Baker Mews CM9 210 A2
Baker Rd IP9 91 A8
Baker St CM2 205 A1
Baker's La
Colchester CO4 109 A2
Great Notley CM77 154 D6
Tolleshunt Major CM9 197 D4
Baker's Rd CO10 12 F2
Bakers Ct
6 Bishop's Stortford CM23 146 A7
Colchester CO1 109 E1
Bakers La Danbury CM3 218 E7
Felsted CM6 152 C4
Bakers Mead CM3 190 F7
Bakery Ct CM24 119 D6
Baldry Cl IP8 16 C1
Baldwin's La CO6 131 E8
Bale Cl CO3 134 E4
Balfe Ct CO4 136 E6
Balkerne Gdns CO1 135 E7
Balkerne Hill CO3 135 E7
Balkerne Pas CO1 135 E7
Ball Alley 3 CO1 135 F7
Ball La Abberton CO2 162 F5
Blackheath CO2 163 B5
Ball's Chace CO8 79 F2
Ball's Chase CO9 76 F1
Ballast Quay Rd
Fingringhoe CO5 164 B6
Wivenhoe CO7 137 D1
Ballingdon Gr CO10 33 D5
Ballingdon Hill CO10 33 C5
Ballingdon Hill Ind Est CO10 33 C6
Ballingdon St CO10 33 D6
Ballingdon Trad Est CO10 33 C6
Balmoral Ave CO15 188 D3
Balmoral Cl IP2 16 F1
Balmoral Ct CM2 205 C2
Balmoral Dr CB9 8 E8
Balton Way CO12 90 F2
Bangs Cl CB1 7 A7
Banham Dr CO10 33 F8
Banister Cl CO16 188 C5
Bank Bldgs 13 CO10 33 E7
Bank Pas CO1 135 E7
Bank Rd IP4 17 E6
Bank St CM7 127 F3
Bankart La CM2 205 F4
Banks Ct CM6 150 D8
Bannister Green Villas CM6 152 E6
Banters La CM3 154 B1
Bantock Way CM8 194 F7
Bantoft Terr IP3 18 C2
Barbary Lodge CM2 205 A2
Barbel Rd CO4 110 F1
Barbour Gdns CO2 134 F2
Barbrook La CO5 179 D6
Barbrook Way CM3 218 E1
Barclay Cl CM2 217 A6
Bardell Cl CM1 204 F6
Bardfield Ctr CM7 72 B1
Bardfield Rd
Bardfield Saling CM7 99 F1
Colchester CO2 136 A1
Thaxted CM6 70 D2
Bardfield Way CO13 170 F6
Barfield Rd CO5 201 C6
Bargate La CO7 85 C3
Baring-Gould Cotts CO5 184 D1
Barker Cl Ipswich IP2 16 D5
Lawford CO11 86 B4
Steeple Bumpstead CB9 27 B6
Barker Rd CO10 15 E2
Barkers Terr CO7 85 A5
Barkis Cl CM1 204 D7
Barkstead Rd CO4 110 C1
Barlee Cl CB11 65 C3
Barley Ct CB11 22 D1
Barley Fields CM8 177 A1
Barley Hills CM23 145 E4
Barley Ho CO10 15 B5
Barley Mead CM3 219 B6
Barley Way CO3 134 E5
Barlon Rd CO11 112 F4
Barlow Road Cotts CB10 6 B2
Barlow's Reach CM2 206 A4
Barn Fields CO3 134 C6
Barn Gn CM1 205 E8
Barn Hall Ave CO2 136 C4
Barn La CO11 112 F7
Barn Mead CM7 128 D2
Barn View Rd CO6 131 A1
Barnaby Rudge CM1 204 F7
Barnard Cl CB11 66 F8
Barnard Rd CM2 216 C2
Barnardiston Rd CO4 110 C1
Barnardiston Way CM8 176 F3
Barnards Field CM6 70 B2
Barnards Yd CB10 22 D1
Barnby Cl CB9 8 C8
Barncroft Cl CO4 110 B3
Barnes Farm Jun & Inf Schs CM2 206 A3
Barnes Mill Rd CM2 205 F2
Barnfield Capel St M IP9 35 B1
Feering CO5 158 D3
Felixstowe IP11 221 B6
Manningtree CO11 86 D4
Barnfield Cotts CM9 210 B5
Barnfield Mews CM1 205 A6
Barnfield Pl CM8 176 F1
Barnfield Rd CO6 109 C6
Barnfields CO5 163 F5
Barnhall Rd CM9 180 D2
Barnham Pl IP5 18 F6
Barnston Gn CM6 151 A4
Baron's Ct 5 CB9 8 E7
Baron's La CM3,CM9 220 E1
Baronia Croft CO4 110 C3
Barons The CM23 145 D5
Baronswood Way CO2 135 D2
Barr Cl CO7 137 C1
Barrack Cnr 5 IP1 17 B6
Barrack La
Great Waltham CM3 190 E8
Harwich CO12 91 E4
Ipswich IP1 17 B6
Barrack Sq 10 CM2 205 B2
Barrack St
Bradfield CO11 114 D8
Colchester CO1 136 B6
Barrel Cl CO7 139 A3
Barrells Down Rd CM23 118 E1
Barrett La 5 CM23 145 F7
Barrington Cl
Great Baddow CM2 217 A6
Little Clacton CO16 168 C2
Barrington Gdns CO15 189 C5
Barrington Rd CO2 136 A5
Barrow Chase CM2 206 B4
Barrow Marsh CM9 211 A4
Barryfields CM7 100 E7
Bartholomew Cl CB10 3 E2
Bartholomew Rd 8 CM23 145 F6
Bartholomew St IP4 17 F6
Bartletts CB10 22 D1
Bartlow Rd
Castle Camps CB1 7 D4
Hadstock CB1 5 D7
Barton Cl IP2 16 E2
Barton Rd IP11 221 F4
Bartram Ave N CM7 128 C3
Bartram Ave S CM7 128 C3
Barwell Way CM8 177 B2
Basbow La 2 CM23 145 F7
Basin Rd CM9 210 E3
Bassetts La CM3,CM9 208 A4
Bassingbourn Rd CM24 121 A3
Bassingham Cres CO5 179 E5
Bateman Rd CO7 185 E8
Bateman's Rd CO16 168 B4
Bates Rd CM9 210 B4
Bath Ct CB9 8 F6
Bath Hill IP11 221 F4
Bath Rd IP11 221 F4
Bath St Ipswich IP2 17 D3
Wivenhoe CO7 164 B8
Bathurst Cl 11 CO2 136 A1
Battery La IP9 91 B8
Battisford Dr CO16 188 A4
Battlesbrook Rd CO2 136 D2
Bawden Way CM2 216 D8
Bawdsey Cl CO16 188 B3
Bawn Cl CM7 128 A4
Bawtree Way CO3 135 A5
Baxters CM3 219 A7
Bay Rd CO12 91 D4
Bay View Cres
Harwich CO12 90 C1
Little Oakley CO12 117 C8
Bayard Ave CO7 185 F7
Bayley St CO9 51 F4
Baynard Ave CM6 151 E7
Baynard's Prim Sch CO5 179 B7
Baynards Cres CO13 170 E6
Bayning Ho CO7 139 F8
Bays Dr CO9 76 E2
Baytree Cl CO11 115 C5
Baytree Ct CM77 126 F2
Beach App CO16 203 B6
Beach Cres CO15 203 F6
Beach Rd
Clacton-on-S CO15 188 F2
Harwich CO12 91 C2
Point Clear B CO16 202 D6
St Osyth CO16 187 B2
West Mersea CO5 201 C5
Beach Rd W IP11 221 D2
Beach Station Rd IP11 221 C1
Beach Way CO15 203 F6
Beach's Dr CM1 204 D3
Beachcroft Ave CO13 170 D6
Beacon Cl CO7 185 E6
Beacon End Ctyd CO3 134 C6
Beacon Field IP11 221 C5
Beacon Hill Maldon CM9 209 E2
Wickham Bishops CM8 196 A6
Beacon Hill Ave CO12 91 E4
Beacon Hill Sch IP2 16 F3
Beacon Hts CO16 186 B2
Beacon Way
Colchester CO3 134 C6
Point Clear B CO16 186 B2
Beaconsfield Ave CO3 135 E6
Beaconsfield Cl CO10 33 E8
Beaconsfield Ct 7 CB9 8 F7
Beaconsfield Rd
Clacton-on-S CO15 188 F3
Ipswich IP1 16 F7
Sudbury CO10 33 E8
Beadel Cl CM8 194 E8
Beadle Way CM3 174 A6
Beadon Dr CM7 128 A1
Bear St CO6 56 A1
Beard's La CB11 41 A4
Beard's Terr CO6 131 A3
Beardsley Dr CM1 205 F7
Bearwalden Bsns Pk CB11 42 F5
Beatrice Ave IP11 221 E5
Beatrice Cl IP3 18 A3
Beatrice Rd
Clacton-on-S CO15 188 E2
Walton-on-t-N CO14 144 D2
Beatty Gdns CM7 128 C4
Beatty Rd IP3 18 B2
Beauchamps Cl CM1 205 F8
Beaufort Ct 5 CB9 8 F7
Beaufort Gdns CM7 128 A4
Beaufort Rd CM2 206 A4
Beaufort St IP1 17 A7
Beaulieu Bvd CM1 206 A7
Beaumont Ave
Brightlingsea CO7 186 A7
Clacton-on-S CO15 188 D3
Beaumont Cl
Colchester CO4 109 F4
Walton-on-t-N CO14 170 F7
Beaumont Ct CB9 9 B6
Beaumont Hill CM6 123 D2
Beaumont Pk CM3 218 C6
Beaumont Pl CM7 128 B3
Beaumont Rd CO12 116 C2
Beaumont Vale CB9 9 B6
Beaumont Wlk CM1 204 D5
Beaver Cl CO3 134 E7
Beche Rd CO2 136 B5
Beck Rd CB11 22 D1
Becker Rd CO3 134 E4
Beckers Green Prim Sch CM7 128 D2
Beckers Green Rd CM7 128 D2
Becketts Ct CM1 205 A3
Becketts La IP7 57 D8
Beckford Rd CO11 87 A4
Beckingham Bsns Pk CM9 197 D3
Beckingham Rd
Great Totham CM9 196 D5
Beckingham Rd *continued*
Tolleshunt D'arcy CM9 198 C4
Beckingham St CM9 197 D3
Becontree Cl CO15 188 F8
Bedells Ave CM77 155 B5
Bedford Cl
Braintree CM7 128 B4
Tiptree CO5 179 D5
Bedford Ct 9 CB9 8 F7
Bedford Rd
Colchester CO4 109 F5
Holland-on-S CO15 189 D5
Bedford St IP1 17 B6
Bedwell Rd CM22 94 B3
Beech Ave Braintree CM7 127 F5
Halstead CO9 77 A2
Wivenhoe CO7 137 B1
Beech Cl Sproughton IP8 16 A6
Takeley CM22 148 C8
Beech Gn CM8 195 F5
Beech Gr
Fordham Heath CO3 107 F1
Haverhill CB9 8 F8
Ipswich IP3 17 F3
Little Oakley CO12 117 B7
Rushmere St A IP5 18 F7
Sible Hedingham CO9 51 D1
Beech Hill CO3 135 A6
Beech Ho IP2 16 D2
Beech Rd
Great Cornard CO10 34 B6
Rivenhall CM8 177 B7
Rushmere St A IP5 18 F7
Beech Rise CM3 194 A3
Beeches Cl
Chelmsford CM1 204 E2
Saffron Walden CB11 43 C7
Beeches Rd
Chelmsford CM1 204 E2
Heybridge CM9 209 F5
Beeches The Ipswich IP3 17 F4
Lawford CO11 86 C3
Wendens Ambo CB11 42 F5
Beechholm 2 IP4 17 E6
Beechlands CM23 145 F5
Beechwood Cl CO2 135 D2
Beehive Cl CO7 59 C3
Beehive Ct CO1 136 A6
Beehive La CM2 216 C5
Beehive Lane Prim Sch CM2 216 D5
Beeleigh Chase CM9 209 D4
Beeleigh Cl CO2 136 A1
Beeleigh Link CM2 205 F3
Beeleigh Rd CM9 209 F3
Begonia Cl CM1 205 F6
Begonia Pl CO16 188 C4
Bekeswell La CM2 215 F2
Bekeswell Pl CM2 216 C2
Bel-Air Beach Cvn Pk CO15 203 C6
Bel-Air Est CO16 203 A6
Belcham's La CB11 93 E8
Belchamp Rd CO9 30 B5
Belchamp St Paul CE Prim Sch CO10 13 A1
Beldams Cl CO16 142 A1
Beldams Gate CM23 146 C6
Beldams La CM23 146 B5
Belgrave Cl
Chelmsford CM2 216 D7
Ipswich IP4 17 E8
Belgrave Ho 6 CM23 146 B8
Bell Cl Colchester CO2 136 D2
Ipswich IP2 17 C4
Bell Coll CB11 43 E8
Bell Farm Ind Pk SG8 39 B2
Bell Gn CO7 186 A7
Bell Hill Danbury CM3 218 C7
Lamarsh CO8 55 C3
Bell La Great Bardfield CM7 72 A2
Ipswich IP2 17 C4
Nuthampstead SG8 39 B2
Panfield CM7 127 A7
Thaxted CM6 70 A3
Bell St CM2 216 F6
Bellamy Cl CO13 170 D6
Bellcroft CM8 177 A3
Belle Vue CM2 205 A1
Belle Vue Rd
Colchester CO1 109 E1
Ipswich IP4 17 F6
Sudbury CO10 33 F7
Wivenhoe CO7 137 C1
Bellevue Terr CO9 76 E2
Bellfield Ave CO7 186 A7
Bellfield Cl CO7 186 A8
Bellingham Bldgs CB10 22 D2
Bellingham Dr CO6 133 E5
Bellingham Pl CO5 158 C3
Bellmead CM1 205 B2
Bells Chase CM2 216 E6
Bells Cl CB11 43 E8
Bells Hill
Bishop's Stortford CM23 145 E7
Bures CO8 80 A4
Bells La CO10 2 C5
Bells Rd CO10 31 F6
Belmans Ct CO12 91 A2
Belmer Rd CM24 120 D4
Belmonde Dr CM1 205 E7
Belmont Cl CM1 205 E7
Belmont Cres CO4 110 C3
Belmont Ct 6 CB9 8 F7
Belmont Hill CB11 43 A1
Belmont Pl CO1 136 C5
Belmont Rd IP2 16 C1
Belsay Ct CB9 8 D8
Belsize Ave CO15 203 D6
Belstead Ave IP2 17 B3
Belstead Rd IP2 17 A3
Belstead Sch IP8 16 C2
Belsteads Farm La CM3 191 E2
Belvawney Cl CM1 204 E6
Belvedere Cl CM3 218 F7
Belvedere Ct
Chelmsford CM2 215 F8
Maldon CM9 220 F8
Belvedere Pl CM9 220 F8
Belvedere Rd
Danbury CM3 218 F7
Ipswich IP4 17 F7
Belvoir Ct 4 CB9 8 E8
Bembridge Cl CO15 188 F8
Bemerton Ct CO13 170 B6
Bemerton Gdns CO13 170 C6
Ben Sainty Ct CM8 177 A2
Benacre Rd IP3 18 A2
Bendalls Ct 18 CO11 86 D4
Bendlowes Rd CM7 72 C1
Benedict Dr CM1 204 E2
Benezet St IP1 17 B6
Benfield Way CM7 128 B2
Benhall Cl CO16 188 A4
Benhooks Ave CM23 145 E5
Benhooks Pl 1 CM23 145 E5
Bennet Ct CO4 136 E6
Bennett Cl
Braintree CM7 155 A8
Walton-on-t-N CO14 171 A8
Bennett Rd IP1 16 D8
Bennett Way CM3 194 A4
Bennett's La CM6 151 E2
Benskins Cl CM23 92 A8
Bensusan Ct CO2 135 B3
Bent Hill IP11 221 E3
Bent La IP4 18 E8
Bentall Cl CO9 103 F8
Bentalls Complex The CM9 210 B5
Bentfield End Cswy CM24 119 D7
Bentfield Gdns CM24 119 D7
Bentfield Gn CM24 119 D8
Bentfield Prim Sch CM24 119 D8
Bentfield Rd CM24 119 D7
Bentleigh Ct 5 CO1 136 D7
Bentley Ave CO15 203 E6
Bentley CE Prim Sch IP9 60 F7
Bentley Cl CM23 145 F5
Bentley Ct CO3 135 C7
Bentley La Belstead IP8 36 C6
Stutton IP9 61 E3
Bentley Rd
Little Bromley CO11 113 D3
Weeley Heath CO7,CO16 167 E6
Witham CM8 176 E4
Benton Cl Cressing CM77 155 E6
Witham CM8 195 A7
Berberis Wlk 5 CO4 136 E7
Berbice La CM6 123 D2
Berechurch Hall Rd CO2 162 D8
Berechurch Rd CO2 135 E2
Berefield Way 6 CO2 136 A1
Bergamot Rd CB9 8 C8
Bergen Ct CM9 220 E8
Bergholt Rd
Brantham CO11 86 B7
Colchester CO4 109 D2
Beridge Rd CO9 76 D2
Beriffe Pl CO7 185 F7
Berkeley Cl IP4 17 E8
Berkeley Gdns CO5 163 F7
Berkeley Rd CO15 188 F5
Berkely Dr CM2 205 F2
Berkley Cl CO4 110 C4
Bermuda Rd IP3 38 E7
Bernard Cl CO13 170 E6
Bernard Cres IP3 18 B2
Berners End CM6 151 B4
Berners St IP1 17 B6
Bernside CM7 127 F2
Berrimans Cl CO4 136 D6
Berry Cl IP3 18 F1
Berryfield Cotts CO1 136 B7
Bertram Ave CO16 168 D1
Berwick Ave CM1 205 B7
Beryl Rd CO12 90 D1
Beslyns Rd CM7 72 A3
Betjeman Cl CM7 155 A8
Betony Wlk CB9 8 D8
Betts Green Rd CO16 168 D5
Betty Cocker Gr CO10 34 B7
Betty Dent's Cnr CO16 141 C5
Beverley Ave CO5 201 E7
Beverley Ct 5 IP4 17 D6
Beverley Dr CO13 170 E7
Beverley Rd
Colchester CO3 135 D6
Ipswich IP4 17 F8
Bevington Mews CM8 177 B2
Bewick Ct CO9 51 E2
Bexhill Cl CO15 203 I8
Bexley Ave CO12 90 F1
Bibb Way IP1 17 A5
Bicknacre Rd CM3 218 F4
Bignells Croft CO4 110 C4
Bigods La CM6 123 D4
Bijou Cl CO5 179 D6
Bilberry End CB1 5 C7
Billers Chase CM1 206 A7
Billy's La CO7 58 D2
Bilsdale Cl CO4 110 C4
Bilton Rd CM1 204 F1

Binley Rd CM2 .... 205 F2
Birch Ave
Great Bentley CO7 .... 166 E8
Harwich CO12 .... 91 B3
Birch Bsns Ctr CO2 ..... 161 A7
Birch CE Prim Sch CO2 . 161 A4
Birch Cl Braintree CM7 ... 127 C2
Brightlingsea CO7 .... 185 E6
Clacton-on-S CO15 .... 188 C3
Witham CM8 .... 177 A4
Birch Dr Brantham CO11 ... 60 D1
Halstead CO9 .... 77 A2
Birch Rd CO2 .... 161 E5
Birch Rise CM8 .... 195 E6
Birch St Birch CO2 .... 161 A3
Nayland CO6 .... 56 A1
Birch Wood Cl CO5 ..... 201 D6
Birchalls CM24 .... 119 E8
Birchanger CE Prim Sch
CM23 .... 119 D2
Birchanger Ind Est
CM23 .... 119 B2
Birchanger La CM23 .... 119 D2
Birches The CO13 .... 170 E6
Birches Wlk CM2 .... 216 A2
Birchway CO2 .... 161 A2
Birchwood CM23 .... 119 D2
Birchwood Cl CO5 ...... 179 F5
Birchwood High Sch
CM23 .... 146 C8
Birchwood Rd
Cock Clarks CM3 .... 219 F2
Dedham CO7 .... 84 B3
Langham CO4 .... 84 A4
Birchwood Way CO5 .... 179 F5
Bird La CO5 .... 179 E4
Birdbrook Rd CO9 .... 28 A3
Birdbush Ave CB11 .... 43 D7
Birds Cl CB10 .... 3 A3
Birk Beck CM1 .... 205 C5
Birkdale Rise CM3 ...... 194 B4
Birkfield Cl IP2 .... 17 A4
Birkfield Dr IP2 .... 16 F2
Birkin Cl CO5 .... 179 C3
Biscay Cl CB9 .... 9 C7
Bishop Hall La CM1 ..... 205 B4
Bishop Mews IP8 .... 16 B2
Bishop Rd
Chelmsford CM1 .... 205 B3
Colchester CO2 .... 135 A3
Bishop William Ward CE
Prim Sch The CO6 ..... 109 B7
Bishop's Ave CM23 ..... 145 F3
Bishop's Cl 8 CB9 .... 8 E8
Bishop's Ct 7 CB9 .... 8 E8
Bishop's Hill IP3 .... 17 E4
Bishop's La CO9 .... 54 B3
Bishop's Stortford Bsns Ctr
CM23 .... 146 A6
Bishop's Stortford Coll
CM23 .... 145 E7
Bishop's Stortford High Sch
The CM23 .... 145 F4
Bishop's Stortford Mus*
CM23 .... 146 A6
Bishop's Stortford Sta
CM23 .... 146 A6
Bishops Ave CM7 .... 128 B3
Bishops Court Gdns
CM2 .... 205 E4
Bishops Dr CO16 .... 203 B6
Bishops Gdns CO16 ..... 203 A6
Bishops La CO5 .... 179 C7
Bishops Park Coll CO16 . 188 A3
Bishops Park Way
CM23 .... 145 B7
Bishops' CE & RC Prim Sch
The CM1 .... 205 F6
Bishopsgarth IP3 .... 17 F4
Bisley Cl CO16 .... 188 B6
Bittern Cl Ipswich IP2 ..... 16 E3
Kelvedon CO5 .... 158 D2
Bixley Dr IP4 .... 18 E5
Bixley La IP4 .... 18 F5
Bixley Rd IP3 .... 18 D3
Black Arches IP8 .... 36 E8
Black Barns IP11 .... 221 A7
Black Boy La CO11 .... 89 A4
Black Bread Cl CM7 .... 128 D3
Black Buoy Hill CO7 ..... 164 B7
Black Chapel La CM6 .... 151 E1
Black Horse La IP1 .... 17 C6
Black La CM7 .... 71 F2
Blackberry Rd CO3 ...... 134 C4
Blackbrook Rd CO6 ..... 109 C7
Blackbushe CM23 .... 119 C1
Blackdown Ave IP5 .... 18 F6
Blackfriars CO10 .... 33 D6
Blackfriars Ct 8 IP4 ...... 17 D5
Blackheath CO2 .... 163 A8
Blackhouse La CO10 ...... 34 C3
Blacklands Cl CB11 ...... 43 C7
Blackley La
Braintree CM3 .... 153 F3
Great Notley CM77 ...... 154 A4
Blacklock CM2 .... 206 A3
Blackman Way CM8 ..... 177 A1
Blacksmith Cl CM1 ..... 205 E8
Blacksmith's Cnr CO6 ... 109 B8
Blacksmith's Cnr CO4 .... 83 D4
Blacksmith's La CO12 .... 90 F2
Blacksmiths Cl CM23 .... 145 B5
Blacksmiths Hill CO10 .... 11 B4
Blacksmiths La
Bulmer Tye CO10 .... 32 F2
Shudy Camps CB1 .... 7 C6
Wickham Bishops CM8 ... 195 E5
Blackthorn Ave CO4 ..... 136 E7
Blackthorn Cl Ipswich IP3 . 18 E1
Writtle CM1 .... 204 A1
Blackthorn Rd
Harwich CO12 .... 90 F2
Witham CM8 .... 176 E4
Blackthorn Way CM9 .... 180 A2
Blackwater Ave CO4 ..... 110 E1
Blackwater Cl
Chelmsford CM1 .... 205 C6
Heybridge Basin CM9 .... 210 E3
Blackwater Dr CO5 ...... 201 A6
Blackwater La CM8 ..... 195 B8
Blackwater Way CM7 .... 128 A4
Blackwell Dr CM7 .... 127 C4
Bladen Dr IP4 .... 18 F5
Bladon Cl Braintree CM7 .. 127 E7
Tiptree CO5 .... 179 E5
Blaine Dr CO13 .... 170 F7
Blair Cl
Bishop's Stortford CM23 .. 145 C7
Rushmere St A IP4 .... 18 E5
Blair Par CB9 .... 8 E8
Blake Cl CO11 .... 86 B4
Blake Dr Braintree CM7 .. 128 C4
Clacton-on-S CO16 ...... 188 D6
Blake Rd CM8 .... 176 F5
Blamsters Cres CO9 .... 103 D8
Blanchard Cl CO13 ...... 170 A7
Blanche St IP4 .... 17 D6
Blandford Rd IP3 .... 18 D3
Blaxhall Ct 17 CB9 .... 8 E7
Blenheim Cl
Bicknacre CM3 .... 218 F2
Braintree CM7 .... 127 E7
Brantham CO11 .... 60 D1
Blenheim Ct
Bishop's Stortford CM23 .. 145 C7
Clacton-on-S CO15 ...... 188 D2
4 Ipswich IP1 .... 17 A7
Blenheim Dr CO2 .... 163 A8
Blenheim Rd
Clacton-on-S CO15 ...... 188 D2
Ipswich IP1 .... 17 A7
Blenheim Way CO5 ..... 179 F5
Blickling Cl IP2 .... 17 B2
Blickling Rd CM77 ...... 154 C8
Blind La Easthorpe CO2 .. 160 B4
Eight Ash G CO6 .... 134 A8
Goldhanger CM9 .... 211 C7
Howe Green CM2 .... 217 F4
Tolleshunt Knights CM9 .. 180 B1
Bliss Cl CM8 .... 194 F7
Blithe Ct CO7 .... 164 B8
Blofield Rd IP11 .... 221 A4
Blois Meadows Bsns Ctr
CB9 .... 27 C8
Blois Rd
Steeple Bumpstead CB9 .... 27 D8
Sturmer CB9 .... 9 F1
Bloom Cl CO13 .... 170 F6
Bloomfield Ave CO13 .... 170 E7
Bloomfield Ho CM7 ..... 128 A3
Bloomfield St IP4 .... 18 B6
Blooms Hall La CO10 ...... 2 F8
Blott Rise CM8 .... 194 F8
Blue Mill La CM9 .... 208 E4
Blue Mills Hill CM8 .... 195 B7
Blue Rd CO5 .... 179 C5
Bluebell Ave CO16 ...... 188 C4
Bluebell Cl Ipswich IP2 .... 16 E4
Witham CM8 .... 176 E3
Bluebell Gn 5 CM1 ..... 205 E7
Bluebell Way CO4 ...... 109 C2
Bluebridge Cotts CO9 .... 77 A1
Bluebridge Ind Est CO9 ... 77 B1
Bluegate La IP9 .... 60 B7
Bluehouse Ave CO16 .... 188 A4
Bluestem Rd IP3 .... 38 E8
Blundens The CO6 .... 56 C6
Blunt's Hall Dr CM8 .... 176 D1
Blunts Hall Rd CM8 .... 176 D1
Blyford Rd CO16 .... 188 A4
Blyford Way IP11 .... 221 A4
Blyth Cl IP2 .... 17 A1
Blyth's Mdw CM7 .... 127 F3
Blyth's Way CM77 ...... 126 F2
Blythe La CO7 .... 164 B8
Blythwood Gdns CM24 .. 119 D6
Boadicea Cotts CO8 ...... 79 F6
Boadicea Way CO2 ...... 135 C4
Boars Tye Rd CM8 ...... 156 D6
Boatman Cl IP8 .... 36 E8
Bobbits La IP9 .... 36 F8
Bobbits Way CO7 .... 164 C8
Bober Ct CO2 .... 163 B7
Bocking Church Street Prim
Sch CM7 .... 127 F8
Bocking End CM7 .... 127 F3
Bocking Pl CM7 .... 127 F3
Bocking's Gr CO16 ..... 188 B5
Bockings Elm Par CO16 . 188 B5
Bodiam Cl IP3 .... 18 D4
Bodiam Rd IP3 .... 18 D4
Bodiam Wlk 3 CB9 .... 8 E8
Bodmin Rd CM1 .... 205 D5
Bogmoor Rd SG8 .... 39 A8
Bohun Cl CM3 .... 173 F7
Bois Field Terr CO9 ...... 76 E2
Bois Hall Gdns CO9 ...... 76 F3
Boley Dr CO15 .... 189 A4
Boley Rd CO6 .... 106 A8
Boleyn Way
Boreham CM3 .... 192 F1
Clacton-on-S CO15 ...... 203 F8
Haverhill CB9 .... 8 D7
Boleyns Ave CM7 .... 127 F6
Bolford St CM6 .... 69 F2
Bolingbroke Cl CM3 .... 173 F7
Bolton La IP4 .... 17 D6
Bond St Chelmsford CM2 .. 205 C2
Ipswich IP4 .... 17 D5
Bonham Cl CO15 .... 189 A5
Bonington Chase CM1 .. 205 E6
Bonneting La CM23 ...... 92 B8
Bonnington Rd IP3 .... 17 F1
Boone Pl CM8 .... 177 A2
Boons Cl CM3 .... 206 E8
Booth Ave CO4 .... 136 C8
Borda Cl CM1 .... 205 A5
Boreham Ind Est CM3 ... 192 F2
Boreham Prim Sch CM3 . 206 F8
Boreham Rd
Great Leighs CM3 .... 174 B7
Little Waltham CM3 ...... 174 B2
Borehamgate CO10 .... 33 F7
Borley Rd CO10 .... 15 B4
Borough La CB11 .... 43 D8
Borradale Ct CB9 .... 27 B6
Borrowdale Ave IP4 ...... 17 E8
Boscawen Gdns CM7 ... 128 C4
Boscombe Ct CO15 ..... 189 F6
Boss Hall Bsns Pk IP1 .... 16 E7
Boss Hall Rd IP1 .... 16 E7
Bostock Rd IP2 .... 17 C1
Boston Rd IP4 .... 17 F7
Boswells Dr CM2 .... 205 C2
Boswells Sch The CM1 .. 205 D6
Botanical Way CO16 .... 187 A5
Botany Dr CM7 .... 128 D3
Botany La CO16 .... 168 B5
Boucheries Pl CO5 ..... 159 D2
Bouchers Mead CM1 .... 205 F7
Bouchiers Barn Visitors Ctr*
CO6 .... 130 D7
Boudicca Mews 5 CM2 .. 205 B1
Boudicca Wlk CO7 ..... 137 C3
Boulton Cotts CM9 ..... 210 B5
Boundary Rd
Bishop's Stortford CM23 .. 146 A5
Colchester CO4 .... 136 F4
Sturmer CB9 .... 9 D5
Wivenhoe CO7 .... 137 A4
Bounderby Gr CM1 ..... 204 E7
Bounstead Hill CO2 ..... 162 C5
Bounstead Rd CO2 ..... 162 D7
Bourchier Ave CM7 ..... 128 D5
Bourchier Way CO9 .... 103 D8
Bourne Cl CO9 .... 103 D8
Bourne Ct Braintree CM7 . 128 D1
Colchester CO2 .... 136 A4
Bourne Hill IP2 .... 37 B7
Bourne Mill* CO2 ...... 136 B4
Bourne Rd
Colchester CO2 .... 136 B4
Haverhill CB9 .... 9 B8
West Bergholt CO6 ...... 108 E2
Bourne Terr IP2 .... 37 B8
Bourne The CM23 ...... 146 A8
Bournebridge Hill CO9 .. 103 B6
Bournemouth Rd CO15 .. 189 F6
Bouverie Rd CM2 .... 216 B8
Bovills Way CO16 ...... 168 C1
Bovingdon Rd CM7 ..... 101 D2
Bowdens La CO6 .... 80 F7
Bower Gdns CM9 .... 209 F3
Bower Hall Dr CB9 .... 27 B6
Bower Hall La CO5 ..... 183 F1
Bowers Cl CM8 .... 156 E3
Bowes Rd CO7 .... 137 D1
Bowland Dr IP8 .... 16 C1
Bowling Cl 14 CM23 .... 145 F6
Bowling Green Ct IP11 .. 221 E4
Bowmans Pk CO9 .... 51 E4
Bowsers La CB10 .... 5 C3
Bowthorpe Cl IP1 .... 17 B7
Box Mill La CO9 .... 76 E3
Boxford Ct
Felixstowe IP11 .... 221 A4
Haverhill CB9 .... 8 E7
Boxhouse La CO7 .... 84 C5
Boxted Ave CO16 .... 188 C4
Boxted CE Prim Sch CO4 . 82 F7
Boxted Church Rd CO6 ... 82 C5
Boxted Rd
Colchester CO4 .... 109 E6
Great Horkesley CO6 ..... 82 C3
Boxted Straight Rd CO4 .. 83 A5
Boyd Cl 1 CM23 .... 146 B8
Boydell's Dairy Farm*
CM7 .... 100 E8
Boydin Cl CM8 .... 194 E8
Boydlands IP9 .... 35 A1
Boyes Croft CM6 .... 123 D1
Boyles Ct CO2 .... 163 B7
Boyne Dr CM1 .... 205 D6
Boyton Rd IP3 .... 18 B1
Boyton Vineyard* CO10 .. 10 D5
Boyton's La CB10 .... 26 A1
Boytons Acre CB11 .... 43 D8
Bracken Way CO5 ...... 163 B2
Brackenbury Cl IP1 ...... 17 B8
Brackenden Dr CM1 .... 205 D7
Brackenhayes Cl IP2 ..... 17 B3
Brackens The CO4 ...... 110 B3
Brackley Cl IP11 .... 221 C5
Bracks La CO6 .... 131 F3
Bradbrook Cotts CO6 ... 108 F4
Bradbury Dr CM7 .... 127 D3
Braddy Ct CO5 .... 158 C2
Bradfield Prim Sch CO11 . 87 E1
Bradfield Rd CO11 ..... 115 B7
Bradford St
Braintree CM7 .... 128 A4
Chelmsford CM2 .... 205 A1
Bradfords Ct CM7 ...... 128 A4
Brading Ave CO15 ..... 189 A7
Bradley Cl CM6 .... 123 C2
Bradley Comm CM23 .... 119 C3
Bradley Mews 1 CB10 .... 22 F2
Bradley St 7 IP2 .... 17 C4
Bradwell Ct CM77 ...... 155 C8
Braemar Ave CM2 ...... 216 B8
Braemore Cl CO4 .... 110 D3
Braggon's Hill IP29 .... 2 B8
Brain Rd CM8 .... 176 E3
Brain Valley Ave CM77 .. 155 B6
Braintree Cnr CO9 .... 75 F6
Braintree Coll CM7 ..... 128 A5
Braintree Ent Ctr CM7 .. 127 D5
Braintree Foyer The 3
CM7 .... 127 F2
Braintree Freeport Sta
CM77 .... 128 B1
Braintree Mus & Heritage
Ctr* CM7 .... 127 F3
Braintree Rd
Cressing CM77 .... 155 E7
Felsted CM6 .... 152 C6
Gosfield CO9 .... 102 E5
Great Bardfield CM7 ...... 72 B1
Great Dunmow CM6 ..... 124 A1
Shalford CM7 .... 100 E6
Terling CM3 .... 174 E5
Wethersfield CM7 .... 73 D2
Witham CM8 .... 176 F4
Braintree Sta CM7 ...... 128 A2
Braintree Town FC CM7 . 128 C2
Braiswick CO4 .... 109 C2
Braiswick La CO4 ...... 109 D4
Braithwaite Dr CO4 .... 109 F2
Bramble Ct CM8 .... 176 E4
Bramble Dr IP3 .... 18 E1
Bramble La CM6 .... 151 F8
Bramble Rd CM8 ...... 176 E4
Brambledown CO5 ..... 201 C7
Brambles CO14 .... 171 B7
Brambles The
Bishop's Stortford CM23 .. 145 C6
Braintree CM7 .... 127 E3
Colchester CO3 .... 134 F3
Bramblewood 1 IP8 ...... 16 C2
Bramford La IP1 .... 16 F8
Bramford Rd IP1 .... 16 E8
Bramhall Cl IP2 .... 16 D1
Bramley Chase IP4 .... 18 B7
Bramley Cl Alresford CO7 . 165 B8
Braintree CM7 .... 128 A1
Colchester CO3 .... 135 B7
Bramley Pl CM2 .... 216 D7
Bramley Rd CB9 .... 8 D7
Bramleys The CO6 ..... 131 A3
Bramston Cl CM2 ...... 216 F8
Bramston Gn CM8 ..... 176 F4
Bramston Wlk CM8 .... 176 F4
Bramwoods Rd CM2 ... 216 E8
Bran End Fields CM6 ... 124 D7
Brancaster Dr CM77 ... 154 C6
Brand Ct CM7 .... 127 F7
Brand Dr CO5 .... 163 B3
Brandon Rd
Braintree CM7 .... 127 D2
Felixstowe IP11 .... 221 A4
Brands Cl CO10 .... 34 C5
Bransby Gdns IP4 .... 17 E7
Branscombe Cl CO13 ... 170 E5
Branston Ct CO16 ..... 188 C4
Branston Rd CO15 ..... 188 D3
Brantham Hill CO11 ..... 86 C8
Brantham Mill Ind Est
CO11 .... 86 B7
Braxted La
Great Braxted CM8 ...... 178 C1
Great Totham CM8,CM9 .. 196 D8
Braxted Park Rd
Rivenhall CM8 .... 177 E4
Tiptree CO5 .... 178 E2
Braxted Rd CM8 .... 196 A6
Braybrooke Gdns CB11 .. 43 D8
Brazier's Wood Rd IP3 ... 38 B8
Braziers Cl CM2 .... 216 C3
Braziers Quay CM23 ... 146 A6
Breach La CM6 .... 97 B2
Breachfield Rd CO2 .... 135 C2
Bream Ct CO4 .... 110 F1
Brecon Cl IP2 .... 17 B2
Bredfield Cl IP11 ...... 221 B5
Bree Ave CO6 .... 132 E3
Brendon Ct CO5 .... 179 D4
Brendon Dr
Halstead CO9 .... 103 F8
Rushmere St A IP5 .... 18 F6
Brendon Pl CM1 .... 204 E1
Brent Cl
Frinton-on-S CO13 ...... 170 F7
Witham CM8 .... 176 E2
Brent Hall Rd CM7 .... 72 B6
Brentwood Rd CO15 .... 189 C6
Brett Cl IP1 .... 16 E8
Bretten Cl CO16 .... 188 A4
Brettenham Cres IP4 .... 17 D8
Bretts Cotts CO5 .... 178 F3
Brewers Cl CM23 ...... 145 C5
Brewery Fields CM2 .... 217 A5
Brewery La CM24 ...... 119 E7
Brewery Yd CM24 ...... 119 F7
Breydon Way IP3 .... 38 D7
Brian Bishop Cl CO14 ... 171 B8
Brian Cl CM2 .... 216 B6
Briar Rd CO7 .... 112 B4
Briardale Ave CO12 ...... 90 F3
Briarfields CO13 .... 170 C8
Briarhayes IP2 .... 17 B2
Briarhayes Cl IP2 .... 17 B3
Briarsford Ind Est CM8 .. 177 B1
Briarswood CM1 .... 205 D7
Briarwood Ave CO15 ... 189 F6
Briarwood End CO4 .... 110 B3
Brices Way CO10 .... 2 B5
Brick Cotts IP9 .... 62 F4
Brick End Villas CM6 ... 121 E8
Brick House La CM3 .... 192 E1
Brick House Rd CM9 ... 197 B7
Brick Kiln Cl CO6 ...... 131 A3
Brick Kiln La
Great Horkesley CO6 .... 109 C7
Rickling Green CB11 ...... 66 D1
Stebbing CM6 .... 124 D7
Thorrington CO7 .... 165 E5
Brick Kiln Rd
Chelmsford CM2 .... 217 C7
Colchester CO1 .... 109 E1
Harkstead IP9 .... 63 C5
Brick Kiln Way CM7 .... 128 D2
Brick Row SG8 .... 19 D3
Brick St CO3 .... 108 B1
Brickbarns CM3 .... 173 F7
Brickburn Cl CM6 ..... 152 C4
Brickfield Cl IP2 .... 17 D3
Brickhouse Cl CO5 ..... 201 B7
Brickhouse Rd CO6 ...... 78 A3
Brickmakers La CO4 .... 109 F2
Brickman's Hill CO11 .... 87 D3
Brickspring La CM9 .... 196 D7
Brickwall Ct CO6 ...... 105 B6
Bridewell Ind Est CO10 ... 12 C8
Bridewell St CO10 .... 12 C8
Bridge Cotts
Cavendish CO10 .... 1 D2
Ridgewell CO9 .... 29 B7
Bridge Croft CM3 ...... 172 F2
Bridge Ct CM9 .... 210 A3
Bridge End CB11 .... 43 A2
Bridge End La CM77 .... 154 C8
Bridge Foot CO10 .... 33 D6
Bridge Hall Rd CM7 .... 129 C3
Bridge Hill CO6 .... 107 C7
Bridge Hospl CM8 ...... 194 E8
Bridge Rd IP11 .... 221 E5
Bridge St
Bishop's Stortford CM23 .. 145 F7
Bures CO8 .... 55 F1
Coggeshall CO6 .... 130 F1
Finchingfield CM7 .... 72 C6
Great Bardfield CM7 ...... 72 B2
Great Yeldham CO9 .... 30 A1
Halstead CO9 .... 76 E2
Ipswich IP1 .... 17 C4
Saffron Walden CB10 ..... 22 D2
Witham CM8 .... 176 F1
Writtle CM1 .... 204 C1
Bridge Terr 1 CO10 ...... 33 F8
Bridgebrook Cl CO4 .... 110 D1
Bridgefield Cl CO4 ..... 136 C7
Bridgeford Ho 13 CM23 . 145 F6
Bridgwater Rd IP2 .... 16 D2
Bridlewalk CO3 .... 134 D6
Bridport Ave IP3 .... 18 D3
Bridport Rd CM1 ...... 205 D5
Bridport Way CM7 ..... 128 D4
Brierley Ave CO5 ...... 201 E7
Brierley Paddocks CO5 .. 201 E7
Bright Cl CO16 .... 188 D6
Brightlingsea Ct CO7 ... 136 F4
Brightlingsea Inf Sch
CO7 .... 185 E6
Brightlingsea Jun Sch
CO7 .... 185 E6
Brightlingsea Mus CO7 .. 185 F6
Brightlingsea Rd
Thorrington CO7 .... 165 E3
Wivenhoe CO7 .... 137 C4
Brighton Rd CO15 ..... 189 F6
Brightside CO13 .... 170 E7
Brightwell Cl IP11 ..... 221 A4
Brimstone Ct CM7 ..... 154 E8
Brimstone Rd IP8 .... 36 E8
Brindley Rd CO15 ..... 189 B8
Bringey The CM2 ...... 217 A6
Brinkley Cres CO4 ..... 110 D2
Brinkley Grove Prim Sch
CO4 .... 110 B5
Brinkley Grove Rd CO4 .. 110 A5
Brinkley La CO4 .... 110 B5
Brinkley Pl CO4 .... 109 F3
Brisbane Rd IP4 .... 18 D6
Brisbane Way CO2 ..... 136 A1
Brise Cl CM7 .... 128 A1
Bristol Ct CM8 .... 156 E3
Bristol Hill IP9 .... 91 B8
Bristol Rd
Colchester CO1 .... 136 A8
Ipswich IP4 .... 18 A7
Bristowe Ave CM2 ..... 217 A6
Britannia Cres CO7 .... 137 B1
Britannia Ct CO7 .... 137 B1
Britannia Pl 3 CM23 ... 145 E5
Britannia Rd IP4 .... 18 B6
Britric Cl CM6 .... 151 F6
Brittania Prim Sch IP4 ... 18 B5
Brittany Way CO2 ..... 136 B4
Britten Cl CO4 .... 136 E6
Britten Cres
Great Baddow CM2 ...... 216 F8
Witham CM8 .... 194 F7
Brixham Cl CO15 ...... 203 I8
Brixton La CB11,CM23 ... 93 B6
Broad La CO6 .... 82 C2
Broad Mdw 3 IP8 .... 16 C2
Broad Oakes Cl CB10 .... 44 E2

Broad Oaks Pk CO4 ... 110 E3
Broad Oke IP1 ... 17 B6
Broad Rd Braintree CM7 ... 128 B7
Wickham St P CO9 ... 53 B8
Broad Street Green Rd
CM9 ... 210 C7
Broadcroft Cres CB9 ... 8 F8
Broadfield CM23 ... 118 F2
Broadfield Rd CM22 ... 148 E7
Broadfields CO7 ... 137 C3
Broadlands CO13 ... 170 E3
Broadlands Way
Colchester CO4 ... 110 B1
Rushmere St A IP4 ... 18 F5
Broadleaf Ave CM23 ... 145 D4
Broadmead Rd CO4 ... 110 E1
Broadmere Cl CO15 ... 189 E7
Broadmere Rd IP1 ... 16 E8
Broadoaks Cres CM7 ... 128 D4
Broadstrood CO16 ... 187 B5
Broadwater Gdns IP9 ... 91 A8
Broadway
Clacton-on-S CO15 ... 203 G7
Glemsford CO10 ... 2 B5
Silver End CM8 ... 156 D4
Broadway Ct CM8 ... 156 D5
Broadway The CM6 ... 123 F3
Brock Cl Tiptree CO5 ... 179 E6
Witham CM8 ... 194 E8
Brockenhurst Way CM3 ... 218 F1
Brockham Cl CO16 ... 188 B6
Brockley Cres IP1 ... 16 D8
Brockley Rd CM2 ... 205 D2
Brocks Mead CM6 ... 122 E7
Brockwell La CO5 ... 158 C1
Brograve Cl CM2 ... 216 D3
Broke Hall Com Prim Sch
IP4 ... 18 E5
Broke Hall Gdns IP3 ... 18 D4
Broman's La CO5 ... 185 A2
Bromfield CB11 ... 43 E8
Bromley Cl
Clacton-on-S CO16 ... 188 D4
Ipswich IP2 ... 17 C3
Bromley Cnr CO11 ... 86 A2
Bromley Cross CO7 ... 112 B3
Bromley Hts CO4 ... 136 F8
Bromley La CB11 ... 43 B1
Bromley Rd
Colchester CO7,CO4 ... 111 C2
Elmstead CO7 ... 138 B5
Frating CO7 ... 139 A4
Lawford CO11 ... 86 B2
Brompton Gdns CM9 ... 220 E8
Bronte Cl CM7 ... 155 A8
Bronte Rd CM8 ... 176 F5
Brook Cl Braintree CM7 ... 127 C2
Great Totham CM9 ... 196 A3
Tiptree CO5 ... 179 F3
Woodham Walter CM9 ... 208 D2
Brook Cotts Boxted CO4 ... 82 E5
Stansted Mountfitchet
CM24 ... 119 E5
Brook End Rd N CM2 ... 206 A4
Brook End Rd S CM2 ... 206 B3
Brook Farm Caravan Pk
CO15 ... 188 E7
Brook Farm Cl CO9 ... 77 A1
Brook Farm La IP9 ... 62 D6
Brook Hall Rd CO5 ... 164 B5
Brook Hill
Little Waltham CM3 ... 191 B6
North End CM6 ... 151 F1
Brook La Chelmsford CM2 ... 206 B2
Felixstowe IP11 ... 221 F5
Galleywood CM2 ... 216 E3
Brook Mdw CO9 ... 51 D1
Brook Mdws CO5 ... 179 C4
Brook Mead CM3 ... 190 E8
Brook Rd Aldham CO6 ... 133 B7
Great Tey CO6 ... 132 C7
Stansted Mountfitchet
CM24 ... 119 E6
Tiptree CO5 ... 179 F3
Tolleshunt Knights CM9,
CO5 ... 180 A2
Brook Service Rd CB9 ... 9 A7
Brook St Chelmsford CM1 ... 205 B3
Colchester CO1 ... 136 B7
Colne Engaine CO6 ... 77 F1
Dedham CO7 ... 84 F7
Glemsford CO10 ... 2 B6
Great Bardfield CM7 ... 72 B2
Great Bromley CO7 ... 112 E1
Little Dunmow CM6 ... 151 D6
Manningtree CO11 ... 86 D4
Wivenhoe CO7 ... 164 C8
Brook Terr CO9 ... 51 E1
Brook Vale CO16 ... 187 B3
Brook View
Chelmsford CM2 ... 217 C6
Stansted Mountfitchet
CM24 ... 119 E5
Thaxted CM6 ... 70 A3
Brook Wlk CM8 ... 194 F8
Brookbank CM2 ... 216 E8
Brooke Ave CB10 ... 22 E2
Brooke Gdns CM23 ... 146 C7
Brooke Sq CM9 ... 210 A1
Brookes Nature Reserve*
CM77 ... 103 E2
Brookfield Rd IP1 ... 16 F8
Brookfields CM6 ... 124 D7
Brookhampton St CB10 ... 3 A5
Brookhill Way IP4 ... 18 F4
Brookhouse Bsns Pk IP2 ... 16 F6
Brookhouse Pl 3 CM23 ... 145 F8
Brookhouse Rd CO6 ... 132 B8
Brookhurst Cl CM2 ... 205 D3
Brookland CO5 ... 179 C4
Brooklands
Clacton-on-S CO15 ... 203 E6
Colchester CO1 ... 136 B7
Brooklands Gdns CO15 ... 203 E6
Brooklands Prim Sch
CO11 ... 86 D8
Brooklands Rd CO11 ... 86 D8
Brooklands Rise CO11 ... 86 D8
Brooklands Wlk CM2 ... 216 A7
Brooklyn Ct CO12 ... 91 C3
Brooklyn Mews CO12 ... 91 C3
Brooklyn Rd CO12 ... 91 C3
Brooks Hall Rd IP1 ... 17 A7
Brooks Malting 3 CO11 ... 86 D4
Brookside Cl CO2 ... 136 B4
Brooksies CB11 ... 40 F6
Brookview IP2 ... 36 E8
Broom Cres IP3 ... 17 F1
Broom Farm Rd CM22 ... 94 C2
Broom Field IP11 ... 221 C5
Broom Hill Rd IP1 ... 17 A8
Broom Knoll CO7 ... 60 C2
Broom St CO10 ... 34 B5
Broom Way
Abberton CO5 ... 163 B2
Capel St M IP9 ... 35 B2
Broomclose Villas CM7 ... 100 E5
Broome Gr CO7 ... 137 B2
Broome Way CO15 ... 203 F6
Broomfield CM8 ... 156 C5
Broomfield Comm IP8 ... 16 B6
Broomfield Cres CO7 ... 137 B2
Broomfield Hospl CM1 ... 191 A3
Broomfield Prim Sch
CM1 ... 191 B1
Broomfield Rd CM1 ... 205 A5
Broomgrove Inf & Jun Schs
CO7 ... 137 B2
Broomhall Cl CM1 ... 191 B2
Broomhall Rd CM1 ... 191 B2
Broomhayes IP2 ... 17 A2
Broomhill IP9 ... 62 D6
Broomhills Ind Est CM7 ... 127 D2
Broomhills Rd CO5 ... 201 D5
Brotherton Ave IP11 ... 221 A8
Broton Dr CO9 ... 76 E2
Brougham Glades CO3 ... 134 D5
Broughton Cl CO2 ... 135 C4
Broughton Rd IP1 ... 17 B7
Brown's End Rd CM6 ... 121 F7
Browning Cl CO3 ... 134 F6
Browning Rd
Braintree CM7 ... 155 A8
Brantham CO11 ... 86 C7
Brownings Ave CM1 ... 205 A5
Brownlow Rd IP11 ... 221 F4
Brownsea Way CO3 ... 135 A4
Bruce Gr CM2 ... 216 A7
Bruce Rd CM1 ... 204 B1
Bruff Cl CO4 ... 109 E2
Bruff Dr CO14 ... 171 A7
Bruges Cl CO12 ... 91 A1
Brundells Rd CO7 ... 139 A5
Brundon La CO10 ... 33 C7
Brunel Ct CO4 ... 110 C6
Brunel Rd Braintree CM7 ... 128 A1
Clacton-on-S CO15 ... 189 B8
Ipswich IP2 ... 16 F6
Brunel Way CO4 ... 110 C6
Brunswick House Cut
CO11 ... 87 A3
Brunswick Rd IP4 ... 17 F8
Brunwin Rd CM77 ... 126 F2
Brussels Cl CO12 ... 91 B1
Bryan Rd CM23 ... 145 F8
Bryanita Ct CO5 ... 179 D5
Bryanstone Mews CO3 ... 134 E5
Bryant Link CM2 ... 206 B4
Bryant's La CM9 ... 219 D7
Bryon Ave IP11 ... 221 A3
Buchan Cl CM7 ... 155 A8
Buck Hill CM77 ... 154 F6
Buck's Horns La IP8 ... 36 B6
Buckenhoe Rd CB10 ... 22 E3
Buckfast Ave CO13 ... 170 D6
Buckfast Cl 5 IP2 ... 17 A2
Buckingham Ct 2 CM2 ... 205 F4
Buckingham Dr CO4 ... 136 E7
Buckingham Rd CB9 ... 8 E6
Bucklesham Rd IP3 ... 18 E2
Buckley's La CO6 ... 131 E6
Buckleys CM2 ... 216 F7
Buckleys Cl CM8 ... 195 E5
Bucks La CO10 ... 12 B7
Buckwoods Rd CM7 ... 128 A1
Buddleia Cl IP2 ... 16 E4
Buddleia Ct CO7 ... 137 A2
Buffett Way CO4 ... 136 E6
Buglers Rise CM1 ... 215 B8
Buick Ave CO15 ... 203 D6
Building End Rd
Chrishall SG8 ... 19 C1
Duddenhoe End SG8 ... 40 B8
Bulford La CM77 ... 155 C5
Bulford Mill La CM77 ... 155 D5
Bull Hill Rd CO15 ... 188 F5
Bull La Langley CB11 ... 40 C2
Long Melford CO10 ... 15 E8
Maldon CM9 ... 210 A3
Tiptree CO5 ... 179 C3
Bullace Cl CO4 ... 110 D3
Bullen Wlk CM2 ... 216 C3
Bullfields CB11 ... 67 A8
Bullfinch Cl
Colchester CO4 ... 136 F8
Harwich CO12 ... 90 E1
Bullfinch Dr CO9 ... 77 A1
Bullock Wood Cl CO4 ... 110 D4
Bullocks La CO10 ... 33 E6
Bulls Cliff IP11 ... 221 D3
Bulls Lodge Cotts CM3 ... 192 B1
Bulmer Rd CO10 ... 33 C6
Bulmer Road Ind Est
CO10 ... 33 C6
Bulmer St CO10 ... 32 D4
Bulrush Cl CM7 ... 128 B1
Bulstrode Rd IP2 ... 17 D4
Bulwer Rd IP1 ... 17 A6
Bumfords La CM3,CM9 ... 208 A7
Bumpstead Rd CB9 ... 9 B4
Bundick's Hill CM1 ... 204 F3
Bung Row CM8 ... 178 C1
Bungalows The CM8 ... 176 F1
Bunting Cl CM2 ... 216 B5
Bunting Rd IP2 ... 16 D3
Buntingford Ct 2 CO2 ... 136 A1
Bunyan Rd CM7 ... 127 E3
Burdun Cl CM8 ... 194 D8
Bure Dr CM8 ... 176 D3
Buregate Rd IP11 ... 221 D2
Bures CE Prim Sch CO8 ... 79 F8
Bures Ct 16 CB9 ... 8 E7
Bures Ho CO8 ... 79 F8
Bures Rd
Great Cornard CO10 ... 34 B3
Nayland CO6 ... 81 B8
Bures Sta CO8 ... 79 E8
Burgate Cl CO16 ... 188 A4
Burgess Field CM2 ... 205 F4
Burghley Ave CM23 ... 145 C7
Burghley Cl
Great Notley CM77 ... 154 B6
4 Ipswich IP2 ... 17 A2
Burghley Way CM2 ... 216 C8
Burgundy Ct CM2 ... 205 C2
Burkitts Ct 8 CO10 ... 33 E7
Burkitts La CO10 ... 33 E7
Burley Rd CM23 ... 146 A4
Burlington Ho IP2 ... 17 B4
Burlington Rd
Colchester CO3 ... 135 E6
Ipswich IP1 ... 17 B6
Burmanny Cl CO15 ... 188 C3
Burnell Gate CM1 ... 206 A7
Burnells Way CM24 ... 119 E7
Burnet Cl IP8 ... 36 D8
Burnham Cl Ipswich IP4 ... 17 F7
Trimley St M IP11 ... 221 A7
Walton-on-t-N CO14 ... 171 B8
Burnham Ct CO15 ... 203 I8
Burnham Rd
Chelmsford CM1 ... 205 D5
Woodham Mortimer CM9,
CM3 ... 219 E5
Burns Ave CO3 ... 134 F6
Burns Cl CM9 ... 210 A1
Burns Cres CM2 ... 216 C8
Burnsall Cl CB11 ... 43 F8
Burnside Cres CM1 ... 205 B7
Burnstie Rd CM6 ... 152 F6
Burnt Dick Hill CO4 ... 82 D7
Burnt Oak Cnr CO7 ... 59 D1
Burnthouse Rd CO6 ... 105 E2
Burr Cl CO12 ... 90 C1
Burrell Rd IP2 ... 17 C4
Burroughs Piece Rd
CO10 ... 33 F7
Burrows Cl
Clacton-on-S CO16 ... 188 D6
Lawford CO11 ... 86 B4
Burrows Rd CO6 ... 105 B7
Burrs Rd CO15 ... 189 A7
Burrsville Com Inf Sch
CO15 ... 188 F6
Burrswood Pl CM9 ... 210 E3
Burstall Cl CO16 ... 188 B4
Burstall La IP8 ... 16 A6
Burton Cl CB9 ... 8 E7
Burton End CB9 ... 8 E7
Burton End Prim Sch CB9 ... 8 D7
Burton Pl CM2 ... 205 F4
Burton's Green Rd CO9 ... 104 B4
Burwood Ct CM2 ... 205 C1
Bury Cl Colchester CO1 ... 136 A8
Marks Tey CO6 ... 132 F4
Bury Fields CM6 ... 152 A5
Bury Gdns CB11 ... 20 A4
Bury La Chrishall SG8 ... 19 D1
Great Waltham CM3 ... 190 D8
Hatfield Peverel CM3 ... 193 F4
Bury Lodge La
Great Hallingbury CM22 ... 147 C7
Stansted Mountfitchet
CM24 ... 120 A2
Bury The CO16 ... 187 A4
Bury Water La CB11 ... 42 E1
Burywater Cotts CB11 ... 42 F1
Burywoods CO4 ... 109 B3
Bush Gr CO10 ... 33 C6
Bush La CB10 ... 46 D2
Bush Rd CB10 ... 46 E2
Bushell Way CO13 ... 170 E6
Bushey Cl IP9 ... 35 A1
Bushey Ley CM7 ... 128 D3
Butcher's Hill CB10 ... 3 A4
Butcher's View CO5 ... 182 E6
Butchers La
Capel St M IP9 ... 35 B1
Walton-on-t-N CO14 ... 171 B7
Butchers Pasture CM6 ... 122 F5
Butchers Row CB10 ... 22 D1
Bute Ct CB9 ... 8 F6
Butler Cl CB11 ... 22 E1
Butler Rd CO9 ... 76 D2
Butler's Hall La CM23 ... 145 B3
Butler's La CO11 ... 88 E1
Butlers Cl CM1 ... 191 B2
Butlers La CB10 ... 23 C5
Butlers Way CO9 ... 30 A1
Butley Cl IP2 ... 36 F8
Butley Ct 1 CB9 ... 8 E6
Butley Rd IP11 ... 221 C3
Butt La Maldon CM9 ... 210 A3
Manuden CM23 ... 92 E2
Butt Rd Colchester CO3 ... 135 E5
Great Cornard CO10 ... 34 B6
Stoke-by-N CO6 ... 56 C5
Butt's Green Rd CM2 ... 217 F3
Butter Market IP1 ... 17 C6
Buttercup Cl IP8 ... 16 C2
Buttercup Wlk CM8 ... 176 E4
Butterfield Rd CM3 ... 206 E8
Butterfly Gdns IP4 ... 18 E5
Buttermarket Sh Ctr 3
IP1 ... 17 C5
Buttermere CM77 ... 154 C7
Buttleys La CM6 ... 149 F8
Butts La CM3 ... 218 F7
Butts Way CM2 ... 215 E3
Buxey Cl CO5 ... 201 B7
Buxton Cotts CO6 ... 132 A3
Buxton Rd
Coggeshall CO6 ... 130 F3
Colchester CO2 ... 136 A3
Bylam La IP9 ... 63 C6
Byland Cl IP2 ... 17 A2
Bylands Cl CM23 ... 145 D6
Byng Cres CO16 ... 142 B1
Byng Ct CO2 ... 136 A1
Byng Gdns CM7 ... 128 C4
Byng Ho CO16 ... 142 B1
Bypass Rd CO16 ... 187 B5
Byrd's Farm La CB10 ... 22 E3
Byron Ave CO3 ... 134 F7
Byron Cl CM7 ... 155 A8
Byron Dr CM8 ... 195 E5
Byron Rd CM2 ... 205 D2
Byrony Cl CM8 ... 176 D4

C

Cadenhouse Mews CO3 ... 134 E7
Cadmus Rd IP1 ... 16 D7
Caernarvon Wlk CB9 ... 8 E8
Cage La Boxted CO4 ... 83 B4
Felixstowe IP11 ... 221 D5
Cairns Rd CO2 ... 136 B2
Caithness Cl IP4 ... 18 B8
Calamint Rd CM8 ... 176 D3
Caldbeck Way CM77 ... 154 C6
Caledonia Rd IP9 ... 91 B8
Calford Dr CB9 ... 8 C8
California Cl CO4 ... 110 B4
California Rd CO11 ... 87 A4
Callis Ct CO10 ... 12 C8
Callis St CO10 ... 12 B8
Callowood Croft CM3 ... 220 D1
Calverley Cl CM23 ... 145 E4
Calves La CO6 ... 56 B8
Cam Way CM8 ... 176 D2
Camberley Rd IP4 ... 18 D7
Camberton Rd CM7 ... 127 E6
Camborne Cl CM1 ... 205 E5
Cambrai Rd CO2 ... 135 D4
Cambria Cl CO11 ... 87 B3
Cambridge Ave CO9 ... 75 E8
Cambridge Ct
Clacton-on-S CO15 ... 188 E4
Frinton-on-S CO13 ... 171 A5
Cambridge Dr IP2 ... 16 F1
Cambridge Ho CB9 ... 9 B6
Cambridge Rd
Clacton-on-S CO15 ... 188 E4
Colchester CO3 ... 135 C5
Felixstowe IP11 ... 221 F4
Frinton-on-S CO13 ... 171 A5
Littlebury CB11 ... 21 F4
Newport CB11 ... 43 A2
Stansted Mountfitchet
CM24 ... 119 E8
Cambridge Way CO8 ... 79 F8
Camden Rd IP3 ... 18 B4
Camellia Ave CO16 ... 188 C4
Camellia Cl 2 CM1 ... 205 F6
Camellia Cres CO16 ... 188 C5
Camellia Ct 5 CO4 ... 136 D8
Camelot Cl CM1 ... 204 F5
Cameron Cl
Braintree CM7 ... 127 F8
Long Melford CO10 ... 15 C6
Camoise Cl CO9 ... 50 B7
Camomile Way CO4 ... 109 C2
Camp Rd CO7 ... 139 A7
Campbell Cl CM2 ... 216 A7
Campbell Ct CO3 ... 135 D6
Campbell Dr CO4 ... 110 E2
Campbell Rd Ipswich IP3 ... 18 C1
Witham CM8 ... 176 F5
Campernell Cl CO7 ... 185 F8
Campion Rd
Colchester CO2 ... 136 A5
Ipswich IP2 ... 16 F4
Campion Way CM8 ... 176 E3
Campions Hill CO6 ... 81 D8
Campions The CM24 ... 119 E8
Camps Rd Bartlow CB1 ... 6 B7
Haverhill CB9 ... 8 F7
Helions Bumpstead CB9 ... 8 B1
Camulodunum Way
CO2 ... 135 C1
Camulus Cl
Braintree CM7 ... 128 A2
Colchester CO2 ... 135 A2
Camwood Gdns IP3 ... 18 B4
Can Bridge Way CM2 ... 205 C1
Canberra Cl
Chelmsford CM1 ... 204 E5
9 Colchester CO2 ... 136 A1
Ipswich IP4 ... 18 D6
Candlet Gr IP11 ... 221 D5
Candlet Rd IP11 ... 221 D6
Candytuft Rd CM1 ... 205 F6
Canes Mill Ct CM7 ... 128 A5
Canfield CM23 ... 145 E8
Canfield Rd CM6 ... 149 D1
Canford Cl CM2 ... 216 E7
Cangle Junc CB9 ... 9 A8
Canham St 8 IP1 ... 17 B6
Canhams Rd CO10 ... 34 C5
Cann Hall Prim Sch
CO16 ... 188 D6
Canning St CO12 ... 91 D5
Cannock Mill Ct CO2 ... 136 C4
Cannon Circ CM7 ... 73 D6
Cannon Leys CM2 ... 216 D3
Cannon Rd CO1 ... 136 B6
Cannon St CO1 ... 136 B6
Cannons Cl
Bishop's Stortford CM23 ... 119 A1
Colchester CO2 ... 135 D4
Cannons Mead CM24 ... 119 D7
Cannons Mill La CM23 ... 119 A1
Cannons The CO2 ... 135 D4
Canonium Mews CO5 ... 158 C2
Canons Cl CM3 ... 218 E1
Cansey La CO11 ... 114 E6
Cant Way CM7 ... 128 C1
Canterbury Cl IP2 ... 36 F8
Canterbury Grange
CM7 ... 127 F8
Canterbury Rd
Colchester CO2 ... 136 A5
Holland-on-S CO15 ... 189 E5
Sudbury CO10 ... 15 C2
Canterbury Way CM1 ... 204 E4
Canuden Rd CM1 ... 204 E2
Canvey Wlk CM1 ... 205 E6
Canwick Gr CO2 ... 136 C4
Cap Pillar Cl CO7 ... 137 B2
Cape Cl CO3 ... 134 F5
Capel Cl Chelmsford CM1 ... 205 B7
Rayne CM77 ... 126 F2
Capel Dr IP11 ... 221 A4
Capel Ho CO4 ... 109 F4
Capel Pk CO13 ... 170 E7
Capel Rd Colchester CO3 ... 135 C5
Rayne CM77 ... 126 F2
Capel St Mary CE Prim Sch
IP9 ... 35 A1
Caper La CO2 ... 160 F4
Capons La CM3 ... 219 A5
Capstan Pl CO4 ... 136 D5
Captains Rd CO5 ... 201 B6
Captains Wood Rd CM8,
CM9 ... 196 A3
Caracalla Way CO4 ... 110 B6
Card's Rd CM2 ... 217 C6
Cardiff Ave IP2 ... 17 B2
Cardigan St IP1 ... 17 B7
Cardinal Cl CO4 ... 137 A7
Cardinal Pk IP1 ... 17 C5
Cardinal St IP1 ... 17 C5
Cardinals Ct IP11 ... 221 E3
Careless Ct 21 CM23 ... 145 F7
Carisbrooke Ave CO15 ... 189 A7
Carleton Ct CO5 ... 163 E8
Carlisle Cl CO1 ... 136 A8
Carlton Cl CO9 ... 30 A2
Carlton Rd CO15 ... 189 B5
Carlton Way IP4 ... 17 E8
Carmarthen Cl IP2 ... 17 A2
Carmel St CB10 ... 3 D2
Carmelite Way CM9 ... 209 F2
Carmen St CB10 ... 3 D3
Carnarvon Rd CO15 ... 188 F3
Carnation Cl CM1 ... 205 F5
Carnation Dr CB10 ... 22 F2
Carolbrook Rd IP2 ... 16 E1
Carolina Way CO5 ... 179 D5
Caroline Cl CO7 ... 137 C3
Carpenters Dr CM77 ... 154 B7
Carpenters The CM23 ... 145 B5
Carr St IP4 ... 17 D6
Carraways CM8 ... 195 B8
Carriage Cl IP11 ... 221 A8
Carriage Dr CM1 ... 205 E7
Carriers Cl CO5 ... 201 A7
Carriers Ct CO7 ... 59 D3
Carrigans CM23 ... 145 E8
Carrington Ct CO5 ... 201 D7
Carrington Ho CO5 ... 201 D7
Carrington Way CM7 ... 127 F8
Carringtons Rd CO7 ... 112 D4
Carrs Rd CO15 ... 188 D3
Carsey Hill CB1 ... 7 B6
Carshalton End CO3 ... 134 F4
Carsons Dr CO10 ... 34 D5
Carstone Pl CM1 ... 204 F2
Cartbridge Cl CO14 ... 171 B8
Carters Cl CO16 ... 188 B3
Carters Croft CB10 ... 6 B1
Carters Hill Boxted CO4 ... 83 A6
Manuden CM23 ... 93 A1
Carters La Henham CM22 ... 94 F5
Wickham Bishops CM8 ... 195 F6
Carters Leys CM23 ... 145 D8

Carters Vineyard* CO4 ....82 E5
Cartwright Wlk CM2 ....205 F2
Case La IP9 ....60 D7
Cassino Rd
  Chelmsford CM1 ......204 E6
  Colchester CO2 ....135 C3
Castle Ave CB9 ....8 E7
Castle Bailey 16 CO1 ..135 F7
Castle Camps CE Prim Sch
  CB1 ....7 E3
Castle Cl
  Castle Hedingham CO9 ...51 E4
  Great Leighs CM3 ......173 F6
Castle Cross CB10 ....22 E2
Castle Ct CO15 ....188 E3
Castle Hill Dedham CO7 ...84 F4
  Saffron Walden CB10 ...22 D2
Castle Hill Mid Sch CB9 ...8 D7
Castle Hill Pk CO16 ....188 E7
Castle Ho* CO7 ....85 A5
Castle La*
  Castle Hedingham CO9 ...51 F4
  Haverhill CB9 ....8 F8
Castle Manor Upper Sch
  CB9 ....8 E8
Castle Mdw CO9 ....51 D2
Castle Rd
  Clacton-on-S CO15 ....188 E3
  Colchester CO1 ....136 A7
Castle St
  Bishop's Stortford CM23 .145 F6
  Colchester CO1 ....136 A7
  Saffron Walden CB10 ...22 D2
Castle View CM23 ....146 A7
Castle Way CO16 ....187 A4
Castle Wlk Haverhill CB9 ...8 E8
  Stansted Mountfitchet
  CM24 ....119 E6
Castlefields CM23 ......173 F7
Castlegate St CO12 .....91 E6
Castleward Cl CO7 .....164 C8
Caswell Mews CM2 .....205 F2
Cat's La CO10 ....34 A7
Catchpole Ct 12 CO10 ...33 E7
Catchpole La CM6 .....196 A4
Catchpool Rd CO1 .....135 F8
Caterham Cl CO16 .....188 C6
Cates Cnr CB10 ....22 E1
Cathedral CE Prim Sch The
  CM1 ....205 C3
Cathedral Wlk CM1 ....205 B3
Catherine Cl CO15 ....189 A5
Catherine Hunt Way
  CO2 ....135 C2
Catherine May Ct CO15 .188 F3
Catherines Cl CM3 ....174 A6
Catons La CO10 ....22 D2
Cattawade St CO11 ....86 C7
Cattermole Ct CO16 ...188 B3
Catts Cl IP9 ....61 F2
Cattsfield IP9 ....61 F2
Cauldwell Ave IP4 .....17 F7
Cauldwell Hall Rd IP14 ..18 A6
Causer Jans CM2 ......152 F1
Causeway Bsns Ctr The 26
  CM23 ....145 F7
Causeway Cl CO10 ......2 C5
Causeway End CO10 ....1 C3
Causeway End Rd CM6 ..152 C3
Causeway Reach CO15 ..188 E7
Causeway The
  1 Bishop's Stortford
  CM23 ....146 A7
  Braintree CM7 ....127 F4
  Colchester CO4 ....110 C1
  Finchingfield CM7 ....72 D6
  Great Baddow CM2 ...216 F7
  Great Dunmow CM6 ...123 D2
  Halstead CO9 ....76 E1
  Harkstead SG9 ....64 B1
  Haverhill CB9 ....8 E7
  Henham CB11 ....68 B7
  Langley CB11 ....40 C3
  Maldon CM9 ....204 D1
  Ridgewell CO9 ....28 F8
  Toppesfield CO9 ......50 B7
  Ulting CM9 ....208 D5
Causton Jun Sch IP11 ..221 C6
Causton Rd CO1 ....135 E8
Caustons Cl CO10 .....34 C5
Cavendish Ave CO2 ...136 C3
Cavendish CE Prim Sch
  CO10 ....1 C2
Cavendish Cl
  2 Haverhill CB9 ....9 B8
  3 Saffron Walden CB10 ...22 F2
Cavendish Dr
  Clacton-on-S CO16 ...188 A4
  Lawford CO11 ....86 B3
Cavendish Gdns
  Braintree CM7 ....128 C5
  Chelmsford CM2 .....205 E3
Cavendish La CO10 .....1 F3
Cavendish Rd Clare CO10 .12 D7
Cavendish St IP3 ......17 F5
Cavendish Way CO10 ...33 F7
Cawkell Cl CM24 ......119 D7
Cawkwell Cl CM2 .....206 A4
Cawley Cl CO10 ....34 C5
Caxton Pl CO9 ....76 E2
Cecil Cl CM23 ....146 D7
Cecil Rd IP1 ....17 B7
Cecilia St IP1 ....17 B5
Cedar Ave
  Brightlingsea CO7 ....185 E7
  Chelmsford CM1 .....205 A3
  Tiptree CO5 ....179 C7

Cedar Ave W CM1 ......205 A3
Cedar Chase CM9 .....210 C5
Cedar Cl Brantham CO11 ..60 D1
  Great Dunmow CM6 ...123 A1
  Walton-on-t-N CO14 ..171 A7
Cedar Cres CO11 ......86 C3
Cedar Ct
  Bishop's Stortford CM23 .118 F1
  West Bergholt CO6 ...108 D5
Cedar Dr CM8 ....177 A5
Cedar Pk CM23 ....149 C7
Cedar Way CO7 ....166 E8
Cedars Rd 8 CO2 .....135 F6
Cedars The CO7 ......102 E7
Celandine Ct CO4 ....109 C2
Cemetery La
  Saffron Walden CB10 ...59 B2
  Ipswich IP4 ....17 E8
Cemetery Rd
  Bishop's Stortford CM23 .145 F6
  Ipswich IP4 ....17 E6
Centaury Cl CO13 ....134 C7
Centenary Way CO15,
  CO16 ....168 E1
Central Arc CB10 .....22 D1
Central Ave
  Frinton-on-S CO13 ...171 A6
  Ipswich IP3 ....38 E8
Central Ho CO12 ......91 D4
Central Maltings The 5
  CO11 ....86 D4
Central Par CO15 .....188 F2
Central Sq 7 CM1 ....205 B2
Centre The
  2 Colchester CO4 ....136 E7
  Halstead CO9 ....76 E2
  Ipswich IP2 ....17 A1
  Tiptree CO5 ....179 D5
Centurion Ho 2 CO2 ..135 F6
Centurion Way CO2 ...135 A3
Chadburn Rd CO10 ....15 D8
Chaffinch Dr CO12 ...91 C5
Chaffinch Gdns CO4 ..136 F8
Chaffinch Way CO9 ...77 A1
Chaffix CM6 ....152 C6
Chaffix Cl CM6 ......152 C6
Chainey Pieces 12 CB9 ...8 F7
Chalfont Rd CO4 .....110 C3
Chalfont Sq 14 IP4 ...17 D6
Chalklands
  Howe Green CM2 ....217 D3
  Saffron Walden CB10 ...22 E3
Chalkners Cl 14 IP9 ...35 A1
Chalks Rd CM8 ....176 F4
Chalkstone Mid Sch CB9 ...9 A8
Chalkstone Way CB9 ...9 D7
Chalky La SG8 ....19 D2
Challenge Way CO1 ...136 A3
Challis La CM7 ....155 A8
Chalon St IP1 ....17 B5
Chamberlain Ave CO16 ..171 B7
Chamberlain Way IP8 ..16 C2
Chamley Ct CO15 .....189 D5
Chancellor Ave CM2 ..206 B4
Chancery Gr CO2 ....163 A8
Chancery Pl CM1 ....204 B1
Chancery Rd IP1 .....17 B5
Chandlers Cl
  Bishop's Stortford CM23 .145 C4
  Clacton-on-S CO16 ..188 B3
  West Mersea CO5 ....201 C7
Chandlers Quay CM9 ..210 A3
Chandlers Row CO1 ..136 C5
Chandlers Way CO7 ..147 D2
Chant Ct CO4 ....110 D3
Chanterelle CO4 .....110 B3
Chantry Cl
  Bishop's Stortford CM23 .145 E8
  Colchester CO1 ......188 E7
Chantry Dr CO6 .....80 E4
Chantry Gn IP9 ......16 D3
Chantry High Sch & Sixth
  Form Ctr IP2 ....16 F3
Chantry Jun & Inf Sch
  IP2 ....16 E3
Chantry La CM3 .....193 A3
Chantry Mount CM23 ..145 E8
Chantry Rd CM23 ....145 E8
Chantry The
  6 Bishop's Stortford
  CM23 ....145 F8
  Colchester CO3 ......135 C7
Chantry View CM8 ....195 A7
Chantry Villas CM3 ..193 A2
Chanute Ave CM7 ....73 D7
Chapel Cl IP9 ....35 A1
Chapel Croft CO11 ...111 E7
Chapel Cut CO11 ....87 A4
Chapel Dr CM3 ......191 B6
Chapel End Way CO9 ..28 B2
Chapel Hill
  Belchamp Walter CO10 ..31 D4
  Braintree CM7 ....128 B2
  Halstead CO9 ....76 D2
  Stansted Mountfitchet
  CM24 ....119 E6
Chapel Hill Bsns & Ret Pk
  CM7 ....128 C1
Chapel Hill Prim Sch
  CM7 ....128 B2
Chapel La Belstead IP8 ...36 C7
  Boxted CO4 ....83 A3
  Colchester CO11 .....111 B1
  Elmstead CO7 ....138 A6
  Great Bromley CO7 ..139 A5
  Great Oakley CO10 ..34 C2
  Heybridge Basin CM9 .210 E2
  Kirby Cross CO13 ...170 A6

Chapel La continued
  Little Baddow CM3 ...207 B3
  Newport CB11 ....67 A8
  St Osyth CO16 ....187 A4
  Tendring CO16 ....140 E8
  Thorington Street CO6 ...57 D6
  Thorrington CO7 .....166 A6
  Washbrook IP8 ....16 A1
  West Bergholt CO6 ...108 E3
Chapel Mews 18 IP4 ...17 D6
Chapel Rd
  Beaumont CO16 .....141 E7
  Boxted CO4 ....83 A3
  Brightlingsea CO7 ...186 A7
  Colchester CO3 ......134 C6
  Great Totham CM9 ...196 D6
  Langham CO4 ....83 D4
  Ridgewell CO9 ....29 B7
  Tiptree CO5 ....179 E4
  Tolleshunt D'arcy CM9 ..198 F4
  West Bergholt CO6 ...108 E4
  Wivenhoe CO7 ....164 B8
Chapel Row 3 CM23 ...145 F6
Chapel St Halstead CO9 ...76 E2
  Rowhedge CO5 ......164 A8
  Steeple Bumpstead CB9 ...27 C7
  Stoke by Clare CO10 .11 A3
Chapel St N 2 CO2 ...135 E6
Chapel St S 3 CO2 ...135 E6
Chapelfields CO13 ....170 E6
Chaplin Cl CM2 ......216 F7
Chaplin Dr CO4 ......110 D1
Chaplin Rd CO7 ......59 D3
Chaplin Wlk CO10 ...34 D5
Chaplins CO13 ......170 F7
Chapman Rd CO15 ...188 F3
Chapmans La CO5 ...201 F8
Chappel & Wakes Colne Sta
  CO6 ....106 D6
Chappel CE Prim Sch
  CO6 ....106 D5
Chappel Cnr CO6 ....106 D6
Chappel Hill CO6 ....106 D6
Chappel Rd
  Bures CO6, CO8 ......79 E3
  Fordham CO6 ....107 D7
  Great Tey CO6 ....106 C1
Charlecote Rd CM77 ..154 C7
Charles Ct
  Colchester CO3 ......134 D6
  Wivenhoe CO7 ......137 C3
Charles Cvn Pk CO16 ..167 E8
Charles Hall CO7 ....109 F4
Charles Pell Rd CO4 ..136 E7
Charles Rd
  Brightlingsea CO7 ...185 F6
  Felixstowe IP11 .....221 C3
Charles St
  Colchester CO1 ......136 A6
  Ipswich IP1 ....17 C6
Charleston Ct CO5 ...201 E6
Charlotte Dr CO13 ...170 E6
Charlotte Way CM8 ..177 B2
Charnock Cl CO13 ...170 F6
Charnwood Ave CM1 ..204 E1
Charnwood Ct IP7 ...17 B4
Charrington Ct CB9 ...9 C6
Charter Cl CO4 ......110 C6
Charter Ho CM9 .....204 C2
Charter Way
  Braintree CM77 .....128 C1
  Colchester CO4 .....109 F4
Chartfield Dr CO13 ..170 D8
Chartwell Cl
  Braintree CM7 ......127 E7
  Ipswich IP4 ....18 A5
Chase Cl CO4 ....136 D7
Chase La CO12 ......90 E2
Chase Lane Prim Sch
  CO12 ....90 E2
Chase Rd E CO7 ....139 C8
Chase Rd W CO7 ...139 B8
Chase The Aldham CO6 ..133 B8
  Barnston CM6 ......151 B4
  Bishop's Stortford CM23 .145 F6
  Boreham CM3 ....206 E8
  Brantham CO11 .....128 A7
  Colchester CO1 .....135 B7
Chase Way The
  Colchester CO1 .....109 C1
  Colchester,Lexden CO3 ..109 B1
Chaser Cl IP3 ....38 C8
Chaseway CM8 ......176 F5
Chaseway The CM7 ..128 D8
Chaters Hill CO10 ...22 E2
Chatham Gn CM3 ...173 D3
Chatham Hall La CM3 ..191 B8

Chatley Rd CM3 ......173 F7
Chatsworth Ave CM77 .154 B7
Chatsworth Cl CM23 ..145 C7
Chatsworth Cres
  Ipswich IP2 ....17 B2
  Trimley St M IP11 ...221 A6
Chatsworth Dr IP4 ...18 E5
Chatsworth Gdns CO15 .188 D2
Chatsworth Rd CO5 ..201 C7
Chatter End CM23 ...118 C7
Chattisham Rd IP8 ...35 C8
Chaucer Cl CO15 ....188 A1
Chaucer Cres CM7 ...155 A8
Chaucer Rd
  Chelmsford CM2 ....205 D1
  Felixstowe IP11 .....221 D3
  Sudbury CO10 ....15 D2
Chaucer Way CO3 ...134 F6
Chauntry Rd CB9 .....8 F7
Chauntry The 2 CB9 ...9 A7
Chedburgh Pl 8 CB9 ...9 A8
Chedworth Pl IP9 ....61 D7
Chelmer Ave CM3 ...191 B5
Chelmer Cl
  Kirby Cross CO13 ...170 E7
  Little Totham CM9 ..197 B4
Chelmer Dr CM6 .....150 F8
Chelmer Lea CM2 ...216 E7
Chelmer Pl CM2 .....205 D3
Chelmer Rd
  Braintree CM7 ......128 D1
  Chelmsford CM2 ....205 D3
  Haverhill CB9 ....9 B8
  Witham CM8 ....176 F2
Chelmer Terr CM9 ...210 B2
Chelmer Valley High Sch
  CM1 ....191 A2
Chelmer Valley Rd CM1 ..205 B5
Chelmer Village Ret Pk
  CM2 ....205 C2
Chelmer Village Way
  CM2 ....206 A3
Chelmerton Ave CM2 ..216 E7
Chelmondiston CE Prim Sch
  IP9 ....63 E7
Chelmsford & Essex
  Regiment Mus* CM2 ..216 A8
Chelmsford Coll
  Chelmsford CM2 ....216 A8
  Chelmsford CM1 ....204 C2
Chelmsford Cty High Sch for
  Girls CM1 ....205 A4
Chelmsford Ho CM6 ..150 E7
Chelmsford Rd
  Barnston CM6 ......151 A4
  Felsted CM6 ....152 B4
  Great Dunmow CM6 ..150 D8
  Great Waltham CM3 ..191 A6
  Ugley CM22 ....93 A6
  Woodham Mortimer CM9 .219 C6
  Writtle CM1 ....204 C1
Chelmsford Road Ind Est
  CM6 ....150 E7
Chelmsford Sta CM1 ..205 B3
Chelsea Cl CO15 ....33 F7
Chelsea Mews 6 CM7 ..127 F2
Chelsea Rd CO10 ....33 F7
Chelsworth Ave IP4 ..18 A6
Chelsworth Rd IP11 ..221 B3
Chelwater CM2 ......216 D8
Chenies Gn CM23 ...145 D6
Chepstow Rd IP11 ...221 D5
Chequers Cl CM21 ..145 C8
Chequers Cr CM8 ...177 B2
Chequers La
  Glemsford CO10 ....150 D8
  Great Dunmow CM6 ..150 D8
  Maldon CM9 ....210 A2
Chequers Rd CO11 ..113 C6
Chequers The CO7 ..165 A7
Cheriton Rd CM7 ...128 C1
Cherry Bglws 1 CM7 ..127 F3
Cherry Blossom Cl IP8 ..16 B2
Cherry Chase CO5 ...179 D4
Cherry Garden La
  Danbury CM3 ....219 B7
  Newport CB11 ......66 F8
Cherry Garden Rd
  Great Waltham CM3 ..190 E7
  Maldon CM9 ....209 E2
Cherry Gdns
  Bishop's Stortford CM23 .146 A8
  Great Notley CM77 ..154 D8
  Haverhill CB9 ....9 A8
Cherry La CO9 ......51 A8
Cherry Lane Gdns IP4 ..18 B7
Cherry Row CO3 ....134 F5
Cherry Tree Ave CO15 ..188 C1
Cherry Tree Cl
  Halstead CO9 ....77 A2
  Little Oakley CO12 ..117 B7
Cherry Tree Ho CO15 ..158 C3
Cherry Tree La
  Alberton CO2 ....162 F6
  Blackheath CO2 .....163 A7
Cherry Tree Prim Sch
  CO2 ....163 A8
Cherry Trees CO15 ..188 F2
Cherrygarden La 1
  CM7 ....216 A8
Cherrytree Ct CO10 ..134 F5
Cherrytree Rd CO10 ..34 B7
Cherrytree Rise CM8 ..177 A5
Cherrywood Dr CO3 ..134 F5
Cherrywoods CO7 ...166 D8
Chervil Cl CO5 ......179 C4
Cherwell Dr CM1 ....204 C5

Cheryl Ct CO15 ......188 D1
Chesapeake Cl IP9 ...63 F7
Chesapeake Rd IP3 ...38 A8
Chesfield Cl CM23 ...145 F5
Chesham Rd IP2 ....17 B4
Chess La CM8 ....177 A2
Chessington Gdns IP1 ..16 F8
Chester Camp CO16 ..188 A4
Chester Cl 4 CB9 ....9 E4
Chester Pl CM1 .....205 A5
Chester Rd IP11 ....221 D5
Chesterton Cl IP2 ...16 F1
Chestnut Ave
  Blackheath CO2 .....163 A8
  Clacton-on-S CO15 ..188 C3
  Gosfield CO9 ....102 E8
  Great Notley CM77 ..154 C7
  Hatfield Peverel CM3 ..194 A3
  Heybridge CM9 .....210 C6
  Jaywick CO16 ......188 A2
  Kirby Cross CO13 ...170 C6
  Littlebury CB11 .....21 C1
Chestnut Cl
  Bishop's Stortford CM23 .145 E6
  Haverhill CB9 ....8 F8
Chestnut Cl CB11 ...67 A8
Chestnut Gr CM7 ...127 C2
Chestnut Rd
  Alresford CO7 ......165 B8
  Glemsford CO10 ....2 B5
Chestnut Terr CO10 ..15 C8
Chestnut View CM6 ..123 C1
Chestnut Way
  Brightlingsea CO7 ...185 E7
  Takeley CM22 ......148 C7
  Tiptree CO5 ....179 C7
Chestnut Wlk
  Chelmsford CM2 ....205 A5
  Felsted CM6 ....152 C6
  Little Baddow CM3 ..207 E1
  Witham CM8 ....177 B4
Chestnuts The IP2 ...16 C2
Chevalier Rd IP11 ...221 F4
Chevallier St IP1 ...17 A7
Cheveley IP11 ......221 E5
Cheveling Rd CO2 ...136 D2
Cheviot Dr CM1 ....204 D6
Chevy Ct CO12 .....90 C2
Cheyne Ct CO10 ...33 E7
Chichester Cl CO3 ..135 A7
Chichester Dr CM1 ..205 C4
Chichester Rd CB11 ..43 E8
Chickney Rd CM22 ..95 C7
Chigborough Rd CM9 ..210 F6
Chilburn Rd CO15 ...189 A7
Childers Field IP11 ..221 B5
Childwell Alley CO1 ..136 A6
Chilford Ct CM7 ....127 D3
Chiltern Cl CO11 ...109 E1
Chilton Cl
  Chelmsford CM2 ....216 D7
  Great Horkesley CO6 ..109 B7
Chilton Cotts CO6 ..80 E4
Chilton Ct Ipswich IP2 ..17 B3
  Sudbury CO10 ......14 D8
Chilton Ind Est CO10 ..34 B8
Chilton Lodge Rd CO10 ..34 A7
Chilton Rd IP3 ......18 C4
Chimney Pot La CM3 ..219 E3
Chimswell Way CB9 ..9 A8
Chimney Cl CM1 ....205 D4
Chingford Ave CO15 ..188 E8
Chinnel La CB11 ....42 D5
Chinnery Hill CM23 ..145 F5
Chinook CO4 ....110 B4
Chippetts La CO3 ...133 C7
Chipping Hill
  2 Halstead CO9 ....76 F2
  Witham CM8 ....176 F4
Chipping Hill Inf Sch
  CM8 ....176 F4
Chippingdell CM8 ..176 F4
Chipstead Wlk CO16 ..188 C6
Chishill Rd SG8 ....19 A4
Chislett Row CM2 ..205 F2
Chittock Cl CO16 ...188 B3
Chitts Hill CO3 ....108 D1
Chivers Rd IP9 ......8 D7
Choat's Cotts CO6 ..107 E1
Choats Wood CO3 ..107 F1
Chrismund Way CO6 ..106 C1
Christ Church Ct CO3 ..135 D5
Christchurch Ct 4 IP4 ..17 D6
Christchurch Mansion
  (Mus)* IP4 ....17 D6
Christchurch Park Hospl
  (private) IP1 ....17 C7
Christchurch St IP4 ..17 D6
Christian Sch The CM22 .148 B7
Christies Warehouse 15
  CM1 ....205 B2
Christina Rd CO4 ...194 E8
Christine Chase CO3 ..134 F5
Christmas Field CO10 ..51 D2
Christopher Ct 9 CO10 ..33 E7
Christopher Dr CO11 ..168 D1
Christopher La CO10 ..135 F4
Christy Ave CM1 ....204 F4
Church Ave CM1 ....205 C4
Church Chase CO5 ..178 A3
Church Cl Cavendish CO10 ..1 A2
  Sproughton IP8 .....16 A6

Church Cl *continued*
West Bergholt CO6 108 E4
Wickham Bishops CM8 195 D5
Church Cnr CM9 208 D2
Church Cotts CM8 195 D5
Church Cres
Clacton-on-S CO15 188 F2
Sproughton IP8 16 A6
Church Dr CM23 92 B8
Church End
Great Dunmow CM6 123 E2
Panfield CM7 127 B7
Church End Villas CM6 123 E3
Church Farm Way CO4 109 E4
Church Field CB11 43 E7
Church Field Rd CO10 34 C8
Church Fields CO9 29 F2
Church Gdns CM6 123 D2
Church Gn Boreham CM3 206 F8
Broomfield CM1 191 B1
Coggeshall CO6 131 A3
Hinxton CB10 3 B7
Little Yeldham CO9 30 D4
Wickham Bishops CM8 195 D5
Church Gr CO6 133 B8
Church Hill Ashdon CB10 24 A8
Earls Colne CO6 105 C6
Finchingfield CM7 72 D6
Harwich CO12 90 B1
Helions Bumpstead CB9 26 C8
Lawford CO11 85 F3
Little Waltham CM3 191 C6
Purleigh CM3 220 E1
Rowhedge CO5 163 F8
White Notley CM8 175 F8
Woodham Walter CM9 208 D2
Church Housen CM3 190 F7
Church La
Beaumont CO16 142 A6
Belstead IP8 36 A7
Bishop's Stortford CM23 145 D3
Braintree CM7 127 F6
Brantham CO11 60 E1
Castle Camps CB1 7 E3
Castle Hedingham CO9 51 E4
1 Chelmsford, Moulsham CM1 205 B2
Chelmsford, Springfield CM1 205 D4
Clare CO10 12 B7
Colchester, Lexden CO3 135 A6
Colchester,Stanway CO3 134 A4
Debden CB11 68 A7
East Mersea CO5 184 E1
Elsenham CM22 120 E8
Felixstowe IP11 221 D6
Ford End CM3 172 B6
Great Henny CO10 54 D8
Great Holland CO13 170 B3
Great Leighs CM3 173 D7
Great Tey CO6 132 C4
Great Wigborough CO5 181 F4
Harkstead IP9 63 B3
Harwich CO12 91 E6
Little Totham CM9 197 B1
Marks Tey CO6 133 A4
Mistley CO11 86 E4
Nayland CO6 56 B1
Ridgewell CO9 29 B6
Sproughton IP8 16 B6
Takeley,Brewer's End CM22 148 B7
Takeley,Little Canfield CM6 149 B7
Toppesfield CO9 50 B7
Washbrook IP8 35 D8
Washbrook,Copdock IP8 35 F7
Weeley Heath CO16 168 A7
Widdington CB11 67 D4
Writtle CM1 204 B1
Church Manor CM23 146 B8
Church Mdws CM7 127 F6
Church Mead CM8 155 F1
Church Mews CO6 56 B1
Church Path Hadstock CB1 5 B6
Saffron Walden CB10 22 D2
Church Pk CO10 11 C3
Church Rd
Alphamstone CO10 54 C6
Alresford CO7 165 B7
Bentley IP9 60 F7
Black Notley CM77 155 A6
Boxted CO4 82 E6
Bradwell CM7 129 E1
Brightlingsea CO7 185 E8
Bulmer CO10 32 F4
Capel St M IP9 35 F1
Chrishall SG8 19 D3
Clacton-on-S CO15 189 A3
Copford CO6 133 E2
Cressing CM77 156 A5
Elmstead CO7 138 A7
Fordham CO6 107 D5
Frating CO7 138 D2
Gosfield CO9 102 E8
Great Cornard CO10 34 A5
Great Hallingbury CM22 146 D3
Great Notley CM77 154 F6
Great Totham CM9 196 E3
Great Yeldham CO9 29 F2
Greenstead Green CO9 104 A5
Hatfield Peverel CM3 194 A3
Hempstead CB10 46 F8
Holbrook IP9 62 D5
Kelvedon CO5 158 C2
Church Rd *continued*
Layer-de-l-H CO2 161 F4
Little Baddow CM3 207 A6
Little Bentley CO7 140 A5
Little Bromley CO11 113 B4
Pattiswick CM7 129 F5
Peldon CO5 182 D6
Rivenhall CM8 157 B1
Shudy Camps CB1 7 C5
Stambourne CO9 28 D2
Stansted Mountfitchet CM24 119 F5
Stutton IP9 62 A2
Tattingstone IP9 61 C7
Terling CM3 175 B2
Thorrington CO7 166 A6
Tiptree CO5 179 D5
Tolleshunt Major CM9 197 F2
Ulting CM9 208 C6
Walton-on-t-N CO14 171 C8
West Mersea CO5 201 B6
Wickham Bishops CM8 195 E5
Wickham St P CO9 53 B6
Wormingford CO6 80 E5
Wrabness CO11 88 F4
Church Rise CB9 26 C8
Church Sq Bures CO8 55 F1
St Osyth CO16 187 A4
Church St
Belchamp St P CO10 13 B3
Bishop's Stortford CM23 145 F7
Boxted CO4 82 F7
Braintree CM7 102 B1
Chelmondiston IP9 63 E7
Chelmsford CM1 205 B2
Clare CO10 12 B7
Coggeshall CO6 131 A2
Colchester CO1 135 E7
Colne Engaine CO6 78 A1
Gestingthorpe CO9 31 E1
Goldhanger CM9 211 E7
Great Baddow CM2 217 A6
Great Chesterford CB10 3 D2
Great Dunmow CM6 123 D2
Great Maplestead CO9 52 D1
Harwich CO12 91 E6
Henham CM22 94 F6
Ickleton CB10 3 B4
Kelvedon CO5 158 B2
Maldon CM9 210 B2
Newport CB11 43 A1
Rowhedge CO5 164 A8
Saffron Walden CB10 22 D2
Sible Hedingham CO9 51 D1
Steeple Bumpstead CB9 27 B7
Stoke-by-N CO6 56 D5
Sudbury CO10 33 D6
Tollesbury CM9 199 D1
Tolleshunt D'arcy CM9 198 D4
Wendens Ambo CB11 42 E5
Witham CM8 176 F4
Church Terr CO10 10 D2
Church View
Ardleigh CO7 111 E7
Colne Engaine CO6 77 F1
Stoke by C CO10 10 D3
Church Wlk
Colchester CO1 135 E7
Littlebury CB11 21 F4
Maldon CM9 209 F3
Sturmer CB9 9 E4
5 Sudbury CO10 33 E7
Churchacre CM9 199 D1
Churchfield Rd
Coggeshall CO6 131 A3
Walton-on-t-N CO14 171 C8
Churchfields
Stansted Mountfitchet CM24 119 F6
Steeple Bumpstead CB9 27 B6
West Mersea CO5 201 B6
Churchfields Ave CO3 134 C4
Churchfields Dr CB9 27 B6
Churchgate
Glemsford CO10 2 C5
Thorpe-le-S CO16 141 F1
Churchill Ave
Halstead CO9 77 A3
Ipswich IP4 18 B5
Churchill Cl CO7 185 F8
Churchill Ct CO12 91 A4
Churchill Dr CO10 15 E2
Churchill Rd
Braintree CM7 127 E7
Tiptree CO5 179 F5
Churchill Rise CM1 205 E7
Churchill Terr CM7 127 E6
Churchill Way CO2 136 B4
Churchmans Ho IP1 17 B5
Churchponds CO9 51 E4
Churchwell Ave CO5 160 A7
Churnwood Cl CO4 110 D1
Churnwood Rd CO4 110 D1
Chuzzlewit Dr CM1 204 E7
Cinnabar Cl IP8 36 E8
Cinque Port Rd CO7 185 F7
Circular Rd E CO2 135 F5
Circular Rd N CO2 135 E5
Circular Rd S CO2 135 E4
Circular Rd W CO2 135 E5
City Rd CO5 201 A6
Civic Dr IP1 17 B6
Civic Ind Est CB9 8 F5
Clachar Cl CM2 206 A3
Clacton & District Hospl CO15 188 E1
Clacton Comm CO15 169 A1
Clacton Cty High Sch CO15 189 A4
Clacton Rd
Bradfield CO11 114 A6
Elmstead CO7 138 C5
Great Holland CO13 170 A2
Holland-on-S CO15 189 F7
Little Oakley CO12 117 B5
Mistley CO11 86 E2
St Osyth CO16 187 B4
Thorrington CO7 166 C4
Weeley Heath CO16 168 A6
Wivenhoe CO7 137 C5
Wix CO11 115 C5
Wix,Stones Green CO12 115 D1
Clacton Sta CO15 188 F3
Claire Ct CO5 201 C7
Claire Rd CO13 170 B6
Clairmont Cl 11 CM7 127 F2
Clairmont Rd CO3 134 E5
Clandon Ho CO13 170 F4
Clapgate Dr CO16 168 C2
Clapgate La IP3 18 A2
Clapton Hall La
Great Dunmow CM6 150 D5
Great Dunmow CM6 150 E6
Clara Reeve Cl CO3 134 F4
Clare Ancient House Mus* CO10 12 C7
Clare Castle Ctry Pk* CO10 12 C7
Clare Cl CO9 103 D7
Clare Com Prim Sch CO10 12 B8
Clare Ct CM6 69 F3
Clare Mid Sch CO10 12 C8
Clare Rd Braintree CM7 127 E2
Ipswich IP4 17 F8
Clare Way CO16 188 B5
Claremont Hts CO1 109 E1
Claremont Rd CO7 164 C8
Clarence Cl CM2 206 A4
Clarence Rd Clare CO10 12 B8
Ipswich IP3 18 B1
Stansted Mountfitchet CM24 119 E7
Sudbury CO10 15 E1
Clarendon Pk CO15 189 B5
Clarendon Rd Haverhill CB9 8 F6
Takeley CM6 148 E7
Clarendon Way CO1 109 E1
Clark Way CM1 191 A1
Clarke's Rd CO12 90 F3
Clarkesmead CO5 179 C4
Clarkia Wlk CO4 136 D7
Clarks Farm Rd CM3 218 F8
Clarks Field Cotts CM3 219 E2
Clarks Wood Dr CM7 128 D3
Clarkson St IP1 17 B6
Clatterbury La
Arkesden CB11 41 E1
Clavering CB11 65 D5
Claud Ince Ave CM77 155 E6
Claude Oliver Cl CO11 86 A2
Claude St IP1 17 C6
Claudian Cl CB9 9 D7
Claudius Rd CO2 136 A5
Claudius Way CM8 194 E8
Clavering Prim Sch CB11 65 C4
Clavering Rd CM7 127 F6
Claverton Way IP4 18 E4
Clay Hill CO10 54 C8
Clay La St Osyth CO16 187 C7
Stebbing CM6 124 D7
Clay Lane Gr CO4 110 D4
Clay Pit Piece CB11 43 E6
Clay Pits CM7 128 D3
Clay Pits Way CM7 128 D3
Claydon Cl CB1 7 E4
Clayhall Rd CO15 189 A5
Clayhive Dr CB9 8 F7
Claypit Hill CM22 120 E5
Claypits Ave CO8 80 A8
Claypits La CO10 14 D5
Claypits Rd CM3 192 F1
Claypits Villas CM6 70 B2
Clayponds CM23 146 B7
Clays Mdw CB11 21 F4
Clays Rd CO14 171 B7
Clayshotts Dr CM8 195 B8
Clayton Rd CO12 90 C2
Claywall Bridge CB9 27 C7
Claywall Cotts CB9 27 C7
Clear Springs Chalet Site CO12 91 A1
Clearing Cl IP8 36 E8
Clearwater CO2 136 B3
Clematis Tye 3 CM1 205 E7
Clematis Way CO4 136 E7
Clement Mellish Ho 10 CO1 135 F7
Clement's La CB9 8 F7
Clementine Gdns IP4 18 B5
Clements Cl
Chelmsford CM2 206 B3
Haverhill CB9 8 F7
Clements Dr CB9 8 F7
Clements Prim Sch CB9 8 F7
Clench Cl 8 IP4 17 D6
Clench Rd IP9 62 D7
Clermont Ave CO10 15 E2
Clevedon Cl CM77 154 C7
Cleveland Cl CO4 110 C4
Cleves Ct CM3 192 E1
Cleves Rd CB9 8 D6
Clicket Hill CO8 80 B8
Cliff Cres CM7 100 E7
Cliff Ct CO13 171 B6
Cliff La IP3 17 F3
Cliff Lane Prim Sch IP3 17 E3
Cliff Par CO14 144 E2
Cliff Rd Harwich CO12 91 D3
Holland-on-S CO15 189 E5
Ipswich IP3 17 E3
Cliff Way CO13 171 B5
Cliffield CM7 100 E7
Clifford Ct 10 CM23 146 A7
Clifford Rd IP4 17 F5
Clifford Road Prim Sch IP4 17 F5
Clifton Terr CO7 164 B8
Clifton Way IP2 16 D2
Clifton Wood IP9 62 D6
Cliftons Farm Dr CO10 12 B7
Clingoe Ct CO4 136 E5
Clive Rd CO1,CO2 136 A6
Cliveden Cl CM1 204 E3
Clobbs Yd CM1 205 B8
Clockhouse Way CM7 128 C2
Cloes La CO16 188 B4
Cloisters The
Braintree CM7 128 A5
Kelvedon CO5 158 B1
Cloncurry Gdns IP11 221 B3
Clopton Dr CO10 15 C6
Close The
Clacton-on-S CO15 203 H7
Cressing CM77 155 E6
Debden CB11 68 B7
Frinton-on-S CO13 170 E5
Great Dunmow CM6 150 E7
Great Holland CO13 170 A3
Harwich CO12 91 A3
Sudbury CO10 33 F8
Tattingstone IP9 61 D7
Clouded Yellow Cl CM7 154 E8
Clough Rd CO4 110 D6
Clovelly Cl IP4 18 F4
Clover Ave CM23 145 B6
Clover Cl IP2 16 F4
Clover Ct Colchester CO3 134 D5
Great Cornard CO10 34 C6
Clover Dr CO7 166 A5
Clover Field CB9 8 D8
Clover Way CO7 111 B5
Cloverlands CO4 110 C2
Clovers 5 CO9 76 D1
Cluanie Orch CO10 1 E1
Club Par CO16 203 B6
Clump Field IP2 16 F2
Clunford Pl CM1 205 F7
Clyde Cres CM1 204 D4
Clydesdale Rd CM7 127 E2
Coach House Way 10 CM8 177 A2
Coach La CM9 209 F3
Coach Rd Alresford CO7 165 B8
Great Horkesley CO6 109 A7
Hempstead CB10 25 F2
Coachman's Paddock IP9 62 D6
Coachmans Ct 6 IP4 17 C5
Coachmans Mead CM7 72 C6
Coan Ave CO15 188 D1
Coast Rd CO5 201 A6
Coastguard Cotts CO14 144 D1
Coates Cl CM9 210 B4
Coates Quay CM2 205 C2
Coats Hutton Rd CO2 135 B3
Cobble Row CO3 134 E6
Cobbold Mews 16 IP4 17 D6
Cobbold Rd IP11 221 E4
Cobbold St IP4 17 D6
Cobbs La CM22 121 F3
Cobbs Pl CM1 205 D3
Cobden Pl IP4 17 D6
Cobham Rd IP3 18 C2
Cock & Bell La CO10 15 C8
Cock & Pye Ct CO1 135 E7
Cock La CB11 64 F3
Cock Rd CO9 53 B1
Cockaynes La CO7 138 A1
Cockett Wick La CO16 187 C1
Cockrell's Rd CO6 81 B4
Codham Little Park Dr CM7 101 C6
Cody Rd IP3 18 C1
Coeur De Lion CO4 109 F2
Coggeshall Rd
Ardleigh CO7 84 F2
Braintree CM7 128 C3
Coggeshall CO6 131 F7
Coggeshall,Marks Tey CO6 131 F3
Earls Colne CO6 105 B3
Great Tey CO6 132 B7
Kelvedon CO5 158 B5
Marks Tey CO6 132 C3
Coggeshall Rd (Feering) CO5 158 D7
Coggeshall Road (Feering) CO6 131 B1
Coggeshall Way CO9 77 A2
Cogmore CB11 41 B8
Cohen Cl CM77 155 B5
Cohort Dr CO2 135 A2
Coke St CO12 91 D5
Cokers Cl CM77 155 C5
Colam La CM3 207 C3
Colbayns High Sch CO15 188 D4
Colchester Boys High Sch CO3 135 E6
Colchester Bsns Pk CO4 110 C6
Colchester Castle* CO1 135 F7
Colchester Castle Mus* CO1 135 F7
Colchester General Hospl CO4 109 E3
Colchester High Sch for Girls CO3 135 B6
Colchester Inst
Clacton-on-S CO15 189 A2
Colchester CO3 135 D8
Colchester Natural History Mus* CO3 135 F7
Colchester Oaks Hospl CO3 135 D7
Colchester Rd
Abberton CO5 163 B1
Ardleigh CO7 111 C6
Bures CO8 79 F8
Chappel CO6 106 E5
Chelmsford CM2 206 A6
Coggeshall CO6 131 D2
Dedham CO7 84 E6
Elmstead CO7 137 F6
Frating CO7 139 E3
Great Bentley CO7,CO16 186 F8
Great Bromley CO7 112 A3
Great Totham CM9 196 D7
Great Wigborough CM9, CO5 181 C2
Halstead CO9 77 A1
Heybridge CM9 210 B5
Holland-on-S CO15 189 D6
Ipswich IP4 18 B8
Lawford CO11 86 C3
Little Horkesley CO6 81 B1
Peldon CO5 183 B6
Salcott-cum-virley CM9 199 A5
St Osyth CO16 187 A5
Thorpe-le-S CO16 141 D2
Tiptree CO5 179 D7
Weeley CO16 140 C2
West Bergholt CO6 108 D6
West Mersea CO5 201 C7
White Colne CO6 105 E6
Witham CM8 177 B3
Wivenhoe CO7 137 B4
Wix CO12 115 B3
Wix,Goose Green CO11 114 E4
Wormingford CO8 80 A6
Colchester Ret Pk CO1 135 E7
Colchester Royal Gram Sch CO3 135 D6
Colchester Sta CO1 109 E1
Colchester Town Sta CO1 136 A6
Colchester Zoo* CO3 134 C1
Cold Hall Chase CO7 138 E6
Cold Store Rd IP11 221 A1
Coldnailhurst Ave CM7 127 F5
Cole End La CB10 44 D5
Cole Gn CO10 13 A1
Cole Hill CM3 174 B5
Cole Ness Rd IP3 38 A8
Colehills CB11 65 C4
Colehills Cl CB11 65 C4
Coleman Ct CO15 188 F3
Colemans La CM3 218 D7
Coleridge Rd CM9 210 A1
Coles La CO14 144 A1
Coles Oak La CO7 84 C6
College Cl CM23 145 D7
College Ct CO11 86 C4
College Ho CM7 127 E2
College Rd
Braintree CM7 127 E2
Clacton-on-S CO15 189 A3
College St IP4 17 C5
Coller Rd CO12 90 F5
Colles Brook Rd CO7 166 F4
Colletts Chase CO6 80 F4
Colley Rd CM2 217 A6
Collier Row CB10 6 B1
Colliers The CM9 210 E3
Collimer Cl IP9 63 E7
Collimer Ct IP11 221 C6
Collindale Gdns CO15 189 C5
Collingwood Ave IP3 18 B3
Collingwood Cl CM7 128 C5
Collingwood Fields CO7 59 B4
Collingwood Rd
Clacton-on-S CO15 188 D1
Colchester CO3 134 E6
Witham CM8 177 A2
Collins Cl 7 CM7 127 F2
Collins Cross CM23 119 B1
Collins Rd CO9 53 D1
Collinson's IP2 16 D5
Collops Villas CM6 125 A4
Colne Bank Ave CO3 135 D8
Colne Chase CM8 176 E2
Colne Com Sch & Colne Coll The CO7 185 E8
Colne Cswy CO2 136 D5
Colne Ct CM7 128 C1
Colne Engaine CE Prim Sch CO6 78 A2
Colne Park Rd CO6 105 D7
Colne Rd
Brightlingsea CO7 185 E6
Bures CO8 79 E8
Clacton-on-S CO15 188 F2
Coggeshall CO6 131 A6
Halstead CO9 77 A2
Sible Hedingham CO9 75 E8
Colne Rise CO5 163 F8
Colne Springs CO9 29 B6
Colne Terr CO7 164 B8
Colne Valley Cl CO9 76 D2
Colne Valley Rd CB9 9 A7

Colne Valley Rly* CO9 ....51 C5
Colne View
Colchester CO2 ....136 D2
Point Clear B CO16 ....186 A2
Colne View Ret Pk CO1 ..110 A1
Colne Way CO16 ....185 F4
Colne Wlk CM7 ....128 D1
Colneford Hill CO6 ....105 D7
Colneis Jun Sch IP11 ...221 F6
Colneis Rd IP11 ....221 F6
Colneys Cl CO10 ....15 D1
Colthorpe Rd CO15 ....188 F8
Colts The CM23 ....145 E4
Coltsfield CM24 ....119 E8
Coltsfoot Ct CO4 ....109 C2
Coltsfoot Rd IP2 ....16 E4
Columbine Gdns
Ipswich IP2 ....16 E5
Walton-on-t-N CO14 ....171 B7
Columbine Mews CO3 ..134 C7
Columbines The CO10 ....1 E2
Colville Cl CM77 ....154 C7
Colvin Chase CM2 ....216 B1
Colvin Cl CO3 ....134 F7
Colyers Reach CM2 ....206 A2
Colyn Pl CB10 ....22 E3
Comac Yd CO15 ....188 E5
Comma Cl CM7 ....127 E1
Commerce Pk CO2 ....136 D4
Commerce Way
Colchester CO2 ....136 D4
Lawford CO11 ....86 C5
Commercial Rd IP1 ....17 B4
Common Hill CB10 ....22 D2
Common La
Duddenhoe End SG8 ....40 B7
Little Baddow CM3 ....207 E2
Woodham Walter CM9 ....208 B3
Common Quay IP2 ....17 D5
Common St CO10 ....12 B8
Common The CM3 ....218 E6
Commons The CO3 ....135 A5
Compasses Rd CM7 ....129 F5
Compton Mews [5] CO4 .136 C8
Compton Rd CO4 ....136 C8
Comyns Cl CO4 ....110 A6
Comyns Pl CM1 ....204 B1
Conan Doyle Cl CM7 ....155 A8
Conder Way CO2 ....136 D4
Conduit La CM9 ....219 E6
Coney Acre CB11 ....93 D8
Conies Rd CO9 ....103 D7
Conifer Cl Alresford CO7 ..164 F7
Colchester CO4 ....136 E8
Conifer Ct [7] CM23 ....145 F8
Coniston Cl CM77 ....154 D6
Coniston Rd IP3 ....18 B2
Coniston Sq IP3 ....18 B2
Connaught Ave CO13 ....170 F4
Connaught Cl CO15 ....189 B3
Connaught Ct CO15 ....189 B3
Connaught Gdns CM7 ...128 B4
Connaught Gdns E
CO15 ....189 B4
Connaught Gdns W
CO15 ....189 B3
Connaught Ho
Clacton-on-S CO15 ....189 B4
Frinton-on-S CO13 ....170 F5
Connaught Rd
Haverhill CB9 ....8 E7
Little Clacton CO16 ....168 C5
Conquerors Cl CM3 ....194 B3
Conrad Rd CM8 ....176 F5
Constable Ave CO16 ....188 C6
Constable Cl
Lawford CO11 ....86 B4
West Mersea CO5 ....201 D7
Constable Ct CO2 ....135 B3
Constable Ho CM7 ....127 E3
Constable Rd
Felixstowe IP11 ....221 F4
Ipswich IP4 ....17 D8
Sudbury CO10 ....33 E8
Constable View CM1 ....205 F6
Constable Way CM77 ....155 B5
Constance Cl
Broomfield CM1 ....191 A3
Witham CM8 ....195 B8
Constantine Rd
Colchester CO3 ....135 D5
Ipswich IP1 ....17 B5
Witham CM8 ....194 E8
Constitution Hill
Ipswich IP1 ....17 B8
Sudbury CO10 ....33 F8
Convalescent Hill IP11 ..221 E3
Convent Hill CM7 ....128 A5
Convent La CM7 ....128 A5
Conway Cl Halstead CO9 ..103 D8
Haverhill CB9 ....8 E8
Ipswich IP2 ....17 B2
Wivenhoe CO7 ....164 C8
Conyer Cl CM9 ....220 F8
Cook Cl CO12 ....90 F1
Cook Cres CO4 ....136 E7
Cook Pl CM2 ....205 F3
Cook's Cnr CO11 ....88 E2
Cook's Hall Rd CO6 ....108 C3
Cook's La Colchester CO3 .134 F7
Colchester,West Bergholt
CO3 ....134 E8
Great Bardfield CM7 ....71 E4
Cooks Cl CO9 ....103 F8
Cooks Hill CO4 ....83 B6
Coolyne Way CO15 ....189 B7
Coombe Lodge CO6 ....105 B6
Coombe Rise CM1 ....205 B7
Cooper Dr CM7 ....127 D4
Cooper Pk CM7 ....127 D4
Cooper's La CO7 ....84 F5
Cooper's Row CM1 ....205 A5
Coopers CM3 ....206 E8
Coopers Ave CM9 ....210 D5
Coopers Cl CM23 ....145 B4
Coopers Cres
Great Notley CM77 ....154 C8
West Bergholt CO6 ....108 F4
Coopers End Rd CM24 ..121 A3
Coopers End Rdbt
CM24 ....121 B3
Coopers La
Clacton-on-S CO15 ....188 C3
Great Leighs CM3 ....173 F7
Coopers Villas CM22 ....121 B2
Coopers Wlk CO4 ....136 D8
Copdock Prim Sch IP8 ...35 F8
Copford CE Prim Sch
CO6 ....133 D2
Copford Ct CO6 ....133 C4
Copland Cl
Broomfield CM1 ....191 A1
Great Baddow CM2 ....216 F8
Copleston High Sch IP4 ..18 C5
Copleston Rd IP4 ....18 B5
Coploe Rd CB10 ....3 A2
Copper Beeches CO3 ...134 D5
Copper Ct CM7 ....127 E1
Copper Gr IP8 ....36 E8
Copperas Rd CO7 ....185 F5
Copperfield Rd
Chelmsford CM1 ....204 E7
Ipswich IP2 ....16 E5
Copperfields CB11 ....43 C8
Coppice Cl CM6 ....123 D1
Coppice End CO4 ....110 B3
Coppice Rd CO7 ....165 B8
Coppice The CO15 ....188 D1
Coppingford End CO6 ...133 D5
Coppins Cl CM2 ....205 E4
Coppins Green Prim Sch
CO15 ....188 E5
Coppins Rd CO15 ....188 D4
Coprolite St IP3 ....17 E5
Copse The
Bishop's Stortford CM23 ..146 C8
Colchester CO4 ....109 F3
Felsted CM6 ....152 F6
Copt Hall La CO5 ....182 C3
Copt Hill CM3 ....218 E6
Copthall Cl CM22 ....146 F4
Copthall La CM6 ....70 B3
Copy Hill CB9 ....8 E3
Coral Dr IP1 ....16 D8
Coralin Wlk CO3 ....134 C6
Cordell Cl CO10 ....15 D8
Cordell Pl CO10 ....15 D8
Cordell Rd CO10 ....15 D8
Corder Rd IP4 ....17 D8
Cordwinders CO7 ....59 F1
Coriander Rd CO5 ....179 C4
Corinda Ho CO13 ....170 F4
Coriolanus Cl CO2 ....135 A3
Cormorant Wlk CM2 ....216 C5
Corn Mill Ct CB11 ....43 E8
Cornard Rd CO10 ....33 F7
Cornel Cl CM8 ....176 D4
Cornelius Vale CM2 ....206 B4
Cornells La CB11 ....67 E3
Corner Pk CB10 ....22 E3
Cornerth Cres CO10 ....34 B6
Cornflower Cl
Colchester CO3 ....134 C7
Ipswich IP2 ....16 E4
Cornflower Dr CM1 ....205 F6
Cornflower Rd CO15 ....203 G7
Cornford Way CO11 ....86 B4
Cornhill
[4] Chelmsford CM1 ....205 B2
[16] Ipswich IP1 ....17 C6
Corniche The CM7 ....72 A1
Cornish Hall End Rd
Stambourne CO9 ....28 A1
Steeple Bumpstead CO9 ....48 E8
Cornwall Cl CO11 ....86 B3
Cornwall Cres CM1 ....205 A7
Cornwall Gdns CM7 ....128 B4
Cornwall Ho CM23 ....145 E4
Cornwall Rd IP11 ....221 D5
Cornwallis Dr CO6 ....132 F3
Cornwallis Pl CB10 ....22 E3
Cornwallis Rd CB9 ....8 F6
Coronation Ave
Braintree CM7 ....127 F2
Colchester CO2 ....136 A2
Coronation Dr IP11 ....221 C3
Coronation Rd
Bishop's Stortford CM23 ..145 E5
Clacton-on-S CO15 ....188 C3
Ipswich IP4 ....18 B5
Coronation Villas CO16 ..141 F7
Coronation Way CM77 ..155 D5
Corporation Ave IP2 ....37 A8
Corporation Rd CM1 ....205 A4
Corriander Dr CM22 ....94 D2
Corry Ct [7] CO4 ....136 D8
Corton Rd IP3 ....18 B1
Cortoncroft Cl CO13 ....170 F7
Cotman Ave CO11 ....86 B4
Cotman Lodge CM1 ....205 F6
Cotman Rd
Clacton-on-S CO16 ....188 D6
Colchester CO3 ....135 A5
Ipswich IP3 ....18 A1
Cotswold Cres CM1 ....204 D6
Cotswold Ct
Clacton-on-S CO15 ....189 A3
Highwoods CO4 ....110 C4
Cotswold Dr CO10 ....15 C6
Cotswold Rd CO15 ....188 F5
Cottage Dr CO2 ....136 D3
Cottage Gn CO16 ....188 C6
Cottage Gr CO16 ....188 C6
Cottage Pl
Chelmsford CM1 ....205 B3
[3] Ipswich IP1 ....17 B6
Cottage Wlk CO16 ....188 C6
Cottey Ho CM2 ....216 B2
Cottingham Rd IP8 ....16 B1
Cottonwood Ct CO2 ....135 D2
Coulsdon Cl CO16 ....188 C6
Council Bglws CM7 ....127 F7
Council Cotts
Great Holland CO13 ....169 F3
Helions Bumpstead CB9 ....8 E1
Council Hos
Bicknacre CM3 ....218 F1
Great Bromley CO7 ....139 A6
Hadstock CB1 ....5 B6
Holbrook IP9 ....62 D6
Peldon CO5 ....182 E5
Shudy Camps CB1 ....7 B6
Thorington Street CO6 ....57 B3
Thorpe-le-S CO16 ....141 E2
Tolleshunt Major CM9 ....197 D3
Wakes Colne CO6 ....79 C1
Council Houses
Cressing CM77 ....156 A4
Great Bentley CO7 ....166 F5
Counting House La
CM6 ....123 D1
County Pl CM2 ....205 B1
Coupals Cl CB9 ....9 C6
Coupals Ct CB9 ....9 C6
Coupals Prim Sch CB9 ....9 D7
Coupals Rd CB9 ....9 E6
Court Cl CM23 ....145 E5
Court Eight CM8 ....176 F5
Court Eighteen CM8 ....176 F5
Court Eleven CM8 ....176 F5
Court Farm CO11 ....61 A1
Court Fifteen CM8 ....176 F5
Court Five CM8 ....176 E5
Court Four CM8 ....176 F5
Court Fourteen CM8 ....176 F5
Court Ind Est CM2 ....205 C2
Court Nine CM8 ....176 F5
Court Nineteen CM8 ....176 F5
Court One CM8 ....176 F5
Court Rd CM1 ....191 A3
Court Seven CM8 ....176 F5
Court Seventeen CM8 ...176 F5
Court Six CM8 ....176 F5
Court Sixteen CM8 ....176 F5
Court St CO6 ....56 A1
Court Ten CM8 ....176 F5
Court Thirteen CM8 ....176 F5
Court Three CM8 ....176 F5
Court Twelve CM8 ....176 F5
Court Twenty CM8 ....176 F5
Court Two CM8 ....176 F5
Courtauld Cl CO9 ....76 F1
Courtauld Homes of Rest
CO9 ....76 E3
Courtauld Rd CM7 ....128 A4
Courtenay Cl CO10 ....15 D2
Courtland Mews CM9 ...220 F8
Courtland Pl CM9 ....220 F8
Courtlands
Chelmsford CM1 ....205 A6
Halstead CO9 ....103 D8
Courts The IP11 ....221 F4
Courtyard The
Braintree CM7 ....128 A4
Maldon CM9 ....209 F2
Coval Ave CM1 ....205 A3
Coval La CM1 ....205 A2
Coval Wells CM1 ....205 A2
Covehite Ct [3] CB9 ....8 E6
Coventry Cl CO1 ....136 A8
Coverdale CM8 ....176 E4
Coverts The
West Mersea CO5 ....201 D6
Writtle CM1 ....204 B1
Cow La
Great Chesterford CB10 ....4 A5
Point Clear B CO16 ....186 C3
Cowdray Ave CO1 ....109 F1
Cowdray Cres CO1 ....135 F7
Cowdray Ctr The CO1 ..110 A1
Cowdrie Way CM2 ....206 B4
Cowell Ave CM1 ....204 E5
Cowell St IP2 ....17 C3
Cowels Farm La CM6 ....97 E5
Cowley Rd IP11 ....221 E4
Cowpar Mews CM7 ....155 A8
Cowper St IP4 ....18 B6
Cowslip Cl IP2 ....16 E4
Cowslip Ct CO3 ....134 C7
Cox La IP4 ....17 D5
Cox Rd CO7 ....165 B8
Cox's Hill CO11 ....86 B4
Coxhall Rd IP9 ....36 E1
Coxs Cl CB9 ....8 D7
Coytes Gdns [2] IP1 ....17 C5
Crabb's Hill CM3 ....193 F2
Crabb's La CO5 ....178 A8
Crabbe St IP4 ....18 A6
Crabs Croft CM7 ....128 D3
Crabtree CO13 ....170 C8
Crabtree Hill CB11 ....67 C3
Crabtree La CO6 ....81 C1
Cracknell Cl CO7 ....137 B2
Crafton Gn CM24 ....119 E7
Craig Ct CO2 ....135 B3
Craig Ho CM7 ....128 A3
Craig's Hill CO8 ....79 E6
Craigfield Ave CO15 ....189 A6
Craigs La CO8 ....79 E6
Craiston Way CM2 ....216 F5
Cramphorn Wlk CM1 ....204 F3
Cramswell Cl CB9 ....8 E6
Cranborne Cl CO4 ....109 F2
Cranbrook La CO10 ....2 F1
Crane Ave CO3 ....134 B4
Crane Hill IP2 ....16 E4
Crane's La CO5 ....157 F1
Cranford Cl CO13 ....170 E5
Cranham Rd CM6 ....95 F3
Cranleigh Cl CO16 ....188 B6
Cranmer Ho CM2 ....215 F7
Cranmer's La CO6 ....131 E6
Cranmere Ct CO1 ....136 A7
Cranmore Cl CM22 ....94 C2
Cranmoregreen La CO10 ...2 F3
Cranwell Cres IP3 ....18 C1
Cranwell Gdns CM23 ....119 C1
Craven Dr CO4 ....110 C3
Crawley End SG8 ....19 D4
Crayfields CM6 ....123 E1
Crayford Cl CM9 ....220 E8
Crayford Rd CO10 ....15 D2
Creance Ct CM2 ....205 A2
Creasen Butt Cl CM9 ....210 A4
Credon Cl CO15 ....188 F7
Credon Dr CO15 ....188 F7
Creek Cotts CO14 ....144 E4
Creek View CO5 ....181 F2
Creekhurst Cl CO7 ....186 A6
Creffield Rd CO3 ....135 D6
Crepping Hall Dr IP9 ....61 F1
Crescent Ct CM9 ....209 F5
Crescent Rd
Bishop's Stortford CM23 ..146 A6
Felixstowe IP11 ....221 E4
Great Baddow CM2 ....217 A7
Heybridge CM9 ....209 F5
Ipswich IP1 ....17 B6
Tollesbury CM9 ....199 E1
Walton-on-t-N CO14 ....171 C8
Crescent The
Clacton-on-S CO15 ....189 B7
Colchester CO4 ....110 C7
Frinton-on-S CO13 ....170 F4
Great Holland CO13 ....170 A4
Great Horkesley CO6 ....82 B1
Great Leighs CM3 ....173 E5
Marks Tey CO6 ....133 A3
Steeple Bumpstead CB9 ....27 B7
Thorpe-le-S CO16 ....141 F2
West Bergholt CO6 ....108 D5
Cress Croft CM7 ....128 D1
Cressages Cl CM6 ....152 F6
Cressing Cty Prim Sch
CM77 ....155 E6
Cressing Rd
Braintree CM7 ....128 C2
Witham CM8 ....176 D6
Cressing Sta CM77 ....155 D5
Cressing Temple Barns*
CM77 ....156 B2
Crestlands CO7 ....165 B7
Cricket Hill Rd IP11 ....221 B5
Cricketers Cl
Broomfield CM1 ....191 C1
Sudbury CO10 ....33 E6
Cricketfield La CM23 ....145 E8
Crispin Cl CB9 ....8 D7
Critchett Terr [1] CM1 ...205 A3
Crittall Cl CM8 ....156 E4
Crittall Dr CM7 ....127 D4
Crittall Rd CM8 ....177 B3
Crix Green Villas CM6 ...153 D6
Croasdaile Cl CM24 ....119 E8
Croasdaile Rd CM24 ....119 E8
Crocklands CO9 ....104 A5
Crocus Cl
Clacton-on-S CO16 ....188 C4
Ipswich IP2 ....16 F4
Crocus Fields CB10 ....22 E3
Crocus Way CM1 ....205 E7
Croft Cl CM7 ....128 A3
Croft Ct CM1 ....205 E8
Croft Ho [3] CO9 ....76 F2
Croft La CB9 ....9 B6
Croft Rd
Clacton-on-S CO15 ....188 D4
Kelvedon CO5 ....158 B2
Sudbury CO10 ....33 E8
Croft St IP2 ....17 C3
Croft The Bures CO8 ....55 F1
Earls Colne CO6 ....105 A6
Elsenham CM22 ....94 C1
Glemsford CO10 ....2 C4
Great Yeldham CO9 ....30 A2
Croft Way CM8 ....177 A3
Crofters Wlk CM77 ....154 D8
Crofton Cl IP4 ....18 B7
Crofton Rd IP4 ....18 B7
Croftside CO8 ....55 F1
Cromar Way CM1 ....204 F1
Cromarty Rd IP4 ....18 B8
Crome Cl CO3 ....135 A5
Crome Rd CO16 ....188 D5
Cromer Rd IP1 ....16 F8
Cromhurst Ct CO3 ....135 E7
Crompton Rd IP2 ....16 F7
Crompton St CM1 ....204 F1
Cromwell Cl
Bishop's Stortford CM23 ..145 B7
Boreham CM3 ....206 D8
Cromwell Ct
[11] Ipswich IP1 ....17 C5
Maldon CM9 ....210 A3
Cromwell Ctr CM8 ....177 B2
Cromwell Hill CM9 ....209 F3
Cromwell Ho CO4 ....109 F4
Cromwell La CM9 ....209 F3
Cromwell Pk CM6 ....152 B5
Cromwell Rd
[16] Colchester CO2 ....135 F6
Saffron Walden CB11 ....43 E7
Cromwell Sq [8] IP1 ....17 C5
Cromwell Way CM8 ....176 F2
Croquet Gdns CO7 ....137 C1
Cross Cotts CO4 ....83 B6
Cross End CO9 ....78 C8
Cross Field Way CO4 ....83 B5
Cross Hill CO12 ....116 D1
Cross La CO5 ....201 F7
Cross Rd Maldon CM9 ....210 A1
Witham CM8 ....176 F5
Cross St Felixstowe IP11 ..221 C6
Saffron Walden CB10 ....22 D1
Sudbury CO10 ....33 D7
Cross The
West Mersea CO5 ....201 E7
Wivenhoe CO7 ....137 B2
Cross Way CO5 ....201 E7
Crossfield Rd CO15 ....188 E3
Crossfield Way CO13 ....170 B6
Crossfields CO6 ....56 C5
Crossgate Field IP11 ....221 C5
Crossley Ave CO15 ....203 E7
Crossroads CO9 ....31 E2
Crosstree Wlk CO2 ....136 A3
Crossways
Chelmsford CM2 ....216 C7
Clacton-on-S CO15 ....203 G8
Colne Engaine CO6 ....77 F1
Crotchets Cl IP9 ....35 A1
Crouch Ct CM7 ....128 D1
Crouch Dr CM8 ....176 E2
Crouch St CO3 ....135 E6
Crouchman's Farm Rd
CM9 ....208 C7
Croutel Rd IP11 ....221 F5
Crow La CO16 ....141 A3
Crow Pond Rd CM3 ....175 C3
Crow St CM22 ....94 F5
Crowe Hall La IP9 ....62 A1
Crowhall La CO11 ....87 E1
Crowhurst Rd CO3 ....135 E7
Crowland Cl [7] IP2 ....17 A2
Crowland Rd CB9 ....8 F8
Crown Bays Rd CO4 ....136 C8
Crown Gate CO4 ....110 D6
Crown Hill CB10 ....6 B1
Crown La Harwich CO12 ...91 D4
Tendring CO16 ....140 D3
Crown La N CO7 ....110 F7
Crown La S CO7 ....111 A4
Crown Mdw CM7 ....128 D4
Crown Rd CO15 ....188 C1
Crown St
Castle Hedingham CO9 ....51 E4
Dedham CO7 ....84 F6
Felixstowe IP11 ....221 C6
Great Bardfield CM7 ....72 B2
Ipswich IP1 ....17 C6
Crown Terr CM23 ....146 A7
Crownfield Rd CO10 ....2 B6
Crownfields CO7 ....84 F6
Croxall Ct CM8 ....176 F2
Crozier Ave CM23 ....145 C8
Crozier Terr CM2 ....206 B4
Cruce Way CO16 ....185 F3
Crummock Cl CM77 ....154 C6
Crunch Croft CB9 ....9 E5
Crusader Way CM7 ....128 D2
Crushton Pl CM1 ....204 F6
Cuckfield Ave IP3 ....18 E3
Cuckoo Hill Bures CO8 ....55 F1
Sible Hedingham CO9 ....75 B8
Cuckoo Way CM77 ....154 C7
Cuckoos La
Great Canfield CM6 ....149 A3
Takeley CM6 ....148 F2
Cudmore Grove Ctry Pk*
CO5 ....185 A1
Culford Pl IP3 ....17 F4
Culford Wlk IP11 ....221 A3
Cullingham Rd IP1 ....17 A5
Culver St E CO1 ....135 F7
Culver St W CO1 ....135 F7
Culver Wlk [21] CO1 ....135 F7
Culvert Cl CO6 ....130 F2
Cumberland Ave CM9 ....209 E1
Cumberland Cl CM7 ....128 B4
Cumberland Cres CM1 ..205 A7
Cumberland Ct
Clacton-on-S CO15 ....189 B5
Colchester CO3 ....135 D6
Cumberland St IP1 ....17 B7
Cumberland Twrs IP1 ....17 A7
Cunningham Cl CO2 ....136 A4
Cunnington Rd CM7 ....128 C3
Cunobelin Way CO2 ....135 A2
Cuppers Cl CM8 ....176 E1
Curds Rd CO6 ....105 A4
Curlew Cl
Clacton-on-S CO15 ....188 F6
Heybridge CM9 ....210 C5
Kelvedon CO5 ....158 D2
Curlew Croft CO4 ....136 F8
Curlew Rd IP2 ....16 D4

Curling Tye La
Maldon CM9 209 A3
Woodham Walter CM9 208 F3
Currants Farm Rd CM7 127 E5
Currents La CO12 91 E6
Curriers' La IP1 17 C5
Curtis Cl
Clacton-on-S CO16 188 B3
Ipswich IP8 16 C1
Curzon Rd CO10 34 B8
Curzon Way CM2 206 A2
Cusak Rd CM2 205 F3
Custerson Ct CB11 22 D1
Custerson Dr CM77 155 B5
Custom House La CO12 91 D6
Cut Hedge CM77 154 C6
Cut The CO5 179 C5
Cut Throat La CM8 177 A4
Cut-A-Thwart La CM9 209 C4
Cuthedge La CO6 157 D7
Cutler St IP1 17 C5
Cutlers Cl CM23 145 D5
Cutlers La CO7 59 D5
Cutmaple CO9 75 E4
Cutmore Pl CM2 215 F8
Cuton Hall La CM2 206 A5
Cutting Dr CO9 76 E1
Cygnet Ct
11 Bishop's Stortford CM23 145 F6
Sible Hedingham CO9 51 E1
Cygnet Wlk CO3 134 C4
Cymbeline Way (Colchester By Pass) CO3 135 B8
Cypress Cl CO15 188 E7
Cypress Ct CM6 123 B1
Cypress Dr CM2 216 C6
Cypress Gr 5 CO4 136 F8
Cypress Mews CO5 201 B7
Cypress Rd CM8 177 A4
Cyril Child Cl CO4 136 E7
Cyril Dowsett Ct CM9 209 E2

D

D'arcy Ave CM9 210 B1
D'arcy Cl CO13 170 F6
D'Arcy Ho CO14 144 D2
D'arcy Hts CO2 136 C3
D'arcy Rd Colchester CO2 136 C3
St Osyth CO16 187 B4
Tiptree CO5 179 F2
D'arcy Way
Brightlingsea CO7 185 E7
Tolleshunt D'arcy CM9 198 E4
Daen Ingas CM3 218 D7
Daffodil Cl IP2 16 E3
Daffodil Way CM1 205 E7
Dagnets La CM77 154 D3
Dahlia Cl
2 Chelmsford CM1 205 F5
Clacton-on-S CO16 188 C4
Dahlia Wlk CO4 136 D7
Daimler Ave CO15 203 D6
Dains Pl IP11 221 A7
Dairy Rd CM2 205 F4
Dairyhouse La CO11 114 F7
Daisleys La CM3 174 A2
Daisy Ct CM1 206 A6
Daisy Green Rd CO3 133 E8
Daisyley Rd CM6 98 B4
Dale Cl Colchester CO3 134 B7
Elmstead CO7 138 A6
Dale Hall La IP1 17 C8
Dale Ho CM7 127 E4
Dale The CO7 164 C8
Dales The CO12 90 F1
Dales View IP8 35 E8
Dales View Rd 1 IP1 17 A8
Daleview Ave CO11 115 C5
Dalham Pl 4 CB9 9 A8
Dallwood Way CM7 128 B3
Dalrymple Cl CM1 205 D3
Daltes La CO16 187 C3
Dalton Gdns CM23 145 E4
Dalton Rd IP1 17 B6
Damant's Farm La CO16 142 D1
Damases La CM3 193 C1
Damask Mews CM7 128 A2
Damask Rd CO3 134 C7
Dame Elizabeth Ct CM1 190 F3
Dame Johane Bradbury's Sch CB10 22 F2
Dammant Ct 8 CO4 136 D8
Dampier Rd CO6 130 F3
Damselfly Rd IP3 38 C8
Danbury Cl CO6 132 F3
Danbury Ctry Pk* CM3 218 B7
Danbury Park Com Prim Sch CM3 218 C7
Danbury Vale CM3 219 A6
Dancing Dicks La CM8 176 A2
Dandalan Cl IP1 16 E8
Dane Acres CM23 145 D8
Dane Ho CM23 145 D8
Dane O'Coys Rd CM23 118 E1
Dane Pk CM23 145 D8
Dane Rd CM1 204 E2
Dane St CM23 146 A7
Danes Ct CO10 34 B4
Daneum Holt CO10 12 A6
Daniel Cole Rd CO2 135 F4
Daniel Way CM8 156 E4
Daniell Cl CO16 188 C6
Daniell Dr CO2 135 B2
Daniells Ho CO6 108 F4
Dansie Ct 7 CO4 136 C8
Daphne Ct CM77 154 C7
Daphne Ct 4 CO4 136 D8
Dapier Dr CM7 128 D3
Darcy Rise CM3 207 E1
Darina Ct CO3 134 B7
Darkhouse La CO5 164 A8
Darnay Rise CM1 204 D6
Darnel Way CO3 134 B7
Darnet Rd CM9 199 E1
Darrell Cl CM1 205 B6
Darrell Rd IP11 221 B1
Darsham Cl IP11 221 B4
Dart Cl CM8 176 D2
Darter Cl IP3 38 C8
Dartmouth Rd CM1 205 E6
Darwin Cl
5 Braintree CM7 127 F1
Colchester CO2 136 B1
Darwin Rd IP4 17 F5
Dashwood Cl IP8 16 D1
Datchet Ho CO3 134 F7
Daundy Cl IP2 16 D5
Davall Cl CO12 90 C1
Davey Cl Colchester CO1 136 D6
Ipswich IP3 17 F1
Davidson Cl CO10 34 D4
Davies Ct CM7 128 A2
Davy Rd CO15 189 C8
Daw St Birdbrook CO9 28 B7
Finchingfield CM7 72 E4
Daw's Hall (Wildfowl Farm)* CO8 55 B6
Dawes La CO5 201 E8
Dawlish Rd CO15 203 I8
Dawnbrook Cl 1 IP2 16 E1
Dawnford Cl CO3 134 C7
Dawnford Ct CO3 134 C7
Daws Cross CO8 78 F6
Dawson Cl CB10 22 F2
Dawson Dr IP11 221 A8
Days Cl CM1 205 B8
Dazeley's La CO7 85 F8
De Bohun Ct CB10 22 E2
De Burgh Rd CO3 134 E6
De Greys Cl CO10 34 C5
De Mandeville Rd CM22 94 C2
De Staunton Cl CO7 165 B7
De Vere Ave CM9 210 B1
De Vere Cl
Hatfield Peverel CM3 194 B3
Wivenhoe CO7 164 B8
De Vere Est CO7 166 D8
De Vere La CO7 164 B8
De Vere Prim Sch CO9 51 E4
De Vere Rd
Colchester CO3 135 A5
Earls Colne CO6 104 F7
De Vere Way CO12 90 F2
De Veres Rd 7 CO9 76 D1
De Vigier Ave CB10 23 A2
De-Marci Ct CM7 128 D3
Dead La Ardleigh CO7 111 C8
Great Bentley CO7 166 F2
Lawford CO11 86 C2
Little Clacton CO16 168 B2
Deadman's La CM2 216 C4
Deal Cl Braintree CM7 127 E6
Clacton-on-S CO15 203 J8
Deal Way CO7 185 E8
Dean Rd CB1 6 B8
Dean Rogers Pl CM7 127 F7
Dean St CO7 185 E7
Dean Way CM1 204 E1
Deane's Cl CO12 91 A2
Deanery Gdns CM7 127 F7
Deanery Hill CM7 127 E7
Deanes Ct CO12 91 A2
Deanhill Ave CO15 189 C5
Deans Wlk CM7 127 F8
Debden CE Prim Sch CB11 68 B7
Debden Dr CB10 44 E2
Debden Rd Newport CB11 67 C8
Saffron Walden CB11 43 D8
Saffron Walden CB11 43 E6
Deben Cl CM8 176 E2
Deben Ct CM7 128 D1
Deben Dr CO10 34 A8
Deben High Sch IP11 221 D4
Deben Rd Colchester CO4 110 F1
Haverhill CB9 9 B8
Deben Way IP11 221 C3
Deben Wlk CO16 188 C6
Dedham Ave CO16 188 B5
Dedham CE Prim Sch CO7 85 A6
Dedham Ct CO2 136 B4
Dedham Meade CO7 84 F3
Dedham Pl 7 IP4 17 D5
Dedham Rd Ardleigh CO7 84 D1
Boxted CO4 83 B6
Lawford CO11 85 E4
Stratford St M CO7 58 E1
Deepdale Rd CO12 91 A4
Deeping Wlk CO16 187 B5
Deer Park Cl CO9 51 F3
Deerhurst Chase CM3 218 F1
Deerleap Way CM7 128 D4
Defoe Cres CO4 109 E4
Deford Rd CM8 194 D8
Delamere Rd
Chelmsford CM1 204 E1
Colchester CO4 110 D3
Delius Wlk CO4 136 E6
Dell La
Bishop's Stortford, Hockerill CM23 146 A7
Bishop's Stortford, Latchmore Bank CM22 146 B1
Dell The Colchester CO1 136 A6
Great Baddow CM2 216 F6
Great Cornard CO10 34 A6
Great Dunmow CM6 123 E1
Dellows La CM22 94 A2
Dells The 11 CM23 145 F7
Dellwood Ave IP11 221 F5
Delvyn's La CO9 52 C6
Demoiselle Cres IP3 38 C8
Dene Ct CM1 204 D5
Dengie Cl CM8 194 F8
Denham Cl CO7 164 C8
Denholm Ct CM8 194 F8
Denmark Gdns IP9 62 D6
Denmark Ho CM2 216 D8
Denny Ct CM23 119 B2
Denton Cl IP2 16 D2
Denton Cres CM77 155 B5
Denton's Terr CO7 164 B8
Derby Cl IP4 18 A5
Derby Rd IP3 18 A4
Derby Road Sta IP3 18 A4
Dereham Ave IP3 17 F3
Dereham Ct CO2 135 C3
Derwent Gdns CO15 189 C6
Derwent Rd
Highwoods CO4 110 C4
Ipswich IP3 17 F3
Derwent Way
Chelmsford CM1 204 D4
Great Notley CM77 154 C7
Desborough Path CM2 205 F8
Devereaux Cl CO14 170 F8
Devereaux Ct 17 IP4 17 D6
Devereaux Pl CO4 109 C3
Devereux Ct CO15 188 F3
Devereux Pl CO4 109 C3
Deverill Cl CM1 191 B2
Devlin Rd IP8 16 B1
Devoils La 9 CM23 145 F7
Devon Rd Colchester CO2 135 B3
Felixstowe IP11 221 D5
Devon Way Harwich CO12 90 D2
Holland-on-S CO15 189 E7
Devonshire Gdns CM7 128 B4
Devonshire Rd IP3 17 F5
Dewberry Cl 3 CO4 136 D7
Dewes Green Rd
Berden CM23 92 A8
Clavering CM23 64 F1
Dewlands CM77 155 B6
Deynes Rd CB11 68 B7
Dhobi Pl IP1 16 F7
Dial Cnr CO7 166 E3
Dial La IP1 17 C6
Dial Rd CO7 166 E3
Diana Ho CO13 170 E5
Diana Way CO15 188 C2
Dickens Cl CM7 155 A8
Dickens Pl CM1 204 D7
Dickens Rd IP2 16 F5
Dicksons Cnr IP1 16 C7
Dicky Moors CM3 190 F7
Didsbury Cl IP2 16 D2
Digby Mews CO5 201 C6
Digby Rd IP4 18 C7
Dilbridge Rd E CO4 136 C8
Dilbridge Rd W CO4 136 C8
Dillestone Ct CB9 9 E5
Dillwyn St IP1 17 A6
Dillwyn St W IP1 17 A6
Dilston CM3 219 A6
Dimsdale Cres CM23 146 B6
Dinants Cres CO6 132 E3
Dinsdale Cl 1 CO4 136 C8
Dinsdale Ct IP11 221 D3
Dismals The CM3 175 B2
Distillery La CO2 136 C4
Ditchingham Gr IP5 18 F6
Dixon Ave
Chelmsford CM1 204 F4
Clacton-on-S CO16 188 C6
Dixon Cl CO11 86 B4
Dixon Way CO7 137 A2
Dobbies La CO6 132 F3
Dock La CO12 117 A4
Dock Rd IP11 221 B2
Dock St IP2 17 C4
Docker Ct CO2 136 B4
Dockfield Ave CO12 90 F3
Dockwra La CM3 219 A7
Doctor's La CO10 11 D2
Docwra Rd CO5 158 C2
Doddenhill Cl CB10 22 E3
Dodmans 7 IP9 35 A1
Doe's Cnr Halstead CO9 76 D5
Hatfield Peverel CM9 194 F1
Dog Chase CM7 73 C3
Dogden La CM23 92 E2
Doggetts La CO6 132 F2
Doghouse Rd CM7 129 F4
Dogs Head St 4 IP4 17 C5
Dogwood Cl IP3 18 D2
Dolby Rise CM2 205 F2
Dolphin Ct CO13 171 B6
Dolphin Way CM23 146 A8
Dombey Cl CM1 204 F7
Dombey Rd IP2 16 F5
Domitian Cl CO4 110 B6
Doms La CM3 175 B2
Domsey Bank CO6 132 E3
Domsey Chase CO5 159 C8
Domsey La CM3 191 F5
Don Ct CM8 176 D2
Donald Way CM2 216 C7
Donard Dr CO6 108 D4
Donne Dr CO15 203 G8
Donyland Way CO5 163 F8
Dooley Rd
Felixstowe IP11 221 A3
Halstead CO9 76 D1
Dorchester End CO2 136 B3
Dorchester Rd IP3 18 D3
Dordell Ct CO9 50 B8
Dorewards Ave CM7 127 F7
Dorking Cres CO16 188 C6
Dorking Wlk CM2 216 E7
Dorothy Curtice Ct CO6 133 E5
Dorothy Sayers Dr CM8 177 A5
Dorset Ave CM2 216 E6
Dorset Cl
Great Baddow CM2 216 E6
Halstead CO9 76 E1
Holland-on-S CO15 189 E6
Dorset Ho 18 CM23 145 F7
Dorset Rd CM9 220 F8
Dorvis La CB10 6 B1
Doubleday Cnr CO6 130 F2
Doubleday Dr CM9 209 F5
Doubleday Gdns CM7 128 B5
Doucecroft Sch CO5 158 C3
Douglas Cl CM2 216 D3
Douglas Gr CM8 176 D2
Douglas Rd
Clacton-on-S CO15 188 C4
Harwich CO12 91 B3
Douglas Wlk 3 CM2 216 A8
Dove Cl
Bishop's Stortford CM23 145 E3
Stansted Mountfitchet CM24 119 E8
Dove Cotts CM22 93 F3
Dove Cres CO12 90 D2
Dove House Rd CB9 9 A8
Dove La CM2 216 A6
Dove St IP4 17 E5
Dove Tree Ct CO3 134 C5
Dovedale IP11 221 B3
Dovedale Gdns CO15 189 C6
Dover Cl Braintree CM7 127 E6
Clacton-on-S CO15 203 J8
Dover Rd
Brightlingsea CO7 185 F8
Ipswich IP3 18 B4
Dovercourt Caravan Pk CO12 91 A1
Dovercourt Sta CO12 91 D4
Doves La CM6 150 B2
Dowches Cotts CO5 158 C2
Dowches Dr CO5 158 C3
Dowches Gdns CO5 158 C3
Dowding Cl CO2 136 A4
Dowling Rd CO8 79 F3
Downham Bvd IP3 38 C8
Downing Cl IP2 16 F2
Downing Prim Sch IP2 16 F2
Downs Cres
Great Dunmow CM6 123 C1
Haverhill CB9 8 F8
Downs Pl 2 CB9 8 F8
Downs Rd CM9 210 B3
Downs Terr CM6 124 D6
Downs The
Felixstowe IP11 221 B5
Great Dunmow CM6 123 D1
Downside Cl IP2 36 F8
Downsway CM1 205 D6
Downton Dr CB9 8 E8
Downton Wlk CO5 179 D6
Dragon's Gn CB10 23 D1
Drake Ave IP3 18 B2
Drake Gdns CM7 128 C4
Drake Sq N IP3 18 B2
Drake Sq S IP3 18 B2
Drakes App CO15 188 A1
Drakes Cnr CO5 181 F2
Drakes La Boreham CM3 192 B7
Little Waltham CM3 191 F7
Drapers Chase
Heybridge CM9 210 D4
Rayne CM7 153 D8
Drapers La CB9 8 B2
Drapery Comm CO10 2 B4
Dray Ct CO6 108 F4
Drayman's Cl CM23 145 B5
Draymans Gr CM77 154 C8
Draymans Way IP3 17 E3
Drays The CO10 15 B5
Drayton Cl 4 CM9 210 A1
Dreys The CB10 44 D8
Driberg Way CM7 128 A1
Driffield Cl CO5 158 D4
Drift The
East Bergholt CO7 60 C2
Great Cornard CO10 34 C5
Ipswich,Priory Heath IP3 18 C1
Ipswich,Rose Hill IP4 18 A6
Stutton IP9 62 C2
Driftway The IP4 18 B6
Drive The
Chelmsford CM1 205 A6
Clacton-on-S CO15 189 B7
Harwich CO12 91 B2
Rivenhall CM8 177 E6
Thaxted CM6 69 F3
Drood Cl CM1 204 F7
Drovers Way CM23 145 C5
Druce The CB11 65 D4
Drum Field CO7 58 D1
Drury Dr CO10 15 F2
Drury La
4 Braintree CM7 127 F3
Ridgewell CO9 29 A6
Drury Rd CO2 135 C5
Dry Dock CO7 164 B8
Du Cane Pl CM8 177 A2
Duchess Cl CM23 145 C7
Duck End CM23 119 F1
Duck St Little Easton CM6 122 F5
Wendens Ambo CB11 42 E5
Duckend Farm La CM6 97 F6
Ducketts Wharf 10 CM23 145 F6
Duddery Ct CB9 9 B7
Duddery Hill CB9 9 A7
Duddery Rd CB9 9 A7
Dudley Cl Boreham CM3 192 E1
Colchester CO2 136 A4
Dudley Rd
Clacton-on-S CO15 188 D3
Earls Colne CO6 104 F7
Fingringhoe CO5 163 E3
Duffield Dr CO4 136 E7
Duffield Rd CM2 216 D6
Duffries Cl CM3 190 E7
Duffs Hill CO10 2 B6
Dugard Ave CO3 134 E4
Duggers La CM7 128 A1
Dugmore Ave CO13 170 C8
Duke St
Brightlingsea CO7 185 E6
Chelmsford CM1 205 B2
Ipswich IP3 17 E4
Dukes La 5 CM2 205 F4
Dukes Orch CM1 204 B1
Dukes Park Ind Est CM2 205 F4
Dukes Priory Hospl The CM1 205 D4
Dukes Rd CM7 127 F5
Dukes Ride CM23 145 C7
Dulverton Cotts CO3 134 C4
Dulwich Ct CO15 189 D4
Dulwich Rd CO15 189 D5
Dumbarton Rd IP4 18 C8
Dumfries Rd IP4 18 C8
Dumney La
Braintree, Hornells Corner CM3 153 E2
Braintree, Thistley Green CM6 153 B3
Great Leighs CM3 173 E8
Dumont Ave CO16 186 B2
Duncan Rd CO2 135 B4
Duncan Rise CO9 29 F2
Dunlin Cl CM9 210 C5
Dunlin Ct CO5 158 C2
Dunlin Rd IP2 16 E2
Dunlop Rd IP2 16 F6
Dunmore Rd CM2 206 A3
Dunmow Rd
Bishop's Stortford CM23 146 C7
Felsted CM6 125 F2
Great Bardfield CM7 98 F8
Great Canfield CM6 149 F1
Great Hallingbury CM22 147 C7
Rayne CM77 126 B2
Takeley CM22 148 C7
Thaxted CM6 97 A7
Dunning Cl CO11 114 C8
Dunnock Way CO4 137 A7
Dunoon Cl CM7 128 D4
Dunster Dr CB9 8 E8
Dunthorne Rd CO4 110 E2
Dunthorpe Rd CO16 188 D6
Duntons Almshouses CO7 84 F6
Dunwich Ct
Colchester CO2 135 F4
Haverhill CB9 8 C8
Ipswich IP1 16 E8
Dupont Cl CO16 188 D6
Durham Cl CM7 72 A1
Durham Sq CO1 136 A7
Duxford Rd CB10 3 A7
Dyehouse Mdw CO10 15 B7
Dyer's Rd Colchester CO3 134 C3
Maldon CM9 210 A2
Dyers Ct CM23 145 C5
Dyers Rd CO9 28 E1
Dyke Rd IP11 221 A2
Dyke St IP1 17 C7
Dykes Chase CM9 209 F3
Dyne's Hall Rd CO9 76 C8

E

Eagle Ave CO14 144 D1
Eagle La CM7 127 F6
Eagle St 3 IP4 17 D5
Eaglegate CO1 136 A7
Eagles Cl IP11 221 D4
Earlhams Cl CO12 90 F1
Earls Cl CM23 145 D6
Earls Colne Prim Sch CO6 105 C6
Earls Colne Rd CO6 106 A1
Earls Gn CB9 8 C8
Earls Hall Dr CO16 187 E5
Earlsfield Dr CM2 205 F3
Earlsmead CM8 176 F3
Earlswood Way CO2 135 D2
East Anglian Rly Mus* CO6 106 D6
East Area IP1 16 C7
East Bay CO1 136 B7
East Bergholt CE Prim Sch CO7 59 B3

East Bergholt High Sch CO7 59 D3
East Bergholt Place Gdn* CO7 59 F1
East Court Ho CO1 136 C7
East Dock Rd CO12 90 F6
East End La CO7 60 C2
East End Rd CO7 60 A3
East Essex Aviation Mus* CO16 185 E4
East Gores Rd CO6 131 F5
East Hanningfield Rd CM2 217 E2
East Haven CO15 188 E5
East Hill CO1 136 A7
East La CO7 85 B5
East Lawn IP4 18 C8
East Mersea Rd CO5 183 E1
East Mill CO9 76 F2
East Mill Gn IP9 60 E6
East Rd
Bishop's Stortford CM23 146 B7
East Mersea CO5 184 D1
West Mersea CO5 201 E7
East Row IP9 62 D6
East Side CO4 83 A4
East St Braintree CM7 128 A3
Coggeshall CO6 131 A2
Colchester CO1 136 B7
Harwich CO12 91 D4
Saffron Walden CB10 22 E1
Sudbury CO10 33 F8
Tollesbury CM9 199 D1
Wivenhoe CO7 164 B7
East Stockwell St CO1 135 F7
East Terr CO14 144 D1
East View CM22 148 C8
East View Cl CB10 45 F8
East Ward Mews CO1 136 C7
Eastacre CB10 22 E2
Eastby Cl CB11 43 F8
Eastcliff Ave CO15 189 B4
Eastcliff Ho CO14 144 D1
Easten Greene CO6 80 E4
Eastend La CM6,CM22 121 C8
Easterford Rd CO5 158 C2
Easterling Cl CO12 91 A4
Eastern App CM2 205 F5
Eastern Ave CB9 8 F8
Eastern Cl IP4 18 F4
Eastern Cres CM1 204 F5
Eastern Prom CO16 185 F3
Eastern Rd CO7 185 E6
Eastgate
Great Chesterford CB10 3 D2
13 Ipswich IP4 17 D6
Eastgate St CO12 91 D6
Easthorpe Rd
Feering CO5 159 D7
Messing CO5 159 F5
Eastland Ct IP11 221 B7
Easton Rd CM8 177 A3
Easton Way CO13 171 B6
Eastway Ent Ctr IP1 16 D8
Eastways CM8 177 B4
Eastwood Dr CO4 110 B3
Eaton Cl IP11 221 A7
Eaton Cotts CO5 179 D7
Eaton Gdns IP11 221 C2
Eaton Ho 5 CM23 146 B8
Eaton Mews CO2 136 B3
Eaton Way CM9 196 E7
Ebenezer Cl CM8 176 E5
Ebenezer Terr CM2 216 F7
Ebony Cl CO2 135 D2
Eccles Rd IP2 16 D1
Eckersley Rd CM1 205 C3
Eden Cl CM8 176 E3
Eden Rd Haverhill CB9 9 A7
Ipswich IP4 18 B5
Eden Way CM1 204 C5
Edens Cl CM23 146 B7
Edenside CO13 170 E7
Edgefield Ave CO11 86 B3
Edgeworth Rd IP2 16 E2
Edgware Rd CO16 188 D5
Edgworth Rd CO10 33 E7
Edinburgh Cl CM8 195 A8
Edinburgh Gdns
Bishop's Stortford CM23 145 E6
Braintree CM7 128 C4
Edison Cl 3 CM7 127 F1
Edison Gdns CO4 110 C1
Edison Rd CO15 189 F6
Edith Borthwick Sch The CM7 127 F8
Edith Cavell Way CB9 27 C6
Edith Rd
Clacton-on-S CO15 188 E2
Kirby-le-S CO13 170 D8
Edmund Cl CB9 8 F8
Edmund Gn CO9 102 E8
Edmund Rd CM8 194 E8
Edward Ave CO7 185 F7
Edward Bowden Ct CB10 22 D1
Edward Bright Cl CM9 210 A2
Edward Cl Ipswich IP1 16 F8
Little Clacton CO16 168 E5
Edward Cordy Ho IP11 221 E3
Edward Dr CM2 216 C7
Edward Marke Dr CO5 163 B3
Edward Rd CO16 168 F7
Edward St CO12 90 E5
Edward Terr CO16 168 E5
Edwards Wlk CM9 209 F3
Egerton Green Rd CO2 135 A3
Egglestone Cl IP2 16 F1
Eggshell La CM7 27 E2
Eglinton Dr CM2 206 B4
Egremont St CO10 2 B3
Egremont Way CO3 134 C4
Egret Cres CO4 137 A8
Ehringshausen Way CB9 9 B7
Eight Acre La CO2 135 C2
Eight Ash Green & Aldham CE Prim Sch CO3 107 F1
Eld La CO1 135 F7
Elder Field CM77 154 B5
Elderberry Gdns CM8 177 B4
Eldon Cl CO4 110 E1
Eldred Ave CO2 135 B3
Eldred Dr CO10 34 C4
Eleanor Cl CO5 179 D6
Eleanor Wlk CO5 179 D6
Eleventh Ave CM24 120 B2
Elgar Dr CM8 194 F7
Elgin Ave CM1 205 A2
Elianore Rd CO3 135 B7
Eliot Way CM9 210 A1
Elizabeth Ave CM8 195 A8
Elizabeth Cl
Highwoods CO4 110 C4
Saffron Walden CB10 22 F2
Elizabeth Ct CO14 144 E3
Elizabeth Rd
Bishop's Stortford CM23 145 E5
Harwich CO12 91 A3
Elizabeth Villas CO5 180 A2
Elizabeth Way
Brightlingsea CO7 185 F6
Felixstowe IP11 221 C3
Halstead CO9 76 E2
Hatfield Peverel CM3 194 A4
Heybridge CM9 210 A5
Saffron Walden CB10 22 F2
Sudbury CO10 33 C5
Wivenhoe CO7 137 C3
Ellen Friend Ho CM23 146 B6
Ellen Way CM77 154 D7
Ellenborough Cl CM23 145 D5
Ellenbrook Gn IP2 16 D1
Ellenbrook Rd IP2 16 D1
Elliot Pl CM7 128 C3
Elliots Dr CO14 171 B8
Elliott St IP1 17 A6
Ellis Rd Boxted CO4 82 F3
Bradfield CO11 114 D8
Clacton-on-S CO15 188 E2
Elm Ave CM9 210 C5
Elm Bglws CM7 127 D4
Elm Cl Alresford CO7 165 B8
Brantham CO11 60 D1
Chelmsford CM1 205 A8
Elsenham CM22 94 C2
Great Baddow CM2 216 F6
Great Bentley CO7 166 E8
Haverhill CB9 8 F8
Sible Hedingham CO9 51 D2
Takeley CM22 148 C7
Tiptree CO5 179 C7
Elm Close Extension CM22 148 C7
Elm Cres CO4 136 D7
Elm Ct Elmdon CB11 20 B4
Sturmer CB9 9 E5
Elm Dr Brightlingsea CO7 185 D7
Halstead CO9 76 F1
Harwich CO12 91 B3
Elm Est CO7 59 C3
Elm Gdns IP11 221 A7
Elm Gr
Bishop's Stortford CM23 146 B7
Clacton-on-S CO15 188 F6
Jaywick CO16 188 A2
Kirby Cross CO13 170 D6
Saffron Walden CB10 22 D1
Wivenhoe CO7 137 B1
Elm Green La CM3 218 C8
Elm Green Prep Sch CM3 207 D3
Elm Ho IP11 221 C4
Elm La Capel St M IP9 35 A1
Marks Tey CO5,CO6 132 B2
Washbrook IP8 35 E8
Elm Rd
Bishop's Stortford CM23 145 F8
Chelmsford CM2 216 A8
East Bergholt CO7 59 C3
Little Clacton CO16 168 C3
Rushmere St A IP5 18 F7
Sudbury CO10 34 A7
Elm Rise CM8 177 A5
Elm St IP1 17 C6
Elm Tree Ave CO13 170 F7
Elm Tree Cl CO13 170 F7
Elm Way CM3 192 E1
Elm Wlk CM77 126 F2
Elmbrook Dr CM23 145 E3
Elmcroft CO7 138 A6
Elmdale Dr CO11 86 D3
Elmden Ct CO15 188 E5
Elmdon Pl 1 CB9 9 B8
Elmfield Cl CO15 189 E7
Elmhurst Cl CB9 9 B7
Elmhurst Dr IP3 17 F3
Elmhurst Rd CO12 91 C3
Elms Dr CM1 205 A4
Elms Hall Rd CO6 104 E8
Elms The
East Bergholt CO7 60 C3
Frinton-on-S CO13 170 F6
Great Chesterford CB10 3 E3
Elmstead Prim Sch CO7 137 F6
Elmstead Rd
Colchester CO4 136 E5
Wivenhoe CO7 137 D4
Elmwood CO3 134 D6
Elmwood Ave CO2 135 B2
Elmwood Dr CO5 201 D7
Elsenham CE Prim Sch CM22 94 D1
Elsenham Cross CM22 94 D1
Elsenham Sta CM22 94 C3
Elsham Dr CM77 154 B6
Elsmere Rd IP1 17 C8
Elthorne Pk CO16 188 D4
Elton Park Bsns Ctr IP2 16 E6
Elton Pk IP2 16 D6
Elton Wlk CO5 179 D6
Elvina Ho CO15 203 F6
Elwes Cl CO4 110 D1
Elwin Rd CO5 179 D5
Elysian Gdns CM9 199 C1
Embassy Ct CM9 210 A2
Emberson Ct CM2 205 F4
Emblems CM6 123 C1
Embra Ct CO2 136 B5
Emily May Ct CO12 91 A3
Emlen St IP1 17 A6
Emmanuel Cl IP2 16 F3
Emperor Circ IP3 38 C8
Empire Ct CO15 188 E3
Empire Rd CO12 91 D3
Empire Wlk 2 CM2 205 C2
Empress Ave CO5 201 E6
Empress Dr CO5 201 D6
Emson Cl CB10 22 D2
Endean Ct CO7 137 A2
Endeavour Cl CM9 199 D2
Endsleigh Ct CO3 135 C7
Endway The
Great Easton CM6 122 F7
Steeple Bumpstead CB9 27 C8
Engaines Prim Sch CO16 168 C2
Engleric SG8 19 D5
Enid Way CO4 109 D2
Ennerdale Ave CM77 154 C6
Enterprise Ct
Braintree CM7 128 B2
Witham CM8 177 A3
Enville Way CO4 110 B4
Epping Cl
Chelmsford CM1 204 E1
Clacton-on-S CO15 188 F8
Epping Way CM8 176 E1
Epsom Cl CO16 188 D6
Erbury Pl CO10 12 B8
Erica Wlk CO4 136 D7
Erick Ave CM1 205 B7
Eridge Cl CM1 205 D7
Eriswell Rd CB9 9 B8
Erle Havard Rd CO6 108 E4
Ernalds Cl CO6 105 B7
Ernest Rd CO7 137 C1
Ernleigh Rd IP4 18 B6
Errington Rd CO3 135 D5
Erskine Rd CO11 86 D4
Esplanade
Frinton-on-S CO13 170 F3
Harwich CO12 91 E4
Esplanade Ct
Frinton-on-S CO13 171 A5
Harwich CO12 91 E6
Esplanade The CO15 189 G6
Essex Ave
Chelmsford CM1 205 A7
Clacton-on-S CO15 203 E6
Sudbury CO10 15 F2
Essex County Cricket Club* CM2 205 B2
Essex Cty Hospl CO3 135 D6
Essex Hall Rd CO1 109 E1
Essex Hill CB11 20 B2
Essex Knowle CO8 55 F1
Essex Rd Braintree CM7 128 B4
Maldon CM9 209 F1
Essex Regiment Way CM3 191 D5
Essex Show Ground CM3 154 A2
Essex Way IP3 18 E1
Essex Yeomanry Way CO3 134 B7
Estate Yd The CM3 175 C2
Estella Mead CM1 204 E7
Estuary Cl CO4 109 E4
Estuary Cres
Clacton-on-S CO15 188 D3
Shotley Gate IP9 91 B8
Estuary Mews CM9 199 D2
Estuary Park Rd CO5 201 E6
Estuary Rd IP9 91 B8
Eton Ct CO13 171 A5
Eton Rd
Clacton-on-S CO15 188 F4
Frinton-on-S CO13 171 A5
Eudo Rd CO2 135 C4
Euro Ret Pk IP3 18 E1
Europa Pk CM8 177 A3
Europa Way Harwich CO12 90 F4
Ipswich IP1 16 D7
Eustace Rd IP1 16 E8
Euston Ave IP4 18 F6
Euston Ct IP11 221 A4
Evabrook Cl IP2 16 E1
Evelyn Pl CM1 204 F1
Evelyn Rd CM3 153 D4
Evelyn Wood Rd CM77 155 E6
Everest Gdns CM23 145 E6
Everest Way CM9 210 B5
Everett Ho CO1 136 B6
Evergreen Dr CO4 110 D4
Everitt Rd CB10 22 F2
Everitt Way CO9 51 E2
Eves Cnr CM3 218 E7
Eves Cres CM1 205 A5
Eves Ct CO12 90 D1
Eves Orch CO8 55 F1
Evesham Cl IP2 17 A2
Ewan Cl CO3 134 C6
Ewan Way CO3 134 C7
Ewell Hall Chase CO5 158 C1
Ewer Ct CO1 136 A6
Exchange Way 5 CM1 205 B2
Exeter Cl Braintree CM7 128 B5
Great Horkesley CO6 109 C7
Exeter Ct 6 CB9 8 E6
Exeter Dr CO1 136 A7
Exeter Rd
Chelmsford CM1 205 E5
Felixstowe IP11 221 D5
Ipswich IP3 18 B4
Exmoor Cl CM1 204 D1
Exmoor Rd IP11 221 D6

F

Faber Rd CM8 194 E8
Fabians Cl CO6 131 A3
Factory Hill CO5 179 E3
Factory La CO11 86 C7
Factory La E CO9 76 E1
Factory La W CO9 76 E1
Factory Terr CO9 76 E2
Faggot Yd CM7 127 F5
Fair Cl CO7 186 A6
Fair Gn CO10 2 B5
Fair Leas CB10 22 E3
Fairbrother Ct 1 CO4 136 D7
Fairclough Ave CO16 188 B3
Fairfax Hall CO4 109 F4
Fairfax Mead CM2 206 A2
Fairfax Rd 17 CO2 135 F6
Fairfield Ave IP11 221 E5
Fairfield Cl CO7 139 A7
Fairfield Gdns 2 CO4 136 C8
Fairfield Inf Sch IP11 221 E5
Fairfield Rd
Braintree CM7 127 F2
Chelmsford CM1 205 A3
Clacton-on-S CO15 188 E4
Ipswich IP3 18 A2
Fairfield Way CO9 76 F1
Fairfields CM3 220 D1
Fairhaven Ave CO5 201 E6
Fairhead Rd N CO4 136 C8
Fairhead Rd S 6 CO4 136 C8
Fairleads CM3 218 F8
Fairlop Cl CO15 188 F8
Fairstead Hall Rd CM3 175 A5
Fairstead Rd CM3 175 C5
Fairway
Bishop's Stortford CM23 146 C6
Chelmsford CM2 216 D7
Fairways CO4 109 B3
Fairways The IP4 18 E5
Fairy Hall La CM77 127 A1
Fairycroft Rd CB10 22 E1
Fal Dr CM8 176 E2
Falcon Cl CB9 9 C8
Falcon Cres CO1 136 B5
Falcon Fields CM9 220 F8
Falcon Mews CM9 220 F8
Falcon Sq CO9 51 F4
Falcon St Felixstowe IP11 221 C6
Ipswich IP1 17 C5
Falcon Way
Chelmsford CM2 216 A6
Clacton-on-S CO15 188 F6
Falconer Rd CB9 9 C5
Falconer St CM23 145 C5
Falcons Mead CM2 205 A1
Falkland Cl CM3 206 E8
Falkland Ct CM7 128 B4
Falkland Gn CM9 219 E6
Falklands Dr 8 CO11 86 D4
Fallowden La CB10 23 F8
Fallowfield Cl CO12 90 F3
Fallowfield Ct 14 CB9 8 E7
Fallowfield Rd CO2 135 C2
Falmouth Rd CM1 205 E5
Falstaff Cotts IP9 60 F8
Fambridge Chase CM8 155 F2
Fambridge Cl CM9 210 A1
Fambridge Rd CM9 209 F2
Fanner's Green Cotts CM3 190 C5
Fanny's La CO16 167 D2
Faraday Cl Braintree CM7 127 F1
Clacton-on-S CO15 169 A1
Faraday Rd IP4 17 F5
Farford Field CO10 34 C5
Farina Cl IP1 16 F7
Farm Rd CO12 116 D3
Farm Wlk CO7 185 E8
Farmadine CB11 22 E1
Farmadine Ct 3 CB11 22 E1
Farmadine Gr CB11 22 E1
Farmadine Ho 5 CB11 22 E1
Farmers Way CO16 188 B3
Farmfield Rd CO6 106 B1
Farmleigh Ave CO15 188 F8
Farnham CE Prim Sch CM23 118 D6
Farnham Gn CM23 118 B7
Farriers Chase CO5 201 D6
Farriers End CO3 134 D5
Farriers Way CM77 154 B7
Farriers Went IP11 221 B7
Farrington Cl 3 CO1 136 C6
Farrow Rd CM1 215 E7
Farthing Cl CM7 128 D4
Farthing Rd IP1 16 C7
Farthing Road Ind Est IP1 16 C7
Farthings Chase CO5 201 E7
Farthings Went IP9 35 B2
Fastnet Cl CB9 9 D8
Faulds Wlk CO2 136 A3
Faulkbourne Rd CM8 176 D4
Faulkeners Way IP11 221 A8
Fawkner Cl CM2 205 F2
Fawley Cl IP4 18 C7
Feathers Field IP11 221 B5
Feedhams Cl CO7 137 C3
Feering CE Prim Sch CO5 158 E4
Feering Hill CO5 158 D3
Feering Mus* CO5 158 B1
Feering Rd CO6 131 B1
Felaw St IP2 17 D4
Felbrigg Cl CM77 154 B7
Felix Rd Felixstowe IP11 221 F4
Ipswich IP3 18 C2
Felixstowe Beach Cvn Pk IP11 221 C2
Felixstowe Cl CO16 188 A4
Felixstowe General Hospl IP11 221 F4
Felixstowe Rd IP3 18 B3
Felixstowe Sta IP11 221 E5
Fell Christy CM1 205 B5
Fell Rd CO9 28 B8
Fellbrigg Ave IP5 18 F6
Fellowes Cl CO4 109 F2
Felnor Wlk IP11 221 E4
Felstead Cl CO2 163 A8
Felsted Almshouses CM6 152 B6
Felsted Prep Sch CM6 152 B5
Felsted Prim Sch CM6 152 D7
Felsted Sch CM6 152 C6
Felsted Vineyard* CM6 151 C7
Feltwell Pl 2 CB9 9 B8
Fen La CO7 84 D1
Fen Mdw IP11 221 A8
Fen St CO6 56 B1
Fen View IP8 35 E8
Fenbridge La CO7 59 B1
Fenman Ct CM22 94 C2
Fenn Cl CO7 139 A3
Fenn Rd CO9 77 A1
Fennell Cl CO5 179 C5
Fennels Cl CB9 9 A7
Fennes Rd CM7 102 A3
Fennings Chase CO1 136 A7
Fenno Cl CO3 134 F4
Fenton Rd CB9 9 B8
Ferdinand Wlk CO4 136 F7
Ferguson Cl CB11 23 A2
Fern Gr CB9 8 E8
Fern Hill CO10 2 B7
Fern Way CO15 203 F7
Ferndale Cl CO15 188 F7
Ferndale Rd CO12 91 D5
Ferndown Rd CO13 170 E5
Ferndown Way CM3 194 B4
Fernhayes Cl IP2 17 A2
Fernie Rd CM7 127 D2
Fernlea CO4 109 C2
Fernlea Rd CO12 91 D5
Fernwood Ave CO15 189 F5
Ferry La IP11 221 A3
Ferry Rd CO5 164 B6
Festival Gdns CM9 198 D4
Feverills Rd CO16 168 D4
Fiat Ave CO15 203 D6
Fiddlers Folly CO3 107 E1
Fiddlers Hill CO3 107 E2
Fiddlers La CO7 59 C3
Field Ct CO4 136 E8
Field Gate La CM22 94 A3
Field View Dr CM9 197 C4
Field Way CO7 137 C2
Field Wlk CO14 171 A8
Fieldgate Dock CO7 185 E5
Fields Cl CO16 167 F6
Fields Farm Rd CO2 162 B4
Fields View CO10 33 F8
Fieldside CB11 43 E7
Fieldview Cl CO4 109 F4
Fifth Ave Chelmsford CM1 205 B6
Frinton-on-S CO13 170 E5
Halstead CO9 77 B1
Stansted Mountfitchet CM24 120 B2
Finbars Wlk IP4 17 F5
Finborough Cl IP4 18 F6
Finch Dr Braintree CM7 127 D4
Great Bentley CO7 139 D1
Finch Hill CO10 33 A7
Finch's CM8 195 F6
Finchdale CO15 188 F6
Finchingfield CE Prim Sch CM7 72 D6
Finchingfield Guildhall Mus* CM7 72 D6
Finchingfield Rd
Stambourne CO9 49 C7
Steeple Bumpstead CB9 27 C6
Finchingfield Way CO2 163 A8
Finchley Ave CM2 216 A8
Finchley Rd IP4 17 E6
Findley Cl IP9 61 F2
Finer Cl CO16 188 C5

Fingringhoe CE Prim Sch
CO5 .....163 F5
Fingringhoe Rd
Abberton CO5 .....163 B3
Colchester CO2,CO5 .....136 D1
Fingringhoe Wick Conservation Ctr*
CO5 .....164 D3
Fingringhoe Wick Nature Reserve & Visitor Ctr*
CO5 .....164 D3
Finham Cl CO4 .....136 F7
Finsbury Pl CO9 .....76 F2
Fir Tree Cl CO4 .....110 B4
Fir Tree Hill IP9 .....62 E4
Fir Tree La CM3 .....207 E1
Fir Tree Rise
Chelmsford CM2 .....216 B6
Ipswich IP8 .....16 C2
Fir Tree Wlk CM9 .....210 C5
Fir Way CO15 .....203 G6
Firebronds Rd IP9 .....62 D5
Firecrest Rd CM2 .....216 C5
Firefly Way IP3 .....38 B8
Firlands CM23 .....145 E6
Firlands Ho CM23 .....145 E6
Firlie Wlk CO2 .....136 A2
Firmins Ct CO6 .....108 D4
Firs Chase CO5 .....201 A6
Firs Chase Cvn Pk CO5 .....201 A7
Firs Cvn Pk CO16 .....168 D2
Firs Dr CM1 .....204 B1
Firs Hamlet CO5 .....201 A6
Firs Jun & Mid Sch The
CM23 .....145 E6
Firs Rd Tiptree CO5 .....179 D4
West Mersea CO5 .....201 B7
Firs The Gosfield CO9 .....102 E8
Layer-de-l-H CO2 .....162 A6
First Ave Chelmsford CM1 .....205 B5
Clacton-on-S CO15 .....189 B4
Frinton-on-S CO13 .....170 E4
Glemsford CO10 .....2 C5
Halstead CO9 .....77 B1
Harwich CO12 .....91 C3
Seawick CO16 .....203 C6
Stansted Mountfitchet
CM24 .....120 B2
Walton-on-t-N CO14 .....144 E3
Weeley CO16 .....140 F1
Firstore Dr CO3 .....134 E7
Firwood's Rd CO9 .....103 E8
Fish Pond Hill IP9 .....63 C3
Fish St CM9 .....211 E6
Fishbane Cl IP3 .....38 B8
Fisher Cl CB9 .....9 D8
Fisher Way CM7 .....128 C4
Fisher's La CO7 .....60 C3
Fishmarket St CM6 .....70 A2
Fishponds Hill CO6 .....81 F4
Fishponds La IP9 .....62 E5
Fisin Wlk CO3 .....134 E3
Fiske Ct CO15 .....188 F2
Fitches Cres CM9 .....210 B1
Fitches Croft CO6 .....133 C4
Fitches Mews CM9 .....210 B1
Fitzgerald Cl CO11 .....86 B4
Fitzgerald Cotts CO12 .....90 F2
Fitzgerald Ct IP4 .....18 A5
Fitzgilbert Rd CO2 .....135 C4
Fitzmaurice Rd IP3 .....18 B3
Fitzpiers CB10 .....22 E2
Fitzroy St 2 IP1 .....17 C6
Fitzwalter La CM3 .....218 D6
Fitzwalter Pl
Chelmsford CM1 .....204 E3
Great Dunmow CM6 .....150 D8
Fitzwalter Rd
Boreham CM3 .....206 F8
Colchester CO3 .....135 B6
Little Dunmow CM6 .....151 E7
Fitzwilliam Cl IP2 .....16 F2
Fitzwilliam Rd CO3 .....135 B7
Five Acres Bicknacre CM3 .....218 F3
Holbrook IP9 .....62 D5
Stansted Mountfitchet
CM24 .....119 E8
Walton-on-t-N CO14 .....171 B8
Five Fields CO4 .....136 E7
Five Ways CO3 .....134 D4
Fiveash La CM7 .....129 E1
Flag Hill CO7 .....186 F8
Flagstaff Rd CO2 .....135 F6
Flail Cl CO7 .....137 F6
Flanders Cl CM7 .....127 E5
Flanders Field CO2 .....136 B3
Flatford Dr CO16 .....188 B5
Flatford Mill (Field Ctr)*
CO7 .....85 D7
Flatford Rd
East Bergholt CO7 .....85 C8
Haverhill CB9 .....8 C8
Flavian Cl CB9 .....9 D7
Flax La CO10 .....2 C3
Fleetwood Ave
Felixstowe IP11 .....221 F5
Holland-on-S CO15 .....189 E7
Fleetwood Cl CO15 .....189 E7
Fleetwood Rd IP11 .....221 F5
Fleming Cl 7 CM7 .....127 F1
Flemish Cotts The CO7 .....84 F6
Flemish Ct CO1 .....135 F8
Fletcher Rd IP3 .....18 A1
Flint Cl IP2 .....17 B2
Flintwich Manor CM1 .....204 E7
Flitch Ind Est The CM6 .....150 D7
Flitch La CM6 .....150 E7
Flixton Cl CO16 .....188 A4
Flood La CO4 .....110 C6
Flora Rd CM8 .....176 D4
Florence Cotts CO7 .....185 F6
Florence Rd CO14 .....144 E2
Florence Wlk 8 CM23 .....145 F8
Florie's Rd CO6 .....131 F8
Flowers Way CO15 .....203 G7
Foley Cotts CM7 .....102 D3
Folkards La CO7 .....185 F8
Folley The CO3 .....134 D5
Folly La IP8 .....35 D4
Folly Mill La CM6 .....96 E6
Folly The
Layer-de-l-H CO2 .....162 A5
Tiptree CO5 .....179 F2
Wivenhoe CO7 .....164 C7
Fonnereau Rd IP1 .....17 C6
Ford End CE Prim Sch
CM3 .....172 B6
Ford La CO7 .....165 A5
Ford Rd CO15 .....188 D3
Ford Road Ind Est CO15 .....188 D3
Ford St CO6 .....107 C2
Fordham All Saints CE Prim Sch CO6 .....107 D4
Fordham Pl IP4 .....18 F5
Fordham Rd
Bures CO6, CO8 .....79 F2
Wormingford CO6 .....80 E2
Fords La CO4 .....109 D5
Fordson Rd CM2 .....206 B6
Fordstreet Hill CO6 .....107 C2
Fordwater Cl CO9 .....10 B3
Fordwich Rd CO7 .....165 E1
Fore Field CM7 .....128 D3
Fore Hamlet IP3 .....17 E5
Fore St IP4 .....17 D5
Forefield Gn CM1 .....205 F7
Foremans CM1 .....204 E3
Foresight Rd CO2 .....136 D2
Forest Dr CM1 .....204 E1
Forest Park Ave CO15 .....188 F7
Forest Rd
Colchester CO4 .....136 D7
Witham CM8 .....177 A5
Forester Cl IP8 .....36 E8
Foresters Ct CO7 .....137 B1
Foresthall Rd CM24 .....119 E4
Forfar Cl IP4 .....18 B8
Forfields Way CM77 .....155 E6
Forge Cotts CO10 .....13 E6
Forge Cres CM7 .....129 D3
Forge St CO7 .....85 A6
Forges Cnr CO10 .....13 E6
Forres CO13 .....170 F4
Forsyth Dr CM7 .....155 A8
Forsythia Cl CM1 .....205 E7
Forties Cl CB9 .....9 D8
Fortinbras Way CM2 .....216 B8
Fortis CM8 .....194 E8
Fortune Cl CM3 .....174 A7
Fossetts La CO6 .....107 F4
Foster Ct 2 CM8 .....177 A2
Foster Rd
Great Totham CM9 .....196 A4
Harwich CO12 .....90 E5
Foster's Cotts CM7 .....129 D2
Foundation St 13 IP4 .....17 C5
Foundry La Copford CO6 .....133 D5
Earls Colne CO6 .....105 B6
Ipswich IP2 .....17 C5
Fountain Ct Harwich CO12 .....91 E5
West Mersea CO5 .....201 D7
Fountain La Copford CO6 .....134 A1
Easthorpe CO6 .....160 F8
Fountains Rd IP2 .....16 F1
Four Acres
Great Chesterford CB10 .....3 E3
Saffron Walden CB11 .....22 E1
Four Ash Hill CO9 .....10 E1
Four Ashes CM7 .....74 C1
Four Sisters CO7 .....59 B5
Fourth Ave
Chelmsford CM1 .....205 B5
Clacton-on-S CO15 .....189 C4
Frinton-on-S CO13 .....170 F4
Glemsford CO10 .....2 B5
Halstead CO9 .....77 B1
Seawick CO16 .....203 B6
Stansted Mountfitchet
CM24 .....120 B2
Fourways CM22 .....94 C1
Fowe's La CO10 .....31 B8
Fowler Ct CM2 .....216 A4
Fowlers Arc CO13 .....170 F4
Fowlmere Rd SG8 .....19 A6
Fox Burrows La CM1 .....204 B2
Fox Cres CM1 .....204 F4
Fox Yd CO9 .....53 C5
Foxburrow Rd IP3 .....18 F1
Foxdells La CM23 .....118 F2
Foxden CM8 .....177 D6
Foxendale Folly CO3 .....134 C7
Foxes Cnr CO6 .....107 D1
Foxes La
Aldham CO3,CO6 .....133 D8
Ashen CO10 .....11 D1
Foxes Rd CO10 .....11 E1
Foxglove Cl
Bishop's Stortford CM23 .....145 C6
Clacton-on-S CO15 .....188 F7
Witham CM8 .....176 D3
Foxglove Cres IP3 .....18 E1
Foxglove Way CM1 .....205 F6
Foxglove Wlk 4 CO4 .....136 E7
Foxgrove La IP11 .....221 F5
Foxhall Cl CO7 .....59 C4
Foxhall Fields CO7 .....59 C3
Foxhall Rd IP3,IP4 .....18 D5
Foxholes Rd CM2 .....216 F6
Foxley Dr CM23 .....146 B8
Foxmead CM8 .....177 D6
Foxtail Rd IP3 .....38 E8
Foxwood Cl CO11 .....85 C2
Foxwood Cres IP4 .....18 F5
Frambury La CB11 .....66 F8
Framlingham Ct 5 IP1 .....17 A8
Framlingham Way
CM77 .....154 C7
Frampton Rd IP3 .....38 A8
Frances Cl CO7 .....137 B2
Frances Gn CM1 .....206 A7
Francis Cl Haverhill CB9 .....8 F8
Tiptree CO5 .....179 C4
Francis Ct CM8 .....156 C5
Francis Rd
Braintree CM7 .....127 D2
14 Sudbury CO10 .....33 E7
Francis St CO7 .....185 F5
Francis Way
Colchester CO4 .....110 D1
Silver End CM8 .....156 C4
Franciscan Way IP1 .....17 C5
Frank Clater Cl CO4 .....136 C8
Frank Naylor Ct 11 CO1 .....135 F7
Franklin Rd IP3 .....18 B2
Fraser Cl CM2 .....216 C8
Fraser Rd IP1 .....16 F7
Frating Abbey Farm Rd
CO7 .....166 C6
Frating Cross CO7 .....166 B7
Frating Ct CM7 .....128 D1
Frating Hill CO7 .....138 D3
Frating Rd Ardleigh CO7 .....111 F6
Great Bromley CO7 .....138 F6
Thorrington CO7 .....166 A7
Frederick Dr CO5 .....179 F5
Fredrick J French Meml Homes CM1 .....205 B6
Fredricks Cl CO11 .....115 B5
Freebournes Ct 5 CM8 .....177 A2
Freebournes Rd CM8 .....177 B2
Freehold Rd IP4 .....18 B6
Freeland Rd CO15 .....188 E1
Freelands CO7 .....186 C6
Freeport Designer Outlet
CM77 .....128 C1
Freewood La CB11 .....20 B3
Freezes Barns CB9 .....27 B7
Fremantle Rd CO2 .....136 B1
French's Wlk 4 CM2 .....205 C2
Frensham Cl CO3 .....134 D7
Frere Ct CM23 .....118 F1
Frere Way CO5 .....164 B6
Freshfields CO12 .....90 F1
Freshwater Cres CM9 .....210 B4
Freshwater La CO15 .....188 F7
Freshwell Gdns CB10 .....22 C2
Freshwell St CB10 .....22 D2
Fresian Cl CM7 .....127 D2
Freston Hill IP9 .....37 E4
Freston Rd IP3 .....38 C8
Freston St IP9 .....37 E3
Friars IP9 .....60 B8
Friars Bridge Rd IP1 .....17 B5
Friars Cl
Clacton-on-S CO15 .....188 E6
Colchester CO4 .....110 C2
Sible Hedingham CO9 .....51 D2
Wivenhoe CO7 .....164 C8
Friars Ct CO2 .....136 C3
Friars Ctyd 1 IP1 .....17 C5
Friars Grove Jun & Inf Schs
CO4 .....110 C2
Friars La Braintree CM7 .....127 F4
Maldon CM9 .....209 F2
Friars St Ipswich IP1 .....17 C5
Sudbury CO10 .....33 E7
Friars Wlk CM2 .....205 B1
Friars Wood CM23 .....146 C8
Friary Fields CM9 .....210 A2
Friday Wood Gn CO2 .....162 F8
Friedberg Ave CM23 .....145 D4
Friends Field CO8 .....55 F1
Friends Sch CB11 .....43 D8
Friends Wlk CB11 .....43 D7
Frietuna Rd CO13 .....170 E6
Frinton Ct CO13 .....170 F3
Frinton Park Ct CO14 .....171 A6
Frinton Rd
Holland-on-S CO15 .....189 E6
Kirby Cross CO13 .....170 D6
Thorpe-le-S CO16 .....142 B1
Frinton Sta CO13 .....170 F5
Frinton-on-Sea Prim Sch
CO13 .....170 E5
Fritillary Cl IP8 .....36 E8
Fritton Cl IP2 .....17 A1
Fritton Ct 10 CB9 .....8 E7
Frobisher Dr CO15 .....187 F1
Frobisher Prim Sch
CO15 .....187 F1
Frobisher Rd
Harwich CO12 .....90 F1
Ipswich IP3 .....17 E1
Frobisher Way CM7 .....128 C4
Frog Hall Cl CO5 .....164 B6
Frog Mdw CO7 .....84 F7
Frogge St CB10 .....3 B3
Fronk's Ave CO12 .....91 C2
Fronk's Rd CO12 .....91 B2
Front Rd IP3 .....38 D8
Frowick La CO16 .....167 B2
Fryatt Ave CO12 .....91 A4
Fuchsia Ct 6 CO4 .....136 D8
Fuchsia La IP4 .....18 A5
Fuchsia Way CO16 .....188 C5
Fulcher Ave CM2 .....205 F3
Fulfen Way CB11 .....43 D7
Fullbridge CM9 .....210 A3
Fuller Ct 3 CM23 .....146 A7
Fuller's Cl CO5 .....158 B2
Fullers Gate CO5 .....158 B2
Fullers Rd CO2 .....136 D2
Fulmar Cl CO4 .....137 A8
Fulton Cres CM23 .....146 C8
Furneaux La CO5 .....163 F5
Furness Cl IP2 .....36 F8
Furriers Cl CM23 .....145 C5
Furrow Cl CO3 .....134 E5
Further Mdw CM1 .....215 A8
Furze Cres CO7 .....165 A7
Furze La CO7 .....139 A5

G

Gablefields CM2 .....217 D6
Gables The CB9 .....9 F4
Gaces Acre CB11 .....43 A1
Gadwall Reach CO5 .....158 D2
Gage's Rd
Belchamp St P CO10 .....13 A1
Little Yeldham C10 .....30 F8
Gager Dr CO5 .....179 E5
Gaiger Cl CM1 .....205 D7
Gainsborough Cl
Clacton-on-S CO16 .....188 B6
West Mersea CO5 .....201 D6
Gainsborough Cres
CM2 .....205 E3
Gainsborough Dr CO11 .....86 C4
Gainsborough La IP3 .....37 F7
Gainsborough Rd
Black Notley CM77 .....155 A4
Colchester CO3 .....135 B5
Felixstowe IP11 .....221 F4
Ipswich IP4 .....17 D8
Sudbury CO10 .....33 E8
Gainsborough St CO10 .....33 E7
Gainsborough's House Mus*
CO10 .....33 E7
Gainsford Ave CO15 .....189 B4
Gainsford End Rd CO9 .....50 B6
Galiots CO5 .....201 A6
Gall End La CM24 .....119 F7
Galleydene Ave CM2 .....216 C3
Galleywood Inf Sch
CM2 .....216 C2
Galleywood Rd
Chelmsford CM2 .....216 A5
Great Baddow CM2 .....216 E5
Galliford Rd CM9 .....210 A4
Galliford Road Ind Est
CM9 .....210 A4
Galloway Cl 1 CM23 .....145 F8
Galloway Dr CO16 .....168 D3
Galloway Rd CM23 .....118 F1
Gallows Green Rd CM6 .....97 F2
Gallows Hill CB11 .....43 C7
Galsworthy Cl CM7 .....155 A7
Gandish Cl CO7 .....59 D1
Gandish Rd CO7 .....59 E2
Ganges Rd IP9 .....91 B8
Gannet Cl CB9 .....9 C8
Gannet Rd IP2 .....16 E3
Gaol La CO10 .....33 E7
Gap The Arkesden CB11 .....41 F1
Holland-on-S CO15 .....189 G6
Garden Ct CO13 .....170 F3
Garden Dr CO3 .....134 E6
Garden Farm CO5 .....201 D7
Garden Field
Felixstowe IP11 .....221 C5
Hatfield Peverel CM3 .....193 F4
Garden Field Cotts CO6 .....81 E5
Garden Fields
Great Tey CO6 .....132 C8
Stebbing CM6 .....124 D6
Garden Pl CO10 .....33 D7
Garden Rd
Clacton-on-S CO15 .....203 G7
Walton-on-t-N CO14 .....171 A7
Garden Terr CO9 .....76 F2
Gardeners CM2 .....216 D5
Gardeners Rd CO9 .....76 F1
Gardeners Row CO6 .....131 A2
Gardenia Pl CO16 .....188 B4
Gardenia Wlk CO4 .....136 E7
Garfield Cl IP11 .....221 D3
Garfield Rd IP11 .....221 D3
Garland Rd CO12 .....90 F5
Garling Wlk CO6 .....108 E3
Garnets Mead CM3 .....175 B3
Garnetts CM22 .....148 B8
Garnetts Bglws CM6 .....152 C5
Garnetts La CM6 .....152 C6
Garnetts Villas CM6 .....152 C5
Garnons Chase CO6 .....81 A5
Garret Pl CO6 .....108 F4
Garrettlands CM2 .....217 F6
Garrison La IP11 .....221 D4
Garrod Ct CO2 .....163 B7
Garrods IP9 .....35 B1
Garthwood Cl CO6 .....108 E4
Gascoigne Rd CO4 .....136 C8
Gasfield 14 CO11 .....86 D4
Gasgoine Ho CO4 .....109 F4
Gaston End CO7 .....59 C3
Gaston St CO7 .....59 C3
Gatacre Ct CO2 .....135 B3
Gatacre Rd IP1 .....17 A7
Gate St CM9 .....209 F3
Gate Street Mews CM9 .....209 F3
Gatefield Cl CO14 .....170 F7
Gatekeeper Cl
8 Braintree CM7 .....127 F1
Ipswich IP8 .....36 E8
Gatwick Cl CM23 .....119 B1
Gauden Rd CM7 .....127 F7
Gavin Way
Colchester CO4 .....110 B5
Colchester,Brinkley Gr
CO4 .....110 A5
Gawlers CM23 .....92 B8
Gay Bowers La CM3 .....218 F6
Gay Bowers Rd CM3 .....218 F4
Gay Bowers Way CM8 .....195 A7
Gaye St 1 IP1 .....17 B6
Gazelle Ct CO4 .....110 C4
Generals La CM3 .....192 B2
Generals Mews IP11 .....221 B5
Genesta Cl CM9 .....199 D2
Geneva Rd IP1 .....17 B7
Genevyll Cl CO10 .....1 D2
Gentian Ct CO4 .....109 C2
Geoff Seaden Cl 2 CO1 .....136 C6
George Ave CO7 .....185 F7
George Cl CO15 .....188 C2
George Ct CM2 .....205 B1
George Cut CO7 .....185 F6
George Frost Cl IP4 .....17 D7
George Gent Cl CB9 .....27 B6
George La CO10 .....2 B3
George Rd CM7 .....127 D2
George St
Chelmsford CM2 .....205 B1
12 Colchester CO1 .....135 F7
Harwich CO12 .....91 D6
Saffron Walden CB10 .....22 D1
George Williams Way
CO1 .....136 A6
George Yd 7 CM7 .....127 F3
Georgian Ct IP11 .....221 D5
Gepp Pl CM2 .....206 B4
Geralds Ave IP4 .....18 A5
Geranium Cl CO16 .....188 C4
Geranium Wlk CO4 .....136 D7
Gerard Ave CM23 .....145 E4
Gerard Rd CO16 .....188 C6
Gernon Cl CM1 .....191 B3
Gernon Rd CO7 .....111 E7
Gershwin Bvd CM8 .....194 F7
Gestingthorpe Rd CO10 .....31 F4
Gibbons Ct CM6 .....123 D1
Gibbons St 3 IP1 .....17 A6
Gibbs Field CM23 .....145 D5
Gibson Cl CB10 .....22 D1
Gibson Gdns CB10 .....22 D1
Gibson Rd CO9 .....51 D1
Gibson Vale CM1 .....205 B8
Gibson Way CB10 .....22 D1
Giffins Cl CM7 .....127 F1
Gifford Cl IP9 .....62 D5
Giffords Pl IP4 .....18 F6
Gilberd Ct CO4 .....110 C6
Gilberd Ho CO3 .....135 A7
Gilberd Rd CO2 .....136 B4
Gilberd Sch The CO4 .....110 B5
Gilbert Rd CO10 .....12 B8
Gilbert Way CM7 .....128 C5
Gilbey Ave CM23 .....146 B6
Gilbey Cotts CM22 .....94 C1
Gilbey Cres CM24 .....119 E8
Gilbey Gn CB11 .....42 F1
Gilchrist Way CM7 .....127 E4
Gilda Terr CM77 .....127 B2
Gilderdale Cl CO4 .....110 D3
Gilders Way CO16 .....188 C5
Gill Cl CM9 .....209 F6
Gilmore Way CM2 .....217 B6
Gilpin Way CM77 .....154 C7
Gilson Cl CM2 .....205 F2
Gilwell Park Cl CO3 .....135 A4
Gimson Cl CM8 .....176 F2
Gippeswyk Ave IP2 .....17 A4
Gippeswyk Rd IP2 .....17 B4
Gipping Cl CB9 .....8 E6
Gipping Way IP8 .....16 B6
Gipsy La CM23,CM24 .....119 C4
Girling St CO10 .....33 E8
Girton Rd CB9 .....9 B7
Girton Way IP2 .....16 F1
Glade The CO4 .....110 F2
Gladeview CO15 .....188 F7
Gladiator Way CO2 .....135 A2
Gladstone Ct CM2 .....205 B1
Gladstone Rd
Colchester CO1 .....136 B5
Ipswich IP3 .....17 F5
Tiptree CO5 .....179 D4
Gladwin Rd CO2 .....135 D4
Glamis Cl CB9 .....8 D8
Glamorgan Rd IP2 .....17 B1
Glastonbury Cl IP2 .....16 F1
Glebe Ave CM7 .....127 F6
Glebe Cl Elmstead CO7 .....138 A6
Sproughton IP8 .....16 B6
Tattingstone IP9 .....61 C7
Wix CO11 .....115 C5
Glebe Cres
Broomfield CM1 .....191 B1
Witham CM8 .....176 E4
Glebe Ct CM23 .....146 B8
Glebe End Capel St M IP9 .....35 B2
Elsenham CM22 .....94 D1
Glebe Gdns CO5 .....158 E5
Glebe La
Chelmondiston IP9 .....63 A8

Glebe La *continued*
Little Easton CM6 122 F5
Woolverstone IP9 38 B1
Glebe Mdw CM3 190 E7
Glebe Rd
Chelmsford CM1 205 B3
Colchester CO2 135 C2
Heybridge CM9 210 C5
Kelvedon CO5 158 B2
Tiptree CO5 179 C5
Glebe The Elmdon CB11 20 A4
Elsenham CM22 94 C1
Peldon CO5 182 E5
Purleigh CM3 220 D1
Saffron Walden CB11 43 E7
Glebe View CM2 216 B3
Glebe Way
Clacton-on-S CO15 203 G7
Frinton-on-S CO13 170 F5
Glebefield Rd CM3 194 B4
Glebelands CO6 82 B1
Glemham Dr IP4 18 F4
Glemsford Cl IP11 221 B3
Glemsford Com Prim Sch CO10 2 B5
Glemsford Pl 3 CB9 9 B8
Glen Ave CO3 135 B7
Glenavon Rd IP4 18 D7
Glencoe Rd IP4 18 C8
Glendale Gr CO4 110 C3
Gleneagles Dr IP4 18 D5
Gleneagles Way CM3 194 B4
Glenfield Ave IP11 221 E5
Glenhurst Ave IP4 18 B8
Glenside CO10 34 A6
Glentress Cl CO4 110 D3
Glenway Ct CO6 82 B1
Glisson Sq CO2 135 B4
Globe Cl CO5 179 D6
Globe Cres CM23 118 D6
Globe Wlk CO5 179 D6
Globe Yd 4 CO10 33 E8
Gloucester Ave
Chelmsford CM2 216 C6
Colchester CO2 135 C3
Maldon CM9 209 F1
Gloucester Cres CM1 205 A5
Gloucester Gdns CM7 128 B4
Gloucester Ho IP11 221 C6
Gloucester Rd
Haverhill CB9 8 F6
Ipswich IP3 18 B2
Gloucester Way CO10 15 D2
Glovers CM3 173 F7
Goat Hall La
Chelmsford CM2 215 F3
Galleywood CM2 216 A3
Goat House La CM3 219 F4
Goat Lodge Rd CM8, CM9 196 A5
Goda Cl CM8 194 D8
Goddard Way
Chelmsford CM2 205 F2
Saffron Walden CB10 22 E3
Godfrey Way CM6 123 C1
Godfreys Mews CM2 205 B1
Godlings Way CM7 127 F2
Godmans La CO6 132 E3
Godric Pl CM7 127 E3
Godric Rd CM8 194 E8
Godwin Cl CO9 76 D1
Godwit Ct CO5 158 D2
Goff's La CO16 141 F8
Goings La CO5 201 D6
Gold Cl CM22 94 B3
Gold St CB10 22 D1
Goldcrest Cl CO4 137 A8
Goldcrest Ct IP2 16 D3
Goldcrest Rd IP2 16 C3
Golden Dawn Way CO4 109 E2
Golden La Radwinter CB10 25 A2
Thorpe-le-S CO16 141 F3
Golden Lion La CO12 91 E6
Golden Noble Hill CO1 136 A6
Goldenacres CM1 205 F8
Goldenlond CO6 56 C5
Goldfinch Cl CO4 136 F7
Goldhanger Ct CM7 128 D1
Goldhanger Rd CM9 210 D4
Golding Thoroughfare CM2 205 F3
Golding Way
Glemsford CO10 2 B4
St Osyth CO16 187 A5
Goldingham Dr CM7 155 A7
Goldings CM23 146 B8
Goldlay Ave CM2 216 C8
Goldlay Gdns CM2 205 C1
Goldlay Rd CM2 205 C1
Golds Nursery Bsns Pk CM22 94 C3
Golf Green Rd CO15 203 G8
Goodchild Way CO9 30 A2
Goodey Cl CO1 136 A6
Goodier Rd CM1 204 F4
Goodlake Cl CO12 90 F2
Goodliffe Pk CM23 119 B2
Goodmans La CM3 173 F4
Goodwin Cl CM2 216 D8
Goodwin Stile CM23 145 D5
Goodwins Cl CB11 21 E3
Goojerat Rd CO2 135 D5
Gordian Wlk CO4 110 B5
Gordon Dr CO4 110 C5
Gordon Rd
Chelmsford CM2 216 A6
Harwich CO12 91 B2
Ipswich IP4 18 A7
Gordon Way CO12 91 B2
Gore La CM77 127 A2
Gore Rd CM77 127 A2
Gore Terr CM77 127 A2
Gorefield Rd CM22,CM24 121 B5
Gorefield Rdbt CM24 121 B4
Goring Ho CO4 109 E4
Goring Rd
Colchester CO4 110 C1
Ipswich IP4 18 C6
Gorse La
Clacton-on-S CO15 189 A8
Tiptree CO5 179 D4
Gorse Lane Ind Est CO15 189 B8
Gorse Rd IP3 18 B2
Gorse Way
Clacton-on-S CO15 203 F7
Colchester CO3 134 D4
Gorse Wlk CO4 136 D7
Gorsehayes IP2 17 B3
Gosbecks Prim Sch CO2 135 A3
Gosbecks Rd CO2 135 A2
Gosbecks View CO2 135 A2
Gosfield Com Prim Sch CO9 102 E8
Gosfield Hall* CO9 102 C8
Gosfield Rd
Blackheath CO2 163 A8
Braintree CM7 102 D3
Gosfield Sch CO9 75 F2
Gosford Cl CO10 12 B8
Goshawk Dr CM2 216 B5
Goslings The CM8 156 C5
Goul La CB10 22 D1
Gouldings Ave CO14 171 B8
Goulds Rd CO8 54 F2
Goulton Rd CM1 191 A1
Government Ct CO12 91 E5
Gower St IP2 17 C4
Gowers Ave CM2 216 E6
Gowers End CO10 2 C5
Goyfield Ave IP11 221 D4
Grace Gdns CM23 145 F4
Grace's Cross CM2 217 C7
Graces Cl CM8 195 A7
Graces La CM3 207 B1
Graces Wlk CO13 171 A6
Grafton Pl CM2 206 A4
Grafton Rd CO12 91 D4
Grafton Way IP1 17 C5
Graham Ave IP1 17 B8
Graham Rd
Felixstowe IP11 221 D5
Ipswich IP1 17 B7
Grailands CM23 145 D8
Grammar School Pl 11 CO10 33 E7
Grampian Gr CM1 204 D6
Granary Barn Mus The* CO7 85 D7
Granary Ct CM6 150 D7
Granary The CO10 12 B6
Grand Ct CO13 170 F3
Grand The CO13 170 F3
Grange Cl
Felixstowe IP11 221 C5
Halstead CO9 103 E7
Walton-on-t-N CO14 171 A7
Grange Com Prim Sch IP11 221 B4
Grange Ct
Chelmsford CM2 215 F7
Clacton-on-S CO16 188 A4
Grange Farm CO2 136 D4
Grange Farm Ave IP11 221 B5
Grange Farm Rd CO2 136 D4
Grange Hill CO6 130 F1
Grange La CM6 151 C7
Grange Mill CO6 130 F2
Grange Pk CM23 118 F1
Grange Rd
Bishop's Stortford CM23 146 A7
Felixstowe IP11 221 B4
Great Horkesley CO6 109 B7
Harwich CO12 91 A3
Ickleton CB10 20 A8
Ipswich IP4 17 E6
Lawford CO11 85 F1
Little Bromley CO11 112 E7
Tiptree CO5 179 A6
Wickham Bishops CM8 195 E4
Grange The CM23 118 F1
Grange Way CO2 136 D3
Grange Way Bsns Pk CO2 136 D3
Grange Wlk CM23 146 A7
Granger Ave CM9 209 F1
Granger Row CM1 204 F6
Grangeside CM23 119 A2
Granta Cl CB10 3 D1
Granta Cotts CB10 3 C2
Grantham Ave CM77 154 B7
Grantham Cres IP2 17 A4
Grantham Ct CO1 136 A7
Grantham Rd CO6 109 B7
Grantley Cl CO6 133 D5
Grants Ct CO14 171 C8
Granville Cl CO6 108 E3
Granville Rd
Clacton-on-S CO15 188 F3
Colchester CO1 136 B5
Felixstowe IP11 221 D3
Granville St 2 IP1 17 B6
Granville Way CO7 186 A7
Grasby Cl CO7 137 B2
Grasmere Cl
Great Notley CM77 154 C6
Ipswich IP3 18 B1
Grasmere Gdns CO13 170 F7
Grassfields CO13 170 E6
Grassmere CO4 110 B5
Gravel Hill CO6 56 A2
Gravel Hill Way CO12 90 F1
Gravel Pit La CO11 60 E2
Gravel The CO6 130 F2
Gray Rd CO3 135 D6
Gray's Cotts CO1 136 B7
Gray's La CM7 73 E4
Grayling Cl CM7 127 E1
Grayling Dr CO4 110 F1
Grayling Rd IP8 36 E8
Grays Cl CO5 201 C6
Grays Ct CM23 145 E8
Grays Mead CO9 51 D2
Great Baddow High Sch CM2 216 D6
Great Bardfield Cage* CM7 72 B2
Great Bardfield Cottage Mus* CM7 72 A1
Great Bardfield Prim Sch CM7 72 B2
Great Bentley Prim Sch CO7 166 E7
Great Bentley Rd CO7 166 A8
Great Bentley Sta CO7 166 E7
Great Bradfords Jun & Inf Schs CM7 128 B4
Great Canfield Rd CM22 148 D5
Great Chesterford CE Prim Sch CB10 3 D2
Great Chesterford Ct CB10 3 C2
Great Chesterford Sta CB10 3 C1
Great Cob CM1 205 E5
Great Colman St 14 IP4 17 D6
Great Cornard Ctry Pk* CO10 34 C4
Great Cornard Mid Sch CO10 34 C4
Great Cornard Upper Sch & Tech Coll CO10 34 B4
Great Dunmow CE Jun Sch CM6 150 C8
Great Dunmow Inf Sch CM6 123 D1
Great Eastern Cl CM23 146 A6
Great Eastern Ct CO14 171 C7
Great Eastern Rd CO10 33 F7
Great Eastern Sq IP11 221 E5
Great Easton CE Prim Sch CM6 123 A8
Great Field IP11 221 A8
Great Gibcracks Chase CM2 218 A2
Great Gipping St IP1 17 B5
Great Hadham Rd CM23 145 C5
Great Harrods CO14 171 A7
Great Holland Common Rd CO13 169 D2
Great Holland Ct CO13 170 A3
Great Leighs Prim Sch CM3 174 A7
Great Notley Ave CM77 154 C5
Great Oak Ct CO9 30 A1
Great Pitchers CO6 105 A7
Great Sampford Prim Sch CB10 47 A3
Great Sq 9 CM7 127 F3
Great Tey CE Prim Sch CO6 106 C1
Great Tey Rd CO6 132 C4
Great Totham Prim Sch CM9 196 A5
Great Totham Rd CM8 195 F5
Great Tufts IP9 35 B1
Great Waltham CE Prim Sch CM3 190 E7
Great Whip St IP2 17 C4
Great Yeldham Rd CO9 50 D7
Greate House Farm Rd CO2 162 A5
Grebe Cl IP2 16 E2
Green Acres Rd CO2 162 A5
Green Cl Chelmsford CM1 205 D4
Hatfield Peverel CM3 194 C3
Writtle CM1 204 B1
Green Cnr CO7 139 E1
Green Ct CO6 104 F7
Green End La CO13 170 B5
Green Farm Rd CO6 78 B2
Green La Aldham CO6 107 C1
Ardleigh CO7 111 D6
Black Notley CM8 155 A2
Boxted CO4 82 D5
Colchester CO4 110 E2
Colchester, Crockleford Heath CO7 111 C1
Great Dunmow CM6 150 C8
Great Horkesley CO6 109 C6
Great Notley CM8 154 F2
Little Totham CM9 197 C4
Stratford St M CO7 58 C4
Tattingstone IP9 61 D7
Tiptree CO5 179 D6
Tolleshunt Knight's CO5 179 E1
Walton-on-t-N CO14 144 D2
Weeley Heath CO16 168 A6
Green Man La CM8 195 F7
Green Mdws CM3 219 A6
Green Oak Glade IP8 36 D8
Green St CM6 148 F2
Green The
Bishop's Stortford CM23 145 F4
Chelmsford CM1 204 F4
Chrishall SG8 19 D3
Clacton-on-S CO16 188 B2
Colne Engaine CO6 78 A2
Feering CO5 158 E5
Great Bentley CO7 166 D8
Little Totham CM9 197 C4
Mistley CO11 86 F4
Saffron Walden CB10 22 D3
Seawick CO16 203 B6
Stanstead CO10 2 E7
Writtle CM1 204 B1
Green Way CO6 78 A2
Green's Yd CO1 135 E7
Greenacres
Clacton-on-S CO15 189 A5
Coggeshall CO6 130 F1
Colchester CO4 109 E3
Greene View CM7 155 B8
Greenfield CM8 177 A1
Greenfield Cotts CO4 82 E6
Greenfield Dr CO6 106 B1
Greenfields
Galleywood CM2 216 C2
Gosfield CO9 102 F7
Stansted Mountfitchet CM24 119 E7
Greenfields Way CB9 8 E6
Greenfinch Ave IP2 16 D3
Greenfinch End CO4 136 F8
Greenford Rd CO15 188 C3
Greengates Mobile Home Pk CO16 168 C4
Greenhill Pk CM23 145 D5
Greenhurst Rd CO7 186 A6
Greenhythe Ct CO4 136 D6
Greenland Gr CO16 186 D3
Greenlawns Cvn Pk CO16 168 C2
Greens The IP4 18 F4
Greens Yd CO13 170 F5
Greensmill CO11 86 C5
Greenspire Gr IP8 16 B2
Greenstead Ct CO1 136 D6
Greenstead Rd CO1 136 D7
Greenstead Rdbt CO4 136 D6
Greenview Pk CO15 189 A7
Greenway
Bishop's Stortford CM23 146 C6
Frinton-on-S CO13 170 F5
Greenway Cl CO15 189 B7
Greenway Gdns CM77 154 D7
Greenway The CO15 189 B7
Greenways
Chelmsford CM1 205 B6
Feering CO5 158 D3
Gosfield CO9 102 F7
Maldon CM9 209 F2
Saffron Walden CB11 43 E7
Greenways Cl IP1 17 B8
Greenways The CO6 131 A3
Greenwich Bsns Pk IP3 17 E2
Greenwich Cl IP3 17 E2
Greenwich Rd IP3 17 E2
Greenwood Cl CB9 8 E7
Greenwood Gr CO4 110 C3
Gregory St CO10 33 E7
Grenadier Rd CB9 8 C8
Grendel Way CO15 189 F6
Grenfell Ave CO15 189 E6
Grenfell Cl CO4 110 C1
Grenville Rd
Braintree CM7 127 E2
Sudbury CO10 15 F2
Gresley Cl CO4 109 F2
Gresley Dr CM7 128 A2
Gresley Gdns IP2 17 C3
Gretna Gdns IP4 18 B8
Greville Cl CO14 144 E2
Grey Friars Rd 10 IP1 17 C5
Grey Ladys CM2 216 B2
Greyhound Hill CO4 83 E5
Greyhound Rd CO10 2 B3
Greys Cl CO10 1 C1
Greys Hollow CB11 93 D8
Greystones Cl CO3 135 A3
Grieves Ct CO3 134 C4
Griffin Ct IP2 17 D3
Grimston Rd CO2 136 A4
Grimston Way CO14 171 B7
Grimwade Cl CO11 86 D7
Grimwade St IP4 17 D5
Grindle The IP8 16 A7
Groom Ho CO15 188 E4
Groom Pk CO15 188 E4
Groome Ct 2 CO4 136 D7
Grooms La CM8 156 E4
Groomside CM7 128 A2
Grosvenor Cl
Bishop's Stortford CM23 145 D4
Chelmsford CM2 216 D7
Ipswich IP4 17 E8
Tiptree CO5 179 D5
Grosvenor Ct IP3 18 B1
Grosvenor Ho 4 CM23 146 B8
Grosvenor Rd CO10 15 D2
Grove Ave
Walton-on-t-N CO14 171 B8
West Mersea CO5 201 C5
Grove Cotts 1 CM8 177 A2
Grove Ctr The CM8 177 A1
Grove Farm Rd
Little Totham CM9 197 C7
Tiptree CO5,CM9 179 A1
Grove Field CM7 102 C1
Grove Hill Belstead IP8 36 C7
Dedham CO7 84 D4
Ipswich IP8 16 E1
Langham CO4 83 F5
Stansted Mountfitchet CM24 119 E7
Grove La
Chelmondiston IP9 63 E5
Ipswich IP4 17 E5
Grove Lea CM9 194 F1
Grove Orch CM7 102 C1
Grove Pl 19 CM23 145 F7
Grove Rd Bentley IP9 60 E6
Brantham CO11 86 D8
Chelmsford CM2 205 B1
Felixstowe IP11 221 E6
Little Clacton CO16 168 D5
Tiptree CO5 179 E6
Grove The Bicknacre CM3 218 F1
Clacton-on-S CO15 188 F2
Earls Colne CO6 105 B6
Great Hallingbury CM22 146 F4
Witham CM8 177 A2
Grove Villas CM7 126 A8
Grove Wlk IP8 36 D8
Gryme's Dyke Ct CO3 134 D6
Gryme's Dyke Way CO3 134 E3
Guelph's La CM6 70 A3
Guernsey Ct CM9 209 F2
Guernsey Way CM7 127 D2
Guildford Rd CO1 136 A8
Guildhall Way CB10 24 A7
Guinea Cl CM7 128 D4
Guisnes Ct CM9 199 A4
Guithavon Ct CM8 176 F2
Guithavon Rd CM8 176 F1
Guithavon Rise CM8 176 F2
Guithavon St CM8 176 F2
Guithavon Valley CM8 176 F2
Gull Cotts CO16 142 D4
Gull Ct CO16 141 F1
Gull's La CO7 85 A3
Gulls Croft CM7 128 D3
Gulpher Bsns Pk IP11 221 D8
Gulpher Rd IP11 221 E8
Gun Hill CO7 84 C7
Gunfleet Cl CO5 201 B7
Gunfleet Ct CO15 189 C4
Gunson Gate CM2 216 D7
Gurdon Rd CO2 135 F3
Gurney Benham Cl CO2 135 B4
Gurton Rd CO6 131 A3
Gusford Com Prim Sch IP2 16 D1
Gutteridge Hall La CO16 167 E7
Gutters La CM1 205 C7
Guy Cook Cl CO10 34 C4
Guys Farm CM1 204 B1
Gwendoline Cl IP4 18 F4
Gwyn Cl CM3 192 E1
Gwynne Rd CO12 91 D4
Gymnasium St IP1 17 B7
Gypsy La CO5 159 C6

H

Ha'penny Field IP9 62 D5
Ha'penny Gdns IP9 62 D5
Hackmans La CM3 219 E2
Haddon Pk CO1 136 C6
Hadfelda Sq CM3 194 A4
Hadfield Dr CM77 155 B5
Hadham Ct CM23 145 E8
Hadham Gr CM23 145 C8
Hadham Rd CM23 145 D8
Hadleigh Ct
Clacton-on-S CO15 189 A3
4 Saffron Walden CB10 22 F2
Hadleigh Rd
Clacton-on-S CO16 188 B4
East Bergholt CO7 59 B3
Frinton-on-S CO13 171 A5
Ipswich IP2 16 D5
Stratford St M CO7 58 A6
Hadleigh Road Ind Est IP2 16 F7
Hadleigh Way CO13 170 F5
Hadley Cl CM7 102 B1
Hadrian Cl
Colchester CO4 110 B6
Haverhill CB9 9 D7
Hadrians Cl CM8 194 E8
Hadrians Way CM9 210 A4
Hadstock Rd CB1 5 B8
Haggars La CO7 138 F3
Haggers Cl CB10 3 D2
Haglemere Dr IP4 17 E7
Haig Ct CM2 205 A1
Hailes Wood CM22 94 D1
Hailes Wood Cl CM22 94 D1
Hainault Gr CM1 204 E1
Hakewill Way CO4 109 E3
Hale Cl IP2 16 D2
Hale Way CO4 110 B6
Halesowen Cl IP2 36 F8
Half Acres CM23 145 F8
Half Moon Yd CO10 12 B7
Halfacres CM8 195 A7
Halford Ct 6 IP8 16 C2
Halfway Cotts CO5 158 B6
Halifax Prim Sch IP2 17 B2
Halifax Rd IP2 17 B2
Halifax Way CO6 104 F2

Hall Barn CO5 201 B6
Hall Bridge Rise CM9 210 C4
Hall Chase CO6 133 B3
Hall Cl
Great Baddow CM2 217 A6
Henham CM22 94 F5
Hall Cres CO15 189 F6
Hall Cut CO7 185 F6
Hall Dr CO9 102 D8
Hall Est CM9 211 E7
Hall Farm Cl CO5 158 E4
Hall Field IP11 221 C5
Hall La Chelmsford CM2 217 C6
Harwich CO12 91 A2
Ridgewell CO9 29 B6
Thorpe-le-S CO16 169 B8
Walton-on-t-N CO14 144 D2
Hall Pond Way IP11 221 C5
Hall Rd
Belchamp Walter CO10 32 A6
Borley CO10 15 A3
Bures CO8 79 E5
Copford CO6 133 E4
Elsenham CM22 94 D1
Fordham CO6 107 D5
Great Bromley CO7 112 C2
Great Totham CM9 196 C3
Maldon CM9 210 B4
Panfield CM7 127 A6
Tiptree CO5 179 C3
Tollesbury CM9 199 D1
West Bergholt CO6 108 D5
Hall Rise Sudbury CO10 33 C6
Witham CM8 194 F8
Hall Road Cotts CO6 108 D6
Hall St Chelmsford CM2 205 B1
Long Melford CO10 15 C8
Hall View Rd CO7 166 E7
Hall Villas CM7 72 B1
Hallcroft Chase CO4 110 C4
Hallett Rd CM6 151 E6
Hallingbury Cl CM22 146 B1
Hallingbury Rd CM22, CM23 146 B4
Halliwell Rd IP4 18 B6
Halstead Hospl CO9 76 E3
Halstead Rd
Braintree CM7 102 E3
Colchester CO3 134 D7
Earls Colne CO6 104 F7
Eight Ash G CO6 134 A8
Fordham CO6 107 B3
Fordham Heath CO6 107 E1
Gosfield CO9 75 F1
Kirby Cross CO13 170 B7
Kirby-le-S CO13 170 C8
Sible Hedingham CO9 76 B6
Halston Pl CM9 220 F8
Halton Cres IP3 18 C1
Hamble Cl CM8 176 E2
Hamel Way CB11 67 D4
Hamford Cl CO14 144 D2
Hamford Dr CO12 116 C3
Hamford Prim Sch CO13 170 F7
Hamilton Ct
Brightlingsea CO7 186 A7
Chelmsford CM1 204 D6
Clacton-on-S CO15 189 E6
Hamilton Gdns IP11 221 F3
Hamilton Ho IP4 18 A7
Hamilton Mews 3 CB10 22 F2
Hamilton Prim Sch CO3 135 D5
Hamilton Rd
Colchester CO3 135 D5
Felixstowe IP11 221 E4
Great Holland CO13 170 A5
Ipswich IP3 18 B3
Sudbury CO10 33 E7
Takeley CM6 148 F7
Wivenhoe CO7 164 B8
Hamilton St
Felixstowe IP11 221 C5
Harwich CO12 90 F5
Hamlet Ct CO8 79 E8
Hamlet Dr CO4 136 F7
Hamlet Rd
Chelmsford CM2 205 B1
Haverhill CB9 9 B7
Hammonds Rd CM3 206 E3
Hampit Rd CB11 41 D2
Hampstead Ave CO16 188 D5
Hampton Rd
Great Baddow CM2 216 E6
Ipswich IP1 16 F7
Hamsters Cl CO9 77 F8
Hanbury Gdns CO4 110 B5
Hanbury Rd CM1 215 E8
Hance La CM77 126 F2
Hanchetts Orch CM6 70 A3
Handel Wlk CO4 136 E6
Handford Cut IP1 17 A6
Handford Hall Prim Sch IP1 17 A6
Handford Rd IP1 17 A6
Handley's La CM8 195 F5
Handy Fisher Ct CO3 135 B4
Hankin Ave CO12 90 C1
Hanlee Brook CM2 216 F6
Hanningfield Way CO4 110 B5
Hanover Bridge CO5 158 F5
Hanover Ct
Braintree CM7 127 F8
Ipswich IP4 17 E6
Sudbury CO10 33 D6
Hanover Ct continued
Walton-on-t-N CO14 171 A8
Witham CM8 177 B1
Hanover Pl CB10 22 C1
Hanover Sq CO5 158 F6
Hanwell Cl CO16 188 D5
Happy Gdns CO5 179 A8
Harborough Hall Rd CO5 159 E2
Harbour Cres CO12 91 E5
Harcourt Ave CO12 91 A4
Hardings Cl CO6 133 B8
Hardings Yd CO7 164 B7
Hardwick Cl
Great Notley CM77 154 B7
Rushmere St A IP4 18 E5
Hardwick Rd CB9 9 B8
Hardy Cl Braintree CM7 155 A8
Brantham CO11 86 C7
Hardy Ct CO10 15 F2
Harebell Cl CO4 110 B3
Harebell Dr CM8 176 E3
Harebell Rd IP2 16 F4
Hares Wlk CO10 33 F8
Harewood Rd CM1 204 E1
Harewood Terr 20 CB9 8 E7
Harfred Ave CM9 210 E3
Hargrave Cl CM24 119 E8
Harkilees Way CM7 127 F5
Harkstead La
Chelmondiston IP9 63 A7
Woolverstone IP9 38 A1
Harkstead Rd IP9 62 F3
Harlings Gr CM1 205 C3
Harman Wlk CO16 188 C5
Harness Cl CM1 205 E7
Harnham Dr CM77 154 C7
Harold Cl CO9 76 F1
Harold Gr CO13 170 F4
Harold Rd Braintree CM7 127 E2
Clacton-on-S CO15 188 F3
Frinton-on-S CO13 170 F4
Harold Rise CM9 209 F5
Harold Way CO13 170 F4
Harp Close Rd CO10 33 F8
Harp Mdw La CO2 135 D4
Harpur's Rd CO10 2 B4
Harrier Cl IP3 18 B1
Harrington Cl
8 Bishop's Stortford CM23 146 A7
Tiptree CO5 179 B5
Harris Gn CM6 150 E7
Harrison Ct CM1 204 F3
Harrison Dr CM7 128 A1
Harrison Rd CO2 135 F3
Harrisons CM23 119 D2
Harrold Ct CO15 189 A2
Harrow Cl IP4 18 B5
Harrow Hill CO9 49 F6
Harrow Rd
Clacton-on-S CO15 188 F4
Haverhill CB9 8 E7
Harrow Way CM2 217 A6
Harsnett Rd CO1 136 B5
Hart St CM2 205 A1
Hart's La CO7 84 B2
Hartest Way CO10 34 B6
Hartley Cl CM2 206 A4
Hartley St IP2 17 C4
Harvard Ct CO4 110 B4
Harvest Cl CO6 133 B4
Harvest Ct Feering CO5 158 E4
Felixstowe IP11 221 F4
Harvest End CO3 134 D5
Harvest Ho IP11 221 F4
Harvest Way
Elmstead CO7 137 F6
Maldon CM9 209 F5
Harvesters CM9 198 D4
Harvesters' Way CO6 132 B8
Harvey Cl CO11 86 C4
Harvey Cres CO3 134 C4
Harvey Ct CO15 203 F6
Harvey Rd
Colchester CO2 135 B2
Great Totham CM9 196 A4
Wivenhoe CO7 137 C1
Harvey St CO9 76 F1
Harvey Way
Hempstead CB10 25 F1
Saffron Walden CB10 22 F2
Harwell Cl CM7 128 D4
Harwich & District Hospl CO12 91 A3
Harwich Com Prim Sch CO12 91 E4
Harwich Crane The* CO12 91 E5
Harwich Ct CO4 136 F4
Harwich Ind Est CO12 90 F5
Harwich International Port CO12 90 F6
Harwich Parkeston Quay Sta CO12 90 F6
Harwich Rd Ardleigh CO7 111 F8
Beaumont CO16 141 F7
Bradfield CO11 87 F2
Colchester CO7 110 F3
Colchester,Greenstead CO1 136 C7
Dedham CO7 84 F1
Great Bromley CO7 139 C6
Great Oakley CO12 116 D5
Lawford CO11 85 C2
Little Bentley CO7 113 E1
Little Clacton CO16 168 E6
Little Oakley CO12 117 C7
Harwich Rd continued
New Mistley CO11 87 B3
Ramsey CO11 89 A2
Wix CO11,CO12 116 A7
Wix,Wix Green CO11 115 D5
Wrabness CO11 88 D2
Harwich Sch The CO12 91 A2
Harwich Town Sta CO12 91 D5
Harwood Cl CO2 136 A4
Haselfoot Rd CM3 206 F8
Haselmere Gdns CO13 170 F7
Haskell Mews CM7 155 A8
Haslemere CM23 146 A4
Haslemere Dr IP4 17 E6
Haslemere Ind Est CM23 146 A4
Hasler Rd CM9 199 D2
Haslers La CM6 150 D8
Hastings Ave CO15 203 J8
Hastings Pl CO7 185 F8
Hastings Rd CO3 135 A4
Hatchcroft Gdns CO7 138 A6
Hatcher Cres CO2 136 C5
Hatchfields CM3 190 F7
Hatfield Forest (Ctry Pk)* CM22 147 D6
Hatfield Forest Nature Trail* CM22 147 E5
Hatfield Gr CM1 204 D1
Hatfield Peverel Sta CM3 193 F5
Hatfield Rd
Hatfield Peverel CM8 194 F4
Ipswich IP3 18 A3
Langford CM9 209 B7
Terling CM3 175 D2
Witham CM8 194 E7
Hatherley Ct CB10 22 E2
Haubourdin Ct CO9 77 A2
Haughley Dr IP4 18 F6
Hauliers Rd IP11 221 B2
Haven Ave CO15 189 G6
Haven Cl IP11 221 B4
Haven Ct CM3 193 F4
Haven Rd CO2 136 D4
Haven The CO12 90 F3
Havencourt CM1 205 B3
Havencroft Ct 3 CO14 171 C8
Havengore CM1 205 F5
Havens The IP3 38 E7
Havergate Rd IP3 38 D8
Haverhill Rd
Castle Camps CB1 7 E5
Helions Bumpstead CB9 8 D1
Steeple Bumpstead CB9 27 C8
Havering Cl
Clacton-on-S CO15 188 E7
Colchester CO4 110 B1
Havers Inf Sch CM23 145 E5
Havers La CM23 145 F5
Havers Par CM23 145 F5
Havisham Way CM1 204 E7
Hawbridge IP9 35 A2
Hawbush Gn CM77 155 F5
Hawes St IP2 17 D3
Hawfinch Rd CO2 162 A5
Hawfinch Wlk CM2 216 B5
Hawke Rd IP3 17 E1
Hawkendon Rd CO16 188 A4
Hawkes La IP11 221 B6
Hawkes Rd CO6 130 F3
Hawkesway CO15 188 F6
Hawkhurst Cl CM1 204 E2
Hawkins Cl CM3 219 E2
Hawkins Ct CO10 15 F2
Hawkins Rd
Alresford CO7 165 B8
Colchester CO2 136 D5
Hawkins Way CM7 128 C4
Hawks Cl CM3 219 A6
Hawkwood Rd CO9 75 D8
Hawlmark End CO6 132 E3
Hawthorn Ave CO4 136 E7
Hawthorn Cl
Chelmsford CM2 216 C6
Halstead CO9 77 A2
Takeley CM22 148 C7
Hawthorn Dr IP2 16 E3
Hawthorn Rd
Clacton-on-S CO15 188 E6
Great Cornard CO10 34 B7
Hatfield Peverel CM3 194 A5
Tolleshunt Knights CM9 180 A2
Hawthorn Rise CM23 145 F3
Hawthorne Rise CM8 177 A5
Hawthornes CM3 220 D1
Hawthorns
Kirby Cross CO13 170 F7
Sible Hedingham CO9 51 D2
Hawthorns The CM3 219 A7
Hay Gn CM3 218 F8
Hay La N CM7 128 C3
Hay La S CM7 128 C3
Haycocks La CO5 183 F1
Haycroft CM23 146 C7
Haye La CO5 163 C4
Hayes Cl CM2 205 B1
Hayes Rd CO15 188 E3
Hayhill Rd IP4 17 E7
Hayhouse Rd CO6 105 A6
Hayley Bell Gdns CM23 145 F3
Hayman Rd IP3 17 F1
Haymeads La CM23 146 C6
Haynes Green Rd CO5 180 A8
Haytor Cl CM7 128 C2
Haywain The CO3 134 D5
Hayward Ct CO1 136 C7
Hayward Sch The CM1 205 A4
Hazel Cl Haverhill CB9 8 E7
Thorrington CO7 166 A5
Witham CM8 177 A4
Hazel Dr IP3 18 F1
Hazel Gr CM7 127 E1
Hazel Mews CO7 185 E7
Hazeldon Cl CM3 191 C6
Hazeleigh Hall La CM3 220 C4
Hazelend Rd CM23 119 B4
Hazell Ave CO2 135 B2
Hazelton Rd CO4 110 D1
Hazelville Cl CO12 90 E1
Hazelwood Cres CO16 168 C1
Hazelwood Ct CM9 210 B6
Hazlemere Jun & Inf Schs CO4 136 E8
Hazlemere Rd CO15 189 C4
Head La CO10 34 B5
Head St Colchester CO1 135 E7
Goldhanger CM9 211 E6
Halstead CO9 76 F2
Rowhedge CO5 163 F8
Headgate CO1 135 E6
Headgate Bldg 1 CO2 135 E6
Headingham Cl 3 IP2 17 A2
Headland Ave CB9 8 E7
Heard's La CM7 48 D5
Heards La CM7 48 C6
Hearsall Ave CM1 205 B7
Heath Cl CO7 59 D3
Heath Cotts CO3 107 F1
Heath Dr CM2 216 B6
Heath La IP4 18 C5
Heath Rd Alresford CO7 165 B8
Bradfield CO11 114 D8
Colchester CO3 134 F5
Colchester,Stanway Green CO3 134 D4
East Bergholt CO7 59 D3
Fordham Heath CO3 108 A1
Ipswich IP4 18 D6
New Mistley CO11 87 B2
Rowhedge CO5 163 F8
St Osyth CO16 167 E1
Tendring CO16 140 E7
Wivenhoe CO7 137 B2
Heath Row CM23 119 B1
Heath Sch The CO3 134 D5
Heath The Dedham CO7 85 A4
Layer-de-l-H CO2 162 A6
Heathcote Sch CM3 218 E7
Heather Ave IP3 18 C3
Heather Cl
Bishop's Stortford CM23 145 D6
Clacton-on-S CO15 189 B7
Layer-de-l-H CO2 161 F5
Heather Ct 10 CM1 205 F6
Heather Dr CO3 134 F5
Heatherhayes IP2 17 A3
Heathfield Rd
Chelmsford CM1 205 B7
Holbrook IP9 62 D5
Heathfields CO6 134 B8
Heathfields Ho CO2 136 C3
Heathgate CM8 195 D6
Heathgate Piece IP11 221 A8
Heathlands CO7 166 A5
Heathlands CE Prim Sch CO6 108 E4
Heathlands Pk IP4 18 E4
Heathside CO6 108 E4
Heathside Sch IP4 18 D6
Heatley Way CO4 136 F8
Heaton Way CO5 179 D6
Heckford's Rd CO7 139 E2
Heckworth Cl CO4 110 C6
Hedge Dr CO2 135 B3
Hedgelands CO6 133 D5
Hedgerows CO3 134 D6
Hedgerows Bsns Pk CM2 206 A6
Hedgerows The CM23 146 B6
Hedingham Castle (remains of)* CO9 51 F4
Hedingham Rd
Bulmer Tye CO10 32 C1
Gosfield CO9 75 E3
Halstead CO9 76 E3
Wickham St P CO9 53 A7
Hedingham Sch CO9 51 D3
Hedingham Pl CO9 51 E1
Heights The CM3 218 D7
Helen How CM3 173 F7
Helena Rd IP3 17 E3
Helena Romanes Sch & Sixth Form Ctr CM6 123 C3
Helford Ct CM8 176 D2
Helions Bumpstead Rd CB9 9 A5
Helions Park Ave CB9 9 A7
Helions Park Gdns CB9 9 A7
Helions Park Gr CB9 9 A7
Helions Rd CB9 27 A6
Helions Service Rd CB9 9 A7
Helions Wlk CB9 9 A7
Helm Cl CO6 109 C7
Helston Rd CM1 205 E6
Hemingway Rd CM8 176 F5
Hemlock Cl CM8 177 A4
Hemmings Ct CM9 220 E8
Hendon Cl CO16 188 D5
Hengrave Cl IP2 17 A2
Henham & Ugley Prim Sch CM22 94 F5
Henham Rd Debden CB11 68 E3
Elsenham CM22 94 E2
Henley Ct Colchester CO3 134 F6
Manningtree CO11 86 C4
Henley Rd IP1 17 C8
Henniker Gate CM2 206 A4
Henniker Rd IP1 16 D8
Henny Back Rd CO8 54 E4
Henny Rd CO8 55 B5
Henrietta Cl CO7 137 C3
Henry Cl CO15 188 C2
Henry Dixon Rd CM8 177 D6
Henry Rd
Chelmsford CM1 205 B4
Ipswich IP3 18 B1
Henslow Rd IP4 18 B5
Henstead Gdns IP3 18 A2
Herald Cl CM23 145 D6
Herbage Park Rd CM9 208 D1
Herbert Rd CO15 188 E3
Hereford Ct
Clacton-on-S CO15 189 E5
Great Baddow CM2 217 A5
Hereford Dr CM7 128 D5
Hereford Rd
Colchester CO1 136 A8
Holland-on-S CO15 189 E6
Hereward Cl CO7 137 C3
Hereward Way CM7 73 C3
Heriot Way CM9 196 B4
Hermitage Ct CM24 119 D7
Hermitage Ho CM24 119 D7
Heron Ct CM23 146 A7
Heron Glade CO15 188 F7
Heron Rd Ipswich IP2 16 E3
Kelvedon CO5 158 D2
Heron Way
Frinton-on-S CO13 170 E6
Heybridge CM9 210 C5
Heronsgate CO13 170 F6
Herrick Pl CO3 135 A6
Herring's Way CO6 107 D6
Herringham Gn CM2 206 A4
Hertford La SG8,CB11 19 E5
Hertfordshire & Essex High Sch The CM23 146 B7
Herts & Essex Hospl CM23 146 B6
Hervey St IP4 17 D7
Hervilly Way CO14 171 B7
Heseltine Ct CO15 189 B3
Hesper Rd CO2 136 C5
Hetherington Cl CO2 163 A8
Hewes Cl CO4 136 F7
Hewitt Rd CO12 90 C1
Hewitt Wlk 6 CM8 177 A2
Hexham Cl 6 IP2 17 A2
Heybridge App CM9 209 F5
Heybridge Ct CO15 189 B3
Heybridge House Ind Est CM9 210 B4
Heybridge Prim Sch CM9 210 C5
Heybridge St CM9 210 B5
Heycroft Dr CM77 155 E5
Heycroft Way
Great Baddow CM2 216 F5
Tiptree CO5 179 D6
Heydon La Chrishall SG8 19 B5
Elmdon CB11 19 F4
Heymeads Ct CM9 210 A5
Heythrop The CM2 205 D4
Heywood Cl IP2 16 E1
Heywood Ct CM9 210 B6
Heywood La CM6 150 D7
Heywood Way CM9 210 B6
Hickford Hill CO10 12 D6
Hickory Ave CO4 136 D7
Hicks Way CB9 9 E5
Hidcote Way CM77 154 B7
High Bridge Rd CM2 205 C1
High Chelmer 8 CM1 205 B2
High Cl SG8 19 A5
High Croft CO6 78 A2
High Cross La CM6 149 B5
High Cross La E CM6 149 E6
High Cross Villas CM6 149 C6
High Easter Rd CM6 150 F2
High Fields CM6 150 D8
High Garrett CM7 102 C2
High La
Bishop's Stortford CM24 119 F8
Stansted Mountfitchet CM24 93 E1
High Lift Villas CO4 83 D8
High Mdw CM6 150 C8
High Oaks CO12 90 B2
High Pasture CM3 207 D3
High Rd CO2 161 F5
High Rd E IP11 221 F5
High Rd W IP11 221 D5
High Ridge CM8 196 C8
High St
Bishop's Stortford CM23 145 F7
Braintree CM7 127 F3
Brightlingsea CO7 185 F6
Bures CO8 55 F1
Castle Camps CB1 7 E3
Cavendish CO10 1 D2
Chelmsford CM1 205 B2
Chrishall SG8 19 D3
Clacton-on-S CO15 188 F2
Clare CO10 12 B7
Clavering CB11 65 D4
Colchester CO1 135 F7
Debden CB11 68 B7
Dedham CO7 84 F7
Earls Colne CO6 105 B6
Elsenham CM22 94 D1
Felixstowe IP11 221 C6
Great Baddow CM2 216 F6
Great Bardfield CM7 72 A1

High St *continued*
Great Chesterford CB10 . . . . .3 E2
Great Chesterford,Little Chesterford CB10 . . . . .21 F8
Great Dunmow CM6 . . . . . .150 D8
Great Oakley CO12 . . . . . .116 C4
Great Yeldham CO9 . . . . .30 A1
Halstead CO9 . . . . .76 E2
Harwich CO12 . . . . .91 D4
Haverhill CB9 . . . . .9 A7
Hempstead CB10 . . . . .25 F1
Henham CM22 . . . . .94 F5
Hinxton CB10 . . . . .3 B7
Ipswich IP1 . . . . .17 C6
Kelvedon CO5 . . . . .158 C2
Langham CO4 . . . . .83 D4
Littlebury CB11 . . . . .21 F4
Maldon CM9 . . . . .210 A2
Manningtree CO11 . . . . .86 D4
Mistley CO11 . . . . .86 F4
Nayland CO6 . . . . .56 B1
Newport CB11 . . . . .67 A8
Rowhedge CO5 . . . . .164 A8
Saffron Walden CB10 . . . . . . .22 D1
Sproughton IP8 . . . . .16 A6
Stebbing CM6 . . . . .124 E5
Thorpe-le-S CO16 . . . . .141 F1
Tollesbury CM9 . . . . .199 D1
Walton-on-t-N CO14 . . . . . .171 C8
West Mersea CO5 . . . . .201 B6
Wethersfield CM7 . . . . .73 C3
Widdington CB11 . . . . .67 D4
Wivenhoe CO7 . . . . .164 B8
High St N CO5 . . . . .201 C7
High Stile CM6 . . . . .150 C8
High Tree La CO14 . . . . . . .144 D2
High View CM23 . . . . .119 D3
High View Ave CO15 . . . . . .188 E6
High View Cl CO15 . . . . . . .188 E6
High View Rd IP1 . . . . .16 D8
High Woods Country Park Visitor Ctr* CO4 . . . . . . .109 F3
High Woods Ctry Pk* CO4 . . . . .110 A4
Higham Hill CO7,IP7 . . . . . .58 A8
Higham Rd CO7 . . . . .58 B3
Highams Chase CM9 . . . . .212 A8
Highbank CO10 . . . . .2 B5
Highbirch Rd CO16 . . . . . . .167 D3
Highbury Terr 1 CO9 . . . . . .76 F2
Highbury Way CO10 . . . . . . .34 B5
Highclere Rd
Colchester CO4 . . . . .110 B4
Great Notley CM77 . . . . . . .154 B6
Highfield CO10 . . . . .12 D7
Highfield Ave
Bishop's Stortford CM23 . .146 C6
Harwich CO12 . . . . .91 B3
Highfield Cl
Braintree CM7 . . . . .128 A6
Danbury CM3 . . . . .218 D6
Highfield Ct CO12 . . . . .91 B3
Highfield Dr CO3 . . . . .135 C7
Highfield Holiday Pk
Clacton-on-S CO16 . . . . . . .188 E8
Little Clacton CO15 . . . . . . .168 F1
Highfield Rd
Chelmsford CM1 . . . . .204 E4
Felixstowe IP11 . . . . .221 E4
Sudbury CO10 . . . . .34 A8
Highfield Stile Rd CM7 . . .128 A6
Highfields Bentley IP9 . . . . .60 E6
Debden CB11 . . . . .68 B7
Great Yeldham CO9 . . . . .30 A2
Halstead CO9 . . . . .103 F8
Henham CM22 . . . . .94 F6
Langley CB11 . . . . .40 D2
Saffron Walden CB10 . . . . . . .22 E2
Highfields La CO5 . . . . . . .178 E7
Highfields Prim Sch CO11 . . . . .86 C4
Highfields Rd CM8 . . . . . . .176 E1
Highland Rd CM23 . . . . . . .145 F3
Highlands CO9 . . . . .75 E1
Highlands Chalet Pk CO15 . . . . .188 F7
Highlands Dr CM9 . . . . . . .209 E2
Highmead CM24 . . . . .119 E8
Highview Cl CO10 . . . . .15 E2
Highwoods App CO4 . . . . . .110 C4
Highwoods Prim Sch CO4 . . . . .110 B4
Highwoods Sq CO4 . . . . . . .110 B4
Hildabrook Cl 2 IP2 . . . . . .16 E1
Hill Cl CO10 . . . . .15 D8
Hill Cotts CO7 . . . . .166 E1
Hill Cres CM2 . . . . .205 D2
Hill Farm La IP9 . . . . .63 F7
Hill House Ct CO7 . . . . . . .186 A7
Hill House Rd IP3 . . . . .17 E5
Hill La CB9 . . . . .9 F4
Hill Rd Chelmsford CM2 . . .205 D2
Clacton-on-S CO15 . . . . . . .188 E6
Coggeshall CO6 . . . . .131 B2
Harwich CO12 . . . . .91 C4
Hempstead CB10 . . . . .46 D8
Ramsey CO12 . . . . .116 E8
Hill Rd S CM2 . . . . .205 D2
Hill St CB10 . . . . .22 D1
Hill Terr CO10 . . . . .12 C8
Hill Top La CB11 . . . . .43 E7
Hill View CM3 . . . . .218 F1
Hill View Rd CM1 . . . . .205 C4
Hillary Cl Bradwell CM7 . . .129 D2
Chelmsford CM1 . . . . .205 D4
Heybridge CM9 . . . . .210 B5
Ipswich IP4 . . . . .18 A5
Hillcrest
Clacton-on-S CO15 . . . . . . .189 A6
Kirby-le-S CO13 . . . . .170 D8
Hillcrest Cotts CO4 . . . . . . .83 E6
Hillcrest Ct CO12 . . . . .91 C3
Hillcrest Rd CO10 . . . . .15 E2
Hillfield CO5 . . . . .158 D4
Hillhouse La CO16 . . . . . . .141 B3
Hilliards Rd CO7 . . . . .113 C2
Hillie Bunnies CO6 . . . . . .105 B7
Hillman Ave CO15 . . . . . . .203 E6
Hillmead Prim Sch CM23 . . . . .145 C7
Hillridge CO4 . . . . .110 B3
Hills Cl CM7 . . . . .127 F4
Hills Cres CO3 . . . . .135 A5
Hills Rd CO9 . . . . .75 D8
Hillside CO13 . . . . .170 E4
Hillside Ave CM23 . . . . . . .146 A7
Hillside Com Prim Sch IP2 . . . . .17 C3
Hillside Cotts
Birchanger CM23 . . . . .119 C3
Sudbury CO10 . . . . .34 A7
Thorpe-le-S CO16 . . . . .142 A2
Hillside Cres
Holland-on-S CO15 . . . . . . .189 C5
Ipswich IP3 . . . . .18 C3
Hillside End CM23 . . . . . . .119 C3
Hillside Gdns CM7 . . . . . . .127 F1
Hillside Gr CM2 . . . . .216 A7
Hillside Ho 2 CM7 . . . . . . .127 F1
Hillside Mews CM2 . . . . . .216 A7
Hillside Rd CO10 . . . . .34 A7
Hillside Specl Sch CO10 . .15 F1
Hillside Terr 1 CM7 . . . . . .127 F1
Hillsleigh Mews CO1 . . . . .136 A7
Hillston Cl CO2 . . . . .136 B2
Hilltop Cl CO2 . . . . .136 D4
Hilltop Cres CO16 . . . . . . .140 F1
Hilltop Rise CO16 . . . . . . .140 E1
HillView Cl CO5 . . . . .163 F8
Hillybroom Gdns CO5 . . .201 D6
Hilton Cl CO11 . . . . .86 D4
Hilton Rd IP3 . . . . .18 C1
Hilton Way CO9 . . . . .75 E8
Hilton Wlk CO9 . . . . .75 E8
Hines Cl CO6 . . . . .133 B8
Hines Rd IP3 . . . . .18 A4
Hintesham Cl IP4 . . . . .18 F5
Hintlesham Dr IP11 . . . . . .221 B5
Hinxton Rd CB10 . . . . .3 A7
Hipkins CM23 . . . . .145 E4
Histon Cl IP5 . . . . .18 F7
Hitch Common Rd CB11 . . .66 F8
Hitcham Rd CO6 . . . . .130 F3
Hitchcock Pl CO10 . . . . .15 E1
Hitchin Mews CM7 . . . . . . .155 B8
Hitherwood Rd CO2 . . . . .135 C2
HMS Ganges Association Mus* IP9 . . . . .91 C8
Hobart Cl CM1 . . . . .204 E5
Hobbs Dr CO4 . . . . .83 A5
Hobbs La CO10 . . . . .2 D2
Hoblongs Ind Est CM6 . . . .150 E6
Hockerill Anglo-European Sch CM23 . . . . .146 B7
Hockerill Ct 7 CM23 . . . . .146 A7
Hockerill St CM23 . . . . . . .146 A7
Hockley Cl CB1 . . . . .7 B5
Hockney Gdns IP3 . . . . .38 A8
Hodges Holt CM8 . . . . . . .195 A7
Hodgkinson Rd IP11 . . . . .221 A3
Hoe Dr CO3 . . . . .135 A5
Hoe La
Great Waltham CM3 . . . . . .190 E6
Pentlow CO10 . . . . .13 F8
Hoe Mill Rd CM9 . . . . .208 E4
Hoffmanns Way CM1 . . . . .205 B4
Hog's La SG8 . . . . .19 D3
Hogarth Cl CO5 . . . . .201 D6
Hogarth Ct CM1 . . . . .205 E6
Hogarth End CO13 . . . . . . .170 E7
Hogarth Rd IP3 . . . . .18 A1
Hogarth Sq IP3 . . . . .18 A1
Holborough Cl CO4 . . . . . .136 F7
Holbrook Cl CO16 . . . . .188 B4
Holbrook Cres IP11 . . . . . .221 B4
Holbrook High Sch IP9 . . .62 D6
Holbrook Prim Sch IP9 . . .62 D6
Holbrook Rd
Harkstead IP9 . . . . .63 A2
Haverhill CB9 . . . . .8 E6
Ipswich IP3 . . . . .17 F1
Stutton IP9 . . . . .62 A2
Holbrooke Wlk CO5 . . . . . .179 E5
Holcombe Cres IP2 . . . . . . .16 D2
Holden Cl Braintree CM7 . .128 A2
Ipswich IP2 . . . . .17 D3
Holden Rd CO4 . . . . .109 F2
Holdsworth Cl CO10 . . . . . . .2 B3
Holkham Cl IP4 . . . . .18 F5
Holland Haven Ctry Pk CO15 . . . . .189 I8
Holland Haven Prim Sch CO15 . . . . .189 E6
Holland Ho CO15 . . . . .189 A3
Holland Lodge CO15 . . . . .188 F3
Holland Park Prim Sch CO15 . . . . .189 B5
Holland Pk CO15 . . . . .189 B4
Holland Rd
Clacton-on-S, Holland on S CO15 . . . . .189 B4
Clacton-on-S, Rush Green CO15 . . . . .188 F2
Felixstowe IP11 . . . . .221 D3
Frinton-on-S CO13 . . . . . . .170 E3
Holland Rd *continued*
Ipswich IP4 . . . . .17 F6
Kirby Cross CO13 . . . . .170 B6
Little Clacton CO16 . . . . . . .168 E2
Hollands Rd CB9 . . . . .9 A6
Holledge Cres CO13 . . . . .170 E6
Hollesley Ave CB9 . . . . .8 C8
Hollies Rd CM7 . . . . .129 C3
Holliland Croft CO6 . . . . . .132 C8
Hollingtons Gr CO2 . . . . .161 A3
Hollis Lock CM2 . . . . .206 A3
Holliwel Cl CO3 . . . . .134 D6
Hollow La Ashen CO10 . . . .11 E3
Broomfield CM1 . . . . .204 E8
Bures CO8 . . . . .55 F3
Chelmondiston IP9 . . . . .63 F7
Hollow Rd Braintree CM6 .153 B4
Chrishall SG8 . . . . .19 D2
Elmdon CB11 . . . . .20 C4
Kelvedon CO5 . . . . .157 F2
Washbrook IP8 . . . . .35 D8
Widdington CB11 . . . . .67 C3
Holloway Rd CM9 . . . . . . .210 A5
Holly Blue Cl IP8 . . . . .36 E8
Holly Bush Cnr CO7 . . . . . . .58 C5
Holly Cl Colchester CO2 . . .135 C2
Ipswich IP3 . . . . .18 F1
Holly Cotts CO7 . . . . .60 C2
Holly Ct CO15 . . . . .188 E4
Holly La Belstead IP8 . . . . . .36 C7
Great Horkesley CO6 . . . . . .82 C4
Stutton IP9 . . . . .61 E3
Holly Oaks CO6 . . . . .80 E4
Holly Rd Colchester CO3 . .134 C4
Ipswich IP1 . . . . .17 B7
Rushmere St A IP5 . . . . .18 F7
Holly Way
Chelmsford CM2 . . . . .216 D7
Elmstead CO7 . . . . .138 A6
Tiptree CO5 . . . . .179 C5
Holly Wlk CM8 . . . . .177 B5
Hollybank CM8 . . . . .176 F1
Hollybush Hill CO7 . . . . . . .166 E3
Hollycroft CM2 . . . . .217 B6
Hollyhock Rd CB10 . . . . .22 E2
Hollymead Cl CO4 . . . . . . .109 F3
Hollytree Ct CO2 . . . . .135 C3
Hollyview Cl CO16 . . . . . . .140 F5
Hollywood Cl CM2 . . . . . . .216 E6
Holm Oak CO2 . . . . .136 A3
Holman Cres CO3 . . . . .135 A4
Holman Rd CO9 . . . . .103 E8
Holmans CM3 . . . . .206 E8
Holmbrook Way CO13 . . .170 E5
Holmes Rd CO9 . . . . .103 E8
Holmoak IP9 . . . . .62 D6
Holmswood House Prep Sch CO3 . . . . .134 D8
Holmwood Cl CO16 . . . . . . .188 B6
Holmwood House Prep Sch CO3 . . . . .134 D8
Holst Ave CM8 . . . . .194 F7
Holt Dr Blackheath CO2 . . .163 A7
Wickham Bishops CM8 . . . .195 E5
Holt's Rd CO6 . . . . .81 B3
Holy Family RC Prim Sch CM8 . . . . .194 F7
Holy Trinity & St Nicholas CE Prim Sch SG8 . . . . .19 C3
Holy Trinity CE Prim Sch CO9 . . . . .76 D2
Holybread La CM3 . . . . . . .207 C4
Holyrood CO12 . . . . .90 F2
Holyrood Cl IP2 . . . . .16 F2
Holywells Cl IP3 . . . . .17 E4
Holywells High Sch IP3 . .18 C1
Holywells Rd IP3 . . . . .17 E3
Home Cl CB9 . . . . .27 C7
Home Farm La
Ardleigh CO7 . . . . .112 A8
Dedham CO7 . . . . .85 A1
Home Farm Prim Sch CO3 . . . . .134 F6
Home Mead
Galleywood CM2 . . . . .216 C2
Writtle CM1 . . . . .204 A1
Homebridge CB10 . . . . .47 A3
Homedale Cotts CO4 . . . . . .83 B6
Homefield IP9 . . . . .35 B1
Homefield Cl CM1 . . . . . . .204 D5
Homefield Rd
Colchester CO2 . . . . .135 C1
Haverhill CB9 . . . . .8 F5
Witham CM8 . . . . .177 A4
Homefield Road Units CB9 .8 F5
Homefield Way
Cressing CM77 . . . . .155 D7
Earls Colne CO6 . . . . .105 B7
Homelands Ct CO14 . . . . . .171 A7
Homelye Chase CM6 . . . . .124 B1
Homeorr Ho IP11 . . . . .221 F4
Homerton Cl CO15 . . . . . . .188 F8
Homestead CM1 . . . . .205 B7
Homestead Sch CO4 . . . . . .83 E4
Homey Bridge Rd CO6 . . .56 C8
Homing Rd CO16 . . . . .168 C4
Honey Cl CM2 . . . . .216 D6
Honey La CB11 . . . . .64 F3
Honey Pot Hall CO15 . . . . .188 F3
Honeybourne CM23 . . . . . .145 E4
Honeycroft CO11 . . . . .86 B3
Honeypot La
Little Clacton CO16 . . . . . . .168 A4
Tolleshunt Knights CM9 . . .180 B1
Weeley Heath CO16 . . . . . .168 B4
Wix CO11 . . . . .114 F3
Honeypots CM2 . . . . .216 C6
Honeysuckle Cl CM23 . . .145 C6
Honeysuckle Gdns IP2 . . .16 E4
Honeysuckle Path 9 CM1 . . . . .205 F6
Honeysuckle Way
Colchester CO4 . . . . .136 E8
Thorrington CO7 . . . . .166 A5
Witham CM8 . . . . .176 D4
Honeywood Ave CO6 . . . .131 A3
Honeywood Rd CO9 . . . . . . .77 A3
Honor Link CM1 . . . . .206 A7
Honorius Dr CO4 . . . . .110 B6
Honywood Cl CO6 . . . . . . .132 E3
Honywood Com Sch The CO6 . . . . .131 A3
Honywood Rd CO3 . . . . . .135 D6
Honywood Way CO13 . . . .170 F7
Hood Gdns CM7 . . . . .128 C4
Hood Rd IP3 . . . . .17 E1
Hop Gardens La CM9 . . . .208 F4
Hop View CO7 . . . . .59 B2
Hopgrounds The CM7 . . . .72 D6
Hopkin's La CO12 . . . . .91 D6
Hopkins Cl
Chelmsford CM2 . . . . .206 A3
Kirby Cross CO13 . . . . .170 F6
Hopkins Mead CM2 . . . . .206 A2
Hopkirk Cl CM3 . . . . .218 F8
Hopping Jacks La CM3 . .218 F7
Hoppit Mead CM7 . . . . . . .127 F1
Hopton Rise CB9 . . . . .8 B8
Horace Eves Cl 1 CB9 . . . . .8 F8
Hordle Pl CO12 . . . . .91 D4
Hordle St CO12 . . . . .91 D4
Horkesley Hill CO6 . . . . . . .82 A7
Horkesley Rd
Great Horkesley CO4 . . . . .109 E8
Nayland CO6 . . . . .56 A1
Horley IP2 . . . . .16 E4
Horley Cl CO16 . . . . .188 C6
Horn Book CB10 . . . . .22 F1
Horn Hill CO9 . . . . .75 C5
Hornbeam Cl
Chelmsford CM2 . . . . .216 A6
Colchester CO2 . . . . .135 D2
Hornbeam Wlk CM8 . . . . .177 A4
Hornbeams The CO12 . . . .117 B7
Horne Row CM3 . . . . .218 D5
Horner Pl 4 CM8 . . . . .177 A2
Hornsea Villas CM6 . . . . .124 D7
Horrocks Cl CO2 . . . . .136 A4
Horse & Groom La CM2 .216 A3
Horse Pond Cl CO10 . . . . . .34 C4
Horseshoe Cl CB11 . . . . . . .20 B4
Horseshoe La CB9 . . . . .8 E7
Horsey Rd CO13 . . . . .170 C8
Horsham Ave IP3 . . . . .18 D3
Horsley Cross CO11 . . . . .114 A3
Horsley Ho IP11 . . . . .221 F4
Hospital App CM1 . . . . . . .191 B3
Hospital Field CM77 . . . . .155 B5
Hospital La CO3 . . . . .135 D6
Hospital Rd CO3 . . . . .135 D6
Hossack Rd IP3 . . . . .38 A8
Houblon Dr CM2 . . . . .216 C2
Houchin's La CO6 . . . . . . .131 E3
Houghton Pl IP4 . . . . .18 F5
House Martins The IP11 . . . . .221 D6
Hove Ct CO15 . . . . .189 F6
Howard Ave CO12 . . . . .90 F2
Howard Cl Braintree CM7 .128 C3
Haverhill CB9 . . . . .8 D7
Howard Dr CM2 . . . . .206 A2
Howard Rd
Holland-on-S CO15 . . . . . . .189 C4
Saffron Walden CB10 . . . . . .22 E2
Howard St IP4 . . . . .18 B6
Howard Vyse Ct CO15 . . .188 E5
Howards Cl CM3 . . . . .206 E8
Howards Croft CO4 . . . . .109 D5
Howbridge CE Jun Sch CM8 . . . . .194 F8
Howbridge Hall Rd
Witham CM8 . . . . .194 F6
Witham CM8 . . . . .194 F7
Howbridge Inf Sch The CM8 . . . . .194 F8
Howbridge Rd CM8 . . . . .194 F8
Howe Ave IP3 . . . . .18 C3
Howe Chase CO9 . . . . .76 E4
Howe Cl CO4 . . . . .136 D7
Howe Green House Sch CM22 . . . . .146 D2
Howe La CB10 . . . . .47 A5
Howlets Terr IP9 . . . . .63 E7
Hoxter Way CO10 . . . . .15 E2
Hoxton Cl CO16 . . . . .188 D5
Hoynors CM3 . . . . .219 A7
Hubbards Chase CO14 . . . .171 B8
Hubert Rd CO3 . . . . .135 B8
Hucklesbury Ave CO15 . . .189 E7
Hudson Cl
Clacton-on-S CO16 . . . . . . .188 C5
Harwich CO12 . . . . .91 A1
Haverhill CB9 . . . . .9 C6
Hudson's Hill CM7 . . . . .73 D4
Hudsons La CO6 . . . . .57 B5
Hugh Dickson Rd CO4 . . .109 E2
Hugh Villas CM23 . . . . . . .146 A5
Hughes Cnr CO7 . . . . .59 A4
Hughes Rd CO7 . . . . .59 A4
Hughes Stanton Way CO11 . . . . .86 B4
Hull La CM3 . . . . .175 A2
Hull's La CM2 . . . . .217 E7
Hulton Cl CM3 . . . . .206 E8
Hulver Ct IP3 . . . . .18 B2
Humber Ave CO15 . . . . . . .203 E6
Humber Doucy La IP4 . . .18 D8
Humber Rd
Chelmsford CM1 . . . . .205 C5
Witham CM8 . . . . .176 D2
Humphrey's Farm La CM3 . . . . .190 C7
Humphry Rd CO10 . . . . . . .33 E8
Hundon Pl 4 CB9 . . . . .9 B8
Hundred La CO4 . . . . .83 C4
Hungerdown La CO11 . . . .85 E1
Hunnable Rd CM7 . . . . . . .127 E2
Hunt Ave CM9 . . . . .210 B5
Hunt Cl CO5 . . . . .158 D4
Hunt Dr CO16 . . . . .188 D6
Hunt Rd CO6 . . . . .105 A6
Hunt Way CO13 . . . . .170 E6
Hunt's Cl CM1 . . . . .215 B8
Hunt's Dr CM1 . . . . .215 B8
Hunter Dr Braintree CM7 .128 C2
Lawford CO11 . . . . .86 A3
Hunter Rd IP3 . . . . .38 C8
Hunter's Chase CO7 . . . . . .84 E2
Hunters Cnr CO3 . . . . .134 F5
Hunters Ct CM22 . . . . .94 C2
Hunters End IP11 . . . . . . .221 A7
Hunters Ridge CO4 . . . . .110 B4
Hunters Way
Chelmsford CM1 . . . . .205 F7
Saffron Walden CB11 . . . . . .43 D7
Hunting Gate CO1 . . . . . . .136 C7
Huntingdon Way CO15 . .188 E6
Huntley's Cvn Pk (E) CO16 . . . . .203 C6
Huntley's Cvn Pk (W) CO16 . . . . .203 B6
Hunts Farm Cl CM9 . . . . .199 D2
Hunts Hill CO10 . . . . .2 B4
Hunts La CB10 . . . . .3 B7
Hunwicke Rd CO4 . . . . . . .136 E7
Hurnard Dr CO3 . . . . .135 A7
Hurrell Down
Boreham CM3 . . . . .192 F1
Highwoods CO4 . . . . .110 A4
Hurrells La CM3 . . . . .206 F3
Hurricane Pl IP3 . . . . .18 C1
Hurst Cl
Bishop's Stortford CM23 . .145 E7
Brightlingsea CO7 . . . . . . .186 A6
Hurst Way CM2 . . . . .205 F2
Hutchinson Cl CO5 . . . . . .179 D4
Hutland Rd IP4 . . . . .17 F7
Huxtables La CO3 . . . . . . .108 A1
Hyacinth Cl
Clacton-on-S CO16 . . . . . . .188 C4
Tollesbury CM9 . . . . .199 E1
Hyacinth Ct 4 CM1 . . . . .205 E7
Hyam's La IP9 . . . . .61 F1
Hyams La IP9 . . . . .62 D5
Hyde Chase
Danbury CM3 . . . . .219 B4
Woodham Mortimer CM9 . .219 D4
Hyde Gn CM3 . . . . .219 B7
Hyde La Danbury CM3 . . . .219 B6
Wethersfield CM7 . . . . .74 B2
Hyde Rd CO10 . . . . .33 E7
Hyde The CB11 . . . . .65 C4
Hydewood Rd CO9 . . . . . . .30 B3
Hyem's La IP11 . . . . .221 F7
Hylands Cl CM6 . . . . .151 A4
Hylands Par CM2 . . . . . . .216 A6
Hylands Sch CM1 . . . . . . .204 D1
Hyldon Ct IP11 . . . . .221 E3
Hyll Cl CB10 . . . . .3 D3
Hyntle Cl IP2 . . . . .16 E5
Hythe Cl Braintree CM7 . . .127 E6
Clacton-on-S CO15 . . . . . . .203 J8
Hythe Gr CO7 . . . . .165 E1
Hythe Hill CO1 . . . . .136 C6
Hythe Quay CO2 . . . . .136 D5
Hythe Sta CO4 . . . . .136 D6
Hythe Station Rd CO2 . . .136 D6
Hythe The CM9 . . . . .210 B2

I

Iceni Way CO2 . . . . .135 B3
Ickleton Pl 5 CB9 . . . . .9 B8
Ickleton Rd Elmdon CB11 . .20 A4
Great Chesterford CB10 . . . . .3 C2
Hinxton CB10 . . . . .3 B6
Icknield Cl CB10 . . . . .3 A3
Ickworth Cl CM77 . . . . . . .154 C7
Ickworth Cres IP4 . . . . .18 F5
Ickworth Ct IP11 . . . . .221 A3
Ilex Cl CO2 . . . . .135 D2
Imogen Cl 4 CO4 . . . . . . .136 F8
Imphal Cl CO2 . . . . .135 C1
Ingarfield Rd CO15 . . . . . .189 E6
Ingelrica Ave CM3 . . . . . . .194 B3
Ingestre St CO12 . . . . .91 D4
Ingham Rd CB9 . . . . .9 B8
Inglenook CO15 . . . . .189 B7
Ingleside Ct CB11 . . . . .22 D1
Inglis Rd CO3 . . . . .135 D6
Ingram Mews CM7 . . . . . .155 B8
Ingram's Piece CO7 . . . . . .111 E8
Ingram's Well CO10 . . . . . .33 F7
Ingram's Well Rd CO10 . . .33 F7
Inkerman Row 3 CO10 . . . .33 E8
Inkerpole Pl CM2 . . . . . . .205 F4
Innes End 4 IP8 . . . . .16 C2
Innham Hill CO9 . . . . .75 C6
Inverness Cl CO1 . . . . . . .136 A8
Inworth La CO6 . . . . .79 D2

Inworth Rd CO5 158 E3
Inworth Wlk 5 CO2 136 A1
Iona Wlk CO5 164 A8
Ipswich High Sch IP9 38 C2
Ipswich Hospl IP4 18 C6
Ipswich Mus* IP1 17 C6
Ipswich Pre Prep Sch IP1 17 B7
Ipswich Rd Ardleigh CO7 83 F1
Brantham CO11 60 E2
Colchester CO4 110 C3
Dedham CO7 84 B6
Harkstead IP9 63 B3
Holbrook IP9 62 E6
Holland-on-S CO15 189 D6
Ipswich IP10 38 F6
Stratford St M CO7 58 E2
Ipswich Sch IP1 17 C7
Ipswich Sta IP2 17 B4
Ipswich Transport Mus* IP3 18 C2
Ireland Rd IP3 17 F1
Ireton Ho CO4 109 F4
Ireton Rd CO3 135 D5
Iris Cl Chelmsford CM1 205 F5
Ipswich IP2 16 F5
Irlam Rd IP2 16 D1
Iron Latch La CO3 134 C8
Irvine Rd CO3 135 C5
Irving Cl CM23 145 D4
Isaac Sq CM2 217 B6
Isbourne Rd CO4 136 F7
Ishams Chase CM8 195 C7
Island Ct CM23 146 A5
Island La CO13 143 E1
Island Rd CO14 143 E4
Ivor Brown Ct CO4 110 B4
Ivry St IP1 17 B7
Ivy Cotts CM6 123 B4
Ivy La CO5 185 B3
Ivy Lodge Rd CO6 109 C8
Ivy Todd Hill CB11 68 A8
Ixworth Rd CB9 8 E6

J

Jacaranda Cl CM1 206 A6
Jack Andrews Dr CO4 110 C5
Jack Branch Ct CO15 188 E2
Jack Hatch Way CO7 137 A3
Jack's La CM22 148 D7
Jackson Ho CO4 110 B6
Jackson Pl CM2 216 D6
Jackson Rd CO15 188 E2
Jackson Sq 10 CM23 145 F7
Jackson Wlk CO2 136 B3
Jackson's La CB10 3 D3
Jackson's Sq CB10 3 D3
Jacobs Ct CO7 185 F6
Jacquard Way CM7 128 A2
Jacqueline Ct CO3 135 A7
Jaggard's Rd CO6 131 A3
James Boden Cl IP11 221 C5
James Carter Rd CO3 134 F3
James Cl CO7 137 C3
James Croft CM2 216 B2
James Gdns CO16 187 B5
James Hatfield Ho IP2 17 D4
James Rd CO15 188 C2
James St
Brightlingsea CO7 185 F6
Colchester CO1 136 A6
Jameson Pl 5 CO10 33 D8
Jameson Rd CO15 188 C3
Janebrook Rd IP2 16 E2
Janmead CM8 177 A3
Janus Cl CB9 9 D6
Japonica Ct CO15 189 C4
Jaques Cl CO10 2 C5
Jarmin Rd CO1 135 F8
Jarndyce CM1 204 F6
Jarvis Field CM3 207 D5
Jasmin Cl CM23 145 C6
Jasmine Cl
2 Chelmsford CM1 205 E7
Colchester CO4 136 E8
Ipswich IP2 16 F3
Jasmine Way CO15 203 G7
Jaspers Green CM7 100 E2
Jay Cl Great Notley CM77 154 D8
Haverhill CB9 9 C7
Jaymar Ct 9 CM7 127 F2
Jayrest Ctr CO3 134 E4
Jays La CO6 132 F3
Jays The CO4 110 C3
Jaywick La CO15,CO16 188 A3
Jaywick Rd CB9 9 A8
Jeans La CM23 145 E7
Jeffcut Rd CM2 205 E2
Jefferies Rd IP4 17 E6
Jefferson Cl CO3 134 E5
Jeffery Rd CM2 217 A7
Jeffrey Cl CO3 134 F5
Jeffrey's Rd CM77 155 E6
Jekylls La CM7 48 D4
Jellicoe Way CM7 128 C4
Jenkins Dr CM22 94 C3
Jenkins La CM22 146 C5
Jenner Cl CM7 127 F1
Jenner Mead CM2 206 A3
Jennings Cl 1 CO1 136 C6
Jermyns Cl IP9 35 B2
Jersey Rd CM9 210 B1
Jersey Way CM7 127 D2
Jervis Cl IP9 62 D5
Jervis Rd CM23 145 F6
Jessica Cl CO4 136 F7
Jessop Cl CO15 189 A8
Jimmy's La CO11 60 F2
Joes Rd CO10 34 F6
John Ball Wlk 2 CO1 135 F7
John Bird Ct CO1 109 F1
John Bramston Sch The CM8 176 F1
John Bunyan Jun & Inf Schs CM7 127 E4
John Dane Player Ct 4 CB10 22 E1
John English Ave CM7 127 E4
John Harper St 4 CO1 135 E8
John Henry Keene Meml Homes CM1 205 A4
John Kavanagh Ct 1 CO1 136 A6
John Kent Ave CO2 135 B2
John King Ct CO7 185 F6
John Raven Ct CO5 158 D3
John Ray Gdns CM77 155 B5
John Ray Jun & Inf Schs CM7 154 F8
John Ray St CM7 128 A3
John St CO7 185 F6
John Tibauld Ct CB9 27 B6
Johns Rd CM23 119 A1
Johnson Cl
Braintree CM7 155 A7
Ipswich IP2 17 C3
Johnson Rd
Great Baddow CM2 217 A5
St Osyth CO16 187 B4
Johnson's Dr CO7 138 A6
Johnsons Yd CB11 22 D2
Johnston Cl
Halstead CO9 103 F8
Holland-on-S CO15 189 E5
Jollyboys La N CM6 152 C6
Jollyboys La S CM6 152 C4
Jonathan Feedham Ct CO7 137 B1
Jonquil Way CO4 109 C2
Joseph Gdns CM8 156 E4
Josse Lyns The IP11 221 A8
Josselin Cl CO6 105 B7
Jovian Way CO4 110 B6
Joyce's Chase CM9 212 A8
Jubilee Ave
Broomfield CM1 191 B2
Clacton-on-S CO16 188 E8
Jubilee Cl
Colchester CO3 134 D6
Harwich CO12 90 E2
Jubilee Ct
Great Dunmow CM6 123 C1
Sible Hedingham CO9 75 E8
Walton-on-t-N CO14 171 C7
Jubilee End CO11 86 C5
Jubilee La CO7 111 C3
Jubilee Rd CO10 33 F8
Jubilee Rise CM3 219 A6
Jubilee Terr CM1 205 A4
Jubilee Way CO13 170 F6
Jubilee Wlk 3 CB9 9 A7
Judge Rd CM2 206 B4
Julian Ave CO4 110 B6
Julian Cl Broomfield CM1 191 B1
Haverhill CB9 9 D7
Julien Court Rd CM7 128 A4
Juniper Cl CO9 103 D8
Juniper Cres CM8 177 A4
Juniper Ct CM6 123 B1
Juniper Dr CM2 216 B6
Juniper Rd Boreham CM3 206 F8
Colchester CO3 134 D5
Juniper Way CO4 136 D8
Juno Mews CO2 135 C1
Jupe's Hill CO6 79 D1
Jupes Hill CO7 85 C4
Jupiter Cl CB9 9 D6
Jupiter Rd IP4 18 B7
Justinian Cl CB9 9 D6
Juvina Cl CM8 194 F7

K

Kale Croft CO3 134 D5
Kangels The CB11 40 D2
Kate Daniels Ho CO16 140 F1
Kate's La CB10 24 C8
Katherine Semar Inf Sch CB11 43 E6
Katherine Semar Jun Sch CB11 43 E6
Kay Cl CM3 174 A7
Kayla Ct 6 CO3 135 E6
Keable Rd CO6 132 E3
Keating Cl CO11 86 B4
Keats Ave CM7 154 F8
Keats Rd CO3 134 F6
Kebbles CO10 2 B6
Keble Cl CO3 135 D6
Kedington Hill CO10 34 B2
Keeble Cl CO5 179 E5
Keeble Ct CO7 166 E7
Keeble Pk CM9 220 F8
Keeble Way CM7 128 A3
Keeble's Yd 7 CB9 9 A8
Keelars La CO7 137 E2
Keelers Way CO6 109 B7
Keene Way CM2 216 B3
Keep The 3 CB9 8 E7
Keepers Gn CO4 109 B3
Keith Cl CO15 189 B8
Kelly Rd IP2 16 E5
Kelso Cl CO6 109 C6
Kelvedon Cl CM1 205 A6
Kelvedon Dr IP4 18 F5
Kelvedon Hall La CO5 178 E5
Kelvedon Rd
Coggeshall CO6 158 A8
Messing CO5 159 C2
Tiptree CO5 179 B7
Tolleshunt D'arcy CM9 198 C6
Wickham Bishops CM8 195 F5
Kelvedon St Mary's CE Prim Sch CO5 158 C2
Kelvedon Sta CO5 158 C3
Kelvin Ct CO13 170 F3
Kemball St IP4 18 A5
Kempe Rd CM7 72 D6
Kempson Dr CO10 34 C5
Kempsters The IP11 221 B7
Kempton Pk CO16 168 B5
Kemsley Rd
Earls Colne CO6 105 A6
Felixstowe IP11 221 D5
Ken Cooke Ct 4 CO1 135 F7
Kendall CE Prim Sch CO1 136 C4
Kendall Rd CO1 136 A6
Kendall Terr CO1 136 A6
Kendall's Almshouses 3 CO1 136 A6
Kenilworth Gr CO16 142 A2
Kenilworth Rd CO15 189 E6
Kennedy Cl IP4 18 A6
Kennedy Way CO15 189 A5
Kennet Way CM1 204 D5
Kensington Rd IP1 17 A8
Kenston Ct CO5 201 B6
Kent Cl CO7 185 F7
Kent Cres CM23 145 E4
Kent Gdns CM7 128 B4
Kent Ho IP11 221 C6
Kent's Ave CO15 189 E6
Kentford Rd IP11 221 A4
Kentings The CM7 127 E2
Kentmere CO4 110 E2
Kents Grass CM9 199 D2
Kents Yd CB11 21 F4
Kentwell Cl IP4 18 F4
Kenworthy Rd CM7 127 F2
Kenyon Cl CO7 58 D1
Kenyon St IP2 17 C4
Kerby Rise CM2 205 F2
Kerridge's Cut CO11 87 A4
Kerry Ct CO1 136 C7
Kersey Ave CO10 34 B6
Kersey Ct CO2 135 C3
Kersey Dr CO16 188 B5
Kersey Rd IP11 221 B3
Kessler Ave CM7 73 D7
Kesteven Rd IP2 17 B4
Kestrel Gdns CM23 145 C6
Kestrel Rd Haverhill CB9 9 C7
Ipswich IP2 16 D3
Kestrel Rise CO9 76 F1
Kestrel Way CO15 188 F6
Kestrel Wlk CM2 216 B5
Keswick Ave CO15 189 C6
Keswick Cl CO13 170 F7
Ketley Cl CO5 179 E5
Ketleys CM2 216 C3
Ketleys View CM7 127 A7
Kettlebaston Way IP4 17 D8
Kew La CO13 170 A4
Key Rd CO15 188 E3
Key St IP4 17 D5
Keyes Way CM7 128 C4
Keymer Way CO3 134 F4
Keynes Way CO12 90 F1
Khartoum Rd IP4 17 F7
Khartoum Villas CO7 111 E8
Kidder Rd CM77 126 F1
Kilburn Gdns CO16 188 D5
Kildermorie Cl CO4 110 D3
Kilmaine Rd CO12 90 F2
Kiln Barn Ave CO15 188 F7
Kiln Cotts
Danbury CM3 218 D6
Dedham CO7 84 F5
Kiln Dr CO10 34 B6
Kiln Field IP11 221 B5
Kiln La CO11 86 D4
Kilns Hill CO6 130 F5
Kiltie Rd CO5 179 E5
Kimberley Cl CM23 146 A5
Kimberley Rd CO1 136 B5
Kincaid Rd CO16 187 A4
King Charles Rd CO5 201 D6
King Coel Rd CO3 134 D7
King Edward Ct CM1 205 A3
King Edward Ind Pk CO2 136 D5
King Edward IV's Almshouses CB11 22 D1
King Edward Quay CO2 136 D5
King Edward Rd IP3 18 B3
King Edward VI Gram Sch CM1 205 A3
King Edward VII Dr IP9 91 C8
King Edward Way CM8 194 E8
King George Rd CO2 135 F4
King George V Memorial Homes IP3 17 F3
King George's Ave CO12 91 B4
King George's Pl CM9 210 A2
King Harold Rd CO3 135 A4
King St
Bishop's Stortford CM23 145 F7
Bradfield CO11 114 C8
Castle Hedingham CO9 51 F4
Felixstowe IP11 221 C6
14 Ipswich IP1 17 C6
Maldon CM9 210 A1
Saffron Walden CB10 22 D1
Sudbury CO10 33 E7
King Stephen Rd CO1 136 B6
King Street Mews 1 CM23 145 F7
King's Cl CO16 187 A3
King's Cotts CM23 146 A6
King's Ct CM6 123 D1
King's Ford Jun & Inf Schs CO2 135 C3
King's Head St CO12 91 E6
King's La Elmdon CB11 20 A3
Long Melford CO10 15 F7
King's Quay St CO12 91 E6
King's Rd
Clacton-on-S CO15 188 D1
Harwich CO12 91 B3
King's Way IP3 18 C2
Kingfisher Ave IP2 16 E3
Kingfisher Cl
Colchester CO4 136 F8
Haverhill CB9 9 C8
Heybridge CM9 210 C5
Kingfisher Dr CO12 90 E1
Kingfisher Gate CM7 128 A5
Kingfisher Lodge CM2 216 F7
Kingfisher Mdws CO9 76 F1
Kingfisher Way
Bishop's Stortford CM23 146 A7
Kelvedon CO5 158 C2
Kingfishers CO15 188 F6
Kings Acre CO6 130 F2
Kings Ave
Clacton-on-S CO15 189 D5
Ipswich IP4 17 E5
Kings Chase CM8 177 A1
Kings Cl CO11 86 C4
Kings Ct
Bishop's Stortford CM23 146 A8
Harwich CO12 91 B3
Holland-on-S CO15 189 E5
Kings Fleet Rd IP11 221 C3
Kings Ford Ct CO2 135 B3
Kings Head Ct 1 CO1 135 E8
Kings Head Wlk 6 CM2 205 C2
Kings Hill CO10 34 A6
Kings Ho CO13 171 A4
Kings La CM7 129 A6
Kings Mead CO9 78 A7
Kings Meadow CO10 34 A6
Kings Meadow Ct CO5 158 C3
Kings Meadow Rd CO1 135 F8
Kings Mews CO7 137 C4
Kings Par CO15 189 E5
Kings Prom CO15 203 J8
Kings Quay St CO12 91 E6
Kings Rd Braintree CM7 127 E6
Chelmsford CM1 204 F4
Glemsford CO10 2 B5
Great Totham CM9 196 D7
Halstead CO9 76 E1
Kings Reach CO14 144 D1
Kings Road Prim Sch CM1 204 F4
Kings Wlk CM9 199 E1
Kingsbridge Cl CM7 127 F8
Kingsbridge Rd CM23 146 A8
Kingsbury Cl CO6 132 F3
Kingsbury Rd IP11 221 A7
Kingsbury Wlk CO10 34 C5
Kingsdale Ind Est The CM1 205 C3
Kingsfield Ave IP1 17 D8
Kingsford Dr CM2 206 B4
Kingsgate Dr IP4 17 F8
Kingsland Beach CO5 201 C5
Kingsland Cl CO5 201 C5
Kingsland Hts CO5 201 C6
Kingsland Rd CO5 201 D6
Kingsman Dr CO16 188 C5
Kingsmead Rd CM23 146 A8
Kingsmere Cl CO5 201 D7
Kingston Ave CM2 205 E3
Kingston Chase CM9 209 F5
Kingston Cres CM2 205 E3
Kingston Mews CO15 188 C3
Kingston Rd IP1 16 F8
Kingsway Harwich CO12 91 D4
Tiptree CO5 179 C6
Kingswode Hoe Sch CO3 135 C7
Kingswood Rd CO4 109 F4
Kingwell Ave CO15 188 E5
Kinlett Cl CO4 110 B4
Kinloch Chase CM8 194 F7
Kino Rd CO14 171 D8
Kipling Cl CM1 205 A5
Kipling Way CM7 155 A8
Kirby Cl IP4 18 A7
Kirby Cross Sta CO13 170 B6
Kirby Hall Rd CO9 51 D5
Kirby Prim Sch CO13 170 B7
Kirby Rd
Great Holland CO13 170 B5
Walton-on-t-N CO14 171 B8
Kirby St IP4 18 A6
Kirk Pl CM2 205 F3
Kirkbaye CO13 170 E6
Kirkham Cl IP2 17 A2
Kirkhurst Cl CO7 186 A6
Kirklees CM1 204 F4
Kirkley Ct CB9 8 C8
Kirkmans Rd CM2 216 D3
Kirkton Cl IP9 91 A8
Kirtling Pl 12 CB9 9 B8
Kitchen Field CM7 128 D3
Kitchen Hill CO10 33 B6
Kitchener Rd IP1 16 F8
Kitchener Way IP9 91 A8
Kittiwake Cl IP2 16 E3
Kittiwake Dr CM9 210 C5
Knapton Cl CM1 205 D7
Knebworth Ct CM23 145 D6
Knevett Cl CO4 109 E3
Knight's Ct 2 CB9 8 E7
Knights Cl
Bishop's Stortford CM23 145 C8
Lawford CO11 86 C4
Tiptree CO5 179 F3
Knights Rd
Braintree CM7 128 D1
Coggeshall CO6 130 F2
Knights Way CM6 123 D1
Knightsbridge Cl CO2 135 C3
Knightsbridge Ct CO15 189 B3
Knole La CB11 41 A7
Knowles Cl CO9 76 E1
Knox Ct CO15 188 E5
Knox Gdns CO15 188 E5
Knox Rd CO15 188 E5
Knutsford Cl IP8 16 C1
Kohima Rd CO2 135 B1
Kreswell Gr CO12 91 B2
Kynaston Pl CM8 177 B2
Kynaston Rd CM7 127 A7

L

La Salle Cl IP2 17 B3
Laburnum Cl
Clacton-on-S CO15 188 C3
Great Bentley CO7 166 F8
2 Ipswich, Chantry IP8 16 C2
Ipswich,Warren Heath IP3 18 E2
Laburnum Cres CO13 170 D6
Laburnum Dr CM2 216 C6
Laburnum Gr CO4 136 E8
Laburnum Way
Hatfield Peverel CM3 194 A3
Witham CM8 177 A5
Lacewing Cl IP8 36 E8
Lacey St IP4 17 E6
Ladbrook Dr CO2 136 A3
Ladbrooke Rd CO16 188 D6
Ladell Cl CO3 134 E3
Lady D'Arcy Charity Almhouses 3 CO1 135 F6
Lady La Chelmsford CM2 216 C8
6 Ipswich IP1 17 B6
Ladygate CB9 8 E6
Ladysmith Ave CO7 185 E6
Ladysmith Cotts CM6 152 C4
Ladywell La CM2 217 B5
Ladywood Rd IP4 18 C7
Laing Rd CO4 136 E6
Lake Ave CO15 188 C3
Lake Way CO15 203 F6
Lake Wlk CO15 188 C3
Lakes Ind Pk CM7 128 B2
Lakes Mdw CO6 131 A2
Lakes Rd CM7 128 B2
Lakeside Cl IP2 16 E2
Lakeside Rd IP2 16 E2
Lakeside Wlk CO3 134 C4
Lakforth CO10 15 D8
Lakin Cl CM2 206 A3
Lamarsh Hill Bures CO8 55 E1
Lamarsh CO8 55 B6
Lamarsh Rd CO8 55 A4
Lamb La CO9 75 D7
Lambert Cross CB10 22 E3
Lambert's Rd CO6 105 F3
Lambeth Cl IP1 16 F8
Lambeth Wlk CO15 188 E5
Lambourne Cl
Clacton-on-S CO15 188 F8
Colchester CO3 134 D4
Lambourne Gr CM9 220 F8
Lammas Dr CM7 128 D3
Lammas Way CO7 137 C2
Lancaster Gdns E CO15 189 A3
Lancaster Gdns W CO15 189 A3
Lancaster Ho IP11 221 C5
Lancaster Rd
6 Ipswich IP4 17 E6
Sudbury CO10 15 D2
Lancaster Way
Bishop's Stortford CM23 145 C8
Braintree CM7 127 E4
Earls Colne CO6 104 F2
Lanchester Ave CO15 203 D6
Lancing Ave IP4 18 A8
Land Cl CO16 188 C5
Land La CO1 136 A7
Landermere Rd CO16 142 B2
Landermere View CO16 142 A2
Landers Ct CM1 204 E5
Landisdale CM3 219 A7
Landscape View CB11 43 D6
Landsdown Rd CO10 34 A8
Landseer Cl IP3 18 A1
Landseer Ct
Clacton-on-S CO15 188 F2
Haverhill CB9 8 F6
Landseer Rd
Colchester CO3 135 B5
Ipswich IP3 17 E2
Lane Rd CO6 106 B7

Lane The Mistley CO11 .....86 F4
West Mersea CO5 ....201 A7
Lanercost Way IP2 ....17 A1
Langdale CM77 ....154 C7
Langdale Dr CO4 ....110 B4
Langdale Gdns CM2 ......216 D8
Langenhoe Com Prim Sch
CO5 ....163 B2
Langenhoe Hall La CO5 .183 C7
Langenhoe Pk CO5 ....163 B2
Langer Park Ind Est
IP11 ....221 D3
Langer Prim Sch IP11 ..221 C2
Langer Rd IP11 ....221 C2
Langford Rd
Heybridge CM9 ....209 F6
Wickham Bishops CM8,
CM9 ....195 C2
Langham Dr CO16 ....188 B4
Langham La CO4 ....83 B2
Langham Prim Sch CO4 ..83 F4
Langham Rd CO4 ....82 F1
Langley Ave
Felixstowe IP11 ....221 C4
Wethersfield CM7 ....73 D7
Langley Cl
Felixstowe IP11 ....221 C5
Harwich CO12 ....91 C3
Langley Hill CO8 ....55 C3
Langleys CO6 ....106 C1
Langstons IP11 ....221 B7
Langton Ave CM1 ....204 E5
Languidic Cl CO10 ....34 C6
Langwood CO5 ....201 C7
Lanham Green Rd
CM77 ....156 A7
Lansdowne Cl CO5 ......179 C6
Lansdowne Rd
Felixstowe IP11 ....221 F6
Ipswich IP4 ....18 A5
Lanvalley Rd CO3 ....134 E6
Lanyards IP11 ....221 F4
Lapwing Dr
Heybridge CM9 ....210 C5
Kelvedon CO5 ....158 D2
Lapwing Rd IP2 ....16 D3
Larch Cl CO4 ....136 D8
Larch Gr Chelmsford CM2 .216 C6
Witham CM8 ....177 A5
Larch Ho IP11 ....221 C4
Larch Way CM6 ....123 B1
Larch Wlk CM9 ....210 C6
Larches The CM3 ....206 E8
Larchwood CM23 ....145 D5
Larchwood Cl IP2 ....16 C5
Lark Rise CO10 ....33 D5
Lark's La Broomfield CM3 .191 A6
Great Waltham CM3 .....190 F5
Larkfield Rd CO7 ....139 D1
Larkhill Rise IP4 ....18 E5
Larkhill Way IP11 ......221 B5
Larkrise Prim Sch CM2 ..216 E6
Larks Cl CB9 ....9 C7
Larks Rise CO9 ....77 A1
Larksfield Cres CO12 .....91 B4
Larksfield Rd IP9 ....62 A2
Larkspur Cl
Bishop's Stortford CM23 ..145 D6
Witham CM8 ....176 E4
Larkspur Ct 3 CM1 .....205 F6
Larkspur Rd IP2 ....16 F3
Larksway
Bishop's Stortford CM23 ..145 C6
Felixstowe IP11 ....221 B3
Larkway CO13 ....170 E7
Larman Ct CO11 ....86 C7
Larneys The CO13 ......170 E7
Latchmore Bank CM22 ..146 B2
Lathcoates Cres CM2 ...216 E8
Lattice Ave IP4 ....18 C6
Launceston Cl CO2 .....136 B1
Laundry Gdns CO10 ......33 D6
Laurel Ave CO12 ....90 F2
Laurel Cl CO15 ....189 B7
Laurel Ct CO4 ....136 E8
Laurel Dr
Great Dunmow CM6 ......123 B1
Long Melford CO10 ....15 C7
Laurel Gr 4 CM2 ....216 A8
Laurelhayes IP2 ....17 A3
Laurels The
Braintree CM7 ....128 A3
Great Notley CM77 ......154 C8
Laurence Ave CM8 ......195 A8
Laurence Cl CO7 ....137 F6
Laurence Croft CM1 ....204 B1
Lauriston Bglws CM9 ...212 C6
Lavender Cl
Bishop's Stortford CM23 ..145 D6
Tiptree CO5 ....179 C4
Witham CM8 ....176 E4
Lavender Ct 1 CM1 .....205 F5
Lavender Field
Haverhill CB9 ....8 D8
6 Saffron Walden CB10 ...22 F2
Lavender Hill IP2 ....16 F4
Lavender Way CO4 ......109 C2
Lavender Wlk CO15 .....203 G7
Lavenham Cl CO16 ......188 B4
Lavenham Ct CO2 ....135 C2
Lavenham Rd IP2 ....16 E5
Lawford CE Prim Sch
CO11 ....86 B2
Lawford La
Chelmsford CM1 ....204 D3
Writtle CM1 ....204 C1
Lawford Mead Inf Sch
CM1 ....204 D5
Lawford Mead Jun Sch
CM1 ....204 D5
Lawford Pl IP4 ....18 F5
Lawling Ave CM9 ....210 C5
Lawn Chase CM8 ....176 F1
Lawn La CM1 ....205 D6
Lawn Way IP11 ....221 C5
Lawns Cl CO5 ....201 C7
Lawns The
Chelmsford CM1 ....205 D5
Ipswich IP4 ....18 C8
Laws Cl CB11 ....43 D7
Lawshall's Hill CO6 ......78 D1
Laxton Ct CO3 ....135 A4
Laxton Gr CO13 ....170 A5
Laxton Rd CO7 ....165 B8
Layer Breton Hill CO2 ...161 B1
Layer Cross CO2 ....161 F5
Layer Ct CO2 ....135 D4
Layer Marney Twr*
CO5 ....180 D8
Layer Rd Abberton CO5 ...162 E4
Abberton CO5 ....163 A3
Colchester CO2 ....135 C3
Great Wigborough CO5 ...181 E5
Haverhill CB9 ....8 E7
Layer-de-la-Haye CE Prim
Sch CO2 ....161 F5
Layzell Croft CO10 ....34 C4
Le Cateau Rd CO2 ......135 E6
Lea Cl
Bishop's Stortford CM23 ..119 B1
Braintree CM7 ....128 D1
Lea Gr CM23 ....119 B1
Lea La CM8 ....177 F2
Lea Side CO5 ....201 D6
Leach Cl CM2 ....217 B7
Leam Cl CO4 ....136 F7
Leapingwell Cl CM2 ....206 A3
Leas La CO2 ....161 D6
Leas Rd
Clacton-on-S CO15 .....188 D2
Colchester CO2 ....135 C1
Leas Sch The CO15 .....188 D2
Leas The CO13 ....171 B6
Leather La
5 Braintree CM7 ....127 F3
Great Yeldham CO9 ....30 A1
Haverhill CB9 ....8 E7
Lee Ct CM2 ....216 E7
Lee Rd Harwich CO12 .....91 C3
Ipswich IP3 ....17 F3
Lee Wick La CO16 ......186 D2
Leech's La CO4 ....109 D4
Leeford CM1 ....204 F6
Leeward Ct IP11 ....221 E5
Leeway The CM3 ....218 F7
Leez La CM3 ....152 E2
Leez Priory* CM3 ......153 A2
Legerton Cotts CO6 ......79 C1
Legg St CM1 ....205 B3
Legions Way CM23 .....146 A8
Leicester Cl
Colchester CO1 ....136 A8
Ipswich IP2 ....16 F1
Jaywick CO15 ....187 F1
Leicester Ct CM8 ....156 D3
Leigh Dr Elsenham CM22 ...94 C1
Wickham Bishops CM8 ...195 D5
Leighs Rd CM3 ....191 E6
Leighton Rd IP3 ....38 A8
Leighton Sq IP3 ....38 A8
Leiston Rd CB9 ....8 E7
Lely Rd IP3 ....37 F8
Lemons Hill IP9 ....61 D8
Leonard Mews CM7 .....155 B8
Leopold Gdns IP4 ....18 B8
Leopold Rd
Felixstowe IP11 ....221 E4
Ipswich IP4 ....18 A8
Les Bois CO2 ....162 A5
Leslie Newnham Ct 1
CM9 ....210 A1
Leslie Rd IP3 ....18 D1
Lethe Gr Blackheath CO2 .163 A8
Colchester CO2 ....162 F8
Letton Cl IP9 ....35 A1
Levels Gn CM23 ....118 C5
Levens Way CM77 ......154 C6
Levington Rd
Felixstowe IP11 ....221 C1
Ipswich IP3 ....18 A3
Lewes Cl IP3 ....18 E3
Lewin Pl CM3 ....206 E8
Lewis Dr CM2 ....216 B6
Lewis La IP9 ....61 E2
Lexden Ct CO3 ....135 C7
Lexden Gr CO3 ....134 F7
Lexden Mews CO3 ......134 F7
Lexden Park Ho CO3 ....135 A7
Lexden Pl CO3 ....134 E7
Lexden Prim Sch CO3 ..134 E6
Lexden Rd
Colchester CO3 ....135 B7
West Bergholt CO6 .....108 D4
Lexden Springs Sch
CO3 ....134 E7
Ley Field Marks Tey CO6 ..132 E3
Takeley CM22 ....148 C7
Ley The CM7 ....128 D1
Leybourne Dr CM1 .....205 E7
Leyfields CM77 ....126 F1
Leys Dr CO16 ....168 C1
Leys Rd CO7 ....137 C3
Leys The Chelmsford CM2 .205 F5
Wimbish CB10 ....45 C3
Leyside CM77 ....126 F2
Leyton Ct CO15 ....188 F8
Leywood Cl CM7 ....128 D2
Lichfield Cl
Chelmsford CM1 ....204 E4
Colchester CO1 ....136 A8
Lidgate Ct IP11 ....221 A4
Lidius Dr CO4 ....110 A5
Lie Field Cl CM7 ....128 D3
Lifchild Cl CM8 ....195 A7
Lilac Ave CO16 ....203 B6
Lilac Cl CM2 ....216 C6
Lilac Ct CO7 ....137 A2
Lilac Tree Ct CO4 ......136 E8
Lilian Impey Dr CO4 ...110 B5
Lilley's La CO7 ....112 D4
Lillies The CM7 ....102 B1
Lilly Cnr CB9 ....27 B6
Lily Cl CM1 ....205 F6
Limbourne Dr CM9 .....210 D5
Lime Ave Colchester CO4 .136 D8
Harwich CO12 ....91 B3
Lime Cl
Clacton-on-S CO15 .....188 C3
Witham CM8 ....177 A5
Lime Gr Haverhill CB9 ......9 C5
Sudbury CO10 ....33 C5
Lime St CO7 ....185 F5
Lime Tree Hill CM6 ....123 D2
Lime Wlk CM2 ....216 C6
Limebrook Way CM9 ...220 E7
Limefields CB10 ....22 D4
Limekiln La CM24 ......119 C5
Limes Cres 4 CM23 ....146 A7
Limes The Ardleigh CO7 ..111 F7
Clacton-on-S CO15 .....189 A3
Galleywood CM2 ....216 B2
Gosfield CO9 ....102 E7
Long Melford CO10 ....15 C7
Tattingstone IP9 ....61 B6
Limetree Dr IP3 ....18 D2
Lincoln Ave CO15 ......203 D6
Lincoln Cl CM23 ....145 D5
Lincoln La CO6 ....82 C1
Lincoln Terr IP11 ......221 D3
Lincoln Way CO1 ....136 A8
Lindbergh Rd IP3 ....18 C2
Linden Cl
Chelmsford CM2 ....216 C7
Colchester CO4 ....110 E1
Lawford CO11 ....86 B3
Linden Dr CO15 ....188 E7
Lindens The
Bishop's Stortford CM23 ..145 F6
Braintree CM7 ....128 A1
Colchester CO3 ....135 B7
Halstead CO9 ....103 F8
Lindisfarne Cl IP2 ....17 A1
Lindisfarne Ct CM9 ....220 E8
Lindsell La CM6 ....98 B2
Lindsey Ave CO10 ....34 B6
Lindsey Cl CM23 ....118 F1
Lindsey Rd
Bishop's Stortford CM23 ..118 F1
Ipswich IP4 ....18 C7
Line Cotts CO4 ....83 A4
Linfold Cl CM7 ....128 D4
Linford Mews CM9 .....220 E8
Ling's La IP9 ....63 D5
Lingwood Cl CM3 ......218 E7
Link Cl CO4 ....109 E4
Link La IP9 ....60 D6
Link Rd
Bishop's Stortford CM23 ..145 F8
Brightlingsea CO7 ......186 A6
Capel St M IP9 ....35 A1
Clacton-on-S CO15 .....188 D2
Halstead CO9 ....103 D8
Link The IP9 ....60 D6
Link Way CM23 ....145 E6
Links Ave IP11 ....221 F6
Links Bsns Ctr The
CM23 ....146 C7
Links Cl CO10 ....2 C5
Links Dr CM2 ....215 F7
Links Rd Cressing CM77 ..156 C7
Seawick CO16 ....203 B6
Linksfield IP5 ....18 F7
Linksfield Gdns IP5 ......18 F7
Linkside CO13 ....170 E3
Linkside Rd CM23 ......146 C6
Linley Gdns CO15 ......188 D2
Linnet Dr CM2 ....216 B6
Linnet Rd IP2 ....16 D4
Linnet Way CO7 ....166 D8
Linnets CO15 ....188 F6
Linnetts La CB9 ....10 A4
Linstead Cl CO16 ......188 A4
Linton Cl CB11 ....43 F8
Linton Pl 13 CB9 ....9 B8
Linton Rd CB1 ....5 B7
Lintons The CM2 ....217 D6
Lion Mdw CB9 ....27 B7
Lion Rd CO10 ....2 B5
Lion St IP1 ....17 C6
Lion Wlk 20 CO1 ....135 F7
Lionel Hurst Cl CO10 ....34 C5
Lionfield Terr CM1 .....205 D3
Lisle Ho
Colchester,Lexden CO3 ...135 A7
Colchester,Mile End CO4 ...109 E4
Lisle Rd CO2 ....136 A5
List Ho CO10 ....15 C8
Lister Rd CM7 ....154 F8
Lister Tye CM2 ....216 C7
Liston La CO10 ....15 B6
Listonhall Chase CO9 ....75 B5
Litchborough Pk CM3 ...218 F8
Litchfield CO12 ....90 E2
Litchfield Cl CO15 .....188 E5
Littell Tweed CM2 .....206 A3
Little & Great Sir Hughes La
CM2 ....217 B2
Little Baddow Rd
Danbury CM3 ....218 E7
Woodham Walter CM9 ...208 C3
Little Bakers CO14 .....171 A7
Little Bentley Rd CO16 ..114 B1
Little Bradfords CM7 ...128 A4
Little Braxted La CM8 ...177 C3
Little Bromley Rd
Ardleigh CO7 ....112 B7
Great Bromley CO7 ......112 F3
Little Bentley CO7 ......113 E1
Little Chishill Rd SG8 ....39 C8
Little Church St CO12 ....91 D6
Little Clacton Rd
Clacton-on-S CO16 .....188 B7
Great Holland CO13 .....169 E2
Little Croft St IP2 ....17 C3
Little Dorrit CM1 ....204 E7
Little Fields CM3 ....219 A7
Little Gipping St 7 IP1 ...17 B6
Little Gr 4 IP9 ....35 A1
Little Gulls 6 IP9 ....35 A1
Little Harrods CO14 ....171 A7
Little Hills CM9 ....209 D8
Little Horkesley Rd CO6 ..81 A4
Little Hyde Cl CO9 ....30 A2
Little Hyde Rd CO9 ......30 A2
Little Larchmount CB11 ..43 D8
Little London Hill CM7 ...72 D8
Little London La CM9 ...208 D4
Little Mdw CM1 ....204 A1
Little Mdws CM9 ....219 E6
Little Nell CM1 ....204 E7
Little Orch IP9 ....62 D5
Little Paddocks CM77 ...126 F1
Little Sq 6 CM7 ....127 F3
Little St Mary's CO10 ....15 C7
Little Stile CM1 ....215 A8
Little Stone Ct CO15 ....203 J8
Little Tey Rd CO5 ......158 F7
Little Totham Rd CM9 ...211 D8
Little Tufts IP9 ....35 B1
Little Walden Rd CB10 ....22 E5
Little Waltham CE Prim Sch
CM3 ....191 B7
Little Waltham Rd CM1 .191 D1
Little Whip St 2 IP2 ......17 C4
Little Wood CO13 ......170 E6
Little Yeldham Rd CO9 ....30 C3
Little's Cres IP2 ....17 C4
Littlebury Gdns CO2 ...136 C4
Littlebury Green Rd
CB11 ....21 D3
Littlecotes CO4 ....109 D4
Littlefield Rd CO2 ......135 C2
Littlegarth Sch CO6 ......82 B7
Livery Mews CM6 ....124 E5
Llewellyn Cl CM1 ......205 D3
Lloyd Rd IP9 ....91 A8
Lloyds Ave 7 IP1 ....17 C6
Loamy Hill Rd
Little Totham CM9 .....197 A7
Tiptree CO5 ....178 F1
Loates Pasture CM24 ...119 D8
Lobelia Cl CM1 ....206 A6
Locarno Rd IP3 ....18 B3
Lock Hill CM9 ....210 E2
Lock Rd CO9 ....103 E8
Lockhart Ave CO3 ......135 C7
Lockram La Witham CM8 .176 F2
7 Witham CM8 ....177 A2
Lockside Marina CM2 ...205 D1
Lodge Ave CM2 ....216 F7
Lodge Cl
Clacton-on-S CO15 .....188 E4
Little Oakley CO12 .....117 C8
Lodge Cres CM3 ....206 E7
Lodge Ct CO6 ....108 F4
Lodge Farm La CO16 ...187 D4
Lodge Farm Rd CO10 ......2 C3
Lodge La Abberton CO5 ...163 D1
Ardleigh CO7 ....111 B6
Ardleigh CO7 ....111 C6
Brightlingsea CO7 ......185 E7
Langham CO4 ....110 D8
Peldon CO5 ....182 E7
Purleigh CM3 ....220 C2
Tendring CO16 ....140 F6
Lodge Rd Braintree CM7 ..127 F1
Brightlingsea CO7 ......185 E8
Little Clacton CO16 .....169 A5
Little Oakley CO12 .....117 C8
Maldon CM9 ....209 F3
Messing CO5 ....159 D3
Thorpe-le-S CO16 ......168 F6
Woodham Mortimer CM3,
CM9 ....220 B5
Writtle CM1 ....215 A8
Lodge The CO15 ....189 F6
Loftin Way CM2 ....216 D7
Lombard Ct IP4 ....17 F7
Lombardy Pl CM1 ......205 B3
Lombardy Rd CO10 ......15 D2
Lonbarn Hill CO11 ....88 A2
London Hill
Chelmsford CM2 ....215 F2
Galleywood CM2 ....216 A2
London Land Cotts CO6 ..80 E4
London Rd
Bishop's Stortford CM23 ..146 A5
Braintree CM7 ....127 E1
Capel St M IP9 ....35 B1
Chelmsford CM2 ....215 E6
Clacton-on-S CO15 .....188 E7
Colchester CO3 ....134 D6
London Rd *continued*
Copford CO3,CO6 ....133 D4
Feering CO5 ....159 B7
Great Chesterford CB10 .....3 D2
Great Horkesley CO6 .....81 F2
Great Notley CM77 ......154 D6
Ipswich IP1 ....17 A6
Ipswich,Chantry IP2 ....16 C3
Ipswich,Chantry IP2 ....16 F5
Kelvedon CO5 ....158 B1
Littlebury CB11 ....21 F2
Maldon CM9 ....209 D3
Marks Tey CO6 ....133 A3
Newport CB11 ....67 A6
Saffron Walden CB11 ......43 D8
Washbrook IP8 ....35 E6
Wendens Ambo CB11 ......42 F4
Wendens Ambo,Littlebury
CB11 ....42 F7
London Stansted Airport
CM24 ....121 A4
Lone Barn Ct IP1 ....16 D8
Long Acres CO5 ....158 F6
Long Border Rd
Great Hallingbury CM22,
CM24 ....147 C8
Takeley CM24 ....120 E1
Long Brandocks CM1 ...204 A1
Long Comm CM9 ....209 F5
Long Croft CM24 ....119 D8
Long Field IP11 ....221 B6
Long Gdns CO9 ....53 F5
Long Gn CM77 ....155 E8
Long Green La CM7 ......99 C2
Long Horse Croft CB11 ...43 E7
Long La Arkesden CB11 ....41 E5
Great Holland CO13 .....170 C3
Rayne CM7 ....153 F8
Long Ley CB11 ....40 D2
Long Mdw
Bishop's Stortford CM23 ..145 D6
Great Notley CM77 ......154 B5
Long Mdws CO12 ....90 F2
Long Melford CE Prim Sch
CO10 ....15 C7
Long Pastures CO10 ....2 C3
Long Perry IP9 ....35 B1
Long Rd CO11 ....86 C3
Long Rd E CO7 ....85 B3
Long Rd W CO7 ....84 E3
Long St IP3 ....17 E5
Long Wyre St CO1 ......135 F7
Longacre
Chelmsford CM1 ....215 E8
Colchester CO4 ....109 E2
Longacre Rd CM77 ......155 E6
Longacres CM7 ....128 A1
Longcroft
Felixstowe IP11 ....221 C6
Hempstead CB10 ....46 E8
Takeley CM22 ....148 C7
Longcroft Rd CO4 ......136 C8
Longedryve CO2 ....135 C4
Longfellow Rd CM9 .....210 A1
Longfield CM8 ....176 E5
Longfield Rd
Capel St M IP9 ....35 B2
Great Baddow CM2 ......216 E8
Longfields CO16 ....187 B4
Longhedges CB11 ....22 E1
Longleaf Dr CM7 ....155 A8
Longleat Cl CM1 ....204 F7
Longmead Ave CM2 .....216 F8
Longmeads CM8 ....195 E5
Longmeads Cl CM1 .....204 A1
Longmore Ave CM2 .....216 E8
Longridge CO4 ....136 F8
Longs La CM3 ....173 F1
Longship Way CM9 ......220 E8
Longshots Cl CM1 ......191 A1
Longstomps Ave CM2 ...216 A7
Longstraw Cl CO3 ......134 D6
Lonsdale 4 IP2 ....17 C4
Lonsdale Cl IP4 ....17 F7
Lonsdale Rd CO16 ......142 A2
Looe Rd IP11 ....221 F5
Loompits Way CB11 ......43 D7
Loppys Hill 1 CM24 .....119 E6
Loraine Way IP8 ....16 A8
Lord Holland Rd CO2 ...135 F3
Lord Mews IP3 ....18 A2
Lord's Croft La CB9 ....9 A8
Lords Ave CM23 ....145 B7
Lords Cl CB10 ....23 D1
Lordship Rd CM1 ....204 B3
Lordsland La CM77 .....103 C1
Lordswood Rd CO2 .....135 C2
Lorkin Way CO6 ....108 F4
Lorkin's La CO10 ....54 C4
Lott's Rd CO16 ....168 B4
Lotus Way CO15 ....203 E7
Louise Cl CO14 ....144 E3
Louse La CO7 ....84 E4
Louvain Dr CM1 ....205 F7
Louvain Rd CO12 ....91 A1
Love La CO7 ....185 F8
Love Way CO16 ....188 C6
Loveday Cl SG8 ....19 D3
Lover's La CO7 ....167 A7
Lovers La IP9 ....63 C4
Loves Wlk CM1 ....204 B1
Lovibond Pl 4 CM2 .....205 F4
Low Lighthouse Maritime
Mus* CO12 ....91 E5
Low Rd CO12 ....90 E1

Low St CO10 2 C6
Lowe Chase CO14 171 B8
Lowefields CO6 105 D5
Lower Anchor St CM2 205 A1
Lower Brook Mews IP1 17 C5
Lower Brook St IP4 17 C5
Lower Cotts SG9 64 A2
Lower Dales IP1 16 F8
Lower Dales View Rd 3 IP1 17 A8
Lower Downs Slade CB9 9 A8
Lower Farm Rd CO4,CO6 57 B1
Lower Gn
Galleywood CM2 216 C2
Stoke by Clare CO10 11 C4
Wakes Colne CO6 79 C1
Lower Harlings IP9 91 A8
Lower Holt St CO6 105 D6
Lower Houses Rd IP9 63 D2
Lower King CM7 128 D1
Lower Langley CO6 106 C1
Lower Marine Par CO12 91 C3
Lower Mill Field CM6 150 E7
Lower Orwell St IP4 17 D5
Lower Park Cres CM23 145 F5
Lower Park Rd CO7 185 E6
Lower Rd Birch CO2 181 A8
Borley CO10 15 B3
Glemsford CO10 2 B2
Peldon CO5 182 D5
Wormingford CO8,CO6 80 B5
Lower Sq CB10 22 D2
Lower St Cavendish CO10 1 D1
Sproughton IP8 16 A7
Stanstead CO10 2 E6
Stansted Mountfitchet CM24 119 F7
Stutton IP9 62 B2
Lowry Gdns IP3 38 A8
Luard Way Birch CO2 161 A3
Witham CM8 176 F1
Lubberhedges La CM6 125 B8
Lucas Ave
Chelmsford CM2 216 C6
Fordham CO6 107 D5
Lucas Hall CO4 109 F4
Lucas Ho CO3 135 A7
Lucas Rd
18 Colchester CO2 135 F6
Sudbury CO10 33 F7
Lucas's La CO16 141 D6
Lucerne Rd CO7 138 A6
Lucerne Way CM1 215 B8
Luces La CO9 51 F4
Lucius Cres CO4 110 B6
Luck's La CM3 172 F2
Lucksfield Way CM2 216 F5
Lucy Cl CO3 134 C6
Lucy La N CO3 134 B7
Lucy La S CO3 134 C7
Ludgores La CM3 218 D5
Ludham Hall La CM77 154 D7
Luff Way CO14 170 F7
Lufkin Rd CO4 109 F3
Lugar Cl CO4 136 E6
Lukin's Dr CM6 150 D7
Lulworth Ave IP3 18 D3
Lulworth Cl CO15 203 I8
Lulworth Dr CB9 8 E8
Lumber Leys CO14 171 A7
Lundy Cl CB9 9 D7
Lunnish Hill CO12 89 F2
Lupin Dr CM1 205 F6
Lupin Mews 1 CM1 205 F6
Lupin Rd IP2 16 E5
Lupin Way CO16 188 C4
Lushington Ave CO13 170 E6
Lushington Rd CO11 86 C4
Luther Dr CO5 179 E5
Luther Rd IP2 17 C4
Lutus Cl CO10 12 A6
Lydgate Cl CO11 86 B4
Lydia Dr CO16 186 A2
Lymington Ave CO15 189 A8
Lyndhurst Ave IP4 18 D5
Lyndhurst Dr CM3 218 F1
Lyndhurst Rd CO15 189 C4
Lynmouth Ave CM2 205 C1
Lynmouth Gdns CM2 205 C1
Lynne Cl CO13 170 E6
Lynton Cl CO12 91 B4
Lynton Ct CM23 145 E4
Lynton Dr CM1 205 E5
Lynwood Ave IP11 221 F5
Lyon Cl
Clacton-on-S CO15 189 A4
Galleywood CM2 216 B3
Lyons Hall Prim Sch CM7 128 D4
Lyons Hall Rd CM7 128 D8
Lysander Rd IP3 38 C8
Lyster Ave CM2 217 A7

M

Mabbitt Way CO4 110 B5
Maberly Ct CB10 22 D2
Macbeth Cl CO4 136 F7
MacDonough Cotts CO12 91 E5
Mace Wlk CM1 204 F3
Mackay Ct CO2 136 B1
Maclarens CM8 196 A6
Macmillan Ct 4 CM2 205 B1
Madeira Rd CO15 189 D4
Madeline Pl CM1 204 E6
Madgements Rd CM7 129 C8
Magazine Farm Way CO3 135 A6
Magdalen Cl CO15 188 E4
Magdalen Ct CO15 188 E4
Magdalen Gn
Colchester CO1 136 B6
Thaxted CM6 70 B2
Magdalen Rd CO15 188 E4
Magdalen St CO1 136 A6
Magdalene Cl IP2 16 F2
Magdalene Cres CM8 156 D3
Magingley Cres IP5 18 F6
Magnaville Rd CM23 145 E4
Magnolia Cl
Chelmsford CM2 216 B6
Witham CM8 177 A5
Magnolia Dr CO4 136 F8
Magnus Dr CO4 110 B6
Magpie Cl Harwich CO12 90 E1
Ipswich IP8 16 C2
Magwitch Cl CM1 204 F7
Maidenburgh St CO1 135 F7
Maidenhall App IP2 17 B3
Maidenhall Gn IP2 17 B2
Maidment Cres CM8 194 F8
Maidstone Inf Sch IP11 221 C5
Maidstone Rd IP11 221 C5
Mailers La CM23 92 F2
Main Rd Boreham CM3 192 F1
Braintree CM3 153 D4
Broomfield CM1 191 B2
Chelmondiston IP9 63 D7
Chelmsford CM2 217 F7
Danbury CM3 218 A7
Danbury CM3 218 D7
Frating CO7 138 E3
Great Holland CO13 170 A3
Great Leighs CM3 173 F7
Harwich, Bath Side CO12 91 E5
Harwich, Dovercourt CO12 91 B3
Ramsey CO12 90 A1
Rushmere St A IP5 18 F8
Woolverstone IP9 38 B2
Wormingford CO6 80 F4
Main St CB1 6 F6
Mais Ct IP2 16 F2
Maitland Ct CO13 170 F4
Maitland Rd CM24 119 E6
Majendie La CO9 51 F4
Makemores CM77 126 F2
Makins Rd CO12 90 F5
Maldon Court Sch CM9 209 F3
Maldon Ct
8 Colchester CO3 135 E6
Great Cornard CO10 34 B7
Maldon District Mus* CM9 210 B2
Maldon Prim Sch CM9 210 A2
Maldon Rd Birch CO2 160 E4
Bradwell Waterside CM0 214 F1
Colchester, Abbey Field CO3 135 D5
Colchester,Stanway Green CO3 134 D1
Danbury, Gay Bowers CM3 219 B5
Danbury, Runsell Green CM3 219 B7
Goldhanger CM9 211 E7
Great Baddow CM2 217 C7
Great Totham CM9 196 B4
Great Wigborough CO5 181 E2
Hatfield Peverel CM3,CM9 194 D3
Kelvedon CO5 158 C1
Langford CM9 209 D6
Tiptree CO5 179 B3
Witham CM8 195 A6
Woodham Mortimer CM9 219 E6
Maldon Way CO16 188 B4
Malin Cl CB9 9 D7
Mallard Cl
Great Notley CM77 154 C5
Kelvedon CO5 158 C3
Layer-de-l-H CO2 162 A5
Tollesbury CM9 199 D2
Mallard Ct IP2 16 F3
Mallard Rd CM2 216 A5
Mallard Way
Great Cornard CO10 34 C5
Ipswich IP2 16 E3
Mallow Wlk CB9 8 D8
Mallowhayes Cl IP2 17 B3
Mallows Field CO9 76 F2
Mallows Green Rd CM23 92 D1
Mallows La CO9 49 F3
Malmesbury Cl IP2 17 A1
Maltese Rd CM1 205 A4
Malthouse Rd CO11 86 D4
Malthouse The CO10 15 B5
Malting Cotts CB9 9 F4
Malting Farm La CO7 84 D2
Malting Green Rd CO2 162 A5
Malting La Clare CO10 12 B7
Kirby-le-S CO13 143 C1
Malting Rd
Colchester CO2 135 C1
Peldon CO5 182 E6
Malting Terr IP2 17 D4
Malting Yd CO7 164 B8
Maltings Cl CO8 55 E1
Maltings Ct CM8 194 F8
Maltings La CM8 194 F8
Maltings Rd
Brightlingsea CO7 165 E1
Great Baddow CM2 217 A5
Maltings The
Cavendish CO10 1 D2
Maltings The *continued*
Great Dunmow CM6 123 D1
Great Easton CM6 96 A2
Ramsey CO12 116 E8
Rayne CM77 127 A2
Saffron Walden CB10 22 D1
Thaxted CM6 70 A2
Maltings View CM7 128 A3
Maltings Wharf CO11 86 D4
Maltings Park Rd CO6 108 F4
Malvern Cl
Chelmsford CM1 204 D6
Ipswich IP3 18 B4
Rushmere St A IP5 18 F7
Malvern Way CO6 109 B7
Malyon Rd CM8 194 F8
Man's Cross CO9 29 E2
Manchester Rd
Holland-on-S CO15 189 E6
Ipswich IP2 16 D2
Mandeville Rd
Marks Tey CO6 132 E3
Saffron Walden CB11 43 D8
Mandeville Way
Broomfield CM1 191 B3
Kirby Cross CO13 170 F6
Mandy Cl IP4 18 A6
Manfield Gdns CO16 187 B5
Manning Rd IP11 221 D3
Mannings Cl CB11 43 E7
Mannings La IP9 38 A2
Mannington Cl IP4 18 F5
Manningtree Ct CO7 136 F4
Manningtree High Sch CO11 86 B3
Manningtree Mus* CO11 86 D4
Manningtree Rd
Brantham CO11 86 A8
Dedham CO7 85 B6
East Bergholt CO7 59 F1
Little Bentley CO7 139 F8
Stutton IP9 61 F2
Manningtree Sta CO11 86 A5
Manor Cl Cavendish CO10 1 C2
Great Horkesley CO6 109 C7
Manor Cres CM3 191 B5
Manor Dr CM2 216 F7
Manor Farm Cl CB9 9 B7
Manor Fields Prim Sch CM23 145 D5
Manor Ho CM3 219 A5
Manor House Way CO7 185 E8
Manor La
Great Chesterford CB10 3 D2
Harwich CO12 91 B2
Stutton IP9 61 E2
Manor Links CM23 146 C7
Manor Pl CM7 128 A3
Manor Rd
Bishop's Stortford CM23 146 A7
Chelmsford CM2 205 C1
Colchester CO3 135 E7
Felixstowe IP11 221 C1
Great Holland CO13 170 A3
Harwich CO12 91 B3
Hatfield Peverel CM3 194 C1
Haverhill CB9 9 B7
Ipswich IP4 17 D8
Little Easton CM6 122 F5
Maldon CM9 209 F4
Stansted Mountfitchet CM24 119 E5
Sudbury CO10 15 E1
West Bergholt CO6 108 E5
Witham CM8 177 A4
Wivenhoe CO7 137 C1
Woodham Walter CM9 208 E5
Manor St CM7 128 A3
Manor Way CO15 189 G6
Manors CM8 156 D4
Manors Way CM8 156 C4
Mansard Ct CO15 189 C5
Mansbrook Bvd IP3 38 D7
Manse Chase CM9 210 A1
Mansfield Twrs CO15 188 F2
Manston Dr CM23 119 B1
Manuden Prim Sch CM23 93 A2
Manwick Rd IP11 221 D2
Maple Ave
Bishop's Stortford CM23 145 D8
Braintree CM7 127 D2
Heybridge CM9 210 C6
Maple Cl
Bishop's Stortford CM23 145 D8
Clacton-on-S CO15 188 C3
Halstead CO9 77 A2
Harwich CO12 91 B3
Ipswich IP2 17 A3
Maple Dr
Chelmsford CM2 216 B6
Kirby Cross CO13 170 D6
Witham CM8 177 A5
Maple Gr CM23 145 D8
Maple Ho IP11 221 C4
Maple La CB10 45 C5
Maple Leaf CO5 179 C7
Maple Rd CO10 34 B5
Maple Spring CM23 145 D8
Maple Way CO2 136 A4
Maples The IP4 18 E8
Maplin Ct CO15 189 D4
Marasca End CO2 163 A7
Maraschino Cres CO2 163 A7
Marbled White Dr IP8 36 E8
Marconi Rd CM1 205 B3
Marcus Cl
Colchester CO4 110 B6
Haverhill CB9 9 D7
Marennes Cres CO7 185 E7
Mareth Rd CO2 135 C2
Margaret Cl CO7 186 A6
Margaret Rd CO1 135 F8
Margaret St
Felixstowe IP11 221 C5
Thaxted CM6 70 A3
Margaret Way CB10 22 D1
Margaretting Rd
Chelmsford CM2 215 F1
Galleywood CM2 216 A2
Writtle CM1 215 A6
Margate Rd IP3 18 C3
Margery Allingham Pl CM9 198 D4
Margrave Gdns 4 CM23 145 E5
Marguerite Way CM23 145 C6
Maria Ct CO2 136 C5
Maria St CO12 91 D5
Marigold Ave
Clacton-on-S CO16 188 C4
Ipswich IP2 16 E3
Marigold Cl
Chelmsford CM1 205 F6
Colchester CO4 136 E8
Marina Gdns
Clacton-on-S CO15 189 C5
Felixstowe IP11 221 C2
Marina Mews 1 CO14 171 C8
Marina Point CO15 188 D1
Marina Rd CM3 194 A4
Marine Ct
Clacton-on-S CO15 188 E1
Frinton-on-S CO13 170 F4
Marine Par CO12 91 D3
Marine Par E CO15 189 B3
Marine Par W CO15 188 E1
Marion Ave CO15 188 E6
Maritime Ave CM9 210 E3
Maritime Ct 12 IP4 17 D5
Market Cl CO1 135 E8
Market End CO6 130 F2
Market Field Sch CO7 138 A5
Market Gr CO9 30 A1
Market Hill Clare CO10 12 B7
Coggeshall CO6 131 A2
Halstead CO9 76 E2
Haverhill CB9 9 A8
Maldon CM9 210 A3
Saffron Walden CB10 22 D2
Sudbury CO10 33 E7
Market Hill Ct CM9 210 A3
Market Pl
11 Braintree CM7 127 F3
Great Dunmow CM6 123 D1
Maldon CM9 209 F2
Saffron Walden CB10 22 D2
Market Rd CM1 205 B2
Market Row CB10 22 D1
Market Sq
6 Bishop's Stortford CM23 145 F7
6 Chelmsford CM1 205 B2
Market St
7 Bishop's Stortford CM23 145 F7
10 Braintree CM7 127 F3
Harwich CO12 91 E6
Saffron Walden CB10 22 D2
Market Wlk CB10 22 D1
Marking's Field CB10 22 E2
Markland Cl CM2 216 C3
Markland Dr CM9 209 E1
Marks Gdns CM7 128 C3
Marks Hall Ctry Est* CO6 130 E7
Marks Hall Rd CO6 130 E6
Marks Tey Rdbt CO6 133 A4
Marks Tey Sta CO6 133 B4
Markwells CM22 94 D2
Marlborough Cl
Bishop's Stortford CM23 145 F5
Clacton-on-S CO15 188 C3
Marlborough Ct
Felixstowe IP11 221 D2
Haverhill CB9 8 E7
Marlborough Dr CO10 33 F8
Marlborough Rd
Braintree CM7 128 A4
2 Chelmsford CM2 205 A1
Ipswich IP4 18 A6
Marlborough Terr CM2 205 A1
Marlowe Cl CM7 155 A8
Marlowe Rd
Clacton-on-S CO15 203 G8
Jaywick CO15 188 A1
Marlowe Way CO3 134 F6
Marlpits Rd CM3,CM9 219 E4
Marne Rd CO2 135 E4
Marney Cl CM2 216 E8
Marney Way CO13 171 B6
Marquis Cl CM23 145 B7
Marram Cl CO3 134 B6
Marsden Ct CO3 134 E4
Marsh Cres CO5 164 A8
Marsh Farm La CO7 166 D3
Marsh Rd CO6,CO7 57 E6
Marsh Way CO7 185 E6
Marshall Cl CO5 158 D4
Marshalls Piece CM6 124 D6
Marshalls Rd CM7 127 E1
Marshbarns CM23 145 C8
Marshy La CO9, C10 30 C7
Marston Beck CM2 206 A2
Martello Cvn Pk CO14 171 C8
Martello Rd 8 CO14 171 C8
Marten's La CO6 56 F8
Martens Mdw CM7 128 D3
Martin End CO2 162 A5
Martin Rd IP2 17 C4
Martin's Rd CO9 76 E1
Martinet Gn IP3 18 C1
Martingale Dr CM1 205 F7
Martinsdale CO15 188 F6
Martyns Rise CO10 15 C5
Marvens CM2 216 D3
Marvens The IP8 16 A1
Mary La N CO7 139 A8
Mary La S CO7 139 B6
Mary McArthur Pl CM24 119 E8
Mary Park Gdns CM23 145 F4
Mary Ruck Way CM77 155 B5
Mary Warner Rd CO7 111 E7
Maryborough Gr CO2 136 B2
Maryland Ct 1 CO2 136 A1
Maryon Rd IP3 18 B1
Mascalls The CM2 216 E8
Mascalls Way CM2 216 E8
Mascot Ct CO15 188 F5
Mascot Sq CO4 136 D5
Masefield Dr CO3 134 F6
Masefield Rd CM7 155 A8
Mashay Rd CO9 30 D5
Mason Cl CO2 135 B3
Mason Rd
Clacton-on-S CO16 188 B3
Colchester CO1 109 F1
Masons Cl IP4 17 F6
Masons Ct CM23 145 E7
Masterman Wharf 12 CM23 145 F7
Matchett Dr CO4 110 B6
Matching La CM23 145 D8
Matfield Cl CM1 205 D7
Mathams Dr CM23 145 D5
Mather Way IP2 17 D4
Mathews Cl CO9 77 A3
Matlock Cl 8 IP2 16 C2
Matson Rd IP1 16 F8
Matthews Cl CO7 58 C1
Maudlyn Rd CO1,CO4 136 C6
Maximus Dr CO4 110 B6
May Rd IP3 18 C2
May Wlk Chelmsford CM2 216 C7
Elsenham CM24 94 A1
May's La CO7 84 E4
Mayberry Wlk CO2 136 A3
Maybury Cl CO6 132 F3
Maybury Rd IP3 18 B1
Mayda Cl CO9 76 D1
Mayes Cl CM23 146 D8
Mayes La
Chelmsford CM2 217 E5
Danbury CM3 218 E6
Harwich CO12 90 C1
Mayes Pl CM6 97 A6
Mayfield Cl CO4 110 C2
Mayfield Pk CM23 145 D3
Mayfield Rd Ipswich IP4 18 C7
Writtle CM1 204 A2
Mayflower Ave CO12 91 E5
Mayflower Cl CO3 134 D6
Mayflower Gdns CM23 145 B6
Mayflower Ho CO12 91 D6
Mayflower Prim Sch CO12 91 B4
Mayflower Way CO10 15 F2
Mayfly Cl IP8 36 E8
Mayford Way CO16 188 B6
Mayland Cl CM9 210 D4
Mayland Rd CM8 177 A2
Maylands Dr CM77 154 D8
Maynard Cl CM6 123 D1
Maynards Villas CM6 122 F5
Mayne Crest CM1 205 E6
Maypole Cl CB11 43 C7
Maypole Dr CO16 187 B4
Maypole Green Rd CO2 135 C1
Maypole Rd Tiptree CO5 179 C6
Wickham Bishops CM8, CM9 195 F2
Maypole The CM6 69 F3
Mays Ct IP11 221 D3
Maysent Ave CM7 127 F5
Maytree Gdns CM22 94 B3
Maze Green Hts CM23 145 C7
Maze Green Rd CM23 145 D7
Mazers Ct 5 CM7 127 F2
Mazoe Cl CM23 145 F5
Mazoe Rd CM23 145 F5
Meachen Rd CO2 136 C5
Mead Ct
Clacton-on-S CO15 188 E3
Stansted Mountfitchet CM24 119 D7
Mead Pastures CM9 208 D3
Mead Path CM2 215 F8
Mead The
Brightlingsea CO7 185 F8
Great Cornard CO10 34 B4
Great Dunmow CM6 123 C2
Thaxted CM6 70 A3
Meadgate Ave CM2 216 D8
Meadgate Prim Sch CM2 216 E8
Meadgate Terr CM2 216 D8
Meadow Brown Ct CM7 127 E1
Meadow Cl
Chelmondiston IP9 63 F7
Clacton-on-S CO15 189 B7
Elmstead CO7 137 F6
Great Bromley CO7 139 A6

Meadow Cl *continued*
Halstead CO9 ... 103 F8
Panfield CM7 ... 127 A7
Meadow Cres IP3 ... 18 F1
Meadow Grass Cl CO3 ... 134 B6
Meadow La Sudbury CO10 ... 33 E7
West Mersea CO5 ... 201 C5
Meadow Rd
Colchester CO2 ... 135 D1
Great Chesterford CB10 ... 3 D3
Meadow Side CM1 ... 205 B3
Meadow View
Bicknacre CM3 ... 218 E1
Great Bardfield CM7 ... 72 B2
Kirby-le-S CO13 ... 143 D1
St Osyth CO16 ... 187 B4
Tiptree CO5 ... 179 B5
Meadow View Cl CO3 ... 134 E5
Meadow View Rd CO10 ... 33 D5
Meadow Way
Abberton CO5 ... 163 B2
Black Notley CM77 ... 155 C5
Clacton-on-S CO15 ... 203 G7
Meadow Wlk 5 CM2 ... 205 C2
Meadowbrook Ct CO1 ... 136 B7
Meadowcroft CM24 ... 119 E7
Meadowcroft Way CO13 ... 170 F7
Meadowford CB11 ... 42 F1
Meadowlands CM23 ... 119 A2
Meadows The
Bishop's Stortford CM23 ... 145 E5
3 Chelmsford CM2 ... 205 C2
Meadowside
Braintree CM7 ... 127 E5
Chelmsford CM2 ... 205 C3
Meadowside Ct CM3 ... 192 E1
Meadowside Gdns IP4 ... 18 E8
Meadowsweet Cl CM23 ... 145 C6
Meadowvale Cl IP4 ... 17 F7
Meads The
Chelmsford CM2 ... 205 A1
Stansted Mountfitchet CM24 ... 119 F6
Wicken Bonhunt CB11 ... 66 A7
Meadside CM7 ... 73 B3
Meadway Gosfield CO9 ... 102 E8
Lawford CO11 ... 86 B3
Maldon CM9 ... 210 B1
Mearns Pl 3 CM2 ... 205 F4
Mede Way CO7 ... 137 C3
Medlar Cl CM8 ... 177 A4
Medley Rd CM77 ... 126 F2
Medusa Ct Harwich CO12 ... 91 B2
Holland-on-S CO15 ... 189 E5
Medway Ave CM8 ... 176 D2
Medway Cl CM1 ... 204 D4
Medway Rd IP3 ... 17 F2
Meekings Rd CO10 ... 34 B8
Meers The CO13 ... 170 E6
Meeson Mdws CM9 ... 220 E8
Meeting Field CO10 ... 15 C7
Meeting La
East Mersea CO5 ... 184 C1
Ridgewell CO9 ... 29 B7
Meeting Wlk CB9 ... 9 B7
Meggy Tye CM2 ... 206 B5
Megs Way CM7 ... 128 B2
Melba Ct CM1 ... 204 C1
Melbourne Ave CM1 ... 204 E5
Melbourne Chase CO2 ... 136 B1
Melbourne Ct CM1 ... 204 E5
Melbourne Par CM1 ... 204 E5
Melbourne Park Prim Sch CM1 ... 204 F6
Melbourne Rd
Clacton-on-S CO15 ... 188 E4
Ipswich IP4 ... 18 D7
Melford Cl IP4 ... 18 F5
Melford Gr CM77 ... 154 B7
Melford Rd Cavendish CO10 ... 1 E2
Sudbury CO10 ... 15 D2
Melford Way IP11 ... 221 A3
Mell Rd CM9 ... 199 E1
Mellis Ct IP11 ... 221 B5
Mellor Chase CO3 ... 134 E7
Melplash Cl IP3 ... 18 E4
Melplash Rd IP3 ... 18 E4
Melrose Gdns
Clacton-on-S CO15 ... 189 C5
Ipswich IP4 ... 18 B8
Melrose Rd CO5 ... 201 C6
Melton Cl CO16 ... 188 A4
Melville Rd IP4 ... 17 F5
Menai Ct IP1 ... 17 B7
Mendip Dr IP5 ... 18 F6
Mendip Rd CM1 ... 204 D6
Mendlesham Cl CO16 ... 188 B4
Menin Rd CO2 ... 135 D4
Menish Way CM2 ... 206 A3
Meon Cl CM1 ... 205 C6
Meopham Ct CO2 ... 136 B4
Mercantile Ho 1 CO1 ... 135 F6
Mercers Ave CM23 ... 145 B4
Mercers Row CB10 ... 22 D1
Mercers Way 2 CO1 ... 135 E8
Mercia Cl CM2 ... 217 A5
Mercury Cl CO2 ... 135 A3
Mercury Pl CM9 ... 209 F5
Merdle Sq CM1 ... 204 F6
Mere Gdns IP4 ... 18 F4
Meredith Rd CO15 ... 188 E3
Merediths Cl CO7 ... 164 B8
Meres Cl CM8 ... 176 F1
Meriden Ct CO15 ... 189 A5
Merivale Cl CO11 ... 86 C3
Merivale Rd CO11 ... 86 B3
Merlin End CO4 ... 110 F1
Merlin Pl CM1 ... 204 F5
Merlin Rd IP2 ... 16 C3
Merriam Cl CO11 ... 86 D8
Merrilees Cres CO15 ... 189 D6
Merrill Pl 2 CM23 ... 145 E5
Merrion Cl 7 IP2 ... 16 C2
Merrymount Gdns CO15 ... 189 B5
Mersea Ave CO5 ... 201 B6
Mersea Ct CO5 ... 201 B7
Mersea Fleet Way CM7 ... 128 C1
Mersea Island Sch CO5 ... 201 C6
Mersea Mus* CO5 ... 201 B6
Mersea Point Nature Reserve* CO5 ... 185 C3
Mersea Rd
Abberton CO2,CO5 ... 163 B5
Colchester CO2 ... 136 A3
Peldon CO5 ... 182 F5
Mersea View CO16 ... 186 A3
Mersey Rd Ipswich IP3 ... 17 F2
Witham CM8 ... 176 E2
Mersey Way CM1 ... 204 C5
Merstham Dr CO16 ... 188 C6
Merton Ct CO2 ... 163 A7
Messines Rd CO2 ... 135 D5
Messing Gn CO5 ... 159 D2
Messing-cum-Inworth Prim Sch CO5 ... 159 C2
Meteor Way CM1 ... 204 F2
Mews Ct CM2 ... 205 B1
Mews The
Bishop's Stortford CM22 ... 146 A3
Felixstowe IP11 ... 221 E4
Frinton-on-S CO13 ... 171 A5
Harwich CO12 ... 91 C3
Panfield CM7 ... 126 A7
Stansted Mountfitchet CM24 ... 119 F7
Meyrick Cres CO2 ... 135 F5
Micawber Way CM1 ... 204 D7
Michaels Rd CM23 ... 119 A2
Michaelstowe Cl CO12 ... 90 C2
Michaelstowe Dr CO12 ... 90 C2
Mickfield Mews IP11 ... 221 B5
Micklegate Rd IP11 ... 221 C1
Middle Gn CO6 ... 79 C1
Middle King CM7 ... 128 D1
Middle Mill Rd CO1 ... 135 F8
Middle Row 5 CM23 ... 145 F6
Middle St CB11 ... 65 C4
Middle Way CO10 ... 15 D8
Middleborough CO1 ... 135 E8
Middlefield CO9 ... 76 F1
Middlefield Rd CO11 ... 87 A3
Middleton Cl
Clacton-on-S CO16 ... 188 D6
Ipswich IP2 ... 16 D2
Middleton Rd CO10 ... 33 D5
Middlewick Cl 4 CO2 ... 136 A1
Midguard Way CM9 ... 220 F8
Midland Cl CO2 ... 135 F4
Midway CO15 ... 203 E6
Midway Rd CO2 ... 135 C2
Milbank CM2 ... 206 B4
Milburn Cres CM1 ... 204 D1
Milch La CM3 ... 153 E6
Milden Rd IP2 ... 16 E5
Mildenhall Pl 14 CB9 ... 9 B8
Mildmay Cl CM6 ... 151 E7
Mildmay Ct 2 CM2 ... 205 B1
Mildmay Jun & Inf Schs CM2 ... 216 B5
Mildmay Rd
Chelmsford CM2 ... 205 B1
Ipswich IP3 ... 18 B1
Mildmays CM3 ... 218 C7
Mile End IP1 ... 17 A6
Mile End Rd CO4 ... 109 E3
Miles Cl CO3 ... 134 C6
Milestones The CM3 ... 194 A4
Milford Cl CO7 ... 137 D1
Military Ct 10 CO1 ... 136 A6
Military Rd CO1 ... 136 A5
Military Way CO12 ... 90 C1
Mill Chase Halstead CO9 ... 76 F2
Steeple Bumpstead CB9 ... 27 C5
Mill Cl Elsenham CM22 ... 94 C1
Felixstowe IP11 ... 221 B4
Great Bardfield CM7 ... 72 B2
Harwich CO12 ... 91 C4
Tiptree CO5 ... 179 C6
Mill Cotts CM2 ... 217 C8
Mill Croft CM23 ... 119 A1
Mill Cswy SG8 ... 19 C5
Mill Ct Braintree CM7 ... 128 B2
Takeley CM6 ... 149 B7
Mill End CM6 ... 70 A2
Mill Field Barnston CM6 ... 151 A4
Chelmondiston IP9 ... 63 E8
Mill Hill Braintree CM7 ... 128 B2
Chelmsford CM2 ... 215 F2
Farnham CM23 ... 118 E5
Harwich CO12 ... 91 C3
Haverhill CB9 ... 9 A7
Lawford CO11 ... 85 D4
Manningtree CO11 ... 86 C4
Purleigh CM3 ... 220 C1
Stansted Mountfitchet CM24 ... 119 E6
Sudbury CO10 ... 33 D7
Wormingford CO6 ... 80 E6
Mill House Cotts CO12 ... 116 D4
Mill La Ardleigh CO7 ... 112 B4
Birch CO2 ... 161 A3
Bradfield CO11 ... 87 D2
Broomfield CM1 ... 191 C1
Cavendish CO10 ... 13 B8
Chelmondiston IP9 ... 63 E7
Coggeshall CO5 ... 131 F1
Mill La *continued*
Colne Engaine CO6 ... 105 B8
Cressing CM77 ... 155 D5
Danbury CM3 ... 219 A6
Dedham CO7 ... 84 F7
Felixstowe IP11 ... 221 C4
Finchingfield CM7 ... 48 F3
Ford End CM3 ... 172 D7
Great Dunmow CM6 ... 123 D1
Great Holland CO13 ... 169 E3
Great Leighs CM3 ... 174 B7
Great Maplestead CO9 ... 76 E8
Harkstead SG9 ... 64 A5
Harwich CO12 ... 91 D3
Hinxton CB10 ... 3 A7
Ickleton CB10 ... 3 B4
Layer-de-l-H CO2 ... 162 B5
Little Baddow CM3 ... 207 E3
Little Yeldham CO9 ... 30 A3
Littlebury CB11 ... 21 F4
Maldon CM9 ... 210 A3
Manningtree CO11 ... 86 D4
Pebmarsh CO9 ... 78 A7
Purleigh CM3 ... 220 C1
Rayne CM7 ... 153 E8
Saffron Walden CB10 ... 22 F2
Salcott-cum-virley CM9 ... 199 B8
Stebbing CM6 ... 124 E5
Stoke-by-N CO6 ... 56 D7
Sudbury CO10 ... 33 D7
Terling CM3 ... 175 A3
Thorington Street CO6 ... 57 C4
Thorpe-le-S CO16 ... 141 F1
Tolleshunt Major CM9 ... 197 E3
Walton-on-t-N CO14 ... 171 C8
Washbrook IP8 ... 16 A1
Weeley Heath CO16 ... 168 A6
Witham CM8 ... 176 F1
Mill Lane Cl CO16 ... 168 A6
Mill Park Dr CM7 ... 128 B1
Mill Rd Birdbrook CO9 ... 10 E2
Boxted CO4 ... 82 F4
Clare CO10 ... 12 C7
Colchester CO4 ... 109 F4
Debden CB11 ... 68 B8
East Bergholt CO7 ... 59 E2
Elder Street CB10 ... 45 B3
Felsted CM6 ... 152 A4
Finchingfield CM7 ... 72 D5
Fordham CO6 ... 107 D4
Foxearth CO10 ... 14 C5
Great Bardfield CM7 ... 72 B2
Great Totham CM9 ... 196 D7
Haverhill CB9 ... 9 A7
Helions Bumpstead CB9 ... 26 C8
Henham CM22 ... 94 E4
Maldon CM9 ... 210 B2
Marks Tey CO6 ... 133 C4
North End CM6 ... 151 F2
Ridgewell CO9 ... 29 B6
Stambourne CO9 ... 28 C3
West Mersea CO5 ... 201 D7
Mill Rise IP9 ... 62 D5
Mill Road Cotts CB10 ... 45 B3
Mill Road Dr IP3 ... 18 F1
Mill Side CM24 ... 119 E6
Mill St
Bishop's Stortford CM23 ... 146 A5
Brightlingsea CO7 ... 186 A6
Colchester CO1 ... 136 A6
Nayland CO6 ... 56 B1
St Osyth CO16 ... 186 F4
Stoke-by-N CO6 ... 56 D8
Mill Tye CO10 ... 34 A4
Mill Vale Lo CM8 ... 176 F2
Mill View CM7 ... 129 D3
Mill Vue Rd CM2 ... 205 F2
Mill Wlk CO5 ... 179 C6
Millars The CM1 ... 191 A3
Millbridge Rd CM8 ... 176 F2
Milldene Prim Sch CO5 ... 179 D6
Millennium Way CM7 ... 155 D8
Miller's Barn Rd CO15 ... 188 A1
Miller's Cl CM6 ... 151 A4
Millers Cl
Bishop's Stortford CM23 ... 145 C5
Braintree CM7 ... 128 A8
Colchester CO3 ... 134 C6
Great Horkesley CO6 ... 109 B7
Millers Croft
Great Baddow CM2 ... 216 F6
Great Dunmow CM6 ... 123 E1
Millers Dr CM77 ... 154 C7
Millers La CO3 ... 134 D6
Millers Mead CO5 ... 158 E4
Millers Reach CO11 ... 87 A4
Millers Row CM7 ... 48 C6
Millers View IP1 ... 16 F7
Millfield Gdns IP4 ... 18 A6
Millfields CO5 ... 179 C6
Millfields Danbury CM3 ... 219 A6
Stansted Mountfitchet CM24 ... 119 E6
Writtle CM1 ... 204 A1
Millfields Prim Sch CO7 ... 137 D1
Millfields Way CB9 ... 9 B8
Millhouse Villas CM6 ... 151 A4
Milligans Chase CM2 ... 216 B1
Milliners Way CM23 ... 145 C4
Mills La CO10 ... 15 C4
Mills Rd CO10 ... 34 A8
Mills The IP4 ... 18 E8
Millside CM23 ... 146 A5
Millson Bank CM2 ... 206 A4
Millways CM9 ... 196 B4
Millwrights CO5 ... 179 C6
Milner Rd CO10 ... 34 B8
Milner St IP4 ... 17 E5
Milnrow IP2 ... 16 C2
Milton Ave CM7 ... 155 A8
Milton Cl CO3 ... 134 F6
Milton Ct CO15 ... 189 E6
Milton Pl CM1 ... 205 A5
Milton Rd Harwich CO12 ... 91 D4
Lawford CO11 ... 86 B2
Witham CM8 ... 176 F5
Milton St IP4 ... 18 B6
Mimosa Cl CM1 ... 205 F6
Mimosa Ct CO4 ... 136 E8
Minden Rd CO10 ... 33 F7
Minerva Cl Harwich CO12 ... 90 F1
Haverhill CB9 ... 9 D6
Minerva End CO2 ... 135 C1
Minos Way IP1 ... 16 D8
Minsmere Dr CO16 ... 188 C6
Minsmere Rd IP3 ... 38 D8
Minsmere Way CO10 ... 34 C6
Minster Way CM9 ... 220 E8
Minters Cotts CO11 ... 115 C5
Miranda Wlk CO4 ... 136 E7
Mirosa Dr CM9 ... 210 B1
Mission La CO7 ... 60 B3
Mistley Norman CE Prim Sch CO11 ... 87 A4
Mistley Place Pk* CO11 ... 86 E4
Mistley Sta CO11 ... 86 F4
Mistley Twrs* CO11 ... 86 F4
Mitchell Ave CO9 ... 76 E1
Mitchell Circ CM7 ... 73 C6
Mitre Gdns CM23 ... 146 A4
Mitre Way IP3 ... 17 F4
Mitton Vale CM2 ... 205 F2
Moat Farm CO9 ... 28 B7
Moat Farm Chase CM8 ... 176 F3
Moat Farm Cl IP4 ... 17 F8
Moat Fields CO6 ... 107 D6
Moat La CO8 ... 55 A4
Moat Rd Birdbrook CO9 ... 28 C7
Fordham CO6 ... 107 D6
Moat Wlk CB9 ... 8 E8
Modlen Rd CO14 ... 171 B7
Moffat Ave IP4 ... 18 B8
Mole Hall La CB11 ... 67 F3
Mole Hall Wildlife Pk* CB11 ... 67 F3
Molehill Green Cotts CM22 ... 121 C6
Molehill Green Rdbt CM22 ... 121 C5
Molrams La CM2 ... 217 B6
Monarch Cl CB9 ... 8 C8
Monarch Way IP8 ... 36 D8
Monk's Cnr CB10 ... 47 B4
Monk's La CO7 ... 84 D4
Monkdowns Rd CO6 ... 131 B3
Monklands Ct 2 CO9 ... 76 D1
Monks Ct CM8 ... 176 E3
Monks Gate IP8 ... 16 A6
Monks Hill CB11 ... 43 F8
Monks Lodge Rd CO9 ... 52 D2
Monks Mead CM3 ... 218 F2
Monks Rd CO6 ... 105 B7
Monks Wlk CM9 ... 213 E8
Monkswood Dr CM23 ... 145 D6
Monkwick Ave CO2 ... 135 F1
Monkwick Jun & Inf Schs CO2 ... 136 A2
Monmouth Cl IP2 ... 17 B1
Mons Rd CO2 ... 135 D4
Montagu Gdns CM1 ... 205 F7
Montague Rd IP11 ... 221 F4
Montbretia Cl CO3 ... 134 D6
Montbretia Ct CO16 ... 188 C4
Montfort Ct 8 CB9 ... 8 F7
Montgomery Cl
Chelmsford CM1 ... 205 E7
Colchester CO2 ... 136 B4
Montgomery Jun & Inf Sch CO2 ... 135 D2
Montgomery Rd IP2 ... 17 B1
Monton Rise IP2 ... 16 D2
Montrose Ct IP3 ... 17 F4
Montrose Rd CM2 ... 206 A4
Moon Hall La CB9 ... 9 A6
Moonhall Bsns Pk CB9 ... 9 A5
Moor Hall La
Bishop's Stortford CM23 ... 145 C3
Bishop's Stortford,Thorley CM23 ... 145 B3
Danbury CM3 ... 218 E2
Moor Rd Great Tey CO6 ... 132 C8
Langham CO4 ... 83 D4
Moor's Farm Chase CM9 ... 197 A3
Moor's La CO7 ... 139 E1
Moorfield Ct CM8 ... 176 F1
Moorhouse Gn CO7 ... 111 E8
Moorings The CM23 ... 146 A5
Moors Cl Feering CO5 ... 158 E5
Great Bentley CO7 ... 139 E1
Moors Croft CM7 ... 128 D3
Moors La
Little Dunmow CM6 ... 151 D7
Rayne CM77 ... 126 D3
Moors The CM6 ... 151 D7
Moorsfield CO10 ... 34 B4
Moorside CO1 ... 136 B7
Mope La CM8 ... 195 D6
Moran Ave CM1 ... 205 B7
Morant Rd CO1 ... 136 B5
Morebarn Rd CO7 ... 112 E2
Morecambe Ct IP4 ... 18 A7
Morella Cl CO7 ... 166 E8
Morello Ct CO2 ... 163 A7
Moretons CM2 ... 216 B2
Morland Ct CO6 ... 82 B1
Morland Prim Sch IP3 ... 38 A8
Morland Rd IP3 ... 37 F8
Morley Rd Halstead CO9 ... 76 F2
Tiptree CO5 ... 179 D4
Morleys Rd CO6 ... 105 A6
Mornington Ave 2 IP1 ... 17 A8
Morris Ave CO15 ... 203 E6
Morris Harp CB10 ... 22 E3
Morris Rd CM2 ... 205 D2
Morrow La CO7 ... 112 A6
Mors End CO7 ... 58 D2
Morses La CO7 ... 165 F1
Morten Rd CO1 ... 135 E8
Mortimer Rd CM3 ... 194 A4
Morton Rd CM9 ... 196 A4
Morton Way CO9 ... 77 A3
Moss Path CM2 ... 216 C3
Moss Rd Colchester CO3 ... 134 E4
Witham CM8 ... 177 B3
Moss Way CO6 ... 108 E3
Moss Wlk CM2 ... 216 B6
Mossfield Cl CO3 ... 135 C6
Mott's La CO6 ... 132 D4
Mottram Cl 9 IP2 ... 16 C2
Motts Cl CM7 ... 127 E4
Motts La CM8 ... 177 B4
Motts Yd CM6 ... 124 E5
Moules La CB1 ... 5 C6
Moulsham Chase CM2 ... 216 C8
Moulsham Dr CM2 ... 216 B8
Moulsham Hall La
Braintree CM3 ... 153 F2
Great Leighs CM3 ... 154 A1
Moulsham High Sch CM2 ... 216 B7
Moulsham Jun & Inf Schs CM2 ... 216 B7
Moulsham St
Chelmsford CM1 ... 205 B2
Chelmsford,Moulsham CM2 ... 205 B1
Moulsham Thrift CM2 ... 216 A6
Moulton Cl CO10 ... 33 F8
Mount Dr Ipswich IP3 ... 18 F1
Stansted Mountfitchet CM24 ... 119 E5
Mount Hill CO9 ... 76 D1
Mount Lodge Chase CM9 ... 196 E6
Mount Pleasant
Halstead CO9 ... 76 E1
Maldon CM9 ... 209 F2
Mount Pleasant Cotts CB11 ... 43 D8
Mount Pleasant Est CM9 ... 196 E6
Mount Pleasant Rd CB11 ... 43 E8
Mount Rd Braintree CM7 ... 128 A3
Coggeshall CO6 ... 131 B2
Haverhill CB9 ... 9 B7
Mount Rise 4 CO9 ... 76 D1
Mount The
Colchester CO3 ... 134 F6
Tollesbury CM9 ... 199 D1
Mountain Ash Cl CO4 ... 110 C2
Mountain's Farm Rd CM6 ... 150 C3
Mountains Rd CM8,CM9 ... 196 C7
Mountbatten Cl CO10 ... 15 F2
Mountbatten Ct 7 IP1 ... 17 A7
Mountbatten Dr CO2 ... 136 B4
Mountbatten Rd
Braintree CM7 ... 128 C4
Sudbury CO10 ... 15 F2
Mountbatten Way CM1 ... 205 E7
Mountfitchet Castle & Norman Village* CM24 ... 119 F6
Mountfitchet High Sch CM24 ... 119 F4
Mountfitchet Rd CM24 ... 119 E5
Mounthill Ave CM2 ... 205 D3
Mountview Rd CO15 ... 189 A5
Moverons La CO7 ... 165 C2
Mowden Hall La
Hatfield Peverel CM3 ... 193 D1
Ulting CM3 ... 208 A8
Mowlands IP9 ... 35 B1
Moy Rd CO2 ... 136 A1
Moze Cross CO12 ... 116 D1
Mulberries The CM7 ... 128 A2
Mulberry Ave CO2 ... 136 A4
Mulberry Ct CM23 ... 146 A5
Mulberry Gdns CM8 ... 177 A4
Mulberry Harbour Way CO7 ... 164 B8
Mulberry Way CM1 ... 205 D4
Mullins Rd CM7 ... 127 F6
Multon Lea CM1 ... 206 A7
Mumford Cl CO6 ... 108 E4
Mumford Rd Ipswich IP1 ... 16 E8
West Bergholt CO6 ... 108 D4
Mumfords La CO13 ... 170 A7
Mundon Rd CM7 ... 128 D1
Munnings Cl IP3 ... 38 B8
Munnings Dr CO16 ... 188 D6
Munnings Rd CO3 ... 135 A5
Munnings Way CO11 ... 86 B5
Munro Rd CM8 ... 176 F5
Murchison Cl CM1 ... 204 E5
Murray Cl CM7 ... 127 F6
Murray Rd IP3 ... 18 A3
Murrayfield Com Prim Sch IP3 ... 18 A2

Murrell Lock CM2 206 A4
Murrills Rd IP3 18 F1
Murton Slade 6 CB9 9 A8
Mus of Power* CM9 209 D6
Muscade Cl CO5 179 D6
Museum St
14 Colchester CO1 135 F7
Ipswich IP1 17 C6
Saffron Walden CB10 22 D2
Musgrave Cl CO12 90 F1
Musk Cl CO3 134 D7
Muswell Wlk CO16 188 D5
Mutlow Cl CB11 42 F5
Mutlow Hill CB11 42 F5
Mychett Cl CO16 188 B6
Myddylton Pl CB10 22 D2
Myland Hall Chase CO4 110 C3
Myland Prim Sch CO4 109 E4
Mynards Way CM3 218 C7
Myneer Pk CO6 131 B2
Myrtle Gr CO2 136 B5
Myrtle Rd IP3 17 E4
Myson Way CM23 146 B7

N

Nabbott Rd CM1 204 E2
Nacton Cres IP3 18 B2
Nacton Rd
Felixstowe IP11 221 C1
Ipswich,Racecourse IP3 18 B2
Ipswich,Rose Hill IP3 18 A3
Nails La 15 CM23 145 F7
Nalla Gdns CM1 205 A6
Nancy Smith Cl CO2 135 F5
Nansen Rd
Holland-on-S CO15 189 D6
Ipswich IP3 18 B2
Napier Ave CO15 203 D6
Napier Ct CM1 204 E5
Napier Rd CO2 135 F6
Narvik Cl CM9 220 E8
Nash Cl Colchester CO3 135 B5
Lawford CO11 86 B5
Nash Dr CM1 191 A3
Nash Gdns IP3 38 B8
Nassau Rd CO16 187 B4
Nathan Ct CO2 163 B8
Nats La CB11 42 E6
Navarre St 4 IP1 17 C6
Navigation Pl CM9 210 B4
Navigation Rd CM2 205 C2
Nayland Dr CO16 188 B4
Nayland Prim Sch CO6 56 A1
Nayland Rd Bures CO8 79 F8
Colchester CO6 109 D6
Felixstowe IP11 221 A4
Great Horkesley CO6 82 B4
Haverhill CB9 8 E6
Little Horkesley CO6 81 F6
West Bergholt CO6 108 D7
Nayling Rd CM7 127 C2
Naze Ct CO14 144 E3
Naze Nature Reserve The*
CO14 144 D6
Naze Nature Trail The*
CO14 144 E4
Naze Park Rd CO14 144 E2
Neale Rd CO9 76 E1
Neale St IP1 17 C6
Neasden Ave CO16 188 D5
Neath Dr IP2 17 A1
Needle Cnr IP9 63 D1
Nelson Ct CO7 186 A7
Nelson Gdns CM7 128 C4
Nelson Gr CM1 204 F3
Nelson Rd
Bishop's Stortford CM23 146 A5
Clacton-on-S CO15 188 E1
Colchester CO3 134 E6
Harwich CO12 91 D4
Ipswich IP4 18 A6
Nelson St CO7 185 F6
Neptune Ct
Chelmsford CM1 204 F4
5 Colchester CO1 136 C6
Neptune Quay IP4 17 D5
Neptune Sq IP4 17 D5
Ness Wlk CM8 176 D2
Nether Ct CO9 77 A1
Nether Hill CO9,CO10 31 D3
Nether Rd CO10 1 D2
Nethergate St CO10 12 B7
Netley Cl IP2 36 F8
Nettleditch CB11 21 E4
Neville Rd CB10 22 E2
New Barn La CM22 146 D1
New Bowers Way CM1 205 F6
New Captains Rd CO5 201 B6
New Cardinal St IP1 17 B5
New Church Rd CO6 108 E4
New Cotts Great Tey CO6 132 C8
Wakes Colne CO6 106 C6
New Cut Bures CO8 79 E8
Glemsford CO10 2 B3
Great Bentley CO7 166 E8
Layer-de-l-H CO2 161 F5
New Cut E IP2,IP3 17 D4
New Cut W IP2 17 D4
New Dukes Way CM2 205 F4
New England Cl CM3 218 F1
New Farm Lodge CO3 134 D5
New Farm Rd CO3 134 D6
New Hall Cotts CO7 58 F7
New Hall Sch CM3 192 A1
New Hall Vineyard*
CM3 220 D2
New House La CB10 24 C3
New Kiln Rd CO3 135 C7
New La Feering CO5 158 F5
Holbrook IP9 63 A5
New Lodge Chase CM3 207 B2
New London Rd CM2 205 A1
New Nabbotts Way CM1 205 E7
New Orleans Flats CO5 201 B5
New Park Gdns CO7 185 F7
New Park St CO1 136 B6
New Pier St 7 CO14 171 C8
New Pk CO9 51 F3
New Place Ho IP2 17 A4
New Pond La CB10 22 C2
New Queens Rd CO10 15 E1
New Rd Aldham CO6 107 B2
Broomfield CM1 191 B1
Colchester CO3 134 D6
Elsenham CM22 94 C2
Gosfield CO9 102 E5
Great Baddow CM2 217 A6
Hatfield Peverel CM3 194 A4
Hinxton CB10 3 B6
Kelvedon CO5 158 C2
Long Melford CO10 15 C7
Messing CO5 159 C1
Mistley CO11 86 E4
Rayne CM77 127 A1
Saffron Walden CB10 22 E1
Shudy Camps CB1 7 C7
Terling CM3 175 C3
Tiptree CO5 179 D5
Tollesbury CM9 199 D2
Trimley St M IP11 221 A7
New Road Terr CM77 126 F1
New St Braintree CM7 127 F2
Brightlingsea CO7 185 F6
Chelmsford CM1 205 B3
Glemsford CO10 2 A5
Great Dunmow CM6 150 D8
Halstead CO9 76 E1
21 Ipswich IP4 17 D5
Maldon CM9 209 F2
Sudbury CO10 33 E8
New Street Fields CM6 150 D8
New Thorpe Ave CO16 142 A2
New Town Rd
Colchester CO1 136 A6
Thorpe-le-S CO16 141 F2
New Village CO11 86 C7
New Way Ipswich IP2 16 F6
Point Clear B CO16 185 F3
New Writtle St CM2 205 B1
Newark Cl IP2 16 F1
Newbarn Rd CO6 106 B1
Newbiggen St CM6 69 F3
Newbourne Gdns IP11 221 B3
Newbridge Hill CO6 108 D2
Newbridge Rd Birch CO5 180 A6
Tiptree CO5 179 F5
Newbury Cl CM23 145 E8
Newbury Ho IP4 18 B6
Newbury Rd IP4 18 C6
Newby Dr IP4 18 F5
Newcastle Ave CO3 134 F4
Newcomen Way CO4 110 C6
Newcourt Rd CM2 205 D3
Newcroft 1 CB10 22 E1
Newgate St 5 CO14 171 C8
Newhaven La CO12 91 D6
Newhouse Rd CO6 104 F5
Newhythe CO3 134 E7
Newington Gdns CO15 188 F8
Newland Ave CM7 72 B1
Newland Pl CM8 177 A1
Newland St CM8 177 A2
Newlands Dr CM8 177 A2
Newlands La CO6 56 B1
Newlands Prec 8 CM8 177 A2
Newlands Spring Prim Sch
CM1 204 D7
Newman Dr CO4 83 A4
Newman's Rd CO10 33 F8
Newmarket Rd CB10 3 C3
Newmill La
Brantham CO11 61 A1
Stutton CO11 87 A8
Newnham Cl CM7 127 E2
Newnham Ct IP2 16 E2
Newnham Gn CM9 209 E3
Newpasture La CM6 125 C5
Newport Cl
Great Baddow CM2 217 B6
Harwich CO12 91 A1
Newport Dr
Clacton-on-S CO15 189 A7
Rickling Green CB11 66 F4
Newport Free Gram Sch
CB11 42 F1
Newport Prim Sch CB11 66 F7
Newport Rd CB11 43 C7
Newport Sta CB11 67 A8
Newport Way CO13 171 A6
Newpots Cl CO5 182 D5
Newpots La CO5 182 E5
Newquay Cl IP5 18 F6
Newry Ave IP11 221 D4
Newson St IP1 17 B7
Newton Cl 4 CM7 127 F1
Newton Croft CO10 34 A7
Newton Gdns CO16 187 A5
Newton Gn CM6 123 C1
Newton Gr CM6 123 B1
Newton Pl 15 CB9 9 B8
Newton Rd Harwich CO12 91 A3
Newton Rd *continued*
Ipswich IP3 18 A4
Sudbury CO10 34 A7
Newton St 10 IP4 17 D6
Newton Way CO16 187 B5
Newtown Rd CM23 145 F6
Nexus The CO1 135 E8
Nicholas Cl CM1 204 B1
Nicholas Ct
Chelmsford, Scot's Green
CM1 204 D6
Witham CM8 176 F2
Nicholas Rd IP11 221 A4
Nichols Cl CO11 86 B3
Nichols Cnr CO7 112 A5
Nichols Ct 1 CM2 205 A1
Nichols Gr CM7 128 C3
Nickleby Rd CM1 204 D6
Nickolsons Gr CO1 136 A6
Nien-Oord CO16 188 C4
Nightingale Cl
Clacton-on-S CO15 188 F5
Colchester CO4 137 A8
Harwich CO12 90 F1
Witham CM8 194 E8
Nightingale Cnr 2 CM9 210 A1
Nightingale Ct CO2 163 A8
Nightingale Hill CO4 83 F6
Nightingale Mews 2
CB10 22 F2
Nightingale Pl CO3 134 C4
Nightingale Rd IP3 38 A8
Nightingale Sq IP3 38 A8
Nightingale Way CO15 188 F5
Nine Acres IP2 16 D5
Nineacres CM7 128 A1
Ninth Ave CM24 120 B2
Noah's Ark La CO10 33 D7
Noak's Cross CM8 178 B2
Noakes Ave CM2 216 E6
Noaks Rd IP7 58 D8
Nobles The CM23 145 D6
Nonsuch Mdw CO10 33 E7
Nook The CO7 164 C8
Norbury Cl CO6 132 F3
Norbury Rd IP4 18 B8
Nordic Lodge CM9 220 F8
Norfolk Ave
Clacton-on-S CO15 189 E7
West Mersea CO5 201 D7
Norfolk Cl CM9 209 E1
Norfolk Cres CO4 110 B1
Norfolk Dr CM1 205 A7
Norfolk Gdns CM7 128 B4
Norfolk Rd Ipswich IP4 17 D6
Maldon CM9 209 E1
Norfolk Way CM23 145 F5
Norman Ave CM23 145 D6
Norman Cl
Marks Tey CO6 132 E3
St Osyth CO16 187 A4
Norman Cres IP3 18 A2
Norman Ct CM24 119 E7
Norman Hill CM3 175 B2
Norman Rd
Clacton-on-S CO15 189 E6
Manningtree CO11 86 D4
Norman Way
Colchester, Lexton CO3 135 B6
Colchester, Shrub End CO3 135 B4
Point Clear B CO16 185 F3
Norman's Way CM24 119 E7
Normandie Way CO8 79 E8
Normandy Ave CO2 136 A3
Normanhurst CO15 188 E1
Normansfield CM6 150 E7
Norris Cl
Bishop's Stortford CM23 146 C7
Braintree CM7 128 C5
North Ave
Chelmsford CM1 204 F5
Haverhill CB9 8 E8
North Cl IP4 17 E8
North Cres CB9 27 B7
North Dell CM1 205 E7
North Dr CM2 216 F7
North End Rd
Gestingthorpe CO9,CO10 31 C2
Hinxton CB10 3 B8
Little Yeldham CO9 30 E2
North Hall Rd CB11 67 A2
North Hill Colchester CO1 135 E7
Little Baddow CM3 207 D5
North Hill Gdns 1 IP4 17 E6
North Hill Rd IP4 17 E6
North Ho CO13 170 F4
North La CO6 133 B5
North Lawn IP4 18 C8
North Mill Pl CO9 76 E3
North Prim Sch CO1 135 E8
North Rd
Belchamp Walter CO10 31 F6
Brightlingsea CO7 185 F7
Clacton-on-S CO15 188 F6
Great Yeldham CO9 30 A2
Takeley CM22 148 C8
Tollesbury CM9 199 C2
North Rise CO10 34 A6
North Sea View CO12 90 F2
North St
4 Bishop's Stortford
CM23 145 F7
Great Dunmow CM6 123 D1
Maldon CM9 210 B2
Manningtree CO11 86 D4
Steeple Bumpstead CB9 27 B7
Sudbury CO10 33 E8
Tolleshunt D'arcy CM9 198 E5
North St *continued*
Walton-on-t-N CO14 171 C8
North Station Rd CO1 135 E8
North Street Par 1 CO10 33 E7
North Terr 5 CM23 145 F8
North View Cotts CO6 109 B7
North Wall CO16 186 A3
Northampton Cl CM7 128 D5
Northampton Mdw CM7 72 B2
Northbourne Rd CO15 188 F4
Northcroft CO10 33 E7
Northend CB11 22 A4
Northern Rd CO10 34 B8
Northfield CM7 72 B3
Northfield Gdns CO4 110 A4
Northfield Rd CB11 43 E8
Northgate End CM23 145 F8
Northgate Prim Sch
CM23 145 E8
Northgate St
Colchester CO1 135 F8
Ipswich IP1 17 C6
Northolt Ave CM23 119 B1
Northumberland Cl
CM7 128 B4
Northumberland Ct 1
CM2 205 F4
Norton Rd
Chelmsford CM1 205 A3
Haverhill CB9 8 E6
Norway Cres CO12 90 F3
Norwich Cl
Clacton-on-S CO16 188 E6
Colchester CO1 136 A8
Norwich Ct 2 IP1 17 A7
Norwich Rd IP1 17 A7
Norwood Ave CO15 189 B5
Norwood Way CO14 171 A7
Notcutts CO7 59 E1
Notley Gn CM77 154 B6
Notley Green Prim Sch
CM77 154 C8
Notley High Sch The
CM7 154 F8
Notley Rd CM7 154 F8
Nottage Cl CO7 164 C8
Nottidge Rd IP4 17 E6
Nottingham Rd CO15 189 E6
Nounsley Rd CM3 194 B1
Nun's Mdw CO9 102 E7
Nunn's Rd CO1 135 E7
Nunnery St CO9 51 D4
Nunns Cl CO6 131 A2
Nuns Wlk CO9 29 F1
Nunty's La
Greenstead Green CO9 104 A1
Pattiswick CM7 129 F8
Nursery Cl
Bishop's Stortford CM23 145 F6
Colchester CO3 134 C5
Nursery Dr CM7 128 A5
Nursery La CM3 218 F8
Nursery Rd
Bishop's Stortford CM23 145 F6
Chelmsford CM2 216 B8
Great Cornard CO10 34 B5
Nursery Rise CM6 150 D7
Nursery Wlk IP11 221 D5

O

Oak Ave CO16 188 A2
Oak Bglws CM7 127 E3
Oak Cl Felixstowe IP11 221 C4
Rushmere St A IP4 18 E7
Thorpe-le-S CO16 142 A1
West Bergholt CO6 108 E4
Oak Cnr Beaumont CO16 141 F8
Woodham Mortimer CM9 219 D6
Oak Cotts CM3 206 E8
Oak Eggar Chase IP8 36 D8
Oak Fall CM8 177 A5
Oak Farm Rd CM9 208 E1
Oak Gr IP8 16 A6
Oak Hall CM23 145 E8
Oak Haven CO12 90 F1
Oak Hill Beazley End CM7 101 A8
Wethersfield CM7 73 F1
Oak Hill La IP2 17 B3
Oak Ho IP2 16 D2
Oak Ind Pk CM6 150 F6
Oak Lodge Tye CM1 206 A6
Oak Rd Chappel CO6 106 B3
Great Cornard CO10 34 B6
Halstead CO9 103 D7
Heybridge CM9 210 B6
Little Maplestead CO9 77 A8
Pebmarsh CO9 77 F8
Rivenhall CM8 177 C6
Tiptree CO5 179 C7
Oak Ridge CO12 117 B7
Oak St CM23 145 F6
Oak Tree Cotts CO6 133 B8
Oak Tree Rd CO7 165 B8
Oak Wlk CO9 51 D2
Oak Yd CO9 76 E2
Oakapple Cl CO2 135 D1
Oakfield CM6 125 A4
Oakfield Dr CO4 83 A5
Oakfield La CM3 175 A2
Oakfield Rd Belstead IP8 36 A7
Washbrook IP8 35 F6
Oakfield Wood* CO11 88 D4
Oakland Rd CO12 91 C3
Oaklands Ave CO3 134 E5
Oaklands Cl
Bishop's Stortford CM23 119 B2
Oaklands Cl *continued*
Great Notley CM77 154 D8
Oaklands Cres CM2 216 B8
Oaklands Dr CM23 119 B2
Oaklands Inf Sch CM2 216 B8
Oaklands Pk CM23 119 B2
Oaklands Way CM3 207 E2
Oaklea Ave CM2 205 E3
Oaklee IP2 17 A1
Oakleigh Ct CM23 145 D8
Oakleigh Rd CO15 188 F8
Oakley Cross CO12 117 B7
Oakley Rd Braintree CM7 127 F7
Harwich CO12 90 D1
Wix CO11 115 E5
Oakmead Rd CO16 186 B3
Oakroyd Ave CM6 150 E8
Oaks Dr CO3 135 D7
Oaks Hospl The CO4 109 E3
Oaks Pl CO4 109 E2
Oaks The CO13 170 F6
Oaksmere Gdns IP2 17 A2
Oakstead Cl IP4 18 A6
Oaktree Cl 14 CM23 145 F7
Oaktrees CM9 197 B5
Oakview CO12 90 F1
Oakwood Ave
Clacton-on-S CO15 189 E7
West Mersea CO5 201 D7
Oakwood Cl CO13 170 E6
Oakwood Dr CO5 201 D7
Oakwood Gdns CO5 201 D7
Oakwood Inf Sch CO15 188 D2
Oasis Ct CM1 205 F5
Oast House Spinney
CM7 127 F6
Oasthouse Ct CB10 22 D1
Oatfield Cl CO3 134 D6
Oatlands CO7 137 F6
Oban St IP1 17 B7
Oberon Cl CO4 136 F7
Obrey Way CM23 145 E3
Observation Ct IP1 17 B5
Observer Way CO5 158 C4
Ockelford Ave CM1 204 F5
Ockendon Way CO14 171 A8
Octavia Dr CM8 194 E7
Oddcroft CO6 77 F1
Odin Lodge CM9 220 F8
Office La CM9 197 A4
Old Barn Rd CO8 80 A6
Old Bell Cl CM24 119 D6
Old Burylodge La CM24 120 A4
Old Cattle Market 5 IP4 17 C5
Old Church La
Bulmer CO10 32 F3
Bulmer Tye CO10 32 F2
West Bergholt CO6 108 D5
Old Clements La CB9 8 F7
Old Coach Rd CO1 136 B7
Old Coastguard Cotts
CM0 214 E4
Old Convent The CO5 158 B1
Old Court Rd CM2 205 D3
Old Ct Chelmsford CM2 205 D3
Long Melford CO10 15 D8
Old Ferry Rd CO7 164 B8
Old Forge CO7 137 C2
Old Forge Rd
Boreham CM3 206 E8
Layer-de-l-H CO2 161 F5
Old Foundry Rd IP4 17 D6
Old Hall Cl CB9 27 C7
Old Hall La Capel St M IP9 35 F3
Tollesbury CM9 199 C5
Walton-on-t-N CO14 144 E3
Old Heath Prim Sch
CO2 136 D3
Old Heath Rd CO1,CO2 136 C4
Old House La CO4 83 B2
Old House Rd CO6 109 A8
Old Ipswich Rd CO7 110 E7
Old London Rd
Capel St M IP9 59 F7
Woodham Walter CM9 208 E1
Old Maltings The 2
CM23 146 A7
Old Market Ct 3 CO10 33 E7
Old Market Pl 2 CO10 33 E7
Old Mead La CM22 94 D4
Old Mead Rd CM22 94 C5
Old Mill Chase CM7 73 C4
Old Mill La CO5 158 D7
Old Mill Rd Langham CO4 83 D5
Saffron Walden CB11 43 E8
Old Parsonage Ct CM8 176 F2
Old Parsonage Way
CO13 170 F5
Old Pier St CO14 171 C8
Old Rd Clacton-on-S CO15 188 E4
Coggeshall CO6,CO5 131 E1
Frinton-on-S CO13 170 F4
Pattiswick CM7 129 F5
Wickham St P CO9 53 D5
Old River La CM23 145 F7
Old Rope Wlk CB9 8 E7
Old Rose Gdns CO4 109 D4
Old School Cl CO16 187 A4
Old School Ct CM3 194 B3
Old School Field CM1 205 E4
Old School Ho IP9 91 B8
Old School Ho The CO5 164 A8
Old School La CO7 138 A6
Old School Yd CB11 43 D8
Old St The IP9 35 B1
Old Vicarage Rd CO12 91 C3
Old Vicarage The CM7 72 D6
Old Way CO13 170 F4

Oldbury Ave CM2 216 F8
Olde Forge CO7 165 E1
Oldfield Rd IP8 16 B1
Oldhouse Villas CM22 148 C8
Olive Gr CO2 135 D2
Oliver Pl CM8 177 B2
Oliver Way CM1 204 F7
Olivers Cl
Clacton-on-S CO15 188 E4
Long Melford CO10 15 D7
Olivers Ct CO15 188 E4
Olivers Dr CM8 195 A7
Olivers La CO2 135 A1
Olivers Rd CO15 188 E4
Oliveswood Rd CM6 150 D7
Olley Wlk CO5 179 E6
Ongar Cl CO16 188 B4
Ongar Rd
Great Dunmow CM6 150 D6
Writtle CM1 204 B1
Ongar Road Trad Est
CM6 150 E7
Onslow Cotts CO5 160 A7
Onslow Cres CO2 136 B1
Opal Ave IP1 16 D8
Ophir Rd CO7 185 F5
Orange St CM6 70 A2
Orange Tree Cl CM2 216 C6
Orchard Ave CO9 76 D2
Orchard Cl
Chelmsford CM2 216 C6
Clacton-on-S CO16 188 C5
Copford CO6 133 D2
Elmstead CO7 138 A6
Great Oakley CO12 116 C3
Hatfield Peverel CM3 194 A4
Haverhill CB9 8 F7
Maldon CM9 209 F2
Newport CB11 66 F8
Ramsey CO12 90 A2
Ridgewell CO9 29 B6
Saffron Walden CB11 43 D7
Thaxted CM6 70 A3
Tollesbury CM9 199 E1
Writtle CM1 204 B1
Orchard Cotts
Boreham CM3 193 A2
Langham CO4 83 F3
Little Horkesley CO6 81 E5
Orchard Ct CO3 135 C7
Orchard Dr
Braintree CM7 128 A1
Great Holland CO13 170 A4
Orchard Field Ct CO5 201 E6
Orchard Gate IP2 16 C5
Orchard Gdns CO4 136 B8
Orchard Gr IP5 18 F7
Orchard Lodge CO5 179 D4
Orchard Mews CO5 179 C4
Orchard Pightle CB1 5 C6
Orchard Rd
Alresford CO7 165 B8
Bishop's Stortford CM23 119 B1
3 Colchester CO1 135 E8
Kelvedon CO5 158 C3
Maldon CM9 209 F2
Orchard St
Chelmsford CM2 205 B1
9 Ipswich 1P4 17 D6
Orchard The CM6 152 C5
Orchard Way CO10 2 B3
Orchards CM8 176 F1
Orchid Ave CM8 176 E4
Orchid Cl IP2 16 E4
Orford Cres CM1 205 D5
Orford Rd
Felixstowe IP11 221 C1
Haverhill CB9 8 F6
Orford St IP1 17 B7
Oriel Cl CO10 34 B6
Oriole Way CM23 145 C6
Orion Way CM7 128 B4
Orkney Cl CB9 9 D7
Orlando Ct CO14 171 C8
Ormonde Cl CO6 108 E4
Orpen Cl CO6 108 D4
Orpen's Hill CO2 161 A5
Orplands Cotts CM0 214 F1
Orsino Wlk CO4 136 F7
Orvis La CO7 59 E1
Orwell Bsns Ctr IP3 17 E2
Orwell Cl CO4 110 E1
Orwell Country Pk*
IP10 38 B6
Orwell Ct 1 IP4 17 D5
Orwell Gdns IP2 17 A3
Orwell High Sch IP11 221 C5
Orwell Ho IP11 221 A4
Orwell Hts IP2 16 E2
Orwell Pl
Chelmondiston IP9 63 F7
2 Ipswich 1P4 17 D5
Orwell Rd
Clacton-on-S CO15 188 F2
Felixstowe IP11 221 D3
Harwich CO12 91 D4
Ipswich IP3 18 A4
Orwell Ret Pk IP2 16 F5
Orwell Rise IP9 63 F8
Orwell Way CO16 188 C6
Orwell Wlk CM8 176 E3
Osbert Rd CM8 194 E8
Osborne Cl CO15 189 A7
Osborne Rd Ipswich IP3 18 A4
West Mersea CO5 201 E6
Osborne St CO2 135 F6
Osbourne Gdns 5
CM23 145 E5
Osbournes Ct CO7 185 F6
Osea Rd CM9 211 B3
Osea Way CM1 205 F5
Osier Pl 3 CB9 8 F8
Osmond Cl CM77 155 B5
Osprey Rd CB9 9 C7
Osprey Way CM2 216 A5
Ospreys CO15 188 F6
Ostler Cl CM23 145 C4
Othello Cl CO4 136 F8
Otho Dr CO4 110 A6
Otley Ct IP11 221 B5
Otten Rd CO10 13 B1
Ottershaw Way CO16 188 B6
Oulton Cl CO12 90 F3
Oulton Rd IP3 17 E2
Our Lady Immaculate RC
Prim Sch CM2 205 A1
Ouse Chase CM8 176 D2
Outpart Eastward CO12 91 E6
Over Hall La CB10 6 D2
Overchurch Cl CB9 8 F7
Overhall Hill CO6 78 C2
Overstone Ct CO2 135 C3
Ovington Pl 16 CB9 9 B8
Owen Ward Cl CO2 135 A3
Owl's Hill CM3 175 B3
Owls Retreat 1 CO4 136 F8
Ox Yd CO9 102 E7
Oxborrow Cl CO13 170 A6
Oxcroft CM23 145 F3
Oxenford Cl CO12 90 F1
Oxford Cl CO10 34 A6
Oxford Cres CO15 188 F4
Oxford Ct
Chelmsford CM2 205 E4
Colchester CO3 135 D6
Earls Colne CO6 105 B6
Oxford Ho CB9 9 B6
Oxford La CO9 51 D2
Oxford Mdw CO9 51 D2
Oxford Pl CO6 105 B6
Oxford Rd
Clacton-on-S CO15 188 F4
Colchester CO3 135 D6
Frinton-on-S CO13 171 A5
Halstead CO9 76 D1
Ipswich IP4 17 E5
Manningtree CO11 86 D4
Oxley Hill Abberton CO5 163 A3
Tolleshunt D'arcy CM9 198 B8
Tolleshunt Knights CM9 180 A1
Oxley Ho CM77 155 B5
Oxley Parker Dr CO4 110 A6
Oxlip Rd CM8 176 E4
Oxney Villas CM6 152 D6
Oxton Cl CO5 164 A8
Oyster Bsns Ctr CM9 199 F2
Oyster Cl CO5 201 C7
Oyster Cotts CM0 213 C1
Oyster Pk CO1 136 D6
Oyster Pl CM2 205 F4
Oyster Tank Rd CO7 185 E5
Ozier Ct CB11 43 E7
Oziers CM22 94 C2

P

Packard Ave IP3 18 B2
Packards La CO6 80 F1
Packe Cl CO5 158 D4
Paddock Cl CO12 91 C4
Paddock Dr CM1 205 E8
Paddock The CM23 145 D3
Paddock Way CO7 137 C3
Paddocks The
Abberton CO5 163 A2
Ashen CO10 11 D1
Bures CO8 79 E8
Great Bentley CO7 166 F5
Great Totham CM9 196 A4
West Mersea CO5 201 D6
Witham CM8 177 A2
Paeony Chase CO5 201 C8
Page Cl CM8 194 D8
Page Rd CO15 188 E3
Pages Cl CM23 145 D5
Pages La CM9 198 F1
Paget Ct CM22 94 C1
Paget Rd Ipswich IP1 17 B7
Rowhedge CO5 163 F8
Wivenhoe CO7 164 C8
Paignton Ave CM1 205 D5
Pakenham Pl 18 CB9 9 B8
Palace Gdns CM23 145 E5
Palfrey Hts CO11 86 D8
Pallister Rd CO15 188 F2
Palm Cl Chelmsford CM2 216 C6
Witham CM8 177 A5
Palmers Croft CM2 206 A2
Palmers La
8 Bishop's Stortford
CM23 145 F7
Chrishall SG8 19 C3
Palmerston Lodge CM2 216 F7
Palmerston Rd
Ipswich IP4 17 E6
Thorpe-le-S CO16 142 A2
Palmerswent Cl CO10 15 D8
Pamela Gdns CM23 145 F3
Pampas Cl CO4 110 A4
Pan Wlk CM1 204 D5
Panfield La CM7 127 E5
Pannells Ash CO10 11 D1
Pannels Cl CO10 2 B4
Pantile Cl CM8 195 A7
Pantlings La CO5 158 A5
Panton Cres 7 CO4 136 E7
Panton Mews CM7 155 A8
Papermill Cotts CO9 76 E2
Papillon Rd CO3 135 E7
Parade Dr CO12 90 C1
Parade Rd IP4 17 F7
Parade The
Colchester CO2 136 A1
Kirby Cross CO13 170 B6
Walton-on-t-N CO14 171 C8
Paradise Rd CM1 215 B8
Pardoe Pl IP4 18 E5
Park Ave
Bishop's Stortford CM23 145 F3
Chelmsford CM1 204 F4
Felixstowe IP11 221 F5
Park Bvd CO15 189 E6
Park Chase CO16 187 C5
Park Cl CO10 34 A8
Park Cotts Gosfield CO9 102 E8
Manningtree CO11 86 D3
St Osyth CO16 187 A5
Park Ct Felixstowe IP11 221 D2
Sible Hedingham CO9 51 D1
Park Dr Braintree CM7 155 A8
Brightlingsea CO7 185 E7
Halstead CO9 76 E1
Maldon CM9 210 B1
Park Drive Par CO7 185 E7
Park Farm Ind Est SG8 39 C2
Park Farm La SG8 39 C2
Park Gate Cotts CM7 101 C6
Park Gate Rd CM8 157 B3
Park La
Bishop's Stortford CM23 145 F4
Bulmer Tye CO10 32 F2
Castle Camps CB1 7 F3
Earls Colne CO6 105 B6
Glemsford CO10 2 D4
Gosfield CO9 102 F7
Langham CO4 83 E3
Langley CB11 40 A3
Saffron Walden CB10 22 D1
Tolleshunt Knights CM9 180 B3
Toppesfield CO9 50 B7
Park Lane Cl CO6 105 B6
Park N IP4 17 D8
Park Rd Ardleigh CO7 111 F3
Chelmsford CM1 205 B2
Clacton-on-S CO15 188 D2
Colchester CO3 135 C6
East Bergholt CO7 60 B2
Elsenham CM22 94 D1
Ford End CM3 172 A3
Great Chesterford CB10 3 E5
Harwich CO12 91 D4
Haverhill CB9 8 D8
Ipswich IP1 17 C8
Little Bentley CO7 139 D8
Little Easton CM6 122 F3
Little Horkesley CO6 82 B8
Maldon CM9 209 F2
Rivenhall CM8 157 A2
Stansted Mountfitchet
CM24 119 E6
Stoke-by-N CO6 56 E4
Sudbury CO10 34 A8
Wivenhoe CO7 164 C8
Wivenhoe, Wivenhoe Park
CO4 137 A4
Park Side CM6 124 D6
Park Sq E
Clacton-on-S CO15 203 G8
Jaywick CO15 188 A1
Park Sq W
Clacton-on-S CO15 203 F8
Jaywick CO15 187 F1
Park St Stoke-by-N CO6 56 D5
Thaxted CM6 70 A2
Park Terr Harwich CO12 91 D4
Long Melford CO10 15 C7
Park The CO11 86 D3
Park Vale Cl CO9 51 E4
Park View CO10 12 C7
Park View Cres CM2 216 F5
Park View Rd IP1 17 B8
Park Way CO15 188 D1
Park Wood La CM9 197 A3
Parkdale CM3 218 C7
Parker Ct CM0 214 F4
Parker Rd CM2 205 C1
Parker Way CO9 103 E8
Parker's Way CO6 56 A1
Parkeston Rd
Felixstowe IP11 221 B4
Harwich, Parkeston CO12 90 F4
Harwich, Upper Dovercourt
CO12 91 A4
Parkfield St CO5 163 F7
Parkfields CO9 51 D1
Parkgate Cnr CO16 169 A2
Parkhall Rd
Beazley End CM7 101 E7
Gosfield CO9 102 B7
Parkins The IP9 35 C2
Parkinson Dr CM1 204 F1
Parkland Ct CO1 136 C5
Parklands Braintree CM7 155 A8
Coggeshall CO6 131 A2
Parklands Cl CO10 2 C5
Parklands Ct CO16 188 B3
Parklands Dr CM1 205 D3
Parklands Way CM2 216 C2
Parkside Haverhill CB9 8 F6
Saffron Walden CB10 22 C1
Parkside Ave IP4 17 D7
Parkside Quarter CO1 135 E8
Parkway
Chelmsford CM1 CM2 205 B2
Shudy Camps CB1 7 C6
Parkway Mid Sch CB9 8 D8
Parkwood IP1 17 C7
Parkwood Ave CO7 137 B1
Parkwood Dr CO10 15 E2
Parliament Rd IP4 18 B5
Parmenter Dr CO10 34 C5
Parnell Cl CO2 136 A2
Parnham Pl IP4 18 F5
Parr Cl CM7 128 D4
Parr Dr CO3 134 E4
Parr Rd CB9 8 D6
Parrington Way CO11 86 A3
Parry Dr CO16 188 C5
Parson's Field CO7 85 A6
Parson's Heath CO4 110 E2
Parson's Hill CO3 135 A6
Parsonage Cl
Broomfield CM1 191 A1
Felixstowe IP11 221 B4
Parsonage Downs CM6 123 C3
Parsonage Farm La CB10 47 B4
Parsonage Farm Trad Est
CM24 119 F3
Parsonage Gdns 6 CB9 8 E7
Parsonage Gr CO8 79 E8
Parsonage La
Barnston CM6 151 D3
Bishop's Stortford CM23 146 C8
Clavering CB11 65 B3
Elder Street CB10 44 F3
Howe Street CM3 172 F2
Little Baddow CM3 207 D2
Stansted Mountfitchet
CM24 119 F4
Tendring CO16 140 E8
Parsonage Rd CM22 148 C8
Parsonage St CO9 76 F1
Parsons Ct 4 CO9 76 F2
Parsons Heath CE Prim Sch
CO4 110 E2
Parsons Hill CO7 138 F8
Parsons La CO1 136 C6
Parsons Yd 10 CO11 86 D4
Partridge Ave CM1 204 F6
Partridge Cl CO12 116 D4
Partridge Dr CO6 107 D5
Partridge Rd IP2 16 E3
Partridge Way CO3 134 C4
Paschal Way CM2 216 F8
Pashlers Alley CO10 12 B7
Paske Ave CB9 8 F7
Pastures The IP4 18 F5
Patching Hall La CM1 205 A6
Paternoster Row 6
CO14 171 C8
Path The CO7 166 E8
Pathfields Rd CO15 188 D4
Pathway The CO13 170 E6
Patmore Cl CM23 145 C8
Patmore Fields CM22 93 E6
Patmore Rd CO4 110 D1
Patricia Gdns CM23 145 E5
Patten Cl CO6 132 F3
Pattern Bush Cl CO11 86 D8
Patteson Rd IP3 17 E4
Patticroft CO10 2 B6
Pattison Cl CM8 195 A8
Pattock's La CO6 106 C2
Pattrick's La CO12 91 C4
Paul Spendlove Ct CO4 110 E1
Paul's Rd IP2 16 F5
Pauline Cl CO15 189 B6
Pauline St 8 IP2 17 C4
Pauls Cres CO7 137 F6
Pauls Way CO15 188 A1
Pavilion Ct CB9 9 B7
Pavitt Mdw CM2 216 C2
Pawle Cl CM2 217 A7
Paxman Ave CO2 135 A3
Paxton Rd CO15 189 B8
Paycocke Way CO6 131 A3
Paycocke's Ho* CO6 130 F1
Payne's La CO11 113 C3
Peace Rd CO3 134 D7
Peacehaven CO13 171 A5
Peacock Cl
Braintree CM7 127 F1
5 Ipswich IP8 16 C2
Peacocks Cl CO10 1 C2
Peacocks Rd CO10 1 C2
Peake Ave CO13 170 A6
Peakes Cl CO5 179 B4
Peal Rd CB11 43 F7
Pear Tree Cl CO9 77 A3
Pearce Manor CM2 215 F8
Pearce Rd IP3 18 A5
Pearl Dr CM7 128 C3
Pearl Rd IP1 16 D8
Pearmain Way CO3 134 C4
Pearmain Wlk CB9 8 C8
Pearmains CM3 173 F7
Pearse Way IP3 18 E1
Pearson Rd IP3 18 C5
Pearsons CO10 2 B4
Peartree Bsns Ctr CO3 134 E4
Peartree Cl
Braintree CM7 128 A1
Goldhanger CM9 211 E6
Peartree Hill CO8 80 A5
Peartree La CM3 218 F3
Peartree Rd CO3 134 E4
Peartree Way CO16 168 C2
Peaslands Rd CB11 43 E8
Pebmarsh Cl CO2 163 A8
Pebmarsh Rd
Alphamstone CO8 54 E2
Colne Engaine CO6 77 F2
Pecockes Cl CO10 34 C5
Peddars Ct CO10 15 C7
Pedder's Cl CO3 134 F3
Pedlars Cl CM3 219 A6
Pedlars Path CM3 219 A6
Pedler''s Cnr CO11 86 D2
Peek's Cnr CO6 105 D5
Peel Cres CM7 127 E3
Peel Rd CM2 205 F4
Peel St 5 IP1 17 C6
Peers Sq CM2 206 A4
Peerswood Rd CO2 135 D2
Peewit Ct IP11 221 B3
Peewit Cvn Pk IP11 221 C2
Peewit Hill IP11 221 B3
Peewit Rd IP2 16 C3
Peg Millar's La CM3 175 E5
Pegasus Way
Braintree CM7 127 E5
Colchester CO4 110 C1
Peggotty Cl CM1 204 F6
Peggy's Wlk CB11 21 E3
Peldon Cres CO5 182 E5
Peldon Rd Abberton CO5 182 E7
Great Wigborough CO5 182 A3
Pelham Cl CO12 90 F2
Pelham Rd CB11 65 C4
Pelham's La 18 CO1 135 F7
Pelican Cl IP2 16 E3
Pelly Ave CM8 195 A8
Pembroke Ave CM9 209 F1
Pembroke Cl
Colchester CO2 136 C3
Ipswich IP2 17 B3
Pembroke Gdns CO15 189 E6
Pembroke Pl
Chelmsford CM1 205 B7
Sudbury CO10 15 D2
Pendleton Rd IP2 16 D1
Penfold Rd
Clacton-on-S CO15 188 E2
Felixstowe IP11 221 E4
Penhaligon Ct 9 CM8 177 A2
Penlan Hall La CO6 107 B5
Penn Cl IP9 35 B2
Penn Mews CM7 155 A8
Pennine Rd CM1 204 D5
Pennington La CM22,
CM24 93 D2
Penningtons CM23 145 C5
Pennsylvania La CO5 179 C5
Penny Cnr IP1 16 C8
Penny La IP3 18 F1
Penny Mdw IP9 35 A1
Penny Royal Rd CM3 218 D6
Pennypot Cnr CO9 103 B6
Pennypot Cotts CO9 103 B5
Pennyroyal Cres CM8 176 E4
Pennyroyal Gdns IP2 16 E4
Pennystone Rd CB11 43 E8
Penrice Cl CO4 136 E6
Penrice Ct CO14 144 D1
Penrose Mead CM1 215 B8
Penshurst Pl CM77 154 B6
Penshurst Rd IP3 18 D4
Penticton Rd CM7 127 D2
Pentland Ave CM1 205 A6
Pentlow Dr CO10 1 E1
Pentlow Hawke Cl CB9 9 B7
Pentlow Hill CO10 14 A8
Pentlow Ridge CO10 13 F6
Penzance Cl
Chelmsford CM1 205 E5
Clacton-on-S CO15 203 I8
Penzance Rd IP5 18 F6
Pepper's Rd CO4 82 E1
Peppercorn Cl CO4 109 F2
Peppercorn Way IP2 17 D3
Pepples La Debden CB10 69 A8
Elder Street CB10 45 A1
Pepys St CO12 91 D5
Percival Rd
Kirby-le-S CO13 143 D1
Walton-on-t-N CO14 144 D2
Peregrine Cl
Bishop's Stortford CM23 145 D6
Clacton-on-S CO15 188 F7
Peregrine Ct CO4 136 F8
Peregrine Dr CM2 216 A4
Perkins Way IP3 17 F1
Perriclose CM1 205 D7
Perrin Pl CM2 205 A1
Perry Hill CM1 205 D3
Perry La CO4 84 A4
Perry Rd Tiptree CO5 179 C5
Witham CM8 177 B1
Perry Way CM8 177 B1
Perryfield CO10 34 B4
Perryfields Jun & Inf Sch
CM1 205 D6
Persardi Ct CO2 163 A7
Pershore End CO3 134 E5
Perth Cl CO2 136 A1
Pertwee Cl CO7 185 E8
Pertwee Dr CM2 216 F6
Pertwee Way CO5 163 B2
Pertwees Ct CO1 136 C6
Pesthouse La CO12 116 D3
Peter Bruff Ave CO16 188 C5
Peter's Gr IP9 35 A1
Peterfield's La CO9 102 F5
Peterhouse Cl IP2 16 F2

Peters Ho CO5 158 C2
Petersfield CM1 205 B7
Peto Ave CO4 109 F2
Petrebrook CM2 206 A3
Petrel Way CM2 216 C6
Petrolea Cl CO4 109 F1
Petronius Way CO4 110 B5
Pettit La CM77 156 A4
Petts La CB10 4 E1
Petunia Cres CM1 205 F6
Petworth Cl
Great Notley CM77 154 B7
Wivenhoe CO7 164 C8
Pevensey Dr CO15 203 I8
Peverel Ave CM3 194 C1
Peverells Rd CB10 44 D1
Pewterers Ave CM23 145 C4
Pharos La CO5 201 C6
Pheasant Rd IP2 16 E3
Pheasant Rise IP8 35 F8
Philip Ave IP11 221 B3
Philip Cl CO14 171 A8
Philip Morant Sch CO3 135 B5
Philip Rd Ipswich IP2 17 C4
Witham CM8 194 E8
Philips Cl CM77 126 F2
Philips Rd CM77 126 F2
Phillip Rd CO7 164 B8
Phillips Chase CM7 128 A5
Phillips Field Rd CO10 34 A5
Philpot End La CM6 150 B4
Phoenix Ct CO2 136 D5
Phoenix Gr CM2 216 A8
Phoenix Rd IP4 18 A7
Piccotts La CM7 126 B8
Pickers Way CO15 189 E7
Pickford Wlk CO4 136 F7
Pickpocket La CM77 154 D6
Pickwick Ave CM1 204 D6
Pickwick Rd IP2 16 E5
Pier App CO14 171 C8
Pier Ave CO15 188 E2
Pier Gap CO15 188 F2
Pier Rd IP11 221 A1
Pierce Glade CO5 179 C5
Pierrefitte Way CM7 127 E3
Pig La CM22 146 A3
Pigeon's La IP8 16 A3
Pightle The Capel St M IP9 35 B2
Finchingfield CM7 72 D6
Haverhill CB9 9 A8
Pightle Way CO14 171 A7
Pigotts Way CM23 145 E5
Pilborough Way CO3 134 E3
Pilcox Hall La CO16 140 D8
Pilgrim Cl CM7 127 F5
Pilgrims Cl CB10 3 D2
Pimblett Row CM22 94 F5
Pimpernel Rd IP2 16 F3
Pin Mill Cl IP2 16 C1
Pincey Rd CM24 120 F3
Pincey Rdbt CM24 121 A3
Pinchpools Rd CM23 93 A3
Pine Ave
Great Dunmow CM6 123 B1
Ipswich IP1 17 B8
Pine Cl Brantham CO11 86 D8
Great Bentley CO7 166 F8
Pine Gr
Bishop's Stortford CM23 146 B6
West Mersea CO5 201 B7
Witham CM8 177 A5
Pine Ho IP11 221 C4
Pine Tree Ct CO4 136 E8
Pine View Rd IP1 17 A8
Pinecroft Gdns CO4 110 B3
Pinecroft Rise CO10 33 D5
Pinelands CM23 118 F1
Pines Hill CM24 119 D5
Pines Rd CM1 204 D5
Pines The CM3 194 A5
Pinetree Cl IP5 18 F7
Pinewood Cl
Clacton-on-S CO15 188 E7
Kirby Cross CO13 170 D6
Pinhoe Dr CB9 8 C8
Pink La CM3 175 D7
Pinkeneys SG8 19 D5
Pinkham Dr CM8 194 F8
Pinkney Cl CB10 44 E2
Pinkuah La CO10 13 F6
Pinmill Rd IP9 63 F8
Pinner's Cross SG8 39 A7
Pintail Cl IP2 16 E3
Pintail Cres CM77 154 C6
Pioneer Pl 8 CO1 136 A6
Pipchin Rd CM1 204 F6
Piper Rd CO3 135 B7
Piper's Tye CM2 216 D3
Piper's Vale Com Prim Sch IP3 17 F1
Piperell Way CB9 9 A5
Piperell Way Units CB9 9 A5
Pipers Cl CB9 9 C6
Pipers Vale Cl IP3 17 E1
Pippins The
Glemsford CO10 2 C4
Halstead CO9 76 D2
Pirie Rd CO6 108 E3
Pit La CO5 179 C6
Pitcairn Rd IP1 16 E8
Pitmire La CO8 55 B6
Pitt Ave CM8 195 A8
Pitt Chase CM2 216 E5
Pitt Gn CM8 195 A8
Pitts End CO7 59 D3
Place Farm Ct CO2 136 D2
Place Farm Prim Sch CB9 8 F8
Plains Farm Cl CO7 110 D6
Plains Field CM7 128 D1
Plains Rd
Great Totham CM9 196 F6
Little Totham CM9 197 A6
Plaistow Green Rd CO9 103 C5
Plaiters Way CM7 128 D3
Plane Tree Cl CM2 216 B6
Plane View Cl CO16 188 B2
Plantation Cl CB11 43 E6
Plantation Rd CM3 192 F1
Planton Way CO7 185 E6
Platters Cl IP3 38 B7
Platters Rd IP11 221 C2
Plaw Hatch Cl CM23 146 B8
Plaw Hatch Cnr CM23 146 D8
Players Ct CM6 152 C6
Playfield Rd IP9 35 B1
Playford Ct 2 CO10 33 E8
Playford Rd IP4 18 E8
Playle Chase CM9 196 B4
Pleasant Rd CM23 145 E8
Pleasant Row 13 IP4 17 D5
Pleasant Valley CB11 43 D7
Pleasants Mews CO5 201 C6
Pleshey Rd CM3 172 B5
Plough Cnr CO16 168 C4
Plough Dr CO3 135 A5
Plough La CO10 33 D7
Plough Rd CO7 166 E6
Plough St IP3 17 E4
Ploughmans Cl CM23 145 C5
Ploughmans Headland CO3 134 E5
Ploughmans La CM77 154 C8
Plover Cl CO13 170 E6
Plover Rd IP2 16 E2
Plover Wlk CM2 216 B5
Plowright Ho 5 CO1 135 E8
Plum St CO10 2 A6
Plume Ave
Colchester CO3 135 A4
Maldon CM9 209 F1
Plume Sch (Lower) CM9 210 A2
Plume Sch (Upper) CM9 209 F2
Plummers Rd CO6 107 E7
Plumptre La CM3 218 D5
Plums La CM7 99 E4
Plumtree Ave CM2 216 F6
Plymouth Rd
Chelmsford CM1 205 E5
Clacton-on-S CO15 203 J8
Felixstowe IP11 221 D6
Pochard Way CM77 154 C5
Pocklington Cl CM2 206 A3
Pod's Brook Rd CM7 127 D2
Pods La CM77 126 D2
Point Clear Bay Holiday Cvn Pk CO16 185 F3
Point Clear Rd CO16 186 D3
Pointwell La CO6 158 A8
Pole Barn La CO13 170 F5
Pole La CM8 155 C3
Polecat Rd CM77 155 F5
Pollard Ct IP2 16 D2
Pollard Wlk CO16 188 C5
Pollard's Gn CM2 205 F2
Pollards Villas CM7 99 D2
Polley Cl CO13 170 E7
Polstead St CO6 56 D5
Polstead Way CO16 188 B4
Pond Chase CO3 135 B4
Pond Cl IP11 221 B5
Pond Cotts IP9 61 E2
Pond Cross Cotts CB11 67 A8
Pond Cross Farm CB11 67 A8
Pond Cross Way CB11 67 A8
Pond House La CO15 189 D8
Ponders Rd CO6 107 C4
Pondfield Rd CO4 110 D1
Pondholton Dr CM8 194 F7
Ponds Rd CM2 216 B1
Pondtail Ct CO13 170 C6
Poney Chase CM8 195 F5
Poney's CM8 195 F5
Pontisbright Cotts CO6 106 E6
Poole Cl IP3 18 D3
Poole St Cavendish CO10 1 C1
Great Yeldham CO9 51 B6
Poore St CB11 65 F8
Poors' Piece Nature Trail* CM3 207 F1
Pope's La CO3 135 E7
Pope's Rd CO6 106 D4
Poperinghe Rd CO2 135 F4
Popes Ct CB9 9 E5
Poplar Ave CO16 188 A2
Poplar Cl
Chelmsford CM2 216 C6
Clacton-on-S CO15 188 B2
Great Yeldham CO9 30 A1
Halstead CO9 103 F8
Witham CM8 177 A5
Poplar Cotts CO5 160 C1
Poplar Ct CO10 34 B7
Poplar Grove Chase CM9 210 B8
Poplar Hall Cl CO1 109 E1
Poplar La IP8 16 B3
Poplar Rd CO10 34 B7
Poplar Way CO13 170 D6
Poplars Cl CO7 165 B7
Poplars The
Brantham CO11 60 D2
Great Dunmow CM6 123 C2
Great Hallingbury CM22 146 F4
Poppy Cl IP2 16 F4
Poppy Gdns CO2 136 C3
Poppy Gn CM1 206 A6
Pork La CO13 169 E5
Port La
Bishop's Stortford CM22 146 B2
Colchester CO1 136 B5
Port Of Felixstowe Rd IP11 221 A4
Portal Prec CO1 135 F7
Porter Rd IP3 18 F1
Porter Way CO16 188 B3
Porter's Cl CO3 107 F2
Porter's Cotts CO3 107 F1
Porter's La CO3 107 F2
Porters Brook Wlk CO4 110 C2
Porters Pk CM3 193 A2
Portland Ave CO12 91 C3
Portland Cl CM7 128 B3
Portland Cres CO12 91 C3
Portland Ho CO13 170 F5
Portland Pl 17 CM23 145 F7
Portland Rd
Bishop's Stortford CM23 145 F7
15 Colchester CO2 135 F6
Portlight Cl CO11 87 A4
Portman Rd IP1 17 B6
Portman Road (Ipswich Town FC) IP1 17 B5
Portman's Wlk IP1 17 A5
Portmans Walk Ind Ctr IP1 17 A5
Portobello Rd CO14 171 C8
Portreath Pl CM1 205 A7
Portsmouth Rd CO15 203 J8
Portway CM2 206 B4
Portway Ct CO9 76 F3
Posford Ct CO4 109 F4
Post Mill Cl IP4 17 F6
Post Office Cnr IP9 61 F2
Post Office La
Glemsford CO10 2 B5
Little Totham CM9 197 B4
Post Office Rd
Chelmsford CM1 205 B8
Woodham Mortimer CM9 219 E6
Postman's La CM3 207 E3
Pot Kiln Chase CO9 31 F2
Pot Kiln Prim Sch CO10 34 B6
Pot Kiln Rd CO10 34 B6
Pot Kilns The CO10 34 C6
Potash Cotts IP9 60 E8
Potash La IP9 60 E8
Potter St
Bishop's Stortford CM23 145 F7
Sible Hedingham CO9 75 E7
Potters Cl CM3 219 A6
Pottery La
Castle Hedingham CO9 51 F3
Chelmsford CM1 205 A5
Poulk Hall La CM3 174 A5
Poulteney Rd CM24 119 E8
Pound Farm Dr CO12 91 A3
Pound Fields CM1 215 B8
Pound Gate CM6 124 D6
Pound Hill Villas CM6 151 E8
Pound La IP9 59 F8
Pound Wlk CB10 22 E2
Poundfield Cl CO7 165 B7
Poundfield Ho CO7 138 A5
Powell Cl CO5 179 E5
Powers Hall End CM8 176 E3
Powers Hall Inf & Jun Sch CM8 176 D3
Powling Rd IP3 18 A2
Pownall Cres CO2 135 F4
Poynter Pl CO13 170 E7
Prail Ct CO6 130 F2
Pratt's La IP9 38 A2
Pratts Farm La CM3 191 D4
Prentice Hall La CM9 213 B8
President Rd CO3 134 E5
Preston Rd CO15 189 D5
Prestwick Dr CM23 119 B1
Pretoria Rd CO9 76 F2
Prettygate Jun & Inf Sch CO3 135 B4
Prettygate Rd CO3 135 A4
Pretyman Rd
Felixstowe IP11 221 C1
Ipswich IP3 18 B3
Prime's Cl CB10 22 D1
Primrose Cl CM23 145 C6
Primrose Hill
Chelmsford CM1 204 F3
Haverhill CB9 8 F7
Holbrook IP9 62 D4
Ipswich IP2 16 F4
Primrose La Ramsey CO12 89 A1
Tiptree CO5 179 C6
Primrose Pl CM8 176 E4
Primrose Rd CO15 189 E6
Primrose Wlk
Colchester CO4 136 E7
Maldon CM9 210 B1
Primula Cl CO16 188 C4
Primula Way CM1 206 A6
Prince Albert Rd CO5 201 D6
Prince Charles Cl
Clacton-on-S CO15 188 C1
Sudbury CO10 33 F8
Prince Charles Rd CO2 136 A2
Prince Of Wales Dr IP2 17 B2
Prince Of Wales Rd CM8,CM9 196 A3
Prince of Wales Rdbt CO6 133 B4
Prince Philip Ave CO15 188 C1
Prince Philip Rd CO2 136 A1
Prince St CO10 33 E8
Prince's Espl CO14 144 D1
Princel La CO7 84 F7
Princel Mews CO7 84 F7
Princes Ct CM23 145 C7
Princes Gate CM23 145 C7
Princes Gdns IP11 221 D4
Princes Rd
Chelmsford CM2 216 B7
Clacton-on-S CO15 189 D5
Felixstowe IP11 221 E4
Harwich CO12 91 B3
Maldon CM9 210 A2
Princes St IP1 17 B5
Princes Well CB10 45 F7
Princess Anne Cl CO15 188 C1
Princess Dr CO4 110 C5
Princess St CO12 90 F5
Princess Way CB9 8 E8
Princethorpe Rd IP3 18 C4
Princeton Mews CO4 110 B4
Prior Cl CO9 103 D8
Prior Way CO4 109 E2
Prior's Hall Barn* CB11 67 D4
Prior's Wood Rd CM22 148 C7
Priors 9 CM23 146 A7
Priors Way CO6 131 A3
Priory Ave CB9 8 F7
Priory Cl Chelmsford CM1 204 E2
Hatfield Peverel CM3 194 B1
Ickleton CB10 3 A3
Seawick CO16 203 A6
Priory Ct
Bishop's Stortford CM23 145 F7
Colchester CO1 135 E7
Hatfield Peverel CM3 194 A4
Ipswich IP10 38 C6
Priory Dr CM24 119 E5
Priory Farm Rd CM3 194 B2
Priory Heath Prim Sch IP3 18 C1
Priory La Bicknacre CM3 218 F1
Great Notley CM77 154 C8
Priory Mews CM3 194 C2
Priory Pk CO16 187 A4
Priory Prim Sch CM3 218 F2
Priory Rd Bicknacre CM3 218 E1
Chappel CO6 106 B3
Clacton-on-S CO15 188 E3
Sudbury CO10 15 D1
Tiptree CO5 178 F3
Priory St Colchester CO1 136 A7
Earls Colne CO6 105 B7
Priory The CM1 215 B8
Priory Wlk
28 Colchester CO1 135 F7
Sudbury CO10 33 E7
Priory Wood CO9 51 E4
Priory Wood Rdbt CM22 147 A8
Prittlewell Cl IP2 16 F1
Proctor Cl CO5 163 B2
Proctor Way CO6 132 E3
Proctors Way CM23 146 A4
Progress Ct CM7 127 E3
Progress Way CO16 168 C1
Promenade
Clacton-on-S CO15 203 D6
Harwich CO12 91 E4
Harwich,Dovercourt CO12 91 C2
Promenade Way CO7 185 E5
Prospect Cl CM3 194 A3
Prospect Hill CO10 34 D3
Prospect Pl CB11 22 F1
Prospect Rd IP1 17 A7
Prospect St 1 IP1 17 A6
Prospero Cl CO4 136 F8
Provence Cl CO3 134 C7
Providence La IP1 17 A7
Providence Pl CO1 136 B6
Providence St 6 IP1 17 C6
Prunus Ct CO2 163 A7
Prykes Dr CM1 205 A2
Pryor Cl CM8 177 A1
Pryors Cl CM23 146 A6
Pryors Rd CM2 216 C2
Pudding La CO2 161 B3
Puffinsdale CO15 188 F5
Pulford Pl CM6 124 D7
Pulpitfield Cl CO14 171 A8
Pump Hill
Great Baddow CM2 216 F6
Harkstead SG9 64 A2
St Osyth CO16 187 D4
Pump Hill Cvn Pk CO16 187 C4
Pump La Chelmsford CM1 205 E6
Danbury CM3 218 D5
Purleigh CM3 220 D1
Punchard Way IP11 221 A8
Punders Field CM7 128 D1
Purbeck Ct
4 Colchester CO1 136 D7
Great Baddow CM2 216 E6
Purcell Cl Colchester CO4 136 E6
Writtle CM1 204 A1
Purdis Ave IP3 18 F2
Purdis Farm La IP3 18 F2
Purleigh Prim Sch CM3 220 D1
Purley Way CO16 188 B6
Purplett Ho IP2 17 D4
Purplett St IP2 17 D4
Purvis Way CO4 110 B5
Putticks La CO7 59 E3
Pye Cnr CO9 51 E4
Pyecat's Cnr CO7 137 C7
Pyefleet Cl
Brightlingsea CO7 185 E7
Fingringhoe CO5 164 C6
Pyefleet Ho CO5 201 D7
Pyefleet View CO5 163 B3
Pyesand CO13 170 C8
Pygot Pl CM7 127 E4
Pyms Rd CM2 216 B3
Pynchbek CM23 145 E3
Pynchon Mews CM1 205 D3
Pyne Gate CM2 216 B1

Q

QM Ind Pk IP3 18 C1
Quadling St IP1 17 C5
Quadrangle Ctr The IP3 18 C1
Quaker's La CB9 9 A7
Quale Rd CM2 206 B4
Quantock Cl IP5 18 F7
Quay Ctyd 2 CO11 86 D4
Quay La Beaumont CO16 142 B5
Kirby-le-S CO13 143 D1
Sudbury CO10 33 E6
Quay St
1 Manningtree CO11 86 D4
Wivenhoe CO7 164 B8
Quay The Harwich CO12 91 D6
Wivenhoe CO7 164 B7
Quay Theatre CO10 33 E6
Quayside Ind Est CM9 210 A4
Queech La IP9 87 C8
Queech The IP9 35 B2
Queen Anne Dr CO5 201 D6
Queen Anne Gdns CO5 201 D6
Queen Anne Rd CO5 201 D7
Queen Edith Dr CB9 27 B6
Queen Elizabeth Ave CO15 188 C1
Queen Elizabeth Way CO2 136 A2
Queen Mary Ave CO2 135 F4
Queen St
Brightlingsea CO7 185 F6
Castle Hedingham CO9 51 E3
Chelmsford CM2 205 A1
Coggeshall CO6 131 A2
Colchester CO1 135 F7
Felixstowe IP11 221 C6
Great Oakley CO12 116 C4
Haverhill CB9 9 A8
Ipswich IP1 17 C5
Maldon CM9 210 A2
Sible Hedingham CO9 75 F6
Queen Victoria Dr IP9 91 B8
Queen's Ave CM9 210 A1
Queen's Cotts CO6 105 B7
Queen's Ct
Clacton-on-S CO15 189 D4
6 Haverhill CB9 8 E8
Queen's Gdns CM7 127 B7
Queen's Head Rd CO4 82 E3
Queen's Ho CO13 170 F4
Queen's Rd
Chelmsford CM2 205 D2
Clacton-on-S CO15 188 D1
Colchester CO3 135 C6
Earls Colne CO6 105 B7
Felixstowe IP11 221 E4
Frinton-on-S CO13 170 F4
Harwich CO12 91 A2
West Bergholt CO6 108 D3
Wivenhoe CO7 164 C8
Queen's Sq IP3 18 B2
Queen's Way IP3 18 B2
Queenborough Gr CM77 154 C8
Queenborough La
Great Notley CM77 154 D8
Rayne CM77 154 B8
Queenbury Cl CO5 201 E6
Queens Cl
Stansted Mountfitchet CM24 119 E8
Sudbury CO10 33 E8
Queens Cnr CO5 201 D7
Queens Cres CM23 145 E5
Queens Ct CO5 201 D7
Queens Mews CO5 201 B6
Queens Rd
Braintree CM7 127 F5
Sudbury CO10 33 E8
Queens Sq 5 CB9 9 A8
Queens Terr CO10 34 A7
Queensberry Rd IP3 18 A1
Queensbury Ave CO6 133 D5
Queenscliffe Rd IP2 17 A3
Queensgate Dr IP4 17 F8
Queensland Cres CM1 204 E5
Queensland Dr CO2 136 A1
Queensway
Clacton-on-S CO15 189 D5
Great Cornard CO10 34 B5
Haverhill CB9 8 E8
Lawford CO11 86 C4
Tiptree CO5 179 C6
Quendon Pl 17 CB9 9 B8
Quendon Way CO13 171 A6
Quentin Cl IP1 16 E8
Quickset Rd CB11 20 C5
Quicksie Hill CB11 41 E2
Quilp Dr CM1 204 F7
Quilter Dr IP8 16 C1
Quilter Rd IP11 221 F4

Quilters Cl C015 ....189 F6
Quince Cl C011 ....60 D1
Quinion Cl CM1 ....204 D7
Quinton's La IP11 ....221 F7
Quintons Cnr C07 ....59 D4
Quintons Rd C07 ....59 D4

R

R A Butler Jun & Inf Schs
CB11 ....22 E1
Rachael Cl **1** CM2 ....205 B1
Rachael Gdns CM8 ....156 E4
Rachel Ct **6** CM4 ....17 D6
Radcliffe Dr IP2 ....16 D2
Radiator Rd C010 ....34 A5
Radwinter Prim Sch
CB10 ....45 F7
Radwinter Rd
Ashdon CB10 ....24 B7
Saffron Walden CB10 ....23 B1
Sewards End CB10 ....23 F1
Raeburn Cl C013 ....170 F7
Raeburn Rd IP3 ....18 A1
Raeburn Rd S IP3 ....17 F1
Raglan Mead C013 ....194 A5
Raglan Rd C013 ....171 A5
Ragley Cl CM77 ....154 B6
Raile Wlk C010 ....15 D8
Railey Rd CB11 ....43 E8
Railway App IP11 ....221 E5
Railway Cotts CB11 ....42 F5
Railway Sq CM1 ....205 A3
Railway St Braintree CM7 ....128 A3
Chelmsford CM1 ....205 A3
Manningtree C011 ....86 D4
Railway Terr
Clacton-on-S C015 ....188 F3
11 Manningtree C011 ....86 D4
Rainbow Cl C012 ....91 D4
Rainbow Mead CM3 ....194 A5
Rainbow Mews CM9 ....209 F5
Rainbow Rd C05 ....201 D6
Rainbow Way C06 ....77 F1
Raine Ave CB9 ....8 D8
Rainham Way C013 ....171 B6
Rainsborowe Rd C02 ....135 C4
Rainsford Ave CM1 ....204 F3
Rainsford La CM1 ....204 F2
Rainsford Rd
Chelmsford CM1 ....204 F3
Stansted Mountfitchet
CM24 ....119 E8
Rambler Cl C03 ....134 D7
Rampart Cotts C06 ....109 B7
Ramparts Cl C06 ....109 B7
Ramplings Ave C015 ....188 E5
Ramsden Cl C015 ....189 A5
Ramsey Cl
Heybridge CM9 ....210 D4
Ipswich IP2 ....17 A1
Ramsey Mews C02 ....136 A4
Ramsey Rd Halstead C09 ....103 D8
Harwich C012 ....90 C2
Ramsey Sch (Priory Hall) The
C09 ....77 A2
Ramsey Sch The C09 ....77 A2
Ramsgate Dr IP3 ....18 B3
Ramshaw Dr CM2 ....205 F3
Rana Cl CM7 ....127 F4
Rana Dr CM7 ....127 F4
Randall Cl CM6 ....123 D1
Randall Ave CM7 ....73 C6
Randolph Cl Ipswich IP4 ....18 B5
Maldon CM9 ....220 F8
Rands Way IP3 ....18 B2
Randulph Terr CM1 ....205 D3
Randwell Cl IP4 ....18 B5
Ranelagh Cr IP11 ....221 E4
Ranelagh Prim Sch IP2 ....16 F5
Ranelagh Rd
Felixstowe IP11 ....221 E4
Ipswich IP2 ....17 A5
Ranger Wlk C02 ....136 B3
Rangoon Cl C02 ....135 B1
Ransom Rd C05 ....179 C5
Ransome Cl IP8 ....16 A6
Ransome Cres IP3 ....18 B2
Ransome Rd IP3 ....18 B3
Ransomes Europark IP3 ....38 E8
Ransomes Way
Chelmsford CM1 ....205 B4
Ipswich IP3 ....38 D8
Ranulph Way CM3 ....194 A3
Raphael Dr CM1 ....205 F7
Rapier St IP2 ....17 C3
Rat Hill IP9 ....63 F2
Ratcliffe Ct
Frinton-on-S C013 ....170 F5
Great Cornard C010 ....158 B2
Ratcliffe Rd C03 ....134 E6
Ravel Ave CM8 ....194 F7
Raven Way C04 ....109 E4
Ravens Ave C09 ....76 F1
Ravens Cres CM6 ....152 C6
Ravensbourne Dr CM1 ....204 E2
Ravenscroft Prim Sch
C016 ....188 B4
Ravensdale C015 ....188 F6
Ravenswood Ave **1** C01 ....136 A6
Ravenswood Ave IP3 ....38 C8
Ravenswood Com Prim Sch
IP3 ....38 C8
Ravenswood Way IP3 ....38 B8
Rawden Cl C012 ....91 B4
Rawlings Cres C04 ....110 B5
Rawstorn Rd C03 ....135 E7

Ray Ave C012 ....91 A3
Ray Ho C05 ....201 D7
Ray La Harwich C012 ....90 E5
Ramsey C012 ....90 A3
Ray Mead CM3 ....190 F7
Ray The CM1 ....205 E5
Raycliff Ave C015 ....188 E7
Raydon Way C010 ....34 C6
Rayfield Cl CM6 ....151 A4
Rayhaven C012 ....90 D2
Rayleigh Cl
Braintree CM7 ....128 C4
Colchester C04 ....110 B1
Rayleigh Mans C02 ....135 C5
Rayleighs The C02 ....135 C5
Rayments Bglws CB10 ....45 E3
Raymouth Ho C02 ....136 C3
Rayne Prim Sch CM77 ....126 F2
Rayne Rd CM7 ....127 D3
Rayner Rd C02 ....135 B4
Rayner Way C09 ....76 E1
Raynham Cl CM23 ....146 C7
Raynham Rd CM23 ....146 B8
Raynhams CB10 ....22 D1
Reaburn Ct CM1 ....205 E6
Reade Rd IP9 ....62 D5
Reader's Cnr CM2 ....216 E5
Readers Ct CM2 ....216 E6
Reading Rd IP4 ....18 B7
Reaper Rd C03 ....135 A5
Rebecca Gdns CM8 ....156 E4
Rebecca Meade CM6 ....122 F8
Rebow Rd Harwich C012 ....91 A2
Wivenhoe C07 ....164 B8
Rebow St C01 ....136 B6
Reckitts Cl C015 ....189 B4
Recreation Cl IP11 ....221 D6
Recreation Ground
CM24 ....119 E6
Recreation La IP11 ....221 D6
Recreation Rd
Clacton-on-S C015 ....188 F3
Colchester C05 ....136 C5
Haverhill CB9 ....8 F7
Sible Hedingham C09 ....75 D8
Recreation Way
Brightlingsea C07 ....185 F7
Ipswich IP3 ....18 B2
Recreation Wlk C010 ....34 B5
Rectory Cl
Bishop's Stortford CM23 ....145 D3
Colchester C04 ....109 E2
Glemsford C010 ....2 B5
Little Waltham CM3 ....191 C6
Littlebury CB11 ....21 F4
Rectory Dr CM23 ....118 D6
Rectory Field IP9 ....63 E7
Rectory Hill
East Bergholt C07 ....59 C1
Stoke-by-N C06 ....56 D7
Wivenhoe C07 ....137 C1
Rectory La Abberton C05 ....163 A3
Ashdon CB10 ....6 A1
Chelmsford CM1 ....205 B4
Farnham CM23 ....118 D6
Great Leighs CM3 ....173 D7
Ramsey C012 ....90 A1
Rivenhall CM8 ....177 A6
Wickham St P C09 ....53 C6
Woodham Mortimer CM9 ....219 F6
Rectory Mdw CM7 ....129 C2
Rectory Mdws C07 ....51 D1
Rectory Rd Aldham C06 ....132 F7
Copford C06 ....133 C1
Frating C07 ....138 F1
Great Henny C010 ....33 E4
Great Holland C013 ....170 A3
Harkstead IP9 ....63 C2
Ipswich IP2 ....17 C4
Langham C04 ....83 F7
Little Bentley C07 ....139 E8
Little Oakley C012 ....117 A7
Rowhedge C05 ....163 E8
Sible Hedingham C09 ....51 D1
Stisted CM7 ....129 B7
Tiptree C05 ....179 C5
Tolleshunt Knights CM9 ....180 C1
Weeley Heath C016 ....167 F3
Wivenhoe C07 ....137 C2
Woodham Walter CM9 ....208 D3
Wrabness C011 ....89 A3
Writtle CM1 ....215 B8
Red Barn La C012 ....116 B2
Red Barn Rd C07 ....185 F8
Red House La
Great Cornard C010 ....34 A4
Sudbury C010 ....33 E7
Red La IP9 ....60 A8
Red Lion Ct **5** CM23 ....146 A7
Red Lion Yd **1** C01 ....135 F7
Red Sleeve **5** IP9 ....35 A1
Redan St IP1 ....17 B7
Redbridge Rd C015 ....188 F8
Redcliffe Rd **2** CM2 ....205 A1
Reddells Cl **3** C010 ....33 E8
Reddings Cl CB11 ....43 E7
Rede Way C010 ....34 C6
Redgate La IP9 ....37 D5
Redgates La CB10 ....23 E3
Redgates Pl CM2 ....205 D4
Redhouse La C04 ....82 D2
Redmayne Pl CM2 ....215 F8
Redmill C03 ....135 A3
Redrose Wlk C016 ....188 C4
Redruth Cl CM1 ....205 E5
Redshank Cl CB9 ....9 C7
Redshank Dr CM9 ....210 C5

Redvers Cl CM23 ....119 A2
Redwing Cl IP2 ....16 D3
Redwood Cl
Colchester C04 ....110 E1
Witham CM8 ....177 A5
Redwood Ct **2** C04 ....136 E8
Reed Cl C010 ....15 D8
Reed Hall Ave C02 ....135 D3
Reedland Way IP11 ....221 B5
Reeds La CB9 ....9 A8
Refinery Rd C012 ....90 E5
Regal Cl CM2 ....216 D8
Regency Cl
Bishop's Stortford CM23 ....145 E7
Chelmsford CM2 ....205 D3
Regency Ct
Heybridge CM9 ....210 A5
Ipswich IP3 ....17 F5
Regency Gn C03 ....135 A4
Regency Lodge C015 ....188 E5
Regent Cl C07 ....185 F8
Regent Ct C015 ....164 A8
Regent Rd C07 ....185 F7
Regent St Ipswich IP4 ....17 E6
9 Rowhedge C011 ....86 D4
Rowhedge C05 ....164 A8
Regents Cl C04 ....110 C5
Regimental Way C012 ....90 C1
Regina Cl IP4 ....18 B5
Regina Rd CM1 ....205 C3
Reigate Ave C016 ....188 D6
Reigate Cl IP3 ....18 B3
Rembrandt Gr CM1 ....205 E6
Rembrandt Way C03 ....135 B5
Rembrow Rd IP9 ....35 A1
Remembrance Ave CM4 ....194 A3
Remercie Rd C011 ....87 A4
Remus Cl C04 ....109 F5
Rendlesham Ct **8** IP1 ....17 A7
Rendlesham Rd
Felixstowe IP11 ....221 B5
Ipswich IP1 ....17 A6
Renfrew Rd CM2 ....206 A4
Rennie Pl CM2 ....206 B3
Renoir Pl CM1 ....205 F7
Retreat The
West Bergholt C06 ....108 D3
Witham CM8 ....177 A1
Reverdy Ho C02 ....136 C3
Reydon Cl CB9 ....8 C8
Reydon Ho IP3 ....18 A2
Reymead Cl C05 ....201 C6
Reynard Copse CM23 ....118 F1
Reynard Ct CM2 ....216 F6
Reynard Hts C04 ....136 C8
Reynards Cl C013 ....170 D6
Reynards Copse C04 ....110 A3
Reynolds Ave
Colchester C03 ....135 B5
Ipswich IP3 ....38 A8
Reynolds Ct IP11 ....221 B5
Reynolds Rd IP3 ....18 A1
Rhodes Ave CM23 ....145 F5
Ribband Rd C04 ....60 B1
Riby Rd IP11 ....221 D3
Rice Bridge Ind Est
C016 ....169 A7
Rich Cl CM3 ....173 F7
Richard Ave
Brightlingsea C07 ....185 F6
Wivenhoe C07 ....137 C3
Richard Burn Way C010 ....15 E2
Richard de Clare Com Prim
Sch C09 ....76 F1
Richard Whittington Prim
Sch The CM23 ....145 E4
Richards Wlk C015 ....188 E6
Richardson Pl CM1 ....204 F4
Richardson Rd C07 ....59 D3
Richardson Wlk
Colchester C03 ....134 F5
Witham CM8 ....177 B2
Richardsons La IP9 ....63 D8
Riche Cl CM6 ....152 B5
Richmond Cl CM23 ....145 C7
Richmond Cres C03 ....134 E6
Richmond Dr C015 ....188 A1
Richmond Ho **20** IP4 ....17 D5
Richmond Rd
Chelmsford CM2 ....206 A4
Ipswich IP1 ....16 F8
West Mersea C05 ....201 D6
Rickling CE Prim Sch
CB11 ....93 E8
Rickling Green Rd
Quendon CB11 ....66 E1
Rickling Green CB11 ....93 E8
Rickling Rd CB11 ....66 B6
Rickstones Rd CM8 ....177 A6
Rickstones Sch The
CM8 ....176 F6
Riddiford Dr CM1 ....204 F4
Riddles Dr C04 ....109 F2
Ridge The Braintree CM7 ....128 B6
Little Baddow CM3 ....207 E2
Walton-on-t-N C014 ....171 B8
Ridgeway C09 ....110 A4
Ridgeway The
Braintree CM1 ....128 A1
Harwich C012 ....91 B3
Ridgewell Ave CM1 ....204 F4
Ridgewell CE Prim Sch
C09 ....29 B6
Ridgewell Rd
Birdbrook C09 ....10 E2
Great Yeldham C09 ....29 E3
Ridgewell Way C02 ....135 F1
Ridings Ave CM77 ....154 B7

Ridings The
Bishop's Stortford CM23 ....145 D4
Great Baddow CM2 ....216 D7
Ridlands Cl CM77 ....155 E6
Ridley Gdns CM22 ....94 C2
Ridley Rd CM1 ....205 B8
Riffhams Chase CM3 ....207 D2
Riffhams Dr CM2 ....217 A7
Riffhams La
Danbury CM3 ....218 C8
Little Baddow CM3 ....207 C1
Rifle Hill CM7 ....127 F1
Rifle Hill Works CM7 ....127 F1
Rigby Ave C011 ....87 A3
Rigby Rd C011 ....87 A4
Rignal's La CM2 ....216 D3
Riley Ave C015 ....203 C6
Rimini Cl C02 ....135 C3
Ringham Rd IP4 ....18 A6
Ripley Cl C016 ....188 B6
Ripple Way C04 ....110 B1
Risby Cl
Clacton-on-S C016 ....188 A4
Ipswich IP4 ....18 B6
Rise The C06 ....134 A8
Ritabrook Rd IP2 ....16 E1
Rivenhall CE Prim Sch
CM8 ....177 B8
River Blackwater Chalet Site
CM9 ....210 C3
River Cl C09 ....76 F1
River Cotts CM3 ....206 F8
River View C05 ....175 A3
River Mead CM7 ....128 A4
River View Braintree CM7 ....127 F1
Holbrook IP9 ....62 D5
Manningtree C011 ....86 C4
Witham CM8 ....195 A8
River View Rd IP9 ....63 B2
Riverbank Cl C010 ....12 C7
Riverdale Ct IP11 ....221 D3
Rivermead Gate CM1 ....205 B4
Rivermead Ind Est CM1 ....205 B4
Rivers Ho C014 ....144 D2
Rivers St IP4 ....17 F7
Riverside
Bishop's Stortford CM23 ....145 F7
Bradwell CM7 ....129 C3
Chelmsford CM1 ....205 C3
Great Dunmow CM6 ....123 E1
Riverside Bsns Pk
Bradwell CM7 ....129 C3
Stansted Mountfitchet
CM24 ....119 E6
Riverside Cotts C011 ....86 C7
Riverside C09 ....76 E2
Riverside Ind Pk IP2 ....17 D3
Riverside Pk CM1 ....205 C3
Riverside Rd IP1 ....16 F7
Riverside Way C05 ....158 C2
Riverside Wlk
10 Bishop's Stortford
CM23 ....145 F7
Colchester C01 ....135 E8
Riverton Dr CM0 ....213 B1
Rivish La C010 ....15 C7
Roach Vale C04 ....110 E1
Roach Vale Prim Sch
C04 ....110 E1
Robeck Rd IP3 ....17 F1
Robert Cl CM2 ....205 F4
Robert Suckling Ct CM9 ....27 B6
Robert Wallace Cl
CM23 ....118 F1
Robert Way C07 ....137 C3
Robert's Hill C08 ....79 F3
Roberts Ct CM2 ....216 E7
Roberts Rd C01,C02 ....136 A5
Robin Cl
Great Bentley C07 ....166 D8
Haverhill CB9 ....9 C7
Robin Cres C03 ....134 B4
Robin Dr IP2 ....16 D3
Robin Hood Rd CM2 ....94 C1
Robin Way
Chelmsford CM2 ....216 B5
Sudbury C010 ....33 C5
Robinia Cl **8** C04 ....136 E7
Robinsbridge Rd C06 ....130 F2
Robinsdale C015 ....188 F6
Robinson Rd C07 ....186 A7
Robjohns Rd CM1 ....205 B6
Robletts Way C06 ....80 E4
Rochdale Way C04 ....136 E6
Rochelle Cl CM7 ....70 A3
Rochester Cl CM7 ....128 D4
Rochester Way C010 ....22 F2
Rochester Way C010 ....15 D7
Rochford Cl CM24 ....119 E6
Rochford Rd
Bishop's Stortford CM23 ....119 C1
Chelmsford CM2 ....205 C1
St Osyth C016 ....187 B4
Rochford Way
Frinton-on-S C013 ....170 F7
Walton-on-t-N C014 ....171 A7
Rockall Cl CM7 ....9 D7
Rockhampton Wlk **10**
C02 ....136 A1
Rockingham Cl C04 ....110 D3
Rodbridge Hill C010 ....15 B5
Rodbridge Nature Reserve*
C010 ....15 A5
Roddam Cl C016 ....135 C6
Roding Ct CM7 ....128 D1

Rodney Gdns CM7 ....128 C4
Rodney Way CM1 ....215 E7
Rogation Cl C03 ....134 D6
Rogers Cl IP11 ....221 D6
Rokell Way C013 ....170 F6
Rolands Cl CM1 ....205 B7
Rollerworld* C01 ....136 B7
Rolley La C05 ....158 C2
Rolph CE Prim Sch
C016 ....141 F1
Rolph Cl C016 ....142 A2
Roman Cl CM9 ....209 F4
Roman Ct Braintree CM7 ....128 C1
Saffron Walden CB11 ....43 F7
Roman Ho **3** CM2 ....205 B1
Roman La CM24 ....120 B2
Roman Rd
Colchester C01 ....136 A7
Little Waltham CM3 ....191 B5
Romans Pl CM1 ....204 B1
Romans Way CM1 ....204 B1
Romanshurst CM9 ....210 A4
Romford Cl C04 ....136 B8
Romney Cl
Braintree CM7 ....127 E6
Brightlingsea C07 ....165 E1
Clacton-on-S C016 ....188 D5
Kirby Cross C013 ....170 E7
Romney Rd IP3 ....38 A8
Romulus Cl C04 ....109 F5
Ronald Rd C09 ....103 E8
Rook End La CB11 ....68 B5
Rookeries The C06 ....133 B4
Rookery Chase C07 ....84 E2
Rookery Cl
Great Chesterford CB10 ....3 D3
Hatfield Peverel CM3 ....194 A5
Rookery La
Great Totham CM9 ....196 E2
Tiptree C05 ....179 C7
Wendens Ambo CB11 ....42 E4
Rookery The
Lawford C011 ....86 C4
Stansted Mountfitchet
CM24 ....119 E8
Rookes CB10 ....22 D3
Rookes Cres CM1 ....215 F8
Rookwood Cl C015 ....188 D7
Rookwood Way CB9 ....9 A6
Roos Hill Debden Rd
CB11 ....43 E5
Roosevelt Way C02 ....136 B4
Roothings The CM9 ....210 B5
Roots La CM6 ....195 E5
Rope Wlk Ipswich IP4 ....17 E5
Maldon CM9 ....210 A1
Roper Ct IP4 ....18 C5
Roper's Chase CM1 ....215 A7
Ropers La C010 ....15 B5
Rosabelle Ave C07 ....137 B3
Rosalind Cl C04 ....136 F7
Rosalind Cl C04 ....136 F7
Rose & Crown Wlk CM7 ....22 D2
Rose Acre C07 ....58 F6
Rose Ave C03 ....134 C4
Rose Cotts
Great Sampford CM7 ....47 E5
Harkstead SG9 ....64 A5
Rose Cres C04 ....109 D2
Rose Ct C02 ....163 B8
Rose Gdns
Braintree CM7 ....128 A2
Seawick C016 ....203 B6
Rose Glen CM2 ....216 C7
Rose Green Cotts C06 ....106 E5
Rose Hill CM7 ....128 A2
Rose Hill Prim Sch IP3 ....18 A4
Rose Ho **20** C01 ....136 A6
Rose La
Great Chesterford CB10 ....3 E2
Ipswich IP1,IP4 ....17 C5
Salcott-cum-virley CM9 ....199 B8
Wivenhoe C07 ....164 B7
Rose Wlk C09 ....29 B6
Roseacres CM22 ....148 C7
Rosebank C012 ....91 A3
Rosebank Ct C015 ....189 A3
Rosebank Rd C05 ....201 B6
Rosebay Cl CM8 ....176 D3
Roseberry Cl CM23 ....146 C6
Rosebery Ave C01 ....136 A7
Rosebery Rd
Chelmsford CM2 ....216 B8
Felixstowe IP11 ....221 F4
Ipswich IP4 ....17 F5
Rosecroft Cl C015 ....188 E6
Rosedale Cotts C03 ....133 F5
Rosehill Cres IP3 ....17 F4
Rosehill Rd IP3 ....17 F4
Roselawn Fields CM1 ....205 B8
Rosemary Ave
Chelmsford CM7 ....127 F4
Felixstowe IP11 ....221 C4
Rosemary Cl
Great Dunmow CM6 ....123 C1
Tiptree C05 ....179 C5
Rosemary Cotts CM3 ....192 E1
Rosemary Cres
Clacton-on-S C015 ....188 F2

Rosemary Cres *continued*
Great Dunmow CM6 .....123 C1
Tiptree CO5 .....179 C5
Rosemary Ct 2 CO4 .....136 D8
Rosemary Gdns CO10 .....15 F2
Rosemary La
Castle Hedingham CO9 .....52 A5
Great Dunmow CM6 .....123 C1
Halstead CO9 .....76 E2
Stebbing CM6 .....124 C7
Thorrington CO7 .....166 B5
Rosemary Rd CO15 .....188 F2
Rosemary Rd W CO15 .....188 E2
Rosemary Way CO15 .....203 G7
Rosemount Ct IP11 .....221 F4
Rosery Mews CO13 .....170 A4
Rosetta Cl CO7 .....137 B2
Rosewood Cl CO4 .....110 A4
Roslings Cl CM1 .....204 D5
Ross Cl Haverhill CB9 .....9 D7
Saffron Walden CB11 .....43 E6
Rossendale CM1 .....204 E1
Rossendale Cl CO4 .....110 D3
Rossland Ct CO15 .....188 F3
Rosslyn Terr CO5 .....158 C3
Rothbury Rd CM1 .....204 D1
Rothesay Ave CM2 .....216 A8
Rothmans Ave CM2 .....216 E6
Roughtons CM2 .....216 C3
Round Cl CO3 .....135 B7
Round Coppice Rd
Great Hallingbury CM24 .....147 A8
Stansted Mountfitchet CM24 .....120 B1
Roundacre CO9 .....103 E8
Roundbush Cnr
Birch CO5 .....160 D3
Great Totham CM9 .....196 D6
Roundbush Rd CO5 .....160 D2
Roundridge Rd IP9 .....35 B2
Roundwood Rd IP4 .....18 A7
Rous Chase CM2 .....216 B1
Routh Ave IP3 .....18 F1
Rover Ave CO15 .....203 E6
Row The Hadstock CB1 .....5 B7
Stratford St M CO7 .....58 C2
Rowallan Cl CO3 .....135 A3
Rowan Chase CO5 .....179 C6
Rowan Cl
Clacton-on-S CO15 .....188 C3
Colchester CO3 .....134 D4
Great Bentley CO7 .....166 F8
Harwich CO12 .....91 B3
Ipswich IP3 .....18 D2
Rowan Dr CM9 .....210 C5
Rowan Pl CO1 .....109 E1
Rowan Way
Hatfield Peverel CM3 .....194 A3
Witham CM8 .....177 A5
Rowanhayes Cl IP2 .....17 B3
Rowhedge Ct CO7 .....136 F4
Rowhedge Ferry Rd
CO7 .....164 A8
Rowhedge Rd CO2,CO5 .....136 E1
Rowherns La CO7 .....139 F4
Rowland Ho IP11 .....221 B5
Rowland's Yd CO12 .....90 E2
Rowley Cl CO11 .....86 D8
Rowley Ct CB9 .....9 E5
Rowley Hill CB9 .....9 E5
Rowney Ave CB10 .....44 E2
Rowntree Way CB11 .....43 D7
Roxborough Cl CO6 .....132 E3
Roxburghe Rd CO16 .....167 F6
Roxwell Ave CM1 .....204 D3
Roxwell Rd
Chelmsford CM1 .....204 C4
Writtle CM1 .....204 A4
Roy Ave IP3 .....18 B5
Royal Ct Colchester CO4 .....110 E1
Maldon CM9 .....210 A1
Royal Hospital Sch IP9 .....62 D3
Royal Oak Gdns 6
CM23 .....145 F6
Royal Sq CO7 .....84 F7
Roydon Way CO13 .....170 F6
Royston Dr IP2 .....16 D2
Royston La CB11 .....20 C6
Royston Rd CB11 .....42 C5
Ruaton Dr CO16 .....188 C4
Rubens Gate CM1 .....205 F7
Rubens Rd IP3 .....18 A1
Rudd Ct CO4 .....110 F1
Rudkin Rd CO4 .....109 F5
Rudlands IP8 .....16 C1
Rudsdale Way CO3 .....134 F5
Rue De Jeunes 2 CM7 .....127 F2
Ruffels Field CM6 .....124 E4
Ruffles Rd CB9 .....9 C7
Rugby Rd CO10 .....34 B4
Rugosa Cl CO3 .....134 C7
Rumballs Ct CM23 .....145 C4
Rumsey Fields CM3 .....218 F7
Rumsey Row CM1 .....204 B1
Runnacles St CM8 .....156 C5
Runnacles Way IP11 .....221 B5
Running Mare La CM2 .....216 A3
Runsell Cl CM3 .....218 F7
Runsell La CM3 .....218 F8
Runsell View CM3 .....219 A7
Rurik Ct CM9 .....220 F8
Rush Cl IP4 .....18 F4
Rush Green Rd CO16 .....188 B2
Rush La CM22 .....94 C1
Rushbury Cl IP4 .....18 B8
Rushes Ct CM23 .....146 A5
Rushleigh Gn CM23 .....145 D4
Rushleydale CM1 .....205 E5
Rushmere Cl CO5 .....201 D6
Rushmere Pl 11 CB9 .....9 B8
Rushmere Rd IP4 .....18 B7
Rushmere St
Ipswich IP4,IP5 .....18 D8
Rushmere St A IP5 .....18 E8
Rushmoor Dr CM7 .....128 B1
Ruskin Cl CO13 .....170 E7
Ruskin Rd
Chelmsford CM2 .....205 E2
Ipswich IP4 .....17 F5
Ruskins The CM77 .....126 F1
Russell Ct
Colchester CO2 .....136 B4
Felixstowe IP11 .....221 C1
Russell Gdns CM2 .....216 A4
Russell Rd
Clacton-on-S CO15 .....189 A3
Felixstowe IP11 .....221 D2
Ipswich IP1 .....17 B5
Russell Way CM1 .....215 E7
Russell's Rd Gosfield CO9 .....76 A1
Halstead CO9 .....103 B8
Russet Cl CM7 .....128 A1
Russets CM2 .....216 D3
Russett Cl CB9 .....8 C8
Rustic Cl CM7 .....128 C3
Rutherfords CM1 .....191 B1
Rutland Ave CO2 .....135 B3
Rutland Ct 11 CB9 .....8 E7
Rutland Gdns CM7 .....128 A4
Rutland Pl CM7 .....72 B2
Rutland Rd CM1 .....205 A7
Rydal Way CM77 .....154 C6
Rydal Wlk IP3 .....18 C2
Ryde Ave CO15 .....189 A8
Rye Cl Brightlingsea CO7 .....165 E1
Colchester CO3 .....134 E5
Hatfield Peverel CM3 .....194 A3
Ipswich IP3 .....18 D4
Rye Ct 3 CB9 .....8 F7
Rye Field The CM3 .....207 D3
Rye Grass Way CM7 .....128 B1
Rye Hills CO9 .....103 F8
Rye La CO2 .....162 A4
Rye Mill La CO5 .....158 D4
Rye St CM23 .....118 F1
Ryes La CO10 .....33 A2
Rygate Rd CO1 .....135 F7
Rylands IP9 .....35 A2
Ryle The CM1 .....215 A8
Rylstone Way CB11 .....43 F8
Rysley CM3 .....207 D4

S

Sackett's Grove Caravan Pk
CO16 .....188 A2
Sacketts Grove Cvn Pk
CO15 .....187 F2
Sackville Cl CM1 .....204 E3
Sackville Way CO6 .....108 D4
Saddle Mews CO3 .....134 E6
Saddle Rise CM1 .....205 E8
Saddlers Cl
Bishop's Stortford CM23 .....145 C4
Great Notley CM77 .....154 B7
Sadds Yd CO15 .....188 F3
Sadler Cl CO2 .....136 B4
Sadlers Cl CO13 .....170 C6
Saffron Bsns Ctr CB10 .....22 F2
Saffron Cl CM7 .....73 C3
Saffron Croft CM9 .....209 E2
Saffron Ct CB11 .....22 D1
Saffron Gdns CM7 .....73 C3
Saffron Walden Cty High Sch
CB11 .....43 C8
Saffron Walden Mus*
CB10 .....22 D2
Saffron Walden YH*
CB10 .....22 D2
Saffron Waldon Hospl
CB11 .....23 A2
Saffron Way CO5 .....179 C4
Saffron Wlk CM7 .....73 B3
Sage Rd CO2 .....136 A2
Sage Wlk CO5 .....179 C4
Sagehayes IP2 .....17 B3
Sages CM22 .....94 F5
Sages End Rd CB9 .....26 B8
Sainty Cl CO7 .....164 C8
St Agnes Way IP5 .....18 F6
St Alban's RC High Sch
IP4 .....18 C7
St Alban's Rd
Clacton-on-S CO15 .....189 A3
Colchester CO3 .....135 D7
St Andrew's Ave CO4 .....137 A5
St Andrew's Ave (Colchester By-Pass Rd) CO4 .....136 D7
St Andrew's CE Jun Sch & Hatfield Peverel Inf Sch
CM3 .....194 B3
St Andrew's CE Prim Sch
Bulmer CO10 .....32 E4
Great Yeldham CO9 .....29 F2
Halstead CO9 .....77 A3
Marks Tey CO6 .....132 E3
Weeley CO16 .....167 F8
Wormingford CO6 .....80 E5
St Andrew's Cotts CM3 .....194 B3
St Andrew's Dr IP9 .....63 E7
St Andrew's Jun & Inf Schs
CO4 .....136 D7
St Andrew's Rd
Clacton-on-S CO15 .....188 E3
Felixstowe IP11 .....221 E5
Hatfield Peverel CM3 .....194 A4
Weeley CO16 .....140 F1
St Andrew's Rise CO10 .....32 E5
St Andrews Cl
Alresford CO7 .....165 B7
Ipswich IP4 .....18 D5
St Andrews Ct 3 CO4 .....136 C8
St Andrews Gdns CO4 .....136 C8
St Andrews Pl CO7 .....165 E1
St Andrews Rd
Boreham CM3 .....192 F1
Great Cornard CO10 .....34 A6
Halstead CO9 .....76 F1
St Anne's Prim Sch CO4 .....110 C1
St Anne's Rd CO4 .....136 C8
St Anne's Sch CM2 .....205 A1
St Annes Cl CO6 .....131 B2
St Annes Ct CM1 .....205 C3
St Anns Rd CO15 .....188 E4
St Anthony's Dr CM2 .....216 C7
St Aubins Ct CO15 .....189 B4
St Aubyns Rd IP4 .....18 A5
St Augustine Cl CM6 .....151 F6
St Augustine Mews
CO1 .....136 A7
St Augustine Rd IP3 .....18 D4
St Augustine's Gdns IP3 .....18 C3
St Austell Rd CO4 .....110 D2
St Austin's La CO12 .....91 E6
St Barbara's Rd CO2 .....135 D4
St Bartholomew Cl CO4 .....110 C3
St Bartholomews La
CO10 .....15 D2
St Benedict RC Coll
CO3 .....135 B6
St Bernard Rd CO4 .....110 D2
St Botolph's Church Wlk 7
CO2 .....135 F6
St Botolph's Cir 8 CO2 .....135 F6
St Botolph's Pl 1 CB9 .....8 F7
St Botolph's St 6 CO2 .....135 F6
St Botolph's Terr 11
CO13 .....171 C8
St Botolph's Way CB9 .....8 F8
St Brelades Ct CO15 .....189 B5
St Bride Ct CO4 .....110 D2
St Catherine's Ct IP2 .....16 E1
St Catherine's Rd
Chelmsford CM1 .....204 E2
Long Melford CO10 .....15 C7
St Catherines Cl CO2 .....135 D1
St Catherines Ct CM23 .....145 E7
St Cedd's Sch CM1 .....205 A4
St Christopher Ct CO4 .....110 D2
St Christopher Rd CO4 .....110 D2
St Christophers Way
CO15 .....203 G7
St Clair Cl CO15 .....188 F8
St Clair's Dr CO16 .....187 B5
St Clair's Rd CO16 .....187 B5
St Clare Dr CO3 .....135 A7
St Clare Rd CO3 .....135 A6
St Clare's RC Prim Sch
CO16 .....188 B4
St Clement Rd CO4 .....110 D2
St Clement's Church La 19
IP4 .....17 D5
St Clement's Ct CO16 .....188 B5
St Clement's Hospl IP3 .....18 B4
St Clements CM6 .....70 A2
St Cleres Hall La CO16 .....187 B3
St Cleres Way CM3 .....218 D7
St Columb Ct CO4 .....110 C2
St Cyrus Rd CO4 .....110 D3
St David's Rd IP3 .....18 B3
St Davids Cl CO4 .....136 C7
St Denis Cl CO12 .....91 A1
St Dominic Rd CO4 .....110 D2
St Edmund's Ct CO4 .....136 C8
St Edmund's Hill CO8,
CO10 .....55 D6
St Edmund's Pl IP1 .....17 C8
St Edmund's Rd
Felixstowe IP11 .....221 D2
Ipswich IP1 .....17 B8
St Edmunds Cl CO12 .....91 A1
St Edmunds Croft CM6 .....123 E1
St Edmunds Fields CM6 .....123 E2
St Edmunds Ho CO4 .....136 E8
St Edmunds La Bures CO8 .....55 F1
Great Dunmow CM6 .....123 E1
St Edmundsbury Ho IP4 .....17 F6
St Fabian's Dr CM1 .....204 E4
St Faith Rd CO4 .....110 D2
St Felix RC Prim Sch CB9 .....8 D7
St Fillan Rd CO4 .....110 D2
St Francis RC Prim Sch
Braintree CM7 .....127 E4
Maldon CM9 .....209 F3
St George's Ave CO12 .....91 C2
St George's CE Prim Sch
CO7 .....112 E1
St George's Cl CO7 .....112 E1
St George's Inf Sch CO2 .....136 A4
St George's Jun Sch
CO2 .....136 A5
St George's St IP1 .....17 C6
St Georges Cl CM9 .....210 E3
St Giles CE Prim Sch
CO9 .....52 D2
St Giles Cl
Great Maplestead CO9 .....52 D2
Maldon CM9 .....209 E2
St Giles Cres CM9 .....209 E2
St Gregory CE Prim Sch
CO10 .....33 D7
St Gregory's Ct CO10 .....33 D8
St Helen's Church La 5
IP4 .....17 E6
St Helen's Gn CO12 .....91 E5
St Helen's La 7 CO1 .....135 F7
St Helen's Prim Sch IP4 .....17 E6
St Helen's St IP4 .....17 D6
St Helena Mews CO3 .....135 D5
St Helena Rd CO3 .....135 D5
St Helena Sch CO3 .....135 D8
St Helens Ave CO15 .....189 A8
St Helier Ct CO15 .....189 B4
St Ives Cl CO16 .....188 B3
St Ives Rd CO5 .....182 E6
St James Ct
Brightlingsea CO7 .....185 E6
Clacton-on-S CO15 .....188 E1
Haverhill CB9 .....8 E8
5 Saffron Walden CB10 .....22 F2
St James Pk CM1 .....204 D4
St James Rd CM7 .....127 F5
St James Way CM23 .....145 C3
St James' CE Prim Sch
CO1 .....136 B7
St James's St CO9 .....51 F4
St Jean Wlk CO5 .....179 D6
St John Gdns CO15 .....188 E6
St John Payne RC Comp Sch
CM1 .....204 F6
St John The Baptist CE Prim Sch CO9 .....78 B8
St John's Ave
Chelmsford CM2 .....216 B8
12 Colchester CO2 .....135 F6
St John's CE Prim Sch
Colchester CO4 .....110 D4
Ipswich IP4 .....18 A7
St John's Cl CO4 .....110 D4
St John's Cres CM24 .....119 E7
St John's Ct Ipswich IP4 .....18 B6
Tollesbury CM9 .....199 C1
St John's Danbury CE Prim Sch CM3 .....218 E7
St John's Gn CM1 .....204 B1
St John's Green Prim Sch
CO2 .....135 F6
St John's Hospl CM2 .....215 F6
St John's La CM24 .....119 E7
St John's Pl 14 CO2 .....135 F6
St John's Rd
Chelmsford CM2 .....216 B8
Clacton-on-S CO16 .....188 C5
Colchester CO4 .....110 D3
Ipswich IP4 .....18 A6
Stansted Mountfitchet CM24 .....119 E7
Wivenhoe CO7 .....164 C7
Writtle CM1 .....204 B1
St John's St
Colchester CO2 .....135 F6
Tollesbury CM9 .....199 C1
St John's Terr CM7 .....72 B2
St Johns Ave CM7 .....127 F2
St Johns Cl
Great Chesterford CB10 .....3 D2
Saffron Walden CB11 .....43 D7
St Johns Ct IP11 .....221 D4
St Joseph Rd CO4 .....110 C3
St Joseph's Coll IP2 .....17 A3
St Joseph's Prim Sch
CO10 .....33 E8
St Joseph's RC Prim Sch
Bishop's Stortford CM23 .....145 E6
Harwich CO12 .....91 B2
St Jude Gdns CO4 .....110 E2
St Judes Cl CO4 .....110 D2
St Julian Gr CO1 .....136 A6
St Lawrence CE Prim Sch
CO2 .....163 F8
St Lawrence Ct 3 CM7 .....127 F3
St Lawrence Dr CM0 .....213 B1
St Lawrence Rd CO4 .....110 D2
St Lawrence St 11 IP1 .....17 C6
St Leonard's Hospl CO10 .....33 F7
St Leonard's Rd CO1 .....136 C6
St Leonards Cl CB11 .....43 A2
St Leonards Rd IP3 .....18 B3
St Leonards School Ho 8
CO1 .....136 C6
St Leonards Terr 7
CO1 .....136 C6
St Luke's CE Prim Sch
CO5 .....179 D5
St Luke's Chase CO5 .....179 D5
St Luke's Cl CO4 .....110 D2
St Margaret's CE Prim Sch
Ipswich IP4 .....17 D6
Toppesfield CO9 .....50 C7
St Margaret's Ct CO16 .....188 C4
St Margaret's Gn 2 IP4 .....17 D6
St Margaret's Plain 1
IP4 .....17 D6
St Margaret's Rd CM2 .....205 E3
St Margaret's Sch CO9 .....102 D8
St Margaret's St IP4 .....17 D6
St Mark Dr CO4 .....110 D2
St Marks RC Prim Sch
IP2 .....16 F3
St Marks Rd CO15 .....188 E4
St Martins Cl CO15 .....188 E4
St Mary Magdalen Ho
CO1 .....136 B6
St Mary's Art Ctr* CO1 .....135 E7
St Mary's Cath* CM1 .....205 B2
St Mary's CE Foundation Prim Sch CM24 .....119 E7
St Mary's CE Prim Sch
Ardleigh CO7 .....111 E7
Saffron Walden CB10 .....22 D2
St Mary's Cl
Great Baddow CM2 .....216 F6
Panfield CM7 .....127 B7
St Mary's Cres IP11 .....221 D6
St Mary's Ct CM9 .....210 B2
St Mary's Dr CM24 .....119 F5
St Mary's La CM9 .....210 B2
St Mary's Pl CM6 .....151 D7
St Mary's RC Prim Sch
IP4 .....17 F7
St Mary's RC Sch CM23 .....145 E7
St Mary's Rd
Braintree CM7 .....128 B3
Clacton-on-S CO15 .....188 E4
Frinton-on-S CO13 .....171 A5
Great Bentley CO7 .....166 F6
St Mary's Rd IP4 .....17 F7
St Mary's Rd
Kelvedon CO5 .....158 C2
Rivenhall CM8 .....177 B7
St Mary's Sch
Colchester CO3 .....135 C7
Copford CO3 .....133 F5
St Mary's Sq CO5 .....158 B1
St Mary's Villas CM7 .....72 B1
St Mary's Wlk CB9 .....27 B6
St Marys Mead CM1 .....191 A1
St Marys Mews
Frinton-on-S CO13 .....171 A5
Tollesbury CM9 .....199 D2
St Marys View CB10 .....22 E4
St Mathew's Ho 4 IP1 .....17 B6
St Matthew's CE Prim Sch
IP1 .....17 B6
St Matthew's St IP1 .....17 B6
St Michael's CE Prim Sch
Bishop's Stortford CM23 .....145 F7
Braintree CM7 .....127 D2
St Michael's Chase CO6 .....133 D2
St Michael's Ct 4 CM7 .....127 F2
St Michael's Hospl CM7 .....127 E3
St Michael's La 1 CM7 .....127 F2
St Michael's Prim Sch
Bishop's Stortford CM23 .....145 E7
Colchester CO2 .....135 C1
St Michael's Rd
Braintree CM7 .....127 F2
Chelmsford CM2 .....216 B8
Harwich CO12 .....91 B2
Thorpe-le-S CO16 .....141 F2
St Michaels Ct 6 CO11 .....86 D4
St Michaels Rd CO2 .....135 D1
St Michaels Wlk CM2 .....216 C2
St Mildreds Rd CM2 .....216 B8
St Monance Way CO4 .....110 D2
St Nazaire Rd CM1 .....204 E6
St Neots Cl CO4 .....110 D2
St Nicholas Cl CM8 .....176 F4
St Nicholas Ct CO12 .....91 D6
St Nicholas Field CM23 .....92 B8
St Nicholas Pas 16 CO1 .....135 F7
St Nicholas Rd CM8 .....176 F4
St Nicholas St
22 Colchester CO1 .....135 F7
Ipswich IP1 .....17 C5
St Nicholas Way CO6 .....131 A3
St Nicholas' Gdns CM7 .....127 F8
St Osyth CE Prim Sch
CO16 .....187 B4
St Osyth CE Sch CO15 .....188 E3
St Osyth Cl IP2 .....36 F8
St Osyth Priory* CO16 .....187 A4
St Osyth Rd
Alresford CO7 .....165 D7
Clacton-on-S CO15 .....188 D3
Little Clacton CO16 .....168 B1
St Osyth Rd E CO16 .....168 C2
St Osyth Rd W CO16 .....168 C1
St Paul's Rd
Clacton-on-S CO15 .....189 A3
Colchester CO1 .....135 E8
St Peter's Ave CM9 .....209 F2
St Peter's CE Prim Sch
Coggeshall CO6 .....131 B2
Sible Hedingham CO9 .....75 D8
St Peter's Cl CM7 .....127 F4
St Peter's Hospl CM9 .....209 F2
St Peter's Rd
Braintree CM7 .....127 F4
Chelmsford CM1 .....204 E2
Coggeshall CO6 .....131 B2
West Mersea CO5 .....201 B6
St Peter's St
Colchester CO1 .....135 F8
Ipswich IP1 .....17 C5
St Peter's Wlk CM7 .....127 F3
St Peter's-In-the-Fields
CM7 .....127 F4
St Peters Cl CM9 .....211 E6
St Peters Ct
Clacton-on-S CO15 .....189 B5
Clare CO10 .....12 B7
Colchester CO1 .....135 E8
10 Sudbury CO10 .....33 E7
St Peters View CO9 .....51 D1
St Philip's Priory Sch
CM2 .....216 A8
St Philomena's Sch
CO13 .....170 F5
St Pius X RC Prim Sch
CM1 .....204 F6
St Runwald St 9 CO1 .....135 F7
St Saviour Cl CO4 .....110 D2
St Stephens La 13 IP1 .....17 C6
St Swithins Cotts CM2 .....217 C3

St Teresa's RC Prim Sch CO3 134 E5
St Thomas Cl CO4 110 E2
St Thomas More RC Prim Sch CB11 43 E8
St Thomas More's RC Prim Sch CO1 136 A7
St Valery CM22 148 C7
St Vincent Chase CM7 128 B5
St Vincent Rd CO15 188 E1
St Vincents Rd CM2 216 B8
Salary Cl CO4 110 F1
Salcombe Rd CM7 128 C1
Salcott Creek Ct CM7 128 D1
Salcott St CM9 199 C8
Salehurst Rd IP3 18 E3
Salerno Cres CO2 135 C2
Salerno Way CM1 204 E6
Saling Hall Gdns* CM7 126 A8
Salisbury Ave CO3 135 E6
Salisbury Cl CM23 145 F5
Salisbury Ct
Clacton-on-S CO15 189 D5
2 Haverhill CB9 8 F7
Salisbury Rd
Clacton-on-S CO15 189 D5
Ipswich IP3 18 A4
Salisbury Terr 1 CO10 33 E8
Sallows Cl IP1 16 F7
Salmon Cl CO3 134 F4
Salmon Par CM1 205 B3
Salmon's Cnr CO6 132 A3
Salmon's La CO6 132 A4
Salmons Cl CM6 151 A5
Saltcote Maltings CM9 210 E4
Salter Pl CM2 205 F2
Salter's Mdw CM9 198 D4
Salters CM23 145 C4
Salters Hall Mews CO10 33 D7
Salthouse St 17 IP4 17 D5
Salvia Cl CO16 188 C4
Samford Cl IP9 62 D7
Samford Ct IP9 61 D7
Samford Pl IP8 16 B6
Samian Cl CM9 209 F5
Samphire Cl CM8 176 D3
Sampson Dr CO10 15 D8
Sampson's La CO5 182 F3
Samson's Cnr CO7 165 D1
Samson's Rd CO7 165 E1
Samsons Cl CO7 185 E8
Samuel Ct IP4 17 D6
Samuel Manor CM2 205 F3
Sanderling Gdns CM9 210 C5
Sanders Cl CM24 119 D7
Sanders Dr CO3 135 B7
Sanderson Mews CO5 163 F8
Sandford Cl CO7 164 C8
Sandford Mill Rd
Chelmsford CM2 205 F2
Chelmsford CM2 206 B2
Great Baddow CM2 217 C8
Sandford Rd CM2 205 E3
Sandhurst Ave IP3 17 F4
Sandle Rd CM23 146 A7
Sandling Cres IP4 18 E5
Sandlings The IP3 18 D1
Sandmartin Cres CO3 134 C4
Sandon Brook Pl CM2 217 E8
Sandon Cl CO6 109 C7
Sandon Hall Bridleway CM2 217 D4
Sandon Hill CM3 172 A6
Sandon Sch The CM2 217 B6
Sandown Cl CO15 189 A8
Sandpiper Cl
Colchester CO4 137 A8
Haverhill CB9 9 C8
Heybridge CM9 210 C5
Sandpiper Rd IP2 16 E2
Sandpiper Wlk CM2 216 C6
Sandpit Cl IP4 18 F5
Sandpit La 8 CM7 127 F3
Sandra Ct 5 CO2 135 E6
Sandringham Cl IP2 16 F2
Sandringham Ct CO10 34 A7
Sandringham Dr CO2 136 A4
Sandringham Gdns 6 CM23 145 E5
Sandringham Pl CM2 205 C2
Sandwich Cl CM7 127 E6
Sandwich Rd
Brightlingsea CO7 185 F8
Clacton-on-S CO15 203 J8
Sandy Hill CO6 80 D5
Sandy Hill La IP3 17 E1
Sandy La Bulmer CO10 32 F5
Sudbury CO10 33 B5
Sapling Pl IP4 18 E5
Sarah's Wlk CM22 148 B7
Saran Ct CO7 137 A2
Sarcel CM7 129 C6
Sargeant Cl CO2 136 B3
Sarre Way CO7 185 E8
Sassoon Way 3 CM9 210 A1
Saul's Ave CM8 195 A8
Sauls Bridge Cl CM8 195 A8
Saunders Ave CM7 127 E3
Saunders Cl CM22 94 C1
Savernake Rd CM1 204 E1
Savill Rd CO2 136 C2
Saville Cl CB11 65 C4
Saville St CO14 144 C1
Sawkins Ave CM2 216 D6
Sawkins Cl Abberton CO5 163 B2
Chelmsford CM2 216 D6
Sawkins Gdns CM2 216 D6
Sawney Brook CM1 204 A1
Sawpit La CM23 92 D7
Sawston Cl IP2 17 A2
Sawyer's Rd CM9 197 C5
Sawyers Cl 3 IP9 35 A1
Saxmundham Way CO16 188 A3
Saxon Bank CM7 128 B2
Saxon Cl Colchester CO3 134 F4
Halstead CO9 76 F2
Saxon Ct CM9 210 A3
Saxon Dr CM8 176 E3
Saxon La IP8 35 D7
Saxon Way
Chelmsford CM1 205 B7
Holland-on-S CO15 189 F6
Maldon CM9 210 B1
Point Clear B CO16 185 F3
Saffron Walden CB11 22 C1
Saxstead Dr CO16 188 A4
Saywell Brook CM2 206 A2
Scarfe Way CO4 136 E6
Scarfe's Cnr CO6 82 B4
Scarletts Cl CM8 195 A7
Scarletts Rd CO1 136 C4
Sceptre Cl CM9 199 D2
School Barn Cotts CO10 13 E7
School Chase CO9 103 E8
School Cl IP9 35 A1
School Ct CO12 91 D4
School Hill Birch CO2 161 A4
Washbrook IP8 35 F8
School Ho
13 Colchester CO1 136 A6
Shalford CM7 100 E5
School La Birch CO2 161 A3
Brantham CO11 60 D1
Broomfield CM1 191 B1
Chelmsford CM1 204 F8
Dedham CO7 84 F7
Duddenhoe End CB11 41 A7
East Bergholt CO7 59 B3
Great Bentley CO7 166 A8
Great Horkesley CO6 82 A2
Great Leighs CM3 173 F8
Great Wigborough CO5 181 F3
Haverhill CB9 8 E7
Henham CM22 94 F5
Lawford CO11 86 A2
Little Horkesley CO6 81 D5
Mistley CO11 86 F4
Newport CB11 42 F1
Stratford St M CO7 58 D2
Takeley CM22 121 D6
West Bergholt CO6 108 E4
School Mews CO6 130 F2
School Rd
Colchester CO2 136 A2
Copford CO6 133 D3
Elmstead CO7 138 A4
Frinton-on-S CO13 170 E5
Great Oakley CO12 116 C3
Great Totham CM9 196 B3
Langham CO4 83 E4
Little Horkesley CO6 81 D4
Little Maplestead CO9 77 B8
Little Totham CM9 197 B3
Little Yeldham CO9 30 D3
Messing CO5 159 D2
Pentlow CO10 13 F6
Rayne CM7 153 E8
Shotley Gate IP9 91 B8
Sible Hedingham CO9 75 D8
Silver End CM8 156 E3
Tattingstone IP9 36 D1
Tendring CO16 140 E6
Wickham Bishops CM8 195 F5
Wickham St P CO9 53 C5
School St Foxearth CO10 14 D6
Great Chesterford CB10 3 D2
Stoke-by-N CO6 56 D5
Sudbury CO10 33 E7
School View CM7 127 E2
School View Rd CM1 204 F3
School Villas
Great Easton CM6 123 A8
Henham CM6 95 F2
Lindsell CM6 97 F4
Takeley CM22 121 C6
School Wlk CM7 127 F3
Schoolfield Birdbrook CO9 28 A6
Glemsford CO10 2 B5
Schreiber Rd IP4 18 B7
Scofield Ct CO10 34 A6
Scotland St CO6 56 E6
Scott Ave CM7 73 D6
Scott Cl CM7 155 A8
Scott Dr CO3 134 F6
Scott Rd
Bishop's Stortford CM23 145 E6
Ipswich IP3 18 B1
Scotts Wlk CM1 204 D5
Scraley Rd CM9 210 E6
Scrip's Rd CO6 158 A7
Scrivener Dr IP2 16 C2
Scurvy Hall La
Howe Street CM3 173 C1
Little Waltham CM3 191 B8
Scylla Cl CM9 210 C6
Scythe Way CO3 134 F4
Sea Cornflower Way CO15 203 G7
Sea Cres CO15 203 F6
Sea Flowers Way CO15 203 G7
Sea Glebe Way CO15 203 G7
Sea Holly Way CO15 203 G6
Sea King Cres CO4 110 B4
Sea Lavender Way CO15 203 G7
Sea Pink Way CO15 203 G6
Sea Rd IP11 221 D2
Sea Rosemary Way CO15 203 G7
Sea Shell Way CO15 203 G6
Sea Thistle Way CO15 203 G7
Sea View Par CM0 213 C1
Sea View Prom CM0 213 B1
Sea Way CO15 203 F6
Seabrook Gdns CM3 192 F1
Seabrook Rd CM2 217 A6
Seafield Ave CO11 87 B4
Seafield Rd CO12 91 B2
Seafields Gdns CO15 189 C5
Seafields Rd CO15 189 C5
Seagers CM9 196 B4
Searle Way CO6 108 B1
Seaton Cl CO11 86 B3
Seaton Rd IP11 221 D5
Seaview Ave
Little Oakley CO12 117 C7
West Mersea CO5 201 E6
Seaview Ct CO15 189 A2
Seaview Cvn Pk CO5 201 F6
Seaview Gdns CO7 185 F7
Seaview Hts CO14 171 C7
Seaview Rd
Brightlingsea CO7 185 F7
Seawick CO16 203 B7
Seaview Terr CO16 186 A3
Seawick Rd CO16 203 B6
Sebastian Cl CO4 136 F7
Seckford Cl IP4 18 F5
Second Ave
Chelmsford CM1 205 B5
Clacton-on-S CO15 189 B4
Frinton-on-S CO13 170 E3
Glemsford CO10 2 C5
Halstead CO9 77 B1
Harwich CO12 91 C3
Seawick CO16 203 C6
Stansted Mountfitchet CM24 120 B2
Sudbury CO10 15 F1
Trimley St M IP11 221 A7
Walton-on-t-N CO14 144 E3
Weeley CO16 167 F8
Seden Ct CO15 169 B1
Sedgefield Way CM7 128 B1
Sedop Cl CB11 43 D7
Seedbed Ctr CO4 110 C6
Seedfield The CO5 201 B6
Selby Cl CO2 135 D1
Seldon Rd CO5 179 D5
Selhurst Ct CO14 170 F7
Selkirk Rd IP4 18 B8
Selsey Ave CO15 203 I8
Selvale Way IP11 221 C4
Selwyn Cl IP2 17 C4
Septimus Dr CO4 110 A5
Serpentine Rd IP3 18 C2
Serpentine Wlk CO1 109 E1
Servite Ho IP4 17 F6
Seven Ash Gn CM1 205 C5
Seven Devils La CB11 43 D6
Seventh Ave
Chelmsford CM1 205 B6
Stansted Mountfitchet CM24 120 B2
Severalls Hospl CO4 109 E5
Severalls La CO4 110 B6
Severn Rd
Clacton-on-S CO15 188 F5
Ipswich IP3 17 F3
Sewell's La CO10 13 B1
Sexton Cl CO2 163 B8
Sextons La CM8 178 B1
Seymore Dr CB9 8 D7
Seymour Rd Ipswich IP2 17 C4
Jaywick CO15 187 F1
Seymour St CM2 205 A1
Shackleton Cl CO12 90 F1
Shackleton Gdns CM23 145 E6
Shackleton Rd IP3 18 B3
Shackleton Sq IP3 18 B3
Shaftenhoe End Rd SG8 39 B8
Shaftesbury Ave CO12 91 B4
Shaftesbury Ct 10 CB9 8 E7
Shaftesbury Sq 4 IP4 17 D5
Shafto Rd IP1 16 E8
Shair La
Great Bentley CO7 167 B8
Weeley CO16 140 B2
Shakespeare Cl CM7 155 A7
Shakespeare Rd CO3 134 F6
Shakeston Cl CM1 215 B8
Shalfleet Ct CO15 188 F8
Shalford Lodge CM1 205 B8
Shalford Prim Sch CM7 100 E5
Shalford Rd CM77 126 E3
Shamrock Ave IP2 16 E4
Shamrock Cl CM9 199 D2
Shamrock Ho CO15 203 J8
Shangani Rd CM23 145 F5
Shanklin Cl CO15 189 A8
Shannon Cl CB9 9 D7
Shannon Rd IP3 38 A8
Shardelow Ave CM1 206 A8
Sharlands Row CM9 199 A8
Sharpington Cl CM2 216 C3
Shatters Rd CO2 161 A1
Shaw Cl CO13 170 F7
Shaw Dr CM7 73 D7
Shaw Rd
Long Melford CO10 15 D8
Witham CM8 176 F5
Shawlands Ave CO10 34 B7
Shearers The CM23 145 C4
Shearers Way CM3 192 F1
Shearman Ct 1 CB9 9 A7
Shears Cres CO5 201 D5
Shears Ct CO5 201 D5
Sheds La CB10 22 E2
Sheene Gr CM7 128 D5
Sheepcoates La CM9 196 F2
Sheepcot Rd CO9 51 F3
Sheepcote La CM23 92 E3
Sheepcotes CM2 206 B5
Sheepcotes La
Little Waltham CM3 191 C7
Silver End CM8 156 E5
Sheepen Pl CO3 135 E8
Sheepen Rd CO3 135 D8
Sheepshead Hill CO10 34 C6
Sheering Wlk CO2 135 F2
Sheerwater Mews CO4 137 A8
Sheldrake Dr IP2 16 E2
Sheldrick Link CM2 206 B4
Shellcroft CO6 77 F1
Shellduck Cres CM77 154 C5
Shelley Ave
Great Cornard CO10 34 B6
Tiptree CO5 179 E5
Shelley La CO16 168 F2
Shelley Rd
Chelmsford CM2 205 D2
Clacton-on-S CO16 188 A5
Colchester CO3 134 F6
Shelley St 6 IP2 17 C4
Shelley Wlk CM7 155 A8
Sheltons The CO13 170 B6
Shenley Rd IP3 18 B1
Shepherd Dr IP8 16 C2
Shepherds Cl CM23 145 C4
Shepherds Croft CO3 134 D5
Shepherds Ct 15 CB9 8 E7
Shepherds La CO10 2 A6
Shepherds Way CB10 22 F2
Sheppard Cl CO16 188 D6
Sheppard Dr CM2 206 A4
Sherborne Rd CM1 205 D5
Sherbourne Cl CO13 170 F7
Sherbourne Rd CO4 136 F7
Sheriffs Way CO15 188 E7
Sheriidan Wlk CO3 134 F6
Sheringham Dr CM77 154 C7
Sherrington Rd IP1 17 A8
Sherwood Cl CO4 136 D7
Sherwood Ct 20 CM23 145 F7
Sherwood Dr
Chelmsford CM1 204 D1
Clacton-on-S CO15 188 E6
Sherwood Way CO5 158 D4
Shetland Cl IP4 18 A8
Shetland Rd CB9 9 D8
Shewell Wlk CO1 135 E7
Shillito Cl CO3 134 F3
Ship La CO11 87 E3
Ship Launch Rd IP3 17 E3
Shipwrights The CO7 164 B8
Shipyard Est CO7 185 F5
Shire Cl CM1 205 F7
Shire Ct 13 CB9 8 E7
Shire Hall Yd 10 IP4 17 D5
Shire Hill CB11 22 F1
Shire Hill La CB10 44 A8
Shire La CO6 108 F4
Shires Cl CM77 154 B7
Shirley Ct CO15 188 A1
Shoebridge's Hill CO7 84 E6
Shop La CO5 184 F3
Shop Rd CO11 113 B6
Shops The CM8 156 D4
Shore La Bradfield CO11 87 E3
Harkstead IP9 63 A2
Shoreham Rd CO15 203 I8
Short Cut Rd CO1 135 E7
Short Wyre St 24 CO1 135 F7
Shortcroft CM23 146 D7
Shortlands IP8 16 D1
Shortlands Pl CM23 145 F8
Shortridge Ct CM8 194 F8
Shotley Cl
Clacton-on-S CO16 188 A3
Felixstowe IP11 221 B4
Ipswich IP2 16 C2
Shotley Mews CB9 8 C8
Shropshire Cl CM2 216 F5
Shrub End Rd CO3 135 B4
Shrubbery Cl IP11 221 D4
Shrubland Ct CO15 189 B5
Shrubland Dr IP4 18 F5
Shrubland Rd
6 Colchester CO2 136 A6
New Mistley CO11 87 A3
Shrublands CB10 22 E3
Shrublands Cl CM2 205 C2
Shums Hill CO13 170 C8
Shut La CO6 105 B6
Siam Pl CO10 33 E7
Sidegate Ave IP4 18 A8
Sidegate La IP4 18 A8
Sidegate Prim Sch IP4 18 A8
Sidings Pl CM7 128 A2
Sidmouth Rd CM1 205 E6
Sidney Pl CM1 206 A7
Sidney Terr CM23 145 F6
Siena Mews CO2 136 B4
Siggin's La CB1 5 D7
Silcock Cl CO4 110 C2
Silcott St CO7 185 E6
Silent St IP1 17 C5
Silk Factory Row CO10 2 B6
Silk Mus* CM7 127 F2
Silks Way CM7 127 F2
Sillett Cl CO16 188 D6
Silvanus Cl CO3 135 D6
Silver Dawn Touring Pk CO16 188 A4
Silver End Prim Sch CM8 156 E3
Silver Leys IP9 60 E6
Silver Row CB11 42 F5
Silver St Maldon CM9 209 F3
Silver End CM8 156 D4
Stansted Mountfitchet CM24 119 D6
Wethersfield CM7 73 B3
Silverdale Ct CO15 189 B5
Silverthorne Cl CO2 136 A3
Silvester Way CM2 206 B4
Simmonds Way CM3 218 F8
Simons Flats CO5 179 C7
Simons La CO1 136 B6
Simpson Cl IP3 17 F1
Simpsons La CO5 179 A3
Sims Cl CO6 105 B7
Sinclair Cl CO4 109 F2
Sinclair Dr IP2 17 C3
Singer Ave CO15 203 E7
Singleton Ct CO10 34 A5
Sinnington End CO4 110 C4
Sioux Cl CO4 110 C4
Sir Alf Ramsey Way IP1 17 B5
Sir Charles Lucas Comp Sch CO4 136 E8
Sir Isaac's Wlk CO1 135 F7
Sirdar Rd IP1 17 A7
Siskin Cl CO4 136 F8
Sittang Cl CO2 135 C1
Sitwell Cl CO11 86 B4
Siward Rd CM8 194 D8
Six Bells Ct CM7 127 F5
Sixth Ave
Chelmsford CM1 205 B6
Stansted Mountfitchet CM24 120 C3
Sixth Form Coll The CO1 135 E7
Skate's Hill CO10 2 B2
Skeins Way CB11 65 C4
Skelmersdale Rd CO15 188 F3
Skelton Cl CO11 86 C4
Skerry Rise CM1 205 B7
Skiddaw Cl CM77 154 D7
Skinner's La CM2 216 B3
Skinners St CM23 145 C4
Skipper Ct CM7 154 F8
Skipper Rd IP8 36 E8
Skitts Hill CM7 128 A1
Skitts Hill Ind Est CM7 128 B1
Skreens Ct CM1 204 D4
Sky Hall Hill CO4 83 D7
Skylark La IP8 16 C2
Skylark Wlk CM2 216 B5
Skyrmans Fee CO13 170 E6
Sladbury's La CO15 189 C6
Sladburys La CO15 189 D8
Slade Rd CO15 189 C6
Slade St 14 IP4 17 D5
Slade The CB10 22 F7
Slade's La CM2 216 A3
Slades Cl CO10 2 C5
Slate CO9 76 F1
Slaters Cl CO13 170 E6
Sleaford Cl IP2 17 A3
Sloe Hill CO9 76 C2
Slough Farm Rd CO9 76 D2
Slough House Cl CM7 128 D1
Slough La Ardleigh CO7 111 D4
Cock Clarks CM3 219 D3
Elmstead CO7 137 B6
Slough Rd
Brantham CO7,CO11 60 D2
Danbury CM3 219 C3
Slushy La IP9 63 B3
Smaley La CO10 15 C8
Smallbridge Entry CO8 80 D8
Smallwood Rd CO2 135 B3
Smart St 11 IP4 17 D5
Smeaton Cl CO4 110 C6
Smeetham Hall La CO10 32 E6
Smith's End La SG8 39 A8
Smithers Cl IP9 35 A1
Smithers Dr CM2 217 A6
Smiths Cotts CM22 93 E4
Smiths Field
Colchester CO1 136 C5
Rayne CM77 126 F2
Smiths Gn CB11 68 A8
Smythe Cl CO16 188 C6
Smythies Ave CO1 136 A7
Snakes La
Stansted Mountfitchet CM24 93 F2
Ugley CM22 94 A2
Snape Cl CO16 188 A4
Snape Way CO13 170 F7
Sneating Hall La CO13 169 E8
Snelling Gr CM2 216 F6
Sniveller's La CO5 157 D3
Snow Hill La CO6 57 D5
Snowberry Ct CM7 128 D4
Snowberry Gr CO2 136 A3
Snowcroft IP9 35 A1
Snowdon Ct 5 CB9 8 E6
Snowdon Rd IP2 17 B2
Snowdrop Cl
Bishop's Stortford CM23 145 C6
Chelmsford CM1 205 E7
Witham CM8 176 E4
Snowley Par CM23 119 B1

Snows Way CO11 86 D8
Soane St IP4 17 D6
Soft Rd CO10 31 F5
Soils The CO12 116 E5
Solway Ct 3 CO4 136 E8
Somers Rd CO3 135 A4
Somerset Cl CO2 135 B3
Somerset Ct 9 CB9 8 E7
Somerset Pl CM1 205 A7
Somerset Rd IP4 17 F8
Somerset Way CO15 187 F1
Somerton Ct IP11 221 F4
Somme Rd CO2 135 E4
Sonell Ct CO7 137 B2
Songers Cotts CO4 83 B6
Sorrel Cl Colchester CO4 109 C2
Ipswich IP2 16 F3
Sorrel Gr CM77 154 B7
Sorrel Horse Mews 22 IP4 17 D5
Sorrel Wlk CB9 8 D8
Sorrell Cl
Goldhanger CM9 211 E7
Little Waltham CM3 191 B6
South Area IP1 16 C7
South Cl Halstead CO9 103 E8
Ipswich IP4 17 E8
St Osyth CO16 187 B4
South Gn CB11 67 D4
South Green Rd CO5 163 F3
South Heath Rd CO7 166 F3
South Hill IP11 221 D3
South Hill Cl CM3 218 D6
South Ho CO13 170 F4
South Primrose Hill CM1 204 F3
South Rd
Bishop's Stortford CM23 146 A5
Saffron Walden CB11 22 E1
Takeley CM22 148 C8
South St
Bishop's Stortford CM23 145 F6
Braintree CM7 127 F2
Colchester CO2 135 E6
Great Chesterford CB10 3 D2
Great Waltham CM3 190 E7
Ipswich IP1 17 B7
Manningtree CO11 86 D4
Tolleshunt D'arcy CM9 198 D4
South St Commercial Ctr 1 CM23 145 F6
South Strand CO11 86 C5
South Suffolk Bsns Pk CO10 34 A7
South View CM6 150 C8
South View Gn IP9 60 E6
Southborough Rd CM2 216 A8
Southcliff CO14 171 C7
Southcliff Ct
Clacton-on-S CO15 189 B4
Walton-on-t-N CO14 171 C7
Southcliff Hall CO15 188 F2
Southcliff Pk CO15 189 A4
Southcliff Prom CO14 171 C7
Southcote Rd CM8 176 F4
Southcroft Cl CO13 170 C6
Southend Rd
Great Baddow CM2 217 B4
Howe Green CM2 217 D2
Woodham Mortimer CM9 219 C5
Southey Cl CM9 210 C4
Southfield CB10 3 A3
Southfields CO7 84 F6
Southgate Cres CO5 179 E5
Southgate Gdns CO10 15 C6
Southgate Rd IP8 16 B1
Southgate St CO10 15 C6
Southgates Ind Pk CB10 43 F7
Southgreen Gdns CO16 188 C4
Southland Cl CO4 110 C1
Southlands Chase CM2 217 E2
Southmill Rd CM23 146 A5
Southmill Trad Ctr CM23 146 A6
Southview Dr
Holland-on-S CO15 189 F6
Walton-on-t-N CO14 171 C7
Southview Rd CM3 218 D6
Southview Sch CM8 176 F6
Southview Terr CM3 218 D6
Southway
Brightlingsea CO7 185 F7
Colchester CO1, CO3 135 E6
Southwold Way CO16 188 A5
Southwood Chase CM3 219 A4
Sovereign Cl CM7 128 D4
Sovereign Cres CO3 135 C6
Sovereign Ctr IP1 16 C7
Sowerberry Cl CM1 204 F7
Spa Dr CM0 213 B1
Spa Rd Feering CO5 158 E4
Witham CM8 176 E2
Spalding Ave CM1 204 E5
Spalding Cl CM7 127 E4
Spalding Ct CM1 205 A3
Spalding Way CM2 216 F8
Spanbies Rd CO7 58 D2
Spansey Ct 1 CO9 76 D1
Spar La CM3 220 C3
Sparepenny La N CB10 47 A4
Sparepenny La S CB10 47 B4
Sparkey Cl CM8 195 A7
Sparks La CO9 29 A6
Sparling Cl CO2 135 C2
Sparlings The CO13 170 C8
Sparrow Cl CO9 75 D8
Sparrow Rd CO10 34 B6
Sparrows Cnr CO12 116 E5
Sparrows Herne CO15 188 F6
Sparrowsend Cotts CB11 43 A4
Sparrowsend Hill CB11 43 A5
Spartan Cl CB9 8 C8
Speckled Wood Cl IP8 36 D8
Speckled Wood Ct CM7 154 E8
Speedwell Cl CM8 176 D4
Speedwell Rd
Colchester CO2 136 D2
Ipswich IP2 16 F4
Spencer Cl
Elsenham CM22 94 C3
Stansted Mountfitchet CM24 119 E6
Spencer Rd
Great Chesterford CB10 3 D3
Thorpe-le-S CO16 142 A2
Spencer Sq CM7 127 F8
Spencers Piece CO4 83 E4
Spendells Cl CO14 144 D2
Spenlow Dr CM1 204 D7
Spennells The CO16 142 A2
Spenser Way CO15 187 F1
Spicers La CO10 15 C8
Spike The 7 CB10 22 F2
Spindle Rd CB9 8 D8
Spindle Wood CO4 110 B4
Spindrift Way CO7 164 B8
Spinks La CM8 176 F1
Spinnaker Cl CO15 203 J8
Spinnaker Dr CM9 210 E3
Spinnel's Hill CO11 88 B1
Spinnel's La Wix CO11 115 D7
Wrabness CO11 88 C1
Spinner Cl IP1 16 D8
Spinney The
Braintree CM7 128 C1
Earls Colne CO6 105 A6
Newport CB11 67 A7
Rushmere St A IP4 18 F4
Stansted Mountfitchet CM24 119 E6
Spinneyfields CO5 179 D6
Spires The
Bishop's Stortford CM23 145 D7
Great Baddow CM2 216 F6
Spital Rd Maldon CM9 209 F2
Maldon CM9 220 D7
Spitfire Cl IP3 18 B1
Sporehams La
Danbury CM3 218 C4
Howe Green CM2,CM3 217 F4
Sportsmans La CM3 194 A2
Sportsway CO1 135 F8
Spots Wlk CM2 216 D3
Spout La CO10 55 D7
Spratts La CO11 113 B4
Spring Chase
Brightlingsea CO7 185 E7
Wivenhoe CO7 137 B2
Spring Cl
Clacton-on-S CO16 188 C5
Colchester CO4 110 C3
Little Baddow CM3 207 D5
Spring Cotts CB9 9 C6
Spring Elms La CM3 207 F3
Spring Gardens Rd CO6 106 E6
Spring Gdns CO10 15 C8
Spring Hill CB11 22 A1
Spring La Colchester CO3 135 A7
Colchester,Lexden Bridge CO3 135 A8
Eight Ash G CO3 108 B1
Great Totham CM9 196 D7
Hatfield Peverel CM3,CM9 194 F2
Maldon CM9 210 B4
West Bergholt CO6 108 E3
Witham CM8 195 A7
Wivenhoe CO7 137 B2
Spring Lane Rdbt CO3 135 A7
Spring Mdw CO10 2 B6
Spring Meadow Prim Sch CO12 91 A3
Spring Pond Cl CM2 216 E8
Spring Rd
Brightlingsea CO7 185 F7
Ipswich IP4 18 A6
St Osyth CO16 187 A3
Tiptree CO5 179 C4
Spring Rise
Galleywood CM2 216 C2
Haverhill CB9 9 C6
Spring Sedge Cl CO3 134 C7
Spring Way CO9 51 E1
Springbank Ave CO11 86 B3
Springbok Ho CM2 216 F5
Springett's Hill CO8 55 D2
Springfield Ave IP11 221 E5
Springfield Basin CM2 205 C2
Springfield Cotts CM9 210 B5
Springfield Ct CM23 145 E8
Springfield Gn CM1 205 E4
Springfield Inf Sch IP1 16 F8
Springfield Jun Sch IP1 16 F8
Springfield La IP1 16 F8
Springfield Lyons App CM2 206 A5
Springfield Park Ave CM2 205 E2
Springfield Park Hill CM2 205 D2
Springfield Park La CM2 205 E2
Springfield Park Par CM2 205 D2
Springfield Park Rd CM2 205 E2
Springfield Pl CM1 205 E5
Springfield Rd
Chelmsford CM1 205 E4
Sudbury CO10 15 E1
Springfield Terr 2 CO10 33 F8
Springfields
Braintree CM77 127 C2
Brightlingsea CO7 185 F7
Great Dunmow CM6 150 D8
Springfields Dr CO2 135 A3
Springhill Cl CO7 138 E8
Springhill Rd CB11 43 D8
Springhurst Cl IP4 17 F6
Springland Cl IP4 18 A6
Springlands Way CO10 15 F2
Springmead CM77 154 D7
Springtail Rd IP8 36 E8
Springvalley La CO7 111 C4
Springwell Rd CB10,CB11 22 A5
Springwood Ct CM7 127 D3
Springwood Dr CM7 127 C4
Springwood Ind Est CM7 127 D3
Sprites End IP11 221 B7
Sprites Jun & Inf Sch IP2 16 C2
Sprites La IP8, IP2 16 C2
Spriteshall La IP11 221 B7
Sproughton Bsns Pk IP1 16 C8
Sproughton CE Prim Sch IP8 16 B6
Sproughton Ct IP8 16 A6
Sproughton Rd IP1 16 D7
Spruce Ave
Colchester CO4 136 E8
Great Dunmow CM6 123 B1
Spruce Cl
West Mersea CO5 201 B7
Witham CM8 177 A4
Spurgeon Cl CO9 51 E1
Spurgeon Pl CO5 158 C2
Spurgeon St CO1 136 C6
Square The
Colchester CO2 135 B3
Heybridge CM9 210 A5
Stansted Mountfitchet CM22 93 F3
West Mersea CO5 201 B6
Widdington CB11 67 D4
Squire's Ct 1 CB9 8 E7
Squires Cl CM23 145 C8
Squirrells Ct CM1 204 F5
Squirrels Cl 2 CM23 145 F8
Squirrels Field CO4 109 F5
Squirrels The IP9 35 A2
Stable Cl Colchester CO3 134 E6
West Mersea CO5 201 E7
Stable Mews CO5 201 E8
Stablecroft CM1 205 E8
Stablefield Rd CO14 171 A7
Stacey Ct 9 CM23 145 F6
Stackyard The CB10 3 A3
Stafford Cl CO13 170 E6
Stafford Cres CM7 128 D4
Stafford Ho CM23 145 F5
Stainers CM23 145 C5
Stalin Rd CO2 136 B4
Stallards Cres CO13 170 E6
Stambourne Rd
Great Yeldham CO9 29 D3
Ridgewell CO9 28 F5
Toppesfield CO9 50 B8
Stambridge Rd CO15 188 C4
Stamford Cl IP2 36 F8
Stammers Rd CO4 109 F4
Standard Ave CO15 203 D6
Standard Rd 9 CO1 136 C6
Standley Rd CO14 144 D1
Standrums CM6 150 D8
Stane Cl CM23 118 F1
Stane Field CO6 132 E3
Stanes Rd CM7 127 F6
Stanfield Cl CO3 134 E3
Stanfield Mdw CM8 155 F1
Stanier Cl CM8 194 F7
Stanley Ave
Brightlingsea CO7 186 A7
Ipswich IP3 18 A4
Stanley Rd
Clacton-on-S CO15 188 C2
Felixstowe IP11 221 E3
Great Chesterford CB10 3 E3
Halstead CO9 76 D2
Sudbury CO10 33 E8
Wivenhoe CO7 137 C1
Stanley Rise CM2 205 F3
Stanley Wood Ave CO10 15 F1
Stanley Wooster Way CO4 136 E7
Stanleys Farm Rd CB11 43 F8
Stanmore Cl CO16 188 D5
Stanmore Way CO16 187 B4
Stannard Way CO10 34 A6
Stanstead Rd CO9 103 F8
Stansted Airport Sta CM24 121 B4
Stansted Cl CM1 204 E1
Stansted Mountfitchet Sta CM24 119 E6
Stansted Rd
Birchanger CM23 119 C4
Bishop's Stortford CM23 119 B2
Colchester CO2 136 A1
Elsenham CM22 94 C1
Stansted Way CO13 171 A6
Stanstrete Field CM77 154 B5
Stanton Pl 9 CB9 9 B8
Stanway Cl CO10 2 C5
Stanway Fiveways Prim Sch CO3 134 D5
Stanway Prim Sch CO3 134 C6
Stanway Sch The CO3 134 D5
Stanwell St 9 CO2 135 F6
Stanwyn Ave CO15 188 E3
Stapleford Cl CM2 205 A1
Staplers Cl CM9 196 B4
Staplers Heath CM9 196 B4
Staplers Wlk CM9 196 B4
Star La
Great Dunmow CM6 123 D1
Ipswich IP4 17 D5
Star Mead CM6 70 A2
Starfield Cl IP4 18 B6
Starling's Hill CO9 75 E4
Starr Rd CM22 94 F5
Start Hill CM22 147 A7
Station App
Braintree CM7 128 A2
Frinton-on-S CO13 170 F5
Station Cotts CO6 133 D2
Station Hill CO8 79 E8
Station La CO12 91 C4
Station Rd Alresford CO7 165 A8
Ardleigh CO7 111 E7
Bentley IP9 60 E6
Birdbrook CO9 10 D1
Bishop's Stortford CM23 146 A7
Bradfield CO11 87 E3
Braintree CM7 127 F2
Brightlingsea CO7 185 E6
Clacton-on-S CO15 188 F3
Clare CO10 12 C7
Colne Engaine CO6 77 F1
Cressing CM8 156 A3
Earls Colne CO6 105 A7
Elsenham CM22 94 C2
Felsted CM6 151 F6
Great Bentley CO7 166 E8
Great Dunmow CM6 150 E8
Harwich, Bath Side CO12 91 E5
Harwich, Dovercourt CO12 91 D4
Harwich, Parkeston CO12 90 F5
Hatfield Peverel CM3 193 F5
Haverhill CB9 9 A8
Kelvedon CO5 158 C3
Kirby Cross CO13 170 B6
Long Melford CO10 15 C5
Maldon CM9 210 A3
Manningtree CO11 86 C5
Marks Tey CO6 133 B4
Newport CB11 67 A8
Rayne CM77 126 F1
Saffron Walden CB11 22 D1
Sible Hedingham CO9 51 E2
Stansted Mountfitchet CM24 119 E6
Sudbury CO10 33 E7
Takeley CM22 148 C7
Thorpe-le-S CO16 168 F8
Thorrington CO7 166 A6
Tiptree CO5 179 C4
Tollesbury CM9 199 D2
Tolleshunt D'arcy CM9 198 E5
Trimley St M IP11 221 A7
Wakes Colne CO6 106 D6
Wendens Ambo CB11 42 F5
White Colne CO6 105 E8
White Notley CM8 155 F2
Wickham Bishops CM8 195 C4
Witham CM8 177 A3
Wivenhoe CO7 164 B8
Wrabness CO11 88 F3
Station Road Ind Est
Great Dunmow CM6 150 E7
Tolleshunt D'arcy CM9 198 E5
Station St Ipswich IP2 17 C3
Saffron Walden CB11 22 D1
Walton-on-t-N CO14 171 C8
Station Terr CM3 193 F5
Station Way CO1 109 E1
Station Yd IP2 17 B4
Steadman Ct CO15 203 D6
Steam Mill Rd CO11 114 B8
Steamer Terr 2 CM1 205 A3
Stebbing Prim Sch CM6 124 E5
Stebbing Rd CM6 152 B7
Steeds Mdw CO10 15 C8
Steele Cl CO6 132 F3
Steele Ho CO12 91 C3
Steeple Bumpstead Prim Sch CB9 27 B6
Steeple Bumpstead Rd CB9 26 E7
Steeple Cl CM9 210 D5
Steeple View CM23 145 F8
Steerforth Cl CM1 204 D7
Stella Maris IP2 16 D5
Stepfield CM8 177 B2
Stephen Cl Haverhill CB9 8 F8
Long Melford CO10 15 B5
Stephen Cranfield Cl CO5 164 A7
Stephen Marshall Ave CM7 72 C6
Stephen Neville Ct CB11 43 D8
Stephen's Ct IP4 18 B6
Stephenson Rd
Braintree CM7 128 A1
Clacton-on-S CO15 189 B8
Colchester CO4 110 D6
Stephenson Rd W CO15 169 A1
Sterling Cl CO3 134 E5
Sterling Complex IP1 16 D7
Stevens Cl CO4 109 E3
Stevens La CM6 152 F6
Stevens Rd CM8 176 E1
Stevens Wlk CO4 136 F7
Stevenson Rd IP1 17 B6
Stewards Cl CO13 170 F7
Stewart Rd CM2 216 A6
Stewarts The CM23 145 E6
Stewarts Way CM23 92 F2
Stilemans Wood CM7 128 D1
Stiles The CM9 210 E3
Stirling Dr CB9 8 E8
Stirrup Cl CM1 205 E7
Stirrup Mews CO3 134 E6
Stisted CE Prim Sch CM7 129 B6
Stivvy's Rd CM9 208 C3
Stock Chase CM9 210 B5
Stock Rd CM2 216 B2
Stock Terr CM9 210 B5
Stockhouse Cl CM9 180 B2
Stockhouse Rd CO5 180 B7
Stocking La SG8 39 C1
Stockley Cl CB9 9 C7
Stockman Terr CM77 154 C8
Stockmen Field CM23 145 C5
Stockmers End 1 IP9 35 A1
Stockwell 5 CO1 135 F7
Stoke Coll CO10 11 C3
Stoke Hall Rd IP2 17 C4
Stoke High Sch IP2 17 C2
Stoke Park Dr IP2 17 A1
Stoke Park Gdns IP2 17 A1
Stoke Quay IP2 17 D4
Stoke Rd Clare CO10 12 A6
Nayland CO6 56 B2
Stoke St IP2 17 C4
Stoke-by-Nayland Mid Sch CO6 56 C6
Stoke-by-Nayland Prim Sch CO6 56 C5
Stokeash Cl CO16 188 A3
Stokebridge Maltings 1 IP2 17 C4
Stokes The CO14 171 B8
Stone Cl CM7 127 F2
Stone Cotts CO9 52 D2
Stone Hall CO10 12 B7
Stone La Tiptree CO5 179 A2
Wrabness CO11 88 F5
Stone Lodge La IP2 17 A3
Stone Lodge La W IP2 16 F3
Stone Lodge Wlk IP2 17 B3
Stone Path Dr CM3 193 F3
Stone Rd CO7 113 B1
Stone's Green Rd CO12 115 E2
Stonebridge Hill CO6 104 E7
Stonechat Rd IP2 16 D2
Stonecrop CO4 109 C2
Stonegrove Rd IP11 221 B1
Stonehall Dr CO16 168 D1
Stonehall La CO12 115 B1
Stoneham St CO6 130 F2
Stonehill Way CO5 201 A6
Stoneleigh Pk CO3 134 F4
Stoney Brook CM24 119 E5
Stoney Comm CM24 119 E5
Stoney Common Rd CM24 119 D5
Stoney La CO7 186 A8
Stoney Pl CM24 119 E5
Stoneyfield Dr CM24 119 E6
Stonham Ave CO16 188 A4
Stony La CM6 70 A2
Stopford Ct 2 IP1 17 A6
Storelands Ho IP11 221 B6
Stores Rd CO5 179 C6
Stores The CO11 86 F4
Storms Way CM2 206 B2
Stort Lodge CM23 145 D8
Stort Rd CM23 145 F6
Stort Valley Ind Pk CM23 119 B2
Stortford Hall Ind Pk CM23 146 B7
Stortford Hall Pk CM23 146 B8
Stortford Hall Rd 3 CM23 146 B8
Stortford Rd
Clavering CB11 65 C4
Great Dunmow CM6 123 C1
Takeley CM6 149 D7
Stour Ave IP11 221 C3
Stour Cl Glemsford CO10 2 C2
Harwich CO12 90 D2
Stour Ct CM7 128 D1
Stour Estuary Nature Reserve* CO12 89 C3
Stour Gdns CO10 34 B4
Stour Gn CO10 12 B6
Stour Rd CO12 91 D5
Stour St Cavendish CO10 13 C8
Manningtree CO11 86 D4
Sudbury CO10 33 E7
Stour Vale Clare CO10 12 A6
Stoke by C CO10 10 D2
Stour Valley Rd CB9 9 B7
Stour View Ct CO12 91 D5
Stour Wlk CO4 110 E2
Stourdale Cl CO11 86 A3
Stourside IP9 91 A8
Stourton Rd CM8 176 E3
Stourview Ave CO11 87 A4
Stourview Cl CO11 87 B4
Stow Ct CO4 109 F5
Stradbroke Rd IP4 18 A7
Straight Rd Boxted CO4 82 F2
Bradfield CO11 87 C1
Colchester CO3 134 F5
Great Bentley CO7 167 A4

Straight Way CO2 ....161 A2
Strand The IP2 ....37 C8
Strasbourg Sq 6 CB9 .....9 B8
Stratford Pl 4 CO14 ....171 C8
Stratford Rd
Clacton-on-S CO15 ....189 D6
Dedham CO7 ....84 D7
Stratford St Mary Prim Sch
CO7 ....58 C1
Straw La CO10 ....33 D7
Strawberry Cl CM7 ....128 A1
Strawberry Fields CB9 ....8 D7
Strawberry La CO5 ......179 F3
Strawbrook Hill CM3 ....173 E4
Street Farm Bglws CO11 .61 A2
Street The Ardleigh CO7 ..111 E8
Ashen CO10 ....11 D1
Belchamp Walter CO10 .....31 C8
Belstead IP8 ....36 C6
Berden CM23 ....92 B8
Birdbrook CO9 ....28 B7
Bradfield CO11 ....87 E1
Bradwell CM7 ....129 D3
Brantham CO11 ....61 A1
Bulmer CO10 ....32 E5
Capel St M IP9 ....35 A1
Chappel CO6 ....106 D5
Cressing CM77 ....156 A6
East Bergholt CO7 ....59 B2
Feering CO5 ....158 E5
Foxearth CO10 ....14 C6
Galleywood CM2 ....216 B2
Gosfield CO9 ....102 E7
Great Hallingbury CM22 ...147 B4
Great Henny CO10 ....33 E3
Great Tey CO6 ....132 C8
Harkstead IP9 ....63 B2
Hatfield Peverel CM3 ......193 F4
Holbrook IP9 ....62 D6
Kirby-le-S CO13 ....143 B1
Little Clacton CO16 ....168 C3
Little Dunmow CM6 ....151 D7
Little Totham CM9 ....197 B5
Little Waltham CM3 ....191 B6
Manuden CM23 ....92 F2
Messing CO5 ....159 D2
Pebmarsh CO9 ....78 A8
Pentlow CO10 ....14 A8
Purleigh CM3,CM9 ....220 F1
Ramsey CO12 ....90 A1
Rayne CM77 ....126 F2
Salcott-cum-virley CM9 ....199 B8
Shalford CM7 ....100 E7
Stisted CM7 ....129 C6
Stoke by Clare CO10 ....11 B3
Stratford St M CO7 ....84 C8
Tendring CO16 ....140 E5
Terling CM3 ....175 C2
Tiptree CO5 ....179 A8
Toppesfield CO9 ....50 B7
Washbrook IP8 ....35 F8
Weeley CO16 ....140 F1
Wherstead IP9 ....37 B6
White Notley CM8 ....155 E1
Wickham Bishops CM8 .....195 F5
Woodham Walter CM9 ......208 D2
Stretford Ct CM8 ....156 D3
Strethall Rd CB11 ....21 C4
Strickmere CO7 ....58 D2
Strood Cl CO5 ....201 B7
Strood The CO5 ....183 C3
Strudwick Cl 10 CM7 .....127 F2
Strutt Cl CM3 ....194 A4
Stuart Cl
Great Baddow CM2 ....217 B6
Ipswich IP4 ....17 F7
Stuart Pawsey Ct CO7 ...137 C1
Stuarts Way CM7 ....128 B2
Stubbs Cl Ipswich IP3 ......18 A1
Kirby Cross CO13 ....170 E7
Lawford CO11 ....86 B4
Stubbs La CM7 ....128 C1
Studd's La CO4 ....109 D4
Stump Cross CB10 ....3 C5
Stump La CM1 ....205 D4
Stump's Cross CO9 ....29 A2
Sturdee Ave IP3 ....18 B3
Sturmer Ct 3 CO2 ....136 A1
Sturmer End Ind Est CB9 ..9 C6
Sturmer Rd Haverhill CB9 ...9 C6
Haverhill, Calford Green CB9 ..9 F7
Sturrick La CO7 ....139 D1
Stutton CE Prim Sch IP9 .62 A2
Stutton Cl IP9 ....62 A2
Stutton Gn IP9 ....62 C1
Stutton La IP9 ....61 C5
Stutton Rd CO11 ....61 A2
Stylemans La CM22 ....146 B5
Styles CM7 ....71 D2
Sub-Station Rd IP11 ....221 B2
Sudbourne Ave CO16 ....188 A4
Sudbourne Rd IP11 ....221 B5
Sudbury Rd Bulmer CO10 ..32 F6
Bures CO8 ....55 F1
Castle Hedingham CO9 ......52 B4
Felixstowe IP11 ....221 A4
Gestingthorpe CO9 ....31 F2
Great Cornard CO10 ....34 F7
Great Maplestead CO9 ....53 C2
Halstead CO9 ....76 F3
Long Melford CO10 ....15 C3
Stoke-by-N CO6 ....56 C6
Sudbury Sta CO10 ....33 F7
Sudbury Upper Sch CO10 .15 F1
Sue Ryder Mus* CO10 ....1 D1
Suffolk Ave CO5 ....201 D7
Suffolk Cl
Clacton-on-S CO15 ....189 E7
Suffolk Cl continued
Colchester CO4 ....110 B1
Suffolk Coll IP4 ....17 E5
Suffolk Coll (Argyll St
Annexe) IP4 ....17 D6
Suffolk Cres CM9 ....209 E1
Suffolk Dr CM2 ....206 A4
Suffolk Ent Pk IP1 ....17 B5
Suffolk Knowle CO8 ....55 F1
Suffolk Rd Ipswich IP4 .....17 D7
Maldon CM9 ....209 E1
Sudbury CO10 ....33 E8
Suffolk Ret Pk IP1 ....17 A6
Suffolk Ski Ctr* IP2 ....37 B8
Suffolk Sq CO10 ....33 E8
Suffolk St CO14 ....171 C8
Sugar La CO9 ....74 E7
Sulleys Hill IP7 ....58 B8
Sullivan Cl CO4 ....136 E6
Summer Hill Rd CB11 ....43 D8
Summercroft Inf Sch
CM23 ....146 C8
Summercroft Jun Sch
CM23 ....146 C8
Summerfield Cl IP4 ....18 D8
Summerfield Ct IP4 ....18 D8
Summerfields CO9 ....51 E1
Summerleaze Ct CM77 ..154 D7
Sun Lido Square Gdns
CM77 ....127 C2
Sunbank CM6 ....150 E7
Sunbeam Ave CO15 ....203 E6
Sunbeam Cl CO5 ....164 A8
Sunbury Way CM9 ....220 F8
Sundale Cl CO15 ....189 F6
Sunfield Cl IP4 ....18 B6
Sunflower Cl 5 CM1 ......205 F6
Sunningdale CM23 ....145 E6
Sunningdale Ave
Felixstowe IP11 ....221 F6
Ipswich IP4 ....18 D5
Sunningdale Dr IP11 ......221 F6
Sunningdale Fall CM3 ....194 B4
Sunningdale Rd CM1 ......204 E4
Sunningdale Way CO13 ..170 E7
Sunny Point CO14 ....144 E3
Sunnyfields Rd CM7 ....102 D2
Sunnyside Braintree CM7 .127 E3
Stansted Mountfitchet
CM24 ....119 E6
Sunnyside Rd CO6 ....107 D5
Sunnyside Way CO16 .....168 C1
Sunnyway Cotts CM3 .....218 E3
Sunray Ave IP11 ....221 F6
Sunrise Ave CM1 ....205 A5
Surbiton Rd IP1 ....16 F8
Surrey Ct CO15 ....189 A2
Surrey La CO5 ....179 C4
Surrey Rd
Felixstowe IP11 ....221 D4
Ipswich IP1 ....17 A6
Sussex Cl CM3 ....206 F8
Sussex Gdns CO15 ....189 E6
Sussex Rd CO3 ....135 C7
Sutherland Ho CM1 ....205 A4
Sutor Cl CM8 ....176 E1
Sutton Mead CM2 ....206 A4
Sutton Park Ave CO3 .....135 A3
Swains Ct CO10 ....32 E5
Swallow Cl Harwich CO12 ..90 E1
Layer-de-l-H CO2 ....162 A5
Swallow Field CO6 ....105 B6
Swallow Path CM2 ....216 B5
Swallow Rd IP2 ....16 C3
Swallow Wlk CO9 ....76 F1
Swallow's Row CO7 ....167 B8
Swallow's Row CO7 ....140 B1
Swallowdale
Clacton-on-S CO15 ....188 F6
Colchester CO2 ....136 C3
Swallowtail Cl IP8 ....36 E8
Swan Chase CO9 ....75 E8
Swan Cl Colchester CO4 ..136 E5
Hatfield Peverel CM3 ......193 F4
Swan Cotts CM3 ....193 F4
Swan Ct
2 Bishop's Stortford
CM23 ....145 F6
Maldon CM9 ....210 B4
New Mistley CO11 ....87 A3
Sible Hedingham CO9 ....75 E8
Swan Dale CO15 ....188 F7
Swan Farm Mews IP8 ......16 A1
Swan Gr CO6 ....106 C5
Swan Hill IP8 ....16 A2
Swan La Haverhill CB9 ....9 A8
Long Melford CO10 ....15 C7
Swan Mdw CO7 ....58 C1
Swan Pas 18 CO1 ....135 F7
Swan Rd CO16 ....141 D5
Swan Side CM7 ....127 F3
Swan St Chappel CO6 .....106 C3
Kelvedon CO5 ....158 D3
Sible Hedingham CO9 ....51 E1
Swan Yd CO6 ....131 A2
Swanfield CO10 ....15 C7
Swans Pasture CM1 ....205 D6
Swanscomb Rd CO6 ....105 F5
Swansea Ave IP2 ....17 B1
Swatchway Cl IP3 ....38 B8
Swaynes CO7 ....58 C2
Sweden Cl CO12 ....90 F4
Swedish Est CO11 ....115 B5
Sweet Briar CM23 ....145 B6
Sweet Briar Rd CO3 ....134 C7
Sweet Mead CB10 ....22 E3
Swift Ave
Clacton-on-S CO15 ....203 F6
Swift Ave continued
Colchester CO3 ....134 C4
Swift Cl CM7 ....155 A7
Swinbourne Dr CM7 ....127 D3
Swinton Cl IP2 ....16 D1
Swiss Ave CM1 ....205 A4
Sworders Yd 3 CM23 ....145 F7
Sycamore Cl Ipswich IP8 ..16 C1
Takeley CM22 ....148 C7
Witham CM8 ....177 A5
Sycamore Gr CM7 ....127 E1
Sycamore Pl CO7 ....166 E8
Sycamore Rd
Colchester CO4 ....136 D8
Great Cornard CO10 ....34 B7
Heybridge CM9 ....210 C6
Sycamore Way
Brantham CO11 ....60 D1
Chelmsford CM2 ....216 C6
Clacton-on-S CO15 ....188 C3
Kirby Cross CO13 ....170 D6
Sycamores The CM23 ....146 B6
Sydner Cl CM2 ....217 A5
Sydney St
Brightlingsea CO7 ....185 F6
Colchester CO2 ....136 B1
Syers Field CM7 ....74 B2
Sylvan Cl CM2 ....216 B6
Symmons Cl CM77 ....126 F1
Syringa Ct 6 CO4 ....136 E7

T

Taber Pl CM8 ....177 B3
Tabor Ave CM7 ....127 E3
Tabor Cl CO7 ....185 F8
Tabor High Sch CM7 ......127 D4
Tabor Rd CO1 ....136 C7
Tabor's Hill CM2 ....216 F7
Tabors Ave CM2 ....216 F8
Tacket St IP4 ....17 D5
Tacon Ct IP11 ....221 C1
Tacon Rd IP11 ....221 C1
Tailors CM23 ....145 B5
Tailors Cl CM77 ....154 C8
Tait Mews CM9 ....210 A2
Takeley Pk CM22 ....148 C6
Takeley Prim Sch CM22 .148 C8
Talbot Ave CO15 ....203 F6
Talbot Rd
Little Clacton CO16 ....168 C4
Sudbury CO10 ....15 F2
Talbot St CO12 ....91 D5
Talbots IP11 ....221 D3
Talcott Rd CO2 ....136 A2
Talisman Cl CO5 ....179 D6
Talisman Wlk CO5 ....179 D6
Tall Trees CO4 ....109 E3
Tally Ho CO4 ....110 B4
Tally Ho Cnr CO7 ....58 D1
Talmash Gdns IP2 ....17 A4
Tamar Ave CM8 ....176 E2
Tamar Rise CM1 ....205 C6
Tamarisk Way
Clacton-on-S CO15 ....203 F6
Colchester CO4 ....136 E8
Tambour Cl CO6 ....132 C8
Tamdown Way CM7 ....127 C4
Tamworth Chase CO2 ....136 A2
Tan La CO16 ....168 F4
Tangerine Cl CO4 ....136 D6
Tanner Cl CO16 ....188 B3
Tanners Mdw CM7 ....128 D2
Tanners View IP1 ....16 F7
Tanners Way CB10 ....22 E1
Tanyard The CM6 ....70 A2
Tapestry Ct CO6 ....105 B6
Tapestry Wlk CM7 ....128 D2
Tapley Rd CM1 ....204 F7
Tapsworth Cl CO16 ....188 D5
Tapwoods CO3 ....135 A7
Tara Cl CO4 ....110 D1
Tarragon Cl CO5 ....179 C4
Tarragona Mews CO2 ....136 B4
Tasman Ct CM1 ....204 E5
Tasman Rd CB9 ....9 C7
Tasmania Rd IP4 ....18 D6
Tattersall Way CM1 ....215 E7
Tattingstone CE Prim Sch
IP9 ....61 D7
Taunton Rd
Chelmsford CM1 ....205 E5
Felixstowe IP11 ....221 D6
Tavern St IP1 ....17 C6
Taverners Wlk CM8 ....176 F4
Tavistock Rd CM1 ....205 E5
Tawell Mews CO5 ....179 D5
Tawney Cl IP9 ....35 A1
Tawneys Ride CO8 ....80 A8
Taylor Ave CM1 ....204 E5
Taylor Ct CO1 ....135 F7
Taylor Dr CO11 ....86 C4
Taylor's Rd CO5 ....163 F8
Taylors End Rd CM24 ....120 E1
Tayspill Ct CO2 ....135 B3
Teak Wlk CM8 ....177 A4
Teal Cl Colchester CO4 ...137 A8
Great Notley CM77 ....154 B5
Ipswich IP2 ....16 D3
Teal Way CO5 ....158 D2
Teapot Cnr IP7 ....57 E8
Tedder Cl CO2 ....136 A4
Tees Cl CM8 ....176 E2
Tees Rd CM1 ....205 C6
Teign Dr CM8 ....176 D2
Telford Pl CM1 ....205 D4
Telford Rd
Braintree CM7 ....128 A1
Clacton-on-S CO15 ....189 C8
Telford Way CO4 ....110 D6
Temperance Yd CO6 ......105 B6
Templar Rd CM7 ....128 D2
Templar's Ct CB9 ....8 E7
Templars Cl CM8 ....176 F4
Templars Jun Sch CM8 ..176 F5
Temple Cl CO13 ....171 A6
Temple Ct CO4 ....110 D2
Temple La CM8,CM77 ....156 C3
Temple Pattle CO11 ....86 C7
Temple Rd
Colchester CO2 ....135 A2
Ipswich IP3 ....18 C4
Temple Way CM9 ....209 F5
Templemead CM8 ....176 F3
Templewood Rd CO4 .....110 E1
Ten Acre App CM9 ....209 F5
Tenby Rd IP2 ....17 B1
Tendring Prim Sch
CO16 ....140 F6
Tendring Rd
Little Bentley CO7 ....140 A8
Tendring CO12 ....114 E2
Thorpe-le-S CO16 ....141 D4
Tendring Tech Coll
Thorpe-le-S CO16 ....142 A1
Walton-on-t-N CO13 ....171 A7
Tennyson Cl CM7 ....154 F8
Tennyson Rd
Chelmsford CM1 ....204 F5
Ipswich IP4 ....17 F5
Tenpenny Hill CO7 ....165 E5
Tenter Cl CM7 ....127 F5
Tenter Field CO7 ....58 D1
Tenterfield CM6 ....150 E8
Tenterfield Rd CM9 ....210 A2
Tenterfields CB11 ....42 F1
Tenth Ave CM24 ....120 C2
Terling CE Prim Sch
CM3 ....175 C3
Terling Cl CO2 ....136 A1
Terling Hall Rd CM3 .....193 C7
Terling Rd
Hatfield Peverel CM3 .....193 F6
Witham CM8 ....176 B3
Terminal Rd N CM22,
CM24 ....121 B4
Terminal Rd S CM22,
CM24 ....121 B4
Termitts Chase CM3 ......194 A7
Tern Cl Haverhill CB9 ....9 C7
Kelvedon CO5 ....158 D3
Tern Mews CO7 ....164 B8
Tern Rd IP2 ....16 E2
Terndale CO15 ....188 F6
Terra Cotta Pl CO10 ....2 E8
Terrace Hall Chase
CO6 ....109 D6
Terrace The
Cavendish CO10 ....1 D1
Felsted CM6 ....152 B5
Hatfield Peverel CM3 .....194 B5
Tew Cl CO5 ....179 D5
Tewkesbury Rd CO15 ....188 F4
Tey Rd Aldham CO6 ....106 E1
Coggeshall CO6 ....131 C4
Earls Colne CO6 ....105 D4
Tey Road Cl CO6 ....105 D6
Thackeray Cl CM7 ....155 A8
Thames Ave CM1 ....204 D4
Thames Cl CM7 ....128 D1
Thanet Rd IP4 ....18 B6
Thanet Wlk CO5 ....164 A8
Thatchers Dr CO7 ....137 F6
Thatchers The CM23 .....145 C5
Thatchers Way CM77 ....154 C8
Thaxted Prim Sch CM6 ...70 A2
Thaxted Rd Debden CB11 ..68 C6
Elder Street CB10 ....44 C4
Saffron Walden CB10 ....43 F8
Thaxted CB10 ....69 E8
Thaxted Wlk CO2 ....163 A8
The Bglws CM7 ....100 F5
Theberton Rd IP3 ....18 B1
Thelsford Wlk CO4 ....136 F7
Thetford Ct CM1 ....204 E1
Thetford Rd 1 IP1 ....17 A7
Thieves' Cnr CM1 ....204 A4
Third Ave
Chelmsford CM1 ....205 B5
Clacton-on-S CO15 ....189 C4
Frinton-on-S CO13 ....170 E4
Glemsford CO10 ....2 C5
Halstead CO9 ....77 B1
Harwich CO12 ....91 C3
Seawick CO16 ....203 B6
Stansted Mountfitchet
CM24 ....120 B2
Walton-on-t-N CO14 ......144 E3
Thirlmere Cl CM77 ....154 D7
Thirslet Dr CM9 ....210 C4
Thirtieth St CM24 ....120 F3
Thirtle Cl CO16 ....188 D6
Thistle Cl IP2 ....16 F4
Thistledown
Highwoods CO4 ....110 B3
Panfield CM7 ....127 A7
Thistley Cl CM9 ....211 E6
Thistley Cres CB11 ....66 E1
Thistley Green Rd CM7 .128 B7
Thomas Ave IP11 ....221 A8
Thomas Bell Rd CO6 .....105 A6
Thomas Cl CM2 ....205 F3
Thomas Heskin Ct 11
CM23 ....146 A7
Thomas Rd CO15 ....188 D4
Thomas St CO7 ....185 F6
Thomas Wakley Cl CO4 ..109 F5
Thomas Wlk CB11 ....20 F1
Thomas, Lord Audley Sch
CO2 ....135 F2
Thompson Ave CO3 ....134 F6
Thompson Rd IP1 ....16 F8
Thorington Cl CM77 ......154 C6
Thorley High CM23 ....145 F2
Thorley Hill CM23 ....145 F5
Thorley Hill Prim Sch
CM23 ....145 F4
Thorley La CM23 ....145 F3
Thorley La E CM23 ....145 D3
Thorley La W CM23 ......145 B4
Thorley Neighbourhood Ctr
CM23 ....145 D4
Thorley Park Rd CM23 ..145 F4
Thorn Gr CM23 ....146 B6
Thorn Grove Prim Sch
CM23 ....146 B6
Thorn Way IP11 ....221 C4
Thornbera Cl CM23 ....145 F4
Thornbera Gdns CM23 ..145 F4
Thornbera Rd CM23 ......145 F4
Thornberry Ave CO16 ....140 F1
Thornbury Rd CO15 ......188 F4
Thornbush La IP8 ....16 A8
Thorncroft CB10 ....22 F2
Thorndon Cl CO16 ....188 A4
Thorne Rd CO5 ....158 B2
Thorney Rd IP9 ....35 A1
Thornfield Ct CO2 ....136 D2
Thornfield Rd CM23 .....145 E8
Thornhayes Cl IP2 ....17 A3
Thornhill CM3 ....220 D1
Thornhill Cl CO13 ....170 F7
Thornley Dr IP4 ....18 C8
Thorns Way CO14 ....171 A8
Thornton Dr CO4 ....109 F2
Thornton Rd CM6 ....148 F7
Thornwood CO4 ....109 F4
Thornwood Cl CO5 ....201 D6
Thoroughfare 9 IP1 ....17 C6
Thoroughgood Rd CO15 .188 F3
Thorpe Cross CO16 ....169 D8
Thorpe Park La CO16 ....169 B7
Thorpe Rd
Beaumont CO16 ....141 B5
Clacton-on-S CO15 ....188 F7
Kirby Cross CO13 ....169 E7
Weeley CO16 ....141 A2
Thorpe Wlk CO4 ....136 F7
Thorpe-le-Soken Sta
CO16 ....168 F7
Thorrington Cross CO7 ..165 F5
Thorrington Rd
Great Bentley CO7 ....166 C8
Little Clacton CO16 ....168 C4
Thorrington Tide Mill*
CO7 ....165 E3
Thracian Cl CO2 ....135 A3
Threadneedle St
2 Chelmsford CM1 ....205 B2
Dedham CO7 ....84 F7
Three Acres CO16 ....187 A4
Three Crowns Rd CO4 ...109 E2
Three Gates Cl CO9 ......103 D8
Three Mile Hill CM4 .....215 C2
Thremhall Ave
Bishop's Stortford CM23 ..146 F8
Great Hallingbury CM22,
CM24 ....147 C8
Takeley CM24 ....121 A2
Threshelfords Bsns Pk
CO5 ....158 E3
Thresher Cl CM23 ....145 C5
Thresher Rise CM77 .....154 C8
Threshers End CO3 ....134 D5
Thrift Wood CM3 ....218 F1
Thriftwood Sch CM2 .....216 B3
Thrimley La CM23 ....118 C6
Thrushdale CO15 ....188 F6
Thurlow Pl 10 CB9 ....9 B8
Thurlston Cl CO4 ....110 D1
Thurstable Cl CM9 ....199 E2
Thurstable Rd CM9 ....199 D2
Thurstable Sch CO5 ......179 D6
Thurstable Way CM9 ....199 E2
Thurston Ct IP11 ....221 A3
Thyme Mews CM8 ....176 E3
Thyme Rd CO5 ....179 C5
Tiberius Cl
Colchester CO4 ....110 B6
Haverhill CB9 ....9 D7
Tiberius Gdns CM8 ....194 E8
Tideswell Cl CM7 ....128 D4
Tidings Hill CO9 ....103 E8
Tiffin Dr CO5 ....179 E5
Tilbury Rd
Great Yeldham CO9 ....30 A3
Ridgewell CO9 ....29 C7
Tildesley Cl CO13 ....170 A6
Tile Barn La CO11 ....85 C2
Tile House Rd CO6 ....109 B8
Tilkey Rd CO6 ....130 F3
Tillwicks Cl CO6 ....105 A7
Timber Hill CO1 ....136 C6
Timbers Cl CM77 ....154 B7
Timsons La CM2 ....205 E4
Tinabrook Cl IP2 ....16 E1
Tindal Sq 3 CM1 ....205 B2
Tindal St CM1 ....205 B2
Tindon End Rd CB10 ......46 D2

Tinker Ave CM7 73 C6
Tinker St CO12 116 D8
Tinnocks La CM0 213 B1
Tintagel Way CM9 220 E8
Tintern Cl IP2 17 A2
Tippett Cl CO4 136 E6
Tiptree Hall La CO5 179 B2
Tiptree Heath Prim Sch CO5 179 B3
Tiptree Mus* CO5 179 E4
Tiptree Rd
  Great Braxted CM8,CM9 196 B8
  Wickham Bishops CM8 195 F6
Titania Cl CO4 136 F7
Titchwell Dr IP3 38 D7
Tithe Cl CM8 176 E3
Titus Way CO4 110 B6
Tobruk Rd
  Chelmsford CM1 204 F6
  Colchester CO2 135 D3
Tofts Chase CM3 207 E5
Tofts Wlk [12] CM7 127 F3
Tog La
  Great Horkesley CO6 82 A3
  Little Horkesley CO6 81 F3
Toga Cl CO2 135 A2
Tokely Rd CO7 139 A3
Tokio Rd IP4 18 A6
Toll Gate Rd IP9 35 A1
Toller Rd IP3 17 E3
Tollesbury Rd CM9 198 F3
Tollesbury Sch CM9 199 D1
Tolleshunt D'arcy Prim Sch CM9 198 D4
Tolleshunt D'arcy Rd CM9 197 F3
Tollgate Ct CO3 134 C6
Tollgate Dr CO3 134 B6
Tollgate E CO3 134 C6
Tollgate Rd CO3 134 C5
Tollgate Rdbt CO3 134 C6
Tollgate W CO3 134 B5
Tolliday Cl CO7 137 A2
Tolly Cobbold Brewery Tours & Brewery* IP3 17 E3
Tolworth Rd IP4 18 A6
Tom Davies Ho [8] CM7 127 F2
Tom Tit La CM9 219 E7
Tom's La CM7 72 A6
Tomline Rd
  Felixstowe IP11 221 E4
  Ipswich IP3 18 A4
Tony Webb Cl CO4 110 C4
Tooley's Ct (Almshouses) [9] IP4 17 D5
Top Rd
  Tolleshunt Knights CM9 180 A2
  Wimbish CB10 45 E3
  Woodham Walter CM9 208 D2
Toppesfield Rd CO9 50 F8
Torquay Rd CM1 205 D5
Torrington Cl CM1 205 E5
Tortoiseshell Cl IP8 36 E8
Tortoiseshell Way CM7 127 E1
Tortosa Cl CO2 136 B4
Torver Cl CM77 154 C6
Tot La CM23,CM24 119 D4
Totham Hill Gn CM9 196 E6
Totlands Dr CO15 189 A7
Totnes Wlk CM1 205 E6
Totteridge Cl CO16 188 D5
Toucan Way CO15 188 F6
Toulmin Rd CM3 194 A4
Tovell's Rd IP4 17 F6
Tower Ave CM1 204 F4
Tower Ct [4] CB9 8 E7
Tower Cut CO7 185 F6
Tower Cvn Pk CO15 203 D6
Tower Est CO16 185 E4
Tower Hill Redoubt Fort* CO12 91 E5
Tower Mill Rd IP1 16 F7
Tower Ramparts IP1 17 C6
Tower Ramparts Ctr [8] IP1 17 C6
Tower Rd
  Clacton-on-S CO15 188 E1
  Felixstowe IP11 221 D3
  Wivenhoe CO7 137 B2
Tower St
  Brightlingsea CO7 185 F6
  Ipswich IP1 17 C6
Towers Rd CM9 210 C5
Towers The CO15 189 A2
Town Croft CM1 205 A5
Town End Field CM8 194 F8
Town St CM6 70 A2
Townfield St CM1 205 B3
Townsend CM2 206 B5
Townsend Rd CO5 179 C7
Towse Cl CO16 188 C5
Traddles Ct CM1 204 F6
Trafalgar Cl IP4 17 F6
Trafalgar Cotts CO12 90 F3
Trafalgar Ct CM7 128 B4
Trafalgar Rd
  Clacton-on-S CO15 188 E1
  Colchester CO3 134 E6
Trafalgar Way CM7 128 B4
Trajan Cl CO4 110 B6
Tredgetts CB10 6 B1
Tree Cl CO15 188 F7
Treetops IP11 221 C6
Treetops Ct CO4 109 F5
Trefoil Cl IP2 16 F4
Trefoil Ct [4] CB9 8 F7
Trelawn CM3 206 E8
Trenchard Cres CM1 205 D8
Trenchard Lodge CM1 205 D7
Trent Rd Chelmsford CM1 204 D5
  Ipswich IP3 17 F2
  Witham CM8 176 E2
Trevose IP11 221 F4
Trews Gdns CO5 158 C3
Triangle Garage CM9 210 B5
Triangle Sh Ctr CO14 170 F7
Trickett Ct CO7 137 B1
Trimley Cl CO16 188 B4
Trimley St Mary Prim Sch IP11 221 A7
Trimley Sta IP11 221 A7
Trinity Ave IP11 221 A4
Trinity Cl
  Bishop's Stortford CM23 145 F6
  Chelmsford CM2 205 D3
  Manningtree CO11 86 D3
  Rushmere St A IP5 18 F7
  West Mersea CO5 201 C7
  Wivenhoe CO7 137 C1
Trinity Ct CO9 76 E2
Trinity Farm Ct [12] CO11 86 D4
Trinity Mews CO5 201 C7
Trinity Rd
  Chelmsford CM2 205 D2
  Halstead CO9 76 D1
  Manningtree CO11 86 D3
Trinity Road Prim Sch CM2 205 D2
Trinity Sq [19] CO1 135 F7
Trinity St
  Bishop's Stortford CM23 145 F6
  Colchester CO1 135 F7
  Halstead CO9 76 D2
  Ipswich IP3 17 E4
Trinity Terr [3] CO9 76 D1
Trinity Way CM23 145 F6
Trinovantian Way CM7 128 A2
Triumph Ave CO15 203 E7
Triumph Cl CO4 136 E5
Troon Gdns IP4 18 B8
Trotters Field CM7 128 B3
Trotwood Cl CM1 204 E7
Troys Chase CM3 175 C6
Trunette Rd CO15 188 C3
Trusses Rd CM0 214 F3
Truswell Terr CO11 86 D7
Tryon Ct [6] CO9 76 D1
Tucker Dr CM8 176 F1
Tucker's Row [4] CM23 145 F6
Tuddenham Ave IP4 17 E7
Tuddenham Rd IP4 17 E8
Tudor CE Prim Sch CO10 15 F1
Tudor Cl
  Brightlingsea CO7 185 E8
  Jaywick CO15 188 A1
  Sudbury CO10 15 E1
  Walton-on-t-N CO14 144 D2
  Witham CM8 176 F1
Tudor Ct CO5 201 C7
Tudor Gn
  Clacton-on-S CO15 203 F8
  Jaywick CO15 187 F1
  Sudbury CO10 15 E2
Tudor Par CO15 203 G8
Tudor Pl [3] IP4 17 D6
Tudor Rd CO10 15 E1
Tudor Rose Cl CO3 134 C7
Tudor Works [12] IP4 17 C5
Tudwick Rd CM9 197 E6
Tufnell Way CO4 109 D2
Tufted Cl CM77 154 C5
Tugby Pl CM1 204 E6
Tukes Way CB11 43 F7
Tulip Cl CM1 205 E7
Tulip Way CO16 188 C4
Tulip Wlk CO4 136 D7
Tumulus Way CO2 135 A3
Tunstall Cl CO16 187 B5
Tupman Cl CM1 204 D6
Turin St IP2 17 C4
Turkentine Cl CO10 34 D5
Turkey Cock La CO3, CO6 133 E7
Turkey Oaks CM1 205 D3
Turner Ave CO11 86 B5
Turner Cl
  Black Notley CM77 155 B4
  Wivenhoe CO7 137 C1
Turner Rd Colchester CO4 109 F3
  Ipswich IP3 38 A8
Turners Cres CM23 145 C4
Turnpike Cl CO7 110 E8
Turnpike Pl CM7 128 A3
Turnstone End [3] CO4 136 F8
Turpins Ave CO15 189 C5
Turpins Cl CO15 189 C5
Turpins Ct CO15 189 C5
Turpins La
  Kirby Cross CO13 170 E7
  Kirby-le-S CO13 170 E8
Turret Green Ct [7] IP1 17 C5
Turret Ho CO15 189 A2
Turret La IP4 17 C5
Turstan Rd CM8 194 E8
Tusser Cl CM8 177 B7
Tusser Ct CM2 216 D8
Tusset Mews CO3 134 E7
Tweed Cl CO9 103 D8
Twelve Acres CM7 128 D3
Twenty First St CM24 120 F3
Twin Oaks CM2 206 A4
Twining Rd CO3 134 E4
Twitten La CM2 216 B2
Twitty Fee CM3 219 A8
Two Acres IP9 35 B2
Twyford Bsns Ctr The CM23 146 A4
Twyford Bury La CM22, CM23 146 A4
Twyford Cl CM23 146 A5
Twyford Gdns CM23 145 F4
Twyford Mill CM22 146 A3
Twyford Rd CM23 146 A5
Tyburn Hill CO6 106 A6
Tydeman Cl CO3 134 C4
Tye Cnr CO10 32 F2
Tye Gn CO10 2 B5
Tye Green Paddocks CO10 2 B5
Tye Green Rd CM22 120 D6
Tye La CO7 137 E3
Tye Rd CO7 137 E7
Tye Rd The CO7 167 B7
Tyed Croft CO3 134 D6
Tyehurst Cres CO4 110 C2
Tyler Ave CO16 188 B3
Tyler St Harwich CO12 90 F5
  Ipswich IP2 17 D4
Tylers CB10 23 E1
Tylers Cl CM2 216 B6
Tylers Gn IP11 221 A7
Tylneys Rd CO9 77 A3
Tymperley Ct [9] CO1 136 A6
Tymperleys Clock Mus* CO1 135 F7
Tyndale Dr CO15 188 A1
Tyndales La CM3 219 B5
Tyne Way CM1 204 D5
Tynedale Ct CO4 110 B4
Tynedale Sq CO4 110 B4
Tyrells Cl CM2 205 E4
Tyrells Way CM2 216 F7
Tyrrells Sch The CM1 205 E5
Tyssen Mead CM3 206 E8
Tythe Cl CM1 205 E8
Tythings The CO9 103 D8

U

Ufford Pl [8] CB9 9 B8
Ullswater Cl CM77 154 C6
Ulting Hall Rd CM9 208 E7
Ulting La CM9 208 E6
Ulting Rd
  Hatfield Peverel CM3 194 C2
  Ulting CM9 208 C8
Una Rd CO12 90 F5
Undercliff Rd W IP11 221 D3
Union Rd CO15 203 G8
Union St [11] IP4 17 D6
Unity Cl CO2 136 B4
Unity St IP3 17 E4
Univ of Essex CO4 136 F4
Upland Cres CO5 201 C7
Upland Dr CO4 110 C2
Upland Rd Ipswich IP4 18 A6
  West Mersea CO5 201 C7
Uplands Com Mid Sch CO10 15 F1
Uplands Cres CO10 15 E1
Uplands Ct CO15 188 D1
Uplands Dr CM1 205 D7
Uplands Rd
  Clacton-on-S CO15 188 D1
  Sudbury CO10 15 E1
Upper Acres CM8 176 F5
Upper Barclay St [12] IP4 17 D6
Upper Branston Rd CO15 188 D4
Upper Bridge Rd CM2 205 A1
Upper Brook St IP4 17 C5
Upper Cavendish St IP3 18 A5
Upper Chapel St CO9 76 E2
Upper Chase [2] CM2 216 A8
Upper East St CO10 33 F8
Upper Farm Rd CO10 29 D8
Upper Fenn Rd CO9 77 A2
Upper Fourth Ave CO13 170 F5
Upper High St [1] IP1 17 C6
Upper Holt St CO6 105 C6
Upper Mill Field CM6 150 E7
Upper Moors CM3 190 F7
Upper Orwell St IP4 17 D5
Upper Park Rd
  Brightlingsea CO7 185 E7
  Clacton-on-S CO15 188 D3
Upper Rd CO10 55 E8
Upper Roman Rd CM2 205 B1
Upper Second Ave CO13 170 E5
Upper Sq CB10 22 D2
Upper St Stanstead CO10 2 E8
  Stratford St M CO7 58 D1
Upper Third Ave CO13 170 E5
Upper Trinity Rd CO9 76 E1
Upperfield Dr IP11 221 F6
Upsheres CB11 43 F8
Upton Cl Ipswich IP4 17 E6
  West Bergholt CO6 108 D4
Urban Rd CM23 146 B7
Usterdale Rd CB10 22 E3
Uxbridge Cres IP3 18 C1

V

Valance Rd CB11 65 A7
Vale Cl CO4 110 E2
Vale End CM2 216 C3
Vale La IP9 61 B4
Valens Cl CO4 110 A6
Valenta Cl CO1 136 C6
Valentine Ct CM7 127 E4
Valentine Way CM8 156 D3
Valentines Dr CO4 110 C1
Valfreda Way CO7 137 B2
Valkyrie Cl CM9 199 D2
Valletta Cl CM1 205 A3
Valley Bridge CM1 205 B6
Valley Cl Brantham CO11 60 D1
  Colchester CO3 134 E3
Valley Cres CO6 108 E3
Valley Ct CM23 145 E5
Valley Farm Camping Ground CO15 189 B5
Valley La Tattingstone IP9 36 F4
  Wherstead IP9 37 A3
Valley Rd Braintree CM7 128 A4
  Clacton-on-S CO15 189 A5
  Colchester CO4 136 F4
  Harwich CO12 90 D2
  Ipswich IP1 17 B8
  Sudbury CO10 34 F8
  Wivenhoe CO7 164 C8
Valley View
  Finchingfield CM7 72 D6
  Stanstead CO10 2 F7
  West Bergholt CO6 108 E3
Valley View Cl CO4 110 A4
Valley Wlk
  Felixstowe IP11 221 D5
  Walton-on-t-N CO14 171 A7
Valleybridge Rd CO15 189 A5
Valleyview Dr IP4 18 F4
Vallis Way CO5 179 E5
Valonia Dr CO7 164 B8
Van Dieman's La CM2 216 C8
Van Dieman's Rd CM2 216 C8
Van Dyck Rd CO3 135 B5
Vandenbury Circ CM7 73 D6
Vandyck Rd IP3 38 A8
Vane Ct CM8 177 A5
Vane La CO6 131 A2
Vanessa Dr CO7 137 B1
Vange Pl [7] CB9 9 B8
Vanguard Way CM7 128 B4
Vanners Rd CB9 9 A7
Vansittart St CO12 91 D5
Varden Cl CM1 204 F6
Vaughan Cl CM77 126 F2
Vaughan St [9] IP2 17 C4
Vaux Ave CO12 90 F1
Vauxhall Ave CO15 203 E6
Vauxhall Dr CM7 127 D2
Vega Cl CO1 136 C6
Vellacotts CM1 205 B7
Venmore Dr CM6 150 E8
Ventnor Dr CO15 189 A8
Ventris Cl IP2 16 D5
Ventura Dr CO1 136 C6
Vermeer Ride CM1 205 F7
Vermont Cl CO15 189 A4
Vermont Cres IP4 17 D7
Vermont Rd IP4 17 D7
Vernon Ct CM23 145 E4
Vernon St IP2 17 C4
Vernon Way CM7 128 C5
Vernon's Cl CM22 94 F4
Vernons Rd CO6 106 E5
Veronica Wlk CO4 136 E7
Vesta Cl CO6 130 F2
Veyses End CO7 58 D2
Viaduct Rd CM1 205 A2
Viborg Gdns CM9 220 E8
Vica Cotts CM3 207 D5
Vicarage Ave CM8 155 F1
Vicarage Cl
  [18] Bishop's Stortford CM23 145 F7
  Panfield CM7 126 A8
  Tolleshunt D'arcy CM9 198 D4
Vicarage Cres CM3 194 B4
Vicarage Ct CO9 76 D2
Vicarage Field CO10 34 B5
Vicarage Gdns CO15 188 E2
Vicarage La Berden CM23 92 B8
  Great Baddow CM2 216 F5
  Thaxted CM6 70 A3
  Thorpe-le-S CO16 141 F2
  Ugley CM22 93 E5
  [2] Walton-on-t-N CO14 171 C8
  Wherstead IP9 37 B5
Vicarage Mdw CO9 76 E1
Vicarage Mead CM6 70 A3
Vicarage Mews CM2 216 F6
Vicarage Rd
  Belchamp St P CO10 13 A1
  Chelmsford CM2 216 B8
  Felixstowe IP11 221 C4
  Finchingfield CM7 72 D6
Vicars Orch CO10 32 E5
Vicerons Pl CM23 145 D4
Viceroy Cl CO2 136 B3
Victor Rd CO1 136 B6
Victoria Ave
  Kirby-le-S CO13 170 D8
  Saffron Walden CB11 22 E1
Victoria Chase CO1 135 E8
Victoria Cl CO7 137 B2
Victoria Cotts CM9 210 A5
Victoria Cres
  Chelmsford CM1 205 A3
  Lawford CO11 86 C4
Victoria Ct
  Braintree CM7 128 A2
  Clacton-on-S CO15 188 F3
  Colchester CO3 134 F7
  Harwich CO12 91 C3
Victoria Espl CO5 201 E5
Victoria Gdns
  Colchester CO4 110 B3
  Saffron Walden CB11 22 E1
Victoria Ho
  Felixstowe IP11 221 E4
  Ipswich IP2 17 B4
Victoria Pl
  Brightlingsea CO7 185 F6
  Colchester CO1 136 B6
Victoria Rd
  Chelmsford CM1 205 B3
  Clacton-on-S CO15 189 A3
  Colchester CO3 135 C6
  Felixstowe IP11 221 D3
  Haverhill CB9 8 D7
  Maldon CM9 210 A2
  Walton-on-t-N CO14 171 C8
  Weeley Heath CO16 168 B5
Victoria Rd S CM1 205 B2
Victoria St
  Braintree CM7 128 A2
  Felixstowe IP11 221 E4
  Harwich CO12 91 D4
  Ipswich IP1 17 A6
Victory Ct CO3 134 E6
Victory Gdns CM7 128 B4
Victory Rd
  Clacton-on-S CO15 188 D3
  Ipswich IP4 18 A7
  West Mersea CO5 201 A6
Vienna Cl CO12 91 A1
Viking Rd CM9 209 E1
Viking Way CO15 189 F6
Villa Ct [4] CO1 136 C6
Villa Ho CO3 134 C6
Villa Rd CO3 134 C5
Village Cl
  Kirby Cross CO13 170 D7
  Little Clacton CO16 168 D1
Village Gate CM2 206 A2
Village Sq CM2 206 A3
Village Way CO13 170 D6
Villiers Pl CM3 206 E8
Villiers-Sur-Marne Ave CM23 145 D4
Vince Cl CO5 201 C6
Vincent Cl IP1 16 E8
Vine Dr CO7 137 C3
Vine Farm Rd CO7 137 C3
Vine Par CO7 137 C3
Vine Rd CO5 179 C6
Vine St CM7 72 B2
Vine Wlk IP9 35 A1
Vinesse Rd CO6 81 D3
Vineway The CO12 91 B4
Vineyard Gate [4] CO2 135 F6
Vineyard St CO2 135 F6
Vineyards The*
  Braintree CM7 153 D6
  Great Baddow CM2 216 F7
Vinnicombe Ct [3] IP2 16 E1
Vint Cres CO3 135 C6
Viola Wlk CO4 136 E7
Violet Cl Chelmsford CM1 205 E7
  Ipswich IP2 16 F4
Virgil Rd CM8 176 F5
Virginia Cl CO15 188 A1
Virley Cl CM9 210 D4
Viscount Dr CO4 110 C5
Visitor Ctr & Country Wlk* CB9 9 C6
Vista Ave CO13 143 D1
Vista Rd CO15 189 A3
Vitllus Cl CO4 110 B6
Vivian Ct CO14 171 C8
Volwycke Ave CM9 220 F8

W

Waddesdon Rd CO12 91 D4
Wade Rd CO15 189 B8
Wade Reach CO14 171 B8
Wadgate Rd IP11 221 C4
Wadhurst Rd IP3 18 D3
Wadley Cl CO5 179 E5
Wagtail Dr CM9 210 C5
Wagtail Pl CO5 158 C2
Wainsfield Villas CM6 70 B2
Wainwright Ave CM77 154 D8
Wainwright St CM23 145 C5
Wakefield Cl
  Colchester CO1 136 A8
  Great Chesterford CB10 3 D3
Wakelin Way CM8 177 B2
Wakes St CO6 106 C6
Wakeshall La C10 30 C8
Waldeck Ct CB11 43 D7
Waldegrave Cl CO11 86 B3
Waldegrave Rd CO11 86 C3
Waldegrave Way CO11 86 B3
Waldegraves Farm Cvn Site CO5 201 G6
Waldegraves La CO5 201 G7
Waldegraves The CO8 79 F8
Walden Ave CB10 44 E2
Walden Castle* CB10 22 D2
Walden Cl CM9 196 A4
Walden Ho CO13 170 F4
Walden House Rd CM8, CM9 196 A4
Walden Pl CB10 22 D2
Walden Rd Ashdon CB10 23 E6
  Great Chesterford CB10 3 E3
  Hadstock CB1 5 B6
  Littlebury CB10 21 F4
  Radwinter CB10 45 D7
  Sewards End CB10 23 D1

Walden Rd *continued*
Thaxted CM6 ...69 F5
Wendens Ambo CB11 ...42 F6
Wendons Ambo CB11 ...43 A6
Walden Way CO13 ...171 A6
Waldgrooms CM6 ...123 C1
Waldingfield Rd CO10 ...33 F8
Walford Cl CO6 ...131 A2
Walford Pl CM2 ...205 F2
Walford Way CO6 ...131 A2
Walk The
Eight Ash G CO6 ...134 A8
Felixstowe IP11 ...221 C5
10 Ipswich IP1 ...17 C6
Walker Cl IP3 ...18 C5
Walkers Cl CM1 ...205 D7
Wall Ct 6 CM7 ...127 F1
Wall La CO11 ...88 D4
Wall St CO16 ...202 D6
Wallace Binder Cl CM9 ...209 F1
Wallace Cres CM2 ...216 D8
Wallace La CM3 ...172 B7
Wallace Rd
Colchester CO4 ...109 E3
Ipswich IP1 ...16 E8
Wallace's La CM3 ...192 F4
Wallasea Gdns CM1 ...205 F5
Waller's Gr IP2 ...16 F4
Wallflower Ct 11 CM1 ...205 F6
Wallis Ct CO3 ...134 E3
Walls The CO11 ...86 E4
Walnut Dr
Bishop's Stortford CM23 ...145 D3
Witham CM8 ...177 A4
Walnut Gr CM7 ...127 E2
Walnut Tree Cotts CM3 ...190 E5
Walnut Tree La
Harkstead IP9 ...63 B2
Sudbury CO10 ...33 D7
Walnut Tree Way
Colchester CO2 ...135 B3
Tiptree CO5 ...179 C7
Walnut Way
Brightlingsea CO7 ...185 E7
Clacton-on-S CO15 ...188 C2
Walnuttree Hospl CO10 ...33 D7
Walsingham Cl CO10 ...34 C5
Walsingham Ct IP2 ...37 A8
Walsingham Rd CO2 ...135 F6
Walter Porter Ct CO4 ...110 D1
Walter Radcliffe Way
CO7 ...164 C7
Walter Way CM8 ...156 D4
Walters Cl CM2 ...216 C3
Walters Yd 6 CO1 ...135 F7
Waltham Cl IP2 ...17 A2
Waltham Glen CM2 ...216 C7
Waltham Rd
Boreham CM3 ...193 A3
Terling CM3 ...175 A2
Waltham Way CO13 ...171 A5
Walton Ave IP11 ...221 A2
Walton Ct Colchester CO4 ...136 F4
Felixstowe IP11 ...221 D6
Walton Hall La CM3 ...220 B1
Walton Ho 4 Ipswich IP1 ...17 A6
Walton-on-t-N CO14 ...171 B8
Walton Maritme Mus*
CO14 ...144 D1
Walton Rd
Clacton-on-S CO15 ...189 A3
Frinton-on-S CO13 ...170 F6
Kirby-le-S CO13 ...170 E8
Thorpe-le-S CO13, CO16 ...142 D2
Walton-on-t-N CO13,CO14 ...171 B7
Walton-On-Naze Sta
CO14 ...171 C7
Walton-on-the-Naze Prim
Sch CO14 ...144 D1
Wantz Chase CM9 ...210 A2
Wantz Haven CM9 ...210 A2
Wantz Rd CM9 ...210 A2
Wapping La CO7 ...165 B2
Warburton Ave CO9 ...75 D8
Ward Cres CM23 ...145 E6
Ward Path CM2 ...206 B4
Ward Rd IP8 ...16 B2
Warde Chase CO14 ...171 B8
Warder Cl CM6 ...123 E1
Wardle Way CM1 ...204 E7
Wardley Cl IP2 ...16 D1
Wards Croft CB11 ...43 D7
Wareham Ave IP3 ...18 D3
Warehouse Rd CM6 ...124 F4
Warehouse Villas CM6 ...125 A4
Wargrave Rd CO15 ...188 D4
Warham Rd CO12 ...90 F1
Warley Cl CM7 ...128 C3
Warley Way CO13 ...171 B6
Warner Cl CM77 ...126 F1
Warner Dr CM7 ...127 D4
Warner Way CO10 ...34 A8
Warners CM6 ...150 D8
Warnham Cl CO16 ...188 B6
Warren Cl
Broomfield CM1 ...191 B3
Takeley CM22 ...148 D7
Warren Ct 12 CB9 ...8 E7
Warren Heath Ave IP3 ...18 D2
Warren Heath Rd IP3 ...18 D2
Warren La CO3 ...134 C2
Warren Lingley Way
CO5 ...179 E6
Warren Rd
Braintree CM7 ...128 C2
Halstead CO9 ...76 D1
Warrens The
Kirby Cross CO13 ...170 E6
Warrens The *continued*
Wickham Bishops CM8 ...195 F5
Warrenside CM7 ...155 A8
Warrington Rd IP1 ...17 B7
Warwick Bailey Cl CO4 ...109 D2
Warwick Cl
Braintree CM7 ...128 B4
Little Easton CM6 ...122 F5
Maldon CM9 ...210 A1
Warwick Cres
Clacton-on-S CO15 ...188 E3
Maldon CM9 ...210 A1
Warwick Ct 2 CB9 ...8 E8
Warwick Dr CM9 ...210 A1
Warwick Rd
Bishop's Stortford CM23 ...146 B6
Clacton-on-S CO15 ...188 E3
Ipswich IP4 ...17 E6
Takeley CM6 ...148 E7
Warwick Sq CM1 ...204 F4
Wash Cnr Aldham CO6 ...107 C3
Ramsey CO12 ...89 E1
Wash La
Clacton-on-S CO15 ...188 D1
Goldhanger CM9 ...211 B7
Washall Dr CM77 ...154 D8
Washford Gdns CO15 ...188 D2
Washington Cl CM9 ...209 E1
Washington Ct
Colchester CO3 ...134 E5
Maldon CM9 ...209 E1
Washington Rd
Harwich CO12 ...91 A2
Maldon CM9 ...209 F1
Wasses Cnr CO16 ...141 D5
Wat Tyler Wlk 1 CO1 ...135 F7
Watch House Rd CM6 ...124 F5
Watchouse Rd CM2 ...216 C3
Water Hall La CM7 ...100 F6
Water La
Bishop's Stortford CM23 ...145 F8
Bures CO8 ...55 E1
Cavendish CO10 ...1 D2
Colchester CO3 ...135 D8
Debden CB11 ...44 B1
Great Easton CM6 ...122 C7
Helions Bumpstead CB9 ...26 D7
Little Horkesley CO6 ...81 F8
Newport CB11 ...43 A1
Pebmarsh CO9 ...78 A7
Radwinter CB10 ...45 E8
Shalford CM7 ...100 F3
Stansted Mountfitchet
CM24 ...119 E6
Steeple Bumpstead CB9 ...27 B6
Stisted CM7 ...129 C5
Stoke-by-N CO6 ...56 E8
Sturmer CB9 ...9 F5
Waterfront Terr CO14 ...144 D1
Waterglade Ret Pk
CO15 ...188 E2
Waterhouse La
Ardleigh CO7 ...112 B5
Chelmsford CM1 ...204 F1
Waterhouse St CM1 ...204 F1
Waterloo La CM1 ...205 C2
Waterloo Rd IP1 ...17 A7
Watermill Rd CO5 ...158 E4
Waterside
Brightlingsea CO7 ...185 F5
Stansted Mountfitchet
CM24 ...119 E6
Waterside Bsns Pk CM8 ...177 B4
Waterside Rd CM0 ...214 F3
Waterson Vale CM2 ...216 C8
Waterville Mews CO2 ...136 B3
Waterwick Hill CB11 ...40 B1
Waterworks Cl CO2 ...161 E3
Waterworks Cotts CO5 ...179 A6
Waterworks Dr CO16 ...188 B5
Waterworks Rd CM9 ...199 D2
Waterworks St 6 IP4 ...17 D5
Watery La
Coggeshall CO6 ...130 A1
Great Dunmow CM6 ...150 A2
Manuden CM23 ...92 C1
Watling La CM6 ...69 F3
Watling St CM6 ...70 A3
Watsham Pl CO7 ...137 C2
Watson Rd CO15 ...188 E3
Watson's Cl CB10 ...47 B4
Watts Cl CM6 ...151 B4
Watts Ct IP4 ...17 D5
Watts Rd CO2 ...135 B2
Watts Yd CM23 ...93 A2
Wavell Ave CO2 ...135 C4
Wavell Cl CM1 ...205 D8
Waveney Dr CM1 ...205 C6
Waveney Rd
Felixstowe IP11 ...221 C3
Ipswich IP1 ...16 E8
Waveney Terr CB9 ...9 A7
Waverley Bridge Ct
CM9 ...210 B5
Wavring Ave CO13 ...170 E7
Way Bank La CO10 ...10 E7
Wayback The CB10 ...22 E2
Wayletts Dr CM23 ...146 B7
Wayside CM3 ...218 E8
Waytemore Castle*
CM23 ...146 A7
Waytemore Rd CM23 ...145 E6
Wear Dr CM1 ...205 D6
Weathervane Cotts CM7 ...72 B1
Weaver Cl IP1 ...16 D8
Weaver St CM23 ...145 C4
Weaverhead Cl CM6 ...70 A3
Weaverhead La CM6 ...70 A3
Weavers Cl
Braintree CM7 ...127 F3
Colchester CO3 ...134 F5
Weavers Ct Halstead CO9 ...76 E1
6 Sudbury CO10 ...33 E7
Weavers Dr CO10 ...2 B4
Weavers Gn CO6 ...107 D6
Weavers La CO10 ...33 E7
Weavers Row CO9 ...76 F1
Weavers Terr 7 CO10 ...33 E7
Weaversfield CM8 ...156 C5
Webb Cl CM2 ...206 B3
Webb St IP2 ...17 C3
Webster Cl CO9 ...75 D8
Weddell Rd CB9 ...9 C6
Wedgewood Dr CO4 ...109 E2
Wedow Rd CM6 ...70 A3
Weeley By-Pass Rd
CO16 ...140 E1
Weeley Rd
Great Bentley CO7 ...166 F8
Great Bentley,Aingers Green
CO7 ...166 F5
Little Clacton CO16 ...168 C4
Weeley Sta CO16 ...167 F8
Weggs Willow CO4 ...136 C7
Weighbridge Ct CB11 ...43 D8
Weight Rd CM2 ...205 C2
Weir La CO2,CO5 ...163 C7
Welbeck Cl IP11 ...221 A7
Welhams Way CO11 ...86 D8
Well Field Halstead CO9 ...103 F8
Writtle CM1 ...204 A1
Well La Clare CO10 ...12 B7
Danbury CM3 ...218 C7
Easthorpe CO5 ...160 A6
Galleywood CM2 ...216 B2
Well Side CO6 ...132 E3
Well St CO7 ...185 E7
Well Terr CM9 ...210 B5
Well's St 3 CM1 ...205 A3
Well-Green Cl CB11 ...43 E7
Welland Ave CM1 ...204 C5
Wellands CM8 ...195 E5
Wellands Cl CM8 ...195 D5
Weller Gr CM1 ...204 E7
Wellesley Ho 7 CO3 ...135 E6
Wellesley Rd
Clacton-on-S CO15 ...188 E4
Colchester CO3 ...135 E6
Ipswich IP4 ...17 F5
Wellfield Way CO13 ...170 D7
Wellington Cl
Braintree CM7 ...128 C4
Chelmsford CM1 ...204 D5
Wellington Ct 5 IP1 ...17 A7
Wellington Rd
Harwich CO12 ...91 E6
Maldon CM9 ...209 F2
Wellington St
Brightlingsea CO7 ...185 F6
4 Colchester CO2 ...135 E6
Ipswich IP1 ...17 A7
Wellington Terr 7 CB9 ...8 E7
Wellmeads CM2 ...216 B8
Wells Cl 4 IP4 ...17 E6
Wells Ct Chelmsford CM1 ...205 D5
Great Dunmow CM6 ...123 C1
Wells Hall Com Prim Sch
CO10 ...34 B4
Wells Hall Rd CO10 ...34 C4
Wells Mead CB11 ...67 D4
Wells Rd CO1 ...136 B8
Wellum Cl 8 CB9 ...8 E7
Welshwood Park Rd
CO4 ...110 F2
Wenden Rd CB11 ...43 B7
Wendy Cl IP9 ...63 F7
Wenham La CO7 ...59 D6
Wenham Rd IP8 ...35 C7
Wenlock Rd CO16 ...167 F6
Wentford Ct CB9 ...8 C8
Wents Cl CO7 ...139 E1
Wentworth Cl CM3 ...194 B4
Wentworth Cres CM7 ...127 F5
Wentworth Dr
Bishop's Stortford CM23 ...145 D6
Ipswich IP8 ...16 C2
Wentworth Mdws CM9 ...209 F2
Wentworth Prim Sch
CM9 ...209 F1
Wentworth Terr 5 CB9 ...8 E8
Wesel Ave IP11 ...221 B3
Wesley Ave CO4 ...136 C8
Wesley End Rd CO9 ...28 D4
Wesley Way IP1 ...16 F8
West Acre Ct CO3 ...135 B7
West Area IP1 ...16 C7
West Ave
Chelmsford CM1 ...204 F5
Clacton-on-S CO15 ...188 E2
West Bank Ferry Terminal
IP2 ...17 C2
West Belvedere CM3 ...218 F7
West Bowers Rd CM9 ...208 C4
West Chase CM9 ...209 F3
West Dock Rd CO12 ...90 E5
West Dr CM7 ...73 C3
West End La CO12 ...91 B1
West End Rd Ipswich IP1 ...17 A5
Tiptree CO5 ...179 A3
West Fields CB11 ...43 E8
West Green Cotts CO11 ...86 A7
West Hanningfield Rd
CM2 ...217 A3
West Lawn
Galleywood CM2 ...216 C2
Ipswich IP4 ...18 C8
West Lodge Rd CO3 ...135 D6
West Mill Gn IP9 ...60 E6
West Quay CO7 ...164 B7
West Rd
Bishop's Stortford CM23 ...145 E6
Clacton-on-S CO15 ...203 H8
Halstead CO9 ...76 E1
Ipswich IP3 ...38 E8
Saffron Walden CB11 ...43 D8
Stansted Mountfitchet
CM24 ...119 E6
West Sq CM9 ...209 F3
West St Coggeshall CO6 ...130 E1
Colchester CO2 ...135 E6
Harwich CO12 ...91 D6
Rowhedge CO5 ...163 F8
Tollesbury CM9 ...199 C1
Walton-on-t-N CO14 ...171 C8
Wivenhoe CO7 ...164 B8
West Station Ind Est
CM9 ...209 E1
West Station Rd CM9 ...209 E1
West Stockwell St CO1 ...135 F7
West View CM22 ...148 C8
West View Cl CO4 ...110 B3
West Wood Hill CO4 ...109 B3
West Yd CO9 ...103 E8
Westbourne Ct 1 CB9 ...9 A8
Westbourne Gr CM2 ...216 D7
Westbourne Rd IP1 ...16 F8
Westbury Cl CO6 ...133 D5
Westbury Rd
Great Holland CO13 ...170 A5
Ipswich IP4 ...18 B8
Westcliff Ct CO15 ...188 E1
Westcott Cl CO16 ...188 D6
Westerdale CM1 ...205 D7
Westerfield Ct IP4 ...17 D7
Westerfield Rd IP4 ...17 D8
Westergreen Mdw CM7 ...127 E1
Westerings
Bicknacre CM3 ...218 F2
Purleigh CM3 ...220 D1
Westerings The CM2 ...216 F5
Westerlings The CM77 ...155 E6
Western Cl
Rushmere St A IP4 ...18 F4
Silver End CM8 ...156 E3
Western Ho CO5 ...158 C2
Western La CM8 ...156 E3
Western Prom
Brightlingsea CO7 ...185 D5
Point Clear B CO16 ...185 E4
Western Rd
Brightlingsea CO7 ...185 E6
Silver End CM8 ...156 F3
Western's End CO11 ...86 D8
Westfield CO10 ...12 A6
Westfield Ave CM1 ...205 A4
Westfield Cl CM23 ...145 E8
Westfield Dr CO6 ...131 A3
Westfield Prim Sch CB9 ...9 B7
Westfield Rd CM23 ...145 E8
Westgate St IP1 ...17 C6
Westholme Rd IP1 ...17 A8
Westlake Cres CO7 ...137 A2
Westlands Com Prim Sch
CM1 ...204 E2
Westleton Way IP11 ...221 B5
Westley La CB10 ...22 D5
Westminster Cl IP4 ...18 B5
Westminster Ct
Clacton-on-S CO15 ...189 B3
Colchester CO2 ...136 C4
Westminster Gdns CM7 ...128 B4
Westmorland Cl CO11 ...87 B3
Weston Rd CO2 ...136 B4
Westridge Rd CO15 ...189 A6
Westropps CO10 ...15 C5
Westside Ctr CO3 ...134 A5
Westway Chelmsford CM1 ...215 E8
Colchester CO1, CO3 ...135 E8
Westwood Ave IP1 ...17 A8
Westwood Ct IP1 ...17 A7
Westwood Dr CO5 ...201 E6
Wet La CO4 ...82 E5
Wetherfield CM24 ...119 D7
Wethersfield CE Prim Sch
CM7 ...73 C3
Wethersfield Rd
Blackheath CO2 ...163 A8
Shalford CM7 ...100 E8
Sible Hedingham CO9 ...51 C1
Wetzlar Ct CO2 ...136 B4
Weymouth Cl CO15 ...203 J8
Weymouth Rd
Chelmsford CM1 ...205 E6
Ipswich IP4 ...17 F6
Whalebone Cnr CO4 ...83 F7
Whaley Rd CO4 ...136 C7
Wharf La CO8 ...79 F8
Wharf Pl CM23 ...146 A6
Wharf Rd
12 Bishop's Stortford
CM23 ...145 F6
Chelmsford CM2 ...205 C2
Heybridge Basin CM9 ...210 F4
Wharfe Cl CM8 ...176 E2
Wharton Dr CM1 ...206 A7
Wheat Croft CM23 ...145 E4
Wheater Ind Est CM8 ...177 B1
Wheatfield Rd CO3 ...134 D5
Wheatfield Way CM1 ...204 F3
Wheatlands Ardleigh CO7 ...111 E7
Elmstead CO7 ...137 F6
Wheatley Ave CM7 ...128 C3
Wheaton Rd CM8 ...177 B2
Wheatsheaf Cl CO11 ...88 D3
Wheatsheaf Ct 14 CO1 ...136 A6
Wheatsheaf La CO11 ...88 D3
Wheeler Cl CO4 ...136 E6
Wheeler's Hill CM3 ...191 D6
Wheelwrights Cl CM23 ...145 C4
Wheelwrights The IP11 ...221 A8
Wherry La 16 IP4 ...17 D5
Wherry Quay IP2 ...17 D5
Wherstead Rd
Ipswich,Maidenhall IP2 ...17 C2
Ipswich,Stoke IP2 ...17 C3
Whinchat Cl IP2 ...16 D3
Whinfield Ave CO12 ...90 F1
Whitbreads Farm La
CM3 ...173 D4
Whitby Rd IP4 ...17 F8
White Arch Pl CO4 ...83 B6
White Barns CM3 ...172 B6
White Bear CM24 ...119 E8
White Caville CB9 ...8 C8
White Cotts CM3 ...174 E5
White Court Prim Sch
CM77 ...154 C6
White Cross CO11 ...89 A2
White Elm Rd CM3 ...219 A2
White Elm St IP3 ...17 E4
White Hart Cotts CM2 ...206 A6
White Hart La
Chelmsford CM1 ...205 F8
West Bergholt CO6 ...108 E5
White Horse Ave CO9 ...103 D8
White Horse Hill IP9 ...36 D1
White Horse La
Maldon CM9 ...209 F2
Newport CB11 ...43 A1
Witham CM8 ...176 F3
White Horse Rd
Capel St M IP9 ...35 B1
East Bergholt CO7 ...59 E1
White Lodge Cres CO16 ...142 C1
White Mead CM1 ...191 B2
White Notley CE Prim Sch
CM8 ...155 F1
White Notley Sta CM8 ...155 F2
White Post Field CM6 ...150 E8
White St CM6 ...150 D8
Whitebeam Cl
Chelmsford CM2 ...215 F7
Colchester CO4 ...109 D5
Whiteditch La CB11 ...42 F2
Whitefriars Way CO3 ...135 A5
Whitegate Rd CO7 ...186 A6
Whitegates CM6 ...97 F4
Whitegates Cl CM77 ...154 C6
Whitehall Cl CO2 ...136 C4
Whitehall Ct CM8 ...177 A2
Whitehall Ind Est CO2 ...136 D4
Whitehall La
Bishop's Stortford CM23 ...118 F1
Thorpe-le-S CO16 ...141 C3
Whitehall Rd
Bishop's Stortford CM23 ...118 E1
Colchester CO2 ...136 D4
Whitehart Ct CO12 ...91 D6
Whitehead Cl CM1 ...215 B8
Whitehouse Cl CO4 ...83 D4
Whitehouse Cres CM2 ...216 D8
Whitehouse Hill CM9 ...199 A7
Whitehouse La
Belchamp St P CO10 ...13 B2
West Bergholt CO6 ...108 D3
Whitehouse Rd CM6 ...124 F5
Whites Field CO7 ...59 B3
Whites La CM3 ...173 E6
Whitesbridge La CM4 ...215 D1
Whiteshot Way CB10 ...22 F2
Whitethorn Cl CO4 ...136 D6
Whitethorn Gdns CM2 ...216 C7
Whitethorn Rd IP3 ...18 F1
Whiteways CB10 ...3 C2
Whiteways Ct CM8 ...176 E3
Whitewell Rd 10 CO2 ...135 F6
Whitfield Link CM2 ...216 D7
Whitland Cl IP2 ...37 A8
Whitlands CO10 ...2 B6
Whitlock Dr CO9 ...29 F1
Whitmore Cres CM2 ...206 B4
Whittaker Way CO5 ...201 B7
Whittington Way CM23 ...145 F3
Whittle Rd IP2 ...16 F6
Whitworth Cl IP2 ...16 D2
Whybrews 4 CO4 ...136 C8
Whyverne Cl CM1 ...205 E6
Wick La Ardleigh CO7 ...111 B8
Fingringhoe CO5 ...164 C3
Harwich CO12 ...91 B2
St Osyth CO7,CO16 ...167 C3
Wick Rd Colchester CO2 ...136 D2
Great Bentley CO7 ...167 B5
Langham CO4 ...83 F3
Thorington Street CO4,CO6 ...57 C2
Wicken Rd Arkesden CB11 ...41 F1
Newport CB11 ...66 F8
Wickfield Ash CM1 ...204 D6
Wickham Bishop Rd
CM3 ...194 D4
Wickham Cres
Braintree CM7 ...128 A2
Chelmsford CM1 ...204 F6
Wickham Hall La CM8 ...195 D3
Wickham Rd
Colchester CO3 ...135 D6
Witham CM8 ...194 F8
Wickham's Chase CM3 ...219 C2
Wickhambrook Ct IP11 ...221 A4

Wickhay Cotts CM3 207 D5
Wicklow Ave CM1 204 D6
Wicks Cl CM7 127 C4
Widford Chase CM2 215 F7
Widford Cl CM2 215 F7
Widford Gr CM2 215 F7
Widford Ind Est CM1 215 E8
Widford Lodge Sch CM2 215 F7
Widford Park Pl CM2 215 F7
Widford Rd CM2 215 F7
Widgeon Cl IP2 16 F3
Widgeon Pl CO5 158 C2
Widleybrook La
Wethersfield CM7 73 F3
Wethersfield,Blackmore End CM7 74 A2
Wigboro Wick La CO16 186 F2
Wigborough Rd
Layer-de-l-H CO2 161 E2
Peldon CO5 182 C5
Wigeon Cl CM77 154 C5
Wiggins View CM2 206 B4
Wigmore Cl IP2 16 F1
Wignall St CO11 85 F3
Wilberforce St IP1 17 A6
Wilbye Cl CO2 135 B4
Wilbye Ho CO3 135 A7
Wild Boar Field CM7 128 D3
Wilding Rd IP8 16 B1
Wilkin Ct CO3 135 A4
Wilkin Dr CO5 179 E5
Wilkinson Gr CM77 155 B5
Wilkinsons Mead CM2 206 A4
Will's Ayley La CB10 23 F2
Willets Pond CO7 59 E1
Willett Rd CO2 135 B3
Willetts Field CB10 47 A3
William Booth Way IP11 221 B5
William Boys Cl 1 CO4 136 D8
William Cl CO7 137 C4
William Dr CO15 188 D2
William Groom Ave CO12 91 A2
William Ho 7 IP4 17 D6
William Julian Courtauld Hospl CM7 127 E2
William Paul Housing Trust 3 IP2 17 C4
William Sparrow Ct CO7 137 C2
William St 3 IP1 17 C6
William's Wlk 8 CO1 135 F7
Williams Dr CM7 127 F4
Williams Rd CM1 191 B1
Williamson Ho 2 CO1 136 A6
Willingale Rd CM7 128 D4
Willingham Way CO4 136 E7
Willis Almshouses CM9 196 B3
Willoughby Ave CO5 201 D6
Willoughby Dr CM2 205 F2
Willoughby Rd IP2 17 B4
Willoughby's La CM7 128 C8
Willow Ave
Kirby Cross CO13 170 D6
Seawick CO16 203 B6
Willow Cl Ardleigh CO7 110 D6
Bishop's Stortford CM23 145 E8
Brightlingsea CO7 185 D6
Broomfield CM1 191 B1
Sudbury CO10 33 E6
Willow Cres CM3 194 A3
Willow Dene CO9 51 D2
Willow Hall La CO11 115 D8
Willow Mdws CO9 75 E8
Willow Pk CO6 133 E5
Willow Rd CM6 123 C1
Willow Rise CM8 177 A5
Willow Springs CM23 145 D8
Willow Tree Ct 1 CO4 136 E8
Willow Tree Way CO6 105 B6
Willow Way
Clacton-on-S CO15 203 G7
Halstead CO9 76 D1
Harwich CO12 90 F2
Willow Wlk
Heybridge CM9 210 C6
Tiptree CO5 179 C7
Weeley CO16 167 F8
Willowbank CM2 216 B3
Willows The
Boreham CM3 206 F8
Chelmsford CM1 205 A2
Colchester CO2 136 A3
Frinton-on-S CO13 170 F5
Great Chesterford CB10 3 D3
Wills Gn CO5 158 F6
Wilmington Rd CO4 110 C2
Wilmslow Dr IP2 16 C2
Wilshire Ave CM2 205 F3
Wilson Cl
Bishop's Stortford CM23 145 F5
Wivenhoe CO7 137 A2
Wilson Ct CO15 189 B8
Wilson Marriage Rd CO4 110 C1
Wilson Rd IP8 16 B1
Wilson's Ct CM9 210 B2
Wilson's La CO6 132 E3
Wilton Cl CM23 146 B7
Wimbish Prim Sch CB10 45 C4
Wimbish Wlk CB10 44 E2
Wimborne Ave IP3 18 E4
Wimbourne Gdns CO13 170 F7
Wimpole Cl IP5 18 F6
Wimpole Rd CO1 136 B5
Wimsey Ct CM8 177 A5
Wincelow Hall Rd CB10 25 E2
Winchelsea Dr CM2 216 E7
Winchelsea Pl CO7 185 F8
Winchester Cl CM23 145 D4
Winchester Ct CO13 171 A5
Winchester Rd
Colchester CO2 136 B5
Frinton-on-S CO13 171 A5
Winchester Way IP2 36 F8
Winckford Cl CM3 191 B6
Windermere Cl IP3 38 B8
Windermere Ct CO15 189 A3
Windermere Dr CM77 154 C6
Windermere Rd
Clacton-on-S CO15 189 C6
Great Notley CM77 154 C7
Sudbury CO10 34 A8
Windham Rd CO10 34 B8
Windhill CM23 145 E7
Windhill Old Rd CM23 145 E7
Winding Piece IP9 35 A1
Windley Tye CM1 204 E3
Windmill Cl Boxted CO4 82 F4
Great Dunmow CM6 123 E1
Ramsey CO12 89 F1
Stansted Mountfitchet CM24 119 D7
Windmill Ct
Clacton-on-S CO15 188 F5
Colchester CO4 109 E4
Copford CO6 133 D4
Windmill Fields CO6 130 F3
Windmill Gdns CM7 128 A8
Windmill Hill CB10,CB11 22 B3
Windmill Pk CO15 188 F5
Windmill Rd
Bradfield CO11 87 C1
Halstead CO9 76 D1
Windmill Row CO10 2 C5
Windmill View CO5 179 C6
Windmills CO6 106 C1
Windmills The CM1 191 B3
Windrush Dr CM1 205 C6
Windsor Ave CO15 188 D3
Windsor Cl CO2 136 A2
Windsor Ct
Brightlingsea CO7 185 F6
6 Colchester CO1 136 C6
Windsor Gdns
Bishop's Stortford CM23 145 C7
Braintree CM7 128 B4
Windsor Ho CO5 201 D7
Windsor Pl CO10 34 A7
Windsor Rd
Clacton-on-S CO15 188 D3
Felixstowe IP11 221 C3
Ipswich IP1 16 F7
West Mersea CO5 201 D7
Windsor Sch The CO15 189 B4
Windsor Terr CB9 8 E8
Windsor Way CM1 204 E1
Winfield Terr CO14 144 D2
Winfrith Rd IP3 18 D4
Wingate Cl CM7 127 E5
Wingfield St IP4 17 D5
Wingrove Ct CM1 205 A6
Winnock Rd CO1 136 A6
Winnock's Almshouses 4 CO1 136 A6
Winnocks 5 CO1 136 A6
Winsey Chase CM7 72 C6
Winsford Way CM2 206 C6
Winsgate Ho 6 IP1 17 A7
Winsley Rd CO1 136 B6
Winsley Sq CO1 136 B4
Winstanley Rd CB11 43 E7
Winston Ave
Colchester CO3 135 B4
Ipswich IP4 18 C8
Tiptree CO5 179 E5
Winston Cl
Braintree CM7 127 E6
Felixstowe IP11 221 B5
Winston Ct CO13 170 F4
Winston Way CO9 77 A3
Winstree Cl CO2 161 F5
Winstree Ct CO3 134 C4
Winstree Rd CO3 134 D5
Winter's Hill CO2 160 F1
Winter's Rd CO5 160 E1
Winterbournes CO14 171 A7
Wisdoms Gn CO6 131 B3
Wistaria Ct 3 CO4 136 E7
Wistaria Pl CO16 188 C5
Wisteria Lodge 7 CM1 205 F6
Wiston Rd CO6 81 D8
Witch Elm CO12 90 F2
Witch La CO6 131 B8
Witchtree La CB10 25 F3
Witham Lodge CM8 194 D7
Witham Rd
Black Notley CM77,CM8 155 B5
Cressing CM77 156 B3
Langford CM9 209 D7
Terling CM3 175 E2
Tolleshunt Major CM9 197 D5
Wickham Bishops CM8 195 E6
Witham Sta CM8 177 A3
Withersfield Rd CB9 8 F8
Withipoll St IP4 17 D6
Withrick Wlk CO16 187 A5
Witting Cl CO16 188 D5
Witton Wood Rd CO13 170 E5
Wivenhoe Cross CO7 137 C2
Wivenhoe Rd
Alresford CO7 165 B7
Wivenhoe Rd *continued*
Colchester CO7 111 C1
Wivenhoe Sta CO7 164 B8
Wix & Wrabness Prim Sch CO11 115 B5
Wix By-Pass CO11 115 C6
Wix Rd Beaumont CO16 141 E8
Bradfield CO11 87 E1
Great Oakley CO12 116 B3
Ramsey CO12 89 F1
Tendring CO11 114 F8
Wix CO11 115 C3
Woburn Ave
Bishop's Stortford CM23 145 C7
Kirby Cross CO13 170 D7
Woburn Ct CM2 205 A1
Wolfe Ave CO1,CO2 136 A5
Wolmers Hey CM3 190 F7
Wolseley Ave CO15 203 E6
Wolseley Rd CM2 205 A1
Wolsey Art Gall* IP4 17 D6
Wolsey Ct IP11 221 E3
Wolsey Gdns IP11 221 E3
Wolsey St 9 IP1 17 C5
Wolton Rd CO2 135 B2
Wolves Hall La CO16 114 F1
Wood Barn La CO11 85 D1
Wood Cnr
Fordham Heath CO6 107 F1
Maldon CM9 209 B2
Wood Dale CM2 216 E6
Wood End CB11 67 D3
Wood Field End CO2 162 A5
Wood Green Est CO7 166 F5
Wood La
Birchanger CM23 119 E2
Fordham Heath CO3 107 F1
Harkstead SG9 64 A6
Heybridge CM9 210 A5
Wood Rd CM9 210 B6
Wood St CM2 216 A7
Wood Way CM77 154 B6
Woodberry Way CO14 171 C7
Woodbridge Gr CO16 188 A4
Woodbridge Rd
Ipswich IP4 17 E6
Ipswich,California IP5 18 B7
Rushmere St A IP5 18 E7
Woodbridge Rd E IP4 18 D7
Woodcock Cl
Colchester CO4 136 E6
Haverhill CB9 9 C7
Woodcock Rd IP2 16 E2
Woodfield Cl
Stansted Mountfitchet CM24 119 E6
Walton-on-t-N CO14 171 A7
Woodfield Cotts CM9 210 C6
Woodfield Dr CO5 201 B7
Woodfield La IP9 61 E3
Woodfield Rd CM7 128 A3
Woodfield Terr CM24 119 E6
Woodfield Way CM3 194 A4
Woodfields CM24 119 E6
Woodford Cl CO15 188 F8
Woodgates IP11 221 B6
Woodgates Rd CO7 59 D5
Woodhall Bsns Pk CO10 15 F2
Woodhall Cl CO10 15 E1
Woodhall Com Prim Sch CO10 15 F2
Woodhall Gr CM23 145 D6
Woodhall Hill CM1 190 C2
Woodhall Par CM1 205 A7
Woodhall Rd
Chelmsford CM1 205 A7
Sudbury CO10 15 E1
Woodham Dr CM3 194 B4
Woodham Mortimer Rd CM9 219 E8
Woodham Walter CE Prim Sch CM9 208 D3
Woodhill Common Rd CM3 218 B5
Woodhill Rd
Chelmsford CM2 217 E6
Danbury CM3 218 B6
Woodhouse La CM3 191 A4
Woodhouse Sq 5 IP4 17 D5
Woodland Chase CO3 107 F1
Woodland Cl CM3 194 A5
Woodland Dr CO3 134 F5
Woodland Rd CM1 205 A4
Woodland Way
Gosfield CO9 102 E8
Wivenhoe CO7 137 B1
Woodlands
Bishop's Stortford CM23 146 C8
Braintree CM7 128 C3
Broomfield CM1 191 A4
Chelmondiston IP9 63 E7
Colchester CO4 110 F2
Great Oakley CO12 116 B2
Great Waltham CM1 190 F4
Ipswich IP8 16 C1
Jaywick CO16 188 A1
Woodlands Cl CO15 189 A8
Woodlands Park Dr CM6 123 B1
Woodlands Rd IP9 62 D7
Woodlands Rise CO16 140 F1
Woodlands Sch CM1 204 F6
Woodlands The CO7 185 E8
Woodlands Wlk CM6 123 B1
Woodlark Cl IP2 16 E1
Woodlyn Ct CO15 189 E6
Woodpecker Cl
Bishop's Stortford CM23 145 C6
Woodpecker Cl *continued*
2 Colchester CO4 136 F8
Woodpecker Rd IP2 16 D3
Woodroffe Cl CM2 206 A3
Woodrolfe Farm La CM9 199 E1
Woodrolfe Pk CM9 199 F2
Woodrolfe Rd CM9 199 E2
Woodrose Lodge 6 CM1 205 F6
Woodrow Way CO4 136 E7
Woodrows La CO16 188 B5
Woodrush End CO3 134 B6
Woodrush Rd IP3 18 E2
Woods Cl CB9 9 E5
Woods Rd CM3 172 B6
Woodside
Bishop's Stortford CM23 146 D8
Great Totham CM9 196 B3
Little Baddow CM3 207 F1
Walton-on-t-N CO14 171 B7
Woodside Cl CO4 110 E1
Woodside Gn CM22 146 F1
Woodside Way CM6 123 A1
Woodspring Cl 2 IP2 17 A2
Woodstock CO5 201 C7
Woodstock Pl CM2 216 F5
Woodview Cl CO4 110 D4
Woodview Cotts CO5 180 C8
Woodview Dr CM3 174 A7
Woodview Rd CM6 150 D8
Woodville Rd IP4 17 F5
Woodward Cl IP2 16 D5
Woodyards CM0 214 F3
Woollards Cl IP1 17 A6
Woollards Gdns CO10 15 C8
Woolner Rd CO16 188 D6
Woolnough Cl CB9 27 B6
Woolpack La CM7 127 F5
Woolpit Downs CO8 79 E8
Woolpit's Rd CM7 99 E1
Woolverstone Cl IP2 16 C1
Woolwich Rd CO16 188 C5
Worcester Cl CM7 128 A1
Worcester Cres CO7 165 B8
Worcester Ct
Clacton-on-S CO15 188 E1
Great Baddow CM2 217 A5
Worcester Ho CB9 9 B6
Worcester Rd
Colchester CO1 136 A8
Ipswich IP3 38 B8
Wordsworth Ct CM1 205 A5
Wordsworth Rd
Braintree CM7 127 F7
Colchester CO3 134 F6
Wordsworths Way CO16 188 A5
Workhouse Cnr CO12 116 C3
Workhouse Hill CO4 82 E4
Workhouse Rd CO6 81 C2
Worlds End La CO5 158 D3
Worrin Rd CM6 151 E6
Worsdell Way CO4 109 F2
Worsley Cl IP2 16 D2
Wortham Pl CB9 9 A8
Worthing Mews CO15 203 I8
Worthington Way CO3 134 F4
Wrabness Local Nature Reserve* CO11 88 D4
Wrabness Rd
Ramsey CO12 90 A2
Wrabness CO12 89 D3
Wrabness Sta CO11 89 A4
Wraglins The CM23 146 B5
Wratting Rd CB9 9 A8
Wren Ave IP2 16 D3
Wren Cl Colchester CO3 134 C4
Great Bentley CO7 139 D1
Wrenbrook Rd CM23 145 F6
Wrendale CO15 188 F6
Wright Ct 2 CM7 127 F3
Wright Mead CM2 206 B4
Wright Rd IP3 18 C2
Wright's Ave CM77 155 E6
Wright's Piece CM22 95 A6
Writtle Cl CO16 188 B4
Writtle Coll CM1 204 B3
Writtle Jun & Inf Schs CM1 215 A8
Writtle Rd CM1 215 E8
Wroxham Cl CO3 135 B6
Wroxham Rd IP3 17 F3
Wryneck Cl CO4 109 F3
Wulvesford CM8 194 D8
Wyatts La CO10 55 D8
Wych Elm CO2 136 A3
Wycke Hill CM9 220 D8
Wycke Hill Bsns Pk CM9 220 E8
Wycke La CM9 213 E8
Wycliffe Gr CO1 109 E1
Wye Rd IP3 18 A3
Wyedale Dr CO3 134 E5
Wykeham Rd CM1 204 B1
Wykes Bishop St IP3 17 E4
Wyncolls Rd CO4 110 D6
Wyndam Cl CO2 163 B8
Wyndham Cres CO15 189 A5
Wynterton Cl IP3 18 B1
Wynyard Rd CB10 22 E2
Wyseman Pl CO11 86 C7
Wyvern Ct CO7 137 B1
Wyvern Rd IP3 18 C1
Wyverne CM6 151 A5

Y

Yale Bsns Pk IP3 38 E8
Yale Mews CO4 110 B4
Yard The CM7 128 A2
Yardley Hall La CM6 69 D6
Yare Ave CM8 176 D2
Yarmouth Cl CO16 188 E6
Yarmouth Pl CB9 9 A8
Yarmouth Rd IP1 17 A6
Yarwood Rd CM2 205 E2
Yeldham Lock CM2 206 A2
Yeldham Pl CB9 9 A8
Yeldham Rd CO9 51 D3
Yeoman Rd IP11 221 B3
Yeomans Cl CM23 145 D6
Yerril Gdn CB9 8 E7
Yew Cl CM8 177 B5
Yew Ct IP2 17 B3
Yew Tree Cl
Colchester CO4 136 E8
Hatfield Peverel CM3 194 A5
Yew Tree Gdns CM2 216 C6
Yew Tree Pl CM23 145 F8
Yew Way CO15 203 F6
Yewtree Gr IP5 18 F7
Yewtree Rise IP8 16 C1
Yonge Cl CM3 192 E1
Yorick Ave CO5 201 C6
Yorick Rd CO5 201 C6
York Cl CO10 33 E8
York Gdns CM7 128 B4
York Mans CO15 189 E5
York Pl CO1 136 A8
York Rd
Brightlingsea CO7 185 E6
Chelmsford CM2 216 A8
Clacton-on-S CO15 189 E5
Earls Colne CO6 105 B6
Felixstowe IP11 221 E4
Haverhill CB9 8 E7
Ipswich IP3 18 A4
Sudbury CO10 33 E8
York St 7 CO11 86 D4
Young Cl CO16 188 C5
Ypres Rd CO2 135 E4

Z

Zambesi Rd CM23 145 F5
Zinnia Mews CO16 188 C4

NG	NH	NJ	NK
NM	NN	NO	NP
NR	NS	NT	NU
NX	NY	NZ	
SC	SD	SE	TA
SH	SJ	SK	TF	TG
SM	SN	SO	SP	TL	TM
SR	SS	ST	SU	TQ	TR
SW	SX	SY	SZ	TV

Any feature in this atlas can be given a unique reference to help you find the same feature on other Ordnance Survey maps of the area, or to help someone else locate you if they do not have a Street Atlas.

The grid squares in this atlas match the Ordnance Survey National Grid and are at 500 metre intervals. The small figures at the bottom and sides of every other grid line are the National Grid kilometre values (**00** to **99** km) and are repeated across the country every 100 km (see left).

To give a unique National Grid reference you need to locate where in the country you are. The country is divided into 100 km squares with each square given a unique two-letter reference. Use the administrative map to determine in which 100 km square a particular page of this atlas falls.

The bold letters and numbers between each grid line (**A** to **F**, **1** to **8**) are for use within a specific Street Atlas only, and when used with the page number, are a convenient way of referencing these grid squares.

Example *The railway bridge over DARLEY GREEN RD in grid square B1*

Step 1: Identify the two-letter reference, in this example the page is in **SP**

Step 2: Identify the 1 km square in which the railway bridge falls. Use the figures in the southwest corner of this square: Eastings **17**, Northings **74**. This gives a unique reference: **SP 17 74**, accurate to 1 km.

Step 3: To give a more precise reference accurate to 100 m you need to estimate how many tenths along and how many tenths up this 1 km square the feature is (to help with this the 1 km square is divided into four 500 m squares). This makes the bridge about **8** tenths along and about **1** tenth up from the southwest corner.

This gives a unique reference: **SP 178 741**, accurate to 100 m.

Eastings (read from left to right along the bottom) come before Northings (read from bottom to top). If you have trouble remembering say to yourself "Along the hall, THEN up the stairs"!

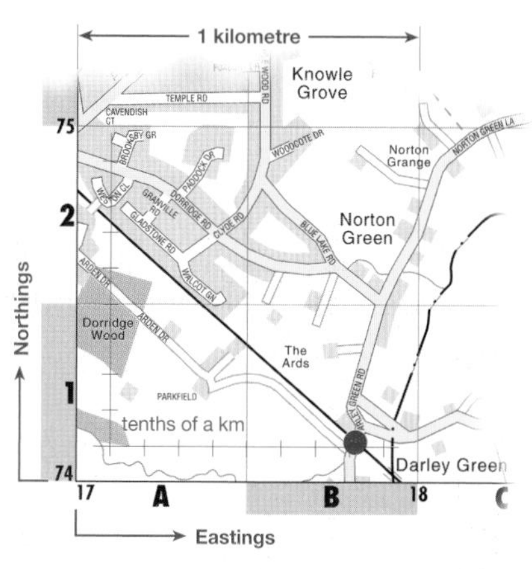

Addresses

Name and Address	Telephone	Page	Grid reference

Addresses

Name and Address	Telephone	Page	Grid reference